CORE TAX ANNUALS

Corporation Tax 2018/19

CORE TAX ANNUALS

Corporation Tax 2018/19

Pete Miller CTA (Fellow)

Satwaki Chanda, Barrister at Law

Donald Drysdale CA CTA (Fellow) TEP MBCS CITP

Eloise Brown CTA ATT (Fellow) BA (Hons)

Series General Editor: Mark McLaughlin CTA (Fellow) ATT (Fellow) TEP

Bloomsbury Professional

LONDON • DUBLIN • EDINBURGH • NEW YORK • NEW DELHI • SYDNEY

Bloomsbury Professional
Bloomsbury Publishing Plc
41–43 Boltro Road, Haywards Heath, RH16 1BJ, UK

British Library Cataloguing-in-Publication Data

A catalogue record for this book is available from the British Library.

ISBN: 978-1-52650-574-3

Typeset by Evolution Design & Digital Ltd (Kent)

Printed and bound by CPI Group (UK) Ltd, Croydon, CR0 4YY

To find out more about our authors and books visit www.bloomsburyprofessional.com. Here you will find extracts, author information, details of forthcoming events and the option to sign up for our newsletters

Preface

Welcome to the new edition of *Corporation Tax 2018/19*, one of Bloomsbury Professional's six Core Tax Annuals.

The aim of this book is to provide a clear, concise guide to the principles and practices of corporation tax, focused on the particular needs of most companies and their advisers. Furthermore, a number of selected tax planning suggestions and cost cutting ideas are listed alphabetically in Chapter 27. However, it has not been possible to cover all circumstances, and readers will need to turn to other texts for in-depth coverage of certain areas such as derivative contracts, leasing and specialised businesses.

After the Introduction (Chapter 1), we deal with the tax treatment of trading companies, dealing with topics such as trading income (Chapter 2), capital allowances (Chapter 3), trading losses and groups (Chapters 4–5).

The following chapters deal with companies with investment business (Chapter 6), with an emphasis on property investment and related matters (Chapters 7-9). In particular, the former chapter on investment business has been split in two, one chapter covering investing in shares and securities (Chapter 6), while the other deals specifically with property matters (Chapter 7).

There then follows more specialised topics such as close companies, loan relationships, and the intangibles regime (Chapters 10–12), as well as topics relating to technology and media such as the UK Patent Box, Research and Development, and the creative sector reliefs (Chapters 13–15).

The next topics deal with chargeable gains, reconstructions and amalgamations, distributions and liquidations (Chapters 16–19), before going on to deal with international matters (Chapters 20–21).

The final sections of the book deal with compliance matters, together with a chapter on accounting (Chapters 22–26).

LATEST DEVELOPMENTS

Finance Act 2017 was substantially shortened, due to the general election in June 2017. Since the last edition, the measures originally announced in March 2017 have finally been enacted in *Finance (No 2) Act 2017*. These are perhaps some of the most radical and complex measures affecting companies in recent years. The new rules on tax relief for corporate losses provide a greater flexibility than was hitherto possible, abolishing the requirement to stream losses, permitting group relief for carry forward losses and giving companies the discretion to choose how much relief to claim and when to claim it. At the same time, there are also new restrictions. A new cap on tax relief for carry forward losses applies where the company's profits exceed £5 million and there are also complex rules for restricting tax relief for corporate borrowings.

Finance Act 2018 has proved a quieter affair for companies as the government concentrates on the UK's departure from the EU and the impact of the so-called Great Repeal Bill. However, the number of consultations has not abated – these include a review of the corporate intangibles regime as well as a proposed 'revenue based' tax for digital businesses.

The law is stated as at 1 June 2018.

ACKNOWLEDGMENTS

Once again, we would like to thank Donald Drysdale, the original author for handing over an excellent manual, which it has been our pleasure to work on. We would also like to thank Ellie Brown of Eloise Brown Taxation for her contribution on the new rules on group relief in Chapter 5, to Steve Collings of Leavitt Walmsley Associates for his work on the accounting chapter 26, and – last but not least – our editor Paul Crick for his patience, support and guidance in helping to deliver this edition.

We hope that you find the book useful. We always welcome readers' comments and suggestions for future editions.

Pete Miller
Satwaki Chanda
June 2018

Contents

Table of examples

[*All references are to paragraph number*]

Chapter 21 Transfer pricing

Chapter 22 Self-assessment

Chapter 23 Rates and payment of corporation tax

Chapter 24 Self-assessment penalties

Chapter 26 Accounting and tax

Table of statutes

[*All references are to paragraph numbers*]

Table of statutory instruments and other guidance

[*All references are to paragraph numbers*]

Table of European Legislation

[All references are to paragraph numbers]

Table of cases

[*All references are to paragraph number*]

S

List of abbreviations

ACCA	Association of Chartered Certified Accountants
ACT	advance corporation tax
ADP	acceptable dividend policy
ADR	alternative dispute resolution
AIA	annual investment allowance
AIM	alternative investment market
AMV	aggregate market value
APA	advance pricing agreement
APC	HMRC Animation Production Company Manual
APR	agricultural property relief
ARC	Accounting Regulatory Committee
ARTG	HMRC Appeals, Reviews and Tribunals Manual
ASB	Accounting Standards Board
ATCA	advance thin capitalisation agreement
ATED	annual tax on enveloped dwellings
ATT	Association of Taxation Technicians
BA	balancing allowance
BEPS	base erosion and profit shifting
BIM	HMRC Business Income Manual
BIS	Department for Business, Innovation & Skills
BMT	bereaved minor trust
BPR	business property relief
CA	HMRC Capital Allowances Manual
CA 2006	Companies Act 2006
CAA 2001	Capital Allowances Act 2001
CCCP	contributions for the current chargeable period
CDFI	community development finance institution
CFC	controlled foreign company
CFM	HMRC Corporate Finance Manual
CG	HMRC Capital Gains Manual
CIHC	close investment holding company
CIOT	Chartered Institute of Taxation
CIRD	HMRC Corporate Intangibles Research & Development Manual
CIS	construction industry scheme
CISR	HMRC Construction Industry Scheme Reform Manual
CITR	community investment tax relief
CPCP	contributions for the previous chargeable period
CRM	customer relationship manager
CSOP	company share option plan
CTA 2009/2010	Corporation Tax Act 2009/2010
CTF	child trust fund
CTM	HMRC Company Taxation Manual
CTNIA	Corporation Tax (Northern Ireland) Act 2015

CTO	Capital Taxes Office
CTSA	corporation tax self-assessment
CTT	capital transfer tax
CVS	corporate venturing scheme
DMBM	HMRC Debt Management and Banking Manual
DOTAS	disclosure of tax avoidance schemes
DPT	diverted profits tax
DT	HMRC Double Taxation Relief Manual
DTR	double taxation relief
EEA	European Economic Area
EIM	HMRC Employment Income Manual
EIS	Enterprise Investment Scheme
EM	HMRC Enquiry Manual
ESC	Extra-statutory Concession
EUFT	eligible unrelieved foreign tax
FA	Finance Act
FATCA	Foreign Accounts Tax Compliance Act (US)
FII	franked investment income
FPC	HMRC Film Production Company Manual
FSMA 2000	Financial Services and Markets Act 2000
FRS	Financial Reporting Standard
FRSME	financial reporting standard for micro-entities
FRSSE	financial reporting standard for smaller entities
FYA	first year allowance
GAAP	generally accepted accounting practice (UK); generally accepted accounting principles (international)
GAAR	general anti-abuse rule
GPA	group payment arrangement
GWR	gift with reservation
HMRC	HM Revenue & Customs
IA	initial allowance
IA 1986	Insolvency Act 1986
IAS	International Accounting Standards
IASB	International Accounting Standards Board
IBA	industrial building allowance
ICAEW	Institute of Chartered Accountants in England and Wales
ICAS	Institute of Chartered Accountants of Scotland
ICTA 1988	Income and Corporation Taxes Act 1988
IFRS	International Financial Reporting Standards
IHT	inheritance tax
IHTA 1984	Inheritance Tax Act 1984
INS	HMRC Insolvency Manual
INTM	HMRC International Manual
IP	intellectual property
ITEPA 2003	Income Tax (Earnings and Pensions) Act 2003
ITTOIA 2005	Income Tax (Trading and Other Income) Act 2005
iXBRL	inline extensible business reporting language
LLP	limited liability partnership
NBCG	HMRC Non-Statutory Business Clearance Guidance Manual

NICs	National Insurance contributions
NRCGT	non-resident capital gains tax
OECD	Organisation for Economic Co-operation and Development
OEIC	open-ended investment company
PET	potentially exempt transfer
PIM	HMRC Property Income Manual
POA	pre-owned asset
R&D	research and development
REIT	real estate investment trust
RIPI	relevant IP income
RPI	retail prices index
RTI	real time information
RTWDV	relevant tax written down value
SDLT	stamp duty land tax
SE	small enterprise
SEIS	Seed Enterprise Investment Scheme
SI	Statutory Instrument
SME	small and medium-sized enterprise
SSAP	Statement of Standard Accounting Practice
SSCBA 1992	Social Security Contributions and Benefits Act 1992
SSE	substantial shareholdings exemption
STEP	Society of Trust and Estate Practitioners
TAAR	target anti-avoidance rule
TCGA 1992	Taxation of Chargeable Gains Act 1992
TIIN	Tax Information and Impact Note
TIOPA 2010	Taxation (International and Other Provisions) Act 2010
TMA 1970	Taxes Management Act 1970
TPC	HMRC Television Production Company Manual
TSI	transitional serial interests
UEL	useful economic life
UITF	Urgent Issue Task Force
UK GAAP	UK Generally Accepted Accounting Practice
UTR	unique taxpayer reference
VCC	venture capital company
VCT	venture capital trust
VOA	Valuation Office Agency
WDA	writing down allowance
WDV	written down value
XBRL	extensible business reporting language

Chapter 1

Introduction to corporation tax

SIGNPOSTS

- Introduction to corporation tax and related company law, including the formation of limited companies (see **1.1–1.3**).
- Fundamentals of corporation tax – including the definition of a company and the extent of the corporation tax charge (see **1.4–1.8**).
- The proposed devolution of certain corporation tax powers to Northern Ireland (see **1.9**).
- Directors' legal duties and obligations – including an overview of the effects of UK GAAP, accounting standards and forthcoming changes, SME status corporation tax assessment procedures, and the continuing hardening of attitudes towards tax avoidance (see **1.10–1.17**).
- HMRC's approach to accounting standards – including a brief overview of policy and attitudes held by HMRC (see **1.18–1.20**).

CORPORATION TAX LEGISLATION

1.1 Corporation tax is a tax levied on the taxable profits of limited companies and other organisations including clubs, societies, associations and other unincorporated bodies. It makes up approximately 8% of the annual tax revenues of the UK government, and is administered by HM Revenue & Customs (HMRC).

First introduced in 1965, the UK corporation tax legislation was re-enacted under the government's tax law rewrite project and is now contained largely within the *Corporation Tax Act 2009 (CTA 2009)*, the *Corporation Tax Act 2010 (CTA 2010)* and the *Taxation (International and Other Provisions) Act 2010 (TIOPA 2010)*. Separately, the government has been undertaking a fundamental reform of aspects of the corporation tax system; many changes have been made and the process is continuing.

The following are the most recent major changes to the corporation tax regime, which were enacted in *Finance (No 2) Act 2017*:

- A major reform to the rules for carrying forward corporate losses to future years. From 1 April 2017 companies have a greater flexibility in using carried forward losses to set against total profits, including the ability to group relieve carry forward losses for the first time (see **Chapters 4** and **5**).
- However, this flexibility is balanced by restrictions on the amount of losses that can be carried forward. A company will only be permitted to relieve losses against 50% of profits in any one year (subject to a £5 million allowance where losses can be relieved freely). Any surplus is available to be carried forward to future years, but subject to the same restrictions;
- Where the company is part of a group, tax relief for finance costs is restricted to 30% of the company's earnings, where the group's net interest expense exceeds £2 million. This follows the OECD's recommendations for best practice as part of the Base Erosion Profit Shifting (BEPS) project. These rules replace the old Debt Cap rules (see **5.31**).
- A major reform to the substantial shareholding exemption for chargeable gains has been enacted with the abolition of the requirement for the investor company to be a trading company or part of a trading group. There is also be a new 'qualifying institutional investor' exemption which allows relief for substantial holdings in non-trading companies (see **6.23**, **16.18**).

These reforms were originally announced during the Spring Budget 2017 but, because of the snap general election in June that year, they only made it to the statute books in November 2017. By comparison, Autumn Budget 2017 and the subsequent *Finance Act 2018* have proved to be a quieter affair for companies, no doubt due to the increasing demands on Parliament as a result of the UK's decision to leave the European Union. There are however, a number of consultations in progress:

- Consultation to charge corporation tax on all non-UK resident companies holding UK property for investment purposes. The charge will apply to both revenue profits and capital gains, irrespective of the type of property held currently subject to income tax within the corporation tax regime. This is aimed mainly at non-resident corporate landlords, with the intention that the new restrictions on interest relief will apply to them (see tinyurl.com/y8rxqnkv and **7.3**, **7.25–7.26**).
- Consultation on the intangibles regime. The modern rules for taxing intellectual property and goodwill in line with a company's accounts date from 2002; the purpose of the consultation is to provide a comprehensive review of the regime and to explore whether there is scope for reform (see tinyurl.com/ybquetx9 and **Chapter 12**).
- Consultation on the design of new rules to extend withholding tax on royalty payments from April 2019 in respect of UK intellectual property

made to connected parties in low or no-tax jurisdictions. These rules are intended to operate irrespective of whether the payer is based in the UK or elsewhere (see tinyurl.com/ycw3vjv7 and **Chapter 12**).

- Consultation on Corporate Tax and the Digital Economy which sets out the government's position on taxing digital businesses where value is created by end users. This includes social media where online platforms are used to facilitate 'user participation' which in turn generates revenues. The government's current thinking is to introduce a revenue-based tax, to be charged by reference to the location of the users rather than the traditional place where the company is resident or has a permanent establishment. This is intended to be an interim measure – it is recognised that a longer-term solution would need to have the agreement of other jurisdictions via the OECD (see tinyurl.com/ybaby57q).

In addition to the corporation tax statutes, there are a number of extra-statutory concessions and statements of practice that are of relevance to companies. Details of concessions may be found at tinyurl.com/kpzbl7x, and statements of practice at tinyurl.com/nnnvocm.

For details of the corporation tax legislation prior to the introduction of *CTA 2009*, *CTA 2010* and *TIOPA 2010*, please refer to *Corporation Tax 2008/09* (Tottel Publishing) and *Corporation Tax 2009/10* (Bloomsbury Professional).

COMPANY LAW ASPECTS

Formation of a UK company

> **Focus**
>
> An understanding of company law is an important step towards gaining an appreciation of how the corporation tax regime works.

1.2 Corporation tax is charged on the profits of UK resident companies (*CTA 2009, s 2(1)*), the vast majority of which are formed in the UK.

A new company may be a private company that is limited by shares or by guarantee, or it may be unlimited. Alternatively, the company may be a public company that is limited by shares. If limited by shares, the members will subscribe to the company's share capital, which in turn forms their initial investment in the company, and the liability of each member is restricted to the amount of his or her investment. A public company can offer its shares to the public, whereas a private company cannot. If a company is to be limited by guarantee, the members make no contribution upon formation or during the company's lifetime, but agree instead to contribute an amount to the company's assets upon winding-up. Members of a private unlimited company have unlimited liability, and the company need not necessarily have a share capital. A company limited by shares is by far the most common structure, and is the arrangement on which the commentary in this book is based.

A UK company is formed by providing Companies House with details of its memorandum and articles of association, directors, company secretary and members and registered office. This may be done in any of the following ways:

- in the case of a private company limited by shares using the standard 'model articles', the Companies House Web Incorporation Service may be used, and the new company may also be registered for corporation tax using this service;
- a third-party company formation agent may be used to incorporate any type of company, and such an agent should also be able to provide specialist advice in connection with the process; or
- a company can be incorporated directly with Companies House using a paper form. Form IN01 (Application to register a company) is to be used for this purpose.

Whichever method of incorporation method is chosen, the Registrar of Companies checks the documents and, if approved, retains them for public inspection.

A company has a separate legal personality from those of its members. A company is required to maintain statutory books to record its constitution and structure, and books of account to record its transactions. Documents notifying changes in structure must be filed at Companies House. Statutory accounts must be prepared, usually at annual intervals, and filed at Companies House. A company is also required to file an annual confirmation statement with the Registrar of Companies.

It is possible to establish a European company or Societas Europaea ('SE') in the UK (*SI 2004/2326; SI 2009/2400*). An SE is treated much like a public limited company (PLC).

See the Companies House website (www.companieshouse.gov.uk) for practical guidance on forming a company.

Companies Act 2006

1.3 UK companies are regulated by companies' legislation that emanates from the nineteenth century. As a result of the Company Law Review 1998, various Law Commission recommendations and EU Directives, this legislation was completely recast and redrafted, and the *Companies Act 2006 (CA 2006)* received Royal Assent on 8 November 2006; its commencement was effectively completed by October 2009 (*SI 2008/2860*). References, where appropriate, are made in this book to *CA 2006*. For previous legislation, see *Corporation*

Tax 2008/09 (Tottel Publishing). *CA 2006* increased the regulation affecting public companies, but reduced that applying to private companies.

CA 2006 provides that information to be supplied to the Registrar of Companies on incorporation includes a memorandum of association, which contains the names and signatures of the subscribers who are forming the company. If a company is to be limited by shares, there must be a commitment that each subscriber will take at least one share. Any person or persons can subscribe to a company. The shareholder reward for investment in the company is a distribution of profits, commonly known as a dividend, and the prospect of growth in the value of the shares.

A company must file its articles of association with the Registrar of Companies, unless it chooses to adopt the model articles of association. The articles of association contain details of how the company is to be run and make provision for the internal management of its affairs.

From April 2016, an unquoted company is required to maintain a register of those persons who have significant control of the company – a 'PSC Register' (*CA 2006, Pt 21A*). The function of the PSC Register is to increase corporate transparency for the purpose of combating tax evasion, money laundering and terrorist financing. There are also similar obligations under the *Fourth EU Anti-Money Laundering Directive* (*EU Directive 2015/849*).

A company must have at least one director who is a natural person (*CA 2006, s 155*), and a public company must have at least two directors (*CA 2006, s 154*). A private company need not appoint a company secretary, although in practice many choose to do so (*CA 2006, s 270*). A public company must appoint a company secretary (*CA 2006, s 271*).

See the Companies House website (www.companieshouse.gov.uk) for further guidance on statutory requirements relating to companies.

THE FUNDAMENTALS OF CORPORATION TAX

Charge to corporation tax

1.4 The profits of a company are brought into charge to tax under the corporation tax regime. Corporation tax is levied directly on the profits of the company and is payable by the company. Profits for this purpose are the company's income less expenses, together with its chargeable gains, all as adjusted in accordance with the relevant provisions of the tax legislation.

A dividend payment is not an expense of the company in computing its profits for corporation tax purposes. Instead, it is a distribution of profits.

Until 5 April 2016, each qualifying distribution to a shareholder carries a tax credit of 1/9th of the distribution, which effectively satisfies the income tax liability of the shareholder if he or she is a basic rate taxpayer, leaving a higher rate or additional rate taxpayer with further income tax to pay. For the new way in which dividends are taxed from 6 April 2016, see **10.32**.

Corporate shareholders are generally not chargeable to corporation tax on distributions from other UK companies.

Corporation tax rates have varied over the years, but have now fallen to their lowest level. The main rate of corporation tax for the financial year 2010 (ie 1 April 2010 to 31 March 2011) was 28%; it gradually reduced to the current rate of 19%. This rate will continue to apply until the financial year 2019, finally reducing to 17% by 2020 (see **Chapter 23** for details).

Historically, a lower rate of corporation tax applied to companies with small profits, and the small profits rate was 20% for the financial year 2014. *FA 2014* repealed the small profits rate provisions for most purposes, and a unified corporation tax rate applied from April 2015.

Companies in which the shares are closely held may also be subject to the close company rules (see **Chapter 10** for details).

> **Focus**
>
> When forming a UK private company, consider whether it will be treated as a close company for tax purposes.

In addition to periodic changes in rates of tax, the corporation tax base is also subject to frequent changes which are brought into effect by *Finance Acts* (usually once each year, but sometimes more in a General Election year) and by secondary legislation. Typically, such changes are designed to target avoidance, provide incentives, or otherwise improve the efficiency and international competitiveness of the UK corporation tax regime. Unfortunately, another effect has been to produce complex and voluminous tax legislation.

Corporation tax was part of the government's tax law rewrite project, which ran from 1997 to 2010 and attempted to modernise the wording of the tax legislation. The new approach made the legislation longer but generally easier to understand.

Bodies liable to corporation tax

1.5 A company is not the only 'person' that may be liable to corporation tax. This is because a company is defined as 'any body corporate or unincorporated association' (*CTA 2010, s 1121(1)*). Therefore, members' clubs, societies and trade and voluntary associations will find themselves within the ambit of corporation tax (see **2.87–2.90**). This *CTA 2010, s 1121* definition of a company excludes a partnership, a local authority or a local authority association. Therefore, partnerships, trustees, local authorities and local authority associations are not chargeable to corporation tax. Please see *Income Tax 2018/19* (Bloomsbury Professional) for partnerships, and *Trusts and Estates 2018/19* (Bloomsbury Professional) or *Trusts and Estates in Scotland 2016/17* (Bloomsbury Professional) for trustees. UK local authorities and local authority associations are exempt from corporation tax and capital gains tax (*CTA 2010, s 984*; *TCGA 1992, s 271(3)*).

The extent of the corporation tax charge

1.6 All UK resident companies are liable to corporation tax on their profits wherever they arise and whether or not they are received in or transmitted to the UK (*CTA 2009, s 5(1)*), except for an exemption available in respect of foreign branches (see **20.33** onwards). For these purposes, the United Kingdom includes Great Britain and Northern Ireland, but not the Irish Republic, the Isle of Man or the Channel Islands.

A company is UK resident if it is incorporated in the UK, ie registered at Companies House (*CTA 2009, s 14*). If it is not incorporated in the UK but is managed and controlled from the UK, it will most likely be resident in the UK for corporation tax purposes. These concepts are discussed in **Chapter 20**.

If a non-UK resident company carries on a trade in the UK through a permanent establishment, it will be liable to corporation tax on the profits directly attributable to the permanent establishment. A permanent establishment could amount to an overseas company's UK branch, UK office or UK agency. Such profits may emanate directly or indirectly from the permanent establishment and will include income from trades, property and intangibles and related gains (*CTA 2009, s 19(2), (3)*).

Taxation of company profits

1.7 *CTA 2009, s 2(2)* brings a company's profits into charge to corporation tax by stating that the profits that are chargeable to corporation tax consist of income and chargeable gains. From 1 July 2009, dividends and distributions received, whether from UK resident or foreign companies, are chargeable to corporation tax unless specifically exempted, although the effect is that most are exempted.

The profits of each accounting period are chargeable to corporation tax (*CTA 2009, s 8(3)*). Corporation tax rates are fixed for financial years. The financial year (for corporation tax) starts on 1 April in one year and ends on 31 March in the next year and is known by the calendar year in which it commences, eg the financial year 2018 starts on 1 April 2018 and ends on 31 March 2019.

Computation of income and gains

1.8 Corporation tax is charged on income and chargeable gains, including any dividends and other distributions which are not specifically exempt.

Each source of income and each chargeable gain are computed separately, in accordance with corporation tax law and practice.

The company's corporation tax computation and its company tax return bring together its total assessable income from trading and other sources, and its chargeable gains. Deductions such as allowable trading losses, charges on income and allowable capital losses are taken into account in arriving at total taxable profits of the period.

The various sources of income and reliefs are discussed in this book as follows:

Source	*Type of income*	*Chapter*
Trading income	Profits from a trade	2
Miscellaneous income	Sundry income	2
Intangible fixed assets	Credits and debits arising from intangible fixed assets	12
Loan relationships	Interest and other income arising from money debts	11
Property income	Profits from rents and other income from property in the UK and overseas	7
Chargeable gains and allowable capital losses	Profits and losses arising from the disposal of capital assets	16
	Type of relief	
Charges on income	Expenditure deducted from total income	4
Loss relief	Relief for excess of expenditure over income against other sources of income	4, 5
Management expenses	Expenses relating to investment business	6

The Northern Ireland rate of corporation tax

1.9 The *Corporation Tax (Northern Ireland) Act 2015 (CTNIA 2015)* received Royal Assent on 26 March 2015. It provides that the Northern Ireland Assembly is to be given power to set the 'Northern Ireland rate' at which corporation tax will be charged on the profits of certain trades and activities of Northern Ireland companies. This power was expected to be brought into effect from April 2018 with a rate set at 12.5% (see tinyurl.com/jb9jau5). The aim is to help Northern Ireland to compete more effectively with the low rate of corporation tax in the Republic of Ireland. However, at the time of writing, no rate has been set and it appears from reports that the Northern Ireland rate is unlikely to come into force in the near future (see tinyurl.com/y8n5ff6r).

The provisions of *CTNIA 2015* give details of what trades and activities will fall within the scope of the Northern Ireland rate, if one is set. The rate will be applied to trading income only, with other sources of income remaining chargeable at the main UK rate of corporation tax.

In most cases, the rate will apply to all trading profits of a corporate SME if its employee time and costs fall largely in Northern Ireland. It will also apply to a corporate partner's share of the profits of a partnership trade if the company and partnership are both SMEs and the partnership's employee time and costs fall largely in Northern Ireland. SMEs which do not meet the employee test will be able to opt for large company treatment (*Finance (No 2) Act 2017 Sch 7*, see below). This will enable them to access the Northern Ireland rate if they at least have a trading presence in the region).

The rate will also apply to the profits of large companies and (in the case of a corporate partner not covered by the SME rules) to a corporate partner's share of the profits of a partnership. In both these cases, it will apply to the trading profits attributed to a 'Northern Ireland regional establishment', computed using internationally recognised principles with some modifications and adaptations.

If a company or partnership is a 'Northern Ireland company' or a 'Northern Ireland firm' in an accounting period, its trading profit or trading loss will be split between 'Northern Ireland profits or losses' of the trade (taxed or relieved at the Northern Ireland rate) and 'mainstream profits or losses' of the trade (taxed or relieved at the main UK rate). Special rules will provide for cases where it makes a mainstream profit combined with a Northern Ireland loss, or a mainstream loss combined with a Northern Ireland profit.

Draft guidance for the Northern Ireland Corporation Tax regime can be accessed at tinyurl.com/hgagw6a.

COMPANY ACCOUNTS AND DIRECTORS' DUTIES

Duty to prepare accounts

1.10 The company's financial results are presented in the company's statutory accounts (often referred to as the 'financial statements'). Preparation of accounts is a statutory duty of the directors. *CA 2006, s 394* states that the 'directors of every company must prepare accounts for the company for each of its financial years'. For this purpose, 'financial year' is defined by *CA 2006, s 390*.

The directors must not approve those accounts unless they are satisfied that they give a true and fair view of the assets, liabilities, financial position and profit or loss of the company (*CA 2006, s 393(1)*). *CA 2006, s 386* states that every company must keep adequate accounting records and stipulates what these should contain. Where a company is required to have an audit, the auditor must also report on whether the company has maintained 'adequate records' (*CA 2006, s 498*).

Choice of accounting framework

1.11 A company's individual accounts may be prepared in accordance with *CA 2006, s 396* ('Companies Act individual accounts') or in accordance with international accounting standards ('IAS individual accounts') (*CA 2006, s 395*).

'Companies Act individual accounts' comprise a balance sheet as at the last day of the financial year, and a profit and loss account for each financial year (*CA 2006, s 396(1)*). The balance sheet must give a true and fair view of the state of the company's affairs as at the end of the financial year, and the profit and loss must give a true and fair view of the profit or loss of the company for the financial year.

'IAS individual accounts' are accounts that comply with international accounting and financial reporting standards. In this case the notes to the accounts must state that the accounts have been prepared in accordance with international accounting standards (*CA 2006, s 397*).

There is a similar choice in determining how group accounts may be prepared – ie in accordance with *CA 2006, s 404* ('Companies Act group accounts') or in accordance with international accounting standards ('IAS group accounts') (*CA 2006, s 403*). Listed companies, as required by *EC Regulation 1606/2002* on the application of international accounting standards, must use IAS when preparing their consolidated accounts (*CA 2006, s 403(1)*). If IAS group accounts are prepared, the directors must state in the notes to those accounts that they have been prepared in accordance with international accounting standards (*CA 2006, s 406*).

Accounting standards

1.12 The Financial Reporting Council (FRC) is the UK's independent regulator responsible for setting accounting standards for the UK for all entities that are not required (and have chosen not) to apply international accounting standards. The FRC has fundamentally revised its accounting standards for accounting periods beginning on or after 1 January 2015. For further details see **Chapter 26**.

The International Accounting Standards Board (IASB) sets the accounting standards to be used by all listed groups. The standards are referred to as

International Accounting Standards (IAS) or International Financial Reporting Standards (IFRS).

UK companies may not use a standard set by the IASB unless it has been adopted by the European Union (referred to here as EU-adopted IFRS) (see **26.1–26.2**). At the time of writing, it is currently unknown how the endorsement process will work in the UK once the UK leaves the EU.

UK GAAP

1.13 The vast majority of UK companies apply UK Generally Accepted Accounting Practice ('UK GAAP'). In recent years there were many changes to UK GAAP, largely due to measures aimed at bringing the UK's accounting standards into closer alignment with the international standards.

> **Focus**
>
> Fundamental changes to UK GAAP are currently dominating the agenda of those responsible for companies' financial reporting and corporation tax affairs.

Following wide-ranging consultation, the FRC published a new financial reporting framework consisting of six new standards:

- FRS 100 *Application of Financial Reporting Requirements* sets out the applicable financial reporting framework for entities preparing financial statements in accordance with legislation, regulations or accounting standards applicable in the UK and Republic of Ireland. It applies to financial statements that are intended to give a true and fair view of the assets, liabilities, financial position and profit or loss for a period;
- FRS 101 *Reduced Disclosure Framework (Disclosure exemptions from EU-adopted IFRS for qualifying entities)* or 'IFRS with reduced disclosures' sets out the disclosure exemptions (a reduced disclosure framework) for the individual financial statements of subsidiaries, including intermediate parents, and ultimate parents that otherwise apply the recognition, measurement and disclosure requirements of EU-adopted IFRS; and
- FRS 102 *The Financial Reporting Standard applicable in the UK and Republic of Ireland* sets out succinct financial reporting requirements based on (but significantly amended from) the IASB's IFRS for Small and Medium-sized Entities (IFRS for SMEs), with reduced disclosures available for 'qualifying entities' reporting under it. FRS 102 is a simplification of the principles in IFRS for recognising and measuring assets, liabilities, income and expenses; in most cases it includes only the

simpler accounting treatment where IFRS permits accounting options, and it requires fewer disclosures. Small companies report under FRS 102 and can apply the presentation and disclosure requirements of Section 1A *Small Entities* if they choose.

- FRS 103 *Insurance Contracts* which sets out the principles for entities which write insurance contracts or hold reinsurance contracts and prepare financial statements in accordance with FRS 102. FRS 103 is likely to be comprehensively revised in the future to reflect the new IFRS 17 *Insurance Contracts* which will replace the current interim standard, IFRS 4 *Insurance Contracts*.
- FRS 104 *Interim Financial Reporting* which provides the guidance for entities that are required, or choose, to prepare interim financial statements (eg half-yearly accounts).
- FRS 105 *The Financial Reporting Standard applicable to the Micro-entities Regime* which applies to the smallest of companies in the UK. FRS 105 is a simplified standard but may not be appropriate to all micro-entities as it is restrictive; for example, it does not allow revaluations or fair values to be used; nor does it provide for any accounting policy choices.

The mandatory effective date for the new financial reporting framework ('new UK GAAP') is for periods of account beginning on or after 1 January 2015. Small and micro-entities were mandatorily required to apply FRS 102, Section 1A or FRS 105 for periods starting on or after 1 January 2016.

The purpose of accounting standards is to enable the financial statements of a reporting entity to give a true and fair view.

Up to periods starting on or after 1 January 2016, smaller companies could adopt the Financial Reporting Standard for Smaller Entities (the FRSSE), which was within UK GAAP. This has essentially been replaced by FRS 102 and small companies must now apply the recognition and measurement principles of full FRS 102, but can apply the presentation and disclosure requirements in Section 1A *Small Entities* in FRS 102 which aim to reduce the level of disclosures witin the financial statements. Large or medium-sized groups cannot use Section 1A and must use full FRS 102 in terms of recognition, measurement, presentation and disclosure.

Unfortunately, the FRSSE (effective January 2015) was a temporary measure which was replaced from 1 January 2016. For accounting periods beginning on or after that date (or earlier if desired), a company that qualifies as a micro-entity is entitled to adopt FRS 105 *The Financial Reporting Standard applicable to the Micro-entities Regime* (or the 'FRSME'), a new financial reporting standard for micro-entities, although this standard is optional and a micro-entity may choose to use FRS 102 if it wishes. A small entity that is not a micro-entity is not allowed to use FRS 105. For further details of these changes, see **Chapter 26**.

In December 2017, the FRC issued amendments to UK GAAP as a result of the first triennial review of the standards. These amendments are aimed to be improvements and clarifications and should not be viewed as wholesale changes, although some of the amendments will have a direct impact on the financial statements themselves. The amendments are mandatorily effective for periods starting on or after 1 January 2019. Revised publications of all six FRSs, incorporating all the amendments made, will be published in the first quarter of 2018.

Micro-entities and small and medium-sized companies

1.14 For financial years beginning on or after 1 January 2016, and a financial year of a company beginning on or after 1 January 2015 but before 1 January 2016 if the directors of the company so decide (*Companies, Partnerships and Groups (Accounts and Reports) Regulations, SI 2015/980*), *CA 2006, ss 382, 383, 384A, 384B, 465* and *466* define micro-entities, small companies and medium-sized companies as those (subject to certain exceptions) which meet at least two of the following criteria respectively (see *SI 2015/980*):

	Micro-entity	*Small company*	*Medium-sized company*
	Not more than	Not more than	Not more than
Turnover	£632,000	£10.2 million	£36 million
Balance sheet total	£316,000	£5.1 million	£18 million
Number of employees	10	50	250

For earlier financial years the limits were as follows:

	Micro-entity	*Small company*	*Medium-sized company*
	Not more than	Not more than	Not more than
Turnover	£632,000	£6.5 million	£25.9 million
Balance sheet total	£316,000	£3.26 million	£12.9 million
Number of employees	10	50	250

The balance sheet total is the aggregate of the company's assets, as shown on the balance sheet, before both current and long-term liabilities. The turnover limits are adjusted proportionately for periods of account longer or shorter than 12 months. Care must be taken not to use net assets as the balance sheet total.

A company qualifies as a micro-entity or a small or medium-sized company (as the case may be) in its first financial year if the qualifying conditions are met in that year. Thereafter, the status of the company will not change unless it fails to meet the appropriate requirements for two consecutive years. For example, if a large company reduces in size so that it satisfies the requirements specified for a small or medium-sized company, it will not be treated as such unless it also met those requirements for the previous year.

These distinctions between large, medium-sized and small companies and micro-entities are dictated by EU law (*Commission Recommendation 2003/361/EC* of 6 May 2003) and apply for *Companies Act* purposes. They have some repercussions for corporation tax purposes, eg where the EU State aid rules are involved.

Small and medium-sized groups

1.15 For financial years beginning on or after 1 January 2016, and a financial year of a company beginning on or after 1 January 2015 but before 1 January 2016 if the directors of the company so decide (SI 2015/980), *CA 2006, ss 383* and *466* contain corresponding definitions of small and medium-sized groups, as follows (see *Companies, Partnerships and Groups (Accounts and Reports) Regulations, SI 2015/980*):

	Small group		*Medium-sized group*	
	Not more than	Not more than	Not more than	Not more than
Aggregate:	Net	Gross	Net	Gross
Turnover	£10.2 million	£12.2 million	£36 million	£43.2 million
Balance sheet total	£5.1 million	£6.1 million	£18 million	£21.6 million
Number of employees	50		250	

For earlier financial years the limits were as follows:

	Small group		*Medium-sized group*	
	Not more than	Not more than	Not more than	Not more than
Aggregate:	Net	Gross	Net	Gross
Turnover	£6.5 million	£7.8 million	£25.9 million	£31.1 million
Balance sheet total	£3.26 million	£3.9 million	£12.9 million	£15.5 million
Number of employees	50		250	

The balance sheet total is the aggregate of the company's assets, as shown on the balance sheet, before both current and long-term liabilities. A parent company, and therefore its group, may satisfy the requirement that its turnover or balance sheet total is below the relevant limit on the basis of either the net or the gross figure. For this purpose 'net' means after any set-offs and other adjustments made to eliminate intra-group transactions, in accordance with either regulations under *CA 2006, s 404* (for Companies Act accounts) or international accounting standards (for IAS accounts). 'Gross' means without those set-offs and other adjustments. Again, care must be taken to use the correct balance sheet total figure (ie gross assets, not net assets).

Corporation tax assessment procedures

1.16 Companies must comply with the corporation tax self-assessment procedures. Companies determine their own corporation tax liability and pay corporation tax to HMRC based on this self-assessment. Compulsory online filing and payment procedures were introduced from 1 April 2011, requiring virtually all companies (however small) to send HMRC their corporation tax return (including accounts and corporation tax computations) online in a prescribed format and to pay their tax online.

> **Focus**
>
> Self-assessment compliance requirements demand that businesses are self-monitoring. Failure to comply will result in fines and penalties.

HMRC are organised into various customer and information units which focus on compliance assurance in order to minimise the risk of loss of tax to the government through taxpayer error, non-payment, evasion and fraud. These activities are reinforced by wide-ranging powers to carry out taxpayer compliance checks, underpinned by a system of penalties based on the taxpayer's degree of culpability.

Further commentary on these topics is to be found in **Chapters 22–25**.

Companies Act directors' duties

1.17 *CA 2006, Pt 10, Ch 2 (ss 170–181)* sets out seven statutory duties of directors (*ss 171–177*):

- a duty to act within powers,
- a duty to promote the success of the company,
- a duty to exercise independent judgment,
- a duty to exercise reasonable care, skill and diligence,

- a duty to avoid conflicts of interest,
- a duty not to accept benefits from third parties, and
- a duty to declare interest in proposed transaction or arrangement.

The directors owe these duties primarily to the company, and in certain circumstances to shareholders. Pre-existing case law on such matters, which was in being before *CA 2006*, still stands (*CA 2006, s 170(4)*).

In promoting the success of the company, it is stated that the directors should consider (*CA 2006, s 172(1)*):

- the likely consequences of any decision in the long term,
- the interests of the company's employees,
- the need to foster the company's business relationships with suppliers, customers and others,
- the impact of the company's operations on the community and the environment,
- the desirability of the company maintaining a reputation for high standards of business conduct, and
- the need to act fairly as between members of the company.

Directors are required to act responsibly in relation to all company dealings; this includes corporation tax compliance and corporation tax planning. They should also look beyond the strict confines of their duties and responsibilities under *CA 2006*. There is widespread public debate on the interaction between law, ethics and morality in relation to tax planning, and the government devotes substantial resources to its efforts to reduce tax evasion and unacceptable tax avoidance. *FA 2013* introduced a general anti-abuse rule (GAAR) to combat abusive tax avoidance schemes. Some bodies have sought to reinforce the call for a responsible approach by companies to their tax affairs (eg *Statement of Tax Principles for Business*, CBI, 8 May 2013), while others have expressed concerns about the legality of certain anti-avoidance measures (eg *Tax and the Rule of Law*, The Law Society, 30 April 2015).

Attitudes to tax avoidance have evolved, and many companies and their directors are concerned about the reputational risks involved. See *obiter dicta* by Lord Walker in *Futter & Anor v HMRC; Pitt & Anor v HMRC* [2013] UKSC 26, in the Supreme Court, at para 135:

> 'Since the seminal decision of the House of Lords in *WT Ramsay Ltd v IRC* [1982] AC 300, [1981] 1 All ER 865, [1981] STC 174 there has been an increasingly strong and general recognition that artificial tax avoidance is a social evil which puts an unfair burden on the shoulders of those who do not adopt such measures.'

The senior accounting officer of a qualifying company (essentially, a large company) is obliged by tax provisions contained in *FA 2009* to ensure that the company's accounting systems are sufficiently robust to provide HMRC with accurate information (see **25.26**).

TAXATION AND ACCOUNTS

The basic premise

1.18 The basic premise is that the accounting profits represent the taxable profits, unless overridden by tax law (*CTA 2009, s 46(1)*). The changes that have recently taken place in UK GAAP (see **Chapter 26**) are not expected to alter this basic premise, but companies should have expected the adoption of new accounting standards to accelerate or defer the recognition of profits in some cases and consequently affect the timing of tax liabilities. Note that there are special provisions dealing with changes of accounting basis and changes of accounting policy (see **2.76, 26.3**).

It is the overriding tax law that we seek to examine in the following chapters. A further discussion of accounting and tax is given in **Chapter 26**, together with additional details of old UK GAAP, new UK GAAP and international financial reporting standards.

Legislation

1.19 While a company may have many sources of income, the vast majority of UK companies carry on trading activities. Over the years, the courts have applied GAAP as the basis for determining the profits of a trade for tax purposes. Where accounts did not comply with GAAP, the courts have held that adjustments should be made to calculate tax liabilities as though the accounts had complied with GAAP: see *Threlfall v Jones (HM Inspector of Taxes); Gallagher v Jones (HM Inspector of Taxes)* [1993] STC 537 and *Tapemaze Ltd v Melluish (HM Inspector of Taxes)* [2000] STC 189.

HMRC acknowledge that profits measured in accordance with GAAP form the starting point for the computation of taxable profits (HMRC Business Income Manual at BIM31005 onwards). Small companies and micro-entities comply with UK GAAP if they choose to adopt the reduced disclosure frameworks available to them. Accounts may also be prepared under international GAAP (ie IFRS), but this is generally done only by large and listed companies.

The assumption is, of course, that accounts based on GAAP will show a true and fair view. Reliance on GAAP in calculating trading profits for corporation tax purposes is embodied in statute by *CTA 2009, s 46*, which states that the profits of a trade must be calculated in accordance with GAAP, subject to any adjustment required or authorised by law in calculating profits for corporation tax purposes. For this purpose, UK GAAP or international GAAP may be used.

HMRC practice

1.20 At BIM31030, HMRC discuss FRS 102, Section 2 *Concepts and Pervasive Principles*, and its predecessor (FRS 18 *Accounting Policies*).

FRS 18 set out the framework for old UK GAAP, and IAS 8 *Accounting Policies, Changes in Accounting Estimates and Errors* is the international equivalent. Under current UK GAAP, FRS 102, Section 2, embodies similar principles.

FRS 102 and IAS 8 provide definitions of accounting policies, estimation techniques and measurement bases: accounting policies are the manner in which certain types of transaction should be presented; estimation techniques are the methods used to arrive at an estimated monetary amount; and measurement bases are the monetary attributes that are reflected in the accounts.

For example, if a company changed its method of stock valuation from average cost to FIFO (ie first in, first out), this would be a change of accounting policy. If, on the other hand, the company changed its method of ascertaining the cost of stock from a percentage of selling price to actual invoiced cost, this would only be a change in estimation techniques. Changes in accounting policy are accounted for retrospectively; while changes in accounting estimate are accounted for in the current period and prospectively (ie going forward – they are not retrospectively applied).

Section 1 *Scope* of FRS 102 requires the standard to be applied to financial statements that are intended to give a true and fair view of the entity's financial position and profit or loss (or income and expenditure) for a period. There is no significant difference between the requirements of Section 1 of FRS 102 and previous UK GAAP.

Paragraphs 2.2 and 2.3 outline the 'objective of financial statements' which is to provide information about the financial position, performance and cash flows of an entity that is useful for economic decision-making by a broad range of users who are not in a position to demand reports tailored to meet their particular information needs. In addition, paragraph 2.3 acknowledges that financial statements also show the results of the stewardship of management.

To that end, the financial statements of an entity must contain certain qualitative characteristics contained in paragraphs 2.4 to 2.14 of FRS 102 which are listed below:

- understandability,
- relevance,
- materiality,

- reliability,
- substance over form,
- prudence,
- completeness,
- comparability,
- timeliness, and
- balance between benefit and cost.

The going concern basis of accounting is always used when preparing the entity's financial statements unless the entity concerned has ceased trading or is to be liquidated. The accruals concept requires that transactions should be reflected in the accounts in the period in which they are incurred rather than the period in which they are received or paid (FRS 102, Section 2, paras 2.36, 3.8, 3.9).

The exercise of prudence (a concept found in FRS 102 but no longer in the *Conceptual Framework for Financial Reporting* in IFRS) does not allow the deliberate understatement of assets or income, or the deliberate overstatement of liabilities or expenses. In short, prudence does not permit bias (FRS 102, Section 2, para 2.9).

FRS 102, Section 32 *Events after the End of the Reporting Period*, requires a company to adjust the amounts recognised in its financial statements, including related disclosures, to reflect events that occur between the end of the reporting period and the date when the financial statements are authorised for issue – if they provide evidence of conditions that existed at the end of the reporting period. At BIM31040, HMRC acknowledge the importance of this by referring to comments in *Symons v Weeks (as personal representative of Lord Llewelyn-Davies)* [1983] STC 195 that 'where facts are available they are to be preferred to prophecies'.

Although HMRC recognise that accounts are to be drawn up in accordance with GAAP, they seem uneasy with the notion of materiality, presumably because *CTA 2009, s 8(3)* states that tax is to be charged on the full amount of profits arising in the accounting period.

Materiality is closely related to the relevance objective. Accounting practice considers that an item would be material to the financial statements if its mis-statement or omission might reasonably be expected to influence the economic decisions of the users of the statements. HMRC recognise materiality as an accountancy concept but not a tax concept (BIM31047). Materiality is a judgement to be made in the light of the circumstances and the event. They suggest that the factual accuracy of any item in the accounts is ultimately for the tribunal to decide. Appeals before the tribunal are discussed in **Chapter 2**.

FRS 102, para 2.8, requires that transactions and other events and conditions are accounted for and presented in accordance with their substance and not merely their legal form, to enhance the reliability of financial statements. The aim is to ensure that the commercial effect of all transactions is recorded in the financial statements. See BIM31055.

Chapter 2

Trading income

SIGNPOSTS

- The meaning of a trade and the commencement and the cessation of trading activities (see **2.1–2.5**).
- The adjustment of trading profits for self-assessment purposes (see **2.6–2.9**).
- The determination of non-trading income (see **2.10–2.11**).
- Expenditure with a restricted deduction (see **2.12–2.30**).
- Additional deductible expenditure (see **2.31–2.34**).
- Deductible expenditure in connection with employees (see **2.35–2.48**).
- Expenses relating to a specific trade – including personal service companies and managed service companies (see **2.49–2.52**).
- Summary of deductible and non-deductible expenditure (see **2.53**).
- Receipts which are not taxable as trading income (see **2.54–2.55**).
- Property income treated as trading income (see **2.56–2.63**).
- Redress payments for mis-selling (see **2.64**).
- Activities treated as a trade by statute (see **2.65–2.67**).
- Barter trades taxable as trading income (see **2.68**).
- Appropriations of profits (see **2.69**).
- Valuation of stocks and work in progress (see **2.70–2.72**).
- The effects of a change in basis of accounting from one valid basis to another (see **2.73–2.76**).
- Charge to corporation tax on post-cessation receipts (see **2.77–2.78**).
- Illustrative computational example (see **2.79**).

- Exempt bodies – charities, mutual companies, members' clubs and community amateur sports clubs – and reliefs for companies supporting them (see **2.80–2.92**).
- Relief for expenditure on grassroots sport (see **2.93**).

INTRODUCTION

2.1 Corporation tax is charged on a company's profits for each financial year, in accordance with the corporation tax statutes (*CTA 2009, s 2(1)*). A company's profits are its income and its chargeable gains of each accounting period, subject to any specific exemptions or reliefs (*CTA 2009, s 2(2)*).

TRADING PROFITS

2.2 The profits of a trade are chargeable to corporation tax (*CTA 2009, s 35*). Normally, it is a question of fact as to whether a trade is being carried on, but certain activities are statutorily deemed to be trades or non-trades, as the case may be.

The profits of a trade must be calculated in accordance with generally accepted accounting practice (GAAP), subject to any adjustment required or authorised by law in calculating profits for corporation tax purposes (*CTA 2009, s 46(1)*). For information about GAAP and changes to UK GAAP, see **Chapter 26**. Losses of a trade are calculated in the same way (*CTA 2009, s 47*)

CTA 2009 imposes no requirement to comply with *CA 2006* or its related subordinate legislation, except as to the basis of calculation; neither does it impose any requirements as to audit or disclosure (*CTA 2009, s 46(2)*). Accounting must be on an accruals basis, and accounting on a cash basis is not acceptable (*CTA 2009, s 48*).

FA 2013, Schs 4, 5, introduced a voluntary cash basis of accounting for small businesses and a range of simplified flat-rate expense deductions, but these do not apply to companies, however small. But see **26.21** for the new substantially abbreviated reporting regime for micro-entities.

In computing taxable profits, adjustments required or authorised by tax law, as interpreted by case law, override GAAP. As a result, a company's total taxable profits of the period will usually differ from the profit shown in the company's profit and loss account or income statement. See **Chapter 26** for the interaction of accounting standards and tax law, and for details of change to UK GAAP.

In the absence of any provision to the contrary, the same calculation rules apply for corporation tax purposes regardless of whether the result is a profit or a loss (*CTA 2009, s 47*).

FA 2016, s 71 introduced provisions to ensure that profits from barter trades are also brought into account as trading profits.

TRADE

Meaning of a trade

2.3 A 'trade' is not specifically defined for corporation tax purposes, but for the purposes of the *Corporation Tax Acts* it includes any venture in the nature of trade, unless otherwise indicated either expressly or by implication (*CTA 2010, ss 1118, 1119*).

Whether or not a trade is being carried on is a question of fact. The Royal Commission on the Taxation of Profits and Income in 1955 identified six 'badges of trade' that indicated whether or not a trade was being carried on. These were:

- the subject matter of the realisation (eg are the goods or services provided by the company of a type that suggests it is trading in the provision of them?);
- the length of the period of ownership (eg is the company typically acquiring and re-selling goods or services over a short timescale?);
- the frequency or number of similar transactions by the same person (eg is the company undertaking such transactions frequently?);
- supplementary work on or in connection with the property realised (eg does the company enhance the goods or services, perhaps adding its own identity or branding?);
- the circumstances that were responsible for the realisation (eg does the company sell its goods or services in a systematic manner which suggests that it is trading?); and
- the motive (eg is the company seeking to make a profit?).

> **Focus**
>
> A company's activities will determine whether or not a trade is being carried on. Case law offers a number of examples.

Case law

2.4 There is a substantial body of long-established case law relating to trading activities, confirming the above badges of trade. The following are a selection of those cases:

Subject matter of transaction. In *Rutledge v CIR* (1929) 14 TC 490, the taxpayer allegedly bought and sold a large quantity of toilet rolls in an isolated transaction. The subject matter of the transaction helped to determine that this was a trading transaction.

Period of ownership. In *Martin v Lowry* (1926) 11 TC 297, an agricultural machinery merchant with no previous connection with the linen trade bought a surplus of government stock of 44 million yards of linen. Negotiations for sale to the linen manufacturers fell through. The taxpayer advertised the linen and eventually all was sold within a year to numerous purchasers. The goods were sold swiftly at a profit. It was held that this was an adventure in the nature of trade.

Frequency of transactions. In *Pickford v Quirke* (1927) 13 TC 251, the taxpayer was a member of four different syndicates involved in buying and selling cotton spinning mills. It was held that the repetition of this transaction implied a trading intention.

In *Leach v Pogson* (1962) 40 TC 585, [1962] TR 289, the taxpayer founded a driving school which he later sold at a profit. He then founded 30 more driving schools. Once the schools were operational he transferred them to companies, partly for shares and partly for cash. Because of the frequency of the transactions, the taxpayer was found to be trading.

Supplementary work. In *Cape Brandy Syndicate v CIR* (1921) 12 TC 358, three wine merchants from different firms bought a quantity of South African brandy. Most of the brandy was shipped to the UK where it was blended with French brandy, re-casked and sold in numerous lots. It was held that the transactions amounted to a trade.

Circumstances or method of realisation. In *West v Phillips* (1958) 38 TC 203, a retired builder owned 2,495 houses, of which 2,208 had been built as investments and 287 for eventual sale. After a period of time, the taxpayer began to sell the houses. It was held that 287 houses were sold as trading stock, but the sale of the remainder held for investment purposes was not a trade.

Motive. In *Wisdom v Chamberlain* (1968) 45 TC 92, the taxpayer made a profit on the purchase and sale of silver bullion. The bullion was bought with borrowed money to protect his wealth against the devaluation of sterling and was resold after a relatively short period. It was held that this was a trading activity because the silver had been purchased for the specific purpose of realising a profit and was not, by its nature, an investment which could produce any income.

Over time, the number of recognised badges of trade has risen to nine, and these were summarised clearly in *Marston v Morton* [1986] STC 463, as follows:

Factor to consider	*Comment*
Was the transaction a one-off transaction?	Frequency of transactions indicate a trade, but a one-off transaction may still constitute a trade depending on intention and other factors.
Was the transaction in some way related to a trade carried on by the taxpayer?	If related to the trade, this will point to a trading transaction.
Was the transaction in a commodity of a kind which is normally the subject matter of trade?	If yes, this will point to a trading transaction.
Was the transaction carried out in a manner typical of a trade in a commodity of that nature?	If yes, this will point to a trading transaction.
How was the transaction financed?	If financed by borrowings, this often indicates that a trade is being carried on.
Was work done on the item before resale?	If yes, it is more likely to be a trading transaction.
Was the item purchased broken down into several lots?	If so, there is an indication that a trading transaction has taken place.
What were the purchaser's intentions at the time of purchase? Was it intended to hold the asset as an investment?	If held as an investment, its resale is unlikely to be a trading transaction.
Did the asset purchased either provide enjoyment for the purchaser, or produce income?	The production of income points to a trading transaction.

Marston v Morton was cited in *Albermarle 4 LLP v Revenue and Customs Commissioners* [2013] UKFTT 083 (TC), where the First-tier Tribunal decided that a trade was being carried on. The *Albermarle 4 LLP* case illustrates the importance of being able to produce contemporaneous documentary evidence of the facts.

The above issues concerning badges of trade can be applied equally to professional income but here, more than likely, the central issue is whether professional skills are sold and marketed for remunerative gain. *CTA 2009* makes no reference to the carrying on of a profession or a vocation, for which there is no statutory definition. A profession is normally understood to mean the provision of services involving a high degree of skill or competence attributed to an individual, for which he or she has undergone specialised training.

Commentary on *CTA 2009* has suggested that a corporate body cannot carry on a profession that depends on the knowledge and skill of the individual. In line with the apparent intentions of *FA 1965*, which first introduced corporation tax, it has long been the HMRC view that a corporate body cannot carry on a profession for corporation tax purposes. Where a corporate body carries on a business consisting of the provision of professional services, the practice is to treat it as carrying on a trade. A vocation is a specific career that can only be undertaken by an individual and requires a personal commitment to a particular activity (*CTA 2009*, Explanatory Notes, Annex 1, Change 2).

In determining whether or not a trade is being carried on, the company's activities must be looked at as a whole. A company may carry one or more trades, and a trading company may also carry on an investment business. Transactions for each activity must be kept separate, as the corporation tax rules for investment business differ from those for trading (see **Chapter 6** for investment business and **Chapter 7** for property investment).

On the premise that a trade is being carried on, the company must establish whether any particular receipt is from the trade and whether it is a capital or a revenue item. It is an established principle that trading income is received when it is recognised in the trader's accounts (HMRC Business Income Manual at BIM40070; see **Chapter 26**). See also HMRC's Toolkit on 'Capital v Revenue Expenditure' at tinyurl.com/63vn6ts, although it is important to be aware that HMRC's Toolkits are based on their view of the legislation and are therefore not definitive.

Commencement of a trade

2.5 A company is treated as starting or ceasing to carry on a trade when it becomes chargeable or ceases to be within the charge to corporation tax in respect of that trade (*CTA 2009, s 41*). Therefore, if the pre-existing business of a sole trader or partnership were to incorporate, the company is treated as starting to carry on the trade from the date of transfer.

Whether or not a company has started or ceased to carry on a trade is a question of fact, as are questions relating to the dates of commencement or cessation. These matters are covered in *Income Tax 2018/19* (Bloomsbury Professional).

SELF-ASSESSMENT OF TRADING INCOME

Company tax return

2.6 The company tax return, consisting of form CT600, the statutory accounts and the company's corporation tax computations, must provide HMRC with information about the reported profits of each trade carried on by the company and the way in which those profits are adjusted for corporation tax purposes. For more about self-assessment see **Chapter 22**.

Adjusted trading profits

2.7 The company must compute its adjusted trading profits, and calculate the capital allowances due. Where more than one trade is carried on, separate computations must be prepared for each trade.

The accounting profits form the basis of the taxable profits, and so the starting point for computing the assessable trading profits for each trade is the reported profits.

In computing the assessable trading profits, it is first necessary to eliminate from the profits any non-trade source income, eg capital items, property income and non-trade loan relationship income.

Loan relationships are subject to corporation tax in accordance with a specific regime (see **Chapter 11**). Special rules also apply to investment business (**Chapter 6**), intangible fixed assets (**Chapter 12**), income from patents (**Chapter 13**), research and development (**Chapter 14**), creative sector reliefs (**Chapter 15**), chargeable gains (**Chapter 16**) and foreign matters (**Chapter 20**). Transfer pricing adjustments can increase taxable profits but never decrease them (**Chapter 21**).

Receipts and expenses

2.8 *CTA 2009* uses the terms 'receipts' and 'expenses' for the accounting credits and debits that are brought into account in calculating trading profits. The use of the word 'receipt' or 'expense' does not mean that an amount has actually been received or paid in cash (*CTA 2009, s 48*).

A receipt can include the receipt of non-monetary consideration. In these circumstances the value of such consideration must be brought into account as well as any cash payment (*Gold Coast Selection Trust Ltd v Humphrey* (1948) 30 TC 209 and now *CTA 2009, s 49A* as inserted by *FA 2016, s 71*).

Capital allowances are treated as an expense, and balancing charges are treated as a receipt of the trade (see **Chapter 3**). Debits and credits arising from the company's trading loan relationships and derivative contracts (**Chapter 11**) and intangible fixed assets (**Chapter 12**) are treated in similar fashion (*CTA 2009, s 49*).

From 1 April 2017, new *TIOPA 2010, Pt 10* (introduced by *F(No 2)A 2017, s 20* and *Sch 5*) restricts relief for interest expenses to 30% of the company or group's earnings before interest, tax, depreciation and amortisation (EBITDA). Only companies with at least £2m of net interest expense are affected (see **5.31**).

Calculation of adjusted trading profits

2.9 If a company is complying with GAAP, there are likely to be relatively few adjustments to the reported trading profits in order to calculate the adjusted trading profits for corporation tax purposes. It should be noted that reported trading profits in accordance with GAAP are the starting point for this calculation, but that adjustments prescribed by tax law take precedence over accounting practice.

If the starting point is taken to be the total profits as shown in the company's accounts, those profits are reduced by any non-trading income and increased by any non-deductible expenses included in the accounts. They are then increased by any trading income and decreased by any deductible expenses not included in the accounts. Appropriations of profits, such as depreciation and dividend payments, are not allowable deductions for corporation tax.

In summary, trading profits are adjusted as follows:

Net profits per accounts	+
Less:	
• Net profits from non-trading activities (see **2.10–2.11**)	–
Trading income per the accounts	
Adjustment for amounts included in the accounts:	
• Expenses with a restricted deduction (see **2.12–2.30**)	+
• Expenses or deemed expenses of a specific trade (see **2.49–2.52**)	–
• Receipts not taxable as trading income (see **2.54–2.55**)	–
• Appropriations of profit (see **2.67**)	+
Adjustment for amounts not included in the accounts:	
• Expenses with a permitted deduction (see **2.31–2.47**)	–
• Expenses or deemed expenses of a specific trade (see **2.49–2.52**)	–
• Receipts taxable as trading income (see **2.56–2.63**)	+
Adjusted trading profits before capital allowances	=

NET PROFITS FROM NON-TRADING ACTIVITIES

2.10 Income and receipts from non-trading sources will include capital items and income assessed according to its own rules (see **2.7**).

Capital versus revenue

2.11 Unless the *Corporation Tax Acts* contain provisions to the contrary, a capital receipt is not to be included in taxable trading profits (*CTA 2009,* *s 93*), and a deduction for capital expenditure in calculating profits of a trade is prohibited (*CTA 2009, s 53*).

> **Focus**
>
> There is a body of case law which has established the revenue versus capital principles. Expenditure on creating an asset, which is intended to provide an enduring benefit to the trade, is capital. Similarly, expenditure on the replacement of an asset will usually be capital expenditure, although there are exceptions, when the replacement can be shown to be effectively a repair to a larger whole, as demonstrated by the examples below.

The cost of repairing a capital asset, carried out during the course of trading activities, is a revenue expense. The cost of putting an asset into working order, or the replacement of an entire asset, is not a revenue expense. In *Law Shipping Co Ltd v CIR* (1923) 12 TC 621, the Court of Session held that expenditure on repairs to a ship in order to make it seaworthy shortly after purchase was capital expenditure. By contrast, in *Odeon Associated Theatres Ltd v Jones* (1971) 48 TC 257, the Court of Appeal held that expenditure incurred on repairs to an already useable cinema over a period of years was revenue expenditure.

In *O'Grady v Bullcroft Main Collieries Ltd* (1932) 17 TC 93, a colliery company built a factory chimney at a cost of £3,067. After several years, it became unsafe. The company built an additional, improved chimney near the site of the old one and claimed £287 of the cost as repairs. No materials from the old chimney were used in constructing the new chimney, and the old chimney was not demolished until after the new chimney had been brought into use. The High Court held that the whole of the cost was capital expenditure because the new chimney was the renewal of the old chimney in its 'entirety'.

In *Samuel Jones & Co (Devondale) Ltd v CIR* (1951) 32 TC 513, the company replaced a factory chimney without making any appreciable improvement, and also incurred costs in respect of the removal of the old chimney. The Court of Session held that the expenditure was an allowable revenue deduction because the old and new chimneys were physically, commercially and functionally an inseparable part of an entire factory, and not separate structures as in the case of *O'Grady v Bullcroft Main Collieries Ltd*.

In *Brown v Burnley Football & Athletic Co Ltd* [1980] STC 424, a stand at the football ground was found to be unsafe. It had been built in 1912 of wood and steel with a brick wall at the back. It was demolished and replaced with a new modern concrete stand. The new stand, with approximately the same capacity, was nearer the pitch but included office and other accommodation not provided by the old stand. The High Court held that the expenditure was capital expenditure because the new stand was a replacement in its entirety.

Brown v Burnley Football & Athletic Co Ltd was cited in *G Pratt & Sons* [2011] UKFTT 416 (TC), in which the First-tier Tribunal held that the complete re-surfacing of a farm driveway was a repair and therefore allowable revenue expenditure rather than capital. Similarly, in *Cairnsmill Caravan Park* [2013] UKFTT 164 (TC), the First-tier Tribunal held that the replacement of a grass surface with a hard-core surface on a caravan site was not an improvement, and was therefore allowable as a revenue expense. And in *Hopegar Properties Ltd* [2013] UKFTT 331 (TC) the First-tier Tribunal held that substantial works carried out on land and buildings amounted to repairs and were deductible.

Expenditure in connection with enduring benefits to a trade is considered to be capital. In *Atherton v British Insulated & Helsby Cables Ltd* (1925) 10 TC 155, a company set up a pension fund and made an initial lump sum contribution to enable the past service of existing staff to rank for pension. The House of Lords held that the expenditure was capital. The principle was established that expenditure was normally capital if it was made not only once and for all but also with a view to bringing into existence an asset or advantage for the enduring benefit of the trade.

In *Van den Berghs Ltd v Clark* (1935) 19 TC 390, the appellant (a UK company) had entered into a profit-sharing agreement with a competing Dutch company in 1908 and this had been intended to last until 1940. The company's payments and receipts under the agreement were treated as trading receipts and expenses. Following disagreement as to the amounts payable following the outbreak of war in 1914, the pooling arrangement was terminated in 1927 on consideration of payment of £450,000 to the UK company 'as damages'. The House of Lords held that the payment was capital and was not taxable as a trading receipt, accepting that the pooling arrangement 'related to the whole structure of the company's profit-making apparatus', and formed 'the fixed framework within which its circulating capital operated'.

In *Tucker v Granada Motorway Services Ltd* [1979] STC 393, the rent which a company paid to the Ministry of Transport for a motorway service area was calculated in part by reference to its gross takings. The gross takings included the duty on sales of tobacco. The lease was not assignable. In order to have the duty on sales of tobacco excluded from the gross takings, the company made a once-and-for-all payment of £122,220 to the Ministry of Transport. The House of Lords held that the expenditure was capital and therefore not deductible from profits. The payment had been made by the company as a once-and-for-all expenditure on an identifiable capital asset (ie the lease), designed to make that asset more advantageous.

In *Beauchamp v F W Woolworth plc* [1989] STC 510, a company entered into two loans (each for 50 million Swiss Francs) for five years, but repayable earlier (at the option of the company) subject to a payment of a graduated premium. The first loan was repaid six months early and the second on the due date, giving rise to an aggregate loss of £11.4 million due to currency exchange transactions. The House of Lords held that the loss was incurred in relation to a capital transaction and was therefore not allowable as a revenue deduction. The company had increased its capital employed and thereby obtained an asset or advantage, which endured for five years and, as such, was a capital asset. A loan is only a revenue transaction if it is part of the day-to-day incidence of carrying on the business, which was not the case in this situation. The loss was not deductible.

There can often be doubt as to whether an item of expenditure is capital or revenue. In *Heather v P-E Consulting Group Ltd* (1972) 48 TC 293, a company undertook to pay 10% of its annual profits, subject to a minimum of £5,000, to a trust set up to enable its staff to acquire shares in the company and to prevent the company from coming under the control of outside shareholders. Accountancy evidence given at the time confirmed that the expenses were of a revenue nature. The Court of Appeal made clear that, although the evidence of accountants as to accountancy practice should be given due weight in determining whether expenditure is of a capital or revenue nature, the question is one of law for the court alone to determine.

In *Rolfe v Wimpey Waste Management Ltd* [1989] STC 454, the company purchased several landfill sites on which to tip waste under a contract with its customers. The company claimed that the purchases were revenue expenditure, on the grounds that it had acquired the land in order to use the airspace above it. The High Court held that the expenditure related to the land and was therefore capital. The sites were used for a sufficiently long period to qualify as capital assets. They were not like the trading stock of a builder, because neither the sites nor any interests in them were disposed of to customers. They were essentially the places where the company carried on its business.

In *Commissioners of Inland Revenue v Coia* (1959) 38 TC 334, the respondent, a garage proprietor, had entered into an agreement with Esso Petroleum whereby Esso undertook to contribute towards the cost of purchasing additional ground, and building extensions to the respondent's garage and workshops, and in return the respondent agreed to purchase all his motor fuels exclusively from Esso for ten years. The sums payable were based on the garage proprietor's past and estimated future sales of petrol as well as on the amount spent on the extension and improvement of his premises. The Court of Session held that the sums were capital, because they represented consideration for the garage proprietor's giving up his freedom of trading and changing the structure of this part of his business.

In *Bolam (HM Inspector of Taxes) v Regent Oil Co Ltd* (1956) 37 TC 56, a petrol marketing company entered into exclusivity agreements under which a number of retailers were reimbursed certain expenditure incurred on repairs etc. The payments were based on sales of petrol, and (depending on the circumstances) were made before or after the expenditure had been incurred. The agreements were originally for a year or less but, later, to counter proposals by competitors, they were for longer periods. The High Court held that the payments were allowable deductions of the petrol marketing company, because they were made to preserve the company's goodwill and did not create capital assets.

In *Shop Direct Group and others v Commissioners for Revenue and Customs* [2014] EWCA Civ 255, the Court of Appeal held that VAT repayments and interest on them were subject to corporation tax, even though the business in respect of which the VAT refunds arose had been transferred.

See BIM35000 onwards for a discussion on the capital/revenue divide. Note that professional fees and other associated costs in connection with capital expenditure are also disallowed in computing trading income.

EXPENSES WITH A RESTRICTED DEDUCTION

2.12 The rules that restrict or allow deductions from trading income are to be found in *CTA 2009, ss 53–92*. Those specifically restricting deductions are to be found in *CTA 2009, ss 53–60A*, and general restrictions on deductions are imposed by *CTA 2009, ss 1288–1309*.

CTA 2009, s 51 governs the relationship between rules which allow trading deductions and others which prohibit such deductions, and provides that certain rules allowing deductions take precedence over those prohibiting deductions. However, in cases involving tax avoidance arrangements entered into on or after 21 December 2012, the order of priority is reversed so that a prohibitive rule has priority over a permissive rule (*CTA 2009, s 51(1A)*).

Where any amount that has been allowed as a deduction is subsequently reversed in the accounts, that reversal will be taxable.

These statutory rules are supported by a body of case law and practice that has been established over a number of years.

Wholly and exclusively

Focus

By far the most important rule restricting deductions is the 'wholly and exclusively' rule. Much of the legislation affecting the deduction of expenditure against chargeable profits is based on this simple premise.

2.13 Expenditure is only allowed as a deduction if it has been incurred 'wholly and exclusively' for the purposes of the trade or profession, and costs or losses that are unconnected with the trade cannot be deducted in calculating the profits of the trade (*CTA 2009, s 54(1)*). Company expenditure must be reviewed from this perspective.

In *McKnight v Sheppard* [1999] STC 669, the House of Lords held that expenditure on preserving a trade from destruction was treated as incurred wholly and exclusively for the purposes of the trade, even where there was an incidental risk to the personal reputation of the person incurring the expense. If part of an expense is incurred wholly and exclusively for the purposes of the trade, that portion will be an allowable deduction from profits. In practice, this means that the allowable portion of the expenditure must be readily identifiable (*CTA 2009, s 54(2)*).

Expenditure with a duality of purpose will not qualify for a deduction from trading profits. In *James Snook & Co Ltd v Blasdale* (1952) 33 TC 244, an agreement for the sale of shares of the company provided, amongst other things, that the purchaser would procure that the company pay compensation for loss of office to the directors and the auditor of the company who, under the sale agreement, were to resign. The purchasing company said that it sought the removal from office of two directors because they were of advanced years and their methods were old-fashioned. The Court of Appeal held that the compensation paid was not an allowable deduction in computing the company's profits, because the duality of purpose in the payment in this case was fatal to the claim for deduction. The mere fact that the compensation was paid on the occasion of the share sale did not make it disallowable, but the two events happening at or about the same time placed the onus on the company to show that it had considered the question of payment wholly untrammelled by the terms of the bargain its shareholders had struck with those who were to buy their shares, and that it had come to a decision to pay solely in the interests of its trade. For HMRC's views on this case, see BIM38340.

In *Vodafone Cellular v Shaw* [1997] STC 734, the Racal Group sought a licence from the DTI to run a cellular mobile telephone network. It applied for this through a joint venture company (the appellant company) which it owned jointly with M, an American company; under a 'fee agreement', M was due to receive 10% of the taxpayer company's pre-tax profits for 15 years. Later, Racal took an opportunity to buy out M's shares in the joint venture, and the fee agreement was ended by the taxpayer paying £30 million to M. The Court of Appeal held that the payment was a revenue item and, on the question of whether it was wholly and exclusively laid out for the taxpayer's trade, decided that the directors' purpose was to rid the group of a trading liability owed to a third party by the taxpayer company alone. As a consequential and incidental effect, the action of the directors benefited other companies in the group, but doing so was not their purpose, so the 'wholly and exclusively' requirement was met. For HMRC's views on this case, see BIM38220.

Trade debts written off

2.14 Trade debts, and any other non-monetary debts that are irrecoverable, are only deductible against trading profits if an impairment loss has been accounted for, or the debt has been released wholly and exclusively for the purposes of the trade as part of a statutory insolvency arrangement. An asset is impaired when its carrying amount exceeds its recoverable amount, and the loss thereon is to be recognised in the income statement using the principles of FRS 102, Section 27 *Impairment of assets* under new UK GAAP, FRS 26 *Financial instruments: recognition and measurement* under old UK GAAP or, where international accounting standards apply, those of IAS 39 *Financial instruments: recognition and measurement* – superseded from 1 January 2018 by IFRS 9 *Financial instruments*. Therefore, by applying GAAP, the company will obtain immediate bad debt relief. See **Chapter 26** regarding changes to UK GAAP.

In *Sere Properties Limited v Revenue and Customs Commissioners* [2013] UKFTT 778 (TC), the First-tier Tribunal considered a claim for relief for a bad debt, and rejected it on the grounds that the appellant company's purpose in not collecting and then subsequently writing off the debt was not solely for its own business purpose.

Repairs

2.15 The cost of a repair is normally allowable expenditure, but the cost of replacing an asset in its entirety, or making a significant improvement to it, is capital expenditure and not allowed as a deduction.

In December 2013, HMRC published a major update to their guidance on their view of what is a repair for the purposes of both trades and property businesses (see BIM46900–BIM46990).

Renewals basis

2.16 Until 31 March 2016, capital expenses incurred on replacing or altering any 'trade tools' (defined as implements, utensils or articles) were allowable as revenue. This treatment is not available after that date (*CTA 2009, s 68*, repealed by *FA 2016, s 72*; see **2.33**).

This treatment only applies to the cost of the renewal. The initial costs of the items remain as capital and therefore non-deductible, except under the capital allowances legislation. The scope of what falls within the definition of 'trade tools' was considered by the Court of Session in *Hyam v The Commissioners of Inland Revenue* (1929) 14 TC 479.

Under a concession that was withdrawn from 1 April 2013, a company incurring capital expenditure on replacing plant or machinery outside the narrow range to which *CTA 2009, s 68* applied was able to claim a revenue deduction for the replacement expenditure, if the company agreed to a number of detailed conditions. This non-statutory renewals basis fell largely into disuse as a result of the availability of 100% first year allowances and, more recently, the annual investment allowance (see **Chapter 3**), and was withdrawn as part of the government's review of all extra-statutory concessions.

Car hire charges

Existing leases that commenced on or after 1 April 2009

2.17 The car hire charges that may be deducted from trading income are restricted by a reduction of 15% (*CTA 2009, s 56*) where they relate to a car which is not:

- a car that was first registered before 1 March 2001,
- a car that has low CO_2 emissions,
- a car that is electrically propelled, or
- a qualifying hire car.

A car has low CO_2 emissions if it was first registered on the basis of a qualifying emissions certificate and its CO_2 emissions figure does not exceed 130g/km (*CTA 2009, ss 56, 57* and *CAA 2001, s 104AA*). Before 1 April 2013, the limit was 160g/km (see *FA 2013, s 68*).

For these purposes, a car is any mechanically propelled road vehicle other than:

(a) a motor cycle (within the meaning of *Road Traffic Act 1988, s 185(1)*);

(b) a vehicle of a construction primarily suited for the conveyance of goods or burden of any description; or

(c) a vehicle of a type not commonly used as a private vehicle and unsuitable for such use (*CTA 2009, s 57(1)*).

A qualifying hire car is a car which:

(i) is hired under a hire purchase agreement under which there is no option to purchase,

(ii) is hired under a hire purchase agreement under which there is an option to purchase exercisable on the payment of a sum of 1% (or less) of the retail price of the car or motor cycle when new, or

(iii) is leased under a long-funding lease (*CTA 2009, s 57(2)*).

Taxis, daily hire cars and cars leased to the disabled are therefore not exempt from the restriction on deductibility.

These rules were introduced by *FA 2009* and the restriction applies where a car is leased for a continuous period of 45 days or more. The rules do not apply to motor cycles (*CTA 2009, s 57*). If the lease includes maintenance, then maintenance costs should be excluded if separately identified in the lease agreement. The lease costs will include the related VAT charge if the company is VAT registered. The restriction does not apply to the hire of low CO_2 emission cars or electric cars if the hire period commences before 1 April 2013 (*CTA 2009, s 58*).

The deductibility of costs of cars purchased by means of a hire purchase agreement is also restricted in this way. *CTA 2010, s 1129* defines a hire purchase agreement as an agreement in respect of which conditions A, B and C are met:

Condition A

- that, under the agreement, goods are bailed (or, in Scotland, hired) in return for periodical payments by the person to whom they are bailed (or hired).

Condition B

- that, under the agreement, the property in the goods will pass to the person to whom they are bailed (or hired) if the terms of the agreement are complied with and one or more of the following events occurs:
  - the exercise of an option to purchase by that person,
  - the doing of another specified act by any party to the agreement, or
  - the happening of another specified event.

Condition C

- that the agreement is not a conditional sale agreement.

A conditional sale agreement is an agreement for the sale of goods whereby the purchase price or part is payable by instalments, and the property in the goods remains with the seller until the conditions specified in the agreement are met. In the meantime, the goods may physically be in the possession of the buyer.

Existing leases that commenced before 1 April 2009

2.18 For leases entered into before 1 April 2009, the previous restriction rules continue to apply for the duration of the lease (*CTA 2009, s 56(2)* before amendment by *FA 2009, Sch 11, para 47*).

Where the retail price of a new car (except an electric car with low CO_2 emissions) or a motor cycle exceeds £12,000 and is hired for the purposes of the trade, the hire charge is reduced for tax purposes by using the formula (£12,000 + RP) / 2RP, where RP is the retail price of the vehicle when new.

Note that motor cycles were subject to a possible restriction under the pre-April 2009 regime but are not thereafter.

Patent royalties

2.19 Patent royalties paid are not deductible against trading profits for corporation tax purposes. Instead, they fall within the intangible fixed assets regime (see **Chapter 12**).

Integral features

2.20 Expenditure on integral features within buildings is not deductible; instead, it may be eligible for capital allowances (see **Chapter 3**).

Business entertainment and gifts

2.21 A company's expenditure on entertainment or gifts is disallowed as a deduction in computing profits, even though it may be incurred in connection with a trade or business that the company carries on (*CTA 2009, s 1298*). This provision overrides the decision in *Bentleys, Stokes and Lowless v Beeson* (1952) 33 TC 491, where a firm of solicitors discussed business affairs with clients at lunch and it had been held that the costs were deductible because there was a business purpose.

The definition of business entertainment includes hospitality of any kind (*CTA 2009, s 1298(5)(b)*). This applies regardless of whether the hospitality is provided free or at a subsidised price. However, in *Celtic Football and Athletic Club Ltd v Customs & Excise Commrs* [1983] STC 470, a case concerning VAT, the Court of Session held that hospitality is not business entertainment if it was given 'pursuant to a legal obligation in return for which it obtains proper and sufficient *quid pro quo*. The *quid pro quo* may be cash or it may be goods or services'. This also extends to a contractual obligation a company may have to provide hospitality (eg as part of a package).

Relief for entertaining expenditure is denied as a deduction not only in calculating trading profits, but also in connection with any business which it carries on. The disallowance applies also in calculating the profits of a property business and in calculating management expenses (*CTA 2009, s 1298(1)–(2)*). The prohibition applies to sums put at the disposal of, or reimbursed to, an employee for meeting the expenditure incurred on entertaining or the provision of a gift (*CTA 2009, s 1298(3)*). Assets used for business entertainment do not qualify for capital allowances. Travel costs associated with business entertainment are not allowable expenses, but exceptions exist such as employees travelling to meet a client.

The entertaining expenditure that any company incurs in entertaining its own staff, including directors and employees, is an exception to the rule regardless of the nature of the company's trade or business. It will be an allowable deduction if incurred wholly and exclusively for the purposes of that trade or business. This does not mean to say that taxable benefits in kind will not arise on the employees concerned (see *Income Tax 2016/17* (Bloomsbury Professional)). The cost of third party entertainment is prohibited as a deduction from business profits of any kind, as is expenditure in entertaining employees if it is incidental to the entertainment of third parties (*CTA 2009, s 1299*).

Another exception occurs if the company's trade consists of the provision of entertainment: any expenses incurred wholly and exclusively for the purposes of that trade, even though of an entertainment nature, will be an allowable deduction from the profits of that trade, eg hospitality provided by restaurants and pubs. In *Fleming v Associated Newspapers Ltd* (1972) 48 TC 382, the House of Lords considered this in relation to a company carrying on the business of publishing newspapers. Although their Lordships held that expenses incurred by its journalists in entertaining their informants were not deductible, their judgments provide helpful analyses of the legislation.

If a company incurs entertainment expenditure in advertising its trade to the public generally, that is an allowable deduction from trading profits. Advertising and promotion costs will normally be allowed, but there can be a fine line between advertising or promotion and hospitality or entertainment. The Special Commissioners considered this in *Netlogic Consulting Ltd v HMRC* [2005] SpC 477, where a company had incurred costs on room hire and entertaining potential customers in order to gain firm orders, and held that the entertaining costs were disallowed but the room hire cost was deductible.

If a company gifts an item that it provides in the normal course of its trade or business to advertise the product to the public generally, the expenditure incurred will be an allowable deduction from trade or business profits. The costs of any other gifts incorporating conspicuous advertisements for the company are deductible, if not exceeding £50 to any one person in any accounting period, but gifts of food, drink, tobacco or tokens or vouchers exchangeable for goods are not deductible in any event.

The costs of providing gifts to employees are deductible in full, unless gifts are also provided to third parties and the gifts to employees are incidental to the gifts to third parties. Where gifts are made to employees, taxable benefits in kind may arise on the employees concerned (see *Income Tax 2016/17* (Bloomsbury Professional)). Gifts made to a charity, the Historic Buildings and Monuments Commission for England or the Trustees of the National Heritage Memorial Fund are deductible in calculating profits (*CTA 2009, s 1300*).

Remuneration

Employees

2.22 Provided the remuneration charged is 'wholly and exclusively' for the purposes of the trade, it should be an allowable deduction (*Copeman v*

Flood (William) & Sons Ltd (1940) 24 TC 53; *LG Berry Investments Ltd v Attwooll* (1964) 41 TC 547). The existence of a contractual obligation to pay the employee will help to substantiate the company's claim to deduct the remuneration and related employment costs, normally at the same time that the remuneration is treated as taxable on the employee.

In order to qualify as a deduction from profits in the accounting period in which it is charged or provided in the company's accounts, remuneration must be paid to the employee no later than nine months after the end of the period of account. If remuneration is not paid by that time, it becomes deductible only in the period of account in which it is paid. If such remuneration is never paid, it never qualifies as deductible (*CTA 2009, ss 1288, 1289*).

Corresponding rules apply to the deductibility of remuneration as management expenses (*CTA 2009, ss 1249, 1250*). If profits are computed for corporation tax purposes earlier than nine months after the end of the period of account, it must be assumed that any remuneration charged or provided in the accounts but not yet paid will not be paid before the end of that period; if such remuneration is then paid before the end of the period, any tax return may be amended accordingly (*CTA 2009, ss 1250(3), 1295*).

The provisions of *ITEPA 2003* will determine when and how the remuneration is to be taxed on the employee (see *Income Tax 2016/17* (Bloomsbury Professional).

Directors

2.23 For company law purposes, a director is any person occupying the position of director by whatever name called (*CA 2006, s 250*), and this includes a 'shadow director' – ie any person in accordance with whose instructions directors are accustomed to act, with the exception of a professional adviser (*CA 2006, s 251*). A similar definition is used for income tax purposes (*ITEPA 2003, s 67*).

The time that remuneration is due and payable to a director is determined by the director's service agreement or contract of employment (if any) or by resolution of the members of the company in general meeting or any equivalent act by the members (eg a resolution by the members approving the company's accounts), while *ITEPA 2003* determines when and how the remuneration is to be taxed on the director.

Directors are treated as having received earnings at the time when they become entitled to be paid them. However, an entitlement to payment is not necessarily the same as the date on which the employee acquires a right to be paid (HMRC Employment Income Manual at EIM42300).

The terms of a service agreement may be written, oral or implied and may give entitlement to a regular salary or a contractual bonus or other sums. The director would then enjoy rights to earnings under the agreement. The time at which entitlement to earnings under a service agreement arises will be governed by the terms of the agreement.

On the practical side, it may be helpful to consider whether employment contracts are in place for directors of close companies. Such directors have the ability to withdraw available funds at will from the company, normally under the rationale that funds are available. Unless this can be proven at the outset by inclusion, say, in a contract, any additional payment may be queried as being not wholly and exclusively for the purposes of the trade.

Remuneration of directors and employees is normally paid under deduction of PAYE (see *Income Tax 2016/17* (Bloomsbury Professional)). By concession, if fees from a directorship are paid directly to a professional partnership or company and treated as part of the income of that partnership or company, HMRC will accept in most cases that PAYE need not be applied (Concession A37; EIM02500). HMRC, when notified, will issue an 'NT' coding: PAYE will not be due on these payments, but the payments will still be liable to Class 1 NICs (EIM02501, EIM03002). Where a partnership is involved in this way, the directorship must be a normal activity of the professional partnership, the fees must be only a small part of the partnership profits, and under the partnership agreement the fees must be pooled for division amongst the partners. Where a company receives the fees, it must have a right to appoint a director to the board of the other company or, if not, it must be a company trading in the UK and not controlled by the director in question and his immediate family, and furthermore the director must have agreed to hand it all his fees from the directorship. In either case the director and the company appointing him should review the situation carefully to ensure that the exact requirements of ESC A37 are met. There is also a possibility that the payment might fall within the IR35 personal services regime, which can apply equally to a partnership as to a company (see **2.50**).

A director or employee may provide services to a company in a separate business capacity. For example, the individual could be carrying on an established business as a solicitor, estate agent, accountant or consultant, whereby services are supplied to the company on terms similar to those given to the individual's other customers. In such circumstances, the payment to the director or employee might not be treated as employment income and thus not be subject to PAYE or NICs (HMRC Employment Status Manual at ESM4040, ESM4022).

Employee benefit trusts

2.24 An employee benefit trust (EBT) is a discretionary trust set up by an employer for the benefit of its employees and directors. EBTs can be resident in the UK or offshore, and can be subject to UK or foreign law. An 'offshore' EBT is only liable to UK income tax on its UK source income and is not liable to UK capital gains tax. An EBT is managed by trustees, who are usually appointed by the company. The trust fund will comprise of: (a) the initial amount settled by the employer to establish the trust, (b) subsequent contributions from the employer, and (c) sums paid to the trustees by third parties. The beneficiaries and (if applicable) the perpetuity period will be defined in the trust deed (BIM44500 onwards).

EBTs are used with employee share schemes, retirement benefit schemes, accident benefit schemes and healthcare trusts. EBTs set up with employee share schemes are called employee share ownership trusts (ESOTs); they can also be known as employee share ownership plan (ESOP) trusts. ESOTs may be used by unquoted companies to provide a market that might otherwise not exist for employees' shares (acquired through employee share schemes), maintain shareholder control and help with business planning and management buy-outs.

Established case law has determined that, where the trust is set up for the benefit of employees, the contributions meet the 'wholly and exclusively' test (*Heather v P-E Consulting Group Ltd* (1972) 48 TC 293; *Rutter v Charles Sharpe & Co Ltd* (1979) 53 TC 163; *Jeffs v Ringtons Ltd* (1985) 58 TC 680; *E Bott Ltd v Price* (1986) 59 TC 437). In *Mawsley Machinery Ltd v Robinson* [1998] STC (SCD) 236 the 'wholly and exclusively' test was not met because the reason for the contributions was to facilitate a share purchase (BIM44565).

There is no corporation tax deduction for amounts put into an EBT by an employer until the amount becomes taxable earnings of the employee. For this to occur, the contributions must be paid to the employee no later than nine months after the end of the period of account in question in a form on which PAYE and NICs are charged (*CTA 2009, s 1290*). Securities and options are included as benefits (*F(No 2)A 2005, s 12, Sch 2*; *MacDonald v Dextra Accessories Ltd* [2005] STC 1111). The same criteria are applied in *JT Dove Ltd v Revenue and Customs Comrs* [2010] UKFTT 16 (TC).

2.25 A deduction can be allowed in a later period of account when the benefits are paid. If a deduction has been disallowed under these provisions because the qualifying benefits had not been paid within nine months of the end of the period of account, a later deduction can only be allowed as long as the associated income tax and NICs are paid within 12 months of the end of the period in which the deduction would otherwise be allowable (*CTA 2009, s 1290* amended by *F(No 2)A 2017, s 37*).

However, where the remuneration is paid more than five years after the end of the period of account in which the contributions are made, no deduction is due for remuneration paid on or after 1 April 2017 (*CTA 2009, s 1290* amended by *F(No 2)A 2017, s 37*).

Pension contributions

2.26 Payments to a pension scheme are a revenue expense and will be deductible from profits in the year in which the premium is paid (*FA 2004, s 196(2)(b)*) if the payment meets the 'wholly and exclusively for the purposes of the trade' test. Under FRS 102, Section 28 *Employee benefits* in new UK GAAP, FRS 17 *Retirement benefits* in old UK GAAP or IAS 19 *Employee benefits* under international accounting standards, the amounts included in the profit and loss account will be based on actuarial assumptions and are unlikely to be the same as the premiums actually paid for the year. Thus, an adjustment will be required for corporation tax purposes that may also be reflected in the deferred tax account (see **Chapter 26**).

Pension contributions paid by a company in respect of its directors or employees are allowable unless there is an identifiable non-trade purpose. HMRC have highlighted the following circumstances where, depending on the facts or the circumstances at the time, there may be a non-trade purpose:

- contributions paid in respect of a controlling director (ie a director who owns more than 20% of the company's share capital) or an employee who is a relative or close friend of the controlling director or proprietor of the business;
- contributions made as part of the arrangements for going out of business, in particular where there is no pre-existing contractual obligation to make such a contribution;
- contribution is required to be made pursuant to *Pensions Act 1995, s 75*;
- where, following the issue of a notice by the Pensions Regulator, a person is required to pay a pension contribution;
- where a contribution is in respect of orphaned liabilities;
- contributions made as part of the bargain struck for the purposes of facilitating the sale of shares in a subsidiary;
- contributions made in connection with the pension deficit of another company's trade where the reputation of the payer's trade or the morale of its staff is not the sole purpose behind the contribution (BIM46030, BIM38250, BIM46065).

Contributions in respect of a controlling director or an employee who is a relative or close friend of the controlling director or proprietor of the business may be queried by HMRC. In establishing whether a payment is for the purposes of the trade, they will examine the company's intentions in making the payment. If the level of the remuneration package is excessive for the value of the work undertaken for the employer by that individual, the contribution may be queried. The pension contribution will be viewed in the light of the overall remuneration package. HMRC acknowledge that employers may make increased pension contributions to remedy under-funding, and will look at the full facts of the case.

HMRC will accept that contributions in respect of a director of a close company, or an employee who is a relative or close friend of the director, are paid wholly and exclusively for the purposes of the trade where the remuneration package paid is comparable with that paid to unconnected employees performing duties of similar value. The proportion of any amount not so expended will be disallowed (BIM46035, BIM47105).

Where there is an undertaking to provide a pension under an employee's contract of employment, the contributions are allowable deductions from profits. Where there is no undertaking to provide a pension, the contributions in doing so are still deductible if they can be shown to have been incurred wholly and exclusively for the purposes of the trade – and, for this purpose, HMRC generally regard contributions made to preserve the reputation and morale of the staff as allowable. However, a contribution for the purpose of going out of business or for any other non-business purpose will not generally be regarded as allowable (BIM46040).

Pension contributions in respect of other group company employees whose current employer can no longer contribute are generally deductible by the payer company. The matter may require further investigation if the current employer is in a position to contribute and the payer company's contribution has not been recharged to the current employer (BIM46065).

Pension contributions paid in connection with the sale or transfer of the shares of a subsidiary company may not necessarily be for the purposes of the trade of the parent company that is paying them. It is important for the parent company to be able to demonstrate that the pension contributions are unrelated to the sale of the company. Again, HMRC regard contributions made to preserve the reputation and morale of the staff as an allowable deduction (BIM46060).

Asset-backed pension contributions

> **Focus**
>
> Special rules aim to ensure that the amount of tax relief given to employers using asset-backed pension scheme arrangements reflects accurately the total amount of payments that the employer makes to the pension scheme directly or through a special purpose vehicle (eg a partnership).

2.27 The legislation in *FA 2004* covering pensions tax relief allows contributions to be deducted as an expense in computing the profits of a trade or investment business. Tax relief is only given for contributions that have actually been paid. Any contributions must be monetary contributions, although it is possible for an employer to enter into an offset arrangement so that the debt for the contribution is offset against a debt to purchase an asset from the employer. In such arrangements, the contribution is paid on the date when the employer and pension offset the two debts.

Certain funding arrangements are structured in such a way that the employer receives a deduction for the contribution paid to a pension scheme upfront, but the pension scheme only receives the cash payments over the term of the arrangement. Where the arrangement involves an asset and this asset generates an income stream to the pension scheme, it had been possible before legislation introduced in *FA 2012* for the employer to obtain both a deduction for the pension contribution upfront and then receive another deduction for income payments derived from the asset – giving them tax relief which the government considered excessive.

Some such asset-backed pension contribution arrangements provide for a 'final bullet payment' to be made at the end of the arrangement period, but only if the pension deficit remains at that time; and, where the final bullet payment has not been made or has been less than the amount of tax relief received upfront, the government also considered that excessive tax relief had been obtained at the outset.

Legislation in *CTA 2010, Pt 16, Ch 2* applies where a company enters into a 'structured finance arrangement' under which, in accordance with UK or international GAAP, 'the borrower' records in its accounts a financial liability in respect of the lump sum advance paid by 'the lender'. Where an asset-backed pension funding arrangement falls within the structured finance arrangement rules, excessive tax relief does not arise.

The government announced on 29 November 2011 that legislation would take effect from that date to ensure that the amount of tax relief given to employers using asset-backed arrangements reflects accurately the total amount of payments the employer makes to the pension scheme, either directly or through a special purpose vehicle (eg a partnership).

Another announcement on 22 February 2012 stated that further legislation would take effect from that later date to ensure that upfront relief is not given unless the total of all asset-backed payments to the pension scheme is fixed from the outset.

The Budget on 21 March 2012 announced additional revenue protection provisions to recover relief when an employer ceases to be chargeable to tax (eg on cessation or migration), anti-abuse provisions to ensure that no person will be placed in a more advantageous tax position as a result of the application of the revenue protection rules published on 22 February 2012, and related amendments to the structured finance legislation within *CTA 2010, Ch 16, Pt 2* or *ITA 2007, Pt 13, Ch 5B*.

All these measures, enacted in *FA 2012* and taking effect variously from 29 November 2011, 22 February 2012 and 21 March 2012, aim to remove any unintended and excessive tax relief being given to an employer in respect of any asset-backed contributions made to their pension schemes, while retaining as much flexibility as possible for employers to continue to be able to use acceptable asset-backed arrangements to help manage their pension deficits (*FA 2012, s 48, Sch 13*).

For a contribution paid on or after 29 November 2011 but before 22 February 2012, if the arrangement is accounted for in accordance with the structured finance rules, then tax relief in the form of an upfront tax deduction is given for the asset-backed contribution in the period of account in which it is paid. Relief is also available under the structured finance rules for the element of subsequent income payments that is accounted for as a finance charge (*FA 2012, Sch 13, Pt 1*).

Transitional rules apply: where an asset-backed arrangement has been established and the employer contribution paid before 29 November 2011, the transitional provisions introduced from 29 November apply to payments that arise from 29 November where the arrangement comes to an end on or after 29 November 2011. A balancing tax charge can arise if the treatment is changed from initially being under the structured finance rules, and anti-avoidance measures will apply where the main purpose of an arrangement to change from the structured finance rules is to obtain excessive relief (*FA 2012, Sch 13, Pt 2*).

If qualifying conditions introduced from 22 February 2012 are met and the arrangement is recognised in the accounts of the employer (or the special purpose vehicle, if used) as a financial liability to which the structured finance arrangement rules apply, then tax relief in the form of an upfront tax deduction is available for an asset-backed contribution paid on or after 22 February 2012, with the relief being given in the period of account in which the contribution is paid. If the arrangement does not meet all the conditions, upfront tax relief is unavailable and relief is only available for subsequent income payments made to the pension scheme under the arrangement (*FA 2012, Sch 13, Pt 3*). Transitional rules apply (*FA 2012, Sch 13, Pt 4*).

Upfront relief continues to be given, provided that the relevant conditions are met. This does not preclude the employer from suspending the regular payments if the value of the pension scheme assets is greater than the value of the pension scheme liabilities. Any suspension or similar change (eg in relation to the original value or schedule of payments) triggers the application of the revenue protection rules, in that a balancing tax charge arises to recover tax relief from the employer by treating the outstanding financial liability immediately before the suspension or change as a profit on a loan relationship. The balancing tax charge is the amount of the outstanding financial liability immediately before it is reduced or no longer recognised in the accounts.

Where the contribution to an asset-backed arrangement was initially accounted for as a financial liability and has gained upfront relief because the arrangement is an acceptable structured finance arrangement, but subsequently changes so that the liability is reduced by an event other than the making of payments by the employer, any excess relief is recovered at the time when the event occurs. If the liability is no longer shown in the accounts, then a balancing tax charge arises similar to the case of payment suspension as mentioned above.

A supplementary provision provides that a reference to a disposal of an asset in the legislation includes (a) anything constituting a disposal of an asset for the purposes of *TCGA 1992* and (b) the taking of any step by virtue of which a person receives an asset, such as the issuing of shares or any instrument creating or acknowledging indebtedness. This is to ensure that all types of asset transfers in relation to asset-backed arrangements are covered (*FA 2004, s 196L(5)*).

The revenue protection provisions taking effect from 21 March 2012 can affect asset-backed arrangements where the contribution is paid:

- before 29 November 2011. For these arrangements, the transitional provisions apply and the revenue protection provisions only have effect on a post-21 March cessation.
- between 29 November 2011 and 21 February 2012. For these arrangements, the transitional provisions apply to payments that arise on or after 22 February and also in circumstances where such an arrangement comes to an end on or after 22 February. The revenue protection provisions only have effect on a cessation that occurs on or after 21 March.
- on or after 22 February 2012. However, for those arrangements where contributions are paid between 22 February 2012 and 20 March 2012, the revenue protection provisions only take effect if the employer ceases to be chargeable to tax on or after 21 March 2012.

For further information on asset-backed pension contribution arrangements, see HMRC's Pensions Tax Manual at PTM043300–PTM043340.

Pension contribution spreading rules

2.28 Contributions paid by an employer to a registered pension scheme in respect of an individual are deductible in the period in which they are paid (subject to the spreading provisions described below) if the company is carrying on a trade, or deductible as management expenses if the company has an investment business (*FA 2004, s 196*).

If the contribution paid in the current chargeable period (CCCP) exceeds 210% of the contribution paid in the previous chargeable period (CPCP), the payments made in the second period may have to be spread forward. To ascertain whether or not spreading is required, the company must calculate its relevant excess contributions by deducting 110% of CPCP from CCCP. If the current and previous chargeable periods are of unequal length, CPCP is adjusted proportionately in order to determine the excess (if any). Note that a chargeable period is defined as a period of account in relation to trading income, but as an accounting period in relation to management expenses of a company with investment business (*FA 2004, s 197*).

The rules for spreading the relevant excess contributions are specified by *FA 2004, s 197(5)* as follows:

Relevant excess contributions	*Relevant excess deductible*
Under £500,000	Current chargeable period (no spreading required)
£500,000 to £999,999	Evenly over current and next chargeable period
£1,000,000 to £1,999,999	Evenly over current and next 2 chargeable periods
£2,000,000 or more	Evenly over current and next 3 chargeable periods

Example 2.1—Whether pension contributions have to be spread

Facts

Wishbone Ltd made pension contributions of £270,000 in the year ended 31 December 2014. In the year ended 31 December 2015, it makes contributions of £797,000.

Analysis

Test 1:

Does CCCP exceed 210% of CPCP? (*FA 2004, s 197(1)*):

	£
CCCP	797,000
210% × CPCP = 210% × £270,000	567,000
Excess	230,000

Conclusion: CCCP exceeds 210% of CPCP, so *FA 2004, s 197* applies.

Test 2:

Are relevant excess contributions less than £500,000? (*FA 2004, s 197(3)*)

	£
CCCP	797,000
Less 110% × £270,000	297,000
Relevant excess contributions	500,000

Conclusion: The relevant excess contributions amount to £500,000 or more, so spreading is required in accordance with *FA 2004, s 197(4)–(5)*.

Example 2.2—Effect of spreading pension contributions

Facts

As in Example 2.1.

Analysis

Wishbone Ltd's pension contribution relief of £797,000 for the year ended 31 December 2015 is spread as follows:

		£
Year ending 31 December 2015	£797,000 – £250,000	547,000
Year ending 31 December 2016		250,000

Employers should note that an employee may suffer adverse tax consequences in the form of an annual allowance charge if the aggregate contributions by the employer and employee in respect of that employee exceed the annual allowance (usually £40,000 in 2016/17, but it can be higher or lower in individual cases). Likewise, if an employee's tax-exempt fund, or its equivalent value in benefits, exceeds the lifetime allowance (usually £1.25m in 2015/16, falling to £1m in 2016/17), it is likely that they will eventually face extra tax in the form of a lifetime allowance charge; however, there have been a number of opportunities to protect higher lifetime allowance limits. For further details, see *Income Tax 2016/17* (Bloomsbury Professional).

Pension contributions on commencement of trade

2.29 The cost of setting up a registered pension scheme is capital expenditure and is not an allowable deduction (*Atherton v British Insulated and Helsby Cables Ltd* (1925) 10 TC 155; *Rowntree and Co Ltd v Curtis* (1924) 8 TC 678).

Pension contributions arising from pension scheme obligations taken over on the purchase of a pre-existing trade as part of the acquisition of the trade are treated as revenue expenditure (*FA 2004, s 196(2)*).

Pension contributions on cessation of trade

2.30 Payments by an employer, who has ceased trading, into a registered pension scheme to satisfy a liability falling due under *Pensions Act 1995, s 75* or *Pensions (Northern Ireland) Order 1995, SI 1995/3213 (NI 22), art 75* are deductible against total taxable profits of the final period of trading. The payment is treated as being made on the last day of trading (*FA 2004, s 199*). Thus, it is not necessary for this income to be relieved under the provisions relating to allowable deductions from post-cessation receipts (*CTA 2009, s 196(1), (2)*).

Under-funding contributions made as a result of a direction issued by the Pensions Regulator are normally allowable against profits; and, if the direction results in the employer making a payment after the trade has ceased, the payment is treated as being made on the last day of trading (*FA 2004, s 199(4)*; BIM46050).

EXPENSES WITH A PERMITTED DEDUCTION

Pre-trading expenses

2.31 Expenditure that a company incurs during the seven years before it starts to carry on a trade, which it cannot relieve because it has no trading income for that trade as yet, but would be allowed if the trade had commenced, is treated as being incurred on the date on which the company starts to carry on that trade (*CTA 2009, s 61*). There is also relief for pre-loan relationship expenditure under the loan relationship rules of *CTA 2009, s 330* (see **11.11**).

Tenants under taxed leases

2.32 The company as tenant or sub-tenant may be required to pay its landlord a capital sum, such as a premium, in respect of a property which it occupies for the purposes of its trade. If so, the landlord will be charged to tax on this receipt, known as a 'taxed receipt', if the remaining duration of the lease or the period for which the sum is payable is 50 years or less (see also **7.14–7.21**). This is essentially a capital receipt that is taxed partly as income – the idea being that the longer the lease, the more the premium is treated as payment for the purchase of an asset, while the shorter the lease, the more it is treated as akin to rent. The legislation is balanced, giving relief to the trading tenant on that part of the premium charged as income of the landlord. The relief is dependent on the amount that has been charged on the landlord, and the period for which the tenant occupies the property for trading purposes. The relief is calculated in the same way as the deduction that would apply if the company were carrying on a property business – see **7.17** (*CTA 2009, ss 62–67*).

A daily amount is calculated according to the formula:

$$\frac{A}{TRP}$$

where A is the landlord's taxable receipt and TRP is the number of days in the taxed receipt period for that particular taxed receipt (*CTA 2009, s 233(6)*).

Example 2.3—Deduction in respect of lease premium

Facts

Golding Ltd has been informed that its landlord has a taxed receipt from the lease premium payment of £7,300. The lease runs from 1 January 2014 for 10 years. Golding Ltd prepares accounts to 31 December each year.

Analysis

The daily deduction for the premium payable is

$$\frac{£7{,}300}{365 \times 10} = £2$$

The annual deduction for the premium payable is £2 × 365 = £730

If the tenant occupies only part of the property for which the landlord paid the premium, the deduction is apportioned according to the proportion occupied.

Before 1 April 2013, where the payment related to a lease of more than 50 years, a premium was also treated as being within this regime if it was unlikely that the lease would continue beyond a period shorter than 50 years and the premium was not substantially greater than it would have been had the lease been for that shorter period (*CTA 2009, s 243(1), Rule 1*). From 1 April 2013, such relief is unavailable to a trader or intermediate landlord that pays a lease premium on a lease that is only deemed to be short because of the operation of *Rule 1* (*CTA 2009, ss 63, 232*).

Replacement and alteration of trade tools

2.33 Expenditure incurred on acquiring, replacing or altering tools used in a trade is capital by nature. However, where this would otherwise mean that no deduction is available, a specific deduction is granted for replacing or altering any implement, utensil or article used in the trade. This deduction is no longer be available for costs incurred after 1 April 2016 (*CTA 2009, s 68*, repealed by *FA 2016, s 72*; see **2.16**).

Flood defence relief

2.34 From 1 January 2015 a company's net contributions of money or services to partnership funding schemes for Flood and Coastal Erosion Risk Management (FCERM) projects are deductible from profits of a trade or property business or as management expenses of an investment business for corporation tax purposes, if no disqualifying benefit has arisen (*CTA 2009, ss 86A, 86B, 210, 1244A, 1253A*, as inserted by *FA 2015, s 35, Sch 5*).

EXPENDITURE IN CONNECTION WITH EMPLOYEES

Payments for restrictive undertakings

2.35 Certain items in relation to employee expenditure are specifically allowable against profits of a trade. Payments to employees in consideration for restricting their conduct or activities, although treated as employee earnings under *ITEPA 2003, ss 225, 226,* are capital by nature. However, a deduction is granted against taxable profits in the accounting period in which the payment is made or is treated as being made (*CTA 2009, s 69*).

Employees seconded to charities and educational establishments

2.36 If a trading company seconds an employee to a charity or an educational establishment on a basis that is stated and intended to be temporary, the costs of that person's employment during the time of his or her secondment are an allowable deduction against the employer company's trading profits. The educational establishment must be situated within the UK and must meet certain pre-defined criteria. For this purpose, there are three differing definitions of 'educational establishment', depending on whether that body is in England and Wales, Scotland or Northern Ireland (*CTA 2009, ss 70, 71*).

Payroll giving – contributions to agents' expenses

2.37 A trading company may operate a payroll deduction scheme, whereby it deducts voluntary charitable donations from its employees' salaries and pays them to an agent who operates the scheme. In these circumstances, the employer is allowed a deduction for expenses incurred in operating the scheme (*CTA 2009, s 72*).

Counselling and retraining expenses

> **Focus**
>
> With the high level of forced redundancies in recent years and the strong emphasis on the need to create new jobs during the current economic recovery, the tax relief available for counselling and retraining costs is important to some employers.

2.38 A trading company may incur expenditure on the provision of counselling and other outplacement services to employees or former employees at or around the time their employment with the company ceases. If the conditions of *ITEPA 2003, s 310* are met, the costs of providing such services are deductible against the employer's trading profits, but the costs are not a taxable benefit on the employee. The conditions are, broadly, that (*CTA 2009, s 73*):

- the services are in connection with a change of employment;
- the services are to assist the person in finding gainful employment or self-employment;
- the services consist of giving advice, improving skills or allowing the use of equipment or facilities;
- the person has been continually employed in the job concerned for a period of two years ending with the earlier of the time when the services began to be provided or, if earlier, the time when the employment ceased;
- the opportunity to receive the services on similar terms is available generally to all employees and former employees or to a particular class or classes of employees; and
- any travelling expenses claimed are such as would have been allowable if the employment had continued and if receiving the services had been one of the duties of that employment.

Retraining courses

2.39 The costs incurred in a retraining course for an employee or former employee are deductible against trading profits if the following conditions are met (*CTA 2009, s 74*):

- the course must last no longer than two years;
- the course is designed to create or enhance employment or self-employment skills;

- the employee commences the course whilst employed by the employer or within one year after the employment ceases;
- the employee ceases to be employed by the employer within a period of two years beginning with the end of the course and is not re-employed by the employer within a period of two years after that employment ceases;
- the employee has been employed by the employer for a period of two years upon commencement of the course or (if earlier) when leaving the employment;
- the opportunity to undertake the course on similar terms is available generally to all employees and former employees or to a particular class or classes of employees; and
- any travelling expenses claimed are such as would have been allowable if the employment had continued and if attendance at the course had been one of the duties of that employment .

The employer must give HMRC notice within 60 days if, subsequently, it becomes clear that the employee retraining conditions are not met – eg if the employee commences the course after one year of leaving the employment, or if the employee does not cease to be employed by the company within a period of two years after the end of the course. HMRC can raise a discovery assessment under *FA 1998, Sch 18, para 41* if the employer fails to provide this notice (*CTA 2009, s 75*).

Redundancy payments

2.40 A statutory redundancy payment is an allowable deduction in the accounting period in which it is paid. If paid after the trade has ceased, it is treated as being paid on the last day of trading (*CTA 2009, s 77*).

If the payment relates partly to the company's trade and partly to one or more other activities, it is to be split on a just and reasonable basis between the two, and the portion allocated to the trade will be deductible against trading income (*CTA 2009, s 78*). If the company employer permanently ceases to carry on a trade or part of a trade and makes a payment to the employee in addition, that payment is also treated as an allowable deduction in the same manner (*CTA 2009, s 79*). Where there are changes in a partnership, the employer is treated as permanently ceasing to carry on the trade unless a company carrying on the trade in partnership immediately before the change continues to carry it on in partnership after the change (*CTA 2009, s 80*). Employee redundancy payments that are payable by an employer, but are in fact paid by the government under the *Employment Rights Act 1996* or the *Employment Rights (Northern Ireland) Order 1996, art 202* and then recovered from the company, are nonetheless allowable deductions for the employer company (*CTA 2009, s 81*).

Contributions to local enterprise organisations or urban regeneration companies

2.41 Contributions by a trading company to a local enterprise organisation or an urban regeneration company are allowable against trading income under *CTA 2009, s 82* even if they would not otherwise be allowable, but the amount so allowed is reduced by the value of any disqualifying benefit arising in connection with the contributions. A benefit is a disqualifying benefit if the costs of obtaining it, had they been incurred by the company contributor directly in a transaction at arm's length, would be disallowed in calculating the profits of the trade. If the value of the qualifying benefits exceeds the amount of the contributions, the excess is treated as a receipt of the trade or, if appropriate, a post-cessation receipt (*CTA 2009, s 82*). Reference should be made to *CTA 2009, ss 83–86* for full details of the qualifying organisations.

Scientific research

2.42 Expenditure of a revenue nature on research and development undertaken by or on behalf of the company that is related to the trade is an allowable deduction (*CTA 2009, s 87*). Expenditure on the acquisition of research and development rights is not included, since this would be capital by nature. Research and development is related to the trade if it may lead to or facilitate an extension of the trade. Research and development expenditure of a medical nature, which has a special relation to the welfare of workers employed in the trade, is also treated as related to the trade. The same research and development expenditure may not be allowed under these provisions in relation to more than one trade (*CTA 2009, s 87*).

If a trading company pays a scientific research association (as defined by *CTA 2010, s 491*) which has as its object the undertaking of research and development that may lead to or facilitate an extension of the class of trade to which the company belongs, or pays an approved university, college, research institute or other similar institution for scientific research related to that class of trade, the sum is allowed as a deduction against trading income for the accounting period in which it is paid (*CTA 2009, s 88*).

See also **Chapter 14** for further details regarding research and development.

Expenses connected with patents, designs or trademarks

2.43 A deduction is allowed for expenses incurred on the grant or extension of a patent's term, or in connection with a rejected or abandoned application, provided such expenditure was incurred for the purposes of the trade (*CTA 2009, s 89*). A deduction is also allowed for expenses incurred in registering a design or trademark, or for extending the term or renewal of registration (*CTA 2009, s 90*). However, see **Chapter 12** in respect of expenditure on intangible fixed assets, in both cases. See also **Chapter 13** for details of the UK Patent Box regime.

Export Credits Guarantee Department and FSMA 2000

2.44 Sums paid to the Export Credits Guarantee Department are deductible if incurred for the purposes of the trade (*CTA 2009, s 91*). Levies payable under the *Financial Services and Markets Act 2000 (FSMA 2000)* are deductible if incurred for the purposes of the trade (*CTA 2009, s 92*). A repayment of a *FSMA 2000* levy is treated as a trading receipt (*CTA 2009, s 104*).

Relief for employee share acquisitions

2.45 Approved share incentive plans are given specific statutory deductions (*CTA 2009, s 985*). The more common schemes are known as SIP (share incentive plans), CSOP (company share option plans), SAYE (savings-related share option schemes) and QUEST (qualifying share ownership trust).

Employing companies receive support for share incentive plans in various ways: deductions are allowed for the cost of setting up plans and for running expenses, as well as payments for the acquisition of shares for the plans.

Deductions are allowed for the costs involved in setting up a plan approved by HMRC. Normally, approval will be given within nine months of the expenses being incurred but, if later, the deduction is allowed in the accounting period in which the company receives the approval (*CTA 2009, ss 987, 999, 1000*).

Deductions for contributions made by a company to trustees of an approved share incentive plan to cover running expenses are allowable. For this purpose, running expenses do not cover the cost of share purchases by trustees other than commission and stamp duty (*CTA 2009, s 988*).

An allowable deduction occurs where the company makes a payment to the trustees of an approved share incentive plan for the purchase of qualifying shares in the company, or a company which controls it. The trustees must use the payment to acquire shares in the company to the amount of at least 10% of the ordinary share capital. These shares cannot be purchased directly from the company and must carry rights to at least 10% of the profits available for distribution to the shareholders and 10% of the assets, in a winding up. For the deduction to be allowed:

- the trustees must acquire the shares within 12 months from the date of the company's payment (*CTA 2009, s 989(4), (7)*),

- at least 30% of the purchased shares must be distributed by the trustees within a period ending five years from the purchase date (*CTA 2009, s 990(2)*), and
- all the acquired shares must be distributed to qualifying employees within ten years from when they were acquired by the trustees (*CTA 2009, s 990(3)*).

Following recommendations by the independent Office of Tax Simplification on the tax treatment of tax advantaged share schemes, *FA 2013* made a number of technical changes to the pre-existing legislation, namely:

- harmonisation of the rules on retirement for SIP, SAYE and CSOP (*FA 2013, Sch 2, Pt 1*);
- greater harmonisation between the provisions for 'good leavers (other than retirees)' for SAYE and CSOP and those already in place for SIP (*FA 2013, Sch 2, Pt 2*);
- tax-free exercise of SAYE and CSOP options, and tax-free payments for SIP shares, on the cash takeover of a business (*FA 2013, Sch 2, Pt 2*);
- removal of the material interest rules for SIP and SAYE and an increase in the material interest percentage for CSOP to 30% (*FA 2013, Sch 2, Pt 3*);
- removal of the current prohibition on the use of certain restricted shares in SIP, SAYE and CSOP (*FA 2013, Sch 2, Pt 4*);
- changes to the basis for determining the number of partnership shares awarded in respect of salary deductions made during a SIP accumulation period (*FA 2013, Sch 2, Pt 5*);
- removal of the limits on SIP dividend reinvestment (*FA 2013, Sch 2, Pt 6*);
- removal of redundant legislation concerning SIP and the acquisition by trustees of shares from an employee share ownership trust (*FA 2013, Sch 2, Pt 7*); and
- extension of the exercise period for enterprise management incentive (EMI) share options following a disqualifying event to 90 days (*FA 2013, Sch 2, Pt 8*).

FA 2014 introduced the following additional changes from 6 April 2014 (*FA 2014, s 51, Sch 8*):

- revised 'purpose tests' for SIP, SAYE and CSOP;
- self-certification requirements for SIP, SAYE and CSOP; and
- mandatory online filing for all employee share scheme returns and information, including EMI and non-tax advantaged arrangements providing employment-related securities (see tinyurl.com/l5z8cw6).

Shares acquired

2.46 Other reliefs are available for certain employee share acquisitions. The employer company receives corporation tax relief on the purchase of non-restricted or non-convertible shares, or on the exercise of options to acquire such shares, on an amount being the difference between the market value of the shares at the time the employee purchases the shares or exercises an option and the price the employee pays (*CTA 2009, ss 1010, 1018*). If, on the other hand, the shares in question are restricted or convertible, the company receives relief on the purchase or the exercise of options based on the amount that counts as employment income of the employee or, in the case of a qualifying option under the enterprise management investment (EMI) scheme, the amount that would have counted as employment income but for the EMI code (*CTA 2009, ss 1011, 1019*). The relief is given in the accounting period in which the option is exercised and the shares acquired (*CTA 2009, ss 1013, 1021*). The relief applies to EMI scheme options, company share option plans (CSOP), unapproved share option plans, and share acquisitions where the employee is subject to tax. The shares must be ordinary shares in a listed company, single company or holding company (*CTA 2009, ss 1008, 1016*).

For accounting periods ending on or after 20 March 2013, no corporation tax deduction is available in relation to an employee share option unless shares are acquired pursuant to that option; and, except in specified circumstances, no other corporation tax deductions are given where statutory corporation tax relief is available (*CTA 2009, ss 1038, 1038A*).

In *Metso Paper Bender Forrest Ltd & Anor* [2013] UKFTT 674 (TC), the First-tier Tribunal held that no corporation tax deduction was available in respect of shares acquired under an option which had replaced another option, since the option exercised was not obtained by reason of employment but had only been deemed to have been so obtained. Following consultation on recommendations by the Office of Tax Simplification, *FA 2014* introduced new provisions extending corporation tax relief from 6 April 2014 for employee share acquisitions that take place by exercise of share options within 90 days of the takeover of a company (*CTA 2009, s 1016(1)(d), (1A)*).

FA 2014 also extended corporation tax relief from 6 April 2015 for employee share acquisitions in certain other cases involving internationally mobile employees. These apply where shares are acquired, or share options are obtained, where an individual is employed by a company not within the charge to corporation tax, and the individual either: (i) works for (but does not have employment with) a company within the charge to corporation tax (for example, during a period of secondment), or (ii) takes up employment with such a company (*CTA 2009, ss 1007A, 1015A, 1015B, 1025A, 1025B, 1030A, 1030B*).

Shares acquired by 'employee shareholders'

2.47 From 1 September 2013, *Growth and Infrastructure Act 2013, s 31* introduced a new employment status of 'employee shareholder', for an employee who agrees to have reduced employment rights and receives fully paid-up shares of a minimum value of £2,000 in the employing company or its parent company, at no cost other than agreeing to become an employee shareholder (*Growth and Infrastructure Act 2013 (Commencement No 3 and Savings) Order 2013, SI 2013/1766*).

Consequential changes to tax law were made by *FA 2013, Sch 23*, also from 1 September 2013. Subject to qualifying conditions, employee shareholders enjoy an income tax advantage (see *Income Tax 2018/19* (Bloomsbury Professional)) and a potentially substantial capital gains tax exemption (see *Capital Gains Tax 2018/19* (Bloomsbury Professional)).

For corporation tax purposes, a company may claim deductions for:

- the acquisition of qualifying shares for employee shareholders; and
- the costs of advice provided to an individual considering an employee shareholder offer (provided these costs are incurred by the company wholly and exclusively for the purposes of its trade).

The corporation tax deduction available on the acquisition of employee shares is usually the market value of the shares acquired by the employee, less any consideration received from the employee. The relief is due when the shares are acquired.

The notional payment of £2,000 which an employee shareholder is deemed to have paid for their shares is ignored for corporation tax purposes – ie the amount of deduction is not reduced by the £2,000 deemed payment.

For further details, see *FA 2013, Sch 23*, particularly *Pt 3* regarding corporation tax; *Finance Act 2013, Schedule 23 (Employee Shareholder Shares) (Appointed Day) Order 2013, SI 2013/1755*; and HMRC guidance at tinyurl.com/qzmrext.

The income tax and capital gains benefits to employees were all removed by *FA 2017, ss 12–14* with effect from 1 December 2016.

Capital allowances

2.48 A company may be able to claim capital allowances on its capital expenditure on plant and machinery, mineral extraction, dredging and research and development (*CAA 2001, s 1*), including an annual investment allowance for plant and machinery expenditure incurred on or after 1 April 2008. Capital allowances are discussed in **Chapter 3**, and the rates of capital allowances are shown at **3.6**.

A company can also claim capital allowances on expenditure incurred prior to 1 April 2002 on patent rights and know-how. For patent rights and know-how acquired on or after 1 April 2002 deductions may be available under the rules for corporate intangibles in **Chapter 12**.

Capital allowances are given by reference to accounting periods. Where an accounting period is less than 12 months, writing down allowances are proportionately reduced. Where a trade begins part of the way through an accounting period, writing down allowances are also proportionately reduced.

EXPENSES OF A SPECIFIC TRADE

Safety at sports grounds before 1 April 2013

2.49 If a company carrying on a trade was liable to pool betting duty and there was a reduction in that duty, and the company made a qualifying payment in consequence of that reduction, the qualifying payment was deductible in computing trading profits for corporation tax. A payment qualified if it was made before 1 April 2013 in order to meet (directly or indirectly) capital expenditure incurred by any person improving the safety or comfort of spectators at a ground to be used for the playing of association football, or made to trustees established mainly for the support of athletic sports or athletic games but with power to support the arts (*CTA 2009, s 138*, before repeal by *FA 2012, Sch 39, para 22*).

Separately from a company's trading income, a charge to corporation tax arises on annual payments received by the company where those would not otherwise be chargeable to corporation tax (*CTA 2009, ss 976, 977*). However, there was a specific exemption for any such payment if it was made before 1 April 2013 in consequence of a reduction in pool betting duty and it was made to meet capital expenditure incurred in improving the safety or comfort of spectators at a ground to be used for the purposes of playing association football (*CTA 2009, s 978*, before repeal by *FA 2012, Sch 39, para 22*).

Providing services through a company

Personal service company

2.50 Individuals who provide their services through a company may fall foul of the IR35 personal service company regime or the managed service company legislation (see *Income Tax 2016/17* (Bloomsbury Professional)).

If IR35 applies, the deemed employment payments and the related employer's National Insurance contributions incurred by the contractor company are deductible from profits in the accounting period during which they are treated as paid (*CTA 2009, s 139*). Deemed payments are calculated for each income tax year ended 5 April.

Example 2.4—Personal service company: deduction for deemed payment

Facts

Mr Persona is an IT consultant who provides his services through Persona Services Ltd. It is understood that the personal services legislation applies. Persona Services Ltd prepares accounts to 28 February each year. Mr Persona's deemed payment for the year ended 5 April 2015 is £50,000, and this is treated as made on 5 April 2015 (*ITEPA 2003, s 50(3)*).

Analysis

Relief for the deemed payment is given against profits for the year ended 28 February 2016.

Managed service company

2.51 A managed service company acts as an umbrella company in raising invoices on a personal service individual's behalf, for which it charges a commission. Managed service companies must account for PAYE and NICs on the full amount invoiced to their clients for the individual's services, rather than the post-commission payment made to the individual. See *Income Tax 2016/17* (Bloomsbury Professional).

The deemed employment payments and the employer's NICs incurred by the managed service company are deductible from profits in the accounting period during which they are treated as paid (*CTA 2009, s 141*).

Waste disposal and site preparation expenditure

2.52 A deduction for site preparation expenditure is available to a company that carries on a trade that includes the deposit of waste materials. This applies to preparation expenditure incurred by either the company itself or its 'predecessor' – being a company or other person who has ceased to carry on trading activities relating to the site and has transferred the whole of the site to the company. The expenditure must have been incurred as a condition of a waste disposal licence or in order to grant or comply with planning permission. Expenditure that qualifies for capital allowances is excluded (*CTA 2009, ss 142–144*).

Relief is calculated by the following formula:

$$RE \times \frac{WD}{SV + WD}$$

where:

- RE is the residual expenditure
- WD is the volume of waste materials deposited on the waste disposal site during the period
- SV is the volume of the waste disposal site not used up for the deposit of waste materials at the end of the period.

The residual expenditure is the total of the site preparation incurred by the company and its predecessor at any time before the end of the accounting period in question, less expenditure allowed as a deduction elsewhere, eg capital expenditure qualifying for capital allowances, any expenditure allowed as a deduction against trading profits of the current or a prior accounting period, and the excluded amount of any unrelieved old expenditure if the company was trading before 6 April 1989.

The excluded amount of unrelieved old expenditure is calculated by applying the following formula to the unrelieved old expenditure:

$$\frac{WD}{SV + WD}$$

where:

- WD is the volume of waste materials deposited on the waste disposal site before 6 April 1989
- SV is the volume of the waste disposal site not used up for the deposit of waste materials immediately before that date.

Relief is also available for site restoration payments, being payments made in connection with the restoration of a site in order to comply with a condition of either a waste disposal licence or planning permission to use the site for the collection, treatment, conversion and final depositing of waste materials or any of those activities (*CTA 2009, s 145*).

In the case of *Dispit Ltd v Revenue and Customs Commissioners* [2007] SpC 579, the Special Commissioners held that restoration expenditure was only deductible from trading profits up to the amount of the payments actually made in the accounting period concerned (see *CTA 2009, s 145(3)*).

Provisions were introduced by *FA 2012* to counter tax avoidance schemes which tried to accelerate relief by making site restoration payments to connected persons many years in advance of future works. These provisions have effect in relation to any site restoration payment made on or after 21 March 2012, other than a payment made under an unconditional contract made before that date (*CTA 2009, s 145*).

DEDUCTIBLE AND NON-DEDUCTIBLE EXPENSES

> **Focus**
>
> Case law and practice on the deductibility of particular types of expenses have become established over many years.

2.53 The following list is a summary of some of the case law and practice regarding the deductibility of various costs:

Item	*Explanation*	*References*
Accounts preparation	Fees incurred for preparing accounts for commercial reasons and for many other accountancy services satisfy the 'wholly and exclusively' test. Normal fees for tax help in agreeing the company's self-assessment are also allowed. Additional costs arising from an enquiry that reveals discrepancies resulting from careless or deliberate inaccuracies are not allowable. See also 'Fee protection insurance' below.	BIM46450, HMRC Enquiry Manual at EM3981
Advertising	Ordinary current expenditure on advertising a company's goods or services is normally allowable.	BIM42550
Animals kept for trade purposes	Animals or other living creatures are accounted for at their capital value on the balance sheet if they are kept wholly or mainly for the work they do in connection with the carrying on of the trade. Otherwise, they are treated as trading stock unless they are part of a herd in relation to which a herd basis election has effect. Part-owned shares in animals or other living creatures are given the same treatment.	*CTA 2009, s 50*

Item	*Explanation*	*References*
Annuities and annual payments	An annuity or an annual payment is disallowed as a business deduction in accounts under *CTA 2009, s 54*. In general terms, an annual payment will be (a) paid under a legal obligation, (b) annually recurring and (c) pure income profit in the hands of the recipient.	*Gresham Life Assurance Society v Styles* (1892) 3 TC 185
Assets in satisfaction of trading debts	Companies can accept assets in satisfaction of trading debts. Where the market value of the asset at the date of acceptance of the asset is less than the amount of the outstanding debt, the shortfall may be allowable as a deduction. However, the company must agree to account for any excess as a trading receipt as a result of the disposal of the asset. The excess is excluded from CGT (*TCGA 1992, s 251(3)*).	BIM42735
Business archives	Costs incurred in maintaining historic business archives will generally be allowable expenses. Company expenditure on the provision of access to archives, and on linked educational services, is also usually allowable.	BIM42501
Capital	Capital payments are disallowed.	
	A company's initial contribution to a staff pension fund was held to be a capital payment because it was made not only once and for all, but also with a view to bringing into existence an asset or an advantage for the enduring benefit of trade.	*Atherton v British Insulated and Helsby Cables Ltd* (1925) 10 TC 155; BIM35320
Company administration	Costs incurred by a company as part of its ordinary annual expenditure on such matters as the keeping of the share register, the printing of annual accounts, and the holding of shareholders' AGMs are normally allowed as trading expenses. Also, the annual cost of a Stock Exchange quotation and the fees paid to newspapers for the inclusion of the company's shares	BIM42510

Item	*Explanation*	*References*
	in the newspaper's report of Stock Exchange prices, and annual fees paid to trustees for debenture holders or mortgagees, are treated as allowable expenses. However, costs incurred by a company to effect changes in its status (eg flotation costs, the initial charges of a Stock Exchange quotation or expenses connected with a purchase of own shares) will not normally be deductible.	
Compensation and damages	The tax deductibility of compensation and damages payments depends on the circumstances of the payment.	BIM42950 onwards
	A compensation payment may be reduced by the reimbursement of trading expenses allowable as a deduction.	
	Compensation and damages payments require to be 'wholly and exclusively' for trade purposes and on 'revenue account'.	BIM42955
	Where compensation relates to normal trading activity and not an identifiable capital asset, it will be an allowable deduction.	BIM42960
	Compensation for termination of an agency was held to be a trading expense where the payments in question were attributable not to fixed but to circulating capital and might properly be debited to revenue account.	*Anglo-Persian Oil Co Ltd v Dale* (1931) 16 TC 253
	Compensation paid by banks for mis-selling etc on or after 8 July 2015 may be disallowed.	*CTA 2009, ss 133A–133M*
	Compensation received for disruption to the business was held to be a taxable receipt.	*John Lints v HMRC* [2012] UKFTT 491 (TC)
Computer software	Expenditure on software may be either capital or revenue expenditure (see **3.14**).	*CAA 2001, ss 71–73* BIM35800 onwards

Item	*Explanation*	*References*
Crime	No deduction is allowed for certain crime-related payments.	*CTA 2009, s 1304* BIM43100 onwards
Defalcations/ embezzlement	Funds misappropriated by a director, then claimed as a remuneration payment on which PAYE was to be paid, were held not to be an allowable deduction for corporation tax purposes.	*Bamford v ATA Advertising* (1972) 48 TC 359
	Defalcations by employees may be allowed as deductions, but misappropriations by a director are not deductible.	*Curtis v Oldfield (J & G) Ltd* (1925) 9 TC 319
	Defalcations allowed for tax and later made good are taxable.	*Gray v Penrhyn (Lord)* (1937) 21 TC 252
Dilapidations	Where the costs of dilapidations (ie repairs at the end of a lease) would be the same if the repairs had been undertaken during the course of the lease period, and are not of a capital nature, they should be allowable (*CTA 2009, s 54*). At the expiry of the lease, the lessee may agree to pay the lessor a sum as compensation in lieu of accrued repairs. This payment is allowable if it does not reflect capital costs.	BIM43250 onwards
Employees' or directors' remuneration	Remuneration wholly and exclusively for the purposes of trade is deductible (see **2.22**, **2.23**). Remuneration paid to connected parties, eg to shareholder's family, must be on arm's-length terms.	*Stott and Ingham v Trehearne* (1924) 9 TC 69; *Earlspring Properties Ltd v Guest* [1993] STC 473; *Robinson v Scott Bader & Co Ltd* [1981] STC 436
Fee protection insurance	Fee protection insurance charges to cover the risk of incurring additional costs are only allowable if the additional costs would have been allowable had they been incurred directly by the business. If the premium covers the costs of an enquiry that reveals discrepancies resulting from careless or deliberate inaccuracies, it is not deductible. Apportionment is not permitted.	BIM46452

Item	*Explanation*	*References*
Fines	Fines are disallowed, as they are not incurred wholly and exclusively for the purpose of trade, but penalties designed to be compensatory rather than punitive may be allowed.	BIM42515 *McKnight v Sheppard* [1999] STC 669
	Penalties for breaches of trading regulations are disallowed.	*CIR v Alexander von Glehn & Co Ltd* (1920) 12 TC 232
	Legal costs in defending a business were held to be allowable.	*McKnight v Sheppard* [1999] STC 669
Fines (parking)	In situations where the employer pays a parking fine that is in fact the liability of the employee, the cost to the employer will be allowable in determining his trading profit, and the employee will be chargeable on the emolument arising.	BIM42515
	Fines paid by the company on vehicles owned by the company are not a benefit for the employee, but neither are they deductible for corporation tax.	
	Fines resulting from civil actions arising out of trade may be allowed if compensatory rather than punitive.	*Golder v Great Boulder Proprietary Gold Mines Ltd* (1952) 33 TC 75
	Parking fines were disallowed even where the appellant argued that their trade of collecting and delivering large amounts of cash required them to park as near as possible to their customers' premises.	*G4S Cash Solutions (UK) Ltd* (2016) TC 05015
Foreign exchange	Foreign exchange gains and losses are taxed or relieved under the loan relationship provisions (see **Chapter 11**).	BIM45875
Franchise payments	An appropriate part of the initial franchise fee will be considered a revenue payment if the items it represents are revenue items and are not separately charged for in the continuing fees. However, franchise fees are more likely to fall within the intangible fixed assets regime (see **Chapter 12**).	BIM57600–BIM57620

Item	*Explanation*	*References*
Guarantee payments	Guarantee payments fall within loan relationships (see **Chapter 11**). However, a payment under a loan guarantee is deductible only if the guarantee was wholly and exclusively for the purposes of the trade and a capital advantage is not secured. Guarantees between group and/or associated companies may not fulfil these conditions.	BIM45301
	Payments under guarantee in respect of an associated company were held to be capital expenditure.	*Milnes v J Beam Group Ltd* [1975] STC 487; *Garforth v Tankard Carpets Ltd* [1980] STC 251; *Redkite v Inspector of Taxes* [1996] STC (SCD) 501
	An exhibition guarantee payment, made in order to secure work, was considered to be an allowable deduction.	*Morley v Lawford & Co* (1928) 14 TC 229; BIM45305
Hire purchase	Revenue payments for the hire of an asset are deductible but capital payments for the purchase of an asset are not.	BIM45351
	Payments under a hire purchase agreement are split between amounts for hire (allowable) and payments for the eventual purchase (capital).	*Darngavil Coal Co Ltd v Francis* (1931) 7 TC 1
	An agreement that transfers ownership immediately is not hire purchase; it is an agreement for purchase by instalments (ie capital expenditure), and none of the expenditure by the purchaser is revenue expenditure.	BIM45351
	Costs of repairs and renewals of hire purchase assets are deductible.	BIM45360
	FRS 102, Section 20 *Leases* deals with accounting for leases, and is substantially the same as SSAP 21 and IAS 17 (see **Chapter 26**).	BIM45355

Item	*Explanation*	*References*
Holding company formation expenses	Holding company formation expenses were held to be capital expenditure and therefore not deductible.	*Kealy v O'Mara (Limerick) Ltd* [1942] 2 ITC 265
Incentive and reward schemes	Expenditure on performance-related awards and incentive schemes may be allowable if (a) the award requires to be based on genuine performance achievement, (b) the employer is obliged to provide the award, and (c) a formal scheme based on known rules is in place.	BIM45080, BIM47010
	Suggestion scheme awards are treated in a similar manner, provided the award is reasonable.	BIM47015
In-house professional fees	A company's in-house professional costs incurred in relation to work involved with the company's capital assets are capital and therefore not allowed as revenue. Fees for the maintenance of a company's assets, facilities or trading rights are normally revenue expenses and allowable, but fees in relation to rights or facilities of a capital nature are capital expenses.	BIM46410
Insurance	Premiums on insurance policies which provide indemnity for loss or damage to fixed assets, intangible assets or current assets (eg trading stock or trade debts), including policies which cover replacement 'new for old', are allowable if incurred wholly and exclusively for business purposes (*CTA 2009, s 54*).	BIM45501, BIM45505, *Green v Gliksten (J) & Son Ltd* (1929) 14 TC 364; BIM45510; *Mallandain Investments Ltd v Shadbolt* (1940) 23 TC 367
	Insurance proceeds for stock lost are assessable as trading income.	*Green v Gliksten (J) & Son Ltd* (1929) 14 TC 364
	Premiums for policies covering (a) fire at company's premises, (b) interruption or loss of use of income-producing assets, (c) interruption or cessation of the supply of raw materials, or (d) events causing loss of profits for	BIM45510

Item	*Explanation*	*References*
	a temporary period, are allowable deductions from trading profits.	
	An indemnity policy premium is allowable where it provides cover for professional negligence. Damages paid as a result of professional negligence are allowable, but not to the extent that they are recoverable under an indemnity policy.	BIM45515
	Premiums paid to indemnify employees against legal action taken against them personally, for actions in the course of the employment, are allowable as a deduction in computing the employer's trading profits.	BIM45520
	The premiums paid on insurance policies taken out wholly and exclusively for the benefit of customers are allowable as a deduction.	BIM45575
Interest on director's property loan	Where interest is paid by a company on a loan (as distinct from an overdraft) taken out by a director to purchase land or buildings occupied rent-free by the company and used for business purposes, it is considered that the company may obtain relief as a trading expense for the interest in the normal way and that the payments would not normally constitute either remuneration or a benefit to the director.	*CTA 2009, s 54* BIM45755
Key employee insurance	Premiums on a term assurance policy in favour of the employer, insuring against death or critical illness of a director, employee or other 'key person', are generally allowable and the proceeds of any such policies are treated as trading receipts, if the sole purpose of the insurance is to meet a loss of trading income that might result from loss of the services of the key person, rather than a capital loss.	BIM45525, BIM45530

Item	*Explanation*	*References*
	Keyman insurance proceeds were held to be taxable as receipts of the trade.	*Keir & Cawder Ltd v CIR* (1958) 38 TC 23; *CIR v Williams' Executor* (1944) 26 TC 23
	Premiums on policies taken out as a condition of loan finance are not deductible (see **11.34**).	*Greycon Ltd v Klaentschi* [2003] STC (SCD) 370
Launch costs	A company may obtain relief for advertising and launch costs of a new product or brand under the intangible assets regime (see **Chapter 12**).	BIM42551
Legal expenses	Legal expenses incurred in maintaining existing trading rights and assets are revenue expenses.	
	The legal costs of defending an overseas branch's title to land in the foreign courts, which it used for the purposes of its trade, was held to be deductible from profits.	*Southern v Borax Consolidated* (1940) 23 TC 598
	Expenditure on defending a company from public ownership, and thereby preventing the seizure of its business and assets, was held to be an allowable business expense.	*Morgan v Tate & Lyle Ltd* (1954) 35 TC 367
Loan finance	See loan relationships (**Chapter 11**).	
Losses	Losses arising in the normal course of trading are allowable. Losses arising from theft or misappropriation by directors are not allowable.	BIM45851, BIM45855 *Curtis v Oldfield (J & G) Ltd* (1925) 9 TC 319; *Bamford v ATA Advertising Ltd* (1972) 48 TC 359
Management expenses	HMRC will accept reasonable management expenses allocations to group companies where expenses are incurred by a group service company on their behalf. HMRC will investigate arrangements where one company incurs expenditure for the purposes of the trade of another that is outside the scope of UK tax.	BIM42140

Item	*Explanation*	*References*
	However, expenses relating to the trade of one group company will not be allowable against the separate trade of another group member.	BIM38230, BIM38250
National Insurance contributions	Secondary Class 1 NICs are deductible in computing profits, as are Class 1A NICs and Class 1B NICs.	*CTA 2009, s 1302*
Onerous contract	Payment of a sum of money to remove a company from an onerous trading contract will usually be considered to be a trading expense.	*Vodafone Cellular v Shaw* [1997] STC 734; BIM38220
	The costs of entering into or terminating a trading contract may be capital where the contract is so fundamental that its loss would cripple or destroy the trade.	*Van den Berghs Ltd v Clark* (1935) 19 TC 390
	A payment by a company to secure release of an option over a trade investment was held to be a trading expense.	*Walker v Cater Securities Ltd* [1974] STC 390
Overseas taxes	Tax of an overseas country charged on the profits arising in that country will be available for tax credit relief in most cases. In certain cases, a deduction may be allowed for taxes of a capital nature.	BIM45901, BIM45905 *Harrods (Buenos Aires) Ltd v Taylor-Gooby* (1964) 41 TC 450
	Interest payable on overseas tax may be admitted as a trading expense, but not if it relates to a penalty in respect of a capital tax or an overseas tax.	
Payments in lieu of notice	Payments in lieu of notice on a cessation of trade were held to be allowable deductions.	*O'Keefe v Southport Printers Ltd* [1984] STC 443
Political expenses	No deductions are allowable for party political expenditure, but costs of a propaganda campaign to prevent the loss of business and protect assets may be allowable.	BIM42528 *Morgan v Tate and Lyle Ltd* (1954) 35 TC 367
Procurement fees	Procuring others to enter into a tax avoidance scheme was not considered to be a trade.	*Ransom v Higgs* [1974] STC 539

Item	*Explanation*	*References*
Professional fees	Professional fees are not allowable if they are of a capital nature or excluded by statute.	BIM46405
	Costs of an unsuccessful planning application were held to be capital expenditure.	*ECC Quarries Ltd v Watkis* [1975] STC 578; *Moore (A & G) & Co v Hare* (1941) 6 TC 572
Professional negligence	Insurance policy premiums to cover professional negligence and employee indemnity risks are usually allowable as a deduction. Damages paid in respect of professional negligence or employee indemnity risks are allowable, but not to the extent that they are recoverable under an indemnity policy.	BIM45515, BIM45520
Provisions	A provision in the accounts may be allowable if (a) it has been estimated with reasonable accuracy, (b) it does not conflict with any statutory rules, (c) it relates to revenue and not capital expenditure, and (d) it agrees with the principles of FRS 102, Section 21 *Provisions and contingencies*, FRS 12 *Provisions, contingent liabilities and contingent assets* or IAS 37 *Provisions, contingent liabilities and contingent assets* (see **Chapter 26**).	BIM46510, BIM46555
	To comply with FRS 102, Section 21, FRS 12 or IAS 37, it may be necessary to discount a provision to its present value if the effect of this is material; in this case, only the discounted provision will be allowable.	BIM46525
	Provisions for capital expenditure have been held to be disallowable.	*RTZ Oil & Gas Ltd v Ellis* [1987] STC 512
	A company's calculation of provisions was held to be insufficiently accurate.	*Owen v Southern Railway of Peru Ltd* (1956) 36 TC 602
Purchase of own shares	Fees in relation to raising equity finance, including purchase of own shares, are capital expenses and are not deductible.	BIM46425

Item	*Explanation*	*References*
Removal expenses	Reasonable employee removal costs due to an employee's change of residence at the employer's request are allowable. If the employer buys and resells the employee's former residence to facilitate the move and the transactions are completed without delay, profits arising are usually taxed as a trading receipt and losses allowed as a deduction.	BIM42531
	Expenses incurred by a company moving to new premises are allowed in most cases.	BIM42530
Renewal of lease	Costs in relation to renewal of a lease are generally capital and may be disallowed. However, they may be allowed where they are relatively small and relate to a short lease (less than 50 years to run).	BIM46420
Rent and rates	Ongoing costs associated with a company's premises, including rent, rates, repairs and insurance, will normally be allowed if incurred wholly and exclusively for the purposes of the trade.	BIM46801, BIM46810
Repairs and renewals	Repair costs are normally regarded as revenue expenditure. The cost of replacement of an entire asset is capital expenditure. Mere replacement of parts that are defective, by the renewal of those parts, is considered to be revenue expenditure. Note the concept of 'entirety' used by the courts. Any repair expenditure resulting in an improvement or upgrade to an asset is capital expenditure (see **2.11**).	BIM46900 onwards *Brown v Burnley Football & Athletic Co Ltd* [1980] STC 424; *Transco plc v Dyall* [2002] STC (SCD) 199
Security expenditure	Where a company needs to protect its employee from a special security threat, because of the nature of the company's business, the revenue expenditure	BIM47301 onwards

Item	*Explanation*	*References*
	incurred in providing the required security measures is likely to be allowed if all the qualifying conditions are met under *ITTOIA 2005, s 81*.	
Sponsorship costs	Sponsorship costs are allowable in arriving at the profits of a company, unless they are considered to be capital expenditure or the expenditure is not made wholly and exclusively for business purposes, in which case it is specifically disallowed. If sponsorship contains an element of hospitality, the cost of which is separately identifiable, this is disallowable under *CTA 2009, ss 1298, 1299*, and the balance of the cost of the sponsorship may be allowed.	BIM42555, BIM42560, BIM42565
	Sums paid as sponsorship to support the personal hobbies and pastimes of a shareholder's family were held not to be deductible from trading profits.	*Executive Network (Consultants) Ltd v O'Connor* [1996] STC (SCD) 29
	Sums paid as sponsorship to a sports club were held not to be deductible because they were not incurred wholly and exclusively to benefit the sponsor's trade but also to benefit the sports club.	*Interfish Ltd v HMRC* [2014] EWCA Civ 876
Take-over costs	The acquirer's fees in relation to take-overs are normally capital and disallowable. The target's fees are capital if in relation to the structuring of the deal, but revenue if in connection with protecting its own trade.	BIM46460, BIM38260 onwards
Tax appeals	The cost of a tax appeal, even if successful, is not deductible. Additional accountancy expenses incurred as a result of 'in-depth' examination by HMRC will be allowed if this results in no discrepancies. If there are discrepancies, the costs are not allowable, even if the investigation reveals no addition to profits.	*Allen v Farquharson Bros & Co* (1932) 17 TC 59 BIM37840

Item	*Explanation*	*References*
	Costs of an appeal before the Special Commissioners (including solicitors' costs, fees of consulting accountants, fees of accountants acting generally for the taxpayers for services specially connected with the appeal, and travelling expenses of witnesses) were disallowed.	*Rushden Heel Co Ltd v Keene* [1948] 2 All ER 378; BIM37060, BIM37300
Tied petrol stations	Exclusivity payments made to retailers by petroleum companies were allowed in computing the petroleum companies' profits.	*Bolam v Regent Oil Co Ltd* (1956) 37 TC 56
	In the hands of a retailer, recurring receipts of this nature that affected only a small part of the retailer's business were held to be trading receipts rather than capital receipts.	*Tanfield Ltd v Carr* [1999] STC (SCD) 213
	In the hands of another retailer, one-off receipts were held to be capital because they represented consideration for the garage proprietor's giving up his freedom of trading and changing the structure of this part of his business.	*Commissioners of Inland Revenue v Coia* (1959) 38 TC 334
Trade organisations etc	Even if not wholly and exclusively for trading purposes, donations are allowable if made to a local enterprise organisation, ie a local enterprise agency, a training and enterprise council, Scottish local enterprise company, or a business link organisation.	BIM47610
Training, education and welfare	A company's expenditure on training, education and welfare is normally allowed.	BIM47080
Travel and subsistence	Reasonable travel and subsistence expenses incurred by itinerant employees (eg commercial travellers), or other employees undertaking business journeys outside the normal pattern, may be allowed.	BIM47705

Item	*Explanation*	*References*
Unsuccessful applications	The expenses of unsuccessful applications for licences were held to be disallowable – the company accepted that expenses of successful applications are capital.	*Southwell v Savill Bros* (1901) 4 TC 430
	Costs of unsuccessful application for variation of an existing licence were held to be disallowable.	*Pyrah v Annis & Co Ltd* (1956) 37 TC 163
Valuations	The costs of valuations for accounts purposes, or as required by the Companies Act, are allowable. Valuations for insurance purposes are allowable. Valuations in connection with a company reconstruction or probate are not allowable.	BIM42540
VAT	In connection with VAT, penalties and interest charged by HMRC are not deductible, and repayment supplement is not taxable. However, interest paid by HMRC in certain cases of official error is taxable.	BIM31610
Website costs	Website maintenance costs are allowable, but costs that create an enduring asset may be treated as capital.	BIM35815 HMRC Corporate Intangibles Research & Development Manual at CIRD25145

RECEIPTS NOT TAXABLE AS TRADING INCOME

Commercial occupation of woodlands

2.54 The commercial occupation of woodlands in the UK is not a trade or part of a trade, and the profits arising are ignored for corporation tax purposes. Woodlands are occupied on a commercial basis if they are managed on a commercial basis, and with a view to the realisation of profits (*CTA 2009, ss 37, 207, 208, 980*). It follows that expenditure incurred in the commercial occupation of woodlands is not deductible for corporation tax purposes, whether it is of a revenue or capital nature. Note that a company occupying land may receive other incidental income such as fishing and shooting rents, which would be subject to corporation tax.

Credit unions

2.55 Credit unions are cooperative financial institutions that are owned and operated by their members. Loans to members and the investment of surplus funds are not regarded as the carrying on of a trade or part of a trade (*CTA 2009, s 40*).

RECEIPTS TAXABLE AS TRADING INCOME

Trade debts released

2.56 If a trade debt that has been written off against trading profits is subsequently released, either in whole or in part, and the release is not part of a statutory insolvency arrangement, the amount released is treated as a receipt in calculating the profits of the trade for the accounting period in which the release is effected (*CTA 2009, s 94*).

Reverse premiums

2.57 If a company tenant receives a payment from its landlord or former landlord (or any person connected with them, or acting as nominee for them, or acting on their directions) as an inducement in connection with a transaction being entered into by the recipient or a person connected with them, whereby the recipient or the connected person becomes entitled to an estate, interest or right over land, the sum is taxable on the company as income (*CTA 2009, s 96*). Payments in connection with the sale of a person's principal private residence, or from sale and leaseback arrangements, are not considered to be reverse premiums. Neither is a receipt that reduces the recipient's expenditure for capital allowances (*CTA 2009, s 97*). A reverse premium is a revenue receipt of the trade if the property transaction was entered into for the purposes of the trade. If no trade is carried on, the premium is taxable as property income – see **7.22** (*CTA 2009, s 98*).

A property transaction not at arm's length between connected parties is treated as taking place at open market value when the transaction is entered into (*CTA 2009, s 99*).

For these purposes, persons are connected if they are connected at any time during the period when the property arrangements are entered into (*CTA 2009, s 100*). 'Connection' is defined in accordance with *CTA 2010, s 1122* (see **10.27**).

Property income treated as trading income

2.58 In general, companies are charged to corporation tax on property income arising from the letting of land and property, and profits and losses from such letting activity are included in the company tax return (see **Chapter 7**).

However, certain property income is treated as trading income (**2.59–2.63**).

Tied premises

2.59 Where a company carries on a trade in tied premises in which it has an interest, receipts and expenses of the premises are brought into account in computing the profits of the trade. Non-trade amounts are apportioned on a just and reasonable basis (*CTA 2009, s 42*).

Caravan sites where trade carried on

2.60 A company that owns a caravan site may carry on activities that amount to a trade, such as a shop or a café; if so, receipts from the letting of caravans and caravan pitches, which would otherwise be treated as arising from a property business, may instead be brought into account in calculating the profits of the trade (*CTA 2009, s 43*).

Surplus business accommodation

2.61 If a company lets or grants a licence to occupy part of a building used to carry on its trade, and the letting income therefrom is 'relatively small', that letting income may be included in the company's trading income. However, this applies only if the premises in question are not part of the company's trading stock and the accommodation let is only temporarily surplus to the company's trading requirements.

A company will meet the 'temporarily surplus to requirements' condition only if:

- the accommodation has been used within the last three years to carry on the trade, or acquired within the last three years,
- the trader intends to use it to carry on the trade at a later date; and
- the letting is for a term of not more than three years.

Accommodation that is temporarily surplus to requirements at the beginning of an accounting period remains so until the end of that period, and all income from the relevant letting must be treated in the same way (*CTA 2009, s 44*; BIM41015, BIM41020).

There is no statutory definition or HMRC guidance on the meaning of 'relatively small'.

Payments for wayleaves

2.62 If a company carries on a trade on some or all of the land to which a wayleave relates, the rental income and the expenses in respect of that wayleave may be included in calculating the profits of the company's trade, even though it would otherwise be assessable as rent receivable for UK electric-line wayleaves under *CTA 2009, s 277* or otherwise as property income. This applies only if no other rent or expenses in respect of the land to which the wayleave relates are included in any property business carried on by the trader.

For this purpose, a wayleave is an easement, servitude or right in or over land in connection with:

- an electric, telegraph or telephone wire or cable (including the supporting pole or pylon and apparatus used),
- a pipe for the conveyance of any thing, or
- any apparatus used in connection with such a pipe (*CTA 2009, s 45*).

Qualifying holiday accommodation

2.63 Where a UK property business consists of or includes the commercial letting of furnished holiday accommodation, that particular activity is treated as a trade for the following corporation tax purposes (*CTA 2009, s 264(2)*):

- relief for property business losses (*CTA 2010, s 65*),
- certain provisions relating to chargeable gains (see *TCGA 1992, s 241*), and
- capital allowances (eg *CAA 2001, ss 248, 249*).

Where a UK property business consists of both the commercial letting of furnished holiday accommodation and other businesses or transactions, it must make separate calculations of the profits of the furnished holiday lettings part and the other part if capital allowances or charges under *CAA 2001, ss 248, 249* apply to either part, or if any loss relief provisions of *CTA 2010, Pt 4* apply, or if a wear and tear allowance is allowed under *CTA 2009, s 248C*. If there is letting of accommodation only part of which is holiday accommodation, just and reasonable apportionments are to be made (*CTA 2009, s 269*).

From April 2011, where an overseas property business consists of or includes the commercial letting of furnished holiday accommodation in one or more EEA states, that particular activity is treated as a trade for some specific corporation tax purposes (*CTA 2009, s 264(2A)*), namely:

- relief for property business losses (*CTA 2010, s 67A*),
- certain provisions relating to chargeable gains (see *TCGA 1992, s 241A*), and

- capital allowances (eg *CAA 2001, ss 250, 250A*).

From April 2011, where an overseas property business consists of both the commercial letting of furnished holiday accommodation in one or more EEA states and other businesses or transactions, it must make separate calculations of the profits of the EEA furnished holiday lettings part and the other part if capital allowances or charges under *CAA 2001, ss 250, 250A* apply to either part, or if any loss relief provisions of *CTA 2010, Pt 4* apply. If there is letting of accommodation only part of which is holiday accommodation, just and reasonable apportionments are to be made (*CTA 2009, s 269*).

For all the above purposes, the commercial letting of furnished holiday accommodation must meet the following conditions:

- the letting is a lease or other arrangement under which a person is entitled to the use of accommodation;
- the accommodation is let on a commercial basis and with a view to the realisation of profits;
- the person entitled to the use of the accommodation is also entitled to the use of furniture; and
- the accommodation is qualifying holiday accommodation.

For holiday accommodation to qualify for an accounting period beginning on or after 1 April 2012, during the 'relevant period' the property must be:

(a) available for holiday letting to the public on a commercial basis for at least 210 days, and

(b) let to the public commercially as holiday accommodation for at least 105 days, and

(c) not normally occupied for more than 31 days by the same person in any period of seven months (*CTA 2009, s 267*).

For accounting periods beginning before 1 April 2012, the numbers of days in (a) and (b) above are 140 and 70 respectively.

The relevant period is normally the accounting period in question. However, if the accommodation was not let by the company as furnished holiday accommodation in the previous accounting period, the 12-month relevant period starts on the first day in the accounting period on which it is let as furnished holiday accommodation. Where the letting ceases, the relevant period is the 12-month period ending on the last day the property is let as furnished holiday accommodation (*CTA 2009, s 266*).

If a company lets both qualifying holiday accommodation and under-used accommodation (ie accommodation that would qualify had it been let for at least 105 days), it can make an averaging election for the accounting period, covering its qualifying holiday accommodation and any or all of its under-used accommodation. The number of actual let days for all elected accommodation in the accounting period is totalled and, if the average is at least 105, the under-used accommodation included in the election is treated as qualifying holiday accommodation. For accounting periods beginning before 1 April 2012, the required average was 70 days (*CTA 2009, s 268*).

Alternatively, where a let property meets the letting condition based on 105 days in one accounting period but fails to do so in the next accounting period or the next two accounting periods, even though there was a genuine intention to meet the letting condition for that period or each of those periods (as the case may be), the company may elect to treat the property as continuing to qualify for either the first or both of those periods. The election may only be made if the averaging election under *CTA 2009, s 268* has not been made in respect of the same year (*CTA 2009, s 268A*).

The provisions of *CTA 2010, Pt 4* for the relief of trading losses are restricted in their application to losses arising from the commercial letting of furnished holiday lettings; and, in particular, losses cannot be relieved against total profits under *CTA 2010, s 37* onwards for accounting periods beginning on or after 1 April 2011 (*CTA 2010, ss 65, 67A*). Group relief is not available (*CA 2009, ss 269(2)(b), 269A(2)(b)*).

REDRESS PAYMENTS FOR MIS-SELLING

2.64 Where a company receives a redress payment as a result of mis-selling, eg for an interest rate hedging product sold to it inappropriately, the sum received is normally but not invariably taxed as income of the accounting period in which it is received. For HMRC guidance on this, see tinyurl.com/lv668cm.

Where a retail or investment bank incurs expenses on or after 8 July 2015 in paying compensation to customers in respect of relevant conduct (ie certain defined acts or omissions on or after 29 April 1988), these expenses are not deductible for corporation tax purposes (*CTA 2009, ss 133A–133M*, as inserted by *F(No 2)A 2015, s 18*).

ACTIVITIES TREATED AS A TRADE BY STATUTE

Farming and market gardening

2.65 Farming or market gardening carried on in the UK is treated as a trade or part of a trade, regardless of whether or not the land is managed on a commercial basis and with a view to the realisation of profits. Furthermore, all farming that a company carries on in the UK is treated as one trade, unless the farming is part of another, non-farming trade (*CTA 2009, s 36*).

This does not apply to farming or market gardening by an insurance company on land which is an asset held by the company for the purposes of its long-term business (*CTA 2009, s 36(3)*).

If the company is a partner in a firm, any farming that is carried on by the firm is not included in any farming trade of the company (*CTA 2009, s 1270(1)*).

Relief for losses arising in a trade of farming or market gardening may be restricted under the 'hobby farming' rules (*CTA 2010, ss 48, 49*; see **4.20**).

Commercial occupation of land other than woodlands

2.66 The commercial occupation of land other than woodlands in the UK is treated as the carrying on of a trade or part of a trade. Land other than woodlands is occupied on a commercial basis if it is managed on a commercial basis and with a view to the realisation of profits (*CTA 2009, s 38*).

Land other than woodlands does not include:

- land used for farming or market gardening (see **2.65**);
- land that is being prepared for forestry purposes;
- commercial woodlands (see **2.54**); or
- land occupied by an insurance company as an asset of its long-term insurance fund.

Profits of mines, quarries and other concerns

2.67 Profits from mines, quarries and other concerns are treated as trades; these activities are detailed as follows:

- mines and quarries (including gravel pits, sand pits and brickfields);
- ironworks, gasworks, salt springs or works, alum mines or works;
- waterworks and streams of water;
- canals, inland navigation, docks and drains or levels;
- rights of fishing;
- rights of markets and fairs, tolls, bridges and ferries; and
- railways and other kinds of way.

However, this does not extend to land occupied commercially other than for woodlands, nor to a concern carried on by an insurance company on land that is an asset of the company's long-term insurance fund (*CTA 2009, s 39*).

BARTER TRADING

2.68 *FA 2016, s 71* introduced provisions that require barter transactions in the course of a trade to be brought into account, in calculating trading profits, if the money's-worth element would not otherwise have been brought into account. This rule is believed to be targeting people who are regular users of barter services, such as Airbnb, where no actual consideration passes but there is potentially valuable reciprocation.

The new rule applies to transactions entered into on or after 16 March 2016.

APPROPRIATIONS OF PROFIT

2.69 Appropriations of profits, ie distributions or dividend payments, are not deductible from profits for corporation tax purposes (*CTA 2009, s 1305*). UK corporation tax payments themselves are not deductible. Depreciation is disallowed, but capital allowances are deductible as a trading expense (*CAA 2001, s 352*).

Depreciation of fixed assets may relate to the production of unsold stock and, for accounting purposes, may not be deducted in arriving at profits until the year in which that stock is disposed of. In such a case, it is only the depreciation charged in the profit and loss account that must be disallowed and therefore added back in the corporation tax computation, regardless of any other entry (*Revenue and Customs Commrs v William Grant & Sons Distillers Ltd; Small (Inspector of Taxes) v Mars UK Ltd* [2007] UKHL 15; see also BIM33190).

VALUATION OF STOCKS AND WORK IN PROGRESS

Meaning of trading stock

2.70 The valuation of closing stock has a direct impact on final profits. The higher the closing stock valuation, the higher are the reported profits.

For this purpose, trading stock includes finished goods and work in progress, and is defined as anything which is sold in the ordinary course of the trade, or which would be so sold if it were mature or its manufacture, preparation or construction were complete, excluding raw materials and services (*CTA 2009, s 156*). In accordance with FRS 102, Section 13 *Inventories* under new UK GAAP, SSAP 9 *Stocks and long-term contracts* under old UK GAAP or IAS 2 *Inventories* under international GAAP, stock valuation should be acceptable for tax purposes, being generally the lower of cost and net realisable value (see **Chapter 26**).

Under old UK GAAP, UITF Abstract 40 *Revenue recognition and service contracts* required companies to make a corporation tax adjustment in respect of their professional work in progress. Under new GAAP this has been superseded by FRS 102, para 23.14.

Valuation of transfers to and from trading stock

2.71 Case law has determined that the market value rule applies where goods are acquired or appropriated into trading stock, other than in the course of a trade (*Sharkey v Wernher* (1955) 36 TC 275). *CTA 2009, ss 157–158* give statutory effect to these rules.

If any stock is used for non-trade purposes, a taxable receipt is deemed to accrue to the company, equal to the market value of that stock at that time, any actual receipt in respect of the same stock is then left out of account (*CTA 2009, s 157*). Similarly, any item which the company already owns, that it transfers as a finished good or work in progress into stock, is to be valued at market value at the date of transfer, and the value of anything given for it is left out of account (*CTA 2009, s 158*).

Generally, the appropriation from fixed assets also gives rise to a chargeable gain or allowable loss (see **16.29** and *Capital Gains Tax 2018/19* (Bloomsbury Professional) at para 4.37). However, an election can be made under *TCGA 1992, s 161(3)* for the asset to be transferred at market value less the gain that would have arisen had there been a market value disposal at the date of the appropriation (*Capital Gains Tax 2018/19* (Bloomsbury Professional) at para 4.38). This means that no chargeable gain arises on appropriation into trading stock, and the amount brought in as cost of stock is reduced by the gain. As a result, the gain or loss on appropriation becomes a trading gain or loss.

For appropriations of assets on or after 8 March 2017, an election can only be made if a chargeable gain would have arisen on appropriation (amendments to *TCGA 1992, s 161* made by *F(No 2)A 2017, s 26*). This is to prevent elections being used to convert allowable capital losses, which are quite restricted in their use, into trading losses, which are much more flexible.

Similar rules apply if an item of stock has been disposed of or acquired by means other than in the normal course of trade (*CTA 2009, ss 159, 160*). Where the transfer pricing rules apply in such circumstances before 8 July 2015, the transfer pricing valuation (which will normally agree with the market valuation) will take precedence (*CTA 2009, ss 160, 161*). Where transfer pricing applies and such a disposal or acquisition takes place on or after 8 July 2015 (unless under an unconditional contractual obligation made before that date), there may also be a further adjustment if necessary to ensure that the full value of the stock is brought into account for tax purposes (*CTA 2009, s 161(1A)–(1C)*, as inserted by *F(No 2)A 2015, s 37*).

Valuation of trading stock on the cessation of a trade

2.72 Subject to any transfer-pricing override, the valuation of the closing stock on the permanent cessation of a trade is dependent upon the seller's relationship to the purchaser (*CTA 2009, s 164*). For this purpose, trading stock includes finished goods, work in progress and raw materials, together with the value of any services included therein. The sale includes the transfer of any benefits and rights which accrue, or might reasonably be expected to accrue, from the performance of any such services (*CTA 2009, s 163*). Incomplete services upon the cessation of a company's trade are included in its trading stock (*CTA 2009, s 163(2)*).

Upon cessation of the trade, trading stock is generally valued at its open market price, but special rules apply to sales to: an unconnected person; a connected person; and a connected person where an election is made.

Sale to unconnected person:

- If the sale is to a person carrying on or intending to carry on a trade in the UK where the stock can be deducted as an expense in calculating the profit, the stock is valued at selling price, being the amount realised on the sale. If the stock is sold with other assets, the amount realised on the sale is apportioned on a just and reasonable basis (*CTA 2009, s 165*).

Sale to connected person:

- If the sale is to a buyer connected with the seller who carries on or intends to carry on a trade in the UK where the stock can be deducted as an expense in calculating the profit, the stock is valued at open market value, being the value which would have been realised if the sale had been between independent persons dealing at arm's length (*CTA 2009, s 166*).

Election by connected persons:

- If the open market value of the stock sold exceeds the acquisition cost and the realised proceeds, the buyer and the seller may jointly elect, within two years after the end of the accounting period in which the cessation occurred, for the stock to be valued at the greater of the acquisition cost and realised proceeds (*CTA 2009, s 167*).

Where transfer pricing applies and the cessation occurs on or after 8 July 2015, there may also be a further adjustment if necessary to ensure that the full value of the stock is brought into account for tax purposes (*CTA 2009, s 162(2A)–(2C)*, as inserted by *F(No 2)A 2015, s 38*).

For these purposes, persons are connected with each other in any one of the following circumstances (*CTA 2009, s 168*):

- within the meaning of *CTA 2010, s 1122* (see **10.27**);
- where a company has a share or the right to a share of the assets of an unincorporated business;
- where a company is controlled by another party;
- where the income and asset sharing rights of two unincorporated businesses belong to a third person;

- where either two companies or an unincorporated business and a company are controlled by the other party or both are under the control of a third party.

Where the basis that the seller adopts in valuing the closing stock on the cessation of its trade is determined in accordance with the above provisions, the buyer will adopt the same value for inclusion as opening stock in its respective trade (*CTA 2009, s 169*). If a transfer of stock is made instead of a sale, the transaction is treated as if it were a sale (*CTA 2009, s 170*). Questions arising from a stock valuation are to be determined in the same way as an appeal (*CTA 2009, s 171*).

CHANGE IN BASIS OF ACCOUNTING

> **Focus**
>
> The fundamental principles establishing how a change in basis of accounting is treated for corporation tax purposes are particularly important, given that most companies are currently making a transition to new financial reporting standards.

2.73 A company may change the basis on which it calculates its trading profits for corporation tax, where the old basis was correct (ie in accordance with prevailing law and practice) for the period of account before the change and the new basis is correct for the succeeding period of account (*CTA 2009, s 180(1)*; see also **2.76**).

Such a change may come about for a variety of reasons, for example (*CTA 2009, s 180*):

- the company may change its accounting policy from UK GAAP to IFRS;
- the company may change its accounting policy from IFRS to UK GAAP;
- the company may change its accounting basis from a realisation basis to a 'mark to market' basis;
- the company may be required to make accounting transition adjustments as a result of changes to UK GAAP. This is currently of particular relevance (see **2.76** and **Chapter 26**); or
- the company may change the tax adjustments applied as a result of a change in view as to what is required or authorised by law.

If the last period of account before the change is calculated on the old basis, and the first period of account after the change is calculated on the new basis, an adjustment will be required to reconcile the two bases.

A positive adjustment is treated as a trading receipt, and a negative adjustment as a trading expense, arising in either case on the first day of the first period of account for which the new basis is adopted. The procedure for calculating the adjustment is contained in *CTA 2009, s 182*. Essentially, receipts and expenses before the change are recalculated on the new basis.

Calculation of the adjustment

2.74 The two bases are compared, and amounts that represent profit understatements and loss overstatements are totalled in Step 1, while amounts that represent profit overstatements and loss understatements are totalled in Step 2.

The amounts are:

	Step 1	*Step 2*
1.	Receipts which would have been brought into account in calculating the profits of the earlier period of account, had they been calculated on the new basis, to the extent that they were not brought into account.	Receipts which were brought into account in the earlier period of account before the change, insofar as they have been brought into account again in calculating the profits on the new basis.
2.	Expenses brought into account in calculating the profits of the later period, insofar as they were brought into account in calculating the profits of the earlier period.	Expenses which were not brought into account in calculating the profits of the earlier period, insofar as they would have been brought into account had the old basis been applied to the later period.
3.	The amount by which the value of the opening stock and work in progress of the later period exceeds the value of the closing stock and work in progress of the earlier period.	The amount by which the value of the opening stock and work in progress of the later period falls below the value of the closing stock and work in progress of the earlier period.
4.	Depreciation charged in the later period not adjusted for corporation tax purposes but would have been required to be adjusted on the new basis.	

Subject to the following additional rules regarding expenses previously brought into account, the adjustment is found by deducting the Step 2 total from the Step 1 total (*CTA 2009, s 182*).

Expenses previously brought into account

2.75 No adjustment is made where the old basis of calculation allowed a tax deduction, but the new basis would have required the deduction to be spread over several periods; the deduction will have been allowed already under the old basis (*CTA 2009, s 183*).

Where there is a change of basis resulting from a tax adjustment affecting the calculation of:

- closing stock in the last period of account before the change of basis,
- opening stock in the first period of account on the new basis, or
- any amount brought into account in respect of depreciation,

then the receipt or expense of the trade is treated as arising only when the asset to which it relates is realised or written off (*CTA 2009, s 184*).

On a change from a realisation basis to a 'mark to market' basis, a company carrying on the trade may elect for any receipt treated as arising to be spread equally over six periods of account. The election must be made within 12 months of the end of the first accounting period to which the new basis applies. If the trade subsequently ceases, any amounts not accounted for are to be brought into account in calculating the profits of the trade immediately before the cessation (*CTA 2009, ss 185, 186*).

Change in applicable accounting standards

> **Focus**
>
> Companies are currently implementing or are about to implement fundamental changes to UK GAAP, and this makes it especially important that appropriate tax adjustments are made to reflect changes of accounting policy.

2.76 Broadly, *CTA 2009, ss 180–183* ensure that expenditure is relieved only once, and income is taxed only once, on changes of specific accounting policies. Accounting policies contained within International Accounting Standards (IAS) and UK GAAP are the only acceptable accounting policies to be used when preparing accounts to be used as the basis for computing taxable profits (*CTA 2010, s 1127*).

Fundamental changes to UK GAAP are taking place, with almost all extant standards being replaced by new Financial Reporting Standards. An updated FRSSE (effective January 2015) set out the financial reporting requirements for smaller entities, but was replaced from 1 January 2016 by an amended FRS 102, including a new Section 1A *Small entities*. There is also a new Financial Reporting Standard for Micro-Entities (FRS 105 or 'the FRSME') for companies entitled to take advantage of the *Small Companies (Micro-Entities' Accounts) Regulations 2013, SI 2013/3008*, which offers micro-entities a substantially abbreviated reporting regime.

To comply with UK GAAP, a company must apply FRS 101, FRS 102, the stop-gap FRSSE or the FRSME for accounting periods beginning on or after 1 January 2015, and early application is permitted. Entities applying FRS 102 for the first time must restate their balance sheet at the beginning and end of the comparative period. Typically, the first period of account of mandatory application of FRS 102 for large companies is the year ending 31 December 2015, with a requirement to restate both the opening balance sheet as at 1 January 2014 and the comparative balance sheet as at 31 December 2014.

Following amendments made by *FA 2012, s 54*, the pre-existing principles of *CTA 2009, ss 180–183* apply to all changes of accounting policy, and in particular to accounting transition adjustments arising from changes to UK GAAP, for accounting periods beginning on or after 1 January 2012 and in relation to adjustments to earlier accounting periods arising from changes in accounting policy on or after 1 January 2012 (*FA 2012, s 54(5)*).

For further details about the changes to UK GAAP, see **Chapter 26**.

POST-CESSATION RECEIPTS

2.77 A post-cessation receipt is an amount that the company receives in respect of its prior trading activities after it has permanently ceased to carry on a trade (*CTA 2009, s 190*).

The recovery of trade debts is included, and allowance is granted for any release (*CTA 2009, ss 192, 193*). Corporation tax is charged on a post-cessation receipt as profits of a trade if it has not been charged elsewhere (*CTA 2009, s 189*).

If the company permanently ceased to carry on its trade and sold the right to receive sums from the trade to a third party, then if that third party does not carry on the trade the company is treated as receiving a post-cessation receipt. On an arm's length sale, the post-cessation receipt is taken to be the sale proceeds and, on a sale not at arm's length, the arm's length value is substituted (*CTA 2009, s 194*).

If the valuation of closing stock and work in progress is brought into account on cessation in accordance with *CTA 2009, ss 162–171* (see **2.72**), a sum realised by its transfer is not a post-cessation receipt (*CTA 2009, s 195*).

Allowable deductions

2.78 Deductions which would have been allowed had the company been trading at the time are allowed against post-cessation receipts (*CTA 2009, s 196*). Losses are deducted from post-cessation receipts from an earlier period before a later period (*CTA 2009, s 197*).

If the company receives a post-cessation receipt in an accounting period beginning not later than six years after the company permanently ceased to carry on the trade, it may elect that the tax chargeable in respect of the receipt is to be charged as if the receipt had been received on the date of the cessation. This election must be made within a period of two years beginning immediately after the end of the accounting period in which the receipt is received, provided there is sufficient income to relieve (*CTA 2009, ss 198, 199*).

If a company makes an election under *CTA 2009, s 198*, the additional tax is payable for the accounting period in which the receipt is received, and not for the accounting period in which the cessation occurred (*CTA 2009, s 200*).

ILLUSTRATIVE COMPUTATIONAL EXAMPLE

2.79 The following example is illustrative of a straightforward corporation tax computation.

Example 2.5—Illustrative corporation tax computation

Sebastian Ltd is a trading company with the following results. There are no associated companies.

Profit and loss account for the year to 31 March 2016:

	£000	*£000*
Gross profit		900
Interest on bank deposit	70	
Property income	30	
Profit on sale of UK quoted shares	10	
		110
		1,010
Less:		
Directors' remuneration	100	
Salaries	80	
Repairs	40	

Advertising and promotion	20	
Depreciation	100	
Miscellaneous expenses	50	
Goodwill amortisation	2	
		392
Profit before tax		618
Miscellaneous expenses:		
Customer entertaining		10
Donation to political party		10
Staff entertaining		14
Christmas gifts:		
5,000 key rings with company name		5
Cigars		1
Other expenses (all allowable)		10
		50

The goodwill was acquired on 1 April 2003 (see **Chapter 12**)

Capital allowances for the year, including the annual investment allowance, amount to £60,000. The net chargeable gains on the sales of UK quoted shares are £5,000. The company received no franked investment income.

Profits for the year ended 31 March 2016 are adjusted as follows:

	£000	*£000*
Trading profits:		
Net profit per accounts		618
Add:		
Depreciation	100	
Customer entertaining	10	
Political donation	10	
Gifts—cigars	1	
		121
		739
Less:		
Bank interest	70	
Profit on sale of shares	10	

Property income	30	
Capital allowances	60	
		170
Adjusted trading profits		569

Corporation tax computation for the year ended 31 March 2016:

	£000
Adjusted trading profits	569
Loan relationship	70
Property income	30
Chargeable gains	5
Total taxable profits of the period	674

Corporation tax payable:

	£
£674,000 at 20%	134,800

BODIES GRANTED EXEMPTION FROM CORPORATION TAX ON TRADING INCOME

Focus

Charities, members' clubs and community amateur sports clubs (CASCs) are granted specific exemptions from corporation tax where certain conditions are met, and companies who support them may enjoy charitable donations relief. Mutual trading is also outside the scope of corporation tax.

Charities

2.80 Various exemptions are available to a company that meets the definition of a charity provided by *FA 2010, Sch 6*. For this purpose, the company must be established for charitable purposes only and must meet specified conditions regarding jurisdiction, registration and management. Regulation of charities is a devolved matter, with separate charity registers established in Scotland and Northern Ireland, but for tax purposes the expression 'charitable purposes' as defined by *Charities Act 2011, s 2* for England and Wales applies for all parts of the UK (*FA 2010, Sch 6, para 1*).

Trading income will be exempt from corporation tax in limited circumstances. The exemption applies if the profits from the trade are applied solely for the purposes of the charitable company (*CTA 2010, s 478*).

The trade must be exercised in the course of carrying out a primary purpose of the charitable company, or the work in connection with the trade must be mainly carried out by the beneficiaries of the charitable company. Where a trade is exercised partly in the course of the actual carrying out of a primary purpose of the charitable company and partly otherwise, or where the work in connection with the trade is carried out partly but not mainly by the beneficiaries, each part is treated as a separate trade, and expenses and receipts are apportioned on a just and reasonable basis (*CTA 2010, s 479*).

Income from those activities that do not meet the charity criteria remain taxable. If a charitable company franchises its trading activities and receives royalty payments which are applied to charitable purposes only, these are exempt from tax on a claim being made (*CTA 2010, s 488*).

In *Helena Partnerships Ltd (formerly Helena Housing Ltd) v Commissioners for HMRC* [2012] EWCA Civ 569, the Court of Appeal unanimously upheld HMRC's view that from 2001 to 2004 the company in question failed to qualify as a charity. Lloyd LJ's judgment provides a valuable review of relevant case law relating to the meaning of 'charitable purpose', including an examination of the 'public benefit' test applied by *Charities Act 2011, s 2* (see *FA 2010, Sch 6, para 1(4)*).

Although the same tax provisions apply to charities throughout the UK, these require compliance with the registration requirements which vary between England and Wales, Scotland and Northern Ireland. The Charity Commission, the Office of the Scottish Charity Regulator and the Charity Commission for Northern Ireland provide guidance on their registration requirements, including matters such as the public benefit test, on their websites at tinyurl.com/kuxckua, www.oscr.org.uk and www.charitycommissionni.org.uk respectively.

Often, a charitable company will form a trading subsidiary for the purpose of carrying out all its trading activities that do not meet the exemption tests. Such a company's income will be taxable but, subject to certain conditions, it can deduct any qualifying charitable donations that it has made (*CTA 2010, s 189*). Such a payment is often (but not necessarily) made to the parent company (see **2.82**).

CHARITABLE DONATIONS RELIEF

2.81 As a general rule, charitable donations made by a company are allowed as deductions from the company's total profits in the accounting period in which they are made, but only so as to reduce the total profits to nil.

There are only two types of transaction that qualify as a charitable donation for corporation tax purposes: payments which are 'qualifying payments', and gifts of investments (subject to certain conditions) (*CTA 2010, s 190*). Both these situations are sometimes described as Corporate Gift Aid.

From 1 April 2014 the tax treatment of money donations out of company profits to registered community amateur sports clubs (CASCs) is on a par with donations of company profits to charity, subject to an anti-abuse rule (*FA 2014, s 35*).

Qualifying payments to charity

2.82 A payment by a company to a charity is a qualifying payment to charity if it meets each of the following six criteria (*CTA 2010, s 191*):

- a payment of a sum of money;
- not subject to a repayment condition;
- made by a non-charitable company;
- not disqualified as an associated acquisition;
- not disqualified as a distribution; and
- not disqualified because of an associated benefit (see **2.83**).

From 1 April 2014 the definition of 'charity' for these purposes includes a registered community amateur sports club (CASC) (*CTA 2010, s 202(aa)*); see **2.89–2.92**).

Special rules were introduced to assist charities that have trading subsidiaries, to ensure that such a subsidiary would be able to donate its entire profits to charity without facing a corporation tax charge.

If a company makes a payment to a charity and the charity makes a repayment to the company, the charitable payment by the company is not 'subject to a condition as to repayment' if, on repayment by the charity to the donor company, the following circumstances apply (*CTA 2010, s 192*):

- the donor company is wholly owned by the charity, or by a number of charities that include the charity;
- the charitable payment is of an amount which the company estimates to be the amount necessary to reduce to nil the company's taxable total profits for the accounting period in which the payment is made, being the relevant period;
- repayment is made solely for the purpose of adjusting the company's taxable total profits to nil for the relevant period; and
- repayment is made no later than 12 months after the end of the relevant period.

Also from 1 April 2014, a repayment by a CASC of any excess payment to its subsidiary to adjust the company's taxable profits to nil is not treated as non-qualifying expenditure for the purposes of *CTA 2010, s 666* (*CTA 2010, s 192(6)(aa)*).

A company is wholly owned by a charity in either of two circumstances: first, if all its ordinary share capital is owned by a charity, and this need not be the same charity; or, secondly, if every beneficiary of a company limited by guarantee is a charity or company wholly owned by a charity (*CTA 2010, s 200*). In the case of a charity which is a CASC, ordinary share capital of a company is treated as owned by a charity if the charity beneficially owns that share capital (*CTA 2010, s 200(4A)*).

A payment is disqualified as an associated acquisition if it:

- is conditional on an acquisition of property by the charity from the company or a person associated with the company;
- is associated with such an acquisition; or
- is part of an arrangement involving such an acquisition.

Only a payment can be disqualified as an associated acquisition; a non-monetary gift cannot be disqualified in this way (*CTA 2010, s 193*).

All payments classed as distributions are disqualified apart from those relating to the transfer of assets and liabilities (see *CTA 2010, s 1020*). The inter-group exceptions detailed in *CTA 2010, s 1002(2)* are ignored in deciding whether a payment is to be regarded as a distribution in these circumstances. Only dividend payments made by a company which is wholly owned by a charity are to be regarded as distributions for these purposes (*CTA 2010, s 194*).

Where a company is wholly owned by a charity, a qualifying payment to charity made in the first nine months of an accounting period can be carried back to the donor company's previous accounting period, provided that a claim is made within two years of the end of the accounting period in which the payment is made, or such longer period as allowed by an HMRC officer (*CTA 2010, s 199*).

Note that the compulsory charges made for all single-use carrier bags provided with goods, are not taxes. Any such charges made by a company should be brought into account in calculating trading profits for corporation tax purposes. If the proceeds are used to fund good causes, relief is only available where the normal rules for charitable donations relief are met.

Restriction on associated benefits

2.83 A payment is disqualified if benefits associated with the payment are received by the donor company or a person associated with it and specified restrictions are breached (*CTA 2010, ss 195–198*). For this purpose, a person is associated with a company if they are connected with either the company itself or a person connected with it (*CTA 2010, s 201*; see also general guidance on Gift Aid, benefits, etc at tinyurl.com/nz9zpmj).

The restrictions are breached if the associated benefits exceed the statutory maxima, which are (*CTA 2010, s 197*):

either

the total value of the benefits associated with the payment exceeds the variable limit, which is set as follows:

Amount of the payment	*Variable limit*
Up to £100	25% of the amount of the payment
£101–£1,000	£25
More than £1,000	5% of the amount of the payment

or

the sum of the following total values is more than £2,500 (or £500 in respect of gifts made in accounting periods ending before 1 April 2011):

- the total value of the benefits associated with the payment; and
- the total value of the benefits (if any) associated with each relevant prior payment.

Amounts are reduced pro rata if the period covered is less than 12 months (*CTA 2010, s 198*).

Certain disposals treated as qualifying charitable donations

2.84 An investment disposal qualifies as a charitable donation if (*CTA 2010, s 203*):

- the company disposes of the whole of the beneficial interest in a qualifying investment to a charity. Note that a registered CASC is not a charity for these purposes, so an investment disposal to a CASC does not qualify;
- the disposal is otherwise than by way of a bargain made at arm's length;
- the company is not itself a charity; and
- the company makes a claim.

A qualifying investment is (*CTA 2010, s 204*):

- any shares or securities which are listed on a recognised stock exchange or dealt in on a designated UK market;
- units in an authorised unit trust;
- shares in an open-ended investment company;
- an interest in an offshore fund; and
- a qualifying interest in land.

As regards land in the UK, a freehold interest (in Scotland, the interest of the owner) or a leasehold interest with a term of years absolute (in Scotland, a tenant's right over or interest in a property subject to a lease) in the land in the UK amounts to a qualifying interest. Relief is available when a company with a qualifying beneficial interest makes a disposal to a charity of the whole of its beneficial interest, and any easement, servitude, right or privilege so far as benefiting the land in question. The granting of a lease to the charity on terms absolute is also regarded as a disposal (*CTA 2010, s 205*).

If the disposal is a gift, the relievable amount is treated for corporation tax purposes as a qualifying charitable donation made by the company in the accounting period in which the disposal is made and is given by the formula:

$$V + IC - B$$

where:

- V is the value of the net benefit to the charity at, or immediately after, the time when the disposal is made (whichever is less)
- IC is the amount of the incidental costs of making the disposal to the company making it
- B is the total value of any benefits received in consequence of making the disposal by the company making the disposal or a person connected with the company.

A different formula is applied for disposals at under-value. The relievable amount is calculated as follows:

$$E + C - B$$

where:

- E is the amount (if any) by which V exceeds the amount or value of the consideration for the disposal
- C is such consideration as would give a no gain, no loss situation in accordance with *TCGA 1992, s 257(2)(a)* less the excess over the value of the actual consideration. If there is no excess, C is the amount of that excess or, if less, the amount of the incidental costs of making the disposal to the company making it. If there is no excess, C is nil

- B is the total value of any benefits received in consequence of making the disposal by the company making the disposal or a person connected with the company.

In either case, negative results are treated as nil (*CTA 2010, s 206*).

The incidental costs of making a disposal amount to (*CTA 2010, s 207*):

- fees, commission or remuneration paid for the professional services of a surveyor, valuer, auctioneer, accountant, agent or legal adviser which are wholly and exclusively incurred by the company for the purposes of the disposal;
- costs of transfer or conveyance wholly and exclusively incurred by the company for the purposes of the disposal;
- costs of advertising to find a buyer; and
- costs reasonably incurred in making any required valuation or apportionment.

The corporation tax relief available under these arrangements is in addition to the relief from corporation tax on chargeable gains for gifts to charity by companies (see **16.16**).

Value of net benefit to charity

2.85 The value of the net benefit to a charity is generally the market value of the qualifying investment; or, if the charity is, or becomes, subject to a disposal-related obligation, the market value of the qualifying investment reduced by the total amount of the disposal-related liabilities of the charity. However, where the donor company acquired the asset within the previous four years as part of a tax avoidance scheme, the acquisition value applies if lower than the market value (*CTA 2010, s 209*).

In most cases, market value for this purpose is the market value as calculated for capital gains tax purposes (*TCGA 1992, ss 272–274*; see **16.16**). However, offshore funds are subject to special rules, being the lowest buying price on the day of disposal or, if none were published on that day, the latest day on which the prices were published before that day (*CTA 2010, s 210*).

There is a disposal obligation to the charity if it is reasonable to suppose either that the disposal of the qualifying investment to the charity would not have been made in the absence of the obligation, or that the obligation (whether in whole or in part) relates to, is framed by reference to, or is conditional on the charity receiving, the qualifying investment or a disposal-related investment (*CTA 2010, s 211*).

A disposal-related liability is a liability of the charity under a disposal-related obligation in relation to the qualifying investment. If the obligation is contingent, the amount to be brought into account is the amount or value of the liability actually incurred if the contingency occurs, or nil if it fails to occur (*CTA 2010, s 212*).

The company cannot make a claim for a qualifying disposal of land unless it has received a certificate given by or on behalf of the charity. The certificate must describe the qualifying interest in land, specify the date of the disposal, and state that the charity has acquired the qualifying interest in land (*CTA 2010, s 213*).

CHARITABLE RECEIPTS

2.86 Charitable companies receiving gifts from individuals under Gift Aid are treated as receiving a gift of an amount equal to the grossed-up amount of the gift (*CTA 2010, s 471*). Donations from companies, even if described as Corporate Gift Aid, are not grossed up.

The total of gifts from charitable or non-charitable companies plus the grossed-up gifts from individuals is treated as income, but is not chargeable to corporation tax so far as it is applied for charitable purposes only (*CTA 2010, ss 472–474*).

MUTUAL COMPANIES

Mutual trading

2.87 As a person cannot trade with himself or herself, a mutual trader is not liable to tax on any profits arising from their 'mutual' trade. This was established by the House of Lords in *Jones v South-West Lancashire Coal Owners' Association Ltd* (1927) 11 TC 790, and affirmed in *Ayrshire Employers Mutual Insurance Association, Ltd v CIR* (1946) 27 TC 331 (see BIM24000 onwards). Mutual trading is a situation whereby an organisation is controlled by the people who use its services. Those, in effect, who contribute to an activity are its sole participators. Arrangements must be in place to ensure that any surplus ultimately finds its way back to the contributors, with no arrangements for it to go to anybody else. Rules that include a winding-up surplus to be gifted to charity will not support mutual trading. Donations to charity are permitted, provided the gift is approved by all members.

In normal circumstances, in the event of the winding up of a company, any surplus available to distribute to members will be distributed pro rata to their shareholdings. Typically, such distribution will only be to the members on the register at that time. By contrast, for mutual trading purposes, it will be necessary for the Articles of Association to state that, on a winding up, any surplus available for distribution will be returned to contributors in a reasonable proportion to their contribution to that surplus, and that any distribution will also need to include contributors who have left in the last five years.

MEMBERS' CLUBS

2.88 Income received by a members' club would not normally constitute trading income. This is because a club is usually established by the members for their own social or recreational objects, and any surplus is for distribution amongst the members. In that respect, they are either mutual trading or not trading.

Goods or services provided commercially to non-members may constitute a trading activity. Expenditure should be allocated on a just and reasonable basis, but costs that relate specifically to members are not deductible against trading income arising from non-members. Other income received, such as interest or rents, will be taxed in the normal way.

COMMUNITY AMATEUR SPORTS CLUBS (CASCS)

CASC conditions

2.89 Reliefs are available to a community amateur sports club which is registered as such with HMRC. The government has powers to change the rules on CASCs through secondary legislation. *The Community Amateur Sports Clubs Regulations 2015, SI 2015/725,* have revised the corporation tax reliefs for CASCs from 1 April 2015, and have made other changes backdated to the start of the CASC regime on 1 April 2010.

Reliefs are available, provided that it is required by its constitution to be a club which:

- is open to the whole community (see *CTA 2010, s 659(2A)*, as inserted by *SI 2015/725, Pt 3*, in relation to costs of membership);
- is organised on an amateur basis (see *CTA 2010, s 660*, as amended by *SI 2015/725, Pt 4*);
- has as its main purpose the provision of facilities for, and the promotion of participation in, one or more eligible sports (*CTA 2010, s 658*); and
- is not one in which the percentage of its members who are 'social members' (ie those not participating, or participating only occasionally, in its sporting activities) exceeds 50% (see *CTA 2010, s 659(2A)*, as inserted by *SI 2015/725, Pt 5*).

The club also has to meet a 'location condition' (ie it must be if it is established in an EU Member State or other relevant territory and its facilities for eligible sports are all located in a single Member State or territory; see *CTA 2010, s 661A*) and a 'management condition' (ie its managers are fit and proper persons to be managers of the club; see *CTA 2010, ss 661A, 661B*).

A club is regarded as open to the whole community if membership of the club is open to all without discrimination. Club facilities must be available to members without discrimination, and any fees must be set at a level that does not pose a significant obstacle to membership, use of the club's facilities or full participation in its activities (*CTA 2010, s 659*).

A club is organised on an amateur basis if it is non-profit making and it provides, for members and guests only, the ordinary benefits of an amateur sports club. The constitution must provide for any net assets on dissolution to be applied for approved sporting or charitable purposes (*CTA 2010, s 660*).

Since CASCs are not meant to be mainly social or commercial, a new 'income condition' imposes a limit of £100,000 on the aggregate trading and property receipts (ie turnover) that a CASC is allowed to generate from non-members in each 12-month accounting period (reduced *pro rata* for shorter periods) to qualify for registration or to maintain its existing registration. If this threshold is likely to be exceeded, HMRC will expect the club to take steps to reduce its non-member trading and property income – which might be achieved, for example, by setting up a trading subsidiary owned by the CASC. If a registered CASC fails to meet the income condition, it will face deregistration, resulting in the loss of all CASC reliefs and a possible tax charge based on the value of its assets (*CTA 2010, s 661CA*, as inserted by *SI 2015/725, Pt 2*).

Those managing CASCs need to look carefully at the recent changes. If a registered CASC fails to meet the new rules, it has until 1 April 2016 to make any necessary changes. If a club no longer wishes to be registered as a CASC but HMRC are satisfied that the club has always met the CASC rules as they were before the changes on 1 April 2015, the club's deregistration date will be 1 April 2016 and there will be no deregistration or exit charge. However, if the club has not met the CASC rules for many years, HMRC will backdate deregistration, resulting in the loss of all CASC reliefs and a possible tax charge based on the value of its assets.

HMRC maintain the register of CASCs (see tinyurl.com/2ypyrv). HMRC's guidance on the tax treatment of CASCs is at tinyurl.com/pmesnyt and tinyurl.com/nahl3v5.

CASC reliefs

2.90 The CASC may apply for exemption from corporation tax on the following income, provided that it is applied for a qualifying purpose – the qualifying purpose being 'providing facilities for and promoting participation in one or more eligible sports' (*CTA 2010, s 658*):

- trading income not exceeding £50,000, or such other limit as may be set by Treasury regulations (*CTA 2010, s 662; Community Amateur Sports Clubs (Exemptions) Order 2014, SI 2014/3327*). Subject to transitional provisions, this limit was £30,000 before 1 April 2015;
- interest income, Gift Aid income and company gift income (*CTA 2010, s 664*);
- rental income not exceeding £30,000, or such other limit as may be set by Treasury regulations (*CTA 2010, s 663; SI 2014/3327*). Subject to transitional provisions, this limit was £20,000 before 1 April 2015; and
- chargeable gains (*CTA 2010, s 665*).

Where any income or gains are incurred for non-qualifying purposes, the tax exemption is reduced proportionately (*CTA 2010, s 666*).

Treasury regulations, which may be retroactive in effect, may provide that a club is not entitled to be registered as a CASC unless it meets one or more conditions relating to income received by the club. Such conditions may include provisions restricting the amount of income, or income of a specified description, that a CASC may receive for a period, or prohibiting a CASC from receiving income of a specified description (*FA 2013, Sch 21, para 8*).

Donor reliefs

2.91 A company that gifts plant, machinery or trading stock to a CASC does not have to bring any disposal amount into account, but can still obtain relief for the cost. Where a company gifts a chargeable asset to a CASC, the disposal is treated as giving rise to neither a gain nor a loss for chargeable gains purposes. There are rules to prevent the donor reliefs from being used for tax avoidance purposes.

From 1 April 2014 a company's money gifts (but not disposals of other assets) to a CASC are treated on a par with Corporate Gift Aid for charities (see **2.81**). However, from the same date, anti-abuse provisions apply to discourage abuse involving companies owned or controlled by CASCs (*CTA 2010, ss 202B–202C*).

Corporation tax self-assessment

2.92 Clubs and mutual companies are required to self-assess for corporation tax, unless they have agreed otherwise with HMRC.

Where the club or unincorporated association is run exclusively for the benefit of its own members and is expected to have an annual corporation tax liability not exceeding £100, HMRC will not issue notices to file returns. Instead, the club or unincorporated association will be treated as dormant, but will be subject to a review that will take place at least once in every five years. For each year of dormancy, the body must have no anticipated allowable trading losses or chargeable assets likely to be disposed of, and no anticipated payments from which tax is deductible and payable to HMRC.

This practice does not apply to: privately owned clubs and unincorporated associations run as commercial enterprises; housing associations or registered social landlords, as designated in the *Housing and Planning Act 1986*; trade associations; thrift funds; holiday clubs; friendly societies; and any company which is a subsidiary of, or wholly owned by, a charity.

A flat-owning property management company is also able to benefit from this practice if the company is not entitled to receive income from land and makes no distributions. The company will be liable to income tax on any interest that it earns from holding service charges on trust received from tenants under *Landlord and Tenant Act 1987, s 42*. The company will be within income tax self-assessment and may be required to make a return to the relevant Trust Office. Income tax is chargeable at the special trust rate (45% for bank interest received in fiscal year 2015/16) except for the first £1,000 which remains chargeable at basic rate (20% for bank interest in fiscal year 2015/16).

A CASC must give details of its income on supplementary pages CT600E, which also enables it to recover income tax on its Gift Aid receipts.

Charities and CASCs can sign up to make their tax repayment claims electronically, using HMRC's Charities Online service (see tinyurl.com/pxjf6wt).

RELIEF FOR EXPENDITURE ON GRASSROOTS SPORT

2.93 From 1 April 2017, qualifying expenditure on grassroots sport will be allowed as a deduction from the company's total profits for the accounting period in which the payment is made (*CTA 2010, Pt 6A*). If a company makes a payment to a qualifying sport body (defined at *CTA 2010, s 217C*), or the paying company is a qualifying sport body, it can claim a deduction against total profits for the amount paid. The only restriction is that the deduction cannot reduce the company's total profits below nil (*CTA 2010, s 217A*).

Where a company makes a direct payment to grassroots sport, not through a qualifying sport body, it can claim a deduction against total profits up to a maximum of £2,500 in any accounting period (proportionately reduced for shorter accounting periods). Once again, the deduction cannot reduce the company's total profits below nil (*CTA 2010, s 217A*).

Chapter 3

Capital allowances (plant and machinery)

SIGNPOSTS

- Rationale for a capital allowances system, and an overview of the expenditure qualifying for relief (see **3.1–3.5**).
- Rates of capital allowance (see **3.6**).
- What qualifies as plant or machinery, with a summary of relevant case law (see **3.7–3.16**).
- Differentiating between plant or machinery on the one hand, and buildings or structures on the other (see **3.17–3.18**).
- The annual investment allowance (AIA) for single companies and groups, including the transitional rules relating to the temporary increase in AIA to £500,000 and the reduction to £200,000 (see **3.19–3.31**).
- First year allowance (FYA), and expenditure on which an FYA may not be claimed (see **3.32–3.42**).
- Interaction of AIA with other capital allowances (see **3.43–3.44**).
- Fixtures and the *FA 2012* fixtures regime (see **3.45–3.51**).
- Computation of capital allowances (see **3.52–3.58**).
- Special rate expenditure and the special rate pool (see **3.59–3.64**).
- Contribution allowances (see **3.65**).
- Leasing – the meaning of a lease, anti-avoidance provisions, and background plant and machinery (see **3.66–3.79**).
- Anti-avoidance (see **3.80**).

TANGIBLE FIXED ASSETS

Accountancy treatment

3.1 A company's fixed assets are disclosed in the balance sheet according to company law requirements and in accordance with generally accepted accounting principles (GAAP).

The GAAP applied will be either:

- FRS 102 *The Financial Reporting Standard applicable in the UK and Republic of Ireland* at Section 17 *Property, Plant and Equipment*, subject to possible reduced disclosure options available under FRS 101 *Reduced Disclosure Framework*, or FRS 102, Section 1A *Small entities*;
- FRS 105 *The Financial Reporting Standard applicable to the Micro-entities Regime* at Section 12 *Property, Plant and Equipment and Investment Property*; or
- IAS 16 *Property, Plant and Equipment* when using international accounting standards.

Investment properties are accounted for under FRS 102, Section 16 *Investment Property,* FRS 105, Section 12 *Property, Plant and Equipment and Investment Property* or IAS 40 *Investment Property.*

For company law requirements, see the *Small Companies and Groups (Accounts and Directors Report) Regulations 2008, SI 2008/409*; the *Large and Medium-sized Companies and Groups (Accounts and Reports) Regulations 2008, SI 2008/410*; and the *Small Companies (Micro-Entities' Accounts) Regulations 2013, SI 2013/3008.*

Company law was amended for periods starting on or after 1 January 2016 by virtue of *The Companies, Partnerships and Groups (Accounts and Reports) Regulations 2015, SI 2015/980.* These amendments made significant changes to the disclosure requirements for small companies.

FRS 102, Section 17 *Property, Plant and Equipment* defines tangible fixed assets as assets with physical substance that are held for use in the production or supply of goods or services, for rental to others, or for administrative purposes, and are expected to be used during more than one period.

See **Chapter 26** regarding changes to UK GAAP.

Tax treatment

3.2 Depreciation calculated for accounting purposes is not an allowable deduction against income for tax purposes. Instead, the tax system grants its own form of depreciation on qualifying assets through the capital allowance system.

Capital allowances were first introduced in 1945 and were designed to assist with the industrial regeneration of the UK's post-World War II economy. The system has been amended by various governments to help UK industry develop. The types of capital expenditure that have been eligible for capital allowances are:

	CAA 2001
Plant and machinery	*Part 2*
Industrial buildings allowances (IBAs) on the construction of industrial buildings, qualifying hotels, commercial buildings in enterprise zones (discontinued with effect from 1 April 2011)	*Part 3*
Business premises renovation (discontinued with effect from 1 April 2017)	*Part 3A*
Agricultural buildings allowances (ABAs) on the construction of agricultural buildings and works (discontinued with effect from 1 April 2011)	*Part 4*
Flat conversions (discontinued with effect from 1 April 2013)	*Part 4A*
Mineral extraction (a specialist topic not covered in this book)	*Part 5*
Research and development	*Part 6*
Know-how (discontinued for companies with effect from 1 April 2002)	*Part 7*
Patents (discontinued for companies with effect from 1 April 2002)	*Part 8*
Dredging	*Part 9*
Assured tenancies (discontinued 1992)	*Part 10*

Focus

By claiming capital allowances on qualifying expenditure, a company can deduct certain capital expenditure from its business profits, usually over a period of years.

Rules based on safeguarding the environment are steadily being introduced into the tax system. Expenditure on energy-saving plant and machinery, environmentally beneficial plant and machinery, ultra low emission cars, zero-emission goods vehicles and gas refuelling stations currently receives generous relief (see **3.33–3.39**). Reliefs are also available for innovative technologies (see **Chapter 14**).

Industrial buildings allowances (IBAs) and agricultural buildings allowances (ABAs) were phased out over the period 1 April 2008 to 31 March 2011. See *Corporation Tax 2010/11* and earlier years (Bloomsbury Professional) for IBA details.

Business premises renovation allowances (discontinued from 1 April 2017) are discussed in **Chapter 8**. Research and development allowances are discussed in **Chapter 14**. Mineral extraction and dredging are not covered in this book. Capital allowances are no longer available on know-how and patents; from 1 April 2002, these were superseded by the intangible fixed assets regime, which is discussed in **Chapter 12**. Capital allowances on assured tenancies are no longer available.

This chapter discusses plant and machinery allowances.

PLANT AND MACHINERY ALLOWANCES

Qualifying activities

3.3 In order to be able to claim capital allowances for plant and machinery, the company must incur qualifying expenditure on a qualifying activity (*CAA 2001, s 11(1)*). Qualifying expenditure is capital expenditure incurred on the provision of plant and machinery, wholly or partly for the purposes of the qualifying activity carried on by the company that incurs the expenditure. As a result of incurring the expenditure, the company 'owns' the asset (*CAA 2001, s 11(4)*).

A qualifying activity of a company may consist of (*CAA 2001, s 15*):

- a trade;
- an ordinary UK property business;
- a UK furnished holiday lettings business;
- an ordinary overseas property business;
- an EEA holidays lettings business;
- a profession;
- a specialist activity falling within the descriptions of mines, quarries and other concerns listed in *CTA 2009, s 39(4)*;
- managing the investments of a company with investment business; or
- special leasing of plant or machinery.

This chapter covers the general capital allowances provisions, with particular emphasis on trades.

Qualifying expenditure

3.4 The tax system maintains the capital/revenue divide for capital assets. This principle was established in *In Re Robert Addie & Sons* 1875,

1 TC 1; *Coltness Iron Co v Black* (1881) 1 TC 287 and *Leeming v Jones* (1930) 15 TC 333.

A company may claim capital allowances on its qualifying capital expenditure (*CAA 2001, s 1*). For corporation tax purposes, relief is given in an accounting period (*CAA 2001, s 6(1)(b)*). Different types and rates of capital allowances have been available on different classes of assets at different times. For plant and machinery, they currently include annual investment allowance (AIA), first year allowance (FYA), writing down allowance (WDA) and balancing allowance. In the past, an initial allowance has also been available. Capital allowances which are clawed back are referred to as balancing charges. Capital allowances must be claimed, otherwise no relief is given (*CAA 2001, s 3(1)*).

Capital allowances can only be claimed on the cost of the plant and machinery itself, not the additional costs of interest or commitment fees (*Ben-Odeco Ltd v Powlson* [1978] STC 460. HMRC allow professional fees and preliminary fees to be included within the cost on an asset for capital allowance purposes only if they relate directly to the acquisition, transport and installation of the plant and machinery (HMRC Capital Allowances Manual at CA20070). Capital allowances are claimed by including the amount of the claim in the company tax return or an amended return.

> **Focus**
>
> A company can select the amount of capital allowances to claim in an accounting period and thus influence both the immediate exposure to tax and the allowances available in subsequent accounting periods.

A company need not claim the full amount of capital allowances available. The company may choose either to make a reduced claim or not to claim at all, eg if it wishes to maximise a loss in a future accounting period (see **Chapter 4**). The claim must be made within the normal self-assessment corporation tax return time limits, being two years after the end of the accounting period concerned (*FA 1998, Sch 18, para 82*). The normal time limit is extended in circumstances where there is an enquiry, amendment or appeal, to 30 days after the respective closure notice, amendment or determination. HMRC have the power to extend the statutory time limits in exceptional circumstances, but have stated that they will not extend the time limits in respect of the following (CA11140):

- a change of mind.
- hindsight showing that a different combination of claims might be advantageous: for example, the group relief available may be lower than the company expected it to be when it claimed capital allowances. The company might then want to claim further capital allowances. But that is not a circumstance beyond the company's control. It could have claimed sooner.

- oversight or error, whether on the part of the company or its tax agent.
- absence or indisposition of an officer or employee of the company unless:
  - the absence or illness arose at a critical time, which delayed the making of the claim;
  - in the case of absence, there was good reason why the person was unavailable at the critical time; and
  - there was no other person who could have made the claim on behalf of the company within the normal time limit.

Capital allowances given in respect of a trade are deducted from trading income as an adjustment (see **2.48**). Balancing charges are added to trading income. Capital allowances in respect of non-trading activities are generally deducted primarily from the source of income to which they relate, eg property income. If the accounting period is less than 12 months, the maximum limit of AIA which can be claimed and the amount of WDAs (but not the amount of FYAs) are time-apportioned accordingly. If the period of account is longer than 12 months, each accounting period (which cannot exceed 12 months) is a separate chargeable period for capital allowance purposes – ie the period of account is divided into one or more 12-month periods and the remaining balance, if any (see **22.5**).

When capital expenditure is incurred

> **Focus**
>
> Consider the accounting period in which the acquisition falls (and, if possible, plan the timing of capital expenditure accordingly) in order to utilise fully the allowances available. The following rules determine the date on which capital expenditure is in fact incurred.

3.5 For the purposes of claiming the allowances, capital expenditure is incurred on the date on which the obligation to pay becomes unconditional, even if there is a later payment date (*CAA 2001, s 5(1)*). Delivery of the goods is normally the time when the obligation to pay becomes unconditional. If the contractual payment period is longer than four months the expenditure is treated as incurred on the payment due date (*CAA 2001, s 5(5)*).

For works under contract, capital expenditure is incurred on the issue of a certificate of work to date. If a certificate is issued within one month of the end of the accounting period but the asset has become the company's property before the end of the accounting period, the expenditure is deemed to have been incurred on the last day of the accounting period concerned (*CAA 2001, s 5(4)*). However, capital expenditure incurred before a trade begins is treated as incurred on the first day of trading.

Capital expenditure still to be incurred under a hire purchase contract at the time when the asset is brought into use is treated as incurred on the date on which the asset is brought into use (CA11800).

If the company incurring the capital expenditure is not registered for VAT and therefore ineligible to claim relief for input VAT, any VAT paid on the cost of the asset is taken into account when calculating the allowances. If the company is partially exempt and only part of the input VAT is relieved, the VAT not so relieved is taken into account when calculating the allowances. If an additional VAT liability is incurred or an additional VAT rebate arises, for example under the operation of the VAT capital goods scheme, this is treated as an adjustment to the capital expenditure, taking place on the last day of the relevant VAT interval (CA11800).

Sales between connected parties are deemed to be made at market value (*CAA 2001, s 567*). Parties under common control may elect for the asset to be transferred at the lower of tax written down value or market value (*CAA 2001, s 569*).

Capital expenditure incurred on plant and machinery for the purposes of a qualifying activity, by a company about to carry on the activity, is treated as if it had been incurred on the first day on which the company carries on the activity (*CAA 2001, s 12*).

Where a company brings plant or machinery into use for the purposes of a qualifying activity but already owns the plant or machinery because it had acquired it for another purpose, the company is treated as incurring capital expenditure of an amount equal to the lesser of its cost and market value at the date on which the change of use occurs (*CAA 2001, s 13*).

RATES OF CAPITAL ALLOWANCES

3.6 Current and recent capital allowance rates for plant and machinery are:

Incurred by	*Expenditure incurred*	*Allowance*	*Rate*
All companies	Annual Investment Allowance		
	• annual limit for expenditure incurred on or after 1 April 2010 but before 1 April 2012	AIA	Maximum £100,000
	• annual limit for expenditure incurred on or after 1 April 2012 but before 1 January 2013	AIA	Maximum £25,000
	• annual limit for expenditure incurred on or after 1 January 2013 but before 1 April 2014	AIA	Maximum £250,000

	• annual limit for expenditure incurred on or after 1 April 2014 but before 1 January 2016	AIA	Maximum £500,000
	• annual limit for expenditure incurred on or after 1 January 2016	AIA	Maximum £200,000
All companies	Energy-saving plant and machinery (with special provisions for energy service providers)	FYA	100%
	Environmentally beneficial plant and machinery	FYA	100%
	Low CO_2 emission cars not exceeding 50g/km/75g/km (see **3.36**)	FYA	100%
	Zero-emission goods vehicles	FYA	100%
	Equipment for refuelling vehicles with natural gas or hydrogen fuel	FYA	100%
	Equipment for electric vehicle charge-points (from 23 November 2016 to 31 March 2019)	FYA	100%
	Plant and machinery for use primarily in a designated assisted area within an enterprise zone	FYA	100%
	North Sea oil ring-fence plant and machinery	FYA	100%
All companies	General plant and machinery		
All companies	Plant and machinery – main rate expenditure:		
	• for accounting periods ending on or before 31 March 2012	WDA	20%
	• for accounting periods ending after 31 March 2012	WDA	18%
	Plant and machinery – special rate expenditure:		
	• for accounting periods ending on or before 31 March 2012	WDA	10%
	• for accounting periods ending after 31 March 2012	WDA	8%

WHAT QUALIFIES AS PLANT OR MACHINERY

The meaning of plant

Focus

Fundamental to any plant and machinery claim is the question as to whether the asset on which the capital allowance is to be claimed is in fact plant and machinery. In practice, the answer is often difficult to determine. Plant owes its meaning to the development of case law to which, in cases of doubt, reference should be made. In general, a business uses plant to earn its profits.

3.7 Plant was first defined in the High Court, in the case of *Yarmouth v France* (1887) 19 QBD 647, as 'whatever apparatus is used by a businessman for carrying on his business – not his stock in trade which he buys or makes for sale but all goods and chattels, fixed or moveable, live or dead, which he keeps for permanent employment in his business'. In other words, the assets that enable a business to be carried on. The Court of Appeal confirmed this as the functional test in the case of *Benson v Yard Arm Club Ltd* [1979] STC 266, where capital allowances were refused on the cost of purchasing and adapting a floating restaurant on the grounds that this was the place where the business was carried on rather than the tools that enabled it to be carried on.

In *Hinton v Maden & Ireland Ltd* (1959) 38 TC 391, the House of Lords (by a majority verdict) held that expenditure on acquiring assets with a life ranging between one and three years was capital, and HMRC have instructed their staff to apply a 'two-year test' (CA21100). Whether the setting in which the business is carried on is plant is a question of fact. In the High Court, lighting that was part of the setting but performed no operational function was held not to be plant in *J Lyons and Co Ltd v Attorney-General* [1944] 1 All ER 477.

Moveable office partitions in a shipping agent's office, which were often moved to enable the trade to be carried on, were held by the Court of Appeal to be plant; the partitions performed a function (*Jarrold v John Good & Sons Ltd* (1962) 40 TC 681). HMRC comment that only moveable partitions that possess mobility as a matter of commercial necessity qualify as plant (CA21120). The functional test was also met in *Leeds Permanent Building Society v Procter* [1982] STC 821, in which the High Court held that decorative screens in a building society window were plant.

CIR v Scottish & Newcastle Breweries Ltd [1982] STC 296, was a landmark case in its time. The House of Lords held that decorative assets in a pub and restaurant were plant because they provided atmosphere and ambience within that trade, thus establishing that assets must be judged within the context of the particular trade. HMRC instructions to their staff state that decorative items only qualify as plant if:

- the trade involves the creation of atmosphere/ambience and in effect the sale of that ambience to its customers, and
- the items on which plant or machinery allowances are claimed were specially chosen to create the atmosphere that the taxpayer is trying to sell.

As an example, HMRC express the view that a painting hanging in an accountant's office would not qualify as plant because selling atmosphere is not part of an accountant's business (CA21130), but this might be arguable.

In *Revenue and Customs Commissioners v Executors of Lord Howard of Henderskelfe (Deceased)* [2014] EWCA Civ 278, a case unrelated to capital allowances, the Court of Appeal upheld an earlier decision by the Upper Tribunal that a valuable painting which had been on display as an important part of the art exhibited in a stately home performed a functional purpose in a trade and therefore qualified as plant (see also **16.6**).

On a specialist point of interest to the agricultural community, HMRC regard most glasshouses and polytunnels as fixed structures, premises or setting rather than as plant or machinery. However, certain glasshouses with integral specialist computer equipment and polytunnels which are moved periodically should qualify for capital allowances as plant and machinery (CA22090).

Lighting installations and other infrastructure

3.8 In *Cole Bros v Phillips* [1982] STC 307, normal lighting installed in a building, comprising no more than the standard equipment of a commercial business, was held by the House of Lords not to be plant; it is part of the building. In that case, lower courts had already held that equipment with a specific functional purpose, and lighting installed into an already useable building to enable a trade to be carried on more effectively, were considered to be plant.

In *Wimpy International Ltd v Warland* [1989] STC 273, the Court of Appeal generally upheld the decision in *CIR v Scottish & Newcastle Breweries Ltd* (above). In particular, the cost of lighting in a restaurant was allowed because it provided atmosphere and ambience. Since then, case law has moved to the functional test and whether the piece of equipment is used within the trade. The tests applied in this case, which HMRC also apply, are:

Questions

1 Is the item stock in trade?

2 Is the item the business premises or part of the business premises (the premises test)?

3 Is the item used for carrying on the business (the business use test)?

Response

- If the answers to questions 1 and 2 are negative and the answer to question 3 is positive, the item is plant (CA21010, CA21140).

In the *Wimpy International Ltd* case, it was suggested that, in order to ascertain whether an asset was part of the premises, the following four factors can be considered:

- Does the item appear visually to retain a separate identity?
- With what degree of permanence has it been attached to the building?
- To what extent is the structure complete without it?
- To what extent is it intended to be permanent or, alternatively, is it likely to be replaced within a short period?

HMRC accept that electrical installation is plant, if the installation is fully integrated, designed and adapted to meet the particular requirements of the trade, functions as apparatus of the trade and is essential for the functioning of the trade. If the installation as a whole fails to qualify as plant, HMRC will adopt a piecemeal approach. The same general and then piecemeal approach is applied to cold water, sewerage and gas systems.

In particular, HMRC will accept that the following elements of an electrical installation are plant:

- the main switchboard, transformer and associated switchgear, provided that a substantial part of the electrical installation – both the equipment and the ancillary wiring – qualifies as plant;
- a standby generator and the emergency lighting and power circuits it services;
- lighting in sales areas, if it is specifically designed to encourage the sale of goods on display;
- wiring, control panels and other equipment installed specifically to supply equipment that is plant or machinery.

Lighting in a sales area will qualify even if there is no other lighting. The public areas in banking businesses are treated as sales areas (CA21180). HMRC also accept that central heating systems, hot water systems, air conditioning systems, alarm and sprinkler systems, ventilation systems, baths, wash basins and toilet suites qualify as plant (CA21200). Flooring and ceilings are generally considered not to be plant, even where they conceal service pipes etc, but there are exceptions – eg where they are temporary, moveable, or form an integral part of heating or ventilation systems (CA22070, CA22080).

Case law summary

3.9 There is a number of decided capital allowance cases, including those mentioned above, and a list of key cases is given below:

Case	*Asset*	*Held*
Yarmouth v France (1887) 19 QBD 647	A horse	Plant
Benson v Yard Arm Club Ltd [1979] STC 266	A floating restaurant	Not plant
J Lyons and Co Ltd v Attorney-General [1944] 1 All ER 477	Lighting – as part of the setting	Not plant
Jarrold v John Good & Sons Ltd (1962) 40 TC 681	Moveable office partitions	Plant
Leeds Permanent Building Society v Proctor [1982] STC 821	Window screens that were particular to the business	Plant
CIR v Scottish & Newcastle Breweries Ltd [1982] STC 296	Lighting and decor providing 'an atmosphere' necessary for the trade	Plant
Cole Bros v Phillips [1982] STC 307	Certain electrical installations	Plant
	Other electrical installations	Not plant
Wimpy International Ltd v Warland [1989] STC 273	Decorative items and certain specialist lighting	Plant
	Shop fronts	Not plant
JD Wetherspoon PLC v Commissioners for HMRC [2012] UKUT 42 (TCC)	Panelling, cornices, architraves and balustrade ends	Not plant
	Incidental expenditure strengthening kitchen floor to take weight of plant	Plant
	Fixed toilet cubicle partitions and flooring	Not plant
Cooke v Beach Station Caravans Ltd [1974] STC 402	Swimming pool used for a holiday caravan park	Plant
Hampton v Fortes Autogrill Ltd [1980] STC 80	False ceilings in a restaurant to conceal pipes and wires, etc	Not plant
Grays v Seymours Garden Centre (Horticulture) [1995] STC 706	An unheated glasshouse – a planteria	Not plant
St John's (Mountford) v Ward [1975] STC 7	A pre-fabricated fixed school building	Not plant
Munby v Furlong (1977) 50 TC 491	A barrister's law books	Plant
Schofield v R & H Hall Ltd [1975] STC 353	Grain silos	Plant
Hinton v Maden & Ireland Ltd (1959) 38 TC 391	A shoe repairer's loose tools, knives and lasts – with an expected life of more than two years	Plant

Case	*Asset*	*Held*
Dixon v Fitch's Garages Ltd [1975] STC 480	A garage canopy to protect customers while refuelling their vehicles	Not plant
Rose & Co (Wallpapers & Paints) Ltd v Campbell (1967) 44 TC 500	Wallpaper pattern books with a useful life of two years	Not plant

Costs which may also qualify as plant and machinery

3.10

> **Focus**
>
> As well as expenditure on the cost of plant itself, certain other expenditure can also be included in a capital allowances claim. This includes expenditure on alterations, demolition, fire precautions, software, thermal insulation and integral features.

Building alterations connected with installations of plant or machinery

3.11 Incidental capital expenditure on alterations to an existing building, for the installation of plant and machinery for the purposes of the qualifying activity, qualifies as plant (*CAA 2001, s 25*). A lift and its necessary machinery and wiring qualify as plant. Installation of a lift shaft to accommodate such a lift in an existing building qualifies as plant, being an alteration to an existing building incidental to the installation of plant or machinery. Installation of a lift shaft in a new building does not qualify as plant, being part of the cost of the building. When plant is relocated, the plant removal and re-installation costs qualify as plant if not allowable as a deduction from trading profits (CA21190).

Demolition costs

3.12 The net demolition cost of plant and machinery that was last used for the purposes of a qualifying activity may be either added to the cost of the new plant, if the plant is replaced, or added to other qualifying expenditure of the same accounting period as the demolition, if the plant is not replaced.

The net demolition costs are the costs of demolition less any money received for the remains of the asset, including any insurance receipts (*CAA 2001, s 26*).

Expenditure on required fire precautions

3.13 Expenditure on fire safety equipment, such as fire alarms and sprinkler systems required by law or otherwise provided for the purposes of a qualifying activity, will normally qualify for tax relief, either as the capital cost of plant and machinery or as revenue expenditure. Whether or not an asset of this kind is plant and machinery is determined in accordance with the normal tests, including principles established by the courts.

Computer software

3.14 Computer software and software rights generally fall within the intangible fixed assets regime (see **Chapter 12**), but not (except as respects royalties) if a company incurs capital expenditure on computer software that falls to be treated for accounting purposes as part of the costs of related hardware (*CTA 2009, s 813*).

Where a company incurs capital expenditure on computer software, it may elect (*CTA 2009, s 815(1)*) to claim capital allowances under rules which treat that particular computer software as plant for this purpose (*CAA 2001, s 71*). Where such an election is made, the intangible fixed assets regime still applies to that asset but with some modifications (*CTA 2009, s 815(2)–(5)*). To be effective, the election under *CTA 2009, s 815(1)* must be made in writing to HMRC not more than two years after the end of the accounting period in which the expenditure was incurred. Once made, the election is irrevocable (*CTA 2009, s 816*).

Thermal insulation of buildings

3.15 Thermal installation is qualifying expenditure for capital allowance purposes, and qualifies for a 'special rate' writing down allowance (see **3.59**) if it is incurred by a company on a building used in carrying on one of the qualifying activities (other than an ordinary UK or overseas property business) within *CAA 2001, s 15* (see **3.3**), or on a building let by an ordinary UK or overseas property business (*CAA 2001, s 28*). If the company is carrying on an ordinary UK or overseas property business, or special leasing of plant or machinery (as defined in *CAA 2001, s 19(1)*), expenditure on the provision of plant or machinery for use in a dwelling house does not qualify for an allowance (*CAA 2001, s 35*); see **8.8** for a discussion of the meaning of dwelling house. If an energy-saving deduction can be made under *CTA 2009, s 251*, by which a landlord may claim a deduction for expenditure on acquiring and installing an energy-saving item in a property or part of a property let as a dwelling-house in the course of his business (see **7.12**), no special rate capital allowance can be claimed (*CAA 2001, s 28(2B)(a)*).

Expenditure on integral features

3.16 A company incurring expenditure on the provision or replacement of integral features on a building or structure, may claim a writing down allowance at the special rate (see **3.59**) if the company meets the following conditions (*CAA 2001, s 33A(1), (2)*):

- it carries on a qualifying activity;
- it uses the building for the purposes of the qualifying activity; and
- it owns the plant and machinery as a result of incurring the expenditure.

Integral features (*CAA 2001, s 33A(5)*) consist of:

- an electrical system (including a lighting system);
- a cold water system;
- a space or water heating system, a powered system of ventilation, air cooling or air purification, and any floor or ceiling comprised in such a system;
- a lift, an escalator or a moving walkway;
- external solar shading.

This list may be varied by Treasury order (*CAA 2001, s 33A(7), (8)*). Insulation expenditure, which is covered in *CAA 2001, s 28* (see **3.15**), is specifically excluded from the list (*CAA 2001, s 33A(6)*). In practice, some of these additions may also qualify as energy-saving or environmentally beneficial plant and machinery (see **3.33**, **3.35**), in which case the option is available to the company to claim 100% FYA.

An integral feature is 'replaced' if expenditure incurred on it within a 12-month period is more than 50% of the cost of replacing it at the time the expenditure is incurred. In other cases, the expenditure is likely to be allowable revenue expenditure on repairs. It may be necessary to apportion the replacement expenditure between two accounting periods (*CAA 2001, s 33B(1)–(4)*). For practical purposes, if it is unknown whether particular expenditure on an integral feature will amount to a replacement and therefore whether the costs are revenue expenditure or capital costs qualifying for a writing down allowance, the return for the earlier accounting period may be filed and appropriate adjustments made at a later date (*CAA 2001, s 33B(5)*).

Differentiating between plant and buildings or structures

What a building includes – Lists A and B

3.17 In general, expenditure on the provision of plant and machinery excludes expenditure on the provision of a building. Certain assets do not fall into this general exclusion but, in order for a company to claim plant and machinery capital allowances, the assets in question still need to qualify as 'plant' in their own right.

For this purpose, a building includes (*CAA 2001, s 21*) an asset which:

- is incorporated in the building,
- is in the building and is of a kind normally incorporated in a building, or
- is in or connected with the building and is in 'List A'.

List A specifies (*CAA 2001, s 21*) that the following assets are treated as buildings:

1. Walls, floors, ceilings, doors, gates, shutters, windows and stairs.
2. Mains services and systems of water, electricity and gas.
3. Waste disposal systems.
4. Sewerage and drainage systems.
5. Shafts or other structures in which lifts, hoists, escalators and moving walkways are installed.
6. Fire safety systems.

Expenditure on the provision of plant and machinery also excludes expenditure on:

- the provision (by construction or acquisition) of a structure or other asset in 'List B', or
- any works involving the alteration of land (which does not include buildings or other structures).

List B stipulates (*CAA 2001, s 22*) the following excluded structures and other assets:

1. A tunnel, bridge, viaduct, aqueduct, embankment or cutting.
2. A way or hard standing (such as a pavement), road, railway, tramway, a park for vehicles or containers, or an airstrip or runway.
3. An inland navigation, including a canal or basin or a navigable river.
4. A dam, reservoir or barrage, including any sluices, gates, generators and other equipment associated with it.
5. A dock, harbour, wharf, pier, marina or jetty and any other structure in or at which vessels may be kept, or merchandise or passengers may be shipped or unshipped.
6. A dike, sea wall, weir or drainage ditch.
7. Any structure not within (1) to (6) other than:

- an industrial structure (but not a building) within the meaning of 'industrial building' as it used to apply for IBA purposes (*CAA 2001, Pt 3, Ch 2, ss 274–285*),
- a structure in use for the purposes of a gas undertaking, and
- a structure in use for a trade consisting of the provision of telecommunication, television or radio services.

Expenditure unaffected by Lists A and B

3.18 Any asset in a category listed in List A or B above does not qualify as plant and machinery except that, if it falls within the following categories, its treatment (as to whether or not it qualifies as plant and machinery) is determined in accordance with the normal tests of what is and what is not plant and machinery, including principles established by the courts:

- thermal insulation of buildings;
- safety at designated sports grounds (incurred on or before 31 March 2013);
- safety at regulated stands at sports grounds (incurred on or before 31 March 2013);
- safety at other sports grounds (incurred on or before 31 March 2013);
- personal security;
- integral features (see **3.16**);
- software and rights to software (*CAA 2001, s 23(2)*); and
- expenditure on any item within List C below.

List C (*CAA 2001, s 23*) specifies items the treatment of which (as to whether or not they qualify as plant and machinery) is unaffected by Lists A and B above. List C is as follows:

1. Machinery (including devices for providing motive power) not within any other item in this list.
2. Gas and sewerage systems provided mainly:
   (a) to meet the particular requirements of the qualifying activity, or
   (b) to serve particular plant or machinery used for the purposes of the qualifying activity.
3. … *[repealed]*
4. Manufacturing or processing equipment; storage equipment (including cold rooms); display equipment; and counters, checkouts and similar equipment.

5. Cookers, washing machines, dishwashers, refrigerators and similar equipment; washbasins, sinks, baths, showers, sanitary ware and similar equipment; and furniture and furnishings.
6. Hoists.
7. Sound insulation provided mainly to meet the particular requirements of the qualifying activity.
8. Computer, telecommunication and surveillance systems (including their wiring or other links).
9. Refrigeration or cooling equipment.
10. Fire alarm systems; sprinkler and other equipment for extinguishing or containing fires.
11. Burglar alarm systems.
12. Strong rooms in bank or building society premises; safes.
13. Partition walls, where moveable and intended to be moved in the course of the qualifying activity.
14. Decorative assets provided for the enjoyment of the public in hotel, restaurant or similar trades.
15. Advertising hoardings; signs, displays and similar assets.
16. Swimming pools (including diving boards, slides and structures on which such boards or slides are mounted).
17. Any glasshouse constructed so that the required environment (namely, air, heat, light, irrigation and temperature) for the growing of plants is provided automatically by means of devices forming an integral part of its structure.
18. Cold stores.
19. Caravans provided mainly for holiday lettings.
20. Buildings provided for testing aircraft engines run within the buildings.
21. Moveable buildings intended to be moved in the course of the qualifying activity.
22. The alteration of land for the purpose only of installing plant or machinery.
23. The provision of dry docks.
24. The provision of any jetty or similar structure provided mainly to carry plant or machinery.
25. The provision of pipelines or underground ducts or tunnels with a primary purpose of carrying utility conduits.

26. The provision of towers to support floodlights.

27. The provision of:

    (a) any reservoir incorporated into a water treatment works, or

    (b) any service reservoir of treated water for supply within any housing estate or other particular locality.

28. The provision of:

    (a) silos provided for temporary storage, or

    (b) storage tanks.

29. The provision of slurry pits or silage clamps.

30. The provision of fish tanks or fish ponds.

31. The provision of rails, sleepers and ballast for a railway or tramway.

32. The provision of structures and other assets for providing the setting for any ride at an amusement park or exhibition.

33. The provision of fixed zoo cages.

Items 1 to 16 above do not include any asset whose principal purpose is to insulate or enclose the interior of a building or to provide an interior wall, floor or ceiling which (in each case) is intended to remain permanently in place (*CAA 2001, s 23(4)*).

HMRC interpret the items in List C narrowly. For example, they state that item 33, which refers to fixed zoo cages, does not apply by analogy to other forms of animal shelter such as kennels or stables (CA22030).

> **Focus**
>
> There are three types of allowance, with differing rules, that can be claimed: annual investment allowance, first year allowance and writing down allowance.

ANNUAL INVESTMENT ALLOWANCE

Introduction

3.19 The annual investment allowance (AIA) largely replaced the plant and machinery first year allowance from 1 April 2008 and can be claimed on expenditure incurred on or after that date (*CAA 2001, s 38A*).

The maximum AIA that can be claimed by a single company in a 12-month accounting period has been changed on several occasions. At the time of writing it is ££200,000 (*CAA 2001, s 51A(5)*).

Changes in the maximum AIA have required transitional provisions. For example, the maximum AIA was cut on 1 April 2012, from £100,000 to £25,000, and special rules were introduced for this. If the company's accounting period straddled 1 April 2012, the maximum AIA was established by determining the maximum AIA that would have applied to each component part (before and after 1 April 2012) and aggregating these; however, the AIA claim in respect of expenditure incurred on or after 1 April 2012 was then restricted to the appropriate proportion of the new £25,000 limit which was attributable to that period (*FA 2011, s 11*; see **3.22**).

The maximum AIA was temporarily increased from £25,000 to £250,000 from 1 January 2013 until 31 December 2014, with complex transitional provisions for accounting periods which would straddle 1 January 2013 or 1 January 2015 and particular complications for accounting periods which straddled both 1 April 2012 and 1 January 2013. However, *FA 2014* introduced a further temporary increase to £500,000 from 1 April 2014 to 31 December 2015, requiring further transitional provisions (*CAA 2001, s 51A(5)*, as amended by *FA 2014, s 10(1)*).

The maximum AIA had been expected to fall to £25,000 from 1 January 2016, until the government announced an increase in the permanent level of the AIA to £200,000 from that date and committed to maintaining it at this level (Budget, 8 July 2015, tinyurl.com/qf7t8ue, para 1.242). On the reduction in AIA from £500,000 to £200,000 on 1 January 2016, the transitional provisions which apply are unchanged from those that were to have applied on the AIA reducing to £25,000 (*FA 2014, Sch 2, paras 4–5; F(No 2)A 2015, s 8*).

In summary, the maximum AIA limits since inception are as follows:

	Maximum AIA for a single company
1 April 2008 to 31 March 2010	£50,000
1 April 2010 to 31 March 2012	£100,000
1 April 2012 to 31 December 2012	£25,000
1 January 2013 to 31 March 2014	£250,000
1 April 2014 to 31 December 2015	£500,000
1 January 2016 onwards	£200,000

AIA is given for a chargeable period, which is the company's accounting period (*CAA 2001, s 6(1)*). If the accounting period is shorter than 12 months, the maximum AIA is reduced proportionately (*CAA 2001, s 51A(6)*). A company may claim all or part of the AIA to which it is entitled (*CAA 2001, s 51A(7)*).

Expenditure incurred on plant and machinery, but not cars, qualifies for AIA (*CAA 2001, s 38B*). Qualifying expenditure retains the meaning adopted for capital allowances, being capital expenditure incurred on the provision of plant and machinery, wholly or partly for the purposes of the qualifying activity carried on by the company that incurs the expenditure and, as a result of incurring the expenditure, the company owns the asset (*CAA 2001, s 11*; see **3.5**).

Although AIA may be claimed by an individual, a partnership or limited liability partnership (LLP) in which all the members are individuals, or a company, it may not be claimed by a trust, or by a mixed partnership or LLP of which a company or a trust is a member (*CAA 2001, s 38A(3)*; see also *Hoardweel Farm Partnership v HMRC* [2012] UKFTT 402 (TC), *Drilling Global Consultant LLP* [2014] TC 04003). For this purpose, a company is any body corporate or unincorporated association (*CTA 2010, s 1121(1)*; see **1.5**).

Special provisions apply to companies in a group, or companies under common control, where only one AIA limit applies (see **3.28–3.31**).

Exclusions from AIA

3.20 Certain types of expenditure incurred are excluded from an AIA claim (*CAA 2001, s 38B*). Expenditure is excluded if it is incurred:

- in an accounting period in which a qualifying activity is permanently discontinued;
- on the provision of a car. A car is any mechanically propelled road vehicle (other than a motor cycle) that is not primarily used for the conveyance of goods or of a type that is not commonly used as a road vehicle (*CAA 2001, s 268A*);
- wholly for the purposes of a ring fence trade (see **23.3**);
- in circumstances which are connected with a change in the nature or conduct of a trade or business carried on by a person other than the company incurring the expenditure, and the obtaining of an AIA is the main benefit, or one of the main benefits, which could reasonably be expected to arise from the making of the change;
- on plant purchased for purposes other than use in the qualifying activity; or
- on plant purchased for long funding leasing.

Expenditure is also excluded from AIA if it is deemed to have been incurred as a result of the owner receiving it as a gift and bringing it into use in the qualifying activity.

Allocation of AIA

> **Focus**
>
> Planning the timing of capital expenditure, and optimising the allocation of AIA to qualifying expenditure, may both play a part in maximising capital allowances.

3.21 Regardless of the number of activities that a company carries on, it may only claim one AIA. The company may claim all the AIA to which it is entitled, or it may choose to claim only part of that amount (*CAA 2001, s 51A(7)*).

A company may allocate its AIA to its relevant qualifying expenditure as it thinks fit (*CAA 2001, s 51B*). This can be crucial in maximising capital allowances because, by allocating the AIA first to expenditure that does not qualify for FYA, the company may still be entitled to some FYA in the same year.

Example 3.1—Allocation of annual investment allowance

Facts

Northco Ltd carries on a manufacturing trade and also runs a property rental business.

During the 12-month accounting period to 31 March 2018, the company's manufacturing division spent £200,000 on new plant and machinery which would qualify for 18% main rate writing down allowance, while the letting business spent £100,000 on plant and machinery which would qualify for 8% special rate writing down allowance.

Analysis

Northco Ltd claims annual investment allowance of £200,000, the maximum for the accounting period, and decides to allocate its AIA as follows:

Eligible for AIA	*£*	*Allocation of AIA*	*£*
Expenditure incurred re			
Manufacturing trade	200,000	Manufacturing trade	100,000
Rental business	100,000	Rental business	100,000
Total claim			200,000

As a result, the balance of £100,000 of expenditure which is not covered by AIA will qualify for ongoing writing down allowances of 18% rather than 8%.

Reduction in maximum AIA at 1 April 2012

3.22 The maximum AIA decreased from £100,000 to £25,000 for expenditure incurred on or after 1 April 2012. Where an accounting period straddled this date ('the relevant day'), transitional provisions required that the maximum AIA claim was apportioned *pro rata* (*FA 2011, s 11*). For example, the maximum claim for a single company with a 31 December 2012 year end amounted to £43,750 (ie (100,000 × 3/12) + (25,000 × 9/12)).

Example 3.2—AIA: period straddling relevant day (1 April 2012)

Facts

Southside Ltd is an engineering company that prepares accounts to 31 December each year. During the year ended 31 December 2012, it purchases the following items of plant and machinery:

Date	*Equipment*	*Cost*
		£
1 February 2012	Mixing machine	5,000
7 April 2012	Saw mill	50,000
30 August 2012	Lathe	15,000

Analysis

The maximum allowance for the period 1 January 2012 to 31 March 2012 is:

£100,000 × 3/12 = £25,000

The maximum allowance for the period 1 April 2012 to 31 December 2012 is:

£25,000 × 9/12 = £18,750

Although the total expenditure amounts to £65,000, the maximum AIA claim for the 12-month accounting period is restricted to £43,750 and, furthermore, the maximum qualifying expenditure in the period 1 April 2012 to 31 December 2012 cannot exceed £18,750. Therefore the company's total AIA for the year amounts to only £5,000 + £18,750 = £23,750.

If the company had planned ahead and bought the saw mill (say) a week earlier, on 31 March, it would have been able to claim AIA of £43,750.

Temporary increase in maximum AIA at 1 January 2013

Focus

The transitional provisions to implement the temporary increase in maximum AIA from 1 January 2013 were widely criticised for their excessive complexity. During the transition, the timing of capital expenditure could have a massive impact on the AIA available.

3.23 The maximum AIA increased from £25,000 to £250,000 for expenditure incurred on or after 1 January 2013 (*FA 2013, s 7, Sch 1*).

Where an accounting period straddled 1 January 2013, the maximum AIA claim for this 'first straddling period' (as defined in *FA 2013, Sch 1, para 1*) was apportioned *pro rata*, but the transitional provisions were more complex than those at 1 April 2012. This was because an accounting period that straddled 1 January 2013 might, or might not, also straddle 1 April 2012 (ie 'the relevant day' when the previous change in maximum AIA took place).

First straddling period beginning before 1 April 2012

3.24 Where a company's first straddling period (ie an accounting period straddling 1 January 2013) began before 1 April 2012, it was necessary to consider (*FA 2013, Sch 1, para 1*):

- so much of the actual chargeable period as fell before 1 April 2012 (referred to here as the 'first period');
- so much of the actual chargeable period as fell on or after 1 April 2012 but before 1 January 2013 (referred to here as the 'second period'); and
- so much of the actual chargeable period as fell on or after 1 January 2013 (referred to here as the 'third period').

The maximum AIA for the first straddling period was the sum of each maximum AIA that would be found if each of the first, second and third periods were treated as separate chargeable periods. However, it was then necessary to consider each of those component periods separately.

In relation to expenditure incurred in the first period, the maximum AIA for that period was limited to the amount that would have been the maximum allowance for the first straddling period, if the temporary increase in the AIA to £250,000 had not been made.

In relation to expenditure incurred in the second period, the maximum AIA for that period was limited to A – B, where:

- 'A' was the amount that would have been the maximum allowance for the period from 1 April 2012 to the end of the first straddling period, assuming that the temporary increase in the AIA to £250,000 had not been made; and
- 'B' was the amount (if any) by which the AIA expenditure incurred in the first period, in respect of which an AIA claim was made, exceeded the maximum allowance for that period, if it were to be treated as a separate chargeable period.

In relation to expenditure incurred in the third period, the maximum allowance for that period was the sum that would be found if the second and third periods were each treated as separate chargeable periods and the maximum allowances for both those periods were aggregated (*FA 2013, Sch 1, para 2*).

Example 3.3—AIA straddling 1 April 2012 and 1 January 2013

Facts

East Road Construction Ltd prepares accounts to 28 February each year. During the year ended 28 February 2013, it spent the following sums on new earth-moving plant and machinery:

Date	*Equipment*	*Cost (£)*
15 March 2012	Plant item 1	50,000
7 July 2012	Plant item 2	15,000
8 February 2013	Plant item 3	55,000

Analysis

First, it is necessary to calculate the maximum AIA for the first straddling period as a whole.

On a straight apportionment basis, the maximum allowance for the 'first period' of the transition from 1 March 2012 to 31 March 2012 is:

£100,000 × 1/12 = £8,333

On the same basis, the maximum allowance for the 'second period' from 1 April 2012 to 31 December 2012 is:

£25,000 × 9/12 = £18,750

Likewise, the maximum allowance for the 'third period' from 1 January 2013 to 28 February 2013 is:

£250,000 × 2/12 = £41,667

Thus, the company's maximum AIA for the whole of this 'first straddling period' is:

£8,333 + £18,750 + £41,667 = £68,750

Then it is necessary to consider each of the three periods separately.

The maximum AIA for the first period is calculated as follows:

£100,000 × 1/12 = £8,333

£25,000 × 11/12 = £22,917

Total £31,250

The maximum AIA for the second period is calculated as follows:

A = £25,000 × 11/12 = £22,917

B = an amount between (£50,000 – £8,333) or £41,667 and Nil

Therefore (A – B) = an amount between £22,917 and Nil

The maximum AIA for the third period is calculated as follows:

£25,000 × 9/12 = £18,750

£250,000 × 2/12 = £41,667

Total £60,417

AIA claims

The actual AIA expenditure incurred in the first period is £50,000, which is more than the maximum of £31,250 for that period, so AIA of up to £31,250 might be claimed.

The actual AIA expenditure incurred in the second period is £15,000. The maximum AIA for that period cannot exceed £22,917, but this limit is reduced by £1 for each £1 by which the AIA claimed in respect of the first period exceeds £8,333.

The actual AIA expenditure incurred in the third period is £55,000, which is less than the maximum of £60,417 for that period, so AIA of up to £55,000 might be claimed.

Thus, the maximum AIA claims that the company could make for expenditure in each component part of the first straddling period, based on the AIA expenditure incurred, would be:

	£
First period	31,250
Second period	15,000
Third period	60,417

However, because of the operation of the (A – B) formula, the aggregate AIA for the first and second periods cannot exceed £31,250.

Overall, the AIA claim for this first straddling period is restricted to £68,750. Within the limits imposed by the maximum AIA limits for each period, the company may allocate its AIA claim to specific relevant qualifying expenditure as it thinks fit (*CAA 2001, s 51B*; see also **3.21**).

The timing of the relevant qualifying expenditure could have a significant impact on the maximum AIA available.

Example 3.4—AIA: expenditure straddling 1 April 2012 and 1 January 2013

Facts

As in Example 3.3, but East Road Construction Ltd incurs the entire £120,000 costs of their new plant on 7 July 2012.

Analysis

Although the maximum AIA for the year to 28 February 2013 (the company's 'first straddling period') is unchanged at £68,750, the maximum AIA for the 'second period' (in which all the expenditure was incurred) must be re-calculated as follows:

A = £25,000 × 11/12 = £22,917 (as before)

B = Nil (because there is no AIA expenditure in the first period, on which AIA is claimed)

Therefore (A – B) = £22,917

AIA claims

In relation to the second period, the maximum AIA that can be claimed for that period is (A – B) = £22,917. The actual AIA expenditure incurred in that period is £120,000, but the maximum AIA that can be claimed is restricted to £22,917. This follows because the entire AIA expenditure was incurred before the maximum AIA was increased on 1 January 2013.

First straddling period beginning on or after 1 April 2012

3.25 If the company's first straddling period began on or after 1 April 2012, there was no 'first period' for the purposes of the above rules, and the calculations were very much more straightforward.

As before, the maximum AIA for the first straddling period was the sum of each maximum AIA that would be found if each of the component periods (ie the parts before, and on or after, 1 January 2013) were treated as separate chargeable periods. However, it was then necessary to consider the first of those periods separately.

In this case, in relation to expenditure incurred in the part of the first straddling period that fell before 1 January 2013, the maximum AIA for that period was limited to the amount that would have been the maximum allowance for the first straddling period, if the temporary increase in the AIA to £250,000 had not been made. In other words, for expenditure incurred before 1 January 2013, only expenditure up to the maximum amount of the £25,000 cap could be covered (*FA 2013, Sch 1, para 3*).

Example 3.5—AIA straddling 1 January 2013

Facts

Westco Ltd, a manufacturing company, prepares accounts to 30 April each year. On 15 December 2012, during the year ended 30 April 2013, it purchases a new milling machine at a cost of £150,000.

Analysis

First, it is necessary to calculate the maximum AIA for the first straddling period as a whole.

On a straight apportionment basis, the maximum allowance for the part of the first straddling period that falls before 1 January 2013 (in this case, the period from 1 May 2012 to 31 December 2012) is:

£25,000 × 8/12 = £16,667

On the same basis, the maximum allowance for the part of the first straddling period that falls on or after 1 January 2013 (in this case, the period from 1 January 2013 to 30 April 2013) is:

£250,000 × 4/12 = £83,333

Thus, the company's maximum AIA for the whole of this 'first straddling period' is:

£16,667 + £83,333 = £100,000

Then it is necessary to consider the part of the first straddling period that falls before 1 January 2013. In relation to expenditure incurred in that part, the maximum AIA is limited to the amount that would have been the maximum allowance for the whole of the first straddling period, if the temporary increase in the AIA to £250,000 had not been made. This is calculated as follows:

£25,000 × 8/12 = £16,667

£25,000 × 4/12 = £8,333

Total £25,000

AIA claims

The actual AIA expenditure incurred in the part of the first straddling period that falls before 1 January 2013 is £150,000, which is more than the maximum of £25,000 for that period, so AIA of up to only £25,000 may be claimed.

No AIA expenditure was incurred in the part of the first straddling period that falls on or after 1 January 2013, so no additional AIA can be claimed.

As before, the timing of the relevant qualifying expenditure could have a significant impact on the maximum AIA available.

Example 3.6—AIA: expenditure straddling 1 January 2013

Facts

As in Example 3.5, but Westco Ltd purchases its new milling machine for £150,000 on 15 January 2013.

Analysis

The maximum AIA for the year to 30 April 2013 (the company's 'first straddling period') is unchanged at £100,000.

There is no AIA expenditure in the part of the first straddling period that falls before 1 January 2013, so it is unnecessary to consider any limit on AIA for that period.

The maximum AIA for the part of the first straddling period that falls on or after 1 January 2013 is limited only by the maximum AIA for the whole of the first straddling period, ie £100,000. In this case, the AIA expenditure exceeds that amount, so AIA on £100,000 can be claimed.

Further temporary increase in maximum AIA at 1 April 2014

> **Focus**
>
> The government's decision to implement a further temporary increase in maximum AIA from 1 April 2014 created the need for additional transitional provisions, but for companies these were not as complex as those which had applied at 1 January 2013.

3.26 The temporary increase in maximum AIA to £250,000 from 1 January 2013 was superseded by a further temporary increase to £500,000 for the period from 1 April 2014 to 31 December 2015 (*FA 2014, s 10*).

Where an accounting period straddles 1 April 2014 (the 'start date'; see *FA 2014, s 10(3)*), the maximum AIA claim for this 'first straddling period' (as re-defined in *FA 2014, Sch 2, para 1(1)*, and not to be confused with the same expression as defined in *FA 2013, Sch 1, para 1*; see **3.23**) is apportioned *pro rata*. The maximum AIA for the whole of the second straddling period is the sum of each maximum AIA that would be found if each of the component periods (ie the parts before, and on or after, 1 April 2014) were treated as separate chargeable periods (*FA 2014, Sch 2, para 1(2)*). However, it is then necessary to consider the first of those periods separately.

In this case, in relation to expenditure incurred in the part of the straddling period that falls before 1 April 2014, the maximum AIA for that part is limited to the amount that would have been the maximum allowance for that part if the increase in AIA from £250,000 to £500,000 had not been made. In other words, for expenditure incurred before 1 April 2014, only expenditure up to the amount of the £250,000 cap can be covered (*FA 2014, Sch 2, para 3*).

These replicate the provisions that applied when AIA was increased from £50,000 to £100,000 on 1 April 2010 (*FA 2010, s 5*).

Example 3.7—AIA straddling 1 April 2014

Facts

New Times Ltd, a trading company, prepares accounts to 31 December each year. On 25 March 2014, during the year ended 31 December 2014, it purchases plant at a cost of £450,000.

Analysis

First, it is necessary to calculate the maximum AIA for this first straddling period as a whole.

On a straight apportionment basis, the maximum allowance for the part of the first straddling period that falls before 1 April 2014 (in this case, the period from 1 January 2014 to 31 March 2014) is:

£250,000 × 3/12 = £62,500

On the same basis, the maximum allowance for the part of the first straddling period that falls on or after 1 April 2014 (in this case, the period from 1 April 2014 to 31 December 2014) is:

£500,000 × 9/12 = £375,000

Thus, the company's maximum AIA for the whole of this first straddling period is:

£62,500 + £375,000 = £437,500

Then it is necessary to consider the part of the first straddling period that falls before 1 April 2014. In relation to expenditure incurred in that part, the maximum AIA is limited to the amount that would have been the maximum allowance for the whole of the first straddling period, if the further temporary increase in the AIA to £500,000 had not been made. This is calculated as follows:

£250,000 × 3/12 = £62,500

£250,000 × 9/12 = £187,500

Total £250,000

AIA claims

The actual AIA expenditure incurred in the part of the first straddling period that falls before 1 April 2014 is £450,000, which is more than the maximum of £250,000 for that period, so AIA of only £250,000 may be claimed.

No AIA expenditure was incurred in the part of the first straddling period that falls on or after 1 April 2014, so no additional AIA can be claimed.

As before, the timing of the relevant qualifying expenditure can have a significant impact on the maximum AIA available.

Example 3.8—AIA: expenditure straddling 1 April 2014

Facts

As in Example 3.7, but New Times Ltd purchases the plant for £450,000 a week later, ie on 1 April 2014.

Analysis

The maximum AIA for the first straddling period to 31 December 2014 remains unchanged at £437,500.

There is no AIA expenditure in the part of the first straddling period that falls before 1 April 2014, so it is unnecessary to consider any limit on AIA for that period.

The maximum AIA for the part of the first straddling period that falls on or after 1 April 2014 is limited only by the maximum AIA for the whole of the first straddling period, ie £437,500. In this case, the AIA expenditure exceeds that amount, so AIA of £437,500 may be claimed.

Reduction in maximum AIA at 1 January 2016

Focus

It was helpful that *FA 2014* contained transitional provisions intended to apply when the temporary increase in AIA came to an end, since this has allowed companies to plan the timing of their capital expenditure to take best advantage of the £500,000 limit while it has lasted. These transitional provisions have not been changed by *F(No 2)A 2015*.

3.27 The temporary increase in maximum AIA to £250,000 from 1 January 2013 was superseded by a further temporary increase to £500,000, for the period from 1 April 2014 to 31 December 2015. The government's stated 'increase in the permanent level of AIA' to £200,000 from 1 January 2016 amounts to a reduction from £300,000 on that date. For accounting periods straddling 1 January 2016, transitional provisions apply (*FA 2014, Sch 2, paras 4–5; F(No 2)A 2015, s 8*).

Where an accounting period straddles 1 January 2016, the maximum AIA claim for this 'second straddling period' (as defined in *FA 2014, Sch 2, para 4(1)*, and not to be confused with the same expression defined in *FA 2013, Sch 1, para 4*, before removal by *FA 2014, Sch 2, para 7(3)*) is apportioned *pro rata*. The maximum AIA for the whole of the second straddling period is the sum of each maximum AIA that would be found if each of the component periods (ie the parts before, and on or after, 1 January 2016) were treated as separate chargeable periods (*FA 2014, Sch 2, para 4(2)*). However, it is then necessary to consider the second of those periods separately.

In this case, in relation to expenditure incurred in the part of the second straddling period that falls on or after 1 January 2016, the maximum AIA for that part is limited to the amount that would have been the maximum allowance for that part if it were treated as a separate chargeable period. In other words, for expenditure incurred on or after 1 January 2016, only expenditure up to the pro-rated amount of the new £200,000 cap can be covered (*FA 2014, Sch 2, para 4(3)*).

This replicates the provisions that applied when AIA was reduced from £100,000 to £25,000 on 1 April 2012 (*FA 2011, s 11*; see **3.22**).

Example 3.9—AIA straddling 1 January 2016

Facts

Compass Ltd is a trading company which prepares its accounts to 31 May annually. During the year to 31 May 2016, it purchases the following items of plant:

Date	*Equipment*	*Cost (£)*
10 October 2015	Packaging machine	80,000
1 April 2016	Assembly conveyor	400,000

Analysis

First, it is necessary to calculate the maximum AIA for this second straddling period as a whole.

On a straight apportionment basis, the maximum allowance for the part of the second straddling period that falls before 1 January 2016 (in this case, the period from 1 June 2015 to 31 December 2015) is:

$$£500,000 \times 7/12 = £291,667$$

On the same basis, the maximum allowance for the part of the second straddling period that falls on or after 1 January 2016 (in this case, the period from 1 January 2016 to 31 May 2016) is:

$$£200,000 \times 5/12 = £83,333$$

Thus, the company's maximum AIA for the whole of this second straddling period is:

$$£291,667 + £83,333 = £375,000$$

Then it is necessary to consider the part of the second straddling period that falls on or after 1 January 2016. In relation to expenditure incurred in that part, the maximum AIA is limited to the amount that would have been the maximum allowance for that part, if it were treated as a separate chargeable period. As above, this is calculated as follows:

$$£200,000 \times 5/12 = £83,333$$

AIA claims

The actual AIA expenditure incurred in the part of the second straddling period that falls on or after 1 January 2016 is £400,000, which is more than the maximum of £83,333 for that period, so AIA of up to only £83,333 may be claimed.

The actual AIA expenditure incurred in the part of the second straddling period that falls before 1 January 2016 is £80,000. AIA may be claimed in full on that expenditure without the total AIA claim (£83,333 + £80,000 = £163,333) exceeding the AIA limit of £375,000 for the whole of the second straddling period.

Once again, the timing of expenditure will have an impact on the availability of AIA.

Example 3.10—AIA: expenditure straddling 1 January 2016

Facts

As in Example 3.9 but the timing of expenditure by Compass Ltd on items of plant is different. The purchases are as follows:

Date	*Equipment*	*Cost (£)*
10 October 2015	Assembly conveyor	400,000
1 April 2016	Packaging machine	80,000

Analysis

The company's maximum AIA for the whole of this second straddling period (ie the year to 31 May 2016) is unchanged at:

£291,667 + £83,333 = £375,000

As before, the maximum AIA for the part of the second straddling period that falls on or after 1 January 2016 is calculated as follows:

£200,000 × 5/12 = £83,333

AIA claims

The actual AIA expenditure incurred in the part of the second straddling period that falls on or after 1 January 2016 is £80,000, which is less than the maximum of £83,333 for that period, so AIA may be claimed in full on the expenditure of £80,000.

The actual AIA expenditure incurred in the part of the second straddling period that falls before 1 January 2016 is £400,000. The maximum for that part is not restricted merely by the fact that it exceeds the amount (£291,667) that would have been the maximum allowance for that part if it were treated as a separate chargeable period.

Thus, the maximum AIA claims that the company could make for expenditure in each component part of the second straddling period, based on the AIA expenditure incurred, would be:

	£
Part before 1 January 2016	400,000
Part on or after 1 January 2016	80,000

However, if this was claimed in full, the total AIA claimed for the whole of the second straddling period would exceed the overall maximum of £375,000. Therefore, the AIA claim must be restricted to £302,084. Within the maximum AIA limits for each period, the company may allocate its AIA claim to specific relevant qualifying expenditure as it thinks fit (*CAA 2001, s 51B*; see also **3.21**). For example, Compass Ltd might choose to claim less than £80,000 of AIA (or even none at all) on the packaging machine, and correspondingly more (up to a maximum of £375,000) on the assembly conveyor.

Observations

By bringing forward substantial AIA expenditure to before 1 January 2016, when the maximum AIA reduces from £500,000 to £200,000, Compass Ltd has increased its AIA claim for the accounting period ending 31 May 2016 from £163,333 to £375,000.

Group companies

3.28 Companies within a group are entitled to claim AIA, but only up to the amount of a single maximum AIA limit, which they may allocate to AIA expenditure incurred by any of them, as they think fit.

For a group, the relevant AIA qualifying expenditure for a financial year is the AIA qualifying expenditure incurred in accounting periods ending within that financial year (*CAA 2001, s 51C(4)*). A financial year commences on 1 April and ends on 31 March.

In determining the existence of a group, the definition of a parent undertaking is applied according to *CA 2006, s 1162* (see also **5.2**). Where the conditions are met, a company is treated as another company's parent undertaking for any financial year in which the other company's accounting period ends (*CAA 2001, s 51C(5)*).

Where accounting periods straddle a date on which the maximum AIA was changed (eg 1 April 2012, 1 January 2013, 1 April 2014 or, prospectively, 1 January 2016), the maximum AIA is calculated as the maximum apportionable to the group, but is subject to the restriction that the maximum statutory claim for the period cannot be exceeded (*CAA 2001, s 51K*; *FA 2011, s 11(9)–(11)*; *FA 2013, Sch 1, para 5*; *FA 2014, Sch 2, para 5*).

Example 3.11—AIA: group of companies with the same accounting dates

Facts

The LMN Group consists of three companies: L Ltd, M Ltd and N Ltd. L Ltd and M Ltd prepared their accounts for the year ended 31 December 2015. N Ltd prepared its accounts for the year ended 28 February 2015 and then for the 10-month period from 1 March 2015 to 31 December 2015.

Company	*Accounting period ending in financial year 2015*	*Individual maximum AIA amounts calculated under FA 2014, Sch 2, paras 1, 3*
		£
L Ltd	12 months to 31.12.2015	500,000
M Ltd	12 months to 31.12.2015	500,000
N Ltd	10 months to 31.12.2015	416,667

Analysis

The companies' individual maximum AIA amounts are as shown in the third column of the table. Their overall maximum AIA, to be shared amongst the group, would be the greatest maximum allowance (namely, £500,000).

Subject to their individual maximum AIA amounts, the companies may vary the AIA claim among themselves, but the overall claim can be no more than £500,000. Thus, if an AIA of (say) £500,000 were allocated to L Ltd, no further AIA could be allocated to the other companies in the group in this particular year.

Alternatively, if an AIA of (say) £416,667 were allocated to N Ltd, and it was agreed that the balance available to the group was to be allocated to L Ltd, no more than (£500,000 – £416,667) = £83,333 could be allocated to L Ltd in this particular year.

Example 3.12—AIA: group of companies with different accounting dates

Facts

The ABCD Group consists of four companies: A Plc, B Ltd, C Ltd and D Ltd. Their accounting dates and their individual maximum AIA amounts for accounting periods ending in the financial year 2014 were as shown:

Company	*Accounting period ending in financial year 2014*	*Individual maximum AIA amounts calculated under FA 2014, Sch 2, paras 1, 3*
		£
A Plc	12 months to 31.12.2014	437,500
B Ltd	12 months to 31.09.2014	375,000
C Ltd	12 months to 30.06.2014	312,500
D Ltd	12 months to 31.03.2015	500,000

Analysis

The companies' individual maximum AIA amounts are as shown in the third column of the table. Their overall maximum AIA, to be shared amongst the group, would be the greatest maximum allowance (namely, £500,000).

Subject to their individual maximum AIA amounts, the companies may vary the AIA claim among themselves, but the overall claim can be no more than £500,000. Thus, if an AIA of (say) £437,500 were allocated to A Plc, no more than (£500,000 – £437,500) = £62,500 could be allocated to the other companies (collectively) in this particular year.

Companies or groups of companies under common control

3.29 Two or more companies or groups of companies under common control in any financial year are only entitled to one AIA, which they may allocate to AIA expenditure incurred by any of them, as they think fit. They are thus governed by the same rules that apply to companies in a group (see **3.28**).

Two or more groups of companies are under common control if they are controlled by the same person and are related to one another (*CAA 2001, s 51D*). Two or more other companies are under common control if they are controlled by the same person and are related to one another (*CAA 2001, s 51E*).

A company is controlled by a person in a financial year if that person controls it at the end of its accounting period ending in that financial year (*CAA 2001, s 51F*). 'Control' means that a person has the power to determine that a company's affairs are conducted in accordance with his wishes (*CAA 2001, s 574(2)*).

For the purposes of these rules, it may be necessary to determine whether companies or activities are related to one another (*CAA 2001, ss 51G, 51J*). Such a relationship exists if, during the financial year, either they share the same premises, or they derive more than 50% of their respective turnovers from qualifying activities within the same NACE common statistical classification. The NACE classification is the first level of the common statistical classification of economic activities in the European Union, established by *Regulation (EC) No 1893/2006* of the European Parliament and the Council of 20 December 2006.

Example 3.13—AIA: companies under common control

Facts

Ashley Ltd runs a retail shop. Burton Ltd operates as an insurance broker. Both companies are controlled by Mr Claridge. Ashley Ltd has an accounting period ending on 30 April 2018. It had sole occupation of Ashley House, its business premises. On 1 July 2018, Burton Ltd, with an accounting period ending on 31 December 2018, moved into Ashley House. Both companies occupied the premises until 31 December 2018.

Analysis

The companies meet the shared premises condition from 1 July to 31 December 2018, and are therefore related to one another during the financial year 2014.

Short accounting periods

3.30 A company that has been a member of a group, or under common control with other companies, for a period of less than one year can only be allocated a proportionately reduced AIA (*CAA 2001, s 51A(6)*).

Example 3.14—AIA: group of companies with short accounting period

Facts

Mr James controls a group of companies comprising Cuthbert Ltd, Damian Ltd and Eldridge Ltd. All three companies have prepared accounts to 31 March 2018. Eldridge Ltd was formed on 1 July 2017. Each company incurs relevant AIA qualifying expenditure of £200,000 in the year to 31 March 2018.

Analysis

The maximum AIA that can be claimed by the group is £200,000, but the maximum AIA that can be allocated to Eldridge Ltd is 9/12 × £200,000 = £150,000.

Multiple accounting periods

3.31 If a company has more than one accounting period ending in a financial year, each accounting period must be examined separately in order to determine whether or not the related activities conditions are met (*CAA 2001, s 51L(2)*).

FIRST YEAR ALLOWANCE

Focus

For many companies, first year allowances have been largely replaced by the AIA. For larger companies, the availability of FYAs on certain capital expenditure can be an important factor in reducing taxable profits – especially given that the maximum AIA per annum was reduced from £500,000 to £200,000 from 1 January 2016.

3.32 Companies that invest in 'new' technologies, being energy-saving or environmentally beneficial plant and machinery, receive a 100% first year allowance (FYA) – generally called an enhanced capital allowance or ECA – on the full cost of their investment, provided all the necessary criteria are met (see **3.33** onwards). From 1 April 2013, expenditure on ships and railway assets is no longer excluded from FYAs (*FA 2013, s 70*).

An FYA can only be claimed in respect of the accounting period in which the expenditure is incurred (*CAA 2001, s 52*; see **3.5** above for the date that expenditure is incurred). If that is also the period in which the qualifying activity is discontinued, no FYA can be claimed.

Energy-saving plant and machinery

3.33 Particular categories of plant or machinery classified as meeting certain energy-saving criteria qualify for 100% FYA, regardless of the size of the company claiming them.

Under statutory powers created in 2001 (*CAA 2001, s 45A(3)*; *Capital Allowances (Energy-saving Plant and Machinery) Order 2001, SI 2001/2541, Capital Allowances (Energy-saving Plant and Machinery) Order 2018, SI 2018/268*), the Government has issued the Energy Technology Criteria List and the Energy Technology Product List. These lists are revised and replaced periodically.

The full lists can be found at tinyurl.com/j6kmp38. The technologies currently included are, broadly, those that fall within a technology class specified in the Energy Technology Criteria List and meet the energy-saving criteria set out in that Criteria List and, in the case of any listed below, are specified in and have not been removed from the Energy Technology Product List or have been accepted for inclusion in that Product List:

- air-to-air energy recovery devices;
- automatic monitoring and targeting (AMT);
- boiler equipment;
- combined heat and power;
- compressed air equipment;
- heat pumps;
- heating, ventilation and air conditioning (HVAC) equipment;
- high speed hand air dryers;
- lighting;
- motors and drives;
- pipework insulation;
- radiant and warm air heaters;
- refrigeration equipment;
- solar thermal systems and collectors;
- uninterruptible power supplies; and
- waste heat to electricity conversion equipment.

No FYAs are available on expenditure incurred on or after 1 April 2012 on plant or machinery which generates electricity or heat (or produces biogas or biofuels) attracting tariff payments under the Feed-in Tariff (FIT) or Renewable Heat Incentive (RHI) schemes, except in the case of combined heat and power equipment (CHP) where the restriction applies from 1 April 2014. 100% FYAs may still be claimed (subject to the other conditions of the FYA scheme) in respect of expenditure on such equipment as long as no tariffs are paid. Any FYAs granted, in respect of expenditure incurred from April 2012 (or April

2014 for CHP installations), will be withdrawn if FITs or RHI tariffs are paid subsequently. From 1 April 2013, these provisions apply also in Northern Ireland (*CAA 2001, s 45AA*, as amended by *FA 2013, s 67*).

Changes are made periodically to the lists of energy-saving technologies which qualify for 100% FYAs.

Expenditure will only qualify for FYA if the energy-saving plant or machinery is unused and not second-hand, is not within a category of assets otherwise excluded from FYAs (eg assets acquired for leasing or letting on hire, cars, sea-going ships and long-life assets), is of a description specified by Treasury order, and meets the energy-saving criteria specified for plant or machinery of that description (*CAA 2001, s 45A*). In certain cases, the government may require that no FYA is available unless a relevant certificate of energy efficiency is in force (*CAA 2001, s 45B*). If a claim is made and a relevant certificate of energy efficiency is later revoked, the company should withdraw the 100% FYA claim (*CAA 2001, s 45B(5)*).

Component parts of an asset may meet the energy-saving criteria. If so, an FYA will be available in respect of those components. A certificate issued to the buyer will indicate the cost of the environmental components, which should be used in calculating the FYA (*CAA 2001, ss 45A, 45C*). If the total expenditure incurred on the asset containing the qualifying component (or components) is less than the amount specified in the order for the component or components incorporated in that asset, the total expenditure qualifies for 100% FYA. If qualifying expenditure is incurred on an asset in stage payments and only part qualifies for FYA under these rules, the part so qualifying is allocated pro rata over the various payments.

Expenditure on energy-saving plant or machinery may qualify for a payable tax credit (see **4.38** onwards).

Expenditure incurred by energy services provider

3.34 If a company which is an energy services provider supplies its client with energy-saving plant or machinery, which is in the technology class 'Combined Heat and Power' specified in the Energy Technology Criteria List (tinyurl.com/nh9mlzu) and which becomes a fixture on the client's land, the parties may be able to elect jointly that the energy services provider becomes entitled to claim an FYA. The parties must not be connected, the plant must not be for use in a dwelling house, and the energy services provider or another organisation with which it is connected must carry out all or substantially all of the operation and maintenance of the plant or machinery (*CAA 2001, s 180A*; *Capital Allowances (Energy-saving Plant and Machinery) Order 2001, SI 2001/2541, art 6, Capital Allowances (Energy-saving Plant and Machinery) Order 2018, SI 2001/268 art 6*).

Environmentally beneficial plant and machinery

3.35 Particular categories of plant or machinery classified as meeting certain environmentally beneficial criteria qualify for 100% FYA, regardless of the size of the company claiming them.

Under statutory powers created in 2003 (*CAA 2001, s 45H(3)*; *Capital Allowances (Environmentally Beneficial Plant and Machinery) Order 2003, SI 2003/2076*), the Department for the Environment, Food and Rural Affairs issued the Water Technology Criteria List and the Water Technology Product List. These lists are revised and replaced periodically.

The full lists can be found at tinyurl.com/l2unmxe. The technologies currently included are, broadly, those that fall within a technology class specified in the Water Technology Criteria List and meet the environmentally beneficial criteria set out in that Criteria List and, in the case of any listed below, are specified in and have not been removed from the Water Technology Product List or have been accepted for inclusion in that Product List:

- cleaning in place equipment;
- efficient showers;
- efficient taps;
- efficient toilets;
- efficient washing machines;
- flow controllers;
- greywater recovery and reuse equipment;
- leakage detection equipment;
- meters;
- rainwater harvesting equipment;
- small scale slurry and sludge dewatering equipment;
- vehicle wash water reclaim units;
- water efficient industrial cleaning equipment;
- water management equipment for mechanical seals; and

Changes are made periodically to the lists of environmentally beneficial plant and machinery which qualify for 100% FYAs.

Expenditure will only qualify for FYA if the environmentally beneficial plant or machinery is unused and not second-hand, is not within a category of assets otherwise excluded from FYAs (eg assets acquired for leasing or letting on hire, cars, sea-going ships and long-life assets), is of a description specified by Treasury order, and meets the environmentally beneficial criteria specified for plant or machinery of that description (*CAA 2001, s 45H*). In certain cases, the government may require that no FYA is available unless a relevant certificate of environmental benefit is in force (*CAA 2001, s 45I*). If a claim is made and a relevant certificate of environmental benefit is later revoked, the company should withdraw the 100% FYA claim (*CAA 2001, s 45I(5)*).

Component parts of an asset may meet the environmentally beneficial criteria. If so, an FYA will be available in respect of those components. A certificate issued to the buyer will indicate the cost of the environmentally beneficial components, which should be used in calculating the FYA (*CAA 2001, ss 45A, 45C*). If the total expenditure incurred on the asset containing the qualifying component (or components) is less than the amount specified in the order for the component or components incorporated in that asset, the total expenditure qualifies for 100% FYA. If qualifying expenditure is incurred on an asset in stage payments and only part qualifies for FYA under these rules, the part so qualifying is allocated pro rata over the various payments.

Expenditure on environmentally beneficial plant or machinery may qualify for a payable tax credit (see **4.38** onwards).

Expenditure on vehicles with low carbon dioxide emissions

Cars

3.36 Expenditure by any size of company on cars with ultra low CO_2 emissions qualifies for an FYA if incurred on or before 31 March 2018. The car must be unused and not second-hand; however, it may have been driven a limited number of miles for the purposes of testing, delivery, test driven by a potential purchaser, or used as a demonstration car (CA23153). It can be either an electric car or a car with CO_2 emissions of not more than 75g/km (95g/km for expenditure incurred before 1 April 2015). From 1 April 2013, no FYA is available if the car is leased (*FA 2013, s 68*). Information regarding a car's CO_2 emissions figure can be found on the vehicle registration document (the 'V5') or on the Vehicle Certification Agency's website at www.dft.gov.uk/vca. Neither the regime for cars costing more that £12,000 nor the car hire or leasing expenses restriction applies to these vehicles (*CAA 2001, s 45D*; *Capital Allowances Act 2001 (Extension of First-Year Allowances) (Amendment) Order 2015, SI 2015/60*; see **2.17**, **2.18** and **3.52**).

The following measures have been enacted to extend the FYA for ultra low emission cars (*Capital Allowances Act 2001 (Cars Emissions) Order 2016, SI 2016/984*):

- an extension to the FYA for ultra low emission cars for a further three years to April 2021;
- from April 2018, the FYA threshold is reduced from 75g/km to 50g/km;

- from April 2018, the main rate threshold is reduced from 130g/km to 110g/km.

A further review for extending the FYA beyond 2021 will take place at Budget 2019.

Goods vehicles

3.37 Expenditure incurred on zero-emission goods vehicles qualifies for an enhanced 100% FYA At the time of writing, the expenditure must be incurred between 1 April 2010 and 31 March 2021 (*CAA 2001, s 45DA(1A)*, as amended by the *Capital Allowances (Extension of First Year Allowances) (Amendment) Order 2017, SI 2017/1304*). A goods vehicle is zero emission if it cannot, under any circumstances, produce CO_2 emissions by being driven. The vehicle must be unused and not second-hand. The vehicle must be registered, but it is immaterial if the vehicle is registered before or after the expenditure is incurred. A 'goods vehicle' is a mechanically propelled road vehicle which is of a design primarily suited for the conveyance of goods or burden of any description (*CAA 2001, s 45DA*).

Certain expenditure is excluded from qualifying, and this includes situations where the expenditure:

- is incurred for the purposes of a business in the fishery or aquaculture sector;
- relates to waste management; or
- has been taken into account for the purposes of receiving a grant or state aid towards that expenditure (*CAA 2001, s 45DB*).

Expenditure on zero-emission goods vehicles qualifying for ECAs is capped at €85 million per undertaking over the eight-year life of the allowances (*CAA 2001, s 212T*). In modernising the EU state aid rules, the EC has revised the existing General Block Exemption Regulation and a new version (*(EU) No 651/2014*) took effect from 1 July 2014. From 17 July 2014, minor technical changes have been made to the qualifying rules for these ECAs to ensure that they continue to comply with the state aid rules (*CAA 2001, s 45DB*, as amended by *FA 2014, Sch 13, para* 2). From 1 April 2015, no FYA is available if another state aid is received towards the expenditure (*CAA 2001, s 45DB*, as amended by *FA 2015, s 45(3)–(9)*).

From 1 July 2016, HMRC have the power to request certain information from a company claiming the allowance. The provision of the information will be a condition for granting the relief. At the time of writing, there is no legislation setting out the specific requirements that must be satisfied, but information that HMRC will be able to request will include the following:

- information about the company and the company's activities;
- information about the subject-matter of the claim for FYA; and

- any other information which relates to the grant of state aid through the provision of the FYA.

(*Finance Act 2016, ss 180–182, Sch 24*; see **25.5**)

Gas refuelling stations

3.38 Expenditure incurred on or before 31 March 2021 on new and unused plant or machinery for a gas refuelling station qualifies for 100% FYAs (*CAA 2001, s 45E(1A*) as amended by the *Capital Allowances (Extension of First Year Allowances) (Amendment) Order 2017, SI 2017/1304*). For this purpose, a gas refuelling station means any premises where vehicles are refuelled with natural gas, biogas (for expenditure incurred on or after 1 April 2008) or hydrogen fuel. The station can be private to a company or open to the public. Eligible expenditure includes storage tanks, compressors, controls and meters, gas connections, and filling equipment (*CAA 2001, s 45E; Capital Allowances Act 2001 (Extension of First-Year Allowances) (Amendment) Order 2015, SI 2015/60*).

Electric vehicle charging points

3.39 From 23 November 2016, a 100% FYA is available to businesses that incur expenditure in acquiring new and unused plant and machinery installed solely for the purpose of charging electric vehicles (*CAA 2001, s 45EA*). For these purposes, an electric vehicle means any road vehicle that can be propelled by electric power, whether or not it can also be propelled by any other kind of power. Accordingly, the relief is equally available for charge-points used to power hybrid vehicles which run on a combination of electric and more conventional fuel sources.

There is currently a short timeframe during which the allowance is available. For corporation tax purposes, the expenditure must be incurred between 23 November 2016 and 31 March 2019 inclusive. However, the Treasury has the power to extend the period for which the relief can be claimed.

Qualifying expenditure in enterprise zones

> **Focus**
>
> Note that the FYAs are available in enterprise zones from 1 April 2012 and are available only for expenditure meeting certain qualifying conditions, and apply only to designated assisted areas within the zones in question (ie not to the entire zones).

3.40 Expenditure qualifies for a 100% FYA – ie an enhanced capital allowance (or ECA) – if:

- it is incurred by a company on the provision of plant or machinery for use primarily in an area which at the time the expenditure is incurred is a designated assisted area, but note that an assisted area may be designated retrospectively (see *CAA 2001, s 45K*). From 1 April 2012 the areas that are to be treated as designated assisted areas are those set out in the *Capital Allowances (Designated Assisted Areas) Order, SI 2014/3183*, which came into force on 23 December 2014; and
- it is incurred during the eight-year period beginning from the date that the area has been designated as an enterprise zone. (*CAA 2001, s 45K(1)(b)* as amended by *Finance Act 2016*). This period may be extended further by Treasury order (*CAA 2001, s 45K(1A)*).

There is a cap on the amount of expenditure, on new plant or machinery in designated assisted areas, that qualifies for ECAs. This is set at €125 million for each 'investment project' (as defined). In modernising the EU state aid rules, the EC has revised the existing General Block Exemption Regulation and a new version (*(EU) No 651/2014*) took effect from 1 July 2014. From 17 July 2014, detailed technical changes were made to the qualifying rules for these ECAs to ensure that they continue to comply with the state aid rules (*CAA 2001, ss 45K, 45M*).

For the ECAs to be available, the following conditions must be met (*CAA 2001, s 45K(6)–(10)*):

- Condition A: the company is within the charge to corporation tax;
- Condition B: the expenditure is incurred for the purposes of a qualifying activity within *CAA 2001, s 15(1)(a)* or *(f)* (trades, mines, quarries etc);
- Condition C: the expenditure is incurred:
  - for the purposes of a business of a kind not previously carried on by the company:
  - for expanding a business carried on by the company; or
  - for starting up an activity which relates to a fundamental change in a product or production process of, or service provided by, a business carried on by the company (but see also the constraints imposed by *CAA 2001, s 45K(8A), (8B)*, from 17 July 2014);
- Condition D: the plant or machinery is unused and not second-hand; and
- Condition E: the expenditure is not replacement expenditure (determined by *CAA 2001, s 45K(11)–(13)*).

For the exclusion of plant or machinery partly for use outside designated assisted areas, and the effect of plant or machinery subsequently being primarily for use outside designated assisted areas, see *CAA 2001, ss 45L, 45N*.

Any qualifying expenditure on plant or machinery not covered by a claim to AIA or FYA qualifies only for writing down allowances at either the main rate of 18% or the special rate of 8% per annum (as appropriate).

The FYA will only be granted on expenditure incurred by trading companies, and expenditure on leased assets is excluded. In compliance with the EU state aid General Block Exemption rules (*Commission Regulation (EU) 651/2014*), the company incurring the qualifying expenditure must not be an undertaking which is (*CAA 2001, s 45M*):

- in difficulty for the purposes of the General Block Exemption Regulation;
- subject to an outstanding recovery order following a European Commission decision declaring an aid illegal;
- engaged in the fisheries and aquaculture sectors, as covered by *Regulation (EU) No 1379/2013 of the European Parliament and of the Council*;
- engaged in any of the coal, steel, shipbuilding or synthetic fibres sectors;
- in the transport sector or related infrastructure;
- relating to energy generation, distribution or infrastructure;
- relating to the development of broadband networks;
- relating to the management of waste of undertakings; or
- engaged in the primary production of agricultural products.

The government has identified the enterprise zones within which certain areas are, or will be, designated for the purposes of 100% FYAs, and they include:

- Black Country;
- Humber Renewable Energy Super Cluster;
- Liverpool;
- North Eastern;
- Sheffield;
- Tees Valley;
- the designated Paull site within Humber Green Port Corridor;
- a designated site in the London Royal Docks enterprise zone;
- designated sites in enterprise areas in Scotland, including Irvine, Nigg and Dundee;
- a designated site at Deeside in North Wales;

- designated sites in the Ebbw Vale and Haven Waterway enterprise zones in Wales; and
- a pilot enterprise zone near Coleraine in Northern Ireland.

Maps of the designated assisted areas have been published at tinyurl.com/pebo4ln.

Details of all such areas should also be readily available from the local authorities in question, and further information can be found:

- for England, at enterprisezones.communities.gov.uk;
- for Scotland, at tinyurl.com/pvj75zt (to be replaced by tinyurl.com/y7rzuv8e);
- for Wales, at business.wales.gov.uk/enterprisezones; and
- for Northern Ireland, at tinyurl.com/zofjkmt.

From 1 July 2016, HMRC have the power to request certain information from a company claiming the enterprise zone allowance. The provision of the information will be a condition for granting the relief. At the time of writing, there is no legislation setting out the specific requirements that must be satisfied, but information that HMRC will be able to request will include the following:

- information about the company and the company's activities;
- information about the subject matter of the claim; and
- any other information which relates to the grant of state aid through the provision of the allowance.

(*Finance Act 2016, ss 180–182, Sch 24*; see **25.5**)

Expenditure on North Sea oil ring-fence plant and machinery

3.41 North Sea gas or oil extraction trades may claim a 100% FYA on equipment purchased for use in the 'ring-fence' trade. (A ring-fence trade is a trade subject to the supplementary charge.)

EXPENDITURE ON WHICH AN FYA MAY NOT BE CLAIMED

3.42 No FYA is available on the purchase of a car unless it is an ultra low emission car – see **3.36** (*CAA 2001, ss 45D, 46*).

Where a company acquires an item of plant or machinery by way of gift and brings it into use for a qualifying activity, capital allowances are available based on the deemed cost of the asset (ie the market value on the date it is brought into use for that purpose) (*CAA 2001, s 13(1)–(3)*), but no FYA is available because the company has not incurred expenditure on acquiring the plant or machinery (*CAA 2001, s 52*).

In most cases, the provision of plant and machinery for leasing is excluded from FYAs. However, expenditure on cars with ultra low CO_2 emissions provided for leasing was eligible for FYA if incurred before 1 April 2013. Also, expenditure qualifies for FYA if incurred on qualifying energy-saving or environmentally beneficial plant or machinery provided for leasing under an excluded lease of background plant or machinery for a building as defined by *CAA 2001, s 76R* (*CAA 2001, s 46*; CA23835).

There is a distinction between the leasing or hiring of an asset and the provision of services that involve the use of an asset. HMRC take the view that plant provided predominantly with an operative is more than mere hire, that the expenditure on the provision of such plant is not for leasing, and therefore that FYAs are available (*Baldwins Industrial Services plc v Barr Ltd* [2003] BLR 176; *MGF (Trench Construction Systems) Limited v Revenue and Customs Commissioners* [2012] UKFTT 739 (TC); CA23115).

No capital allowances are given on assets used for business entertainment (*CAA 2001, s 269*).

The general rule is that no FYA may be claimed on assets purchased from connected parties (*CAA 2001, s 217*). This rule does not apply where the asset is produced by the seller, is unused, and is sold in the ordinary course of the seller's business (*CAA 2001, s 230*). 'Connection' for these purposes is determined by *CTA 2010, s 1122* (see **10.27**).

See **3.44** for provisions common to FYA and AIA.

INTERACTION OF AIA WITH OTHER CAPITAL ALLOWANCES

Allowance claims

> **Focus**
>
> If a company's qualifying expenditure on plant and machinery exceeds the amount of AIA available, the company should not overlook the possibility that it might be able to claim some FYAs by allocating its AIA primarily to expenditure not qualifying for FYA.

3.43 A company may not claim AIA and FYA in respect of the same expenditure (*CAA 2001, s 52A*).

Example 3.15—When to claim FYA or AIA

Facts

In the year to 31 March 2018, Roderick Ltd incurs £25,000 on an item of new plant and machinery that appears on the energy-saving technology list and therefore qualifies for a 100% FYA.

Analysis

Roderick Ltd may claim either 100% FYA on the energy-saving plant and machinery, or £25,000 AIA.

The company's decision will depend upon its other capital expenditure on plant and machinery. It would generally be best to claim 100% FYA where available, and allocate the AIA claim against expenditure not qualifying for FYA – ideally against special rate (8%) plant before main rate (18%) plant, thus maximising capital allowances in this and following accounting periods.

The expenditure on which AIA is claimed must be added to the appropriate plant and machinery pool(s), and the AIA must be deducted from the same pool(s), to ensure proper treatment of subsequent disposals (*CAA 2001, s 58(4A)*).

Example 3.16—AIA: impact on qualifying expenditure pools

Facts

Holbein Ltd is a single company. On 1 November 2018, during its accounting period ending 31 December 2018, it incurs expenditure of £80,000 on general plant and machinery and £20,000 on integral fixtures. The values of qualifying capital expenditure brought forward at 1 January 2015 are £350,000 in the main pool and £200,000 in the special rate pool.

Analysis

Although the company would have been entitled to AIA of up to £200,000, the amount it can claim is restricted to the amount of the qualifying expenditure incurred. The adjustment to the pool is as follows:

	Pools of qualifying expenditure	*Main*	*Special rate*	*Total allowances claimed*
		£	*£*	*£*
1 January 2018	Written down values brought forward	350,000	200,000	

	Add: qualifying expenditure	80,000		20,000		
	Less: AIA (restricted)	(80,000)		(20,000)		100,000
	Additions to the pools		0		0	
			350,000		200,000	
	WDA @ 18%		(63,000)			63,000
	WDA @ 8%				(16,000)	16,000
31 December 2018	Written down values carried forward		287,000		184,000	179,000

Where plant and machinery is of a type that qualifies for FYAs, then FYAs are available on expenditure which is above the maximum AIA limit or on which AIA has not been claimed, which would otherwise qualify for WDAs in the main or special rate pools.

Example 3.17—AIA and FYA: impact on qualifying expenditure pools

Facts

Western Ltd carries on a manufacturing trade. During its 12-month accounting period ending 31 December 2018, the company spends £225,000 on general plant and machinery, £30,000 of which is energy-saving plant qualifying for 100% FYA. It also spends £50,000 on integral fixtures. The values of qualifying capital expenditure brought forward at 1 January 2018 are £55,000 in the main pool and £25,000 in the special rate pool.

Western Ltd is entitled to maximum AIA of £200,000 for the accounting period. The company chooses to maximise its capital allowance claim for the year ended 31 December 2018 by allocating AIA first to its special rate plant and then to the general plant which is not energy-saving plant, thus maximising WDAs in following years, while gaining an immediate benefit by leaving its energy-saving plant to be covered by 100% FYA.

Analysis

The calculation of capital allowances is as follows:

	Pools of qualifying expenditure			*Main*		*Special rate*	*Total allowances claimed*
				£		*£*	*£*
1 January 2018	Written down values b/f			55,000		25,000	
	Add: FYA expenditure	30,000					
	Less: 100% FYA	(30,000)					30,000
	Add: non-FYA qualifying expenditure		195,000		50,000		
	Less: AIA		(150,000)		(50,000)		200,000
				45,000		0	
				100,000		25,000	
	WDA @ 18%			(18,000)			18,000
	WDA @ 8%					(2,000)	2,000
31 December 2018	Written down values c/f			82,000		23,000	
	Total allowances claimed						550,000

Observations

Western Ltd has gained the benefit of FYA of £30,000 in addition to its maximum AIA claim of £200,000. The company has allocated £50,000 of its AIA claim to special rate plant, thus ensuring that it maximises its WDA claims in subsequent accounting periods.

Provisions common to FYAs and AIA

3.44 There are aspects of the legislation common to FYAs and the AIA:

- the allowances are to be reduced to a just and reasonable amount, if the expenditure has been incurred for non-business purposes (*CAA 2001, s 205*);
- the allowances are to be reduced if a subsidy is received (*CAA 2001, s 210*);
- no allowance is given for disposals to connected persons, for transactions entered into for avoidance reasons, and in sale and leaseback transactions (*CAA 2001, s 217*); and
- any additional VAT liability related to the original expenditure on which an allowance has been claimed is deemed to be incurred at the same time as the expenditure, and will also qualify for the allowance (*CAA 2001, s 236*; *FA 2008, Sch 24, para 6*).

FIXTURES

Persons who are treated as owners of fixtures

3.45 For capital allowances purposes, a 'fixture' is plant or machinery that is so installed or otherwise fixed in or to a building, or otherwise to land, so as to become part of that building or land. This specifically includes any boiler or water-filled radiator installed in a building as part of a space or water heating system (*CAA 2001, s 173*). In practice, the definition of 'fixture' excludes moveable items, but includes lighting and other electrical systems, lifts and lift machinery, hot and cold water systems, alarm systems, heating and air conditioning plant, etc.

If plant and machinery purchased for the purposes of a qualifying activity becomes a fixture and the company holds a relevant interest in the land, the company will be able to claim the capital allowances. Where more than one party meets the necessary conditions, the party entitled to claim is normally the party with the lowest interest in the land (*CAA 2001, s 176*; CA26150).

Lessors and lessees of equipment fixtures used for a qualifying activity of the lessee may jointly elect for the fixture to be treated as belonging to the equipment lessor, thus enabling the lessor to claim the capital allowances (*CAA 2001, s 177*). The election must be made within two years of the end of the accounting period in which the capital expenditure was incurred.

Where a taxpayer incurs significant expenditure in a chargeable period on a number of properties that contain fixtures that qualify for plant and machinery allowances, HMRC may accept claims based on statistically acceptable sampling methodologies (CA20075).

The FA 2012 fixtures regime

> **Focus**
>
> Companies buying or selling property should study carefully the provisions for determining the value at which they acquire fixtures and for ensuring that they will eventually be able to pass on entitlement to capital allowances on fixtures to a subsequent owner.

3.46 The purchase or sale of a property generally includes fixtures contained within buildings on which capital allowances may be claimed. Where an item of property is disposed of together with other property, capital allowances are to be calculated on the basis of a just and reasonable apportionment of the sale proceeds or consideration (*CAA 2001, s 562*). The courts have considered this from the perspective of a seller (see *Wood and Another v Provan* (1967) 44 TC 701) and a buyer (see *Mr & Mrs Tapsell & Mr Lester (as partnership 'The Granleys')* [2011] UKFTT 376 (TC); *Bowerswood House Retirement Home Ltd* [2015] UKFTT 94 (TC)).

Allowances are limited to the lower of original cost (*CAA 2001, s 62*) and the last disposal value that has been brought into account by any previous owner of the fixture (*CAA 2001, s 185*). The seller and purchaser can jointly elect for any part of the sale price to be attributed to fixtures – subject always to the cap of the seller's original cost (*CAA 2001, ss 198, 199*). In practice, before the *FA 2012* changes took effect, late claims often used to arise because no time limit was laid down to govern when a seller and purchaser should agree the part of the sale price of a property that should be attributed to the fixtures.

FA 2012 reinforced the intention of pre-existing rules in preventing capital allowances from being given more than once on the original cost of a fixture, by making the availability of capital allowances to a purchaser of second-hand fixtures conditional on:

- the pooling of relevant expenditure prior to the transfer; and
- either:
  - the seller and purchaser formally agreeing a value for fixtures within two years of the transfer, or
  - formal proceedings to agree the value being commenced within two years of the transfer.

HMRC guidance on capital allowances on second-hand fixtures can be found at CA26470–CA26486.

The pooling requirement

3.47 From 1 April 2014, to pass on an entitlement to claim capital allowances to a subsequent owner, a company that is the current owner must meet the 'pooling requirement' by pooling their expenditure on fixtures at any time after acquisition, as long as this is before the fixtures are eventually sold on, disposed of, or transferred to another person. Following any such change in ownership, this pooling requirement is met in respect of any fixture if the immediate past owner has claimed FYA on their qualifying expenditure relating to the fixture, or has allocated it to a pool, whether or not they have claimed AIA or WDA (*CAA 2001, s 187A(4)*; for more on the meaning of pooling, see **3.52** onwards).

The fixed value requirement

3.48 From 1 April 2012, where existing fixtures are disposed of, a time limit is imposed within which the 'fixed value requirement' must be met. Within two years of the sale, the seller and purchaser must adopt or invoke one of two pre-existing procedures to fix their agreement about the value of the fixtures. These procedures are:

- the *CAA 2001, s 198/199* facility for the seller and purchaser to jointly elect, within two years of a sale, to determine the amount of the sale price that is to be attributed to fixtures (subject always to the cap of the seller's original cost); or, if the parties cannot reach an agreement
- the *CAA 2001, s 563* facility to refer the matter to the First-tier Tribunal for an independent determination. *CAA 2001, s 563* was amended so that this procedure may be invoked by either party if the matter appears material to their tax liability. If the parties are unable to agree, the purchaser has to invoke this procedure within two years in order to claim allowances. The tribunal does not have to reach its determination within the two-year limit (*CAA 2001, s 187A(5)–(9)*).

Persons not entitled to claim capital allowances (such as charities not chargeable to tax) buying property from 'past owners' are entitled to make a *CAA 2001, s 198/199* election or apply to the tribunal for a determination of the fixtures value. However, this could impact harshly on some bodies that are unaware of the capital allowances rules. In these circumstances the fixed value requirement can be met if the current owner obtains written statements made by the past owner (eg the charity):

- that relevant apportionment under *CAA 2001, s 187A(6)(a)* has not been made and is no longer capable of being made; and
- of the amount of the disposal value that the past owner in fact brought into account (*CAA 2001, s 187A(8)*).

The disposal value statement requirement

3.49 Exceptionally, there are certain specified circumstances in which the fixed value requirement is not available. These may include a sale of the qualifying interest at less than market value, or a cessation of ownership where the qualifying interest continues, or would continue but for merging with another interest. Alternatively, it may not be feasible to meet the fixed value requirement, eg where the owner's qualifying activity is permanently discontinued without any immediate change of ownership of the fixture (*CAA 2001, s 187A(10)*).

Where such circumstances arise from 1 April 2012 onwards, the 'disposal value statement requirement' must be met instead of the fixed value requirement. This requires the past owner, within two years after their later sale of the property, to make a written statement of the amount of the disposal value of fixtures which they are or have been required to bring into account (for example, when they permanently ceased business). It also requires the current owner to obtain this statement or a copy of it (*CAA 2001, s 187A(11)*).

Fixtures on which certain other capital allowances are made

3.50 A company is not generally entitled to claim capital allowances on a fixture if any other person has claimed a capital allowance on the same item except as plant and machinery. However, this restriction does not apply in the case of fixtures on which there has already been a claim for industrial buildings allowance, research and development allowance or (from 1 April 2012) business premises renovation allowance (*CAA 2001, ss 9(1)–(2), 185–187*). For further information on R&D allowance see **Chapter 14**; for business premises renovation allowance, see **Chapter 8**.

Where capital allowances have been claimed on a fixture, no-one is entitled to make a later claim for an allowance on the same item except as plant and machinery (*CAA 2001, s 9(3)*).

Practical implications of the *FA 2012* fixtures regime

3.51 As a result of the changes introduced by *FA 2012, Sch 10*, it is prudent to ensure that a *CAA 2001, s 198/199* election agreement is a standard provision of all sale and purchase agreements for commercial property interests in cases where the seller was entitled to claim capital allowances. A standard practice of reaching and recording this apportionment agreement before the sale, or as part of the sale negotiations, is clearly the best way forward for all concerned. This does not detract in any way from the right of either the seller or the purchaser to insist on a just and reasonable apportionment of the sale value of a property to its fixtures; if either side feel that the other is not 'playing fair', they can invoke the tribunal facility.

The tribunal process is generally likely to benefit the buyer more than the seller, since the seller is likely to have all their allowances clawed back as balancing charges where the property has been sold at a gain, and there will often be a partial clawback where the property is sold at a loss.

The focus on fixtures within buildings is concentrating minds on the need to maintain accurate records of expenditure on fixtures, but in this regard *FA 2012* was not exactly a sea change. Businesses were already under pressure to create and maintain accurate records arising from transactions on property and other large assets to ensure accuracy in accounting and in computing their tax liabilities.

COMPUTATION OF CAPITAL ALLOWANCES

The pool

3.52 Most qualifying expenditure is pooled in a multi-asset pool. Special rate pools are maintained for expenditure on 'expensive cars', being non-low emission cars costing more than £12,000, incurred before 1 April 2009 (*CAA 2001, ss 74–78*, but see further below), and short-life assets (*CAA 2001, s 86*; see **3.55**). A separate pool was maintained for expenditure incurred on long-life assets prior to 1 April 2008 (*CAA 2001, s 101*; see **3.56**).

The provisions relating to expenditure incurred on expensive cars (*CAA 2001, ss 74–78*), whereby writing down allowance on each such car is restricted to £3,000 per annum, were repealed for expenditure incurred on or after 1 April 2009. Subject to commencement provisions, the new rules based on CO_2 emissions apply to expenditure incurred on cars on or after 1 April 2009 (*FA 2009, Sch 11, paras 26–29*). Transitional provisions apply to pre-existing expensive car pools; in most cases, the remaining balance in any such pool at the end of a 'transitional chargeable period', which was the accounting period that began before 1 April 2014 and ended on or after 31 March 2014, was transferred to the main pool (*FA 2009, Sch 11, paras 30–32*).

Allowances

3.53 Four types of capital allowances are available: annual investment allowance (AIA), first year allowance (FYA), writing down allowance (WDA), and a balancing adjustment. AIA or FYA can only be claimed in the year of purchase.

Expenditure eligible for FYA cannot be allocated to a pool for the year in which it is incurred, but the balance (if any) of that expenditure after claiming the FYA is generally allocated to a pool in the next accounting period (*CAA 2001, s 58(5)*).

Expenditure eligible for AIA must be allocated to the appropriate pools for the year in which it is incurred, and each pool then reduced by the appropriate part of the AIA claimed, in order to arrive at the available qualifying expenditure (*CAA 2001, s 58(4A)*).

WDAs are claimed annually on a reducing balance basis. The WDA is applied to the unrelieved pool of qualifying expenditure at the beginning of the year, adjusted for disposals and additions but not expenditure eligible for FYA. From 1 April 2012 the main rate of WDA is 18% (previously 20%), except for ring fence trades (*CAA 2001, s 56*).

Special rate expenditure includes expenditure on long-life assets, thermal insulation, integral features and expenditure incurred on or after 1 April 2009 on cars with CO_2 emissions of more than 110g/km (or 130g/km before April 2018) (see **3.55** onwards). From 1 April 2012 the special rate of WDA is 8% (previously 10%), except for ring fence trades (*CAA 2001, ss 104D*).

Where the amount of any main pool or special rate pool on which WDA falls to be calculated is less than or equal to £1,000, the full amount of that pool may be claimed as WDA (*CAA 2001, s 56A*).

Example 3.18—Writing down allowance

Facts

Sailaway Ltd's accounting period begins on 1 January 2018 and ends on 31 December 2018. The balance brought forward in the main capital allowance pool amounts to £340,000, and in the special rate pool amounts to £20,000. There is also an expensive car on which the balance of unrelieved expenditure amounts to £50,000.

Analysis

The writing down allowances for the year ended 31 December 2014 will be as follows:

Period 01.01.18–31.12.18		*Main Pool*	*Special Rate Pool*	*Expensive Car*	*Total Allowances*
		£	£	£	£
Balance of expenditure b/f		340,000	20,000	50,000	
WDA	18%	(61,200)			61,200
	8%		(1,600)		1,600
WDA (restricted)				(3,000)	3,000
		278,800	18,400	47,000	

Transfer of expensive car to main pool	47,000		(47,000)	
Balance of expenditure c/f	325,800	18,400	0	
Total allowances				65,800

The rates of writing down allowance were reduced from 1 April 2012 onwards. Where a company's period of account straddles this date, the main rate WDA and the special rate WDA are each apportioned according to the following formulae:

Main rate writing down allowance (*CAA 2001, s 56(1)*; *FA 2011, s 10*):

$$X = \frac{(20 \times BRD)}{CP} + \frac{(18 \times ARD)}{CP}$$

where:

- BRD is the number of days in the financial year 2011
- ARD is the number of days in the financial year 2012
- CP is the number of days in the accounting period
- X (rounded up to two decimal points) is the WDA percentage to be applied for that accounting period.

Special rate writing down allowance (*CAA 2001, s 104D(1)*; *FA 2011, s 10*):

$$Y = \frac{(10 \times BRD)}{CP} + \frac{(8 \times ARD)}{CP}$$

where:

- BRD is the number of days in the financial year 2011
- ARD is the number of days in the financial year 2012
- CP is the number of days in the accounting period
- Y (rounded up to two decimal points) is the WDA percentage to be applied for that accounting period.

Example 3.19—Hybrid rates of WDA for periods straddling 1 April 2012

Facts

Hybrid Ltd's accounting period begins on 1 January 2012 and ends on 31 December 2012.

Analysis

The calculation of the hybrid rates of WDAs will be as follows:

Periods	*No of days*	*Rate*	*Calculation*	*Hybrid Rate*
Main rate WDA				
01.01.12–31.03.12	91	20%	91/366 × 20%	4.97%
01.04.12–31.12.12	275	18%	275/366 × 18%	13.52%
Rate for the period	366			18.49%
Special rate WDA				
01.01.12–31.03.12	91	10%	91/366 × 10%	2.49%
01.04.12–31.12.12	275	8%	275/366 × 8%	6.01%
Rate for the period	366			8.50%

On previous occasions when WDA rates had changed and businesses had to calculate hybrid rates for straddling periods, HMRC made a ready reckoner available on their website. Unfortunately, against a background of public expenditure cuts, no such utility was made available by HMRC in connection with the rate changes on 1 April 2012.

Disposal proceeds

3.54 An asset is treated as disposed of for capital allowances purposes if the person who incurred the qualifying expenditure on the plant and machinery:

- ceases to own the plant or machinery; or
- loses possession of the plant or machinery in circumstances where it is reasonable to assume that the loss is permanent.

The asset is also treated as being disposed of if the plant and machinery:

- has been in use for mineral exploration and access and the person abandons it at the site where it was in use for that purpose;

- ceases to exist as such (as a result of destruction, dismantling or otherwise);
- begins to be used wholly or partly for purposes other than those of the qualifying activity;
- begins to be leased under a long funding lease; or
- if the qualifying activity is permanently discontinued (*CAA 2001, s 61(1)*).

When an asset is disposed of, the disposal proceeds (up to the amount of the original cost) are deducted from the balance on the appropriate expenditure pool. If a positive balance remains after the deduction on a multi-asset or long-life asset pool, the balance continues to be written off on a reducing balance basis, except in the final period of trading when it becomes a balancing allowance that may be deducted from chargeable profits. If a negative balance would otherwise arise on the pool after the deduction, this becomes a balancing charge that must be added to the company's assessable profits. In the case of a single-asset pool, a positive balance, after the deduction for sale proceeds, is allowed as a deduction from profits as a balancing allowance, whereas a negative balance becomes a balancing charge – in each case, in the period in which the disposal occurs (*CAA 2001, s 55*).

Example 3.20—Disposal proceeds

Facts

The written down value of Sebastian Ltd's main plant pool, after deduction of capital allowances for the year to 31 March 2018, was £6,660.

In July 2018 the company sold an asset on which capital allowances had been claimed, receiving sale proceeds of £300.

Analysis

The capital allowance claim for the year to 31 March 2016 is as follows:

	Main pool	*Capital allowances*
	£	£
WDV b/f	6,660	
Sales proceeds (July 2018)	(300)	
	6,360	
WDA @ 18%	(1,145)	1,145
WDV c/f	5,215	
Allowances		1,145

If the assets concerned have not been the subject of a capital allowance claim, it is not necessary to deduct the disposal proceeds from the pool. However, this exclusion does not generally apply if the asset was originally acquired from a connected person or by means of a series of transactions between connected persons and any one person has brought the disposal value into account (*CAA 2001, s 64*). The definition of 'connection' follows *CTA 2010, s 1122* (*CAA 2001, s 575;* see **10.27**).

Expenditure on an asset that is partly used for a qualifying activity and partly for other purposes is put into a separate pool. The expenditure is apportioned on a just and reasonable basis and the allowances are reduced accordingly. If there is a significant change of circumstances and, at the end of an accounting period, the market value of the asset in the pool exceeds the pool value by more than £1 million, the asset is deemed to have been disposed of at market value at the end of that accounting period and reacquired at the beginning of the following accounting period for an amount equal to that disposal value (*CAA 2001, ss 206–208*).

Short-life assets

Focus

A company with assets which are likely to have a useful life of less than eight years should consider the possible benefit of electing for these to be treated as short-life assets.

3.55 A company acquiring plant or machinery eligible for capital allowances may elect for individual assets to be treated as short-life assets (*CAA 2001, s 83*) unless the particular item is excluded from short-life asset treatment (*CAA 2001, s 84*). Typically, companies elect to apply this treatment to technology assets and other assets which are expected to have a relatively short life.

The company may make an irrevocable election for an asset to be treated as a 'short-life asset', and this must be made within two years of the end of the accounting period in which the expenditure was incurred (*CAA 2001, ss 83(b), 85*). The asset is then allocated to a single asset short-life pool until the earlier of its disposal or the eighth anniversary of the end of the accounting period in which the expenditure was incurred on its acquisition. If the asset is disposed of, the single asset pool ends and a balancing charge or a balancing allowance arises. Alternatively, if the short-life asset in question remains unsold at the relevant cut-off date, the single asset pool ends and the remaining balance of expenditure in it is transferred back to the main pool or, in the case of a car which is not a main rate car, to the special rate pool (*CAA 2001, s 86*).

For expenditure incurred on short-life assets before 1 April 2011, the fourth anniversary applied instead of the eighth (*CAA 2001, s 86*, before amendment by *FA 2011, s 12*). The change in this time limit from four to eight years greatly increased the relevance of the short-life assets regime, and companies with assets which are expected to have a useful life of less than eight years should consider electing for these to be treated as short-life assets where this is likely to accelerate their capital allowances.

If a company owns a large number of assets, it may not be practicable to identify each asset separately and maintain individual capital allowance computations for each short-life asset. In Statement of Practice 1 (1986), HMRC set out options that can be adopted to simplify the process (see tinyurl.com/o5k83yp).

Long-life assets

3.56 In certain circumstances, expenditure on plant and machinery with an expected useful life of 25 years or more must be added to a special rate pool on which writing down allowance is limited to 8% (10% until 31 March 2012) (*CAA 2001, s 91*; see **3.59**).

Expenditure is excluded from this long-life asset treatment if (*CAA 2001, ss 93, 96, 98*):

- it is on plant, machinery and fixtures in a house, hotel, shop or showroom;
- it is on cars; or
- it amounts to no more than a specified monetary limit.

The monetary limit is £100,000 for a 12-month accounting period, but is proportionately reduced where the company claiming the writing down allowance has an accounting period of less than 12 months (*CAA 2001, s 99(3)*).

Until 31 March 2015 the limit is also proportionately reduced where the company has one or more associated companies, by dividing it by one plus the number of associated companies, and 'associated company' is defined as it is for the purposes of the small profits rate of corporation tax (*CTA 2010, ss 25–30*; *CAA 2001, s 99(4)–(5)*; see **23.14** onwards).

From 1 April 2015 the pre-existing associated company rules are repealed as a result of unification of the main and small profits rates of corporation tax. However, these rules have been relied upon for ring fence marginal relief (which will continue), quarterly instalment payments by large companies and certain other corporation tax purposes, including the capital allowances provisions for long-life assets. For the financial year 2015 onwards, these rely instead on a new simplified 'related 51% group company' test (*CTA 2010, s 279F*, as inserted by *FA 2014, Sch 1, para 5*; see **23.22**).

Reduced allowances

3.57 If the accounting period is shorter than 12 months, the writing down allowance and the maximum annual investment allowance are reduced proportionately (but not the first year allowance). Capital allowances must be claimed, otherwise no relief is given (*CAA 2001, s 3(1)*), but a company may choose to claim no capital allowances or less than its full entitlement for a particular accounting period. The tax written down value is carried forward to the next accounting period and will be available for writing down allowance accordingly (*CAA 2001, ss 57(1)(b), 59*).

Assets acquired under hire purchase

3.58 A company is eligible to claim capital allowances on capital expenditure incurred on the provision of plant or machinery for a qualifying activity or corresponding overseas activity if it is incurred under a contract providing that the company shall or may become the owner of the plant or machinery on the performance of the contract (*CAA 2001, s 67*).

Where a contract falls to be treated as a lease in accordance with GAAP, the plant or machinery can only be treated as owned by the company if the contract is treated under GAAP as a finance lease. If it fails this test because it is treated under GAAP as an operating lease, it cannot be treated for capital allowance purposes as owned by any other person at the relevant time (*CAA 2001, s 67*). Companies that are lessees reporting under IFRS 16 *Leases*, which replaces IAS 17 *Leases* mandatorily for periods starting on or after 1 January 2019 (early application is permissible) do not distinguish between finance and operating leases (although lessors do) as IFRS 16 essentially removes the concept of operating leases for lessees, with some limited exceptions for short-life leases and leases of low-value equipment. Nevertheless, under government proposals it will still be possible to claim allowances if the lease 'transfers substantially all the risks and rewards incidental to ownership' of the plant or machinery to the person claiming the relief (Consultation Paper 'Plant and machinery lease accounting changes' published on 1 December 2017, paras 3.34–3.36, 3.64–3.65; see **3.69** below and **Chapter 26** regarding changes to UK GAAP).

Two or more agreements can be read together if, had they constituted a single contract, the effect would be that the expenditure is incurred under a contract providing that the company shall or may become the owner of the plant or machinery on the performance of the contract (*CAA 2001, s 67(6)*).

It was confirmed in *Darngavil Coal Co Ltd v Francis* (1913) 7 TC 1 that payments under a hire purchase contract must be apportioned between:

- revenue payments for hire, deductible in calculating the lessee's taxable profits, and

- capital payments for the purchase or option to purchase, which are not deductible but may qualify for capital allowances under *CAA 2001, s 67* (CA23300 onwards).

The disposal value to be brought into account when the asset ceases to be owned is the amount of disposal proceeds received, together with any unpaid capital instalments (*CAA 2001, s 68*; CA23330).

A company may only claim capital allowances on plant or machinery if the assets belong to the company at some time (*CAA 2001, s 11(4)(b)*). This can apply to circumstances other than hire purchase. If there is a contractual relationship that states that 'a company may become the owner of the plant or machinery on the performance of the contract' and the purchasing company incurs capital expenditure on plant or machinery that is not supplied, thus incurring abortive capital expenditure, it will nonetheless meet the conditions set out in *CAA 2001, s 67(1)(a)–(b)* and therefore capital allowances are available (CA23350). When the company ceases to be entitled to the benefit of the contract without becoming the owner of the asset, *CAA 2001, s 67(4)* treats the taxpayer as ceasing to own the asset and the company must bring a disposal value into account (CA23330, CA23350).

Where capital expenditure is incurred under hire purchase on the provision of plant or machinery which becomes a fixture in a building, the fixtures rules in *CAA 2001, s 176* (see **3.45**) take precedence over the normal hire purchase rules explained here (*CAA 2001, s 69*; CA23320).

SPECIAL RATE EXPENDITURE AND THE SPECIAL RATE POOL

Special rate writing down allowance

3.59 The special rate writing down allowance is applied to expenditure on the following types of assets (*CAA 2001, s 104A*):

- thermal insulation expenditure (see **3.15**);
- integral fixtures (see **3.16**);
- long-life assets (see **3.56**);
- special rate car (ie any car that is not a main rate car – see **3.61**); and
- solar panels (expenditure incurred on or after 1 April 2012).

If part only of any particular capital expenditure on plant and machinery is special rate expenditure, and part is not, just and reasonable apportionments are to be made (*CAA 2001, s 104B*).

The special rate expenditure must be allocated to a special rate pool or (if appropriate) a single asset pool (see **3.52**) (*CAA 2001, s 104C*). An 8% rate of writing down allowance (10% until 31 March 2012) is applied to the balance of qualifying expenditure less disposal receipts. The same rate applies to special rate expenditure that has been allocated to a single asset pool (*CAA 2001, s 104C*).

Disposal value of special rate assets

3.60 If a disposal results from a scheme or arrangement entered into to avoid tax, and the actual disposal value is less than the notional written down value, the notional written down value is taken as the disposal value. This is the expenditure incurred less the special rate allowances which the company could have claimed for this expenditure (*CAA 2001, s 104E*).

Cars

Main rate car

3.61 Expenditure on a main rate car is allocated to the general pool of expenditure and qualifies for an annual writing down allowance of 18% (20% until 31 March 2012).

A car is a mechanically propelled vehicle other than:

- a motor cycle;
- a vehicle constructed in such a way that it is primarily suited for transporting goods or burden of any kind; or
- a vehicle of a type not commonly used as a private vehicle and unsuitable for such use.

A double cab pick-up with a payload of one tonne or more is treated as a commercial vehicle, not a car (CA23510).

A car is classified as main rate if (*CAA 2001, s 104AA*):

- it is first registered before 1 March 2001;
- it has low CO_2 emissions – no more than 130g/km (160g/km until 31 March 2013); or
- it is electrically propelled.

A car has low CO_2 emissions if it is first registered on the basis of a qualifying emissions certificate and its applicable CO_2 emissions do not exceed the relevant limit. A qualifying emissions certificate is either an EC certificate of conformity or a UK approval certificate that specifies the emissions in terms of grams per kilometre driven for each type of fuel. Bi-fuel vehicles will have separate emission factors for different fuels (these are cars that run on a combination of road gas and either petrol or diesel).

For non bi-fuel vehicles, if only one emissions figure is specified on the certificate, that is the figure to be applied; but, if more than one figure is specified, the combined amount is the figure to be applied (*CAA 2001, s 268C*).

A car is classified as electrically propelled if it is propelled solely by external electrical power or from a storage battery that is not connected to any source of power when the vehicle is in motion (*CAA 2001, s 268B*).

Expenditure on a special rate car, ie a car which does not qualify as a main rate car, is added to the special rate pool and qualifies for a special rate annual writing down allowance (see **3.59**).

Special rate cars – discontinued activities

3.62 Where a car, which is used wholly for business purposes and included in the main pool or the special rate pool, is disposed of, there is no balancing adjustment unless the business ceases; and, in the case of the special rate pool, the allowances may continue over a particularly long period of time. Anti-avoidance legislation exists to prevent businesses from contriving to wind up their activities in these circumstances to generate a balancing adjustment that would not otherwise be due.

If a company discontinues a qualifying activity that consisted wholly or partly of car hire or leasing (other than incidentally) in relation to a special rate car, the balancing allowance available can be restricted. This applies if a company, to which group relief would be available (whether or not a claim is made), carries on a qualifying activity that consists wholly or partly of car hire or leasing (other than incidentally) in relation to a special rate car at any time during the six months after the company's qualifying activity is permanently discontinued (*CAA 2001, s 104F*).

It is necessary to make the following calculations:

- the balancing allowance on the special rate pool (SBA);
- the total of the balancing charges (BC) arising on all assets for the period; and
- the total of the balancing allowances (OBA) on all other assets except the special rate pool.

The amount of the balancing allowance that the company then becomes entitled to in respect of the special rate pool is reduced to:

BC – OBA

On the day after the cessation, the group company that continues the qualifying activity (or, if more than one, the company nominated by the company that has ceased or, failing that, by HMRC) is treated as having incurred notional expenditure of an amount by which SBA exceeds:

(BC – OBA)

Where any part of this accounting period in which this deemed expenditure would be treated as incurred overlaps the penultimate accounting period of the company that has ceased, a proportionate part of the deemed expenditure cannot be taken into account until the continuing company's following accounting period.

Example 3.21—Special rate cars: discontinued activities

Facts

Oswald Ltd, which prepared its accounts annually to 30 September, carried on a car hire trade which it ceased on 31 December 2018. Percival Ltd, a company in the same group, continued to carry on a similar activity thereafter. Percival Ltd prepares its accounts to 30 June each year.

The capital allowances computation for Oswald Ltd's car hire activity for the period ended 31 December 2018 is as follows:

	Special rate car	*Short-life assets*	*Plant and machinery pool*
	£	£	£
WDV	45,000	7,000	18,000
Sale proceeds	30,000	5,000	26,000
Balancing (charge) or allowance	15,000	2,000	(8,000)
	SBA	OBA	BC

Analysis

Oswald Ltd's balancing allowance on the special rate car is restricted to:

£8,000 – 2,000 = £6,000

Percival Ltd is deemed to have incurred expenditure of:

£15,000 – 6,000 = £9,000

This deemed expenditure would normally be treated as incurred on the day after Oswald Ltd had ceased to trade, ie 1 January 2019. However, a three-month part of this accounting period of Percival Ltd overlaps the penultimate accounting period of Oswald Ltd (ie the year ended 30 September 2018), so a proportionate part (ie 3/12ths) of the deemed expenditure cannot be taken into account until Percival Ltd's following accounting period.

Therefore, Percival Ltd's capital allowances computation will reflect qualifying expenditure of:

- £9,000 × 9/12 = £6,750 on 1 January 2019; and
- £9,000 × 3/12 = £2,250 in the accounting period ending 30 June 2020.

Sale between connected persons

3.63 A special rate allowance cannot be claimed on sales and subsequent re-sales of integral features between connected parties, where the buyer incurred the original expenditure before 1 April 2008 or incurred expenditure after that date that was not qualifying. The expenditure will be qualifying if the original expenditure was qualifying expenditure or the buyer's expenditure would have been qualifying had it been incurred at the time the original expenditure was incurred (*FA 2008, Sch 26, para 15*). The definition of 'connection' follows *CTA 2010, s 1122* (*CAA 2001, s 575*); see **10.27**.

Intra-group transfers

3.64 Group members may elect to transfer integral features between them at written down value, where the expenditure was incurred before 1 April 2008. If the expenditure is of a type on which allowances can be claimed, it will be added to the purchasing company's main pool, and not to the special rate pool (*FA 2008, Sch 26, paras 16* and *17*). The definition of a 'group' is as for chargeable gains purposes (see **16.24–16.25**).

CONTRIBUTION ALLOWANCES

3.65 As a general rule, a business may claim capital allowances on a contribution that it makes, for the purposes of its business, to certain qualifying capital expenditure incurred by another business. The recipient of the contribution is prevented from claiming capital allowances on the same sum (*CAA 2001, s 537*).

For contributions made on or after 29 May 2013, in relation to pooling of expenditure (on a new or amended tax return) and new capital allowances claims, the rules have been tightened to prevent abuse, by clarifying that such contribution allowances on plant and machinery are not available in the recipient's hands. In this case, the contributor's capital contribution is treated as capital expenditure on the provision of plant and machinery for use in the contributor's business, and it is the contributor who can claim capital allowances, not the recipient. In certain circumstances, if the recipient of a contribution has previously pooled expenditure which would be ineligible to be pooled under the amended legislation, the unrelieved portion of that expenditure is brought into account as a disposal value (*CAA 2001, s 538*).

LEASING

> **Focus**
>
> Although a company's financial statements are the starting point on which its corporation tax computation is based, the way in which leasing contracts are reflected in the accounts can be particularly complex, and significant adjustment may be required for tax purposes. The new IFRS 16 on leases, which replaces IAS 17 for annual reporting periods beginning on or after 1 January 2019, is likely to cause further complications.

Accounting classification of leases

Introduction

3.66 Under UK GAAP, FRS 102, Section 20 *Leases*, follows broadly the pattern of SSAP 21 *Accounting for lease and hire purchase contracts* under old UK GAAP, by classifying a lease as either a finance lease or an operating lease, although the criteria are changed and rather more judgement will be required under FRS 102 in distinguishing between finance and operating leases. For example, the 90% 'bright line test' – which was in SSAP 21 and stated that, if the present value of the minimum lease payments equates to 90% or more of the fair value of the leased asset, the lease is a finance lease – is removed. Paragraph 20.5(d) requires more judgement as this states that if, at the inception of the lease, the present value of the minimum lease payments amounts to at least substantially all of the fair value of the leased asset, this indicates the lease is a finance lease. Readers will notice that the 90% test is replaced by the phrase 'substantially all'.

When substantially all of the risks and rewards of ownership are transferred from lessor to lessee, there is a finance lease, and the asset appears on the finance lessee's statement of financial position (balance sheet) with a corresponding finance lease creditor. Where the risks and rewards of ownership remain with the lessor, there is an operating lease, and the operating lessee charges rentals to profit or loss as incurred.

Accounting for finance leases

3.67 A finance lease is essentially a lending arrangement between two companies. The finance lessor company (the lender) retains ownership of the leased asset. The leased asset is not disclosed as a fixed asset on the finance lessor's statement of financial position but as a loan, which is normally the cost of the leased asset. The finance lessor's return is interest and loan repayment.

Interest is recorded in profit and loss as income. Capital repayments reduce the amount of outstanding debt.

Although the finance lessee company (the borrower) does not own the asset, it records the asset in its statement of financial position under FRS 102, Section 20 *Leases*, following the principle of substance over form (FRS 102, Section 2 *Concepts and Pervasive Principles* para 2.8). This is because, in substance, the lessee has acquired an asset which it has financed through a leasing arrangement. Capital owed to the finance lessor is shown as a creditor and is split between the amount falling due within one year and the amount falling due after more than one year in the statement of financial position and in the notes. Interest payable in the finance lease, calculated using the effective interest method under FRS 102, is charged to profit and loss. The finance lessee company charges depreciation on the asset.

See **Chapter 26** regarding changes to UK GAAP.

Accounting for operating leases

3.68 Under an operating lease, the accounting treatment recognises that the operating lessor company retains ownership of the leased asset. The operating lessor company records the leased asset in its statement of financial position under FRS 102, Section 20 *Leases*. The operating lessor company charges depreciation on the asset.

The operating lessee company recognises lease payments under an operating lease as an expense over the lease term. Alternative bases to the straight-line method can be used if the alternative is more representative of the time pattern of the lessee's benefit, even if the payments are not on that basis.

See **Chapter 26** regarding changes to UK GAAP.

Changes to lease accounting

3.69 In January 2016, the IASB issued a new accounting standard on leases, IFRS 16, to replace IAS 17. The new standard applies to accounting periods beginning on or after 1 January 2019, although a company can elect for it to apply before that date.

The key change is that for lessees, the distinction between operating and finance leases is to be abolished. Apart from short leases of 12 months or less and leases of low-value assets, all leases are to be treated as finance leases for accounting purposes, irrespective of whether or not the risks of holding the asset falls on the lessee. As a consequence, operating lessees will be required to recognise the asset on the balance sheet and charge depreciation over the period of the lease, in addition to an interest charge, calculated using the effective interest method, in the statement of profit or loss.

Lessors will continue to account for the lease either as an operating lease or a finance lease.

In August 2016, the government published a Consultation Paper (Lease accounting changes – tinyurl.com/zylmsst) exploring options for changing the tax treatment of leasing in response to IFRS 16. As a result of this consultation, the government has decided to maintain the current system of lease taxation, by making legislative changes that enable the rules to continue to work as intended (Overview of Tax Legislation and Rates March 2017, para 2.12).

These proposals are discussed further in the consultation paper 'Plant and machinery lease accounting changes' published on 1 December 2017: tinyurl.com/y7mx8x8q). In summary (Consultation Paper para 3.16):

- For lessors using either IFRS 16 or FRS 102 and for lessees using FRS 102 (both of which groups will continue to distinguish between operating and finance leases), the existing rules will apply in determining the tax treatment for leases.
- For lessees using IFRS 16, the long funding lease rules will apply (or not as the case may be) in accordance with the substance of the lease arrangements, but using the reporting of the relevant assets, liabilities and costs that is available in the accounts as they are drawn up under the new standard.
- Where the long funding lease rules do not apply, the application of generally accepted accounting practice (whether IFRS 16 or FRS 102) will (subject to existing exceptions) continue to give the quantum of the rental payments that are allowable deductions for tax purposes.

Tax treatment of leases

Introduction

3.70 A company's financial statements, prepared in accordance with GAAP, are the starting point on which its corporation tax computation is based. However, in the case of a company that is involved in leasing contracts, significant adjustment may be required for tax purposes.

For all leases, the tax treatment may depend upon whether the lease is a finance lease or an operating lease. In addition, since 1 April 2006, the tax treatment of leases of plant or machinery depends upon whether or not the lease is a 'long funding lease'.

Accounting standards are revised from time to time. Provisions in *FA 2011* ensure that any changes on or after 1 January 2011 to accounting standards for leases, if they diverge from the way in which leases were accounted for under IFRS for SMEs as it was on 1 January 2011, are to be disregarded for tax purposes (*FA 2011, s 53*).

However, the government intends to repeal this provision for accounting periods beginning on or after 1 January 2019 to coincide when the new accounting standard IFRS 16 comes into force (Consultation Paper 'Plant and machinery lease accounting changes' published on 1 December 2017, Chapter 4: see **3.69** and **Chapter 26** regarding changes to UK GAAP).

It is expected that the measure will mainly affect leases classified as operating leases under IAS 17, that are not long-funding leases. This is because accounting adjustments will be required on transitioning to IFRS 16 which will in turn require adjustments to be made for tax purposes. However, *FA 2011, s 53* will continue to apply to businesses that adopt IFRS 16 before the relevant legislative changes come into effect. In these circumstances, no accounting adjustment will be brought into account for tax purposes in the year of transition.

HMRC's guidance on the tax treatment of leases is contained in their Business Leasing Manual.

Finance leasing tax treatment

3.71 Until 31 March 2006, the tax legislation regarded the finance lessor as owner of the leased asset with entitlement to capital allowances. The lessor could only claim a 25% writing down allowance, and no first year allowance was available. Plant leased to companies not resident in the UK and whose activities are not charged exclusively to UK tax only qualify for a 10% WDA during the designated period (*CAA 2001, s 105*). The designated period is ten years from the time that the plant and machinery is first brought into use. The equipment is placed in a separate pool.

FA 2006, Sch 8 introduced the concept of long funding leases, which applies from 1 April 2006 except in certain circumstances where a written agreement was in place before 21 July 2005. A long funding lease is essentially a lease with a life of more than seven years. The effect is that the lessor company takes the finance element of the rentals arising under the lease as income. The lessee company deducts the finance element of the rentals payable over the life of the lease as an expense and is entitled to capital allowances if it so chooses (*FA 2006, s 81, Sch 8*).

Long funding leases

3.72 The lessor in a plant and machinery long funding lease arrangement is not entitled to capital allowances, but the lessee may be entitled to them (*CAA 2001, s 34A*). The lessee company must report the long funding lease on its tax return (*CAA 2001, s 70H*).

In brief, a 'long funding lease' is a funding lease (see **3.74**) which meets the following conditions:

- it is not a short lease (see **3.73**);
- it is not an excluded lease of background plant or machinery for a building (see **3.77**);
- it is not excluded because it is plant or machinery of a low percentage value leased with land (see **3.78**) (*CAA 2001, s 70G*).

For leases entered into on or after 13 December 2007, if the lessee of any plant and machinery is also the lessor of a long funding lease, both leases are treated as non-funding (*FA 2008, Sch 20, para 8*; *CAA 2001, s 70H(1A), (1B)*).

A lessee of plant or machinery under a long funding lease who claims capital allowances is required to bring in a disposal value at the end of the lease according to a specified formula. *FA 2012* introduced measures to counter tax avoidance schemes by ensuring that businesses are required to bring all relevant expenditure and receipts into account in arriving at a disposal value (*CAA 2001, s 70E*).

Short lease

3.73 A short lease is any lease with a term of five years or less. If the lease term is more than five years but less than seven years, the lease is a short lease if the following three conditions A, B and C are met (*CAA 2001, s 70I*):

Condition A

The lease is one which, under generally accepted accounting practice, falls (or would fall) to be treated as a finance lease.

Condition B

The residual value of the plant or machinery which is implied in the terms of the lease, is not more than 5% of the market value of the plant or machinery at the commencement of the term of the lease, as estimated at the inception of the lease.

Condition C

Under the terms of the lease, the total rentals falling due in the 12 months beginning on the day following the commencement of the lease amount to at least 90% of the total rentals falling due in the following 12 months, and the total rentals falling due in the final year or in any successive 12-month period after the second 12-month period are no greater than 110% of the total rentals falling due in the second 12-month period.

If plant and machinery is the subject of a lease and finance leaseback arrangement, it is not a short lease.

The government is planning to simplify the rules on short leases by removing Conditions A, B and C and providing that a lease is a short lease if its term is seven years or less (Consultation Paper 'Plant and machinery lease accounting changes' published on 1 December 2017 para 3.32, see **3.69**).

A funding lease

3.74 A 'funding lease' is a plant or machinery lease (see *CAA 2001, s 70K*) which, at its inception, meets one or more of the following tests:

- the finance lease test – a lease which under GAAP falls to be a finance lease (*CAA 2001, s 70N*). This test is to be amended to take into account changes to accounting practice upon the introduction of IAS 16 (Consultation Paper 'Plant and machinery lease accounting changes' published on 1 December 2017, para 3.35: see **3.69** and **Chapter 26** regarding changes to UK GAAP);
- the lease payments test – the present value of the minimum lease payments is equal to 80% or more of the fair value of the assets. The present value is calculated by using the interest rate implicit in the lease (*CAA 2001, s 70O*); and
- the useful economic life test – the term of the lease is more than 65% of the remaining useful economic life of the asset. The remaining useful economic life is the period beginning with the commencement of the term of the lease and ending when the asset is no longer used and no longer likely to be used by any person for any purpose as a fixed asset of the business (*CAA 2001, ss 70, 70P*).

The minimum lease payments are the minimum lease payments over the entire term of the lease after deducting certain amounts such as VAT and any residual amount at fair value reasonably expected to be recovered by the lessor at the end of the lease (*CAA 2001, s 70YE*).

A non-funding lease

3.75 A non-funding lease is outside of the scope of the funding lease regime and the relevant asset may be treated as belonging to the hirer (*CAA 2001, s 70J(3)*). A lease is not a funding lease if, prior to the commencement of the term of the lease, the relevant asset has been leased under one or more other leases, the aggregate terms of which exceed 65% of the remaining useful economic life of the asset at the commencement term of the lease, provided none of the earlier leases was itself a funding lease (*CAA 2001, s 70J(4)*).

A lease is not a long funding lease of the lessor if prior to 1 April 2006 the asset had been leased out under one or more leases for an aggregate period of at least

10 years and the lessor was also the lessor of the asset on the last day it was leased before 1 April 2006 (*CAA 2001, s 70J(6)*).

Anti-avoidance

3.76 Anti-avoidance provisions introduced by *FA 2006* are concerned with a qualifying change of ownership of a company carrying on a business of leasing plant or machinery, or changes in a company's interest in such a business after 4 December 2005. The provisions in question were changed by *FA 2012* to protect the Exchequer against risk of loss of tax when such a company moves from corporation tax into tonnage tax (*CTA 2010, ss 385, 394ZA*). Tonnage tax is an alternative to corporation tax, applicable to certain shipping companies commercially and strategically managed within the UK, and is outside the scope of this book.

There is an anti-avoidance provision under which capital payments in respect of leases can be treated as income. Any receipt not already included in income, which the provision terms as a 'capital payment', will be included in the lessor's accounts as lease income of the accounting period in which the payment is made. Where there is an unconditional obligation to make a 'capital payment', the lessor is treated as receiving lease income of the same amount in the accounting period in which the obligation arises. A deduction may be claimed in the accounts if it is expected that the amount will not actually be paid (*CTA 2010, ss 890(1)–(4), 892(3)*).

Anti-avoidance provisions designed to remove the advantages of sale and leaseback schemes are included in *FA 2009, Sch 32* and *FA 2011, s 33*.

FA 2010, Sch 6 introduced anti-avoidance legislation which applies in two situations: the first is in relation to companies with little leasing income that are potentially able to claim capital allowances, thus creating tax losses; and the second is where a lessor claims capital allowances in the initial loss-making phase of a lease of plant or machinery and avoids tax on the income that arises when the lease moves into the profitable phase (*CAA 2001, ss 228MA–228MC*).

Finance Act 2016 introduced a further anti-avoidance provision which applies when the lessee assigns its lease obligations to a third party who receives as consideration a payment which is not subject to a tax charge. The effect of the payment is that the assignee receives the benefit of the tax deductions on the lease without having incurred the full economic expenditure. In these circumstances the consideration received by the assignee or to anyone connected to it, is to be taxable as a revenue receipt. The new rules apply to transactions taking place on or after 25 November 2015 (*CTA 2010, s 894A*).

In March 2013, HMRC updated their published guidance on the leasing anti-avoidance legislation introduced from 2004 onwards (see HMRC Business Leasing Manual at BLM60000 onwards).

Background plant and machinery

3.77 Background plant and machinery contributes to the functionality of a building. Background plant and machinery leased with a building is excluded from the funding lease regime if it corresponds with any of a number of prescribed examples, as follows (*CAA 2001, ss 70R–70T*; *Capital Allowances (Leases of Background Plant or Machinery for a Building) Order 2007, SI 2007/303, art 2*):

(a) heating and air-conditioning installations;

(b) ceilings which are part of an air-conditioning system;

(c) hot water installations;

(d) electrical installations that provide power to a building, such as high and low voltage switchgear, all sub-mains distribution systems and standby generators;

(e) mechanisms, including automatic control systems, for opening and closing doors, windows and vents;

(f) escalators and passenger lifts;

(g) window cleaning installations;

(h) fittings such as fitted cupboards, blinds, curtains and associated mechanical equipment;

(i) demountable partitions;

(j) protective installations such as lightning protection, sprinkler and other equipment for containing or fighting fires, fire alarm systems and fire escapes; and

(k) building management systems.

The following types of plant or machinery are deemed to be background plant or machinery (*CAA 2001, ss 70R–70T*; *SI 2007/303, art 3*):

(a) lighting installations including all fixed light fittings and emergency lighting systems;

(b) telephone, audio-visual and data installations incidental to the occupation of the building;

(c) computer networking facilities incidental to the occupation of the building;

(d) sanitary appliances and other bathroom fittings including hand driers, counters, partitions, mirrors, shower and locker facilities;

(e) kitchen and catering facilities for producing and storing food and drink for the occupants of the building;

(f) fixed seating;

(g) signs;

(h) public address systems; and

(i) intruder alarm systems and other security equipment including surveillance equipment.

The following descriptions of plant or machinery are deemed not to be background plant or machinery (*CAA 2001, ss 70R–70T*; *SI 2007/303, art 4*):

(a) storing, moving or displaying goods to be sold in the course of a trade, whether wholesale or retail;

(b) manufacturing goods or materials;

(c) subjecting goods or materials to a process;

(d) storing goods or materials:

  (i) which are to be used in the manufacture of other goods or materials;

  (ii) which are to be subjected, in the course of a trade, to a process;

  (iii) which, having been manufactured or produced or subjected in the course of a trade to a process, have not yet been delivered to any purchaser; or

  (iv) on their arrival in the United Kingdom from a place outside the United Kingdom.

Plant and machinery leased with land: low percentage value

3.78 An exclusion applies to low percentage value plant and machinery leased with land where:

- the plant and machinery is affixed to the building or otherwise installed on the land;
- the plant and machinery is not background plant and machinery for any building situated in or on the land; and
- the plant or machinery is leased with the land under a mixed lease, the sole purpose of which is to secure a tax advantage.

In these circumstances, the lease is not a long funding lease if the aggregate market value (AMV) does not exceed both 5% of the market value of the land (including fixtures and fittings) and 10% of the aggregate value of the background plant and machinery (*CAA 2001, s 70U*). AMV is the aggregate of the relevant plant and machinery and the market value of all other plant and machinery leased with the land (*CAA 2001, s 70U*).

Change of company ownership

3.79 As a result of the impact of capital allowances, a lessor company's profits chargeable to corporation tax are likely to be lower in the earlier years of a leasing contract than in the later years. Where there is a change of ownership of a single company, group company (see **5.6**) or consortium company (see **5.7**), or changes in a company's partnership share of an interest in a business, the available loss relief may be restricted under the 'sales of lessors' provisions.

For corporation tax purposes, an accounting period ends and a new accounting period commences on the date of the change. On that date ('the relevant day'), an adjustment is calculated which is treated as income for the accounting period prior to the change and as an expense of the accounting period after the change. The legislation then restricts losses arising after the relevant day from being carried back under *CTA 2010, s 37(3)(b)* against profits before the relevant day (*CTA 2010, s 385*, before and after amendment by *FA 2012, s 24*). If this results in the expense giving rise to a loss that cannot be used in the accounting period immediately after the change, *CTA 2010, s 386* governs how this may be carried forward to subsequent accounting periods, subject to adjustments in its value.

For these purposes, a company is considered to be a lessor company or carrying on a leasing business if at least half the accounting value of its plant or machinery is relevant plant or machinery, or at least half of the company's income in the period of 12 months ending with the date of the change derives from plant or machinery that it or its qualifying associate has leased out under a plant and machinery lease, but not an excluded lease of background plant or machinery for a building. The qualifying associate must have leased the plant and machinery to someone other than the relevant company. An associate is anyone connected with the relevant company, but a qualifying associate is anyone who is an associate at the start of the relevant period or at any time within the previous 12 months, whether or not the plant and machinery was leased out (*CTA 2010, s 387*).

Relevant plant or machinery on a particular date is the accounting value of the company's plant and machinery at the beginning of the relevant day, plus the amounts of any plant and machinery transferred to it by its associates during that day (*CTA 2010, ss 388–389*). Long funding leases and hire purchase are excluded (*CTA 2010, s 390*). Qualifying leased plant and machinery is plant and machinery bought wholly or partly for the purposes of the business, on which the company is entitled to plant and machinery capital allowances and which is leased at any time during the 12 months prior to the date of the change. Plant and machinery in let buildings owned by a property investment company does not fall into this category.

If the relevant company is owned by a consortium, or is a qualifying 75% subsidiary of a consortium, any person connected with the relevant company includes any member of the consortium and any person connected with such a member (*CTA 2010, s 387*).

The adjustment that is to be made is calculated according to the formula:

PM – TWDV

where:

- PM is the amount of plant and machinery and the net investment in finance leases shown on the company's balance sheet at the start of the relevant day, together with that of its associates at the end of the relevant day
- TWDV is the total of the tax written down value of the single asset pools, the class pools and the main pool at the start of the relevant accounting period following the date of the change.

If the result is negative, it is assumed to be nil (*CTA 2010, ss 399–404*).

Example 3.22—Leasing: change of company ownership

Facts

James plc prepares accounts to 31 December each year. On 1 July 2018, the company is taken over by Frank plc. At 30 June 2018, the balance sheet shows net investment in leased assets of £1,200 million. The same assets have a tax written down net book value of £640 million.

Analysis

For corporation tax purposes:

(i) James plc has two accounting periods: the six months to 30 June 2018, and the six months to 31 December 2018.

(ii) The required adjustment is £(1,200 – 640) million = £560 million.

(iii) If the income adjustment in the period to 31 December 2018 results in a profit, James plc will not be able to reduce that profit by carrying back any amount of loss arising in the new accounting period that follows the change of ownership.

These rules will continue to apply where there is a transfer of trade under *CTA 2010, ss 939–952*.

ANTI-AVOIDANCE

3.80 Anti-avoidance rules exist to restrict capital allowances where plant or machinery is bought or acquired on hire purchase and the two parties are connected, where there is a sale and leaseback or where the capital allowances were the sole or main benefit expected to accrue. However, there is an exception to this rule where the plant or machinery is acquired directly from the manufacturer or supplier in the normal course of business. Further restrictions apply for expenditure incurred on or after 12 August 2011, but the pre-existing exception continues to apply unless the transaction has an avoidance purpose (*CAA 2001, ss 213–230*).

From 1 April 2012 there was a tightening of other pre-existing anti-avoidance rules which can operate to restrict the capital allowances available to a purchaser of plant or machinery (*CAA 2001, ss 215, 218ZA, 268E*).

From 26 February 2015, *FA 2015, Sch 10*, introduced a new restriction in certain circumstances where the person disposing of the asset, or a person with whom they are or have previously been connected, acquired the asset without incurring either capital expenditure or 'qualifying revenue expenditure'. Qualifying revenue expenditure is expenditure of a revenue nature incurred at an arm's length price or, where the person who acquired the asset is a manufacturer, reflecting all the normal costs of manufacture. Where the new restriction applies, the person acquiring the asset will be treated, for the purposes of plant and machinery allowances, as having no qualifying expenditure. The types of transaction potentially affected are:

- long funding leasebacks (*CAA 2001, s 70DA*);
- transactions between connected persons, or sale and leaseback transactions (*CAA 2001, s 218*); or
- transfers followed by hire-purchase etc (*CAA 2001, s 229A*).

A further tightening of the anti-avoidance rules applies where the parties to a transaction seek to artificially reduce the disposal value of the plant and machinery. The new rules apply to transactions taking place on or after 25 November 2015 (*CAA 2001, ss 213, 215*, as amended by *Finance Act 2016*).

Chapter 4

Single company trading losses

SIGNPOSTS

- Criteria for carrying a trading loss forward for relief against future profits of the same trade (see **4.1–4.15**).
- Loss relief for all companies is restricted from 1 April 2017. While this strictly only applies to companies with profits in excess of £5 million, all companies, however small, are subject to the onerous compliance regime (see **4.3**).
- Criteria for setting a trading loss against total profits of the same accounting period and the previous 12 months (see **4.16–4.20**).
- Trading losses arising from 1 April 2017 can be set against total profits of future accounting periods (see **4.4** and **4.5**).
- Relief for qualifying charitable donations (see **4.21**).
- Loss relief available on a cessation of trade (see **4.22** and **4.23**).
- Restrictions on loss relief due to a change in ownership of the company and in other situations (see **4.24–4.31**).
- Self-assessment loss claim procedures and elections and HMRC amendments (see **4.32–4.37**).
- The entitlement to first-year tax credits, claim procedures and clawback (see **4.38–4.52**).

TRADING PROFITS AND LOSSES

Computation

4.1 The vagaries of business life mean that many companies can make losses in their trading ventures just as easily as they can make profits.

A trading loss is computed in exactly the same way as a trading profit (*CTA 2009, s 47*). When a company incurs a trading loss, it must prepare its corporation tax computation in the normal way to send to HMRC, together with form CT600 and the statutory accounts. If a trading loss is incurred during the accounting period, the chargeable profits are recorded as 'nil'.

By default, a trading loss arising before 1 April 2017 is carried forward against future profits of the same trade (see **4.2**). However, the legislation allows the company to claim relief for the loss against its other profits of the same accounting period and then of other accounting periods falling within the previous 12 months (see **4.16–4.22**).

Losses arising on or after 1 April 2017 can be set against total profits of future accounting periods, subject to satisfying a number of conditions (see **4.4** and **4.5**).

A company may be entitled to claim tax credits under a variety of different provisions and, if these give rise to surrenderable losses, may surrender such losses to HMRC in return for a repayable tax credit (see **4.39–4.52**).

See HMRC's Toolkit on 'Company Losses' at tinyurl.com/63vn6ts.

CARRY-FORWARD OF TRADING LOSS

> **Focus**
>
> A trading loss incurred before 1 April 2017 is automatically set against future profits from the same trade, unless the company claims otherwise.
>
> Losses arising on or after 1 April 2017 can be used more flexibly, and can be set against total profits of later years, so long as the trade continues.
>
> Time limits apply to both claims.

Loss claim before 1 April 2017

4.2 Unless a trading loss is utilised in other ways, it will automatically be carried forward to set against profits of the same trade in the next and subsequent accounting periods. The loss can only be used if there are available profits and, once used, it cannot be used again. There is no facility to disclaim the whole or even part of the loss, which must be matched consecutively year on year to available profits until fully utilised (*CTA 2010, s 45(4)*).

Relief for a trading loss is only available if the trade continues to be carried on when the loss is to be relieved (*CTA 2010, s 45(4)(a)*). What is more, the trade has to be the same trade but, unlike *CTA 2010, s 37(3)* (see **4.17**), there is no requirement for the trade to continue to be carried on in the UK.

Exceptionally, companies that are in financial difficulties may enter into an agreement with the Treasury or another government department or agency, and part of the terms of the agreement may be the forfeiture of their right to tax losses. If such an arrangement is in place, no tax relief is given by virtue of the tax relief forgone under the arrangement (*FA 2009, s 25*).

In the case of banking companies (including building societies and savings banks), the proportion of their profits from 1 April 2015 that can be covered by relevant reliefs carried forward from before that date is limited to 50% until 31 March 2016, after which the restriction will be 25%. Building societies and savings banks benefit from a special £25 million allowance (*CTA 2010, ss 269A–269CN*), and other financial organisations may be exempt from this rule if they qualify as an excluded entity under *CTA 2009, s 133F.*

Many businesses shift naturally from unprofitable to profitable sources and, as business life moves swiftly, it is often difficult to determine whether a new activity is in fact an extension of the existing trade or a new trade. Loss relief will be allowed when the same trade is carried on, but will be denied where the loss-making trade has been superseded by a new trade. The courts have considered such cases (see **4.9**).

> **Focus**
>
> A company seeking to use carried-forward losses must state on the face of the corporation tax return how much of the £5 million allowance is allocated to the use of trading losses. Failure to do so will lead to the loss of the £5 million allowance for the period in question.

> **Focus**
>
> All groups, however small and however low their profits, are required to comply with the detailed rules for allocating the £5 million allowance between the group members and complying with the detailed rules for supplying HMRC with the appropriate statement.

General restriction on loss relief from 1 April 2017

4.3 From 1 April 2017 the maximum loss relief that a company will be able to claim will be restricted where the company's profits exceed £5 million (the 'deductions allowance'; *CTA 2010, s 269ZL*).

In such cases, the general rule is that the company's maximum deductions cannot exceed £5 million plus 50% of the excess profits over £5m. For an example, a company with profits of £8 million would only be entitled to use carried-forward losses of £7m, being the £5m deductions allowance and half the excess, ie another £2 million.

The deductions allowance is proportionately reduced for short accounting periods (*CTA 2010, s 269ZL(3)*), and is also apportioned within a group of companies (*CTA 2010, s 269ZK(3)*).

The detailed rules are in new *CTA 2010, Pt 7ZA*, introduced by *F(No 2)A 2017*.

A major compliance point that smaller companies and groups need to look out for is that the £5 million allowance has to be 'claimed' by any company wishing to set off carried-forward losses against profits of a later year. The legislation provides that every company should state on its return the amount of its trading profits deductions allowance, for the purposes of the use of carried-forward trading losses. Failure to state the amount on the face of the return will, strictly, mean that the company has no trading profits deductions allowance, so that the use of any carried-forward losses will be restricted by 50% (*CTA 2010, s 269ZB(7)(b)*).

Similarly, there is no de minimis level for the requirement to allocate the £5 million allowance between companies in a group (*CTA 2010, s 269ZK(3)*). This means that even the smallest companies comprising a holding company and a trading company must strictly nominate one of the companies to provide the relevant statement to HMRC, with all of the other information on it that the legislation requires.

HMRC have not indicated any sensible policy explanation as to why even the smallest companies must comply with these requirements. The concern is that a great many companies will not realise that this legislation applies to them, so that they will be denied the use of losses for no good reason. Alternatively, this will add time to every corporate self-assessment, so that the time required to submit company returns will be increased. While this might be a small amount of time for each individual return, the combined extra time required for an accountant with, say, 1,000 corporate clients will be huge.

Loss claim after 1 April 2017 – pre-1 April 2017 losses

4.4 From 1 April 2017, it will be necessary to segregate losses arising up to 31 March 2017 and losses arising after that date. Unused losses at 31 March 2017 are then carried forward under *CTA 2010, s 45(4)(a)* and set against future profits of the same trade, as was always the case. However, *CTA 2010, s 45A*, introduced by *Finance Act 2017*, allows the company to claim how much, if any, of the profit of the trade is reduced by the carried-forward losses. Such a claim can only apply to accounting periods starting on or after 1 April 2017 (including the later part of a straddling accounting period). The claim must be made within two years of the end of the accounting period, or a longer period if permitted by HMRC.

The new rules apply to accounting periods starting on or after 1 April 2017. Accounting periods straddling this date are treated as two accounting periods, one ending on 31 March 2017 and another starting on 1 April 2017.

> **Focus**
>
> Relief for carried-forward losses against future total profits of the company must be claimed. The relief is not given automatically.
>
> Claims must be made within two years of the end of the accounting period, or a longer period if permitted by HMRC. We assume that the use of losses in a corporation tax computation will be an acceptable form of claim.

Loss claim after 1 April 2017 – Losses arising on or after 1 April 2017

4.5 New rules apply for trading losses arising on or after 1 April 2017. The basic premise remains the same, however, in that trading losses are carried forward by default to future accounting periods. The main difference is that the carried-forward loss can be set against the total profits of the company in the later period (*CTA 2010, s 45A*).

The new rules for carry forward will still require that the company continues to carry on the same trade in the future accounting period. The further conditions are:

- the trade is not a ring fence trade;
- the trade did not become small or negligible in the loss-making period;
- relief against total profits of the loss-making period were not denied by *CTA 2010, s 37(5)* (trade carried on wholly outside the UK), *44* (trade not commercial or carried on for statutory functions – see **4.20**), *48* (farming or market gardening) or *52* (dealing in commodity futures);
- relief against total profits of the loss-making period were not denied by various provisions of *CTA 2009* relating to the creative sector reliefs;
- relief against total profits of the future period would not be denied by *CTA 2010, s 44* (trade not commercial or carried on for statutory functions) in the later period, if the carried-forward loss were a loss of the later period.

The unrelieved loss can then be carried forward to the future accounting period, and the whole loss or any part of it can be used against the company's total profits of that later period. The relief must be claimed for the amount of loss to be used in the later period, and the claim must be made within two years of the end of the accounting period, or a longer period if permitted by HMRC.

4.6 If the losses are not all used in the later period, they are carried forward again (*CTA 2010, ss 45A* and *45C*), so long as:

- the company continues to carry on the same trade in the future accounting period;
- the trade did not become small or negligible in the previous period;
- relief against total profits of the future period would not be denied by *CTA 2010, s 44* (trade not commercial or carried on for statutory functions) in the later period, if the carried-forward loss were a loss of the later period.

If the trade did become small or negligible in the previous period, or relief against total profits of the future period would not be denied by *CTA 2010, s 44* in the later period, unused losses can be carried forward to relieve future profits of the same trade (*CTA 2010, s 45D*, see **4.8**).

4.7 In certain cases, a carried-forward loss can still only be set against the future trading profits of the company (*CTA 2010, s 45B*). The conditions are:

- the trade is a ring fence trade;
- the trade became small or negligible in the loss-making period;
- relief against total profits of the loss-making period was denied by *CTA 2010, s 37(5)* (trade carried on wholly outside the UK), *44* (trade not commercial or carried on for statutory functions – see **4.20**), *48* (farming or market gardening) or *52* (dealing in commodity futures);
- relief against total profits of the loss-making period was denied by various provisions of *CTA 2009* relating to the creative sector reliefs;
- relief against total profits of the future period would be denied by *CTA 2010, s 44* (trade not commercial or carried on for statutory functions) in the later period.

In such cases, the carried-forward loss can only be used to relieve the profits of the same trade, if any, in the later accounting period.

This use of the loss is automatic, unless a claim is made not to use some or all of the available loss. As always, the claim must be made within two years of the end of the accounting period, or a longer period if permitted by HMRC. Otherwise, the whole loss is used, so far as possible.

Any unused losses can be carried forward to be used against the future profits of the same trade in the same way and subject to the same rules of set-off and claim (*CTA 2010, ss 45B* and *45E*).

4.8 Where a loss is carried forward under *CTA 2010, s 45A* but the trade became small or negligible in the previous period, or relief against total profits of the future period would be denied by *CTA 2010, s 44* in the later period, those unused losses can be used to relieve the profits of the same trade (*CTA 2010, s 45D*).

The rules for relief and claims are the same as those for *CTA 2010, s 45B*.

Case law – same trade or different?

4.9 Gordon & Blair Ltd traded as brewers. The company's activities consisted of brewing and selling beer to third parties. After a period of time, Gordon & Blair Ltd stopped brewing beer and engaged another company to brew to its specification. Gordon & Blair Ltd continued to sell the beer. The Court of Session held that the brewing trade had ceased and a new trade of beer selling had commenced, with the effect that the brewing trade's losses could not be set against the beer sales profits (*Gordon & Blair Ltd v CIR* (1962) 40 TC 358).

Bolands Ltd, an Irish company, traded in Ireland as millers and bakers. The company owned two mills and, in its own bakeries, it used about half of the flour it produced. The company hit dire times, incurred losses and closed the mills. A year later, it reopened one of the mills, mainly to supply the bakeries. It was held that a single trade was carried on throughout. Therefore, it was able to utilise its trading losses (*Bolands Ltd v Davis* (1925) 1 ITC 91).

In contrast, JG Ingram & Sons Ltd manufactured and sold surgical goods. At that time, the company used rubber in its manufacturing process. The company suffered large losses. A receiver was appointed, the plant sold and the factory closed. The company continued to sell surgical goods under its own brand that were made by an associated company. A year later, a change of ownership took place and the company recommenced manufacturing but used plastic rather than rubber in its production process. The sale of surgical goods continued. The company claimed that it carried on the continuing trade of the sale of surgical goods. The Court of Appeal disagreed and decided that a new trade had commenced with the production of plastic surgical goods (*JG Ingram & Sons Ltd v Callaghan* (1968) 45 TC 151).

More recently, in *Kawthar Consulting Ltd v HMRC* [2005] STC (SCD) 524, the *JG Ingram* argument was used. Kawthar Ltd's trade was the provision of computers and monitors. Unfortunately, the company's client went into liquidation and Kawthar Ltd suffered large losses. Two to three years later, the company won a lucrative contract for the supply of compliance software. The company regarded itself as an IT company and set the earlier trading losses against the current profits under *ICTA 1988, s 393(1)*. The Special Commissioners decided that the company's trade of dealing in computers had ceased and a new trade of providing IT consultancy services had begun, with the result that Kawthar Ltd was unable to utilise its brought-forward trading losses against its current profits.

Corporation tax self-assessment

4.10 As the carry-forward of loss relief under *CTA 2010, s 45(4)* is automatic, the legislation requires no formal claim. In order to satisfy the corporation tax self-assessment filing requirement, the company, when completing form CT600, is required to state the amount of the loss that is to be relieved. Only the actual amount to be set against profits should be entered on the CT600. A separate loss calculation should be supplied with the company tax return to explain how the loss has been utilised. In particular, if more than one trade is being carried on, the computation should clearly show how the trading losses are utilised against the income of each particular trade. As soon as a trade ceases, it will no longer be possible to carry forward any unused loss that arose in that trade.

The company in its corporation tax self-assessment submission must distinguish between an existing trade and a new or different trade when claiming loss relief. This is where potential difficulties may lie. From the case law examples cited above, it is apparent that, if a company changes its activities during the course of its existence, it may wish to demonstrate that these activities are sufficiently uninterrupted and interrelated to constitute a continuing trade; otherwise, a claim to carry forward the loss will fail.

Losses and HMRC enquiries

4.11 The fact that a company incurs a loss rather than a profit during its accounting period has no effect on HMRC's powers of enquiry; they remain the same (see **Chapter 22**). A brought-forward trading loss shown on a corporation tax computation cannot be enquired into under *FA 1998, Sch 18, para 25* if the time limit of two years after the end of the accounting period in which the loss was incurred has expired. If HMRC wished to enquire into earlier losses, they would have to open a discovery enquiry under *FA 1998, Sch 18, para 43*.

A discovery assessment or determination can only be made if tax was understated as a result of the careless or deliberate actions of the company, its representative or anyone who was in partnership with the company at the relevant time. Alternatively, an enquiry may be opened into the use of a trading loss where there is a reconstruction (*CTA 2010, s 944(3)*) or a change of ownership (*CTA 2010, s 674(2)*). *Section 944* permits losses to be transferred from one company to another company with substantially the same ownership, as discussed in **17.26–17.27**. *Section 674* can prevent loss utilisation where there is a change of ownership (see **4.24**). HMRC have also stated that they may enquire into the use of a trading loss carried forward in a later accounting period where there is a dispute about whether a trade has continued, or whether it has ceased and a new trade commenced (HMRC Company Taxation Manual at CTM04150).

Within the charge to corporation tax

4.12 In order to be granted loss relief, not only must the company be carrying on the same trade but it must also be within the charge to corporation tax (*CTA 2010, s 36(3)*). This requirement is most likely to affect companies who become resident in the UK after having been resident abroad.

When a company becomes UK resident, it falls within the charge to corporation tax if it has a source of income. If the company becomes UK resident while continuing to carry on the same trade as it carried on before, its loss relief capacity is restricted. The company, now resident in the UK, is not entitled to relief for trading losses incurred whilst non-UK resident against profits earned after it became UK resident.

On the other hand, a non-UK resident company that is carrying on a trade in the UK through a permanent establishment is within the charge to corporation tax (*CTA 2009, ss 5(2), 19(1)*). A permanent establishment may consist of a branch or agency. Therefore, the branch or agency will obtain relief for any UK losses it incurs against the UK income that it earns. If the accounts and records are kept in a foreign currency, the loss should be converted to sterling using the same exchange rate as used for the profits conversion (see **20.48** onwards).

Corporation tax computation

4.13 The following example details the presentation of a corporation tax computation in circumstances where there are trading losses brought forward to set against future trading income from the same trade under *CTA 2010, s 45(4)*.

Example 4.1—Carry-forward of trading loss (1)

Facts

The Abracadabra Trading Company Ltd has the following results for the year ended 31 March 2016:

	£000
Trade profits	200
Property income	1,600
Loan relationship	400
Chargeable gains	300
Loss brought forward under *CTA 2010, s 45(4)*	5,000

Analysis

The company calculates its profits chargeable to corporation tax and its trading loss carried forward as follows:

Corporation tax computation for the year ended 31 March 2016

	£000
Trade profits	200
Less: Loss brought forward under *CTA 2010, s 45(4)*	(200)
	0
Property income	1,600
Loan relationship	400
Chargeable gains	300
Total profits	2,300
Total taxable profits of the period	2,300

Loss utilisation

	£000
Loss brought forward	5,000
Used against trading income of the year	(200)
Loss carried forward under *CTA 2010, s 45(4)*	4,800

In contrast, look at the position if the losses arose after 1 April 2017.

Example 4.2—Carry-forward of trading loss (2)

Facts

The Abracadabra Trading Company Ltd has the following results for the year ended 31 March 2020:

	£000
Trade profits	200
Property income	1,600
Loan relationship	400
Chargeable gains	300
Loss brought forward under *CTA 2010, s 45A*	5,000

Analysis

The company calculates its profits chargeable to corporation tax and its trading loss carried forward as follows:

Corporation tax computation for the year ended 31 March 2020

	£000
Trade profits	200
Property income	1,600
Loan relationship	400
Chargeable gains	300
Total profits	2,500
Less: Loss brought forward under *CTA 2010, s 45A*	(2,500)
Total taxable profits of the period	Nil

Loss utilisation

	£000
Loss brought forward	5,000
Used against trading income of the year	(2,500)
Loss carried forward under *CTA 2010, s 45A*	Nil

Relief for trading losses against interest and dividends

4.14 Where a company has insufficient profits in a later period against which to set a trading loss from an earlier period, *CTA 2010, s 46(2)* allows the inclusion, as though they were trading income, of interest and dividends that would be included as trading income but for the fact that tax has been deducted at source. Dividends from UK companies are excluded. In practice, this treatment will only be applied where the investment forms part of the trade, and it was refused by the Court of Session in *Bank Line Ltd v CIR* [1974] STC 342 and by the House of Lords in *Nuclear Electric plc v Bradley* [1996] STC 405 (CTM04250; see also HMRC Business Income Manual at BIM40805).

Companies entering into partnership

4.15 A company may form links with other companies to further its trading activities. Groups are discussed in **Chapter 5**. A company engaged in a particular trading activity, whilst carrying on this trade, might enter into partnership with another company or individual. HMRC have confirmed that the company can carry forward any losses incurred by it in that trade before the formation of the partnership, and relieve losses under *CTA 2010, s 45(4)* against its share of the partnership trading income, but only if the partnership continues to carry on the same trade that was previously carried on by the company (CTM04200).

FA 2014 introduced complex anti-avoidance measures affecting partnerships, including LLPs, in the following circumstances:

- Where the partnership is mixed (ie those involving individuals and non-individuals, usually companies) and there is an 'excess profit allocation scheme' or an 'excess loss allocation scheme' designed to exploit the differences in marginal tax rates payable by the partners. More specifically:
  - From 6 April 2014, provisions may be invoked to reallocate excess profits, attributed initially to a non-individual partner, and ascribe them instead to an individual where certain conditions are met – eg where the non-individual's share is excessive and a UK individual partner has the power to enjoy the non-individual's share or there are deferred profit arrangements in place (an 'excess profit allocation scheme'). The legislation may also reallocate excess profits to an individual who is not a partner (*CTA 2009, s 1264A*).
  - From 6 April 2014, certain income tax loss reliefs and capital gains relief may be denied where a loss is allocated to a UK taxpaying individual who is party to arrangements designed to secure that some or all of the loss is allocated, or otherwise arises, to the individual instead of a non-individual with a view to the individual obtaining relief (an 'excess loss allocation scheme') (*ITA 2007, ss 116A, 127C*).
- Also from 1 April 2014, if a company is involved in the transfer of assets or income streams through arrangements that seek to manipulate the flexibility of a partnership (whether mixed or not) to reduce tax by exploiting the differing tax attributes of the partners, it may face a charge to corporation tax on income (*CTA 2010, ss 757A, 757B, 779A, 779B*).

For further details of the *FA 2014* changes, see HMRC's Technical Note 'Partnerships: A review of two aspects of the tax rules', 27 March 2014, at tinyurl.com/nnno7ny.

SET TRADING LOSS AGAINST TOTAL PROFITS

4.16 As an alternative to carrying forward the whole of any trading loss to set against future trading profits, the company may claim to offset the loss against its other profits (*CTA 2010, s 37(3)(a)*).

Example 4.3—Set-off of trading loss against total profits

Facts

A Ltd's results for the year ending 31 March 2018 show:

	£
Trading loss	(10,000)
Property income	3,000
Loan relationship	4,000
Chargeable gains	7,200

Analysis

The loss may be relieved as follows:

	£
Property income	3,000
Loan relationship	4,000
Chargeable gains	7,200
	14,200
Deduct trading loss	(10,000)
Total taxable profits of the period	4,200

4.17 The profits that are eligible are the total profits for the same accounting period as the loss, followed (if the company's claim so requires) by the total profits of the immediately preceding 12 months, provided that the trade was being carried on throughout that period (*CTA 2010, s 37(3)(b)*). The relief (if claimed) must be taken in that order, and the relief for the same accounting period must be taken in full, up to the amount of the chargeable profits. It is not possible to make a partial claim. Only after this relief is taken can the balance of the loss be set against the total profits of previous accounting periods so far as they fall wholly or partly within the previous 12 months, and in that case the loss must be relieved against a later period before an earlier period. No claim is allowed if the company carried on the trade wholly outside the UK in the loss-making period. Furthermore, during the period in which the losses are relieved, the company must carry on the trade and must not do so wholly outside the UK (*CTA 2010, s 37(5), (6)*).

Focus

It is up to the company to decide whether to set its trading loss against other profits of the same accounting period and, if it wishes, against total profits of the previous 12 months.

Example 4.4—Carry-back of trading loss against previous 12 months' profits

Facts

A company made a trading loss of £35,000 in the accounting period 1 January 2018 to 31 December 2018. Other corporation tax profits of the period amounted to £20,000. The company continues to trade. The corporation tax profits of earlier accounting periods were as follows:

	£
1 July 2017 to 31 December 2017	10,000
1 July 2016 to 30 June 2017	20,000

The trade in which the loss was incurred was carried on throughout the whole of the period from 1 July 2016 to 31 December 2018. The company claims under *CTA 2010, s 37(3)* to extend the relief to the 'preceding period', ie the 12-month period which ends on 31 December 2017.

Analysis

Relief is given as follows:

Against profits of the accounting period	£
1 January 2018 to 31 December 2018	20,000
1 July 2017 to 31 December 2017	10,000
1 July 2016 to 30 June 2017	5,000
Total amount of profits relieved	35,000

Note that relief has been given against the whole of the profits of the accounting period to 31 December 2017 before any relief is given against the profits of the earlier accounting period.

The maximum relief available for the period 1 July 2016 to 30 June 2017 is 6/12ths of the profits of that period, as only 6 months of the period falls within the 12-month period immediately prior to the loss period. In this case, up to £10,000 of the profits could thus be relieved; but see Example 4.5.

Example 4.5—Carry-back of trading loss: restriction to 12 months

Facts

The facts are the same as those in Example 4.4, except that the trading loss for the period from 1 January 2018 to 31 December 2018 was £45,000.

Analysis

Relief is given as follows:

Against profits of the accounting period	£
1 January 2018 to 31 December 2018	20,000
1 July 2017 to 31 December 2017	10,000
1 July 2016 to 30 June 2017	10,082
Total amount of profits relieved	40,082

The set-off for the accounting period ended 30 June 2017 is limited by *CTA 2010, s 38* to the proportion (184/366 × £20,000 = £10,082) of the profits of that period which fall within the 12 months ending on 31 December 2017. The unused balance of the loss for the accounting period ending 31 December 2018 (£4,918) is available for carry-forward under *CTA 2010, s 45(4)* (CTM04540).

Profits for the accounting period ended 30 June 2017 have been apportioned on a time basis. Exceptionally, there might be a possibility of apportioning the profits on an actual basis if this gives a more accurate result; see **22.7** for a discussion on *Marshall Hus & Partners Ltd v Bolton* [1981] STC 18.

4.18 It is not compulsory to take relief under *CTA 2010, s 37(3)*. The relief can be ignored and the loss can be carried forward in an automatic *CTA 2010, s 45(4)* set-off. If *CTA 2010, s 37(3)* relief is claimed, current year relief under *CTA 2010, s 37(3)(a)* must always be taken first. If (but only if) the company's claim so requires, relief is then given under *CTA 2010, s 37(3)(b)* against profits of the previous 12 months.

Where there are losses arising in consecutive accounting periods and relief is claimed under *CTA 2010, s 37(3)* for each accounting period, the order of set-off is:

(i) loss of the first accounting period against total profits of the same accounting period;

(ii) loss of the first accounting period against the preceding 12 months' profits;

(iii) loss of the second accounting period against total profits of the same accounting period;

(iv) loss of the second accounting period against profits of the preceding 12 months, which in effect amounts to the 'first accounting period'.

This can often result in insufficient profits against which to make a carry-back election for the second accounting period.

Example 4.6—Carry-back of trading loss: order of set-off

Facts

A company commenced trading on 1 January 2017 and prepares six-monthly accounts for its first two years of trading. It makes trading losses of £25,000 in its six-month accounting period ended 30 June 2018, and £40,000 in its six-month accounting period ended 31 December 2018. The corporation tax profits of the preceding periods were as follows:

	£
Accounting period 6 months to 31 December 2017	20,000
Accounting period 6 months to 30 June 2017	10,000

Analysis

Relief for the £25,000 loss for the accounting period ended 30 June 2018 is given before relief for the £40,000 loss for the accounting period ended 31 December 2018. Relief is therefore given as follows:

Loss for the period to 30 June 2018

	Profit	*Loss relief*	*Net taxable*
	£	£	£
Against profits of the accounting period			
• 6 months to 31 December 2017	20,000	20,000	—
• 6 months to 30 June 2017	10,000	5,000	5,000
Total	30,000	25,000	5,000

Loss for the period to 31 December 2018

This loss cannot be carried back, because the only profits for accounting periods falling wholly or partly into the 12 months immediately preceding the accounting period ended 31 December 2018 (that is, the six months to 30 June 2017 and the six months to 31 December 2017) have already been covered by loss relief from an earlier period.

It would have suited the company better had it been allowed to claim relief for the period ended 31 December 2018 first, before the claim in respect of the period ended 30 June 2018. However, the legislation does not allow this (CTM04550).

4.19 The loss can be set against the total profits of each accounting period falling wholly or partly within the previous 12 months if, and only if, the trade in question was carried on at some time in that accounting period. It is not necessary for the trade to have been carried on for the whole of the preceding 12-month period. If the trade was carried on for only part of the previous 12 months, the loss will still be relievable against total profits of that period (CTM04510). The loss up to the full amount of the total profits must be utilised or, if less, the full amount of the loss. The balance of any unused loss is available to carry forward under *CTA 2010, s 45(4)*.

A claim must be made within two years of the end of the accounting period in which the loss is incurred. The claim can be made on the company's corporation tax return and by giving full details of the loss and the trade to which it refers (*CTA 2010, s 37(2)*).

Commercial basis with a view to profit

4.20 Relief under *CTA 2010, s 37*, in respect of a trading loss is available only if, during the loss-making period, the trade in question is conducted on a commercial basis, and with a view to making a profit or so as to afford a reasonable expectation of making a profit (*CTA 2010, s 44*; CTM04600).

Wannell v Rothwell [1996] STC 450 concerned a taxpayer trading in commodity futures from his home. In dismissing the taxpayer's appeal, the High Court noted his lack of commercial organisation and held that, even though he was trading, he was not doing so on a commercial basis.

In *Kerr (Re Grantham House) v Revenue & Customs* [2011] UKFTT 40 (TC), the taxpayer leased a National Trust property for £45,000 per annum, spent £22,000 on repairs and wages, and then made total sales of only £80 in the first year from opening the property to the public. Nonetheless, the First-tier Tribunal held that the trade was commercial with a view to making a profit.

In *Glapwell Football Club Ltd v Revenue & Customs* [2013] UKFTT 516 (TC), the First-tier Tribunal held that the directors' hopes and intentions of future income were not supported by sufficient convincing objective evidence to establish that the trade was being carried on so as to afford a reasonable expectation of making a profit.

If a trade of farming or market gardening makes a loss for five consecutive years, the next year's loss can only be carried forward against future profits of the same trade, and not used in any other way. This is known as the 'hobby farming' rule. However, this restriction does not apply if the carrying on of the trade forms part of or is ancillary to a larger trading undertaking, or if the trade is carried on with a reasonable expectation of profits (*CTA 2010, s 48*; see CTM04710 onwards; also *French v HMRC* [2014] UKFTT 940 (TC).

RELIEF FOR QUALIFYING CHARITABLE DONATIONS

4.21 Relief for qualifying charitable donations is given under *CTA 2010, s 189*. Such payments are not related to a company's trading activity, so they are known as 'non-trade' charges. They can only be relieved against total profits of the current accounting period after any relief for trading losses, including loss relief carried back under *CTA 2010, s 37(3)(b)*.

Example 4.7—Carry-back of trading loss: unrelieved non-trade charges

Facts

Wizard Ltd prepares accounts to 30 June each year. The company has recently changed its accounting date from 31 December.

Wizard Ltd's results, both actual and forecast, are as follows:

	Year ended 31 December 2016	*Six months ended 30 June 2017*	*Year ended 30 June 2018*	*Year ended 30 June 2019*
	£000	*£000*	*£000*	*£000*
Trade profit/(loss)	35	20	(120)	90
Property income	5	3	6	4
Chargeable gain	10	0	8	0
Charitable donations	(3)	(2)	0	0

Analysis

CTA 2010, s 37(3)(a) claim for the year ended 30 June 2018:

	Year ended 30 June 2018
	£000
Property income	6
Chargeable gain	8
	14

Less: loss claim	(14)
Total taxable profits of the period	0

CTA 2010, s 37(3)(b) claim for the previous 12 months:

	Year ended 31 December 2016	*Six months ended 30 June 2017*
	£000	*£000*
Trade profit	35	20
Property income	5	3
Chargeable gain	10	0
	50	23
Less: loss claim	(25)	(23)
	25	0
Charitable donations	(3)	0
Total taxable profits of the period	22	0

The qualifying charitable donations for the six months ended 30 June 2017 remain unrelieved, because the loss relief must be given first.

CTA 2010, s 45(4) loss carried forward against future trading profits:

	Year ended 30 June 2019
	£000
Trade profit/(loss)	90
Less: loss claim	(58)
	32
Property income	4
Chargeable gain	0
Total taxable profits of the period	36

Summary of loss utilisation:

	£000
Trading loss for the year ended 30 June 2018	120
Less: *CTA 2010, s 37(3)(a)* claim for the current year	(14)
	106

Less: *CTA 2010, s 37(3)(b)* claim for the previous 12 months:	
• Six months to 30 June 2017	(23)
• Six months to 31 December 2016	(25)
Loss carried forward (*CTA 2010, s 45(4)*)	58
12 months to 30 June 2019	(58)
Balance of loss unrelieved	0

Example 4.8—Trading losses carried forward and back

Facts

B Ltd has carried on the same trade for many years. Total profits for the year ended 30 September 2012 were nil, so no loss can be carried back to that year. The results for the years ended 30 September 2013, 2014 and 2015 are shown below:

Year ended 30 September	*2013*	*2014*	*2015*
	£000	*£000*	*£000*
Trade profit/(loss)	(23)	20	(25)
Loan relationship	5	3	5
Chargeable gains	5.6	4.7	4
Charitable donations	—	(1)	—

Analysis

The losses may be relieved as follows:

Year ended 30 September	*2013*	*2014*	*2015*
	£000	*£000*	*£000*
Trade profits		20	
Deduct loss brought forward		(12.4)	
		7.6	
Loan relationship	5	3	5
Chargeable gains	5.6	4.7	4
	10.6	15.3	9
Trading losses of same period	(10.6)		(9)

Deduct trading loss carried back from year ended 30 September 2015		(15.3)	
Total taxable profits of the period	nil	nil	nil
Charitable donations		1	

Summary of loss utilisation:

Year ended 30 September	*2013*	*2014*	*2015*
	£000	*£000*	*£000*
Trading loss	23		25
Charitable donations		1	
	23		25
Losses used in current year	(10.6)		(9)
Carried back to year ended 30 September 2014			(15.3)
Losses carried forward and used in year ended 30 September 2014	(12.4)		
Balance of unrelieved losses carried forward at 30 September 2015			0.7

TERMINAL LOSS RELIEF

Cessation of trade – pre-1 April 2017

4.22 When a company ceases trading, it is most likely to cease at some stage during the accounting period that had been anticipated, rather than on its normal year-end. The legislation recognises this and allows the loss of the last 12 months of trading to be utilised in a carry-back claim. This 'terminal loss' will most likely include two components; namely, the loss (if any) of the last trading period, which will usually be an accounting period of less than 12 months ending on the date of cessation of trading, and a proportionate part of a loss (if any) that falls into the preceding accounting period (*CTA 2010, s 39(3)*). Relief for the loss of the earlier period is given before relief for the loss of the later period (CTM04520, CTM04530).

Terminal loss relief claims can now include amounts carried forward to the terminal period, so long as the losses arose on or after 1 April 2017 (*CTA 2010, s 45F*); see **4.23**.

> **Focus**
>
> In calculating terminal loss relief, the order in which the components of the loss are applied is crucial.

For the purposes of terminal loss relief, the loss carry-back period of *CTA 2010, s 37(3)(b)* is extended from a 12-month period to a three-year period by *CTA 2010, s 39(2)*, provided the trade was being carried on at that time. Within that three-year period, losses are set off against profits of later accounting periods before those of earlier accounting periods.

If, on a company ceasing to carry on a trade, any of the activities of that trade begin to be carried on by a person or persons outside the charge to corporation tax, terminal loss relief is not available if the cessation is part of a scheme or arrangement the main purpose or one of the main purposes of which is to secure terminal loss relief (*CTA 2010, s 41*).

Example 4.9—Terminal trading loss: three-year carry-back

Facts

Hardwood ceased trading on 30 April 2016. It had the following results:

Accounting period ended	*Months*	*Trade profit*	*Trade loss*
		£	£
30 April 2016	4		30,000
31 December 2015	12		60,000
31 December 2014	12		3,000
31 December 2013	12	60,000	
31 December 2012	12	50,000	
31 December 2011	12	2,000	

Analysis

The terminal loss relief claim under *CTA 2010, s 39* is made as follows:

	£
Loss arising in the accounting period falling wholly in the 12-month period prior to cessation—4 months to 30 April 2016	30,000
Proportion of the loss arising in the accounting period falling partly in the 12-month period prior to cessation—8 months to 31 December 2015: (8/12) × 60,000	20,000
Total	70,000

The losses are relieved as follows:

Accounting period ended	*Months*	*Trade profit*	*Loss utilised*	*Profit assessed*	*Loss reliefs*	
					CTA 2010, s 39	*CTA 2010, s 37(3)(b)*
		£	£	£	£	£
30 June 2016	6				(30,000)	
31 December 2015	12				(40,000)	(20,000)
31 December 2014	12					(3,000)
31 December 2013	12	60,000	(3,000)	Nil		3,000
			(40,000)		40,000	
			(17,000)		17,000	
31 December 2012	12	50,000		50,000		
			(30,000)		30,000	
31 December 2011	12	2,000		2,000		
Total		112,000	(60,000)	52,000		
Balance unrelieved					(13,000)	(20,000)

The £3,000 loss of the year to 31 December 2014 is set back against the profit of the year to 31 December 2013 under the normal loss carry-back provisions of *CTA 2010, s 37(3)(b)*.

Of the terminal loss, the £40,000 loss for the period to 31 December 2015 is utilised before the £30,000 loss for the later period to 30 April 2016. The £40,000 loss is fully relieved against the profit of the year to 31 December 2013, and had there been any excess loss it could have been set back against the profit of the year to 31 December 2012. Part of the £30,000 loss can be relieved against the remaining profit of £17,000 for the year to 31 December 2013, but the balance of £13,000 terminal loss cannot be carried back more than three years so it remains unrelieved.

Note that one-third of the loss incurred in the year ended 31 December 2015 (ie the £20,000 loss arising in the first four months of that year) fell outside the terminal loss relief calculation. It is not possible to utilise that £20,000 loss under the normal loss carry-back provisions of *CTA 2010, s 37(3)(b)*, because there are no profits in the year ended 31 December 2014 against which it can be set.

Cessation of trade – from 1 April 2017

4.23 Under *CTA 2010, s 45F*, there are new rules applicable to losses carried forward to the period of cessation of a trade (the 'terminal period'). Where losses have been carried forward to the terminal period under *CTA 2010, ss 45, 45A* or *45B*, a claim can be made to use those losses against profits of the company in the terminal period and in the three-year period ending with cessation (*CTA 2010, s 45F*). However, the losses cannot be carried back to the period in which the loss arose, or an earlier period, or any period beginning before 1 April 2017.

Where the losses were carried forward under *CTA 2010, s 45A*, they can be used to relieve total profits of the company for the relevant periods. Otherwise, the losses can only be set against the profits of the same trade.

The relief must be claimed and the claim must be made within two years of the end of the terminal period, or a longer period if permitted by HMRC.

LOSS RELIEF RESTRICTIONS

Changes in situation

4.24 Longstanding anti-avoidance provisions exist to prevent the buying and selling of tax losses. (See also **17.28–17.39** for restrictions on capital allowance buying and transfer of deductions.)

Loss relief carry-forward and carry-back are denied where (*CTA 2010, ss 673, 674*):

- there is a change in the ownership (see **4.25**) of a company, *and*
  - for accounting periods ending on or before 31 March 2017, within any period of three years in which the change in ownership occurs there is a major change in the nature or conduct of a trade (see **4.26**) carried on by the company (Condition A),
  - for accounting periods starting on or after 1 April 2017, within any period of five years in which the change in ownership occurs, starting not more than three years before the change of ownership, there is a major change in the nature or conduct of a trade (see **4.26**) carried on by the company (Condition A),*or*
  - the change in ownership occurs at any time after the scale of activities in a trade carried on by the company has become small or negligible and before any significant revival of the trade (Condition B).

In such circumstances, the accounting period in which the change in ownership occurs is treated as two separate accounting periods, the first ending with the change and the second consisting of the remainder of the period. No loss reliefs may be carried forward or back across the change in ownership. From 1 April 2017, this applies to losses carried forward under *CTA 2010, ss 45, 45A* and *45B*.

These provisions are substantially expanded by *Finance (No 2) Act 2017*, with effect from 1 April 2017. The existing gateway provision is amended to change the period mentioned in the first bullet point, above, so that it refers to the change in the nature or conduct of the trade occurring within a five-year period starting no more than three years before the change of ownership. However, both the change of ownership and the change of the trade must occur on or after 1 April 2017.

If these rules apply, terminal loss relief cannot be given for losses incurred after a change of ownership by carrying back those losses to periods before the change of ownership (*CTA 2010, s 674(1A)*).

Change in company ownership

4.25 A change in ownership of a company arises if a single person or a group of persons acquires more than half the ordinary share capital of the company. Holdings below 5% are ignored, unless the acquisition is an addition to an existing holding and the two holdings together amount to at least 5% (*CTA 2010, s 719*). To determine whether such a change has taken place, any two points in a three-year period may be compared; and this does not have to be the same three-year period as is referred to in Condition A in **4.24** but can be any three-year period which includes the date of the change in ownership. Connected persons' holdings are included. The definition of 'connected' persons in *CTA 2010, s 1122* is used (see **10.27**). Shares acquired under a will or on intestacy are left out of account. Any gift of shares which is unsolicited and made without regard to the provisions of *CTA 2010, Pt 14* (Change in company ownership) is also left out of account (*CTA 2010, s 720*).

If the company is a 75% subsidiary, changes in ownership are ignored if it remains a 75% subsidiary of the same ultimate parent, but a change in ownership of a holding company will extend to the subsidiary (*CTA 2010, s 724*).

From 1 April 2014 the change in company ownership provisions were amended to allow a holding company to be inserted at the top of a group of companies without triggering the restrictions which would otherwise apply. This applies to a change of ownership of a company (C) where there is a share acquisition or a scheme of reconstruction involving a share cancellation and, broadly, the shareholders and shares of the new company after the acquisition or scheme are the same as the shareholders and shares of C before the change. To prevent abuse of this easing of constraints, the pre-existing restrictions continue to apply to the holding company shareholders throughout the transaction (*CTA 2010, s 724A*).

Major change in the nature or conduct of the trade

4.26 What constitutes a major change in the nature or conduct of the trade is largely a question of fact, but *CTA 2010, s 673(4)* states that it includes the following:

- a major change in the type of property dealt in, or services or facilities provided, in the trade; or
- a major change in customers, outlets or markets of the trade.

The effect of the change is to restrict the loss relief both before and after the change, with the activity before and the activity after the change being treated as two separate accounting periods. Balancing adjustments will be calculated for capital allowance purposes.

Examples of what HMRC would or would not constitute major changes in the conduct or nature of trade are detailed in Statement of Practice 10 (1991) at tinyurl.com/o37d4ut.

These are:

Examples where a major change would be regarded as occurring:

(i) A company operating a dealership in cars switches to operating a dealership in tractors (a major change in the type of property dealt in).

(ii) A company owning a public house switches to operating a discotheque in the same, but converted, premises (a major change in the services or facilities provided).

(iii) A company fattening pigs for their owners switches to buying pigs for fattening and resale (a major change in the nature of the trade, being a change from providing a service to being a primary producer).

Examples where a change would not in itself be regarded as a major change:

(i) A company manufacturing kitchen fitments in three obsolescent factories moves production to one new factory (increasing efficiency).

(ii) A company manufacturing kitchen utensils replaces enamel by plastic, or a company manufacturing time pieces replaces mechanical by electrical components (keeping pace with developing technology).

(iii) A company operating a dealership in one make of car switches to operating a dealership in another make of car satisfying the same market (not a major change in the type of property dealt in).

(iv) A company manufacturing both filament and fluorescent lamps (of which filament lamps form the greater part of the output) concentrates solely on filament lamps (a rationalisation of product range without a major change in the type of property dealt in).

Changes in situation from 1 April 2017

4.27 Further provisions restrict relief for trading losses where *CTA 2010, s 674* (see **4.24**) is not in point. First, new *CTA 2010, Pt 14, Ch 2A* applies where, on or after 1 April 2017 (*CTA 2010, s 676AA*):

- there is a change in the ownership (see **4.25**) of a company; *and*
- there is a major change in the business of the company or of a co-transferred company, either within a five-year period starting no more than three years before the change of ownership.

A major change is defined as a major change in the nature or conduct or scale of any trade or business carried on by the company, or beginning or ceasing to carry on a trade or business (*CTA 2010, s 676AC*).

A major change in the nature or conduct of a trade or business means a major change in the type of property dealt in, or services or facilities provided, a major change in customers, outlets or markets, or a major change in the nature of the investments of a company's investment business. These definitions also apply where there is a gradual process of change beginning before the five-year period in the legislation.

Where *CTA 2010, Pt 14, Ch 2A* applies, carried-forward trading losses from before the change of ownership cannot be used against 'affected profits' (*CTA 2010, s 676AF*). These are profits arising in the period ending five years after the change of ownership, and which can be attributed, on a fair and reasonable basis, to the activities or sources of income relating to the major change in the business (*CTA 2010, s 676AE*).

Transfers of assets from 1 April 2017

4.28 New *CTA 2010, Pt 14, Ch 2B* applies where, on or after 1 April 2017, there is a change in ownership of a company (*CTA 2010, s 676BA*) and:

- the company acquires an asset under the intra-group transfer rules such that no gain or loss arises on the transfer, and, within five years of the change in ownership, that company makes a gain on the disposal of the asset; or
- a gain is transferred to the company in accordance with *TCGA 1992, ss 171A* and *171B*.

Carried-forward trading losses under CTA 2010, ss 45A or 45F cannot be used to relieve the gains if the losses arose before the change of ownership (*CTA 2010, s 676BC*).

This Chapter refers to both gains arising on chargeable assets and non-trading gains arising on chargeable intangible assets.

Government investment written off

4.29 It has been part of the government's policy to invest in certain companies. Where shares owned by the government are cancelled or the government writes off any debt lent to the company out of public funds, the company's losses carried forward as at the end of the accounting period are reduced by an equivalent amount. If the amount written off exceeds those losses, any excess is carried forward to reduce a loss of the next accounting period, and so on until the whole of the written-off amount has been set off (*CTA 2010, s 92*).

These losses affected are divided into five types, with set-off being made against Types 1 to 4 before Type 5:

Type 1

- *CTA 2010, s 62* – UK property trade losses carried forward against future UK property trade profits
- *CTA 2010, s 66* – Overseas property trade losses carried forward against future overseas property trade profits
- *CTA 2010, s 63* – Losses treated as management expenses for the next accounting period are included

Type 2

- *CTA 2009, s 1223(3)* – Excess management expenses carried forward for deduction to the next accounting period

Type 3

- *CAA 2001, s 260(2)* – Special leasing allowance carried forward for deduction to the next accounting period

Type 4

- *CTA 2010, s 99(1)(d)* – Qualifying charitable donations made by the company so far as they exceed the company's profits of the accounting period and are available for surrender for the next accounting period as group relief

Type 5

- *TCGA 1992, s 8* – Capital losses so far as not allowed for the accounting period or any previous accounting period.

Where, before the write-off, a claim has already been made to set the loss against current profits under *CTA 2010, s 37* (trading loss set against profits of the same or earlier accounting period), *CAA 2001, s 260(3)* (special leasing allowance to be set against current profits) or *CTA 2010, s 99* (group relief), it will not be disturbed (*CTA 2010, s 95*).

Tax avoidance involving carried-forward losses

4.30 From 18 March 2015, *CTA 2010, ss 730E–730H* (as inserted by *FA 2015, Sch 3*) deny the use of carried-forward trading losses under *CTA 2010, s 45*, where:

- a company receives profits from which it can deduct any of the relevant carried-forward reliefs, and it is reasonable to assume that the profit would not have arisen to that company but for the arrangement;
- the company, or a company connected with it, is entitled to bring a deductible amount into account as a consequence of the arrangement; and
- the main purpose, or one of the main purposes, of entering the arrangement is to obtain a tax advantage involving both the deduction and the use of the carried-forward reliefs.

Broadly, these provisions target arrangements to use the carried-forward relief whilst creating newer and more versatile relief. They were extended from 8 July 2015 to ensure that they apply also to arrangements involving the avoidance or reduction of a controlled foreign company (CFC) charge (*CTA 2010, ss 730G, 730H*, as amended by *F(No 2)A 2015, s 36*; for more about CFCs, see **Chapter 20**).

The restrictions will not generally apply unless the tax value (ie the corporation tax advantage and related economic benefits) of the tax arrangements would be greater than the non-tax value (ie any other economic benefits) of the tax arrangements (*CTA 2010, s 730G(6)–(8)*, as inserted by *FA 2015, Sch 3*).

Targeted anti-avoidance rule for corporate losses

4.31 A new targeted anti-avoidance rule for corporate losses was introduced as *CTA 2010, s 19*. It allows HMRC to counteract any loss-related tax advantage arising from relevant tax arrangements, by making just and reasonable adjustments. Adjustments may be made by way of an assessment, the modification of an assessment, the amendment or disallowance of a claim, or otherwise.

Relevant tax arrangements must satisfy two conditions. Condition A is that one of the main purposes of the arrangements is to obtain a 'loss-related tax advantage'. Condition B is that it is reasonable to regard the arrangements as circumventing the intended limits of relief under the relevant provisions or otherwise exploiting shortcomings in those provisions. All of the relevant circumstances are to be taken into account in determining whether condition B is satisfied. This will include considering whether the arrangements include contrived or normal steps, or steps with no genuine commercial purpose.

A 'loss-related tax advantage' means a tax advantage as a result of a deduction or increased deduction under a variety of provisions, including, specifically, the trading loss provisions at *CTA 2010, ss 37, 45, 45A, 45B* and *45F*.

SELF-ASSESSMENT

Loss claims and elections

4.32 If a company makes a loss claim, it must quantify the amount of the loss at the time (*FA 1998, Sch 18, para 54*). This means that the company must express the claim in figures; it is not acceptable to express the claim as a formula (CTM90605). For an example of failure to quantify a claim (albeit relating to income tax), see *Robins v Revenue & Customs* [2013] UKFTT 514 (TC).

There is a general time limit of four years from the end of the accounting period to which the claim relates (*FA 1998, Sch 18, para 55*). Subject to transitional provisions, this limit was six years before 1 April 2010.

The normal four-year time limit is overridden if the legislation prescribes a longer or shorter time limit. In particular, a loss claim under *CTA 2010, s 37(3)(b)* must be made within two years of the end of the accounting period in which the loss arises. Similarly, the rules for carrying forward losses from 1 April 2017 all require a claim to be made within two years of the end of the accounting period in which they are to be relieved, unless HMRC allow a longer period.

Normally, loss relief is claimed on the company tax return CT600 and corporation tax computation for the year of the loss and this fulfils the claim requirement. If, for any reason, the CT600 is delayed, a separate quantified loss claim should be submitted to HMRC. Any errors in a claim or election can be corrected within the claim time limits (*FA 1998, Sch 18, para 56*).

The legislation differentiates between:

- claims affecting a single accounting period (*FA 1998, Sch 18, para 57*);
- claims or elections involving more than one accounting period (*FA 1998, Sch 18, para 58*); and
- all other claims and elections (*FA 1998, Sch 18, para 59*).

Claims affecting a single accounting period

4.33 As stated above, claims are usually included within the company tax return. If the company does not include the claim with the company tax return but submits it at a later date, although still within the company tax return filing date period, the claim will be treated as an amendment to the return (*FA 1998, Sch 18, para 15*). The amendment should be made formally by letter, the relief sought must be given a brief description, and the amount of the claim must be quantified. If the 12-month period after the year end amendment period has expired, a claim (if still within time) can be made under *TMA 1970, Sch 1A* (CTM90625).

Claims or elections involving more than one accounting period

4.34 In this scenario, a company makes a claim for an accounting period, which affects more than one accounting period. This will occur where a company claims to carry-back a trading loss under *CTA 2010, s 37(3)(b)* against its profits of the previous 12 months. The claim is made for the accounting period but it affects the previous accounting period. If the claim is made within the amendment period for the first accounting period, which contains the profits against which the losses are to be set, it will be treated as an amendment to the return. If the amendment period is past, it is treated as an amendment under *TMA 1970, Sch 1A*. Depending on the circumstances, the corporation tax repayment will either reduce the current year liability or be repaid direct to the company (CTM90630).

All other claims and elections

4.35 The corporation tax self-assessment enquiry period only runs to 12 months after the end of the filing date of the return. Some claims and elections may be submitted after this. This would mean that HMRC would be unable to enquire into the claim or election. Hence, such elections fall under *TMA 1970, Sch 1A*. HMRC have similar powers of enquiry but they are extended to one year and the quarter day after the claim is filed (*TMA 1970, Sch 1A, para 5*). HMRC can amend obvious errors within 12 months of the claim being made (*TMA 1970, Sch 1A, para 3(a)*), and the company may amend the claim at any time within 12 months of the claim, provided that it is not under enquiry (CTM90635).

Amendments to returns, claims and elections

4.36 HMRC have the following powers to amend returns (CTM90650):

- Amendment of a company tax return under *FA 1998, Sch 18, para 34(2)(a)*.
- Discovery assessment made under *FA 1998, Sch 18, para 41*.
- An assessment to recover excess group relief under *FA 1998, Sch 18, para 76*.

In turn, where this happens, the company may make, revoke or vary certain claims (*FA 1998, Sch 18, para 61*) outside the normal time limit. The extended time limit is one year from the end of the accounting period in which the HMRC adjustment was made (*FA 1998, Sch 18, para 62(1)*).

Certain liabilities can be reduced by the claim. These are:

- the increased liability resulting from the amendment or assessment;
- any other tax liability for the accounting period to which the amendment or assessment relates; or
- any other tax liability for any subsequent accounting period, which ends not later than one year from the end of the relevant accounting period (*FA 1998, Sch 18, para 62(3)*).

However, the claim cannot reduce the eventual liability by more than the additional assessment (*FA 1998, Sch 18, para 64*).

Where the claim affects another person's tax liability, the company must obtain that other person's consent (*FA 1998, Sch 18, para 62(3)*).

In situations of fraud or neglect, a company can make additional claims but only those that can be given effect in HMRC's assessment. The claims must be made before the assessment is raised or in the appeal period (*FA 1998, Sch 18, para 65(1), (2)*; CTM90665).

Assessments under appeal

4.37 If an HMRC amendment to a company tax return or an HMRC assessment is under appeal, claims cannot be made through the claims procedures under *FA 1998, Sch 18, para 54* etc. Any claims that the company wishes to make must be made through an application to the First-tier Tribunal presiding over the appeal for a determination of the amount that is to be repaid, pending the final determination of the liability. The application is heard in the same way as an appeal (see **22.23–22.30**) (*TMA 1970, s 59DA(4), (5)*; CTM92110).

ENTITLEMENT TO FIRST-YEAR TAX CREDITS

Focus

First-year tax credits under the capital allowances code offer the company a tax repayment. The company can claim a credit on qualifying expenditure incurred on energy-saving and environmentally beneficial plant and machinery that qualified for a first year allowance by surrendering a qualifying loss, which is restricted to the lower of the first year allowance and the unrelieved loss. Various conditions apply, as detailed below. Of particular note is the meaning of an unrelieved loss.

4.38 If a company incurs relevant first year expenditure (**4.40**) on or after 1 April 2008, it may claim a first-year tax credit for an accounting period in which it has a surrenderable loss (**4.42**), unless it is an excluded company (**4.41**) for that accounting period (*CAA 2001, Sch A1, para 1*).

Surrenderable loss

4.39 A company has a surrenderable loss for an accounting period if, in that period:

- a first-year allowance is made to the company in respect of relevant first-year expenditure (see **4.40**) incurred for the purposes of a qualifying activity the profits of which are chargeable to corporation tax; and
- the company incurs a loss in carrying on that qualifying activity.

The amount of the surrenderable loss is equal to the lower of:

- the unrelieved loss; and
- the first-year allowance made in respect of the relevant first-year expenditure in the chargeable period in question.

Any first-year tax credit claimed reduces the amount of the loss carried forward (*CAA 2001, Sch A1, para 19*).

Relevant first-year expenditure

4.40 Relevant first-year expenditure is expenditure incurred on or before 31 March 2018, regardless of the special rule in *CAA 2001, s 12* (see *CAA 2001, Sch A1, para 3(1)(b), (2)*), on:

- energy-saving plant or machinery (*CAA 2001, s 45A*) (see **3.33**); or
- environmentally beneficial plant or machinery (*CAA 2001, s 45H*) (see **3.35**).

Additional expenditure attributable to a VAT liability under *CAA 2001, s 236*, is excluded (*CAA 2001, Sch A1, para 3(1)*).

Excluded company

4.41 A company is an excluded company if it is disregarded for corporation tax purposes, being a co-operative housing association (*CTA 2010, s 642*) or a self-build society (*CTA 2010, s 651*). The company is also excluded if it is a charity (*CTA 2010, s 474*) (see **2.80**) or a scientific research association (*CTA 2010, s 469*; *CAA 2001, Sch A1, para 1(4)*).

Amount of first-year tax credit

4.42 If a company has a surrenderable loss for the accounting period, it is entitled to claim a first-year tax credit of an amount equal to the lower of:

- 19% of the amount of the surrenderable loss for the accounting period; and
- the upper limit (*CAA 2001, Sch A1, para 2(1)*).

The upper limit is the greater of:

- the total amount of the company's PAYE and NICs liabilities for payment periods ending in the accounting period; and
- £250,000 (*CAA 2001, Sch A1, para 2(2)*).

A company may claim the whole or part of the amount that it is entitled to claim.

Total amount of company's PAYE and NIC liabilities

4.43 The total amount of the company's PAYE and NICs liabilities for payment periods ending in the accounting period is:

- PAYE due to HMRC for the period, disregarding child tax credit and working tax credit deductions; and
- Class 1 NICs due to HMRC for that period, disregarding statutory sick pay, statutory maternity pay, child tax credit and working tax credit deductions.

A payment period is a period which ends on the fifth day of a month and for which the company is liable to account for income tax and NICs to HMRC (*CAA 2001, Sch A1, para 17*).

Meaning of 'unrelieved loss'

Trade or furnished holiday lettings business

4.44 For a qualifying activity that is a trade or a furnished holiday lettings business, the unrelieved loss is calculated as follows (*CAA 2001, Sch A1, para 11(3)*):

Trading loss for the period

less

any relief:

- available under *CTA 2010, s 37(3)(a)*, against profits of same accounting period (see **4.16**);
- obtained under *CTA 2010, s 37(3)(b)* or *42(3)*, against profits of previous accounting period (see **4.17**);
- available under *CTA 2010, s 99*, group relief (see **5.10**);
- surrendered under a tax credit provision, of:
  - *CTA 2009, s 1043* (research and development) (see **14.26**);
  - *CTA 2009, ss 1143–1158* (remediation of contaminated land) (see **14.63**);
  - *CTA 2009, ss 1085–1142* (expenditure on vaccine research) (see **14.45**);
  - *CTA 2009, s 1201* (film tax credits) (see **15.11**);
  - *CTA 2009, s 1216CH* (television tax credits) (see **15.19**);
  - *CTA 2009, s 1217CH* (video game tax credits) (see **15.27**);
  - *CTA 2009, s 1217K* (theatre tax credits) (see **15.36**);
  - *CTA 2009, s 1217RH* (orchestra tax credits) (see **15.45**); or
  - *CTA 2009 s 1218ZCH* (museums and galleries tax credits).
- set off against the loss under *CTA 2010, s 92*, government investment write-off (see **4.29**) (*CAA 2001, Sch A1, para 11(2)*).

No account is to be taken of any loss:

- brought forward from an earlier accounting period under *CTA 2010, s 45(4)* (see **4.2**);
- carried back from a later accounting period under *CTA 2010, s 37(3)(b)* or *42(3)* (see **4.16**); or
- incurred on a leasing contract (*CTA 2010, s 53*).

Example 4.10—Calculation of first-year tax credit

Facts

On 1 June 2014, during its 12-month accounting period ending 31 March 2015, Radius Ltd invests in a solar-powered energy system that qualifies for a first year allowance of £100,000. The company has traded at a loss, but its prospects have now improved. Radius Ltd is not a member of a group. It has PAYE and NIC liabilities for the year of £18,000. It surrenders a loss for the year ended 31 March 2015 in return for a first-year tax credit. Its results are as follows.

Year ended 31 March 2015:

	£
Trade loss	(500,000)
Property income	80,000
Loan relationship	5,000
First year allowance	100,000

There were no profits for the year ended 31 March 2014.

Analysis

The surrenderable loss for the year ended 31 March 2015 is calculated as follows:

		£	£
Loss for the year			500,000
Less relief against profits of the same accounting period			
Property income		80,000	
Loan relationship		5,000	85,000
Maximum surrenderable loss			415,000
Tax credit based on first year allowance		100,000	
The tax credit is restricted to the lower of:			
19% of the first year allowance and			
the upper limit which is the greater of			
(i)	the total of the PAYE and NIC liabilities for the year (ie £18,000) and		
(ii)	£250,000		
The company claims a tax credit of		19,000	
Loss restriction			100,000
Loss carried forward			315,000

Note that Radius Ltd was unable to carry back its trading loss to the previous year because of the absence of profits. However, before surrendering a loss for the year ended 31 March 2015 in return for a first-year tax credit at 19%, it should compare the effect of this with the alternative of carrying forward the whole of its loss against future profits.

Lettings business other than furnished holiday lettings

4.45 For a qualifying activity that is a lettings business other than a furnished holiday lettings business, the unrelieved loss is calculated as follows (*CAA 2001, Sch A1, para 12(2)*):

Loss from lettings for the period

less any relief:

- available under *CTA 2010, s 62*, property income losses (see **7.13**);
- available under *CTA 2010, s 99*, group relief (see **5.10**);
- surrendered under a tax credit provision, of *CTA 2009, ss 1143–1158* (remediation of contaminated or derelict land) (see **14.48**); and
- set off against the loss under *CTA 2010, s 92* (government investment write-off – see **4.29**).

No account is to be taken of any property income losses brought forward from an earlier accounting period under *CTA 2010, s 62(5)* (see **7.13**) (*CAA 2001, Sch A1, para 12(3)*).

Overseas property business

4.46 For a qualifying activity that is an overseas property business trade or a furnished holiday lettings business, the unrelieved loss is calculated as follows (*CAA 2001, Sch A1, para 13(2)*):

Loss from lettings for the period

less any relief:

- set off against the loss under *CTA 2010, s 92* (government investment write-off – see **4.29**).

No account is to be taken of any loss brought forward from an earlier accounting period under *CTA 2010, s 66(3)* (losses from an overseas property business).

Management of investments

4.47 For a qualifying activity that is the management of investments, the unrelieved loss is calculated as follows (*CAA 2001, Sch A1, para 15(2)*):

Excess management expenses for the period

less any relief:

- available under *CTA 2010, s 99(1)*, group relief (see **5.10**); and
- set off against the loss under *CTA 2010, s 92* (government investment write-off – see **4.29**).

No account is to be taken of any loss brought forward from an earlier accounting period under *CTA 2009, s 1223(2), (3)* (management expenses – see **6.15**) (*CAA 2001, Sch A1, para 15(3)*).

Payment in respect of first-year tax credit

4.48 A first-year tax credit may be either repaid to the company or, together with any repayment interest (see **23.30**), used to discharge any of the company's corporation tax liabilities (*CAA 2001, Sch A1, para 18(1)–(3)*).

If the return is under enquiry, HMRC are under no obligation to make a repayment until the enquiry is complete. However, they may make a repayment of an amount that they consider to be appropriate (*CAA 2001, Sch A1, para 18(4)–(5)*).

HMRC are precluded from making a repayment if any PAYE or Class 1 NIC is outstanding (*CAA 2001, Sch A1, para 17(6)*).

A payment in respect of a first-year tax credit is not chargeable to corporation tax (*CAA 2001, Sch A1, para 23*).

Clawback of first-year tax credit

Circumstances in which first-year tax credit clawed back

> **Focus**
>
> The first-year tax credit is clawed back if the equipment on which it is claimed is disposed of less than four years after the end of the accounting period for which the tax credit was paid.

4.49 If a company disposes of an item on which a first-year tax credit is paid before the end of the clawback period, the loss is restored and the first-year tax credit is treated as if it never should have been paid (*CAA 2001, Sch A1, para 24*). The clawback period begins when the relevant first-year expenditure on the item is incurred, and ends four years after the end of the accounting period for which the tax credit was paid (*CAA 2001, Sch A1, para 25(10)*).

A company disposes of an item of tax-relieved plant or machinery if the circumstances for a disposal of plant and machinery are met (see **3.54**) or the business is in new ownership. The disposal value of the item is the actual amount received, but this is replaced by market value if the disposal is made to a connected person for less than its market value, or the business is in new ownership (*CAA 2001, Sch A1, para 25*). Broadly, this is one where there has been a transfer of a business and, for the purposes of making allowances and charges under *CAA 2001*, anything done to or by the transferor is treated as having been done to or by the transferee.

Amount of restored loss

4.50 The amount of the restored loss is determined by the following formula (*CAA 2001, Sch A1, para 26*):

$$(LS - OERPM) - (OE - DV) - ARL$$

where:

- LS is the amount of the loss surrendered in the accounting period for which the first-year tax credit was paid
- OERPM is the amount (or the aggregate of the amounts) of the original expenditure on the retained tax-relieved plant and machinery after the item is disposed of
- OE is the aggregate of the amount of the original expenditure on the item disposed of, and the amounts of the original expenditure on any items of tax-relieved plant and machinery, which the company has previously disposed of
- DV is the aggregate of the disposal value of the item disposed of, and the disposal values of any items of tax-relieved plant and machinery which the company has previously disposed of
- ARL is the amount of the restored loss (or the aggregate of the amounts of prior restored losses).

If the result is less than nil, the amount of the restored loss is nil.

Example 4.11—Loss restored on clawback of first-year tax credit

Facts

For the accounting period ended 31 December 2014, Nonsuch Ltd incurred expenditure of £60,000 on plant that qualified as relevant first year expenditure. It surrendered a loss of £60,000 in return for a first-year tax credit. During the accounting period ended 31 December 2016, the company sells part of the plant for £15,000. The original cost of the plant unsold was £10,000. There have been no other disposals or tax credit claims.

Analysis

Nonsuch Ltd's restored loss is calculated as follows:

(LS – OERPM) – (OE – DV) – ARL

£(60,000 – 10,000) – (50,000 – 15,000) – 0 = £15,000

Company's duty to notify clawback

4.51 If, after submitting its corporation tax return, a company becomes aware that a claim to first-year tax credit has been included incorrectly in the tax return and the return is now incorrect, it must notify HMRC and give details of the amendment required. The notice must be given within three months beginning with the day on which the company becomes aware that a clawback is required (see **4.49**) (*CAA 2001, Sch A1, para 27*).

Tax credit claim

4.52 A tax credit claim must be included in the corporation tax return.

The following details must be given (*FA 1998, Sch 18, para 83ZA(1), (2)*):

- the plant or machinery on which the claim is made;
- the relevant first-year expenditure incurred; and
- the date on which that expenditure was incurred.

The company must also provide a certificate, as applicable, for energy-saving plant and machinery (*CAA 2001, s 45B*) or environmentally beneficial plant and machinery (*CAA 2001, s 45I*).

A claim is to be disregarded if arrangements are entered into wholly or mainly for a disqualifying purpose, ie if their main object is to obtain a first-year tax credit to which the company would not otherwise be entitled, or of a greater amount than that to which it would otherwise be entitled (*CAA 2001, Sch A1, para 28*).

The company will be liable to a penalty for an incorrect tax return if it fraudulently or negligently makes a claim for a first-year tax credit which is incorrect, or discovers that a claim for a first-year tax credit made by it (neither fraudulently nor negligently) is incorrect and does not remedy the error without unreasonable delay (*FA 2007, Sch 24*; see **24.2–24.12**).

Chapter 5

Groups

SIGNPOSTS

- A review of group business structures together with an introduction to the accounting requirements and tax reliefs (see **5.1–5.4**).
- General restriction on use of losses from 1 April 2017 (see **5.5**).
- Requirements that are to be met to enable a company to claim group and consortium relief (see **5.6–5.10**).
- Use of brought-forward losses in group relief claims for post-31 March 2017 losses (see **5.11**).
- Group relief claim conditions, limitations and restrictions (see **5.12–5.16**).
- UK losses and overseas losses used in a group relief claim (see **5.17–5.22**).
- Conditions required to be met regarding a consortium relief claim (see **5.23–5.24**).
- Compliance issues covering the company tax return, corporation tax repayments, quarterly instalment repayments and group income (see **5.25–5.30**).
- Restriction on the deductibility of group finance costs under the 'corporate interest restriction' provisions (see **5.31**).
- The worldwide debt cap, which has effect for accounting periods of worldwide groups ending before 1 April 2017 (see **5.32–5.65**).
- Anti-avoidance provisions aimed at transfers of corporate profits within groups (see **5.66**).

BUSINESS STRUCTURES

5.1 As a company's business grows and its affairs develop, the company may consider whether a simple single company structure remains appropriate for its activities or whether it should consider other forms of organisation.

Single company

From a tax perspective, the single company offers a degree of simplicity and a number of specific advantages.

Until 31 March 2015 the absence of associated companies meant that the small profits rate was not unduly dissipated (see **23.2**). From 1 April 2015 the absence of 'related 51% group companies' offers advantages for the purposes of quarterly instalment payments by large companies and certain other corporation tax purposes (see **23.22**).

Chargeable gains and allowable capital losses within a single company can be set against one another in most cases (see **Chapter 16**).

All of the single company's trading activities fall within one company and may form one trade. If similar trading activities were split amongst two or more group companies, they would comprise separate trades.

Retaining activities in one company also avoids the practicalities of preparing company tax returns and group relief claims for each separate entity.

Group of companies

Tax does not and should not rule the commercial world, and separate business structures may be required. The company may consider buying or forming another company (see **17.1**). Acquisition of another company's shares may bring about a group situation.

In some cases, a separate limited company may be considered advisable to isolate a high-risk venture from other activities. Given the rapid changes encountered in the business world, a business structure best suited to today's circumstances may not be appropriate tomorrow.

> **Focus**
>
> Group structures may evolve in an unplanned manner as groups expand over time, and management should review them periodically to ensure that tax repercussions are fully understood and any adverse implications minimised.

A company committed to growth may form or acquire other companies and thus create a group structure.

Specific tax provisions and compliance issues affect groups of companies. Before entering into a group arrangement, the company may be well advised to consider a partnership or a joint venture, which it may find simpler to operate.

Partnership

Where there is a partnership, a corporate partner's share of the firm's profits or losses is calculated as though the partnership trade were chargeable to corporation tax (*CTA 2009, s 1259*). The company's share of a partnership loss is available to the company to set against its other income of the same accounting period or the previous 12 months, if the partnership and its trade existed at that time, or to carry forward against the company's share of future trading income of the partnership.

The partnership accounts need not comply with *CA 2006*, but they must be in accordance with GAAP. If a corporate partner exercises a dominant influence, the 'parent and subsidiary' provisions of *CA 2006, s 1162*, FRS 102, Section 9 *Consolidated and separate financial statements* under new UK GAAP, FRS 2 *Accounting for subsidiary undertakings* under old UK GAAP and IFRS 10 *Consolidated financial statements* under international GAAP must be considered, as appropriate (see **Chapter 26** regarding changes to UK GAAP).

Each corporate partner will have joint liability for the debts of the partnership if it is constituted as a general partnership, or joint and several liability in Scotland (*Partnership Act 1890, s 9*). With this in mind, the business partners may decide on a limited liability partnership (LLP) under the *Limited Liability Partnerships Act 2000*.

FA 2014 introduced complex anti-avoidance measures affecting mixed partnerships, including LLPs, where profit allocations have been manipulated (see **4.15**).

Joint venture

A joint venture between a company and its business associates may be a simpler structure. No special legal form is required, and the appropriate proportions of the business activities are included within the accounts of each party to the joint venture, thus simplifying the use of losses.

ACCOUNTING AND TAX TREATMENT OF GROUPS

Accounting

5.2 For company law, a group consists of parent and subsidiary undertakings (*CA 2006, ss 474, 1162*). For these purposes, an undertaking can be a body corporate, a partnership or an unincorporated association carrying on a business with a view to profit (*CA 2006, s 1161*). Groups of companies must prepare consolidated accounts unless they are exempted by the small group exemptions (*CA 2006, s 399*). Each company within the group must prepare its own individual company accounts (*CA 2006, s 394*).

Specific accounting standards address the financial reporting obligations of parent companies and their subsidiaries. These are FRS 102, Section 9 *Consolidated and separate financial statements* under new UK GAAP, FRS 2 *Accounting for subsidiary undertakings* under old UK GAAP and IFRS 10 *Consolidated financial statements* under international GAAP. See **Chapter 26** regarding changes to UK GAAP.

Tax

5.3 For corporation tax purposes, each company within a group must submit its company tax return to HMRC, including its corporation tax return form CT600, corporation tax computation and statutory accounts (see **22.2**). Group accounts may be submitted as supporting information and it is normal practice for a parent company to submit these. Corporation tax is calculated in respect of each individual company's profits. Hence, there is no requirement to prepare a group company tax return. The group situation is brought into account when calculating the individual company's liability and when granting reliefs. Companies must prepare the supplementary form CT600C where group relief or eligible unused foreign tax is claimed or surrendered.

Tax reliefs available to groups

5.4 The tax legislation recognises that a group is essentially one large business entity made up of several components. Although each group company makes its own self-assessment return in its own name and is responsible for its own corporation tax liability, the tax legislation permits a degree of loss sharing and certain other tax privileges amongst group members. Group companies have the opportunity to transfer losses to other group members to be relieved against those members' profits, and to transfer chargeable assets within the group without chargeable gains arising. Chargeable gains or allowable capital losses may be reallocated wholly or partly between companies within the same group (see **16.27**). Group companies may also surrender eligible unused foreign tax (see **Chapter 20**). There are different definitions of a group applying to revenue losses, capital losses and consortium situations. These definitions apply for tax purposes and do not always concur with those in *CA 2006*.

General restriction on loss relief from 1 April 2017

5.5 For losses arising on or after 1 April 2017 the maximum loss relief that a company will be able to claim for carried-forward losses is restricted where the company's profits exceed £5m (the 'deductions allowance'; *CTA 2010, s 269ZH*). The detailed rules are in *CTA 2010, Pt 7ZA*.

In such cases, the general rule is that the company's maximum deductions cannot exceed £5m plus 50% of the excess profits over £5m. For an example, a company with profits of £8m would only be entitled to use carried-forward losses of £7m, being the £5m deductions allowance and half the excess, ie another £2m.

For groups of companies, the deductions allowance is to be allocated between those group companies that are within the charge to corporation tax (*CTA 2010, s 269ZH*). Very broadly, a 'nominated company' in a group must allocate the deductions allowance between the group companies and is responsible for informing HMRC (*CTA 2010, ss 269ZH–269ZK*).

There are also computational rules for the deductions allowance for a company that joins or leaves a group during an accounting period, which can include apportioned deductions allowances for periods when the company was a member of a group or more than one group, as well as an appropriate proportion of the deductions allowance for any time that the company was not a member of a group during the accounting period (*CTA 2010, s 269ZG*).

The deductions allowance is proportionally reduced for short accounting periods (*CTA 2010, s 269ZH(4)*).

GROUP RELIEF

Definition of a group

> **Focus**
>
> Tax law grants significant privileges to groups and consortia, allowing favourable arrangements under which (for example) losses can be relieved or assets transferred. However, care needs to be taken to ensure that the appropriate group or consortium relationships exist.

5.6 Various conditions must be satisfied before losses can be transferred between group members. The first condition is that a group actually exists for group relief purposes.

A group exists if one company is a 75% subsidiary of the other company or both companies are 75% subsidiaries of a third company (*CTA 2010, s 152*). Shares held by share dealing companies as stock in trade are ignored (*CTA 2010, s 151(3)*). A 75% subsidiary is a company whose ordinary share capital (see **5.8**) is owned directly or indirectly by another company. 'Own' in this context means possessing the beneficial ownership (*CTA 2010, s 1154*).

Ownership within a group, or a consortium (see **5.7**), is determined by reference not only to ordinary share capital held, but also to beneficial entitlement to profits available for distribution to equity holders, and assets available for distribution to equity holders in a winding up. For these purposes, equity holders include ordinary shareholders, subject to the special definition at *CTA 2010, s 160* (see **5.9**), and loan creditors in relation to loans other than normal commercial loans, as defined at *CTA 2010, s 162*. The definition of 'normal commercial loan' is extended to include loans made on or after 21 March 2012 that carry a right to conversion into shares or securities in quoted companies that are not connected to the company that issues the loan (*CTA 2010, ss 162, 164*).

The provisions referred to in this section apply to group relief for carried-forward losses by virtue of *CTA 2010, s 188FB*.

Group relationships can be formed by reference to companies resident anywhere in the world, and UK branches of non-resident subsidiaries may also claim or surrender group relief (HMRC Company Taxation Manual at CTM80150, CTM80305).

Example 5.1—75% direct or indirect ownership

Facts

A Ltd owns 100% of the ordinary share capital of B Ltd. B Ltd owns 80% of the ordinary share capital of C Ltd.

Analysis

A Ltd, B Ltd and C Ltd are a group, because A Ltd owns 100% of B Ltd and indirectly 80% of C Ltd (100% × 80%).

Example 5.2—Identifying separate 75% groups

Facts

A Ltd owns 75% of the ordinary share capital of B Ltd. B Ltd owns 80% of the ordinary share capital of C Ltd.

Analysis

A Ltd and B Ltd are a group, because A Ltd owns 75% of B Ltd.

A Ltd and C Ltd are not a group, because A Ltd only effectively owns 60% of C Ltd (75% × 80%).

B Ltd and C Ltd are a separate group, because B Ltd owns 80% of C Ltd.

Definition of a consortium

5.7 A company is owned by a consortium if the company is not a 75% subsidiary of any company, and if 75% or more of its ordinary share capital is beneficially owned by companies each of which beneficially owns at least 5% of that capital. The consortium member's share is measured by the lowest of the member's percentage interests in shares, profits or assets. Where these have varied over the year, a weighted average is used, taking into account the lengths of time involved (Statement of Practice C6, at tinyurl.com/pzbodv4).

A 90% trading subsidiary of a company which is itself a consortium-owned company is also owned by the consortium (*CTA 2010, s 153*).

Example 5.3—A company owned by a consortium

Facts

P Ltd has an issued share capital of 1,000 ordinary shares, beneficially owned as follows:

Q Ltd	200
R Ltd	100
S Ltd	100
T Ltd	100
U Ltd	100
V Ltd	100
W Ltd	50
Total	750

The remaining shares are held by shareholders who are individuals.

Analysis

P Ltd is owned by a consortium, because it is not a 75% subsidiary of any company, and 75% of its ordinary share capital is beneficially owned by companies of which none owns less than 5%.

Example 5.4—A company not owned by a consortium

Facts

Z Ltd has an issued share capital of 1,000 ordinary shares, beneficially owned as follows:

Q Ltd	200
R Ltd	100
S Ltd	100
T Ltd	100
U Ltd	100
V Ltd	50

W Ltd	50
Total	700

The remaining shares are held by shareholders who are individuals.

Analysis

Z Ltd is not owned by a consortium because, although it is not a 75% subsidiary of any company, less than 75% of its ordinary share capital is beneficially owned by companies of which none owns less than 5%.

Definition of ordinary share capital

5.8 The phrase 'ordinary share capital' is defined as all the issued share capital (by whatever name called) of the company, other than capital the holders of which have a right to a dividend at a fixed rate but have no other right to share in the profits of the company (*CTA 2010, s 1119*). This definition therefore includes all of the issued share capital of a company, apart from capital carrying a right to a dividend at a fixed rate. For a detailed exposition on the meaning of this definition, see *South Shore Mutual Insurance Co Ltd v Blair* [1999] STC (SCD) 296.

There is some uncertainty about whether shares that do not carry a dividend are shares that carry 'a right to a dividend at a fixed rate but have no other right to share in the profits of the company' or are, instead, part of the ordinary share capital of the company. The received wisdom (and HMRC's view) is that zero-coupon shares are part of the ordinary share capital of a company, a view affirmed by the First-tier Tribunal in the case of *Castledine* [2016] UKFTT 145 (TC). The Upper Tribunal's decision in *McQuillan and another v Revenue and Customs Commissioners* [2017] UKUT 344 (TCC) was consistent with the FTT in *Casteldine.* The existence of non-voting redeemable shares with no rights to dividends meant that Mr and Mrs Casteldine's own shareholdings were less than 5% of ordinary share capital. In reaching its decision, the UT overturned the decision of the FTT (incidentally, this was the same Tribunal as in *Casteldine*), which had decided that the non-voting redeemable preference shares were shares with a fixed right to a dividend at 0%, and hence were not part of the ordinary share capital. The McQuillans have applied to appeal to the Court of Appeal, and so it remains to be seen whether the current (relatively clear) position changes. The UT did not opine on the wider implications of its decision, but it did acknowledge that, if the FTT's decision had stood, 'the repercussions of its construction of *s 989* could be unexpected and far reaching'.

Definition of equity holders: shares that are not treated as ordinary shares

5.9 For the special purposes of determining who is an equity holder of a company, a different definition applies. An equity holder is the holder of any 'ordinary shares' of a company, and all shares are 'ordinary shares' apart from restricted preference shares.

Restricted preference shares are shares that meet the following conditions (*CTA 2010, s 160*):

- issued for new consideration in whole or in part;
- carry no conversion rights except to shares in the company or its parent;
- carry no rights to the acquisition of shares or securities;
- carry no right to a dividend or carry a restricted right to a dividend; and
- on repayment, do not carry rights to an amount exceeding the new consideration given, except so far as those rights are reasonably comparable with those generally carried by fixed dividend shares listed on a recognised stock exchange.

Shares carry a restricted right to a dividend if the dividends represent no more than a reasonable commercial return on the consideration given for the issue of the shares, and the company cannot reduce the dividend rate or be excused from payment except in special circumstances that include its own financial difficulties or its necessity to comply with the law of a regulatory body relevant to its circumstances (*CTA 2010, s 161*), thus ensuring that the external investors receive their fixed return.

The provisions referred to in this section apply to group relief for carried-forward losses by virtue of *CTA 2010, s 188FB*.

Group relief – surrender of losses arising before 1 April 2017

5.10 Group relief is the surrender and claim of group and consortium members' trading losses.

Surrenderable losses arising up to 31 March 2017 are losses of the current year only. Losses incurred on or after 1 April 2017 are available for surrender as group relief when carried forward as well where detailed conditions are met and subject to a number of restrictions (*CTA 2010, Pt 5A*; see **5.11**).

Under the pre-*Finance (No 2) Act 2017* rules, surrenderable losses include (*CTA 2010, s 99*):

- trading losses,
- excess capital allowances,

- non-trading loan relationship deficits,
- qualifying charitable donations,
- UK property business losses,
- management expenses, and
- a non-trading loss on intangible fixed assets.

Trading losses, excess capital allowances and non-trading loan relationship deficits may be set off against the claimant company's profits even though the surrendering company has other profits for the same accounting period against which they could otherwise have been set.

Where (subject to transitional provisions) the surrender period of the surrendering company ends on or after 20 March 2013, qualifying charitable donations, UK property business losses, excess management expenses and a non-trading loss on an intangible fixed asset are only available for surrender if, in total, they exceed the surrendering company's 'profit-related threshold'; for earlier surrender periods, this restriction was based on the surrendering company's gross profits of the surrender period rather than on the profit-related threshold (*CTA 2010, s 105(1)–(3)*, before and after amendment by *FA 2013, s 29*).

If a surrender is made, the order of set-off is as follows (*CTA 2010, s 105(4)*):

(i) qualifying charitable donations,

(ii) UK property business losses,

(iii) management expenses, and

(iv) a non-trading loss on an intangible fixed asset.

The surrendering company's 'profit-related threshold' is the sum of:

- the surrendering company's gross profits of the surrender period, and
- chargeable profits of a controlled foreign company (CFC) for an accounting period ending in the surrender period, apportioned to the surrendering company (for more about CFCs, see **Chapter 20**).

The surrendering company's gross profits of the surrender period are its profits for that period before deducting any trading losses, excess capital allowances, non-trade loan relationships deficits, qualifying charitable donation, property business losses or management expenses, and without any deduction for losses, allowances or other amounts in respect of any other accounting periods (*CTA 2010, s 105(5)*).

Generally, all losses arising from carrying on a trade in the UK are available for group relief. However, losses from trades not carried out on a commercial basis and farming and market gardening losses within the *CTA 2010, s 48* restriction are not eligible for group relief (*CTA 2010, s 100(2)(b)*; see **5.19**).

Excess capital allowances are allowances that are required to be set in the first instance against a specified class of income, eg special leasing (*CTA 2010, s 101*).

A non-trading loan relationship deficit is discussed in **11.26**. Qualifying charitable donations are those paid by the company during the period.

A UK property business loss must be a commercial loss and must not include any loss brought forward from a previous period (*CTA 2010, s 102*).

The expression 'management expenses' means the annual amount deductible by the company for the accounting period, but does not include amounts brought forward from earlier periods (*CTA 2010, s 103*).

A non-trading loss on an intangible fixed asset is the loss arising for the period concerned (*CTA 2010, s 104*).

A claimant company must use its own trading losses brought forward before it makes a group relief claim (*CTA 2010, s 45(4)*).

The way in which losses are surrendered within a group can have a particular impact on tax liabilities for periods up to 31 March 2015, when the small profits rate of corporation tax was available to certain companies. For further analysis, see 2017/18 and earlier editions of this book.

Example 5.5—Losses carried forward and back, and group relief – losses arising prior to 1 April 2017

Facts

A Ltd (a group member) has the following results:

	Year ending 31 December 2015	*Year ending 31 December 2016*
	£	£
Trading profit/(loss) brought forward	(500)	—
Trading profit/(loss)	1,000	(1,000)
Loan relationship	500	500

Analysis

For the accounting period ended 31 December 2015:

- The loss brought forward must be relieved in priority to group relief. The maximum amount of group relief claimable will be £1,000.
- If relief for this period is claimed for so much of the trading loss of the following period as cannot be relieved in that period, ie £500,

such relief would be displaced by a group relief claim, and would then be available for carrying forward.

For the accounting period ending 31 December 2016:

- No group relief is obtainable, whether or not the trading loss is carried back.

Group relief – surrender of losses on or after 1 April 2017

5.11 Losses arising on or after 1 April 2017 are available for surrender as group relief when carried forward (*CTA 2010, Pt 5A*), so long as the company is still carrying on the same trade or continues to hold income-producing assets and subject to detailed restrictions and anti-avoidance legislation discussed further in the following sections.

Surrenderable losses are (*CTA 2010, s 188BB*):

- trading losses carried forward under *CTA 2010, s 45A*,
- non-trading loan relationship deficits carried forward under *CTA 2009, s 463G*,
- UK property business losses carried forward under *CTA 2010, ss 62(5)(a)* and *63(3)(a)*,
- management expenses carried forward under *CTA 2009, s 1223*, and
- non-trading deficits on intangible fixed assets under *CTA 2009, s 753(3)*.

There are a number of restrictions on the ability to surrender carried-forward losses:

- Where losses have been brought forward from before 1 April 2017, they are not eligible for relief under *CTA 2010, Pt 5A* (*CTA 2010, s 188BC*).
- Non-trading loan relationship deficits, management expenses and UK property business losses cannot be surrendered in a year where the company's investment business became small or negligible before the beginning of the surrender period (*CTA 2010, s 188BD*).
- Losses cannot be surrendered if the surrendering company has not utilised its own 'relevant maximum deductions' (*CTA 2010, s 188BE*). 'Relevant maximum deductions' is the deductions allowance of £5m, plus 50% of relevant profits (*CTA 2010, s 188DD*).
- Losses cannot be surrendered if the surrendering company does not have any income-generating assets at the end of the surrendering period (*CTA 2010, s 188BF*).

- Losses of a UK resident company cannot be surrendered if they arise from a non-UK permanent establishment and are deductible from, or allowable against, non-UK profits of a person other than the surrendering company (*CTA 2010, s 188BG*).
- A non-UK company carrying on a trade of dealing in or developing UK land or carrying on a trade in the United Kingdom through a permanent establishment cannot surrender losses, except that companies resident in the EEA during the loss-making period may surrender losses if the activities were within the charge to corporation tax in the loss-making period and those activities are not double taxation exempt (*CTA 2010, s 188BH*).
- A dual-resident company cannot surrender losses (*CTA 2010, s 188BJ*).

Example 5.6—Group relief for losses carried foward

Apple Ltd had trading losses of £12 million for the year ended 30 June 2018. In the following year to 30 June 2019, it has trading profits of £8 million.

Apple Ltd's 100% subsidiary, Ball Ltd, has trading profits of £7.3 million for the year ending 30 June 2019. It has non-trading deficits on loan relationships brought forward from the year ended 30 June 2018 of £3 million.

Year ended 30 June 2019

	Apple Ltd taxable profits £ million
Qualifying total profits (£8m less nil ('in year reliefs'))	8
Deductions allowance (maximum)	(5)
Relevant total profits	3
Maximum deduction for losses (50%)	(1.5)
Taxable profits	1.5

	Ball Ltd taxable profits £ million
Qualifying total profits	7.3
Deductions allowance (none)	(0)
Relevant total profits	7.3
Non-trading loan relationship deficits brought forward	(3)
Carried-forward losses available for surrender from Apple Ltd	(4.3)
Taxable profit	nil

Apple Ltd loss memorandum

	Trading losses
	£ million
Losses brought forward from year ended 30 June 2018	12
Utilised:	
Apple Ltd profits	(6.5)
Ball Ltd profits	(4.3)
Carried forward	1.2

GROUP RELIEF CLAIMS

Conditions

Focus

Group relief is available for claim by the claimant company only if specific conditions are met. Furthermore, there are limitations on the amount of group relief that can be claimed.

5.12 For losses arising in the year of claim (ie not carried-forward losses) three requirements must be satisfied for a company to make a valid group relief claim (*CTA 2010, s 130*):

Requirement 1 – Consent

- the surrendering company consents to the claim.

Requirement 2 – Period

- there is a period ('the overlapping period') that is common to the claim period and the surrender period.

Requirement 3 – Either the group condition is met or any of the consortium conditions 1 to 3 is met

Group condition

The group condition is met if:

- at a time during the overlapping period, the companies are members of the same group and are either UK resident or are carrying on a trade in the UK through a permanent establishment (*CTA 2010, s 131*).

Consortium condition 1

Consortium condition 1 is met if (*CTA 2010, s 132(1)*):

- the *surrendering* company is a trading company or a holding company;
- the *surrendering* company is owned by a consortium;
- the *claimant* company is a member of the consortium; and
- both companies are either UK resident or carrying on a trade in the UK through a permanent establishment.

Consortium condition 1 is also met if (*CTA 2010, s 132(2)*):

- the *claimant* company is a trading company or a holding company;
- the *claimant* company is owned by a consortium;
- the *surrendering* company is a member of the consortium; and
- both companies are either UK resident or carrying on a trade in the UK through a permanent establishment.

However, consortium condition 1 is not met if any profit on the potential sale of shares by a member of shares held in a consortium company would be treated as a trading receipt of the member (*CTA 2010, s 132(3)*).

Consortium condition 2

Consortium condition 2 is met if (*CTA 2010, ss 133(1)* as amended by *F(No 2) A 2015, s 34*):

- the surrendering company is a trading company or a holding company;
- the surrendering company is owned by a consortium;
- the claimant company is not a member of the consortium;
- the claimant company is a member of the same group of companies as a third company ('the link company');
- the link company is a member of the consortium;
- the surrendering company and the claimant company are both 'UK related' (ie either UK resident or carrying on a trade in the UK through a permanent establishment; see *CTA 2010, s 134*) and
- in the case of accounting periods beginning before 10 December 2014, the link company (see **5.23**) is either UK related or established in the European Economic Area (for a list of countries that are members of the EEA, see the table in **5.18**).

Consortium condition 3

Consortium condition 3 is met if (*CTA 2010, ss 133(2)* as amended by *F(No 2) A 2015, s 34*):

- the claimant company is a trading company or a holding company;
- the claimant company is owned by a consortium;
- the surrendering company is not a member of the consortium;
- the surrendering company is a member of the same group of companies as a third company ('the link company');
- the link company is a member of the consortium;
- the surrendering company and the claimant company are both UK related; and
- in the case of accounting periods beginning before 10 December 2014, the link company is either UK related or established in the EEA.

The last two bullets points of each of consortium conditions 2 and 3 above are as modified by *F(No 3)A 2010*, following *Philips Electronics UK Ltd v HMRC* [2009] UKFTT 226 (TC), in an attempt to bring them into line with EU law for accounting periods beginning on or after 12 July 2010 (see **5.23**). Furthermore, since the link company no longer needs to be in the UK or the EEA for accounting periods beginning on or after 10 December 2014, the requirements for a UK link company and one based in another jurisdiction are the same (*F(No 2)A 2015, s 34*).

Consortium conditions 2 and 3 are not met if any profit on the potential sale by the link company of shares held in a consortium company would be treated as a trading receipt of the link company (*CTA 2010, s 133(3)–(4)*).

For accounting periods beginning before 10 December 2014, a company is established in the EEA if it is constituted under the law of the UK or an EEA territory and it has a registered office, central administration or principal place of business within the EEA (*CTA 2010, s 134A,* before repeal by *F(No 2) A 2015, s 34*).

5.13 For carried-forward losses generally, three requirements must be satisfied for a company to make a valid group relief claim (*CTA 2010, s 188CB*):

Requirement 1 – Consent

- the surrendering company consents to the claim.

Requirement 2 – Period

- there is a period ('the overlapping period') that is common to the claim period and the surrender period.

Requirement 3 – Either the group condition is met or any of the consortium conditions 1 or 2 is met.

In certain consortium cases, another two consortium conditions, 3 and 4 are introduced, too (*CTA 2010, s 188CC*).

Group condition

The group condition is met if at a time during the overlapping period, the companies are members of the same group and are either UK resident or are carrying on a trade in the UK through a permanent establishment (*CTA 2010, ss 188CE, 188CJ*).

Consortium condition 1

Consortium condition 1 is met if (*CTA 2010, s 188CF*):

- the *claimant* company is a trading company or a holding company;
- the *claimant* company is owned by a consortium;
- the *surrendering* company is a member of the consortium; and
- both companies are either UK resident or carrying on a trade in the UK through a permanent establishment.

However, consortium condition 1 is not met if any profit on a sale of shares by the surrendering company would be treated as a trading receipt of that company.

Consortium condition 2

Consortium condition 2 is met if (*CTA 2010, s 188CG*):

- the claimant company is a trading company or a holding company;
- the claimant company is owned by a consortium;
- the surrendering company is not a member of the consortium;
- the surrendering company is a member of the same group of companies as a third company ('the link company');
- the link company is a member of the consortium; and
- the surrendering company and the claimant company are both UK related.

Consortium condition 2 is not met if any profit on the potential sale of shares by the link company would be treated as a trading receipt of that company.

Consortium condition 3

Consortium condition 3 is met if (*CTA 2010, s 188CH*):

- the *surrendering* company is a trading company or a holding company;
- the *surrendering* company is owned by a consortium;
- the *claimant* company is a member of the consortium; and
- both companies are either UK resident or carrying on a trade in the UK through a permanent establishment.

Consortium condition 3 is not met if any profit on the sale of shares by the claimant company would be treated as a trading receipt of that company.

Consortium condition 4

Consortium condition 4 is met if (*CTA 2010, s 188CI*):

- the surrendering company is a trading company or a holding company;
- the surrendering company is owned by a consortium;
- the claimant company is not a member of the consortium;
- the claimant company is a member of the same group of companies as a third company ('the link company');
- the link company is a member of the consortium; and
- the surrendering company and the claimant company are both either UK resident or carrying on a trade in the UK through a permanent establishment.

Consortium condition 2 is not met if any profit on the potential sale of shares by the link company would be treated as a trading receipt of that company.

Group relief limitations

5.14 For accounting periods beginning on or after 12 July 2010, group relief is reduced by 50% in a claim based on consortium condition 1 or 2 where the surrendering company is owned by the consortium, and arrangements are in place during the overlapping common accounting period that prevent the claimant or the link company respectively, either alone or together with one or more other companies that are members of the consortium, from controlling the surrendering company, and these arrangements form part of a scheme the main purpose of which, or one of the main purposes, is to enable the claimant company to obtain a tax advantage (*CTA 2010, s 146A*).

Also for accounting periods beginning on or after 12 July 2010, group relief is reduced by 50% in a claim based on consortium condition 1 or 3 where the claimant company is owned by the consortium, and arrangements are in place during the overlapping common accounting period that prevent the surrendering company or the link company respectively, either alone or together with one or more other companies that are members of the consortium, from controlling the claimant company, and these arrangements form part of a scheme the main purpose of which, or one of the main purposes, is to enable the claimant company to obtain a tax advantage (*CTA 2010, s 146B*).

Restrictions for the claimant company

5.15 The amount which a company can claim as current year group relief must not exceed its total profits as reduced by the following current and past losses:

- any relief whatsoever for a loss from a previous period;
- relief for any trading loss brought forward from a previous accounting period under *CTA 2010, s 45*;
- relief available to the company (whether claimed or not) for any trading loss of the same accounting period under *CTA 2010, s 37(3)(a)*;
- relief for UK property income losses of the same accounting period under *CTA 2010, s 62*;
- relief for qualifying charitable donations (*CTA 2010, s 189*);
- relief available to the company (whether claimed or not) for an excess of capital allowances under *CAA 2001, s 260(3)(a)* in respect of special leasing of plant or machinery in the same accounting period; and
- relief for non-trading loan relationship deficits under *CTA 2009, s 461* of the same accounting period.

The amount that can be claimed by way of group relief is not restricted by reference to losses arising in any later period (*CTA 2010, s 137*).

A company cannot claim group relief for surrendered carried-forward losses if the claimant company has not used its own carried-forward losses in the year of claim, or has claimed that unused trading losses or loan relationship deficits are not to be used in the period (*CTA 2010, ss 188CD, 188BB(1)*).

Group relief for carried-forward losses – calculation of relevant maximum

5.16 The amount of group relief which can be claimed for carried-forward losses for an overlapping period is restricted by reference to a company's 'relevant maximum'. The steps for calculating a claimant company's 'relevant maximum' are set out in *CTA 2010, s 188DD* and may be summarised as follows:

Step 1 – Calculate the claimant company's relevant maximum as 50% of relevant profits plus the deductions allowance of £5m (*CTA 2010, s 269ZD(4)*).

Step 2 – Deduct from the result of step 1 the sum of the following amounts, if there are any:

- trading losses which arose prior to 1 April 2017 or 'non-qualifying' trade losses arising on or after 1 April 2017 (set off against trading profits), other than certain specified losses such as creative industry losses and losses from furnished holiday lettings (*CTA 2010, ss 45(4)(b), 45B(4)*);
- non-trading loan relationship deficits which arose prior to 1 April 2017 or non-qualifying non-trading loan relationship deficits arising on or after 1 April 2017 (set off against non-trading profits) (*CTA 2009, ss 457(3), 463H(5)*); and

- any other deductions from total profits which are specified in the legislation, other than group relief for carried-forward losses.

For the detail of which amounts to deduct or exclude, the legislation at *CTA 2010, s 188DD* must be carefully followed.

Step 3 – Take the proportion of the claim period included in the overlapping period and apply that proportion to the amount arrived at under step 2.

If the claimant company's relevant profits are lower than the amount of deductions allowance allocated to it, there are different steps to the calculation, which may be summarised as follows (*CTA 2010, s 188DD(3)*):

Step 1 – Calculate the claimant company's relevant maximum as relevant profits (*CTA 2010, s 269ZD(5)*) plus the deductions allowance of £5m.

Step 2 – Deduct all brought-forward amounts from 'relevant profits'.

Step 3 – Take the proportion of the claim period included in the overlapping period and apply that proportion to the amount arrived at under step 2 (this step is unchanged).

The legislation ensures that surrendering companies do not surrender excessive amounts of carried-forward losses where there have been prior claims. The 'unused part of the surrenderable amount' is the surrenderable amount (based on the proportion of the period of surrender in the overlapping period) for the overlapping period less the amount of 'prior surrenders' for that period (*CTA 2010, s 188DC(1)–(2)*).

Steps set out in *CTA 2010, s 188DC(3)–(6)* then prescribe how to determine the amount of prior claims (ie earlier valid claims relating to the same amounts) for each claimant. There are equivalent provisions which ensure that claimant companies cannot claim excess relief for carried-forward losses (*CTA 2010, ss 188DB–188DE*).

AVAILABILITY OF GROUP RELIEF

UK losses

5.17 Assuming that losses have been incurred, it is necessary to determine whether group relief is available.

A UK resident surrendering company may not surrender a loss or other amount attributable to a permanent establishment through which the company carries on a trade outside the UK; neither may it surrender a loss that is relievable against another company's non-UK profits (*CTA 2010, ss 106, 108*; *CTA 2010, s 188BH(8)* in relation to group relief for carried-forward losses).

A non-UK resident company resident outside the EEA and carrying on a trade in the UK through a permanent establishment may only surrender a loss or other amount for group relief if that loss or other amount:

- is attributable to activities of the surrendering company in respect of which it is within the charge to corporation tax for the surrender period;
- is not attributable to activities of the surrendering company that are double tax exempt for the surrender period; and
- does not correspond to, and is not represented by, an amount deductible from or otherwise allowable against non-UK profits of any person (*CTA 2010, s 107(2), (6)*; *CTA 2010, s 188BI* in relation to group relief for carried-forward losses).

On the other hand, a non-UK resident company resident *within the EEA* and carrying on a trade in the UK through a permanent establishment may only surrender a loss or other amount for group relief if that loss or other amount:

- is attributable to activities of the surrendering company in respect of which it is within the charge to corporation tax for the surrender period;
- is not attributable to activities of the surrendering company that are double tax exempt for the surrender period; and
- does not correspond to, and is not represented by, an amount which is (in any period) *deducted* from or otherwise *allowed* against non-UK profits of any person (*CTA 2010, s 107(1A), (6A), (6B)*, as inserted by *FA 2013, s 30* following the ECJ decision in *HMRC v Philips Electronics UK Ltd* (Case C-18/11); *CTA 2010, s 188BI(2), (8), (9)* in relation to group relief for carried-forward losses).

It is arguable that UK law on group relief discriminates against companies resident in other EEA states with UK permanent establishments, as compared with UK resident companies.

If the surrendering company is UK resident and is also within a charge to non-UK tax under the law of a territory because:

- it derives its status as a company from that law;
- its place of management is in that territory; or
- it is for some other reason treated under that law as resident in that territory for the purposes of that tax,

it may not surrender its losses or other amounts if any of the following conditions are met (*CTA 2010, s 109*; *CTA 2010, s 188BJ* in relation to group relief for carried-forward losses):

- *Condition A*: the surrendering company is not a trading company throughout the surrender period.
- *Condition B*: in the surrender period, the surrendering company carries on a trade consisting wholly or mainly of one or more of the following activities:

  - Activity 1: acquiring and holding shares, securities or investments of any other kind (whether directly or indirectly);
  - Activity 2: making payments that are classified as loan relationships debits;
  - Activity 3: making payments which are qualifying charitable donations;
  - Activity 4: making payments similar to qualifying charitable donation payments that are deductible in calculating the profits of the surrendering company for corporation tax purposes; and
  - Activity 5: obtaining funds for any of Activities 1 to 4.

- *Condition C*: in the surrender period, the surrendering company carries on one or more of these activities in addition to its main trade to an extent which does not appear to be justified.

Overseas losses

> **Focus**
>
> Following the *Marks & Spencer* case before the European Court of Justice in 2006, changes were made to allow non-UK resident companies resident or carrying on a trade in the EEA to surrender certain group losses and other amounts (but not consortium losses).

5.18 In *Marks & Spencer v David Halsey* (Case C-446/03) the European Court of Justice held that the UK group relief rules discriminated unfairly against overseas subsidiaries. The law was amended following that decision and, for accounting periods beginning on or after 1 April 2006, a 'qualifying overseas loss' may be surrendered for group relief (*CTA 2010, ss 111–128*). A subsequent EC challenge to the amended law was rejected by the ECJ in *European Commission v United Kingdom* (Case C-172/13).

Subject to the requirements detailed in **5.19**, non-UK resident companies that are resident or carrying on a trade in the EEA may surrender certain group losses and other amounts (but not consortium losses) in the same way as UK resident companies (*CTA 2010, s 111(1)*). The surrendering company must be:

- a 75% subsidiary of a UK resident claimant company, or
- together with the claimant company, 75% subsidiaries of a third company that is UK resident (*CTA 2010, s 121*).

The following countries are members of the EEA:

Austria	Estonia	Ireland	Netherlands	Spain
Belgium	Finland	Italy	Norway	Sweden
Bulgaria	France	Latvia	Poland	UK
Croatia	Germany	Liechtenstein	Portugal	
Cyprus	Greece	Lithuania	Romania	
Czech Republic	Hungary	Luxembourg	Slovakia	
Denmark	Iceland	Malta	Slovenia	

Relief in respect of overseas losses of non-resident companies

5.19 If the surrendering company is a non-UK resident company resident or trading in the EEA, the following requirements must be met (*CTA 2010, ss 135, 136*):

Requirement 1 – Consent

- the surrendering company consents to the claim;

Requirement 2 – Period

- there is a period ('the overlapping period') that is common to the claim period and the surrender period;

Requirement 3 – The EEA group condition

- either the surrendering company is a 75% subsidiary of the claimant company, and the claimant company is UK resident; or
- both the surrendering company and the claimant company are 75% subsidiaries of a third company, and the third company is UK resident.

The loss must meet the following conditions in relation to the EEA territory:

(a) The equivalence condition: The loss must be of a kind that would be available for relief by a UK company (*CTA 2010, s 114*).

(b) The EEA tax loss condition:

For EEA resident companies:

- the loss is calculated under the laws of the EEA territory, and
- the loss is not attributed to a UK permanent establishment of the company.

For non-EEA resident companies:

- the company carries on a trade through a permanent establishment in the EEA territory,

- the loss is calculated under the laws of the EEA territory, and
- the activities are not exempt under a double tax treaty, as these would be ignored (*CTA 2010, ss 115, 116*).

(c) The qualifying loss condition:

- The loss cannot be given qualifying relief for any period ('the current period') or any past or future period, and
- the loss has not been given any other qualifying relief under the law of any territory outside the UK (other than the EEA territory concerned) (*CTA 2010, ss 117, 118*).

(d) The precedence condition: The loss cannot be relieved in any other grouping (*CTA 2010, s 121*).

The relevant accounting period concerned is the accounting period the company would have if it were UK resident (*CTA 2010, s 168*). The loss will not qualify for relief if it arose from artificial arrangements (*CTA 2010, s 127(3), (4), Sch 2, para 52*). The qualifying loss condition must be satisfied at the date on which the company makes the group loss relief claim, as confirmed by the Supreme Court in *Commissioners for HM Revenue & Customs v Marks and Spencer plc* [2013] UKSC 30, approved in February 2015 by the European Court of Justice in *European Commission v United Kingdom* (Case C-172/13). The correct method of calculating the loss available to be surrendered was established in *Revenue and Customs Commissioners v Marks and Spencer plc* [2014] UKSC 11. Furthermore, the ECJ held in *A Oy* (Case C-123/11), concerning a Finnish company, that national legislation should allow a parent company the chance to show that its subsidiary had exhausted the possibilities of taking the losses into account in its state of residence.

Application of UK rules to non-resident company

5.20 The corporation tax computation must be recalculated using the applicable UK tax rules. The calculated loss cannot exceed the non-resident company's actual loss; and, if the result is a profit, no relief is available (*CTA 2010, s 113(2)*).

On preparing the computation, it is necessary to assume that the company is UK resident and that its trade is carried on wholly or partly in the UK. Rental income and income from land is calculated on the assumption that the land is based in the UK and on property income principles. The accounting period on which the computation is based is assumed to begin at the beginning of the loss period. If plant and machinery is purchased, it is assumed that capital allowances are available (*CTA 2010, s 126*).

Further details of claims procedures in respect of overseas losses of non-UK resident companies can be found at CTM81600 onwards.

Arrangement for transfer to another group or consortium

5.21 If two companies would otherwise be members of the same group of companies, they are not treated as such if arrangements exist whereby (*CTA 2010, s 154*):

- one of the companies could cease to be a member of the same group of companies as the second company and could become a member of the same group of companies as a third (unrelated) company;
- at some time during or after the current period, a person (other than either of those companies) has or could obtain control of the first company but not the second company; or
- at some time during or after the current period, an unrelated third company could start to carry on the whole or part of a trade that, at a time during the current period, is carried on by the first company.

If a trading company would otherwise be owned by a consortium, it is not treated as such if arrangements exist whereby (*CTA 2010, s 155*):

- the trading company or its successor could become a 75% subsidiary of a third company;
- a person, or persons together, who own less than 50% of the ordinary share capital of the trading company have or could obtain control of the trading company;
- any person, alone or with connected persons, holds or could obtain at least 75% of the qualifying votes in the trading company or controls or could control the exercise of at least 75% of those votes; or
- a third company could start to carry on the whole or a part of the trade as direct or indirect successor to the trading company.

This ineligibility for group relief or consortium relief will last only for the period in which the arrangements exist, with apportionment of accounting periods as appropriate (*Shepherd v Law Land plc* [1990] STC 795).

Where shares or securities carry temporary rights, all such rights are deemed to have been exercised at the earliest possible date. If rights differ over the ownership period, the lowest common denominator is applied to the holdings to ascertain whether group relief is available (*CTA 2010, s 172(3)*).

Some statutory public bodies set down conditions or requirements for companies, who may happen to be members of wider groups, and these might be caught inadvertently within the definition of arrangements that would prevent group relief but for their exclusion from this definition for accounting periods ending on or after 1 April 2013 (*CTA 2010, s 156*, before and after amendment by *FA 2013, s 31*). For accounting periods ending on or after 1 January 2015, conditions agreed or imposed by a minister or statutory body, which provide that at some point in the future one company's right over the profits or assets of another could change, will not prevent claims to group relief (*CTA 2010, s 169*). Care is needed in respect of earlier accounting periods when these exclusions did not apply.

Certain arrangements entered into in accounting periods beginning on or after 1 March 2012, where they involve joint venture companies or mortgages of shares or securities, are excluded from the application of the restrictions on group relief and consortium relief contained in *CTA 2010, ss 154, 155*, by virtue of *CTA 2010, ss 155A, 155B*, which replaced Concession C10.

Group relief: non-coterminous accounting periods

5.22 A group relief claim can only be made for a corresponding accounting period. Often, group member accounting periods are not coterminous and the available profits and losses must be apportioned.

The rules for carried-forward losses (*CTA 2010, ss 188DA–188EK*) are broadly similar. See **5.25** for further computational aspects of group relief claims for carried-forward losses.

The amount that may be surrendered is the smaller of:

- the unused part of the surrenderable amount for the overlapping period, and
- the unrelieved part of the claimant company's total profits for the overlapping period.

The overlapping period is the period common to both companies (*CTA 2010, ss 139–142*).

Example 5.7—Group relief: non-coterminous accounting periods – losses arising prior to 1 April 2017

Facts

Mu Ltd owns 90% of the ordinary share capital of Nu Ltd.

Mu Ltd has prepared annual accounts to 30 June 2016.

Profits for the year amount to £48,000.

Nu Ltd has prepared annual accounts to 31 December 2016.

The trading loss for the year amounts to £56,000.

Analysis

Although Mu Ltd and Nu Ltd are a group for group relief purposes, they can only claim and surrender losses pro rata to their common accounting periods.

Nu Ltd's maximum loss surrender

(1 January 2016 to 30 June 2016) ÷ (1 January 2016 to 31 December 2016) = 6/12

£56,000 × 6/12 = £28,000

So the group loss surrendered by Nu Ltd to Mu Ltd for the corresponding period from 1 January 2016 to 30 June 2016 cannot exceed £28,000. However, this may have to be restricted further.

Mu Ltd's maximum profits against which loss may be surrendered

(1 January 2016 to 30 June 2016) ÷ (1 July 2015 to 30 June 2016) = 6/12

£48,000 × 6/12 = £24,000

Therefore, only £24,000 of Nu Ltd's £56,000 trading loss for the corresponding period from 1 January 2016 to 30 June 2016 can be group relieved against Mu Ltd's profits. The remaining £4,000 is available for relief against Nu Ltd's other income.

This restriction also applies to a group relief claim made by a consortium.

Consortium relief claim

5.23 There are, broadly, four types of loss relief that can apply within a consortium:

1. consortium company surrenders its loss to the consortium members;
2. consortium member surrenders its loss to the consortium company (*CTA 2010, s 132*);
3. mixed group and consortium relief; and
4. relief via a link company (*CTA 2010, s 133*).

The claimant company, the surrendering company and (in the case of accounting periods beginning before 10 December 2014) the link company, must be UK resident or, if non-resident, be carrying on a trade in the UK through a permanent establishment or established in the EEA.

If a consortium-owned company makes a loss, it may surrender that loss to the consortium members. The only difference between this and full group relief is that each member is entitled to claim only its share (by reference to its percentage holding of ordinary shares) of the consortium-owned company's loss (*CTA 2010, s 143*).

Similarly, if one of the consortium members makes a loss, it may surrender that loss against its percentage share of the consortium-owned company's profits (*CTA 2010, s 144*).

A link company is a company which is both a member of a consortium and a member of a group and may act as a conduit for loss relief between the consortium member and the group/consortium (*CTA 2010, ss 133, 146*). If the loss is claimed via a link company, the relief that is available amounts to that which would be available to the link company on the assumption that the link company is UK related (*CTA 2010, s 146(3)*).

The member's interest in the surrendering company, claimant company or link company (as applicable) for the purpose of a consortium claim or surrender is the lower of the percentage of (*CTA 2010, ss 143–145*):

- ordinary share capital;
- profits available for distribution;
- assets on a winding up; and
- the proportion of the voting power.

If the percentages fluctuate over the period, the average is taken (*CTA 2010, ss 143(4), 144(4)*).

In *BUPA Insurance Ltd* [2014] UKUT 262 (TCC), the Upper Tribunal held that contractual arrangements between the various parties had not deprived the link company of beneficial entitlement to any distribution made by the surrendering company for consortium relief purposes.

Example 5.8—Consortium relief: surrender by consortium-owned company

Facts

Delta Ltd is a consortium-owned company, which is owned 60% by Alpha Ltd, 20% by Beta Ltd and 20% by Gamma Ltd. All companies prepare accounts to 31 December each year. In the accounting period ended 31 December 2018, Delta's trading loss amounts to £75,000.

Analysis

The maximum loss claim is as follows:

		£
Alpha Ltd	60%	45,000
Beta Ltd	20%	15,000
Gamma Ltd	20%	15,000
		75,000

Loss relief up to these limits can be claimed by any of the consortium members that have sufficient profits.

Example 5.9—Consortium relief: claim by consortium-owned company

Facts

The companies and their relationships are as detailed in Example 5.8.

In the accounting period ended 31 December 2018, Delta Ltd makes a profit of £80,000. Alpha Ltd makes a loss of £120,000, Beta Ltd makes a loss of £30,000 and Gamma Ltd makes a profit of £60,000.

Analysis

The maximum surrenderable losses are calculated as follows:

		£	£
Delta Ltd	Profit		80,000
	Losses surrendered:		
Alpha Ltd	Loss made	(120,000)	
	Maximum surrender is 60% of £80,000	48,000	(48,000)
	Not available for current-year surrender	(72,000)	
Beta Ltd	Loss made	(30,000)	
	Maximum surrender is 20% of £80,000	16,000	(16,000)
	Not available for current-year surrender	(14,000)	
Gamma Ltd	Not applicable		
	Total taxable profits		16,000

Example 5.10—Consortium relief and group relief

Facts

A Ltd owns 100% of the share capital of B Ltd.

B Ltd owns 40% of the share capital of D Ltd.

C Ltd owns 60% of the share capital of D Ltd.

D Ltd owns 100% of the share capital of E Ltd.

D Ltd owns 100% of the share capital of F Ltd.

The companies have the following results for the year ended 31 July 2018:

A Ltd	£100,000	profit
B Ltd	(£30,000)	loss
C Ltd	Nil	
D Ltd	(£20,000)	loss
E Ltd	£10,000	profit
F Ltd	(£3,000)	loss

Analysis

There are two groups:

- A and B; and
- D, E and F.

D is owned by a consortium of B and C. All companies have the same accounting periods. None of the companies has any losses brought forward.

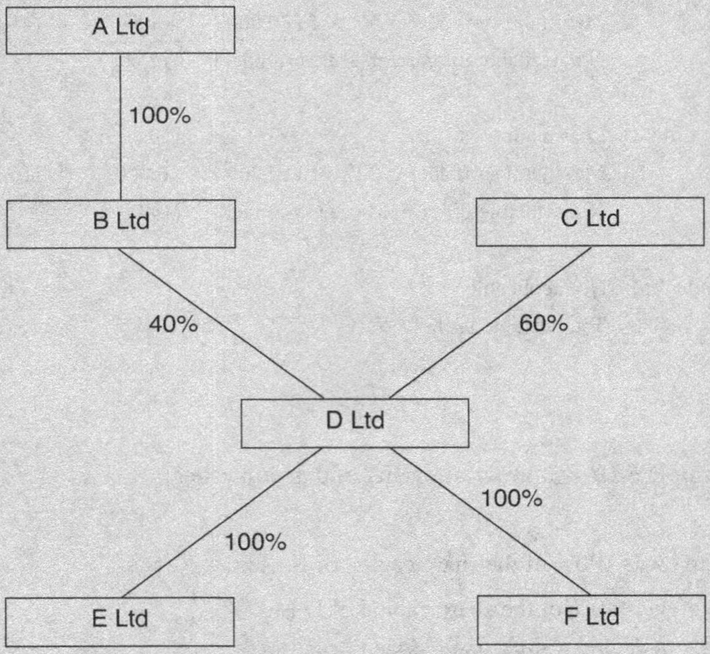

E Ltd claims current-year group relief (in priority to consortium relief) as follows:

	£	£
Profit		10,000
Deduct:		
Group relief: loss surrendered by F Ltd	3,000	
Group relief: loss surrendered by D Ltd	7,000	
		(10,000)
		—

A Ltd can claim group relief first and then consortium relief as follows:

	£	£
Profit		100,000
Deduct:		
Group relief: loss surrendered by B Ltd	30,000	
Consortium relief: loss surrendered by D Ltd (£20,000 – £7,000) × 40%	5,200	
		(35,200)
		64,800

Example 5.11—UK/overseas group and consortium relationships

Facts

A Ltd is the UK subsidiary of a Dutch holding company, K BV. B Ltd is the UK branch of an associated Dutch company, L BV. The respective link companies have no liability to UK corporation tax.

Analysis

A Ltd makes a consortium claim for group relief against L BV in respect of the losses incurred by L's UK branch. If the claim were made in respect of accounting periods that began before 12 July 2010, HMRC would have refused the claim because the link company was not within the charge to corporation tax.

In *Philips Electronics UK Ltd v HMRC* [2009] UKFTT 226 (TC), it was decided that such a restriction was contrary to the freedom of establishment principle and should not be applied to restrict such a claim. Since this case was decided, changes were made by *F(No 3)A 2010* for accounting periods beginning on or after 12 July 2010 in an attempt to ensure that relief would be available (see **5.12**).

The matter was considered again in *HMRC v Philips Electronics UK Ltd* (Case C-18/11), when the European Court of Justice decided that it was contrary to EU law for the UK to deny relief for losses simply because some of them were deductible against the profits of the EU company in its head office jurisdiction. Accordingly, *FA 2013, s 30* modified the restriction that applies for EEA resident companies, and from 1 April 2013 this is based on whether their losses are relieved in another country in any period, rather than on whether they could potentially be relieved in another country (see **5.17**).

Group relief claimant company

5.24 The claimant company sets the relief against its total profits for the year to reduce its overall corporation tax liability. The claimant company is not required to pay the surrendering company for utilisation of the loss. There is no tax effect if a payment is made of any sum up to the amount of the loss, as distinct from the tax value of the loss (*CTA 2010, s 183*).

Group relief and changes of ownership

5.25 The extended group relief rules introduced by *Finance (No 2) Act 2017* are also the subject of some anti-avoidance legislation, largely to prevent pre-acquisition losses being available for carried-forward group relief in post-acquisition periods.

Where there has been a change of ownership of a company, which therefore becomes a member of a group, losses arising in the company prior to the change of ownership cannot be part of group relief claims for carried-forward losses in accounting periods following the change of ownership (*CTA 2010, s 676CB*). There are three exceptions to this general rule:

- Cases where consortium condition 1 or 2 was previously met (*CTA 2010, s 676CC*). Where the claimant company is the transferred company, group relief for carried-forward losses is restricted to the amounts available based on the ownership proportions before the change of ownership. This restriction applies for the five-year period mentioned in *CTA 2010, s 676CE* (below).
- Cases where consortium condition 3 or 4 was previously met (*CTA 2010, s 676CD*). Where the surrendering company is the transferred company, group relief for carried-forward losses is restricted to the amounts available to surrender by the surrendering company based on the ownership proportions before the change of

ownership. This restriction applies for the five-year period mentioned in *CTA 2010, s 676CE* (below).

- The restriction falls away completely after the fifth anniversary of the change of ownership (*CTA 2010, s 676CE*).

Group relief and transfers of assets

5.26 Where, on or after 1 April 2017, there is a change in ownership of a company (*CTA 2010, s 676DA*) and:

- the company acquires an asset under the intra-group transfer rules such that no gain or loss arises on the transfer, and, within five years of the change in ownership, that company makes a gain on the disposal of the asset; or
- a gain is transferred to the company in accordance with *TCGA 1992, ss 171A* and *171B*,

carried-forward trading losses under *CTA 2010, s 45A* or *45F* cannot be used to relieve the gains if the losses arose before the change of ownership (*CTA 2010, s 676DC*).

This chapter refers to both gains arising on chargeable assets and non-trading gains arising on chargeable intangible assets.

GROUP RELIEF COMPLIANCE

Company tax return

5.27 Details of the group relief claim are included on supplementary pages CT600C. Both claimant and surrendering companies must complete their respective CT600C pages, which formalise the claim. The claimant company includes the amount of group relief and consortium relief claimed on its form CT600. The claim must be made within the normal self-assessment time limits, ie two years after the end of the chargeable period for which the claim is made. A claim made out of time can be refused (*Farmer v Bankers Trust International Ltd* [1990] STC 564; *R (on the application of the Bampton Property Group Ltd and others) v King* [2012] All ER (D) 259 (Dec)). Likewise, an application to withdraw a claim out of time can be refused (*R (on the application of GMGRM North Ltd & Ors) v Ritchie (an officer of Revenue and Customs Commissioners) & Anor* [2013] EWHC 4115 (Admin)).

Alternatively, 'an authorised group company', normally the holding company, may request HMRC in writing to grant it the power to furnish group relief claims and surrender notices on behalf of the other group and consortium companies. The application should include:

- the name and the tax office reference of the authorised company,
- the names and the tax office references of the authorising companies,
- details relating to the authorised company and each of the authorising companies that are sufficient to demonstrate that the company concerned is a member of the group of companies or, as the case may be, a consortium company, and
- a statement by the authorised company and the authorising companies that they agree to be covered by the arrangements and bound by claims, surrenders and withdrawals made under the arrangements.

The application must be accompanied by:

- a specimen copy of a group relief claim and surrender statement that the authorised company proposes to use for the purpose of making and withdrawing surrenders and claims on behalf of itself and the authorising companies; or
- in the case of a company that is a consortium company, an agreement, signed by each member of the consortium and the consortium company, consenting to the authorised company acting on their behalf in relation to the arrangements.

The application must be signed on behalf of each of the companies concerned by an officer of the company, normally the company secretary, and sent to the tax office dealing with the tax affairs of the authorised company (*FA 1998, Sch 18, para 77*; *Corporation Tax (Simplified Arrangements for Group Relief) Regulations 1999, SI 1999/2975*).

Repayments of corporation tax

5.28 Companies within the same group may elect jointly for repayment due to one company to be surrendered to another company in payment towards its corporation tax liability. The facility is aimed at reducing the group's exposure to interest on overdue tax. The companies involved must have the same accounting period and must be members of the same group throughout the accounting period. Any inter-company tax payment up to the amount of the tax is ignored. There is no prescribed format for the election. A letter to HMRC will suffice with details of the company and tax district reference numbers. Each company should appoint an authorised person to sign the form on its behalf.

The joint notice is not given on the form CT600, but must be made separately. The surrendering company should use the 'repayment' section of its form CT600 to claim its refund and show how much is to be surrendered. A copy of the joint notice should be submitted with the form CT600 (*CTA 2010, s 963*; CTM92440).

See also **23.36** regarding corporation tax group payment arrangements.

Refunds of quarterly instalments

5.29 The intra-group arrangement is also available for quarterly instalments of corporation tax (*Corporation Tax (Instalment Payments) Regulations 1998, SI 1998/3175*; see **23.11**). A refund of tax that is paid under the instalment arrangements can be surrendered to fellow group members at the date of payment. Again, the aim is to reduce the group's exposure to interest by netting off the debit and credit interest to eliminate the differential interest that would otherwise arise from underpaid and overpaid instalments of tax.

For this purpose, *CTA 2010, ss 963–964* apply (with modifications set out in *SI 1998/3175, reg 9*) when a tax refund is due to be made to the surrendering company, whether under *SI 1998/3175, reg 6* or *TMA 1970, s 59D(2)*. HMRC guidance at CTM92740 explains that:

- payments made during the quarterly instalment payment period may be retrospectively allocated between group members to mitigate the interest position of the group, beyond that limited circumstance,
- *SI 1998/3175, reg 9* (as amended) only applies in relation to CT paid on account of the surrendering company's own liability, and
- a group is unable to make a global payment in the name of a dormant company or one that will have no CT liability, and then reallocate it between group members retrospectively.

The surrendering company must give notice to HMRC, at the time when the joint surrender notice is given, specifying the payment(s) out of which the refund is to be treated as made (*CTA 2010, s 963(3)*; or *CTA 2010, s 963(6C)* by virtue of *SI 1998/3175, reg 9*). The surrendering company then has 30 days in which to bring its specification into line with the amount of the repayment due. If it fails to do so within that time, the repayment can be made as if no notice of surrender had been given (*CTA 2010, s 964(6C), (6D)*, by virtue of *SI 1998/3175, reg 9*).

Example 5.12—Groups: repayments of corporation tax

Facts

Red Ltd and Blue Ltd are within the same group and they both qualify under the special rules of *CTA 2010, s 963*.

Both companies have 31 December year ends and each company makes the following quarterly payments in respect of the year ending 31 December 2017:

	Red Ltd	*Blue Ltd*
	£	£
14 July 2017	500,000	500,000
14 October 2017	500,000	500,000
14 January 2018	250,000	500,000
14 April 2018	150,000	500,000
Total paid	1,400,000	2,000,000

The actual corporation tax liability for the year is as follows:

	Red Ltd	*Blue Ltd*
	£	£
Corporation tax liability year ending 31 December 2017	10,000	3,500,000

Analysis

Red Ltd makes a repayment claim for £1,390,000 under *SI 1998/3175, reg 6* because it is now known that no instalment tax was due.

Blue Ltd should have paid quarterly instalments of £875,000 in each quarter.

So, Blue Ltd's cumulative underpayment of instalments is:

	Instalments due	*Instalments paid*	*Shortfall*
	£	£	£
14 July 2017	875,000	500,000	375,000
14 October 2017	875,000	500,000	375,000
14 January 2018	875,000	500,000	375,000
14 April 2018	875,000	500,000	375,000
	3,500,000	2,000,000	1,500,000

Red Ltd makes a repayment claim for the overpaid instalments.

Red Ltd and Blue Ltd give joint notice of surrender under *CTA 2010, s 964(6B)*, so that the instalment tax paid by Red Ltd is treated as paid by Blue Ltd with Red Ltd's payment dates.

Red Ltd is treated as if the overpaid tax had been repaid to it on those dates.

The claim results in Red Ltd not making any quarterly payments. Its corporation tax of £10,000 is now due by 1 October 2018, and it pays this separately by that date. Blue Ltd has to make a further instalment payment as soon as possible of £100,000, which is calculated as follows:

	£
Corporation tax due year ending 31 December 2017	3,500,000
Quarterly instalments paid by Blue Ltd	(2,000,000)
Quarterly instalments paid by Red Ltd	(1,400,000)
Net amount due	100,000

Information regarding instalment payments

5.30 *Corporation Tax (Instalment Payments) Regulations 1998, SI 1998/3175, reg 10,* empowers HMRC, at any time after the filing date, to require a company to furnish such information as may reasonably be required about:

- the computation of any instalment payment,
- the reasons it omitted to make quarterly instalment payments, and
- a *SI 1998/3175, reg 6* repayment claim.

The time allowed for providing the information must be not less than 30 days and must be shown on the notice.

SI 1998/3175, reg 11 empowers HMRC to require the company to produce 'books, documents and other records in its possession or power' for the purposes of *SI 1998/3175, reg 10.* HMRC accept photocopies, as long as the originals are available for inspection. These powers are not part of the enquiry procedures.

CORPORATE INTEREST RESTRICTION

Introduction

Focus

The principle of the corporate interest restriction is to restrict tax deductions in respect of excessive debt owed by UK members of a group.

> The measure applies whether the UK group companies are members of a UK or non-UK headed group. The amount of interest allowed as a deduction is restricted by reference to one of two ratios, subject to an overriding restriction.

5.31 New *TIOPA 2010, Pt 10* contains legislation which took effect for accounting periods beginning on or after 1 April 2017, replacing the worldwide debt cap legislation (see **5.32** onwards). Further reporting requirements are introduced in new *TIOPA 2010, Sch 7A*.

The new rules only apply to companies with an interest deduction in excess of £2m, referred to as the 'de minimis' amount (*TIOPA 2010, s 392*).

From 1 April 2017, two possible ratios are applied to determine the amount of interest that a company can deduct, the fixed ratio or the group ratio.

Under the fixed ratio mechanism, the basic interest allowance of a worldwide group for a period of account of the group is generally restricted to 30% of the aggregate tax-EBITDA of the group for the period (*TIOPA 2010, s 397*). However, the interest deduction also cannot exceed the adjusted net group-interest expense (*TIOPA 2010, s 400*), which broadly means the net interest expense of the worldwide group, subject to certain statutory adjustments (*TIOPA 2010, s 413*).

If preferred, an election can be made to use the group ratio mechanism. Under these rules, the basic interest allowance of a worldwide group for a period of account of the group is generally restricted to the group ratio percentage of the aggregate tax-EBITDA of the group for the period (*TIOPA 2010, s 398*). Very broadly, this is the ratio of the group's qualifying interest expense to the group's EBITDA for the period (*TIOPA 2010, s 399*). Again, the interest deduction also cannot exceed the adjusted net group-interest expense (*TIOPA 2010, s 400*), which broadly means the net interest expense of the worldwide group, subject to certain statutory adjustments (*TIOPA 2010, s 413*).

Where interest cannot be deducted in an accounting period, it can be carried forward indefinitely.

Where a company has excess capacity for interest deductions, ie the amount of deductible interest is less than the relevant limit, the excess capacity can be carried forward for up to five years (*TIOPA 2010, s 395*).

In most cases, affected companies will be members of a group, usually a multinational group. Only members of a group that are subject to corporation tax are affected by these rules. There are detailed rules about the allocation of restrictions between group companies and the reporting requirements for the group (in *TIOPA 2010, Sch 7A*).

DEBT CAP

Introduction

> **Focus**
>
> The principle of the worldwide debt cap is to restrict tax deductions in respect of excessive debt owed by UK members of a group. The measure applies whether the UK group companies are members of a UK or non-UK headed group. The amount of debt regarded as excessive is established by comparing the costs of borrowing, rather than snapshots of debt. For this purpose, costs of borrowing are particular defined finance expenses.
>
> The debt cap is repealed with effect from 31 March 2017.

5.32 *TIOPA 2010, Pt 7,* contains legislation, which took effect for accounting periods beginning on or after 1 January 2010, to cap the tax deduction for finance expenses payable by the UK members of a worldwide group of companies. The amount of the deduction is restricted to the consolidated gross finance expense of the group. Finance expenses and finance income are payments of interest and interest-like amounts. In brief, the restriction is calculated by comparing the UK group members' cost of borrowing with the cost of borrowing of the worldwide group. The restriction (where it applies) is allocated to one or more of the UK group companies, leading to a disallowance of part or all of their finance expenses. If other UK members of the group have net finance income, then this can be exempted up to the amount of the total disallowance.

The debt cap rules apply, broadly, where the UK net debt of the group exceeds 75% of the worldwide gross debt of the group. There are two important reliefs: for companies with net debt below £3 million; and for dormant companies.

From 1 April 2017, the debt cap rules have been repealed and replaced with the new corporate interest restriction regime (outlined in **5.31**).

The debt cap rules continue to apply for accounting periods of worldwide groups ending before 1 April 2017. The remainder of this chapter gives details of the rules in force for accounting periods ending prior to 1 April 2017.

Guidance on the worldwide debt cap is to be found in HMRC's Corporate Finance Manual at CFM90000 onwards.

Meaning of a worldwide group

5.33 A worldwide group is any large group that contains one or more relevant group companies (*TIOPA 2010, s 337*). A group has the same meaning as used for international accounting standards. If a group has more than one ultimate parent, each of those ultimate parents, together with its subsidiaries, is to be treated as a separate group. An entity that is a parent of the ultimate parent of a group is not to be treated as a member of the group (*TIOPA 2010, s 338*).

An ultimate parent must be:

- a member of the group (*TIOPA 2010, s 339(1)(a)*); and
- either a corporate entity (but not a limited liability partnership (LLP) or – for periods of account of the worldwide group ending on or after 17 July 2012 – an entity formed under the law of a territory outside the UK that would be a partnership if formed in the UK) or a relevant non-corporate entity (*TIOPA 2010, s 339(1)(b)*).

An ultimate parent must not be:

- a collective investment scheme (*TIOPA 2010, s 339(1)(c), (2)*); or
- a subsidiary company (*TIOPA 2010, s 339(1)(d)*).

A group is large if any member of the group is not within the category of micro, small and medium-sized enterprises, as defined in the *Annex* to *Commission Recommendation 2003/361/EC* of 6 May 2003 (see **14.23**, **21.11**). However, the rights of the liquidator or administrator are to be left out of account if the group member is in liquidation or administration (*TIOPA 2010, s 344*).

A UK group company is defined as any company that is either:

- UK resident, or
- non-resident in the UK but carrying on a trade in the UK through a permanent establishment.

In each case the company concerned must be either the ultimate parent of the worldwide group or a relevant subsidiary of the ultimate parent of the worldwide group.

A relevant subsidiary of the ultimate parent of the worldwide group is a company:

- which is a 75% subsidiary of the ultimate parent;
- whose ultimate parent is beneficially entitled to at least 75% of any profits available for distribution to equity holders of the company; or
- whose ultimate parent would be beneficially entitled to at least 75% of any assets of the company available for distribution to its equity holders on a winding up.

Throughout the relevant period, the company must not be a securitisation company (*TIOPA 2010, s 345*).

Arrangements to secure that a company is not treated as a member of a group are ignored (*TIOPA 2010, s 305A*; see **5.65**).

Foreign currency accounts are to be converted to sterling at the average rate of exchange for the period calculated from daily spot rates (*TIOPA 2010, s 350*).

Regulations may provide that any company which has entered into capital market arrangements may jointly elect, with another group company, for that other company to take over its corporation tax liabilities. This is because the company may not meet the securitisation criteria and be left out of account. Uncertainty about future tax liabilities may have an adverse effect on the arrangements (*TIOPA 2010, s 353A*). In this connection, a draft statutory instrument (*Tax Treatment of Financing Costs and Income (Capital Market Arrangements) (Elections) Regulations 2012*) was issued in November 2012 for consultation, but no final version has been brought into effect.

For periods of account of a worldwide group starting on or after 5 December 2013, a UK resident company which has no ordinary share capital (eg a company limited by guarantee) can be a relevant group company subject to the debt cap. From the same date, the definition of a 75% subsidiary has been modified to allow indirect ownership to be traced through intermediate entities which have no ordinary share capital (*TIOPA 2010, s 345*).

Application of the debt cap rules

Focus

The 'gateway test' determines whether the worldwide debt cap rules are to apply in respect of excessive debt owed by UK members of a group.

5.34 The rules apply to a worldwide group where, for any period of account, its UK net debt exceeds 75% of its worldwide gross debt of the group. This is commonly referred to as the 'gateway test'. The percentage that applies for this test may be varied for future accounting periods by Treasury order (*TIOPA 2010, s 261*).

Worldwide gross debt is established from the worldwide group's financial statements, which are the consolidated financial statements of the ultimate parent and its subsidiaries (*TIOPA 2010, s 346*). Accounts are acceptable if they are drawn up under IAS, UK GAAP or GAAP operated in any of the following territories: Canada, China, Japan, South Korea, USA or India (*Corporation Tax (Tax Treatment of Financing Costs and Income Acceptable Financial Statements) Regulations 2009, SI 2009/3217*). Accounts are non-compliant if they are not drawn up under GAAP on an acceptable basis and the amounts disclosed are materially different from what they would be if IAS had applied (*TIOPA 2010, s 347*). See **Chapter 26** regarding changes to UK GAAP.

If financial statements of the worldwide group are not drawn up in respect of a relevant period, the debt cap rules apply as if IAS accounts had been drawn up. If the relevant period is more than 12 months, it is treated for this purpose as one or more periods of 12 months followed by any remaining balance of the relevant period. For periods of account of a worldwide group ending on or after 17 July 2012, if the group becomes or ceases to be a worldwide group in a period of account, the accounts prepared for that period are ignored, and the part of the period for which the worldwide group is in existence is treated as a relevant period for which financial statements have not been drawn up (*TIOPA 2010, s 348*).

The debt cap rules do not apply to a qualifying financial services group (*TIOPA 2010, s 261(2)*). A qualifying financial services group is essentially a group that is engaged in financial services activities, including insurance and dealing in financial instruments or a group securitisation company (*TIOPA 2010, s 266*). A financial instrument is anything that is a financial instrument for any purpose of the FCA Handbook or the PRA Handbook, or an option, future or contract for differences (*TIOPA 2010, s 270*).

For HMRC guidance on the gateway test, see CFM90600 onwards.

Business combinations and demergers

5.35 Where, for periods of account of a worldwide group ending on or after 17 July 2012:

- a relevant event occurs in that the worldwide group is a party to a business combination or demerger,
- as a result of which there is a change in the ultimate parent of the worldwide group or any other group that is party to the relevant event, and
- there is a straddling period of account during which the financial statements of the worldwide group are drawn up (or treated as drawn up),

financial statements are treated as not having been drawn up and there is no requirement for the worldwide group to draw up financial statements for that period. Instead, financial statements are deemed to have been drawn up in respect of each of the following:

- the period beginning at the same time as the straddling period and ending immediately before the relevant event; and
- the period beginning with the relevant event and ending at the same time as the straddling period.

In effect, any worldwide group involved in the relevant event is required to finalise its debt cap computation for the period before the relevant event and begin a new debt cap computation from the date of that event (*TIOPA 2010, s 348A*).

Net debt below £3m treated as nil

5.36 UK net debt is the total of the UK net debt amounts of each group member during the accounting period. The net debt amount of each group member is the average of the net debt at the beginning and at the end of the accounting period. An averaged amount of less than £3 million in respect of a company is treated as nil (*TIOPA 2010, s 262(3)*).

The net debt of a company that is a 'dormant company' at all times, beginning with that company's start date and ending with that company's end date, is also treated as nil. The company's start date is the first day of the period of account of the worldwide group, or the date the company joined the group (if later). The company's end date is the last day of the period of account of the worldwide group, or the date the company ceased to be a group company (if earlier). For periods of account of the worldwide group ending on or before 17 July 2012, a dormant company was defined more specifically as dormant within the meaning of *CA 2006, s 1169* (*TIOPA 2010, s 262*).

In practice, the UK debt might not be measured on the same basis as the worldwide debt. Mismatches between the tax treatment and the accounting treatment of an item are corrected in accordance with the *Tax Treatment of Financing Costs and Income (Correction of Mismatches) Regulations 2010, SI 2010/3025*. The amount referred to in the accounts ('the accounts amount') is the amount disclosed in the financial statements of the worldwide group; and, if it is not disclosed, it is nil. The 'tax amount' is the deductible amount for corporation purposes (*TIOPA 2010, s 336A*).

Mismatches between tax and accounting treatment

5.37 A mismatch may occur if the amount disclosed in the financial statements of the worldwide group in respect of a liability differs from the amount accounted for in respect of the same liability by the UK member of the worldwide group. A series of regulations in the *Tax Treatment of Financing Costs and Income (Correction of Mismatches) Regulations 2010, SI 2010/3025*, deals with such mismatches. A worldwide group has the option to elect for any (or all) of certain regulations, or pairs of regulations, not to apply to it.

Regulations 3 and 4: Mismatches arising as a result of the use of fair value accounting or hedge accounting:

- If the computed available amount (see **5.45**) exceeds the loan relationship amount, the available amount is decreased by the fair value adjustment made or the excess, whichever is lower.
- If the loan relationship amount exceeds the available amount, the available amount is increased by the fair value adjustment or the excess, whichever is lower.
- If the loan relationship amount is negative, it is treated as zero.

Regulations 5 to 8: Correction of mismatches which occur where interest is treated for loan relationship purposes as not accruing until it is paid:

- An amount in respect of a debit relating to interest so treated is included in the available amount in the period of account in which it is paid, to the extent that it is not included in that amount under another provision.
- An amount in respect of accrued interest is included in the available amount in the period of account in which it accrues, rather than that in which it is paid.

Regulations 9 to 12: Correction of mismatches occurring where a debit in respect of a debtor relationship which is represented by a deeply discounted security is brought into account in the period in which the security is redeemed:

- A debit is to be included in the available amount to the extent that it is not included in that amount under another provision.
- Where an amount in respect of a debtor relationship represented by a deeply discounted security is included in the available amount in the period of account other than that in which it is redeemed, the amount is excluded from the available amount in that period of account.

Regulations 13 and 14: Loan relationships with embedded derivatives:

- Such part of the debit as is directly attributable to the requirement that it be measured at amortised cost shall be included in the available amount to the extent that it is not included in that amount under another provision.

Regulations 15 and 16: Debt restructuring:

- An amount equal to such part of the debit as is directly attributable to the requirement that it be measured at amortised cost shall be included in the available amount to the extent that it is not included in that amount under another provision.

Elections may be made under *SI 2010/3025, reg 17,* to disapply any or all of the following regulations or pairs of regulations:

- *reg 3*;
- *regs 5* and *7*;
- *regs 9* and *11*;
- *reg 13*; or
- *reg 15*.

Any election made is irrevocable. It must be made within a year of the end of the first period of account of the worldwide group beginning on or after 1 January 2010, or by 31 March 2011 if later, and must be made by the reporting body (see **5.46**) and signed by the appropriate person.

Calculation of a company's net debt

5.38 A company's net debt at any date is the difference between the total of its relevant liabilities and the total of its relevant assets, as disclosed in accordance with GAAP on the company's balance sheet at that date. The result can be negative.

Relevant liabilities are:

- all borrowings (whether by way of overdraft or other short-term or long-term borrowing);
- liabilities in respect of finance leases;
- long-term arrangements that have the economic effect of loans; or
- any other amounts as specified by regulation.

Short-term borrowings are borrowings which, at the outset, are stipulated to expire within 12 months of the arrangement being entered into.

Relevant assets are (*TIOPA 2010, s 263*):

- cash and cash equivalents;
- amounts loaned (by overdraft or short- or long-term loan);
- net investments, or net cash investments, in finance leases;
- UK or foreign government securities;
- other financial assets which produce a return economically equivalent to interest; or
- such other amounts as may be specified by regulation.

Any amount that is shown on the company's balance sheet as its own share capital or shareholding held in another company is neither a relevant asset nor a relevant liability.

An amount is economically equivalent to interest if it is a payment for the time value of money, charged at a reasonable commercial rate, and at the time the arrangement was made it was understood to be continuing.

Calculation of a worldwide group's gross debt

5.39 The worldwide gross debt of the worldwide group for a period of account of the group is the average of:

- the sum of the relevant liabilities of the group as at the day before the first day of the period, and
- the sum of the relevant liabilities of the group as at the last day of the period (*TIOPA 2010, s 264*).

Relevant liabilities take the same definition as in **5.38**. If the computation of relevant liabilities for the individual company and the group differ because of different accounting treatments, the method to be used in deciding whether the debt cap applies is the method used for the consolidated accounts (*TIOPA 2010, s 265A*).

Disallowance of deductions: computation

Total disallowed amount

5.40 Worldwide groups may suffer a disallowed finance expense. This is known as the total disallowed amount ('TDA'), being the difference between the tested expense amount ('TEA') and the available amount ('AA') (*TIOPA 2010, s 274*).

Tested expense amount

5.41 The tested expense amount for a period of account of the worldwide group is the sum of the net financing deductions of each relevant group company.

The net financing deduction of a company is:

- the sum of the company's financing expense amounts for the period (**5.43**),

  less

- the sum of the company's financing income amounts for the period (**5.44**).

Transactions undertaken when the company is not a relevant group company for debt cap purposes are ignored.

If the net financing deduction of a company would otherwise be a negative result, it is treated as nil (*TIOPA 2010, s 329(4)*).

If the net financing deduction of a company would otherwise be small (ie less than £500,000 or such other sum as may be set by Treasury order), it is treated as nil (*TIOPA 2010, ss 329(5), 331*).

For periods of account of a worldwide group ending on or after 17 July 2012, the worldwide group can elect out of this *TIOPA 2010, s 329(5)* 'small amounts' rule. The election must be made by the reporting body of the worldwide group and applies to both net financing deductions and net financing income (see **5.42**). An election or the withdrawal of such an election must be made to HMRC in writing within 12 months of the end of the first period of account for which it has effect (*TIOPA 2010, s 331ZA*).

Tested income amount

5.42 The tested income amount for the period of account of the worldwide group is the sum of the net financing incomes of each UK group company.

The net financing income of a company is:

- the sum of the company's financing income amounts for the period (**5.44**),

  less

- the sum of the company's financing expense amounts for the period (**5.43**).

If the net financing income of a company would otherwise be a negative result, it is treated as nil (*TIOPA 2010, s 330(4)*).

If the net financing income of a company would otherwise be small (ie less than £500,000 or such other sum as may be set by Treasury order), it is treated as nil (*TIOPA 2010, ss 330(5), 331*).

For periods of account of a worldwide group ending on or after 17 July 2012, the worldwide group can elect out of this *TIOPA 2010, s 330(5)* 'small amounts' rule, and the election applies for both net financing deductions and net financing income (*TIOPA 2010, s 331ZA*; for further details, see **5.41**).

Financing expense amounts

5.43 An amount is essentially a financing expense amount if it meets Condition A, B or C below (*TIOPA 2010, s 313*).

Condition A, B or C applies where, were it not for the worldwide debt cap rules, amounts would be accounted for respectively as:

Condition A

- a debit under a trading or non-trading loan relationship (see **Chapter 11**), but not a debit excluded by reason of it being:
  - an impairment loss;
  - an exchange loss; or
  - a related transaction.

Condition B

- financing cost implicit in payments made under finance leases.

Condition C

- financing cost payable on debt factoring or any similar transaction.

Debit or other amounts that do not fall entirely into the accounting period of the worldwide group are reduced *pro rata*. For periods of account of the worldwide group ending on or after 17 July 2012, adjustments are made on a just and reasonable basis, and amounts can be reduced to nil (*TIOPA 2010, s 313(6), (6A)*).

Financing income amounts

5.44 An amount is essentially a financing income amount if it meets Condition A, B, C or D below (*TIOPA 2010, s 314*).

Condition A, B, C or D applies where, were it not for the worldwide debt cap rules, amounts would be accounted for respectively as:

Condition A

- a credit under a loan relationship (see **Chapter 11**), but not a credit excluded by reason of it being:
  - the reversal of an impairment loss;
  - an exchange gain; or
  - a profit from a related transaction.

Condition B

- financing income implicit in amounts received under finance leases.

Condition C

- financing income receivable on debt factoring or similar transactions.

Condition D

- income receivable from another company in consideration of the provision of a guarantee or borrowings.

The credit arising under Condition A can be accounted for as a trading or non-trading loan relationship (see **Chapter 11**), but it must not be an excluded credit by reason of it being:

- the reversal of an impairment loss;
- an exchange gain; or
- a profit from a related transaction (*TIOPA 2010, s 314*).

Credit or other amounts that do not fall entirely into the accounting period of the worldwide group are reduced *pro rata*. For periods of account of the worldwide group ending on or after 17 July 2012, adjustments are made on a just and reasonable basis, and amounts can be reduced to nil (*TIOPA 2010, s 314*).

Furthermore, for accounting periods of controlled foreign companies (CFCs) beginning on or after 1 January 2013, where a CFC charge applies, an appropriate proportion of the CFC's relevant finance profits or loan relationship profits may be taken to be a financing income amount of the chargeable company for debt cap purposes (*TIOPA 2010, s 314A*). This is treated as exempt for debt cap purposes (*TIOPA 2010, s 292* onwards; for more about CFCs, see **Chapter 20**).

Available amount

5.45 The available amount for a period of account of the worldwide group is the sum of the amounts disclosed in the financial statements of the group for that period in respect of:

- interest payable on borrowing;
- amortisation of discounts relating to amounts borrowed;
- amortisation of premiums relating to amounts borrowed;
- amortisation of expenses ancillary to borrowing;
- the financing expense implicit in payments made under finance leases;
- the financing expense relating to debt factoring; and
- amounts of such other description as may be specified in regulations made by HMRC (*TIOPA 2010, s 332(1)*).

Expenses are ancillary to borrowing if they are incurred in bringing the borrowing into existence, altering its terms or making payments in respect of borrowing. Abortive expenses ancillary to borrowing are treated in the same way (*TIOPA 2010, s 332(1A), (1B)*).

The *Tax Treatment of Financing Costs and Income (Available Amount) Regulations 2010, SI 2010/2929*, cater for the following more detailed situations:

- interest payable in respect of a relevant non-lending relationship;
- alternative finance return under alternative finance arrangements;
- manufactured interest; and
- finance charges in connection with a stock sale and repurchase arrangement 'repos' and deemed loan relationships.

Dividends payable in respect of redeemable preference shares that are recognised as a liability in the financial statements of the group for the period are ignored (*TIOPA 2010, s 332*). Special rules apply to companies with income from oil extraction, shipping and ring fenced tax exempt business (*TIOPA 2010, ss 333, 334*). Income from securitisation companies is not included in the calculation (*TIOPA 2010, s 332A*).

Where a member of a worldwide group is a member of a partnership which has entered into borrowing arrangements, the company's available amount is calculated on the assumption that each member of the partnership borrowed an amount and incurred an expense in proportion to its profits share (*TIOPA 2010, ss 332B, 332C*).

Example 5.13—Worldwide debt cap calculations

Facts

The Frank Group has a French holding company, one subsidiary in Malta and two subsidiaries in the UK. Accounts are made up to 31 December each year according to GAAP. It is necessary to find the disallowed finance expense amount for the year ended 31 December 2015. The following information is to hand.

Extracts from the individual company financial statements:

Balance Sheets		Income Statements	
Net Debt		Tested Expense Amount	
		Finance expenses less finance income	
31.12.2015			
	£m		*£m*
UK Subsidiary 1	4,400	UK Subsidiary 1	1,300
UK Subsidiary 2	3,600	UK Subsidiary 2	1,250

Extracts from the group consolidated financial statements:

Consolidated Balance Sheet		Consolidated Income Statement	
Gross Debt		External Gross finance expense	
	£m		*£m*
31.12.2015	11,000	Gross finance income	500
31.12.2014	10,000	Gross finance expense	1,000

Analysis

Does the UK debt exceed 75% of the worldwide debt?

The UK debt is the total net debt of the UK companies at 31.12.2015. It amounts to

£4,400m + £3,600m = £8,000m

The worldwide debt is the group average gross debt for the year. It amounts to

(£11,000m + £10,000m) ÷ 2 = £10,500m

75% of the worldwide debt amounts to

£10,500m × 75% = £7,875m

Therefore, the UK debt exceeds 75% of the worldwide debt, and the debt cap rules are to be applied.

If the tested expense amount (TEA) is £2,550m and the available amount (AA) is £1,000m (AA), the disallowed amount is £1,550m (TDA) which is to be allocated to the two UK companies up to the amount of the net finance expense.

Disallowance of deductions: compliance

Appointment of authorised company

5.46 Statements of allocated disallowances have to be made by a reporting body. For this purpose, all relevant group companies within the worldwide group, instead of reporting jointly, may appoint one of their number as an authorised company to comply with the reporting obligations.

Where such an appointment is made, all the relevant companies must give their written consent, signed by the appropriate person, being either a director, a company secretary or other authorised person. Companies that are dormant throughout the relevant period of account are relieved of this reporting responsibility for periods of account of the worldwide group ending on or after 17 July 2012 (*TIOPA 2010, ss 276, 277*).

Companies to which the exemption of financing income rules apply may also appoint their own reporting body, and similar rules apply (see **5.55**).

Statement of allocated disallowances: requirements

5.47 Within 12 months of the end of the accounting period concerned, HMRC must receive a statement of allocated disallowances for that period from the reporting body. HMRC will accept revised statements within 36 months of the end of the accounting period concerned. Revised statements must show how they differ from the previous statement (*TIOPA 2010, ss 278, 279*). All statements submitted must be signed by all companies concerned, or by the one reporting company if so appointed (*TIOPA 2010, s 280(2)*).

The statement of allocated disallowances must show:

- the tested expense amount;
- the available amount; and
- the total disallowed amount.

The statement must also list the companies to which the disallowance applies, and specify the relevant details for each disallowed amount (*TIOPA 2010, s 280(3), (4)*).

The relevant details in relation to a financing expense amount are which of the conditions (A, B or C) in *TIOPA 2010, s 313* (see **5.43**) is met and the relevant accounting period in which, were it not for the worldwide debt cap rules, the amount would be brought into account (*TIOPA 2010, s 280(5)*).

For periods of account of a worldwide group ending on or after 17 July 2012, an amount may not be specified in relation to a company if it accrues at a time when the company is not a relevant group company (*TIOPA 2010, s 280(5A)*).

Statement of allocated disallowances: effect

5.48 Any financing expense that is included in the statement of disallowances is disallowed as a deduction when computing the company's corporation tax liability. If the statement is submitted after the company tax return, the company is treated as having amended its tax return (*TIOPA 2010, s 282*).

Failure to submit statement of allocated disallowances

5.49 If a reporting body fails to submit a statement of allocated disallowances or fails to submit a statement that complies with the requirements (see **5.46**), each company with a net financing deduction for the accounting period concerned must reduce the amounts that it brings into account in relevant accounting periods in respect of financing expense amounts (*TIOPA 2010, s 284*).

This reduction is calculated by the formula:

$$\frac{NFD \times TDA}{TEA}$$

where:

- NFD is the net financing deduction of the company for the relevant period of account, being the sum of the company's financing expense amounts for the period less the sum of the company's financing income amounts for the period (see **5.43**, **5.44**)
- TEA is the tested expense amount for the relevant period of account, being the sum of the net financing deductions for each relevant group company (see **5.41**)

- TDA is the total disallowed amount (see **5.40**). Regulations may be issued to determine how the particular financing expense amounts are to be reduced.

Different formulae apply for determining the total of the reductions required where one or more dual resident investing companies are involved (see *TIOPA 2010, s 284A*). The total reductions are determined as follows, where X is the total of the net financing deductions of the dual resident investing companies:

- If the company in question is not a dual resident investment company, either

  NFD / TEA – X × TDA

  or NFD if lower.

- If the company in question is a dual resident investment company, either

  NFD / X × (TDA – (TEA – X))

  or nil if the result is negative or zero.

Exemption of financing income: computation

Introduction

5.50 If a worldwide group suffers a disallowed finance expense, known as the total disallowed amount (ie the difference between the tested expense amount (see **5.41**) and the available amount (see **5.45**)), it is necessary to calculate the extent to which the financing income of the UK group companies will be exempt from corporation tax (*TIOPA 2010, ss 286–298A*).

Intra-group financing income where payer denied deduction

5.51 Financing income amounts (see **5.44**) received after introduction of the worldwide debt cap are not chargeable to corporation tax if the payer and the recipient are both members of the same worldwide group, subject to satisfying all of the following conditions (*TIOPA 2010, s 299*):

- *Condition A*

  at the time the payment is received, the payer is a relevant associate of the recipient (see **5.52**).

- *Condition B*

  at the time the payment is received, the payer is tax-resident in an EEA territory. A payer is tax-resident in a territory if it is liable, under the law of that territory, to tax by reason of domicile, residence or place of management (*TIOPA 2010, s 301*); and

the payer is liable to a tax of that territory that is chargeable by reference to profits, income or gains arising to the payer.

- *Condition C*

  qualifying EEA tax relief for the payment is not available to the payer in the period in which the payment is made ('the current period') or any previous period (see **5.53**); and

  qualifying EEA tax relief for the payment is not available to the payer in any period after the current period (see **5.54**).

Meaning of 'relevant associate'

5.52 The payer is a relevant associate of the recipient if the payer is (*TIOPA 2010, s 300*):

- a parent of the recipient,
- a 75% subsidiary of the recipient, or
- a 75% subsidiary of a parent of the recipient.

Qualifying EEA tax relief in current or past periods

5.53 Qualifying EEA tax relief for a payment is not available to the payer in the current period or a previous period if Conditions A and B are both met in relation to the payment:

Condition A

- no deduction calculated by reference to the payment can be taken into account in calculating any profits, income or gains that:

  (a) arise to the payer in the current period or any previous period, and

  (b) are chargeable to any tax of the UK or another EEA territory, for the current period or any previous period.

Condition B

- no relief determined by reference to the payment can be given in the current period or any previous period for the purposes of any tax of the UK or another EEA territory by:

  (a) the payment of a credit,

  (b) the elimination or reduction of a tax liability, or

  (c) any other means of any kind.

This is on the proviso that all steps have been taken to secure the reliefs, and no double tax provisions have been disregarded (*TIOPA 2010, s 302*).

Qualifying EEA tax relief in future period

5.54 Qualifying EEA tax relief for a payment is not available to the payer in a period after the current period if both the following conditions are met in relation to the payment:

- no deduction calculated by reference to the payment can be taken into account in calculating any profits, income or gains that:
  - (a) might arise to the payer in any period after the current period, and
  - (b) would, if they did so arise, be chargeable to any tax of the UK or another EEA territory for any period after the current period; and
- no relief determined by reference to the payment can be given in any period after the current period for the purposes of any tax of the UK or another EEA territory by:
  - (a) the payment of a credit,
  - (b) the elimination or reduction of a tax liability, or
  - (c) any other means of any kind.

This is on the proviso that all steps have been taken to secure the reliefs, and no double tax provisions have been disregarded (*TIOPA 2010, s 303*).

Exemption of financing income: compliance

Appointment of authorised company

5.55 Statements of allocated exemptions have to be made by a reporting body. For this purpose, all UK companies within the worldwide group, instead of reporting jointly, may appoint one of their number as an authorised company to comply with the reporting obligations.

Where such an appointment is made, all the UK companies must give their written consent, signed by the appropriate person, being either a director, a company secretary or other authorised person. Companies that are dormant throughout the relevant period of account are relieved of this reporting responsibility for periods of account of the worldwide group ending on or after 17 July 2012 (*TIOPA 2010, ss 288, 289*).

For the purpose of reporting on allocated disallowances, all relevant companies within the worldwide group may also appoint their own reporting body, and similar rules apply (see **5.46**).

Statement of allocated exemptions: requirements

5.56 Within 12 months of the end of the accounting period concerned, HMRC must receive a statement of allocated exemptions for that period from the reporting body. HMRC will accept revised statements within 36 months of the end of the accounting period concerned. Revised statements must show how they differ from the previous statement (*TIOPA 2010, ss 290, 291*). All statements submitted must be signed by all companies concerned, or by the one reporting company if so appointed (*TIOPA 2010, s 292(2)*).

The statement of allocated exemptions must show:

- the tested expense amount;
- the available amount; and
- the total disallowed amount.

The statement must also list the companies to which the exemption applies, and specify the relevant details for each exempted amount; in the case of an amount under *TIOPA 2010, s 314A*, a proportion of the amount may be specified (*TIOPA 2010, s 292(3), (4), (5C)*).

For periods of account of the worldwide group ending on or after 17 July 2012, an amount may not be specified in relation to a company if it accrues at a time when the company is not a relevant group company (*TIOPA 2010, s 292(5A)*).

The relevant details in relation to a financing income amount are (*TIOPA 2010, s 292(5)*):

- either
  - which of the conditions (A, B, C or D) in *TIOPA 2010, s 314* is met, or
  - the fact that *TIOPA 2010, s 314A* applies (see **5.44**); and
- the relevant accounting period in which, were it not for the worldwide debt cap rules, the amount would be brought into account.

Statement of allocated exemptions: effect

5.57 Any financing income that is included in the statement of exemptions is non-taxable. If the statement is submitted after the company tax return, the company is treated as having amended its tax return (*TIOPA 2010, s 294*).

Failure to submit statement of allocated exemptions

5.58 If a reporting body fails to submit a statement of allocated exemptions or fails to submit a statement that complies with the requirements (see **5.56**), the financing income amount of each company is reduced to nil. However, for periods of account of the worldwide group ending on or after 17 July 2012, this does not apply to a financing income amount if it accrues to the company in question at a time when it is not a UK group company (*TIOPA 2010, s 296*).

If the total of the unrestricted reductions exceeds the lower of the total disallowed amount and the tested income amount, referred to as 'the excess', each unrestricted reduction is reduced by an amount as calculated by the formula:

$$\frac{UR \times X}{TUR}$$

where:

- UR is the unrestricted reduction in question
- TUR is the total of the unrestricted reductions
- X is 'the excess' referred to above.

Regulations may be issued to determine how the particular financing income amounts are to be reduced (*TIOPA 2010, s 297*).

Group treasury companies

> **Focus**
>
> The debt cap rules include special measures recognising the role of group treasury companies, and these were made more restrictive from 2012 onwards.

5.59 A group treasury company can elect, within three years after the end of the relevant accounting period, whether or not it requires the debt cap rules to apply.

A company is a group treasury company in the relevant period if:

- it is a member of the worldwide group;
- it undertakes treasury activities for the worldwide group in the relevant period (whether or not it also undertakes other activities); and
- at least 90% of the relevant income of the company for the relevant period is group treasury revenue.

For periods of account of a worldwide group beginning on or after 11 December 2012, a company is not a group treasury company unless it makes an election in respect of the relevant period (*TIOPA 2010, s 316(2)*). The same amended definition of group treasury company also applies for CFC purposes (see **20.27**).

For periods of account of the worldwide group ending on or after 17 July 2012, it is no longer necessary for all group treasury companies within a worldwide group to make an election under these provisions in order for any of them to be valid (*TIOPA 2010, s 316(4)*, as repealed by *FA 2012, Sch 5, para 11*).

Where an election has effect for a period of account of a worldwide group beginning on or after 11 December 2012, then (*TIOPA 2010, s 316(4)–(7)*):

- if, throughout the relevant period, all or substantially all of the activities undertaken by a group treasury company consist of treasury activities undertaken by it for the worldwide group, and all or substantially all of the assets and liabilities of the company relate to such activities,
  - the relevant amount, and all other amounts that are relevant amounts in respect of the group treasury company and the relevant period, are treated as not being a financing expense amount or a financing income amount of the group treasury company;
- otherwise,
  - those relevant amounts are treated as not being a financing expense amount, or a financing income amount of the group treasury company only to the extent that they relate (determined on a just and reasonable basis) to treasury activities undertaken by the company for the worldwide group.

Treasury activities (*TIOPA 2010, s 316(9)*) consist of:

- managing surplus deposits of money or overdrafts,
- making or receiving deposits of money,
- lending money,
- subscribing for or holding shares in another company which is a UK group company and a group treasury company,
- investing in debt securities, and
- hedging assets, liabilities, income or expenses.

Group treasury revenue is revenue arising from the treasury activities that a company undertakes for the group, but dividends or other distributions are not group treasury revenue unless received from a UK group treasury company (*TIOPA 2010, s 316(10), (11)*).

Intra-group short-term finance: financing expense

5.60 A paying company can elect for its intra-group short-term financing expense not to be treated as a financing expense amount. An election must be made jointly by both parties to the loan relationship, and can only be made if they are both members of the same worldwide group. The election must be made within 36 months of the end of the accounting period of the worldwide group to which the relevant amount relates. The election is irrevocable. If this election is made, the respective income of the recipient company is not treated as a financing income amount (*TIOPA 2010, ss 319, 320*).

A short-term relationship is essentially a money debt that cannot or does not last for longer than 12 months (*TIOPA 2010, s 321*). Regulations specify that a relationship is not short-term if any part of the funding is used for long-term purposes or the financing relates to a long-term aggregated finance arrangement (*Corporation Tax (Exclusion from Short-Term Loan Relationship) Regulations 2009, SI 2009/3313*).

Stranded non-trading deficits

Introduction

5.61 Where a group has a debt cap disallowance, it may become much more difficult to use non-trading loan relationships deficits that are being carried forward, because such deficits can only be used against non-trading profits of the same company. Without some special provision, deficits might become stranded in particular companies almost indefinitely.

Stranded deficits in non-trading loan relationships

5.62 A paying company may elect for the 'relevant amount' of a financing expense to be treated as non-deductible. An election must be made jointly by both parties to the loan relationship, and can only be made if they are both members of the same worldwide group. The election must be made within 36 months of the end of the accounting period of the worldwide group to which the relevant amount relates (*TIOPA 2010, s 322(1)–(4), (8)*).

The recipient must be resident in the UK or, if non-resident, be carrying on a trade in the UK through a permanent establishment. The recipient must carry forward an amount equal to or greater than the relevant amount as a non-trading deficit and set it off against non-trading profits of an accounting period that falls wholly or partly within the period of account of the worldwide group (*TIOPA 2010, s 322(5)–(7)*).

In these circumstances, the relevant amount is treated as not being financing income of the recipient (*TIOPA 2010, s 323*).

Stranded management expenses in non-trading loan relationships

5.63 A company may elect for the 'relevant amount' of a financing expense to be treated as non-deductible. An election must be made jointly by both parties to the loan relationship, and can only be made if they are both members of the same worldwide group. The election must be made within 36 months of the end of the accounting period of the worldwide group to which the relevant amount relates (*TIOPA 2010, s 324(1)–(4), (9)*).

The recipient must be a company with investment business. It must be resident in the UK or, if non-resident, be carrying on a trade in the UK through a permanent establishment. The recipient must carry forward an amount equal to or greater than the relevant amount as management expenses in respect of an accounting period that falls wholly or partly within the period of account of the worldwide group. Furthermore, the recipient's calculation of total profits for the relevant period for corporation tax purposes must result in a loss if the recipient's credit is not included in that calculation (*TIOPA 2010, s 324(5)–(8), (10)*).

In these circumstances, the relevant amount is treated as not being financing income of the recipient (*TIOPA 2010, s 325*).

Relevant accounting change

5.64 The debt cap rules may be amended by regulation if, on or after 17 July 2012, there is a 'relevant accounting change' resulting from a change in accounting standards. For this purpose, a relevant accounting change is a change in the way that a company is required or permitted to present or disclose amounts in its consolidated financial statements. A change in accounting standards includes the issue, revocation, amendment, recognition or withdrawal of recognition of accounting standards by an accounting body. The regulations may include an election. The regulations may apply to a pre-commencement period, which is defined as an accounting period or part of an accounting period that begins before the regulations are made, to enable the regulations to apply to early adopters of the changes in accounting standards if necessary (*TIOPA 2010, s 353AA*).

Under this power, the *Tax Treatment of Financing Costs and Income (Change of Accounting Standards: Investment Entities) Regulations 2015, SI 2015/662*, came into effect from 2 April 2015 for accounting periods beginning on or after that date, or earlier, and increase the measure of a worldwide group's gross finance costs by certain amounts relating to funding from sources external to the worldwide group. These are amounts which are taken into account in the calculation of a UK company's net finance expenses or income, but not in the amount of gross finance costs of the group as a whole for the purposes of the debt cap calculations, as a result of changes to international GAAP from 1 January 2014 or UK GAAP from 1 January 2015.

See **Chapter 26** regarding changes to UK GAAP.

Anti-avoidance

5.65 For periods of account of the worldwide group ending on or after 17 July 2012, anti-avoidance legislation applies if a large group attempts to remove itself from the application of the debt cap rules by ensuring that the group does not have any relevant group companies in the period of account. If a group does not have any relevant group companies, it is not a worldwide group for the purposes of the debt cap. However, if the following conditions are met:

- Condition A: during a period of account, the group entered into a scheme, and the main purpose (or one of the main purposes) for entering into the scheme or being a party to the scheme is to secure that the group does not contain any relevant group companies, and
- Condition B: the scheme is not an excluded scheme,

the debt cap applies to the group as it would have applied had the scheme mentioned in condition A not been entered into (*TIOPA 2010, s 305A*).

Widely drawn anti-avoidance provisions also exist to counteract schemes entered into:

- to avoid the debt cap regime by artificially keeping a period of account of the worldwide group out of *TIOPA 2010, s 261(1)* (the gateway test; see **5.34**) (*TIOPA 2010, s 306*);
- to reduce a disallowance by manipulating any or all of the tested expense amount, the tested income amount or the available amount (*TIOPA 2010, ss 307–310*); or
- to manipulate the rules on intra-group financing income (*TIOPA 2010, s 311*).

For all of these anti-avoidance measures, a 'scheme' includes any scheme, arrangements or understanding of any kind whatever, whether or not legally enforceable, involving a single transaction or two or more transactions. An 'excluded scheme' is one that is excluded by regulations (*TIOPA 2010, s 312*).

For HMRC guidance on the debt cap anti-avoidance provisions, see CFM92600 onwards.

From 4 December 2013, certain stipulated types of scheme are excluded from the debt cap anti-avoidance rules, but only in cases where the scheme is not notifiable by any member of the worldwide group under the DOTAS rules (*Tax*

Treatment of Financing Costs and Income (Excluded Schemes) Regulations 2013, SI 2013/2892; for details of DOTAS, see **25.32–25.41**).

ANTI-AVOIDANCE: TRANSFERS OF CORPORATE PROFITS

5.66 *FA 2014* introduced an anti-avoidance provision which targets situations where two companies within the same group are party to any scheme, arrangement or understanding (whether or not at the same time) which, in substance, transfers all or a significant part of the profits of any business within the group and the main purpose or one of the main purposes of the arrangements is to secure a tax advantage. For payments made on or after 19 March 2014 (where this applies), the profits of the transferring company are calculated for corporation tax purposes as if the transfer had not occurred (*CTA 2009, s 1305A*). HMRC guidance on the provision is contained in a Technical Note, updated in July 2014 and published at tinyurl.com/n25emrd.

This provision does not extend to certain intra-group anti-avoidance arrangements involving total return swaps or other derivative contracts, which are targeted by a separate anti-avoidance measure from 5 December 2013 (*CTA 2009, s 695A*).

Chapter 6

Investment business

SIGNPOSTS

- A basic investment business corporation tax computation (see **6.1–6.2**).
- Management expenses – including unallowable expenses, restricted deductions and group companies (see **6.3–6.20**).
- Investments in securities – including share loss relief, substantial shareholdings exemption, loan stocks and specialist investment companies (see **6.21–6.28**).
- Community investment tax relief – including accreditation, conditions and rules (see **6.29–6.41**).

INTRODUCTION

Focus

Relief for management expenses is available to most companies whose business consists wholly or partly of making investments. Management expenses can be relieved against current and future income, or used in a group relief claim. Special criteria determine the availability of this relief.

6.1 A company's income from its investment business is chargeable to corporation tax. There are special rules to relieve expenditure as 'management expenses'.

INVESTMENT INCOME

6.2 Typically, a company's investment income may come from a variety of sources, such as property (taxed as the profits of a property business), stocks (normally exempt), bonds (taxed under the loan relationships rules) or derivatives. A deduction for management expenses is available to companies with investment business.

Example 6.1—Investment business tax computation

Facts

XYZ Ltd draws up accounts to 31 March each year. Results for the year ended 31 March 2018 show the following:

	£000
Rents receivable	197
Interest receivable accrued (gross)	5
Chargeable gains	48
Management expenses	
• attributable to property	25
• attributable to management	40
Capital allowances	
• attributable to property	5
• attributable to management	1
Charitable charges on income	10

The company has unrelieved management expenses brought forward from previous accounting periods of £42,000.

Analysis

XYZ Ltd's corporation tax computation for the year ending 31 March 2018 is as follows:

	£000	*£000*
Profits of a property business		197
Less:		
Capital allowances	5	
Management expenses	25	
		(30)
		167
Loan relationship		5
Chargeable gains		48
		220

Less:		
Management expenses unrelieved brought forward for year		
• Unrelieved brought forward	42	
• For year	40	
Capital allowances	1	
		(83)
		137
Less charges		(10)
Total taxable profits		127

MANAGEMENT EXPENSES

Definitions

6.3 A company with investment business is a company whose business consists wholly or partly of making investments, except that a credit union is excluded (*CTA 2009, s 1218B*). Companies trading in the purchase and sale of investments are also excluded.

The meaning of 'business of making investments' was considered by the High Court in *CIR v Tyre Investment Trust Ltd* (1924) 12 TC 646, and, more recently, in *Cook v Medway Housing Society Ltd* [1997] STC 90. Both cases related to predecessor legislation concerning investment companies, but remain relevant (see HMRC Company Taxation Manual at CTM08050).

In calculating total profits, expenditure of a revenue nature is deductible as management expenses if it relates to the company's business of making investments. The investments must not be held for an unallowable purpose, and there is no deduction for capital expenditure. In general, if expenditure can be charged against the company's other income it cannot be included in management expenses, but there are exceptions (see **6.7**). Any apportionment of expenditure is to be done on a just and reasonable basis (*CTA 2009, s 1219*).

Unallowable purpose

6.4 Investments are held for an unallowable purpose during an accounting period if they are held for a purpose that is not a business or other commercial purpose of the company, or if they are held for the purpose of activities in respect of which the company is not within the charge to corporation tax. In this regard, investments are not held for a business or other commercial purpose if they are held directly or indirectly in consequence of, or otherwise in connection with, any arrangements for securing a tax advantage (*CTA 2009, s 1220*).

Expenses in connection with investments held for a non-business or non-commercial purpose, or for the purpose of activities not within the charge to corporation tax, are not chargeable as management expenses (*CTA 2009, s 1219(2)(b)*). Such activities will include:

- investments held by a company for social or recreational purposes;
- provision of services and facilities by a members' club to its members;
- UK branch expenses of a non-resident company in respect of activities not connected with the UK branch; and
- mutual trading activities.

However, a company that merely receives dividends from UK companies that are exempt from corporation tax in its hands will still be classed as a company with investment business, as will any company whose capital gains are covered by the substantial shareholding exemption or collective investment scheme gains exempt under *TCGA 1992, s 100(1)* (CTM08225).

Capital expenditure

6.5 Capital expenditure is specifically excluded from deductible management expenses (*CTA 2009, s 1219(3)(a)*). HMRC's view is that expenditure incurred on appraising the purchase or sale of an investment up to the decision point is revenue, and expenditure following the decision to acquire or dispose of an investment is capital (CTM08260).

In HMRC's view, success fees that are payable only when the deal goes through are likely, by their nature, to be capital and are therefore excluded from management expenses, but the contrary may be arguable in some instances. It is necessary to examine the facts of each case and to apply the same criteria to abortive expenditure. The capital costs associated with purchase and sale, whether successful or abortive, are not regarded as management expenses. In *Capital and National Trust Ltd v Golder* (1949) 31 TC 265 and *Sun Life Assurance Society v Davidson* (1957) 37 TC 330, brokerage and stamp duties were not allowed as management expenses (CTM08190).

Cost of asset valuations for accounts purposes (*Small Companies and Groups (Accounts and Directors' Report) Regulations 2008, SI 2008/409*, and *Large and Medium-sized Companies and Groups (Accounts and Reports) Regulations 2008, SI 2008/410*) are considered to be management expenses, but valuations related to the acquisition and disposal of assets are not (CTM08420).

A useful summary of relevant case law can be found in the case of *Howden Joinery Group Plc; Howden Joinery Ltd* [2014] UKFTT 257 (TC), which concerned whether certain payments and provisions were expenses of management and whether or not they were capital. ..

Capital expenditure on assets used for the purpose of management qualifies for capital allowances. The capital allowances are a management expense, and balancing charges are income of the investment business (*CAA 2001, ss 18, 253*; see **6.6**).

Management expenses deduction

> **Focus**
>
> The courts have drawn a distinction between costs of managing a company's investment business, which qualify as management expenses, and costs of managing the investments, which do not.

6.6 A deduction for management expenses for an accounting period is allowed against the total profits of the accounting period. No management expenses deduction is allowed for expenses that are otherwise deductible from total profits, or in calculating any component of total profits. No management expenses deduction is allowed for expenses of a capital nature, although capital allowances may be claimed on capital expenditure (*CTA 2009, s 1219*; see **6.5**).

The definition of the expression 'expenses of management' is specific and, unlike the *CTA 2009, s 54* 'wholly and exclusively' trading company criteria, it cannot extend to just about any general administration costs. It covers (*CTA 2009, s 1219(2)*) only expenses of management of a company's investment business so far as:

- they are in respect of so much of the company's investment business as consists of making investments, and
- the investments concerned are not held for an unallowable purpose during the accounting period to which the expenses are referable.

In *Dawsongroup plc v Revenue & Customs Comrs* [2010] EWHC 1061 (Ch), the High Court held that the costs of buying out the external shareholders when de-listing were not deductible as expenses of management because they related, not to the management of the company's investment business, but to the management of individual investments. In his judgment, Mann J (at para 71) stated:

> 'The expenditure was intended to improve the business in a broad sense. It did so by making sure that there were more assets within the business, and by giving the directors more freedom in making business decisions. Those decisions did not relate to the management of the investment business. They

> related to the management of the investments. The extra retained money would remain in the subsidiaries and make them more valuable, or would be applied in their growth, and again make them more valuable. Or they could be retained by the holding company and applied elsewhere to improve the investments. These characterisations demonstrate that the expenditure was not in order to manage the business; it was to improve the investments, or even (in substance, if not literally) to acquire more investments.'

Running costs in connection with managing the company's investment business, including reasonable directors' remuneration, staff salaries and pension contributions are allowed as management expenses (*LG Berry Investments Ltd v Attwooll* (1964) 41 TC 547). The same timing rules for remuneration payments apply as for trading profits (*CTA 2009, s 1249*; see **2.22**). Company secretarial costs, such as maintaining the share register, printing annual accounts and holding an AGM, are regarded as expenses of management. Entertaining expenditure and expenditure involving crime are specifically prohibited (*CTA 2009, ss 1298, 1304*).

No relief is given if the expenses are incurred for an unallowable purpose (**6.4**).

Management expenses are deductible from investment income of UK resident companies, and from that of non-resident companies with a permanent establishment in the UK from where the income is derived (*CTA 2009, s 1222*).

Management expenses are the amounts shown in the accounts prepared under GAAP. If the accounts are not prepared under GAAP or are not prepared at all, the management expenses are calculated as if GAAP had applied (*CTA 2009, ss 1225–1227*). Credits in respect of management expenses first reduce the management expenses for the year and are then brought into charge as other income. In practice, company expenditure may relate to a number of activities, in which case it should be allocated between them on a just and reasonable basis. See **Chapter 26** regarding changes to UK GAAP.

Amounts treated as expenses of management

6.7 The exclusion of capital expenditure from management expenses does not apply to any amounts that are treated as management expenses under any of the following provisions (*CTA 2009, s 1221(1)*):

- share incentive plans (*CTA 2009, s 985(3)*);
- costs of setting up an SAYE option scheme or an CSOP scheme (*CTA 2009, s 999(4)*);
- costs of setting up an employee share ownership trust (*CTA 2009, s 1000(3)*);
- employee share acquisitions: relief if shares acquired by employee or other person (*CTA 2009, s 1013(3)*);

- employee share acquisitions: relief if employee or other person acquires option to obtain shares (*CTA 2009, s 1021(3)*);
- employers' contributions to pension schemes (*FA 2004, s 196*); and
- manufactured dividend (*CTA 2010, s 814C*); before 1 January 2014, this referred to manufactured overseas dividends (*CTA 2010, s 791(4)*).

The following amounts are treated as management expenses, but only so far as they cannot be deducted from the company's other profits (*CTA 2009, ss 1219, 1221(2)–(3), 1232*):

- deduction for costs of setting up SAYE option scheme or CSOP scheme (*CTA 2009, s 999(4)*);
- deduction for costs of setting up employee share ownership trust (*CTA 2009, s 1000(3)*);
- excess capital allowances (*CTA 2009, s 1233*; see **3.3**);
- payment to employees for restrictive undertakings that are treated as employee earnings (*CTA 2009, s 1234*);
- employees seconded temporarily to charities and educational establishments (*CTA 2009, s 1235*);
- payroll deduction schemes (*CTA 2009, s 1236*);
- counselling and other outplacement services to an employee in connection with the cessation of employment (*CTA 2009, s 1237*);
- retraining courses (*CTA 2009, s 1238*);
- redundancy payments and approved contractual payments (*CTA 2009, ss 1239–1243*);
- additional payments (*CTA 2009, s 1242*);
- contributions to local enterprise organisations or urban regeneration companies (*CTA 2009, s 1244*); any related disqualifying benefit is taxed as a receipt of the investment business (*CTA 2009, s 1253*);
- payments to Export Credits Guarantee Department (*CTA 2009, s 1245*); and
- levies under *FSMA 2000* (*CTA 2009, s 1246*); any related repayment under *FSMA 2000* is taxed as a receipt of the investment business (*CTA 2009, s 1254*).

Deductions restricted

6.8 The following provisions prohibit or restrict the deduction of management expenses (*CTA 2009, s 1247*):

- employee benefit contributions (*CTA 2009, s 1290*);
- business entertainment and gifts (*CTA 2009, s 1298*);
- social security contributions (*CTA 2009, s 1302*);
- penalties, interest and VAT surcharges (*CTA 2009, s 1303*);
- crime-related payments (*CTA 2009, s 1304*);
- sums in connection with the cost of providing benefits under a registered pension scheme other than contributions paid by the employer (*FA 2004, s 200*);
- restriction of deduction for non-contributory provision (*FA 2004, s 246*);
- employers' contributions: power to restrict relief (*FA 2004, s 196A*);
- expenses in connection with arrangements for securing a tax advantage (*CTA 2009, s 1248*);
- unpaid remuneration, as far as not paid within nine months of the end of the account period for which due (*CTA 2009, ss 1249, 1250*); and
- car hire (*CTA 2009, s 1251*; see **2.17**).

Credits that reverse debits

6.9 Credits for management expenses first reduce the management expenses for the year and any excess management expenses brought forward from a previous year; the remainder is then brought into charge as taxable income (*CTA 2009, ss 1229, 1230*).

Income from a source not charged to tax

6.10 A company's management expenses are reduced by any untaxed income that the company may have in connection with its investment business (*CTA 2009, s 1222*).

Group companies

6.11 Group companies often recharge other group members with expenses such as administration costs. Provided the allocation is done on a reasonable basis, this will result in each group member deducting its share of administration costs from its relevant trade or activity (see **2.53**; HMRC Business Income Manual at BIM42140; CTM08180).

Management activities

6.12 Management expenses cannot be claimed unless the company is within the charge to corporation tax. This would, for example, exclude a mutual trading company, as its profits are not chargeable to corporation tax (see **2.87**). In order for a company to be within the charge to corporation tax, it must have an activity, otherwise it would be totally dormant. On the assumption that the company had no other business, activities that would be regarded as sufficient to bring a company with investment business within the charge to corporation tax would be the holding of shares in another non-dormant company or the disposal of an asset resulting in a chargeable gain or allowable loss (CTM08225). The management expenses claim for the year and the management expenses carried forward are included in the company's corporation tax return.

Insurance premiums

6.13 Premiums paid on assets used in the management of the company are considered to be management expenses, but premiums paid on the insurance of the investments are not. This is because the view is taken that the expenses incurred must relate to management of the investment business, and not to general administration (CTM08320). Depending on the circumstances, such premiums may be classed as capital expenditure.

Self-assessment

6.14 Under self-assessment, a company with investment business is required to show totals of its investment income and its management expenses claim on form CT600 within its corporation tax return. The company's corporation tax computation would normally show supporting details of the company's income and gains from its investment activity, and details of the management expenses claimed.

Management expenses set-off

Set-off against current year profits

6.15 Management expenses are allowed as a deduction from the company's total profits for the accounting period in which the expense is incurred (*CTA 2009, s 1219*). The whole of the expense must be deducted as far as possible against current year profits with any excess being automatically carried over and treated as a management expense of the subsequent accounting period (*CTA 2009, s 1223*). The deduction against current year profits is given priority over any other deduction allowable against total profits (*CTA 2009, s 1219(1A)*).

Carry forward of excess management expenses

6.16 Where management expenses cannot be wholly deducted against total profits, the excess is carried forward and treated as a management expense of the subsequent accounting period (*CTA 2009, s 1223*).

However, for accounting periods beginning on or after 1 April 2017, tax relief for carry forward expenses is no longer automatic, but must be claimed. The claim must be made within two years after the end of the period in question or within such further period as HMRC may allow (*CTA 2009, ss 1223(3B), (3D)*). Furthermore, there is no longer a requirement to deduct the full amount which is carried forward. The company can elect to relieve only part of the amount or even decide not to make a deduction for the period in question, with any unrelieved amount being carried forward to later accounting periods (*CTA 2009, s 1223(3C)*).

The requirement to deduct carry forward management expenses in priority to other deductions is also abolished for accounting periods beginning on or after 1 April 2017 (*CTA 2009, s 1223(3E)*).

However, carry forward expenses are subject to the restrictions under the corporate loss rules which have effect for accounting periods beginning on or after 1 April 2017. These rules limit the total amount of losses that can be carried forward to £5 million plus 50% of profits in excess of that figure, with any surplus losses being carried forward to the next accounting period. The limit applies not to the total of all losses from a variety of sources such as trading losses, property losses, non-trading loan relationship deficits, management expenses, non-trading deficits on intangible assets as well as deductions for carry-forward group relief. The restrictions apply to losses carried forward from periods prior to 1 April 2017 as well as losses incurred on or after that date (*CTA 2009, s 1223(7)* and *CTA 2010, Part 7ZA* see **Chapter 4).**

For the purpose of applying the above rules, an accounting period that straddles 1 April 2017 is treated as two accounting periods, one ending on 31 March 2017 and another starting on 1 April 2017, with profits and losses apportioned between the two (*F(No 2)A 2017, Sch 4 para 190*).

Group relief claims

6.17 A company may surrender, as group relief, its surplus management expenses for the accounting period, ie only those that exceed its gross profits for the period (*CTA 2010, ss 99, 103*).

For accounting periods before 1 April 2017, the relief is not available to any amounts that have been carried forward from a previous year (*CTA 2010, s 103(2)*).

For accounting periods beginning on or after this date, carry-forward expenses can be group relieved, provided that (*CTA 2010, Pt 5A, ss 188BB–188BD, 188BF,* see **Chapter 5**):

- the expense has not been carried forward from a pre-1 April 2017 accounting period;
- the company's investment business has not become small or negligible before the beginning of the surrender period; and
- the company still has income producing assets at the end of that period.

Where a group relief claim is made, the order of set-off is first qualifying charitable donations, then UK property business losses, then management expenses, and finally a non-trading loss on intangible fixed assets (*CTA 2010, s 105(4)*: see **5.10**).

Example 6.2—Set-off of management expenses

Facts

Kappa Ltd owns 90% of the ordinary share capital of Lambda Ltd. Kappa Ltd is the group investment holding company.

Both companies prepare accounts to 31 December each year.

Results for the year ended 31 December 2019 are as follows:

	Kappa Ltd	*Lambda Ltd*
	£000	*£000*
Trading profits		50
Profits of a property business	10	20
Loan relationship	40	30
Qualifying charitable donations		2
Management expenses for the year (*CTA 2009, s 1219(1)*)	100	
Management expenses brought forward (*CTA 2009, s 1223(3)*)	5	

Analysis

Kappa Ltd's corporation tax computation, after management expenses and group relief, is as follows:

	Kappa Ltd
	£000
Management expenses	
Management expenses for the year (*CTA 2009, s 1219(1)*)	100
Management expenses brought forward (*CTA 2009, s 1223(3)*)	5
	105
Excess management expenses for group relief	
Management expenses for the year (*CTA 2009, s 1219(1)*)	100
Less:	
• Profits of a property business	(10)
• Loan relationship	(40)
Excess management expenses for group relief	50
Group relief	(50)
	0
Excess management expenses brought forward and carried forward	5
Group relief (carry forward)*	(5)
	0

Lambda Ltd corporation tax computation after group relief is as follows:

	Lambda Ltd
	£000
Trading profits	50
Profits of a property business	20
Loan relationship	30
	100
Less charges	(2)
Total profits	98
Group relief (management expenses)	(50)
Total taxable profits before management expenses carried forward	48
Carry-forward group relief (management expenses)*	(5)
Total taxable profits	43

*Group relief is available for the brought-forward management expenses of £5,000 only to the extent that this amount was incurred on or after

1 April 2017. This example assumes that the entire amount was incurred on or after this date.

If only part of the £5,000 was incurred on or after 1 April 2017, then only part is available for group relief; the remainder can only be set against Kappa's future profits. No group relief is available for the brought-forward management expenses if the entire amount was incurred prior to 1 April 2017.

Anti-avoidance

6.18 Claims to relieve management expenses are subject to TAAR-related legislation which counteracts loss related tax advantages. This legislation applies to tax advantages arising in respect of accounting periods beginning on or after 1 April 2017 and affects current year and carry forward claims as well as claims for group relief (*F(No 2)A 2017, s 19*).

Companies ceasing to trade

6.19 Practical considerations may arise when a company ceases to trade. In *Jowett v O'Neill & Brennan Construction Ltd* (1998) 70 TC 566, the High Court held that the holding of a static bank account after trading had ceased was not enough to prevent a company from being regarded as 'dormant'. In such circumstances, it would be necessary for a company to show that it intends to continue with an investment activity if it wishes to claim management expenses for that period. The same criteria will apply to a company that is in liquidation. It will be necessary to show that it is 'making investments'.

Pensions paid to former employees by a company that ceases to trade, and becomes a company with investment business, are not expenses of management if the former employees were not at any time employees of the company after it ceased to trade. This is because the pension payments relate to the former trade and not to the investment activity.

Where the investment business of an employer making the payment has ceased, the payment, if it is allowable, will be treated as paid on the last day of the business and allowed accordingly (CTM08345).

Restriction on management expenses

6.20 Management expenses are restricted where there is a change of ownership and any of the following occur (*CTA 2010, Pt 14, Ch 2A, 3–5*):

(A) there is a major change in the nature or conduct of the business which takes place within any of the following periods beginning three years before the change in ownership:

(a) the period is six years where either the change in ownership or the change in the business occur before 1 April 2017;

(b) in all other cases, the period is eight years;

(B) prior to the change in ownership, the scale of the company's activities has become small or negligible, with no subsequent revival prior to the change;

(C) after the change in ownership, there is a significant increase in the company's capital;

(D) none of A, B and C apply, and the company becomes subject to a tax charge on the disposal or realisation of an asset which was:

(a) acquired after the change in ownership from another group member on a tax neutral basis (either under *TCGA 1992, s 171* for capital assets or *CTA 2009, s 775* for intangibles); and

(b) disposed of or realised within three years after the change in ownership where the change occurs before 1 April 2017 and. five years where the change occurs on or after that date.

The restrictions apply to limit the carry forward of management expenses, whether in whole or in part. From 1 April 2017, there are also restrictions on group relief for management expenses carried forward (*CTA 2010, Pt 14, Chs 2C, 2D,*).

A change of ownership occurs where:

(i) a single person acquires more than half the ordinary share capital of the company; or

(ii) two or more persons each acquire a holding of 5% or more of the ordinary share capital of the company, and those holdings together amount to more than half the ordinary share capital of the company; or

(iii) two or more persons each acquire a holding of the ordinary share capital of a company, and those holdings together amount to more than half the ordinary share capital of the company. Holdings of less than 5% are disregarded unless it is in addition to an existing holding and the two holdings together amount to 5% or more of the ordinary share capital (*CTA 2010, s 719*); or

(iv) in certain cases, there is also a change in ownership of a company C if, as a result of a person acquiring ordinary share capital in C, another company A becomes a fellow group member of C, and provided that both companies are UK related (*CTA 2010, s 719(4A), Chs 2B–2D*).

A company is UK related if it is either UK resident, or non-resident but carrying on a trade in the UK through a permanent establishment (*CTA 2010, ss 188CE, 188CJ,*).

The 5% threshold means there is no need to examine very small shareholdings, particularly those of public companies. However, note that it is possible for more than half of a company's shares to change hands and yet not trigger a change of ownership if the shares are purchased by a number of unconnected persons, each of whom acquires a holding of less than 5%.

From 1 April 2014, there is a significant increase in a company's capital where it increases by at least £1 million *and* 25%; up to 31 March 2014, there was a significant increase where the capital increased by at least £1 million *or* 100% (*CTA 2010, ss 688–691*, before and after amendment of *s 688* by *FA 2014, s 37*).

A major change in the nature or conduct of the business includes a major change in the nature of the investments held, even if that change was the result of a gradual process which began before the period of six years within which the change has to take place (*CTA 2010, s 677(5)*).

INVESTMENTS IN SHARES OR LOAN STOCK

Investment in other companies

6.21 An investment in another company will bring about share ownership for the company. The subsequent disposal of the shares will bring about a chargeable gain or capital loss (see **Chapter 16**). Income (if any) from the shares will take the form of dividend receipts. UK dividends have, in effect, already borne corporation tax and are not taxed on the recipient company (see **18.40–18.50**), and foreign dividends are also generally exempt (see **18.51–18.57**).

There are special reliefs for share disposals, as follows:

- share loss relief on shares in unquoted trading companies (see **6.22**), and
- substantial shareholdings exemption (see **6.23** and **16.18–16.23**).

There are also certain types of companies whose business is to invest in other companies, and which enjoy special tax status (see **6.28**).

Share loss relief

6.22 In certain specific circumstances, an investment company may claim 'share loss relief' against income for capital losses arising on the disposal of shares in unquoted qualifying trading companies, which had been subscribed for by the investment company. The loss, which is calculated under normal chargeable gains rules, may be set off against income (before management expenses and charges) of the same and (in some cases) preceding accounting periods (*CTA 2010, s 71*).

This share loss relief is available to an investment company, whether or not it is a close investment-holding company (a status which ceases to have relevance for corporation tax from 1 April 2015, see **10.29–10.31**). The relief must be claimed, in writing, within two years after the end of the accounting period in which the loss was incurred.

The company obtains relief for its capital loss by set-off against its income chargeable to corporation tax. The loss relief is set first against income of the accounting period in which the loss is incurred. If a balance of the loss remains unused, this can then be set against income of previous accounting periods ending within the 12 months immediately preceding the accounting period in which the loss was incurred. Where an accounting period falls partly within and partly outside the 12-month period, only a proportion of its income can be relieved.

The loss relief against income is given before deduction of charges on income and expenses of management. Where loss relief is given under these provisions, the loss is ignored for the purpose of corporation tax on chargeable gains (see **Chapter 16**).

The main conditions to be satisfied in order to qualify for share loss relief are as follows (*CTA 2010, s 69*):

- The company subscribing for shares and incurring the capital loss must, generally, have been an investment company for the whole of the previous six years.
- The shares subscribed for must be share capital of a qualifying trading company as defined in *CTA 2010, ss 78–85*.
- The investment company must not control the trading company, the two companies must not be under common control, and the two companies cannot be members of the same group.

For the purposes of share loss relief:

- a trading company (*CTA 2010, s 79*) is one which:
  - ignoring any incidental purposes, exists wholly for the purpose of carrying on one or more qualifying trades, or
  - is a parent company and the business of the group does not consist wholly or substantially in the carrying on of non-qualifying activities;
- and an investment company (*CTA 2010, s 90(1)*) is one:
  - whose business consists wholly or mainly in the making of investments, and

– which derives the principal part of its income from the making of investments.

A share loss relief claim may also be made where the necessary conditions are met and an asset consisting of subscribed shares in an unquoted qualifying company has become of negligible value (*TCGA 1992, s 24*; see **16.5**).

Substantial shareholdings exemption

> **Focus**
>
> The substantial shareholdings exemption provides that a gain on a disposal by a company of shares in another company (or an interest in shares, or certain assets related to shares) will not be a chargeable gain, provided certain stringent conditions are met. The exemption is aimed primarily at corporate holdings in trading ventures. However, from 1 April 2017, the relief is extended, to cover investments in non-trading companies held indirectly by qualifying institutional investors.

6.23 From 1 April 2017, there are effectively two sets of tax relief from chargeable gains available to a company holding a substantial shareholding in another company (*TCGA 1992, Sch 7AC* and **16.18–16.23**):

- The main substantial shareholding exemption ('SSE') which applies to corporate investors holding a significant stake in a trading company or group. This exemption has been available since 1 April 2002.
- A relief for companies holding a significant stake in a non-trading company, where qualifying institutional investors ('QIIs') hold at least a 25% interest in the investing company (the 'QII exemption'). This relief is available for disposals made on or after 1 April 2017.

For a holding to be substantial, either one of two conditions must be satisfied ((*TCGA 1992, Sch 7AC, paras 8, 8A*):

- The investing company must hold a stake of at least 10% of the ordinary share capital of the investee company, together with the associated entitlement to profits available for distribution and assets on a winding up.
- From 1 April 2017, it is also possible to hold less than a 10% interest if QIIs hold at least 25% of the investing company. In these circumstances relief will apply if the investing company has invested at least £20 million in acquiring shares or an interest in shares in the investee company. This condition applies equally to the main SSE exemption (see **6.24**) and the QII exemption (see **6.25**).

The main SSE exemption provides a complete exemption. Provided that all the relevant conditions are met, any gains arising on such holdings are exempt, while losses are unallowable.

The QII exemption, which applies from 1 April 2017, provides a partial or complete exemption on disposal, depending on the size of the stake in the investing company held by QIIs.

The main SSE exemption

6.24 The exemption is aimed primarily at holdings in trading ventures. The main conditions are that:

- for disposals made before 1 April 2017, the investing company must be a trading company or member of a trading group (*TCGA 1992, Sch 7AC, para 18*, repealed by *F(No 2)A 2017, s 27(2)* for disposals made on or after that date;
- the investee company must be a trading company or the holding company of a trading group (*TCGA 1992, Sch 7AC, para 19*); and
- the investing company or group must have held the stake in the investee company for a continuous 12-month period within the previous two years for disposals made before 1 April 2017, and within the previous six years for disposals made on or after that date (*TCGA 1992, Sch 7AC, paras 7–8A*).

Until 1 April 2017, it was not generally possibly for an investment company to qualify for the main SSE exemption. However, there was a narrow exception where the company was part of a wider trading group. This is because it was sufficient for the investee company to be a *member* of a trading group – unlike the conditions for the investee company, there was no requirement for this company to trade in its own right, or to be the holding company of a trading group.

An example where an investment company could benefit from the SSE is where the company was the venture capital arm of a banking group, holding stakes in high-growth enterprises. The company itself was not a trading company, but it benefited from the trading status of the wider group of which it was a member.

From 1 April 2017, the requirement that the investing company satisfy the trading conditions is withdrawn (*TCGA 1992, Sch 7AC, para 18*, repealed by *F(No 2)A 2017, s 27(2)*).

The QII exemption

6.25 From 1 April 2017, the QII exemption is available for companies holding substantial shareholdings in non-trading companies. In order to qualify, the investing company must itself have a significant proportion of its own ordinary share capital in the ownership of 'qualifying institutional investors' (QIIs). (*TCGA 1992, Sch 7AC, para 3A*).

The relief makes sense when one considers that the investing company is effectively a vehicle through which QIIs hold their stake in the investee company. A QII is normally tax exempt in its own right and would not expect to pay tax on disposals of directly held investments. The QII exemption affords a complete or partial relief when the disposal is made by an intermediate (investing) company.

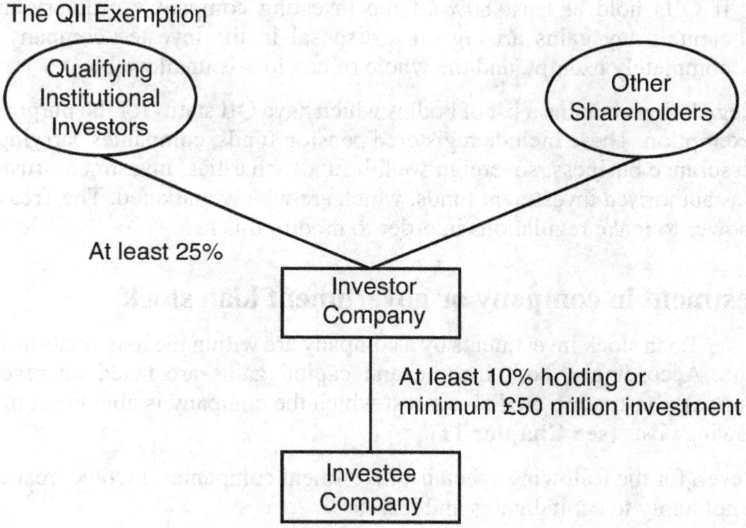

In most cases, the QII exemption is likely to be claimed by unquoted companies. The relief does not apply if the investing company is listed on a recognised stock exchange unless it is also a qualifying institutional investor or a qualifying UK REIT. In the latter circumstances the investing company already has the benefit of a separate tax exemption by virtue of its special status – the QII exemption may therefore appear to be redundant. However, there may be special instances where a listed investing company is unable to rely on its special tax status – in these circumstances, the QII exemption may offer an alternative relief if the relevant conditions are satisfied. For example, a REIT cannot claim an exemption from chargeable gains on equity holdings, as these do not form part of the company's property rental assets (*CTA 2010, s 535*; see **7.27**).

As with the main exemption, the investing company must have held the stake in the investee company for a continuous 12-month period within the previous six years (*TCGA 1992, Sch 7AC, para 7*).

The stake in the investing company held by QIIs (there can be more than one) must be at least 25% in order to benefit from a partial relief, and 80% for a complete exemption. In particular:

- If the holding is at least 25% but less than 80% of the investing company's ordinary share capital, the amount of any gain that is taxable is reduced in proportion to the percentage of ordinary share capital held by QIIs. For example, if QIIs hold 75% of the investing company, the latter's gain on disposing of a holding in the investee company is reduced by 75%. Accordingly, the investing company will only pay tax on 25% of the gain. A similar rule applies to reduce allowable losses.
- If QIIs hold at least 80% of the investing company's ordinary share capital, any gains arising on a disposal in the investee company are completely exempt, and the whole of any loss is unallowable.

The legislation contains a list of bodies which have QII status for the purpose of the exemption. These include registered pension funds, companies carrying on life assurance business, sovereign wealth funds, charities, investment trusts as well as authorised investment funds, which are widely marketed. The Treasury has power to make regulations in order to modify this list.

Investment in company or government loan stock

6.26 Loan stock investments by a company are within the loan relationships regime. Accordingly, both income and capital gains are taxed on revenue account as non-trading credits, against which the company is able to set off its borrowing costs (see **Chapter 11**).

However, for the following specialist investment companies, income treatment does not apply to capital gains and losses:

- investment trusts (*CTA 2009, s 395*);
- venture capital trusts (*CTA 2009, s 396*); and
- authorised investment funds such as authorised unit trusts and open-ended investment companies (*Authorised Investment Funds (Tax) Regulations 2006, SI 2006/964, reg 10*).

These companies all enjoy a tax exemption on chargeable gains (*TCGA 1992, s 100*; see also **6.28**). This exemption includes capital gains arising on debt investments which continue to be taxed as capital rather than as income profits under the general loan relationships rules.

Investments in derivatives

6.27 A derivative is a contract between two or more parties whose value is based on the value of an underlying asset or a variable such as stock indices or interest rates. Common examples of derivatives include:

- an option to purchase a specific amount of shares in a public company at a specified price (an 'option');
- a contract made by an airline company to purchase a specific amount of oil at a date in the future, but at a specified price (a 'future');
- a contract whereby, at certain specified dates, one party agrees to pay to the other party a fixed rate of interest on a notional sum of money, while the other party agrees to pay a floating rate of interest (an 'interest swap').

Companies invest in derivatives for a variety of reasons. They may be acquired in order to provide protection against certain commercial risks, or they can be acquired as investments in their own right.

For companies, derivatives are taxed under the legislation set out in *CTA 2009, Part 7*. The legislation applies to any contract satisfying the following criteria (*CTA 2009, s 576(1)*):

- the contract is either an option, a future or a contract for differences (a 'swap') (*CTA 2009, ss 577, 580–582*);
- the contract is treated as a derivative for accounting purposes under FRS 25 (*CTA 2009, s 579*); and
- it is not on the excluded list due to the nature of its subject matter (*CTA 2009, s 589*).

As with loan relationships, the general rule is that all receipts and expenses relating to derivatives are calculated in accordance with generally accepted accounting practice and taxed on revenue account (*CTA 2009, ss 571, 595*). However, there are various exceptions to this rule.

Firstly, for the following specialist investment companies, income treatment does not apply to capital gains and losses:

- investment trusts (*CTA 2009, s 637*);
- venture capital trusts (*CTA 2009, s 638*); and
- authorised investment funds such as authorised unit trusts and open-ended investment companies (*Authorised Investment Funds (Tax) Regulations 2006, SI 2006/964, reg 11*).

These companies all enjoy a tax exemption on chargeable gains (*TCGA 1992, s 100*; see also **6.28**). This exemption includes capital gains arising on derivative investments which continue to be taxed as capital rather than as income profits under the general rules.

Secondly, capital gains treatment applies to certain types of contract falling within the following categories:

- Contracts which are taxed under the derivatives legislation but with the general rule being disapplied for capital gains. These contracts include derivatives relating to land and tangible moveable property, property return swaps and certain derivatives embedded within a loan relationship such as convertible bonds (*CTA 2009, Chapter 7*).

- Certain types of contract which would otherwise satisfy the necessary conditions are taken out of the derivatives legislation altogether. These contracts include contracts relating to intangibles and shares in a company (*CTA 2009, s 589*).

The effect of these exceptions is to avoid any mismatch between the company's tax position and any economic profit or loss which may arise on payments made under a derivative.

Example 6.3—Using derivatives to hedge a share portfolio

Willis Shepherd Ltd ('Willis Shepherd') is a company whose business consists of investing in smaller, listed companies on both AIM and the London Stock Exchange. The company has acquired a holding of 100,000 ordinary shares in Blue Moon Enterprises plc ('Blue Moon') for a sum of £100,000 at a price of £1 per share.

In order to protect its investment, Willis Shepherd pays £10,000 to take out a put option on Blue Moon. If exercised, the terms of the option require the counterparty to pay a sum equal to the fall in value (if any) of the company's holding in Blue Moon.

The Blue Moon shares subsequently fall to 70p per share, and Willis Shepherd exercises the option. At the same time, it sells its entire holding in Blue Moon for £70,000.

	£	£
Sale of shares		
Sale proceeds	70,000	
Purchase price	(100,000)	
Loss		(30,000)
Exercise of option		
Option proceeds (£1 – £0.70) × 100,000	30,000	
Option price	(10,000)	
Profit		20,000
Overall profit/loss		(10,000)

The company has made an economic loss of £10,000, which is also equal to its loss for tax purposes. This is because the profit on the option is taxed as a capital gain which is relieved entirely by the loss on the shares. This set-off would not be permitted if the profit on the option were taxed as income under the general rules governing derivative transactions. In these circumstances, the company would have been taxed on a profit of £20,000, in spite of having made an overall loss of £10,000.

Specialist investment companies

6.28 There are two types of company that specialise in investing in shares or securities, both of which have been granted special tax treatment:

- investment trusts, which are companies that are listed on the London Stock Exchange – until 2012, they were required to invest mainly in shares or securities, but are now permitted to invest in a wider class of alternative assets, such as property, commodities and gold bullion; and
- venture capital trusts (VCTs), which are also listed on the London Stock Exchange, and are companies that invest in smaller, high-growth companies.

Both types of company are aimed at retail investors in order to provide the latter with a diversified portfolio of investments. The work of selecting and managing the investments is normally undertaken by a fund manager.

Both investment trusts and VCTs are exempt from corporation tax on chargeable gains (*TCGA 1992, s 100*). The exemption permits the fund manager to make investment decisions which are not distorted by tax considerations. Furthermore, the retention of gains within the company permits further investment with funds that would otherwise be unavailable, thereby boosting investment returns.

In order to qualify for special status, both investment trusts and VCTs are required to satisfy strict conditions. These include the requirement to be listed on a recognised investment exchange, to distribute at least 85% of income profits, and, for VCTs, conditions regarding the companies making up the investment portfolio. The rules for investment trusts are contained in *CTA 2010, Ch 3A* and the *Investment Trust (Approved Company) (Tax) Regulations 2011, SI 2011/2999.* The rules for VCTs are contained in *ITA 2007, Pt 3, Ch 3.*

For VCTs, individual shareholders are entitled to a variety of tax incentives, provided the relevant conditions are satisfied (see *Venture Capital Tax Reliefs*, 2nd Edition, Bloomsbury Professional).

COMMUNITY INVESTMENT TAX RELIEF (CITR)

Eligibility for tax relief

> **Focus**
>
> The CITR scheme aims to encourage investment in disadvantaged communities by giving tax relief to investors who back businesses and other enterprises in such areas by investing in accredited community development finance institutions (CDFIs).

6.29 Companies that make investments in an accredited community development finance institution (CDFI) may obtain community investment tax relief (CITR) (*CTA 2010, s 219(1)*). The investor company itself cannot be a CDFI (*CTA 2010, s 233*). There must be no tax avoidance purposes (*CTA 2010, s 235*). The investment may take the form of a secured or unsecured loan, or a subscription to a securities or share issue, but not the form of an overdraft (*CTA 2010, s 221*).

The relief is given over a five-year period, beginning with the day the investment is made (*CTA 2010, s 223*).

For investments made by companies on or after 1 April 2013, CITR was changed from notifiable EU state aid to a *de minimis* unnotified state aid. To meet the conditions of this, the amount that a company can invest in CDFIs and other unnotified state aid is limited to no more than the equivalent of €200,000 in any three-year period, and earlier references to equity investments as 'relevant investments' have been removed (*Community Investment Tax Relief (Accreditation of Community Development Finance Institutions) Regulations 2003, SI 2003/96*, as amended by *SI 2013/417*). For the purpose of the €200,000 limit, account must be taken of all CITR and other *de minimis* aid to which the company is entitled on or after 1 April 2013.

For further guidance, see tinyurl.com/ng3laot and tinyurl.com/pd8w2k2.

The relief

6.30 The investing company must claim on form CT600 for its corporation tax liability to be reduced by the smaller of 5% of the invested amount and the amount which reduces its corporation tax liability to zero. The claim can be made for the accounting period in which the investment is made and in each of the following four accounting periods (*CTA 2010, s 220*). The company must have received a tax relief certificate relating to the investment from the CDFI.

For accounting periods beginning on or after 1 April 2013, unused CITR can be carried forward to a later accounting period in which the investor is entitled to relief in respect of the investment (*CTA 2010, s 220A*).

CDFI accreditation

6.31 The intending CDFI must apply for accreditation in order to provide funding to encourage business growth by SMEs in disadvantaged communities. SMEs in disadvantaged communities include both SMEs located in disadvantaged areas, and SMEs owned or operated by, or designed to serve, members of disadvantaged groups (*SI 2003/96*; *SI 2008/383*).

No claim can be made unless the company is an accredited CDFI (*CTA 2010, s 238*). If the investor company itself becomes a CDFI, no claim is possible (*CTA 2010, s 239*). When granted, a period of accreditation will last for three years (*ITA 2007, s 341*).

For an accreditation period starting on or after 1 April 2013, a CDFI must notify the Secretary of State in writing of the date when the first investment is made in the CDFI in that period, no later than three months after that date (the 'first investment date'). Regulations stipulate the proportions of the investment fund to be invested by the CDFI in relevant investments in qualifying enterprises at the first, second and third anniversaries of the first investment date and at all times thereafter. The first investment date is also used as the reference point for periodic reporting purposes.

Conditions to be satisfied in relation to loans

6.32 There are conditions related to loans. First, the CDFI either receives the full amount of the loan on the investment date, or the draw down period must commence no later than 18 months after the investment date. Secondly, the loan must not carry any present or future rights for conversion to shares or securities redeemable within the five-year period beginning with the day the investment is made. Thirdly, the loan must not be repayable during the first two years; no more than 25% of the loan outstanding at the end of the first two years can be repaid in the third year; no more than 50% of the loan capital can be repaid before the end of the fourth year; and no more than 75% of the loan capital can be repaid before the end of the loan period. Other normal commercial conditions may be imposed (*CTA 2010, s 226*).

Conditions to be satisfied in relation to securities

6.33 Any securities issued must be subscribed wholly in cash and be fully paid for on the investment date. The securities must not carry any present or future right to be redeemed within the five-year period beginning with the day the investment is made, or any present or future right to be converted into or exchanged for a loan which is, or securities, shares or other rights which are, redeemable within that period (*CTA 2010, s 227*).

Conditions to be satisfied in relation to shares

6.34 Shares must be subscribed wholly in cash, and be fully paid up on the investment date. In addition, akin to the rule for securities above, the shares must not be redeemable *per se* or redeemable in exchange for a loan for other securities within the five-year period beginning with the day the investment is made. Shares are not fully paid up on the investment date if there is any undertaking to pay cash to the CDFI at a future date in connection with the acquisition of the shares (*CTA 2010, s 228*).

Tax relief certificates

6.35 Tax relief certificates may be issued by the CDFI in respect of retail investments made in the CDFI in that period with an aggregate value exceeding £10 million, and in any other case, in respect of investments made in the CDFI in that period with an aggregate value exceeding £20 million (*CTA 2010, s 229*). The investment consists of the amount of the loan or the investment in shares. There is a £3,000 penalty for any tax relief certificates issued fraudulently or negligently.

There can be no pre-arranged protection against the normal commercial risks that would be associated with such an investment, other than an arrangement that might reasonably be expected if the investment were made by a banking business – eg where a loan by an investor to a CDFI is secured by means of a charge on a property owned by the CDFI (*CTA 2010, s 230*; HMRC Community Investment Tax Relief Manual CITM4050).

At any time during the five-year period beginning with the day the investment is made, the investor or a connected party must not control the CDFI. When considering control, all future rights and powers are attributed to the investor, and the investor must be the sole beneficial owner of the investment or loan repayment entitlement when it is made (*CTA 2010, s 231*).

Investment

6.36 As regards securities or shares, the invested amount for a tax year or accounting period is the amount subscribed by the investor for the securities or shares. The shares must have been held by the investor throughout the accounting period (*CTA 2010, s 237*).

The amount of a loan investment is determined according to its average capital balance. The average capital is the mean of the daily balances of capital outstanding during the period. The investment is as follows:

- for the tax year or accounting period in which the investment date falls, the average capital balance for the first year of the five-year period beginning with the day the investment is made;
- for the tax year or accounting period in which the first anniversary of the investment date falls, the average capital balance for the second year of that five-year period;
- for any subsequent tax year or accounting period:
  - the average capital balance for the period of one year beginning with the anniversary of the investment date falling in the tax year or accounting period concerned; or
  - if less, the average capital balance for the period of six months beginning 18 months after the investment date (*CTA 2010, s 222*).

The loan must be outstanding at the end of the accounting period concerned (*CTA 2010, s 236*).

Where more than one investment is made, the relief is attributed pro rata (*CTA 2010, s 240*).

Withdrawal of relief

6.37 If the relief is withdrawn or reduced for any reason, an income assessment will be made on the company for the accounting period for which the relief was obtained (*CTA 2010, ss 254, 255*). An assessment may be made at any time not more than six years after the end of the accounting period for which the relief was obtained; but, if a loss of tax is brought about deliberately by the company or a related person, this period is extended to 20 years (*FA 2008, Sch 39, para 48*).

In the case of a loan, the relief is withdrawn if, within the five-year period beginning with the day the investment is made, the investor disposes of the whole or part of the loan (*CTA 2010, s 243*) otherwise than by a 'permitted disposal', ie:

- a distribution on dissolution or winding up of the CDFI;
- a deemed disposal on a claim under *TCGA 1992, s 24(1)* (entire loss, destruction, dissipation or extinction of asset); or
- a disposal made after the CDFI has ceased to be accredited.

For this purpose, full or partial repayment of the loan is not treated as a disposal (but see **6.38**).

In the case of shares or securities, the relief is withdrawn if, within the five-year period beginning with the day the investment is made (*CTA 2010, s 244*):

- the investor disposes of the whole or any part of the investment;
- the CDFI has not ceased to be accredited;
- the disposal does not arise as a result of a repayment, redemption or repurchase of shares included in the investment; and
- the disposal is a 'qualifying disposal', ie one that is either:
  - made by way of a bargain made at arm's length, or
  - a 'permitted disposal' (as above).

Repayments of loan capital

6.38 The relief is withdrawn if loan capital is repaid and the average capital balance of the loan for the period of six months beginning 18 months after the investment date is less than the prescribed percentage, being 75% for the third year, 50% for the fourth year, and 25% for the final year. The relief is not withdrawn if the amount does not exceed £1,000.

The average capital is the mean of the daily balances of capital outstanding during the period disregarding any non-standard repayment.

A repayment is non-standard if it is made at the choice or discretion of the CDFI and not as a direct or indirect consequence of a contractual obligation (*CTA 2010, s 245*). The same situation applies if value is received in repayment of a loan (*CTA 2010, s 246*).

Excessive returns to an investor

6.39 Relief is withdrawn, or pro rata partially withdrawn, if the investor receives excess value from the company during the first three years of the period of six years beginning one year before the investment date (the period of restriction). Amounts of less than £1,000 are ignored.

Relief is also withdrawn if the aggregate amount of value received by the investor before the beginning of the fifth year of the period of restriction (as mentioned above) is more than 25% of the invested capital or 50% before the final year and 75% during the final year. Amounts of less than £1,000 are ignored (*CTA 2010, s 247*).

Value received

6.40 An investor receives value from a CDFI at any time when the CDFI:

(a) repays, redeems or repurchases any securities or shares included in the investment;

(b) releases or waives any liability of the investor to the CDFI or discharges, or undertakes to discharge, any liability of the investor to a third person (a CDFI shall be treated as having released or waived a liability if the liability is not discharged within 12 months of the time when it ought to have been discharged);

(c) makes a loan or advance to the investor, which has not been repaid in full before the investment is made (a loan is treated as made by the CDFI to the investor if there is a debt incurred by the investor to the CDFI, other than an ordinary trade debt, or a debt due from the investor to a third person which has been assigned to the CDFI);

(d) provides a benefit or facility for:

  (i) the investor or any associates of the investor; or

  (ii) if the investor is a company, directors or employees of the investor or any of their associates.

(e) disposes of an asset to the investor for no consideration or for a consideration which is or the value of which is less than the market value of the asset;

(f) acquires an asset from the investor for a consideration which is or the value of which is more than the market value of the asset; or

(g) makes a payment to the investor other than the following:

  (i) any payment by any person for any goods, services or facilities provided by the investor (in the course of his trade or otherwise) which is reasonable in relation to the market value of those goods, services or facilities;

  (ii) the payment by any person of any interest, which represents no more than a reasonable commercial return on money, lent to that person;

  (iii) the payment by any company of any dividend or other distribution which does not exceed a normal return on any investment in shares in or securities of that company;

  (iv) any payment for the acquisition of an asset, which does not exceed its market value;

  (v) the payment by any person, as rent for any property occupied by the person, of an amount not exceeding a reasonable and commercial rent for the property; and

  (vi) a payment in discharge of a trade debt for goods or services supplied in the ordinary course of a trade or business with credit terms of not more than six months and not longer than that normally given to customers of the person carrying on the trade or business (*CTA 2010, s 249*).

HMRC notification

6.41 If the relief is to be withdrawn, the investor company must inform HMRC within the period of 12 months beginning with the end of the accounting period in which the event occurred (*CTA 2010, s 260*). An investor must notify HMRC of value received by any person no later than 60 days from the date when the investor comes to know of that event, if this is later than the period of 12 months beginning with the end of the accounting period.

Chapter 7

Property investment

SIGNPOSTS

- Introduction (see **7.1**).
- Trading or investing? (see **7.2**).
- Profits of a property business – deductions, interest costs, capital allowances, repairs and renewals, energy-saving items (see **7.3–7.11**).
- Property losses (see **7.13**).
- The lease premium rules – lease premiums, grant at an undervalue, sale and reconveyance (see **7.14–7.21**).
- Reverse premiums (see **7.22**).
- Annual tax on enveloped dwellings and related capital gains tax (see **7.23–7.24**).
- Non-UK residents' gains on UK residential property (see **7.25–7.26**).
- Specialist investment companies – real estate investment trusts (see **7.27**).

INTRODUCTION

Focus

Property investment is a specialised topic which has its own particular rules in addition to the general rules that apply to companies with an investment business.

7.1 The acquisition of land, with a view to letting it out at a profit, has certain features that are not shared with other types of investment activity. While tax relief is available for management expenses, a company with a property business will also be concerned with obtaining deductions for its finance costs, capital allowances and the costs of maintaining the properties in its asset portfolio.

In addition, there are special rules imposing tax charges when a landlord is paid a premium, as opposed to rent, for the property. The effect of these rules is to turn part of a capital sum into an income receipt.

For corporate landlords investing in residential property, regard must be had to the Annual Tax on Enveloped Dwellings ('ATED'). While most property investors will fall outside the ATED regime, there are still important filing requirements that need to be complied with.

In certain circumstances, non-UK resident corporate landlords are also subject to capital gains tax in respect of gains arising on their property assets. The charge is levied on 'closely held' companies disposing of residential property, and can lead to complications when the ATED regime also applies. From April 2019, all non-UK resident companies will be subject to corporation tax on gains arising on all UK property holdings, irrespective of whether the property is for residential or commercial use (see **7.25**, **7.26**).

TRADING OR INVESTING?

7.2 The question whether a company is trading or investing is normally determined by reference to case law and the so-called 'badges of trade' (see **2.3–2.4**). It is also possible for a company to be deemed to be trading by specific statutory provisions. In particular, the rules relating to transactions in UK land, introduced by *FA 2016*, may apply to treat a gain arising on a disposal of property as an income receipt arising from a trade (*CTA 2010, Part 8ZB*). These rules are targeted at situations where land is developed or exploited with a view to selling at a profit. The legislation is drafted widely and could, in theory, apply to property letting businesses, on the basis that the rules can be triggered if the main purpose, or one of the main purposes, of acquiring the land was to realise a profit or gain on disposal (*CTA 2010, s 356OB(4)*). However, this is unlikely to be the case in practice, as HMRC have stated that the intention behind the legislation is to tax activities which are, in substance, trading activities and not to alter the treatment of activities which clearly amount to property investment (HMRC Guidance 8 December 2016, BIM60555; see tinyurl.com/hmrcdevelopland).

If a company invests in property, it is a company with investment business and is likely to be entitled to relief for management expenses (see **6.3**). It will show the property as a fixed asset on the balance sheet and will record letting income as property income. Property disposals will fall within the rules for chargeable gains. Letting income will be assessable as profits of a property business (*CTA 2009, ss 202–291*).

Alternatively, a company could be trading as a property dealer or developer, in which case the property cost is shown as trading stock or work in progress on the balance sheet. Such a company earns its income primarily from the sale of properties, whether with or without development, and such profits are assessed as trading profits (see **Chapter 2**).

If a property-dealing or development company sells a property, which it has held as trading stock, to a property investment company within the same group which will hold it as a fixed asset, the transferor is treated as appropriating the property (at market value) from trading stock and then immediately transferring it intra-group on a no gain/no loss basis (*TCGA 1992, s 161(2)*; see **16.26**, **16.31**).

If a property investment company sells a property, which it has held as a fixed asset, to a property-dealing or development company within the same group which will include it as trading stock, the transferor is treated as transferring it intra-group on a no gain/no loss basis (see **16.24**) and the transferee as then immediately appropriating it to trading stock (see **16.27**). However, the transferee may elect to bring the property into its trading stock at its market value at the time of the appropriation. Such election must be made within two years after the end of the accounting period in which the property is so appropriated (*TCGA 1992, s 161*).

One of the most significant differences between trading and investing activities is the tax treatment of losses. A trading company has a greater range of options for utilising its losses – in particular, terminal losses can be carried back up to three years from the last accounting period in which the business ceases. By contrast, terminal losses are unavailable to a property investment company (see **7.13**).

PROFITS OF A PROPERTY BUSINESS

Income from UK land and buildings

7.3 UK resident companies are charged to corporation tax on income arising from the letting of land and property situated in the UK and abroad. The income generated from land situated in the UK is treated as a single property business (*CTA 2009, s 205*), and the income generated from land situated overseas is treated as a single overseas property business (*CTA 2009, s 206*).

Generating income from land is defined as exploiting an estate, interest or right in or over land as a source of rents or other receipts. Rents include not only the periodical payments referred to in a lease, but also any payments that a tenant makes for work carried out in maintaining or repairing the leased premises, which the lease does not require him to carry out.

Other receipts include:

- payments for a licence to occupy, use or exercise a right over land;
- rent charges, ground annuals, feu duties and other annual payments in respect of land; and

- income from furnished lettings, including furnished holiday lettings; and income from caravans or houseboats where their use is confined to one location in the UK (*CTA 2009, s 207*).

Profits of a property business are included on form CT600 within the company tax return.

Certain activities carried out on land are treated as a trade: farming or market gardening in the UK; certain commercial occupation of UK land; and mining and quarrying (*CTA 2009, s 208*; see **2.65–2.67**). Income from other activities may be treated as income of a trade: tied premises; caravan sites where a trade is carried on; surplus business accommodation; and payments for wayleaves (*CTA 2009, s 213*; see **2.59–2.62**).

Income derived from the occupation of commercially managed woodlands in the UK is specifically exempt from corporation tax (*CTA 2009, s 980*; see **2.54**).

Non-UK resident companies investing in UK property do not currently pay corporation tax, but are subject to income tax at basic rate on their rental profits (*ITA 2007, s 11*; *CTA 2009, s 5*). In addition, there is a complete exemption from chargeable gains on non-residential property ((*TCGA 1992, s 2(1), (1A)*). However, residential property holdings are potentially subject to tax on capital gains under the ATED and NRCGT regimes (*TCGA 1992, ss 2B–2F, 14B–14G, Sch 4ZZA, 4ZZB*; see **7.23–7.25**).

At Spring Budget 2017, the government announced its intention to bring non-UK resident corporate landlords within the charge to corporation tax on their rental profits (see Overview of Tax Legislation and Rates March 2017, para 2.19 and Consultation Paper at tinyurl.com/ljplstw). This was subsequently confirmed during the Autumn Budget 2017 – draft legislation will be published in the summer of 2018 with the intention of applying the new corporation tax charge from April 2020 (Overview of Tax Legislation and Rates November 2017, para 2.32). One consequence of charging non-resident corporate landlords to corporation tax instead of income tax is that they will be subject to the same restrictions on obtaining tax relief on their borrowings as apply to UK companies under the corporate interest restriction rules (*TIOPA 2010 ,Pt 10* inserted by *Finance (No 2) Act 2017, Sch 5*, see **4.4–4.5**, **5.31**).

The rules for chargeable gains are also changing as the government proposes to bring all gains on property held by non-UK resident companies within the corporation tax net from April 2019 (see **7.25**).

Computation of property business profits

General principles

7.4 The profits of a property business are calculated in the same way as the profits of a trade (see **Chapter 2**). The trading profits provisions (*CTA 2009,* *ss 61* and *68–92)*, that allow a deduction against trading income, also apply to property income. The general calculation rules that restrict deductions (see **2.12**) also apply.

CTA 2009, s 214, governs the relationship between rules which permit property business deductions and others which prohibit such deductions, and provides that certain rules allowing deductions take precedence over those prohibiting deductions. However, in cases involving tax avoidance arrangements entered into on or after 21 December 2012, the order of priority is reversed so that a prohibitive rule has priority over a permissive rule (*CTA 2009, s 214*).

Expenditure must be revenue and incurred wholly and exclusively for the purpose of the business.

7.5 There are two key principles that apply to determine whether expenses incurred in the business are tax deductible:

- expenses must be incurred wholly and exclusively for the purpose of the letting business (*CTA 2009, ss 210, 54*); and
- expenses must be of a revenue or income nature, as opposed to capital nature (*CTA 2009, s 53*).

The following types of revenue expenses are normally deductible in calculating the profits of the property business:

- finance costs such as interest and fees in respect of bank borrowings taken out to acquire the property assets;
- any rent required to be paid if the property constitutes a leasehold rather than a freehold interest;
- ongoing maintenance costs such as repair work (but not if this constitutes a capital item);
- rates such as business and water rates, and council tax where the landlord has agreed to pay for these in the lease;
- insurance premiums;
- professional fees paid to letting agents for managing the property; and
- legal and accounting fees for submitting tax returns.

Capital allowances are the exception to the rule that capital expenditure is not deductible against income profits. These are only available for expenses incurred in respect of commercial property (see **7.8**). For residential property, a deduction may be allowed for the cost of replacing furnishings (see **7.9**).

The largest expense of the business is the acquisition cost of the properties involved. Since these costs constitute capital expenditure, they are not allowable to be set off against rental receipts. As a consequence, the following incidental costs are also unallowable in computing income profits:

- stamp duty land tax payable on acquiring the properties;
- estate agent and legal fees incurred on the purchase;
- the cost of obtaining a survey or valuation; and
- the cost of major renovation works.

However, these costs may be deductible in calculating the chargeable gains arising on a subsequent disposal of the property.

Interest and finance expenses

7.6 Although loan relationships are specifically excluded from computing the profits of a property business, this does not mean that tax relief is unavailable for finance costs (*CTA 2009, s 211(1)*). Relief is given by first computing the property profits and then setting off the relevant interest expenses, which are treated as non-trading debits (*CTA 2009, ss 299–301, Part 5, Ch 16*).

Although the result in most cases is technically the same, the following example shows that this is not always the case.

Example 7.1—How interest relief is calculated for corporate landlords

The first table shows the profits of a property investment company for three consecutive years, and assumes that it is in fact permitted to include interest costs in calculating taxable profits.

	2017	*2018*	*2019*
	£	*£*	*£*
Property profits before deducting interest expense	30,000	1,000	3,000
Interest expense	(5,000)	(10,000)	(3,000)
Property profits	25,000	(9,000)	Nil
Interest income (bank and intercompany loan)	14,000	Nil	Nil
Taxable profits	39,000	Nil	Nil

In 2018, the property business has made a loss of £9,000, which can either be set against current year profits or carried forward. But there are no other profits for the year and no profits in the following year to set against. It is not possible to carry back the loss into the preceding year 2017 (see **7.13**).

The second table shows the actual position as required by the legislation, whereby interest costs are not regarded as part of the profits of the property business, but deducted only after those profits have been determined.

	2017	*2018*	*2019*
	£	*£*	*£*
Property profits	30,000	1,000	3,000
Interest income (bank and intercompany loan)	14,000	Nil	Nil
Interest expense	(5,000)	(10,000)	(3,000)
Net interest income/expense	9,000	(10,000)	(3,000)
Interest relief (current year profits)		(9,000)	Nil
Interest relief (carry back against net interest income)	(9,000)		
Taxable profits	30,000	Nil	Nil

For the year 2018, the property business made a profit of £1,000, even though there is an overall loss of £9,000. This is because the interest expense cannot be deducted in calculating the profits of the business.

However, the expense can be deducted against the profits once those profits have been determined, leaving an excess of £9,000 available for relief. Because the £9,000 excess is a loan relationship deficit, and not a property loss, it can be carried back to set against the interest income arising in the previous year.

For further details of how a company obtains relief under the loan relationship rules, see **Chapter 11** and, in particular, **11.27–11.32**.

Note that there are rules restricting the deduction of finance costs. Until 31 March 2017, the debt cap rules applied to restrict deductions where the company's, or (if the company is part of a group) the group's, UK net debt was at least £3 million and exceeded 75% of the group's worldwide gross debt.

From 1 April 2017, the debt cap rules are replaced by new rules whereby interest expenses are restricted to 30% of the company or group's earnings before interest, tax, depreciation and amortisation. These restrictions only apply where the group's net interest expense is at least £2 million (*TIOPA 2010, Pt 10,* introduced by *Finance (No 2) Act 2017*; see **5.31**). However, the restrictions do not apply to interest expenses incurred by a company engaged in property investment, provided that the following conditions are satisfied (the 'public infrastructure exemption' under *TIOPA 2010, ss 432–439*):

- the properties involved must be let on short leases to tenants that are unrelated to the company. For these purposes, a short lease is one with an effective duration of 50 years or less under the rules relating to leases set out in *CTA 2009, Part 4* (see **7.15**);
- all, or all but an insignificant proportion, of the company's income and assets must derive from the letting of property or ancillary activities;
- the properties must be recognised as assets on the company's or group balance sheet;
- the lender's recourse in relation to the loan must only be to the income, assets or shares of the company or of another company qualifying under the public infrastructure exemption. This means that guarantees by third parties are forbidden. However, guarantees provided before 1 April 2017 are disregarded, as are non-financial guarantees by related parties such as guarantees relating to the performance of services; and
- the company is 'fully taxed' in the UK, whereby every source of income that the company has is within the charge to corporation tax, and it has not made any claim for double taxation relief. For non-resident companies, a source of income is ignored if it is regarded as insignificant.

The company or group must make an election to ensure that the exemption applies. If an election is made, no restriction on interest deductions will apply where the creditor is unrelated. The election must be made before the end of the relevant accounting period, although elections for any period beginning before 1 April 2018 can be made at any time before that date (*TIOPA 2010, s 434*; *F(No 2)A 2017, Sch 5, para 32*; *FA 2018, Sch 8, paras 7, 23*). An election can be made on a group basis (*TIOPA 2010, s 435*).

Management expenses

7.7 Since it is a company with investment business, a property investment company is permitted to deduct its management expenses (see **6.3–6.20**).

Capital allowances

7.8 Capital allowances are available in respect of non-residential property only (*CAA 2001, s 35*). The most common items for which allowances may be available are fixtures and fittings, such as electrical systems for heating, lighting and ventilation, or fire and burglar alarms.

To the extent that these items are already in place when purchasing the property, the landlord should be able to apportion part of its acquisition cost in order to make a capital allowance claim. The apportionment must be made on a just and reasonable basis (*CAA 2001, s 562*). Allowances are limited to the lower of original cost and the last disposal value that has been brought into account by any previous owner of the relevant fixtures – note that this is not limited to the seller of the property but includes the seller's predecessors (*CAA 2001, ss 62, 185*).

It is common for both seller and purchaser to make a joint election to fix the sale price attributable to the fixtures. The amount is normally the seller's tax written down value in order that the latter can avoid a balancing charge (see **3.4**). However, the parties are free to negotiate any price, as long as it is capped by the seller's original cost (*CAA 2001, ss 198, 199*). The parties must also have regard to the special rules relating to claiming for fixtures that came into force in 2012 (see **3.46**).

A company may use the same asset, on which it claims capital allowances, in an ordinary UK property business, a UK furnished holiday lettings business, an ordinary overseas property business or an EEA furnished holiday lettings business (*CAA 2001, s 15(1)(a)–(d)*). For accounting periods beginning on or after 1 April 2011, where the company uses plant or machinery in succession for different types of property business, whilst still retaining ownership, the company is treated as if the plant or machinery was different plant or machinery in each instance, and as if the amount of qualifying expenditure was the market value of the plant or machinery, or the amount of the original expenditure if lower (*CAA 2001, s 13B*).

Residential property deductions for furnished dwellings

7.9 A furnished letting provides a tenant with the use of premises and furniture. Capital allowances are not available for plant let for use in a dwelling house (*CAA 2001, s 35(2)*).

Until 31 March 2016, there was a range of statutory options under which a landlord could claim a deduction for various items of furniture and other plant:

- *CTA 2009, s 248* allowed a deduction for any expenses incurred in connection with providing furniture, irrespective of whether the cost was revenue or capital in nature. In practice, relief was normally given by allowing 10% of rental income (net of the landlord's outlay on council tax and water rates, if any) as a wear and tear deduction.
- Alternatively, relief could be claimed under the statutory renewals basis (for replacement of assets falling within the scope of 'implements, utensils or articles'; *CTA 2009, s 68* repealed by *FA 2016, s 71*). Before

1 April 2013, the replacement of other assets could be claimed under the non-statutory renewals basis (see **2.16**).

- The landlord could make an election for a statutory wear and tear allowance amounting to 10% of net rental income under *CTA 2009, ss 248A–248C*, irrespective of the actual amount of expenditure incurred on furniture or replacement costs.

For accounting periods beginning on or after 1 April 2016 the position is as follows (*FA 2016, ss 72–74*):

- A deduction for furniture expenses under *CTA 2009, s 248* is restricted to costs of a revenue nature.
- Both the statutory renewals deduction and wear and tear allowance are abolished.
- In their place is a new relief allowing a deduction for the actual costs of replacing furnishings in unfurnished, part-furnished and furnished let residential properties. The new relief does not apply to furnished holiday letting businesses or letting of commercial properties, where capital allowances are available (*CTA 2009, s 250A*).

Repairs and renewals

7.10 The question of whether a tax deduction is available for expenditure on work done to the property depends on whether such work constitutes a repair or a renewal. In general, repairs are allowable as revenue expenditure; but, if the work consists of improving the relevant asset beyond its condition prior to the repair, this will be deemed a capital expense and disallowable. Expenditure incurred in repairing the subsidiary parts of an asset is classed as revenue expenditure (HMRC Property Income Manual at PIM2020 and Business Income Manual BIM46900–BIM46990).

The distinction between what constitutes a repair and what is a renewal is set out in case law):

> 'Repair is restoration by renewal or replacement of subsidiary parts of a whole. Renewal, as distinguished from repair, is reconstruction of the entirety, meaning by the entirety, not necessarily the whole, but substantially the whole subject matter under discussion'

(*Lurcott v Wakely v Wheeler* [1911] 1 KB 905 per Buckley LJ at 923–924)

For example, works such as replacing faulty light bulbs, fixing a broken window or a leaky roof, or whitewashing the walls, do not materially alter the nature of the assets in question. By contrast, the work involved in transforming a fast food café into an upmarket restaurant is likely to mean that most of the costs are of a capital nature. Such costs are not allowable, except to the extent that capital allowances are available (see **7.8**).

Legal fees

7.11 Legal fees of a revenue nature, wholly and exclusively in connection with the rental business, are deductible.

The expenses incurred in connection with the first letting or sub-letting of a property for more than one year are capital expenditure and therefore not allowable. The expenses may include legal expenses, lease preparation costs, agent's and surveyor's fees, and commission. If the lease is for less than one year, the expenses are deductible.

Legal and professional costs incurred in respect of the renewal of a lease for less than 50 years are allowable. Legal costs in relation to the payment of a premium on the renewal of a lease are not deductible.

Legal expenses in connection with letting arrangements that closely follow the terms of previous arrangements are considered to be a revenue expense and will not be disallowable, except for the legal or other costs that relate to the payment of a premium on the renewal of a lease.

Legal costs in connection with a change of use of the premises in between lets will be treated as a capital expense and hence disallowable.

HMRC have identified the following legal and professional costs as allowable:

- costs of obtaining a valuation for insurance purposes,
- the normal accountancy expenses incurred in preparing rental business,
- subscriptions to associations representing the interests of landlords,
- the cost of arbitration to determine the rent of a holding, and
- the cost of evicting an unsatisfactory tenant in order to re-let the property.

The following costs are disallowable:

- legal costs incurred in acquiring, or adding to, a property,
- costs in connection with negotiations under the *Town and Country Planning Acts*, and
- fees pursuing debts of a capital nature, for example, the proceeds due on the sale of the property.

Normal recurring legal and accountancy costs incurred in preparing accounts are deductible, including, by concession, agreeing the tax liabilities. However, legal costs in connection with acquisition of a property or costs in connection with negotiations under the *Town and Country Planning Acts* are not deductible.

Expenditure on energy-saving items

7.12 Until 31 March 2015 a company which operated a residential property letting business, either in the UK or overseas, could deduct the cost of acquiring and installing certain energy-saving items in the residential properties which they let, from the rental business profits assessable to corporation tax (*CTA 2009, s 251(2)*).

There was a maximum amount of allowable expenditure of £1,500 for each dwelling house. Any contributions received from persons not entitled to a deduction reduced the amount of the deduction. The limit applied to each separate dwelling; for example, the £1,500 limit was applied to each flat in a block of separate apartments, rather than to the entire building.

The qualifying expenditure in question was capital expenditure, which did not qualify for capital allowances or the annual investment allowance, but was incurred 'wholly and exclusively' for the purposes of the letting business and was of an energy-saving nature. The qualifying expenditure was expenditure on hot water system insulation, draught proofing, cavity wall insulation, solid wall insulation, floor insulation and loft insulation.

If a landlord incurred qualifying expenditure that benefited more than one property, this was apportioned amongst the relevant properties on a just and reasonable basis (*CTA 2009, s 251(4)*). No deduction for the cost of the energy-saving item was permitted if it was installed in the property during the course of construction. The landlord had to have a legal title to the property. If the energy-saving item was installed whilst the landlord was in the course of acquiring a legal title or changing that legal title, no deduction was permitted. No deduction was permitted in respect of property used in a commercial letting of furnished holiday accommodation (see **2.63**). The expenditure only qualified as pre-trading expenditure under *CTA 2009, s 61* if it was incurred no more than six months before the residential letting business commenced. In addition, the acquisition and the installation expenditure must have been incurred solely for the purposes of the dwelling-house (*CTA 2009, s 252*).

In practice, more than one party could have a legal interest in the property, and any apportionment of the relief or the expenditure should be made on a just and reasonable basis. The company has the right of appeal in the event of a dispute (*CTA 2009, s 251*; *SI 2008/1520*; *SI 2008/1521*).

PROPERTY LOSSES

> **Focus**
>
> The treatment of property losses has some important differences compared with trading losses. In particular, terminal losses cannot be carried back when the business comes to an end.

7.13 A company's UK property losses are given relief in the following order:

- Firstly, losses are set against the company's total profits for the same accounting period.
- If there are insufficient profits to relieve the loss, it is carried forward to subsequent accounting periods, to be set against total profits.
- Excess losses are carried forward in this way until the property business ceases. If there is still an excess loss at this point, it can be carried forward and treated as a management expense.
- For accounting periods beginning on or after 1 April 2017, a claim must be made to relieve any amounts carried forward, either as property losses or losses converted to management expenses. Claims may be made for the whole or part of the loss or expense and must be made within two years after the end of the period in question, or within such further period as HMRC may allow (*CTA 2010 ss 62(5C), 63(6)*).
- For accounting periods beginning on or after 1 April 2017, the total amount of losses that can be carried forward is restricted to £5 million plus 50% of profits in excess of that figure, with any surplus losses being carried forward to the next accounting period. The limit applies to the total of all losses from a variety of sources such as trading losses, property losses, non-trading loan relationship deficits, management expenses, non-trading deficits on intangible assets as well as deductions for carry-forward group relief. The restrictions apply to losses carried forward from periods prior to 1 April 2017 as well as losses incurred on or after that date.(*CTA 2009, s 1223(7)* and *CTA 2010, Pt 7ZA*, see **Chapter 4**).
- Losses can also be surrendered to other group companies under the group relief provisions. However, carry-forward group relief which applies only to losses incurred on or after 1 April is only available if the company has income producing assets at the end of the relevant surrender period and the business has not become small or negligible. Accordingly, careful planning is required when winding down the company's business;
- For the purpose of applying the loss relief rules, an accounting period that straddles 1 April 2017 is treated as two accounting periods, one ending on 31 March 2017 and another starting on 1 April 2017, with profits and losses apportioned between the two (*F(No 2)A 2017, Sch 4, para 190*).

(*CTA 2010, ss 62, 63, 99(1)(e)*, and *ss 188BB–188BD, 188BF*).

Note that claims for loss relief are subject to TAAR-related legislation which counteracts loss-related tax advantages. This legislation applies to tax advantages arising in respect of accounting periods beginning on or after 1 April 2017 (*F(No 2)A 2017, s 19*).

For investment in overseas property, the rules are modified so that losses are automatically carried forward to subsequent accounting periods. There is no set-off against total profits, as is the case with a UK property business (*CTA 2010, s 66*).

Note that there are two important differences between the treatment of property losses and trading losses:

- There is no facility to carry back a property loss to a previous accounting period.
- In particular, terminal losses cannot be carried back to the three previous accounting periods, as is the case with trading losses. Terminal losses are therefore stranded, unless the company has another business, in which case the terminal loss is treated as a management expense, which can then be carried forward.

The following table illustrates the differences between trading losses and property losses:

	Trading Losses	**Property Losses**
Carry forward	Yes. Pre-1 April 2017 losses only against same trade (*CTA 2010, s 45*). Post-1 April 2017 losses may be set against total profits (*CTA 2010, s 45A*).	Overseas property business – automatic carry forward against property profits (*CTA 2010, s 66*). UK property business – carry forward against total profits but only after current year set-off (*CTA 2010, s 62*).
Set-off against total profits	Yes – current year and carry back for one year (*CTA 2010, s 37*). Post-1 April 2017 losses may be carried forward for set-off against total profits (*CTA 2010, s 45A*).	Yes for UK property business, but not for overseas property business (*CTA 2010, s 62*).
Carry back	Yes – one year/three years (*CTA 2010, ss 37, 39*).	No.
Group relief	Yes (*CTA 2010, s 99(1)(a), s 188C*).	Yes (*CTA 2010, s 99(1)(e), s 188C*).
Terminal losses	Yes – can carry back losses for three years (*CTA 2010, s 39*). Post-1 April 2017 losses carried forward to terminal year may also be carried back (*CTA 2010, s 45F*).	No – terminal loss is treated as a management expense to be carried forward in the event that the company has another business (*CTA 2010, s 63*).

There are further restrictions where the company's business consists of furnished holiday accommodation. Although this is treated as a trade, losses can only be carried forward to subsequent accounting periods – no set-off against total profits or carry back to previous years is permitted (*CTA 2010, ss 65, 67A*). However, group relief is still available under *CTA 2010, Pts 5, 5A*.

Property losses are also subject to restrictions where there has been a change of company ownership and any of the following occur (*CTA 2010, Pt 14, Chs 3–5*):

(A) there is a major change in the nature or conduct of the business which takes place within any of the following periods beginning three years before the change in ownership:

- (a) the period is six years where either the change in ownership or the change in the business occur before 1 April 2017;
- (b) in all other cases, the period is eight years.

(B) prior to the change in ownership, the scale of the company's activities has become small or negligible, with no subsequent revival prior to the change;

(C) after the change in ownership, there is a significant increase in the company's capital; or

(D) none of A, B and C apply, and the company becomes subject to a tax charge on the disposal or realisation of an asset which was:

(a) acquired after the change in ownership from another group member on a tax neutral basis (either under *TCGA 1992, s 171* for capital assets or *CTA 2009, s 775* for intangibles); and

(b) disposed of or realised within three years after the change in ownership where the change occurs before 1 April 2017 and five years where the change occurs on or after that date..

For these purposes, a change of ownership occurs where:

(i) a single person acquires more than half of the ordinary share capital of the company; or

(ii) two or more persons each acquire a holding of 5% or more of the ordinary share capital of the company, and those holdings together amount to more than half of the ordinary share capital of the company; or

(iii) two or more persons each acquire a holding of the ordinary share capital of a company, and those holdings together amount to more than half of the ordinary share capital of the company. Holdings of less than 5% are disregarded, unless it is in addition to an existing holding and the two holdings together amount to 5% or more of the ordinary share capital (*CTA 2010, s 719*); or

(iv) in certain cases, there is also a change in ownership of a company C if, as a result of a person acquiring ordinary share capital in C, another company A becomes a fellow group member of C, and provided that both companies are UK related (*CTA 2010, s 719(4A), Chs 2B–2D*). A company is UK related if it is either UK resident, or non-resident but carrying on a trade in the UK through a permanent establishment (*CTA 2010, ss 188CE, 188CJ*).

The 5% threshold means there is no need to examine very small shareholdings, particularly those of public companies. However, note that it is possible for more than half of a company's shares to change hands and yet not trigger a change of ownership if the shares are purchased by a number of unconnected persons, each of whom acquires a holding of less than 5%.

From 1 April 2014, there is a significant increase in a company's capital where it increases by at least £1 million *and* 25%; up to 31 March 2014, there was a significant increase where the capital increased by at least £1 million *or* 100% (*CTA 2010, ss 688–691*, before and after amendment of *s 688* by *FA 2014, s 37*).

A major change in the nature or conduct of the business includes a major change in the nature of the property investments held, even if that change was the result of a gradual process which began before the period of six years within which the change has to take place (*CTA 2010, s 677(5)*).

The restrictions apply to limit the carry forward of property losses, whether in whole or in part. From 1 April 2017, there are also restrictions on group relief for carry forward losses (*CTA 2010, Pt 14, Chs 2C, 2D* inserted by *Finance (No 2) Act 2017, Sch 9*).

These rules also apply to restrict the ability to carry forward management expenses (see **6.20**) and non-trading loan relationship debits. Accordingly, care needs to be taken in any type of restructuring following the takeover of the company.

THE LEASE PREMIUM RULES

Focus

The lease premium rules are a highly complex set of rules which effectively turn a capital payment into a rental receipt. The effect of these rules is to deprive the landlord from using the acquisition cost of the property to relieve a taxable gain when a premium is paid in respect of a short lease.

Tax treatment of landlord

7.14 When a lease is granted for a premium, the landlord is treated, for chargeable gains purposes, as making a part disposal of its interest in the property, with the premium taxed as a capital receipt (*TCGA 1992, Sch 8, para 2(1)*). As a consequence, the landlord is able to deduct part of the property's base cost, together with any professional fees incurred in negotiating the lease (*TCGA 1992, s 38(1)*).

The amount that the landlord can deduct is calculated by multiplying the original base cost of the property by the following factor:

$$P/(P + R)$$

where P is the value of the premium and R is the value of the landlord's reversionary interest, together with the capitalised value of the rentals under the lease (*TCGA 1992, Sch 8, para 2(1)*).

These rules are modified when the landlord grants a short lease, being a lease with a term of 50 years or less *(CTA 2009, s 216*). In these circumstances, the premium is split into two parts – one part is taxed as capital, the remainder as an income receipt constituting a payment of rent (*CTA 2009, s 217*; *TCGA 1992, Sch 8, para 5*).

The idea behind the lease premium rules is to prevent landlords from effectively charging rent upfront, disguising it as a premium. The effect would be to permit the landlord to offset revenue income, in the form of rent, against the cost of the property which constitutes capital expenditure.

The amount that is taxed as income is given by the formula:

$$P \times [(50 - Y)/50]$$

where Y is the number of complete years that the lease is to run, less the first year. This amount can be rewritten as:

$$P - [(P \times Y)/50]$$

The amount taxed as capital is therefore:

$$[(P \times Y)/50]$$

In calculating the landlord's chargeable gains, further adjustments are made to the property's base cost. There are also special rules that apply when the landlord grants a sub-lease out of a short lease (*TCGA 1992, Sch 8, para 5(1), (2)*).

A premium is not limited to a cash payment and includes benefits of non-monetary value. More specifically, the landlord is treated as receiving a premium where the tenant has an obligation under the lease to carry out works on the premises (*CTA 2009, s 218*). This is calculated as:

- the value of the landlord's estate or interest immediately after the commencement of the lease; less
- the value that the landlord's interest would have been at that time, if the terms of the lease did not impose the obligation on the tenant to carry out the works.

In effect, the landlord is taxed, not on the actual cost of works undertaken, but on the benefit received, being the growth in value of the reversionary interest. However, no tax charge arises if the tenant carries out works that the landlord would have obtained a deduction for if the latter had done the work itself.

Duration of the lease for tax purposes

7.15 The effective lease term is the length of time that the lease is expected to last for that tenancy, given the current state of affairs and conditions that existed at the time that the lease was entered into. This may not necessarily be the length of time that is stated in the agreement (*CTA 2009, s 243*). For example:

- A lease for 99 years but with an option to terminate after seven years can be treated as a seven-year lease, if circumstances make it likely that the lease will be terminated. It is necessary that the premium paid by the tenant is similar to the premium one would expect for the shorter lease.
- A lease for 35 years, with an option to extend for another 60 years, can be treated as a 95-year lease, if circumstances make it likely that the lease will be extended.
- At the end of the lease, the tenant is entitled to be granted a further lease of the same premises, or even part of the premises. This can be considered as an extension of the original lease. This includes the case where it is a connected party, rather than the tenant, who moves into the property.

Relief for lease premium under the additional calculation rule

7.16 The additional calculation rule applies when the landlord itself holds a short leasehold interest in the property, for which it has paid a premium to the superior landlord. In these circumstances, the lease premium rules apply twice:

(a) On granting the headlease, the superior landlord is required to treat part of the premium paid by the landlord as rent.

(b) On granting the sub-lease, the landlord is required to treat part of the premium paid by its own tenant as rent.

In these circumstances, the landlord's liability under (b) can be offset by part of the rent that it is deemed to have paid to the superior landlord under (a). Relief is given by the following formula (*CTA 2009, ss 227, 228*):

A × LRP/TRP

where:

- A is the unreduced amount of the taxed receipt – broadly, this is the income element of the premium paid to the superior landlord;
- LRP is the receipt period of the receipt under calculation – broadly equivalent to the term for which the landlord lets the property to the sub-lessee; and
- TRP is the receipt period of the taxed receipt – broadly equivalent to the term of the headlease held by the landlord.

From 1 April 2013, corporate tenants are not entitled to relief for any part of a lease premium in circumstances where a lease of more than 50 years is treated as a short lease for tax purposes (*CTA 2009, ss 63, 232, 243*).

If the lease does not extend to the whole premises, the formula can be adjusted on a just and reasonable basis (*CTA 2009, s 229*).

Example 7.2—Premiums on lease and sub-lease of property

Facts

Horatio Ltd and Eustace Ltd are property companies. Horatio Ltd granted a 30-year lease of a property to Eustace Ltd on 1 January 2015 with a £50,000 premium and £60,000 annual rent. Horatio Ltd prepares accounts to 31 December each year.

On 1 January 2018, Eustace Ltd grants a 21-year sub-lease of the same property to Ferrero Ltd with a £40,000 premium and £35,000 annual rent. Eustace Ltd prepares accounts to 31 December each year.

Analysis

Horatio Ltd's property business receipts for the year ended 31 December 2015 are as follows:

Profits of a property business	£
Income portion of the premium receivable	
£50,000 × (50 – 29)/50	21,000
Plus: rent for the year ended 31 December 2015	60,000
Profits of the property business	81,000

Eustace Ltd's property business receipts for the year ended 31 December 2018 are as follows:

Profits of a property business	£
Income portion of premium receivable	
£40,000 × (50 – 20)/50	24,000
Less: relief for income portion of premium paid to Horatio Ltd	
£21,000 × 21/30	(14,700)
	9,300
Plus: rent for the year ended 31 December 2018	35,000
Profits of the property business	44,300

Tax treatment of tenant

7.17 A corporate tenant using the premises for business purposes is able to deduct the income element of the premium against its taxable profits. The deduction is spread over the following periods (*CTA 2009, ss 62, 231–234*):

- For a tenant that uses the property for trading purposes, the period of the lease for which the tenant is in occupation of the premises.
- For a tenant that is a corporate landlord, the period of the lease for which the landlord either sublets the property or occupies the property itself for the purpose of the rental business.

The deduction is given by allocating a daily amount calculated according to the following formula:

A/TRP

where:

- A is the taxable receipt – broadly, this is the income element of the premium paid to the landlord; and
- TRP is the number of days in the receipt period of the taxed receipt – which normally equates to the number of days in the lease.

Relief is given for each day that the tenant is in occupation of the premises or (where the tenant is also a landlord) for each day that the property is sublet. Note that, for a tenant that sub-lets the property as part of its own property business, the additional calculation rules may apply if a premium has been paid to the landlord under a short lease, and the tenant has subsequently charged a premium to its own sub-tenant (see **7.16**). In these circumstances, the deduction for the premium paid to the superior landlord is made in the following order (*CTA 2009, s 233*):

(a) The premium paid to the superior landlord is first netted off against the premium received from the sub-lessee under the additional calculation rules.

(b) Any remainder is then deducted over the length of the lease, using the formula for the daily calculation.

As explained in **7.16** above, from 1 April 2013, company tenants are not entitled to relief for any part of a lease premium in circumstances where a lease of more than 50 years is treated as a short lease for tax purposes (*CTA 2009, ss 63, 232, 243*; see also **2.32**).

If the lease does not extend to the whole premises, the formula is adjusted on a just and reasonable basis (*CTA 2009, s 234*).

Variations on the lease premium rules – grant at an undervalue and sale and reconveyance rules

7.18 The legislation contains other provisions to prevent the parties from structuring a lease transaction so as to avoid the charge to income on the payment of a premium:

- where the lease is granted at an undervalue and assigned to a third party (*CTA 2009, s 222*); and
- where, instead of granting a lease, the landlord sells its interest in the property to the tenant, but with a right to a reconveyance at a later date (*CTA 2009, ss 224, 225*).

Both provisions are aimed at transactions where the premium, or a substantial amount of what is effectively the premium, is paid not on the grant of a lease but on the transfer of an existing property interest.

Grant at an undervalue

7.19 The following diagram illustrates the position when a lease is granted at an undervalue:

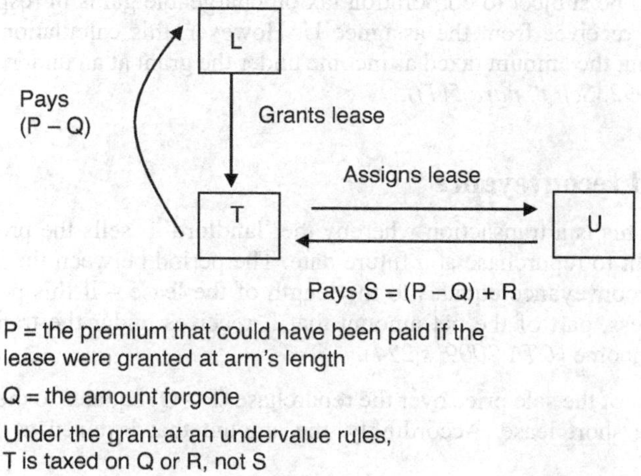

The idea behind this structure is that, because the premium paid on the grant of the short lease is at an undervalue, there is a minimal charge to corporation tax on income under the lease premium rules. The subsequent assignment by T to U is not caught, because T is not granting a lease – T will therefore be able to benefit from capital treatment. T will normally be connected to the landlord L, which permits the shortfall on the premium (Q) to be kept within the landlord's family (however, the legislation does not require the two to be connected).

This structure is caught by the provisions in *CTA 2009, s 222*. Under these provisions, T is subject to corporation tax on income – not on the amount it receives from U the assignee, but on the amount of the premium forgone (Q), or on the profit element (R), whichever is smaller. Note that, if R is equal to Q, T receives the full market premium (P) from U, with the net result that the whole of P becomes subject to the lease premium rules:

- L is subject to corporation tax on income on the appropriate part of the premium (P – Q) that it receives on granting the short lease to T:

  $$(P - Q) \times [(50 - Y)/50]$$

  where Y is the number of complete years that the lease is to run, less the first year.

- T is taxed on the remainder Q, with the income element being calculated as:

  $$Q \times [(50 - Y)/50]$$

Adding the two gives the result:

$$P \times [(50 - Y)/50]$$

which is the amount that would have been treated as a rental receipt if L had granted the lease for the full market value premium.

T will also be subject to corporation tax on chargeable gains in respect of the amount it receives from the assignee U. However, this calculation will take into account the amount taxed as income under the grant at an undervalue rules (*TCGA 1992, Sch 8, para 5(1)*).

Sale and reconveyance

7.20 This is a transaction whereby the 'landlord' L sells the property, but with a right to repurchase at a future date. The period between the initial sale and the reconveyance equates to the length of the lease – if this period is 50 years or less, part of the net amount that L receives under the transaction is taxed as income (*CTA 2009, s 224*).

The excess of the sale price over the repurchase (P – Q) equates to the premium paid for a short lease. Accordingly, the amount that is taxed as income is given by:

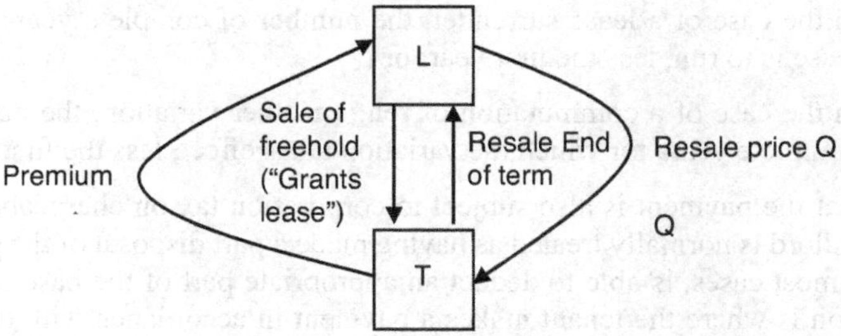

(P – Q) × [(50 – Y)/50]

where Y is the number of complete years between the sale and the reconveyance, less the first year.

There are similar provisions where, instead of a reconveyance, the property is leased back to the original owner (*CTA 2009, s 225*).

Variations on the lease premium rules – payments on a variation or lease surrender

7.21 In addition, there are rules under which various transactions between landlord and tenant are treated as if a premium has been paid. In these circumstances, the landlord may be required to treat part of the payment as an income receipt:

- Under the terms of the lease, the tenant pays a sum in lieu of rent. If the period for which the rent has been commuted is 50 years or less, part of the sum is treated as an income receipt – this applies irrespective of whether the lease itself is a long or short lease (*CTA 2009, s 219*).
- Under the terms of a short lease, the tenant pays a sum to surrender the lease (*CTA 2009, s 220*).
- The tenant pays a sum to vary or waive the terms of the lease (other than rent). If the period of the waiver or variation is 50 years or less, part of the payment is taxed as an income receipt. As with payments in lieu of rent, it is the length of the waiver/variation period that determines whether income treatment applies, and not the length of the lease itself (*CTA 2009, s 221*).

The formula for calculating the income element of the payment is similar to that which applies when a premium is paid on the grant of a short lease, and is given by (*CTA 2009, ss 218–221*):

S × [(50 – Y)/50]

where S is the sum payable by the tenant, and Y is either:

(a) in the case of a lease surrender, the number of complete years that the lease is to run, less the first year; or

(b) in the case of a commutation of rent, or other variation, the number of complete years for which the variation takes effect, less the first year.

Note that the payment is also subject to corporation tax on chargeable gains. The landlord is normally treated as having made a part disposal of the property and, in most cases, is able to deduct an appropriate part of the base cost. The exception is where the tenant makes a payment in accordance with the terms of the lease for its surrender. In these circumstances, the landlord is treated as making a disposal of its interest in the lease itself and not the freehold or superior interest out of which the lease was granted. In these circumstances, it cannot make use of the base cost of the property to set against any chargeable gain (*TCGA 1992, Sch 8, para 3*).

The chargeable gains computation is adjusted to take into account the amount of the payment that is taxed as income (*TCGA 1992, Sch 8, para 5*).

REVERSE PREMIUMS

7.22 Where a landlord pays a sum to induce a tenant (or a person connected with the tenant) to take a lease, this sum is known as a 'reverse premium'. Unless it reduces expenditure qualifying for capital allowances, a reverse premium is generally treated as a receipt in calculating the revenue profits of the tenant's trade if the latter has entered into the lease for trading purposes (*ITTOIA 2005, ss 99–103; CTA 2009 ss 96–100*). Otherwise, the tenant is deemed to be carrying on a property business and the reverse premium is treated as notional rent (*ITTOIA 2005, s 311; CTA 2009, s 250*). Other benefits, such as the grant of a rent-free period, are not taxable under these rules.

If the landlord is a property-dealing or development company, the payment of a reverse premium will be a deduction against trading profits. If the landlord is a property investment company, the payment will be treated as a capital payment that may enhance the value of the underlying asset, provided that the enhancement is reflected in the asset at the time of its disposal (*TCGA 1992 s 38(1)(b)*). The premium will not be deductible from rental income (see BIM41060).

ANNUAL TAX ON ENVELOPED DWELLINGS (ATED)

7.23 As part of measures to counter avoidance of stamp duty land tax (SDLT), *FA 2013* introduced an annual tax on enveloped dwellings (ATED) from 1 April 2013. This is chargeable on companies, collective investment schemes and partnerships with company members who hold UK residential dwellings valued above a specified threshold on specified valuation dates (*FA 2013, Pt 3*).

The threshold was set initially at £2 million but was progressively reduced to £500,000 by April 2016.

ATED is based initially on the market valuation of properties at 1 April 2012. Thereafter, properties are revalued every five years, with each valuation applying to the next five chargeable periods beginning one year later (*FA 2013, s 102(2A)*, as inserted by *FA 2015, s 71*). Additional valuations are required on the occasion of significant acquisitions or disposals.

For the chargeable periods beginning 1 April 2013 to 1 April 2018, the annual chargeable amount payable for a single-dwelling interest is as follows:

Taxable value of property interest	More than £500,000 but not more than £1m	More than £1m but not more than £2m	More than £2m but not more than £5m	More than £5m but not more than £10m	More than £10m but not more than £20m	More than £20m
Chargeable period (1 April to 31 March						
2013–14	n/a	n/a	£15,000	£35,000	£70,000	£140,000
2014–15	n/a	n/a	£15,400	£35,900	£71,850	£143,750
2015–16[1]	n/a	£7,000	£23,350	£54,450	£109,050	£218,200
2016–17[2]	£3,500	£7,000	£23,350	£54,450	£109,050	£218,200
2017–18[3]	£3,500	£7,050	£23,550	£54,950	£110,100	£220,350
2018–19[4]	£3,600	£7,250	£24,250	£56,550	£113,400	£226,950

[1] *FA 2015, s 70*

[2] *FA 2014, s 110*

[3] *FA 2013, s 101; Annual Tax on Enveloped Dwellings (Indexation of Annual Chargeable Amounts) (No 2) Order 2016, SI 2016/1244*

[4] *FA 2013, s 101; Annual Tax on Enveloped Dwellings (Indexation of Annual Chargeable Amounts) Order 2017, SI 2017/1246*

For the chargeable period ending 31 March 2014, ATED was payable on or before 31 October 2013. For subsequent chargeable periods beginning on 1 April, ATED is generally payable on or before 30 April during the chargeable period.

For the chargeable period ending 31 March 2016, ATED was payable on or before 30 April 2015, except in the case of dwellings in the new £1 million to £2 million band where the tax is payable on or before 31 October 2015.

The ATED charge accrues day by day and, if it transpires that the payer is not chargeable for the full year, a repayment claim can be made. Late payment interest is charged on ATED paid late to HMRC, and repayment interest arises on ATED repaid late by HMRC (*FA 2009, ss 101–103*).

The amounts of annual tax payable are indexed each year in line with increases in the consumer price index (CPI). However, there is no provision for indexing the taxable value bandings, so there is an expectation that more and more properties will fall within the scope of ATED as values rise.

There are a number of reliefs and exemptions from ATED. For example, there are reliefs for residential dwellings which are leased out in a property rental business, held for sale in a property development or trading business, exploited in a trade of permitting the public to visit, stay in or otherwise enjoy the property, or provided for employees to use in the owner's trade. There are also reliefs for charities, exemptions for public and national bodies, and exemptions for dwellings which are conditionally exempt from inheritance tax. From 1 April 2015 the ATED filing obligations and information requirements have been simplified in respect of properties eligible for reliefs (*FA 2015, s 73*).

With the progressive lowering of ATED thresholds and increases in ATED rates, ultimate owners of enveloped properties should look carefully at the range of reliefs available or consider the alternative of de-enveloping to avoid future ATED charges. Dismantling an existing enveloped structure should be approached with care, as it is likely that adverse tax implications may arise, including the possibility of significant chargeable gains and ATED-related capital gains emerging.

While ATED was introduced to counter avoidance of SDLT, it continues to apply throughout the UK, even though SDLT was replaced in Scotland by land and buildings transaction tax (LBTT) from 1 April 2015.

For HMRC's technical guidance on ATED, see tinyurl.com/o7vw46w; and, for the ATED return form and guidance, see tinyurl.com/o37mx33. For further information on ATED and the related capital gains tax charge (see below), refer to *Capital Gains Tax 2018/19* (Bloomsbury Professional).

ATED-related capital gains tax charge

7.24 *FA 2013* introduced a new charge to capital gains tax (CGT) on both UK and non-UK resident 'non-natural persons' (NNPs) in respect of gains accruing on the disposal of interests in high-value residential property that are subject to ATED (see **7.23**). For a company, this new charge is a CGT charge that is levied in respect of a fiscal year ended 5 April, and not an accounting period (*FA 2013, Sch 25*). It is distinct from the corporation tax to which the company may be liable in respect of its chargeable gains (see **Chapter 16**), although the same element of a gain will not be subject to both taxes.

The new CGT charge applies to gains on such disposals on or after 6 April 2013. A form of rebasing applies for this CGT charge (though not for computing the non-ATED-related chargeable gain for corporation tax purposes), to ensure that pre-6 April 2013 increases (and decreases) in the value of affected properties are outside the scope of the ATED-related CGT charge but remain subject to corporation tax. Gains and losses within the scope of the ATED-related CGT charge are excluded from the scope of corporation tax (*CTA 2009, s 2(2A)*).

This CGT is charged at 28% on disposals of UK residential property which have been subject to ATED, where the consideration exceeds a specified threshold (*TCGA 1992, s 4(3A)*). The threshold is being progressively reduced, as follows:

Fiscal year	*ATED-related CGT threshold* £
6 April 2013 to 5 April 2014	2 million
6 April 2014 to 5 April 2015	2 million
6 April 2015 to 5 April 2016	1 million*
6 April 2016 to 5 April 2017 onwards	500,000*

* *FA 2015, Sch 8, paras 3–4*

The threshold is reduced proportionately where the company owns only part of the property or disposes of part of it, thus ensuring that the charge cannot be avoided through fragmentation.

For HMRC's guidance on their interpretation of the CGT charge on enveloped dwellings, see CG73600–CG73670. For further information on ATED and the related capital gains tax charge, refer to *Capital Gains Tax 2018/19* (Bloomsbury Professional).

NON-UK RESIDENTS' GAINS ON UK PROPERTY

Capital gains tax charges on residential property

7.25 Traditionally, non-resident companies that do not trade in the UK through a permanent establishment have benefited from an exemption from chargeable gains on their UK property holdings. This position is gradually changing, firstly with the introduction of ATED-related capital gains tax charges in 2013 (see **7.24** above) and the non-resident capital gains tax charge (NRCGT) on residential properties in 2015. From April 2019, non-resident companies will be fully chargeable to corporation tax, irrespective of the type of property held (see **7.26** below).

The NRCGT charge applies from 6 April 2015 and is levied on gains accruing on disposals of UK residential property by non-UK residents, including companies.

A non-UK resident company may be subject to NRCGT on a gain arising on the disposal of UK residential property (*TCGA 1992, ss 14B–14H*, as inserted by *FA 2015, Sch 7, para 11*), if the gain is not otherwise taxable as either:

- a chargeable gain on a non-resident company with a UK permanent establishment (*TCGA 1992, s 10B*; see **20.5**); or
- an ATED-related gain (*TCGA 1992, Sch 4ZZB, Pt 4*, as inserted by *FA 2015, Sch 7, para 39*; see **7.23**).

The NRCGT charge applies where the non-resident company is controlled by five or fewer persons, except where the company itself (or at least one of the controlling persons) is a qualifying institutional investor (*TCGA 1992, Sch C1*, as inserted by *FA 2015, Sch 7, para 37*).

NRCGT is charged at 20% on net NRCGT gains arising in a fiscal year ended 5 April, and not an accounting period. A non-resident company disposing of UK residential property must report the disposal to HMRC on an NRCGT return no later than the filing date – normally 30 days after completion, which is usually the date of conveyance – and must pay the NRCGT (or a withholding tax) by that filing date (*TMA 1970, ss 12ZA–12ZN*, as inserted by *FA 2015, Sch 7, para 43*).

NRCGT is charged only on gains that are treated as accruing from 6 April 2015 onwards. Where a gain accrues over a period which straddles this date, there are usually three possible computation options (see *TCGA 1992, Sch 4ZZB, Pt 2*, as inserted by *FA 2015, Sch 7, para 39*):

- rebasing to market value at 5 April 2015 (the default method);
- time apportionment (unavailable if the disposal is also subject to ATED-related CGT); or
- the entire gain or loss over the whole period of ownership.

In the first and third of these options, all or part of the gain from 6 April 2013 onwards may be liable to ATED-related CGT, if relevant. Thus, for enveloped dwellings there are now two separate CGT regimes that may apply to a gain realised by a closely held non-resident company. Where all or part of a gain is subject to the ATED-related CGT charge levied at 28% (see **7.24**), this takes priority and the NRCGT charge at 20% does not apply to that gain (or part).

Example 7.3—NRCGT gain/(loss) computed by time apportionment

Facts

A closely held non-resident company buys a UK let residential property for £1m on 5 April 2010 and sells it for £1.4m on 5 April 2020. The market value of the property on 5 April 2015 is £800,000. There is no ATED-related gain because let property is exempt from ATED.

Analysis

The NRCGT gain (ignoring indexation allowance) is calculated as follows:

Computation options	*Gain/(loss)*
Default based on market value at 5 April 2015	600,000
Time apportioned gain/(loss) (available because no ATED-related gain)	200,000
Gain/(loss) over the whole period of ownership	400,000

If an election is made under *TCGA 1992, Sch 4ZZB, para 2(1)(a)* for time apportionment to apply, the NRCGT gain is £200,000.

Example 7.4—NRCGT gain/(loss) computed over whole period of ownership

Facts

As in Example 7.3, but the cost of the property is £1.4m and the selling price is £1m.

Analysis

Computation options	*Gain/(loss)*
Default based on market value at 5 April 2015	200,000
Time apportioned gain/(loss) (available because no ATED-related gain)	(200,000)
Gain/(loss) over the whole period of ownership	(400,000)

If an election is made under *TCGA 1992, Sch 4ZZB, para 2(1)(b)* for the gain or loss to be determined over the whole period of ownership, the NRCGT loss is £400,000.

Further apportionment is needed where there are consecutive changes between residential and non-residential use. For concurrent mixed use, a just and reasonable apportionment must be made.

NRCGT losses are ring-fenced for use against the company's NRCGT gains of the same fiscal year, with any unused balance being available to carry forward to later years. Where the company later becomes UK resident, any unused ring-fenced losses will become available to use against its chargeable gains in general. A UK resident company which becomes non-resident will be able to carry forward unused UK residential property losses against future UK residential property gains.

Companies within a group that are subject to NRCGT may treat the assets of the group on a 'pooled' basis, with the ability to offset NRCGT gains and losses of different non-resident group members within the same tax year, carry forward unrelieved losses, transfer properties within the group on a tax-neutral basis, and nominate a group member as the group's representative company (*TCGA 1992, ss 188A–188K*, as inserted by *FA 2015, Sch 7, para 30*).

For HMRC guidance on NRCGT, see tinyurl.com/o8cvw6d and tinyurl.com/osmvo9k.

Proposals to extend corporation tax to gains on all UK property

7.26 From April 2019, corporation tax will apply to all property gains made by non-resident companies. This proposal was announced during the Autumn Budget 2017 (see Consultation Paper 22 November 2017 at tinyurl.com/y8rxqnkv) and extends the Government's initial plan to simply bring the current NRCGT charge on residential property within the corporation tax regime (see Consultation Paper 20 March 2017 para 2 at tinyurl.com/ljplstw).

Accordingly, the following changes will take place:

- The NRCGT charge on residential property gains will be replaced by a corporation tax charge. This charge will not be limited to closely held companies but will apply to all non-UK companies irrespective of the size of the investor base.
- Where ATED is relevant, ATED-related gains charge will be 'harmonised' within the corporation tax framework.
- Corporation tax will also apply to gains on non-residential properties. The charge will apply to all non-resident companies holding UK property.

As with the ATED and NRCGT charges, there will be a rebasing exercise to ensure that only post-April 2019 gains and losses are captured. However, companies will have the option to bring all the gain or loss within the tax charge. An election is likely to be made where there is a post-April 2019 gain, but the taxpayer has suffered an overall loss on its investment. Unlike the NRCGT regime there will not be an option to calculate the gain on a time-apportioned basis (see **7.24**).

Gains and losses will be subject to all the normal rules that apply to corporation tax on chargeable gains. Unlike the NRCGT regime, there will be no ring-fencing – thus gains and losses on property holdings may be netted against losses and gains on other chargeable assets. Furthermore, all the applicable reliefs will apply.

In addition to the tax on directly held property, non-residents will also be taxed on gains where property is held indirectly through an intermediate vehicle such as a company or partnership or other entity. This ensures that property gains can still be taxed where the non-resident company disposes of its interest in the relevant entity by selling its shares or partnership interest. The charge on disposals of indirect property holdings will apply in the following circumstances:

- At the time of the disposal, the non-resident company holds, or has held a 25% stake in the entity at any point within the previous five years. The stake need not be held directly, but with other persons such as fellow group members;
- The entity is 'property-rich' at the time of the disposal. An entity is property-rich if at least 75% of its gross asset value derives from UK land. The latter test applies on a 'look-through' basis so as to take into account property held through other entities such as in a corporate group structure, or a layer of partnership interests.

Where the non-resident company holds its interest through another corporate vehicle, relief is potentially available under the substantial shareholdings provisions if all the relevant conditions are satisfied. For example:

- The main exemption may apply if the underlying business is a trading venture, as would be the case where the properties are held for development purposes or otherwise held as trading stock; or
- If the properties are held mainly for investment purposes, relief will be available if the non-resident company is owned mainly by qualifying institutional investors.

(See **6.24–6.25**, **16.18–16.23**.)

For both direct and indirect property disposals, the non-resident company will need to register for UK corporation tax as well as to report the disposal electronically to HMRC in the same way as currently applies for the NRCGT charge.

As always, there will be anti-avoidance provisions:

- first, a 'standard' targeted anti-avoidance rule (TAAR) to apply generally; and
- for indirect property disposals, anti-forestalling rules apply to any arrangements established on or after 22 November 2016 in order to take advantage of any favourable tax treaty in the event that a disposal occurs after the new tax charge comes into force.

SPECIALIST INVESTMENT COMPANIES: REAL ESTATE INVESTMENT TRUSTS

7.27 A real estate investment trust ('REIT') is a listed company, resident in the UK, whose business consists of letting out property. REITs have a special tax status, in that both rental profits and capital gains on their rental assets are exempt from corporation tax. Instead, the tax is effectively transferred to shareholders, who are treated as if they had invested directly in the underlying property.

There are various conditions that apply for a company to qualify as a REIT. As with investment trusts and VCTs (see **6.28**), a substantial amount of the REIT's rental profits (at least 90%) must be distributed to shareholders, and there are rules to ensure that the property portfolio is sufficiently diversified. Unlike investment trusts and VCTs, the tax exemption on gains does not extend to all the assets held by the REIT, but is limited to those assets that are used for the purpose of the rental business. REITs are able to undertake other activities such as development work, but these activities are constrained within statutory limits and are taxable in the normal way.

The legislation for REITs can be found at *CTA 2010, Part 12*.

Chapter 8

Business premises renovation allowance

SIGNPOSTS

- This chapter looks at the special reliefs for buildings and structures (see **8.1**).
- The business premises renovation allowance is available up to March 2017 only (see **8.2–8.17**).

INTRODUCTION

8.1 In general, there is no relief against revenue profits for the capital cost of the purchase or construction of a building. Special reliefs, were available in the past, but these have been gradually withdrawn. This chapter deals with the relief that was available on expenditure incurred on renovation of business premises (**8.2–8.17**). This relief was withdrawn for corporation tax purposes from 1 April 2017.

Relief was also available (on or before 31 March 2013) for the conversion of business premises into flats; see *Corporation Tax 2015/16* (Bloomsbury Professional).

Relief was also available on or before 31 March 2011 on capital expenditure incurred on the purchase or construction of industrial buildings; see *Corporation Tax 2010/11* (Bloomsbury Professional).

INTRODUCTION TO BUSINESS PREMISES RENOVATION ALLOWANCE

8.2 A company that incurs qualifying expenditure on or before 31 March 2017 (**8.3**) on the conversion of a qualifying building (**8.5**) to qualifying business premises (**8.7**), or incurs qualifying expenditure on the renovation of a qualifying building, may be entitled to business premises renovation allowances if all conditions are satisfied (*CAA 2001, s 360A*). The company incurring the expenditure must have a relevant interest in the building. If that company acquires an interest after incurring the expenditure, it will be treated as having the interest when the expenditure was incurred (*CAA 2001, s 360F*). The allowances are given as receipts or expenses of the trade or property business (*CAA 2001, ss 360Z–360Z1*).

FA 2014 narrowed the scope of expenditure that qualifies for business premises renovation allowance (see **8.3**), and tightened up some of the other conditions for the relief.

From 1 July 2016, HMRC have the power to request certain information from a company claiming the business premises renovation allowance (*Finance Act 2016, ss 180–182, Sch 24*, see **25.5**). The provision of the information is a condition for granting the relief. At the time of writing, there is no legislation setting out the specific requirements that must be satisfied. However, it is unlikely that there will be any information requests given that the relief has expired and will not be renewed (Budget 2016, para 2.91, 'Overview of Tax Legislation and Rates 2016', para 2.12).

Focus

Up to 100% initial allowance and/or a 25% writing down allowance can be claimed on certain capital expenditure incurred on the conversion of a building to business premises or the renovation of a building. Various conditions apply as to the type of expenditure incurred and as regards the building itself. The expenditure must be incurred on or before 31 March 2017 in order to qualify.

Qualifying expenditure

8.3 Originally the scheme was to expire on 11 April 2012 but it was extended. To qualify, the expenditure must be incurred on or before 31 March 2017, and there is an upper limit of €20 million on the total expenditure that may qualify for business renovation allowances on any one project (*Business Premises Renovation Allowances (Amendment) Regulations 2012, SI 2012/868*).

From 1 April 2014 the scope of the expenditure that qualifies for the business premises renovation allowance was narrowed. From that date, the only costs qualifying for relief are the actual costs of construction and building work and certain specified activities (eg architectural and surveying services), plus additional associated but unspecified activities (eg project management services) up to a limit of 5% of the sums incurred on building works.

To qualify, expenditure must be on (*CAA 2001, s 360B(2A)*):

(a) the conversion of a qualifying building into qualifying business premises;

(b) the renovation of a qualifying building if it is or will be qualifying business premises; or

(c) repairs to a qualifying building or, where the building is part of a building, to the building of which the qualifying building forms part, to the extent that the repairs are incidental to expenditure within (a) or (b).

The expenditure must be incurred on (*CAA 2001, s 360B(2B), (2C)*):

- building works;
- architectural or design services;
- surveying or engineering services;
- planning applications;
- statutory fees or statutory permissions; or
- other matters up to a limit not exceeding 5% of the aggregate qualifying expenditure incurred on the building works, architectural or design services and surveying or engineering services referred to above.

However, certain expenditure is specifically excluded from qualifying (see **8.4**).

Non-qualifying expenditure

8.4 Certain types of expenditure do not qualify for the business premises renovation allowance (*CAA 2001, s 360B(3)*). These include expenditure on:

- the acquisition of land or rights in or over land;
- the extension of a qualifying building (except to the extent required for the purpose of providing a means of getting to or from qualifying business premises);
- the development of land adjoining or adjacent to a qualifying building; or
- the provision of plant and machinery, unless it is or becomes a legally recognised fixture of the building (within *CAA 2001, s 173(1)(a)*) and falls within the following list, which may be varied by Treasury order (*CAA 2001, s 360B(3A)*):
  - integral features within *CAA 2001, s 33A* (see **3.16**);
  - automatic control systems for opening and closing doors, windows and vents;
  - window cleaning installations;
  - fitted cupboards and blinds;
  - protective installations such as lightning protection, sprinkler and other equipment for containing or fighting fires, fire alarm systems and fire escapes;
  - building management systems;

- cabling in connection with telephone, audio-visual data installations and computer networking facilities, which are incidental to the occupation of the building;
- sanitary appliances, and bathroom fittings which are hand driers, counters, partitions, mirrors or shower facilities;
- kitchen and catering facilities for producing and storing food and drink for the occupants of the building;
- signs;
- public address systems; and
- intruder alarm systems.

Expenditure is also excluded if and to the extent that it exceeds the market value amount for the works, services or other matters to which it relates. The 'market value amount' assumes costs incurred at arm's length in the open market in market conditions prevailing at the time (*CAA 2001, s 360B(3B), (3C)*).

Furthermore, expenditure is excluded if the qualifying building was used at any time during the 12 months ending with the day on which the expenditure is incurred (*CAA 2001, s 360B(3D)*).

Building repair expenditure not available for relief for tax purposes against the profits of a property business or a trade, profession or vocation is treated as capital expenditure (*CAA 2001, s 360B(4)*).

Where qualifying expenditure has been incurred, the works, services or other matters to which it relates must be completed within 36 months; otherwise, the expenditure for those not completed will be treated as not having been incurred. If and when those works are eventually completed, the expenditure will be treated as being incurred at that time (*CAA 2001, s 360BA*).

No business premises renovation allowance is made if the same expenditure, or the same building or single investment project, results in the receipt of any other state aid or such other grant as may be specified by Treasury order (*CAA 2001, s 360L*). In these circumstances, the company would have to decide which aid to receive. This applies to relevant grants made at any time towards expenditure incurred on or after 1 April 2014, and those made on or after 1 April 2014 towards expenditure incurred before that date (see *FA 2014, s 66(11)*). For earlier expenditure, see **8.10**, **8.11**.

A qualifying building

8.5 To be a qualifying building, the following conditions must be met at the date on which the conversion or renovation work begins. The building itself can be any building or structure, or part of a building or structure. The conditions (*CAA 2001, s 360C*) are that the building:

- is situated in a designated disadvantaged area;
- was unused throughout the period of one year ending immediately before the date on which the conversion or renovation work began;
- had last been used:
  - for the purposes of a trade, profession or vocation; or
  - as an office or offices (whether or not for the purposes of a trade, profession or vocation);
- had not last been used as, or as part of, a dwelling; and
- in the case of part of a building or structure, on that date had not last been occupied and used in common with any other part of the building or structure, other than a part that was unused for a year before that date or which had last been used as a dwelling.

In *Senex Investments Ltd* [2015] UKFTT 107 (TC04312), the First-tier Tribunal held that a former church was a qualifying building, and that the church vestry qualified as an office.

For expenditure incurred before 11 April 2012, premises are not qualifying business premises where:

(a) the person entitled to the relevant interest in the premises (see *CAA 2001, ss 360E, 360F*) is carrying on a relevant trade; or

(b) the premises are used, or used in part, for the purposes of such a trade,

and, for this purpose, 'relevant trade' means a trade or part of a trade in any sector in relation to which *Commission Regulation (EC) 1628/2006* on the application of *Articles 87* and *88* of the *Treaty* to national regional investment aid does not apply by virtue of *para 2* of *Article 1* of that *Regulation* (*Business Premises Renovation Allowances Regulations 2007, SI 2007/945*).

For expenditure incurred on or after 11 April 2012, 'relevant trade' means a trade:

- in any sector in relation to which *Commission Regulation (EC) 800/2008* declaring certain categories of aid compatible with the common market in the application of *Articles 87* and *88* of the *Treaty* ('General Block Exemption Regulation') does not apply by virtue of *para 3* of *Article 1* of that *Regulation*; or
- carried on by any undertaking (as defined for the purposes of *CAA 2001, s 45DB* (exclusions from allowances under *CAA 2001, s 45DA*) which:
  - is subject to an outstanding recovery order made by virtue of *Article 108* of the *Treaty on the Functioning of the European Union*; or

- it is reasonable to assume would be regarded as a firm in difficulty for the purposes of the Community Guidelines on State Aid for Rescuing and Restructuring Firms in Difficulty.

Broadly, a relevant (ie prohibited) trade is a trade in any of the following sectors (HMRC Capital Allowances Manual at CA45300):

- fisheries and aquaculture,
- shipbuilding,
- the coal industry,
- the steel industry,
- synthetic fibres,
- the primary production of certain agricultural products, and
- the manufacture or marketing of products which imitate or substitute for milk and milk products.

In modernising the EU state aid rules, the EU revised the existing General Block Exemption Regulation and a new version (*(EU) 651/2014*) took effect from 1 July 2014. From 17 July 2014 the following additional activities are excluded from business premises renovation allowance (*Business Premises Renovation Allowances (Amendment) Regulations 2014, SI 2014/1687*):

- energy generation, distribution and infrastructure;
- broadband network development; and
- the transport sector and related infrastructure.

A disadvantaged area

8.6 The Treasury has designated the areas that are to be treated as disadvantaged (*CAA 2001, s 360C(2)*; from 1 July 2014, see the *Assisted Areas Order 2014, SI 2014/1508*; before 1 July 2014, see the *Assisted Areas Order 2007, SI 2007/107*). If a building is situated partly in a disadvantaged area, a just and reasonable apportionment of the expenditure will be made (*CAA 2001, s 360C(6)*).

Qualifying business premises

8.7 Business premises can be any building or structure or part of a building or structure (*CAA 2001, s 360D(2)*), but must be a 'qualifying building' as defined, so use for a relevant trade is still prohibited (see **8.5**). The premises must be used or be available and suitable for letting for use for the purposes of a trade, profession or vocation, or as an office or offices. There is no requirement for any office to be used for the purposes of a trade, profession or vocation, therefore, a charitable organisation would qualify. Temporary periods of unsuitability are ignored if the building qualified in the immediate prior period (*CAA 2001, s 360D*). The premises must not be used or available for use as a 'dwelling' or part of a dwelling.

A dwelling

> **Focus**
>
> Because premises used as a dwelling or part of a dwelling are excluded from business premises renovation allowance, the definition of 'dwelling' is important. Where a building contains multiple dwellings, common areas may still qualify for business premises renovation allowance.

8.8 From 22 October 2010, 'dwelling house' is defined for business premises renovation allowance and capital allowances generally according to the services that it provides, namely 'a dwelling house provides its occupants with the facilities for day-to-day domestic existence' (Revenue & Customs Brief 45/2010, 22 October 2010, tinyurl.com/ous98qy, see also HMRC Capital Allowances Manual at CA11520, CA20020). The question is essentially one of fact, so unusual or controversial cases may need to be considered in the light of their individual circumstances.

The definition is of particular relevance in relation to multi-occupancy buildings. In the case of university halls of residence, for example, HMRC consider that each flat in multiple occupation comprises a dwelling house, but that an individual study bedroom is not because it would not afford the occupants the facilities required for day-to-day private domestic existence. A communal kitchen and lounge etc serving a number of occupants within a flat are part of their dwelling house, but common parts of the building block such as the common entrance lobby, stairs or lifts are not (Revenue & Customs Brief 45/2010).

Included within the general definition of a dwelling house are second or holiday homes. Hospitals, prisons, nursing homes or hotels, run as a trade and offering services, whether by the owner-occupier or by the tenant, are not dwelling houses. On-site university accommodation with no direct access to kitchen and dining facilities is probably an institution and not a dwelling house, while student bedrooms with en-suite facilities and shared kitchens are likely to be dwelling houses (CA11520).

Expenditure on plant and machinery for use in a dwelling house does not qualify for plant and machinery allowances (*CAA 2001, ss 15, 35*). In a building with multiple occupation, the expenditure can be apportioned between common areas and dwelling houses. Thus a block of flats is not a dwelling house, although the individual flats may be. A lift or central heating system serving only the common parts of a building which contains two or more dwelling houses, will not comprise part of any of the dwelling house. A central heating system serving an individual residential flat does not qualify for plant and machinery allowances. Expenditure on central heating systems serving the whole of the building containing two or more dwelling houses should be apportioned between the common parts, which qualify for plant and machinery allowances, and the residential flats or individual dwelling houses, which do not (CA20020).

The principles to be followed for business premises renovation allowance are similar to those that restrict capital allowances for plant and machinery within dwelling houses.

Example 8.1—Plant in dwellings and common areas

Facts

Property Company Ltd owns a block of residential flats and a nursing home. It incurs expenditure on a new fire alarm system for the block of flats, new cookers for the flats, and new beds for the nursing home.

Analysis

If the fire alarm system protects the common areas and the individual dwelling houses, the company will be able to claim plant and machinery allowances on the proportion of the cost that relates to the common areas. It will not be able to claim plant and machinery allowances on the proportion of the alarm that relates to the individual flats, or on the new cookers, because each flat in itself constitutes a dwelling house. It will be able to claim plant and machinery allowances on the new beds, because a nursing home is not a dwelling house.

It is unclear whether a 'dwelling', as referred to for business premises renovation allowance purposes, includes not only the separate unit of living accommodation but also any attached garden, yard, garage or other outbuildings.

Example 8.2—Business premises renovation allowance in a mixed building

Facts

Office Blocks Ltd owns a foundry in a disadvantaged area. The building has not been used for two years. The company incurs qualifying expenditure on renovation of this building within its original shell, creating ground floor offices with residential flats above.

Analysis

The company will be able to claim business premises renovation allowance on the qualifying renovation expenditure attributable to the offices, but not on the expenditure relating to the dwellings (CA45300).

Relevant interest

8.9 The relevant interest is the interest held by the company that incurred the qualifying expenditure or that incurs expenditure on conversion. If the company was entitled to more than one interest, of which one was a reversionary interest, the reversionary interest becomes the relevant interest. If the company held a leasehold interest which was extinguished on it acquiring a reversionary interest, the interest into which the leasehold interest merges becomes the relevant interest (*CAA 2001, ss 360E, 360F*).

Initial allowances

8.10 The company incurring the expenditure on qualifying business premises may claim an initial allowance of up to 100% of that expenditure in the accounting period in which it is incurred, provided it continues to own the relevant interest at the time of the claim. Part or all of the initial allowance may be disclaimed (*CAA 2001, s 360G*).

No initial allowance is made if, when the premises are first occupied or let, the qualifying building does not constitute qualifying business premises (see **8.7**) (*CAA 2001, s 360H*).

Up to 31 March 2014, no initial allowance is made in respect of expenditure to the extent that it is taken into account for any other state aid or such other grant as might be specified by Treasury order (*CAA 2001, s 360L*, before substitution by *FA 2014, s 66(8)*; see also **8.4**).

Writing down allowances

8.11 A company may claim a writing down allowance of 25% of the balance of unrelieved qualifying expenditure at the end of the chargeable period, if all the relevant conditions continue to apply, which are that:

- the company is entitled to the relevant interest in the qualifying building;

- the company has not granted a long lease (ie longer than 50 years) of the qualifying building out of the relevant interest in consideration of the payment of a capital sum; and
- the qualifying building constitutes qualifying business premises.

The writing down allowance is proportionately increased or reduced if the chargeable period is more or less than a year (*CAA 2001, s 360J*). Part or all of the writing down allowance may be disclaimed (*CAA 2001, ss 360I, 360J*).

Up to 31 March 2014, no writing down allowance is made in respect of expenditure to the extent that it is taken into account for any other state aid or such other grant as might be specified by Treasury order (*CAA 2001, s 360L,* before substitution by *FA 2014, s 66(8)*; see also **8.4**).

Balancing events

> **Focus**
>
> The disposal of a property on which a business premises renovation allowance has been claimed may trigger a balancing event. In general, there is no balancing event if the disposal occurs more than five (previously seven) years after the renovated premises were first used for business purposes.

8.12 When a balancing event takes place, a balancing adjustment, ie a balancing charge or allowance, is made on the company that incurred the expenditure. From 1 April 2014, there is no balancing adjustment if the balancing event occurs more than five years after the time when the renovated premises were first used, or were suitable for letting, for the purposes of a trade, profession or vocation, or as an office or offices, whether or not for the purposes of a trade, profession or vocation. Up to 31 March 2014, this time limit was seven years (*CAA 2001, s 360M,* before and after amendment by *FA 2014, s 66(9)*).

A balancing event occurs in the following circumstances (*CAA 2001, s 360N*):

- the relevant interest in the qualifying building is sold; a long lease (ie a lease longer than 50 years) of the qualifying building is granted out of the relevant interest in consideration of the payment of a capital sum; if the relevant interest is a lease, the lease ends otherwise than on the person entitled to it acquiring the interest reversionary on it;
- the qualifying building is demolished or destroyed;
- the company is wound up; or

- the qualifying building ceases to be qualifying business premises (without being demolished or destroyed).

The proceeds from a balancing event are as follows (*CAA 2001, s 360O*):

Balancing event	*Proceeds from event*
1 The sale of the relevant interest.	The net proceeds of the sale.
2 The grant of a long lease out of the relevant interest.	If the capital sum paid in consideration of the grant is less than the commercial premium, the commercial premium (ie an arm's length premium). In any other case, the capital sum paid in consideration of the grant.
3 The coming to an end of a lease, where a person entitled to the lease and a person entitled to any superior interest are connected persons.	The market value of the relevant interest in the qualifying building at the time of the event.
4 The death of the person who incurred the qualifying expenditure.	The residue of qualifying expenditure immediately before the death.
5 The demolition or destruction of the qualifying building.	The net amount received for the remains of the qualifying building, together with: (a) any insurance money received in respect of the demolition or destruction; and (b) any other compensation of any description so received, so far as it consists of capital sums.
6 The qualifying building ceases to be qualifying business premises.	The market value of the relevant interest in the qualifying building at the time of the event.

Balancing adjustment

8.13 A balancing allowance is equal to the excess of the proceeds over the asset's tax written down value (termed as the 'residue') before disposal. A balancing charge arises if the proceeds are more than the tax written down value.

A balancing charge cannot exceed the total amount of capital allowances granted to the company making the disposal (*CAA 2001, s 360P*).

If proceeds received for a relevant interest are partly attributable to assets qualifying for business premises renovation allowance and partly for other assets, a just apportionment is made (*CAA 2001, s 360Z2*; CA45940).

Writing off qualifying expenditure

8.14 Initial allowances are written off the qualifying expenditure at the time when the qualifying business premises are first used, or suitable for letting for use. Writing down allowances are written off at the end of each chargeable period for which such an allowance is made. Where a balancing event occurs at the end of a chargeable period, the amount written off in that period is taken into account in calculating any balancing adjustment (*CAA 2001, s 360R*).

Demolition costs

8.15 If the company which is entitled to the allowances also incurs the cost of demolition, the net cost of the demolition (ie demolition costs less sale proceeds) is added to the residue of qualifying expenditure immediately before the demolition (*CAA 2001, s 360S*).

VAT

8.16 Where the company was entitled to an initial allowance and later incurs an additional VAT liability in respect of the expenditure, it is entitled to an initial allowance on the amount of that additional VAT liability in the accounting period in which it accrues (*CAA 2001, s 360U*).

An additional VAT rebate is a balancing event that will not give rise to a balancing allowance, but it can give rise to a balancing charge (*CAA 2001, s 360X*). This occurs when the amount of the VAT rebate is more than the amount of the residue of qualifying expenditure or there is no residue (*CAA 2001, ss 360T–360Y*).

Termination of lease

8.17 Depending on the circumstances, the termination of a lease may be treated as a disposal or a continuation of the relevant interest.

The relevant interest continues in the following circumstances (*CAA 2001, s 360Z3*):

- If, with the consent of the lessor, the lessee of the qualifying building remains in possession of the qualifying building after the termination without a new lease being granted to him, the relevant interest continues as long as the lessee remains in possession.
- If, on the termination, a new lease is granted to a lessee as a result of the exercise of an option available to him under the terms of the first lease, the second lease is treated as a continuation of the first.

- If, on the termination:
  - another lease is granted to a different lessee; and
  - in connection with the transaction that lessee pays a sum to the person who was the lessee under the first lease,

  the two leases are to be treated as if they were the same lease, which had been assigned by the lessee under the first lease to the lessee under the second lease in consideration of the payment.

The relevant interest ceases in the following circumstance:

- If, on the termination, the lessor pays a sum to the lessee in respect of business premises comprised in the lease, the lease is treated as if it had come to an end by surrender in consideration of the payment.

Chapter 9

The Construction Industry Scheme

SIGNPOSTS

- Introduction to CIS (see **9.1**).
- Main definitions – including construction contract, operations, sub-contractors and contractors – and the importance of determining employment status (see **9.2–9.7**).
- Tax deductions from payments to sub-contractors – including tax rates, payments and surcharges (see **9.8–9.14**).
- Registration for gross payment – including the business, turnover and compliance tests, and information to be provided to HMRC (see **9.15–9.21**).
- Verification procedure – and sub-contractor penalties (see **9.22–9.24**).
- Record-keeping – including HMRC's inspection powers (see **9.25–9.26**).
- Monthly return procedures – including content and submission of monthly contractor returns, and information to be provided to sub-contractors (see **9.27–9.29**).
- Cancellation of registration for gross payment, and the serious implications this can have for sub-contractors (see **9.30–9.32**).
- Application of sums deducted from contract payments (see **9.33**).
- CIS penalties on contractors – including failure to file, disclose or pay (see **9.34–9.39**).
- Security deposit legislation (see **9.40**).

INTRODUCTION

9.1 Companies whose trade involves construction or building may find that they are required to comply with the Construction Industry Scheme (CIS).

Such businesses will include construction businesses, property developers, speculative builders and construction work gang leaders. *FA 2004* introduced the current Construction Industry Scheme, which came into effect on 6 April 2007. Legislation is contained in *FA 2004, ss 57–77* and *Sch 11*. Secondary legislation is contained within *Income Tax (Construction Industry Scheme) Regulations 2005, SI 2005/2045*. CIS applies not only to companies but also to individuals, partnerships and other bodies.

A company may have to comply with CIS in its capacity as a contractor or sub-contractor, or in both capacities.

Each month, a company that is a contractor is required to make a return of all payments made to sub-contractors in that month. The contractor must account to HMRC each month for all tax which it has deducted from payments to its sub-contractors. Where no payments are made to subcontractors in a particular month, nil returns used to be required but from 6 April 2015 these are no longer necessary (*Income Tax (Construction Industry Scheme) (Amendment) Regulations 2015, SI 2015/429, reg 2(2)*).

A company that acts as a sub-contractor is required, subject to conditions, to register for gross or net payments. A contractor using a sub-contractor must confirm each month that all their sub-contractors are independent businesses, or (if individuals) are properly self-employed and have not been taken on under terms that would make them employees. A contractor company engaging a sub-contractor must verify with HMRC whether to make payment gross or net in accordance with regulations.

Where a contractor company has a recent connection with the sub-contractor, it need not carry out any verification procedures. The rule is, broadly, that a contractor does not have to verify a sub-contractor if they last included that sub-contractor on a return in the current tax year (ending 5 April) or either of the two immediately preceding tax years. HMRC will notify any change in the payment status of the sub-contractor to any contractor who has engaged that sub-contractor in the current year or the previous two years.

HMRC guidance on CIS can be found at tinyurl.com/jwrzwpd and in HMRC's Construction Industry Scheme Reform Manual at CISR00000 onwards.

The dangers of failing to comply with CIS are well illustrated by *Island Contract Management (UK) Ltd v HMRC* [2015] UKUT 472 (TCC), an Upper Tribunal case in which a UK company that had engaged construction workers through its Isle of Man parent to avoid CIS was found liable to tax of over £42 million.

EMPLOYMENT STATUS

9.2 It is a responsibility of the contractor to ensure that none of their sub-contractors are employees.

Whether an individual is employed or self-employed is a matter determined by the terms and conditions on which they are engaged, and by complex legislative provisions. A worker is generally self-employed if they are in business on their own account and bear the responsibility for their business's success or failure. There are a number of factors which typically indicate whether or not a worker is self-employed, and HMRC guidance on these can be found at tinyurl.com/qfy4pr2 (see also Consultation Paper: Employment Status 7 February 2018 at tinyurl.com/y8yd75rq).

To help contractors, HMRC also provide an online 'employment status indicator' (ESI) tool on their website at tinyurl.com/9munln, but this provides only a general guide and is not binding on HMRC.

In cases of doubt, HMRC can provide a contractor with a written opinion about a particular worker's employment status for tax and National Insurance contributions purposes. To obtain such an opinion, the contractor should contact the CIS Helpline on 0300 200 3210 (from abroad +44 161 930 8706; Textphone 0300 200 3219 see tinyurl.com/y7eracyw). If the contractor disagrees with the opinion given, HMRC will reconsider it in the light of any additional information available and, failing agreement, the contractor has a right of appeal.

CONSTRUCTION CONTRACT

Meaning of a construction contract

9.3 For the purposes of CIS, a construction contract is a contract relating to construction operations carried out in the UK, which is not a contract of employment (*FA 2004, s 57(2)*). The UK for this purpose consists of England, Scotland, Wales and Northern Ireland and their territorial waters, but not the Channel Islands or the Isle of Man (*FA 2004, s 74(1),* CISR11090).

For a construction contract to exist for CIS purposes, there must be a contract and a sub-contractor. CIS requires that certain payments under construction contracts are to be made under deduction of sums on account of tax (*FA 2004, s 57(1)*). Reverse premium payments (see **7.22**) are not payments under a construction contract (*Income Tax (Construction Industry Scheme) Regulations 2005, SI 2005/2045, reg 20*).

Sub-contractor

9.4 The status of a sub-contractor is determined by the construction contract. If a party to a contract relating to construction operations (whether that party is an individual, a partnership or a company) has a duty to the contractor under the contract to carry out the operations, or to furnish their own labour (in the case of a company, the labour of the employees or officers of the company) or to furnish the labour of others or is answerable to the contractor for the work of others, that party is considered to be a sub-contractor for these purposes (*FA 2004, s 58*).

Construction operations

> **Focus**
>
> Companies should check whether any of the activities which they carry out are construction operations within the CIS scheme.

9.5 Activities falling under one of more of the following headings are considered to be construction operations (*FA 2004, s 74(2)*):

1. The construction, alteration, repair, extension, demolition or dismantling of buildings or structures (whether permanent or not), including offshore installations.
2. The construction, alteration, repair, extension or demolition of any works forming, or to form, part of the land, including (in particular) walls, roadworks, power-lines, electronic communications apparatus, aircraft runways, docks and harbours, railways, inland waterways, pipe-lines, reservoirs, water-mains, wells, sewers, industrial plant and installations for purposes of land drainage, coast protection or defence.
3. The installation in any building or structure of systems of heating, lighting, air-conditioning, ventilation, power supply, drainage, sanitation, water supply or fire protection.
4. The internal cleaning of buildings and structures, so far as carried out in the course of their construction, alteration, repair, extension or restoration.
5. The painting or decorating the internal or external surfaces of any building or structure.
6. Operations which form an integral part of, or are preparatory to, or are for rendering complete, such operations as are previously described in this subsection, including site clearance, earth-moving, excavation, tunnelling and boring, laying of foundations, erection of scaffolding, site restoration, landscaping and the provision of roadways and other access works.

The following activities are not construction operations (*FA 2004, s 74(3)*):

1. The drilling for, or extraction of, oil or natural gas.
2. The extraction (whether by underground or surface working) of minerals and tunnelling or boring, or construction of underground works, for this purpose.

3 The manufacture of building or engineering components or equipment, materials, plant or machinery, or delivery of any of these things to site.

4 The manufacture of components for systems of heating, lighting, air-conditioning, ventilation, power supply, drainage, sanitation, water supply or fire protection, or delivery of any of these things to site.

5 The professional work of architects or surveyors, or of consultants in building, engineering, interior or exterior decoration or in the laying-out of landscape.

6 The making, installation and repair of artistic works, being sculptures, murals and other works, which are wholly artistic in nature.

7 Signwriting and erecting, installing and repairing signboards and advertisements.

8 The installation of seating, blinds and shutters.

9 The installation of security systems, including burglar alarms, closed circuit television and public address systems.

HMRC's CIS Helpline (see **9.2**) can provide clarification in cases of doubt over a particular activity.

Contractors

9.6 A company carrying on a business which includes construction operations is a contractor. Any public body, government department or agency or NHS trust is also a contractor (*FA 2004, s 59(1)(a)*).

Any other business is a contractor if its average annual expenditure on construction operations in the period of three years ending with the end of the last period of account before that time exceeds £1 million, or (where it was not carrying on the business at the beginning of that three-year period) if one-third of its total expenditure on construction operations for the part of that period during which the business was carried on exceeds £1 million (*FA 2004, s 59(1)(b)–(l)*). For this purpose a payment is ignored if the property is used for the purposes (other than for sale, letting or investment) of the business in question, another company in the same group (see **5.6**) or another company of which that company owns 50% or more of the shares, and incidental use of the property is ignored (*Income Tax (Construction Industry Scheme) Regulations 2005, SI 2005/2045, reg 22*).

Except in the case of companies carrying on businesses which include construction operations and certain contracts relating to social housing (see *FA 2004, s 59(1)(a), (g)*), a body ceases to be a contractor if, since the last period of three financial years (ended 31 March) during which it had average annual expenditure on construction operations of more than £1 million, there have been three successive financial years in each of which its annual expenditure on construction operations was less than £1 million (*FA 2004, s 59(2), (3)*).

A contractor may elect to be treated as different contractors in relation to different groups of sub-contractors, with the result that for each group the contractor is a different contractor. The election must give information to identify the groups of sub-contractors, and contain a certificate that there are no other sub-contractors besides those identified. The election must be made before the beginning of the tax year for which it is to have effect. If a contractor company acquires the whole or part of any business from another contractor, the company may elect within 90 days of the acquisition to be treated as a different contractor in relation to the acquired sub-contractors, or to add some or all of the acquired sub-contractors to existing groups of sub-contractors in respect of whom an election is already in force. The election continues in effect until it is revoked. For a revocation to be effective, it must be given before the beginning of the tax year for which it is to apply (*SI 2005/2045, reg 3*).

Transfer of a trade

9.7 For the purposes of *FA 2004, s 59(1)–(3)* (see **9.6**), if a company transfers the whole or part of its trade to another company and *CTA 2010, s 944* applies to the transfer (see **17.26**), the transferee company is deemed to have incurred the expenditure actually incurred by the transferor. Where only part of the trade is transferred, the expenditure is to be apportioned in such manner as appears to HMRC (or, on appeal, the Tribunal) to be just and reasonable (*FA 2004, s 59(4)*).

TAX DEDUCTIONS FROM CONTRACT PAYMENTS TO SUB-CONTRACTORS

> **Focus**
>
> It is necessary to establish the identity of the sub-contractor, and the nature of the payments made, to establish whether tax should be deducted at source from those payments.

Contract payments

9.8 A contract payment is any payment made by the contractor under a construction contract to the sub-contractor, a person nominated by the sub-contractor or the contractor, or a person nominated by a sub-contractor under another contract in connection with all or some of the construction operations.

A payment is not a contract payment if it is treated as employment earnings of an employed person or an agency worker (*FA 2004, s 60*). A payment does not include the cost of materials, VAT or an amount in respect of the Construction Industry Training Board (CITB) levy; but, depending on the terms of the contract, it may include payments for subsistence and/or travelling expenses (CISR11100).

Deductions on account of tax from contract payments

9.9 It is necessary to be able to distinguish between the direct cost of materials for the construction operation and all other costs. The contractor must deduct tax when making a contract payment to the sub-contractor which does not relate to the direct material costs (*FA 2004, s 61*). The sum deducted and payable to HMRC is treated as a payment towards the sub-contractor's liability for NICs, PAYE and other taxes if a company (see **9.33**), or income tax if an individual (*FA 2004, s 62*).

There is no requirement to deduct tax from a contract payment if the contractor is an approved public body or an approved business, other than one which includes construction operations as highlighted in **9.6** (*FA 2004, s 59(1)(b)–(l)*), and the total payments (excluding the direct cost of materials) are, or are likely to be, lower than £1,000. Similarly, there is no requirement to deduct tax if the contractor is an approved business which includes construction operations on land owned by the company, and the total payments (excluding the direct cost of materials) are, or are likely to be, lower than £1,000 (*Income Tax (Construction Industry Scheme) Regulations 2005, SI 2005/2045, regs 18, 19*).

From 6 April 2010, penalties introduced by *FA 2009, Sch 56*, apply for failure to pay CIS tax on time (see **9.39**).

Rate of tax on deductions from contract payments

9.10 The rate of tax applied to the payment to the sub-contractor depends on the sub-contractor's status. For registered and verified sub-contractors, the rate is 20%; for unregistered or unverified sub-contractors, the rate is 30% (*Finance Act 2004, Section 61(2), (Relevant Percentage) Order 2007, SI 2007/46, art* 2; CISR11100). The rate is nil for those sub-contractors that are registered for gross payment (CISR16050).

Monthly payment

9.11 The return period is the tax month, ie the period of one month ending on the fifth day of each calendar month.

Payment is due within 17 days of the end of the tax month (ie the 22nd of the calendar month) if the payment is made electronically and within 14 days (ie the 19th) if the payment is made by any other means (*Income Tax (Construction Industry Scheme) Regulations 2005, SI 2005/2045, reg 7*). If HMRC have not received payment in full within 17 days, they may issue a notice requiring a return to be completed. HMRC may also make an estimation based on past payment criteria (*SI 2005/2045, regs 10, 11*).

If the contractor makes an error in good faith or, after enquiry, genuinely believed that the scheme did not apply, any amounts not deducted by the contractor company can be recovered from the sub-contractor. Also, the contractor may ask HMRC to issue a direction that the contractor is not liable to any excess tax. If there is a dispute between the contractor and the sub-contractor, HMRC may make a determination of the amount due. Both contractor and sub-contractor have the right of appeal (*SI 2005/2045, regs 9, 13*).

Interest on CIS tax paid late

9.12 For CIS tax payments due on or after 19 May 2014, a contractor is charged interest under *FA 2009, s 101* and *Sch 53*, on CIS tax paid late in respect of 2014/15 and subsequent tax years (*Finance Act 2009, Sections 101 and 102 (Interest on Late Payments and Repayments), Appointed Days and Consequential Provisions Order 2014, SI 2014/992*). Such interest is deductible in computing profits for corporation tax purposes.

Interest on CIS tax paid late in respect of 2013/14 and earlier tax years is charged from 19 April after the end of the tax year until the date of payment (*Income Tax (Construction Industry Scheme) Regulations 2005, SI 2005/2045, reg 14*). Such interest is not deductible for corporation tax purposes (*CTA 2009, s 1303*).

From 6 October 2011, late payment interest rates were harmonised over most taxes and duties, including CIS tax (*FA 2009, s 103*; *Finance Act 2009, Section 103 (Appointed Day) Order 2011, SI 2011/2401*). For earlier periods, see *Corporation Tax 2010/11* (Bloomsbury Professional).

From 31 October 2011 the rate of late payment interest is fixed at 2.5% above the Bank of England rate (*Taxes and Duties, etc (Interest Rate) Regulations 2011, SI 2011/2446*).

HMRC have power to bring proceedings against the contractor for unpaid tax and unpaid interest (*SI 2005/2045, regs 14, 16*).

Interest on CIS tax overpaid

9.13 For CIS tax payments due on or after 19 May 2014 in respect of 2014/15 and subsequent tax years and later repaid by HMRC, a contractor is entitled to interest under *FA 2009, s 102* and *Sch 54*, on overpaid tax (*Finance Act 2009, Sections 101 and 102 (Interest on Late Payments and Repayments),*

Appointed Days and Consequential Provisions Order, SI 2014/992). Such interest is taxable for corporation tax purposes.

A contractor is entitled to interest on overpaid CIS tax in respect of 2013/14 and earlier tax years (*Income Tax (Construction Industry Scheme) Regulations 2005, SI 2005/2045, reg 15*). Such interest is not taxable for corporation tax purposes.

From 6 October 2011, repayment interest rates were harmonised over most taxes and duties, including CIS tax (*FA 2009, s 103*; *Finance Act 2009, Section 103 (Appointed Day) Order 2011, SI 2011/2401*). For earlier periods, see *Corporation Tax 2010/11* (Bloomsbury Professional).

From 31 October 2011, interest paid on overpayments is fixed at 1% below the Bank of England rate, subject to a minimum rate of 0.5% (*Taxes and Duties, etc (Interest Rate) Regulations 2011, SI 2011/2446*).

Quarterly payment

9.14 A contractor company may pay quarterly if it has reasonable grounds for believing that the average monthly amount it has to pay by way of PAYE and CIS payments will be less than £1,500 and the company chooses to pay quarterly. In such a case the tax is payable by reference to the quarters of the fiscal year (ie for the quarters ending 5 July, 5 October, 5 January and 5 April). For example, in the case of the tax for the quarter ending 5 July, payment is due within 17 days of the end of the tax quarter (ie by 22 July) if the payment is made electronically and within 14 days (ie by 19 July) if the payment is made by any other means (*Income Tax (Construction Industry Scheme) Regulations 2005, SI 2005/2045, reg 7*).

The average monthly amount is the average, for tax months falling within the current tax year, of the amounts that would be payable using the following formula (*SI 2005/2045, reg 8*):

$$(P + N + L + S) - (SP + CD)$$

where:

- P is the PAYE due for the period less any PAYE repayments as calculated according to *Income Tax (Pay As You Earn) Regulations 2003, SI 2003/2682, reg 67G* or *68*
- N is the employees' class 1 primary contribution, disregarding any secondary contributions transferred from the employer to the employee under an *SSCBA 1992, Sch 1, para 3B(1)* election
- L is the Student Loan repayments less tax credits under *Education (Student Loans) (Repayment) Regulations 2009, SI 2009/470, reg 54(1), (3)*

- S is the CIS tax due by the contractor for the tax month (*SI 2005/2045, reg 7*)
- SP is the statutory sick pay, statutory maternity pay, ordinary statutory paternity pay, additional statutory paternity pay and statutory adoption pay under *SSCBA 1992*
- CD is, where the contractor is a company, the amount which others would deduct from payments to it, in its position as a sub-contractor, under *FA 2004, s 61*.

REGISTRATION FOR GROSS PAYMENT

Focus

For a sub-contractor, gross payment registration has cash flow advantages. However, the circumstances in which registration for gross payment is allowed are narrowly defined and strictly applied.

Registration of sub-contractors

9.15 HMRC will register a sub-contractor company for gross payment on submission of the relevant information and documentation. The company is required to comply with the business, turnover and compliance test conditions in order to be eligible for gross payments.

In turn, the Board of HMRC may direct that the conditions shall apply to:

- the directors of the company,
- if the company is a close company, the beneficial owners of shares in the company, or
- specified persons,

as if each were an applicant for gross payment registration (*FA 2004, s 64(5)*). In other circumstances, the company will be registered for net payment.

Gross payment tests

9.16 If a company applies for gross payment registration, it must satisfy the business test, the turnover test and the compliance test (*FA 2004, Sch 11, para 9*).

The business test

9.17 The company must satisfy HMRC that:

- it is carrying on a business in the UK; and
- the business consists of or includes the carrying out of construction operations or the furnishing or arranging for the furnishing of labour in carrying out construction operations, and is substantially carried on through a bank account (*FA 2004, Sch 11, para 10*).

The following evidence must be supplied to HMRC (*Income Tax (Construction Industry Scheme) Regulations 2005, SI 2005/2045, reg 27*):

- the company's address;
- invoices, contracts or purchase orders for construction work carried out by the company;
- details of payments for construction work;
- the books and accounts of the company; and
- details of the company bank account, including bank statements.

The turnover test

9.18 The company must either satisfy HMRC with evidence that it is likely to receive the minimum turnover in the year in which the application is made, or satisfy HMRC that the only persons with shares in the company are companies, which are limited by shares, and are themselves registered for gross payment.

The minimum turnover for the period is the smaller of:

- £30,000 × number of relevant persons for the company, or
- £200,000 for tax years up to and including 2015/16 and £100,000 thereafter (the *Income Tax (Construction Industry Scheme) (Amendment) Regulations 2016, SI 2016/348*).

Company directors are relevant persons. Beneficial owners of shares in a close company are also relevant persons (*FA 2004, Sch 11, para 11*).

The company must be able to supply evidence of turnover and relevant payments, together with documentary evidence to demonstrate that operations during the period amounted to construction operations. In the case of a new business, evidence of turnover and relevant persons during the qualifying period should be supplied. Evidence should also be supplied of construction contracts entered into by the company, including payment schedules where the aggregate value of these contracts exceeds £100,000 and payments of at least £30,000 have been made.

If a company's business does not consist mainly of construction operations, HMRC will treat the turnover test as satisfied, if not actually satisfied, if the following conditions are met (*Income Tax (Construction Industry Scheme) Regulations 2005, SI 2005/2045, regs 29, 31*):

- in the year prior to making the application, the total turnover of the business exceeded the relevant turnover threshold; and
- in the year following the making of the application, the company is likely to receive relevant payments in relation to construction operations which are incidental to the company's main business.

The compliance test

9.19 Within 12 months of the registration application, the company must have complied with all HMRC requests concerning information and documentation (*FA 2004, Sch 11, paras 12, 14*). HMRC will treat the following prescribed obligations as being satisfied by the following prescribed circumstances (*Income Tax (Construction Industry Scheme) Regulations 2005, SI 2005/2045, reg 32* as amended by the *Income Tax (Construction Industry Scheme) (Amendment) Regulations 2016, SI 2016/348*).

The following prescribed obligations apply for tax years up to and including 2015/16:

Prescribed obligations	**Prescribed circumstances**
Obligation to submit monthly contractor return within the required period	1 Return is submitted not later than 28 days after the due date, and 2 the company: (a) has not otherwise failed to comply with this obligation within the previous 12 months, or (b) has failed to comply with this obligation on not more than two occasions within the previous 12 months
Obligation to pay: (a) the tax deducted from payments made during that tax period, or (b) tax liable to be deducted under the *PAYE Regulations, SI 2003/2682*	1 Payment is made not later than 14 days after the due date, and 2 the company: (a) has not otherwise failed to comply with this obligation within the previous 12 months, or (b) has failed to comply with this obligation on not more than two occasions within the previous 12 months

Obligation to pay income tax	1 Payment is made not later than 28 days after the due date, and 2 the applicant has not otherwise failed to comply with this obligation within the previous 12 months
Obligation to submit Forms P11D and P9D within the required period (*PAYE Regulations, SI 2003/2682, reg 85*)	Return is submitted after the due date
Obligation to pay corporation tax for which the applicant or company is liable	1 Payment is made not later than 28 days after the due date, and 2 any shortfall in that payment has incurred an interest charge but no penalty
Obligation to submit a self-assessment return within the required period	Return is submitted after the due date
Obligations and requests to supply information in support of the compliance test	The failure to comply occurred before 6 April 2007 but complied with previous requirements
Obligation to make a payment under the *Tax Acts* or *TMA 1970*	Late payment or non-payment of an amount under £100

From 2016/17 onwards, the prescribed obligations are as follows:

Prescribed obligations	**Prescribed circumstances**
Obligation to submit monthly contractor return within the required period	1 Return is submitted not later than 28 days after the due date, and 2 the company has failed to comply with this obligation on not more than two occasions within the previous 12 months
Obligation to pay: (a) the tax deducted from payments made during that tax period, or (b) tax liable to be deducted under the *PAYE Regulations, SI 2003/2682*	1 Where the amount not paid by the due date is under £100, or 2 where the amount not paid by the due date is at least £100, and: (a) the payment is made not later than 14 days after the due date; and

	(b) the applicant or company has failed to comply with this obligation in respect of an amount of at least £100 on not more than two occasions within the previous 12 months
Obligation to submit a self-assessment return within the required period	Return is submitted not later than 28 days after the due date

From 6 April 2015 a sub-contractor company does not need to meet the compliance test if one or more of its members is/are already registered for gross payment and they possess or are entitled to acquire at least 50% of the share capital or voting rights, or so much of the share capital or rights as would on a winding up entitle them to receive at least 50% of the assets or the amounts available for distribution (*Income Tax (Construction Industry Scheme) (Amendment of Schedule 11 to the Finance Act 2004) Order 2015, SI 2015/789*).

A sub-contractor company receiving gross payments is subject to an annual review of its compliance record by HMRC. This is called a 'Scheduled Review', also known as an 'Ongoing TTQT' (Tax Treatment Qualification Test), and is an automated check on whether the sub-contractor has complied with all its tax obligations as a taxpayer including, if appropriate, as an employer or contractor. For further information on the Ongoing TTQT, see CISR49600.

Information to be supplied to HMRC

9.20 On application for gross payment status, a sub-contractor company must supply the following information to HMRC (*Income Tax (Construction Industry Scheme) Regulations 2005, SI 2005/2045, reg 25*):

- the name, address, National Insurance number and unique taxpayer reference of each of the directors of the company and, if the company is a close company, each of the persons who are the beneficial owners of shares in the company,
- utility bills,
- council tax bills,
- current passports,
- driving licences,
- company registration number, and
- company's memorandum and articles of association.

From 6 October 2011, penalties introduced by *FA 2009, Sch 55* apply if the information is not submitted on time (see **9.34–9.38**).

Company change of control

9.21 If there has been a change in the control of a company that is applying for gross payment registration, HMRC may ask for information regarding the changes in control of the company (*FA 2004, s 65*).

The definition of 'control' for this purpose is set out in *CTA 2010, s 1124* (see **21.5**).

Where there is a change of control of a private company limited by shares which is a close company, either registered as a sub-contractor for gross payment or applying to be so registered, and that change of control occurs by reason of an issue or transfer of shares in the company to a person who was not a shareholder in the company immediately before the issue or transfer, the company must notify HMRC within 30 days of the issue or of receiving information as to the transfer. The company must supply HMRC with details of the name and address of the person to whom the shares were issued or transferred (*Income Tax (Construction Industry Scheme) Regulations 2005, SI 2005/2045, reg 53*).

VERIFICATION, RECORD-KEEPING AND PENALTIES

9.22 HMRC may make regulations requiring the contractor company to verify the status of the sub-contractor company (*FA 2004, s 69*).

A contractor must verify with HMRC the status of the sub-contractor to whom gross payments are to be made and, if applicable, a nominee appointed by the sub-contractor.

The contractor company must provide details of:

- the company name, unique taxpayer reference (UTR), accounts office reference and employer's reference, and
- in relation to the person to whom it is proposing to make the payment and, where that person has appointed a nominee, his nominee:
  - (i) if that person or nominee is an individual, his name, UTR and National Insurance number;
  - (ii) if that person or nominee is a partner in a firm, the name of the firm and the partner, the UTR of the firm; and, if the partner is an individual, his UTR or National Insurance number or, if the partner is a company, the UTR or the company registration number; or
  - (iii) if that person or nominee is a company, the name of the company, UTR and the company registration number.

Verification is not possible until a contract is in place (*Income Tax (Construction Industry Scheme) Regulations 2005, SI 2005/2045, reg 6(1)–(3)*).

From 6 April 2017, online verification is mandatory via the government website page at tinyurl.com/gpkvodc or the for Electronic Data Interchange (EDI) services provided through the Construction Industry Scheme Online (*Income Tax (Construction Industry Scheme) Regulations 2005, SI 2005/2045, reg 6A(2A)–(2C)*, inserted by the *Income Tax (Construction Industry Scheme) (Amendment) Regulations 2016, SI 2016/348*).

Situations where verification is not required

9.23 Verification is not required if the contractor:

(a) has included the sub-contractor in a sub-contract return in the current or previous two tax years;

(b) has elected under *Income Tax (Construction Industry Scheme) Regulations 2005, SI 2005/2045, reg 3* (see **9.6**); or

(c) acquired the contract under which the payment is to be made in a transfer of a business as a going concern in one of the situations described in (a) or (b) above (*SI 2005/2045, reg 6(4)*).

Sub-contractor penalties

9.24 A sub-contractor company may be liable to a £3,000 penalty if it knowingly or recklessly makes a false statement, or provides a false document (*FA 2004, s 72*).

RECORD-KEEPING

9.25 HMRC may make regulations requiring contractor companies that make payments under construction contracts to:

- make returns to HMRC,
- keep records as prescribed relating to the payments, or
- provide such information as may be prescribed to the persons to whom the payments are made (*FA 2004, s 70*).

Records must be kept for three years after the end of the tax year to which they relate (*Income Tax (Construction Industry Scheme) Regulations 2005, SI 2005/2045, reg 51(10)*).

In particular, the company making the return must state that none of the contracts to which the return relates is a contract of employment, the regulations have been complied with, and the returns contain all the necessary information, and confirm that the verification status requirements of the sub-contractor have been complied with (*SI 2005/2045, reg 6*). The sub-contractor need not seek verification if the sub-contractor has been included in a monthly return in the current or previous two years of the same company or group company. For this purpose, *SI 2005/2045, reg 6*, defines a group, as for group relief purposes, in accordance with *CTA 2010, s 152* (see **5.6**).

Inspection of records of contractors and sub-contractors

9.26 A contractor or sub-contractor must produce records for the previous three years to HMRC when required to do so. HMRC may make copies, remove or make extracts from these records. HMRC will issue a receipt for all documents removed and provide copies on request free of charge to the contractor or sub-contractor from whom the documents were removed (*Income Tax (Construction Industry Scheme) Regulations 2005, SI 2005/2045, regs 51, 52*).

MONTHLY RETURN PROCEDURES

Content of monthly contractor returns to HMRC

9.27 Contractor companies are required to submit monthly returns to HMRC within 14 days of the end of each tax month. Until 5 April 2016, these could be lodged either online or on paper; but, after that date, online filing is mandatory. The contractor company may appoint another company in the same group as the scheme representative (*Income Tax (Construction Industry Scheme) Regulations 2005, SI 2005/2045, reg 5*).

The monthly return must show:

- the contractor's name,
- the contractor's unique taxpayer reference (UTR) and Accounts' Office reference,
- the tax month to which the return relates, and
- in respect of each sub-contractor to whom, or to whose nominee, payments under construction contracts were made by the contractor during that month:
  - (i) the sub-contractor's name;
  - (ii) the sub-contractor's national insurance number (NINO) or company registration number (CRN), if known;
  - (iii) the sub-contractor's UTR;
  - (iv) if the sub-contractor is registered for gross payment, the total amount of payments which would be contract payment exceptions

(see **9.8**) made by the contractor to the sub-contractor during the tax month;

(v) if the sub-contractor is registered for payment under deduction of tax, the total amount of the contract payments (see **9.8**) made by the contractor to the sub-contractor during the tax month, the total amount included in those payments which the contractor is satisfied represents the direct cost to any person other than the contractor of materials used or to be used in carrying out the construction contract to which the contract payment relates, and the amount of tax deducted; and

(vi) if the sub-contractor is not registered for gross payment or payment under deduction of tax, the total amount of the contract payments (see **9.8**) made by the contractor to the sub-contractor during the tax month, the total amount included in those payments which the contractor is satisfied represents the direct cost to any person other than the contractor of materials used or to be used in carrying out the construction contract to which the contract payment relates, and the amount of tax deducted, together with the verification reference for higher rate deduction.

On each monthly return, the contractor company must declare that none of the contracts to which the return relates is a contract of employment, and must indicate whether it has verified each sub-contractor's status.

Submission of contractor returns

9.28 From 6 April 2016, online verification is mandatory, either through the government's online service at tinyurl.com/gpkvodc or (for large businesses) though the Electronic Data Interchange (EDI). It is no longer be possible to submit paper returns (*Income Tax (Construction Industry Scheme) Regulations 2005, SI 2005/2045, reg 4(4)* as amended by the *Income Tax (Construction Industry Scheme) (Amendment) Regulations 2016, SI 2016/348*).

For periods up to 5 April 2015, if no payments were made and the contractor made (or should have made) a return for the previous tax month, a nil return was required, unless the contractor had notified HMRC that it would make no further payments under construction contracts within the following six months. From 6 April 2015, nil returns are no longer necessary (*Income Tax (Construction Industry Scheme) (Amendment) Regulations 2015, SI 2015/429, reg 2(2)*).

From 6 October 2011, penalties introduced by *FA 2009, Sch 55* apply if the return is not submitted on time (see **9.34–9.38**).

Most contractor and sub-contractor companies also have direct employees in respect of which they are obliged to account for PAYE under the online real time information (RTI) regime. The total that must be accounted for to HMRC for the month (or quarter, if applicable) is calculated as:

- the PAYE charge shown on the company's Full Payment Summary (FPS) returns, if it has direct employees,

plus

- the CIS charge shown on the company's CIS300 returns, if it is a contractor,

minus

- the CIS deductions suffered, as shown on the company's Employer Payment Summary (EPS), if it is a sub-contractor (see **9.33**).

Information to be provided to sub-contractors

9.29 In all cases where payment has been made under deduction, the contractor must provide each sub-contractor with details of the payments (or total payments) made to it during each tax month, not later than 14 days after the end of the tax month to which the payments relate (*Income Tax (Construction Industry Scheme) Regulations 2005, SI 2005/2045, reg 4*).

If the sub-contractor is registered for payment under deduction, the details must include:

- the contractor's name;
- the contractor's employer's reference;
- the tax month to which the payments relate or the date of the payment;
- the sub-contractor's name;
- the sub-contractor's unique taxpayer reference (UTR);
- the total amount of contract payments made by the contractor to the sub-contractor during the tax month;
- the total amount included in those payments which the contractor is satisfied represents the direct cost to any person other than the contractor of materials used or to be used in carrying out the construction contract to which the contract payment relates; and
- the total tax deducted.

If the sub-contractor is not registered under CIS, so that tax has been deducted at the higher rate of 30% (see **9.10**), the information provided must also include the verification reference for this higher rate deduction.

There is no obligation on contractors to issue statements to sub-contractors who are paid gross, but HMRC suggest that it is good practice to do so.

CANCELLATION OF REGISTRATION FOR GROSS PAYMENT

> **Focus**
>
> Loss of gross payment status can be a very serious blow for a sub-contractor because of the adverse cash flow repercussions. If HMRC move to withdraw registration for gross payment, the sub-contractor should take immediate action to try to persuade them not to do this, or should seek to appeal against the decision.

Reasons for cancellation

9.30 HMRC may issue a determination stating the reasons to cancel a sub-contractor's (eg a sub-contractor company's) gross payment registration if, at any time, it appears to them that:

- if an application to register the company for gross payment were to be made at that time, the Board would refuse so to register it,
- the company has made an incorrect return or provided incorrect information (whether as a contractor or as a sub-contractor) under any provision of *FA 2004, Pt 3, Ch 3* or regulations made under it, or
- it has failed to comply (whether as a contractor or as a sub-contractor) with any such provision.

The gross payment cancellation takes effect from the end of a prescribed period of 90 days after HMRC have notified the sub-contractor of the making of the determination. On receipt of the determination, the sub-contractor must register for net payment. The sub-contractor is then debarred from re-applying for gross payment registration for a year from cancellation (*FA 2004, s 66*; *Income Tax (Construction Industry Scheme) Regulations 2005, SI 2005/2045, reg 26*).

Fraudulent conduct

9.31 HMRC may issue a determination, stating the reasons, to cancel a person's (eg a company's) gross payment registration if, at any time, they have reasonable grounds to suspect that the company:

- became registered for gross payment on the basis of information which was false;

- has fraudulently made an incorrect return or provided incorrect information (whether as a contractor or as a sub-contractor) under any provision of *FA 2004, Pt 3, Ch 3* or of regulations made under it; or
- has knowingly failed to comply (whether as a contractor or as a sub-contractor) with any such provision.

In such circumstances, the cancellation takes immediate effect on the issue of the determination. On receipt of the determination, if HMRC think fit, the sub-contractor company may register for net payment. Again, the sub-contractor company is debarred from re-applying for gross payment registration for a year from cancellation (*FA 2004, s 66*).

Right of appeal against cancellation of registration

9.32 Withdrawal of a sub-contractor company's registration for gross payment may have a swift and serious adverse impact on the company's business. In many cases, the cash flow repercussions may put the company out of business within a very short period. Thus a company needs to take immediate action if its registration for gross payment has been withdrawn inappropriately.

The company has the right of appeal to the Tribunal against the determination. The appeal must give the full grounds and be made within 30 days after the refusal or cancellation. A refusal or cancellation under appeal does not take effect until the later of:

- the abandonment of the appeal,
- the determination of the appeal by the Tribunal, or
- the determination of the appeal by the Upper Tribunal or a court (*FA 2004, s 67*).

John Kerr Roofing Contractors v Commissioners of Revenue & Customs [2013] UKFTT 135 (TC) concerned the jurisdiction of the First-tier Tribunal to review HMRC's exercise of their discretion to cancel a contractor's registration for gross payment status. The Tribunal held that HMRC had erred in cancelling the registration without taking into account its possible impact on the taxpayer's future trade.

This contrasted with the more recent case of *J P Whitter (Water Well Engineers) Ltd v Revenue and Customs Commissioners* [2015] UKUT 392 (TCC), in which the taxpayer had successfully appealed against withdrawal of gross payment status on two previous occasions. On this the third time, the Upper Tribunal upheld the cancellation of gross payment status, concluding that the financial consequences were not a relevant factor to be taken into account by HMRC.

APPLICATION OF SUMS DEDUCTED FROM CONTRACT PAYMENTS

9.33 Companies that have CIS deductions taken from their income as sub-contractors can set these off against their monthly or quarterly PAYE liabilities. This may be done only by sub-contractors that are companies, and not by sub-contractors that are partnerships or individuals.

The PAYE RTI regime is used to report the deductions to HMRC so that these set-offs can be made. Even if the sub-contractor company has no employees during the tax year, it must submit an Employer Payment Summary (EPS) to HMRC within 14 days after the end of the tax month, reporting the sums withheld. Form CIS132 is a form provided by HMRC, not for submission to HMRC, but simply to help the sub-contractor record the sums to be reported.

The deductions suffered by the sub-contractor company are applied by HMRC against liabilities of the sub-contractor in the following order:

- employee Class 1 NICs;
- additional statutory paternity pay under *Additional Statutory Paternity Pay (Birth, Adoption and Adoptions from Overseas) (Administration) Regulations 2010, SI 2010/154, regs 4–7*;
- employer Class 1 NICs;
- PAYE;
- student loan deductions;
- refund to HMRC of any funding payment made in respect of statutory sick pay, statutory maternity pay, ordinary statutory paternity pay, additional statutory paternity pay or statutory adoption pay; and
- construction industry deductions from its sub-contractors.

If there is an excess of tax suffered by the sub-contractor, either it is set off against any outstanding corporation tax due by the sub-contractor, or it is repaid to the sub-contractor. In most cases HMRC will not make any such repayment to the sub-contractor until after the end of the tax year in which the deductions were made and the sub-contractor has submitted its final EPS or Full Payment Summary (FPS) for the tax year (*Income Tax (Construction Industry Scheme) Regulations 2005, SI 2005/2045, reg 56*).

From 6 April 2015, by virtue of *Income Tax (Construction Industry Scheme) (Amendment) Regulations 2015, SI 2015/429, reg 2(3)*, HMRC may repay any excess deduction to the sub-contractor company during the tax year in which the deduction was made if:

(a) the sub-contractor is subject to a winding-up under *IA 1986, Pt 4*; and

(b) the sub-contractor has:

(i) ceased trading,

(ii) permanently ceased making contract payments in its capacity as a contractor, or

(iii) ceased trading and permanently ceased making such payments.

HMRC have been notoriously slow in repaying CIS tax to sub-contractor companies. In April 2014, they published a Helpcard providing guidance for companies and their agents on the CIS repayment procedures (see tinyurl.com/kwes43y).

CIS PENALTIES ON CONTRACTORS

Focus

There are a number of different circumstances in which a contractor may face penalties under the CIS regime.

Returns outstanding for less than 12 months

9.34 From 6 October 2011, penalties introduced by *FA 2009, Sch 55, paras 7–13,* apply for monthly returns submitted late.

Initial failure to meet due date

If a return is not received by HMRC by its due date of the 19th of the calendar month, a penalty of £100 is charged.

Return still outstanding two months after due date

If the return has still not been received by HMRC two months after its due date, a further penalty of £200 is charged.

Return still outstanding six months after due date

If the return is still outstanding six months after its due date, a 'tax-geared' penalty becomes due. This penalty is the greater of 5% of any deductions shown on the outstanding return and £300.

Returns outstanding for more than 12 months

Returns affecting the contractor's liability for CIS deductions

9.35 If, by failing to make the return within 12 months after the due date, the contractor withholds information which would enable or assist HMRC to assess its own (the contractor's) liability to tax, a range of penalties may be charged. Some of these are fixed penalties. Others are tax-geared penalties, some of which depend on whether or not the withholding of information is deliberate or concealed and on the timing and quality of the contractor's disclosure to HMRC.

If the withholding of information on the return has been deliberate and concealed, the penalty is the greater of 100% of any deductions shown on the return and £3,000.

If the withholding of information on the return has been deliberate but not concealed, the penalty will be the greater of 70% of any deductions shown on the return and £1,500.

In cases where the withholding of information has been deliberate, these tax-geared penalties can be reduced, depending on the timing and quality of the contractor's disclosure to HMRC.

In all other cases, ie where the information on the return has not been withheld deliberately, the penalty will be the greater of 5% of any deductions shown on the return and £300.

Information relating to gross payment sub-contractors

9.36 If information relating to sub-contractors registered for gross payments (see **9.15**) remains outstanding for 12 months beginning with the penalty date, an additional fixed-rate penalty may be charged. If, by failing to make the return, the contractor withholds information which relates to such persons, the penalty arising depends on whether the withholding of information is deliberate or concealed.

If the withholding of information is deliberate and concealed, the penalty is £3,000.

If the withholding of information is deliberate but not concealed, the penalty is £1,500.

Reductions in penalties

9.37 Some of the above penalty details (see **9.34–9.36**) refer to the level of penalty being affected by the timing and quality of the contractor's disclosure to HMRC.

The timing of a disclosure is crucial. There are reductions in the penalties charged for unprompted disclosure. An unprompted disclosure can be made at any time when the person making it has no reason to believe that HMRC have discovered or are about to discover the inaccuracy or under-assessment. In all other cases, the disclosure is prompted.

The quality of a disclosure is an assessment of the contractor's helpfulness in telling HMRC of the information withheld, helping HMRC to work out correctly any outstanding liability to make payments, and giving HMRC access to their records to achieve this.

In summary, the tax-geared penalties for a return still outstanding 12 months after the due date are based on a percentage of the total tax deductions shown on the return, and this percentage can vary as follows:

Type of behaviour (ie way information was withheld)	*Unprompted disclosure*	*Prompted disclosure*	*Normal minimum penalty*
Non-deliberate	5%	5%	£300
Deliberate but not concealed	20% to 70%	35% to 70%	£1,500
Deliberate and concealed	30% to 100%	50% to 100%	£3,000

HMRC have discretion to reduce a penalty if they consider that special circumstances apply. The special circumstances do not include the contractor's inability to pay, or the fact that a potential loss of revenue from one taxpayer is balanced by a potential over-payment by another. HMRC also have discretion not to bring proceedings in relation to a penalty, and to agree a compromise during any proceedings that should take place (*FA 2009, Sch 55, para 16*).

These penalties are reduced by any other penalty or surcharge applied to the same tax liability (*FA 2009, Sch 55, para 17(1)*).

For a contractor that has not submitted any previous CIS returns and is filing its first CIS returns late, there will be an upper limit of £3,000 on the total fixed-rate penalties that may accrue. This capping of the total fixed penalties does not extend to any 'tax-geared' penalty except that, where it applies, it removes the £300 minimum on the penalty that would otherwise be charged where the tax-geared penalty is less than £300. Note that the capping only applies in respect of contractors new to CIS that have not sent in their first returns on time, and does not apply to contractors that have already filed returns previously.

Assessing the penalty

9.38 In order to charge the penalty, HMRC must raise an assessment, notify the contractor, and state in the notice the period in respect of which the penalty is assessed. The contractor must pay the penalty within 30 days beginning with the day on which notification of the penalty was issued (*FA 2009, Sch 55, para 18*). The time limit for assessing the penalty is the last day of the period of two years beginning with the filing date. If there is an appeal, the time limit is the last day of the period of 12 months beginning with either the end of the appeal period for the assessment of the liability to tax which would have been shown in the return or, if there is no such assessment, the date on which that liability is ascertained or it is ascertained that the liability is nil (*FA 2009, Sch 55, para 19*).

An insufficiency of funds is not a reasonable excuse, unless it is attributable to events outside the contractor's control. Where the contractor relies on another person to do anything, that fact is not a reasonable excuse unless the contractor took reasonable care to avoid the failure; in *Nigel Barrett v Commissioners of Revenue & Customs* [2015] UKFTT 329 (TC), an appeal against CIS late filing penalties succeeded where the taxpayer had been unaware of the CIS scheme and had relied on his accountant.

Where the contractor had a reasonable excuse for the failure, but the excuse has ceased, the contractor is treated as having continued to have the excuse if the failure is remedied without unreasonable delay after the excuse ceased (*FA 2009, Sch 55, para 23*).

Penalties for failure to pay tax

9.39 From 6 April 2010, penalties introduced by *FA 2009, Sch 56,* apply for failure to pay CIS tax on time.

HMRC may charge a penalty on late payment of deductions on account of corporation tax from contract payments payable under *FA 2004, s 62* (see **9.9**). The penalty is based on the number of defaults made during the tax year, being the contractor's failure to pay tax on time in full:

Number of failures to pay tax in full and on time	*Number of defaults resulting during the tax year*	*Penalty*	*Amount on which penalty is based*
1	0	0%	Nil
2, 3 or 4	1, 2 or 3	1%	Total amount of defaults 1–3
5, 6 or 7	4, 5 or 6	2%	Total amount of defaults 1–6
8, 9 or 10	7, 8 or 9	3%	Total amount of defaults 1–9
11	10 or more	4%	Total amount of defaults in the period

The amount of a default is the amount of tax which the contractor fails to pay, and a default is still counted for penalty purposes even if the default is remedied before the end of the tax year.

If any amount of the tax is unpaid after the end of the period of six months beginning with the penalty date, the contractor is liable to an additional penalty of 5% of that amount. If any amount of the tax is unpaid after the end of the period of 12 months beginning with the penalty date, the contractor is liable to an additional penalty of 5% of that amount (*FA 2009, Sch 56, paras 5, 6*).

The penalty may be reduced for special circumstances, and there is an appeals procedure (see **22.23–22.30**).

In *Oddy (t/a CMO Bird Proofing Specialists) v HMRC* [2014] UKFTT 673 (TC), the First-tier Tribunal upheld the taxpayer's appeal against penalties levied under previous legislation in respect of late CIS monthly contractor returns, finding that the taxpayer's systematic record-keeping of the submission of returns on time were more credible than HMRC's records.

SECURITY DEPOSIT LEGISLATION

> **Focus**
>
> The government proposes that, from April 2019, a contractor registered under the CIS will be required to provide a security deposit where HMRC believe that there is a risk to the revenue.

9.40 The new proposals are part of the government's Consultation Paper on extending the security deposit legislation to corporation tax and CIS (*Consultation Paper: Extension of Security Deposit Legislation* 13 March 2018 at tinyurl.com/y8kp8axg; see also **23.47**). Security will be required from contractors who have a history of non-compliance – in particular, the following two situations are targeted:

- non-compliant businesses, where there is a history of persistent late filing or payment, or a failure to pay a large tax liability on time, and where the business has not requested time to pay or does not respond to contact from HMRC to discuss possible ways of managing the debt;
- cases of 'phoenixism', where a business owner has a practice of closing one business down and leaving behind its tax debts, and subsequently beginning a similar business, usually from the same trading premises, with the same personnel and the same clients.

The new rules will not be applicable where the taxpayer has been unable to pay due to financial difficulties or is a party to a 'time to pay' or other debt management arrangement. The rules are targeted at those who are unwilling to pay. It is proposed that a criminal offence is committed when a contractor pays a subcontractor under a construction contract when he has been required to give security but has failed to do so.

The security need not be limited to cash payments, but may include guarantees in the form of a performance bond issued by a financial institution.

Chapter 10

Close companies and connected issues

SIGNPOSTS

- How close company status is determined, including the meaning of a participator, principal member, director, loan creditor and associate (see **10.2–10.13**).
- How loans, advances or benefits to participators are treated for tax purposes, and the self-assessment requirements (see **10.14–10.26**).
- Determination of whether one company is connected with another (see **10.27**).
- Consequences of close investment-holding company categorisation (see **10.29–10.31**).
- Companies owned by spouses or civil partners (see **10.32**).

INTRODUCTION

10.1 Ownership of a company is vested in its shareholders. A share in a company is a bundle of rights, namely voting rights, dividend rights, and a right to assets in a winding up. Companies owned by a small number of individuals are in a position to control a company to their advantage. The corporation tax legislation looks through these relationships and modifies the corporation tax rules, in particular in relation to:

- close companies;
- close investment-holding companies (up to 31 March 2015); and
- loans, advances and certain other benefits provided to 'participators'.

CLOSE COMPANIES

> **Focus**
>
> Close company legislation is, in effect, complex anti-avoidance legislation designed to prevent individuals from gaining a tax advantage through owning shares in a closely held company. This legislation has been in course of development over a period of half a century. Current close company rules are far more generous than those first enacted. In practice, a good knowledge of the company and its shareholders is a prime requirement in determining close company status.

Consequences

10.2 The close company provisions were included within the corporation tax provisions that were first introduced in 1965, and similar legislation had been in existence before that time.

The effect of the provisions (if all the related conditions apply) is to widen the scope of distributions to include benefits to shareholders and members of their families (see **Chapter 18** for distributions). The provisions regard some loans and certain specific benefits to shareholders as extractions of profits and seek to tax the company on these. Close investment-holding companies were prevented from taking advantage of the small profits rate of corporation tax until it was abolished with effect from 1 April 2015.

Status

10.3 A company is a close company if either condition A or condition B is met (*CTA 2010, s 439*):

Condition A

The company is under the control of:

- five or fewer participators, or
- participators who are directors.

Condition B

Five or fewer participators, or participators who are directors, together possess or are entitled to acquire (*CTA 2010, s 439*):

- such rights as would, in the event of a winding up, entitle them to receive the greater part of the assets of the relevant company which would then be available for distribution among the participators, or

- such rights as would, in that event, so entitle them if there were disregarded any rights which any of them or any other person has as a loan creditor (in relation to the relevant company or any other company).

For the purpose of the notional winding up referred to above, the part of the assets available for distribution among the participators which any person is entitled to receive is the aggregate of:

- any part of those assets which the person would be entitled to receive on the winding up of the relevant company; and
- any part of those assets which the person would be entitled to receive if any other company which is a participator in the relevant company were also wound up and its assets distributed among its participators (*CTA 2010, s 440*).

For this purpose, a person is treated as a participator in, or director of, a company if the person is a participator in or director of any other company which would be entitled to receive assets in the company's notional winding up (*CTA 2010, s 441(2)*).

In determining whether a company is a close company under *CTA 2010, s 439*, no account is taken of a participator which is a company unless that company possesses or is entitled to acquire its rights as a participator in a fiduciary or representative capacity (*CTA 2010, s 441(3)*), but this rule is disapplied when determining assets under *CTA 2010, s 440* for the purposes of a notional winding up (*CTA 2010, s 441(4)*).

Control

10.4 *CTA 2010, s 450* prescribes that a person controls a company if that person:

- exercises,
- is able to exercise, or
- is entitled to acquire,

direct or indirect control over the company's affairs.

A 'person' can be a natural person or a body of persons corporate or unincorporate, eg another company (*Interpretation Act 1978, Sch 1*).

A person is treated as having control of a company if that person possesses or is entitled to acquire:

- the greater part of the company's share capital or issued share capital,
- the greater part of the voting power in the company,
- so much of the company's issued share capital as would, on the assumption that the whole of the company's income were distributed

among the participators, entitle that person to receive the greater part of the amount so distributed (for this purpose, the rights of loan creditors are disregarded), or

- such rights as would entitle the person, in the event of the company's winding up or in any other circumstances, to receive the greater part of the company's assets which would then be available for distribution among the participators.

If two or more persons together satisfy any of the above conditions, they are regarded as having control of the company (*CTA 2010, s 450*).

'Entitlement to acquire' includes actual and future entitlement (*CTA 2010, s 451(2)*).

'Possession' includes any rights or powers held on behalf of another person and those that a person may be required to exercise on the direction of another or on their behalf (*CTA 2010, s 451(3)*).

Additional rights and powers may also be attributable to that person (*CTA 2010, s 451(4)*), namely the rights and powers of any:

- company or companies of which the person has, or the person and associates of the person have, control,
- associate of the person, or
- two or more associates of the person.

A person is not attributed with the rights and powers of associates of that person's associates (*CTA 2010, s 451(5)*).

Non-close companies

10.5 There are exceptions, and a company satisfying the following criteria is not a close company:

- a company not resident in the UK (although a number of tax provisions relevant to close companies also specify a company that would be close if it were UK resident);
- a registered industrial and provident society or building society (*CTA 2010, s 442*);
- a company controlled by or on behalf of the Crown (*CTA 2010, s 443*);
- a company controlled by one or more non-close companies, where it cannot be treated as a close company except by including a non-close company as one of its five or fewer participators (and, for this purpose, a close company includes a company which would be close if it was UK resident) (*CTA 2010, s 444(2)*);

- a company that can only be treated as a close company by including non-close company loan creditors among its participators on a notional winding up (and, for this purpose, a close company includes a company which would be close if it was UK resident) (*CTA 2010, s 444(3)*);
- a company whose shares are held on trust for a registered pension scheme, unless the scheme has been established wholly or mainly for the benefit of the directors, employees, past directors or past employees of the company or their respective dependants. This exception applies to the company itself and to the company's associated companies. It also applies to companies which are under the control of a director, the associate of a director, or two or more directors or associates acting jointly (*CTA 2010, s 445*);
- a quoted company where:
  - shares carrying at least 35% of the voting power in the company have been allotted unconditionally to, or acquired unconditionally by, and are at that time beneficially held by, the public; and
  - within the preceding 12 months, those voting shares have been the subject of dealings on a recognised stock exchange (*CTA 2010, ss 446(1), 447(4)*); and
  - the total voting power of the company's 'principal members' does not exceed 85% (*CTA 2010, s 446(2)*).

For this purpose, shares include stock but do not include those entitled to a fixed rate of dividend (*CTA 2010, s 446(6)*). For the meaning of principal member, see **10.8**. A recognised stock exchange is any HMRC-designated market of a UK or overseas recognised investment exchange (*CTA 2010, s 1137*; *ITA 2007, s 1005*; see tinyurl.com/pac87uz).

Shares held beneficially by the public

10.6 Shares in a company are beneficially held by the public if they are:

- beneficially held by a UK-resident company which is not a close company, or by a non-UK resident company which would not be a close company if it were UK resident,
- held on trust for a registered pension scheme, or
- not comprised in a principal member's holding (*CTA 2010, s 447(1)*).

Shares are not beneficially held by the public if they are held:

- by a director of the company's director,
- by an associate of such a director,
- by a company which is under the control of one or more directors or associates,

- by an associated company, or
- as part of a fund the capital or income of which is applicable or applied wholly or mainly for the benefit of employees, directors, past employees or past directors of the company or any associated company or company controlled by one or more directors or associates (*CTA 2010, s 447(2), (3)*).

For this purpose, a principal member's holding consists of the shares which carry the voting power possessed by him (*CTA 2010, s 447(5)*). Shares held includes shares the rights or powers of which are held on behalf of, or under the direction of, another person (*CTA 2010, s 447(6)*). Shares include stock (*CTA 2010, s 447(8)*).

Associated company

10.7 Where the term 'associated company' arises for the purposes of determining whether a company is a close company (see **10.5**, **10.6**), a company is another's 'associated company' at a particular time if, at that time or at any other time within the preceding 12 months, one of them has control of the other, or both are under the control of the same person or persons (*CTA 2010, s 449*). When deciding if a person or group of persons has control of a company, account must always be taken of the rights which the persons and their nominees possess or are entitled to acquire (*CTA 2010, s 450(2)–(3)*; HMRC Company Taxation Manual at CTM03740).

This definition of 'associated company' should not be confused with the same expression as used up to 31 March 2015 for the purposes of the small profits rate marginal relief, where the concept of a person's associates applies more narrowly (see **23.5**, **23.15**).

Principal member

10.8 A principal member is a person holding more than 5% of the voting power in the company or, where there are more than five such persons, one of the five who possess the greatest percentages. Where two or more persons hold equal percentages so that the greatest percentages are held by more than five persons, a principal member is any one of that number (*CTA 2010, s 446(3), (4)*).

Director

10.9 A director includes any person occupying the position of director, whatever name is given to him, and any person in accordance with whose directions or instructions the directors are accustomed to act. A director also includes any person who is a manager of the company or otherwise concerned in the management of the company's trade or business and is the beneficial owner of, or is directly or indirectly able to control, at least 20% of the company's ordinary share capital (*CTA 2010, s 452*).

Close company tests

> **Focus**
>
> The five tests applied by HMRC are useful in determining whether or not a company is a close company.

10.10 In order to determine whether a company is close, HMRC apply five tests (CTM60102):

Test	*Answer*	*Result*
1. Is the company within one of the specific exceptions that exclude it from being a close company?	Yes	The company is not close.
	No	Consider further tests.
2. Who are the participators in the company and what powers or rights do they possess or are they entitled to acquire?		
3. What rights and powers of other persons are attributable to the participators?		
4. Having regard to the rights etc of each participator, and other persons' rights etc which are attributed to the participator, do:		
(i) five or fewer participators control the company, or	Yes	The company is close.
	No	Consider further tests.
(ii) participators who are directors control the company?	Yes	The company is close.
	No	Consider further tests
5. Would more than half the assets of the company be ultimately distributed to five or fewer participators, or to participators who are directors, in the event of the company being wound up?	Yes	The company is close
	No	The company is not close

The result as to which participators control the company should always be inferred from the minimum controlling holding. X, Y and Z may each own 33.33% of the company. Therefore, control in applying the tests is given to X and Y, or Y and Z, or X and Z, but never X, Y and Z (*CTA 2010, s 450(5)*).

Participator

10.11 HMRC's Test 2 (above) requires the identity of each participator to be determined. The full definition of a participator is given as (*CTA 2010, s 454*):

'… "participator", in relation to a company, means a person having a share or interest in the capital or income of the company ¼ and includes:

(a) a person who possesses, or is entitled to acquire, share capital or voting rights in the company,

(b) a loan creditor of the company,

(c) a person who possesses a right to receive or participate in distributions of the company or any amounts payable by the company (in cash or kind) to loan creditors by way of premium or redemption,

(d) a person who is entitled to acquire such a right as is mentioned in paragraph (c), and

(e) a person who is entitled to secure that income or assets (whether present or future) of the company will be applied directly or indirectly for the person's benefit.'

Generally speaking, a participator is anyone who has a financial interest in a close company, ie who has invested in the company's share capital or who has provided loan finance. A participator is 'entitled to acquire' or 'entitled to secure' if he has a contractual right to do so (see *R (on the application of Newfields Developments Ltd) v IRC* [2001] STC 901 on this point).

Loan creditor

10.12 A loan creditor is also a participator and is defined as (*CTA 2010, s 453(1), (2)*):

'(1) … "loan creditor", in relation to a company, means a creditor–

(a) in respect of any debt within subsection (2), or

(b) in respect of any redeemable loan capital issued by the company …

(2) Debt is within this subsection if it is incurred by the company–

(a) for any money borrowed or capital assets acquired by the company, or

(b) for any right to receive income created in favour of the company, or

(c) for consideration the value of which to the company was (at the time when the debt was incurred) substantially less than the amount of the debt (including any premium on the debt).'

Normal company trade creditors are not included in the definition. A holder of a beneficial interest in debt or loan capital is treated as a loan creditor to the extent of that interest, provided the person is not a loan creditor in any other way (*CTA 2010, s 453(3)*). Hire purchase arrangements are not regarded as part of loan capital. Arrangements where a person makes annual payments to a company in exchange for a capital sum at some future date result in the person being treated as a participator.

Loans made in the normal course of a banking business do not bring about a loan creditor relationship (*CTA 2010, s 453(4)*).

Associate

10.13 A person's associates include the following (*CTA 2010, s 448*):

- any 'relative': relative includes spouse or civil partner (even if separated), parent or remoter forebear, child or remoter issue, and brother or sister (including half-brother or half-sister); relative excludes former spouse or civil partner (following divorce or dissolution), aunt or uncle, nephew or niece, and step-brother or step-sister;
- any business partner;
- the trustee(s) of any settlement in which the person (or any living or dead relatives of the person) is or was a settlor; and
- the trustee(s) of a settlement or personal representatives of an estate holding company shares in which the person has an interest (and, where the person is a company, any other company interested in those shares is also an associate).

Benefits to participators

> **Focus**
>
> The definition of 'distribution' is extended to include certain benefits provided by a close company to its participators or their associates.

10.14 Benefits or facilities of any kind, including living or other accommodation, entertainment and domestic or other services, are treated as a distribution to the participator of an amount equal to the expense, less any part of the expense that the participator makes good to the company (*CTA 2010, s 1064*). The amount of the expense is equal to the cash equivalent that would arise under *ITEPA 2003, Pt 3, Ch 6, 7* or *10* (*CTA 2010, s 1064*; see also *Income Tax 2016/17* (Bloomsbury Professional)). Payments made by companies acting in concert are also within these provisions, the payment being deemed to be received by the person concerned from the company in which he or she is a participator (*CTA 2010, s 1067*).

Payments will not be treated as a distribution (*CTA 2010, s 1065*) if they are paid to:

- a participator who is employed and the benefits are assessable to income tax as employment income under *ITEPA 2003, Pt 3, Ch 6, 7* or *10* (cars, vans, loans and other benefits) or *ITEPA 2003, s 223* (payments on account of director's tax), or would be so assessable without the exclusion provided by *ITEPA 2003, s 216* for lower-paid employees;
- any person in respect of living accommodation within the meaning of *ITEPA 2003, Pt 3, Ch 5* and provided by reason of the person's employment; or
- the spouse, civil partner, children or dependants of a person employed by the company, in respect of a pension, annuity, lump sum, gratuity or other like benefit to be given on the employee's death or retirement. Note that this exception is not removed by *FA 2013, s 11*, which from 6 April 2013 denied exemption from income tax and National Insurance contributions relief for contributions paid into a registered pension scheme of an employee's family member as part of the employee's flexible remuneration package (see *Income Tax 2016/17* (Bloomsbury Professional)).

Where the participator is a company, a benefit that arises on a transfer of assets or liabilities by the company to the participator, or to the company by the participator, or in connection with such a transfer, is not treated as a distribution if the company and the participator are both UK resident and one is a 51% subsidiary of the other, or both are 51% subsidiaries of a third UK resident company. For this purpose, shares owned as trading stock and shares held in non-resident companies are ignored in determining the 51% subsidiary relationship (*CTA 2010, s 1066*).

Loans to participators

Focus

Where close companies fail to exercise strict financial disciplines, and especially where they fail to keep their financial affairs clear and distinct from those of their proprietors, it is not unusual for them to find that they have made loans or advances to participators (sometimes inadvertently) and thereby incurred liabilities to tax under *CTA 2010, s 455*.

10.15 If, in an accounting period, a close company makes a loan or advances money to a relevant person who is a participator or an associate of a participator, and this is not done in the ordinary course of a business which includes the lending of money, the company must pay tax, as if it were corporation tax (*CTA 2010, s 455*). For this purpose, a relevant person may be an individual, or a company receiving a loan or advance in a fiduciary or representative capacity (*CTA 2010, s 455(1)*).

For loans or advances made before 6 April 2016, the amount of tax payable is equal to 25% of the loan or advance outstanding at the end of the accounting period. For loans or advances made on or after 6 April 2016, however, the rate increases to the higher rate payable on dividends under the new dividend tax rules, currently 32.5%. If and when the loans are repaid or forgiven, the tax can be repaid (*CTA 2010, s 458*).

This tax is intended to deter the owners of the business from extracting cash in a tax free manner, rather than receiving taxable remuneration or dividends.

In *RKW Limited v Revenue & Customs* [2014] UKFTT 151 (TC), the First-tier Tribunal rejected HMRC's contention that an individual previously unconnected with a close company, agreeing to subscribe by instalments for a controlling interest in fully issued shares in it and subsequently failing to make the required payments, was thereby receiving a loan or advance on which the company should pay tax under what is now *CTA 2010, s 455*.

Aspect Capital Ltd v Revenue and Customs Commissioners [2014] UKUT 81 (TCC) concerned a complex arrangement in which the taxpayer company made funds available under an employee participation scheme; the Upper Tribunal held that the facility amount was a loan or debt caught by *CTA 2010, s 455*.

To counter schemes which attempted to sidestep the tax charge under *CTA 2010, s 455*, the charge was extended from 20 March 2013 onwards (*CTA 2010, s 455(1)(b), (c)*) to include a loan or advance by a close company to:

- the trustees of a settlement, one or more of the trustees or actual or potential beneficiaries of which is a participator in the company or an associate of such a participator, or
- a limited liability partnership (LLP) or other partnership, one or more of the partners in which is an individual who is either a participator in the company or an associate of an individual who is such a participator.

HMRC consider these changes to have been clarifications, rather than changes of law, so they may challenge arrangements in existence in place before 20 March 2013, too.

Example 10.1—Close company loan via partnership

Facts

P, an individual, is a participator in close company A Ltd.
P and A Ltd become partners in an LLP.
A Ltd makes a loan to the LLP.

Analysis

Close company A Ltd has made a loan to an LLP in which there is an individual partner who is also a participator in the close company, so a tax charge arises under *CTA 2010, s 455(1)(c)* – unless any specific exemption applies.

The legislation also catches certain indirect or reciprocal arrangements if they are not made in the ordinary course of a business (*CTA 2010, s 459*). A loan is treated as having been made to a participator (or his associate) where:

- a close company makes a loan or advance which would not otherwise give rise to tax under *CTA 2010, s 455*; and
- a person other than that close company makes a payment or transfers property to, or releases or satisfies (in whole or part) a liability of, a relevant person who is a participator in the company, or an associate of a participator (*CTA 2010, s 459*).

Caution is required, as this provision can apply in cases where no abusive extraction is intended. For example, following a management buy-out, a typical structure will have a trading company owned by a holding company, which owes the proceeds of sale to the vendor shareholder. If cash is loaned from the trading company to the holding company, to allow some or all of the debt to be repaid, *CTA 2010, s 459* strictly applies!

Example 10.2—Indirect or reciprocal close company loan

Facts

A is an individual. A Ltd and B Ltd are both close companies.

Analysis

	Results
A is a shareholder of A Ltd	A is a participator in A Ltd
A Ltd owns all the shares in B Ltd	A is treated as a participator in B Ltd (*CTA 2010, s 459(4)*)
B Ltd makes a loan to A	The loan is within *CTA 2010, s 455*

Payment and repayment of tax

10.16 The company must self-assess tax liabilities arising under *CTA 2010, s 455* in respect of any loans or advances made in any of the above circumstances during the accounting period, in accordance with the corporation tax self-assessment provisions. The tax is due and payable nine months and one day following the end of the accounting period in question (*CTA 2010, s 455(3)*).

The following reliefs from tax under *CTA 2010, s 455* are provided by *CTA 2010, s 458(3)–(5)*:

- the tax under *s 455*, or a proportionate part of it, need not be paid if the loan or advance or part of it has been repaid, released or written off within nine months and one day following the end of the accounting period (*CTA 2010, s 458(2)*);
- where the loan or advance is repaid, released or written off more than nine months after the end of an accounting period, the tax paid under *s 455* can be repaid nine months after the end of the accounting period in which the repayment, release or writing off takes place (*CTA 2010, s 458(3)–(5)*).

The above reliefs under *CTA 2010, s 458* are subject to restrictions imposed by *CTA 2010, ss 464C, 464D* (see **10.18**).

Repayment of tax paid can only be made on a formal claim by the company, which must be made within four years of the end of the financial year (NB not the accounting period) in which the loan or advance is repaid, written off or released (*CTA 2010, s 458(3)*).

Other arrangements conferring benefit on a participator

Focus

From 20 March 2013, close companies can face tax charges if they enter into tax avoidance arrangements which benefit participators or their associates.

10.17 If, at any time on or after 20 March 2013, a close company becomes a party to tax avoidance arrangements, as a result of which value is extracted from the company and the benefit is (directly or indirectly) conferred on an individual who is a participator or an associate of a participator without a charge to income tax falling on the individual (or a charge to tax under *CTA 2010, s 455* falling on the company), the company must pay tax, as if it were corporation tax (*CTA 2010, s 464A*).

For benefits conferred before 6 April 2016, the amount of tax payable is equal to 25% of the value of the benefit. From 6 April 2016, however, the rate increases to 32.5% in line with the higher rate payable on dividends under the new dividend tax rules.

If a company controls another company, a participator in the first company is treated for this purpose as being also a participator in the second company (*CTA 2010, s 464A(5)*).

Arrangements (including any arrangements, scheme or understanding of any kind, whether or not legally enforceable, involving a single transaction or two or more transactions) are 'tax avoidance arrangements' if their main purpose, or one of their main purposes, is:

- to avoid or reduce, or obtain a relief or increased relief from, a charge to tax on the company under *CTA 2010, s 455*, or
- to obtain a tax advantage (as defined in *CTA 2010, s 1139*) for the participator or associate.

'Tax advantage' means (*CTA 2010, s 1139*, as applied by *CTA 2010, s 464A(7)*):

- a relief from income tax or increased relief from income tax;
- a repayment of income tax or increased repayment of income tax;
- the avoidance or reduction of a charge to income tax or an assessment to income tax; or
- the avoidance of a possible assessment to income tax.

Example 10.3—Close company arrangements: benefit to participator

Facts

Q, an individual, is a participator in close company B Ltd.

Q and B Ltd are partners in a partnership. Under the partnership agreement, 80% of the profits for the year ended 31 March 2016 are allocated to B Ltd and charged on B Ltd at the corporation tax rate.

B Ltd leaves its profits undrawn on capital account in the partnership, and Q draws on them.

Analysis

There is a benefit conferred on Q because (i) Q has received funds from B Ltd, a company in which Q is a participator, and (ii) there was no *CTA 2010, s 455* charge on B Ltd and no income tax charge on Q. If the funds had been transferred directly from B Ltd to Q, they would have been chargeable to income tax on Q (if transferred as remuneration or a dividend) or *CTA 2010, s 455* tax on B Ltd (if transferred as a loan). A charge will arise on B Ltd under *CTA 2010, s 464A*.

Note: Because the arrangement applied on or after 6 April 2014, HMRC have an additional option of countering the tax avoidance by invoking *CTA 2009, s 1264A* (as inserted by *FA 2014, Sch 17, para 10*), to reallocate excess profits attributed initially to B Ltd and ascribe them instead to Q (see **4.15**).

The tax charge under *CTA 2010, s 464A* operates in a similar manner to that under *CTA 2010, s 455*. The company must self-assess tax liabilities arising under *CTA 2010, s 464A* in respect of any relevant benefits conferred on a participator or associate in any of the above circumstances during the accounting period, in accordance with the corporation tax self-assessment provisions. The tax is due and payable nine months and one day following the end of the accounting period in question (*CTA 2010, s 464A(4)*).

The procedures for claiming relief are broadly similar to those under *CTA 2010, s 458*. If a benefit has given rise to tax on a close company under *CTA 2010, s 464A*, relief is given from that tax, or a proportionate part of it, if a payment is made to the company in respect of the benefit and no consideration is given for that return payment (*CTA 2010, s 464B*). If this has happened:

- within nine months and one day following the end of the accounting period in which the benefit was conferred, relief from the tax under *CTA 2010, s 464A* can be claimed and it need not be paid (*CTA 2010, s 464B(2)*); or
- later than nine months and one day following the end of the accounting period in which the benefit was conferred, the tax paid under *CTA 2010, s 464A* can be reclaimed nine months after the end of the accounting period in which the return payment is made (*CTA 2010, s 464B(3)–(5)*).

The above reliefs are subject to restrictions imposed by *CTA 2010, ss 464C, 464D* (see **10.18**).

Restrictions on relief

10.18 From 20 March 2013, restrictions can apply to relief otherwise available to companies under *CTA 2010, ss 458, 464B*. These create a substantial trap, particularly for close companies that had been accustomed to circumventing the tax charge under *CTA 2010, s 455* by 'bed and breakfasting', ie arranging for loans and advances to be repaid before a tax charge arose and then replacing them with new loans or advances (see also **10.22**).

Where:

- in any period of 30 days, a company receives repayments of at least £5,000 repaying loans chargeable under *CTA 2010, s 455*, or benefits chargeable under *CTA 2010, s 464A*, which have not previously been matched with a chargeable payment under *CTA 2010, s 464C*, and
- within the same 30-day period but in a later accounting period, the company provides the same participator or their associate with new chargeable payments which are not repaid within that 30-day period and have not previously been matched with a repayment under *CTA 2010, s 464C*,

the repayments are matched as far as possible with the new chargeable payments, and can only be set against the original chargeable payments to the extent that the repayments are in excess of the new chargeable payments (*CTA 2010, s 464C(1), (2)*).

Where a person owes the company £15,000 or more and, at the time the repayment is made, arrangements had been made for one or more chargeable payments to be made to replace some or all of the amount repaid, more stringent conditions apply to ensure that the repayment is treated as far as possible as a repayment of the new chargeable payment rather than the original chargeable payment (*CTA 2010, s 464C(3)*).

The above restrictions do not apply in relation to a repayment which gives rise to a charge to income tax on the participator or associate by reference to whom the loan, advance or benefit was a chargeable payment (*CTA 2010, s 464C(6)*). Therefore, arrangements where the loan is repaid by a bonus or dividend are not caught by these new restrictions.

The limits of £5,000 and £15,000 referred to in *CTA 2010, s 464C* may be varied by Treasury order.

Example 10.4—Close company restrictions on 'bed and breakfasting' loans

Facts

R, an individual, is a participator in close company C Ltd.

During C Ltd's accounting period to 31 March 2017, R borrows £20,000 from C Ltd.

If the loan is not repaid by 1 January 2018, C Ltd will have to pay tax of £6,500 (= 32.5% of £20,000) under *CTA 2010, s 455*.

On 27 November 2018 (ie 35 days before the tax under *s 455* becomes due and payable), R borrows a further £25,000 from C Ltd and immediately uses £20,000 of this to repay the original loan.

Analysis

It is likely in this situation that the repayment of £20,000 would be treated as a repayment of £20,000 of the new £25,000 loan, by virtue of *CTA 2010, s 464(3)*. As a result, the original loan would be treated as not repaid by 1 January 2018, so the tax under *s 455* would become due and payable.

Example 10.5—Close company: countering of arrangements

Facts

S, an individual, is a participator in close company D Ltd.

During D Ltd's accounting period to 30 June 2017, S borrows £30,000 from D Ltd.

If the loan is not repaid by 1 April 2018, D Ltd will have to pay tax of £9,750 (= 32.5% of £30,000) under *CTA 2010, s 455*.

On 17 March 2018 (ie 15 days before the tax under *CTA 2010, s 455* becomes due and payable), S borrows £30,000 from his bank on a 40-day loan and uses this immediately to repay D Ltd.

On 22 April 2018 (ie 36 days after repaying D Ltd), S borrows a further £30,000 from D Ltd and uses this immediately to repay his bank loan.

Analysis

There are clear arrangements here, so the original loan would be treated as not repaid and the tax under *CTA 2010, s 455* would become due and payable.

Self-assessment disclosure

10.19 Relevant loans or advances made to participators or their associates during the accounting period, and relevant arrangements giving rise to benefits conferred on participators or their associates, must be disclosed on the corporation tax return. Supplementary page CT600A is used for this purpose and is to be filed online as part of the corporation tax return. Details of the name of the participator or associate to whom the loan or advance was made, and the amount of the loan or advance outstanding at the end of the accounting period for which the return has been made, must be disclosed. Where the provisions of *CTA 2010, s 464A*, apply in respect of benefits conferred, similar details have to be disclosed.

HMRC have prepared a Directors' Loan Accounts Toolkit to assist companies and their tax agents in monitoring compliance, and they updated this in May 2015 (see tinyurl.com/63vn6ts).

Where one or more participators have balances owing to or by a close company, care should be taken to account correctly for tax under *CTA 2010, s 455* in respect of each loan or advance. Separate loan accounts should not be aggregated or 'netted off' for *CTA 2010, s 455* purposes, and each such account should be considered individually. There is a charge to tax under *CTA 2010, s 455* when the close company makes a loan or advance, irrespective of whether the same director or participator has a credit balance on another account with the company. In exceptional cases, there may be a joint loan account between the company and two or more participators, but this would be unusual except where the participators are spouses, civil partners or otherwise closely related individuals.

If the loan has been repaid, released or written off within nine months and one day after the end of the accounting period, details of the name of the participator or associate whose loan has been repaid, released or written off, together with the amount and date repaid, released or written off, must be disclosed. In such a case, HMRC will be able to follow these through to the tax affairs of each individual to ensure that loan releases or write-offs to directors or employees (or their associates) have been included in payroll or correctly declared on forms P11D. For further information on benefits in kind, see *Income Tax 2018/19* (Bloomsbury Professional).

Relief by formal claim can only be given for the tax already paid by the company, or a proportionate part of it, if the loan, advance or debt is repaid, released or written off in full or in part (*CTA 2010, s 458(1), (2)*). The claim must be made within four years from the end of the financial year in which the repayment is made or the release or writing off occurs (*CTA 2010, s 458(3)*). If the repayment, release or writing off occurs later than nine months and one day after the end of the accounting period during which the loan or advance is made, the tax relief is due nine months after the end of the accounting period in which the repayment, release or writing off occurred (*CTA 2010, s 458(4), (5)*).

Any tax due under *CTA 2010, s 455* becomes payable with the company's main corporation tax liability. Any late payment falls within the normal interest provisions. Interest is charged on any outstanding liability from the due date until the earlier of the payment of the *CTA 2010, s 455* tax and the date that the loan or part is repaid, released or written off (*TMA 1970, ss 87A(1), 109(3A)*). If the repayment, release or write-off of a loan takes place earlier than nine months and one day after the end of the accounting period in which the loan was made, repayment interest will accrue from the later of nine months after the end of that accounting period and the date the tax was paid. If the loan is repaid, released or written off more than nine months after the end of the accounting period in which the loan was made, interest will accrue from the later of nine months after the end of the accounting period in which the loan was cleared and the date the tax was paid (*ICTA 1988, s 826(4)*). HMRC may make enquiries into the loan accounts as part of their corporation tax self-assessment enquiries.

Similar self-assessment procedures apply to benefits to participators and their associates which are assessable on the company under *CTA 2010, s 464A*.

Loans within CTA 2010, s 455

10.20 Loans to employee share schemes and employee benefit trusts are within *CTA 2010, s 455*. The section is applied at the time of the loan if the trust is a shareholder or individual trustees are participators in the company. HMRC state that *CTA 2010, s 455* may apply when the trustees make payments to existing shareholders in respect of their shares (CTM61525).

Loans to a tax-transparent partnership, where a participator is a member, are within *CTA 2010, s 455*. However, there were exceptions up until 19 March 2013 in the case of loans to a Scottish general partnership (which has a separate legal *persona*) or where a company lent money to a partnership of which the company itself was a member (see **10.15**, **10.21**).

Loans or advances that a company makes to its participators and/or their associates, other than in the ordinary course of business, are within *CTA 2010, s 455*. The following also fall within the scope of *CTA 2010, s 455*:

- any debt due by the participator or associate to the company (*CTA 2010, s 455(4)(a)*);
- any debt due by the participator or associate to a third party, which has been assigned by the third party to the company (*CTA 2010, s 455(4)(b)*); or
- the provision of goods or services in the ordinary course of trade or business to a participator on credit terms that exceed six months or are longer than normally given to the company's customers (*CTA 2010, s 456(2)*).

As regards debts due to a third party, HMRC acknowledge that a debt can only be assigned by the third party. If the debtor (the person to whom the money is lent) and the close company of which he is a participator agree that the close company will pay the debt on his behalf, *CTA 2010, s 455(4)* cannot apply. However, when the close company pays the debt to the third party on the participator's behalf, a debt due from the participator to the close company may arise and this will fall under *CTA 2010, s 455(4)(a)*. Indeed, depending on the facts of the case, HMRC may treat the amount as remuneration or a distribution (CTM61535).

As regards the provision of goods or services, HMRC acknowledge the presumption that a debt is incurred at the time the goods are delivered or the services are provided and that credit runs from that time until payment (*Grant (Andrew) Services Ltd v Watton* [1999] STC 330; CTM61535).

Loans not within CTA 2010, s 455

10.21 There is no charge under *CTA 2010, s 455* in the following situations (*CTA 2010, s 456*):

- A money lending business makes a loan in the ordinary course of its business. This principle was tested in *Brennan v Deanby Investment Co Ltd* [2001] STC 536, and resulted in the comment that 'business requires some regularity of occurrence'. It would seem that, without doubt, a commercial lending bank's business includes lending money.
- A close company supplies goods or services in the ordinary course of its trade or business, unless the credit given exceeds six months or is longer than that normally given to the company's customers.
- A close company makes a loan or advance to a charitable trust where the funds are to be applied solely to the purpose of the charity (applicable to loans or advances made on or after 25 November 2015.
- A close company makes a loan or advance to one of its directors or employees, or to a director or employee of an associated company, subject to all of the following three conditions being satisfied:
  1. The amount of the loan or advance, when taken as a single transaction or when taken together with any other outstanding loans and advances made to the borrower by the close company or any of its associated companies, does not exceed £15,000. Individuals who are spouses or civil partners, if employees of the company, have their own £15,000 limits.
  2. The borrower works full-time for the close company or any of its associated companies. HMRC interpret 'full-time' as not less than three-quarters of the normal working hours of the close company (CTM61540).
  3. The borrower does not have a material interest in the close company or in any of its associated companies. If a material interest is acquired during the time that the loan is outstanding, the close company is treated as making a loan to the borrower of the amount outstanding at that time.

For these purposes, a person has a material interest in a company in either of the following situations:

- the person, either alone or with associates, is the beneficial owner of, or directly or indirectly able to control, more than 5% of the ordinary share capital of the company; or
- the person, either alone or with associates, possesses or is entitled to acquire such rights as would, in the event of the winding up of the company or in any other circumstances, give an entitlement to receive

more than 5% of the assets which would then be available for distribution among the participators (*CTA 2010, s 457*).

HMRC state that they will look for the following characteristics to determine whether there is a money-lending trade:

- Money-lending advertisements aimed at the general public.
- Interest rate publication.
- Receipt of loan applications from the public.
- Commercial interest rate charge.
- *In situ* debt collection personnel and procedures.
- Legally enforceable written repayment term contracts.
- A reasonable number of existing loans (usually 200+) enabling, inter alia, loan set-off.
- Matched time period borrowing and lending.

If there is a money-lending business, the loan to the participator must still be made on the same commercial lending terms (regarding size, terms and conditions) as those which would normally apply to other customers in order to avoid a charge to tax under *CTA 2010, s 455* (CTM61530).

Until 19 March 2013, loans to a Scottish general partnership were not treated as falling within *CTA 2010, s 455*, because a Scottish partnership (as distinct from an LLP) has a separate legal *persona* from the persons carrying on the partnership (CTM61520).

HMRC's guidance before the *FA 2013* changes stated that they would not apply *CTA 2010, s 455* where money was lent to a partnership of which the company is a member and there was a genuine partnership with *bona fide* arrangements. Following the *FA 2013* changes, the guidance now states (CTM61520) that *CTA 2010, s 455* applies to a loan or advance made on or after 20 March 2013 to any partnership (including LLPs) in which at least one of the partners/members is an individual:

- who is a participator in the company making the loan; or
- who is an associate of an individual who is a participator in the company making the loan.

Where any doubts exist, HMRC may invoke *CTA 2010, s 459(1), (2)*, which enables them to assess a loan not made by the close company but by arrangements not in the ordinary course of business to a relevant person who is a participator in the company or an associate of such a participator (CTM61515).

Payments by a company to a director in respect of the director's private business were held by the High Court to be within *CTA 2010, s 455* in *Grant (Andrew) Services Ltd v Watton (Inspector of Taxes)* [1999] STC 330.

Loan accounts

> **Focus**
>
> Particular care is needed to ensure that any ongoing loan accounts with directors or shareholders are disclosed correctly for the purposes of *CTA 2010, s 455*.

10.22 For accounts purposes, if a loan is made to a participator, the company will record the loan in its nominal ledger as a 'loan account'. Director loan accounts are a common feature of owner-managed companies, which are invariably close companies. HMRC will not accept that the netting off of one loan or advance against another reduces exposure to tax under *CTA 2010, s 455*, even where both accounts are with the same participator and one account is in debit while the other is in credit. Each loan or advance must be considered separately. If a genuine posting is made to clear the two loan accounts, this is treated as though the loan had been repaid under *CTA 2010, s 458*. The posting date is the repayment date (CTM61565).

Actual repayment by the participator or a third party takes place on the date that payment is made. A director's loan account may be cleared by a bonus payment. *ITEPA 2003, s 18* onwards determines the date that the bonus is received by the director for income tax purposes. For *CTA 2010, s 455* purposes, the date of repayment is the date that the bonuses are voted or the date on which PAYE was operated, if earlier.

The director/participator may wish to use a dividend payment to clear the loan account. A dividend may only be declared if there are sufficient distributable profits. In practice, the company's constitution should be examined for any matters that may affect dividend payments.

A dividend is generally treated as paid when it is due and payable (*CTA 2010, s 1168(1)*); but, for *CTA 2010, s 458* purposes, in HMRC's view, *CTA 2010, s 1168(1)* does not apply. HMRC's explanation is that the question for *s 458* purposes is not when the dividend was paid but rather when the debt was repaid to the company, so that 'until the dividend is actually paid, the debt remains outstanding'(CTM61600). Also in HMRC's view, 'a dividend is not paid and there is no distribution, unless and until the shareholder receives money or the distribution is otherwise unreservedly put at their disposal, perhaps by being credited to a loan account on which the shareholder has the power to draw' (CTM20095). Evidence of the payment or credit should be shown in the company's books of account. If a dividend is paid unlawfully and the shareholder knew or was in a position to know of this fact, he or she is liable to return the distribution to the company (*CA 2006, s 847*; *It's a Wrap (UK) Ltd (in liquidation) v Gula* [2006] EWCA Civ 544).

HMRC acknowledge that, in many small private companies, the directors and shareholders are one and the same. A final dividend is treated as due and payable on the date of the resolution by the company to pay the dividend unless some future date for payment is specified. An interim dividend is treated as paid only when the money is placed unreservedly at the disposal of the directors/shareholders as part of their current accounts with the company, so payment is not made until such a right to draw on the dividend exists (presumably) when the appropriate entries are made in the company's books; if, as may happen with a small company, such entries are not made until the annual accounts preparation process or audit, and this takes place after the end of the accounting period in which the directors resolved that an interim dividend be paid, then the 'due and payable' date is in the later rather than the earlier accounting period.

A director or participator may clear their loan account shortly before the company's year end by borrowing from an external third party, only to reinstate the loan at the beginning of the next accounting period. In such circumstances, it has always been possible that HMRC might contend that there is nonetheless a *CTA 2010, s 455* liability; and, if the company has failed to report this, HMRC might regard the company as supplying a false document under the *FA 2007* penalty regime; see **24.2–24.11** (HMRC Enquiry Manual EM8565). From 20 March 2013, there are restrictions on relief to combat the effectiveness of many such 'bed and breakfast' arrangements (see *CTA 2010, ss 464C, 464D*; see also **10.18**).

Repayment of tax paid under CTA 2010, s 455 or 464A

10.23 When the loan giving rise to tax paid under *CTA 2010, s 455* is repaid, or when the company receives a return payment in respect of the benefit giving rise to tax paid under *CTA 2010, s 464A*, the company may become entitled to repayment of the tax that it has already paid under *CTA 2010, s 455* or *464A* (see **10.15**, **10.17**), subject to the restrictions introduced by *FA 2013* (see **10.18**).

Any such tax is not due for repayment until nine months after the accounting period in which the loan is repaid or the return payment received (*CTA 2010, ss 458(5), 464B(5)*). There is no facility for earlier repayment. The claim to repayment must be made under *TMA 1970, Sch 1A* within four years from the end of the financial year (NB not the accounting period) in which the loan is repaid, and repayment will not be due until nine months after the end of the accounting period in which the loan is repaid or the return payment received.

Section 455 loan released

10.24 If the loan is released or written off, the same procedures apply to the company as for repayment, but the individual participator will be treated under *ITTOIA 2005, ss 415–417*, as receiving the sum as a net distribution. Prior to

6 April 2016, the amount subject to tax was grossed up at the dividend ordinary rate prescribed by *ITA 2007, s 8(1)* (see **10.32**). This charge takes precedence over the employment income charge. Nonetheless, where the amount released or written off is remuneration, it will attract Class 1 National Insurance contributions. The release or write-off is not deductible for corporation tax purposes (CTM61655, CTM61660).

Circuitous and indirect loans

10.25 The legislation also catches certain indirect or reciprocal arrangements if they are not made in the ordinary course of a business. A loan is treated as having been made to a participator (or his associate) where:

- a close company makes a loan or advance which would not otherwise give rise to tax under *CTA 2010, s 455*, and
- a person other than that close company makes a payment or transfers property to, or releases or satisfies (in whole or part) a liability of, a relevant person who is a participator in the company, or an associate of a participator (*CTA 2010, s 459*; see also CTM61540).

From 20 March 2013 the restrictions on relief under *CTA 2010, ss 464C* and *464D* apply equally to such indirect or reciprocal arrangements (*CTA 2010, s 459(2)*).

HMRC give the following examples of indirect or reciprocal arrangements:

Example 10.6—Close company: circuitous and indirect loans

Facts

Company D is a close company. Instead of making a loan directly to P, an individual participator, it makes it to an associated company, Company E. Company E then passes the loan to P.

Analysis

The loan by one company to the other is treated as if it had been made directly by close company D to its participator P.

Example 10.7—Close company: reciprocal loans

Facts

Company T, a close company, makes a loan to A. A is an individual participator in Company W but not in Company T. Company W, acting in concert with Company T, then makes a loan to D, an individual participator in Company T.

Analysis

Company T and Company W have made loans to one another's participators and are treated as if they had made loans to their own participators.

Such loans should be assessed to tax under *CTA 2010, s 455* in the normal way, except where the arrangements have arisen in the ordinary course of business, or the total income of the person concerned includes, in respect of the arrangements, an amount not less than the loan or advance (CTM61550, CTM61555).

This can be a particular problem in management buy-out situations, where the target company passes funds to the holding company by way of loan, not dividend. The cash is then used to pay off the ex-shareholders.

Example 10.8—Close company: management buy-out

Facts

Company X, a close company, is sold to BidCo, a company set up by the management team for the buy-out. The ex-shareholders are also issued some shares in BidCo, as well as receiving cash and loan notes. Company X lends cash to BidCo, and BidCo uses this money to pay what it owes to the ex-shareholders of Company X.

Analysis

Company X has made a loan to which *CTA 2010, s 455* does not apply. BidCo has then made a payment to a relevant person. Such loans should be assessed to tax under *CTA 2010, s 455* in the normal way.

Anti-avoidance

10.26 Loans made by companies controlled by a close company or subsequently controlled by a close company are treated as being made by the close company itself, unless it can be shown that no avoidance arrangements exist (*CTA 2010, s 460*). Loans made in the ordinary course of business are ignored (*CTA 2010, s 461*).

If a close company makes a loan or advance to a person who is not a participator, and a person other than the close company makes a payment, transfers property, or releases or satisfies (in whole or in part) a liability of a relevant person who is a participator or his or her associate, that loan or advance is treated as having been made to the relevant person. For this purpose, a person is also treated as a participator in any company controlled by the relevant company. Loans made within the ordinary course of a business and loans included within the relevant person's total income are ignored (*CTA 2010, s 459*).

CONNECTED PERSONS

Conditions

10.27 *CTA 2010, s 1122* defines when a company is connected with another company or a person, and uses the identifier 'A' to denote the particular person.

The company is connected with another company if any of the following circumstances are met (*CTA 2010, s 1122(2)*):

- the same person has control of both companies;
- a person (A) has control of one company, and persons connected with A have control of the other company;
- A has control of one company, and A together with persons connected with A have control of the other company, or
- a group of two or more persons has control of both companies and the groups either consist of the same persons or could be so regarded if (in one or more cases) a member of either group were replaced by a person with whom the member is connected.

The company is connected with another person (A) if any of the following circumstances are met (*CTA 2010, s 1122(3)*):

- A has control of the company, or
- A, together with persons connected with A, have control of the company.

In relation to a company, any two or more persons acting together to secure or exercise control of the company are connected with one another, and any person acting on the directions of any of them to secure or exercise control of the company.

CTA 2010, s 1122 further defines how an individual is connected with another individual, a trust or a partner.

An individual 'A' is connected with another individual 'B' if:

- A is B's spouse or civil partner,
- A is a relative of B,
- A is the spouse or civil partner of a relative of B,

- A is a relative of B's spouse or civil partner, or
- A is the spouse or civil partner of a relative of B's spouse or civil partner.

A relative is any brother, sister, ancestor or lineal descendant.

A person, in the capacity as trustee of a settlement, is connected with:

- any individual who is a settlor in relation to the settlement;
- any person connected with such an individual;
- any close company whose participators include the trustees of the settlement;
- any non-UK resident company which, if it were UK resident, would be a close company whose participators include the trustees of the settlement;
- any body corporate controlled by a close company or non-UK resident company that would be close were it to be resident;
- if the settlement is the principal settlement in relation to one or more sub-fund settlements, a person in the capacity as trustee of such a sub-fund settlement, and
- if the settlement is a sub-fund settlement in relation to a principal settlement, a person in the capacity as trustee of any other sub-fund settlements in relation to the principal settlement.

A person who is a partner in a partnership is connected with:

- any partner in the partnership;
- the spouse or civil partner of any individual who is a partner in the partnership, and
- a relative of any individual who is a partner in the partnership.

Partnership connections are not, however, taken into account in relation to acquisitions or disposals of assets of the partnership pursuant to genuine commercial arrangements.

Control

10.28 A person controls a company or any body corporate if that person has the power to secure that the body corporate's affairs are conducted in accordance with his wishes, either:

- by means of the holding of shares or the possession of voting power in relation to that or any other body corporate, or
- as a result of any powers conferred by the articles of association or other document regulating that or any other body corporate.

A person controls a partnership if that person has the right to a share of more than half the assets, or of more than half the income, of the partnership (*CTA 2010, s 1124*).

CLOSE INVESTMENT-HOLDING COMPANIES

Consequences

10.29 Trading uncommercially or letting property to connected parties may mean that a close company becomes a 'close investment-holding company'.

Up to 31 March 2015 the small profits rate of corporation tax could be available to a close company, but not to a close investment-holding company. A close investment-holding company must pay corporation tax at the main rate, regardless of its profit levels (*CTA 2010, s 18(b)*).

With the abolition of the small profits rate of corporation tax on non-ring fence profits from 1 April 2015 (see **23.2**), the relevance of close investment-holding company status ceases to have any significance for corporation tax purposes. However, it is retained for the purposes of the rules which allow income tax relief on loans to buy interests in certain close companies, and the expression 'close investment-holding company' was redefined for this purpose from 6 April 2014 (*ITA 2007, s 393A*; see *Income Tax 2018/19* (Bloomsbury Professional)).

Status

10.30 For corporation tax purposes up to 31 March 2015, *CTA 2010, s 34* determines whether or not a close company, referred to for this purpose as 'the candidate company', is a close-investment holding company. For income tax purposes, *ITA 2007, s 393A* adopts similar terms (see *Income Tax 2018/19* (Bloomsbury Professional)).

For corporation tax, a company is *not* a close investment-holding company in an accounting period if, throughout the period in question, it exists wholly or mainly for one or more of the following permitted purposes:

- for the purpose of carrying on a trade on a commercial basis;
- for the purpose of making (either directly, or by one or more qualifying companies, or by a company which has control of the candidate company) investments in land or estates or interests in land in cases where the land is or is intended to be let commercially to persons other than:
  - any person connected with the candidate company,
  - any person who is the spouse or civil partner of such a connected person, or

  - a relative (or spouse or civil partner of a relative) of such a connected person;
- for the purpose of holding shares in and securities of, or making loans to, one or more companies each of which is a qualifying company or a company which:
  - is under the control of the relevant company or of a company that has control of the relevant company, and
  - itself exists wholly or mainly for the purpose of holding shares in or securities of, or making loans to, one or more qualifying companies;
- for the purpose of co-ordinating the administration of two or more qualifying companies; and
- for the purpose of a trade or trades carried on on a commercial basis by one or more qualifying companies or by a company that has control of the candidate company (*CTA 2010, s 34(1), (2)*).

In general terms, a 'qualifying company' is a company which is under the control of the candidate company or a company which has control of the candidate company and is a trading company or a property investment company (*CTA 2010, s 34(6)*).

The courts have decided that, if a company intends to carry on a trade or property investment business but fails to do so, the close investment-holding company provisions need not apply.

In *Herts Photographic Bureau Ltd v Revenue & Customs Comrs* [2010] UKFTT 629 (TC), a close company ceased to trade and leased its surplus business premises in a property investment business. Four years later, the premises were sold and the company intended to use the proceeds to purchase residential properties for use in its property investment business. The financial crisis intervened, the proceeds were placed on an interest-earning bank deposit account, and corporation tax was payable on the interest received. The First-tier Tribunal held that the company was a close investment-holding company and therefore not prevented from claiming the small profits rate of corporation tax in the year in question, because of its intention to use the funds for future investment.

Letting of land to a connected person

10.31 Letting of land by a company to a connected person (or their spouse, civil partner or relative) may bring a close company into the close investment-holding company regime and thereby restrict the availability of the small profits rate of corporation tax up to 31 March 2015 (*CTA 2010, s 34(3)*). 'Connection' is defined in *CTA 2010, s 1122(3)* (see **10.27**).

Example 10.9—Close investment-holding company: letting to a relative

Facts

Joe is married to Mary. Joe owns 100% of Joe Ltd, a building and construction company in the South of England. Joe would like to provide Mary's mother, Mrs K, with a home where she could reside independently of Joe and Mary.

On 1 January 2017, Joe formed Mrs K Ltd, a 100% subsidiary of Joe Ltd. The subsidiary bought a plot of land with development value on which stood Plum Cottage, a Victorian property. Mrs K moved into the cottage and paid her landlord, Mrs K Ltd, a full market rent for the property. Mrs K maintained her independence and paid for the upkeep of Plum Cottage herself.

Analysis

The facts appear to fall under *CTA 2010, s 34(3)*.

This would bring the company within the close investment-holding company regime.

Joe formed the company in order to buy a property suitable for his mother-in-law's occupation, and it was merely incidental that the land on which the property stood had development value.

If, alternatively, Mrs K Ltd had bought the land with development value for the purposes of a building and construction trade, and the temporary occupation of Plum Cottage by Mrs K was merely incidental to the trading purpose, there might be an argument that Mrs K Ltd existed mainly for the purpose of carrying on a trade on a commercial basis, either by Mrs K Ltd or by Joe Ltd. As a result, Mrs K Ltd might escape the close investment-holding company regime.

COMPANIES OWNED BY SPOUSES OR CIVIL PARTNERS

10.32 Under independent taxation, spouses or civil partners each have their own personal allowances for income tax purposes. In normal circumstances, where spouses or civil partners jointly own and manage a private company, each will bear tax independently on any income they draw from the company. However, in some such cases, HMRC regard all the income as falling to the income-producing spouse by means of a settlement. This is only likely to arise where the other spouse is seen as taking no part in the function of the business, and possesses a holding that reflects only a right to income. This situation was tested in *Jones v Garnett (Inspector of Taxes)* [2007] STC 1536, and the House of Lords found that a settlement did indeed exist, but the exemption for gifts between spouses also applied, so dividends paid were not income arising under a settlement but were taxable on each spouse who received them. However, each case must be reviewed on its merits. See *Income Tax 2018/19* (Bloomsbury Professional).

Where a company is closely controlled and particularly where it is wholly owned by an individual, a couple or within a family, there is often scope for varying the levels of remuneration and dividends withdrawn. Many companies have habitually paid modest salaries and high dividends to reduce the tax and national insurance contributions ultimately payable. However, from April 2016 the dividend tax credit is abolished. Instead, there is a tax-free dividend allowance of £5,000 a year for all taxpayers, and new dividend income tax rates: 7.5% (basic rate), 32.5%(higher rate) and 38.1% (additional rate). This will reduce the incentives to incorporate and to remunerate through dividends rather than salaries to reduce tax liabilities.

Chapter 11

Loan relationships

SIGNPOSTS

- How loan finance affects a company's corporation tax liability, whereas equity finance has no direct effect (see **11.1–11.6**).
- Criteria applied to determine the existence of a money debt (see **11.7–11.9**).
- The accounting treatment recognition of loan relationship credits and debits (see **11.10–11.15**).
- How the loan relationship rules apply to close companies (see **11.16–11.17**).
- The meaning of a trading loan relationship and the 'unallowable purpose' test (see **11.18–11.25**).
- The meaning of a non-trading loan relationship and relief for non-trading deficits, including set-off against the income of current, previous and future years (see **11.26–11.32**).
- Pre loan relationship expenditure and pre-trading expenditure (see **11.33**).
- Relief for the costs of finance (see **11.34–11.35**).
- Connected companies relationships and their consequences (see **11.36–11.45**).
- The effects of the loan relationship rules on groups and consortia (see **11.46–11.47**).
- The inclusion of exchange gains and losses within the loan relationship regime (see **11.48**).
- Anti-avoidance legislation, including group mismatch schemes and tax mismatch schemes (see **11.49–11.54**).
- Loan relationship debits and credits to be included on the company tax return (see **11.55**).

COMPANY FINANCE

Equity versus loan finance

11.1 Companies raise finance by borrowing, issuing shares and exploiting their assets. A debt has a legal right to repayment whereas shares have no such rights. Various controls are exercised on a company's activities through the *Financial Services and Markets Act 2000*, the *Companies Act 2006* and the Stock Exchange.

For tax purposes the basic premise is that equity finance, which relates to the issue of shares, will have no direct effect on the company's corporation tax liability. UK distributions received are not taxable on a company. On eventual disposal the vendor's profit or loss will be a chargeable gain or capital loss.

By contrast, loan finance does have an effect on the company's corporation tax liability. Lenders are rewarded by an interest payment, albeit at low rates in recent years. Lenders generally look for some form of asset security or guarantee regarding the loan repayment. Interest payments are deductible against a company's corporation tax liability, and interest receipts are taxable.

Development of the loan relationship regime

11.2 The loan relationship rules governing the corporation tax treatment of corporate debt, principally aimed at aligning the tax treatment of loan finance with the accounting treatment, were collated and redrafted under the government's tax law rewrite project and are now contained in *CTA 2009, Pt 7, ss 292–710*. The aim of *CTA 2009* was not to change the earlier legislation but to make it clearer. For the previous legislation, see *Corporation Tax 2008/09* (Tottel Publishing).

In the Budget of 20 March 2013 the government announced plans to modernise the loan relationship regime to make it simpler and clearer and, at the same time, more robust against tax avoidance. Following consultation, reforms were made by *FA 2015* and (to a greater extent) *F(No 2)A 2015*.

The main areas of change are:

- clarifying the relationship between tax and accounting, and basing taxable loan relationship profits on accounting profit and loss entries (see **11.3**, **11.10–11.13**);
- new 'corporate rescue' rules to provide tax relief where loans are released or modified in cases of debtor companies in financial distress (see **11.13**, **11.17**); and
- new regime-wide anti-avoidance rules for both loan relationships and derivative contracts (see **11.54**).

The changes apply for accounting periods beginning on or after 1 January 2016, except for the new corporate rescue rules and anti-avoidance provisions which apply on and after 18 November 2015. For details of the loan relationships regime before these changes, see *Corporation Tax 2014/15* (Bloomsbury Professional).

The reforms announced in 2013 were also expected to result in unification of the regimes for loan relationships and derivative contracts, but in the event this aspect was not taken forward. The derivative contracts regime and changes made to it in 2015 are specialist topics outside the scope of this book.

Ambit of the loan relationship provisions

> **Focus**
>
> For loan relationship purposes, capital and revenue receipts are treated alike. A careful analysis is required of transactions that fall within the loan relationship rules.

11.3 A company has a 'loan relationship' if it stands in the position of debtor or creditor in respect of any 'money debt' which arises from the lending of money (*CTA 2009, s 302*). For this purpose, a 'money debt' is defined by *CTA 2009, s 303* and includes (broadly) a debt which is or has been one that falls to be settled by:

- the payment of money;
- the transfer of a right to settlement under a debt which is itself a money debt; or
- the issue or transfer of shares in any company.

The loan relationship rules treat capital and revenue receipts in a like manner and show no distinction between realised and unrealised amounts (*CTA 2009, s 293(3)*).

Matters in respect of which amounts are to be brought into account under the regime are profits, losses, interest and expenses arising to a company on its loan relationships (*CTA 2009, s 306A(2)*, as substituted for *CTA 2009, s 307(4)* by *F(No 2)A 2015, Sch 7, paras 3, 4*).

Profits and deficits are calculated according to the basis adopted in the accounts, and are termed 'credits' and 'debits'. Changes have been made, removing the requirement that credits and debits brought into account should 'fairly represent' profits and gains arising from loan relationships (now considered unnecessary because of the introduction of new regime-wide anti-avoidance rules), and introducing a new rule for apportionment of amounts where an accounting period of a company does not coincide with a period of accounts (*CTA 2009, s 296*; also *s 307* as amended by *F(No 2)A 2015, Sch 7, para 4*).

In a new approach for accounting periods beginning on or after 1 January 2016, subject to transitional provisions, only amounts recognised in profit or loss (and not the other equity statements) will be brought into account for tax purposes. On an on-going basis this will include amounts previously recognised in other comprehensive income and later transferred to profit or loss (*CTA 2009, s 308*, as amended by *F(No 2)A 2015, Sch 7, para 5*; see also *paras 114–118*).

All amounts recognised as items of other comprehensive income will be brought into account at some point (*CTA 2009, s 308(1A), 320A*, as inserted by *F(No 2)A 2015, Sch 7, paras 5, 14*).

Profits and losses from related transactions are also included within the meaning of a loan relationship (*CTA 2009, s 293(1), (2)*). A related transaction is any disposal or acquisition, in whole or in part, of rights or liabilities under the relationship. A disposal or acquisition includes the transfer or discharge by an outright sale, gift, exchange, surrender, redemption or release of any rights or liabilities under the loan relationship (*CTA 2009, s 304*).

Rights and liabilities under a loan relationship refer to the arrangements as a result of which that relationship subsists. Rights and liabilities attached to any security that is issued in relation to the money debt are also included (*CTA 2009, s 305*).

A debtor (borrower) may choose to settle an interest liability to a creditor (lender) by an issue of funding bonds. If so, the market value of the bonds at their issue date is treated as being the amount of interest paid. The later redemption of these bonds will not be treated as interest paid. Funding bonds can include any bonds, stocks, shares, securities or certificates of indebtedness (*CTA 2009, s 413*).

The loan relationship rules apply to trading and non-trading companies, unincorporated associations subject to corporation tax, UK branches of overseas companies and controlled foreign companies. The rules apply to companies that are members of a partnership but not to individuals. Non-resident companies come within the loan relationship rules if they trade in the UK through a branch or agency and the loan relationship is held for trading purposes by that branch or agency.

Trading credits and debits

11.4 Trading credits and debits are included respectively as receipts and expenses of the trade, which are to be brought into account in calculating a company's profits for that period in the computation of trading income (*CTA 2009, s 297(2), (3)*). Note that these amounts can be subject to adjustment either under the loan relationship rules themselves or the transfer pricing rules.

From 1 April 2017, the amount of interest expense that can be deducted from a company or group's profits is restricted to 30% of EBITDA, where the net interest expense is at least £2m (*TIOPA 2010, Pt 10,* see **5.31**). This rule replaces the debt cap rules which applied before that date (*TIOPA 2010, Pt 7,* see **5.32**).

Non-trading debits and credits

11.5 Non-trading debits and credits are netted off against each other. An excess of non-trading credits over non-trading debits results in a non-trading profit. Conversely, an excess of such debits over such credits results in a non-trading deficit (*CTA 2009, s 301*). Note that these amounts can be subject to adjustment either under the loan relationship rules themselves or the transfer pricing rules. From 1 April 2017, the amount of interest expense that can be deducted from a company or group's profits is restricted to 30% of EBITDA, where the net interest expense is at least £2m (*TIOPA 2010, Pt 10,* see **5.31**). This rule replaces the debt cap rules which applied before that date (*TIOPA 2010, Pt 7,* see **5.32**).

Creditor and debtor loan relationship

11.6 The first issue that a company will want to address is whether a debt arrangement into which it has entered constitutes a loan relationship. In most situations, this will be the case. A loan relationship exists where:

- the company stands in the position of a creditor or debtor as respects any money debt (whether by reference to a security or otherwise), and
- that debt is one arising from a transaction for the lending of money,

and references to a loan relationship and to a company's being a party to a loan relationship are construed accordingly (*CTA 2009, s 302(1)*).

For a company to be within the loan relationship provisions, it must have a money debt. Where the company is creditor or debtor in the case of a normal trade debt, this is not a loan relationship since it does not arise from a transaction for the lending of money.

A creditor relationship is a loan relationship where the company stands in the position of a creditor as respects the debt in question, ie the lender (*CTA 2009, s 302(5)*). A debtor relationship is a loan relationship where the company stands in the position of a debtor as respects the debt in question, ie the borrower (*CTA 2009, s 302(6)*).

In *MJP Media Services Ltd v HMRC* [2012] EWCA Civ 1558, the Court of Appeal upheld an earlier finding by the Upper Tribunal that, in the absence of clear evidence to the contrary, the recording of inter-company debt and its subsequent write-off by accounting entry did not constitute a loan relationship.

Money debts

11.7 A money debt is a debt which falls to be settled by:

- the payment of money;
- the transfer of a right to settlement under a debt which is itself a money debt; or
- the issue or transfer of any share in a company.

A money debt is also any debt that has at any time fallen to be so settled or could at the option of the debtor or the creditor be so settled. If the debt can be settled in any other way this is ignored in deciding whether there is a money debt. If an instrument has been created that represents the rights under the debt, this will be within the loan relationship rules (*CTA 2009, s 303(3)*).

Examples of debts that are included within loan relationships are: overdrafts, mortgages, advances, gilts, bank loans and deposits, building society shares and deposits, debentures, certificates of deposit, company securities and Eurobonds, government stock, discounts, premiums, bills of exchange and promissory notes.

For corporation tax purposes, a qualifying corporate bond (QCB) is a loan relationship. A QCB is a security which at all times has represented a normal commercial loan and which is only redeemable in sterling (*TCGA 1992, s 117*). A convertible loan note is not a QCB (*Weston v Garnett* [2005] STC 1134). A loan note or security that contains a currency conversion option on issue is not a QCB, even if the option were to lapse in the meantime (*Harding v Revenue and Customs Comrs* [2008] EWHC 99 (Ch)).

Certain relationships are treated as loan relationships: relevant non-lending arrangements; OEICs (open ended investment companies); unit trusts and offshore funds; building societies; industrial and provident societies; alternative finance arrangements; shares with guaranteed returns; returns from partnerships; manufactured interest; repos; and investment life insurance contracts. These are all specialist topics beyond the coverage of this book.

A debt arising from share rights granted in a company does not bring about a money debt (*CTA 2009, s 303*). For this purpose, a share in a company is any share that gives entitlement to a distribution (*CTA 2009, s 476(1)*).

Money debts brought within the loan relationship rules

11.8 A money debt is not necessarily a loan relationship. Certain money debts are brought within the loan relationship rules as relevant non-lending relationships (*CTA 2009, ss 478–486*). A relevant non-lending relationship is a loan relationship that does not arise from the lending of money (*CTA 2009, s 479(1)*), but is a kind of debt on which interest is payable to or by the company, or an exchange gain or loss arises to the company, or there is an impairment loss resulting from an unpaid business debt. Such items will include interest on late payment for goods and services, interest on judgment debts, late payment interest on completion, and late payment of tax. In such cases, only the interest and exchange gains and losses are brought into account within the loan relationship rules and included as debits or credits. Interest imputed under transfer pricing (see **21.23–21.24**) is also included within loan relationships (*CTA 2009, ss 483, 484*). Whether the interest is trading or non-trading depends on whether it is receivable or payable for the purposes of the trade. Interest receivable from or payable to HMRC is always non-trading (*CTA 2009, s 482(1)*).

Interest in excess of a reasonable commercial return does not fall within the loan relationship provisions, because the regime excludes any amount which falls to be treated as a distribution except for credits arising from anti-avoidance arrangements (*CTA 2009, s 465*).

Discounts on money debts are also loan relationships (*CTA 2009, s 480(1)*), but discounts that are treated as distributions are not.

Circumstances that are not loan relationships

11.9 From the above, it may be difficult to judge what arrangement can be considered not to be a loan relationship. However, the following are accepted as not being loan relationships as they do not derive from the lending of money: trade debts arising from the purchase of goods and services; finance leases; HP agreements; court settlements; loan guarantees; and contingencies.

ACCOUNTING TREATMENT

> **Focus**
>
> In most cases, generally accepted accounting practice (GAAP) determines how assessable profits or allowable losses are derived from loan relationships.

Amounts brought into account for tax purposes

11.10 The amounts that a company must bring into account as credits and debits are those that are recognised in determining the company's profit or loss for the accounting period in question in accordance with GAAP (*CTA 2009, s 307(2)* as amended by *F(No 2)A 2015, Sch 7, para 4*). See **Chapter 26** regarding changes to UK GAAP.

The amounts that the company must bring into account as regards its loan relationships are (*CTA 2009, s 306A(1)* as substituted for *CTA 2009, s 307(3)* by *F(No 2)A 2015, Sch 7, paras 3, 4*):

- all profits and losses from its loan relationships and related transactions, but excluding interest and expenses;
- all interest under those relationships; and
- all expenses incurred under or for the purposes of those relationships and transactions.

Expenses are only treated as incurred if they are incurred directly in (*CTA 2009, s 306A(2)* as substituted for *CTA 2009, s 307(4)* by *F(No 2)A 2015, Sch 7, paras 3, 4*):

- bringing the loan relationship into existence;
- entering or giving effect to any of the related transactions;
- making payments under any of those relationships or as a result of any of those transactions; or
- taking steps to ensure the receipt of payments under any of those relationships or in accordance with any of those transactions.

GAAP and accounting bases

11.11 If a company has drawn up accounts which are not GAAP-compliant, or has not drawn up accounts at all, its results are re-calculated for loan relationship purposes as if GAAP-compliant accounts had been drawn up for the period of account in question and any relevant earlier period (*CTA 2009, s 309*). See **Chapter 26** regarding changes to UK GAAP.

Any basis of accounting may be adopted for bringing debits and credits into account, provided it complies with GAAP, including any amortised cost basis or a fair value basis, but particular accounting bases are required in the following circumstances:

Amortised cost basis:

- connected companies relationships (*CTA 2009, s 349* as amended by *F(No 2)A 2015, Sch 7, para 28*);
- discounts arising from a money debt under a relevant non-lending relationship (*CTA 2009, s 482(2)*).

Fair value accounting:

- determination of credits and debits where amounts are not fully recognised for accounting purposes (*CTA 2009, s 312(5), (6)*);

- company partners using fair value accounting (*CTA 2009, s 382(2)*);
- index-linked gilt-edged securities (*CTA 2009, s 399(2)*);
- connected parties deriving benefit from creditor relationships (*CTA 2009, s 453(2)*);
- reset bonds etc (*CTA 2009, s 454(4)*);
- holdings in OEICs, unit trusts and offshore funds (*CTA 2009, s 490(3)*); and
- application of shares as rights under a creditor relationship by virtue of *s 523* (*CTA 2009, s 534(1)*).

Meaning of amortised cost and fair value accounting

11.12 The amortised cost basis of accounting is where an asset or liability representing the loan relationship is measured in the company's balance sheet at its amortised cost using the effective interest method, but with that amortised cost being adjusted as necessary where the loan relationship is the hedged item under a designated fair value hedge (*CTA 2009, s 313(4), (4A)*, as amended/inserted by *F(No 2)A 2015, Sch 7, para 7(5), (6)*).

Fair value accounting is where assets and liabilities are measured in the company's balance sheet at their fair value and changes in the fair value of assets and liabilities are recognised as items of profit or loss (*CTA 2009, s 313(5)*, as amended by *F(No 2) A 2015, Sch 7, para 7(7)*).

The Treasury may by regulations provide that, where there is a change in accounting basis from amortised cost to fair value, the Treasury may by regulations provide that debits and credits continue to be dealt with on an amortised cost basis (*CTA 2009, s 314*).

A change in accounting policy from one acceptable basis to another – eg on a change from old UK GAAP to new UK GAAP (see **Chapter 26**), a change from UK GAAP to international GAAP or *vice versa,* or a change to comply with tax rules (eg the requirement under *CTA 2009, s 349*, to apply an amortised cost basis of accounting to connected companies relationships) – may bring about a change in the 'tax-adjusted carrying value' of an asset or a liability between one accounting period and the next. If so, an adjusting debit or credit (as appropriate) is to be brought into the later accounting period (*CTA 2009, ss 315, 316,* as amended/inserted by *F(No 2)A 2015, Sch 7, paras 9, 10*). (See also *Fidex Ltd v HMRC* [2016] EWCA Civ 385 – a case where a debit resulting from a change in accounting practice was disallowed under the unallowable purpose rules, discussed at **11.23**.)

A similar adjustment is required if there is a change in value following the cessation of a loan relationship (*CTA 2009, s 318* amended by *F(No 2)A 2015, Sch 7, para 12*).

The tax-adjusted carrying value of an asset or liability includes accruals, payments in advance and impairment losses, together with provisions for bad or doubtful debts, and is equal to the carrying value in the company's accounts, adjusted as a result of particular statutory provisions (*CTA 2009, s 465B* as substituted for *CTA 2009, s 317* by *F(No 2)A 2015, Sch 7, para 52*). In this context an impairment loss is a debit resulting from the impairment (including uncollectability) of a financial asset (*CTA 2009, s 476(1)*).

The Treasury may by regulations make provision for cases where there is a change of accounting policy in drawing up a company's accounts from one period of account to the next which affects the amounts to be brought into account for accounting purposes in respect of the company's loan relationships (*CTA 2009, s 319*).

Under GAAP (eg under FRS 102 *The Financial Reporting Standard applicable in the UK and Republic of Ireland* at Section 25 *Borrowing Costs* or under IAS 23 *Borrowing Costs*), some loan relationship debits or credits may be treated as capital: in these circumstances they are treated for tax purposes under the loan relationships regime as though they had been brought into account in determining the company's profit or loss under GAAP (*CTA 2009, s 320* as amended by *F(No 2)A 2015, Sch 7, para 13*).

See **Chapter 26** regarding changes to UK GAAP.

Debits with no complementary credits

11.13 For accounting purposes, debits and credits complement each other but, if a debt is released, no complementary credit needs to be recognised in the accounts (*CTA 2009, s 322*, as amended by *F(No 2)A 2015, Sch 7, para 16*) if:

- the release is part of a statutory insolvency arrangement;
- the release is in consideration of shares forming part of the ordinary share capital of the debtor company, or in consideration of any entitlement to such shares;
- the debtor company meets one of the insolvency conditions and the debtor relationship is not a connected companies relationship (see **11.17**). The insolvency conditions are that the company is in insolvent liquidation, in administration or in insolvent administrative receivership, or if an appointment of a provisional liquidator is in force. Any of the insolvency conditions may be met in the UK or there may be corresponding circumstances in a jurisdiction outside the UK (*CTA 2009, s 322(6)*); or

- the release occurs on or after 18 November 2015 in circumstances where there is a material risk that within 12 months of the release the company would be unable to pay its debts (the corporate rescue exception), *CTA 2009, s 322(5B)*, as inserted by *F(No 2)A 2015, Sch 7, para 16(4)*). For the meaning of 'unable to pay its debts' see *CTA 2009, s 323(1A)*, as inserted by *F(No 2)A 2015, Sch 7, para 17*; the corporate rescue exception is intended to apply only where a debtor company is in significant financial distress.

If an asset is revalued, no debit is to be brought into account, with the exception of an impairment loss or a debit resulting from a release by the company of any liability under the relationship, or a debit in respect of valuation changes in respect of hedged assets and liabilities. Credits, which correspond to the disallowed debits, are also not brought into account. This treatment does not apply if the company adopts fair value accounting (*CTA 2009, ss 324, 325* as amended by *F(No 2)A 2015, Sch 7, para 19*)).

Where a government debt is written off under *CTA 2010, s 94* (see **4.29**) by the release of a liability to pay an amount under a debtor relationship, no credit is required to be brought into account (*CTA 2009, s 326*).

There is no relief for a loss incurred when the loan relationship was not subject to UK tax (*CTA 2009, s 327*).

Loan relationships and non-market loans

11.14 As a result of changes to UK accounting standards, companies can now be required to recognise interest-free loans and other loans made on 'non-market' terms at a discount to the par value of the loan. The effect of unwinding the discount during the life of the loan is to create an interest cost in the accounts, in spite of the fact that this does not reflect the actual interest paid. From 1 April 2016, tax deductions in respect of such notional interest expenses are restricted (*CTA 2009, s 446A*).

Loan relationships and transfer pricing

11.15 As a result of changes to UK accounting standards, a company can be required to recognise amounts in their financial statements which subsequently reverse. This can have adverse consequences where a loan relationship debit is restricted under a transfer pricing adjustment. When the debit is reversed in the accounts, the full amount is recognised and potentially taxable as a credit, even though only a partial deduction was obtained on the corresponding debit. From 1 April 2016, a credit that arises on a reversal of a previous debit is only taxed to the extent that the debit was deductible for tax purposes (*CTA 2009 s 447* as amended by *Finance Act 2016*).

CLOSE COMPANIES

Release of loans to participators

11.16 If a loan made by a close company to a participator results in a tax charge under *CTA 2010, s 455* (see **Chapter 10**) and the whole of the debt is written off, there is no corresponding loan relationship debit (*CTA 2009, s 321A*). Before 24 March 2010, such a write-off could bring about a loan relationship debit.

Connected company debts released

11.17 Special rules apply to connected companies relationships. For the meaning of connected companies, see **11.36**.

Where a debt between connected parties is released, the company is only required to bring a credit into account in respect of the release if it is a deemed release (*CTA 2009, s 358* as amended by *F(No 2)A 2015, Sch 7, para 33*). This is a release which is deemed to occur because of:

- an acquisition of creditor rights by a connected company at undervalue (*CTA 2009, s 361,* as amended by *F(No 2)A 2015, Sch 7, para 35*); or
- previously unconnected parties to a loan relationship, as debtor and creditor respectively, becoming connected (*CTA 2009, s 362*, as amended by *F(No 2)A 2015, Sch 7, para 38*). For details of how this applied before 1 April 2012, see *Corporation Tax 2014/15* (Bloomsbury Professional).

There are two exceptions from the deemed release under *CTA 2009, s 361*, as follows:

- equity-for-debt; and
- corporate rescue.

Both these exceptions require an arm's length transaction.

The equity-for-debt exception requires that consideration given for the loan consists only of shares forming part of the ordinary share capital of the acquiring company or its connected company (*CTA 2009, s 361C*).

The corporate rescue exception applies to the credit that arises on a deemed release otherwise imposed on a debtor company under *CTA 2009, s 361* when an impaired debt is acquired by a creditor company connected to the debtor (*CTA 2009, s 361D*, as inserted by *F(No 2)A 2015, Sch 7, para 37*), or under *CTA 2009, s 362* where the parties to an impaired debt become connected (*CTA 2009, s 362A*, as inserted by *F(No 2)A 2015, Sch 7, para 38*). In each case the exception applies where there is a material risk that, within 12 months of the event in question, the debtor company would be unable to pay its debts (for the meaning of this, see **11.13**).

Example 11.1—Release of connected company debt

Facts

D Ltd is a struggling company that owes £100,000 to its parent company E Ltd. F Ltd is an unconnected company which believes it can turn round D Ltd's business. In February 2018, F Ltd comes to an arrangement with E Ltd to buy from it (a) the shares in D Ltd and (b) its loans to D Ltd. D Ltd then becomes completely independent of its former parent, E Ltd. F Ltd pays an arm's length price of £40,000 for the loans, and in its accounts it does not recognise any credits in respect of the acquired debt. Later F Ltd releases the entire £100,000 debt so that D Ltd is not required to pay it.

Analysis

On the assumption that F Ltd's acquisition of the debt of D Ltd meets the conditions for the corporate rescue exception in *CTA 2009, s 361A*, there will be no 'deemed release' on D Ltd of £60,000.

On subsequent release of the debt by F Ltd, there will be a 'release of relevant rights' of £60,000 under *CTA 2009, s 354* (see **11.44**).

TRADING AND NON-TRADING LOAN RELATIONSHIPS

Introduction

Focus

For corporation tax purposes, there is a need for both borrowers and lenders to distinguish between trading and non-trading loan relationships.

11.18 It is necessary to distinguish between a trading and a non-trading loan relationship. Essentially, if a company owes a sum or is owed a sum for the purposes of its trade, it is within a trading loan relationship (*CTA 2009, s 297(1)*). In the case of a sum owed by the company, if this arises as a result of borrowing for the purposes of its trade, including the purchase of capital assets for use in that trade, it is a trading loan relationship.

In the case of the creditor company, a more stringent test applies, and it is only within a trading loan relationship if it entered into the loan 'in the course of activities forming an integral part of its trade' (*CTA 2009, s 298(1)*). In practice, only companies within the financial sector, such as banks, insurance companies and other financial businesses which lend funds as an integral part of their trade, will meet this requirement. In some cases, group treasury companies and group finance companies may also meet this test.

In *Nuclear Electric plc v Bradley* (1996) 68 TC 670, the House of Lords held that money lending was not an integral part of the trade of an electrical energy producer and supplier; therefore, interest earned on money set aside to meet future liabilities was deemed to relate to a non-trading loan relationship.

TRADING LOAN RELATIONSHIPS

Trading income

11.19 The appropriate accounting method will result in all credits and debits arising from profits, gains and losses, both capital and revenue, interest, charges and expenses, together with exchange gains and losses relating to the company's loan relationships, being brought into the corporation tax computation. Credits and debits resulting from a trading loan relationship are included as receipts or expenses of the trade (*CTA 2009, s 296*). Any consequent profits or losses arising are assessable or relievable accordingly under the trading income rules.

The loan relationship legislation overrides the capital expenditure exclusion (*CTA 2009, s 53*; see **2.11**), the 'wholly and exclusively' requirement (*CTA 2009, s 54*; see **2.13**) and the patent royalties exclusion (*CTA 2009, s 59*; see **2.19**) regarding trading income (*CTA 2009, s 297(4)*).

Example 11.2—Accounting and tax treatment of trading loan relationship

Facts

Aurora Ltd is a small trading company that requires additional finance for the purposes of its trade. On 1 January the bank grants the company an additional £1 million fixed interest loan facility at 5% per annum, which is an arm's length rate. The company is charged legal fees and other professional costs of £5,000 in relation to obtaining the loan. The company prepares its accounts annually to 31 December, in accordance with FRS 102, Section 1A.

Analysis

The loan is a trading loan relationship as it has been taken out for trading purposes. As the company applies FRS 102, Section 1A, the finance costs of borrowings are allocated to the accounting periods over the term of the borrowings at a constant rate on the carrying amount calculated using the effective interest method. The amounts charged will form the allowable debits and no adjustment to profits is required when preparing the corporation tax computation. The expenses will be allowable by reason of *CTA 2009, s 306(2)* – see **11.34**.

Example 11.3—Credit not recognised in profit or loss

Facts

Q plc acquires shares in a new subsidiary for £10 million. It pays the vendor company £8 million in cash, and issues loan notes for the remaining £2 million. Subsequently, Q plc discovers problems regarding the financial position of its new subsidiary that had not come to light in the due diligence process. Discussions with the vendor company follow, as a result of which it is agreed that the purchase price should be reduced by £1 million. Accordingly, loan notes to the value of £1 million issued by Q plc are cancelled. It accounts for the transaction as:

Debit	Creditors (loan notes)	£1 million
Credit	Cost of investment	£1 million

Analysis

For tax purposes, the loan notes are loan relationships because, although there has been no lending of money, an instrument has been issued representing security for the creditor's rights under the £2 million money debt. The cancellation of £1 million of the notes does not, however, give rise to a tax charge under the loan relationships rules. Although a credit appears in the company's books, there is no amount that has been recognised in determining the company's profit or loss for the period. Nothing, therefore, falls within *CTA 2009, s 307(2)*, as amended by *F(No 2)A 2015, Sch 7, para 4*.

Note that there are different computational rules for non-trading loan relationships (see **11.26** onwards).

LOAN RELATIONSHIPS WITH AN UNALLOWABLE PURPOSE

Focus

The rules that restrict credits and debits when a loan relationship has an unallowable purpose were originally contained in *FA 1996, Sch 9, para 13*, but are now set out in *CTA 2009, s 441*. However, until 2011 there was little or no judicial guidance on what constituted an unallowable purpose. Since then, a series of cases have been decided, and it is not unlikely that more cases will follow.

Introduction

11.20 The rules apply if, in any accounting period, a company has a loan relationship with an unallowable purpose (*CTA 2009, s 441(1)*). If the conditions are satisfied, restrictions apply to both credits and debits. In particular:

- the company cannot bring into account any credits in respect of any exchange gains arising from the loan relationship to the extent that those credits are attributable to an unallowable purpose (*CTA 2009, s 441(2)*); and
- the company cannot bring into account any debits in respect of the loan relationship to the extent that those debits are attributable to an unallowable purpose (*CTA 2009, s 441(3)*);
- the unallowable purpose rules extend to transactions that are deemed to be loan relationships, such as when the return on equity holdings is economically equivalent to a commercial rate of interest (*CTA 2009, Ch 6A, s 521E*; see also *Travel Document Service and Ladbroke Group International v HMRC* [2017] UKUT 45 (TCC)).

In practice, most unallowable purpose issues will relate to the question of whether tax relief is available for a debit. It is easy to overlook the fact that credits are also subject to restrictions, although the scope of the rules is narrower than for debits, applying only to exchange gains arising from the relevant loan relationship.

The fact that a transaction does not result in any overall loss of tax to the Treasury does not save it from being struck down by the unallowable purpose rules. In *Travel Document Service and Ladbroke Group International v HMRC* [2015] UKFTT 582 (TC), debits on a loan were denied tax relief, in spite of the fact that they were balanced by credits elsewhere within the corporate group.

Meaning of unallowable purpose

11.21 A loan relationship has an unallowable purpose if the purposes for which the company is a party to the relationship or a related transaction include a purpose which is not amongst the company's business or other commercial purposes that are within the charge to corporation tax (*CTA 2009, s 442(1)–(2)*).

A related transaction is a transaction that consists of a disposal or acquisition of any rights or liabilities arising under an existing loan relationship (*CTA 2009, s 304*). For the unallowable purpose rules, this definition is extended to include anything which, in substance, equates to a related transaction (*CTA 2009, s 442(1A)*).

The most obvious type of unallowable purpose is a tax avoidance purpose. A tax avoidance purpose becomes an unallowable purpose when it is the main purpose or one of the main purposes for which the company is a party to the relationship or enters into a related transaction (*CTA 2009, s 442(3)–(4)*).

Example 11.4—Unallowable purpose: tax avoidance

Facts

A company, B Ltd, borrows £50 million from a finance company, F Ltd, at arm's length. B Ltd becomes insolvent and disposes of all its assets, leaving it with an outstanding debt of £40 million owed to F Ltd. B Ltd is not liquidated and interest continues to accrue on the debt. F Ltd either omits to accrue the interest receivable or it accrues the interest and then writes it off as a bad debt. B Ltd accrues the interest and makes a deficit on which group relief claims are made.

Analysis

B Ltd has no activity which is within the charge to corporation tax (*CTA 2009, s 442(2)*). It would appear that the only purpose of the loan relationship in the current accounting period is to generate group relief, thereby attempting to secure a tax advantage for another group company (*CTA 2009, s 442(5)*). The purpose of the loan relationship is therefore specifically excluded from being a business or commercial purpose and it is an unallowable purpose. In addition, although the loan relationship was originally *bona fide*, its continued existence is not commercial. The continuing debits relating to the loan relationship are disallowed.

The use of funds to secure or finance a tax avoidance scheme is an unallowable purpose (*CTA 2009, s 442*; CFM38140). This is illustrated in the case of *Explainaway Ltd & Ors v Revenue & Customs* [2011] UKFTT 414 (TC), where funds were borrowed to finance a transaction which was designed to generate a capital loss involving the use of derivatives (this case was subsequently appealed, but no further argument was heard on the unallowable purpose issue – see *Explainaway Ltd and others v HMRC* [2012] UKUT 362 (TCC)).

The *Explainaway* case also illustrates the proposition that the tax advantage need not arise from the loan relationship. The tax advantage in that case was the capital loss generated to shelter a significant chargeable gain by another group company.

The tax avoidance purpose need not be the purpose of the company that is party to the loan relationship. A tax avoidance purpose can include the securing of a tax advantage for another person (*CTA 2009, s 476(1)*; *CTA 2010, s 1139*).

Unallowable purpose not restricted to tax avoidance

11.22 It should, however, be noted that the absence of a tax avoidance motive does not necessarily mean that a loan relationship has an allowable purpose. All that is required is that the purpose does not fall within the company's 'business or other commercial purposes'. In theory, it is therefore possible for a purpose to be unallowable without tax avoidance being involved; but, in practice, tax avoidance is the most likely reason for a challenge by HMRC.

Example 11.5—Non-business (no tax avoidance)

Dale Ltd is a manufacturing concern based in Yorkshire, which exports goods to South America. The company borrows money to buy a property in London in which to house visiting buyers from abroad and to hold meetings with them. The interest payments on the loan are clearly allowable since the loan has been taken out for the purpose of the company's business.

The property is used from time to time by the managing director's son, who is going to university in London. The interest costs which are recognised in the accounting periods in which the property is used in this way arise from a non-business purpose. These costs must therefore be apportioned on a just and reasonable basis, and the debits relating to the non-business use of the property are disallowed.

(This example is taken from counsel's argument in *Fidex Ltd v Revenue & Customs* [2011] UKFTT 713 (TC) at para 179.)

Example 11.6—Unallowable purpose: non-business

Facts

Chekov is the UK branch of Zagrev, a non-UK resident Russian holding company. The company uses British banks to fund its global activities. A £12 million loan is raised from the CASH Bank plc to fund Zagrev's activities in Guatemala, which are not within the charge to UK corporation tax. Chekov has no involvement in these activities but agrees to pay the interest.

Analysis

The interest charged is deemed to be an 'unallowable purpose' for Chekov, and hence is disallowable (*CTA 2009, s 442(2)*).

Unallowable purpose must relate to an accounting period

11.23 Timing issues are important in considering whether a credit or debit is to be disallowed:

- There must be an unallowable purpose which exists in an accounting period.
- However, only those credits and debits arising in that same accounting period can be disallowed.

Furthermore, a loan relationship need not have an unallowable purpose at the outset – it can have various purposes throughout the life of the loan. It is only when a purpose is an unallowable purpose that the rules apply, and only in respect of accounting periods during which that purpose exists.

These principles are illustrated in the case of *Fidex Ltd v HMRC* [2016] EWCA Civ 385. In *Fidex,* the company held a pre-existing bond portfolio, which it was intending to divest, as part of a group restructuring. This was achieved by matching four of its bonds with four classes of preference shares issued to an outside party, effectively giving the latter the right to the income from the bonds. By changing its accounting standards, the company was required to derecognise the bonds from its balance sheet, giving rise to a loan relationship debit in the region of €84 million, which was surrendered as group relief.

The initial purpose of the company in acquiring the bonds was for use as collateral for its business of issuing commercial paper. A tax avoidance purpose did not arise until a few years later when the company issued the preference shares and changed its accounting standards. At the First Tier Tribunal (*Fidex Ltd v Revenue & Customs* [2011] UKFTT 713 (TC)), the court ruled in favour of the company on the basis that:

- the debit was recognised in the 2005 accounting period; but
- the tax avoidance purpose arose in the previous 2004 accounting period; that purpose had been achieved by the end of that year.

The debit was therefore allowed, since there was a mismatch between the accounting period in which the debit was recognised and the accounting period in respect of which there was an unallowable purpose.

This decision was overturned both by the Upper Tribunal and the Court of Appeal on the basis that the unallowable purpose carried over into the beginning of the 2005 accounting period.

Credits and debits must be attributable to the unallowable purpose

11.24 It is not sufficient for the loan relationship to have an unallowable purpose – the credits or debits must be attributable to that purpose. If the latter is wholly attributable to the unallowable purpose, the entire amount is disallowed. If there is more than one purpose, and some of those purposes are allowable, an apportionment is made on a just and reasonable basis.

Example 11.7—Unallowable purpose: apportionment

Facts

The CASH Bank plc grants the Village Tennis Club a loan to finance the construction of a new club house, which is to be used by members and non-members.

Analysis

For corporation tax purposes, the club's interest expense is apportioned between allowable and non-allowable elements *pro rata* to its taxable income from non-members and non-taxable income from members.

However, the fact that a 'bad' loan relationship has one or more allowable purposes does not automatically mean that only part of the debit will be disallowed. In *Fidex* (see **11.23**), it was accepted by the court that the bonds were held for commercial purposes as well as for tax avoidance reasons.

But the key issue is: to what extent is the debit attributable to the unallowable purpose? Both appellate courts held that the debit was wholly attributable, in spite of the fact that there was a commercial purpose in holding the bonds. In particular, the Upper Tribunal held that, since the commercial purpose arose *after* the debit was recognised, no attribution could be made to that purpose, while the Court of Appeal held that the debit would never have arisen had it not been for the company entering into the tax avoidance scheme in the first place.

Whose purpose?

11.25 On the face of it, the purpose must be that of the company that is a party to the loan.

The words of the legislation require that the loan relationship has an unallowable purpose, and that purpose is defined in terms of the company that is party to that loan relationship, or a related transaction (*CTA 2009, ss 441(1), 442(1)*). The legislation goes on to define a tax avoidance purpose as being that of the company, albeit the tax advantage accrues to someone else (*CTA 2009, s 442(4)–(5)*).

However, in *AH Field (Holdings) Ltd v HMRC* [2012] UKFTT 104 (TC), the court took a wider approach and considered not only the purpose of the company concerned, but that of its shareholders and advisers, stating that the purpose of the directors of the appellant company could not be 'divorced from and treated as discrete from the purposes of all the members of and advisers to the company' (at para 118). It remains to be seen whether this is good law and, if so, what criteria should apply if the purpose of persons outside the loan relationship is to be taken into account.

NON-TRADING LOAN RELATIONSHIPS

11.26 A company is party to a non-trading loan relationship if it is party to the relationship for purposes other than the purposes of its trade. A property business or an overseas property business is not a trade for these purposes. For many trading companies, their only non-trading income will be bank interest received from the investment of surplus funds (*Nuclear Electric plc v Bradley* (1996) 68 TC 670; see **11.18**).

Non-trading loan relationship debits and credits are aggregated to result in a non-trading profit or deficit. A non-trading profit is chargeable to corporation tax.

Example 11.8—Non-trading loan relationship

Facts

On 1 January 2016, Borealis Ltd bought £20,000 nominal gilt-edged stock at £95 per £100 nominal stock. The investment was not for the purposes of trade. The securities are redeemable on 31 December 2020 at par. Interest at 3% is payable annually on 31 December.

Analysis

As the investment has no relationship to the trade, it amounts to a non-trading loan relationship, and the interest and discount are chargeable to corporation tax as profits from a non-trading loan relationship.

The accounting treatment and the assessable amounts are as follows:

Year ended 31 December	*2016*	*2017*	*2018*	*2019*	*2020*
	£	*£*	*£*	*£*	*£*
Interest received	600	600	600	600	600
Discount	200	200	200	200	200
Non-trading loan relationship profit	800	800	800	800	800

RELIEF FOR NON-TRADING DEFICITS

Basic rule – deficit carried forward to subsequent accounting periods

11.27 The tax treatment depends on whether the deficit is in relation to an accounting period beginning before 1 April 2017 (a 'pre-1 April 2017 deficit'), or an accounting period beginning on or after that date (a 'post-1 April 2017 deficit'). Accounting periods straddling this date are treated as two accounting periods, one ending on 31 March 2017 and another starting on 1 April 2017, with profits and losses apportioned between the two (*F(No 2)A 2017, Sch 4 para 190*).

The basic rule is for the non-trading loan relationships deficit to be carried forward and set off against profits of the company for accounting periods after the deficit period.

For pre-1 April 2017 deficits, the carry-forward is restricted to being set against non-trading profits (*CTA 2009, s 457(1)*). For post-1 April 2017 deficits, carry-forward relief is available against total profits (*CTA 2009, ss 463G, 463I*). However, relief against total profits is unavailable for a charitable company, a company with an investment business that has become small or negligible and in certain circumstances restrictions also apply to insurance companies. In these circumstances, the company is restricted to carrying forward the deficit against non-trading profits only (*CTA 2009, ss 456(1)(b(ii), 457(1), 463A(1)(b), 463H*). Note that there are special anti-avoidance rules that prevent a company from 'buying in' profits in order to relieve a carried forward non-trading deficit (*CTA 2010, s 730F*; see **4.30**).

For pre-1 April 2017 deficits, carry forward relief is automatic unless a claim is made for an alternative method of relief (see **11.28**). The company may also elect to claim relief for only part of the amount carried forward, with the remainder being carried forward to later accounting periods. The company may even disclaim relief in respect of the accounting period following the year in which the deficit arose, and elect that the entire amount is carried forward to later accounting periods. A claim must made within two years after the end of the first accounting period that follows the period in which the deficit arose (*CTA 2009, s 458*).

For post-1 April 2017 deficits, carry forward relief must be claimed, either for the whole or part of the amount of the deficit. As with pre-1 April 2017 deficits, it is possible to skip an accounting period and claim for the relief to be carried forward to the next accounting period. A claim must made within two years after the end of the first accounting period that follows the period in which the deficit arose, but this time limit can be extended at HMRC's discretion (*CTA 2009, ss 463G(7), (10), 463H(7), (8),*).

Where a non-trading deficit is carried forward into a post 1 April 2017 accounting period, relief is subject to the corporate loss restrictions which have effect for accounting periods beginning on or after 1 April 2017. These restrictions apply where the company's profits exceed the £5 million 'deductions allowance' (which may be adjusted for accounting periods shorter than 12 months and which can be split and allocated between group members). In these circumstances, the total amount of losses that can be carried forward against future profits is limited to £5 million plus 50% of profits in excess of that figure. If it is not possible to set off the whole of the carried forward loss, the excess may be carried forward to the next accounting period, where the cap continues to apply. For these purposes, the term 'losses' is not limited to non-trading loan relationship deficits, but includes losses from a variety of sources such as trading losses, property losses, management expenses, non-trading deficits on intangible assets as well as deductions for carry-forward group relief. The restrictions apply in respect of losses incurred prior to 1 April 2017 as well as losses incurred on or after that date.

(*CTA 2010, Pt 7ZA*; see **Chapter 4).**

Example 11.9—Single company: partial claim for deficit brought forward

Facts

Josephine Ltd only carries on an overseas property business. A double tax agreement is in place. The profits for the year ended 31 March 2016 amounted to £90,000. The overseas tax paid was £12,000. Many years ago, Josephine Ltd incurred a non-trading loan relationship deficit. The balance brought forward under *CTA 2009, s 457* at 31 March 2015 is £100,000.

Analysis

Josephine Ltd claims under *CTA 2009, s 458* that only part of the deficit is to be set against the current year's income, with the following result:

	Year ending 31 March 2016
	£
Overseas property business	90,000
Non-trading loan relationship part deficit	(30,000)
Total taxable profits	60,000
Corporation tax @ 20%	12,000
Overseas tax paid	12,000

The balance of deficit available to carry forward is £70,000.

Alternative methods of relief for non-trading deficits

11.28 Relief for non-trading deficits is also available as follows:

(a) by claim for group relief – for accounting periods beginning on or after 1 April 2017 this includes a claim to group relieve post-1 April 2017 deficits carried forward into a subsequent accounting period, unless the company is a company with investment business which has become small or negligible (*CTA 2010, s 99*, and *s 188BB*, see **Chapter 5**); or

(b) by claim:

   (i) to set against other profits of the company for the deficit period, in whole or in part (*CTA 2009, s 459(1)(a)*, and *s 463B(1)(a)*); or

   (ii) carried back and set against the chargeable loan relationship profits of the previous 12 months, in whole or in part (*CTA 2009, s 459(1)(b)*, and *s 463B(1)(b)*); or

(c) any remaining amount will be carried forward to succeeding accounting periods (*CTA 2009, s 457*, and *s 463G*, see **11.27**).

The company can claim relief for all or part of the deficit.

A claim for group relief can be made at any time up to the first anniversary of the filing date of the return (*FA 1998, Sch 18, para 74*). A claim to relieve the deficit against either current year profits or to carry back against the previous year must be made within two years after the deficit period ends (*CTA 2009, s 460(1)*, and *s 463C*).

Note that loss relief claims in respect of loan relationships deficits are subject to TAAR related legislation which counteracts loss related tax advantages. This legislation applies to tax advantages arising in respect of accounting periods beginning on or after 1 April 2017 (*F(No 2)A 2017, s 19*).

Example 11.10—Single company: pre-1 April 2017 deficit (no deficit in previous years)

Facts

Admiral Ltd's results are shown below. Admiral Ltd has a non-trading deficit for the year ended 31 December 2015 of £10,000. There are no group companies.

Year ended 31 December	*2012*	*2013*	*2014*	*2015*	*2016*
	£	*£*	*£*	*£*	*£*
Trade profits	10,000	20,000	30,000	700	900
Non-trading loan relationship profits	1,000	1,000	5,000		300
Total taxable profits	11,000	21,000	35,000	700	1,200

Analysis

Relief for the non-trading deficit for the year ended 31 December 2015 is obtained as follows:

	£	£
Total loss		10,000
Set against other profits of the company for the deficit period (*CTA 2009, s 459(1)(a)*)	700	
Carried back and set against non-trading loan relationship profits of the previous 12 months (*CTA 2009, s 459(1)(b)*)	5,000	
Carried forward and set against non-trading loan relationship profits in the next accounting period (*CTA 2009, s 457*)	300	
Loss utilised		6,000
Balance available to carry forward to subsequent accounting periods		4,000

Example 11.11—Single company: post-1 April 2017 deficit (no deficit in previous years)

Facts

Admiral Ltd's results are shown below. Admiral Ltd has a non-trading deficit for the year ended 31 December 2019 of £10,000. There are no group companies.

Year ended 31 December	*2016*	*2017*	*2018*	*2019*	*2020*
	£	£	£	£	£
Trade profits	10,000	20,000	30,000	700	900
Non-trading loan relationship profits	1,000	1,000	5,000		300
Total taxable profits	11,000	21,000	35,000	700	1,200

Analysis

Relief for the non-trading deficit for the year ended 31 December 2018 is obtained as follows:

	£	£
Total loss		10,000
Set against other profits of the company for the deficit period (*CTA 2009, s 463B(1)(a)*)	700	

Carried back and set against non-trading loan relationship profits of the previous 12 months (*CTA 2009, s 463B(1)(b)*)	5,000	
Carried forward and set against total profits in the next accounting period (*CTA 2009, s 463G*)	1,200	
Loss utilised		6,900
Balance available to carry forward to subsequent accounting periods		3,100

Example 11.12—Group company: no deficit in previous years

Facts

Horatio Ltd has the following results for the years ended 30 June 2014, 2015 and 2016:

Year ended 30 June	*2014*	*2015*	*2016*
	£	£	£
Trade profits	5,000	15,000	40,000
Non-trading loan relationship profit	10,000	10,000	
Non-trading loan relationship deficit			(5,000)

Analysis

Horatio Ltd has the option of utilising the £5,000 deficit for the year ended 30 June 2016 in:

(i) a group relief claim (*CTA 2010, s 99*),
(ii) against total profits for the year ending 30 June 2016 (*CTA 2009, s 459(1)(a)*),
(iii) against loan relationship profits for the year ending 30 June 2015 (*CTA 2009, s 459(1)(b)*), or
(iv) carry forward against non-trading profits in succeeding periods (*CTA 2009, s 457*).

Example 11.13—Single company: partial loss claim for current year

Facts

Nelson Ltd has the following results for the year ended 31 March 2016 and makes a partial claim to set its non-trading deficit against profits of the same period:

	£
Trade profits	78,000
Profits of a property business	40,000
Non-trading deficit	152,000

Analysis

Nelson Ltd's partial loss claim is as follows:

	Trade profits	*Profits of a property business*	*Total*	*Non-trading loan relationship deficit*
	£	£	£	£
Income	78,000	40,000	118,000	(152,000)
Partial deficit claim (*CTA 2009, s 459(1)(a)*)	(78,000)	(10,000)	(88,000)	88,000
Total taxable profits	0	30,000	30,000	
Corporation tax @ 20%			6,000	
Deficit available:				
(i) to carry back under *CTA 2009, s 459(1)(b)*, or				64,000
(ii) to carry forward (*CTA 2009, s 457*)				

Order of relief: current year

11.29 If the non-trading loan relationships deficit is set against total profits of the current period, the order of set-off is as follows (*CTA 2009, s 461(5), (6),* and *s 463D(4)*):

(i) after relief for any deficit brought forward from any earlier accounting period (for pre-1 April 2017 deficits), but

(ii) before relief for:

(a) losses of a property business set against profits for the same period (*CTA 2010, s 62(3)*),

(b) trading losses set against profits for the same period, or carried back from a later period (*CTA 2010, s 37*), or

(c) a non-trading deficit carried back from a later period (*CTA 2009, s 459(1)(b),* and *s 463B(1)*).

Order of relief: carry back to previous year

11.30 If the non-trading loan relationships deficit is carried back and set against loan relationship profits of the previous 12-month accounting period, the claim can only be made after any claims that relate to (*CTA 2009, ss 462, 463(5)*, and *ss 463E, 463F(5)*):

(i) deficits of the claim period to be set off against total profits (*CTA 2009, s 459(1)(a), s 463B(1)(a)*),

(ii) losses or deficits from any period before the deficit period, or that are treated as coming from an earlier period,

(iii) relief for charitable donations made for trading purposes (*CTA 2010, Pt 6*),

(iv) trading losses set against profits of the same or preceding year under *CTA 2010, s 37,* and

(v) if the company is a company with investment business:

- management expenses under *CTA 2009, s 1219* (see **Chapter 6**);
- charitable donations relief under *CTA 2010, Pt 6* (see **Chapter 16**); and
- plant and machinery allowances under *CAA 2001, Pt 2* (see **Chapter 3**).

Example 11.14—Group company: deficit in previous year

Facts

See Example 11.12, but assume that Horatio Ltd's results for the years ended 30 June 2014, 2015 and 2016 had been as follows:

Year ended 30 June	*2014*	*2015*	*2016*
	£	£	£
Trade profits	–	15,000	40,000
Non-trading loan relationship profit		10,000	
Non-trading loan relationship deficit	(8,000)		(5,000)

Analysis

Horatio Ltd can still use the £5,000 deficit for the year ended 30 June 2016 by surrendering it as group relief or setting it against other profits, but can only relieve £2,000 of the deficit in the year to 30 June 2015 because the brought-forward deficit of £8,000 has priority.

Example 11.15—Single company: deficit in previous years

Facts

Kiora Ltd is a single company, prepares accounts to 31 March each year and has the following actual and forecast results:

Year ended 31 March	*2015*	*2016*	*2017*
	£000	*£000*	*£000*
Trade loss brought forward	(90)		
Trade profits	400	200	500
Profits of a property business	50	50	20
Chargeable gain	100	100	2
Non-trading loan relationship:			
Interest accrued credits	10	8	20
Interest accrued (debits)		(400)	(400)
Net deficit		(392)	(380)

Analysis

The non-trading loan relationship deficit can be relieved as follows:

Year ended 31 March	*2015*	*2016*	*2017*
	£000	*£000*	*£000*
Trade profits	400	200	500
Loss: *CTA 2010, s 45(4)* brought forward	(90)		
Trade profits (after loss relief)	310	200	500
Profits of a property business	50	50	20
Chargeable gain	100	100	2
Non-trading loan relationship credits	10		
Total non-trading profits	160	150	22

Total profits	470	350	522
Set-off against current profits of whatever description (*CTA 2009, s 459(1)(a)*)		(350)	(380)
Set-off against loan relationship profits of the previous 12 months (*CTA 2009, s 459(1)(b)*)	(10)		
Carry forward to set against future non-trading profits (*CTA 2009, s 457*)			(22)
Total relief	(10)	(350)	(402)
Total taxable profits	460	0	120
Non-trading deficit memorandum			
Net deficit		392	380
Current year relief		(350)	(380)
Prior year relief		(10)	
Future year relief		(22)	
Balance carried forward		10	0

Restriction on change in ownership of shell companies

11.31 In parallel with long-standing provisions which restrict the carry-forward of a company's trading losses on a change of ownership (see **4.24** onwards), measures restrict relief for certain non-trading loan relationship deficits of a shell company (ie one not carrying on a trade, property or investment business). These apply on a change of ownership on or after 20 March 2013 (*CTA 2010, ss 705A–705G*). The effect is to restrict:

- the non-trading loan relationship debits to be brought into account for the period before the change in ownership; and
- the carry-forward of non-trading deficits to periods after the change in ownership.

11.32 The accounting period in which the change of ownership takes place is treated as two separate accounting periods, and there are detailed rules for apportioning amounts between the two accounting periods (*CTA 2010, s 705F*).

PRE LOAN RELATIONSHIP AND PRE-TRADING EXPENDITURE

11.33 Pre loan relationship expenses and abortive expenses are classed as non-trading debits, and are deductible if they would have been so deductible had the loan relationship been entered into at that time (*CTA 2009, s 329*).

If a company intends to trade, any interest or other loan relationship expenses that it incurs before commencement of trading are also classed as a non-trading debit. If such a debit would be allowed as a trading debit had trading commenced, the company may elect under *CTA 2009, s 330(1)(b)*, within two years of the end of the accounting period in which the debit arose, that it is not to be brought in as a non-trading debit. Instead, it is to be treated as a trading debit for the accounting period in which the company commences to trade. This is on the proviso that the company has a source of income and therefore an accounting period at the time the expenditure is incurred, that it begins to carry on the trade within seven years of the end of the accounting period in which the expenditure was incurred, and that the expenditure is of a type that would be deductible from trading income had the trade been carried on at that time (*CTA 2009, s 330*; CFM33060, CFM32100). A trading company may wish to make this election because non-trading deficits carried forward can only be set against future non-trading income, which may not accrue to the company.

COSTS OF OBTAINING LOAN FINANCE

11.34 For trading and non-trading loan relationships, the following expenses directly incurred in connection with loan finance are allowed as debits under the appropriate provisions of *CTA 2009* (the examples quoted are provided by HMRC; see CFM33060):

Provision	*Expense*	*Examples*
s 306A(2)(a)	Bringing a loan relationship into existence	Arrangement fees with banks. Fee or commission for a loan guarantee. BIS fees for investing surplus cash in liquidation.
s 306A(2)(b)	Entering into, or giving effect to, a related transaction	Broker's fees on purchase or sale of existing securities. Legal fees on the transfer of a security.
s 306A(2)(c)	Making a payment under a loan relationship or related transaction	Cost of making interest payments. Early redemption penalties.
s 306A(2)(d)	Pursuing payments due under a loan relationship or related transaction	Solicitor's fees incurred in pursuing a debt defaulter.
s 329	Attempting to bring a loan relationship into existence	This covers abortive expenditure. As long as the expense would have been allowable had the company raised the loan, it is still allowable even if the loan never exists.

Note that the statutory references to *CTA 2009, s 306A(2)* above are derived from *CTA 2009, s 307(4)*, as substituted by *F(No 2)A 2015, Sch 7, paras 3, 4*.

Expenditure not directly incurred in connection with the loan relationship does not qualify as loan relationship debits. As examples, HMRC state that key person insurance premiums, other insurance policies or general investment advice are not considered to be directly incurred (CFM33060).

Costs of finance included in accounts under GAAP

11.35 Where interest and loan expenses on a fixed capital asset or project have been capitalised in accordance with UK or international GAAP, they are relieved against profits chargeable to tax by adjusting the corporation tax computation (*CTA 2009, s 320*, as amended by *F(No 2)A 2015, Sch 7, para 13*). This treatment is mandatory where interest is capitalised into the value of assets falling within the chargeable gains regime (see **Chapter 16**), but does not apply to an equivalent debit taken into account in arriving at the cost of an intangible fixed asset (see **Chapter 12**).

The above treatment does not apply where interest is charged to work in progress. This follows from the fact that such interest has been charged in the profit and loss account, albeit this is counterbalanced by an increase in work in progress (CFM33160).

Where, under GAAP, the incidental costs of loan finance to purchase shares in a subsidiary are spread over more than one accounting period, relief is granted in each respective accounting period. However, where the shareholding is held as a fixed asset and the costs are capitalised in accordance with GAAP, relief is given by adjusting the corporation tax computation as explained above (*CTA 2009, s 320*, as amended by *F(No 2)A 2015, Sch 7, para 13*; CFM33160).

See **Chapter 26** regarding changes to UK GAAP.

CONNECTED COMPANIES RELATIONSHIPS

Meaning of connection

Focus

Special rules apply where loan relationships exist between connected companies, and when debtor and creditor companies become connected with one another or cease to be connected.

11.36 A company has a connected companies relationship if, as debtor company in the relationship, it has a connection with the creditor company, or if, as creditor company, it has a connection with the debtor company. A company can be in the connected companies relationship through a direct connection with the respective creditor or debtor company or indirectly through a series of loan relationships or relevant money debts. If there is a connected companies loan relationship at any time during an accounting period, it is treated as being in place for the whole of that accounting period (*CTA 2009, s 348*).

There is a connection between two companies if one controls the other, or both are under the same control (*CTA 2009, s 466(2)*; for the meaning of 'control', see **11.37**). Unless specifically provided otherwise (see *CTA 2009, ss 467–471, 1316(1)*), this definition does not disapply the definition given in *CTA 2009, s 1316(1)*, which refers back to the following definition in *CTA 2010, s 1122(2)*:

> 'A company is connected with another company if—
>
> (a) the same person has control of both companies,
>
> (b) a person ("A") has control of one company and persons connected with A have control of the other company,
>
> (c) A has control of one company and A together with persons connected with A have control of the other company, or
>
> (d) a group of two or more persons has control of both companies and the groups either consist of the same persons or could be so regarded if (in one or more cases) a member of either group were replaced by a person with whom the member is connected.'

Although unable to be a party to a loan relationship, an individual or a partnership may be considered to stand indirectly in the position of debtor or creditor and so bring about a loan relationship (*CTA 2009, s 467*; CFM35160).

Meaning of control

11.37 'Control' in relation to a company means the power of a person to secure that the affairs of the company are conducted in accordance with the person's wishes:

(a) by means of the holding of shares or the possession of voting power in or in relation to the company or any other company; or

(b) as a result of any powers conferred by the articles of association or other document regulating the company or any other company (*CTA 2009, s 472(2)*).

Shares held as trading stock are ignored (*CTA 2009, s 472(3)*). Creditors who are financial traders are generally exempt from being treated as connected (*CTA 2009, ss 469, 470*).

This definition of 'control' does not disapply the definition given in *CTA 2009, s 1316(2)*, which refers back to the definition in *CTA 2010, s 1124*, on which *CTA 2009, s 472* seems to be based.

A partnership's property, rights or powers are apportioned between the partners in their profit-sharing ratios (*CTA 2009, s 467(4)*).

Example 11.16—Connected companies relationship: direct

Facts

Mr Link controls Right Ltd and Left Ltd.

Analysis

If Right Ltd lent money directly to Left Ltd, there would be a connection under *CTA 2009, s 466(2)*, because both companies are under the control of the same person. There is thus a connected companies relationship between Right Ltd and Left Ltd.

Example 11.17—Connected companies relationship: indirect

Facts

Following on from Example 11.16, Right Ltd lends money to Ms Wrong, who then lends it to Mr Wright who in turn lends it to Left Ltd. Right Ltd and Left Ltd are connected because Mr Link controls them, but neither company is connected with Ms Wrong or Mr Wright.

Analysis

As a result of *CTA 2009, s 348(5)*, Left Ltd stands indirectly in the position of debtor in relation to Right Ltd's loan relationship in this series of loans. There is thus a connected companies relationship between Right Ltd and Left Ltd. Note that there are no consequences for Ms Wrong or Mr Wright.

Example 11.18—Connected companies relationship: indirect series

(a) *Facts*

Norman Ltd controls Saxon Ltd, and lends money to Saxon Ltd.

Analysis

There is a connected companies relationship between Norman Ltd and Saxon Ltd under *CTA 2009, s 466(2)* because one company is controlled by the other.

(b) *Facts*

Angle Ltd is not connected to either Norman Ltd or Saxon Ltd. In an attempt to avoid the connected companies loan relationship, Norman Ltd lends £50,000 to Angle Ltd and then Angle Ltd lends £50,000 to Saxon Ltd on identical terms.

Analysis

There is no connection between Norman Ltd and Angle Ltd, so *CTA 2009, s 348* does not apply to the loan relationship.

There is no connection between Angle Ltd and Saxon Ltd, so *CTA 2009, s 466* does not apply to the loan relationship.

However, in relation to Norman Ltd's loan relationship, Saxon Ltd stands indirectly in the position of debtor through a series of loan relationships. There is thus a connected companies relationship between Norman Ltd and Saxon Ltd by virtue of *CTA 2009, s 348(5)*.

CONSEQUENCES OF CONNECTION

Amortised cost basis of accounting

11.38 Where a loan relationship debtor and creditor are connected, certain rules are applied to the accounting treatment.

Regardless of the accounting method used in the company's accounts, the debits and credits brought into account must be determined according to an amortised cost basis of accounting (*CTA 2009, s 349,* as amended by *F(No 2) A 2015, Sch 7, para 28*).

The amortised cost of a financial asset or a financial liability is the amount at which the asset or liability is measured at initial recognition (usually its cost) less any repayments of principal, less any reduction for impairment or lack of collectability, plus or minus the cumulative amortisation of the difference between that initial amount and the maturity.

The amortisation is calculated using the effective interest rate. The effective interest rate is the internal rate of return (IRR), ie the rate at which the net present value of the instrument is nil.

Example 11.19—Amortisation: effective rate of return

Facts

A £200,000 bond will pay £231,525 on maturity in three years' time.

Analysis

The IRR is r, where £200,000 × $(1 + r)^3$ = £231,525

$r^3 = [(231{,}525 - 200{,}000) \div 200{,}000]$

$= 0.157625$

$r = \sqrt[3]{0.157625}$

$= 0.05$

$= 5\%$

The future value of £200,000 @ 5% = £200,000 × $(1 + 0.05)^3$ = £231,525

The present value of £231,525 = £231,525 × $\{1 \div (1 + 0.5)^3\}$ = £200,000

The present value of £200,000 less the initial investment of £200,000 equals the net present value, which is nil.

Therefore, the effective rate of return is 5%.

Credits and debits are excluded from tax where there is a related transaction involving a connected company loan relationship. This does not prevent credits and debits from being brought into account where those amounts are attributable to interest rate movements on an arm's length borrowing, but no credit is subsequently brought into account to the extent that it represents a reversal of a loss which gave rise to the reduction of debits (*CTA 2009, ss 352, 352A*, as amended/inserted by *F(No 2)A 2015, Sch 7, paras 30, 31*).

Companies beginning and ceasing to be connected

11.39 Before 1 January 2016, where there was a change in accounting basis brought about by companies becoming connected during the year, such that a fair value basis was used before the connection and an amortised cost basis after the connection, the resulting differences in the valuation of an asset or a cost of a liability between the two periods had to be brought into account as a debit or a credit, as appropriate. A similar rule in reverse operated for companies ceasing to be connected during the accounting period (*CTA 2009, ss 350, 351* before repeal by *F(No 2)A 2015, Sch 7, para 29*). Those provisions are no longer required, because amended rules now apply in circumstances where a company changes its basis of accounting for loan relationship credits and debits. If this results in a difference between the tax-adjusted carrying value of an asset or liability at the one accounting period and the corresponding value at the beginning of the next, a credit or debit (as the case may be) of an amount equal to the difference must be brought into account in the later period (*CTA 2009, ss 315, 316*, as amended/substituted by *F(No 2)A 2015, Sch 7, paras 9, 10*; see **11.12**).

If the creditor company is connected to the debtor in exempt circumstances, ie in the course of its financial trade, it is not required to apply the amortised cost basis of accounting or to follow the other provisions that apply to connected persons. In spite of this, the debtor company must apply the connected persons rules (*CTA 2009, s 469*).

Example 11.20—Connected companies relationship: exempt circumstances

Facts

The CASH Bank plc issues listed security bonds worth £10 million, which it places with Rowbothams plc, its security trader subsidiary company. Rowbothams plc is to place the bonds with unconnected investors.

The market is slow and Rowbothams plc holds the bonds for three months whilst it finds buyers. The bonds are part of its trading stock. It applies GAAP when preparing its accounts.

Analysis

The parties are connected under *CTA 2009, s 466(2)*. Without the *CTA 2009, s 469* exemption, Rowbothams plc would have to account for the bonds using the amortised cost basis of accounting. However, this is an ordinary commercial arrangement, with Rowbothams plc buying and selling the bonds as part of its trade. By applying *CTA 2009, s 469*, Rowbothams plc can continue to account for the debt as trading stock. The CASH Bank plc is not exempted by *CTA 2009, s 469* and will therefore use the amortised cost basis when accounting for the securities (CFM35130).

Unpaid interest

11.40 'Late-paid interest' rules exist to prevent exploitation of tax mismatches.

Provisions which defer or deny relief for:

- unpaid interest on debt issued to a UK company by a connected company tax resident in a non-qualifying territory (or effectively managed in a non-taxing non-qualifying territory), or
- unpaid interest in certain circumstances where a loan relationship connection exists as a result of the creditor having a major interest in the debtor,

were repealed from 3 December 2014 in respect of loans entered into on or after that date, with transitional rules up to 31 December 2015 for interest accrued on such loans existing before 3 December 2014 (*CTA 2009, ss 374, 377*, as repealed by *FA 2015, s 25*). Following the repeal, deferred interest is subject to the normal loan relationship rules and is generally brought into account as it accrues in a company's accounts.

A non-qualifying territory is any territory with which the UK does not have a double tax agreement with a suitable non-discrimination clause (*CTA 2009, s 374*). This means that, in the majority of cases, unless the creditor company is located in a tax haven, normal loan relationship principles have been applied already and interest is deductible as it accrues in the accounts rather than when it is paid. For HMRC's latest guidance on the late interest rules, see CFM35960.

Restrictions on relief for accrued unpaid interest also apply in certain circumstances where a loan relationship connection exists through participation in a close company, and these have not been repealed (*CTA 2009, s 375*).

Discounted securities

11.41 Where the parties have a connection, provisions under which relief on securities issued at a discount is deferred until redemption (rather than being allowed as a debit over the life of the loan) were also repealed from 3 December 2014 in respect of loan relationships entered into on or after that date, with transitional rules up to 31 December 2015 for discounts accrued on such relationships existing before 3 December 2014 (*CTA 2009, ss 407, 408*, as repealed by *FA 2015, s 25*). Following the repeal, deferred discounts are subject to the normal loan relationship rules and are generally brought into account as they accrue in a company's accounts.

Creditor relationships: benefit derived by connected persons

11.42 A benefit directly or indirectly received in respect of any time before 19 July 2011 by a company that is connected with a company that has a third-party creditor loan relationship as a result of the loan relationship is treated as a credit, using fair value accounting of the creditor company, if the actual return that the creditor company receives is below a commercial rate of interest (*CTA 2009, s 453*).

Bad debt relief and impairment losses generally

11.43 The loan relationship rules, in general, grant relief automatically for bad debts. Impairment losses in respect of financial instruments are accounted for in accordance with FRS 102, Section 11 *Basic Financial Instruments* and Section 12 *Other Financial Instruments issues* under new UK GAAP, or, where international accounting standards apply, IAS 39 *Financial Instruments: Recognition and Measurement* (superseded by IFRS 9 *Financial Instruments* for periods starting on or after 1 January 2018 (this date supersedes the original effective date of periods starting on or after 1 January 2015).

The accounting standards prescribe rules for identifying and measuring impairment losses at the year end. If the company correctly applies the relevant standard to arrive at a debit for impairment losses (or a credit for reversal of impairment losses), the debit will be allowable (or the credit taxable) in accordance with the normal computational provisions of *CTA 2009, s 308*.

See **Chapter 26** regarding changes to UK GAAP.

Connected parties: bad debt relief and impairment losses

11.44 Special rules apply to bad debt relief and impairment losses for connected parties. The general rule is that bad debt or impairment loss relief is denied if the companies to the loan relationship are connected (*CTA 2009, s 354*, as amended by *F(No 2)A 2015, Sch 7, para 32*).

Impairment loss relief is not denied if the connection only arises because the debt is exchanged for equity, provided that the companies were not connected when the creditor company acquired possession of or entitlement to the shares (*CTA 2009, s 356(1)–(3)*). Neither is it denied if the creditor company goes into insolvent liquidation (*CTA 2009, s 357*).

The corresponding creditor company is not required to include a credit for the loss or bad debt relief reversal (*CTA 2009, s 360*), whether or not the companies are still connected when the reversal takes place.

If any rights or liabilities (known as related transactions) are acquired at a non-arm's length price, they are accounted for as though they were a transaction between independent persons (*CTA 2009, s 444*).

Release of trade debts between connected companies

11.45 Where debts between connected companies have arisen from a trade or a property business and are then waived, they are taxed under the loan relationship provisions, the result being that there is no charge on the debtor on the release and no tax relief for the creditor on the cancellation (*CTA 2009, ss 479, 481*).

GROUPS AND CONSORTIA

11.46 Group companies are connected under the loan relationship rules.

Consortium companies may not be connected under *CTA 2009, s 466(2)*, but consortium members are in a position to obtain not only consortium relief but also bad debt or impairment relief. Therefore there are restrictions on the available amount of bad debt relief where there has been a claim to group relief. The group impairment losses and subsequent credits are first netted off against each other to result in the net consortium debit for the year. The effect of the restriction is to reduce the net consortium debit by the amount of the group relief claimed (*CTA 2009, s 365*; CFM35640).

Example 11.21—Consortium-owned company: impairment loss

Facts

Winston Ltd is a consortium-owned company with £1,000 issued ordinary shares.

Its ownership is as follows:

	No of shares
A Ltd	400
B Ltd	400
C Ltd	200

All of the companies prepare accounts to 31 December.

Winston Ltd incurs a loss of £40,000 for the year ended 31 December 2018 which is used in a group relief claim by the consortium members. A Ltd's share of this group relief is £16,000.

On 1 January 2018, A Ltd made a £50,000 loan to Winston Ltd. At 31 December 2018, it seems unlikely that Winston Ltd will be able to repay the whole of A Ltd's loan, so A Ltd writes off £25,000 as bad.

Analysis

CTA 2009, s 365 will restrict A Ltd's impairment loss by the amount of the group relief claim, ie £16,000. Therefore, only £9,000 (£25,000 – £16,000) may be claimed. The group relief claim remains intact, and the £16,000 restricted amount is carried forward, to be considered for future group and impairment loss claims.

The position for the year ended 31 December 2018 may be summarised as follows:

Impairment loss	*Group relief*	*Impairment loss granted*	*Group relief allowed*	*Impairment loss carry-forward*
£	£	£	£	£
25,000	16,000	9,000	16,000	16,000

Implications of transfers within groups

11.47 Loan relationship intra-group transfers are tax neutral, and in such cases the loan relationship is transferred at a notional carrying value (*CTA 2009, ss 336, 340, 341*).

Where one group company has replaced another as a party to a loan relationship and then leaves the group within the next six years, there is a deemed disposal and reacquisition of the loan relationship for its fair value immediately before the transferee company leaves the group. As a consequence, amounts may arise under the loan relationships rules as credits and debits (*CTA 2009, ss 344–346*).

From 1 April 2014, conditions which had previously restricted the application of the degrouping rule to loan relationship credits were removed, so the degrouping event now brings into account both credits and debits (*CTA 2009, ss 345, 346*).

FOREIGN EXCHANGE GAINS AND LOSSES

11.48 Exchange gains and losses are within the loan relationship regime. Credits and debits are brought into the corporation tax computation following generally accepted accounting principles (but see **Chapter 26** regarding changes to UK GAAP). Amounts arising on the retranslation of a business from its functional currency into a different currency are excluded (*CTA 2009, s 328*, as amended by *F(No 2)A 2015, Sch 7, para 20*).

All relevant capital and revenue profits, gains and losses must be included, together with charges and expenses for the year (*CTA 2009, s 329(1), (2)*).

HMRC have published guidance on the tax treatment of Bitcoin and similar digital or virtual 'cryptocurrencies', and the general rules on foreign exchange and loan relationships apply (see **26.26**).

Many companies use derivatives (such as options, futures and swaps) to mitigate or hedge commercial risks that they face as a result of movements in interest rates, foreign currency exchange rates, commodity prices, etc. Some companies trade in derivatives, while others hold them as investments. Such activities are likely to generate profits or losses, and their tax treatment is addressed in *CTA 2009, Pt 7, ss 570–710*. The 'Disregard Regulations' (the *Loan Relationships and Derivative Contracts (Disregard and Bringing into Account of Profits and Losses) Regulations 2004, SI 2004/3256*, as amended) allow certain profits and losses from loan relationships and derivative contracts to be left out of account, to be brought into account in a different way or to be brought into account at a later date. These are specialist transactions which are outside the scope of this book.

ANTI-AVOIDANCE LEGISLATION

Group mismatch schemes

11.49 Loan relationship credits and debits are calculated according to the basis adopted in the accounts, and some companies and groups had used the rules to their advantage through 'group mismatch schemes', which aimed to ensure that a loan relationship debit was not matched by a loan relationship credit, with the result that the loss created for tax purposes was not reflected by a genuine economic loss.

HMRC v DCC Holdings (UK) Limited [2010] UKSC 58 was a case in point, where the legal form of the transaction differed from the economic reality and the Supreme Court rejected the taxpayer's appeal, ruling that recognition of the debits and credits should be symmetrical.

Anti-avoidance legislation exists within the loan relationship rules to combat group mismatch schemes (*CTA 2010, Pt 21B, ss 938A–938N*). A scheme is a group mismatch scheme if it involves members of the same group (as defined for this purpose in *CTA 2010, s 938E*) and either of the following conditions is met:

- Condition A: when the scheme is entered into, there is no practical likelihood that it will fail to secure a relevant tax advantage (ie an economic profit arising from asymmetries in loan relationship debits and credits) of £2 million or more (this limit may be increased by Treasury order); or
- Condition B: that:
  - the purpose or one of the main purposes of any member of the scheme group on entering into the scheme is to secure a relevant tax advantage of any amount, and
  - when the scheme is entered into, there is no chance that it will secure a relevant tax disadvantage (ie an economic loss arising from asymmetries in loan relationship debits and credits), or there is such a chance but the value of the scheme is nevertheless a positive amount.

If a company is, at any time, a party to a group mismatch scheme and is a member of the scheme group, detailed provisions aim to ensure that no scheme loss or profit arising in connection with defined asymmetry conditions is brought in under the loan relationship rules, but must still be treated (for other corporation tax purposes) as though it were so brought into account.

Tax mismatch schemes

> **Focus**
>
> Tax mismatch provisions introduced by *FA 2013* were based on the pre-existing anti-avoidance rules for group mismatch schemes but have a significantly wider reach.

11.50 *FA 2013* introduced anti-avoidance provisions to block 'tax mismatch schemes', being other arrangements where a company (not necessarily within a group) benefits from a tax advantage by creating a mismatch using a loan relationship (*CTA 2010, Pt 21BA, ss 938O–938V*).

These measures apply to, but are not limited to, schemes where a company enters into a loan relationship with a partnership of which it is a member and a loan is accounted for differently by the company and the partnership to create a tax advantage.

The definition of a tax mismatch scheme is based closely on that of a group mismatch scheme (**11.49**). A scheme is a tax mismatch scheme if either of the following conditions is met:

- Condition A: when the scheme is entered into, there is no practical likelihood that it will fail to secure a relevant tax advantage of £2 million or more (this limit may be increased by Treasury order); or
- Condition B: that:
  - the purpose or one of the main purposes of any member of the scheme group on entering into the scheme is to secure a relevant tax advantage of any amount, and
  - when the scheme is entered into, there is no chance that it will secure a relevant tax disadvantage, or there is such a chance but the value of the scheme is nevertheless a positive amount.

If a company is, at any time, a party to a tax mismatch scheme and is a member of the scheme group, detailed provisions aim to ensure that no scheme loss or profit arising in connection with defined asymmetry conditions is brought in under the loan relationship rules, but must still be treated (for other corporation tax purposes) as though it were so brought into account.

The provisions on tax mismatch schemes apply to accounting periods beginning on or after 5 December 2012, with a new period of account being treated as beginning on that date.

Disguised interest

11.51 The 'disguised interest' rules (*CTA 2009, ss 486A–486E*) exist to ensure that, where a company receives an interest-like return, that return is taxed under the loan relationships legislation. The legislation applies, broadly, where:

- a company becomes party to an arrangement which produces a return for the company on any amount which is economically equivalent to interest; or
- two or more persons are party to an arrangement which produces a return which is economically equivalent to interest for the persons taken

together but not for either of them individually, and a company becomes party to the arrangement.

Where a company is a party to such an arrangement, its share of the return (determined on a just and reasonable basis) is treated as a profit arising from a loan relationship, subject to exclusions for:

- any part of the return otherwise taxable (*CTA 2009, s 486C*),
- arrangements that have no tax avoidance purpose (*CTA 2009, s 486D*), and
- excluded shares (*CTA 2009, s 486E*).

Amounts not fully recognised

11.52 Where, on or after 6 December 2010, a company is (or is treated as) party to a creditor loan relationship and, as a result of tax avoidance arrangements, an amount (in accordance with GAAP) is not fully recognised in respect of the creditor loan relationship, the company is required to recognise the full amount of any credits arising on the creditor loan relationship during the relevant accounting period. A company is not allowed to recognise any debits arising in respect of such creditor loan relationship where it became a party to the tax avoidance arrangements in question on or after 23 March 2011 (*CTA 2009, ss 311, 312*). See **Chapter 26** regarding changes to UK GAAP.

Debts becoming held by connected company

11.53 *FA 2012* modified the rules that apply when the parties to a loan relationship become connected, introducing an anti-avoidance provision to ensure that the pre-existing rules relating to deemed releases (*CTA 2009, ss 361, 362*; see **11.17**) could be circumvented. Where arrangements (including any agreement, understanding, scheme, transaction or series of transactions, whether legally enforceable or not) are entered into on or after 27 February 2012 (and in some cases, under transitional provisions, before that date) and the main purpose or one of the main purposes of any party in entering into them is:

- to avoid an amount being treated as released under *CTA 2009, s 361* or *362*, or
- to reduce the amount which is treated as released under *CTA 2009, s 361* or *362*,

an amount (or a greater amount) will be released so that the arrangements will not achieve their intended effect (*CTA 2009, s 363A*).

CTA 2009, ss 361, 362, have been subject to consequential amendments by *F(No 2)A 2015, Sch 7, paras 35, 38*. See also **11.17**.

Counteraction by just and reasonable adjustments

11.54 *F(No 2)A 2015* repealed a number of specific anti-avoidance measures that were contained in *CTA 2009, ss 443, 454, 455*, and introduced a new regime-wide anti-avoidance rule. This counteracts 'loan-related tax advantages' arising from 'relevant avoidance arrangements' by requiring just and reasonable adjustments to be made to loan relationship credits and debits (*CTA 2009, ss 455B, 455C*, as inserted by *F(No 2)A 2015, Sch 7, para 51*). For this purpose, relevant avoidance arrangements exclude arrangements aimed at obtaining tax advantages which can reasonably be assumed to have been intended under the loan relationships legislation (*CTA 2009, s 455C(4)*).

The regime-wide anti-avoidance legislation provides a non-exhaustive list of examples of results which might indicate that the exclusion from the definition of 'relevant avoidance arrangements' in *CTA 2009, s 455C(4)*, should not apply. However, these are relevant only where it is reasonable to assume that the result in question was not the anticipated outcome at the time of enactment of any provisions of the loan relationships regime pertinent to the arrangements (*CTA 2009, s 455D*, as inserted by *F(No 2)A 2015, Sch 7, para 51*).

COMPANY TAX RETURN

11.55 Under self-assessment, companies must include trading loan relationship credits and debits within their trading results (see **11.4**). In addition, they are required to include the totals of their non-trade profits and deficits on loan relationships within specific boxes on form CT600 within their corporation tax return, and supporting details should be supplied by means of the corporation tax computation and the accounts.

Chapter 12

Intangible fixed assets

SIGNPOSTS

- The importance of establishing whether the intangible fixed asset was acquired before 1 April 2002, or on or after that date (see **12.1–12.4**).
- The meaning of an intangible fixed asset (see **12.5–12.8**).
- The treatment of debits and credits, including the treatment of acquired goodwill after 3 December 2014 or 8 July 2015 (see **12.9–12.16**).
- The adjustments required resulting from an impairment review, the reversal of a previous accounting gain and the realisation of an intangible fixed asset (see **12.17–12.21**).
- Sale of a chargeable intangible asset, and roll-over relief on realisation and reinvestment (see **12.22–12.25**).
- Group treatment including inter-asset transfers and reconstructions (see **12.26–12.37**).
- International matters including the effect of a company ceasing to be UK resident (see **12.38–12.39**).
- A consultation between February and May 2018 considers major changes to some of the rules.

SCOPE PRE- AND POST-*FA 2002*

12.1 The intangible fixed assets regime was introduced from 1 April 2002 by *FA 2002*, and applies to companies only, not to unincorporated businesses. Under this regime, a company is taxed on receipts arising from its intangible fixed assets and intellectual property (IP) and can claim tax relief on expenditure on these assets (*CTA 2009, Pts 8–9, ss 711–931*), including amortisation.

> **Focus**
>
> It is important to establish whether an intangible fixed asset came into existence before 1 April 2002, or on or after that date, as different rules apply. There were also transitional rules that applied at that time.

Pre-FA 2002 assets

12.2 The pre-1 April 2002 rules had been in existence for many years before 1 April 2002, and are referred to in the 2002 legislation as 'the law as it was before 1 April 2002'. Those rules continue to apply to assets in existence before that date (*CTA 2009, s 882(1)*). The legislation refers to these assets as 'pre-*FA 2002* assets' (*CTA 2009, s 881*).

Chargeable intangible assets

12.3 The *FA 2002* intangible fixed asset rules apply to assets which are:

- intangible fixed assets created by the company on or after 1 April 2002; or
- intangible fixed assets that the company acquired on or after 1 April 2002, from a third party who was unrelated to the company at the time of the acquisition (*CTA 2009, s 882(1)*); or
- intangible fixed assets that the company acquired on or after 1 April 2002, from a related party that created the asset on or after 1 April 2002 or that acquired the asset from a person who was unrelated to the company at the time of the acquisition (*CTA 2009, s 882(1)*).

The legislation refers to these assets as 'chargeable intangible assets', being assets on whose realisation any gain would be a chargeable realisation gain on the company (*CTA 2009, s 741(1)*). A chargeable realisation gain in relation to an asset means a gain on the realisation of that asset that gives rise to a credit to be accounted for under the intangible fixed asset rules (*CTA 2009, s 741(2)*).

The intangible fixed asset regime also applies to chargeable intangible assets acquired from related parties in the following circumstances (*CTA 2009, s 882(3)–(5)*):

- immediately before the acquisition, the asset was a chargeable intangible asset of the company from which it was acquired;
- if the asset was acquired from an intermediary who acquired the asset on or after 1 April 2002 from a third person, at the time of the intermediary's acquisition the third person was neither a related party of the intermediary nor of the company; or

- the asset was created on or after 1 April 2002, either by the person from whom it was acquired or by any other person.

A consultation on the corporate intangibles regime was launched on 19 February 2018, running until 11 May 2018. One aspect discussed is whether the commencement rules create an artificial boundary for tax purposes that causes problems when companies are carrying out commercial activities or transactions. The consultation document considers whether pre-2002 intangible fixed assets should now be brought into the regime.

Goodwill

12.4 As above, the intangible fixed asset regime does not apply to pre-*FA 2002* assets, ie assets held by the company on 1 April 2002 or acquired from a related party who held them on 1 April 2002.

There is a special rule for goodwill, which is regarded as being created before 1 April 2002 if the business was carried on at any time before 1 April 2002 by the company or by a related party; it is regarded as created on or after 1 April 2002 in any other case (*CTA 2009, s 884*; CIRD11680). HMRC Corporate Intangibles Research & Development Manual (at CIRD10145) provides a useful key to HMRC Manual references applying to pre-1 April 2002 assets (ie grandfathered assets).

In *Mertrux Ltd v Revenue and Customs Commissioners* [2013] EWCA Civ 821, the Court of Appeal overturned a decision by the First-tier Tribunal and held that a payment received by the taxpayer for the sale of its motor dealership did not represent consideration for the disposal of a pre-*FA 2002* asset (ie goodwill) in respect of which chargeable gains roll-over relief (see **16.8–16.15**) would otherwise have been available.

Claims to write off the cost of goodwill under the intangible fixed assets regime have been rejected by the First-tier Tribunal, where it was held that the goodwill had been acquired from a connected party and had been in existence before 1 April 2002 (see *Pennine Drilling & Grouting Services Ltd v HMRC* [2013] UKFTT 200 (TC); *Blenheims Estate and Asset Management Ltd v HMRC* [2013] UKFTT 290 (TC)).

Example 12.1—Goodwill created before 1 April 2002

Facts

Ted set up a delivery company that started trading on 1 March 2002. For commercial reasons the trade was transferred on 1 November 2014 from the delivery company to a related company (a specialist distribution company also owned by Ted) for consideration of £500,000 for tangible fixed assets and £200,000 for goodwill, in each case equal to open market value.

Analysis

Although the goodwill was transferred after 1 April 2002, it was in existence prior to 1 April 2002 and was transferred between related parties. The goodwill is not within the intangible fixed assets regime while it is owned by either of the companies.

This example is continued in Example 12.3.

Example 12.2—Goodwill created on or after 1 April 2002 but before 3 December 2014

Facts

Bill set up a design company that started trading on 1 May 2002. For commercial reasons the trade was transferred on 1 November 2014 from the design company to a related company (an advertising company also owned by Bill) for consideration of £300,000 for tangible fixed assets and £250,000 for goodwill, in each case equal to open market value.

Analysis

The trade was not carried on by Bill's company or a related party on 1 April 2002, so the goodwill falls within the intangible fixed assets regime. This applies during its ownership by each of the companies.

This example is continued in Example 12.3.

Case law has confirmed that the same criteria apply to group companies. In *Greenbank Holidays v HMRC* [2011] STC 1582, two companies, Greenbank Holidays Ltd (G) and Keyline Continental Ltd (K), were members of the same group of companies. On 30 September 2003, G acquired K's business and, in its books of account, treated the excess cost of K's net assets as the purchase price of acquired goodwill. G claimed relief under the intangible fixed assets regime. HMRC denied such relief on the grounds that, although the intangible fixed assets regime applies to internally generated assets, the goodwill concerned existed within K prior to 1 April 2002. On appeal, the Upper Tribunal held that HMRC's interpretation was correct.

'Split' assets

If only part of the expenditure on the creation or acquisition of an asset is incurred on or after 1 April 2002, the asset is treated for the purposes of the transitional provisions as though it were two separate assets, one a pre-*FA 2002* asset and the other created on or after 1 April 2002, and any apportionment for these purposes must be made on a just and reasonable basis (*CTA 2009, s 883*). Apportionment may also be required where an asset created or acquired on or after 1 April 2002 represents expenditure which, under the law as it was before 1 April 2002, was not qualifying expenditure for capital allowances purposes (*CTA 2009, s 885*; *FA 2009, s 70*).

Anti-avoidance

New rules apply to corporate members of partnerships and LLPs from 25 November 2015 (*FA 2016, s 52* amending *CTA 2009, s 882*). In considering whether a person is a related party in relation to another person, it is now necessary to consider whether the participation condition in *TIOPA 2010, s 148* is satisfied. The legislation is not entirely clear but it appears that the participation condition is satisfied if one of the persons directly or indirectly participates in the management, control or capital of the other person, or if the same person or persons directly or indirectly participates in the management, control or capital of both parties.

The new rule was introduced because HMRC had 'identified arrangements that use bodies such as partnerships or LLPs to transfer assets in ways that aim to bring the assets within the new rules without an effective change of economic ownership' (Explanatory Notes to *Finance Bill 2016*).

MEANING OF AN INTANGIBLE ASSET

> **Focus**
>
> For corporation tax purposes, the intangible fixed assets regime adopts the accountancy meaning of 'intangible asset'. This means that the definition changes on transition from old UK GAAP to new UK GAAP. Note that the accounting treatment adopted can be crucial in determining whether an asset is an intangible fixed asset.

Accountancy definition

12.5 For tax purposes, 'intangible asset' is given the same meaning as it has for accounting purposes, and includes an internally generated intangible asset (*CTA 2009, s 712(1)*). See **Chapter 26** regarding changes to UK GAAP.

Under old UK GAAP, FRS 10 *Goodwill and intangible assets* defines intangible assets as:

> 'Non-financial fixed assets that do not have a physical substance but are identifiable and are controlled by the entity through custody or legal rights. An asset is identifiable if it is capable of being disposed of or settled separately, without disposing of a business of the reporting entity.'

Under new UK GAAP, the definition of 'intangible asset' for accounting purposes under FRS 102, Section 18 *Intangible assets other than goodwill* is:

> 'An identifiable non-monetary asset without physical substance. Such an asset is identifiable when:
>
> (a) it is separable, ie capable of being separated or divided from the entity and sold, transferred, licensed, rented or exchanged, either individually or together with a related contract, asset or liability; or
>
> (b) it arises from contractual or other legal rights, regardless of whether those rights are transferable or separable from the entity or from other rights and obligations.'

This definition differs from that in FRS 12 in that an asset need not be separable from the business in order to be recognised as an intangible asset under new UK GAAP. Consequently, either on transition to new UK GAAP or on subsequent business combinations, more intangible assets may be recognised under FRS 102 than would have been recognised under FRS 10.

CA 2006, s 396, and the *Large and Medium-sized Companies and Groups (Accounts and Reports) Regulations 2008, SI 2008/410*, include intangible fixed assets under the following sub-headings:

- development costs;
- concessions, patents, licences, trademarks and similar rights and assets; and
- goodwill.

The assets may only be included in the balance sheet if they were acquired for valuable consideration or, with the exception of goodwill, were created by the company itself.

For example, a company may include intangible assets under the following headings within intangible assets:

- patents, trademarks and other product rights;
- brand names;
- goodwill;
- publishing copyrights, rights and titles;
- newspaper titles;
- programmes, film rights and scores;

- databases;
- know-how agreements;
- development costs;
- betting office licences;
- trade value of retail outlets; and
- exhibition rights and other similar intangible assets.

For tax purposes, intangible assets specifically include intellectual property (*CTA 2009, s 712(2)*), which includes UK and overseas patents, trademarks, registered designs, copyright or design rights, plant breeders' rights, together with rights under *Plant Varieties Act 1997, s 7*, and the overseas equivalent. Assets owned outright and by licence are included, as are assets that are not protected by a legal right but which have an industrial, commercial or other economic value. Options or rights to acquire or dispose of an intangible asset are also included (*CTA 2009, s 712(3)*).

The intangible fixed assets regime applies to goodwill, and for this purpose 'goodwill' is given the same meaning as it has for accounting purposes, and includes internally generated goodwill (*CTA 2009, s 715*).

Under old UK GAAP, FRS 10 defines purchased goodwill as:

> 'The difference between the cost of an acquired entity and the aggregate of the fair values of that entity's identifiable assets and liabilities. Positive goodwill arises when the acquisition cost exceeds the aggregate fair values of the identifiable assets and liabilities. Negative goodwill arises when the aggregate fair values of the identifiable assets and liabilities of the entity exceed the acquisition cost.'

Under new UK GAAP, the definition of 'goodwill' for accounting purposes under FRS 102 is:

> 'Future economic benefits arising from assets that are not capable of being individually identified and separately recognised.'

For the purposes of the intangible fixed assets regime, 'goodwill' includes internally generated goodwill – not merely purchased goodwill. Goodwill is treated as created in the course of carrying on the business in question (*CTA 2009, s 715*; *FA 2009, s 70*).

For further discussion of the constituent parts of goodwill, see HMRC Capital Gains Manual (at CG68000 onwards) and *Balloon Promotions Ltd v HMRC* [2006] SpC 524.

Note that the accounting treatment adopted can be crucial in determining whether an asset is an intangible fixed asset. A company which is the controlling partner in a general partnership may include in its financial statements its proportional share of the partnership's assets, including intangible fixed assets, but in *Armajaro Holdings Ltd* [2013] UKFTT 571 (TC) the First-tier Tribunal held that this did not apply in the case of a limited liability partnership (LLP).

Excluded assets

12.6 For tax purposes, assets wholly excluded from the intangible fixed assets regime comprise rights over land or tangible moveable property, oil licences, financial assets, assets representing production expenditure on films, shares in a company, trust and partnership rights and powers and assets neither held for a business nor a commercial purpose (*CTA 2009, ss 803–809*). 'Financial asset' is given the same meaning as it has for accounting purposes (*CTA 2009, s 806(2)*). See **Chapter 26** regarding changes to UK GAAP.

Under old UK GAAP, FRS 13 *Derivatives and other financial instruments: disclosures* defines 'financial asset' as:

> 'cash, a contractual right to receive cash or another financial asset from another entity, a contractual right to exchange financial instruments with another entity under conditions that are potentially favourable or an equity instrument of another entity.'

Under new UK GAAP, FRS 102 defines 'financial asset' as:

> 'Any asset that is:
>
> (a) cash;
>
> (b) an equity instrument of another entity;
>
> (c) a contractual right:
>
> (i) to receive cash or another financial asset from another entity, or
>
> (ii) to exchange financial assets or financial liabilities with another entity under conditions that are potentially favourable to the entity; or
>
> (d) a contract that will or may be settled in the entity's own equity instruments and:
>
> (i) under which the entity is or may be obliged to receive a variable number of the entity's own equity instruments; or
>
> (ii) that will or may be settled other than by the exchange of a fixed amount of cash or another financial asset for a fixed number of the entity's own equity instruments. For this purpose the entity's own equity instruments do not include instruments that are themselves contracts for the future receipt or delivery of the entity's own equity instruments.'

Assets excluded in certain situations

12.7 Apart from royalties, all assets owned by a life assurance business or any mutual trade or business are excluded from the definition of intangibles (*CTA 2009, ss 810, 902*). Expenditure on films, sound recording and computer software expenditure (when accounted for with the hardware) is also excluded, apart from expenditure on royalties (*CTA 2009, ss 810–813*). If the computer software is bought separately, the company may elect for the software to be removed from the intangible fixed assets regime (*CTA 2009, ss 815, 816*; see **3.14**).

Royalties and licences granted over pre-*FA 2002* assets from related parties are themselves treated as pre-*FA 2002* assets (*CTA 2009, s 896*).

Research and development expenditure

12.8 Research and development (R&D) expenditure incurred by companies has its own tax regime (see **Chapter 14**). The proceeds from the sale of R&D (but not the corresponding costs) are included within the intangible fixed assets regime (*CTA 2009, s 814*).

CORPORATION TAX TREATMENT

Debits and credits

12.9 Under the intangible fixed assets regime, gains and losses relating to chargeable intangible assets held for the purposes of a business carried on by the company are generally taxed as revenue items. Within the legislation, costs are known as 'debits' and income receipts as 'credits'.

The treatment of the debits and credits in calculating the taxable profits will depend on whether the assets are held for the purposes of a trade, a property business, certain mines, quarries, etc, or if the company is not carrying on any of these businesses.

Debits and credits in respect of assets held for the purposes of a trade (ie trading debits and credits) are treated as expenses and receipts of the trade in calculating the profits of the trade for tax purposes (*CTA 2009, s 747*). Likewise, debits and credits held for a property business are treated as expenses and receipts of that property business (*CTA 2009, s 748*). A property business includes an ordinary property business, a furnished holiday lettings business or an overseas property business. Finally, debits and credits held for a business within *CTA 2009, s 39(4)* – mines, quarries and a variety of other land-based businesses – are treated as expenses and receipts of that trade.

If a company is not involved in any of these types of business, the debits and credits are 'non-trading' debits and credits (*CTA 2009, s 746*, and are subject to specific rules (see **12.17**).

Expenditure and the reversal of an earlier gain are deductible from profits as they are written off in the accounts. Amortisation is allowed on an accounting basis or on a revenue fixed rate basis (*CTA 2009, ss 726(1)(b), 729*). However, restrictions apply in the case of goodwill and certain customer-related intangibles (see **12.11**).

In the case of a company which is a member of a group, HMRC will look to consistency with UK group accounting policies to determine whether the individual company's accounting treatment may be adopted for tax purposes (*CTA 2009, s 718*).

Example 12.3—Amortisation of goodwill

Facts

Assume the same facts as in Examples 12.1 and 12.2.

Analysis

The goodwill acquired by Ted's specialist distribution company is not within the intangible fixed assets regime, so the company will be unable to write off the cost of the goodwill in its accounts.

On the other hand, Bill's advertising company will be able to write off the cost of the goodwill it has acquired. Assuming that the company adopts a 10% amortisation rate, the annual write off is £25,000 (10% × £250,000).

But see **12.10** for restrictions imposed on certain goodwill, etc. from 3 December 2014 or 24 March 2015 until 7 July 2015, and new rules for the treatment of goodwill etc. acquired on or after 8 July 2015.

As a result of these new rules, if Bill had sold the assets to the advertising company in August 2016, no amortisation would have been due in respect of the goodwill.

Treatment of acquired goodwill

Focus

FA 2015 and *F(No 2)A 2015* have introduced new restrictions on relief for amortisation and impairment debits for acquired goodwill.

12.10 Prior to 3 December 2014, deductions were permitted for the amortisation or impairment of acquired goodwill, regardless of source, unless it was acquired from a related party. Between 3 December 2014 and 8 July

2015, there were restrictions on the amortisation of goodwill acquired on incorporation of a company. From 8 July 2015 onwards, no relief was given for amortisation or impairment of goodwill acquired from any source.

This restriction is also discussed in the February 2018 consultation document.

Restrictions to goodwill deductions on incorporation

12.11 From 3 December 2014 to 7 July 2015, relief was restricted where a company acquired internally generated goodwill or certain other 'relevant assets' (ie certain customer-related intangible assets and unregistered trademarks normally associated with goodwill) from a related individual, or from a partnership involving a related individual, except where these were 'acquired third party assets'.

The restriction applied to relevant assets acquired, on incorporation of a pre-existing business or otherwise, from 3 December 2014 onwards, unless acquired under an unconditional contractual obligation made before that date. For the avoidance of doubt, the legislation specifies that it applies to acquisitions made 'directly or indirectly' from such related parties from 24 March 2015 onwards, unless acquired under an unconditional contractual obligation made before that date. It is thought that HMRC might contend that, even before 24 March 2015, the restrictions apply equally to direct and indirect acquisitions.

Where these provisions apply, no debits in respect of amortisation or impairment (see 'Restrictions to goodwill deductions on acquisition' below) are allowed until disposal of the intangible asset, and even then the debit is treated as a non-trading debit (*CTA 2009, ss 746(2)(ba), 849B–849D*, as inserted by *FA 2015, s 26*; see also **12.15**).

Where the related transferor had acquired some of the relevant assets from an unrelated third party, the transferee company is allowed to claim, as trading debits, a proportion of the debits (such as amortisation and impairment debits) that would otherwise have applied under the old (pre-*FA 2015*) rules, based broadly on the GAAP-compliant accounting value of those acquired third party assets as a proportion of the total value of assets acquired. In these circumstances, the allowable trading debits are (*CTA 2009, s 849C(4), (6)*):

$$D \times AM$$

where:

- D is the amount of the debit that would otherwise have applied, and
- AM (the appropriate multiplier) is the lesser of 1 and RAVTPA ÷ CEA, where:
  - RAVTPA is the relevant accounting value of third party acquisitions, and

– CEA is the expenditure incurred by C on acquisition of the relevant assets.

On eventual realisation of such relevant assets, a non-trading debit is recognised equal to (*CTA 2009, s 849C(5), (6)*):

D – TD

where:

- D is the amount of the debits that would otherwise have been brought into account, and
- TD is the amount of the trading debits already allowed.

Note that an acquisition is not treated as a third party acquisition if its main purpose, or one of its main purposes, is for any person to obtain a tax advantage (*CTA 2009, s 849B(9)*).

Restrictions to goodwill deductions on acquisition

12.12 After only a few months, the above restrictions imposed from 3 December 2014 or 24 March 2015 were followed by a much wider restriction, from 8 July 2015. No corporation tax deductions, such as amortisation or impairment debits, are allowed at all in respect of any goodwill and other relevant assets (as defined above), whether acquired from a related or unrelated party on or after 8 July 2015 (unless acquired under an unconditional contractual obligation made before that date) or created by the company, until disposal of the intangible asset. On eventual disposal, any loss arising is treated as a non-trading debit (*CTA 2009, s 816A*, as inserted by *F(No 2)A 2015, s 32*).

Annual payments and patent royalties

12.13 Annual payments and patent royalties relating to chargeable intangible assets are deducted as debits on an accruals basis (*CTA 2009, s 728(5)*).

If a royalty is payable to or for the benefit of a related party and the payment is not made within 12 months after the end of the accounting period, it cannot be allowed as a deduction for that period (*CTA 2009, s 851*). See **12.33** regarding related parties.

Amortisation for tax purposes

Focus

Whether or not an intangible fixed asset is written down for accounting purposes, the company may elect to write down the cost for tax purposes at a fixed rate, but this choice is irrevocable.

12.14 A company may depreciate an intangible fixed asset for tax purposes in line with its accounting treatment or it may choose to adopt the fixed rate basis set out in the legislation. If using the fixed rate basis, it must make a written election to HMRC no later than two years after the end of the accounting period in which the asset is created or acquired. The asset is then amortised on a straight-line basis at 4% per annum, reduced *pro rata* for accounting periods shorter than 12 months.

The election applies to all expenditure on the asset that is capitalised for accounting purposes, and is irrevocable (*CTA 2009, ss 730, 731*). Once the election is made, the company is also giving up the right to future impairment losses, so there is no further relief if the asset becomes materially devalued, unless and until it is actually disposed of.

Furthermore, if the asset is later fragmented, perhaps through a change in accounting treatment, the election also applies to the fragmented assets.

The continued usefulness of this facility is discussed in the February 2018 consultation.

Non-trading debits and credits

12.15 Broadly, non-trading debits and credits are aggregated and an aggregate credit balance is charged to corporation tax (*CTA 2009, ss 751, 752*).

An aggregate debit balance can be relieved against the company's total profits for the accounting period, surrendered by way of group relief under *CTA 2010, s 99* (see **5.10**) or carried forward and treated as a non-trading debit of the later period (*CTA 2009, s 753*).

Changes to the loss relief rules in *F(No 2)A 2017* mean that carried-forward non-trading losses on intangible fixed assets can now be surrendered for group or consortium relief purposes under the new rules in *CTA 2010, Pt 5A* (see **5.11**).

Restriction on change in ownership of companies

12.16 In parallel with long-standing provisions which restrict the carry-forward of a company's trading losses on a change of ownership (see **4.24** onwards), relief for certain non-trading losses on intangible fixed assets may also be restricted.

Relief may not be due if there is a change of ownership of a company carrying on investment business and one of the following conditions is satisfied (*CTA 2010, s 677*):

- Condition A is that, after the change in ownership, there is a significant increase in the amount of the company's capital.

- Condition B is that, within the period of eight years beginning three years before the change in ownership, there is a major change in the nature or conduct of the business carried on by the company. Prior to 1 April 2017, the period was six years.
- Condition C is that the change in ownership occurs at any time after the scale of the activities in the business carried on by the company has become small or negligible and before any significant revival of the business.

If any of these conditions applies, non-trading losses on intangible fixed assets cannot be carried forward from before the change of ownership and used in accounting periods after it (*CTA 2010, s 681*).

In parallel with long-standing provisions which restrict the carry-forward of a company's trading losses on a change of ownership (see **4.24** onwards), relief for certain non-trading losses on intangible fixed assets of a shell company (ie one not carrying on a trade or a property or investment business) is restricted on a change of ownership on or after 20 March 2013 (*CTA 2010, ss 705A–705G*). The effect is to restrict:

- the allocation of relief for non-trading losses on intangible fixed assets to periods before and after the change in ownership; and
- the carry-forward of non-trading losses on intangible fixed assets to periods after the change in ownership.

The accounting period in which the change of ownership takes place is treated as two separate accounting periods, and there are detailed rules for apportioning amounts between the two accounting periods (*CTA 2010, s 705F*).

PRESCRIBED DEBIT AND CREDIT ADJUSTMENTS

Focus

There are certain events that trigger a corporation tax adjustment. These include an impairment review, a reversal of a previous accounting gain, a realisation or a part realisation.

Impairment review

12.17 An impairment review may arise under old UK GAAP, new UK GAAP or international accounting standards. See **Chapter 26** regarding changes to UK GAAP.

FRS 102, Section 19 *Business combinations and goodwill* under new UK GAAP is broadly comparable with FRS 6 *Acquisitions and mergers* and FRS 7 *Fair values in acquisition accounting* under old UK GAAP. However, some differences exist:

- because the definition of an intangible asset differs, an acquisition may result in a different balancing figure being assigned to goodwill on a business combination under FRS 102;
- there is a change in the measurement of the consideration given where that consideration is contingent;
- the 'look back period' in which provisional fair values can be amended is different (in FRS 102, it is 12 months since the acquisition date); and
- there is a change in step acquisitions in some circumstances.

These standards are relevant in UK tax law only where the carrying value of an asset or liability acquired in a business combination is relevant for tax purposes.

The acquisition of an intangible asset may be part of an impairment review because the acquisition cost is more than fair value. This could happen, for example, if a subsidiary was acquired in stages and deferred values were obtained. The following formula is used to calculate the deductible debit in the year of acquisition (*CTA 2009, s 729(3)*):

$$L \times (E + CE)$$

where:

- L is the amount of the loss recognised for accounting purposes
- E is the amount of expenditure on the asset that is recognised for tax purposes
- CE is the amount capitalised in respect of expenditure on the asset.

In subsequent periods of account, the following adjustment is made (*CTA 2009, s 729(5)*):

$$L \times (WDV + AV)$$

where:

- L is the amount of the loss recognised for accounting purposes
- WDV is the tax written down value of the asset immediately before the amortisation charge is made or, as the case may be, the impairment loss is recognised for accounting purposes
- AV is the value of the asset recognised for accounting purposes immediately before the amortisation charge or, as the case may be, the impairment review.

Reversal of a previous accounting gain

12.18 If an accounting loss is recognised where the tax value and the accounting value of the asset differ, the amount of the loss is adjusted in accordance with the following formula:

$$RL \times (PC + RG)$$

where:

- RL is the amount of the loss recognised for accounting purposes
- PC is the amount of the credit previously brought into account for tax purposes in respect of the gain
- RG is the amount of the gain that is (in whole or in part) reversed (*CTA 2009, s 732*).

This could occur on a change in accounting policy (see **2.73–2.76**, **26.3**).

Income taxable

12.19 Receipts, revaluations, negative goodwill credits and reversals of any previous debits are all taxable as income on an accounting basis as they accrue (*CTA 2009, ss 720, 721*). Apart from assets for which an election has been made for the 4% fixed rate amortisation, accounting adjustments brought about by a revaluation of intangible fixed assets or the restoration of past losses are adjusted by the following formula:

$$I \times (WDV + AV)$$

where:

- I is the amount of the increase in the accounting value of the asset
- WDV is the tax written down value of the asset immediately before the revaluation
- AV is the value of the asset by reference to which the revaluation is carried out (*CTA 2009, s 723*).

Any gain recognised in calculating negative goodwill is apportioned to the intangible fixed assets on a just and reasonable basis and included in income accordingly (*CTA 2009, s 724*).

Accounting gain reversals of previous losses recognised in the company's accounts are adjusted as follows:

$$RG \times (D + RL)$$

where:

- RG is the amount of the gain recognised for accounting purposes

- RL is the amount of the loss that is (in whole or in part) reversed
- D is the amount of the tax debit previously brought into account in respect of the loss (*CTA 2009, s 725*).

Realisation of chargeable intangible assets

12.20 Amounts arising from asset sale (proceeds less incidental costs of realisation) or balance sheet writing off are compared to the asset's tax written down value and the resultant net debit or credit is included in calculating profits chargeable to corporation tax (*CTA 2009, s 738*).

Abortive expenditure costs are allowed as a deduction (*CTA 2009, s 740*).

In the case of a part realisation, the tax written down value is apportioned by the following formula:

$$\frac{(AVB - AVA)}{AVB}$$

where:

- AVB is the accounting value immediately before the realisation
- AVA is the accounting value immediately after the realisation (*CTA 2009, s 737*).

Cost is substituted for tax written down value (WDV) if the asset has not been depreciated (see **12.17**). Where there is no balance sheet valuation for the asset, possibly because it was created by the company, the full sale proceeds are brought into the profit and loss account as income.

Where the asset has been written down on an accounting basis, the tax written down value is calculated as follows:

Tax cost – Total net debits

where:

- 'Tax cost' is the cost of the asset recognised for tax purposes
- 'Total net debits' are total debits less total credits as previously brought into account for tax purposes.

Debits are the total amount of the debits, eg depreciation, previously brought into account for tax purposes; and credits are the total amount of any credits, eg revaluation amounts, previously brought into account for tax purposes (*CTA 2009, s 742*).

The comparable adjustment for assets that have been written down on the fixed rate basis (see **12.14**) is as follows:

Tax cost – Debits

where:

- 'Tax cost' is the cost of the asset recognised for tax purposes
- 'Debits' are the total amount of the depreciation debits previously brought into account for tax purposes on the fixed rate basis (*CTA 2009, s 743*).

Part realisation of an asset

12.21 If there has been a partial sale of a chargeable intangible asset, the tax written down value of the asset immediately after the part realisation is calculated as follows:

WDVB × (AVA + AVB)

where:

- WDVB is the tax written down value of the asset immediately before the part realisation
- AVA is the accounting value of the asset immediately after the part realisation
- AVB is the accounting value immediately before the part realisation (*CTA 2009, s 744*).

An asset may cease to be a chargeable asset during its lifetime, in which case there is a deemed disposal for the company (*CTA 2009, s 859*).

SALE OF A CHARGEABLE INTANGIBLE ASSET

Sale proceeds

12.22 The proceeds of realisation of chargeable intangible assets must be brought into account as credits for tax purposes. For this purpose, proceeds of realisation means the proceeds of disposal recognised for accounting purposes, less the amount so recognised as incidental costs of realisation (*CTA 2009, ss 738, 739*). Relief is also given for abortive costs of sale (*CTA 2009, s 740*).

The rules were amended by *FA 2018, s 20* for non-monetary receipts on realisations on or after 22 November 2017. In such cases, the amount to be brought into account for tax purposes is the open market value of the non-monetary consideration, and not the amount brought in for accountancy purposes.

Roll-over relief on realisation and reinvestment

> **Focus**
>
> On realisation of an intangible fixed asset, reinvestment relief can allow corporation tax on the resulting credit to be deferred indefinitely against the cost of replacement intangible fixed assets.

12.23 When a company sells a chargeable intangible asset it may be able to claim reinvestment relief, provided all the necessary conditions are met. The effect is that, for tax purposes, it can defer the credit in respect of the proceeds of realisation (ie the disposal proceeds less incidental costs of realisation) (*CTA 2009, s 754*).

There are two specific conditions which must be met in relation to the 'old' asset (ie the asset disposed of):

- the old asset must have been within the intangible fixed assets regime throughout its ownership. Where the old asset was within the intangible fixed assets regime at the time of disposal and for a substantial period (but not the whole) of the ownership, it will be treated as a separate asset for the time that it so qualified, and disposal proceeds are apportioned on a just and reasonable basis; and
- the proceeds on disposal of the old asset must be greater than the original cost of that asset, or greater than the adjusted cost where there has been a part realisation (*CTA 2009, s 755*).

The 'other assets' (ie the replacement assets) must be chargeable intangible assets of the company as soon as they are acquired (as recognised for accounting purposes), and the expenditure on them must be capitalised for accounting purposes. Expenditure on the replacement assets must be incurred in the period beginning 12 months before and ending three years after the disposal of the old asset, or within such longer period as an officer of HMRC may by notice allow (*CTA 2009, s 756*).

Any claims to HMRC must be in writing, must specify the old assets, must identify the expenditure on replacement assets, and must state the amount of the relief claimed (*CTA 2009, s 757*).

A company may make a provisional claim for relief if it has sold a chargeable intangible asset and intends to replace it with new chargeable intangible assets. The provisional claim continues until the earlier of its being withdrawn, its being superseded by a new claim, or the expiry of four years after the end of the accounting period in which the realisation took place. All necessary adjustments are then made, by assessment or otherwise, regardless of time limits that might otherwise have prevented these (*CTA 2009, s 761*).

The effect of the claim is to reduce the realisation proceeds and the tax cost of the replacement assets by the same amount. Thus, the credit that would otherwise have been recognised on the realisation is deferred, in some cases virtually indefinitely.

The relief is calculated as follows (*CTA 2009, s 758*):

- If the new expenditure on replacement assets is equal to or greater than the proceeds of realisation of the old asset, the amount available for relief is the amount by which the proceeds of realisation exceed the tax cost of the old asset.
- If the amount of the new expenditure on replacement assets is less than the proceeds of realisation of the old asset, the amount available for relief is the amount (if any) by which the expenditure on the new assets exceeds the tax cost of the old asset.
- If the new expenditure does not exceed the tax cost of the old asset, no relief is given.

Example 12.4—Reinvestment relief

Facts

P Ltd makes up accounts to 31 December each year. The following accounting transactions take place:

Year ended 31 December		*Sale proceeds*	*Cost*	*Profit and loss account*		*Net book value*
		£000	*£000*	*£000*		*£000*
2016	Bought copyright A with an estimated life of five years		50	10 debit	Annual depreciation	40
2017	Sold copyright A	70		30 credit	Profit on sale	Nil
	Bought copyright B with an estimated life of five years		75	15 debit	Annual depreciation	60

Analysis

For corporation tax purposes, the company wishes to claim reinvestment relief on realisation of copyright A. In order to do this, it must first analyse the gain arising:

Year ended 31 December	*Total gain*	*Arising from depreciation*	*Gain available for reinvestment relief*	*Actual new chargeable intangible asset purchased*	*Tax cost of new asset purchased*
	£000	*£000*	*£000*	*£000*	*£000*
2017	30	10	20	75	55

The corporation tax deductions on these transactions are as follows:

Year ended 31 December		*Purchase and sale transactions*	*Reinvestment relief*	*Opening tax value*	*Adjustment to profits for corporation tax*	*Closing tax value*
		£000	*£000*	*£000*	*£000*	*£000*
2016	Bought	50			10 debit	40
2017	Sold	70	20		10 credit	Nil
	Bought	75	20	55	11 debit	44

Part realisation and reinvestment

12.24 On a part realisation, the adjusted cost is calculated as follows:

$$\frac{(\text{AVB} - \text{AVA})}{\text{AVB}}$$

where:

- AVB is the accounting value immediately before the part realisation
- AVA is the accounting value immediately after the part realisation (*CTA 2009, s 759*).

If a company realises an asset and subsequently reacquires it, the disposal and reacquisition are treated as separate assets, and reinvestment relief may be available (*CTA 2009, s 762*).

Deemed realisations are generally not recognised for reinvestment relief (*CTA 2009, s 763*).

Interaction with chargeable gains roll-over relief

12.25 *FA 2014* corrected an error made during the government's tax law rewrite project. For claims made on or after 19 March 2014, companies cannot claim chargeable gains roll-over relief (**16.8–16.15**) where the proceeds on disposal of a tangible asset are reinvested in an intangible fixed asset (*TCGA 1992, s 156ZB*). To prevent tax relief from being given twice, for accounting periods beginning on or after 19 March 2014 (subject to transitional provisions) the tax cost of the replacement intangible fixed asset is adjusted where roll-over relief was given for claims made on or after 1 April 2009 and before 19 March 2014 (*CTA 2009, s 870A*).

GROUPS

> **Focus**
>
> The existence of a group relationship allows certain intra-group transfers of intangible fixed assets to be made without any tax impact; it can also facilitate reconstructions, and allow reinvestment relief on a group-wide basis. Where a company leaves a group owning a chargeable intangible asset acquired by intra-group transfer within the past six years, a degrouping charge may arise.

Meaning of a group

12.26 'Group' for intangible fixed assets purposes adopts the chargeable gains definition: see **16.24**.

Thus, a company (referred to here as the 'principal company') and its 75% subsidiaries (whether UK resident or not) form a group. If any of those subsidiaries have 75% subsidiaries, the group includes them and their 75% subsidiaries, but not so as to include a company that is not an effective 51% subsidiary of the principal company (*CTA 2009, ss 765, 766*).

A company is an 'effective 51% subsidiary' of the principal company if (and only if) the latter:

- is beneficially entitled to more than 50% of any profits available for distribution to equity holders of the subsidiary, and

- would be beneficially entitled to more than 50% of any assets of the subsidiary available for distribution to its equity holders on a winding up (*CTA 2009, s 771*).

The anti-avoidance rules in *CTA 2010, ss 158, 160* apply to determine the meaning of equity holders.

A company (A) cannot be the principal company of a group if it is itself a 75% subsidiary of another company (B). The exception to this rule is where A is prevented from being a member of B's group because it is not an effective 51% subsidiary of B. In this case, A can be the principal company of another group, unless this enables a third company (C) to be the principal company of a group of which A would then be a member (*CTA 2009, s 767*).

A company cannot be a member of more than one group. Where a company could otherwise belong to two or more groups, four criteria are applied to determine to which group the company belongs, in the following order: voting rights; profits available for distribution; assets on a winding up; and percentage of directly and indirectly owned ordinary shares (*CTA 2009, s 768*).

A group of companies remains the same group as long as the same company is the principal company of the group. If the principal company of a group becomes a member of another group, the groups are treated as the same group, and the question whether a company has ceased to be a member of a group is determined accordingly. The passing of a resolution for the winding up of a member of a group is not regarded as the occasion of that or any other company ceasing to be a member of the group (*CTA 2009, s 769*).

Intra-group asset transfers

12.27 Intra-group transfers of chargeable intangible assets have no tax effect except for tax-exempt friendly societies, dual resident investing companies, and (from 19 July 2011) transferor companies that have elected under *CTA 2009, s 18A* for exemption in respect of foreign permanent establishments (see **20.33**). Instead, the transferee company adopts the asset and stands in the shoes of the transferor company (*CTA 2009, ss 775, 776*).

Reinvestment relief (see **12.23–12.25**) on a group-wide basis is also available to group members, other than dual resident investing companies. Where the old asset is disposed of by one group company and the replacement assets are acquired by another, both companies involved are required to claim in respect of reinvestment relief. Group reinvestment relief is not available on intra-group asset transfers (*CTA 2009, s 777*).

Purchase by a company of the controlling interest in a non-group company that subsequently becomes a member of the group is treated for reinvestment relief purposes as a purchase of the underlying assets on which relief is available. In such a case, expenditure incurred by the company on its new purchase is treated as the lesser of the tax written down value of the underlying assets immediately before acquisition and the consideration paid for the controlling interest. If reinvestment relief applies, the tax value of the underlying chargeable intangible assets is reduced by the amount of the relief (*CTA 2009, ss 778, 779*).

Leaving a group

12.28 When a company leaves a group, having acquired a chargeable intangible asset by intra-group transfer within the past six years, there is a degrouping charge on the transferee based on a deemed disposal and reacquisition of the relevant asset by the transferee at its market value at the date of that intra-group transfer. A debit or credit adjustment is made in the accounting period in which the company leaves the group (*CTA 2009, s 780*).

The February 2018 consultation considers whether the degrouping charge should be brought into line with the capital gains legislation, so that degrouping gains would be added to the proceeds of a share sale, rather than generating a gain in the company holding the asset.

Note that there is no distinction (as there is for chargeable gains; see **16.33**) between a company leaving a group as a result of a disposal of its shares or in any other circumstances. Thus any tax reliefs or exemptions that apply to such a disposal of shares (eg the substantial shareholdings exemption; see **16.18–16.22**) do not apply also to the degrouping charge.

For intra-group transfers on or after 19 July 2011, there is no degrouping charge where two associated companies, who have made intra-group transfers of assets between them within the past six years, leave the group at the same time, provided that both companies are members of the same group or sub-group at all times from when the asset is transferred until immediately after they leave the original group. Before 19 July 2011, this exception from the degrouping charge applied on a narrower basis (*CTA 2009, ss 780, 783*).

There is no degrouping charge if the entire group becomes a member of another group. However, if the transferee ceases to qualify as a member of the new group within six years of having acquired a chargeable intangible asset by intra-group transfer, it is treated as having sold and reacquired the asset at the time of that intra-group transfer. Any adjustment is included in the corporation tax computation for the period in which the company leaves the new group (*CTA 2009, s 785*).

No degrouping charge arises where a transferee company ceases to be a member of a group as part of a merger, where the merger is carried out for genuine commercial reasons and the avoidance of tax is not its main purpose or one of its main purposes (*CTA 2009, s 789*).

A degrouping charge arising to a transferee company can, by joint election between that transferee company and any other member of the relevant group at the relevant time, be passed to that other group company to be treated as accruing to it as a non-trading credit. The company taking on responsibility for this credit must be either resident in the UK, or carrying on a trade in the UK through a permanent establishment that is not exempt from corporation tax on income or chargeable gains under *TIOPA 2010, s 2(1)*, and it must not be a friendly society or a dual resident holding company (*CTA 2009, ss 792, 793*).

Unpaid tax may be recovered from any group members or controlling directors of non-UK resident companies carrying on a trade in the UK, if not paid by the relevant company (*CTA 2009, s 795*).

If payments are made between group companies in respect of group reinvestment relief or the reallocation of a degrouping charge, they are left out of account for corporation tax purposes, provided they do not exceed the amount of relief (*CTA 2009, s 799*).

Reconstructions

12.29 In general, reconstructions avoid a tax charge. In order to ensure this effect, a clearance procedure is available (*CTA 2009, s 832*).

In a scheme of reconstruction where the whole or part of a business of one company is transferred to another company and the transferor receives no part of the consideration (otherwise than by the transferee taking over the whole or part of the liabilities of the business), and where the transfer includes assets which are chargeable intangible assets of the transferor immediately before and of the transferee immediately after the transfer, the transfer of the chargeable intangible assets is tax-neutral. Neither transferor nor transferee may be a friendly society or a dual resident investing company. The reconstruction must be effected for genuine commercial reasons, and must not form part of a scheme or arrangements of which the main purpose, or one of the main purposes, is avoidance of corporation tax, capital gains tax or income tax (*CTA 2009, ss 818, 831*).

There are similar provisions to ensure that transfers of chargeable intangible assets may be tax-neutral on the transfer of the whole or part of the UK business of an EU company resident in one EU member state to an EU company resident in another EU member state, provided that the transfer is wholly in exchange for securities issued by the transferor to the transferee. The chargeable intangible asset is transferred to the transferee company complete with its tax history (*CTA 2009, ss 819, 820*).

Where a UK company's overseas permanent establishment transfers all or part of a trade to a non-UK resident company, the gain on chargeable intangible assets included in the transfer may be deferred. The transfer of trade must include the whole of the assets used for the purposes of the trade or part trade, or the whole of those assets other than cash. The transfer must be made wholly or partly in exchange for securities which comprise at least one quarter of the ordinary share capital of the transferee or bring the transferor's total holding in the transferee to at least that level. The transfer must be effected for genuine commercial reasons, and must not form part of a scheme or arrangements of which the main purpose, or one of the main purposes, is avoidance of corporation tax, capital gains tax or income tax (*CTA 2009, ss 827, 828, 831*). If the securities are later sold otherwise than by intra-group transfer, a credit equal to the deferred gain must be brought into account by the transferor. Also, if at any time within six years after the transfer the transferee disposes of the relevant chargeable intangible assets, a credit must be brought into account by the transferor equal to the deferred gain (*CTA 2009, ss 829, 830*). Relief for any foreign tax is available if there is no deferral of the gain (*TIOPA 2010, s 117*).

Where a pre-*FA 2002* asset (see **12.2**) is transferred under a reconstruction to which *TCGA 1992, s 139, 140A* or *140E* applies, the asset remains a pre-*FA 2002* asset in the hands of the transferee (*CTA 2009, ss 892–900*).

Transfers between related parties

12.30 Transfers of chargeable intangible assets between related parties that are not companies within the same group take place at market value for most tax purposes, whether or not the related party is a company, subject to the transfer pricing provisions (*CTA 2009, ss 845, 846*). Where transfer pricing applies and the transfer takes place on or after 8 July 2015 (unless acquired under an unconditional contractual obligation made before that date), there may be a further adjustment if necessary to ensure that the full market value of the asset is brought into account for tax purposes (*CTA 2009, s 846(1A)–(1C)*, as inserted by *F(No 2)A 2015, s 39*).

Exceptions to the market value rules

12.31 The market value rule for transfers between related parties does not apply in the following situations:

- Where a transfer pricing adjustment must be considered, because the provision is not on arm's-length terms, even if no adjustment is actually made. Where transfer pricing applies and the transfer takes place on or after 8 July 2015 (unless acquired under an unconditional contractual obligation made before that date), there may be a further adjustment if necessary to ensure that the full market value of the asset is brought into account for tax purposes (*CTA 2009, s 846(1A)–(1C)*, as inserted by *F(No 2)A 2015, s 39*).

- These rules were extended by *FA 2018, s 21*, introducing *CTA 2009, ss 849AB–849AD*, so that the grant of a licence by a company to a related party, or *vice versa*, is deemed to be made at market value. This rule applies as long as the asset is a chargeable intangible asset of the grantor, or the licence or right is a chargeable intangible asset of the grantee, immediately after the right or licence is granted.

- Where the transfer is to an employee at undervalue or from an employee at overvalue (*CTA 2009, s 847*). If the market value rule applied, the transfer would be deemed to be at market value and there would be no taxable benefit under the earnings and benefits rules for income tax purposes.
- Where the transfer is to a shareholder at undervalue or from a shareholder at overvalue (*CTA 2009, s 847*). If the market value rule applied, the transfer would be deemed to be at market value and there would be no distribution for income tax purposes.

Related parties and gift relief

12.32 Where a chargeable intangible asset is transferred to a company and the transferor (being an individual) claims capital gains tax hold-over relief under *TCGA 1992, s 165*, in respect of a gift of business assets (see *Capital Gains Tax 2018/19* (Bloomsbury Professional)), the transfer is treated as taking place at market value less the amount of the reduction in the transferor's chargeable gain (*CTA 2009, s 849*).

Example 12.5—Related parties and hold-over relief

Facts

In 2005, Colin personally acquired the rights to certain intellectual property rights (IPR). These rights are used by his company, Colin Ltd, and on 1 January 2015 he transferred the rights to the company for no consideration, claiming hold-over relief under *TCGA 1992, s 165*, on his gift of business assets.

Analysis

On his disposal, Colin's capital gain is held over. For corporation tax purposes, Colin Ltd is treated as having acquired intangible fixed assets (ie the IPR) for their open market value less the amount of the gain that was held over. Accordingly, this reduced transfer value is used as the basis for calculating the company's amortisation of the patent rights for tax purposes.

Roll-over relief on realisation and reinvestment is not available to a company where there is a part realisation and, resulting from it, an acquisition by a related party (*CTA 2009, s 850*). Royalty payments to a related party, not paid within 12 months of the accounting period in which they are accrued and not brought in as a credit by the recipient company, are not allowed as a deduction by the payee (*CTA 2009, s 851*).

See **12.10** for details of restrictions imposed from 3 December 2014 or 24 March 2015 until 7 July 2015 where a company acquired internally generated goodwill or certain other 'relevant assets' from a related individual, or from a partnership involving a related individual.

Related parties

12.33 Parties are 'related parties' in the following circumstances:

Case 1

P Ltd and C Ltd are related parties if either company has control of, or a major interest in, the other company (*CTA 2009, s 835(2)*).

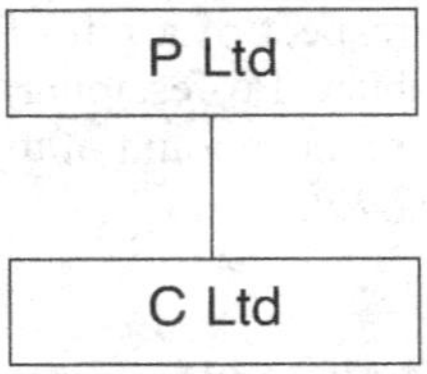

For this purpose, P Ltd controls C Ltd if P Ltd has power to secure that the affairs of C Ltd are conducted in accordance with the wishes of P Ltd, whether (*CTA 2009, s 836*):

- by means of the holding of shares or the possession of voting power in or in relation to C Ltd or any other company; or
- as a result of powers conferred by the articles of association or other document regulating C Ltd or any other company.

P Ltd has a major interest in C Ltd if (*CTA 2009, s 837*):

- P Ltd and another person together have control of C Ltd; and
- the rights and powers by means of which they have such control represent, in the case of each of them, at least 40% of the total.

Case 2

P Ltd and C Ltd are related parties if they are companies under the control of the same person, whether or not that third person is a company (*CTA 2009, s 835(3)–(4)*).

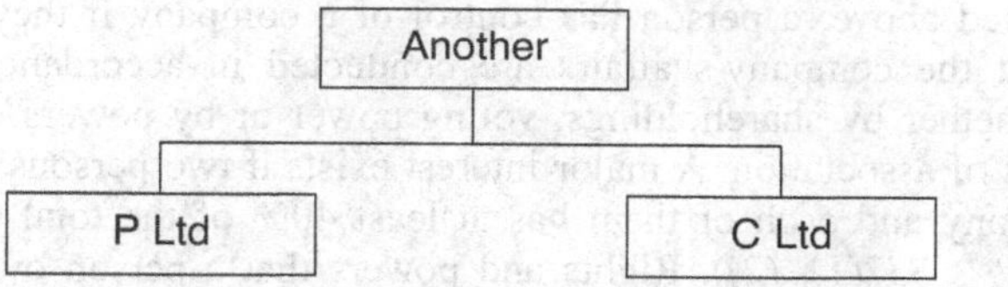

However, P Ltd and C Ltd are not related parties by virtue of the fact that they are both under the control of:

- the Crown;
- a Minister of the Crown or a government department;
- the Scottish Ministers;
- the National Assembly for Wales;
- a Minister within the meaning of the *Northern Ireland Act 1998* or a Northern Ireland department;
- a foreign sovereign power; or
- an international organisation.

Case 3

P and C Ltd are related parties if C Ltd is a close company and P is (*CTA 2009, s 835(5)*):

- a participator or an associate of a participator in C Ltd (*CTA 2010, s 454*; close company definitions apply: see **10.9**, **10.11**); or
- a participator in a company that has control of, or holds a major interest in, C Ltd.

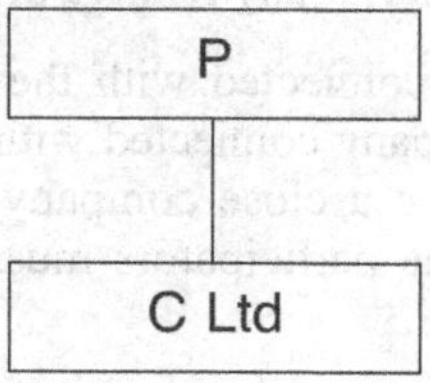

Case 4

P Ltd and C Ltd are related parties if they are companies in the same group (*CTA 2009, s 835(6)*).

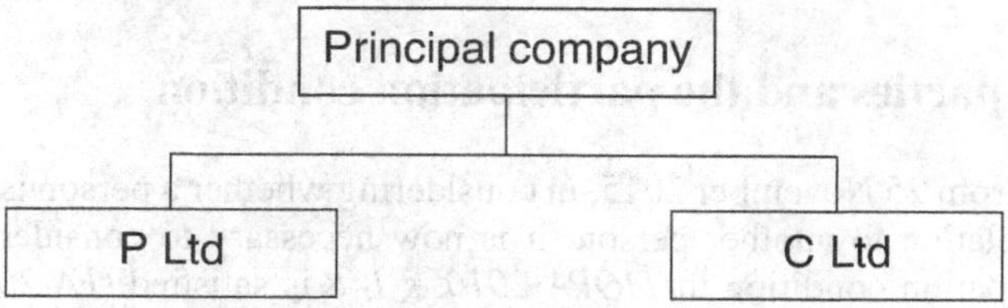

As explained above, a person has control of a company if they are able to secure that the company's affairs are conducted in accordance with their wishes, whether by shareholdings, voting power or by powers conferred by the articles of association. A major interest exists if two persons have control of a company and each of them has at least 40% of the total shareholding (*CTA 2009, s 837(1), (2)*). Rights and powers that a person owns singly or jointly are taken into account; these include rights and powers that he is entitled to acquire at a future date or will, at a future date, become entitled to acquire and other rights and powers that can be exercised on his behalf, under his direction or for his benefit. Rights and powers of a person connected with him are also taken into account, but not persons connected to a connected person (*CTA 2009, ss 838, 839*). Loan security arrangements are not taken into account (*CTA 2009, s 838(7)*). Rights and powers of a person as a member of a partnership are only taken into account if the person has a major interest (40%) in the partnership (*CTA 2009, s 840*).

Connected persons

12.34 In relation to a person, connected persons include (*CTA 2009, s 843*; CIRD45190):

- their spouse or civil partner;
- their relatives (ie brothers, sisters, ancestors and lineal descendants);
- the spouse or civil partner of any relative;
- any relative of their spouse or civil partner; and
- the spouse or civil partner of any relative of their spouse or civil partner.

A trustee of a settlement is connected with the settlor, a person connected with the settlor and any company connected with the settlement, and for this purpose the company must be a close company (or only not close because it is not UK resident) and the participators must include the trustees of the settlement (*CTA 2009, s 843*).

A person is connected with a company if they are related parties because of common control, and for this purpose a company includes any body corporate or unincorporated association (*CTA 2009, s 843*; *CTA 2010, s 1121(1)*; see also **1.2**).

Related parties and the participation condition

12.35 From 25 November 2015, in considering whether a person is a related party in relation to another person, it is now necessary to consider whether the participation condition in *TIOPA 2010, s 148* is satisfied (*FA 2016, s 53,* amending *CTA 2009, s 845*). The draft legislation is not entirely clear but it appears that the participation condition is satisfied if one of the persons directly or indirectly participates in the management, control or capital of the other person, or if the same person or persons directly or indirectly participates in the management, control or capital of both parties.

The result of the new rule is that a gain on an intangible fixed asset arising to a partnership or LLP is a chargeable realisation gain, to the extent that it is attributed to the corporate member under *CTA 2009, s 1259*.

The rule was introduced because HMRC had 'identified arrangements that use bodies such as partnerships or LLPs to transfer assets in ways that aim to bring the assets within the new rules without an effective change of economic ownership', in a way that circumvented the market value rule (Explanatory Notes to *Finance Bill 2016*).

OTHER ASPECTS

Grants

12.36 Regional development grants and certain Northern Ireland grants are not treated as credits under the intangible fixed assets regime. All other grants received directly or indirectly towards expenditure on chargeable intangible assets and recognised in the company's profit and loss account are treated as taxable credits (*CTA 2009, ss 852, 853*).

Finance lessors

12.37 Finance lessors are within the intangible fixed assets regime for assets leased under finance leases to other companies. However, neither fixed rate amortisation nor reinvestment relief is available (*CTA 2009, ss 854, 855*; *Corporation Tax (Finance Leasing of Intangible Assets) Regulations 2002, SI 2002/1967*).

INTERNATIONAL ASPECTS

Company ceasing to be UK resident

12.38 There is a deemed disposal of a chargeable intangible asset at market value when the company owning it ceases to be UK resident. A UK holding company and a 75% subsidiary may jointly elect for the gain to be postponed on assets used for the purposes of the trade of the branch or agency where market value exceeds cost (*CTA 2009, ss 859, 860*).

The gain, being the excess of market value over cost, is chargeable as a non-trading credit on the UK holding company if the now non-resident subsidiary company disposes of the asset within six years of becoming non-resident.

In the case of a part realisation, the tax written down value is apportioned by the following formula (*CTA 2009, s 861*):

$$\frac{\text{MVB} - \text{MVA}}{\text{MVB}}$$

where:

- MVB is the market value of the asset immediately before the part realisation
- MVA is the market value of the asset immediately after the part realisation.

The gain becomes chargeable on the holding company if, at any subsequent time, it ceases to be UK resident or the company owning the asset ceases to be its subsidiary (*CTA 2009, s 862*).

For further details of this exit charge and the circumstances in which it may be postponed, see **20.20**, **20.21** and **20.23**.

Chapter 13

UK Patent Box

SIGNPOSTS

- An elective regime for companies exploiting patented inventions was introduced from 1 April 2013, with the benefit of the special IP rate of corporation tax being phased in over five years (see **13.1–13.2**).
- Current regime is open to new entrants for accounting periods ending on or before 30 June 2016 and will remain in place until 30 June 2021 (see **13.1** and **13.17**).
- There is a modified regime for new entrants from 1 July 2016, which will apply to everyone from 1 July 2021. Other companies may elect into the new regime early (see **13.16**).
- The meaning of qualifying company and qualifying IP rights (see **13.3–13.5**).
- How to calculate the relevant IP profits or losses of a trade (see **13.6–13.7**).
- The small claims election (see **13.8**).
- The alternative 'streaming' approach (see **13.9–13.10**).
- Mandatory streaming (see **13.11**).
- The treatment of relevant IP losses of a trade (see **13.12**).
- Making or revoking a Patent Box election (see **13.13**).
- Anti-avoidance provisions (see **13.15**).
- Modified regime from 1 July 2016 (see **13.16–13.19**).

INTRODUCTION

> **Focus**
>
> The Patent Box regime is voluntary, and a qualifying company may choose whether or not to opt into it. If a company carries on more than one trade, an election to apply the Patent Box will have effect in relation to all those trades.

13.1 *FA 2012* introduced a new regime known as the UK Patent Box, which provides a reduced tax rate for companies (but not unincorporated businesses) from 1 April 2013. It applies to companies exploiting patented inventions or certain other medicinal or botanic innovations (*CTA 2010, Pt 8A*).

The Patent Box offers companies the chance to elect into what is potentially a very generous tax regime, but there are stringent conditions to be met and the computation of the relief is complex.

HMRC guidance on the Patent Box provisions can be found in their Corporate Intangibles Research & Development Manual at CIRD200000 onwards. They advise that companies with specific queries on the Patent Box should first approach their HMRC Customer Relationship Manager or Customer Co-ordinator, if they have one. Other companies should contact the Maidstone R&D Unit, Medvale House, Mote Road, Maidstone, Kent, ME15 6AF, telephone 01622 760405.

The Patent Box is available to all companies within the scope of corporation tax which:

- elect into the regime;
- hold a qualifying patent or other qualifying intellectual property (IP); and
- receive income relating to that patent or IP.

If a company carries on more than one trade, an election into the Patent Box applies to all of them. Profits falling within the regime will effectively (by means of a deduction from trading profits) be subject to a corporation tax rate that could be as low as 10% in some cases, instead of the main corporation tax rate.

Profit eligible for the Patent Box is calculated according to a structured process specified in the legislation, designed to strip out (a) profit that would have been made even if the company did not hold valuable IP, and (b) value attributable to the company's brand rather than the patented technology. For some parts of the calculations, the legislation provides a pre-determined formula; but, for others, companies must make their own assessment requiring a degree of judgement. There is a simplified process in relation to calculating brand value for companies which only have small claims to make.

The Patent Box regime applies to profits attributable to qualifying patents, and certain other IP rights, starting from 1 April 2013. There are transitional rules phasing in the benefits over the first five financial years of the regime, as follows:

Financial year	*Proportion of Patent Box benefit available*
2013	60%
2014	70%
2015	80%
2016	90%
2017 onwards	100%

Focus

The Patent Box in its present form will be closed to new entrants for accounting periods ending after 30 June 2016 and replaced by a modified version from 1 July 2016. Therefore, elections for relief under the old regime must be made by 30 June 2018.

The Patent Box and other IP tax regimes are changing as part of the Organisation for Economic Co-operation and Development (OECD) Base Erosion and Profit Shifting (BEPS) project (see **21.2**). Following discussions among the G20 nations in November 2014, such preferential IP tax regimes will be closed to new entrants by 30 June 2016 and abolished by 30 June 2021. Replacement schemes must have a direct nexus between the income receiving the tax benefits and the R&D expenditure contributing to that income in the jurisdiction in which the preferential regime exists. The UK's proposals appear to go further than this and link the availability of relief only to R&D expenditure by the claimant company.

The original Patent Box regime is described in **13.2** to **13.14**. The modified nexus regime is described in **13.16** onwards.

SCOPE AND NATURE OF THE PATENT BOX

13.2 The reduced rate of corporation tax applies to a proportion of the profits derived from:

- licensing or sale of the patent rights;
- sales of the patented invention or products incorporating the patented invention;

- use of the patented invention in the company's trade; or
- infringement and compensation.

In addition to qualifying patents, the regime also applies to other qualifying IP rights, such as regulatory data protection (also called data exclusivity), supplementary protection certificates and plant variety rights.

The Patent Box regime is expected to benefit a wide range of companies which receive royalties in respect of qualifying IP rights, or sell products, or use patented processes as part of their business. Other non-qualifying profits in these companies will continue to be taxed at the main rate of corporation tax.

Where a company has elected into the regime, any relevant IP profits of a trade of the company for an accounting period for which it is a qualifying company are chargeable at a lower rate of corporation tax. This lower rate is given effect by allowing a deduction to be made in calculating the profits of the trade for that period for corporation tax purposes.

The amount of the deduction is

$$RP \times \frac{(MR - IPR)}{MR}$$

where:

- RP is the relevant IP profits of the trade of the company
- MR is the main rate of corporation tax
- IPR is the special IP rate of corporation tax (*CTA 2010, s 357A(1)–(3)*).

The special IP rate of corporation tax has been set initially at 10% (*CTA 2010, s 357A(4)*).

QUALIFYING COMPANY

13.3 *CTA 2010, Pt 8A, Ch 2* is concerned with qualifying companies. A company must be a qualifying company for the purposes of the Patent Box regime in order to elect into the regime (*CTA 2010, s 357A*).

A company is a qualifying company if it either:

- holds a qualifying IP right or an exclusive licence in respect of a qualifying IP right at some time during the accounting period; or
- has previously held a qualifying IP right or an exclusive licence in respect of a qualifying IP right, and is taxable in the accounting period on income in respect of that right. That income must be attributable to events occurring wholly or partly during a period when the company

was a qualifying company and had made an election under *CTA 2010, s 357A*, eg where damages for a patent infringement are received after expiry of a patent but the company had made a Patent Box election at the time of the infringement (*CTA 2010, s 357B(1)–(3)*).

In addition, for a company that is a member of a group to be a qualifying company (*CTA 2010, s 357B(5)*), it must also satisfy the 'active ownership' condition (*CTA 2010, s 357BE*). This allows the company to qualify even if another group company has undertaken the qualifying development. A company meets this for an accounting period if all or almost all of the qualifying IP rights held by the company in that accounting period are rights in respect of which either of the following conditions is met:

- Condition A is that, during the accounting period, the company performs a significant amount of management activity in relation to its qualifying IP rights portfolio, including the formulation of plans and decision-making in relation to the development or exploitation of the IP rights.
- Condition B is that the company meets the development condition in relation to the rights by virtue of *CTA 2010, s 357BC(2)* or *(3)* (see **13.4**, Conditions A and B).

For the purposes of Condition A above, it is thought that 'management activity' would include such involvement as granting licences, ensuring that the IP is protected, and looking for other ways to exploit the IP. The expression 'significant' is not defined, and whether what is done is a significant amount of management activity is determined (CIRD210210) in the light of all the relevant circumstances, given:

- the resources that the company employs,
- the breadth of its responsibilities for the IP,
- the nature of the IP rights held and the amount of management they require, and
- the significance and impact of the decisions and plans that it (as opposed to other group companies, if any) makes in relation to that IP.

QUALIFYING IP RIGHTS

Focus

The new Patent Box regime focuses primarily on patents granted by the UK Intellectual Property Office and the European Patent Office, but other intellectual property rights are also covered.

13.4 The Patent Box regime is aimed primarily at patents granted by the UK Intellectual Property Office and the European Patent Office (EPO), but qualifying IP also includes:

- supplementary protection certificates;
- regulatory data protection granted in respect of medicinal, veterinary and plant protection products;
- UK and EC plant variety rights;
- patents that would have been granted but for a prohibition on publication on the grounds of national security or public safety (eg nuclear technology); and
- marketing exclusivity granted to orphan status medicines and medicines for paediatric use.

The Patent Box extends to patents granted in other EEA Member States that have comparable patentability criteria and search and examination practices to the UK (*Profits from Patents (EEA Rights) Order 2013, SI 2013/420*), namely:

Austria	Finland	Romania
Bulgaria	Germany	Slovakia
Czech Republic	Hungary	Sweden
Denmark	Poland	
Estonia	Portugal	

The regime applies to new and existing rights and is available to both those who own a patent outright and those who hold an exclusive licence to use a patent.

IP rights to which the Patent Box regime applies are defined in the legislation (*CTA 2010, s 357BB*) and include:

(a) a patent granted under the *Patents Act 1977*,

(b) a patent granted under the *European Patent Convention*,

(c) a right of a specified description which corresponds to a right within paragraph (a) or (b) and is granted under the law of a specified EEA state,

(d) a supplementary protection certificate,

(e) any plant breeders' rights granted in accordance with *Part 1* of the *Plant Varieties Act 1997*, and

(f) any Community plant variety rights granted under *Council Regulation (EC) 2100/94*.

For an IP right to be a qualifying IP right in relation to a company, it is also necessary that the company meets the 'development' condition (*CTA 2010, ss 357BC, 357BD*) in relation to the right. This essentially involves the company creating or contributing to the creation of the protected invention or a product incorporating the patented invention, or performing a significant amount of development activity to that end. For this purpose, the term 'significant' is not defined, but might be assessed by reference to (say) time, cost or effort, or the value or impact of the contribution (CIRD210190).

Where the patented device is incorporated as an essential component within a larger product, the income from that larger product falls within the 'gross income' definition for the Patent Box.

Example 13.1—Patented device within a larger product

Facts

A patented printer cartridge is designed to be inserted in a printer and, once installed, not to be removed until empty, at which point it will be replaced.

Analysis

The patented cartridge is regarded as incorporated in the printer. Income from the sale of a printer including the cartridge (whether the cartridge is installed or included separately in the box with the printer as part of a single package) can therefore qualify as relevant IP income, even if there is no patent over the printer itself.

Example 13.2—Product to be incorporated in patented device

Facts

A printer includes a patented invention, but the printer cartridge bespoke to that printer does not. The company holding the relevant patents sells cartridges bespoke to that printer, both with the printer and on their own.

Analysis

The cartridge is regarded as an item wholly or mainly designed to be incorporated into the patented printer, and income of that company from the sale of the cartridges (whether with the printer or on their own) can therefore qualify as relevant IP income.

Example 13.3—Patented product for use with various unpatented devices

Facts

A patented DVD, supplied in a package with an unpatented DVD player, is designed to work with a wide variety of DVD players and is intended to be removed after each use.

Analysis

The DVD is not regarded as incorporated in the DVD player, or designed to be incorporated in it. The mere fact of including the patented DVD with the unpatented DVD player does not result in income from the sale of the DVD player qualifying as relevant IP income.

Similarly, if the DVD player was patented and the DVD was not, sale of the DVDs (whether with the DVD player or on their own) would not produce relevant IP income.

For these and further examples, see CIRD220190.

If the company is a member of a group of companies and acts as an IP holding company, it must also show that it actively manages the IP rights. A company can meet the development condition by meeting any of the following conditions:

- *Condition A* is that the company has at any time carried out qualifying development in relation to the particular IP rights during the accounting period, and has not ceased to be, or become, a controlled member of a group since that time (*CTA 2010, s 357BC(2)*).
- *Condition B* is that the company has at any time carried out qualifying development in relation to the particular IP rights during the accounting period, and has ceased to be, or become, a controlled member of a group since that time, and for the succeeding 12 months has performed activities of the same description as those that constituted the qualifying development, and remains a member of that group or (as the case may be) does not become a controlled member of any other group (*CTA 2010, s 357BC(3)*).
- *Condition C* is that the company is a member of a group, another company that is or has been a member of the group has carried out qualifying development in relation to the right, and that other company was a member of the group at the time it carried out the qualifying development (*CTA 2010, s 357BC(4)*).
- *Condition D* is that the company is a member of a group, another company ('T') that is or has been a member of the group has carried out qualifying

development in relation to the right, that other company or its successor in trade has, while carrying on that trade as a member of the group, performed activities of the same description as those that constituted the qualifying development, and those activities of those companies, taken together, have been performed for a period of 12 months beginning with the day on which T became a member of the group (*CTA 2010, s 357BC(5)*).

A company carries out qualifying development in relation to a right if it creates or significantly contributes to the creation of the invention, or if it performs a significant amount of activity for the purposes of developing the invention or any item or process incorporating the invention. In other words, the company must have made a significant contribution to the creation or development of the invention claimed in the patent, or a product incorporating this invention.

If the company licenses the patent rights, the licence must give it exclusivity for those rights, at least countrywide. However, HMRC takes the view that the exclusivity requirement does not preclude different companies having licences over the same technology in the same jurisdiction, if the rights are for sufficiently different commercial applications.

An exclusive licence, in relation to a right ('the principal right'), means a licence which:

- is granted by the person who holds either the principal right or an exclusive licence in respect of the principal right ('the proprietor'), and
- confers on the person holding the licence ('the licence-holder'), or on the licence-holder and persons authorised by it:
  (a) one or more rights conferred to the exclusion of all other persons (including the proprietor) in one or more countries or territories, although this does not necessarily exclude the possibility of third parties owning other rights over some or all of the same innovation for use (say) in different fields; and
  (b) the right (i) to bring proceedings without the consent of the proprietor or any other person in respect of any infringement of the rights within paragraph (a), or (ii) to receive the whole or the greater part of any damages awarded in respect of any such infringement.

There is no specific requirement for the licence to be a formal document. In cases where the arrangements between the parties are sufficient to form an implicit licence, it is considered that Patent Box relief should potentially be available.

Where a company has claimed Patent Box benefit on the basis of a reasonable but mistaken belief that an item qualifies, there will be no retrospective withdrawal of those benefits, but no further claims can be made from the point at which it became reasonably apparent that the belief was mistaken. This would apply equally to rights held under an exclusive licence (CIRD210180).

Companies may wish to look carefully at the IP that they own, to assess whether it would be worthwhile seeking new patents in order to bring the related income within the Patent Box regime. Applying for a patent is not necessarily an expensive process, and relief can begin to accumulate as soon as the patent is applied for, even though it cannot be claimed until the patent is granted. However, it should be noted that, in some circumstances, increasing the flow of patent royalties into the company might alter the company's status as a 'trading company' for the purposes of other tax reliefs.

Patents pending

13.5 A company cannot benefit immediately from the Patent Box on profits from items pending patent approval. But, for up to six years before grant, the company can calculate what the relevant IP profits (RP) of its trade would have been had the patent been granted at that time. These amounts are aggregated over the six years, and then they can be added to the RP of the year in which the patent is granted when calculating the Patent Box deduction.

Profits from patents pending can only qualify in this way if they relate to periods on or after 1 April 2013 during which the company had elected into the Patent Box, and if the company had made an election (on a patent-by-patent basis) for this relief to be granted (*CTA 2010, s 358CQ(2)*; CIRD 220540; see also Step 7 in **13.7**). If the company had elected into the Patent Box but was not a qualifying company during any of the earlier periods in question, it is treated for this purposes as though it were a qualifying company (*CTA 2010, s 358CQ(8), (9)*).

RELEVANT IP PROFITS OR LOSSES OF A TRADE

13.6 *CTA 2010, Pt 8A, Ch 3* is concerned with the calculation of relevant IP profits for the purposes of the Patent Box regime. A company wishing to elect into the regime, or assess whether to do so, should ensure that their IP records and accounting systems produce all the information required, so that they can take a properly informed decision and (if appropriate) support their calculations made under the regime.

The calculation starts by identifying how much of the company's total gross income includes relevant IP income ('RIPI'), which is income derived from its qualifying patents. Broadly, five specific types of income can qualify as RIPI, but additionally, companies that generate income outside these categories can treat a part of their turnover (measured by reference to an arm's length royalty rate) as RIPI if they use patented inventions in providing services or in their business processes.

> **Focus**
>
> Calculation of relevant IP income ('RIPI') is central to the application of the Patent Box regime. The calculation is complicated, and the related compliance burdens may deter some companies from electing into the Patent Box.

RIPI includes (*CTA 2010, ss 357CC–357CF*):

- income from worldwide sales of the patented item, or an item incorporating it, including in territories where the item is not protected by a patent or whose patents would not themselves qualify for the Patent Box;
- worldwide licence fees and royalties from:
  - rights that the company grants others out of its qualifying patents or over the patented item or process, including licences in territories outside the protection of the qualifying patents over the item or process; and
  - other non-patent rights granted for the same purpose as the patent rights;
- income from the sale or disposal of UK or other qualifying EPO or national patent rights;
- amounts received from others accused of infringing the qualifying patent; and
- other compensation, including damages, insurance proceeds and compensation for lost income that would have been relevant IP income. Again, this applies wherever the RIPI would have arisen worldwide.

For these purposes, finance income is not part of the company's gross income. Additionally, neither ring-fence oil extraction income nor income from exploiting non-exclusive patent rights can qualify.

The company can normally choose one of two routes to calculate how much of its profits derive from its RIPI. Either:

- it can apportion its total corporation tax profits according to the ratio of RIPI to total gross income; or
- it can allocate its expenses on a just and reasonable basis to the two 'streams' of income (RIPI and non-qualifying income) to arrive at an appropriate profit derived from its RIPI stream.

Profits apportioned or expenses attributed must exclude finance income and expenses, and any R&D expenditure credit received. They must also exclude any additional deduction above actual cost for R&D costs under the R&D tax credits regime.

Two further stages are necessary in the calculation. The first is to remove a routine return on certain specified expenses from the apportioned or streamed patent-derived profits (*CTA 2010, s 357CI*). This leaves an amount called qualifying residual profit ('QRP'). The relevant costs include corporation tax deductions made in respect of personnel, premises (if tax-deductible), plant and machinery (including capital allowances) and miscellaneous services (*CTA 2010, s 357CJ*). Expenditure qualifying for R&D expenditure credits, R&D tax credits, R&D relief or patent allowances is excluded, as are loan relationship and derivative contract debits (*CTA 2010, s 357CK*). The return is set at 10% of the relevant expenses, and the profit is reduced by this amount.

The final stage is either:

- to remove a return on marketing assets used to derive RIPI, by deducting a notional marketing royalty for use of the assets (*CTA 2010, ss 357CN–357CP*); or
- provided that the company's QRP is less than a maximum amount of £3 million, to apply small claims treatment to the QRP; the small claims treatment removes 25% of QRP as a deemed marketing return, leaving the remaining 75% (up to a maximum £1 million small claims threshold) inside the Patent Box (*CTA 2010, ss 357CL–357CM*).

In either case, the result is a profit figure called relevant IP profits ('RP') which can benefit from the Patent Box. This figure is used to calculate the appropriate amount of the deduction from the profits of the trade which gives effect to the lower rate of corporation tax (*CTA 2010, s 357A*).

The steps to calculating relevant IP profits

13.7 The calculations explained above, to determine the relevant IP profits of a trade, are set out clearly in the legislation (*CTA 2010, s 357C*).

Step 1 specifies that the total gross income of a trade must be calculated, including revenue, compensation, adjustments, proceeds from intangible fixed assets, and profits from patent rights, but excluding finance income (see *CTA 2010, ss 357CA, 357CB*).

Step 2 determines the percentage ('X%') of the company's total gross income that is relevant IP income under the headings of sales income, licence fees, proceeds of sale etc, damages for infringement, and other compensation, including notional royalty income, but excluding ring fence income and income attributable to non-exclusive licences (*CTA 2010, ss 357CC–357CE*), using the following formula:

$$\frac{RIPI}{TI} \times 100$$

where:

- RIPI is so much of the total gross income of the trade for the accounting period as is relevant IP income (see *CTA 2010, ss 357CC, 357CD*)
- TI is the total gross income of the trade for the accounting period.

For this purpose, mixed income is apportioned on a just and reasonable basis (*CTA 2010, s 357CF*).

Step 3 apportions the total profit or loss of the trade between that attributed to activities of the trade involving the exploitation of qualifying IP rights and other matters. This is achieved by applying the percentage, X%, computed at Step 2 to the total profit or loss of the trade for corporation tax purposes, subject to various adjustments relating to loan relationships, derivatives, R&D reliefs and expenditure credits, and finance income (*CTA 2010, s 357CG*).

Step 4 determines any qualifying residual profit figure by deducting an amount representing a routine return, calculated under *CTA 2010, s 357CI*, from the result of Step 3. Where this is a positive figure, this is the qualifying residual profit, which represents the additional profit over and above a routine return attributed to the exploitation of all of the company's intangible assets. If the routine return figure is greater than X% of the total profit then, subject to Step 7, there will be a relevant IP loss for the period. No further adjustment is necessary under Steps 5 and 6 where there is a loss at this stage in the calculation.

Companies with a qualifying residual profit now make a decision regarding how to calculate the amount of this qualifying residual profit that is attributed to the qualifying IP rights.

Step 5 sets out that, where the company has not made an election for small claims treatment, it should proceed to Step 6; alternatively, if the company has elected for small claims treatment, it should use the simplified procedure to calculate the small claims amount in relation to the trade (*CTA 2010, ss 357CL, 357CM*).

Step 6 deducts from any qualifying residual profit an amount to be attributed to marketing assets (*CTA 2010, ss 357CN–357CP*). Whilst it is possible that the result of deducting the marketing assets return figure from the qualifying residual profits creates a loss, in practice a company in that position will always be better off making a small claims election and using the alternative method set out in *CTA 2010, ss 357CL–357CM*, so long as it is eligible (see **13.8**).

Step 7 allows an adjustment in respect of patents granted in the year. A company cannot benefit immediately from the Patent Box on profits from items pending patent approval. But, for up to six years before grant (though not before 1 April

2013), the company can calculate what the RP would have been from each such patent had it been granted at that time. These amounts are aggregated over the six years, and then they can be added to the RP of the year in which the patent is granted when calculating the Patent Box deduction (*CTA 2010, s 357CQ*; see **13.5**).

Small claims election

13.8 The small claims election provides a simpler method for calculating the relevant IP profits (RP) of a company where its profits are small. It allows a company that qualifies for this treatment to use a formulaic approach in the computation of RP instead of following Step 6 in *CTA 2010, s 357C(1)*. However, it should be noted that, while simplification might seem attractive, a company may not qualify for such generous relief with the small claims election as it would without.

A company may elect for small claims treatment for an accounting period if it meets one of the following conditions:

- *Condition A* is that the aggregate of the amounts of qualifying residual profit of all of its trades for the accounting period does not exceed £1,000,000.
- *Condition B* is that:
  - the aggregate of the amounts of qualifying residual profit of all of its trades for the accounting period does not exceed the relevant maximum, and
  - the company did not take Step 6 in *CTA 2010, s 357C(1)* or *357DA(1)* for the purpose of calculating the relevant IP profits of any trade of the company for any previous accounting period beginning within the period of four years ending immediately before the accounting period in question (*CTA 2010, s 357CL(2)–(3)*).

For the purposes of Condition B, the 'relevant maximum' for a 12-month accounting period is £3,000,000, proportionately reduced for an accounting period shorter than 12 months. Until 31 March 2015 the limit is also proportionately reduced where the company has one or more associated companies, by dividing it by one plus the number of associated companies which have elected for the Patent Box regime for the accounting period, and 'associated company' is defined as it is for the purposes of the small profits rate of corporation tax (*CTA 2010, ss 25–30, 357CL*; see **23.15**).

From 1 April 2015 the pre-existing associated company rules are repealed as a result of unification of the main and small profits rates of corporation tax, so the legislation relies instead on the 'related 51% group company' test. Thus from 1 April 2015 the relevant maximum is proportionately reduced where the company has one or more related 51% group companies, by dividing it by one plus the number of related 51% group companies which have elected for the Patent Box regime for the accounting period (*CTA 2010, s 279F*, as inserted by *FA 2014, Sch 1, para 5*; see **23.22**).

Where any amount of qualifying residual profit of a trade of the company is not greater than nil, it is disregarded in calculating whether the relevant maximum has been exceeded (*CTA 2010, s 357CL(8)*).

Where an election for small claims treatment is made by a company with only one trade, the amount of its relevant IP profits is the lower of (a) 75% of the qualifying residual profit of the trade and (b) the small claims threshold.

Where a company has more than one trade, the qualifying residual profits of all the trades are aggregated to determine whether the small claims threshold has been exceeded, with any negative amounts of qualifying residual profit in a trade being ignored. Where the total does not exceed £1,333,333, the relevant IP profits are 75% of the qualifying residual profit in each trade; otherwise, the relevant IP profit figure for each trade is the amount given by

$$\frac{SCT}{T}$$

where:

- SCT is the small claims threshold
- T is the number of trades of the company (*CTA 2010, s 357CM(2)(b)*).

For these purposes the 'small claims threshold' for a 12-month accounting period is £1,000,000, proportionately reduced for an accounting period shorter than 12 months. As with the relevant maximum (see above), until 31 March 2015 the small claims threshold is also proportionately reduced where the company has one or more associated companies, by dividing it by one plus the number of associated companies which have elected for the Patent Box regime for the accounting period, and 'associated company' is defined as it is for the purposes of the small profits rate of corporation tax (*CTA 2010, ss 25–30, 357CM*; see **23.15**). From 1 April 2015 the new simplified 'related 51% group company' test applies instead, and the small claims threshold is proportionately reduced where the company has one or more related 51% group companies which have elected for the regime (*CTA 2010, s 279F*, as inserted by *FA 2014, Sch 1, para 5*; see **23.22**).

No formal procedure is prescribed for a small claims election. The company may simply include the election for small claims treatment by way of a note to the computations in its corporation tax return (or an amended return) for the accounting period. The election is intended to relieve companies with smaller profits from the administrative burden of carrying out a full analysis of its marketing assets return, as required by Step 6 in *CTA 2009, s 357C(1)*.

ALTERNATIVE 'STREAMING' APPROACH

Focus

Streaming offers the company an opportunity to allocate profits to RIPI using a method that may avoid unfair distortions, but this can work both ways and in some circumstances the company may be required to use this approach to protect the Exchequer.

13.9 In certain circumstances, apportioning the profits of a trade by using the overall ratio of relevant IP income to total gross income, as required by Step 3 in *CTA 2010, s 357C(1)*, may give rise to a distorted result. This may occur, for example, where the relative proportions of income from the exploitation of IP rights and other income differ markedly from the relative proportions of profits derived from such income.

Such a distortion could work to a company's disadvantage, eg where it has a significant amount of non-IP income that produces relatively little profit, and a smaller proportion of income that is relevant IP income but produces a much larger level of profit.

Example 13.4—Streaming advantageous for a taxpayer company

Facts

Inventor A Ltd derives turnover of £900,000 and net profits of £50,000 from manufacturing and selling a range of established products, none of which incorporate items protected by qualifying IP. The company also owns qualifying IP which it developed many years ago and has licensed out to other businesses in return for annual licence fees of £100,000.

Analysis

If the trade profits of £150,000 were apportioned by the ratio of RIPI to total gross income, the relevant IP profits eligible for the Patent Box would be:

£100,000 / £1,000,000 × £150,000 = £15,000.

However, on a streaming basis it is clear that the £100,000 profit from licence fees would all qualify as relevant IP profits, so the company is likely to opt for the streaming method.

There may also be converse situations where a company could gain unfairly, eg where it manufactures and sells items which rely on qualifying IP rights and also receives licence royalties in respect of non-qualifying IP.

Example 13.5—Streaming disadvantageous for a taxpayer company

Facts

Inventor B Ltd generates receipts of £1 million and net profits of £200,000 from exploiting qualifying IP rights. The company also receives licence income of £1 million from non-qualifying IP.

Analysis

If the trade profits of £1,200,000 were apportioned by the ratio of RIPI to total gross income, the relevant IP profits eligible for the Patent Box would be:

£1,000,000 / £2,000,000 × £1,200,000 = £600,000.

In this example, £400,000 of profit from non-qualifying IP would potentially qualify as relevant IP profits. It is understandable that HMRC would wish to restrict this.

Electing for streaming

13.10 A company may make a 'streaming election' for the purpose of determining the relevant IP profits of any trade of the company for an accounting period. Such an election has effect for the accounting period for which it is made and for each subsequent accounting period, unless there is change of circumstances relating to the trade, in which case the company can vary or cease its streaming election in relation to that trade (*CTA 2010, ss 357D, 357DB*).

Step 1 directs that any credits taken into account in computing the corporation tax profits of the trade in the accounting period (including transfer pricing adjustments), net of any finance income, are divided into two 'streams' of income: relevant IP income (including any notional royalty), and income that is not relevant IP income.

Step 2 requires that all debits taken into account in calculating the corporation tax profits of the trade in the accounting period should be allocated on a just and reasonable basis against one or other of the streams of income. Debits in respect of trading loan relationships, derivatives, and certain research and development items are not to be allocated; the effect of this is that they do not reduce relevant IP profits, so that they attract relief at the full corporation tax rate.

The aim of Step 2 is that debits that arise in generating the relevant IP income are allocated against the relevant IP income stream, and debits that arise in generating the other income are allocated against that other income stream. What is just and reasonable depends on the specific circumstances. However, all debits must be allocated, so, for example, R&D which may relate to future income must still be allocated fairly to the current income streams.

Step 3 requires that the debits allocated against the relevant IP income stream are deducted from that income stream to give a figure to carry forward to Step 4.

Step 4 requires that the 10% routine return percentage be applied to any routine deductions included in the debits allocated against the relevant IP income stream, including any routine deductions incurred on the company's behalf by other group members, and that the resulting figure be deducted from the figure produced by Step 3 to give the figure of qualifying residual profit.

Steps 5, 6 and *7* follow broadly the same approach as in the normal (non-streaming) calculation of relevant IP profits (see **13.7**), the only difference being in the treatment of any actual marketing royalty in Step 6. The aggregate of all actual marketing royalty amounts allocated to the relevant IP stream is deducted from the notional royalty in calculating what should be deducted from qualifying residual profit. This is instead of deducting a *pro-rata* amount of such a royalty from the notional marketing royalty, as required for the non-streaming calculation.

The following is an example of a streaming calculation.

Example 13.6—Streaming calculation

Facts

Inventor C Ltd develops, manufactures and sells a range of branded patented products in the UK. It also licenses out the right to manufacture the products in other countries using its patented technology, know-how and brand.

C Ltd also uses its excess manufacturing capability to provide manufacturing services on a contract basis to other group companies.

The company allocates its cost of goods on a direct basis.

It determines that other manufacturing costs are incurred equally, whether patented or non-patented goods are being manufactured. It therefore determines that these costs should be allocated based on the number of units produced.

C Ltd allocates all its R&D department costs to the RIPI stream. Note that it does not matter how these costs are allocated to manufacturing and licensing within this stream, as both produce fully qualifying income.

All 'other manufacturing costs' but none of the cost of goods are 'routine deductions'. R&D costs are outsourced.

For its accounting period ending 31 March 2018 (assuming that the Patent Box has been fully phased in), the company has elected into the Patent Box and has elected for small claims treatment. Assume that the main rate of corporation tax is 20%, and the IP rate is 10%.

Analysis

		RIPI		*Non-RIPI*
	Total	*Full risk manufacturing*	*Licensing*	*Contract manufacturing*
Income	100,000	60,000	10,000	30,000
Cost of goods	40,000	29,000	–	11,000
Gross profit	60,000	31,000	10,000	19,000
Other manufacturing costs	13,000	6,000	–	7,000
Profit before R&D costs	47,000	25,000	10,000	12,000
R&D costs	27,000	27,000		–
Profits chargeable to corporation tax	**20,000**	**8,000**		**12,000**

Streamed Profit & Loss Account of C Ltd

C Ltd's Streaming Calculation

Step 1 RIPI is calculated as £60,000 + £10,000 = £70,000

Step 2 Total debits of £62,000 are allocated against RIPI (£29,000 + £6,000 + £27,000)

Step 3 Deduct debits from RIPI, leaving stream profits of £8,000

Step 4 Apply routine return of 10% to routine expenses of £6,000 included in RIPI stream. Deduct this £600 from the £8,000 to give £7,400 QRP

Step 5 The company elects for small claims treatment, so its RIPI is 75% of QRP, or £5,550

The company's Patent Box tax deduction is therefore £5,550 × (20 – 10) / 20 = £2,775

So, the company's corporation tax profits are reduced from £20,000 to £17,225, and its corporation tax payable at the main rate of 20% is reduced from £4,000 to £3,445.

Mandatory streaming

13.11 If any one of three mandatory streaming conditions is met in relation to a trade of a company for an accounting period, the company must apply the streaming provisions for the purposes of determining the relevant IP profits of the trade for that accounting period. These conditions are as follows.

Condition A is met for an accounting period where the accounts of the company for the period do not recognise a substantial amount of revenue from the trade that is taken into account in computing the profits of the period for corporation tax purposes. This might happen, for example, when there are accounting adjustments affecting prior years' statements of income, or where additional income is recognised for tax purposes on the basis of a transfer pricing adjustment covering several periods (*CTA 2010, s 357DC(1)–(4)*).

Condition B is met for an accounting period where the company's total gross income from the trade includes both relevant IP income and a substantial amount of licensing income that is not relevant IP income (*CTA 2010, s 357DC(5)–(6)*).

Condition C is met for an accounting period where the company's total gross income from the trade includes income that is not relevant IP income, as well as a substantial amount of relevant IP income in the form of licence fees or royalties received under an agreement granting rights to another person over IP rights where the company itself only holds an exclusive licence in respect of those IP rights. This assumes that the relevant IP income received would result in little profit after allowing for royalties paid, so an apportionment process to determine relevant IP profits would not be appropriate in these circumstances (*CTA 2010, s 357DC(7)–(8)*).

TREATMENT OF RELEVANT IP LOSSES OF A TRADE

Focus

Special rules apply where a company makes a 'relevant IP loss' – ie where the calculation of relevant IP profits produces a negative result.

13.12 Particularly in the early stages of IP development, a company may derive income from its qualifying IP rights but not yet return a profit; or it may produce a profit which is less than a routine return on the costs of earning the income. In such cases, the calculation of relevant IP profits results in a negative figure, referred to in the legislation as a 'relevant IP loss'. A consequence of this for the company is that there is no amount of RP. As a result, the company is taxed on its actual profits, or will be able to relieve its losses, as if it had made no election into the Patent Box.

Where a company has a relevant IP loss, the company has a 'set-off amount' which is equivalent to this loss (*CTA 2010, s 357E*).

Where a company has a set-off amount and the company has another Patent Box trade with RP, the set-off amount must be reduced by the RP of that other trade. The RP that has been used to reduce the set-off amount is then excluded from the amount of RP that is used to calculate the Patent Box deduction for the accounting period (*CTA 2010, s 357EA*).

If, after any reduction of the set-off amount under *CTA 2010 s 357EA*, there is still a set-off amount remaining, the excess is reduced by any RP of other relevant group companies for the relevant accounting period. An accounting period of a company that has a set-off amount is a relevant accounting period if it ends at the same time as, or within an accounting period of, another group member. The other group member is a relevant group member if it has made a Patent Box election that has effect in relation to that period. Again, any RP of another relevant group member used to reduce the set-off amount is no longer eligible to be included in calculating that relevant group member's Patent Box deduction for that accounting period.

Where there is more than one company within the group with RP which are subject to set-off, the group may determine in which order the set-off is to be made; otherwise, the set-off amount is reduced by the company with the greatest amount of RP first, then the next largest, and so on. Tax-free payments can be made between group companies to compensate for RP being reduced by set-off amounts of other group companies; provided that they do not exceed the reduction in the relevant IP profits as a result of the set-off, they are not taken into account in calculating the company's taxable profits or treated as distributions of profits (*CTA 2010, ss 357EB, 357EF*).

If, after the application of *CTA 2010, ss 357EA–357EB*, the company has remaining set-off amounts, it can carry these forward against any RP arising in the following accounting period. If the set-off amount brought forward exceeds the RP of the company for that accounting period and the company is a member of a group, the balance of the set-off should be reduced by RP of other relevant group members. Again, any RP which is used to reduce the carried forward set-off amount is no longer eligible for the Patent Box deduction. Any set-off amounts which still remain unreduced are carried forward and reduced by RP of future accounting periods, as described above (*CTA 2010, s 357EC*).

If a company ceases to carry on a trade, ceases to be within the charge to corporation tax in respect of the trade, or the Patent Box election ceases to have effect, any unreduced set-off amounts are first transferred to set off against the relevant IP profits of any other trade carried on by the company. If there are remaining set-off amounts, the amounts are transferred to any other group member that is a qualifying company at the relevant time. The group can decide which group members with RP are to be allocated the set-off amount; otherwise, the sum goes in order to the companies with largest relevant IP profits of the relevant accounting period. If there are no companies with RP, the set-off amount is allocated to the company with the largest set-off amount of its own (*CTA 2010, s 357ED*).

If, in an accounting period, the trade is transferred to another group company, the set-off amount goes to the transferee (*CTA 2010, s 357EE*).

MAKING OR REVOKING A PATENT BOX ELECTION

13.13 To opt into the Patent Box regime, a company must give notice to HMRC in writing, specifying the first accounting period for which the election is to apply. This must be submitted no later than the last day on which the company would be entitled to amend its tax return for that accounting period under *FA 1998, Sch 18, para 15*. In practice, an election may be made in the computations or by separate notice.

The election has effect from the start of the accounting period stated in the notice. An election applies equally to all trades of the company and for all subsequent accounting periods until it is revoked (*CTA 2010, s 357G*).

A company does not have to be a qualifying company at the time it makes the election. This can be valuable because, in the accounting period in which the patent is granted, the company may then obtain the benefit of the Patent Box on profits arising from exploiting the patented invention during the patent pending period (*CTA 2010, s 357CQ*; CIRD220540; see **13.5**).

A company may opt back out of the Patent Box regime by giving HMRC notice in writing, specifying the first accounting period for which the revocation is to have effect. The time limit for this is the same as for an election into the regime (see above). The revocation has effect from the start of the accounting period stated in the notice, and applies equally to all trades of the company and for all subsequent accounting periods until it is revoked. Following revocation, the company may not elect back into the regime for at least five years (*CTA 2010, s 357GA*).

ANTI-AVOIDANCE PROVISIONS

13.14 The Patent Box legislation contains a number of specific anti-avoidance provisions.

CTA 2010, s 357F applies where licences are entered into for non-commercial reasons, ie where the main purpose, or one of the main purposes, of conferring any right in respect of a protected item is to ensure that the licence meets the definition of exclusive licence for the purposes of the Patent Box. This may apply, for example, in cases where the exclusivity provided by the agreement was in respect of a spurious commercial right. In such cases, even though the licence may confer the right to the exclusion of all other persons, it is not regarded as an exclusive licence for the purposes of the Patent Box regime.

CTA 2010, s 357FA applies where a qualifying item is incorporated into a larger item to ensure that income from the sale of that larger item will be relevant IP income. Where the main purpose, or one of the main purposes, of the inclusion of the item is to make income from the sale of the larger item relevant IP income, such income will not be relevant IP income.

CTA 2010, s 357FB is a targeted anti-avoidance provision which limits or denies a Patent Box deduction to a company that is party to a 'tax advantage scheme', ie a scheme entered into in order to secure a tax advantage.

For this purpose, a relevant tax advantage arises where:

- relevant IP profits are increased as a result of the scheme; and
- the scheme is of a specified type.

Specified types of tax advantage scheme are:

- schemes designed to avoid the application of any provision of the Patent Box regime;
- schemes designed to create a mismatch between the expense of acquiring or developing a qualifying IP right (or an exclusive licence over a qualifying IP right) and the income arising from that right or licence. Such a mismatch would occur, for example, if the expense is incurred whilst the company (or a company with which it is grouped) is outside the regime, whilst the income arises once the company has elected into the regime; and
- schemes designed to inflate artificially the amount of relevant IP income brought into account in calculating the profits of the trade. This might happen, for example, if a single agreement is made for the sale of both qualifying and non-qualifying items, and the sale proceeds are allocated unreasonably towards the qualifying items; or where the company enters into an agreement to generate relevant IP income that will be substantially matched by an increase in debits that correspond to that income.

Undertaking practical and commercially appropriate transactions will not be taken to be tax advantage schemes, even if they have the effect of creating or enhancing Patent Box benefits. For example, the following transactions are not tax advantage schemes:

- making a Patent Box election under *CTA 2010, s 357A*;
- delaying an election under *CTA 2010, s 357A* until such time as the company begins to make relevant IP profits rather than relevant IP losses;
- electing out of the regime once relevant IP profits become relevant IP losses (although, of course, no further *CTA 2010, s 357A* election will be possible within five years);
- creating IP holding companies to crystallise income from qualifying IP in the form of royalties;

- separating trades with profitable qualifying IP income streams and those with non-profitable income streams into different companies to allow decisions about whether or not to elect into the regime to be made more easily; and
- bringing qualifying IP into the UK.

Companies may wish to make changes to their commercial arrangements in order to take advantage of the Patent Box regime. In general, where the resulting arrangements would not have been taken to be tax advantage schemes if set up from scratch, then reasonable and commercially appropriate steps taken to restructure group arrangements to maximise benefits from the Patent Box are not taken to be a tax avoidance scheme to which *CTA 2010, ss 357F–357FB* apply. For examples of transactions which HMRC have stated that they will not regard as tax advantage schemes, see CIRD250130.

TRANSFERRING TRADES

13.15 *FA 2016, s 63* introduces a new rule into the Patent Box regime, allowing for continuity of treatment where a company transfers a trade or part of a trade to another company (*CTA 2010, s 357GCA*). In effect, the R&D history of the transferor is inherited by the transferee. This allows the transferee company to claim Patent Box relief in the same way as the transferor did, including retaining its status as not being a new entrant, etc.

PATENT BOX FROM 1 JULY 2016

13.16 The essence of the revised scheme for Patent Box relief is that the income streams for each patent are inspected separately and relief is granted based on the extent to which the claimant company carried out the relevant research and development. So streaming effectively becomes mandatory in every case, on a patent-by-patent or product-by-product basis.

The new legislation is in *CTA 2010, Pt 8A, Chs 2A, 2B, 3* and *4*. *Chapter 2A* covers the situation where the first accounting period for which the company's election (or most recent election) begins on or after 1 July 2016 (a 'new entrant', per *CTA 2010, s 357A(11)*) and also to all accounting periods starting on or after 1 July 2016 (*CTA 2010, ss 357A(6)* and *357BF(1)*). *Chapters 2B, 3* and *4* apply to accounting periods starting before 1 July 2021, where the company has elected into the Patent Box regime before 1 July 2016 and is therefore not a new entrant (*CTA 2010, ss 357A(7)* and *357BO(1)*).

Where a company's accounting period straddles 1 July 2016, the new rules apply as if the company had two accounting periods, one ending on 30 June 2016 and another starting on 1 July 2016 (*FA 2016, s 64*).

Chapter 2A: new entrants, etc

Calculating relevant IP profits

13.17 The calculations are again carried out as a series of numbered steps, much as in the original regime (*CTA 2010, s 357BF*).

Step 1: Divide the company's taxable income (except finance income, defined at *CTA 2010, s 357BG*) into the 'relevant IP income stream' (essentially the same as for the original regime but specifically defined in *CTA 2010, ss 357BH* to *357BHC*) and the 'standard income stream'.

Step 2: Divide the relevant IP income stream into sub-streams attributable to specific IP rights (an individual IP right sub-stream), to a specific IP item (a product sub-stream) or to income derived from a specific IP process (a process sub-stream).

An IP item is an item in respect of which the company has a qualifying intellectual property right or an item that incorporates such an item.

An IP process is a process in respect of which the company has a qualifying intellectual property right or a process that incorporates such a process.

Step 3: Allocate the allowable trading expenses between the standard income stream and the relevant IP income sub-streams on a just and reasonable basis.

Step 4: Deduct the appropriate expenses (as determined in step 3) from each relevant IP income sub-stream. Then deduct the routine return for that sub-stream. The routine return deduction is 10% of the aggregate of the various heads of expenditure, which are, again, broadly similar to those for the original regime (*CTA 2010, ss 357BJ* to *357BJB*). The resulting figure is the qualifying residual profit (QRP) for the sub-stream.

Step 5: If the small claims treatment for the marketing return is required (*CTA 2010, s 357BNA* onwards, inserted by *FA 2016, s 64*), the company can elect to make a notional royalty election, a small claims figure election or a global streaming election. A company can make one of these elections if it carries on only one trade during the accounting period and its qualifying residual profit does not exceed the larger of £1 million in the period and the relevant maximum for the period. This is £3 million (reduced for short accounting periods) divided by the total number of companies in the 51% group (reduced for short accounting periods).

A company is excluded from making any of the elections if it was within the new regime in the previous four years, its QRP exceeded £1 million and it had not made one of the elections for that previous accounting period. Similarly, a company is excluded from making such an election if it was within the old regime in the previous four years, its QRP exceeded £1 million and it had not made a small claims election (under the old regime: see **13.8**) for that previous accounting period.

A notional royalty election applies only where the company is claiming relief on the basis that it does not sell patented items but it uses a patented process or items to produce what it sells, whether goods or services. If the election is made, 75% of the company's IP-related income is treated as relevant IP profits for the period.

If a small claims figure election is made, the QRP of the trade is compared to the small claims threshold, which is £1 million, reduced by a factor of (1 + N) where the claimant company has N 51% group companies (see *CTA 2010, s 357BNC* introduced by *FA 2016, s 64*). If the QRP is less than 75% of the small claims threshold, the routine return small claims figure for the sub-stream is 25% of the sub-stream QRP. Otherwise, the small claims figure for the sub-stream is given by A – (A * SCT)/QRP, where:

- A is the amount of the sub-stream following the deductions required by Step 4 in *s 357BF(2)*;
- QRP is the qualifying residual profit of the trade of the company for the accounting period; and
- SCT is the small claims threshold.

If a global streaming election is made, it appears that the company can claim Patent Box relief as if it had a single stream of relevant IP profit, rather than having to do separate calculations for each IP sub-stream or product sub-stream. This will be a tremendous boon to smaller businesses that might otherwise not have claimed Patent Box due to the complexity of the new regime.

A company cannot make a global streaming election if it also has Patent Box assets to which the old regime applies. So this might be a case where a company with mixed old and new regime claims might prefer to elect fully into the new regime.

Step 6: If a small claims election has not been made, the marketing assets return is computed by *CTA 2010, s 357BL* and deducted from the sub-stream QRP. The marketing assets return is the notional marketing royalty less the actual marketing royalty for the sub-stream.

The notional marketing royalty for a sub-stream is the proportion of the relevant IP income sub-stream that would be paid to a third party on arm's length terms for the right to use the relevant IP assets (*CTA 2010, s 357BLA*). The actual marketing royalty is any royalty paid for the use of the relevant IP assets that is allocated to the sub-stream at step 3 (*CTA 2010, s 357BLB*).

If the actual marketing royalty exceeds the notional marketing royalty, or the actual marketing royalty is less than 10% of QRP, no adjustment is required.

Step 7: The resultant figure is multiplied by the R&D fraction, which is given by *CTA 2010, s 357BM*. This is the restriction of the relief to take into account the R&D actually carried out by the company in respect of the relevant IP asset.

The R&D fraction is the lesser of 1 and the fraction [(D + S1) * 1.3]/(D + S1 + S2 + A), where:

- D is the company's qualifying expenditure on relevant R&D undertaken in-house (*CTA 2010, s 357BMB*). This specifically excludes expenditure by a foreign permanent establishment in respect of which an election under *CTA 2010, s 18A* (profits of foreign PEs excluded from scope of UK corporation tax) has been made (*CTA 2010, s 537BMB(3A)*);
- S1 is the company's qualifying expenditure on relevant R&D sub-contracted to unconnected persons (*CTA 2010, s 357BMC*);
- S2 is the company's qualifying expenditure on relevant R&D sub-contracted to connected persons (*CTA 2010, s 357BMD*), which is 65% of the R&D expenditure in the period that is sub-contracted to a connected party (as defined by *CTA 2010, s 1122*); expenditure by a foreign permanent establishment in respect of which an election under *CTA 2010, s 18A* (profits of foreign PEs excluded from scope of UK corporation tax) has been made is included under S2 as well (new *CTA 2010, s 537BMB(3A)* inserted by *FA 2016, s 61*); and
- A is the company's qualifying expenditure on the acquisition of relevant qualifying IP rights (*CTA 2010, s 357BME*).

Essentially, the fraction takes the proportion of the R&D spend incurred by the claimant company, either directly or sub-contracted to unconnected third parties, over the total R&D spend plus costs of acquiring the relevant IP assets, with a 30% enhancement. In many cases, therefore, the R&D fraction will be 1.

Step 8: Add together the total amounts obtained for each sub-stream.

Step 9: Add any amounts arising in respect of earlier years, before a patent was granted, as computed under *CTA 2010, s 357BN*. This works in much the same way as the pre-grant allowances under the original regime (see **13.5**).

The overall result is the relevant IP profit for the period (or relevant IP loss, if less than 0).

Chapters 2B to 4: non-new entrants

13.18 These provisions apply if the company's accounting period begins on or after 1 July 206 and the company is not a new entrant, ie it has already elected into the Patent Box regime before 1 July 2016, but it has a new qualifying IP right contributing to its relevant IP income (*CTA 2010, s 357BO(1)*).

A new qualifying IP right is one which was granted or issued to the company following an application on or after the relevant date, was assigned to the company on or after the relevant date or where an exclusive licence was granted to the company on or after the relevant date. Any other qualifying IP right is therefore an old qualifying IP right (*CTA 2010, s 357BP*).

The relevant date is usually 1 July 2016. However, it is 2 January 2016 if a qualifying IP right was assigned to the company, or an exclusive licence was granted to the company, by a connected person (by *CTA 2010, s 1122*) that was not within the charge to corporation tax or to a designated foreign tax, and one of the main purposes of the assignor, in being a party to the assignment or grant, was the avoidance of a foreign tax. For example, if a company's shareholder owns the qualifying IP right and decided to license the rights to the company to avoid German tax, these new rules would apply if the licence were granted on or after 2 January 2016. If there were no tax avoidance motive, the original rules would apply to the new licence instead.

If a company is not a new entrant and a qualifying IP right was assigned to it, or an exclusive licence was granted to it, between 2 January 2016 and 1 July 2016 (inclusive), then the original Patent Box rules apply to income accruing to the company in respect of those rights between 1 January 2016 and 1 January 2017 (*FA 2016, s 64(12), (13)*).

Calculating relevant IP profits

13.19 Under these provisions, steps 1 to 9 (see **13.17**) apply, with the addition of a further sub-stream of income attributable to old qualifying IP rights, called 'an old IP rights sub-stream' (*CTA 2010, s 357BQ(3)*).

If the rules are being applied on a product basis to a multi-IP item (see **13.17**, step 2), there are special rules where the product comprises both old and new IP:

- If the value of the multi-IP item is wholly or mainly attributable to the old IP or the old IP percentage is at least 80%, the item can be dealt with wholly under the original Patent Box rules (*CTA 2010, s 357BQ(8)*).
- If the old IP percentage is at least 20% but less than 80%, that amount of income can be dealt with under the original Patent Box rules, with the remaining income being treated as a separate product sub-stream (*CTA 2010, s 357BQ(9)*).

The old IP percentage is based on the number of qualifying IP rights incorporated into the multi-product item (*CTA 2010, s 357BQ(10)*).

Chapter 14

Research and development

SIGNPOSTS

- Introduction; the meaning of research and development (see **14.1–14.2**).
- How relief for R&D capital expenditure is given through the capital allowances system (see **14.3–14.9**).
- Relief for R&D revenue expenditure incurred on R&D (see **14.10–14.22**).
- The rules specific to SMEs, including subsidised and capped expenditure (see **14.23–14.34**).
- The rules specific to large companies (see **14.35–14.39**).
- The 'above-the-line' expenditure credit for large companies (see **14.40–14.42**).
- Restrictions on R&D and other reliefs, including the going concern requirement, and film, television, video games and theatre tax reliefs (see **14.43–14.44**).
- Tax relief for expenditure on vaccine research, repealed with effect from 1 April 2017 (see **14.45**).
- Claiming R&D reliefs: time limit for claims, and HMRC R&D contact details (see **14.46–14.47**).
- Relief for expenditure incurred on the remediation of contaminated or derelict land (see **14.48–14.67**).

INTRODUCTION

14.1 Relief is available for capital expenditure on research and development (R&D) through the capital allowance rules (*CAA 2001, ss 437–450*), and for revenue expenditure on R&D through the provisions for additional relief for expenditure on in-house and contracted-out R&D (*CTA 2009, ss 1039–1084*).

Similar relief is available for revenue expenditure on vaccine or medicine research (*CTA 2009, ss 1085–1112*).

FA 2013 introduced changes which offer large companies a taxable 'above-the-line' R&D 'expenditure credit' to encourage R&D activity (*CTA 2009, ss 104A–104Y*). The expenditure credit was available at a rate of 10% of qualifying revenue expenditure incurred from 1 April 2013. This was increased to 11% from 1 April 2015 (*CTA 2009, s 104M*, as amended by *FA 2015, s 27(2)*) and to 12% from 1 January 2018 (*CTA 2009, s 104M*, as amended by *FA 2018, s 19(1)*).

This new regime ran as an alternative option alongside the pre-existing additional relief for R&D expenditure incurred by large companies, but replaced it completely with effect from 1 April 2016 (see **14.40–14.42**).

Focus

In order to claim relief for either capital or revenue R&D expenditure, the company must be carrying on a trade connected with the R&D. Therefore, company and group structures must be considered carefully when considering R&D allowances. The reliefs are generous, but often the time taken to generate revenue from an R&D activity is protracted. Careful planning should ensure that a company optimises its cash position, and that it does not accumulate R&D losses and allowances which it is unable to use until an unknown future date.

Meaning of research and development

14.2 For capital allowances purposes, R&D is defined in *CAA 2001, s 437*, and includes oil and gas exploration and appraisal. For relief in respect of revenue expenditure, R&D is defined differently by *CTA 2010, s 1138*, and generally excludes oil and gas exploration and appraisal.

For both capital and revenue purposes, an activity is treated as R&D if normal accounting practice treats it as R&D and it satisfies the conditions set out in Guidelines produced by the Department for Business, Innovation & Skills (BIS) and last updated on 6 December 2010; see HMRC Corporate Intangibles Research and Development Manual at CIRD81300, CIRD81900.

The definition of R&D follows generally accepted accounting practice. This is FRS 102, Section 18 *Intangible assets other than goodwill* under new UK GAAP, SSAP 13 *Accounting for research and development* under old UK GAAP, or IAS 38 *Intangible assets* under international accounting standards. See also **Chapter 26** for changes to UK GAAP.

The definitions in FRS 102 and IAS 38 are as follows:

> 'Research is original and planned investigation undertaken with the prospect of gaining new scientific or technical knowledge and understanding.'
>
> 'Development is the application of research findings or other knowledge to a plan or design for the production of new or substantially improved materials, devices, products, processes, systems or services before the start of commercial production or use.'

The SSAP 13 definition is as follows:

> 'Research and development expenditure means expenditure falling into one or more of the following broad categories (except to the extent that it relates to locating or exploiting oil, gas or mineral deposits or is reimbursable by third parties either directly or under the terms of a firm contract to develop and manufacture at an agreed price calculated to reimburse both elements of expenditure):
>
> (a) Pure (or basic) research: experimental or theoretical work undertaken primarily to acquire new scientific or technical knowledge for its own sake rather than directed towards any specific aim or application.
>
> (b) Applied research: original or critical investigation undertaken in order to gain new scientific or technical knowledge and directed towards a specific practical aim or objective.
>
> (c) Development: use of scientific or technical knowledge in order to produce new or substantially improved materials, devices, products or services, to install new processes or systems prior to the commencement of commercial production or commercial applications, or to improve substantially those already produced or installed.'

HMRC recommend that the tests in the BIS Guidelines are applied before the tests under UK or international GAAP. Essentially, a project qualifies as an R&D project if it is carried on in a field of science or technology and is undertaken with an aim of extending knowledge in a field of science or technology to which the relief applies (CIRD81300).

The BIS Guidelines are reproduced at CIRD81900. Paragraph 19 of the Guidelines defines the meaning of a project:

> 'A project consists of a number of activities conducted to a method or plans in order to achieve an advance in science or technology. It is important to get the boundaries of the project correct. It should encompass all the activities that collectively serve to resolve the scientific or technological uncertainty associated with achieving the advance, so it could include a number of different sub-projects. A project may itself be part of a larger commercial project, but that does not make the parts of the commercial project that do not address scientific or technological uncertainty into R&D.'

Therefore, most research activity needs to be broken down into its separate parts to ascertain whether or not it qualifies as R&D.

In practice, it can be difficult to distinguish between qualifying R&D undertaken in connection with the development of a new product, and other non-qualifying production costs. BIS emphasise that catching up with what many other businesses can already do is not R&D. They say that the work needs to involve a genuine advance, though not necessarily a huge one, in developing scientific or technological knowledge that is not already commonly available. It should involve scientific or technological challenges that have had to be overcome, ie uncertainties that competent professionals cannot readily resolve, where solutions are not common knowledge.

Tax practitioners often make the mistake of assuming that, if a scientific or technical process looks complicated, it must qualify as R&D. This is a misleading approach, usually arising more from practitioners' lack of understanding of the science involved than their true appreciation of whether the work involves a genuine advance in developing scientific or technical knowledge. In many cases, the opinion of a scientific or technical specialist can be invaluable.

R&D CAPITAL EXPENDITURE

Research and development allowances

14.3 R&D allowances may be claimed by any size of company but only if the company carries on a trade. If the company does not already carry on a trade, it will only qualify if it sets up and commences a trade connected with the R&D after incurring the expenditure (*CAA 2001, s 439(1)*). The company need not carry on the R&D itself; a third party may carry on the R&D on the company's behalf. The R&D must be related to the trade that is being carried on, known as 'the relevant trade'. R&D capital allowances are treated as an expense of the trade, and any balancing charge as a receipt of the trade (*CAA 2001, s 450*). Capital R&D expenditure qualifies for a 100% capital allowance (not designated as a 'first year allowance') in the accounting period in which it is incurred (*CAA 2001, s 441*).

Trade-related R&D

14.4 The trade-related R&D may be of a sort that may lead to or facilitate an extension of the company's trade, or it may be of a medical nature which has a special relation to the welfare of workers employed in that trade (*CAA 2001, s 439(5)*).

If the R&D is carried on by a third party on the company's behalf, the company must retain responsibility for the R&D and the expenditure must be undertaken directly.

Example 14.1—Research not directly undertaken

Facts

In *Gaspet Ltd v Ellis* [1987] STC 362, S Ltd had a part share in a petroleum exploration licence. It arranged for G Ltd to provide the funds and the equipment to conduct operations. In return, S Ltd gave G Ltd the rights to the ownership of all the petroleum won and saved to which it was entitled. G Ltd claimed that the expenditure incurred under that agreement qualified as R&D capital expenditure because it was incurred on scientific research directly undertaken on its behalf.

Analysis

G Ltd was not entitled to the R&D capital allowance because the R&D was not directly undertaken by or on behalf of G Ltd.

Medical R&D

14.5 Medical research undertaken for the benefit of the community as a whole may qualify for R&D allowance if it may lead to or facilitate an extension of the trade. For example, medical research undertaken by a drug company for the purpose of its trade may qualify because it is related to its trade of manufacturing drugs (HMRC Capital Allowances Manual at CA60400). R&D expenditure also extends to payments made to clinical trial volunteers for taking part in such tests (*CTA 2009, Sch 2, para 124*).

Qualifying expenditure

14.6 Relief may be claimed on the capital costs of providing facilities to carry out the research (*CAA 2001, s 438*). Land does not qualify for relief, nor does the cost of a dwelling that amounts to more than 25% of the cost of the building (*CAA 2001, s 438(4)*). Expenditure on the acquisition of rights in R&D or rights arising out of R&D does not qualify as R&D (*CAA 2001, s 438(2)*).

Example 14.2—Qualifying research expenditure

Facts

N plc is engaged in a qualifying research project and incurs the following expenditure:

- A building for £2.5 million excluding the cost of the land. The cost of the building is apportioned between research laboratories (£2 million) and living accommodation (£500,000).

- A car for each researcher who is required to travel about the country carrying out research activities.
- The patent rights to a patented invention that N plc considers may be of assistance with the current project.

Analysis

The building, including the living accommodation, will qualify for R&D allowance in full. This is because the cost of the living accommodation is less than 25% of the cost of the whole building.

The costs of the cars will qualify for R&D allowance in full. Note that the restrictions that generally prevent cars from qualifying for 100% first year allowances (see **3.42**) are of no relevance for this purpose.

The cost of acquiring the patent rights does not qualify for R&D allowance because it is expenditure incurred in acquiring rights arising out of R&D.

Any additional VAT liability incurred on the R&D asset after acquisition will also qualify for R&D allowance, provided that the company which incurred the original expenditure on the asset still owns it and the asset has not been demolished or destroyed (*CAA 2001, s 447*; see also CA60750).

Allowances

Focus

If the full 100% R&D allowance is not claimed in the year in which the qualifying capital R&D expenditure is incurred, no further allowances are available on that expenditure.

14.7 An R&D allowance of 100% may be claimed on the expenditure during the accounting period in which the expenditure is incurred. A reduced claim may be made (*CAA 2001, s 441(3)*) but there is no facility to claim further allowances (such as writing down allowances) in subsequent accounting periods.

If ownership of the asset changes hands or if it is destroyed, a disposal value must be included within the company's corporation tax computation. If the asset is sold at not less than market value, the disposal value to be brought into account is the net proceeds of sale. If the asset is lost or destroyed, the disposal value to be brought in is the net amount received for the remains of the asset, together with any insurance money or other capital compensation received. In any other case, the disposal value to be brought in is the market value of the asset at the time of the event (*CAA 2001, s 443*).

In the accounting period of disposal, a balancing charge may arise. The amount of the balancing charge is the smaller of:

- the amount by which the disposal value to be brought into account exceeds any part of the allowance to which the company was entitled but did not claim, and
- the allowance made (*CAA 2001, s 442*).

There is no facility in the legislation for claiming a balancing allowance.

R&D allowances and balancing charges are treated respectively as expenses and receipts of the trade (*CAA 2001, s 450*).

Example 14.3—R&D balancing charge

Facts

In the year of acquisition of a research building on which it would have been entitled to claim R&D allowance of £2.5 million, N plc claims R&D allowance of only £1 million. Some years later, it sells the building for £5 million.

Analysis

The balancing charge is the smaller of:

- the difference between the disposal value and the balance of unclaimed expenditure:

  £5m – £(2.5m – 1m) = £3.5m

and

- the R&D allowance claimed:

  £1m

The balancing charge is therefore £1 million, ie the amount of the R&D claim made.

Change of use

14.8 No R&D allowance is due where an asset, acquired and used for other purposes, begins to be used later for R&D purposes.

If a company acquires an asset for R&D purposes and claims the R&D allowance, and later ceases to use the asset for the R&D purpose, this is not a disposal for R&D purposes and the R&D allowance is not clawed back at this stage – it is only clawed back on the eventual sale of the asset. Following the change of use, the asset may qualify for plant and machinery allowances (see **Chapter 3**).

Disposal value

14.9 If an R&D asset on which an R&D allowance has been claimed is demolished and the demolition costs exceed the disposal value (which, in many cases, may be nil), the excess demolition costs may qualify for R&D allowance. They will only qualify if the asset has not begun to be used for any purpose other than R&D (*CAA 2001, s 445*). The excess is not to be treated as expenditure on any property that replaces the demolished asset.

Any additional VAT rebate arising on the cost of the asset after acquisition will be treated as a disposal value, provided that the company that incurred the original expenditure on the asset still owns it and the asset has not been demolished or destroyed. If there is no unclaimed R&D allowance, the VAT rebate is treated as a balancing charge. If the additional VAT rebate is more than the unclaimed R&D allowance, the difference is treated as a balancing charge. If there is unclaimed R&D allowance and the additional VAT rebate is less than the unclaimed R&D allowance, the additional VAT rebate is deducted from the unclaimed R&D allowance, leaving a reduced unclaimed R&D allowance for the purpose of future disposal events (*CAA 2001, ss 448, 449*; see also CA60750).

R&D REVENUE EXPENDITURE

Revenue deduction

14.10 Tax relief for qualifying revenue expenditure on R&D may be claimed by all companies, regardless of size.

If a company carrying on a trade incurs expenses of a revenue nature on R&D related to its trade and directly undertaken by or on behalf of the company, the expenditure is deductible in computing trading profits (*CTA 2009, s 87*; see also **2.42**).

In *The Vaccine Research Ltd Partnership (the 'Partnership') v Revenue and Customs Commissioners* [2014] UKUT 389 (TCC), a case involving a tax avoidance scheme, the Upper Tribunal restricted a claim for R&D relief to the expense incurred on the relevant R&D activities, while disallowing a substantial fee relating to the tax avoidance scheme as a whole.

Enhanced deduction

14.11 Additional tax relief for qualifying revenue expenditure on R&D may be claimed by all companies, regardless of size. This enhanced deduction is often referred to as the 'super-deduction'.

The rules applying to small or medium-sized companies (SMEs) are contained in *CTA 2009, ss 1043–1073*, and the rules applying to large companies are contained in *CTA 2009, ss 1074–1079*.

Subject to the rules governing the respective schemes, an SME or large company that claims the enhanced deduction receives it as a deduction from trading profits, and this may create or augment a trading loss. If an SME has a 'surrenderable loss' as a result of the enhanced deduction, it may claim an R&D tax credit (ie a cash payment) from HMRC (see **14.26**).

For SMEs, from 1 July 2016, HMRC has the power to request certain information from a company claiming the enhanced deduction or tax credit. The provision of the information will be a condition for granting the relief. These provisions are only exercisable in relation to EU obligations relating to state aid and the information that HMRC will be able to request will include the following:

- information about the company or the company's activities;
- information about the subject matter of the claim; and
- any other information which relates to the grant of state aid through the provision of the relief.

(*FA 2016, ss 180–182, Sch 24*, see **25.5**)

Above-the-line relief

14.12 From 1 April 2013, *FA 2013* introduced a new taxable above-the-line R&D expenditure credit which may be claimed by large companies. This new regime initially ran as an alternative option for large companies, alongside the super-deduction. From 1 April 2016, this mechanism replaced the super-deduction for large companies. For further details of the above-the-line expenditure credit, see **14.40–14.42**.

These reliefs apply only to companies and, for this purpose, the definition of 'company' given in *CTA 2010, s 1121(1)* applies: 'company means any body corporate or unincorporated association but does not include a partnership, a local authority or a local authority association'. The company must be within the charge to corporation tax. A company that participates in a joint venture is eligible in respect of the R&D expenditure which the company itself incurs (CIRD81200). There are special rules for companies in partnership (CIRD81220).

For accounting periods ending before 1 April 2012, a company qualified for the enhanced deduction if R&D expenditure incurred was more than £10,000 in the accounting period; for accounting periods ending on or after 1 April 2012, this threshold no longer applies, thus making the enhanced deduction more accessible to companies with relatively small qualifying R&D spend (*CTA 2009, s 1050*, repealed by *FA 2012, Sch 3, para 3*).

The enhanced deduction is taken into account in computing the adjusted trading profits for tax purposes. A company claims this enhanced relief in its corporation tax return.

Qualifying expenditure 'for an accounting period' is that which is allowable as a deduction in calculating the taxable trading profits for that period. For this purpose, certain pre-trading expenses are treated as incurred on the date on which the trade begins (*CTA 2009, s 61*; see also **2.31**). For expenditure incurred by SMEs before 1 April 2012, the provisions of *CTA 2009, s 61(1)(a)* (pre-trading expenses treated as incurred when trading begins) were ignored (*CTA 2009, s 1099*, repealed by *FA 2012, Sch 3, para 26*).

Relevant research and development

> **Focus**
>
> In practice, claims for the enhanced deduction for expenditure on R&D can be complicated to establish. Companies should ensure that they have full documentation to support their claims.

14.13 The enhanced deduction for revenue expenditure on R&D can be claimed only on 'relevant R&D'. This is defined in *CTA 2009, s 1042(1)* to mean R&D that is related to a trade carried on by the company, or from which it is intended that a trade to be carried on by the company will be derived.

The R&D expenditure related to an existing trade carried on by the company includes R&D expenditure which may lead to or facilitate an extension of that trade, as well as R&D expenditure of a medical nature which has a special relation to the welfare of workers employed in that trade (*CTA 2009, s 1042(2)*). However, the special provisions which provide relief for certain vaccine or medicine research apply regardless of whether or not there is any special relation to the welfare of workers employed in the trade (*CTA 2009, ss 1042(3), 1085–1112*; see **14.45**).

From 1 April 2012, relief for vaccine or medical research is only available to large companies – it is no longer available to SMEs (*FA 2012, Sch 3, para 16*).

Qualifying R&D expenditure on in-house direct R&D

14.14 The rules to determine which in-house R&D revenue expenditure qualifies for both SMEs and large companies are similar but not identical. They can be summarised broadly as follows:

- the expenditure must be incurred on staffing costs (see **14.15**), software or consumable items (see **14.16**), qualifying expenditure on externally provided workers (see **14.17**), or on relevant payments to the subjects of a clinical trial (see **14.18**);

- the expenditure must be attributable to relevant R&D directly undertaken by the company or on its behalf;
- the expenditure must not be incurred by the company in carrying on activities which are contracted out to the company by any third party (except, in the case of the large company scheme, either (a) another large company or (b) any person otherwise than in the course of a trade, profession or vocation the profits of which are chargeable to tax as profits of a trade); and
- the expenditure must not be subsidised (SME scheme only; see **14.19**).

The requirements for qualifying expenditure on in-house direct R&D are set out in the legislation – for SMEs in *CTA 2009, s 1052*, and for large companies in *CTA 2009, s 1077*.

Staffing costs

14.15 For SMEs and large companies, staffing costs of directors or employees for R&D purposes include earnings in money, secondary Class 1 National Insurance contributions (NICs), employer's contributions to a UK staff pension fund and compulsory contributions under the social security legislation of another EEA state or Switzerland. Benefits in kind are not included (*CTA 2009, s 1123*).

Staffing costs attributable to R&D include the staffing costs for all directors and employees actively engaged in the R&D. Staffing costs for employees only partly engaged in research are apportioned appropriately. Secretarial and administrative costs are excluded (*CTA 2009, s 1124*).

The expenditure must be incurred by the company making the claim. In *Gripple Ltd v Revenue and Customs Comrs* [2010] EWHC 1609 (Ch), a company made a salary payment to a director for R&D work and recharged the payment to the company within the group that was actually carrying out the R&D. The company carrying out the R&D was denied relief because it had not made the salary payment to the director.

Software or consumable items

14.16 Expenditure on computer software and consumable or transformable items is relevant R&D expenditure. Consumable or transformable materials include water, fuel and power (*CTA 2009, ss 1125, 1126*).

From 1 April 2015, new rules restrict the extent to which costs of materials and other consumable items are eligible for relief. In the circumstances where the R&D activity results in goods or services sold in the normal course of a company's business, the cost of consumable items reflected in those goods or services do not attract tax credits. Qualifying expenditure on consumable items is limited to the cost of only those items fully used up or expended by the R&D activity itself, and not any that go on to be sold as part of a commercial product. The restriction does not apply where the product of the R&D is transferred as waste, or where it is transferred but no consideration is received (*CTA 2009, ss 1126A–1126B*, as inserted by *FA 2015, s 28*).

Externally provided workers

14.17 Externally provided workers are individuals engaged on the project who are not employed by the company but are under the company's supervision. From 1 April 2012 the rules defining an externally provided worker were extended to recognise the possible involvement of a 'staff controller' separate and distinct from the 'staff provider', to allow for cases where additional parties are involved in providing workers (*CTA 2009, ss 1127–1132*). Self-employed consultants are not externally provided workers, although their costs may form part of sub-contracted R&D (CIRD84100).

If the company and the staff provider (or, from 1 April 2012, the company, the staff provider and (if different) the staff controller (or staff controllers)) are all connected, and in accordance with GAAP:

- the whole of the staff provision payment has been brought into account in determining the staff provider's profit or loss for a relevant period, and
- all of the relevant expenditure of each staff controller has been brought into account in determining the staff controller's profit or loss for a relevant period,

the company may claim R&D tax credit on the lower of:

- the qualifying payment for staff that it makes to the staff provider, and
- the aggregate of the amounts that the staff controllers include as relevant revenue expenditure in their accounts (*CTA 2009, s 1129*).

For this purpose, the relevant period is a period ending not more than 12 months after the end of the accounting period in which the company claiming the R&D allowance makes the payment.

If the company and the staff provider (or, from 1 April 2012, the company, the staff provider and (if different) the staff controller (or staff controllers)) are not all connected, only 65% of the staff provision payment cost is treated as qualifying expenditure on externally provided workers. However, in such circumstances they may jointly elect in writing, within two years of the end of the accounting period in which the contract arrangement is entered into, for the connected persons treatment to apply; this election has effect in relation to all staff under the same arrangement (*CTA 2009, ss 1130, 1131*).

Relevant payments to the subjects of a clinical trial

14.18 Relevant payments to the subjects of clinical trials are payments made to individuals for the purposes of participating in an investigation in human subjects undertaken in connection with the development of a health care treatment or procedure (*CTA 2009, s 1140*).

Subsidised expenditure

14.19 A company's expenditure is treated as subsidised if a notified state aid is, or has been, obtained in respect of the whole or part of the expenditure, or any other expenditure (whenever incurred) attributable to the same R&D project. 'Notified state aid' is a state aid notified to and approved by the European Commission (*CTA 2009, s 1138*). The subsidised expenditure requirement only applies to SMEs. Therefore, an SME that fails the subsidised expenditure test may be entitled to claim large company relief (see **14.27**).

Intellectual property

14.20 'Intellectual property' includes (*CTA 2009, s 1139*):

- any industrial information or technique likely to assist in:
  - the manufacture or processing of goods or materials; or
  - the working of a mine, oil well or other source of mineral deposits, or the winning of access thereto; or
  - the carrying out of any agricultural, forestry or fishing operations;
- any patent, trademark, registered design, copyright, design right or plant breeder's right or overseas equivalent.

The intellectual property, if vested, should be vested at the time when the intellectual property is created.

Qualifying expenditure on contracted-out R&D incurred by an SME

14.21 An SME's payments to its sub-contractors are qualifying expenditure if they meet all of the following conditions (*CTA 2009, s 1053*):

- the expenditure is attributable to relevant R&D undertaken on behalf of the company;
- the expenditure is not incurred by the company in carrying on activities which are contracted out to the company by any person; and

- the expenditure is not subsidised.

Qualifying expenditure on contracted-out R&D incurred by a large company

14.22 A large company's expenditure on contracted-out R&D is qualifying expenditure if all of the following conditions are met (*CTA 2009, s 1078*):

- the expenditure is incurred in making payments to:
  - a qualifying body,
  - an individual, or
  - a firm, each member of which is an individual,

  in respect of R&D contracted out by the company to the body, individual or firm;
- the R&D is undertaken by the body, individual or firm itself;
- the expenditure is attributable to relevant R&D in relation to the company; and
- if the contracted-out R&D is itself contracted out to the company, it is contracted out by a large company, or by any person otherwise than in the course of carrying on a chargeable trade.

RULES SPECIFIC TO SMES

14.23 An SME is defined in accordance with the *European Recommendation*, as detailed in *CTA 2009, ss 1119(1)–(2), 1120(2)–(7)* and *Sch 2, para 118(1)–(3)*.

The following definitions of medium, small and micro-size companies apply for R&D purposes:

	Medium	*Small*	*Micro*
If the company has fewer than	500 employees	50 employees	10 employees
And			
either an annual turnover not exceeding	€100m	€10m	€2m
Or			
a balance sheet total not exceeding	€86m	€10m	€2m

(*Commission Recommendation 2003/361/EC* of 6 May 2003)

Basis of definition of an SME

14.24 The staff head count is based on the number of full-time person years attributable to people who have worked within or for the concern during the year in question. Part-time, seasonal and temporary workers are included on a pro-rata basis.

'Employees' includes actual employees, persons seconded to the enterprise, owner-managers and partners (other than sleeping partners). Apprentices or students engaged in vocational training with an apprenticeship or vocational training contract are excluded, as also are any periods of maternity or parental leave.

Turnover is taken per the accounts (net of VAT).

The balance sheet total is the gross amount of assets shown in the accounts. Results are converted from sterling to euros to ascertain whether the tests are met.

The EC defines the enterprise as either autonomous, linked or partner. Autonomous means that there are no partner or linked enterprises. A linked enterprise is an enterprise whereby one company is able to exercise control directly or indirectly over the other. A partner enterprise exists where the enterprises are not linked but where one enterprise is able to exercise control either directly or indirectly over the affairs of the other. If a company has partner or linked enterprise relationships, the results are aggregated (see flowchart at CIRD92850).

The conditions are relaxed for public investment corporations, venture capital companies (VCCs), 'business angels' (provided the total investment of those business angels in the same enterprise is less than €1.25 million), universities or non-profit research centres, and institutional investors, including regional development funds and autonomous local authorities with an annual budget of less than €10 million and fewer than 5,000 inhabitants. The case of *Pyreos Ltd v Revenue and Customs Commissioners* [2015] UKFTT 123 (TC) concerned VCC status in this context. The case of *Monitor Audio Ltd v Revenue and Customs Commissioners* [2015] UKFTT 357 (TC) did likewise and also considered institutional investor status.

Over time, as the company's trade and business activities develop and it increases its staff and its financial performance, it may find that its status changes from SME to large company. In this case, a transition period allows the SME status to be retained until the limits have been exceeded for two consecutive accounting periods. Similarly, if a large company decreases in size or demerges from a larger group of entities, it will not attain SME status until the head count and the financial limits have been met for two consecutive accounting periods.

The situation is different where an SME is taken over by a single large company or a collection of smaller entities which, when taken together, are regarded as large. Where such an event occurs during an accounting period, the company loses its SME status for the whole of the accounting period concerned (Revenue & Customs Brief 55/2008, 17 November 2008, tinyurl.com/oclnzl7).

Tax relief for expenditure on research and development

14.25 An SME qualifies for an enhanced deduction from trading profits on its qualifying R&D expenditure amounts (*CTA 2009, s 1044*).

Qualifying expenditure is expenditure that would be allowable as a deduction in computing the taxable profits of a trade carried on by the company, or would have been allowable if the trade were being carried on at the time that the expenditure was incurred. See **14.11** regarding pre-trading expenditure incurred by an SME before 1 April 2012.

The SME is allowed tax relief for its qualifying R&D expenditure in accordance with the ordinary rules for revenue expenditure, plus an additional deduction in calculating its profits, and these amount in total to an enhanced deduction which is expressed as a percentage of the R&D expenditure (*CTA 2009, s 1044*; *FA 2012, Sch 3, para 2*):

Date expenditure incurred	*Enhanced deduction*
On or after 1 April 2015 (*FA 2015, s 27*)	230%
1 April 2012 to 31 March 2015	225%
1 April 2011 to 31 March 2012	200%
1 August 2008 to 31 March 2011	175%
Before 1 August 2008	150%

For the SME to obtain the enhanced deduction, it must make a claim for this on its corporation tax return (*CTA 2009, s 1044(6)*; see **14.46, 14.47**).

For accounting periods ending before 1 April 2012, the enhanced deduction was only available if R&D expenditure incurred was more than £10,000 in the accounting period (*CTA 2009, s 1050*, repealed by *FA 2012, Sch 3, para 3*).

Following a consultation on improving access to R&D tax credits for smaller companies, the government has announced that it will introduce voluntary advanced assurances lasting three years for smaller businesses making a first claim from autumn 2015, reduce the time taken to process claims from 2016, and produce new standalone guidance aimed specifically at smaller companies (Budget, 18 March 2015, tinyurl.com/oewrc3l, para 2.128).

R&D deemed trading losses and payable tax credits

14.26 If an SME incurs qualifying R&D expenditure but has not yet started the trade to which it relates, it may elect to treat the enhanced R&D deduction as a trading loss of the accounting period in which the expenditure was incurred. In this case, the normal treatment of pre-trading expenditure under *CTA 2009, s 61* does not apply (*CTA 2009, s 1045*). The deemed trading loss may not be set off against profits of a preceding accounting period (where *CTA 2010, s 37(3)(b)* applies) unless it is also entitled to a deemed trading loss for that earlier period (*CTA 2009, s 1048*). The election must be made in writing to an officer of HMRC within two years of the accounting period to which the loss relates (*CTA 2009, s 1045*).

Where an SME has a 'surrenderable loss' for an accounting period, it may claim a payable R&D tax credit. A company has a surrenderable loss if it incurs a loss which includes R&D relief for direct expenditure incurred in that period, or is treated as incurring a loss in respect of pre-trading expenditure. The amount of the surrenderable loss for the purposes of a claim to R&D tax credit is:

- so much of the trading loss as is unrelieved, or
- if less, the enhanced deduction in respect of the qualifying R&D expenditure in respect of which the relief was obtained (*CTA 2009, s 1055*).

For this purpose, the amount of a trading loss that is unrelieved is the amount of that loss reduced by:

- any relief that was or could have been obtained by the company making a claim to set the loss against total profits of the same accounting period;
- any other relief obtained by the company in respect of the loss, including relief against profits of an earlier accounting period; and
- any loss surrendered to group or consortium members.

Losses brought forward to, or carried back from, the accounting period in question are disregarded (*CTA 2009, s 1056*).

Where an SME makes a claim for an R&D tax credit to which it is entitled for an accounting period, HMRC must pay the amount of the tax credit to the company. The amount of the R&D tax credit is a specified percentage of the surrenderable loss for the period, as follows (*CTA 2009, ss 1054–1060*):

Date expenditure incurred	*Rate of R&D tax credit*
On or after 1 April 2014	14.5%
1 April 2012 to 31 March 2014	11%
1 April 2011 to 31 March 2012	12.5%
1 August 2008 to 31 March 2011	14%
Before 1 August 2008	16%

HMRC need not make any payment in respect of an R&D tax credit if the SME has any outstanding PAYE and NIC liabilities for the period in question (*CTA 2009, s 1060(6)*).

For accounting periods ending before 1 April 2012, the payment of R&D tax credit to an SME cannot exceed the total of the company's PAYE and NIC liabilities for payment periods ending in the accounting period. Employee child tax credits, working tax credit, statutory sick pay and statutory maternity pay are ignored in these calculations. For accounting periods ending on or after 1 April 2012, this restriction to the level of the company's PAYE and NIC liabilities no longer applies, thus making the R&D tax credit more accessible to a wider range of SMEs (*CTA 2009, s 1059*, repealed by *FA 2012, Sch 3, para 15*).

The time limit for an SME to make a claim for R&D tax credit is two years from the end of the relevant accounting period, and the relief is claimed on the company's corporation tax return (see **14.46**, **14.47**). Receipt of an R&D tax credit is not treated as income of the company for any tax purposes (*CTA 2009, s 1061*).

These R&D tax credits are only available to SMEs. If the SME is owned by a consortium, no R&D relief may be surrendered to any group company that is not an SME (*CTA 2009, s 1049*).

Relief for SMEs: subsidised and capped expenditure on R&D

Additional deduction in calculating profits of trade

> **Focus**
>
> In certain circumstances, an SME may claim R&D relief under the rules relating to large companies.

14.27 An SME may incur R&D expenditure that would have qualified for relief under the SME scheme but fails to qualify only because it is:

- subsidised expenditure (see **14.19**) on in-house direct R&D (*CTA 2009, s 1071*; see **14.28**);
- subsidised expenditure on contracted-out R&D (*CTA 2009, s 1072*; see **14.29**); or
- capped R&D expenditure (*CTA 2009, s 1073*; see **14.30**).

In these circumstances, the SME can either:

- claim an additional 30% of this expenditure (if incurred before 1 April 2016) as a deduction from its trading profits under the large company scheme if the expenditure would have been allowable had the SME been a large company (*CTA 2009, s 1068*; CIRD89000; see **14.35–14.39**). For accounting periods ending before 1 April 2012, this enhanced deduction was only available if R&D expenditure incurred was more than £10,000 in the accounting period (*CTA 2009, s 1050*, repealed by *FA 2012, Sch 3, para 3*); or
- claim an 'above the line' R&D expenditure credit in respect of the expenditure (if incurred on or after 1 April 2013) under the new scheme for large companies (see **14.40–14.42**) under the provisions for subsidised or capped R&D expenditure (*CTA 2009, ss 104F–104I*).

Subsidised qualifying expenditure on in-house direct R&D

14.28 An SME's subsidised qualifying expenditure on in-house direct R&D is expenditure that meets all the following conditions (*CTA 2009, s 1071*):

- the expenditure is subsidised (see **14.19**);
- the expenditure is:
  - incurred on staffing costs (see **14.15**),
  - incurred on software or consumable items (see **14.16**),
  - qualifying expenditure on externally provided workers (see **14.17**), or
  - incurred on relevant payments to the subjects of a clinical trial (see **14.18**);
- the expenditure is attributable to relevant R&D undertaken by the company itself; and
- the expenditure is not incurred by the company in carrying on activities which are contracted out to the company by any person.

Subsidised qualifying expenditure on contracted-out R&D

14.29 An SME's subsidised qualifying expenditure on contracted-out R&D is expenditure that meets all the following conditions (*CTA 2009, s 1072*):

- the expenditure is subsidised (see **14.19**);
- the sub-contractor is:
  - a qualifying body,

   - an individual, or
   - a firm each member of which is an individual;
- the body, individual or firm concerned undertakes the contracted-out R&D itself; and
- the expenditure is not incurred by the company in carrying on activities which are contracted out to the company by any person.

Capped R&D expenditure

14.30 Capped R&D expenditure is any expenditure on which the company is not entitled to relief because of a cap on R&D aid (see **14.34**), which is not qualifying R&D sub-contracted expenditure, and which would have qualified as large company expenditure had the company been a large company throughout the accounting period in question (*CTA 2009, s 1073*).

R&D sub-contracted to an SME

Additional deduction in calculating profits of trade

14.31 An SME that incurs expenditure relating to sub-contracted in-house or external R&D, contracted out to it by a large company, or any person that is not carrying on a trade, can claim an additional 30% of this expenditure as a deduction from its trading profits (*CTA 2009, ss 1063, 1065*). For accounting periods ending before 1 April 2012, the enhanced deduction was only available if R&D expenditure incurred was more than £10,000 in the accounting period (*CTA 2009, s 1050*, repealed by *FA 2012, Sch 3, para 3*).

Expenditure on sub-contracted R&D undertaken in-house

14.32 Three conditions are to be met in order for expenditure to qualify as sub-contracted R&D undertaken in-house (*CTA 2009, s 1066*):

- the R&D is undertaken by the SME itself;
- the expenditure is:
   - incurred on staffing costs (see **14.15**),
   - incurred on software or consumable items (see **14.16**),
   - qualifying expenditure on externally provided workers (see **14.17**), or
   - incurred on relevant payments to the subjects of a clinical trial (see **14.18**); and

- the expenditure is attributable to relevant R&D in relation to the company (see **14.13**).

Expenditure on sub-contracted R&D not undertaken in-house

14.33 Three conditions are to be met in order for expenditure to qualify as sub-contracted R&D not undertaken in-house (*CTA 2009, s 1067*):

- the expenditure is incurred in making payments to:
  - a qualifying body,
  - an individual, or
  - a firm, each member of which is an individual,

  in respect of R&D contracted out by the company to the body, individual or firm;
- the R&D is undertaken by the body, individual or firm itself; and
- the expenditure is attributable to relevant R&D in relation to the company (see **14.13**).

Cap on 'R&D aid'

14.34 The maximum 'R&D aid' that an SME may claim in respect of R&D expenditure incurred on an R&D project is restricted to €7.5 million (*CTA 2009, ss 1113–1118*). Note that this limit also extends to vaccine research relief claimed by a large company (*CTA 2009, s 1113(4)(b)*; see **14.45**).

The total R&D aid in respect of expenditure by a company attributable to an R&D project is calculated according to the following formula:

$$A = (TC + R + (P \times CT)) - N \times CT)$$

where:

- A is total R&D aid
- TC is total tax credits paid to the claimant in respect of expenditure attributable to that project, plus claims made but not paid or applied unless refused by HMRC
- R is actual reduction in tax liability in respect of expenditure attributable to that project for all accounting periods concerned, including such reductions for all companies concerned if a group or consortia exists and group relief has been claimed
- P is potential relief, being the aggregate of all relief other than a tax credit, for which the claimant has made a claim or election, unless refused by HMRC

- CT is the main rate of corporation tax at the time when the total R&D aid is calculated
- N is notional relief that the company could have claimed if it were a large company throughout the accounting period.

From 1 April 2016, large companies must claim the R&D expenditure credit. Accordingly, the formula is adjusted to:

$$A = (TC + R + (P \times CT)) - N$$

where N is notional R&D expenditure credit that the company could have claimed if it were a large company throughout the accounting period (*FA 2016, s 48*).

Example 14.4—R&D aid cap

Facts

The Wonderco Ltd is an SME that makes up accounts to 31 March each year. It incurs expenditure on one project that qualifies for R&D. The company wishes to know the amount of R&D relief available for the year ended 31 March 2016.

The company has received the following R&D relief:

Year ended 31 March 2013	R&D reduction in tax liability	£2m
Year ended 31 March 2014	R&D tax credit	£1m
Year ended 31 March 2015	R&D reduction in tax liability	£3m

The rate of corporation tax for the year ended 31 March 2016 is 20%. The £/€ exchange rate is 1/1.36.

If the company were to have been a large company, it could have qualified for aggregate relief of £4 million for the years ended 31 March 2013 and 2015. There are no claims outstanding.

Analysis

The company's total R&D aid is calculated as follows:

$$\text{Aid} = £(1 + 7 + (0 \times 20\%)) - (4 \times 20\%)\text{m} = £5.2\text{m}$$

Converted to euros, this total R&D aid amounts to:

$$€(5.2\text{m} \times 1.36) = €7{,}072{,}710$$

This falls short of the limit of €7.2m by €127,290 = £(127,290 ÷ 1.36) = £93,596

The maximum R&D relief available for the year ended 31 March 2016 is therefore £93,596.

RULES SPECIFIC TO LARGE COMPANIES

Tax relief for expenditure on research and development

14.35 For expenditure incurred on or before 31 March 2016, a large company may claim an enhanced deduction from trading profits of 130% of its qualifying R&D expenditure – much less generous than the SME scheme (see **14.25**). For accounting periods ending before 1 April 2012, the enhanced deduction was only available if R&D expenditure incurred was more than £10,000 in the accounting period (*CTA 2009, s 1050*, repealed by *FA 2012, Sch 3, para 3*).

Qualifying expenditure is expenditure that would be allowable as a deduction in computing the taxable profits of a trade carried on by the company, or would have been allowable if the trade were being carried on at the time that the expenditure was incurred.

For relevant R&D expenditure incurred on or after 1 April 2013, an above-the-line expenditure credit is available to a large company as an alternative to the enhanced deduction (see **14.40–14.42**). The enhanced deduction ceased to be available to large companies with effect from 1 April 2016.

Qualifying R&D expenditure

14.36 Large company R&D includes not only direct R&D expenditure (as discussed in **14.10** onwards) but also sub-contracted R&D and contributions to independent R&D (*CTA 2009, s 1076*).

Sub-contracted R&D

14.37 R&D sub-contracted by a large company may qualify for relief if it is sub-contracted to an individual, or a partnership made up of individuals. It may also qualify for relief if it is sub-contracted to a qualifying body. A qualifying body is a charity, a higher education institution, a scientific research organisation or a health service body.

The research carried out must be relevant research directly undertaken on the company's behalf. In addition, if the sub-contracted work is itself contracted out to the company, it must be contracted out by a large company or by a person otherwise than in the course of that person's trade (*CTA 2009, s 1078*).

Contributions to independent research and development

14.38 Contributions by a large company to independent R&D qualify for relief if the expenditure in question (known as 'the funded R&D') is incurred in making payments to an individual, or a partnership made up of individuals, or a qualifying body (see **14.37**). The company must not be connected with the individual or any individual in the partnership when the payment is made. In addition, the funded R&D must not be contracted out to the qualifying body, the individual or the partnership concerned by another person (*CTA 2009, s 1079*).

Location

14.39 There is no statutory provision restricting the location of the R&D work carried out. In *Laboratoire Fournier SA v Direction des Verifications Nationales et Internationales* (Case C-39/04), the ECJ ruled that *Art 49* of the *EC Treaty* precluded legislation of a member state which restricted the benefit of an R&D tax credit to R&D carried out in that member state.

'ABOVE-THE-LINE' EXPENDITURE CREDIT FOR LARGE COMPANIES

Introduction

Focus

By encouraging large companies to account for R&D 'expenditure credit' in calculating their pre-tax profits, and by offering a payable credit to large companies with no corporation tax liabilities, the government believes that the above-the-line credit makes R&D relief more effective at influencing large company investment decisions and will help to increase the overall level of R&D activity in the UK.

14.40 For R&D expenditure incurred on or after 1 April 2013, large companies could claim an 'above-the-line' R&D expenditure credit. As previously explained, this became mandatory from 1 April 2016 but was an alternative to the super-deduction between 1 April 2013 and 31 March 2016.

The computed amount of the R&D expenditure credit is payable in cash to companies that have no corporation tax liability. This contrasts with the pre-existing R&D enhanced deduction, under which companies must wait until they enter profit before they receive any benefit.

Key features of the above-the-line R&D expenditure credit are as follows:

- a direct cash credit reduces the R&D cost in the company's accounts;
- the value of the credit depends on the company's qualifying R&D expenditure;

- a payable credit is available to loss makers; and
- increased pre-tax profits for companies, which could attract internationally mobile R&D capital.

The expenditure credit is calculated directly from a large company's eligible R&D revenue expenditure, instead of being an adjustment to the company's taxable profit, as under the pre-existing R&D tax credit.

The underlying rules for identifying qualifying activity and calculating qualifying revenue expenditure remain unchanged from the pre-existing R&D scheme for large companies, and the new expenditure credit is calculated as a percentage by reference to the amount of qualifying expenditure on R&D.

For relevant R&D expenditure incurred on or after 1 January 2018, the above-the-line expenditure credit is available to large companies at a pre-tax rate of 12% (*CTA 2009, s 104M*, as amended by *FA 2018, s 19(1)*). From 1 April 2015 to 31 December 2017 the rate was 11% (*CTA 2009, s 104M*, as amended by *FA 2015, s 27(2)*). On expenditure from 1 April 2013 to 31 March 2015, the rate was 10%. The expenditure credit is taxable.

For expenditure from 1 April 2016 onwards, the expenditure credit replaced the enhanced deduction for large companies. From 1 April 2013 to 31 March 2015, the expenditure credit was an alternative to the enhanced relief for R&D expenditure.

For expenditure incurred on or after 1 August 2015, institutions of higher education (as defined by *CTA 2009, s 1142(1)(b)*) and charities are ineligible for R&D expenditure credit, and the Treasury has power to prescribe other companies as ineligible (*CTA 2009, s 104WA*, as inserted by *F(No 2)A 2015, s 30*).

Following consultation, the government stated in 2013 that it was not proposing to replace the existing SME R&D tax credit regime with a taxable above-the-line R&D expenditure credit, and it was not planning to reduce the level of R&D tax relief available to SMEs.

Entitlement to R&D expenditure credit

14.41 A company carrying on a trade and incurring qualifying R&D expenditure may claim an R&D expenditure credit, to be brought into account as a receipt in calculating the profits of its trade for an accounting period (*CTA 2009, s 104A*).

For this purpose:

- where the company is an SME at any time in the accounting period, its qualifying R&D expenditure is:
  - its qualifying expenditure on sub-contracted R&D,
  - its subsidised qualifying expenditure, and

  - its capped R&D expenditure, or
- where the company is a large company throughout the accounting period, its qualifying R&D expenditure is:
  - its qualifying expenditure on in-house direct R&D,
  - its qualifying expenditure on contracted-out R&D, and
  - its qualifying expenditure on contributions to independent R&D.

A company may not claim both an R&D expenditure credit and an enhanced deduction under the pre-existing R&D scheme, in respect of the same expenditure (*CTA 2009, s 104B*). Once a company has claimed R&D expenditure credit for the first time, the R&D enhanced deduction ceases to be available to it from the beginning of the accounting period in question; it has effectively elected into the expenditure credit regime and that election is irrevocable (*FA 2013, Sch 15, para 29*; CIRD89705).

The R&D expenditure credit regime adopts, without change, the definitions of all the underlying terms and the conditions which must be met in order to claim the pre-existing enhanced deduction (*CTA 2009, ss 104C–104L*, as inserted by *FA 2013, Sch 15, para 1*). It does so by incorporating pre-existing R&D provisions from *CTA 2009, Pt 13, Chs 3–5* until their repeal with effect from 1 April 2016.

Example 14.5—Comparison of enhanced deduction and expenditure credit

Facts

In the year to 31 March 2016, Research Co plc spends £2 million on an R&D project, of which £1 million is eligible for R&D tax relief. It then receives a total of £2.4 million in income from the project.

Research Co plc could choose to claim R&D enhanced deduction under the pre-existing large company R&D scheme. Alternatively, it could opt to claim above-the-line R&D expenditure credit, which provides pre-tax financial support worth 11% of the eligible R&D spend, taxable at the main corporation tax rate of 20%.

If Research Co plc claims the new expenditure credit equal to £100,000 for the project, its reported profit would be increased by the amount of the above-the-line credit, assuming that this treatment is in accordance with GAAP.

Analysis

The relative impacts of the pre-existing enhanced deduction and the new expenditure credit can be compared as follows:

	Pre-existing R&D tax relief (£000)		*'Above the line' credit (£000)*	
Turnover		2,400		2,400
R&D expenditure	(1,000)		(1,000)	
Above-the-line credit 11%	–		110	
	(1,000)		(890)	
Other expenditure	(1,000)		(1,000)	
		2,000		1,890
Profit/(loss)		400		510
Enhanced deduction 30%		(300)		–
Taxable profit/loss		100		510
Tax @20%		20		102
Benefit to company compared:				
Profit/(loss) less tax		380		408
Tax saving on enhanced deduction		60		
Above-the-line credit after tax at 20%				88

If the company had been loss-making, the above-the-line expenditure credit could nonetheless provide benefit by allowing the company to claim a repayable expenditure credit under *CTA 2009, s 104S* (see **14.42**).

How R&D expenditure credit is given

Focus

As with the enhanced deduction, claims for the above-the-line R&D expenditure credit are complex to establish, and companies should ensure that they have full documentation to support their claims. The steps involved in working out how the expenditure credit is given are also complicated.

14.42 The amount of the R&D expenditure credit for an accounting period is the relevant percentage of the company's qualifying R&D expenditure for that period. The percentage is 49% for a ring fence trade (as defined by *CTA 2010, s 277* for oil-related activities). In all other cases, the percentage is 12% from 1 January 2018, 11% for expenditure incurred from 1 April 2015 to 31 December 2017, and 10% for expenditure incurred from 1 April 2013 to

31 March 2015. The rates of expenditure credit may be changed by Treasury order (*CTA 2009, s 104M*).

Where a company is entitled to an R&D expenditure credit for an accounting period, the amount of the credit ('the set-off amount') is treated in the following way (*CTA 2009, ss 104N, 104NA*):

Step 1

The set-off amount is applied in discharging any liability to corporation tax for the accounting period.

Step 2

If any balance remains:

- first determine 'the net value of the set-off amount' under *CTA 2009, s 104N(2A)* by deducting from the set-off amount the corporation tax that would be chargeable on it if it had not included any amount treated as R&D expenditure credit by virtue of Step 3 (below), using the main rate of corporation tax (or, in the case of ring fence profits, the ring fence rate and the supplementary charge);
- if the balance remaining after Step 1 exceeds the net value of the set-off amount, the balance carried forward to Step 3 (below) is to be reduced to the net value of the set-off amount, and
- the excess ('the Step 2 amount'), if any, may be used in accordance with complex rules set out in *CTA 2009, s 104NA*; broadly, it may be surrendered in whole or in part to other group companies (if any) to the extent that this is effective (see *CTA 2009, s 104Q*), or otherwise applied in discharging any liability of the company to pay corporation tax for any subsequent accounting period. Any surrender is not taken into account in determining the profits or losses of either company for corporation tax purposes, and is not to be regarded as a distribution.

Step 3

If any remaining amount is greater than the company's total PAYE and NIC in respect of R&D, it is capped at that latter amount, and the amount thus disallowed is treated as an amount of R&D expenditure credit for the next accounting period. The government claims that this cap is designed as a safeguard against abuse in cases where expenditure credit is paid to companies with no corporation tax liability; in practice, it could severely restrict R&D claims involving large costs other than payroll (eg sub-contractors, materials or software) and claims in respect of foreign branches.

Step 4

If any balance remains, it is applied in discharging any corporation tax liability of the company for any other accounting period.

Step 5

If any balance remains and the company is a member of a group, it may (if it wishes) surrender the whole or any part of the balance to any other member of the group to the extent that this is effective (see *CTA 2009, s 104Q*).

Step 6

If any balance remains, it is applied in discharging any other liability of the company to pay any sum to HMRC, whether under any enactment or under a contract settlement.

Step 7

If any balance remains, it is paid to the company by HMRC, subject to the following restrictions (*CTA 2009, s 104S*):

- If the company was not a going concern at the time of its claim, the amount at Step 7 is not payable but is extinguished, unless the company becomes a going concern on or before the last day on which an amendment of the company's tax return for the accounting period could be made under *FA 1998, Sch 18, para 15*.
- In the case of an enquiry into the company's tax return for the accounting period, the HMRC officer may withhold the amount at Step 7 or may make a provisional payment of such amount as he thinks fit.
- No payment of the amount at Step 7 need be made if the company has outstanding PAYE and NIC liabilities for the accounting period.

Specific provisions address the treatment of group companies and insurance companies (*CTA 2009, ss 104U–104W*).

Any transaction attributable to arrangements entered into wholly or mainly for a disqualifying purpose is disregarded for the purpose of calculating R&D expenditure credit. Arrangements include any scheme, agreement or understanding, whether legally enforceable or not, that are entered into wholly or mainly for a disqualifying purpose if their main object, or one of their main objects, is to enable a company to obtain or augment an R&D expenditure credit (*CTA 2009, s 104X*).

R&D expenditure credit is administered and settled through the tax system, and companies that claim it are responsible for self-assessing it. HMRC guidance on the R&D expenditure credit can be found at CIRD89700–CIRD89950.

RESTRICTIONS ON R&D AND OTHER RELIEFS

Going concern

14.43 R&D tax credits for SMEs, vaccine research tax credits for SMEs (until they were abolished with effect from 1 April 2012) and R&D expenditure credits may be claimed only if the claimant company is a going concern. If a company ceases to be a going concern after its claim is made but before it has been paid or applied, the claim is treated as though it had not been made (*CTA 2009, ss 104S, 104T, 1057, 1106*).

A company is a going concern for this purpose if its latest published accounts were prepared on a going concern basis and nothing in those accounts indicates that they were only prepared on that basis because of an expectation that the company would receive R&D relief or R&D tax credits. 'Publication' is interpreted in accordance with the *Companies Act* in that the accounts are circulated in a way that invites members of the public or a class of members of the public to read them (*CA 2006, s 436(2)*; *CTA 2009, s 1106*).

For the purposes of R&D tax credit claims and elections made by SMEs on or after 1 April 2012, and R&D expenditure credits since their inception on 1 April 2013, a company in liquidation or administration under UK or equivalent foreign law is not a going concern (*CTA 2009, ss 104T(2)–(4), 1057(4A)–(4C)*).

Film, television, video games and theatre tax reliefs

14.44 Where a company has incurred expenditure on which it is entitled to an R&D expenditure credit, or on which it has obtained an enhanced R&D deduction, then in respect of the same expenditure it is not entitled to claim (*CTA 2009, ss 104BA, 1040ZA*):

- film tax relief (*CTA 2009, s 1195(3A)*; see **15.2–15.10**),
- television tax relief (*CTA 2009, s 1216C(4)*; see **15.11–15.19**),
- video games tax relief (*CTA 2009, s 1217C(4)*; see **15.20–15.27**), or
- theatre tax relief (*CTA 2009, s 1217JA(2)*; see **15.28–15.36**).

TAX RELIEF FOR EXPENDITURE ON VACCINE RESEARCH

14.45 For expenditure incurred on or after 1 April 2012, relief for qualifying vaccine or medical research ('vaccine research relief') is available to large companies in accordance with rules broadly similar to those which apply for R&D relief (*CTA 2009, s 1085* onwards). For expenditure incurred before 1 April 2012, vaccine research relief was also available to SMEs (*CTA 2009, s 1085*, before amendment by *FA 2012, Sch 3, para 21*).

For large companies (and, before 1 April 2012, SMEs), vaccine research relief is an additional relief, over and above R&D relief, for expenditure incurred on qualifying R&D of specified types of vaccine. Vaccine relief expired on 31 March 2017 (*FA 2016, s 47*).

For expenditure before 1 April 2012, if a 'larger SME' (see **14.23**) obtained an R&D tax credit in respect of normal (ie non-vaccine) R&D expenditure, it was entitled to vaccine research relief only on qualifying expenditure that had not otherwise qualified for R&D relief. Subject to this, for SMEs (including larger SMEs), the amount of the vaccine research relief was a specified percentage of the expenditure on qualifying vaccine or medical research for the accounting period, as follows (*CTA 2009, s 1089*):

Date expenditure incurred	*SME vaccine research relief*
On or after 1 April 2012	Abolished
1 April 2011 to 31 March 2012	20%
1 August 2008 to 31 March 2011	40%
Before 1 August 2008	50%

If an SME incurs a trading loss in an accounting period in which it is entitled to R&D tax relief or vaccine research relief, it may claim a tax credit in respect of its surrenderable loss (*CTA 2009, ss 1092, 1103–1105*; see **14.26**).

For large companies, the amount of the vaccine research relief is also a specified percentage of the expenditure on qualifying vaccine or medical research for the accounting period, as follows (*CTA 2009, s 1091*):

Date expenditure incurred	*Large vaccine research relief*
On or after 1 August 2008	40%
Before 1 August 2008	50%

A large company submitting a claim for vaccine research relief must include a declaration that the availability of the relief has resulted in an increase in:

- the amount, scope or speed of the company's R&D, or
- the company's expenditure on R&D (*CTA 2009, s 1088*).

From 1 July 2016, HMRC has the power to request certain information from a company claiming the vaccine relief. The provision of the information will be a condition for granting the relief (*FA 2016, ss 180–182, Sch 24*; see **25.5**). At the time of writing, there is no legislation setting out the specific requirements that must be satisfied. However, it is unlikely that there will be any information requests, given that the relief is due to expire (*FA 2016, s 47*). The reason for abolishing the relief is that the take-up has been very low, being claimed by fewer than ten companies each year (*Finance Bill 2016*, Explanatory Notes, cl 43).

CLAIMING R&D RELIEFS

Time limit for claims

14.46 Under the SME and large company R&D schemes, a claim for the enhanced deduction (see **14.25** and **14.35**), R&D tax credit (see **14.26**), R&D expenditure credit (see **14.40**) or vaccine research relief (see **14.45**) can only be made by being included in a company tax return. The claim must specify the amount of the relief claimed, and may be made at any time up to two years after the end of the accounting period (*FA 1998, Sch 18, paras 10, 83A–83F*).

Specialist HMRC units for R&D tax credit claims

> **Focus**
>
> In spite of the government's best intentions to promote R&D activity, HMRC are a tax-collecting authority with a historical reluctance to provide reliefs if they can avoid doing so. Getting the right advice on how to set out a claim for R&D relief, and presenting the claim to HMRC in the most persuasive manner, may be crucial to the success of a claim.

14.47 The Large Business Service and five specialist R&D tax credit units deal with the R&D and vaccine research relief claims. These units should be approached if there are any queries.

Companies and agents should send corporation tax returns with R&D tax credit claims to the specialist unit dealing with the postcode for the location of the main R&D activity of the company, apart from companies dealt with by the Large Business Service and companies dealt with by the specialist pharmaceutical units in Manchester.

Contact details for the units are as follows (CIRD80350):

Croydon R&D Unit,
Local Compliance S1137,
PO Box 3900,
Glasgow,
G70 6AA

Telephone: 03000 511811
Email: Croydon.RandD@hmrc.gsi.gov.uk

Leicester R&D Unit,
Local Compliance S0563,
PO Box 3900,
Glasgow,
G70 6AA

Telephone: 03000 515236
Email: Leicester.RandD@hmrc.gsi.gov.uk

Manchester R&D Unit,
Local Compliance S0717,
PO Box 3900,
Glasgow,
G70 6AA

Telephone: 03000 510190
Email: randd.manchester@hmrc.gsi.gov.uk

Portsmouth R&D Unit,
Local Compliance S0793,
PO Box 3900,
Glasgow,
G70 6AA

Telephone: 03000 528835
Email: Portsmouth.RandD@hmrc.gsi.gov.uk

Cardiff R&D Unit (Wales, Scotland and Northern Ireland),
Local Compliance S0970,
PO Box 3900,
Glasgow,
G70 6AA

Telephone: 03000 582420
Email: Cardiff.randd@hmrc.gsi.gov.uk

Companies whose main R&D activities are located in one of the following postcodes should send their corporation tax returns containing R&D tax credit or relief claims to the appropriate office listed below (CIRD80360):

Postcode	*Office*	*Postcode*	*Office*	*Postcode*	*Office*
AB	Cardiff	HA	Cardiff	PR	Manchester
AL	Cardiff	HD	Manchester	RG	Portsmouth
B	Cardiff	HG	Manchester	RH	Portsmouth
BA	Cardiff	HP	Portsmouth	RM	Leicester
BB	Manchester	HR	Cardiff	S	Leicester
BD	Manchester	HS	Cardiff	SA	Cardiff

BH	Portsmouth	HU	Manchester	SE	Croydon
BL	Manchester	HX	Manchester	SG	Leicester
BN	Portsmouth	IG	Cardiff	SK	Manchester
BR	Croydon	IP	Leicester	SL	Portsmouth
BS	Cardiff	IV	Cardiff	SM	Croydon
BT	Manchester	KA	Cardiff	SN	Portsmouth
CA	Manchester	KT	Croydon	SO	Portsmouth
CB	Leicester	KW	Cardiff	SP	Portsmouth
CF	Cardiff	KY	Cardiff	SR	Manchester
CH	Manchester	L	Manchester	SS	Leicester
CM	Leicester	LA	Manchester	ST	Manchester
CO	Leicester	LD	Cardiff	SW	Croydon
CR	Croydon	LE	Leicester	SY	Cardiff
CT	Croydon	LL	Cardiff	TA	Cardiff
CV	Leicester	LN	Leicester	TD	Cardiff
CW	Manchester	LS	Manchester	TF	Cardiff
DA	Croydon	LU	Leicester	TN	Portsmouth
DD	Cardiff	M	Manchester	TQ	Portsmouth
DE	Leicester	ME	Croydon	TR	Portsmouth
DG	Cardiff	MK	Leicester	TS	Manchester
DH	Manchester	ML	Cardiff	TW	Croydon
DL	Manchester	N	Croydon	UB	Croydon
DN	Leicester	NE	Manchester	W	Croydon
DT	Portsmouth	NG	Leicester	WA	Manchester
DY	Cardiff	NN	Leicester	WC	Croydon
E	Croydon	NP	Cardiff	WD	Cardiff
EC	Croydon	NR	Leicester	WF	Manchester
EH	Cardiff	NW	Croydon	WN	Manchester
EN	Cardiff	OL	Manchester	WR	Cardiff
EX	Portsmouth	OX	Portsmouth	WS	Leicester
FK	Cardiff	PA	Cardiff	WV	Cardiff
FY	Manchester	PE	Leicester	YO	Manchester
G	Cardiff	PH	Cardiff	ZE	Cardiff
GL	Cardiff	PL	Portsmouth		
GU	Portsmouth	PO	Portsmouth		

REMEDIATION OF CONTAMINATED OR DERELICT LAND

> **Focus**
>
> The government sees relief for expenditure on remediation of contaminated or derelict land as an important element in supporting the housing and construction sectors through planning reforms and the release of large areas of publicly owned land for development.

Introduction

14.48 Provided all conditions apply, a company may be able to obtain relief for expenditure incurred on the remediation of contaminated or derelict land.

Capital expenditure and 150% of the revenue expenditure is relievable against the profits of a UK property business or against the profits of a trade (see **14.49**). Alternatively, if the company has a loss from a UK property business or trade, it can claim a repayable tax credit. Legislation is contained in *CTA 2009, ss 1143–1179*. There is no entitlement to relief for artificial arrangements (*CTA 2009, s 1169*).

Deduction for capital expenditure

14.49 In order to qualify for a deduction for capital expenditure, the company must have acquired a major interest in land situated in the UK for the purposes of its trade or UK property business that it carries on. A major interest in land can be either freehold or leasehold. Land includes buildings on the land (*Interpretation Act 1978*).

Property law varies across the UK, and the definition of a 'major interest in land' in *CTA 2009, s 1178A*, is intended to ensure that the effect is the same irrespective of where in the UK the land is situated, as follows (CIRD69015):

- a company that owns the land has a major interest in the land;
- a company that is granted a lease of at least seven years over the land has a major interest in the land; and
- a company that is assigned a lease with at least seven years remaining has a major interest in the land.

At the time of the acquisition, all or part of the land must be either in a contaminated or a derelict state or both, and the company incurs qualifying land remediation expenditure. If Japanese Knotweed is present, there is no such requirement (*Corporation Tax (Land Remediation Relief) Order 2009, SI 2009/2037*). If the land is in a derelict state, in order to qualify it must be in a derelict state throughout the period beginning with the earlier of 1 April 1998 and the date the company, or a person connected with the company, acquired the major interest in that land (*CTA 2009, s 1147*).

The company may elect by notice in writing, to an HMRC officer, for this expenditure to be allowed as a deduction in computing total taxable profits of the period. The election must state the accounting period in which the relief is to be claimed and should be given within the normal time limit, ie within two years after the end of the accounting period concerned (*CTA 2009, s 1148*). Expenditure is treated as incurred when it is recognised in the accounts drawn up under GAAP.

Expenditure incurred before trading commences is treated as being incurred on the first day of trading (*CTA 2009, s 1147(7)*).

Additional deduction for qualifying land remediation expenditure

14.50 In order to qualify for the enhanced relief, the company must have acquired a major interest in land situated in the UK for the purposes of its trade or UK property business. The company must carry on a trade of UK property business during the accounting period in which it makes the acquisition.

At the time of the acquisition, all or part of the land must be either in a contaminated or in a derelict state or both. If Japanese Knotweed is present, there is no such requirement (*Corporation Tax (Land Remediation Relief) Order 2009, SI 2009/2037*). If the land is in a derelict state, it must have been in a derelict state throughout the period beginning with the earlier of 1 April 1998 and the date the company, or a person connected with the company, acquired the major interest in that land. The enhanced relief is available on expenditure that the company incurs in respect of that land that qualifies as a deduction in calculating the profits of the business or the trade for corporation tax purposes (*CTA 2009, s 1149*).

The land remediation relief is given in the accounting period in which the expenditure qualifies as a deduction from profits. The claim should be included in the online corporation tax return.

Denial of relief

14.51 A company has no entitlement to relief for capital expenditure (see **14.49**) or revenue expenditure (see **14.48**) if the land is in a contaminated state or derelict state, wholly or partly as a result of a deed or omission brought about by the company or a person with a relevant connection to the company (*CTA 2009, s 1150*).

For the purposes of remediation of contaminated or derelict land, a person has a relevant connection to the company if the person was connected with the company (*CTA 2009, s 1178*):

- at the time of the deed or omission;
- at the time of the land acquisition; or
- when the remediation work is undertaken.

A relevant interest in land includes an interest (or an option) in a right over, or licence to occupy, the land, or the person has disposed of any estate or interest in the land for a value that reflects on the value of the remediation, contamination or dereliction (*CTA 2009, s 1179*).

Qualifying land remediation expenditure

14.52 In order to qualify, there are various conditions applying to the expenditure incurred (*CTA 2009, s 1144*; *FA 2009, Sch 7, para 4*):

- either all or part of the land must be in a contaminated or a derelict state;
- the expenditure must be incurred on relevant land remediation directly undertaken by the company or on its behalf;
- the expenditure must be incurred on relevant contaminated land remediation undertaken by the company or derelict land remediation so undertaken (see **14.55** and **14.56**);
- the expenditure must be incurred:
  - on employee costs, or
  - on materials,

  or is qualifying expenditure on relevant land remediation contracted out by the company to an unconnected person, or qualifying expenditure on connected sub-contracted land remediation;
- the expenditure would not have been incurred had the land not been in a contaminated or derelict state;
- the expenditure is not subsidised; and
- the expenditure is not incurred on landfill tax.

Contaminated and derelict state

Contaminated state

14.53 Land can only be in a contaminated state if relevant harm is being caused by something in, on or under the land, or there is a serious possibility that relevant harm will be caused (*CTA 2009, s 1145*). Relevant harm is defined as:

- death of living organisms or significant injury or damage to living organisms;
- significant pollution of controlled waters;
- a significant adverse impact on the ecosystem, or
- structural or other significant damage to buildings or other structures or interference with buildings or other structures that significantly compromises their use.

> **Focus**
>
> Subject to a number of specific exceptions, land is not generally regarded as being in a contaminated state unless it has been contaminated by industrial activity.

In most cases, such land will have been contaminated by industrial activity. Land cannot generally qualify as being in a contaminated state by reason of any living organisms or decaying matter deriving from living organisms, air or water living in or under it or any other such cause (*CTA 2009, s 1145(2)*). However, from 1 April 2009 the presence of arsenic, arsenical compounds, Japanese Knotweed or radon in, on or under the land enables the land to qualify as contaminated land (*Corporation Tax (Land Remediation Relief) Order 2009, SI 2009/2037*), but only in relation to:

- that part of the land where the items in question are present, and
- expenditure incurred for the purpose of remedying or mitigating the effects of relevant harm caused by the presence of the items in question.

A nuclear site is not treated as land in a contaminated state or in a derelict state (*CTA 2009, s 1145B*).

In *Dean & Reddyhoff Ltd v Revenue & Customs* [2013] UKFTT 367 (TC), the taxpayer incurred expenditure on the seabed, foreshore and land above the tidal high water mark in the course of constructing a marina. The First-tier Tribunal held that work on the contaminated foreshore qualified for land remediation relief (the contamination in this case being by reason of wave, tidal surge and flood damage) but rejected the other claims, holding that the seabed was not 'land' and the land above the high tide mark was not contaminated.

Derelict state

14.54 Land is in a derelict state only if it is not in productive use, and cannot be put into productive use without the removal of buildings or other structures (*CTA 2009, s 1145A*; see also CIRD62001, CIRD62005, CIRD62030).

Relevant contaminated land remediation

14.55 The activities that a company carries out together with any relevant preparatory activities will be relevant remediation if the following two conditions are met:

- the activities comprise the doing of any works, the carrying out of any operations or the taking of any steps in relation to:
  - (a) the land in question,
  - (b) any controlled waters affected by that land, or
  - (c) any land adjoining or adjacent to that land; and
- the purpose of the activities is:
  - – to prevent or minimise, or remedy or mitigate the effects of, any relevant harm by virtue of which the land is in a contaminated state; or
  - – any other specified activity introduced by the Treasury.

From 1 April 2009 the removal of material which contains or may contain Japanese Knotweed from the land in question to a licensed landfill site constitutes a specified activity. In accordance with *Corporation Tax (Land Remediation Relief) Order 2009, SI 2009/2037, art 4, a* licensed landfill site is a site in respect of which a permit has been granted under one of the following regulations:

(i) the *Environmental Permitting (England and Wales) Regulations 2007*;

(ii) the *Pollution Prevention and Control (Scotland) Regulations 2000*;

(iii) the *Pollution Prevention and Control (Northern Ireland) Regulations 2003*; and

(iv) *Council Directive 1999/31/EC* of 26 April 1999 on the landfill of waste.

A relevant preparatory activity must be connected to the company's remedial activities, and involves an assessment of the conditions of the land in question, any controlled waters affected by that land, or any land adjoining or adjacent to that land.

Controlled waters can only be affected by land in a contaminated state if something in, on or under the land causes the land to be in such a condition that significant pollution of those waters is being caused, or there is a serious possibility that significant pollution of those waters will be caused (*CTA 2009, s 1146*).

Relevant derelict land remediation

14.56 The activities that a company carries out, together with any relevant preparatory activities, will be relevant remediation if the following two conditions are met:

- the activities comprise the doing of any works, the carrying out of any operations or the taking of any steps in relation to the land in question; and
- the purpose of the activity is specified by Treasury Order.

A relevant preparatory activity must be connected to the company's remedial activities and involves an assessment of the conditions of: the land in question, any controlled waters affected by that land, or any land adjoining or adjacent to that land (*CTA 2009, s 1146A*).

The purposes specified in *Corporation Tax (Land Remediation Relief) Order 2009, SI 2009/2037, art 6*, are the removal of:

- post-tensioned concrete heavyweight construction;
- building foundations and machinery bases;
- reinforced concrete pilecaps;
- reinforced concrete basements; or
- redundant services that are located below ground.

Employee costs

14.57 Only the employee costs of directors or employees directly and actively engaged in the relevant land remediation can be attributed to the relevant land remediation. Administration and support services are not included. Employee costs consist of all salaries and benefits to the company's directors or employees, employer's Class 1 NI contributions and company pension fund contributions.

Employee costs of those not working full-time on the land remediation are calculated pro-rata except for two circumstances. If a director or employee spends less than 20% of his total working time on land remediation work, none of the employee costs relating to him are treated as attributable to relevant land remediation. If a director or employee spends more than 80% of his total working time on land remediation work, the whole of the employee costs relating to him are treated as attributable to relevant land remediation (*CTA 2009, ss 1170, 1171*).

Expenditure on materials

14.58 Expenditure on materials is attributable to relevant land remediation if the materials are employed directly in that relevant land remediation (*CTA 2009, s 1172*).

Expenditure incurred because of contamination

14.59 If expenditure incurred on the land is increased only because the land is in a contaminated state, that increased amount is relevant land remediation expenditure (*CTA 2009, s 1173*).

Subsidised expenditure

14.60 Land remediation expenditure is treated as subsidised if a grant or subsidy is obtained or it is met by another person. Any receipt not allocated to a particular payment will be allocated on a just and reasonable basis (*CTA 2009, s 1177(1), (2)*).

Expenditure where company and sub-contractor connected

14.61 The company may incur sub-contracted expenditure on land remediation. If the company and the sub-contractor are connected persons, the amount of the sub-contractor payment which is qualifying expenditure on connected sub-contracted land remediation may be limited by reference to the sub-contractor's 'relevant expenditure' (*CTA 2009, s 1175*). Connection is determined under *CTA 2010, s 1122* (see **10.27**).

For the purposes of remediation of contaminated or derelict land, a person has a relevant connection to the company if the person was connected with the company (*CTA 2009, s 1178*):

- at the time of the deed or omission;

- at the time of the land acquisition; or
- when the remediation work is undertaken.

Treatment of sub-contractor payment in other cases

14.62 Where the company is not connected to the sub-contractor, the whole of the amount of the sub-contractor payment is treated as qualifying expenditure on sub-contracted land remediation (*CTA 2009, s 1176*).

Entitlement to land remediation tax credit

14.63 If the company incurs a UK property business or trading loss in the same business or trade for which the contaminated land was acquired, it may claim a land remediation tax credit if it has a 'qualifying land remediation loss' in an accounting period.

The 'qualifying land remediation loss' is the lower of:

- 150% of the related qualifying land remediation expenditure; and
- the unrelieved UK property loss or trading loss (*CTA 2009, s 1152*).

The 'unrelieved' UK property loss or trading loss is the loss for the accounting period as reduced by the amount of any UK property loss (*CTA 2010, s 62*) or trading loss (*CTA 2010, s 37(3)(a)*) claim that could be made in that accounting period and any other relief claimed by the company in respect of the loss for that accounting period. This will include losses relieved against profits of an earlier accounting period (*CTA 2010, s 37(3)(b)*) and losses surrendered to group or consortium members (*CTA 2010, s 99*).

UK property losses (*CTA 2010, s 62*) and trading losses (*CTA 2010, s 45(4)*) brought forward from an earlier accounting period, and any trading losses carried back from a later accounting period (*CTA 2010, s 37(3)(b)*), are ignored for this purpose.

The corresponding loss carried forward is reduced accordingly (*CTA 2009, s 1153*).

Amount of land remediation tax credit

14.64 A company's entitlement to land remediation tax credit is 16% of the qualifying land remediation loss for the period (*CTA 2009, s 1154*). This is not income of the company for any tax purposes (*CTA 2009, s 1156*). The credit is claimed in the company's corporation tax return.

Example 14.6—Calculation of land remediation tax credit

Facts

Arthur plc incurs land remediation expenditure of £80,000 in the accounting period ended 30 September 2015. The expenditure is deductible against trading profits, and the company claims land remediation relief.

The company's results for the year are as follows:

	£
Trading loss	(140,000)
Loan relationship	40,000

The company makes a claim to surrender the full amount of its qualifying land remediation loss in exchange for a payment of land remediation tax credit. It makes no other loss relief or group relief claims for the period.

Analysis

The 'qualifying land remediation loss' is the lower of:

	£
150% of the qualifying land remediation expenditure (£80,000 × 150%) and	120,000
The company's unrelieved trading loss for the accounting period (£140,000 less £40,000)	100,000
Therefore the qualifying land remediation loss is	100,000
The tax credit payable (£100,000 × 16%)	16,000
Trading loss available to carry forward to future accounting periods (£140,000 less £40,000 less £100,000)	Nil

Payment in respect of land remediation tax credit

14.65 HMRC may use the tax credit to settle any outstanding corporation tax liability (*CTA 2009, s 1155(2)*).

The credit may be applied in discharging any liability of the company to pay corporation tax and, to the extent that it is so applied, HMRC's obligation under *CTA 2009, s 1155(1)* is discharged. If a return is under enquiry, the tax credit will not be paid until the enquiry is complete, although an HMRC officer has discretionary powers to pay a provisional amount.

HMRC are not required to pay a land remediation tax credit for an accounting period if the company has outstanding PAYE and NIC liabilities for the same accounting period (*CTA 2009, s 1155*).

Certain qualifying land remediation expenditure excluded for purposes of chargeable gains

14.66 Qualifying land remediation expenditure that has been used in a tax credit claim is excluded expenditure for chargeable gains purposes (*CTA 2009, s 1157(1), (2)*). Capital expenditure on qualifying land remediation allowed as a deduction in computing the profits (losses) of a trade or UK property business is not an allowable deduction for chargeable gains purposes (*TCGA 1992, s 39*).

Penalties

14.67 The company is liable to a penalty if it makes an incorrect claim for a land remediation tax credit or discovers that a claim is incorrect but fails to inform HMRC (see **Chapter 24**).

Chapter 15

Creative sector tax reliefs

SIGNPOSTS

- Introduction to the reliefs (see **15.1–15.2**).
- Film tax relief (see **15.3–15.11**).
- Television tax relief (see **15.12–15.20**).
- Video games tax relief (see **15.21–15.28**).
- Theatre tax relief (see **15.29–15.37**).
- Orchestra tax relief (see **15.38–15.46**).
- Museums and galleries exhibitions tax relief (see **15.47**).
- Special rules for losses (see **15.48**).

INTRODUCTION TO THE RELIEFS

Focus

Although the creative tax reliefs are based closely on film tax relief, there are significant differences between them. A company seeking to claim any of the creative sector tax reliefs should have careful regard to the respective legislation.

15.1 Although film tax relief was introduced in 2006, government support for the British film industry had been available long before that time. From the 1980s, favourable capital allowance treatment in the form of 100% first year allowances were available. When the first year allowances were phased out, they were replaced by special reliefs whereby the production and acquisition costs could be written off at accelerated rates (*F(No 2)A 1992, s 40*; *F(No 2) A 1997, s 48*).

However, as pointed out in the HMRC Business Income Manual, the reliefs were rarely accessed directly by film producers themselves (BIM56005,

BIM56010). More often, banks and other financial intermediaries would market film schemes to wealthy individuals as a means of mitigating their personal tax liabilities. By offering a suitable level of gearing, investors were enabled to make inflated claims for income tax relief, without incurring the associated commercial risks in the venture.

As a result, various anti-avoidance rules were introduced from 2004, until eventually the old reliefs were abolished and the new film tax relief was introduced in 2006.

As with the old regime, the aim of the new film tax relief is to encourage sustainable film production in the UK and maintain the industry's creative and technical skills. However, the rules have been designed to ensure that it is the film producers rather than investors who can benefit from the reliefs.

Since 2013 a range of additional tax reliefs have been introduced to encourage and support other aspects of the creative sector. These subsequent reliefs are all modelled broadly on the pre-existing film tax relief, but there are significant differences.

All the creative sector tax reliefs allow eligible companies (but not unincorporated businesses) to claim an additional deduction based on certain qualifying expenditure when computing their taxable profits for corporation tax purposes and gives them the option, where that additional deduction results in a loss, to surrender that loss in return for a payable tax credit.

The newer creative sector tax reliefs are:

- a tax relief for television production, covering culturally British high-end television production and animation, which came into effect from 1 April 2013. To encourage the production of culturally British children's television programmes in the UK, relief has been extended to children's programming where expenditure is incurred on or after 1 April 2015 (*CTA 2009, Pt 15A*; see **15.12–15.20**);
- a tax relief for culturally British video games development, which had been intended to come into effect from 1 April 2013 but was delayed because of difficulties in obtaining EU state aid approval. It eventually came into effect from 1 April 2014 (*CTA 2009, Pt 15B*; see **15.21–15.28**);
- a tax relief for theatrical production, covering the production of plays, musicals, opera, ballet and dance, which came into effect from 1 September 2014 subject to EU state aid approval (*CTA 2009, Pt 15C*; see **15.29–15.37**); and
- a tax relief for orchestras from 1 April 2016, modelled on theatre tax relief (see **15.38–15.46**);
- a tax relief for museums and galleries from 1 April 2017, modelled on orchestra tax relief (see **15.47**);

The reliefs for television and video games were originally set to expire in 2018 under state aid rules, but have since been extended to 2023 (see tinyurl.com/ybpkdv5e and tinyurl.com/y7qyd7lc).

From the outset, the government has sought to prevent abuse, maintain the long-term sustainability of the creative sector tax reliefs and ensure that they remain effective and sufficiently targeted. In addition to specific anti-avoidance provisions in the legislation, regulations may be brought forward to prevent:

- artificially inflated claims for tax credit; and
- wrongful disclosure.

From 1 July 2016, HMRC have the power to request certain information from a company claiming the creative tax reliefs. Until 5 February 2018, there was an exception for video games relief, but this is no longer the case (Video Games Tax Relief (Amendment of Tax Advantages in Schedule 24 to the Finance Act 2016) Regulations 2018, SI 2018/28). The provision of the information will be a condition for granting the relief. At the time of writing, there is no legislation setting out the specific requirements that must be satisfied, but information that HMRC will be able to request will include the following:

- information about the company and the company's activities;
- information about the subject-matter of the claim; and
- any other information which relates to the grant of state aid through the provision of the relief.

(*Finance Act 2016, ss 180–182, Sch 24*; see **25.5**)

In addition to HMRC's detailed technical guidance as it becomes available, they have published more general guidance on the creative industry tax reliefs at tinyurl.com/pzrrade.

Common themes to the creative sector reliefs

15.2 There are a number of common themes which inform the way in which the creative sector reliefs are designed:

- First, there must be a defined project – a specific film, television programme, video game to be produced, or a theatrical or musical piece to be performed, or an exhibition to be displayed.
- There must be a production company to produce and develop the project. It is this company that is to claim the benefit of the tax reliefs on offer.
- Each project constitutes a single trade. If the production company has other projects in the pipeline, these constitute separate trades. For the theatrical and orchestral reliefs, however, it is possible for a series of performances to constitute a single trade.

- As a consequence, the profits and losses of each project are segregated from each other. One cannot automatically set expenses of one project against the revenue receipts of another.
- In particular, there are special rules governing the way that losses can be utilised. There are restrictions on loss relief during the production stages – only when the project is complete can losses be relieved in the normal way (see **15.48**).

FILM TAX RELIEF

> **Focus**
>
> Companies should note that, although film tax relief has been available since 2006, the rules for the relief were amended in 2014 and 2015.

Introduction

15.3 Film tax relief was introduced by *FA 2006*. The relief offers an additional deduction against profits for corporation tax purposes and, in some cases, a payable tax credit. It is available to companies but not unincorporated businesses. The relevant legislation is at *CTA 2009, Pt 15, ss 1180–1216*.

Changes were made by *FA 2014* for films on which the principal photography was not completed before 1 April 2014 (see *Finance Act 2014, Section 32 (Film Tax Relief) (Appointed Day) Order 2014, SI 2014/2880*). Further changes were made by *FA 2015* for films on which the principal photography is not completed before 1 April 2015 and are being brought into effect from that date.

There is no cap on the amount of film tax relief which can be claimed (other than an upper limit set on EU state aid), but only companies that are eligible 'film production companies' can claim the relief.

Where a company has incurred expenditure on which it is entitled to an R&D expenditure credit, or on which it has obtained an enhanced R&D deduction, it is not entitled to claim film tax relief in respect of the same expenditure (*CTA 2009, ss 104BA, 1040ZA, 1195(3A)*; for further details of R&D reliefs, see **Chapter 14**).

HMRC's guidance on film tax relief is in their Film Production Company Manual at FPC10000 onwards.

Definition of a film

15.4 A film includes any record, however made, of a sequence of visual images that is capable of being used as a means of showing that sequence as a moving picture. References to a film include its soundtrack. Special provisions determine whether or not a series of films is treated as separate films. A film is completed when it is first in a form in which it can reasonably be regarded as ready for copies of it to be made and distributed for presentation to the general public (*CTA 2009, s 1181*).

Film production company

15.5 A company that meets the definition of a film production company is subject to special tax rules, and can qualify for film tax relief if certain conditions are met (*CTA 2009, ss 1180–1216*).

A film production company is a company that is responsible for the pre-production, principal photography and post-production of a film, as defined (*CTA 2009, s 1181*). The company must also be engaged actively in production planning and decision-making during those stages, as well as having responsibility for delivery of the completed film, negotiations, contracts and payments for rights, goods and services in relation to the film. Whilst a film production company might also have responsibility for the development, marketing and distribution of the film, there is no requirement that it does so. The definition of a film production company is tightly drawn to ensure that only the actual producers of a film (rather than investors) fall within the special tax rules.

For any one film, there can only be one film production company (except in the case of 'qualifying co-productions'). If there is more than one company satisfying the film production company requirements in relation to a particular film, the film production company is the one most directly engaged in the activities. If there is no company satisfying the film production company requirements in respect of a film, there is no film production company for that film and therefore no film tax relief may be claimed. A company may elect not to be regarded as the film production company in relation to a film, and such an election has effect in relation to films which commence principal photography in that or any subsequent accounting period (*CTA 2009, s 1182*; FPC10110).

Separate film trade

15.6 For corporation tax purposes, the film production company's activities in relation to a film are treated as a trade separate from any other activities of the company, including any activities in relation to any other film. If a film production company makes more than one film, each film is considered as a separate film trade, so that profits or losses are calculated separately for each film that the company produces. So, for tax purposes, the company needs to identify separately the income and expenditure on film-making activities in connection with each film. The separate film trade is treated as beginning when pre-production begins or, if earlier, when any income from the film is received by the company (*CTA 2009, s 1188*).

Qualifying co-productions

15.7 A 'qualifying co-production' is a film that is treated as a national film in the UK by virtue of an agreement between the UK government and any other government, international organisation or authority. A co-producer can be treated as a film production company if it makes an effective creative, technical and artistic contribution to the film, but not if it makes only a financial contribution (*CTA 2009, ss 1182(4), 1186*).

Conditions for claiming film tax relief

15.8 The film production company may be eligible for film tax relief if all four of the following conditions are met:

- There must be a 'film' (*CTA 2009, s 1181*).
- At the end of the accounting period in question and at the end of all previous accounting periods during which the company has been carrying on film-making activities in relation to the film, the film must be intended for 'theatrical release' (*CTA 2009, ss 1195, 1196*).
- The film must be certified as a 'British film' (*CTA 2009, ss 1195, 1197*). There are three ways in which a film can qualify as British (FPC40030). It may:
  - satisfy the 'cultural test' specified in *Films Act 1985, Sch 1*, as amended from 29 January 2015 by the *Films (Definition of 'British Film') Order 2015, SI 2015/86*, for films starting principal photography on or after 1 April 2014, subject to transitional provisions. For guidance from the British Film Institute (BFI), which administers the certification scheme on behalf of the Department for Culture, Media and Sport (DCMS), see tinyurl.com/q742wh6;
  - meet the terms of one of the UK's bilateral co-production treaties; or
  - meet the terms of the European Convention on Cinematic Co-Production.
- Of the 'core expenditure' (ie expenditure on pre-production, principal photography and post-production) incurred on the film by the film production company (or by the co-producers, if applicable), at least 10%

(or 25% for films the principal photography of which was completed before 1 April 2014; see *FA 2014, s 32(2)*) must be expenditure on goods or services used or consumed in the UK (*CTA 2009, ss 1185, 1195, 1198*).

There is no requirement under tax law for the film production company to hold any intellectual property rights in connection with the film, or for any such rights to be held in the UK.

Calculating film tax relief

The additional deduction

15.9 If film tax relief is available, the film production company may claim an 'additional deduction' (or 'enhancement') which increases the amount of expenditure that is allowable as a deduction for corporation tax purposes, reducing the company's taxable profits or creating or augmenting a tax loss (*CTA 2009, s 1199*).

This additional deduction is calculated (*CTA 2009, s 1200*) as:

$$E \times R - P$$

In the above formula:

- E (the enhanceable expenditure) is the lower of:
  - UK qualifying expenditure incurred to date, and
  - 80% of total qualifying expenditure incurred to date.
- R (the rate of enhancement) is:
  - 100% for a limited-budget film, ie a film with core expenditure of £20 million or less. 'Core expenditure' means production expenditure on pre-production, principal photography and post-production; or
  - 80% for any other film.

  However, from 1 April 2015 the rate of enhancement is 100% for all films (*CTA 2009, s 1200(3)*, as substituted by *FA 2015, s 29(3)*).
- P is the total of additional deductions given for previous periods of account (so P is Nil for the first period of account of the separate film trade).

Special rules apply to determine how trading losses from a separate film trade may be used including the treatment of terminal losses (*CTA 2009, ss 1208–1211* and **15.48–15.53**).

Film tax credit

15.10 If film tax relief is available, the film production company may claim a film tax credit (ie a cash payment from HMRC) for an accounting period in which it has a surrenderable loss. See *CTA 2009, ss 1201–1203* for further details on how the surrenderable loss is calculated and how the tax credit is given.

Before 1 April 2014, the tax credit for a limited-budget film was 25% of losses surrendered, and for other films the rate was 20% (see FPC55000 onwards). From 1 April 2014, the distinction between limited-budget films and other films was removed; instead, the tax credit for all films became 25% on the first £20 million of qualifying production expenditure and 20% on expenditure in excess of that limit (*CTA 2009, s 1202(2), (3)*, as substituted by *FA 2014, s 32(3)*).

From 1 April 2015, the rate of payable tax credit has become 25% for all films and the category of limited-budget film has been removed (*CTA 2009, s 1202(2), (3)*, as amended by *FA 2015, s 29(4)*).

How to claim film tax relief

15.11 A claim for film tax relief must be included in the company's tax return for an accounting period. It can be made in respect of any accounting period during which the film production company carries on the separate film trade. Normally, a claim is made for the accounting period in which the film is completed or abandoned. A claim can also be made in a subsequent accounting period after the film is completed if, in that period, the film production company has trading activity; for example, if the company has to make additional payments to the director and actors due to the success of the film. For guidance on claims, see FPC60000 onwards.

Before a claim for the relief is made, the Secretary of State must certify that the film is a British film. An interim certificate as well as a final certificate can be obtained. Interim claims are made on the assumption that the required conditions have been met, and there have been separate provisions for interim claims made for the more generous relief available for a limited-budget film. If the company abandons film-making activities in relation to the film, its tax return for the period in question may be accompanied by an interim certificate, and the abandonment does not affect entitlement to special film relief (see **15.9**) for that film in respect of that or any previous period. However, if the company completes the film, its tax return for the completion period must be accompanied by a final certificate; otherwise, all entitlement to special film relief for that film for any period is forfeited. If any of the conditions are not actually met on completion of the film, the position is adjusted to reflect the outcome, including (if appropriate) repayment of the film tax credit to HMRC with interest. Interim claims cannot be made outside the corporation tax company return process (*CTA 2009, ss 1197, 1213, 1215*).

A general anti-avoidance provision denies film tax relief arising from artificially inflated claims. Where a transaction is attributable to arrangements, the main object or one of the main objects of which is to enable a company to obtain film tax relief (whether the additional deduction or film tax credit), or to enhance its entitlement to film tax relief, that transaction is disregarded in determining the amount of film tax relief due (*CTA 2009, s 1205*).

TELEVISION TAX RELIEF

> **Focus**
>
> From 1 April 2015, television tax relief has been extended to include certain types of children's television programmes.

Introduction

15.12 Television tax relief was introduced from 1 April 2013 to cover high-end television and animation, and was extended to children's programmes from 1 April 2015. The rules for television tax relief are based closely on those for the pre-existing film tax relief (see **15.3–15.11**).

The relief allows qualifying companies engaged in the production of relevant programmes intended for broadcast to the general public to claim an additional deduction in computing their taxable profits and, where that additional deduction results in a loss, to surrender that loss for a payable tax credit. The relevant legislation is at *CTA 2009, Pt 15A, ss 1216A–1216EC*.

There is no cap on the amount of television tax relief which can be claimed (other than an upper limit set on EU state aid), but only companies that are eligible 'television production companies' can claim the relief.

Where a company has incurred expenditure on which it is entitled to an R&D expenditure credit, or on which it has obtained an enhanced R&D deduction, it is not entitled to claim television tax relief in respect of the same expenditure (*CTA 2009, ss 104BA, 1040ZA, 1216C(4)*; for further details of R&D reliefs, see **Chapter 14**).

Relief for animation is simply a type of television tax relief. However, because the rules and procedures differ, HMRC have published their guidance in two separate manuals. Their guidance on television tax relief can be found in their Television Production Company Manual at TPC10000 onwards, and the implications for animation are addressed in their Animation Production Company Manual at APC10000 onwards.

Definition of a relevant programme

> **Focus**
>
> The rules defining a relevant television programme are complex. Depending on the individual circumstances, factors to be considered may include programme content, slot length, average core expenditure, intended audience, cost of prizes, and a long list of exclusions.

15.13 To qualify for relief, a television programme must be a 'relevant programme' produced to be seen on television or the internet. This includes drama, documentary, animation and (from 1 April 2015) children's programmes. Except in the case of animation or a children's programme, the programme must be commissioned to fill a 'slot length' greater than 30 minutes at an average core expenditure per hour of not less than £1 million (*CTA 2009, s 1216AB*, as amended by *FA 2015, s 30*).

A drama or documentary that includes animation is treated as animation if the core expenditure on the completed animation constitutes at least 51% of the total core expenditure on the completed programme (*CTA 2009, s 1216AC(2)*).

A children's programme is one for which, when production begins, the anticipated primary audience is expected to be under the age of 15 (*CTA 2006, s 1216AC(2A)*, as inserted by *FA 2015, s 30*).

Programmes are excluded from the relief (*CTA 2009, s 1216AD*, as amended by *FA 2015, s 30*) if they are:

(a) advertisements or promotions;

(b) news, current affairs or discussions;

(c) quiz, game, panel, variety or chat shows or similar entertainment;

(d) competitions or contests, or the results of such events;

(e) broadcasts of live events or theatrical or artistic performances given otherwise than for the purpose of being filmed; or

(f) training programmes;

unless (from 1 April 2015) they are children's programmes which:

- are quiz shows, game shows or programmes within (d) above, and
- if they have prizes, the programme total of these does not exceed £1,000 (or such other amount as may be set by Treasury regulations).

Television production company

15.14 A company that meets the definition of a television production company is subject to special tax rules in respect of programmes qualifying for television tax relief, and can qualify for this relief if certain conditions are met (*CTA 2009, ss 1216A–1216EC*).

A television production company is a company that is responsible for the pre-production, principal photography and post-production of a relevant programme. It must also be engaged actively in production planning and decision-making during those stages, as well as having responsibility for delivery of the completed programme, negotiations, contracts and payments for rights, goods and services in relation to the programme. The definition of a television production company is tightly drawn to ensure that only the actual producers of a programme (rather than investors) fall within the special tax rules.

For any one programme, there can only be one television production company (except in the case of 'qualifying co-productions'). If there is more than one company satisfying the television production company requirements in relation to a particular programme, the television production company is the one most directly engaged in the activities. If there is no company satisfying the television production company requirements in respect of a programme, there is no television production company for that programme, and therefore no television tax relief may be claimed. A company may elect not to be regarded as the television production company in relation to a programme, and such an election has effect in relation to relevant programmes which commence principal photography in that or any subsequent accounting period (*CTA 2009, ss 1216AE, 1216AF*; TPC10110; APC10110).

Separate programme trade

15.15 For corporation tax purposes, the television production company's activities in relation to each 'qualifying relevant programme' (ie each relevant programme in relation to which the conditions for television tax relief are met) are treated as a trade separate from any other activities of the company, including any activities in relation to any other qualifying relevant programme. For the meaning of 'relevant programme', see **15.13**. If a television production company makes more than one qualifying relevant programme, each qualifying relevant programme is considered as a separate programme trade, so that profits or losses are calculated separately for each qualifying relevant programme that the company produces. So, for tax purposes, the company needs to identify separately the income and expenditure on programme-making activities in connection with each qualifying relevant programme. The separate programme trade is treated as beginning when pre-production begins or, if earlier, when any income from the programme is received by the company (*CTA 2009, s 1216B*).

Qualifying co-productions

15.16 A 'qualifying co-production' is a programme that is eligible to be certified as British as a result of an agreement between the UK government and any other government, international organisation or authority. A co-producer can be treated as a television production company if it makes an effective creative, technical and artistic contribution to the programme, but not if it makes only a financial contribution (*CTA 2009, ss 1216AE(4), 1216AI*).

Conditions for claiming television tax relief

15.17 The television production company may be eligible for television tax relief if all four of the following conditions are met:

- There must be a 'relevant programme' (*CTA 2009, ss 1216AA–1216AD*; see **15.13**).
- When production activities begin, the programme must be intended for broadcast to the general public (*CTA 2009, ss 1216C, 1216CA*).
- The programme must be certified as a 'British programme' (*CTA 2009, ss 1216C, 1216CB*; TPC40030; APC40030). The points-based cultural test to be applied for this purpose was updated from 23 July 2015 to bring it more closely into line with the cultural test for film tax relief (see *Cultural Test (Television Programmes) Regulations 2013, SI 2013/1813*, as amended by *Cultural Test (Television Programmes) (Amendment) Regulations 2015, SI 2015/1449)*. For guidance from the British Film Institute (BFI), which administers the certification scheme on behalf of the Department for Culture, Media and Sport (DCMS), see tinyurl.com/owmaqby regarding high-end television or tinyurl.com/qjhrawr regarding animation programmes.
- Of the 'core expenditure' (ie expenditure on pre-production, principal photography and post-production) incurred on the programme by the television production company (or by the co-producers, if applicable), at least 10% (or 25% for programmes the principal photography of which was completed before 1 April 2015; see *FA 2015, s 31(1)*) must be expenditure on goods or services used or consumed in the UK (*CTA 2009, ss 1216AH, 1216C, 1216CE*).

There is no requirement under tax law for the television production company to hold any intellectual property rights in connection with the programme, or for any such rights to be held in the UK.

Calculating the television tax relief

The additional deduction

15.18 If television tax relief is available, the television production company may claim an 'additional deduction' (or 'enhancement') which increases the amount of expenditure that is allowable as a deduction for corporation tax purposes, reducing the company's taxable profits or creating or augmenting a tax loss (*CTA 2009, s 1216CF*).

This additional deduction is calculated as:

$$E - P$$

where:

- E (the enhanceable expenditure) is the lower of:
  - UK qualifying expenditure incurred to date
  - 80% of total qualifying expenditure incurred to date
- P is the total of additional deductions given for previous periods of account (so P is Nil for the first period of account of the separate programme trade) (*CTA 2009, s 1216CG*).

Special rules apply to determine how trading losses from a separate programme trade may be used including the treatment of terminal losses (*CTA 2009, ss 1216D–1216DC* and **15.48–15.53**).

Television tax credit

15.19 If television tax relief is available, the television production company may claim a television tax credit (ie a cash payment from HMRC) for an accounting period in which it has a surrenderable loss. See *CTA 2009, ss 1216CH–1216CJ*, for further details on how the surrenderable loss is calculated and how the tax credit is given. The tax credit is 25% of losses surrendered. See also TPC55000 onwards and APC55000 onwards.

How to claim television tax relief

15.20 A claim for television tax relief must be included in the company's tax return for an accounting period. It can be made in respect of any accounting period during which the television production company carries on the separate programme trade. Normally, a claim will be made for the accounting period in which the programme is completed or abandoned.

Before a claim for the relief is made, the Secretary of State must certify that the programme is a British programme. An interim certificate as well as a final certificate can be obtained. Interim claims are made on the assumption that the required conditions have been met. If the company abandons programme-making activities in relation to the programme, its tax return for the period in question may be accompanied by an interim certificate, and the abandonment does not affect entitlement to special television relief (see **15.18**) for that programme in respect of that or any previous period. However, if the company completes the programme, its tax return for the completion period must be accompanied by a final certificate; otherwise, all entitlement to special television relief for that programme for any period is forfeited. If any of the conditions are not actually met on completion of the programme, the position is adjusted to reflect the outcome, including (if appropriate) repayment of the television tax credit to HMRC with interest. Interim claims cannot be made outside the corporation tax company return process (*CTA 2009, ss 1216CB, 1216EA, 1216EB*). For guidance on claims, see TPC60000 onwards and APC60000 onwards.

A general anti-avoidance provision denies television tax relief arising from artificially inflated claims. Where a transaction is attributable to arrangements, the main object or one of the main objects of which is to enable a company to obtain television tax relief (whether the additional deduction or television tax credit), or to enhance its entitlement to television tax relief, that transaction is disregarded in determining the amount of television tax relief due (*CTA 2009, s 1216CL*).

VIDEO GAMES TAX RELIEF

Introduction

15.21 Video games tax relief was introduced by *FA 2013*, and the rules for this relief are based closely on those for the pre-existing film tax relief (see **15.3–15.11**).

The relief had been intended to come into effect from 1 April 2013 but was delayed because of difficulties in obtaining EU state aid approval. That approval was eventually obtained, and the provisions for video games tax relief came into effect from 1 April 2014 by virtue of the *Finance Act 2013, Schedules 17 and 18 (Tax Relief for Video Games Development) (Appointed Day) Order 2014, SI 2014/1962*.

The relief allows qualifying companies engaged in the development of qualifying video games intended for supply to the general public to claim an additional deduction in computing their taxable profits and, where that additional deduction results in a loss, to surrender that loss for a payable tax credit. The relevant legislation is at *CTA 2009, Pt 15B, ss 1217A–1217EC*.

There is no cap on the amount of video games relief which can be claimed (other than an upper limit set on EU state aid), but only companies that are eligible 'video games development companies' can claim the relief.

To qualify for relief, a video game must not include:

- anything produced for advertising or promotional purposes, or

- anything produced for the purposes of gambling (within the meaning of the *Gambling Act 2005*).

References to a video game include the game's soundtrack (*CTA 2009, s 1217AA*).

Where a company has incurred expenditure on which it is entitled to an R&D expenditure credit, or on which it has obtained an enhanced R&D deduction, it is not entitled to claim video games tax relief in respect of the same expenditure (*CTA 2009, ss 104BA, 1040ZA, 1217C(4)*; for further details of R&D reliefs, see **Chapter 14**).

HMRC's guidance on video games tax relief is in their Video Games Development Company Manual at VGDC10000 onwards.

Definition of a video game

> **Focus**
>
> Video games tax relief is targeted at video game software. HMRC do not regard a 'video game' as extending to the hardware on which it is played, even if that hardware is designed solely for use in playing video games.

15.22 The term 'video game' is not defined in the legislation, so it must be given its normal meaning. HMRC regard a video game as an electronic game that is played through a video device; the video game is the software and other electronically stored content and information, rather than the hardware it is played on, even if the two are sold as a single product (VGDC10100).

A video game does not include anything produced for advertising or promotional purposes, or anything produced for the purposes of gambling. References to a video game include its soundtrack. A video game is completed when it is first in a form in which it can reasonably be regarded as ready for copies to be made and supplied to the general public, even if it is supplied and sent back for changes, or never supplied at all (*CTA 2009, s 1217AA*; VGDC10150).

Video games development company

15.23 A company that meets the definition of a video games development company is subject to special tax rules in respect of video games qualifying for video games tax relief, and can qualify for this relief if certain conditions are met (*CTA 2009, ss 1217A–1217EC*).

A video games development company, in relation to a video game, is a company which (otherwise than in partnership):

- is responsible for designing, producing and testing the video game,
- is actively engaged in planning and decision-making during the design, production and testing of the video game, and
- directly negotiates, contracts and pays for rights, goods and services in relation to the video game.

The definition of a video games development company is tightly drawn to ensure that only the actual producers of a video game (rather than investors) fall within the special tax rules.

For any one video game, there can only be one video games development company. If there is more than one company satisfying the video games development company requirements in relation to a particular game, the video games development company is the one most directly engaged in the activities. If there is no company satisfying the video games development company requirements in respect of a game, there is no video games development company for that game, and therefore no video games tax relief may be claimed. A company may elect not to be regarded as the video games development company in relation to a game, and such an election has effect in relation to video games which begin to be produced in that or any subsequent accounting period (*CTA 2009, ss 1217AB, 1217AC*; VGDC10110).

Unlike film tax relief and television tax relief, the video games tax relief rules contain no provision allowing for a co-production to be treated as British by virtue of an agreement between the UK government and any other government, international organisation or authority (see **15.7**, **15.16**).

Separate video game trade

15.24 For corporation tax purposes, the video games development company's activities in relation to each qualifying video game (ie each video game in relation to which the conditions for video games tax relief are met) are treated as a trade separate from any other activities of the company, including any activities in relation to any other qualifying video game. As to which video games qualify, see **15.21**. If a video games development company makes more than one qualifying video game, each qualifying game is considered as a separate video game trade, so that profits or losses are calculated separately for each qualifying game that the company produces. So, for tax purposes, the company needs to identify separately the income and expenditure on video game development activities in connection with each qualifying game (*CTA 2009, s 1217B*).

Conditions for claiming video games tax relief

15.25 The video games development company may be eligible for video games tax relief if all four of the following conditions are met:

- There must be a video game (*CTA 2009, s 1217AA*).
- When production activities begin, the video game must be intended for supply to the general public (*CTA 2009, ss 1217C, 1217CA*).
- The video game must be certified as a culturally British product (*CTA 2009, ss 1216C, 1217CB*). The *Cultural Test (Video Games) Regulations 2014, SI 2014/1958,* set out a points-based cultural test for video games, with points awarded on the basis of the setting, content, language and British cultural aspects of the game, where certain work on the game is carried out, and the residence or nationality of the personnel involved in the making of the video game. For guidance from the British Film Institute (BFI), which administers the certification scheme on behalf of the Department for Culture, Media and Sport (DCMS), see tinyurl.com/pqpd55p.
- At least 25% of the 'core expenditure' incurred on the video game by the video games development company must be expenditure on goods or services that are provided from within the EEA. 'Core expenditure' means expenditure on designing, producing and testing the video game, but does not extend to expenditure incurred in designing the initial concept, debugging a completed game or carrying out any maintenance (*CTA 2009, ss 1217AD, 1217AE* (as amended by *FA 2014, s 34(3)*), *1217C, 1217CE*).

There is no requirement under tax law for the video games development company to hold any intellectual property rights in connection with the video game, or for any such rights to be held in the UK.

Calculating the video games tax relief

The additional deduction

15.26 If video games tax relief is available, the video games development company may claim an 'additional deduction' which increases the amount of expenditure that is allowable as a deduction for corporation tax purposes, reducing the company's taxable profits or creating or augmenting a tax loss (*CTA 2009, s 1217CF*).

This additional deduction is calculated as (*CTA 2009, s 1217CG*):

$$E - P$$

where:

- E (the enhanceable expenditure) is the lower of:
  - EEA qualifying expenditure incurred to date (before 1 April 2014, this was UK qualifying expenditure)
  - 80% of total qualifying expenditure incurred to date

- P is the total of additional deductions given for previous periods of account (so P is Nil for the first period of account of the separate video game trade).

However, for these purposes 'qualifying expenditure' excludes any subcontractor payments in excess of £1 million in respect of design, production or testing (*CTA 2009, s 1217CF(3A), (5)*).

Special rules apply to determine how trading losses from a separate video game trade may be used including the treatment of terminal losses (*CTA 2009, ss 1217D–1217DC* and **15.48–15.53**).

In certain circumstances, a video games development company that has ceased to carry on its separate video game trade in respect of one game, and carries on a separate video game trade in respect of another game, may elect to carry forward its unused terminal loss from the first game against the profits from the second game. The legislation uses the expression 'special video games relief' to refer collectively to video games tax relief and this ability to transfer terminal losses (*CTA 2009, ss 1217DC, 1217E*).

Video game tax credit

15.27 If video games tax relief is available, the video games development company may claim a video game tax credit (ie a cash payment from HMRC) for an accounting period in which it has a surrenderable loss. See *CTA 2009, ss 1217CH–1217CJ*, for further details on how the surrenderable loss is calculated and how the tax credit is given. The tax credit is 25% of losses surrendered. See also VGDC55000 onwards.

How to claim video games tax relief

15.28 A claim for video games tax relief must be included in the company's tax return for an accounting period. It can be made in respect of any accounting period during which the video games development company carries on the separate video game trade. Normally, a claim will be made for the accounting period in which the video game is completed or abandoned.

Before a claim for the relief is made, the Secretary of State must certify that the game is a British game. An interim certificate as well as a final certificate can be obtained. Interim claims are made on the assumption that the required conditions have been met. If the company abandons video games development activities in relation to the game, its tax return for the period in question may be accompanied by an interim certificate, and the abandonment does not affect entitlement to special video games relief (see **15.26**) for that game in respect of that or any previous period. However, if the company completes the video game, its tax return for the completion period must be accompanied by a final certificate; otherwise, all entitlement to special video games relief for that game for any period is forfeited. If any of the conditions are not actually met on completion of the video game, the position is adjusted to reflect the outcome, including (if appropriate) repayment of the video game tax credit to HMRC with interest. Interim claims cannot be made outside the corporation tax company return process (*CTA 2009, ss 1217CB, 1217EA, 1217EB*). For guidance on claims, see VGDC60000 onwards.

A general anti-avoidance provision denies video games tax relief arising from artificially inflated claims. Where a transaction is attributable to arrangements, the main object or one of the main objects of which is to enable a company to obtain video games tax relief (whether the additional deduction or video game tax credit), or to enhance its entitlement to video games tax relief, that transaction is disregarded in determining the amount of video games tax relief due (*CTA 2009, s 1217CL*).

THEATRE TAX RELIEF

Introduction

15.29 A tax relief for theatrical production (generally referred to as 'theatre tax relief') was introduced by *FA 2014* to support the production of plays, musicals, opera, ballet and dance. This relief applies from 1 September 2014 (*FA 2014, Sch 4, para 17(1)*; see also *Finance Act 2014, Schedule 4 (Tax Relief for Theatrical Production) (Appointed Day) Order 2014, SI 2014/2228*). The rules for this relief are based on those for the pre-existing film tax relief, television tax relief and video games tax relief, but with significant differences (see **15.3–15.28**).

The relief allows qualifying companies within the charge to corporation tax (but not unincorporated businesses) engaged in the production of certain theatrical productions to claim an additional deduction in computing their taxable profits and, where that additional deduction results in a loss, to surrender that loss for a payable tax credit. The relevant legislation is at *CTA 2009, Pt 15C, ss 1217F–1217OB*.

There is no cap on the amount of theatre tax relief which can be claimed (other than an upper limit set on EU state aid), but only a company that is an eligible 'production company' in relation to a qualifying 'theatrical production' can claim the relief.

Where a company has incurred expenditure on which it is entitled to an R&D expenditure credit, or on which it has obtained an enhanced R&D deduction, it is not entitled to claim theatre tax relief in respect of the same expenditure (*CTA 2009, ss 104BA, 1040ZA, 1217JA(2)*; for further details of R&D reliefs, see **Chapter 14**).

HMRC's guidance on theatre tax relief is in their Theatre Tax Relief Manual at TTR10000 onwards.

Definition of a theatrical production

> **Focus**
>
> Unlike the rules for film tax relief, television tax relief and video games tax relief, those for theatre tax relief contain no cultural test and no requirement that the production must be certified as British.

15.30 Subject to a number of exclusions, 'theatrical production' includes a dramatic production and this extends to any type of ballet whether or not it is also a dramatic production.

'Dramatic production' means a production of a play, opera, musical, or other dramatic piece (whether or not involving improvisation) in relation to which (*CTA 2009, s 1217FA*):

- the actors, singers, dancers or other performers are to give their performances wholly or mainly through the playing of roles;
- each performance in the proposed run of performances is to be live. A performance is 'live' if it is to an audience before whom the performers are actually present; and
- the presentation of live performances is the main object or one of the main objects of the company's activities in relation to the production.

'Dramatic piece' may also include, for example, a show that is to be performed by a circus.

A dramatic production or ballet is not regarded as a theatrical production if (*CTA 2009, s 1217FB*):

- the main purpose, or one of the main purposes, for which it is made is to advertise or promote any goods or services;
- the performances are to consist of or include a competition or contest;
- a wild animal performs or is shown in any performance;
- the production is solely or principally of a sexual nature; or
- the making of a recording for public release or broadcast is the main object or one of the main objects of the company's activities in relation to the production.

Production company in relation to a theatrical production

15.31 A company that meets the definition of a production company in relation to a theatrical production is subject to special tax rules in respect of productions qualifying for theatre tax relief, and can qualify for this relief if certain conditions are met (*CTA 2009, s 1217FC*).

A theatrical production company is a company that is directly involved in a theatrical production. The definition of a production company is tightly drawn to ensure that only the actual producers of a production (rather than investors) fall within the special tax rules. For this purpose, 'directly involved' means that the company (acting otherwise than in partnership):

- is responsible for producing, running and closing the theatrical production;
- is actively engaged in decision-making during the production, running and closing phases;
- makes an effective creative, technical and artistic contribution to the production; and
- directly negotiates for, contracts for and pays for rights, goods and services in relation to the production.

For any one theatrical production, there can only be one production company. If there is more than one company satisfying the production company requirements in relation to a particular theatrical production, the production company is the one most directly engaged in the activities detailed above. If there is no company satisfying the production company requirements in respect of a theatrical production, there is no production company for that production, and therefore no theatre tax relief may be claimed (*CTA 2009, s 1217FC(2)–(4)*).

Unlike the rules for film tax relief, television tax relief and video games tax relief, those for theatre tax relief contain no provision for a company to elect not to be regarded as the production company in relation to a theatrical production.

Conditions for claiming theatre tax relief

15.32 A company qualifies for theatre tax relief if (*CTA 2009, s 1217G*):

- it is the production company in relation to a theatrical production;
- the 'commercial purpose condition' is met (namely, that at the beginning of the production phase the company intends that all or a high proportion of the live performances that it proposes to run will be to paying members of the general public or provided for arm's length educational purposes); and

- the 'EEA expenditure condition' is met (namely, that at least 25% of the core expenditure on the production incurred by the company is on goods or services provided from within the EEA). For this purpose, 'core expenditure' means that incurred in producing and closing the production, and may extend to substantial recasting or redesign; it does not extend to the ordinary running of the production, or any matters not directly involved in the production (eg financing, marketing, legal services or storage).

There is no requirement under tax law for the production company to hold any intellectual property rights in connection with the theatrical production, or for any such rights to be held in the UK.

Core expenditure

> **Focus**
>
> It is important to differentiate between core costs incurred in producing and closing the production, which qualify for theatre tax relief, and ongoing running costs of the production and indirect costs, which do not.

15.33 In order to qualify for the relief, expenditure must be directly incurred in the theatrical production and integral to the production process. Qualifying expenditure can be incurred in any country, but it is a qualifying condition for the production that at least 25% of the core expenditure incurred on goods or services are provided from within the EEA. Indirect expenditure, such as costs of marketing or financing, are not eligible (*CTA 2009, s 1217GC*).

The definition of qualifying expenditure will change depending on the stage of production, with no qualifying expenditure in the running period. The following table sets out the production periods and provides examples of qualifying expenditure at each stage:

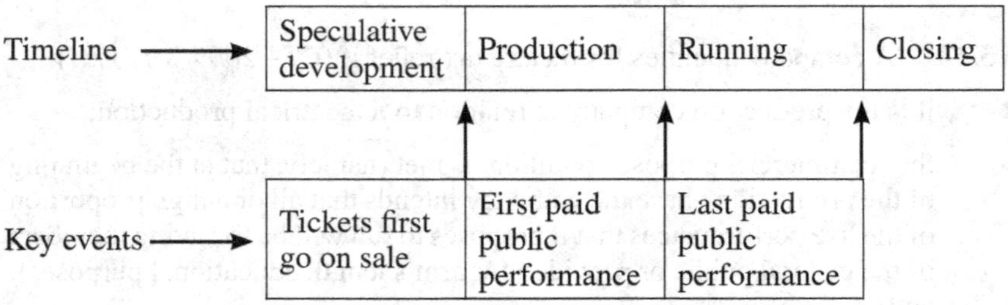

Production stage	Costs qualifying for additional deduction	Costs not qualifying for additional deduction
Speculative development	None	Speculative development costs if the production does not enter the next stage
Production	Expenditure directly incurred in theatre production and integral to the production process, eg Script fees and development Casting Rehearsal costs • theatre costs / rent • cast and crew wages • travel and subsistence • direction and development Labour and materials • props • sets and backdrops • costumes • equipment hire Visual and sound effects	Expenditure indirectly incurred in theatre production, eg Marketing / advertising Costs of financing Fees (legal, accounting) Speculative development Entertaining
Running	Further development • substantive recasting • substantive changes to stage sets	
Closing	Closing costs • striking the set	Administration Costs of financing Fees (legal, accounting) Entertaining

Separate theatrical trade

15.34 For corporation tax purposes, the theatre production company's activities in relation to each theatrical production (ie each production in relation to which the conditions for theatre tax relief are met) are treated as a trade separate from any other activities of the company, including any activities in relation to any other qualifying production (*CTA 2009, s 1217H*).

The company is treated as beginning to carry on the separate theatrical trade when the production phase begins or, if earlier, at the time of the first receipt by the company of any income from the theatrical production.

If a theatre production company makes more than one qualifying production, each qualifying production is considered as a separate theatrical trade, so that profits or losses are calculated separately for each qualifying production that the company produces. So, for tax purposes, the company needs to identify separately the income and expenditure on production activities in connection with each qualifying production.

A company may cease a separate theatrical trade at any time. If the company ceases to meet the necessary qualifying conditions in relation to the production, it is treated as ceasing to carry on the separate trade at that time.

Special provisions stipulate how the profits or losses of a separate theatrical trade are to be calculated for corporation tax purposes (*CTA 2009, s 1217I*). For each period of account, the production costs incurred (and represented in work done) to date are recognised as a debit, and the proportion of the estimated total income treated as earned at the end of the period is brought in as a credit.

The proportion of the estimated total income treated as earned at the end of a period of account is:

$$\frac{C}{T} \times I$$

where:

- C is the total to date of costs incurred (and represented in work done)
- T is the estimated total cost of the theatrical production
- I is the estimated total income from the theatrical production.

See *CTA 2009, ss 1217IB–1217IF*, for further details on how income and costs of production are to be computed. Expenditure which would normally be treated as capital, only because it is incurred on the creation of an asset (ie the theatrical production), is treated as being of a revenue nature.

Calculating the theatre tax relief

The additional deduction

15.35 If theatre tax relief is available, the production company may claim an 'additional deduction' which increases the amount of expenditure that is allowable as a deduction for corporation tax purposes, reducing the company's taxable profits or creating or augmenting a tax loss (*CTA 2009, s 1217H*).

This additional deduction is calculated as:

$$E - P$$

where:

- E (the enhanceable expenditure) is the lower of:
  - EEA qualifying expenditure incurred to date, and
  - 80% of total qualifying expenditure incurred to date
- P is the total of additional deductions given for previous periods of account (so P is nil for the first period of account of the separate theatrical trade) (*CTA 2009, s 1217J*).

Special rules apply to determine how trading losses from a separate theatrical trade may be used including the treatment of terminal losses (*CTA 2009, ss 1217M–1217MC* and **15.48–15.53**).

Theatre tax credit

15.36 If theatre tax relief is available, the production company may claim a theatre tax credit (ie a cash payment from HMRC) for an accounting period in which it has a surrenderable loss. See *CTA 2009, ss 1217K–1217KC*, for further details on how the surrenderable loss is calculated, how the tax credit is given, and a limitation on the EU state aid that an undertaking may receive in any year. The tax credit is:

- 25% of losses surrendered if the production is a touring production, or
- 20% of losses surrendered if it is not a touring production.

For this purpose a production is a 'touring production' only if the company intends at the beginning of the production phase to present at least 14 performances of the production in two or more different premises, or any number of performances in at least six or more different premises (*CTA 2009, s 1217K(6)*).

How to claim theatre tax relief

15.37 A claim for theatre tax relief must be included in the production company's tax return for an accounting period. It can be made in respect of any accounting period during which the production company carries on the separate theatrical trade. Normally, a claim will be made for the accounting period in which the production closes.

Interim claims may be made in a company tax return if it states the amount of planned core expenditure on the theatrical production that is EEA expenditure, and that the amount is such as to indicate that the EEA expenditure condition will be met in relation to the production. The company is then provisionally entitled to the additional deduction, theatre tax credits and terminal losses.

Interim relief is clawed back if it subsequently appears that the EEA expenditure condition will not be met on the company's ceasing to carry on the separate theatrical trade.

When a company which has made an interim claim for theatre tax relief ceases to carry on the separate theatrical trade, the company's corporation tax return for the period in which that cessation occurs must state that the company has ceased to carry on the separate theatrical trade, and must be accompanied by a final statement of the amount of the core expenditure on the production that is EEA expenditure. If this shows that the EEA expenditure condition is not met, the company is not entitled to the additional deduction, theatre tax credits and terminal losses relief, and any relief already granted is withdrawn.

Interim claims cannot be made outside the corporation tax company return process (*CTA 2009, ss 1217N–1217NA*).

A general anti-avoidance provision denies theatre tax relief arising from artificially inflated claims. Where a transaction is attributable to arrangements, the main object or one of the main objects of which is to enable a company to obtain a tax advantage (as defined by *CTA 2010, s 1139*), or to obtain theatre tax relief (whether the additional deduction or theatre tax credit), or to enhance its entitlement to theatre tax relief, that transaction is disregarded in determining the amount of theatre tax relief due (*CTA 2009, ss 1217LA–1217LB*).

ORCHESTRA TAX RELIEF

Focus

Finance Act 2016 introduced a tax relief for orchestral performances. The relief is based on theatre tax relief.

15.38 Orchestra tax relief is available from 1 April 2016 to companies, including charitable companies, but not to unincorporated businesses. Where qualifying conditions are met, it will offer an enhanced deduction based on core creative and production costs of live orchestral performances but not day-to-day running costs, and a tax credit of 25% based on surrenderable losses. The relevant legislation is at *CTA 2009, Pt 15D, ss 1217P–1217U*.

The relief allows qualifying companies within the charge to corporation tax (but not unincorporated businesses) engaged in the production of orchestral concert productions to claim an additional deduction in computing their taxable profits. Where the additional deduction results in a loss, it is possible to claim a payable tax credit instead.

There is no cap on the amount of theatre tax relief which can be claimed (other than an upper limit set on EU state aid). Only a company that is an eligible 'production company' in relation to a qualifying 'orchestral concert can claim the relief.

Where a company has incurred expenditure on which it is entitled to any of the other creative tax reliefs, it is not entitled to claim orchestra tax relief in respect of the same expenditure (*CTA 2009, s 1217RF*).

Definition of an orchestral concert

> **Focus**
>
> As with theatre tax relief, the rules for orchestra tax relief contain no cultural test and no requirement that the production must be certified as British.

15.39 An orchestral concert is a concert by an orchestra, ensemble, group or band consisting wholly or mainly of instrumentalists who are the primary focus of the concert (*CTA 2009, s 1217PA(1)*).

However a concert is not regarded as an orchestral concert if (*CTA 2009, s 1217PA(2)*):

- the main purpose, or one of the main purposes of the concert is to advertise or promote any goods or services;
- the concert is to consist of or include a competition or contest;
- the main object or one of the main objects of the company's activities in relation to the production is the making of a recording for public release or broadcast, or to be used as part of another media product for the consumption of the general or paying public. This includes using the recording as a soundtrack to a television or radio broadcast, in a video game, or in a film.

It should be noted that there are no definitions in the legislation for what constitutes an orchestra, or group or band, or any criteria for determining who is an instrumentalist.

Production company in relation to a concert

15.40 A company that meets the definition of a production company in relation to an orchestral concert will be subject to special tax rules in respect of concerts qualifying for orchestra tax relief, and will be able to qualify for this relief if certain conditions are met (*CTA 2009, s 1217PB*).

The definition of a production company is tightly drawn to ensure that only the actual producers of a production (rather than investors) fall within the special tax rules. A company will be a production company if (acting otherwise than in partnership), it:

- is responsible for putting on the concert from the start of the production process to the finish, including employing or engaging the performers;
- is actively engaged in decision-making in relation to the concert;
- makes an effective creative, technical and artistic contribution to the concert; and
- directly negotiates for, contracts for and pays for rights, goods and services in relation to the concert.

For any one concert, there can only be one production company. If there is more than one company satisfying the production company requirements in relation to a particular concert, the production company is the one most directly engaged in the activities detailed above. If there is no company satisfying the production company requirements, there is no production company for that concert. In these circumstances no orchestra tax relief may be claimed (*CTA 2009, s 1217PB(2)–(4)*).

Unlike the rules for film, television and video games relief, the rules for orchestra tax relief contain no provision for a company to elect not to be regarded as the production company in relation to an orchestral concert.

Conditions for claiming orchestra tax relief

15.41 A company will be able to qualify for orchestra tax relief if (*CTA 2009, ss 1217RA, 1217RB*):

- it is the production company in relation to a qualifying orchestral concert or a series of qualifying orchestral concerts;
- the company intends that the concert of concert series will be performed live before the paying public or for educational purposes; and
- the 'EEA expenditure condition' is met. This requires at least 25% of the core expenditure on the production to be incurred on goods or services provided from within the EEA.

A concert is a qualifying orchestral concert if the number of instrumentalists is at least 12 and none of the musical instruments to be played, or a minority of those instruments, is electronically or directly amplified (*CTA 2009, s 1217RA(3)*). A qualifying orchestral concert series is a series of at least two orchestral concerts, with a high proportion of the concerts being qualifying orchestral concerts (*CTA 2009, s 1217RA(5)*).

There is no requirement for the production company to hold any intellectual property rights in connection with the production, or for any such rights to be held in the UK.

Core expenditure

15.42 In order to qualify for the relief, expenditure must be incurred on those matters that are directly involved in producing the concert or concert series. This will include expenses such as travelling to and from a venue other than the usual venue that the company normally uses to stage their concerts. However, matters that are not directly associated with putting together the concert or series such as financing, marketing, legal services or storage will be excluded, as are speculative expenses. Any expenditure on the actual performance itself, such as payments to the musicians will also be excluded (*CTA 2009, s 1217RC*).

Separate orchestral trade

15.43 For corporation tax purposes, the production company's activities in relation to each concert will be treated as a trade separate from any other activities of the company, including any activities in relation to any other qualifying concert (*CTA 2009, s 1217Q*). However, it will also be possible for the company to elect to treat a series of concerts as constituting a single trade, separate from any other concerts or concert series that the company may be producing. The election is required to be made in writing to HMRC before the date of the first concert in the series, and once made, is irrevocable (*CTA 2009, ss 1217Q(4), 1217QA*).

The company will be treated as beginning to carry on the separate orchestral trade either (*CTA 2009, ss 1217Q(7), 1217QA(4)*):

- at the beginning of the pre-performance stage of the concert, or the first concert in the series; or
- if earlier, at the time of the first receipt of any income from the concert or concert series.

A company may cease a separate orchestral trade at any time. If the company ceases to meet the necessary qualifying conditions in relation to the concert or concert series, it is treated as ceasing to carry on the separate trade at that time.

Special provisions stipulate how the profits or losses of a separate orchestral trade are to be calculated for corporation tax purposes (*CTA 2009, s 1217QB*). For each period of account, the production costs incurred (and represented in work done) to date are recognised as a debit, and the proportion of the estimated total income treated as earned at the end of the period is brought in as a credit.

The proportion of the estimated total income treated as earned at the end of a period of account is:

$$\frac{C}{T} \times I$$

where:

- C is the total to date of costs incurred (and represented in work done)
- T is the estimated total cost of the production of the concert or concert series
- I is the estimated total income from the production of the concert or concert series.

See *CTA 2009, ss 1217QB–1217QG* for further details on how income and costs of production are to be computed. Expenditure which would normally be treated as capital, only because it is incurred on the creation of an asset (the concert or concert series), is treated as being of a revenue nature.

Calculating the orchestra tax relief

The additional deduction

15.44 If orchestra tax relief is available, the production company will be able to claim an additional deduction. This increases the amount of expenditure that is allowable as a deduction for corporation tax purposes, reducing the company's taxable profits or creating or augmenting a tax loss (*CTA 2009, s 1217RD*).

This additional deduction is calculated as:

$$E - P$$

where:

- E (the enhanceable expenditure) is the lower of:
  - EEA qualifying expenditure incurred to date, and
  - 80% of total qualifying expenditure incurred to date; and
- P is the total of additional deductions given for previous periods of account (so P is nil for the first period of account of the separate orchestral trade) (*CTA 2009, s 1217RE*).

Special rules apply to determine how trading losses from a separate orchestral trade may be used including the treatment of terminal losses (*CTA 2009, ss 1217S–1217SC* and **15.48–15.53**).

Orchestra tax credit

15.45 If orchestra tax relief is available, the production company will be able to claim a cash payment in the form of an orchestra tax credit for an accounting period in which it has a surrenderable loss. See *CTA 2009, ss 1217RG–1217RI*, for further details on how the surrenderable loss is calculated, how the tax credit is given, and a limitation on the EU state aid that an undertaking may receive in any year. The tax credit is 25% of losses surrendered.

How to claim orchestra tax relief

15.46 A claim for orchestra tax relief is required to be included in the production company's tax return for an accounting period. It can be made in respect of any accounting period during which the production company carries on the separate orchestral trade.

Interim claims may be made in a company tax return if it states the amount of planned core expenditure on the concert or concert series that is EEA expenditure, and that the amount is such as to indicate that the EEA expenditure condition will be met in relation to the production. The company is then provisionally entitled to the additional deduction, orchestra tax credits and terminal losses.

Interim relief is clawed back if it subsequently appears that the EEA expenditure condition will not be met on the company ceasing to carry on the separate orchestral trade. In these circumstances, the company's corporation tax return for the relevant period must state that the company has ceased to carry on the separate orchestral trade, and must be accompanied by a final statement of the amount of the core expenditure on the production that is EEA expenditure.

Interim claims cannot be made outside the corporation tax company return process (*CTA 2009, ss 1217T–1217TA*).

A general anti-avoidance provision denies orchestra tax relief arising from artificially inflated claims. Where a transaction is attributable to arrangements, the main object or one of the main objects of which is to enable a company to obtain a tax advantage (as defined by *CTA 2010, s 1139*), or to obtain orchestra tax relief, or to enhance its entitlement to the relief, that transaction is disregarded in determining the amount of relief due (*CTA 2009, ss 1217RL–1217RM*).

MUSEUMS AND GALLERIES EXHIBITIONS TAX RELIEF

> **Focus**
>
> From 1 April 2017, charitable companies can claim museums and galleries exhibitions tax relief under provisions introduced by *Finance (No2) Act 2017*. The rules are broadly similar to the theatre and orchestra tax reliefs.

15.47 From 1 April 2017, companies that are engaged in the production of exhibitions are able to access tax relief in respect of their qualifying expenditure. As with the other creative sector reliefs, there are two sets of relief available:

- An additional (super) deduction amounting to the EEA qualifying expenditure incurred, capped at 80% of the total core expenditure (*CTA 2009, s 1218ZCF*,);
- A payable tax credit in the event that the additional deduction results in a loss. As with theatre tax relief, the credit is equal to 25% of the surrendered loss for touring exhibitions and 20% for other exhibitions (*CTA 2009, s 1218ZCH*):

Unlike the other reliefs, the tax credit is capped at a maximum of £100,000 for each touring exhibition and £80,000 for other exhibitions (*CTA 2009, s 1218ZCK*).

The relief is only available to a company if it is either (*CTA 2009, s 1218ZCA(3)*):

- a charity that maintains a museum or gallery; or
- a wholly owned subsidiary of such a charity; or
- a company wholly owned by a local authority that maintains a museum or gallery.

The detailed conditions of the relief are broadly similar to theatre and orchestra tax relief (*CTA 2009, Pt 15E*).

SPECIAL RULES FOR LOSSES

> **Focus**
>
> Special rules apply to restrict losses while the project is undergoing production. There are, however, also valuable reliefs available for terminal losses.

15.48 The usual loss relief rules are modified for companies engaging in a creative sector trade. These rules are contained in the following legislative provisions:

Creative relief	Legislation
Film tax relief	*CTA 2009, ss 1208–1211*
Television tax relief	*CTA 2009, ss 1216D–1216DC*
Video games tax relief	*CTA 2009, ss 1217D–1217DC*
Theatre tax relief	*CTA 2009, ss 1217M–1217MC*
Orchestra tax relief	*CTA 2009, ss 1217S–1217SC*
Museums and galleries exhibitions tax relief	*CTA 2009, ss 1218ZD–1218ZDC*

For each creative sector relief, the company's accounting periods fall into one of two categories:

(1) a pre-completion period, being the period when the project is still in the production phase, and has not been completed; and

(2) post-completion periods, being all subsequent accounting periods.

In the case of films, television and video games, the legislation defines the completion period as the period in which the project is either completed or abandoned. For other reliefs, the completion period is simply the accounting period in which the trade comes to an end. The reason for the differences is that for films, television and video games, the project's earning power arises after completion. By contrast, a live theatrical or musical performance, whether a single performance or a series, comes to an end at the same time that the production is complete – there are no fees to be earned in subsequent accounting periods.

Companies in the creative sector industries also benefit from a more flexible tax treatment of terminal losses.

Pre-completion losses

15.49 Losses are restricted in the pre-completion period. They can only be carried forward against future profits of the same trade. No set off is available against profits made on other projects for that period, and no group relief or carry back is available against the previous year's total profits.

For the purpose of determining whether loss relief is restricted under *CTA 2010, s 269ZB* (see **4.3**), pre-completion losses carried forward against the same trade are disregarded.

Post-completion losses

15.50 On completion or abandonment of the project, the restrictions are relaxed. There are two types of post-completion loss:

- losses incurred in pre-completion periods and which have been carried forward to a post-completion period; and
- losses incurred in post-completion periods (including the one where the project is finished or abandoned).

In both cases, restrictions still apply to that part of the loss which is attributable to a creative sector tax relief. A loss is attributable to a creative tax relief if it includes an amount that has been claimed as an additional deduction (including an addition deduction claimed in an earlier accounting period and brought forward). The amount attributable to the creative sector relief can only be carried forward against profits of the same trade (subject to the rules on terminal losses). However, this part of the loss is disregarded for the purpose of the loss restriction rules losses in *CTA 2010, s 269ZB* (see **4.3**).

Pre-completion losses carried forward to a post-completion period

15.51 Pre-completion losses may continue to be carried forward against profits from the same trade. However, to the extent that such losses are not attributable to the relevant creative tax relief, they are treated as having been incurred post-completion and may also be relieved as follows:

- set off against total profits of the same period and/or carried back to the previous accounting period under *CTA 2010, s 37*. However, losses cannot be carried forward to subsequent accounting periods to be set against total profits under CTA 2010, s 45A;
- group relieved under *CTA 2010, Pt 5*. The loss is surrendered to another group member to set against profits arising in the same post-completion accounting period to which the loss was first carried forward. However, losses cannot be carried forward to subsequent accounting periods for 'carry forward' group relief under *CTA 2010, Pt 5A*..

Losses incurred in post-completion periods

15.52 These are normal losses, and all of the standard reliefs apply with the caveat that the following are not available to the extent that the loss is attributable to the relevant creative sector tax relief:

- carry forward against total profits under *CTA 2010, s 45A*;

- set against total profits and/or carried back under *CTA 2010, s 37*; or
- group relieved under *CTA 2010, Pt 5*.

Terminal losses

15.53 Special rules apply where a loss is terminal, including a loss incurred during the period in which a project was abandoned. In these circumstances, losses can be carried back for three years under the standard rules (*CTA 2009, s 39*). In addition, the following special treatment applies:

(a) The loss (or part of the loss) can be carried forward against another creative trade carried on by the company (provided it is the same type of creative trade);

(b) The loss (or part of it) can be surrendered to another group company. Unlike the standard group relief provisions, the company benefiting from the loss can carry any excess into subsequent accounting periods, provided that this company is carrying on the same type of creative sector trade and it is this trade that utilises the loss;

(c) In these two situations, there is no need to exclude any part of the loss that is attributable to the relevant creative sector relief.

(d) Note that a terminal loss can still be group relieved under the standard rules, where the fellow group company does not carry out the same type of creative sector trade. However, in this case, the group company to which the loss is surrendered cannot carry the loss forward or back under current legislation.

Losses that are carried forward as a consequence of these special provisions are ignored for the purpose of the corporate loss restriction rules losses in *CTA 2010, s 269ZB* (see **4.3**). The 'disregard' applies to the entire loss and is not restricted to the part that is attributable to the relevant creative sector tax relief.

Chapter 16

Chargeable gains

SIGNPOSTS

- Introduction and basic chargeable gains computation – including indexation and losses; indexation allowance frozen at 31 December 2017 (see **16.1–16.7**).
- Roll-over relief – including partial replacement and personal assets used in the trade (see **16.8–16.15**).
- Gifts to charities, and to the nation (see **16.16–16.17**).
- The substantial shareholdings exemption and amendments made by *F(No 2)A 2017* (see **16.18–16.23**).
- Intra-group transfer issues – including relief, elections and non-resident transfer (see **16.24–16.28**).
- Special transfer issues – including assets to and from trading stock and companies leaving the group (see **16.29–16.35**).
- Anti-avoidance value-shifting rules and application (see **16.36–16.39**).
- Capital losses – including those attributable to depreciatory transactions, such as dividend stripping, changes in ownership and restrictions on purchase of gains or losses (see **16.40–16.51**).
- Attribution of gains to members of non-resident companies (see **16.52**).

INTRODUCTION

Chargeable gains for companies

16.1 Companies are not liable to capital gains tax (CGT), with two notable exceptions which have no direct bearing on the way in which a company is subject to corporation tax on its chargeable gains.

Companies pay corporation tax on their chargeable gains at the same rate as on trading profits and other income. Gains arising on the disposal of fixed assets are chargeable gains, except where exemptions apply (*TCGA 1992, s 1*). From a company's perspective, disposals that are most likely to fall within the chargeable gains net are disposals of land and property held on capital account, and shareholdings not qualifying for the substantial shareholdings exemption (see **16.18–16.23**). Disposals of loan stock come within the loan relationship rules (see **Chapter 11**), and disposals of intangible fixed assets come within the intangible fixed assets regime (see **Chapter 12**).

Chargeable gains are computed, broadly, in accordance with normal CGT principles (see *Capital Gains Tax 2018/19* (Bloomsbury Professional)), although reliefs for individuals, such as retirement relief, taper relief or entrepreneurs' relief have never applied to companies. Nor has there ever been an annual exempt amount for companies.

A company's chargeable gains are adjusted by indexation allowance to allow for the effect of inflation since March 1982. The repeal of indexation allowance for individuals and other payers of CGT from 6 April 2008, did not extend to the chargeable gains of companies. However, indexation allowance for companies was frozen at 31 December 2017, meaning that no allowance is due on assets acquired on or after 1 January 2018 (*FA 2018, s 26*).

Gains on the disposal of a company's chargeable assets are included within the company's self-assessment corporation tax return. See also HMRC's Toolkit on 'Chargeable Gains for Companies' at tinyurl.com/63vn6ts.

Focus

The chargeable gains legislation offers a number of reliefs and allowances, and contains some special computational rules. It should also be noted that there are a number of anti-avoidance provisions which may trap the unwary.

The principal reliefs and allowances are addressed in the following sections:

Negligible value claims	**16.5**
Roll-over relief on replacement of business assets	**16.8–16.15, 16.32**
Intra-group asset transfers	**16.24–16.27**
Losses on shares in unquoted trading companies	**6.22**
Substantial shareholdings exemption	**16.18–16.23**
Asset transfer to a non-resident company	**16.28**
Reorganisations	**17.7–17.13**

Special computational provisions apply to:

Transfers of assets to trading stock	**16.29–16.30**
Transfers of assets from trading stock	**16.31**
Replacement of business assets by members of a group	**16.8–16.15, 16.32**
Companies leaving a group	**16.33–16.35**

Some of the anti-avoidance provisions are discussed as follows:

Value shifting	**16.36–16.37**
Depreciatory transactions	**16.40**
Dividend stripping	**16.41**
General restrictions on capital losses	**16.42**
Pre-entry losses	**16.44**
The targeted anti-avoidance rules (TAARs)	**16.45–16.51**
Attribution of gains to members of non-resident companies	**16.52**

Exceptionally, a company is subject to CGT (rather than corporation tax) on disposals of UK residential property where:

- the property has been subject to the ATED-related CGT charge introduced by *FA 2013* (see **7.24**); or
- the disposal is made on or after 6 April 2015 by a non-UK resident company controlled by five or fewer persons, except where the company itself, or at least one of the controlling persons, is a qualifying institutional investor (see **7.25**).

BASIC CHARGEABLE GAINS COMPUTATION

16.2 A chargeable gain (or, as the case may be, an allowable capital loss) is calculated by taking the gross sale proceeds and deducting allowable items of expenditure and (where applicable) indexation allowance. Allowable items include the costs of acquisition and enhancement, and incidental costs of acquisition and disposal (*TCGA 1992, s 38*). Indexation based on acquisition and enhancement costs is available to companies from the date on which such costs are incurred, or 31 March 1982 if later, until the date of disposal (*TCGA 1992, s 52A* onwards) or 31 December 2017, if sooner (*FA 2018, s 26*).

Gilt-edged securities, qualifying corporate bonds, and options to acquire or dispose of such assets are exempt from corporation tax on chargeable gains (*TCGA 1992, s 115*).

The disposal of an asset otherwise than under a bargain at arm's length is generally treated as taking place at market value (*TCGA 1992, s 17*). For chargeable gains purposes generally, the market value of an asset means the price which it might reasonably be expected to fetch on a sale in the open market (*TCGA 1992, s 272(1)*). Note that, until 5 April 2015, listed securities were usually valued at 'one-quarter up' between the respective values of the lowest and highest bargains made during the day. From 6 April 2015 onwards, they are valued at the mid-point between the closing 'buy' and 'sell' quoted at the end of the day (*TCGA 1992, s 272*, as amended by the *Market Value of Shares, Securities and Strips Regulations 2015, SI 2015/616*).

When preparing the chargeable gains computation, the incidental costs of sale are deducted from sale proceeds and may include such items as valuation fees, auctioneers' or estate agency fees, costs of advertising or legal costs. These costs do not qualify for indexation allowance, regardless of when they are incurred (*TCGA 1992, ss 38(1)(c), 53(2)(b)*).

Thus, allowable expenditure includes:

(a) the original cost of the asset;

(b) any enhancement expenditure; and

(c) the incidental costs of disposal.

All of the expenditure allowed under (a) and (b) above qualifies for indexation allowance, where applicable.

Where any capital sum is derived from an asset, there is a disposal for the purposes of the chargeable gains legislation. This is subject to exceptions in the case of certain compensation and insurance monies and mortgage arrangements (*TCGA 1992, s 22*).

On the entire loss, destruction, dissipation or extinction of an asset, there is disposal for the purposes of the chargeable gains legislation, whether or not any capital sum is received. For this purpose, a building or structure may be regarded as an asset separate from the land on which it is situated (*TCGA 1992, s 24*).

Where a capital sum was received before 27 January 2014 as compensation or damages in respect of a right to take court action (eg under an agreement to settle a case out of court) which had no connection with a chargeable asset, it was exempt from tax on chargeable gains by concession. However, from 27 January 2014 this concession is limited to the first £500,000 of any such sum; the balance will normally be taxed as a chargeable gain, but this may be a matter for negotiation with HMRC (Concession D33). HMRC have since consulted on the possibility of primary legislation to replace the concessionary limit by an absolute limit of £1 million, although no amendments were enacted by any of the 2015 or 2016 *Finance Acts* (see tinyurl.com/kkp762m).

Enhancement expenditure

16.3 Enhancement expenditure is capital expenditure incurred for the purpose of enhancing the value of the asset, being expenditure reflected in the state or nature of the asset at the time of the disposal (*TCGA 1992, s 38(1)(b)*). Expenditure deductible on revenue account, such as repairs, maintenance and insurance, is excluded since such costs only maintain the value of an asset. Conversely, capital expenditure that has not qualified as a deduction on revenue account may qualify as a deduction for chargeable gains purposes, so long as it enhances the value of the underlying asset.

In *Aberdeen Construction Group Ltd v CIR* 52 TC 281 at the Court of Session, Lord Emslie stated that what the legislation 'is looking for is, as the result of relevant expenditure, an identifiable change for the better in the state or nature of the asset, and this must be a change distinct from the enhancement of value'.

In *Blackwell v Revenue and Customs Commissioners* [2015] UKUT 418 (TCC), the Upper Tribunal held that a payment made by the taxpayer to release him from an agreement with a prospective purchaser was not deductible as enhancement expenditure on subsequent sale of his shares, as the state or nature of the shares themselves was unaffected by the expenditure. A capital contribution to a company was disallowed for similar reasons in *Trustees of the F D Fenston Will Trusts* (SpC 589).

For details of how HMRC interpret the rules on enhancement expenditure, see HMRC Capital Gains Manual at CG15180 onwards.

Indexation

16.4 Indexation allowance is calculated by multiplying the relevant allowable expenditure by the indexation factor. The indexation factor is computed (*TCGA 1992, s 54*) by expressing the following fraction as a decimal (to three decimal places):

$$(RD - RI)/RI$$

where:

- RD is the retail prices index (RPI) for the month of disposal
- RI is the RPI for the later of:
  - March 1982; and
  - the month in which the expenditure was incurred.

If there is a decrease in RPI between the base month and the month of disposal, the indexation allowance is nil. If expenditure is incurred on two or more dates, a separate indexation calculation is required for each component of the expenditure.

Indexation allowance cannot create or augment a loss. Therefore, no indexation is available if proceeds less costs result in a loss before indexation (*TCGA 1992, s 53(2A)*). If the deduction of indexation allowance would have turned a gain before indexation into a loss, the gain is reduced to nil instead (*TCGA 1992, s 53(1)(b)*).

See **Appendix 1** for the RPI from March 1982 onwards. Indexation allowance tables showing the indexed rise in respect of disposals taking place in particular months can be found at tinyurl.com/nwf65d8 (for months up to 31 March 2014) and at tinyurl.com/jgeevzr.

Negligible value claims

16.5 Where an asset becomes of negligible value, a claim may be made to treat the asset as though it had been sold and immediately reacquired for consideration equal to the value specified in the claim, either at the time of the claim or at an earlier time specified in the claim and falling on or after the first day of the earliest accounting period ending not more than two years before the time of the claim (*TCGA 1992, s 24*).

For a negligible value claim to be made, either of the following conditions must be met:

- Condition A: the asset has become of negligible value while owned by the current owner; or
- Condition B: the asset had become of negligible value at an earlier time, since when there had been no disposals other than no gain/no loss disposals.

An earlier time may not be specified in a negligible value claim if a loss arising on a deemed disposal at the time of the claim would fall within the substantial shareholdings exemption (see CG53210; also **16.18–16.23**).

A negligible value claim can be used to establish a capital loss in the accounting period in which the claim is made or, as explained above, in an earlier accounting period. Careful choice of the period in which the loss is established may be crucial in determining when the loss can be relieved.

There is no statutory definition of 'negligible' for this purpose. HMRC take the view that it means 'worth next to nothing' (CG13124).

HMRC publish a list of shares formerly quoted on the London Stock Exchange, which have been declared of negligible value, and this is updated periodically (see tinyurl.com/p2q4uql).

In *Brown v Revenue & Customs* [2014] UKFTT 208 (TC), the First-tier Tribunal upheld the taxpayer's contention that shares had become of negligible value even though, in the particular circumstances of the case, the company continued to trade, the majority shareholder subscribed for further shares and the taxpayer said that he would not consider selling his shares for less than 10 pence each.

Exemption for certain wasting assets

16.6 Where a wasting asset is tangible movable property, its disposal is exempt from tax on chargeable gains. However, this exemption does not extend to plant or machinery that has been used by a business which has, or could have, claimed capital allowances (*TCGA 1992, s 45*).

Following HMRC's defeat in *Revenue and Customs Commissioners v Executors of Lord Howard of Henderskelfe (Deceased)* [2014] EWCA Civ 278, the law has been changed from 1 April 2015 so that this wasting asset exemption applies only if the vendor has used the asset as plant in its own business (*TCGA 1992, s 45(3A)–(3D)*, as inserted by *FA 2015, s 40*).

Relief for capital losses

16.7 The company's chargeable gains for the accounting period are reduced by allowable capital losses of the same period, and any unrelieved allowable capital losses brought forward from previous accounting periods. Capital losses may only be set against chargeable gains of the current accounting period or carried forward to set against future chargeable gains.

Unused capital losses are carried forward for offset against chargeable gains of subsequent accounting periods. There are no provisions allowing for the carry back of capital losses, the surrender of capital losses between group companies, or the offset of capital losses against trading or other income, with the following exceptions:

- limited provisions which allow capital loss relief against income on disposals of shares in qualifying trading companies (see **6.22**); and
- provisions which allow a chargeable gain or allowable loss to be reallocated wholly or partly between companies within the same group (see **16.27**).

Under self-assessment, the total of a company's allowable capital losses are required to be shown on form CT600 within the company tax return.

Example 16.1—Computation of chargeable gain

Facts

The West End Trading Co Ltd prepares accounts to 31 March each year. On 3 December 2015 the company disposes of an office block for £40 million.

The incidental costs of sale are £1 million. The block was purchased in January 2008 for £15.5 million. Incidental costs of acquisition amounted to £0.5 million. In January 2009 a new frontage was added to the building at a cost of £2 million, and this was considered to be capital expenditure.

Analysis

The chargeable gain to be included within the corporation tax computation for the year ended 31 March 2016 is calculated as follows:

		£000	*£000*
December 2015	Gross sale proceeds		40,000
	Less: Incidental costs of sale		1,000
	Net sale proceeds		39,000
	Less: Relevant allowable expenditure:		
January 2008	Acquisition cost	15,500	
January 2008	Incidental costs of acquisition	500	
January 2009	Enhancement expenditure	2,000	
			18,000
	Un-indexed gain		21,000
	Less: Indexation allowance		
	Cost 16,000 × 0.249	3,984	
	Enhancement 2,000 × 0.247	494	
			4,478
	Chargeable gain		16,522

Workings: calculation of indexation factor

RPI	December 2015	262.0
RPI	January 2008	209.8
RPI	January 2009	210.1

Factor

Cost	(RPI December 2015 – RPI January 2008) ÷ RPI January 2008	0.249
Enhancement	(RPI December 2015 – RPI January 2009) ÷ RPI January 2009	0.247

ROLL-OVER RELIEF ON REPLACEMENT OF BUSINESS ASSETS

Focus

Roll-over relief enables a company to defer a gain on replacement of a chargeable business asset – sometimes indefinitely, if the business continues.

16.8 Assets sold in excess of cost may bring about a chargeable gain, assessable upon the company. If the assets are within any of a number of classes and if new 'replacement' assets also within any of those classes are purchased, the gain may qualify for roll-over relief under *TCGA 1992, s 152*. This will enable the gain to be deferred against the cost of the new asset.

The assets that can qualify for relief are listed under *TCGA 1992, s 155*.

For companies, there are three relevant classes of asset as follows:

Class 1

Assets within heads A and B are given below.

Head A

(i) Any building or part of a building and any permanent or semi-permanent structure in the nature of a building, occupied (as well as used) only for the purposes of the trade.

(ii) Any land occupied (as well as used) only for the purposes of the trade. Head A has effect subject to *TCGA 1992, s 156*.

Head B

Fixed plant or machinery which does not form part of a building or of a permanent or semi-permanent structure in the nature of a building.

Class 2

Ships, aircraft and hovercraft ('hovercraft' having the same meaning as in the *Hovercraft Act 1968*).

Class 3

Satellites, space stations and spacecraft (including launch vehicles).

There are additional relevant classes of assets for unincorporated businesses – namely goodwill and various agricultural quotas. For companies, such assets have fallen within the intangible fixed assets regime since 1 April 2002 (see

Chapter 12), but a chargeable gain realised by a company on disposal of a pre-*FA 2002* intangible asset falling within these classes could still qualify for roll-over relief under *TCGA 1992, s 155*.

FA 2014 corrected an error made during the government's tax law rewrite project. For claims made on or after 19 March 2014, companies cannot claim chargeable gains roll-over relief where the proceeds on disposal of a tangible asset are reinvested in an intangible fixed asset (*TCGA 1992, s 156ZB*; see **12.25**).

Roll-over relief on replacement of business assets can be claimed by a group of companies on a group-wide basis, so that a gain by one member of the group can be rolled over against new assets acquired by other group members. For this purpose, all the trades carried on by the members of the group are treated as a single trade. Where a company leaves the group owning an asset against which a gain from another group company has been rolled over within the past six years, a degrouping charge can arise (see **16.33–16.35**).

Conditions affecting the old assets and the new assets

16.9 The old assets must have been used solely for the purposes of the trade throughout the period of ownership. The consideration received must be used in acquiring new assets or an interest therein. Upon acquisition the new assets must also be used solely for the purposes of the trade. The new assets must be acquired for the purpose of their use in the trade, and not (eg as in the case of an investment or trading stock) wholly or partly for the purposes of realising a gain from their disposal, ie as an investment or trading stock (*TCGA 1992, s 152(5)*).

The trading company can then claim that the consideration on the sale of the old assets be regarded as reduced by an amount that results in their disposal producing neither a gain nor a loss after indexation allowance, or by such lesser amount that is invested in the new assets. The acquisition cost of the new asset is reduced by the same amount.

There is no requirement that a new asset is, in fact, a specific replacement for an old asset. It is only necessary to show that the assets each fall within any of the relevant classes of asset (and not necessarily within the same classes), and that the new asset was acquired within a specified time period. The new asset must be acquired during the period commencing 12 months before and ending three years after the disposal of, or of the interest in, the old asset, or at such earlier or later time as HMRC may by notice allow. A provisional claim may be made if the company enters into an unconditional contract for purchase (CG60620–CG60660).

An apportionment is required if the old asset is not used for the purposes of the trade throughout the period of ownership, or if only part of an asset is used for the purposes of a trade. Periods before 31 March 1982 are ignored in calculating the period of ownership.

Assets only partly replaced

16.10 If only part of the proceeds of disposal of the old assets is reinvested in new assets, but the amount not reinvested is less than the chargeable gain, part of the gain can still be rolled over. The amount of gain that can be rolled over is the total amount of the gain less the sum that is not reinvested (*TCGA 1992, s 153*).

In *Pems Butler Ltd and Others v Revenue and Customs Commissioners* [2012] UKFTT 73 (TC), a trading company sold a farm but reinvested only part of the disposal proceeds in a replacement asset, which was then used only partly by the company, so the company's claim for roll-over relief was sharply reduced.

New assets which are depreciating assets

16.11 If the new asset is a depreciating asset, the chargeable gain is not deducted from the cost of the new asset but is held over and becomes chargeable (*TCGA 1992, s 154*) at the earliest of the following events:

- the new asset is disposed of;
- the asset is no longer used for the purposes of the trade; or
- ten years have elapsed since the acquisition of the new asset.

A depreciating asset is any asset that will become a wasting asset within ten years of acquisition. A wasting asset is an asset with a predictable life of 50 years or less (*TCGA 1992, s 44*). Fixed plant and machinery installed in a building with a life of more than 60 years to run is not a depreciating asset. A leasehold building with less than 60 years of the lease still to run is a depreciating asset (CG60360).

Land and buildings: roll-over relief

16.12 Land on the one hand and buildings on the other are treated as separate assets for roll-over relief purposes. HMRC wish to see separate computations to support a claim, together with an appropriate apportionment of costs (CG60970). No roll-over relief is available for land held or property dealt with in the course of trade by a property dealing or development company, other than land and buildings that it used as a fixed asset for the purposes of the trade. Lessors of tied premises are treated as occupying and using the premises for the purposes of their trade (*TCGA 1992, s 156(4)*).

New assets not purchased

16.13 By concession, roll-over relief may be claimed where proceeds from the disposal of old assets are used to enhance the value of qualifying assets already held. Those assets already held must have been used only for the purposes of the company's trade and, on completion of the enhancement work, the assets must be taken back immediately into use in the trade (Concession D22).

Similarly, by concession, if proceeds from the sale of old assets are used to acquire a further interest in another asset that is already being used for the purposes of the trade, that new interest is treated as a new asset if it is taken into use for the purposes of the trade (Concession D25).

New asset not brought immediately into trading use

16.14 If a new asset is not taken into use for the purposes of the trade immediately it has been acquired, roll-over relief will still be available by concession in the following circumstances (Concession D24):

- the owner proposes to incur capital expenditure for the purposes of enhancing its value;
- any work arising from such capital expenditure begins as soon as possible after acquisition and is completed within a reasonable time;
- on completion of the work the asset is taken into use for the purpose of the trade and for no other purpose; and
- the asset is neither let nor used for any non-trading purpose in the period between acquisition and taking into use for trade purposes.

Assets owned personally and used for personal company's trade

16.15 If an individual exercises no less than 5% of the voting rights of a company, which uses an asset owned by that individual for the purposes of its trade, the company and the individual will be treated as one person for the purpose of determining whether the conditions for roll-over relief are satisfied (*TCGA 1992, s 157*).

GIFTS TO CHARITIES, ETC

16.16 Where a company disposes of an asset, otherwise than under a bargain at arm's length, to a charity, a registered Community Amateur Sports Club (CASC) or one of a number of other bodies approved in connection with gifts for national purposes, etc, the usual 'market value' rule (see **16.2**) is disapplied. Instead, if the consideration by the charity, CASC or approved body does not exceed the donor company's allowable expenditure, no chargeable gains arises. If it does, the disposal is treated as made for the actual consideration given, and the resulting chargeable gain, after indexation allowance, is taxable if not otherwise exempted or relieved (*TCGA 1992, s 257*).

The relief from corporation tax on a chargeable gain in these circumstances is in addition to the corporation tax relief available on gifts of certain investments to charities but not to CASCs (see **2.84**).

GIFTS OF PRE-EMINENT OBJECTS TO THE NATION

16.17 A company that is the sole owner of a pre-eminent object, a collection of objects, or an object associated with a particular historic building, may offer to gift it to the nation under an arrangement that is also known as the 'cultural gifts scheme'. From 1 April 2012 and subject to detailed qualifying conditions (which include acceptance of the donor company's offer), the company is entitled to corporation tax relief amounting to up to 20% of the value of the gift, given in the accounting period in which its offer was registered under the scheme. On acceptance, any gain made by the donor is not treated as a chargeable gain (*FA 2012, Sch 14*). This scheme does not extend to land or buildings. For further details of the relief, *see Capital Gains Tax 2016/17* (Bloomsbury Professional).

SUBSTANTIAL SHAREHOLDINGS EXEMPTION (SSE)

The nature of the exemption

> **Focus**
>
> The substantial shareholdings exemption provides that a gain (or loss) on a disposal by a company of shares in another company (or an interest in shares, or certain assets related to shares) is not a chargeable gain (or allowable capital loss, as the case may be) if certain conditions are met.
>
> The relief is substantially simplified by *F(No 2)A 2017* from 1 April 2017.

16.18 Provided all relevant conditions are met, the gain on the disposal of shares or an interest in shares held by a company in another company is not a chargeable gain. Conversely, a loss arising in such circumstances is not an allowable capital loss and cannot therefore be offset against chargeable gains on other disposals (*TCGA 1992, Sch 7AC*).

The exemption does not apply where a disposal is deemed to be a no gain/no loss transfer for chargeable gains purposes under *TCGA 1992, s 171* (see **16.26**).

Where the necessary conditions are met, the substantial shareholdings exemption applies automatically and the company cannot opt out of it. No claim is required.

Definition of a substantial shareholding

16.19 Essentially, the investing company must hold a 'substantial shareholding' in the company invested in throughout a continuous period of at least 12 months beginning not more than two years before the disposal (*TCGA 1992, Sch 7AC, para 7*). For this purpose, a substantial shareholding (*TCGA 1992, Sch 7AC, para 8*) comprises shares or interests in the shares of a company, by virtue of which the investing company:

- holds not less than 10% of the investee company's share capital; and
- is entitled to at least 10% of that company's profits available for distribution to equity holders; and
- is entitled to at least 10% of that company's assets available to equity holders on a winding up.

From 1 April 2017, the period of holding has been extended to a continuous period of at least 12 months beginning not more than six years before the disposal, for disposals on or after 1 April 2017 (*F(No 2)A 2017, s 27*). This will give vendors substantially greater flexibility in the use of the exemption.

Group member holdings can be aggregated in order to calculate whether the 10% holding criteria are met (*TCGA 1992, Sch 7AC, para 9*). The chargeable gains group definition applies, but is modified so that the requirement of one company being a 75% subsidiary of another is replaced by the requirement to be a 51% subsidiary instead (*TCGA 1992, Sch 7AC, para 26(1)(b)*; see **16.24** for the definition of a chargeable gains group).

Even if shares are vested in a liquidator, the company continues to be treated as the beneficial owner of the assets (*TCGA 1992, Sch 7AC, para 16*).

The period of ownership looks back through no gain/no loss transfers and share reorganisations in determining whether the necessary 12-month period of ownership has been achieved (*TCGA 1992, Sch 7AC, paras 10, 14*). For intra-group transfers from 1 April 2017, the aggregated period of ownership includes periods of ownership by non-resident companies (*TCGA 1992, Sch 7AC, para 10* as amended by *F(No 2)A 2017, s 27(4)*).

However, for deemed sales and reacquisitions, the time of ownership commences with the reacquisition of the holding (*TCGA 1992, Sch 7AC, para 11*).

Repurchase agreement arrangements treat the time of ownership as that commencing with the original owner (*TCGA 1992, Sch 7AC, para 12*). Similarly, stock lending arrangements have no effect on the original ownership time span (*TCGA 1992, Sch 7AC, para 13*). A demerger that is treated as a reorganisation (*TCGA 1992, s 192*) is also looked through when calculating the period of ownership (*TCGA 1992, Sch 7AC, para 15*).

The substantial shareholdings exemption conditions are deemed satisfied in certain circumstances where trading assets have been transferred intra-group to a newly incorporated company by the investing company or another group company (*TCGA 1992, Sch 7AC, para 15A*). This extends the holding period to include previous use of trading assets by another company while it was a member of a group, and facilitates a hive-down before a company leaves a group as a result of a disposal of its shares on or after 19 July 2011 (or, in some cases, 1 April 2011). See also **16.33–16.35** regarding degrouping charges.

Conditions affecting the investing company

16.20 The conditions affecting the investing company are completely repealed for disposals on or after 1 April 2017 (*F(No 2)A 2017, s 27(2)*).

For disposals up to 31 March 2017, the investing company must be a sole trading company or a member of a qualifying group (broadly, this means a trading group but can also be a group with material not for profit activities, as those activities are usually ignored in determining whether a group is a trading group) throughout the period beginning at the start of the latest 12-month period referred to in **16.19** and ending with the time immediately after the disposal (*TCGA 1992, Sch 7AC, para 18(1)*; see **6.23**).

This requirement can also be met in a group situation where the company holding the shares does not qualify, if there is another member of the group that could have done so had the investment been transferred to it by intra-group transfer under *TCGA 1992, s 171* and it had then made the disposal.

Where there is a deferral of the completion date on disposal, the investing company must qualify at the time of completion and immediately afterwards (*TCGA 1992, Sch 7AC, para 18(5)*).

If the investing company has any doubts about its own status as this affects its eligibility for the relief, it may be possible to request HMRC's opinion through the non-statutory clearance service (see CG53120; also tinyurl.com/pvc4j2h).

Conditions affecting the investee company

16.21 For disposals up to 31 March 2017, the company invested in must be a qualifying company (ie a trading company or a holding company of a trading group or a trading subgroup) throughout the period beginning at the start of the latest 12-month period (referred to in **16.19**) and ending with the time immediately after the disposal (*TCGA 1992, Sch 7AC, para 19(1)*).

There are special provisions dealing with transfers of shares which have occurred within the group (*TCGA 1992, Sch 7AC, para 15*).

Where there is a deferral of the completion date on disposal, the investee company must qualify at the time of completion (*TCGA 1992, Sch 7AC, paras 15, 19(3)*).

For disposals on or after 1 April 2017, the requirement will only have to be satisfied throughout the period beginning at the start of the latest 12-month period (referred to in **16.19**) and ending with the time of the disposal, so there will no longer be a requirement to satisfy the condition immediately after the disposal (*TCGA 1992, Sch 7AC, para 10* as amended by *F(No 2)A 2017, s 27(5)*).

There are two exceptions to this change, whereby it will still be necessary for the company to continue to trade immediately after the disposal:

- where the disposal is to a person connected with the investing company; or
- where the requirement in *TCGA 1992, Sch 7AC, para 7* is met by virtue of *TCGA 1992, Sch 7AC, para 15A* (see **16.19**).

It is the responsibility of the investor company to determine whether a company, in which shares (or interests in shares or assets related to shares) are held and since disposed of, was a qualifying company. However, in cases of uncertainty, it may be possible for the investee company to request HMRC's opinion through the non-statutory clearance service (CG53120; also tinyurl.com/pvc4j2h).

Trading activities

16.22 A 'trading company' is defined as a company carrying on trading activities whose activities do not include (to a substantial extent) activities other than trading activities (*TCGA 1992, Sch 7AC, para 20*).

The generation of investment income does not necessarily mean that a company is not trading. For example, the company may set aside funds in the short term for the expansion of the business, or a cyclical business may hold large funds from time to time that it requires for settling its trading debts.

Trading activities, for these purposes, include activities carried on by a company:

- in the course of, or for the purposes of, a trade it is carrying on;
- for the purposes of a trade it is preparing to carry on;
- with a view to it acquiring or starting to carry on a trade; or
- with a view to it acquiring a significant interest in the share capital of a trading company, or the holding company of a trading group or subgroup (subject to the restrictions outlined below).

A company's purpose is understood to mean its actual or its intended activities; this will mean examining the directors' intentions. The company's view to acquire or start a trade, or its view to acquire a shareholding, must materialise as soon as is reasonably practical in the circumstances; 'significant' for this purpose only refers to ordinary share capital, and the company to be acquired must not already be a member of the same group.

Any non-trading activities should be insubstantial. As to the meaning of this and HMRC's views thereon, see **6.23**.

A holding company of a trading group is 'a company whose business (disregarding any trade carried on by it) consists wholly or mainly of the holding of shares in one or more companies which are its 51% subsidiaries'. HMRC interpret 'wholly or mainly', in this context, as more than half of whatever measure is reasonable in the circumstances of the case. Intra-group activities are disregarded for the purpose of the financial tests.

Trading activities also include a qualifying interest in a joint venture company (*TCGA 1992, Sch 7AC, para 20*).

Example 16.2—Substantial shareholdings exemption

Facts

Atlantic Ltd is a trading company, with two wholly owned subsidiary companies, India Ltd and China Ltd.

On 1 July 2014, Atlantic Ltd acquired a 25% holding in the ordinary share capital of Pacific Ltd.

On 1 September 2014, Pacific Ltd was taken over by Adriatic Ltd in return for the issue of new shares by Adriatic Ltd.

Atlantic Ltd received an exchange of shares under the no gain/no loss treatment. *TCGA 1992, s 135* (exchange of securities for those in another company) applied *TCGA 1992, s 127* (equation of original shares and new holding). As a result, Atlantic Ltd owned 20% of Adriatic Ltd.

On 1 March 2015, Atlantic Ltd transferred its 20% holding in Adriatic Ltd to its 100% subsidiary, India Ltd, on a no gain/no loss basis. *TCGA 1992, s 171* (transfers within a group) applied.

On 1 July 2015, India Ltd sold its 20% holding in the ordinary share capital of Adriatic Ltd to an unconnected third party.

Analysis

The holding in Pacific Ltd was bought on 1 July 2014 and sold on 1 July 2015. It is necessary to look back through the period of ownership of the holding to ascertain whether the substantial shareholdings exemption applies (*TCGA 1992, Sch 7AC, para 10*). Since 1 July 2014 the only disposals have been no gain/no loss disposals, so India Ltd is treated as having owned the shares for an unbroken period of 12 months prior to disposal; therefore, the substantial shareholdings exemption applies.

SUBSTANTIAL SHAREHOLDINGS EXEMPTION FOR QUALIFYING INSTITUTIONAL INVESTORS

The nature of the exemption

Focus

The substantial shareholdings exemption is extended, from 1 April 2017, to qualifying shareholdings in companies with qualifying institutional investors holding at least 25% of their ordinary share capital.

16.23 *F(No 2)A 2017* introduced a new exemption within the SSE, for companies partly held by qualifying institutional investors (QIIs) (*F(No 2) A 2017, s 28*). The main requirements for relief are that the investor company must have a substantial shareholding (see **16.19**) and the investee company must fail trading company or trading group tests in *TCGA 1992, Sch 7AC, para 19* (new *TCGA 1992, Sch 7AC, para 3A(2)* introduced by *F(No 2)A 2017, s 28(2)*).

If a shareholder company does not have a substantial shareholding, it can still qualify through a value-based rule, whereby a shareholding qualifies for the exemption if, despite being less than 10%, it cost at least £20 million when acquired (new *TCGA 1992, Sch 7AC, para 8A* introduced by *F(No 2) A 2017, s 28(3)*). The investor company must also be entitled to not less than a proportionate percentage of the profits available for distribution to equity holders of the company invested in, and to not less than a proportionate percentage of the assets of the company invested in available for distribution to equity holders on a winding up, unless the difference is insignificant (*TCGA 1992, Sch 7AC, para 8A(5)*).

There are no rules as to the activities of the investing company or the company invested in. However, the investing company must not be a disqualified listed company (*TCGA 1992, Sch 7AC, para 3A(2)(c)*). A company is a disqualified listed company if any of its shares are listed on a recognised stock exchange, it is not itself a QII and it is not a qualifying UK REIT (within the meaning of *CTA 2010, Pt 12*) (*TCGA 1992, Sch 7AC, para 3A(5)*).

If at least 80% of the shares of the investing company are held by QIIs, a chargeable gain on the disposal by the investing company is exempt (*TCGA 1992, Sch 7AC, para 3A(3)*). If between 25% and 80% of the shares of the investing company are held by QIIs, any chargeable gain on the disposal by the investing company is reduced by the percentage of the ordinary share capital of the investing company which is owned by the qualifying institutional investors (*TCGA 1992, Sch 7AC, para 3A(4)*).

A qualifying institutional investor is defined by new *TCGA 1992, Sch 7AC, para 30A* as:

- a pension scheme;
- a life assurance business;
- sovereign wealth funds;
- charities;
- investment trusts;
- authorised investment funds; or
- exempt unauthorised unit trusts.

INTRA-GROUP ASSET TRANSFER

Focus

Group companies are able to transfer chargeable assets amongst themselves without crystallising chargeable gains or allowable capital losses.

Group structure

16.24 A company (referred to here as the 'principal company') and its 75% subsidiaries (whether UK resident or not) form a group for chargeable gains purposes. If any of those subsidiaries have 75% subsidiaries, the group includes them and their 75% subsidiaries, but not so as to include a company that is not an effective 51% subsidiary of the principal company (*TCGA 1992, s 170(3)*).

A company is an 'effective 51% subsidiary' of the principal company if (and only if) the latter:

- is beneficially entitled to more than 50% of any profits available for distribution to equity holders of the subsidiary, and
- would be beneficially entitled to more than 50% of any assets of the subsidiary available for distribution to its equity holders on a winding up (*TCGA 1992, s 170(7)*).

The concept of equity holders is largely the same as for group relief purposes (*TCGA 1992, s 170(8)*; see **5.6** and **5.9**).

Example 16.3—Definition of group for chargeable gains purposes

Facts

A Ltd owns 75% of the ordinary share capital of X Ltd. X Ltd owns 80% of the ordinary share capital of Y Ltd.

Analysis

A Ltd, X Ltd and Y Ltd are a group because:

- A Ltd owns at least 75% of X Ltd;
- X Ltd owns at least 75% of Y Ltd; and
- A Ltd controls over 50% of Y Ltd.

A company (A) cannot be the principal company of a group if it is itself a 75% subsidiary of another company (B). The exception to this rule is where A is prevented from being a member of B's group because it is not an effective 51% subsidiary of B. In this case, A can be the principal company of another group, unless this enables a third company (C) to be the principal company of a group of which A would then be a member (*CTA 2009, s 767*).

A group of companies remains the same group as long as the same company is the principal company of the group. If the principal company of a group becomes a member of another group, the groups are treated as the same group and the question as to whether a company has ceased to be a member of a group is determined accordingly. The passing of a resolution for the winding up of a member of a group is not regarded as the occasion of that or any other company ceasing to be a member of the group (*CTA 2009, s 769*).

Company cannot be a member of more than one group

16.25 Where a company could otherwise belong to two or more groups, four criteria are applied to determine to which group the company belongs, in the following order (*TCGA 1992, s 170(6)*):

- voting rights;
- profits available for distribution;
- assets on a winding up; and
- percentage of directly and indirectly owned ordinary shares.

Example 16.4—Definition of group: indirect holdings

Facts

A Ltd owns 75% of the ordinary share capital of F Ltd. F Ltd owns 80% of the ordinary share capital of G Ltd. G Ltd owns 75% of the ordinary share capital of H Ltd. H Ltd owns 75% of the ordinary share capital of I Ltd.

Analysis

A Ltd, F Ltd and G Ltd are a group.

A Ltd and H Ltd are not a group, because A Ltd effectively owns only 45% of H Ltd (75 × 80 × 75).

H Ltd and I Ltd are a group.

Relief

16.26 For chargeable gains purposes, intra-group transfers of assets are always deemed to be made at a price which, taking account of indexation up to the date of the transfer, results in neither a gain nor a loss for the transferee company (*TCGA 1992, s 171*; *Innocent v Whaddon Estates Ltd* [1982] STC 115). See also *Gemsupa Ltd & Another v Revenue & Customs Commissioners* [2015] UKFTT 97 (TC), in which *TCGA 1992, s 171* applied, even on an intra-group transfer which was part of tax avoidance arrangements.

The relief is automatically applied and given without claim, but does not apply where a transfer arises in satisfaction of a debt, a disposal of redeemable shares on redemption, a disposal by or to an investment trust, venture capital trust (VCT) or qualifying friendly society, or a disposal to a dual resident investing company. On a share exchange where *TCGA 1992, s 135* applies (see **17.8**), *TCGA 1992, s 135* takes preference so *TCGA 1992, s 171* does not apply.

Although a non-UK company can be a member of the group, it cannot be a party to an intra-group no gain/no loss transfer unless it trades in the UK through a permanent branch or agency and the asset in question is used for the purposes of that branch or agency (*TCGA 1992, s 171(1A)*). For the no gain/no loss rule to apply, the following conditions must be met:

- the group company disposing of the asset is resident in the UK at the time of the disposal, or the asset is a chargeable asset in relation to that company immediately before the disposal; and
- the group company acquiring the asset is resident in the UK at the time of the disposal, or the asset is a chargeable asset in relation to that company immediately after the disposal.

When a company in the group eventually disposes of the asset to a third party, the company making the disposal adopts, as its base cost, the price used for the purposes of its intra-group acquisition of the asset, and applies indexation allowance to this from the date of that transfer.

Election to reallocate gain or loss to another group member

16.27 A chargeable gain or allowable loss arising on or after 21 July 2009 may be reallocated wholly or partly between companies within the same group (*TCGA 1992, ss 171A–171C*). This applies where:

- a chargeable gain or allowable loss in respect of an asset accrues to a company (A);
- at the time the gain or loss accrues to A, A and another company (B) are members of the same group; and
- had A disposed of the asset to B immediately before the time of accrual, that transfer would have been a no gain/no loss disposal under *TCGA 1992, s 171(1)*.

Negligible value claims (**16.5**) and (from 19 July 2011) degrouping charges (**16.33–16.35**) may be reallocated in this way.

The companies must jointly elect for this treatment within two years of the end of the chargeable period in which the gain or the loss accrues (*TCGA 1992, s 171A(5)*).

Any payment made between A and B in connection with the election is not to be taken into account for corporation tax and is not to be treated as a distribution, provided that it does not exceed the gross amount (as distinct from the tax value) of the chargeable gain or allowable loss in question (*TCGA 1992, s 171B*).

Asset transfer to a non-resident company

16.28 Corporation tax on gains arising from the transfer of a UK company's assets of an overseas branch to a non-resident company, in exchange for securities consisting of shares or loan stock issued by the transferee company, are postponed until the disposal of the securities or of the underlying assets. The disposal of the underlying assets or of the securities will create a deemed gain that is chargeable to tax (*TCGA 1992, s 140*). Where there is a disposal of the underlying securities, the charge only arises if this is within six years of the original transfer.

SPECIAL COMPUTATIONAL PROVISIONS

> **Focus**
>
> Assets owned by a company may be held as fixed assets, including investments, or as trading stock. Careful attention needs to be given to transfers between fixed assets and trading stock.

Appropriation from fixed assets to trading stock

Election to convert chargeable gain into trading profit

16.29 Where a company appropriates an asset to trading stock, a chargeable gain or allowable capital loss arises as if the asset had been disposed of at market value (*TCGA 1992, s 161(1)*).

Similarly, where a group company acquires a capital asset from another member of the group and appropriates that asset to trading stock, the intra-group asset transfer will be at no gain/no loss. However, as soon as the asset is transferred to stock, a chargeable gain or allowable capital loss arises on the transferee. The transferee adopts the transferor's asset base cost and indexation (*TCGA 1992, s 173(1)*).

As an alternative, the company can elect under *TCGA 1992, s 161(3)* to treat the asset as acquired at market value less the chargeable gain that would otherwise have arisen, and the deferred gain will then arise (perhaps in a later accounting period) as part of the trading profit on disposal of the asset.

See also **2.71**.

Example 16.5—Intra-group transfer: appropriation to trading stock

Facts

O Ltd transfers a fixed asset to its holding company N Ltd, which then appropriates the asset to its trading stock. The indexed cost of the asset was £12,500 to O Ltd, and the market value on transfer is £20,000. N Ltd eventually sells the asset to a third party for £30,000.

Analysis

Without an election under *TCGA 1992, s 161(3)*, the position is as follows:

N Ltd	£
Market value	20,000
Indexed cost	12,500
Chargeable gain	7,500
Sale proceeds	30,000
Deemed cost	20,000
Trading profit	10,000

By contrast, with an election under *TCGA 1992, s 161(3)*, the position is as follows:

N Ltd	£
Sales proceeds	30,000
Indexed cost	12,500
Trading profit	17,500

Election to convert allowable capital loss into trading loss

16.30 Until 7 March 2017, the transferee could also elect under *TCGA 1992, s 161(3)* when a capital loss would otherwise have arisen on appropriation of the asset to trading stock. This had the potential to turn a capital loss into a trading loss. However, the loss could only be allowed if there was a true trading intention (*Coates v Arndale Properties Ltd* [1984] STC 637).

This facility is no longer available. For appropriations of assets on or after 8 March 2017, an election can only be made if a chargeable gain would have arisen on appropriation (*F(No 2)A 2017, s 26*). This is to prevent elections from being used to convert allowable capital losses, which are quite restricted in their use, into trading losses, which are much more flexible.

Example 16.6—Intra-group transfer: *TCGA 1992, s 161(3)* election where loss arises

Facts

O Ltd wishes to sell a run-down shop property which it has held as a fixed asset, but has encountered difficulties in finding a buyer. It transfers the property intra-group to T Ltd, a land dealing company, which appropriates the asset to its trading stock. The indexed cost of the asset was £50,000 to O Ltd, and the market value on transfer is £20,000. T Ltd eventually sells the asset to a third party for £22,500.

Analysis

Without an election under *TCGA 1992, s 161(3)*, the position is as follows:

T Ltd	*£*
Market value	20,000
Indexed cost	50,000
Capital loss	30,000
Sale proceeds	22,500
Deemed cost	20,000
Trading profit	2,500

By contrast, with an election under *TCGA 1992, s 161(3)*, the position is as follows:

T Ltd	*£*
Sales proceeds	22,500
Indexed cost	50,000
Trading loss	27,500

Appropriation from trading stock to fixed assets

16.31 Where a company appropriates an asset that it holds as trading stock to another purpose, the asset is deemed to be transferred at market value in the transferor's books, giving rise to a trading profit (*CTA 2009, s 157*). When the company sells the asset, it adopts the market value of the asset at the date of appropriation as its base cost for chargeable gains purposes, and for calculating indexation allowance (*TCGA 1992, s 161(2)*).

Similarly, where a group company transfers an asset that it holds as trading stock to another member of the group that then holds it as a fixed asset, the asset is deemed to be transferred at market value in the transferor's books, giving rise to a trading profit (*CTA 2009, s 157*). When the transferee company sells the asset outside the group, it adopts the market value of the asset when it was transferred from the transferor company as its base cost for chargeable gains purposes, and for calculating indexation allowance (*TCGA 1992, s 173(2)*).

Example 16.7—Intra-group transfer: appropriation from trading stock

Facts

N Ltd transfers an asset from its trading stock to its subsidiary company O Ltd. For O Ltd the asset will be a chargeable fixed asset. The cost of the asset was £10,000, and the market value on transfer is £30,000. O Ltd then sells the asset to a third party for £40,000. The indexation from the time of transfer is £500.

Analysis

The respective tax positions of N Ltd and O Ltd are:

	£	£
N Ltd		
Market value		30,000
Cost		10,000
Trading profit		20,000
O Ltd		
Sale proceeds		40,000
Deemed cost	30,000	
Indexation	500	
		30,500
Chargeable gain		9,500

Replacement of business assets by members of a group

16.32 *TCGA 1992, s 152* roll-over relief is extended to group situations. For this purpose, all group assets and trades are treated as one. The new assets must be purchased outside the group (*TCGA 1992, s 175*). See **16.8** onwards.

Companies leaving the group

> **Focus**
>
> Although a chargeable gain does not arise on an intra-group transfer, the gain thus avoided may crystallise in the form of a degrouping charge when a company subsequently leaves the group.

16.33 If a company leaves a group within six years of an intra-group transfer, a chargeable gain known as a degrouping charge arises on any retained asset acquired on a no gain/no loss basis from another group member within the previous six years (*TCGA 1992, s 179*). This is designed to prevent a company from avoiding a chargeable gain on a disposal by a simple enveloping method. Were it not for the degrouping charge, a company wishing to sell an asset could transfer the asset to a newly incorporated company and then sell the company, rather than directly selling the asset, so that there would be no gain.

The degrouping charge is the gain or loss arising on the company's deemed disposal and reacquisition of the asset at its market value at the time of the original intra-group transfer (*TCGA 1992, s 179(3)*).

Example 16.8—Degrouping charge after intra-group transfer

Facts

In 1990, N Ltd acquired a freehold property for £280,000. In 2010, when the market value was £500,000 and the indexation to date was £20,000, N Ltd transferred the property to P Ltd, a fellow group member. P Ltd leaves the group on 1 January 2015 when the property is worth £650,000. Both companies prepare accounts to 30 June each year.

Analysis

The *TCGA 1992, s 179* gain for the year ended 30 June 2015 is calculated as follows:

	£
P Ltd	
Market value	500,000
Indexed cost	300,000
Chargeable gain	200,000

Where a company leaves a group on or after 19 July 2011 (or, in some cases, 1 April 2011) as a result of a disposal of its shares, the disposal consideration for those shares is increased (or reduced) by the degrouping gain (or loss) (see **16.35**): as a result, any tax reliefs or exemptions that apply to the disposal of shares (eg the substantial shareholdings exemption) apply also to the degrouping charge. However, if the company leaves the group in any other circumstances, the degrouping gain (or loss) arises in that company itself in the accounting period in which it leaves the group.

Where a company left a group before 19 July 2011 (or 1 April 2011, as applicable), the degrouping charge accrued to the company leaving the group.

Exception to charge on companies leaving the group

16.34 Where two companies that have transferred an asset between them in the previous six years leave a group at the same time, a degrouping charge may be avoided under *TCGA 1992, s 179(2)*.

In *Johnston Publishing (North) Ltd v Revenue & Customs Commissioners* [2008] EWCA Civ 858, which looked at the legislation before changes were made by *FA 2011*, the Court of Appeal held that not only must companies be associated at the time of leaving the group, but also the same group of companies must be associated at the time of the acquisition of the asset, for the exemption in *TCGA 1992, s 179(2)* to apply.

Following this case, the rule was 'clarified' by the enactment of *TCGA 1992, s 179(2ZA)* and *(2ZB)* with effect from 23 March 2011. Two companies are associated for this purpose if one is a 75% subsidiary and effective 51% subsidiary of the other at the time of the intra-group transfer until the time of the degrouping event, or if both are 75% subsidiaries and effective 51% subsidiaries of another company at the time of the intra-group transfer until the time of the degrouping event.

The legislation can override the exception for companies leaving the group at the same time if the companies join a second group that is connected with the original group; in this case, the degrouping charge is reapplied if the transferee company leaves the second group within six years of acquiring the asset or, if earlier, when the two groups cease to be connected. For these purposes, a connection between the groups is established by looking at the control of the two groups (*TCGA 1992, s 179(2A)–(2B)*).

Issues arising on degrouping by disposal of shares

16.35 As explained in **16.33**, no immediate degrouping charge arises if the disposal occurs as a result of the company's shares being sold by another group member (*TCGA 1992, s 179(3A)(a)*). This rule applies to companies within the charge to corporation tax and to persons charged to tax as members of a non-resident company by *TCGA 1992, s 13* (see **16.52**).

For this purpose, the rule equating the new shareholding with the original shareholding under *TCGA 1992, s 127* (see **17.7**) is disapplied (*TCGA 1992, s 179(3C)*). If the substantial shareholdings exemption also applies (see **16.18–16.23**), the degrouping gain or loss will result in an adjustment to the exempt gain or loss of the group company disposing of shares (*TCGA 1992, s 179(3D)*). If the substantial shareholdings exemption does not apply, the degrouping gain or loss will accrue on a future disposal of the asset received in exchange for the shares. This is achieved by reducing the allowable cost of the asset received in the exchange. Where a degrouping gain exceeds the allowable cost of the asset, the excess will result in a separate gain accruing at the time the asset is sold (*TCGA 1992, s 179(3E)*).

Where more than one company is involved in the share disposal, the companies concerned may elect for the adjustment to be shared amongst them in whatever proportion they choose, otherwise it will be shared equally. The election must be made within two years of the end of the first accounting period in which the chargeable gain or loss accrues. Similarly, if a company leaves a group as a result of a company making a disposal of more than one class of shares, the company may allocate the adjustment between each class of shares as it wishes (*TCGA 1992, s 179(3F)–(3H)*).

The company can claim for the degrouping charge to be reduced by an amount that is just and reasonable, with the result that the reduction in the gain is reflected in the cost of the asset (*TCGA 1992, s 179ZA)*).

Example 16.9—Degrouping charge: companies leaving group together

Facts

P is the principal company of a chargeable gains group. Q is one of its 100% subsidiaries.

Q has a 100% subsidiary, R, which in turn has two 100% subsidiaries, A and B.

A also has an 80% subsidiary, S.

A transfers an asset to B; *TCGA 1992, s 171* applies and no gain or loss arises.

Later, R is liquidated and its shareholdings passed to Q.

S is then transferred elsewhere in the group.

B then acquires a new 100% subsidiary, T.

P plans to sell Q, along with its subsidiaries, to a third party.

Analysis

If P sells Q, along with its subsidiaries at that time, to a third party, there will be no degrouping charge in respect of the asset transferred from A to B. This is because Q, A and B formed a group of companies by themselves when the asset transfer took place (A and B were both 100% indirect subsidiaries of Q) and at the time when P left the main group (A and B were both 100% direct subsidiaries of Q).

TCGA 1992, s 179(2) defines a group by reference to actual and retained membership of the same group or sub-group.

(HMRC Brief, 17 December 2008 – Example updated)

Example 16.10—Calculation of degrouping charge

Facts

X Ltd owns all the shares in A Ltd and B Ltd. On 1 January 2014, X Ltd transferred a chargeable asset to B Ltd. *TCGA 1992, s 179* applied. Were it not for the group relationship, a gain of £50,000 would have arisen.

X Ltd disposes of its shares in B Ltd on 1 January 2016 to Z Ltd, an unconnected company, for £2 million. The substantial shareholdings exemption does not apply. The shares were bought for £1 million in 2000. Indexation amounts to £500,000.

Analysis

The gain on the sale of the shares is calculated as follows:

	£	£
Sale proceeds		2,000,000
Add gain on asset transfer within six years of sale		50,000
		2,050,000
Less		
Cost	1,000,000	
Indexation	500,000	
		1,500,000
Net gain		550,000

Example 16.11—Degrouping: substantial shareholdings exemption

Facts

X Ltd owns all the shares in A Ltd and B Ltd. On 1 January 2014, X Ltd transferred a chargeable asset to B Ltd. *TCGA 1992, s 179* applied. Were it not for the group relationship, a gain of £50,000 would have arisen.

X Ltd disposes of its shares in B Ltd on 1 January 2016 to Z Ltd, an unconnected company, for £2 million. The substantial shareholdings exemption applies. The shares were bought for £1 million in 2000. Indexation amounts to £500,000.

Analysis

The base cost of the shares acquired by Z Ltd is calculated as follows:

	£
Cost	2,000,000
Less gain on asset transfer within six years of sale	50,000
	1,950,000

ANTI-AVOIDANCE

Value shifting

16.36 The shareholders own a company through its share structure. A share or security is a chargeable asset for chargeable gains purposes (*TCGA 1992, s 21*). Transactions that affect the value of these shares could fall within the chargeable gains rules for value shifting, found in *TCGA 1992, ss 29–31*, or the depreciatory transaction rules found in *TCGA 1992, ss 176–181*.

The value shifting rules affecting the disposal of shares were simplified by *FA 2011*. For details of previous rules, see *Corporation Tax 2010/11* (Bloomsbury Professional).

General application

16.37 If a person having control of a company exercises his control so that value passes out of shares in the company owned by him or a person with whom he is connected, or out of rights over the company exercisable by him or by a person with whom he is connected, and passes into other shares in or rights over the company, this is treated as a disposal of the shares or rights in question for consideration equal to the market value of what is acquired (*TCGA 1992, s 29(2)*). A loss arising in such circumstances is not an allowable loss (*TCGA 1992, s 29(3)*). A company falls within the definition of 'person', so the value shifting rules are applicable to all companies.

Disposal of shares or securities by a company

16.38 Where shares or securities in another company are sold on or after 19 July 2011 (*TCGA 1992, s 31*), the value shifting rules are applied if:

- arrangements have been made so that the value of those shares or securities or any relevant asset are materially reduced (or increased, if a disposal of shares or securities precedes their acquisition);
- the main purpose, or one of the main purposes, of the arrangements is to obtain a tax advantage, either for the disposing company or for any other person; and
- the arrangements do not consist wholly of the making of an exempt distribution.

The disposal proceeds in such an event are to be increased by an amount that is just and reasonable, having regard to the arrangements so made and their effect on the corporation tax charge or relief. A relevant asset is any asset that is owned, at the time of the disposal, by a member of the same group as the disposing company. Share disposals that are chargeable because of the general value shifting rules (*TCGA 1992, s 29*; see **16.37**) remain so chargeable, even where arrangements are in place such that the value of the shares has been materially reduced and the main purpose, or one of the main purposes, is to obtain a tax advantage, either for the company or for some other person. See **18.40** onwards for exempt distributions.

Tax-free benefits

16.39 A disposal of an asset at market value is deemed to take place (*TCGA 1992, s 30(1)*) where, as a result of a scheme or arrangements:

- the value of the asset has been materially reduced; and
- a tax-free benefit has been or will be conferred on the person making the disposal or a person with whom he is connected (or, where there is a tax avoidance motive, any other person). Where avoidance of tax was not the main purpose or one of the main purposes of the scheme or arrangements in question, any tax-free benefit to 'any other person' is to be disregarded.

A company falls within the definition of 'person'.

A benefit arises when a person becomes entitled to any money or money's worth, when the value of an asset increases or when a liability is reduced or cancelled (*TCGA 1992, s 30(3)*).

Following a deemed disposal under the value shifting provisions, a new base cost of the asset is established for future chargeable gains purposes.

These rules do not apply to group asset transfers groups (*TCGA 1992, s 171(1)*) (see **16.26**) or companies ceasing to be a member of a group (*TCGA 1992, ss 178, 179*) (see **16.33**).

LOSSES ATTRIBUTABLE TO DEPRECIATORY TRANSACTIONS

Depreciatory transactions within a group

16.40 Without appropriate anti-avoidance legislation, a loss on a disposal of shares or securities outside a group could be created or enhanced by a 'depreciatory transaction', ie a transaction that takes value out of the shares or securities, typically by the payment of a dividend or the transfer of a fixed asset from a subsidiary company for less than full value.

If assets are transferred to a group member at below market value, this could artificially deflate the value of the transferor company. If its shares were later sold outside the group, the market price would reflect the deflated value and therefore a capital loss might arise. The use of such loss as an allowable loss is likely to be restricted under the depreciatory transactions rules (*TCGA 1992, s 176*).

Example 16.12—Restriction of loss on depreciatory transaction

Facts

B Ltd owns fixed assets worth £1,000,000.

A Ltd buys 100% of the share capital of B Ltd for £1,000,000.

A Ltd buys the entire fixed assets of B Ltd in an intra-group transaction for the nominal consideration of £1.

A Ltd sells 100% of the share capital of B Ltd to an unconnected third party for £1.

Analysis

A Ltd would like to claim the allowable loss of £999,999 that it has apparently suffered on the purchase and sale of B Ltd.

Instead, the allowable loss is restricted by virtue of the depreciatory transaction that has been undertaken, and only allowed to the extent considered by HMRC to be just and reasonable – presumably nil in this case.

TCGA 1992, s 176 deals with depreciatory transactions within groups of companies, and applies where there is a disposal of shares or securities (referred to in the legislation as 'the ultimate disposal') and the value of the shares or securities has been materially reduced within the previous six years by a depreciatory transaction (*TCGA 1992, s 176(1)*).

For disposals on or after 22 November 2017, the rule applies if the depreciatory transaction was on or after 31 March 1982 (*TCGA 1992, s 176(1)* amended by *FA 2018, s 28*). This extended period also applies where the disposal is treated as made before 22 November 2017 as a result of a negligible value claim made on or after that date.

Examples of transactions which can be depreciatory transactions include:

- the payment of a dividend (but not where paid out of profits generated since the company was acquired by the group);
- the transfer of an asset or liability at more or less than its market value;
- the cancellation of loans or debts; and
- excessive payments for services, use of assets or group relief (but absence of payment for group relief or payment at below the tax advantage obtained is not treated as a depreciatory transaction).

The depreciatory transactions rules restrict the allowable loss on a disposal of shares or securities but do not convert a loss into a gain or increase the amount of a gain.

HMRC interpret 'materially reduced' as meaning that the value of the shares or securities is reduced other than by a negligible amount (CG46550).

Dividend stripping

16.41 The 'dividend stripping' rules are an extension of those that apply to depreciatory transactions within a group. They adopt the same general approach by invoking the application of *TCGA 1992, s 176*, but there is no need for any group relationship to exist; instead, they cover depreciatory distributions to a company with at least a 10% interest in the class of shares or securities to which the distribution relates (*TCGA 1992, s 177*).

This legislation is aimed at situations where a company might hold 10% or more of the same class of securities of another company in a non-dealing non-group situation. A distribution is then made, the effect of which materially reduces the value of the other company. If the shares are then sold, the loss can be expected to be much greater as a result of the depreciatory distribution, but the extent to which that loss is allowable will be restricted under *TCGA 1992, ss 176, 177*.

RESTRICTIONS ON ALLOWABLE CAPITAL LOSSES

General restrictions on capital losses

16.42 A capital loss can be valuable to a company, as it can be carried forward indefinitely and set against future chargeable gains (see **16.7**). Provisions exist to target improper utilisation of capital losses.

A loss is not an allowable capital loss if it accrues to a company in such circumstances that, if a gain had accrued, it would be exempt from corporation tax (*TCGA 1992, s 8(2)*).

Furthermore, a capital loss is not an allowable capital loss if it accrues directly or indirectly in consequence of or in connection with any arrangements of which the main purpose, or one of the main purposes, is to secure a tax advantage. The rationale is that capital loss relief should only be available in circumstances where there has been a true commercial disposal of an asset accompanied by a genuine commercial loss because of economic conditions existing at that time. Losses created by schemes that result in a tax loss greater than the actual loss, or that leave the economic ownership of the asset virtually intact, are not allowed (*TCGA 1992, s 16A*; see also CG40240 onwards).

Capital losses after a change in ownership

16.43 Legislation exists to prevent capital losses incurred before a company joined a group from being relieved against a gain realised after the company joined the group (see **16.44**). Provisions are also in force to prevent capital loss buying – ie the acquisition of a company merely to gain access to its capital losses, whether actual or latent (see **16.46–16.51**).

Pre-entry losses

16.44 There are provisions restricting the set-off of pre-entry losses against chargeable gains, to prevent a company from buying another company in order to use its capital losses (*TCGA 1992, Sch 7A*). These provisions were simplified from 19 July 2011, and their scope reduced because they have been superseded by anti-avoidance rules on loss-buying (see **16.46**) except in cases where there is no arrangement for avoiding tax.

The rules on pre-entry losses apply when a company joins a relevant group. Relief for a pre-entry loss is restricted so that it cannot be set against gains realised after joining the relevant group. The amount of the pre-entry loss is, broadly:

- for set-off in an accounting period ending on or after 19 July 2011, any allowable loss realised by the company on a disposal which took place before it joined the group; or
- for set-off in an accounting period ending before 19 July 2011, a loss realised by the company before it joined the group, plus the pre-entry proportion of a loss accruing on the disposal of a pre-entry asset after the company joined the group.

Targeted anti-avoidance rules

16.45 Measures to counter 'bed and breakfast' arrangements used to exist, to prevent companies from selling and re-buying shareholdings within a short space of time to utilise capital losses. These were replaced by targeted anti-avoidance rules (TAARs) aimed at:

(1) the buying of capital losses and gains (*TCGA 1992, ss 184A–184F*; see **16.46–16.48**);

(2) the conversion of an income stream into a chargeable gain, or a chargeable gain matched by an income stream, thus covering the gain with an allowable loss (*TCGA 1992, s 184G*; see **16.49**, **16.51**); and

(3) the artificial generation of capital losses (*TCGA 1992, s 184H*; see **16.50–16.51**).

Restriction on buying capital losses

Tax avoidance schemes (TCGA 1992, s 184A)

16.46 By reallocating chargeable gains or allowable capital losses wholly or partly between companies within the same group (*TCGA 1992, ss 171A–171C*; see **16.27**), a group company is effectively able to secure relief for its allowable capital losses against the chargeable gains of other group companies.

This is denied by *TCGA 1992, s 184A* where:

- there is a direct or indirect change of ownership of a company;
- a loss accrues to the company or any other company on the disposal of an asset acquired prior to the change in ownership (a 'pre-change asset') (see *TCGA 1992, s 184A(3)*);
- the change of ownership is connected with any arrangements the main purpose or one of the main purposes of which is to secure a tax advantage; and

- the advantage involves the deduction of a qualifying loss from any chargeable gains, whether or not any other transactions or events are involved.

The resulting loss is not deductible from chargeable gains accruing to the company (*TCGA 1992, s 184A(2)*). The legislation targets a change of ownership of a company with latent losses, and only applies where there is an arrangement to avoid tax. It takes precedence over the restrictions on the use of pre-entry losses (*TCGA 1992, Sch 7A*; see **16.44**), except in cases where there is no arrangement for avoiding tax.

Arrangements include any agreement, understanding, scheme, transaction or series of transactions, whether or not they are legally enforceable. It is irrelevant as to whether the loss accrues before or after the change of ownership. It is irrelevant whether there are any chargeable gains at the time against which it can be utilised or whether the tax advantage accrues to the company to whom the loss has accrued or to any other company (*TCGA 1992, s 184A(4)–(5)*).

A qualifying change of ownership occurs at any time that (*TCGA 1992, s 184C*):

- a company joins a group of companies,
- the company ceases to be a member of a group of companies, or
- the company becomes subject to different control.

Whether a company is a member of a group is determined in accordance with *TCGA 1992, s 170* (*TCGA 1992, s 184C(2)*; see **16.24**).

Group off-set of losses is only available if both the companies in question were members of the same group immediately before the disposal and have remained members until immediately after the disposal (*TCGA 1992, s 184C*).

A tax advantage means relief or increased relief from corporation tax or repayment or increased repayment of corporation tax. It also means the avoidance or reduction of a charge to corporation tax or an assessment to corporation tax or the avoidance or a possible assessment to corporation tax (*TCGA 1992, s 184D*).

Example 16.13—Change of company ownership: restriction of loss relief

Facts

Sam Arkwright and Bill Weatherspoon each own 50% of Solo Ltd, a single company with substantial capital losses. Solo Ltd owns Nevercourt, a property that it is in negotiations to sell.

Solo Ltd issues ordinary shares that amount to 30% of the nominal value of the ordinary share capital to Alfonso Roderigo (an unconnected third party). Mr Roderigo's shares only have dividend rights.

Sam Arkwright and Bill Weatherspoon then sell the original shares in Solo Ltd to the Multi Group plc. Although, in economic terms, Solo Ltd has joined the Multi Group plc, it has not joined the Multi Group plc's chargeable gains group, because Multi Group plc owns less than 75% of the issued share capital.

Multi Group plc intends to transfer all of its assets that have not yet risen in value, but that it expects to rise in value, to Solo Ltd in the expectation that any resulting chargeable gains could be covered by the purchased losses.

Analysis

The issue of shares in Solo Ltd to Alfonso Roderigo is clearly intended to prevent Solo Ltd from joining the Multi Group plc when the original shareholders sell their shares. This prevents *TCGA 1992, Sch 7A* (Restriction on set-off of pre-entry losses) from applying.

Solo Ltd has neither left nor joined a chargeable gains group but it has become subject to a different control. There has, therefore, been a qualifying change of ownership as defined by *TCGA 1992, s 184C*. Solo Ltd has accrued losses on pre-change assets.

The change of ownership has occurred in connection with arrangements, the main purpose of which is to secure a tax advantage for the Multi Group plc. *TCGA 1992, s 184A* applies and Solo Ltd's losses are qualifying losses which cannot be deducted from any gains arising to the company, except those accruing to Solo Ltd on a disposal of pre-change assets.

If Nevercourt, the property owned by Solo Ltd at the time of the change of ownership, is then sold, giving rise to a chargeable gain, the losses in question may be offset against that gain.

For these purposes, *TCGA 1992, ss 184E–184F* contain provisions relating to the treatment of pre-change assets (see **16.48**).

Restriction on buying chargeable gains

Tax avoidance schemes (TCGA 1992, s 184B)

16.47 By reallocating chargeable gains or allowable capital losses wholly or partly between companies within the same group (*TCGA 1992, ss 171A–171C*; see **16.27**), a group company is effectively able to secure that its chargeable gains are relieved by allowable capital losses of other group companies.

This is denied by *TCGA 1992, s 184B* where:

- there is a direct or indirect change of ownership of a company;

- a gain accrues to the company or any other company on the disposal of an asset acquired prior to the change in ownership (a 'pre-change asset') (see *TCGA 1992, s 184B(3)*);
- the change of ownership is connected with any arrangements the main purpose or one of the main purposes of which is to secure a tax advantage; and
- the advantage involves the deduction of a loss from a qualifying gain, whether or not any other transactions or events are involved.

The resulting gain cannot be offset against a loss accruing to the company (*TCGA 1992, s 184B(2)*).

The same definitions and criteria apply in relation to this restriction as they do for the restriction on buying losses (*TCGA 1992, s 184A*; see **16.46**).

For these purposes, *TCGA 1992, ss 184E–184F* contain provisions relating to the treatment of pre-change assets (see **16.48**).

Disposal of pre-change assets

16.48 Special rules contained in *TCGA 1992, s 184E* apply for the purposes of the anti-avoidance restrictions on buying capital losses and chargeable gains (*TCGA 1992, ss 184A–184B*; see **16.46–16.47**) where:

- a company has disposed of a pre-change asset but retains an asset or rights representing the pre-change asset; or
- a chargeable gain on disposal of a pre-change asset has been deferred against another asset still owned by the company.

The chargeable gain on the following disposals may be deferred:

- Reconstructions involving transfers of business (*TCGA 1992, s 139*).
- Postponement of charge on transfer of assets to non-resident companies (*TCGA 1992, s 140*).
- Transfer of a UK trade (*TCGA 1992, s 140A*).
- Merger leaving assets within UK tax charge (*TCGA 1992, s 140E*).
- Replacement of business assets (*TCGA 1992, ss 152, 153*).
- Postponement of charge on deemed disposal under *TCGA 1992, s 187* (*TCGA 1992, s 185*).

In all of these circumstances, any gain or loss accruing as a result of any subsequent event is treated as accruing on a pre-change asset.

Where a pre-change asset consists of a holding of securities of the same class, the pre-change securities are pooled separately from any post-change securities. A disposal of securities after the change is matched first with the post-change pool, then with the pre-change pool, and only then in accordance with the usual share identification rules (*TCGA 1992, s 184F*).

Schemes converting income to capital (*TCGA 1992, s 184G*)

16.49 HMRC may serve notice on a company where they consider that all of the conditions specified in *TCGA 1992, s 184G* are satisfied, namely:

- Condition A: a receipt or (from 30 January 2014) other amount arises to a company directly or indirectly in connection with any arrangements;
- Condition B: that amount falls to be taken into account in calculating a chargeable gain (the 'relevant gain') which accrues to the relevant company, and losses accrue (or have accrued) to the relevant company (whether before or after or as part of the arrangements);
- Condition C: but for the arrangements, a measure of income would have fallen to be taken into account wholly or partly instead of that amount; and
- Condition D: the main purpose or one of the main purposes of the arrangement is to obtain a capital loss deduction from the gain, irrespective of any other purpose.

Conditions A and B were widened by *FA 2014* in relation to arrangements made on or after 30 January 2014, and in relation to earlier arrangements to the extent that any chargeable gain accrues on a disposal which occurs on or after that date.

For the consequences of an HMRC notice under these provisions, see **16.51**.

Schemes securing deductions (*TCGA 1992, s 184H*)

16.50 HMRC may serve notice on a company where they consider that all of the conditions specified in *TCGA 1992, s 184H* are satisfied, namely:

- Condition A: a chargeable gain accrues to a company directly or indirectly in consequence of or in connection with any arrangements and losses accrue (or have accrued) before or after the first asset's disposal as part of the arrangements;
- Condition B: the relevant company, or a company connected with it, becomes entitled to an income deduction directly or indirectly in connection with the arrangements;
- Condition C: the main purpose or one of the main purposes of the arrangements is to obtain that income deduction, and a capital loss deduction from the relevant gain, irrespective of any other purpose; and

- Condition D: the arrangements are not 'excluded arrangements'. Arrangements are excluded if they are made between unconnected persons dealing at arm's length, they relate to land, and they fall within *CTA 2010, ss 835(1), 836(1)* (sale and leaseback).

Conditions A and B were widened by *FA 2014* in relation to arrangements made on or after 30 January 2014, and in relation to earlier arrangements to the extent that any chargeable gain accrues on a disposal which occurs on or after that date.

For the consequences of an HMRC notice under these provisions, see **16.51**.

HMRC notices under *TCGA 1992, ss 184G, 184H*

16.51 If HMRC consider on reasonable grounds that the necessary conditions are satisfied, they may issue the company with a notice under *TCGA 1992, s 184G* or *184H*. If all the conditions are satisfied, no loss accruing to the relevant company at any time may be deducted from the relevant gain.

If a company submits its tax return within a 90-day period after the receipt of the notice, it may disregard the notice in preparing the return and, within the 90-day period, amend the return in order to comply with the notice.

If the company has already submitted its company tax return, HMRC can only give the company a notice in respect of these anti-avoidance schemes if a notice of enquiry has also been given to the company in respect of the return for the same period.

HMRC may give the company a notice after any enquiries into the return have been completed if two conditions are satisfied. First, that at the time the enquiries into the return were completed HMRC could not have been reasonably expected, on the basis of information made available to them before or at that time or to an officer of theirs before that time, to have been aware that the circumstances necessitated the issue of a notice. The second condition is that the company or any other person was requested to produce or provide information during an enquiry into the return for that period and, if the request had been duly complied with, HMRC could have been reasonably expected to give a notice in relation to that period.

ATTRIBUTION OF GAINS TO MEMBERS OF NON-RESIDENT COMPANIES

16.52 A UK resident company or individual can be taxed on chargeable gains attributed to them as a result of their participation in a non-resident closely controlled company.

These provisions are designed to prevent companies and individuals from avoiding tax on chargeable gains by sheltering them overseas. From 6 April 2012 (or 1 April 2013 for those who elect accordingly), changes were made to secure compatibility with EU law by introducing an exclusion for assets used in genuine business activities, clarifying the treatment of furnished holiday accommodation, and raising the threshold at which the charge applies to unconnected minority participators.

ATED-related gains (see **7.24**) and non-UK residents' gains on UK residential property (see **7.25**) are also excluded from the provisions (*TCGA 1992, s 13*, as amended by *FA 2015, Sch 7, para 10*).

Chapter 17

Buying and selling companies

SIGNPOSTS

- Matters to consider when buying or selling a corporate business (see **17.1–17.4**).
- Chargeable gains tax exemptions for reconstructions (see **17.5–17.14**).
- The treatment of trading losses on a change of ownership (see **17.15–17.26**).
- Capital allowances – including capital allowance buying (see **17.27–17.39**).
- Restrictions on transfer of deductions (see **17.40**).
- Impact of reconstructions on the UK Patent Box (see **17.41**).
- European mergers and reconstructions (see **17.42**).
- Transactions in securities (see **17.43**).
- Non-statutory and statutory clearance procedures (see **17.44–17.50**).

BUYING AND SELLING A CORPORATE BUSINESS

Focus

Growing the business of a company often involves acquiring other existing businesses. Share purchase may result in a new group structure and offer the benefit of the substantial shareholdings exemption on a subsequent sale. At the opposite extreme, an asset purchase may offer the company the simplicity of remaining a singleton company without the need to administer a group structure, but the possibility of a chargeable gain on a subsequent sale may need to be anticipated.

Buying a company

17.1 Purchase of another company's share capital requires careful consideration. Depending on the percentage acquired, the new acquisition will become a subsidiary or an investment of the acquiring company. All tax aspects of the transaction must be considered, not only corporation tax but also other taxes – particularly VAT (see *Value Added Tax 2018/19* (Bloomsbury Professional)) and stamp duty (see *Stamp Taxes 2018/19* (Bloomsbury Professional).

In buying all or part of the share capital of an existing company, the purchasing company should recognise that the tax history, liabilities and contingent liabilities of the target company remain with that company under its new ownership. For this reason, the purchaser of all or a significant proportion of the share capital will wish to seek warranties and indemnities from the vendor.

The situation whereby some or all of a company's activities, assets or liabilities are transferred from the existing company to a subsidiary (typically a newly formed subsidiary) is commonly known as a 'hive-down'. Such a transaction is used to facilitate a company sale, so that only the chosen activities, assets and liabilities are taken over, and it should be feasible for the purchaser to avoid inadvertently taking over contingent liabilities. Such a transaction may also be used to facilitate the division of a group's activities. Regarding hive-downs, see also **16.19**, **16.33** and **16.35**.

Asset purchase

17.2 As an alternative to buying share capital, the company may wish to consider an asset purchase. In this case, the assets acquired from the target company are absorbed into the acquiring company rather than being maintained within a separate corporate entity. Importantly, the purchaser avoids the automatic takeover of any of the vendor's tax history, liabilities or contingent liabilities. Apart from the normal funding and synergy issues, the acquiring company will need to consider a variety of issues affecting the tax impact of the transaction.

All tax aspects of the transaction must be considered, not only corporation tax but also other taxes – particularly VAT (see *Value Added Tax 2018/19* (Bloomsbury Professional)) and stamp duty land tax (SDLT) (see *Stamp Taxes 2018/19* (Bloomsbury Professional) and, for property in Scotland, *Land and Buildings Transaction Tax* (Bloomsbury Professional).

The purchased tangible and intangible fixed assets will be included within the company's fixed assets as shown on the balance sheet. In particular, the excess of the purchase price of the business acquired over the value of the identifiable assets – namely, the goodwill – will also be shown on the balance sheet. This, in turn, will form an intangible fixed asset which is subject to the intangibles legislation in *CTA 2009, Pt 8* (see **12.9**).

The company may also be able to use the newly acquired assets in roll-over relief claims for replacement of fixed assets (see **16.8**) and reinvestment in intangible fixed assets (see **12.23**). The assets may be established at relatively high base costs for the purpose of computing future chargeable gains on disposal of tangible fixed assets, or credits on disposal of intangible fixed assets, because the gains or credits to date will have been assessed on the predecessor company.

The acquisition of trading stock and work in progress will be a deduction from trading profits.

For capital allowances purposes, the assets in question are disposed of by the vendor (with balancing adjustments arising, if applicable) and acquired by the successor; for an explanation of balancing adjustments, see **3.54**. If the companies are connected within the definition given by *CTA 2010, s 1122*, then special provisions for a company reconstruction with continuity of trading and no change of ownership may apply (*CTA 2010, Pt 22, Ch 1, s 940A* onwards; see **17.15**). If *CTA 2010, s 940A* does not apply, both companies may elect for the assets to be transferred at tax written-down value. If this occurs during an accounting period, the allowances are apportioned *pro rata* (*CAA 2001, ss 266, 569*). Consideration should be given to the anti-avoidance legislation on capital allowance buying (see **17.28–17.39**).

To ensure the availability of capital allowances on the acquisition of second-hand fixtures or leased fixtures within an existing building, the purchaser will wish to pay particular attention to the requirements for the pooling of relevant expenditure by the vendor before the transfer, and for fixing the value to be placed on the fixtures within two years of the transfer (*CAA 2001, ss 187A–187B*; see **3.45–3.51**). The value allocated to a second-hand fixture must not exceed the seller's original cost or the actual sale price (*CAA 2001, ss 198(3)(a), 199(3)(a)*).

Acquisition finance costs

17.3 Regardless of whether the acquiring company undertakes a share or asset purchase, it will often require the use of borrowed funds to finance the acquisition. Any interest or finance costs incurred in acquiring assets for the purposes of the company's trade, including capital assets for use in that trade, are trading debits within the loan relationship regime. However, any interest or finance costs charged in acquiring a company are non-trading debits, because they are not costs incurred for the purposes of the trade of the acquiring company (see **11.34** for relief for costs of obtaining loan finance).

Selling a corporate business

17.4 Many of the same factors need to be considered, but from the opposite perspective, when selling a corporate business and deciding whether to sell the assets or the company.

If the assets are to be sold, chargeable gains may arise within the company. The company may be cash rich, which then presents a problem for cash extraction. If the company is owned by individuals, they will need to consider their own capital gains tax position if the company is to be wound up or sold (see *Capital Gains Tax 2016/17* (Bloomsbury Professional)). In practical terms, the sale may be facilitated by means of a reconstruction to make use of the *CTA 2010, s 940A* relief, as described in **17.15** onwards.

If shares are to be sold by a company, the substantial shareholdings exemption may apply (see **16.18–16.23**). If the substantial shareholdings exemption is unavailable, the intending vendor company may wish to consider the payment of a pre-sale dividend by the company that is about to be sold. This, in effect, reduces the value of the company to be sold, but results in tax-free funds being received by the vendor company; hence the sale price must be renegotiated accordingly.

Under company law a pre-sale dividend is permitted financial assistance for the company's purchase of its own shares (*CA 2006, s 681(2)(a)*). In this respect, it is necessary to consider the chargeable gains anti-avoidance provisions in relation to value shifting (see **16.36–16.39**).

COMPANY RECONSTRUCTIONS AND AMALGAMATIONS

Focus

As opposed to an outright sale or purchase of an existing business or as a precursor to such a deal, a company may choose to reorganise its structure. No chargeable gains or allowable capital losses will arise if the changes being made meet the conditions of the reconstruction reliefs contained in *TCGA 1992, ss 126–131*.

Introduction

17.5 The development of a company's trading activity may mean that it has to change its structure. Shares in a corporate structure can be bought or sold, or created or cancelled. Shares may be owned by individuals or other companies. A change in a company's capital structure may be necessary to enable it to carry on its future activities. Such changes will have tax consequences. This might involve, for example, the formation of a new company and the transfer of the predecessor's assets to the new company, the result being that the ownership of the business remains in the same hands but is carried on through a different corporate structure; in these circumstances, the shareholders would normally receive a share for share exchange.

Company law

17.6 It is, of course, imperative to ensure that any transactions are permissible under company law, before tax legislation can be considered. And, of course, the company's articles of association must also permit the transactions or must be amended, first.

Generally, the rules in *CA 2006* that permit reconstructions and amalgamations, subject to certain conditions are:

- the availability of distributable reserves (*CA 2006, s 830 et seq*), which are essential for 'exempt distribution' demergers (*CTA 2010, s 1074 et seq*: see **18.14–18.21**);
- a court order under *CA 2006, Pt 26* may be required to sanction an arrangement with the members (or creditors) of the company, provided this is voted on with 75% agreeing to the scheme at the company meeting (*CA 2006, ss 899, 907* and *922*);
- *Insolvency Act 1986, s 110* permits a liquidator to transfer the company's business or property to another company. The liquidator will receive shares for the distribution. Any dissenting members may require the liquidator to purchase their shares; and
- a reduction of capital (*CA 2006, s 641 et seq*) may be required to drive a scheme of reconstruction or to create distributable reserves for a transaction.

Chargeable gains

Reorganisation of share capital

17.7 A reorganisation of share capital, whereby the shareholder receives new shares or debentures in more or less the same proportion as the old shares, is tax neutral, and no chargeable gains arise. There is deemed to be no disposal of the original shares and the new shares or debentures are deemed to have been acquired at exactly the same time as the old shares and at the same price (*TCGA 1992, ss 127–131*). If the original shares or the new holding consist of or include qualifying corporate bonds, *TCGA 1992, s 116(5)* disapplies *TCGA 1992, ss 127–130*.

Any cash received is treated either as a capital distribution or as a part disposal (*TCGA 1992, ss 122, 128*). Any additional consideration given for the new holding is treated as being given for the original holding, but is indexed from the time that it is given rather than from the time that the original shareholding was acquired, for companies only. Indexation for individuals was repealed in 2008 and indexation for companies was frozen at 31 December 2017.

Share exchanges

17.8 The no disposal and no acquisition treatment contained in *TCGA 1992, ss 127–131* will also apply to a share exchange where a company issues shares or debentures to a person in exchange for shares or debentures which that person owns in another company and (*TCGA 1992, s 135*):

- as a result of the exchange, the successor company holds or will hold more than 25% of the ordinary share capital of the original company;
- the successor company issues shares or debentures as a result of a general offer made conditional upon the successor company acquiring control over the original company to the members of the successor company or any class of them; or
- the successor company holds or will hold as a result of the exchange the greater part of the voting power of the original company.

For this type of transaction, there is no requirement in tax law that the shares or debentures issued be in proportion to the original holdings. Where they are not, however, it may be necessary to consider the stamp duty position and whether the relief at *FA 1986, s 77* will be available.

Schemes of reconstruction

17.9 The no disposal and no acquisition treatment contained in *TCGA 1992, ss 127–131* will also apply where, pursuant to a scheme of reconstruction, the shareholders or debenture holders (or a class of shareholders or debenture holders) in a company (A) are issued with shares or debentures in another company (B) in respect of and in proportion to their relevant holdings in A, and their shares or debentures in A are either retained by them or cancelled (*TCGA 1992, s 136*). The shareholders will benefit from this treatment provided that the scheme meets Condition 1 and Condition 2, and either Condition 3 or Condition 4, as follows:

Condition 1. The successor must only issue ordinary shares to the original company's ordinary shareholders and not to any other party (*TCGA 1992, Sch 5AA, para 2*).

Condition 2. The original ordinary shareholders in the same class all obtain the same proportional entitlement to ordinary shares in the new company

(*TCGA 1992, Sch 5AA, para 3*). These two conditions apply after any preliminary reorganisation of share capital, and disregard subsequent issues of shares or debentures by the successor (*TCGA 1992, Sch 5AA, paras 6, 7*).

Condition 3. There must be continuity of the business. More or less the whole of the business of an original company must be carried on by one successor company, or by two or more successor companies of which the original company may be one (*TGCA 1992, Sch 5AA, para 4*).

Condition 4. The scheme is carried out in pursuance of a compromise arrangement under *CA 2006, Pt 26* or foreign equivalent, and no part of the business is transferred to any other person (*TCGA 1992, Sch 5AA, para 5*).

Bona fide commercial arrangements

17.10 The reliefs provided by *TCGA 1992, s 135* or *136* (see **17.8**) only apply if the scheme in question is made for *bona fide* commercial purposes and where a main purpose is not the avoidance of corporation tax or capital gains tax. This restriction does not apply to holders of less than 5% of the shares. If the conditions are not met, HMRC can collect the tax from any of the shareholders concerned (*TCGA 1992, s 137*).

A tax avoidance purpose was found in *Snell v HMRC Comrs* [2006] EWHC 3350 (Ch). In accordance with professional advice which he had received, the vendor (an individual) became non-UK resident to avoid a capital gains tax liability. The High Court supported the finding of the Special Commissioners that, although the exchange of shares was undertaken for bona fide commercial reasons, it was nonetheless part of a tax avoidance arrangement, so *TCGA 1992, ss 135, 127–131*, did not apply.

The company may apply to HMRC for advance clearance that the proposed reconstruction or reorganisation is for *bona fide* commercial purposes. The full facts of the transaction should be given to HMRC, who have 30 days to reply. If HMRC refuse a clearance application, or if they fail to respond within the statutory 30 days, the company may refer its case to the Tribunal (*TCGA 1992, s 138*). See **25.41** and **17.44** onwards for further details regarding clearance procedures.

Reconstruction involving transfer of business

17.11 Where, pursuant to a scheme of reconstruction, the whole or part of a company's business is transferred to another company for no consideration, apart from taking over the liabilities, the transfer of chargeable assets is deemed to take place for such consideration that provides neither gain nor loss (*TCGA 1992, s 139*).

Again, for this treatment to apply, the transfer must be made for *bona fide* commercial purposes and a main purpose must not be the avoidance of corporation tax, income tax or capital gains tax (*TCGA 1992, s 139(1)*). An advance clearance procedure is available under *TCGA 1992, s 139(5)* and works in exactly the same way as a clearance under *TCGA 1992, s 138*.

Similar provisions apply to the transfer of intangible fixed assets in such circumstances (*CTA 2009, s 818*) and, for that purpose, an advance clearance procedure is also available (*CTA 2009, ss 832, 833(1)*). Where a pre-*FA 2002* intangible fixed asset (see **12.2**) is transferred under a reconstruction to which *TCGA 1992, s 139* or *140A* applies, the asset remains a pre-*FA 2002* intangible fixed asset in the hands of the transferee (*CTA 2009, s 892*).

A scheme of reconstruction can be used to break up an existing business into separate undertakings. This may involve the liquidation of the original company (see **Chapter 19** for liquidations).

Company reconstruction examples

17.12

Example 17.1—Company reconstruction: Solution 1

Facts

The issued share capital of Union Ltd is of one class of share and is held as follows:

Shareholders	*£1 Ordinary Shares*
	£
Jack	50,000
Jill	50,000
	£100,000

The company has two businesses: it rents holiday homes in the UK; and it arranges tours of Great Britain, mainly for overseas visitors.

Original structure

It is proposed to separate the two businesses. There are several possible solutions that will satisfy the conditions of *TCGA 1992, Sch 5AA* (see **17.8**). First, there are three mechanisms that can be used:

- liquidation;
- distribution *in specie* (see **18.15** onwards); or
- reduction of capital.

Each of these can then be carried out in such a way that Jack and Jill continue to have a 50% share of each business, or they can be carried out so that Jack owns one business and Jill owns the other.

Solutions 1 and 2 both involve the liquidation of Union Ltd, with solution 1 leaving Jack and Jill with a 50% share of each business and solution 2 segregating the shareholders.

Solutions 3 and 4 both use the distribution route, with solution 3 leaving Jack and Jill with a 50% share of each business and solution 4 segregating the shareholders.

Reconstructions using a reduction of capital are more complex in implementation, but they look similar in structure to solutions 3 and 4.

Reconstruction Solution 1

Union Ltd enters into a scheme under *Insolvency Act 1986, s 110*. The original shares in Union Ltd are organised into A shares and B shares. The holdings are now as follows:

Shareholders	*Total*	*£1 A Ordinary Shares*	*£1 B Ordinary Shares*
	£	£	£
Jack	50,000	25,000	25,000
Jill	50,000	25,000	25,000
	100,000	50,000	50,000

The assets and liabilities of the holiday home rental business are allocated to the A shares. The assets and liabilities of the tours of Great Britain business are allocated to the B shares.

Union Ltd is placed in liquidation. The liquidator transfers the holiday home rental business to a new company, Country Homes Ltd (a successor company). Country Homes Ltd issues ordinary shares to the holders of the A shares in proportion to their respective holdings. The tours of Great Britain business is transferred to a new company Roving Ltd (a successor company) which issues ordinary shares to the holders of the B shares in proportion to their respective holdings. Now Jack and Jill each own 50% of each of the two companies.

Structure post Reconstruction 1

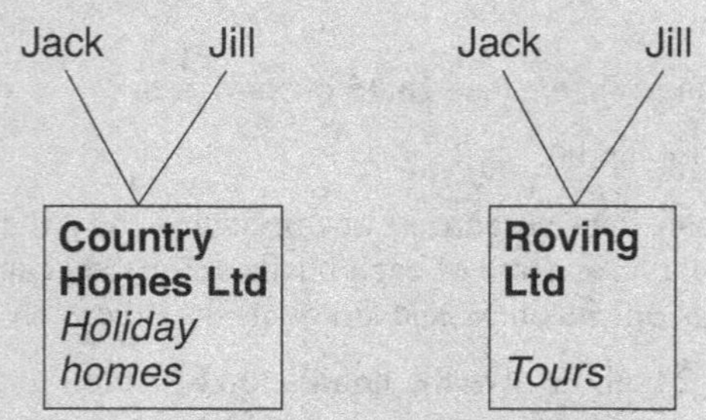

Example 17.2—Company reconstruction: Solution 2

Facts

As in Example 17.1.

Reconstruction Solution 2

This time, the new A shares are issued to Jack and the new B shares are issued to Jill. The new shareholdings are as follows:

Shareholders	*Total*	*£1 A Ordinary Shares*	*£1 B Ordinary Shares*
	£	£	£
Jack	50,000	50,000	—
Jill	50,000	—	50,000
	100,000	50,000	50,000

The assets and liabilities of the holiday home rental business are allocated to the A shares. The assets and liabilities of the tours of Great Britain business are allocated to the B shares.

Union Ltd is placed in liquidation. The liquidator transfers the holiday home rental business to a new company, Country Homes Ltd (a successor company). Country Homes Ltd issues ordinary shares to the holders of the A shares in proportion to their respective holdings. The tours of Great Britain business is transferred to a new company Roving Ltd (a successor company) which issues ordinary shares to the holders of the B shares in proportion to their respective holdings. Now Jack and Jill each own 100% of their respective companies.

Structure post Reconstruction 2

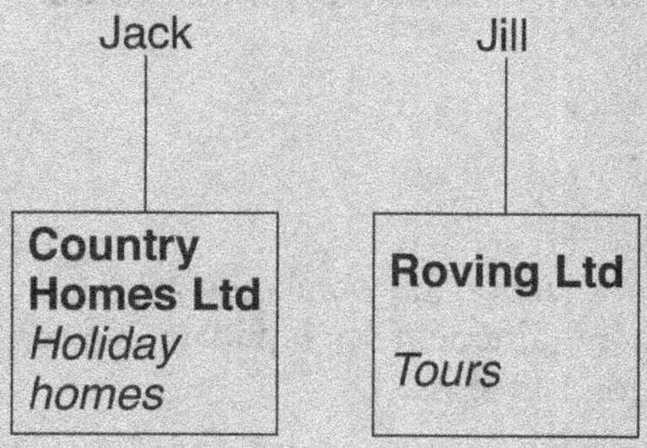

Example 17.3—Company reconstruction: Solution 3

Facts

As in Example 17.1.

Reconstruction Solution 3

As in Example 17.2, the new A shares are issued to Jack and the new B shares are issued to Jill, but it is not necessary to liquidate Union Ltd.

Instead, Union Ltd declares a dividend on the B shares, which it pays by transferring the assets and liabilities of the touring business to Roving Ltd. Roving Ltd then issues Jill with ordinary shares. Jill's B shares in Union Ltd are now worthless, so they can be cancelled or Jill can sell them to Jack for £1. Jack now owns all the shares in Union Ltd which holds the holiday home business, so Jack and Jill each own 100% of their respective companies.

Structure post Reconstruction 3

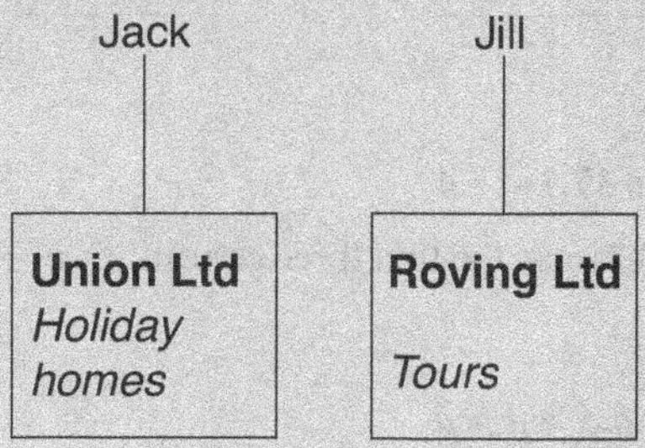

Example 17.4—Company reconstruction: Solution 4

Facts

As in Example 17.1.

Reconstruction Solution 4

Solution 4 takes place under the demerger rules (see Example 18.3 in **18.17**). There is no requirement to liquidate Union Ltd. The original shareholdings in Union Ltd are:

Shareholders	*£1 Ordinary Shares*
	£
Jack	50,000
Jill	50,000
	100,000

A new company, Roving Ltd, is formed, with Jack and Jill each owning 50% of the issued ordinary share capital. The tours of Great Britain business is transferred to Roving Ltd by distribution *in specie*. The holiday home letting business continues to be operated by Union Ltd. Now Jack and Jill each own 50% of each of the two companies.

Structure post Reconstruction 4

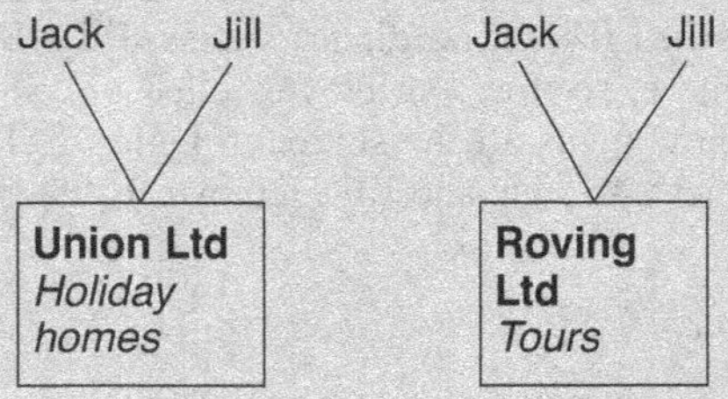

Analysis of Examples 17.1–17.4

17.13 In all four solutions, the first three conditions of *TCGA 1992, Sch 5AA* (see **17.8**) are met:

Reconstruction—Conditions satisfied

Condition 1

The successor companies have issued ordinary shares to the holders of ordinary shares in the share classes of the original company, which are involved in the scheme of reconstruction and to no other person. *TCGA 1992, Sch 5AA, para 2*

Condition 2

The original ordinary shareholders in the same class all obtain the same proportional entitlement to ordinary shares in the new company. *TCGA 1992, Sch 5AA, para 3*

Condition 3

If the activities of the successor companies are taken together they carry on the whole of the business of the original company. *TCGA 1992, Sch 5AA, para 4*

The result is that the disposal of Jack and Jill's holdings in Union Ltd in Solutions 1 and 2, and the disposal of Jill's holding in Solution 3, and the acquisition of the respective new holdings, are no disposal and no acquisition transactions (*TCGA 1992, s 136*). In Solution 4, there is no disposal of the original holding, so this does not matter.

The liquidator's transfer of the two businesses to Holiday Homes Ltd and Roving Ltd in Solutions 1 and 2 are no gain/no loss disposals (*TCGA 1992, s 139*).

In practice, these steps would not be taken in isolation from other factors; in particular, the stamp taxes and company procedural matters must be considered. Furthermore, if the business activities have accumulated losses, the utilisation of these losses will be hampered if there is cessation of the relevant activities concerned.

Solutions 1 and 2 will involve cessation of Union Ltd's activities. Solution 1 offers the protection of *CTA 2010, s 940A* (see **17.15**), but Solution 2 does not because the same ownership structure pre- and post-reconstruction is not retained.

Solutions 3 and 4 involve continuation of Union Ltd's holiday home activity, but cessation of the touring trade. Protection under *CTA 2010, s 944* (see **17.26**) will be given to Roving Ltd in Solution 4, but not in Solution 3 where the same ownership structure pre and post reconstruction is not retained.

The choice of reconstruction method would require careful consideration, and would be influenced by the future plans of Jack, Jill and each of the businesses.

Groups

17.14 A transfer of tangible fixed assets between companies which are in a group relationship (see **16.24** for the definition of a 'group') does not give rise to any chargeable gains, as the transfer is deemed to be at such consideration as generates neither a gain nor a loss (*TCGA 1992, s 171*). When the company that acquired the asset leaves the group within six years after the acquisition, a degrouping charge will arise, the nature of which depends on whether the company leaves the group on or after 19 July 2011 (or, in some cases, 1 April 2011), whether this is as a result of a disposal of its shares, or in any other circumstances (*TCGA 1992, s 179*; see **16.33–16.35**).

Subject to anti-avoidance provisions, the degrouping charge in respect of chargeable assets under *TCGA 1992, s 179* does not apply to intra-group asset transfers between associated companies who subsequently cease to be group members at the same time (*TCGA 1992, s 179(2)*; see **16.34**). The companies must have been associated at the time that the asset transfer was made (*Johnston Publishing (North) Ltd v Revenue and Customs Comrs* [2007] All ER (D) 240 (Mar)). The companies must remain associated after they leave the group. For this purpose, 'associated companies' are defined as companies that would themselves form a group (*TCGA 1992, s 179(10)*).

There is also an exemption from the charge under *TCGA 1992, s 179* where the company that acquired the asset intra-group subsequently ceases to be a member of the group in the course of a merger carried out for *bona fide* commercial reasons and not for tax avoidance (*TCGA 1992, s 181*).

Similarly, intangible fixed assets can be transferred between companies which are in a group relationship without giving rise to any credits on disposal (*CTA 2009, ss 775, 776*). When the company that acquired the asset leaves the group within six years after the acquisition, a degrouping charge will arise, based on a deemed disposal of the asset at its market value at the date of the original intra-group transfer (*CTA 2009, s 780*; see **12.28** for further details, including exceptions from the degrouping charge).

TRADING LOSSES

> **Focus**
>
> Where a succession takes place without a change of ownership and the same trade continues, there are provisions that allow unused trading losses of the predecessor company to be carried forward to the successor company if certain conditions are met.

Company succession without a change of ownership

17.15 Where there is a company succession with continuity of trading and no change of ownership, the losses incurred by the previous company are generally available to set against profits earned by the new company, provided the ownership condition (**17.16**) and the tax condition (**17.17**) are both satisfied (*CTA 2010, s 940A* onwards; HMRC Company Taxation Manual at CTM06005 onwards).

A company does not have to claim the *CTA 2010, s 940A* reliefs, because they are mandatory in cases where the necessary conditions are met. The successor is automatically given relief under *CTA 2010, s 944* for any losses carried forward from the predecessor, subject to any claims made by the predecessor to set such losses against its total profits under *CTA 2010, s 37* (see **4.17**) and a reduction under *CTA 2010, s 945* for any excess of liabilities transferred. The predecessor is not entitled to terminal loss relief under *CTA 2010, s 39* (see **4.22**).

Where *CTA 2010, s 940A* applies, capital allowances continue uninterrupted (*CTA 2010, s 948*). But see also **17.28–17.39** for restrictions on capital allowance buying and transfer of deductions.

CTA 2010, s 940A can apply only where there is no change of ownership. Note that, where there is a change of ownership and a change in the nature or conduct of the trade, the use of trading losses is restricted (*CTA 2010, s 673*), as discussed in **4.24–4.26**.

The carry-forward of the predecessor company's losses to the successor company is also restricted (*CTA 2010, s 676*) where there is a reconstruction, with continuity of trading and no change of ownership, and it is either:

- followed by a change in ownership of the successor; or
- preceded by a change in ownership (on or after 20 March 2013) of the predecessor.

Ownership condition

17.16 The ownership condition is that, on the transfer of the transferred trade or at some time during the period of two years beginning immediately after the transfer, a 75% interest in the transferred trade belongs to certain persons and, at some time during the period of one year ending immediately before the transfer, a 75% interest in the transferred trade belonged to the same persons (*CTA 2010, s 941*).

If two or more companies carry on a trade, the interests in the trade belonging to them are taken to correspond to the shares of the trade's profits to which they are entitled, and an interest in a trade belonging to trustees (but not for charitable or public purposes) is treated as belonging to the persons for the time being entitled to the income under the trust.

Persons who are beneficiaries under a trust are treated as a single person. Persons who are relatives of one another are treated as a single person. 'Relative' means a spouse, civil partner, ancestor, lineal descendant, brother or sister.

The interest in the trade belonging to the company may be determined in accordance with any of the following options (*CTA 2010, s 942*):

Option 1

The interest in the trade is taken to belong to the persons owning the ordinary share capital of the trading company in proportion to the amount of their holdings of that capital.

Option 2

If the trading company is the subsidiary of another company, the interest in the trade is taken to belong to:

(a) the trading company's parent company; or

(b) the ordinary shareholders of the parent company in proportion to their holdings.

Option 3

If a person has management control over a company to which, by applying Option 1 or 2, an interest in the trade can be taken to belong, that interest is instead taken to belong to that person.

75% ordinary share ownership by one company of another determines a parent and subsidiary relationship, unless both companies are subsidiaries of a third company.

Management control is the power to secure that the affairs of the company are conducted in accordance with a person's wishes. Power derives from a holding of shares or the possession of voting rights in or in relation to any company, or a document regulating any company. Ordinary share capital ownership can be direct, indirect or a combination of the two.

In *Barkers of Malton Ltd v Revenue and Customs Commissioners* [2008] SpC 689, it was held that trading should continue for some time, to demonstrate that the successor company actually carries on the trade. In that case, a trade was transferred to a group company that was then sold. The trade was then hived up to the new parent company, and succession to the trade, and hence to its losses, was claimed by the new owner of the trade. The claim was refused on the basis that the intermediary company had only owned the trade for a matter of an hour or so, and could not be said to have carried on the trade in that time.

Tax condition

17.17 The tax condition is met if the trade has been carried on by companies within the charge to corporation tax within the prescribed period of ownership, being two years immediately after the transfer and one year immediately prior to the transfer, as set out in *CTA 2010, s 941(1)*. The situation not only applies to UK resident companies but also to non-resident companies chargeable to corporation tax in respect of a trade carried on by a UK branch or agent. The relief applies to a 'trade' and will also apply if only part of a trade is transferred (*CTA 2010, s 951(3)*).

Beneficial ownership

Definition of beneficial ownership

17.18 For the above purposes, ownership of the ordinary share capital of a company is the beneficial ownership. Ordinary share capital is defined in *CTA 2010, s 1119* and means all the issued share capital of the company, by whatever name it is called, other than capital whose holders have only a right to a dividend at a fixed rate but have no other right to share in the profits.

A beneficial owner is not necessarily the person in whose name the ordinary shares are registered. A person who holds shares as a nominee is not a beneficial owner. Beneficial ownership is established by looking through to the ultimate owners (CTM06030).

Establishing beneficial ownership

17.19 The ownership of a trade is established whenever the conditions of *CTA 2010, s 941* are met. Ownership can fall to the holders of the ordinary share capital of the company carrying it on under *CTA 2010, s 942(1), Option 1*, or to the parent of the company carrying on the trade under *CTA 2010, s 942(1), Option 2(a)*. Ultimately, the holders of the ordinary share capital of the parent under *CTA 2010, s 942(1), Option 2(b)* may be the beneficial owners of the company. Finally, as will apply in most owner-manager controlled companies, the person or persons who by voting power or other means can direct or control the affairs of a company, which directly or indirectly owns the ordinary share capital of the company carrying on the trade, may own the company (*CTA 2010, s 942(1), Option 3*). HMRC will look to the person who can control the company 'by other means', which seems to imply that they might accept an arrangement not formalised by a written document (CTM06020).

A 75% parent and subsidiary ownership relationship is required for *CTA 2010, s 942(1)* above (see *CTA 2010, s 942(2)*). Persons who are relatives of one another are treated as a single person, and relative includes spouse, civil partner, ancestor, lineal descendant or sibling.

Example 17.5—Common ownership: shares in same ownership

Facts

Matthew, Mark and Luke each own 33.33% outright of the ordinary share capital of the publishing company W Ltd. H Ltd takes over the publishing trade from W Ltd. Following this takeover, Matthew, Mark, Luke and John each own 25% of H Ltd.

Analysis

Common ownership of the trade is achieved, because the same group of persons owns not less than 75% of both companies.

Example 17.6—Common ownership: spouses and civil partners

Facts

Sleekstyles Ltd manufactured hairdressing products but is now dormant following the takeover of its trade by Crazystyles Ltd on 1 January 2015. The percentage ownership of the ordinary shares of both companies is as follows:

	Sleekstyles Ltd	*Crazystyles Ltd*
	%	%
William	60	40
Nathan	20	40
Roger	10	8
Susan	5	7
Clementine	3	3
Nadia	2	2
Total	100	100

William and Nathan formalised their relationship by entering into civil partnership on 5 December 2012. Roger and Susan became engaged to be married on 1 January 2014. Clementine and Nadia are senior employees.

Analysis

William and Nathan's shares are aggregated. Without the need to look any further, common ownership of the trade is achieved because the same group of persons owns not less than 75% of both companies.

Beneficial ownership at the relevant time

17.20 For the *CTA 2010, s 940A* reliefs to apply, beneficial ownership of the shares must be in place at the relevant time.

In *Wood Preservation Ltd v Prior* (1969) 45 TC 112, the carry-forward of loss relief was denied because Wood Preservation Ltd's trade was transferred after its parent company lost beneficial ownership of the company's shares.

Beneficial ownership passes from vendor to purchaser when an unconditional contract for the sale of the shares is made. If the contract is subject to a condition precedent, beneficial ownership does not pass until the condition is satisfied. An oral agreement can be an unconditional contract (CTM06030). Therefore, a potential vendor should be particularly vigilant with respect to the point in time at which beneficial ownership is transferred.

Transfer of trade

17.21 To determine whether *CTA 2010, s 940A* applies, HMRC have identified the following four practical situations where either a trade or part of a trade is transferred between companies (*CTA 2010, s 951(1)*; see CTM06060):

- a succession to an entire trade, arising under *CTA 2010, s 939(2)*, where a company ceases to carry on a trade and another company begins to carry it on;
- a transfer of the activities of a trade under *CTA 2010, s 951(3)*, where a company ceases to carry on a trade and another begins to carry on the activities of that trade as part of its trade;
- a transfer of the activities of part of a trade, where a company ceases to carry on part of a trade and another company begins to carry on the activities of that part as its trade, again under *CTA 2010, s 951(3)*; or
- where a company ceases to carry on part of a trade and another company begins to carry on the activities of that part as part of its trade.

Succession

17.22 In practical terms, for a company to succeed to the trade formerly carried on by the predecessor, sufficient of the predecessor's trading activities must be transferred to the new company.

In Example 17.6, if Sleekstyles Ltd transferred its factory, its manufacturing operations and its employees to Crazystyles Ltd without its book debts or its sales distribution unit, this might be a sufficient transfer of trading activity to qualify as a succession. In *Malayam Plantations Ltd v Clark* (1935) 19 TC 314, the acquisition of a rubber plantation and its employees without the book debts or the selling organisation was considered to be a 'succession'. The fact that one company actually succeeds to the trade of another company within the same ownership will bring about the *CTA 2010, s 940A* reliefs, as in *Wadsworth Morton Ltd v Jenkinson* (1966) 43 TC 479.

Activities of a trade

17.23 The *CTA 2010, s 940A* reliefs also apply if the predecessor's trade is added to the successor's trade in an identifiable form.

In *Laycock v Freeman Hardy and Willis Ltd* (1938) 22 TC 288, for example, two shoe-manufacturing companies supplied shoes wholesale to their parent company for retail sale. The parent company wound up the subsidiaries. It took over the factories and the staff, and manufactured the shoes itself. The parent company was denied use of the subsidiaries' losses because, although the manufacturing activities continued, the wholesale activities failed to continue. The Court of Appeal held that the trade was not carried on in the same identifiable form as before the transfer.

In *Rolls Royce Motors Ltd v Bamford* [1976] STC 162, activities treated for tax purposes as a single trade were transferred in two parts of very unequal size to two successor companies. The High Court held that the smaller successor trade was different from that of the predecessor, and *CTA 2010, s 944* loss relief was denied.

In *Falmer Jeans Ltd v Rodin* [1990] STC 270, a company manufacturing jeans and casual clothing made trading losses. A company with which it was associated marketed its merchandise. The marketing company bought the manufacturing company and carried on its trade. The High Court held that the trading losses were available for relief after transfer because all the essential activities of the previous manufacturing trade were still carried on, even though the profits were no longer earned separately.

Likewise, in *Briton Ferry Steel Co Ltd v Barry* (1939) 23 TC 414, the Court of Appeal held that the appellant company had continued to carry on trades previously carried on by certain subsidiary companies, and there was a succession to those trades.

The above judgments were considered in *Leekes Ltd* [2015] UKFTT 93 (TC), where the First-tier Tribunal held that there was no need to stream the losses when the old and the new trades form part of the same trading activities, albeit enlarged. The case was successfully appealed by HMRC to the Upper Tribunal, who agreed with HMRC that the legislation did not grant Leekes the opportunity to set the losses acquired with the Coles trade against its own (ie Leekes's) profits. Loss relief had to be limited to the amounts that could have been set off if the succession had not occurred. Since the Coles element of the trade continued to be loss-making, no loss relief was allowed.

Activities of part of a trade

17.24 *CTA 2010, s 951* refers to 'part of a trade' (see **17.21**), but there is no definition of this expression within the legislation. HMRC's guidance states that it is a severable part of a company's trading activity that is capable of being a free-standing apparatus and making profits or losses in its own right. A part of a trade does not have to amount to anything as distinctive as a branch or a division (CTM06060).

Later events

17.25 When a trade is subject to successive transfers between companies, there are provisions which may allow the transfer of losses from the first company through to the ultimate successor company if certain conditions are met (*CTA 2010, s 953*).

Practical effects of section 944 relief

Trading losses carried forward

17.26 If all the necessary conditions are met so that *CTA 2010, s 940A* applies, the successor is able to use all or part of the predecessor's trading loss brought forward under *CTA 2010, s 45* against future profits from the same trade (*CTA 2010, s 944(3)*). Following the Upper Tribunal decision in *Leekes Ltd* [2016] UKUT 320 (TCC), it appears that any losses transferred to a company that already has a trade can only be use against future profits of the trade that was transferred, not against the profits of the combined trade after the transfer. This streaming of the losses will require of the profits of the two trades to be monitored separately for tax purposes.

The amount of the loss that can be used in this way is the unused loss that would have been available to the predecessor, reduced by the relevant liabilities restriction. The relevant liabilities restriction is a factor dependent on the retained relevant liabilities, the retained relevant assets and the consideration (*CTA 2010, s 945*).

The relevant liabilities are taken at their actual value immediately before the predecessor ceased to trade. Relevant liabilities exclude share capital, share premium, reserves or relevant loan stock and any liabilities transferred to the successor. Intra-group debts are included in relevant liabilities (*CTA 2010, s 946(1)*). Relevant loan stock can be secured or unsecured, but does not extend to the stock of a person carrying on a trade of moneylending (*CTA 2010, s 946(8), (9)*).

Relevant assets are the assets that the company owned immediately before it ceased to trade (*CTA 2010, s 947(4)*) and are valued at market value (*CTA 2010, s 947(3)*).

The consideration is the amount given to the predecessor by the successor of the trade. Liabilities assumed by the successor are not included within the consideration (*CTA 2010, s 945*). However, if a liability is transferred to the successor and the creditor agrees to accept less than the full amount due in settlement of the outstanding debt, the shortfall is treated as a liability for the purposes of the restriction.

If losses exceed the net relevant liabilities, there is no restriction. Any losses disallowed are not available to the predecessor company (*CTA 2010, s 945(5)*). Where part of a trade is transferred, a just apportionment of receipts, expenses, assets or liabilities is to be made for this purpose (*CTA 2010, s 952*). The restriction only applies to trading losses and not to capital allowances and balancing charges.

The release of a trading debt will be a taxable receipt of the trade (*CTA 2009, s 94*).

Example 17.7—Carry forward of trading loss under *CTA 2010, s 944*: relevant liabilities restriction

Facts

Alfonso Ltd took over the trade and assets of Bertino Ltd on 1 January 2016. *CTA 2010, s 940A* relief applies. Bertino Ltd's unutilised trading losses amount to £150,000. Neither cash nor trade creditors are included in the sale. The balance sheet at 31 December 2015 directly before transfer is shown below. What is the loss relief restriction (if any) if Bertino Ltd sells the business to Alfonso Ltd for (i) £10,000 or (ii) £100,000?

Bertino Ltd: Balance sheet at 31 December 2015

	£000	*£000*
Fixed assets		
Plant and machinery		60
Current assets		
Stock	20	
Debtors	10	
Cash	5	
	35	
Current liabilities		
Trade creditors	30	
		5
		65
Shareholders' funds		
Share capital		50
Profit and loss account		15
		65

Analysis

The restriction is calculated as follows:

(i) Sale proceeds: £10,000

	£000
Trade creditors	30
Less cash	(5)
	25
Less sale consideration	(10)
Loss relief restriction	15

Therefore the losses that are available for relief are £150,000 – 15,000 = £135,000

(ii) Alternative sale proceeds: £100,000

	£000
Trade creditors	30
Less cash	(5)
	25
Less sale consideration	(100)
Loss relief restriction	(75)

As the sale consideration exceeds the value of the liabilities and assets not taken over, there is no loss restriction.

If only £50,000 of the plant had been taken over, the restriction would be calculated as follows:

Sale proceeds	£10,000	£100,000
	£000	£000
Trade creditors	30	30
Less plant retained	(10)	(10)
Less cash	(5)	(5)
	15	15
Less sale consideration	(10)	(100)
Loss relief restriction	5	(85)

If the company is sold for £10,000, the losses that are available for relief are:

£150,000 – £5,000 = £145,000

If the company is sold for £100,000, there is no loss restriction, as the sale consideration continues to exceed the value of the liabilities and assets not taken over.

CAPITAL ALLOWANCES

17.27 Where there is a company reconstruction with continuity of trading and no change of ownership and the conditions of *CTA 2010, s 940A* apply, the transfer is ignored for capital allowances purposes; the successor company gets the same allowances and suffers the same charges as the predecessor would have got if it had continued to carry on the trade. Where the whole of a trade is transferred, writing down allowances are calculated as though the predecessor has an accounting period ending on the transfer date and the successor has an accounting period beginning on that date (see HMRC Capital Allowances Manual at CA15400), and are reduced proportionately for accounting periods shorter than 12 months (see **3.57**). When the assets are eventually sold, any balancing charge or allowances will fall upon the company carrying on the trade at the time, ie the successor, as if it had always owned the assets (*CTA 2010, s 948(2)*).

This contrasts with the situation where the trade of a company is sold to a successor company in circumstances such that the predecessor's trade ceases. In that case, the assets are deemed to be sold to the new company at market value (*CAA 2001, s 559*), and balancing adjustments (see **3.54**) will ensue for the predecessor.

Restrictions on capital allowance buying

Introduction

Focus

Anti-avoidance legislation exists which may prevent capital allowances from being used in a group relief claim after a change of ownership.

17.28 A company purchase, sale or reconstruction may trigger the capital allowance-buying anti-avoidance legislation, which has been designed to prevent unused capital allowances arising before the transfer of a trade from being used in a group relief claim to new group members after the transfer. It applies to situations where a company in a group has not claimed all the capital allowances to which it was entitled and is then subject to a 'qualifying change'. Transfers of entitlement to postponed allowances on ships are within the scope of these rules (*CAA 2001, ss 212A–212S*).

From 20 March 2013 (subject to transitional provisions), these restrictions apply not only to trades but to all 'qualifying activities' under *CAA 2001, s 15*.

See also **17.40** for restrictions on transfer of deductions.

Application of capital allowance-buying legislation

17.29 The legislation needs to be considered in situations where all the following conditions are met (*CAA 2001, s 212B*):

- a company (C) carries on a qualifying activity, either alone or in a partnership (P);
- there is a qualifying change in relation to C on any day (the relevant day being the day of the transfer);
- C (or P, if applicable) has an excess of allowances in relation to that activity; and
- the qualifying change has an unallowable purpose.

Whether or not the company carries on a qualifying activity will be a question of fact. The legislation sets out conditions that determine whether there is a qualifying change, an unallowable purpose and an excess of allowances.

Qualifying change

17.30 There is a qualifying change (*CAA 2001, s 212C*) if any of the following four conditions are met by the company (C) itself or by its principal company:

Condition A

- C's principal company or companies at the beginning of the relevant day is not, or are not, the same as at the end of that day; or
- C has no principal company at the beginning of the relevant day but there is one, or more than one, at the end of the relevant day.

Condition B

- any principal company of C is a consortium principal company (CPC), whose ownership proportion at the end of the relevant day is more than at the beginning of the relevant day.

Condition C

- the relevant activity is a trade and on the relevant day, C ceases to carry on the whole or part of the relevant activity; and
- it begins to be carried on in partnership by two or more companies, in circumstances in which *CTA 2010, s 940A* (transfers of trade without change of ownership) applies in relation to the transfer of the relevant activity.

Condition D

- at the beginning of the relevant day, C carried on the relevant activity either alone or in partnership; and
- C's relevant percentage share in the relevant activity at the end of the relevant day is less than at the beginning of the relevant day (or is nil).

Example 17.8—Capital allowance buying: Condition A

Facts

C is a wholly owned member of the Y Group and, on the relevant day, C is sold to the X Group.

Analysis

C's Ownership before change *C's Ownership after change*

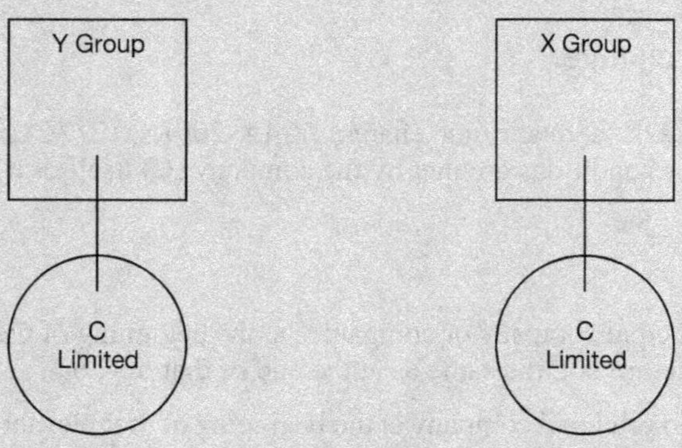

Condition A is met because, at the end of the relevant day, the Y Group is no longer C's principal company.

Example 17.9—Capital allowance buying: Condition B

Facts

C is a consortium-owned company and is owned equally by the A and X Groups. The A Group sells 30% of its 50% shareholding to the X Group.

Analysis

C's Ownership before change *C's Ownership after change*

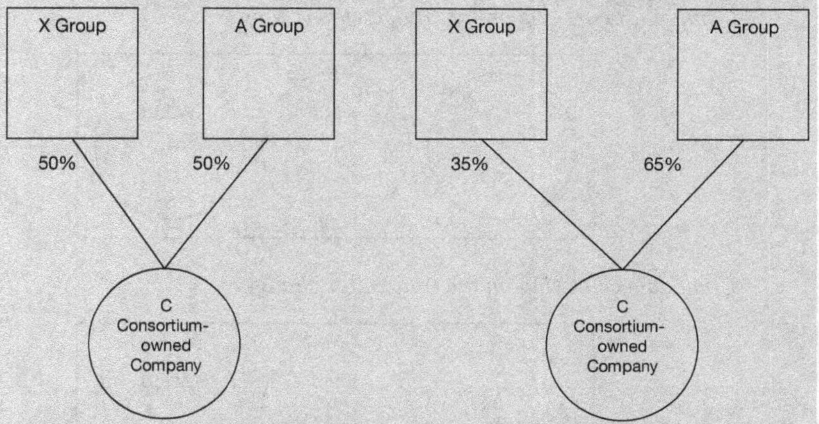

Condition B is met, because the X Group's ownership proportion has increased from 50% to 65%.

Example 17.10—Capital allowance buying: Condition C

Facts

C ceases to carry on the relevant activity (a trade), which begins to be carried on in partnership by A and B, in circumstances where *CTA 2010, s 944* applies on the transfer.

Analysis

Ownership of trade before change *Ownership of trade by partnership after change*

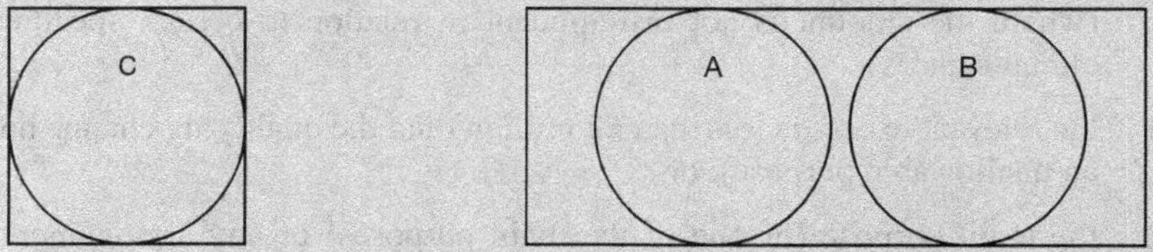

In these circumstances, Condition C applies.

Example 17.11—Capital allowance buying: Condition D

Facts

Three companies carrying on a relevant activity in partnership are C, X Ltd and W Ltd. C's percentage share at the start of the relevant day is 70%, and at the end of that day it is 30%.

Analysis

Companies carrying on the trade before change

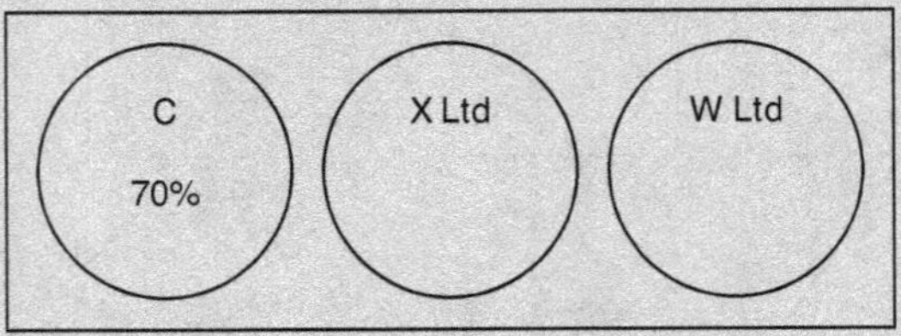

Companies carrying on the trade after change

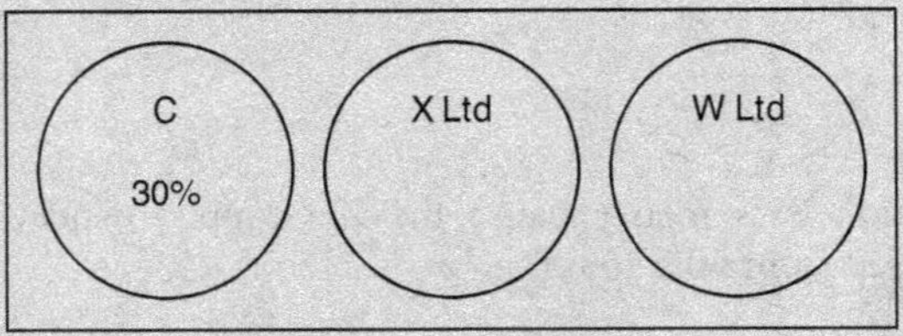

Condition D is met, because C's relevant percentage share in the relevant activity at the end of the relevant day is less than at the beginning of the relevant day.

From 20 March 2013 the definition of 'qualifying change' was amended and it must now meet at least one of four 'limiting conditions' (*CAA 2001, s 212LA*), namely:

(a) the relevant excess of allowances (see **17.32**) is £50 million or more (in any circumstances);

(b) the relevant excess is £2 million or more and less than £50 million (where the amount is not insignificant in relation to certain specified circumstances);

(c) the relevant excess is less than £2 million (and the qualifying change has an unallowable purpose); or

(d) the main purpose (or one of the main purposes) of any arrangements is to procure that conditions (a) or (b) above or the £2 million limit in condition (c) above is not met.

Definitions

17.31 For the purposes of the capital allowance-buying anti-avoidance rules, *CAA 2001, s 212E* gives precise definitions of what is meant by a 'principal company', a 'consortium', a 'qualifying subsidiary' and other related expressions.

Principal company

In six separate scenarios, 'U', 'V', 'W', 'X', 'Y' and 'Z' are each C's principal company in the following situations:

1. C is a qualifying 75% subsidiary of U, and U is not a qualifying subsidiary of another company (*CAA 2001, s 212E(1)*).
2. C is a qualifying 75% subsidiary of U, and U is a qualifying 75% subsidiary of V, and V is not a qualifying subsidiary of another company (*CAA 2001, s 212E(2)*).
3. V is a qualifying 75% subsidiary of another company W. W is a principal company of C unless W is a qualifying 75% subsidiary of another company, and so on (*CAA 2001, s 212E(3)*).
4. X is a consortium principal company of C if C is owned by a consortium of which X is a member, or C is a qualifying 75% subsidiary of a company owned by a consortium of which X is a member and is not a qualifying 75% subsidiary of another company (*CAA 2001, s 212E(4)*).
5. Y is a consortium principal company of C if C is owned by a consortium of which X is a member, or C is a qualifying 75% subsidiary of a company owned by a consortium of which X is a member, and X is a qualifying subsidiary of Y but Y is not a qualifying 75% subsidiary of another company (*CAA 2001, s 212E(5)*).
6. If Y is a qualifying 75% subsidiary of another company Z, Z is a consortium principal company of C unless Z is a qualifying 75% subsidiary, and so on (*CAA 2001, s 212E(6)*).

Consortium

A company can only be owned by a consortium if it is not the qualifying subsidiary of another company. A consortium consists of other companies each beneficially owning no less than 5% of the ordinary share capital of the consortium company (*CAA 2001, s 212F*).

Qualifying 75% subsidiary

A company is a 75% subsidiary of another if its parent company is beneficially entitled to at least 75% of any profits available for distribution to equity holders of the subsidiary company, and would be entitled to at least 75% of the subsidiary's assets available for distribution to its equity holders on a winding up, where (*CAA 2001, s 212G*) either:

- the subsidiary company has ordinary share capital and is a 75% subsidiary of the parent company (see *CTA 2010, s 1154(3)*); or
- the subsidiary company has no ordinary share capital and the parent company has control over the subsidiary.

Ownership proportion

The ownership proportion is (*CAA 2001, s 212H*) the lowest of:

- the percentage of the ordinary share capital of C that is beneficially owned by the consortium principal company (CPC);
- the percentage to which CPC is beneficially entitled of any profits available for distribution to equity holders of C; and
- the percentage to which CPC would be beneficially entitled of any assets of C available for distribution to its equity holders on a winding up.

Relevant percentage share

The relevant percentage share is C's percentage share in the profits or losses of the activity, which at any time are determined on a just and reasonable basis (*CAA 2001, s 212I*).

Relevant excess of allowances

17.32 A company has a relevant excess of allowances if the relevant tax written down value (RTWDV) of the assets concerned is greater than their balance sheet value (BSV) (*CAA 2001, s 212J*).

The RTWDV is essentially the sum of the unrelieved qualifying expenditure included in the single asset pools, the class pools and the main pool that is available to be carried forward and used in calculating the profits of the relevant activity. Ship-owning businesses are required to add the amount on which any allowances have been postponed. The unrelieved pool is calculated on the assumption that all available expenditure has been allocated to the pool (*CAA 2001, s 212K*).

Balance sheet value

17.33 The balance sheet value (BSV) is the sum of the net book value (or carrying amount) of the relevant assets and the net investment value in respect of finance leases, as disclosed in the appropriate balance sheet. The value of any fixture included within the value of any land or in a finance lease is to be determined on a just and reasonable basis. The balance sheet has to be drawn up in accordance with GAAP and is adjusted to reflect relevant plant disposals on the relevant day (*CAA 2001, s 212L*). Finance leases are leases treated as such for GAAP. A fixture is any installed plant and machinery that forms a legal part of the property, and includes boilers and hot water radiators. See **Chapter 26** regarding changes to UK GAAP.

Unallowable purpose

17.34 An unallowable purpose exists if the main purpose or one of the main purposes of change arrangements is to obtain a relevant tax advantage for any person. Change arrangements are any arrangements made to bring about or otherwise connected with the qualifying change. Arrangements in this context include any agreement, understanding, scheme, transaction or series of transactions, regardless of whether or not they are legally enforceable. A relevant tax advantage is obtained if, for corporation tax purposes, the person concerned becomes entitled to a reduction in profits, or an increase in losses, as a result of a capital allowance claim in respect of the relevant plant and machinery or qualifying expenditure (*CAA 2001, s 212M*).

Change in accounting periods

17.35 If the capital allowance-buying anti-avoidance rules apply, the existing accounting period ends on the relevant day and a new accounting period commences on the following day. There are specific variations to this rule where the company concerned carries on the relevant activity in partnership with another company or other companies (*CAA 2001, s 212N*).

Excess of allowances

17.36 A relevant pool has an excess of allowances if 'PA' exceeds the 'BSVP'. PA is the unrelieved qualifying expenditure included within the relevant pool, and the BSVP is so much of the balance sheet value (BSV) that can be attributed to that pool on a just and reasonable basis. If the BSVP exceeds the PA for any relevant pool, this can be taken into account, provided it has not been taken into account elsewhere (*CAA 2001, s 212O*).

Example 17.12—Capital allowance buying: excess of allowances

Facts

Plantation Ltd leaves the X Group and joins the Y Group on 1 January 2016, and the capital allowance-buying anti-avoidance legislation applies to the transfer. At the date of the change, the unrelieved qualifying expenditure in respect of plant and machinery in its main pool is £100 million, and the corresponding balance sheet value is £90 million.

Analysis

The excess of allowances is calculated as follows:

	£m
PA	100
BSVP	(90)
Excess of allowances	10

Effect of excess of allowances on pools

17.37 If there is an excess of allowances, each relevant pool's unrelieved qualifying expenditure is reduced at the beginning of the new period by the amount of the excess in relation to that pool, and the excess is then treated as qualifying expenditure in a new pool of the same type as the relevant pool.

After the qualifying change has taken place, any qualifying activity that is transferred and begins to be carried on by the company (whether or not in partnership) is treated as a separate activity from the original activity of the company or partnership for the purposes of claiming allowances in respect of qualifying expenditure in the new pool. Losses arising from an allowance claimed in respect of qualifying expenditure in the new pool may only be set against the profits of a qualifying activity carried on by the company, or any company that is a member of the partnership, at the beginning of the relevant day. In addition:

- the loss cannot exceed the amount of the loss which would have been available for such set-off but for the qualifying change;
- the loss cannot be set off by way of group relief, unless it would have been available for set-off but for the qualifying change; and
- the amount of the loss available for such set-off by the claimant company is not to exceed the amount of the loss which would have been available for such set-off but for the qualifying change.

In order to qualify for relief, the company or partnership must carry on the activities on the relevant day (*CAA 2001, s 212P*).

Only the company or partnership is entitled to claim an allowance in respect of the plant or machinery after the transfer (*CAA 2001, s 212S*).

Example 17.13—Capital allowance buying: allocation of qualifying expenditure

Facts

On joining the Y Group, Plantation Ltd's qualifying expenditure is allocated in accordance with *CAA 2001, s 212P*, as follows:

	Relevant pool	*New pool*
	£m	*£m*
Balance of pool expenditure	90	10

Analysis

New pool capital allowances are not available to set off against Plantation Ltd's original trade.

Postponed capital allowances on ships

17.38 From 9 December 2009, postponed allowances on ships are treated in broadly the same way as excess allowances, but a number of special provisions apply (*CAA 2001, s 212Q*).

Apportionment of proceeds from relevant plant and machinery

17.39 Disposal proceeds from the sale of relevant plant and machinery are to be apportioned between the new pool and the relevant pool on a just and reasonable basis (*CAA 2001, s 212R*).

RESTRICTIONS ON TRANSFER OF DEDUCTIONS

17.40 From 20 March 2013 (subject to transitional provisions), there are two particular restrictions that may prevent certain 'deductible amounts' from being brought into account following a 'qualifying change' in relation to a company (*CTA 2010, s 730A*). For this purpose, 'qualifying change' is defined as for the capital allowance-buying anti-avoidance rules (see **17.30**).

The 'deductible amounts' (ie trading expenses, property business expenses, management expenses, or non-trading debits within the loan relationships, derivatives or intangible fixed assets regimes) are those which, at the date of the qualifying change (the 'relevant day'), can be regarded as 'highly likely' to arise as deductions for an accounting period ending on or after that day. What is highly likely on the relevant day is to be determined having regard to any arrangements made and events that take place on or before that day (*CTA 2010, s 730B*).

One such restriction is on relevant claims – namely, claims to set trading losses against total profits, and claims to group relief. Deductible amounts may not be included in such claims, where the purpose or one of the main purposes of arrangements connected to the qualifying change is for the deductible amounts to be the subject of, or brought into account as a deduction in, such a claim (*CTA 2010, s 730C*).

The other restriction is in respect of deductible amounts where there are 'profit transfer arrangements' – namely, arrangements which result in an increase in the total profits (or a reduction of any loss or other relievable amount) of the company in question or a company connected with it. In such cases, deductible amounts may not be brought into account as deductions by any of those companies, where the purpose or one of the main purposes of those arrangements is to bring the deductible amounts into account as deductions (*CTA 2010, s 730D*).

On a qualifying change on or after 1 April 2014, these restrictions do not apply to capital expenditure crystallising as research and development allowances (*CTA 2010, s 730B(1)*; see also **14.3–14.9**).

UK PATENT BOX

17.41 On any reconstruction, amalgamation or group reorganisation involving a company that has opted into the Patent Box, care should be taken to ensure that the necessary conditions for ongoing relief under that regime are maintained. It may be particularly important to ensure that the development condition and the active ownership condition are still met (see **Chapter 13**).

Following amendments introduced by *FA 2016, s 64*, it is possible to transfer the trade of a company that claims the Patent Box relief and for the Patent Box claim to be transferred with the trade (see **13.15**).

EUROPEAN MERGERS AND RECONSTRUCTIONS

17.42 Reconstructions and mergers that involve a company resident in another member state are, in general, tax neutral (*TCGA 1992, ss 140A et seq*; *CTA 2009, ss 817–833*; *CTA 2010, s 1078*).

TRANSACTIONS IN SECURITIES

17.43 Anti-avoidance provisions exist to counteract corporation tax advantages from transactions in securities (*CTA 2010, ss 731–751*). However, it is generally assumed that these provisions have no practical effect.

Where a company is in a position to obtain or has obtained a corporation tax advantage and any one of certain conditions are satisfied, HMRC have power to counteract that advantage by making such adjustments as they may specify in a notice to the company (*CTA 2010, s 733*).

These provisions may apply where the company receives consideration:

- representing a company's assets, future receipts or trading stock, in consequence of a transaction whereby another person receives an abnormal amount by way of dividend ('circumstance C') (*CTA 2010, s 736*);
- in connection with the distribution, transfer or realisation of assets of a relevant company, as defined ('circumstance D') (*CTA 2010, s 737*); or
- in connection with the direct or indirect transfer of assets of a relevant company, as defined, or any transaction in securities in which two or

more relevant companies are concerned ('circumstance E') (*CTA 2010, s 738*).

Note that an ordinary liquidation (in which a company is wound up following the complete cessation of its business or the transfer of that business to a person unconnected with its original shareholders) is outside the scope of these provisions (see, for example, *Laird Group PLC v CIR* 74 TC 399). However, the legislation can apply to counteract a tax advantage obtained in consequence of the combined effect of a transaction in securities and the liquidation of a company (*CTA 2010, s 733(3)*; CTM36850).

The transactions in securities anti-avoidance provisions do not apply if the company shows that the transaction or transactions meet conditions A and B, as follows (*CTA 2010, s 734*):

- the transaction or transactions are effected for genuine commercial reasons, or in the ordinary course of making or managing investments (condition A); and
- enabling corporation tax advantages to be obtained is not the main object or one of the main objects of the transaction or, as the case may be, any of the transactions (condition B).

There are detailed provisions for:

- the issue of a preliminary notification by HMRC to the company that *CTA 2010, s 733* may apply (*CTA 2010, s 743*);
- a statutory declaration by the company within 30 days after issue of the notification, stating the grounds on which it opposes the notification (*CTA 2010, s 744*); and
- determination by the Tribunal where agreement cannot be reached (*CTA 2010, s 745*).

Counteraction by HMRC may take the form of an assessment, the nullifying of a right to repayment, the return of a repayment already made or the calculation or recalculation of profits or gains or liability to corporation tax (*CTA 2010, s 746*).

HMRC have published guidance on the transactions in securities provisions relating to corporation tax (see CTM36800 onwards).

CLEARANCE PROCEDURES

Introduction

17.44 Non-statutory clearances, statutory clearances, statutory approvals or technical clarification from HMRC are often required in connection with reconstructions and amalgamations, and in many other situations.

The purpose of a tax clearance is to provide certainty for UK taxpayers, as a useful practical service at a level whereby speed of response from HMRC can be reasonably assured.

Non-statutory clearances

17.45 HMRC provide a Non-Statutory Clearance Service for all taxpayers and their advisers. To make the service as useful as possible, HMRC focus their efforts on where the benefit is greatest. They try to ensure that, as far as possible, those issues brought forward for clearance are the ones that have the greatest impact on the businesses concerned.

A non-statutory clearance is written confirmation of HMRC's view of the application of tax law to a specific transaction or event. HMRC aim to provide clearances across all taxes:

- within 28 days as the norm, although they may take longer in complex cases;
- on areas of material uncertainty arising from any new legislation introduced within the last four *Finance Acts*; and
- on legislation older than the last four *Finance Acts* where there is material uncertainty around the tax outcome of a real issue of commercial significance to the taxpayer.

On application, HMRC provide non-statutory clearances:

- pre-transaction, where evidence is supplied that the transaction is genuinely contemplated; and/or
- post-transaction.

HMRC will not provide a non-statutory clearance where:

- the application does not contain all the necessary information;
- they do not agree that there are genuine points of uncertainty. In such cases, they will explain why they think this and will direct the applicant to the relevant online guidance;
- the application seeks tax planning advice, or approval for tax planning products or arrangements;
- the application is about the treatment of transactions which, in their view, are for the purposes of avoiding tax;
- the application relates to a period for which they have already opened an enquiry;
- the application relates to a period for which the 'enquiry window' has already closed or the tax return is final; or
- a statutory clearance procedure is available for the transaction in question.

HMRC publish checklists of information required in support of non-statutory clearance applications, and they ask that the appropriate checklist be used as a cover sheet or that the order of the checklist be adhered to in any covering letter. For these and general guidance on their non-statutory clearance service, see tinyurl.com/n2upf27.

Companies should submit non-statutory clearance applications to HMRC as follows (see tinyurl.com/p5s52ef):

- If the company has a Customer Relationship Manager at HMRC, or if the company or its agent is already in contact with an HMRC clearance team:

  Directly to the HMRC Client Relationship Manager (CRM) assigned to the business, or the clearance team in question. In the case of market-sensitive information, the company should make contact in advance.

- Other companies:

  HMRC Non-Statutory Clearance Team, 5th Floor, Alexander House, 21 Victoria Avenue, Southend-on-Sea, Essex, SS99 1AA

  Or by email to: hmrc.southendteam@hmrc.gsi.gov.uk

  In the case of market-sensitive information, telephone 01733 317030 in advance.

For HMRC's internal guidance on how they handle applications for non-statutory clearances, see their Other Non-Statutory Clearance Guidance Manual at ONSCG1000 onwards.

Statutory clearances

17.46 There are a number of statutory provisions, relating variously to corporation tax and other taxes, which set out procedures for HMRC to give 'statutory clearances' relating to specific points. These are referred to as 'statutory clearances'.

The following is a list of specific statutory clearances:

Clearance category	**Statutory reference**
Demergers*	*CTA 2010, s 1091*
Demergers: Chargeable payments*	*CTA 2010, s 1092*
Purchase of own shares*	*CTA 2010, s 1044*
EIS shares: acquisition by new company*	*ITA 2007, s 247(1)(f)*
Employee share schemes	*ITEPA 2003, Schs 2–4*

Transactions in securities*	*ITA 2007, s 701*; *CTA 2010, s 748*
Share exchanges*	*TCGA 1992, s 138(1)*
Share exchanges: continuity of SEIS relief*	*ITA 2007, s 257HB(1)(f)*
Reconstructions involving the transfer of a business*	*TCGA 1992, s 139(5)*
Transfer or division of a UK business between EU member states*	*TCGA 1992, s 140B*
Transfer or division of non-UK business by a UK company to a company resident in another EU member state	*TCGA 1992, s 140D*
Intangible assets*	*CTA 2009, s 831*
Loan relationships: transfers*	*CTA 2009, s 427*
Loan relationships: mergers*	*CTA 2009, s 437*
Derivative contracts: transfers*	*CTA 2009, s 677*
Derivative contracts: mergers*	*CTA 2009, s 686*
Targeted Anti Avoidance Rule 3 (Capital Gains)*	*TCGA 1992, ss 184G–184H*
Company migrations	*TMA 1970, s 109B*
Insurance companies: Transfer of business	*TA 1988, s 444AED*
Insurance companies: Transfer of long-term business on or after 1 January 2013	*FA 2012, s 133*
Insurance companies: Transitional rules	*FA 2012, Sch 17, para 18*
Assignment of lease at undervalue*	*ITTOIA 2005, s 300*; *CTA 2009, s 237*
Transactions in land*	*ITA 2007, s 770*; *CTA 2010, s 831*; *CTA 2009, s 237*; *ITTOIA 2005, s 300*
Offshore funds:	
(a) Reporting fund status	*SI 2009/3001, reg 54(2)*
(b) Equivalence and genuine diversity of ownership requirements	*SI 2009/3001, reg 78*
Stamp Duty Adjudication	*SA 1891, s 12A*

For specific guidance from HMRC on particular statutory clearances and details of where to send applications, see the appropriate topics at tinyurl.com/28f7sh.

Clearance applications under more than one of the provisions marked * above may be submitted to HMRC as a single application, by email, fax or letter, as follows:

- By letter:

  HM Revenue and Customs
  CTIS Clearance S0483
  Newcastle
  NE98 1ZZ

- By email:

  reconstructions@hmrc.gsi.gov.uk

The facilities to apply by fax or to telephone the unit have been withdrawn.

It helps HMRC if applications for statutory and non-statutory clearances are submitted separately. However, if one clearance application letter covers both, copies should be sent to all relevant teams, and the covering letter should state clearly to which teams it has been sent.

Market sensitive applications should be addressed to the Team Leader at the postal address above. HMRC will not reply to market sensitive applications by email.

Statutory approvals

17.47 A statutory approval is different from a statutory clearance. Approval may be required in advance for a particular tax treatment to apply to a particular issue that can have far-reaching consequences, and the tax treatment changes according to whether an approval has been given or not, eg statutory approval for the beneficial tax treatment of certain employee share schemes.

For contact details on statutory approvals, see the appropriate topics at tinyurl.com/28f7sh.

HMRC contact details

17.48 HMRC publish (at tinyurl.com/lf9sgdw and tinyurl.com/ll8qwdt) their contact details for general advice and specialist areas of tax, covering a wide range of topics. These include:

- annual tax on enveloped dwellings;
- charities and Community Amateur Sports Clubs;
- Construction Industry Scheme (CIS);
- corporation tax – forms ordering;
- corporation tax – general enquiries;
- corporation tax – payments;

- creative industry tax reliefs;
- employers – general enquiries;
- FATCA – UK–US Automatic Exchange of Information Agreement;
- group payment arrangements;
- IR35;
- Northern Ireland corporate tax office;
- oil and gas large businesses;
- online services helpdesk;
- payment problems (ie Business Payment Support Service);
- pension schemes;
- settlement opportunities – tax avoidance schemes;
- shares and assets valuation; and
- tax avoidance schemes.

Additional HMRC contact details, or references to specific HMRC guidance relating to particular specialist topics, are given in appropriate chapters throughout this book.

Post-transaction valuation checks for chargeable gains

17.49 This service allows taxpayers (including companies) to ask HMRC to check valuations required to compute chargeable gains. It can be used after a disposal, or after a deemed disposal following a claim that an asset has become of negligible value, but before the related tax return is submitted. If HMRC have agreed a valuation, they will not challenge the subsequent use of it in a tax return.

Form CG34 (tinyurl.com/9batvkn) must be completed for each valuation which HMRC are asked to check, and submitted together with the information listed on the form.

Applicants should allow at least two months for HMRC to check valuations. Companies should submit the application to the appropriate office dealing with the company's affairs.

Inheritance tax clearance service for business owners

17.50 This service allows the owners of companies and other businesses (or their advisers) to make clearance applications in respect of IHT business property relief (BPR), if HMRC are satisfied that there is material uncertainty over the application of the law and that the issue is commercially significant to the business itself. Applications can be made post-transaction, or pre-transaction if evidence is supplied that the transaction is genuinely contemplated.

HMRC will also provide a view on the tax consequences of a transfer of value that involves a change of ownership of a business (succession) where this transfer (ignoring BPR) would result in an immediate IHT charge. Clearances in these succession cases will only remain valid for a limited period of six months.

For further details, see tinyurl.com/n2upf27, particularly Annex C.

Chapter 18

Distributions

SIGNPOSTS

- The meaning of a distribution and the various transactions that are classed as distributions (see **18.1–18.10**).
- Non-qualifying and qualifying distributions (see **18.11**).
- Small company dividend payments (see **18.12**).
- Payments not treated as distributions (see **18.13**).
- Exemptions from the distribution rules – including demergers, and the purchase by a company of its own shares (see **18.14–18.30**).
- Striking off a defunct company, and distributions in anticipation of dissolution (see **18.31–18.36**).
- Surplus ACT (see **18.37–18.38**).
- Distributions received by a company are generally exempt from corporation tax (see **18.39–18.50**).
- Where distributions are not exempt, double tax relief may be due if foreign source dividends are out of taxed profits (see **18.51–18.57**).

INTRODUCTION

18.1 A dividend is a shareholder's expected reward from the company for investing in its shares. Under company law, a company may declare and distribute a dividend out of its realised profits. The dividend is then payable to the shareholders *pro rata* to their shareholdings (*CA 2006, Pt 23*).

A distribution can take a variety of forms, including dividends, and may include capital or assets. For corporation tax purposes, the distribution rules apply whenever cash or assets (other than a repayment of share capital) are passed to the members of the company. For corporation tax purposes, distributions are defined in *CTA 2010, s 1000 et seq*.

It is axiomatic that a distribution must be 'in respect of shares' held by the recipient. If, for example, a payment or benefit provided to the shareholder by the company relates to the member's services to the company, it is not a distribution but a payment for services performed for the company; such a payment will be chargeable on the member as employment income under the rules of *ITEPA 2003* or as self-employed income under a contract for services, and any payments so made should be deductible by the company for corporation tax purposes.

For a shareholder that is itself a company, a distribution constitutes franked investment income (if non-group); for a shareholder who is an individual, dividend income is assessable under *ITTOIA 2005, s 384* (see *Income Tax 2016/17* (Bloomsbury Professional)).

There is a general rule that a company is chargeable to corporation tax on all the income distributions that it receives unless the distribution is exempt (*CTA 2009, Pt 9A*). In practice, most distributions received are exempt. For further details, see **18.40–18.50**.

The significance for the paying company is that no corporation tax deduction is available for any dividends or other distributions (*CTA 2009, s 1305*).

PAYMENTS CLASSED AS DISTRIBUTIONS

Focus

It is important to determine whether or not a payment is classed as a distribution for tax purposes. Legislation is detailed on this point.

18.2 *CTA 2010, s 1000* defines a distribution as anything which falls within the following transaction criteria:

	Transaction	*Criteria*
A	Dividends	Any dividend paid by the company, including a capital dividend (see **18.3**).
B	Distributions in respect of shares	Any distribution from the company's assets in respect of shares, except that part which represents a repayment of capital or new consideration received by the company for the distribution (see **18.4**).
C	Redeemable shares	Any redeemable share capital issued by the company in respect of shares in, or securities of, the company, and otherwise than for new consideration (see **18.5**).
D	Issued securities	Any security issued by the company in respect of shares in, or securities of, the company, and otherwise than for new consideration (see **18.6**).

E	Distributions on non-commercial securities	Any interest or other distribution out of assets of the company in respect of non-commercial securities, except any amount that represents the principal secured by the securities or a reasonable commercial return for the use of the principal (see **18.7**).
F	Distributions on special securities	Any interest or other distribution out of assets of the company in respect of securities of the company which are special securities, except any amount that represents the principal secured by the securities, and interest treated as a distribution elsewhere (see **18.8**).
G	Transfer of assets or liabilities	Any amount treated as a distribution, being a transfer of assets or liabilities (see **18.4**).
H	Bonus issues	Any amount treated as a distribution, being a bonus issue following repayment of share capital (see **18.9**).

Close companies are subject to special rules in addition to the above. Expense payments made and certain benefits provided to a participator in a close company are also classed as distributions, unless the participator is also an employee to whom the earnings and benefits code of *ITEPA 2003* applies (*CTA 2010, ss 1064–1065* and see **Chapter 10**).

Dividend

18.3 In general, a dividend paid by a company, including a dividend out of a capital profit (referred to as a 'capital dividend'), is a distribution for tax purposes (*CTA 2010, s 1000(1)(a)*). Exceptions are stock dividends and dividends paid by building societies and industrial or UK provident societies or UK agricultural or fishing co-operatives (*CTA 2010, ss 1054, 1055, 1057*).

HMRC guidance explains the tax treatment of payments to individuals and other non-corporates following a reduction in the share capital of a company, and their interpretation of 'new consideration' (see tinyurl.com/nzgetm4). Essentially, a dividend is treated as income of the recipient regardless of the source of the distributable reserves (*CTA 2010, s 1027A*). So if a company reduces its capital and creates distributable reserves, dividends out of those reserves will be income dividends, despite the fact that the ultimate source of the payment was from capital. This is distinct from a reduction of capital paid directly to shareholders, which is a capital payment (albeit subject to the transactions in securities rules for income tax payers). Share capital includes share premium where the share capital was issued at a premium representing new consideration.

In determining whether a reserve arises from a reduction of share capital of a limited company incorporated outside the UK, the local legislation governing the capital reduction must correspond with *CA 2006* requirements. For an unlimited company incorporated outside the UK, the local legislation governing the capital reduction must correspond with the equivalent UK legislation under which an unlimited company may reduce its share capital (*CTA 2010, s 1027A*).

Premiums paid on redemption of share capital are not treated as repayments of share capital (*CTA 2010, s 1024*). However, where the share capital was issued at a premium, that share premium is treated as being part of the share capital for the purposes of *CTA 2010, s 1024*, by virtue of *s 1025*.

Generally, distributions following a bonus issue (ie where no new consideration was given for the new shares) are not treated as repayments of share capital (*CTA 2010, s 1026*). The only exception is where the distribution is made more than ten years after the issue of the share capital, is in respect of share capital other than redeemable share capital, and the company is listed on the main list of the London Stock Exchange (*CTA 2010, ss 739 and 1026(3)*).

Distributions in respect of shares/transfers of assets and liabilities

18.4 There is a high degree of overlap between *CTA 2010, s 1000(1)B*, distributions in respect of shares, and *s 1000(1)G*, transfers of assets or liabilities.

Any value passing from a company to a member is prima facie a distribution if the value is derived from the assets of the company, except to the extent that the distribution is in return for new consideration from the member or it is the repayment of share capital, including any premium on subscription (*CTA 2010, s 1000(1)B*). Thus a distribution can be a payment to a member or the transfer of an asset.

If a company transfers an asset to a member, the amount of the distribution is the market value of the asset less the market value of any new consideration given by the member (*CTA 2010, s 1020*). Similarly, if a liability is transferred to a company by a member for undervalue, the amount of the distribution is the value of the liability less the market value of any new consideration given by the member.

If the person to whom an asset is passed is also a director, it is a matter of fact whether he or she receives the asset as shareholder or as employee. If received as an employee, the amount is assessable as employment income. In practice, however, we generally expect HMRC to argue that the transfer of an asset (or assumption of a liability) is in respect of the employment. Arguably, the same might be said of a cash payment, but we have never seen HMRC challenge the payment of a dividend as being, in reality, employment income, except in complex tax avoidance cases.

Until 17 July 2012, a transfer of an asset (except cash) or a liability by one company to another was not a distribution (*CTA 2010, s 1002*, now repealed) if:

- both companies were UK resident;
- neither company was a 51% subsidiary of a non-UK resident company; and
- the two companies were not under the control of the same person or persons, either at the time of the transfer or as a result of it.

Redeemable share capital

18.5 The issue of redeemable share capital other than wholly for new consideration is a distribution (*CTA 2010, s 1000(1)C*). The value of the distribution is the sum of the amount of the share capital and any premium payable on redemption, in a winding up or in any other circumstances, less any new consideration given for the issue (*CTA 2010, s 1003*).

The shares can be issued directly or issued from bonus redeemable shares or securities received from another company.

If shares are issued as stock dividends, this provision does not apply (*CTA 2010, s 1049*).

Prior to 6 April 2016, an issue of redeemable share capital was called a non-qualifying distribution (*CTA 2010, s 1136*, repealed by *FA 2016, s 5*).

Securities issued otherwise than for new consideration

18.6 The issue of securities other than wholly for new consideration is a distribution (*CTA 2010, s 1000(1)D*). The value of the security is the sum of the amount of the principal secured and any premium payable – whether at maturity, in a winding up or in any other circumstances (*CTA 2010, s 1004*).

The securities can be issued directly or issued from bonus redeemable shares or securities received from another company.

Prior to 6 April 2016, an issue of redeemable share capital was called a non-qualifying distribution (*CTA 2010, s 1136*, repealed by *FA 2016, s 5*).

Distributions in respect of non-commercial securities

18.7 A non-commercial security is any security for which the company provides more than a reasonable commercial return for the use of the principal secured (*CTA 2010, s 1005*). A distribution is any interest or other distribution paid out of the assets of the company that exceeds the amount of the principal secured for the security or that represents more than a reasonable commercial return for the use of the principal secured (*CTA 2010, s 1000(1)E*).

At its simplest, if the interest payable on such securities is in excess of a commercial return for the capital secured, the excess is a distribution. Similarly, if the amount repaid exceeds the principal secured, the excess is a distribution. There are, however, a number of overlapping rules relating to the amount that is taken as being the principal secured.

The phrase 'principal secured' would normally takes its general meaning of the minimum amount the holder of the security is entitled to receive on maturity of the security under the terms of issue (HMRC Company Taxation Manual at CTM15501). But this is subject to specific further tax rules.

First, the principal secured is restricted to the amount of new consideration given for the securities (*CTA 2010, s 1006*). The value of the principal secured is not taken to exceed the issue price if the securities are unlisted and the issue price is less than the amount repayable, unless the securities are issued on terms reasonably comparable with the terms of issue of securities listed on a recognised stock exchange (*CTA 2010, s 1117(6)*). This is only relevant where the new consideration given and the issue price are different (as explained in CTM15501).

If the security is issued at a premium, ie an amount that must be paid on redemption or conversion of the security under the terms of the security, then the principal secured includes any premium (*CTA 2010, s 1007* and CTM15501).

But *CTA 2010, s 1007* does not apply where the consideration received exceeds the principal secured. The difference here is that the new consideration exceeds the amount repayable, in contrast to a premium, which is an amount that is repayable on maturity. In this situation, the principal secured is still treated as increasing the principal for these purposes (*CTA 2010, s 1008*) but this rule is subject to an exception in *CTA 2010, s 1002*. In practice, *CTA 2010, s 1008* is mainly likely to be relevant to banks and similar institutions (CTM15503).

The exception occurs if the security reflects, to a significant extent, dividends or other distributions in respect of, or fluctuations in the value of, shares, and those shares are in one or more companies, each of which is the issuing company or an associated company of the issuing company. There are separate rules for banking businesses (*CTA 2010, ss 1009, 1010*).

For this purpose, two or more companies are associated with one another if one has control of the other, or both are under the control of the same person or persons (*CTA 2010, s 1011*). A person controls a company if that person has the power to secure that the affairs of the company are conducted in accordance with that person's wishes, and that power is derived from:

- holding shares in the company or any other company;
- possessing voting power in relation to the company or any other company; or
- any powers conferred by:

– the articles of association of the company or any other company; or

– any other document regulating the company or any other company.

Shares held by a company, and any voting power or other powers arising from the shares, is ignored if a profit on the sale of those shares would be treated as a trading receipt of a trade carried on by the company, and the shares are not assets of an insurance company's long-term insurance fund.

The existence of hedging arrangements modifies these rules (*CTA 2010, ss 1012–1014*).

Distributions in respect of special securities

18.8 Securities are 'special' if they meet any of the following conditions detailed in *CTA 2010, s 1015*:

- Condition A: The securities are issued otherwise than for new consideration.
- Condition B: The securities are convertible or carry a right to receive shares in or securities of the company, and are neither listed on a recognised stock exchange nor issued on terms which are reasonably comparable with the terms of issue of securities listed on a recognised stock exchange.
- Condition C: The consideration given by the company for the use of the principal secured depends (to any extent) on the results of the company's business, or any part of the company's business. But a consideration based on the reciprocal of results is to be ignored (ie the interest goes up if the results are poor or vice versa) (*CTA 2010, s 1017(1)*).
- Condition D: The securities are connected with shares in the company. Connection arises if, as a consequence of the nature of the rights attaching to the securities or shares and, in particular, any terms or conditions attaching to the right to transfer the securities or shares, there is a necessity or advantage, when disposing of or acquiring the securities, to dispose of or to acquire a proportionate holding of the shares (*CTA 2010, s 1017(2)*).
- Condition E: The securities are equity notes issued by the company and held by a company which is associated with the issuing company, or is a funded company. A company will be treated as a funded company under arrangements whereby it is or it will be put in funds either directly or indirectly by the issuing company, or a company associated with the issuing company (*CTA 2010, s 1017(3)*). Whether or not a security is an equity note is determined by its redemption conditions; if any of the following criteria are met, either in the terms or through the issuing house, a security is an equity note (*CTA 2010, s 1016*):

- no particular deadline redemption date;
- redemption terms determine that redemption date is more than 50 years after issue; or
- redemption depends on a likely event more than 50 years after issue.

A distribution is any interest or other distribution paid out of the assets of the company that exceeds the amount of the principal secured for the security or that falls into paragraph E (*CTA 2010, s 1000(1)F*).

At its simplest, any interest payable on such securities is a distribution.

Similarly, if the amount repaid exceeds the principal secured, the excess is a distribution. There are, however, a number of overlapping rules relating to the amount that is taken as being the principal secured for this purpose.

First, the principal secured is restricted to the amount of new consideration given for the securities (*CTA 2010, s 1018(1)*). The value of the principal secured is not taken to exceed the issue price if the securities are unlisted and the issue price is less than the amount repayable, unless the securities are issued on terms reasonably comparable with the terms of issue of securities listed on a recognised stock exchange (*CTA 2010, s 1117(6)*). This is only relevant where the new consideration given and the issue price are different (as explained in CTM15501).

If the security is issued at a premium, ie an amount that must be paid on redemption or conversion of the security under the terms of the security, then the principal secured includes any premium (*CTA 2010, s 1018(2), (3)* and CTM15501).

There is no equivalent rule to *CTA 2010, s 1008* for paragraph F.

There are rules that prevent a relevant alternative finance return within the meaning of *CTA 2009, s 513* from being treated as a distribution (*CTA 2010, s 1019*).

Bonus issue following repayment of share capital

18.9 Following a repayment of ordinary share capital, share capital which is issued within ten years thereafter in excess of new consideration can be attributed to a distribution (*CTA 2010, ss 1000(1)H, 1022, 1023*).

The distribution is calculated as follows (CTM15420):

- the nominal amount of the bonus issue up to the amount of the capital repaid,

  minus

- any new consideration received,

  minus

- any amounts in respect of the same repayment of capital already treated as distributions under *CTA 2010, s 1022*.

Example 18.1—Bonus issue following repayment of share capital

Facts

In July 2006, A Ltd repays £200,000 of its share capital.

In June 2014 the company issues 100,000 fully paid £1 ordinary shares at 30p per share. In August 2015, it issues 500,000 fully paid £1 preference shares for no new consideration.

Analysis

The issue of ordinary shares in June 2014 results in a distribution of:

$$100{,}000 \times (£1 - £0.30) = £70{,}000$$

The second (bonus) issue, in August 2015, is of shares with par value of £500,000 (500,000 × £1).

This distribution is restricted to a maximum of the repayment of share capital less the earlier distribution. The amount of this distribution is, therefore:

$$£200{,}000 - £70{,}000 = £130{,}000$$

Interest and other situations

18.10 Interest payments in excess of a normal commercial rate of return may be treated as a distribution (see **18.7**). HMRC have previously confirmed that there is no requirement to deduct income tax at source under the CT61 procedures (*ITA 2007, s 874*; see **23.37–23.39**) from interest payments treated as distributions (Revenue & Customs Brief 100/09, 12 January 2010, tinyurl.com/pu3npf5). This Brief is now archived but, logically, there cannot be a requirement to deduct tax from an amount that is a distribution for corporation tax purposes, because it is not interest.

Distributions in a winding up are not income distributions and are subject to tax on chargeable gains (*TCGA 1992, s 122*).

QUALIFYING AND NON-QUALIFYING DISTRIBUTIONS (NOW DISTRIBUTIONS TO WHICH *CTA 2010, S 1100* APPLIES AND OTHER DISTRIBUTIONS)

18.11 Until 5 April 2016, bonus issues of redeemable shares or of securities within *CTA 2010, s 1000(1)C* and *D* (*CTA 2010, s 1136*, repealed by *FA 2016, s 5*) were described as 'non-qualifying distributions'. Now they are simply described as distributions that are not within *CTA 2010, s 1100*. Where such a distribution is made, the company must notify HMRC on form CT2 within 14 days after the end of the quarter in which the non-qualifying distribution is made (*CTA 2010, s 1101* and CTM15910).

All other distributions were called 'qualifying distributions' (*CTA 2010, s 1136*, repealed by *FA 2016, s 5*). To the extent that any distinction is required, they are now referred to as being distributions other than those within *CTA 2010, s 1000(1)C* and *D* (as in *CTA 2010, s 1100(4A)*).

Until 5 April 2016, a tax credit of 1/9th generally attached to a dividend or other qualifying distribution. For a shareholder who is an individual, this 10% tax credit satisfies their basic rate income tax liability on the gross distribution and, depending on their circumstances, they may be charged also at the 32.5% higher rate or the 37.5% additional rate. For the new way in which dividends are to be liable to income tax from 6 April 2016, see **10.32**.

SMALL COMPANY DIVIDEND PAYMENTS

> **Focus**
>
> *CA 2006* rules regarding the payment of dividends are contained in the statutory model articles. These are of particular interest to smaller companies in determining when payments are made to directors and/or shareholders.

18.12 Owner managers of small private companies generally take their reward from their companies in the form of dividends and/or remuneration. Remuneration is deductible for corporation tax purposes. Dividend payments are not tax deductible. See also **10.32**.

Under *CA 2006, s 19*, statutory model articles apply from 1 October 2009; see the *Companies (Model Articles) Regulations 2008, SI 2008/3229, Sch, arts 30–36* concerning dividends and other distributions.

Dividends may be declared by the company in general meeting but no dividend shall exceed the amount recommended by the directors (*SI 2008/3229, art 30*).

Interim dividends may be paid by decision of the directors from time to time (*SI 2008/3229, art 30*).

The timing of the dividend payment may have a marked impact on the directors' and shareholders' personal tax situation. A dividend is not paid until the shareholder receives the funds direct or the dividend amount is put unreservedly at his or her disposal, for example by a credit to a loan account on which the shareholder has the power to draw.

Final dividends are normally due and payable on the date of the resolution unless a future date is set for payment. Interim dividends are not an enforceable debt and can be varied or rescinded prior to payment. Interim dividends are due when paid or when the funds are placed at the disposal of the director/shareholders as part of their current accounts with the company. HMRC state that:

> 'payment is not made until such a right to draw on the dividend exists (presumably) when the appropriate entries are made in the company's books. If, as may happen with a small company, such entries are not made until the annual audit, and this takes place after the end of the accounting period in which the directors resolved that an interim dividend be paid, then the "due and payable" date is in the later rather than the earlier accounting period.' (CTM20095)

For tax purposes, an 'illegal dividend' will be treated in the same way as a legal dividend. If a shareholder knew, or was in a position to know, that a dividend was illegal at the time of payment, it is refundable to the company (*CA 2006, s 847(2)*; see also **10.22**). In these circumstances, an unlawful dividend can create a debt due from the shareholder to the company, triggering a charge under the loans to participator rules, *CTA 2010, s 455(4)* (see **10.20**). Conversely, if the shareholders have taken reasonable steps to ensure that dividends are lawful, they are not liable to repay the funds and no participators' loans arise. See, for example, *Richard and Julie Jones v HMRC* [2014] UKFTT 1082 (TC).

There is also the possibility that, if the directors were to pay an interim dividend during an accounting period and it is not possible to demonstrate that the interim dividend payment was paid out of available profits (or, alternatively, as a repayment of loans due from the company), HMRC could attack the nature of the payment, classing it as remuneration and assessing the company for PAYE and NICs for which it should have accounted. This form of challenge should be strongly resisted, as it does not have any basis in law.

For a dividend waiver to be effective for the purposes of tax on the shareholder, a final dividend may be waived at any time before entitlement to it becomes effective – either on approval by the company in general meeting or (if later) on the date that the dividend is payable. In the case of an interim dividend, the waiver must be made before payment, because payment and entitlement arise at the same time. If a waiver takes place afterwards, it is not an effective waiver but merely a transfer of after-tax income.

Under GAAP, a company may not recognise a dividend in its financial statements unless it is a liability at the reporting date. See FRS 21 *Events after the balance sheet date*, IAS 10 *Events after the reporting period* and FRS 102, Section 4. See also **Chapter 26** regarding changes to UK GAAP.

PAYMENTS NOT TREATED AS DISTRIBUTIONS

Focus

Just as the tax legislation defines certain payments that are to be treated as distributions, so also it defines others that are not classed as distributions.

Special reliefs have been granted to demergers, purchases of own shares and the winding up of a private company.

18.13 Certain payments are not treated as distributions for tax purposes. They include:

- distributions in respect of share capital on a winding up (these are taken into account instead for chargeable gains purposes) (*CTA 2010, s 1030*; *TCGA 1992, s 122*);
- certain distributions in anticipation of a winding up (*CTA 2010, s 1030A*; see **18.33**).
- a distribution as part of a cross-border merger (*CTA 2010, s 1031*);
- interest, etc. paid in respect of certain securities (*CTA 2010, s 1032*);
- a purchase by an unquoted trading company of own shares (*CTA 2010, s 1033*; see **18.22–18.30**);
- stock dividends (*CTA 2010, s 1049*);
- building society payments (*CTA 2010, s 1054*);
- industrial and provident societies: interest and share dividends (*CTA 2010, s 1055*);
- a dividend or bonus relating to transactions with a registered industrial and provident society (*CTA 2010, s 1056*);
- UK agricultural or fishing co-operatives: interest and share dividends (*CTA 2010, s 1057*);
- exempt distributions (*CTA 2010, ss 1075–1078*; see **18.14–18.21**); and
- a transfer of a building society's business to a company: qualifying benefits (*FA 1988, Sch 12, para 6*).

From 6 April 2015 a shareholder offered a choice of a distribution or an alternative receipt is treated as though they receive a qualifying distribution (*ITTOIA 2005, s 396A*; *CTA 2010, s 1100(7)*, as inserted by *FA 2015, s 19*; see *Income Tax 2016/17* (Bloomsbury Professional)).

DEMERGERS

Introduction

18.14 The demerger provisions exist to facilitate certain transactions by which trading activities carried on by a single company or group are divided so as to be carried on (*CTA 2010, s 1074*):

- by two or more companies not belonging to the same group; or
- by two or more independent groups.

Transactions to achieve this would normally involve the making of a distribution by a company. However, where certain general conditions and other additional conditions are met, the distribution in question is an 'exempt distribution' – ie one that is not treated as a distribution for corporation tax purposes (*CTA 2010, s 1075*). Nonetheless, other adverse tax repercussions may arise as a result of transactions in a demerger, so careful planning is always needed.

For HMRC guidance on demergers, see CTM17200 onwards.

General demerger conditions

18.15 All companies involved in the transactions must be resident in an EU member state at the time of the distribution (*CTA 2010, s 1081(1)*). The distributing company and any company whose shares are distributed must be a trading company or a member of a trading group (*CTA 2010, s 1081(2)*). The distribution must be made wholly or mainly for the benefit of some or all of the trading activities formerly carried on by a single company or group and, after the distribution, carried on by two or more companies or groups (*CTA 2010, s 1081(3)*). The distribution must not form part of a scheme or arrangement for:

- the avoidance of tax;
- the making of a chargeable payment;
- the transfer of control of a relevant company to persons other than members of the distributing company; or
- the cessation of a trade or its sale after the distribution (*CTA 2010, s 1081(4)–(7)*).

Types of demerger

18.16 *CTA 2010* facilitates three types of transaction where, subject to the general conditions mentioned above and to additional conditions, such a transaction is treated as an exempt distribution. Statement of Practice 13 (1980) at tinyurl.com/npzk2gm provides additional interpretation and guidance. Exempt distributions may consist of:

Direct demerger

A distribution by a company of its shares in one or more 75% subsidiaries (CTA 2010, s 1076)

Conditions are that (*CTA 2010, s 1082*):

- the distributed shares:
  - must not be redeemable;
  - must constitute the whole or substantially the whole of the distributing company's holding of the ordinary share capital of the subsidiary; and
  - must confer the whole or substantially the whole of the distributing company's voting rights in the subsidiary;

and

- after the distribution, the distributing company must either be:
  - a trading company, or
  - the holding company of a trading group,

  but this is not necessary if:
  - the distributing company is a 75% subsidiary of another company (see further below), or
  - the transfer relates to two or more of the distributing company's 75% subsidiaries, and the distributing company is dissolved devoid of net assets available for distribution on a winding up or otherwise.

Indirect demerger

A transfer of a company's trade to one or more companies in consideration for the issue of shares in the transferee company (CTA 2010, s 1077)

Conditions are that (*CTA 2010, ss 1083–1084*):

- if a trade is transferred, the distributing company must either:
  - not retain any interest in that trade; or
  - retain only a minor interest in it;

- if shares in a subsidiary are transferred, those shares:
  - must constitute the whole or substantially the whole of the distributing company's holding of the ordinary share capital of the subsidiary; and
  - must confer the whole or substantially the whole of the distributing company's voting rights in the subsidiary;
- the only or main activity of the transferee company, or each transferee company, after the distribution must be:
  - the carrying on of the trade; or
  - the holding of the shares transferred to it;
- the shares issued by the transferee company or each transferee company:
  - must not be redeemable;
  - must constitute the whole or substantially the whole of its issued ordinary share capital; and
  - must confer the whole or substantially the whole of the voting rights in that company;

and

- after the distribution, the distributing company must be either a trading company or the holding company of a trading group,

  but this is not necessary if:
  - the distributing company is a 75% subsidiary of another company (see further below), or
  - there are two or more transferee companies each of which has transferred to it either a trade or shares in a separate 75% subsidiary of the distributing company, and the distributing company is dissolved devoid of net assets available for distribution on a winding up or otherwise.

For direct and indirect demergers, the following additional conditions must be met if the distributing company is a 75% subsidiary (*CTA 2010, s 1085*):

- the group (or, if more than one, the largest group) to which the distributing company belongs at the time of the distribution must be a trading group; and
- the distribution (known as the original distribution) must be followed by one or more other distributions (known as further distributions) which:
  - are exempt distributions, and
  - result in members of the holding company of the group (or largest group, if more than one group) to which the distributing company

belonged at the time of the original distribution becoming members of:

- the transferee company or each transferee company to which a trade was transferred by the distributing company;
- the subsidiary or each subsidiary whose shares were transferred by the distributing company; or
- a company (other than the holding company) of which the transferee or the subsidiary company are 75% subsidiaries.

Cross-border demerger

A division of a business in a cross-border transfer, being the transfer of part of a business to one or more companies in consideration for the issue of shares in the transferee company or companies (CTA 2010, s 1078)

Among the conditions are that (*CTA 2010, s 1078(2)*; *TCGA 1992, s 140A(1A)* or *140C(1A)*):

either:

- a company resident in one EU member state transfers the whole or part of a business carried on by it in the UK to a company resident in another member state;
- the transfer is wholly in exchange for shares or debentures issued by the transferee to the transferor;
- the transferor is resident in one member state;
- the part of the transferor's business which is to be transferred is carried on by the transferor in the UK;
- at least one transferee is resident in a member state other than that in which the transferor is resident;
- the transferor company continues to carry on a business after the transfer;
- the relief is claimed by the transferor and the transferee; and
- additional conditions are met in relation to the transferee; or:
- the part of the transferor's business which is to be transferred is carried on, immediately before the time of the transfer, by the transferor in a member state other than the UK through a permanent establishment;
- at least one transferee is resident in a member state other than the UK;
- the transferor company continues to carry on business after the transfer;
- the transfer includes the whole of the assets of the transferor used for the purposes of the business or part (or the whole of those assets other than cash);

- the aggregate of the chargeable gains accruing to the transferor on the transfer exceeds the aggregate of the allowable losses;
- the relief is claimed by the transferor; and
- the transfer is made in exchange for the issue of shares in or debentures of each transferee company to the persons holding shares in or debentures of the transferor, or fails to comply with this only because of a prohibition on acquiring its own shares.

In either case, it is a condition that the transfer is effected for bona fide commercial reasons and does not form part of a scheme or arrangements of which the main purpose, or one of the main purposes, is avoidance of income tax, corporation tax or capital gains tax.

Examples of demergers

18.17

Example 18.2—Direct demerger under *CTA 2010, s 1076(a)*

Facts

A distribution by a company of its shares in one or more 75% subsidiaries (*CTA 2010, s 1076(a)*) is a direct demerger.

In this case B Ltd, a group company, leaves the group but its ultimate ownership remains with A and B.

Analysis

Before the demerger:

- A and B owned A Ltd, and
- A Ltd owned B Ltd and C Ltd.

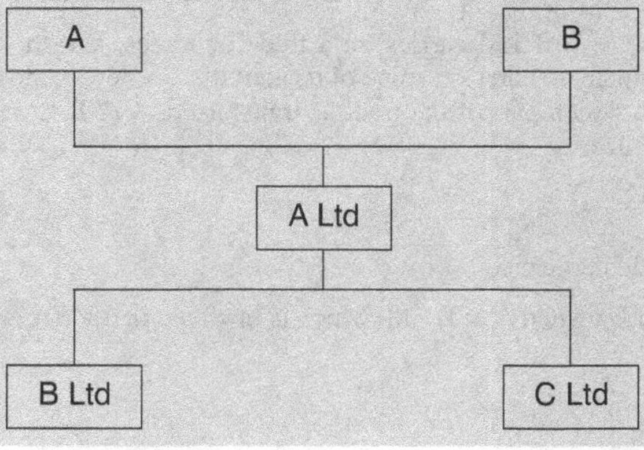

After the demerger:

- A and B own A Ltd and B Ltd, and
- A Ltd owns C Ltd.

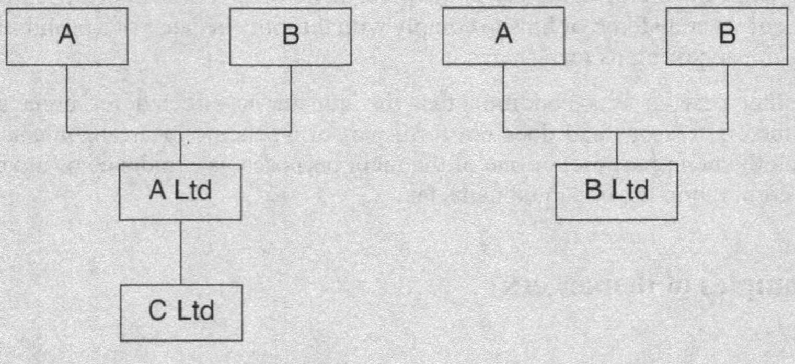

In particular, in this situation, the B Ltd shares that are distributed by A Ltd to A and B must be non-redeemable and must be the whole or substantially the whole of the ordinary shares and voting rights that A Ltd holds in B Ltd (*CTA 2010, s 1082(1)*). 'Whole' is interpreted as around 90% or more (Statement of Practice 13 (1980)).

Example 18.3—Indirect demerger under *CTA 2010, s 1077*

Facts

A distribution of a company's trade or shares in one or more 75% subsidiary companies in consideration for the issue of shares in the transferee company (*CTA 2010, s 1077*) is a form of indirect demerger.

In this case, A & B Ltd carries on a trade or trades, and the aim is for another company to carry on some of its activities. A new company, B Ltd, is formed to which part of the trade is transferred. A & B Ltd remains in active existence.

Analysis

Before the demerger:

- A and B owned A & B Ltd, which is involved in trade A and trade B.

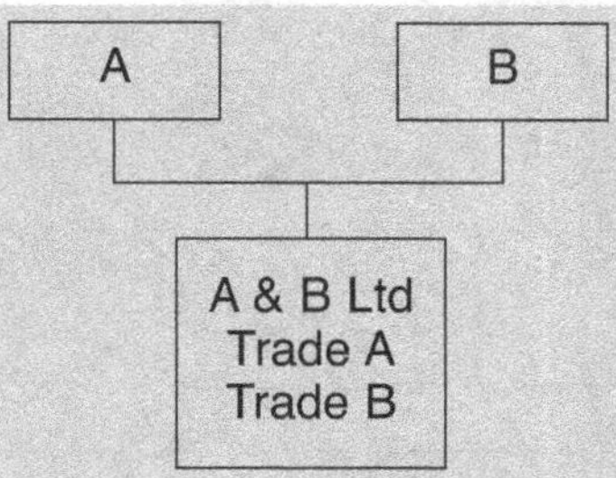

After the demerger:

- A and B own A & B Ltd, which is involved in trade A, and
- A and B own B Ltd, which is involved in trade B.

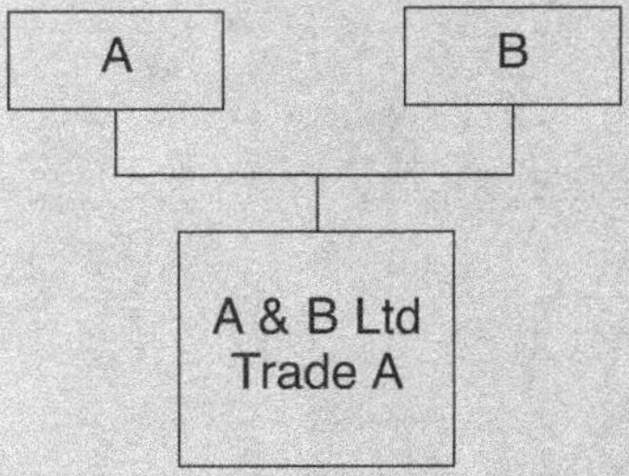

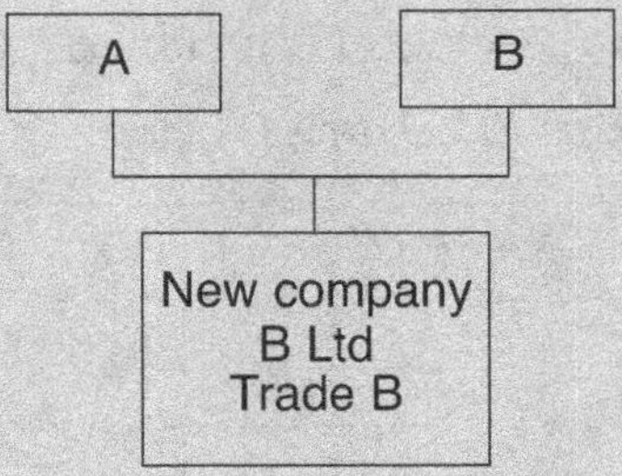

Example 18.4—Indirect demerger under *CTA 2010, s 1078*

Facts

A distribution of shares in a 75% subsidiary or subsidiaries to one or more companies, which issue their shares to the members of the distributing company (*CTA 2010, s 1078*) is another form of indirect demerger.

In this case, B Ltd, a subsidiary company, leaves the group to be within the ownership of a newly formed company but remains within A and B's ultimate ownership.

Analysis

Before the demerger:

- A and B owned A Ltd, and
- A Ltd owned B Ltd and C Ltd.

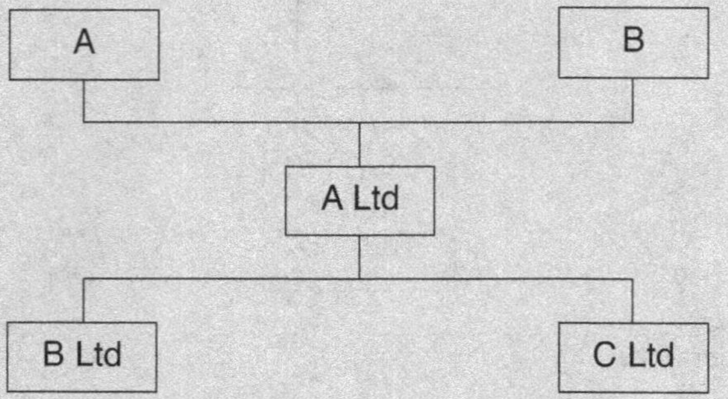

After the demerger:

- A and B own A Ltd and the new company D Ltd,
- A Ltd owns B Ltd, and
- D Ltd owns C Ltd.

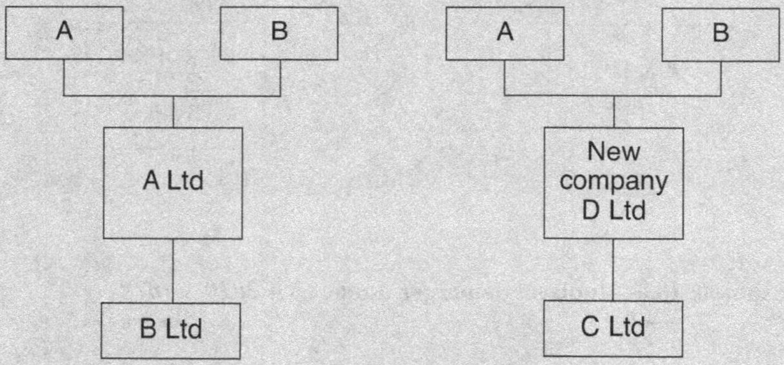

Demerger reliefs

18.18 Where the demerger reliefs apply, the share transfer is an exempt distribution and is not taxable on the recipient shareholders (*CTA 2010, s 1075*).

The direct demerger is not treated as a capital distribution under *TCGA 1992, s 122,* but instead is treated as a reorganisation under *TCGA 1992, ss 126–130* (see *TCGA 1992, s 192(2)*). Thus the capital gains base cost is usually apportioned to the shares in the transferee company and in the distributing company in proportion to their values at the time of any subsequent disposal of any of the shares (*TCGA 1992, s 129*).

In the case of an indirect demerger, capital gains relief is generally obtained in practice under *TCGA 1992, s 136,* because the demerger is usually a scheme of reconstruction (see HMRC Capital Gains Manual at CG52720, CG52721, CG33920A and **Chapter 17**).

In the case of an exempt distribution demerger, whether direct or indirect, degrouping charges under *TCGA 1992, s 179* do not arise (*TCGA 1992, s 192(3)*). However, if there is subsequently a chargeable payment (see **18.19**), the degrouping charge is reinstated (*TCGA 1992, s 192(4)*).

Chargeable payments

18.19 A chargeable payment is, broadly, a payment of any kind by a company to its members, or to anyone by an unquoted company, directly or indirectly, which is a money payment or the transfer of money's worth, except for:

- distributions;
- exempt distributions;
- payments made to a company in the same group; and
- payments made for genuine commercial reasons and not as part of a tax avoidance scheme (*CTA 2010, ss 1088, 1089*).

To be a chargeable payment, however, the payment must also be made in connection with the shares of a company.

As a measure to discourage the use of demergers for tax avoidance purposes, a chargeable payment is treated as a distribution by the company if made during the five-year period after an exempt distribution. Individuals receiving a chargeable payment will be charged to income tax in full. Companies receiving a chargeable payment will be charged to corporation tax on the full amount of the receipt (*CTA 2010, s 1086*).

Demerger clearance procedure

18.20 Clearance procedures are available for the distributing company and also for any person considering making a chargeable payment within five years of an exempt distribution (*CTA 2010, ss 1091, 1092*).

A company may make an application before making a distribution, and HMRC will notify the company whether or not the payment is to be treated as exempt (*CTA 2010, s 1091*). Likewise, a person intending to make a payment may make an application before the payment is made, and HMRC will notify the applicant whether or not the payment is a chargeable payment (*CTA 2010, s 1092*).

In each case, the application must be in writing and contain particulars of the relevant transactions. Within 30 days of receipt, HMRC can require the applicant to provide further particulars for the purpose of enabling them to make their decision. The Commissioners must notify their decision to the applicant within 30 days of receiving the application, or within 30 days of their request to provide further information. HMRC decisions made in respect of applications that do not fully and accurately disclose all facts and circumstances material for the decision are void. HMRC are not required to make a decision should their request for further information be ignored (*CTA 2010, s 1093*).

Returns

18.21 Within 30 days of making an exempt distribution, a company must make a return to HMRC giving details of the distribution and the reason why it is exempt (*CTA 2010, s 1095*).

If the demerger is in accordance with transactions for which a clearance has been obtained, the return should simply confirm this. Before receiving the return, the HMRC office dealing with the company's tax affairs will already have received a copy of the clearance.

Within 30 days of making a chargeable payment within five years after an exempt distribution, the payer must make a return to HMRC giving details of the chargeable payment (*CTA 2010, s 1096*). In certain circumstances, the payer may be a company not directly involved in the demerger, or a person other than a company (see CTM17290).

PURCHASE BY A COMPANY OF ITS OWN SHARES

Effects of the legislation

18.22 *CA 2006* permits a company to purchase and redeem its own share capital. In the absence of relieving legislation, a distribution would arise under *CTA 2010, s 1000* on the difference between the subscribed capital and the purchase or redemption proceeds.

Relief is given under *CTA 2010, s 1033* for payments made by an unquoted trading company or the unquoted holding company of a trading group on the purchase or redemption of their own shares. The excess of the payment above the refund of share capital is treated as a distribution. If certain conditions are complied with, there is no distribution treatment. Instead, the disposal receives chargeable gains treatment in the hands of the vendor shareholder.

In some cases it may suit a company to undertake a series of transactions to purchase some of its own shares on a phased basis. This can be achieved, but care is needed to meet the qualifying conditions so that favourable tax treatment is secured.

In *Baker v Revenue & Customs* [2013] UKFTT 394 (TC), a purported purchase of own shares had not satisfied the company law requirements and so was void; the First-tier Tribunal held that the taxpayer was under an obligation to repay the sum received from the company in respect of the shares, and therefore the receipt was not a distribution for tax purposes.

For HMRC guidance on the provisions relating to the purchase by a company of its own shares, see CTM17500 onwards, Statement of Practice 2 (1982) at tinyurl.com/n7dgfk8, and HMRC's helpsheet at tinyurl.com/pxee4x5.

Note that a quoted company is 'a company whose shares are listed in the official list of the Stock Exchange'. An unquoted company is a company which is neither a quoted company nor a 51% subsidiary of a quoted company (*CTA 2010, s 1048(1)*). Shares listed on the Alternative Investment Market are not listed in the official list of the UK Stock Exchange and are therefore unquoted for these purposes (CTM17507). Payments on purchase and redemption by quoted companies remain within the distribution legislation.

Conditions – purpose

Focus

To qualify for beneficial tax treatment, the purchase of a company's own shares must be wholly or mainly to benefit the trade of the company or a subsidiary, or to raise funds to meet an inheritance tax liability of the seller.

18.23 The transaction must be undertaken wholly or mainly to benefit the company's trade or a trade carried on by any of its 75% subsidiaries. It must not form part of a scheme or arrangement to enable a shareholder to participate in company profits without receiving a dividend, or any other form of tax avoidance (*CTA 2010, s 1033(2)*). HMRC will review the circumstances of each case.

The case of *Allum v Marsh* [2004] SpC 446 began with such scrutiny from HMRC. Mr and Mrs A owned 99% of the ordinary shares in A Ltd, an unquoted trading company, and their son owned the remaining 1%. Mr and Mrs A and their son were all directors. The company owned a property from which the business was carried out and there was a large loan due to the directors. The company approved a contract for the sale of the property and, when the sale had been completed, it voted to purchase Mr and Mrs A's shares in A Ltd. Mr and Mrs A resigned as company directors. A new company secretary was appointed and the board voted to make voluntary payments to Mr and Mrs A in appreciation of their services to the company. Their shareholdings were duly purchased by the company. The next year, the company's activities became small and negligible, and the company could not find suitable premises from which to carry on its activities. Mr and Mrs A were assessed to a distribution on the basis that the exemption under *CTA 2010, s 1033* did not apply because the purchase of the shares was not made wholly or mainly for the purpose of benefiting the company's trade. The voluntary payments were assessed as emoluments. This case illustrates how important it is to demonstrate that the purchase takes place for the benefit of the trade.

Alternatively, where the transaction is not undertaken wholly or mainly to benefit the company's trade or a trade carried on by any of its 75% subsidiaries, it is sufficient to show that the whole of the payment (apart from any sum applied in paying capital gains tax charged on the redemption, repayment or purchase) is applied by the recipient in discharging a liability of his or hers for inheritance tax charged on a death and is so applied within the period of two years after the death (*CTA 2010, s 1033(3)*).

Conditions – shareholder residence

18.24 The seller shareholder must be resident in the UK in the year of assessment in which the purchase is made. If the shares are held through a nominee, the nominee must also be so resident (*CTA 2010, s 1034*).

Conditions – period of ownership

18.25 The shares must have been owned by the seller throughout the period of five years ending with the date of the purchase (*CTA 2010, s 1035(1)*). For an individual, a period of ownership by their spouse or civil partner is also taken into consideration, provided that the spouse or civil partner was living with the seller at that time (*CTA 2010, s 1036*).

If the seller acquires shares of the same class at different times, shares acquired earlier are taken into account before shares acquired later. Disposals are matched, however, to shares acquired later rather than to those acquired earlier. In certain circumstances, the capital gains tax share identification rules of *TCGA 1992, Pt 4, Ch 2* (reorganisation of share capital, conversion of securities etc) will apply instead (*CTA 2010, s 1035(2), (3)*).

Shareholder's interest in the company

18.26 Immediately after the purchase, the shareholder's interest (or, if applicable, his interest combined with those of his associates) must be substantially reduced (*CTA 2010, s 1037(1), (2)*). By this, it is meant, first, that the total nominal value of the shares owned by him immediately after the purchase, expressed as a fraction of the issued share capital of the company at that time, must not exceed 75% of the corresponding fraction immediately before the purchase (*CTA 2010, s 1037(3)*). Second, his share of profits available for distribution immediately after the purchase must not exceed 75% of the corresponding fraction immediately before the purchase. Unless both these conditions are met, the shareholding will not be treated as substantially reduced (*CTA 2010, s 1038*).

In a group situation, other group members' and associates' interests are also taken into account (*CTA 2010, ss 1039, 1040*). 'Group' for these purposes is a 51% relationship (*CTA 2010, s 1041*).

After the purchase, the seller must not be connected with the company making the purchase, or with any company that is a member of the same group as that company (see **18.27**, **18.28**). The purchase must not be part of a scheme or arrangement which is designed, or is likely, to result in the seller, or an associate of the seller, not having substantially reduced his or her interest in the company. A transaction occurring within one year after the purchase will be treated as part of a scheme or arrangement of which the purchase is also part (*CTA 2010, s 1042*).

Associated persons

18.27 Associated persons include spouses or civil partners who are living together and children under the age of 18 together with their respective associates. It follows that where there is a husband and wife owned company, this mechanism cannot be used to allow one of the shareholders to retire, as the remaining shares will be held by a connected person.

Two or more companies are connected if they are both under the same control. Trustees are connected with the settlor, the beneficiaries and their respective associates.

A person connected with a company is an associate of the company and of any company controlled by it, and the company and any company controlled by it are his associates. Trustees are associated with the settlor or an associate of his or the beneficiaries if any one of the beneficiaries has an interest of more than 5%. Personal representatives are associated with any beneficiary who has an interest of more than 5% in the estate.

If one person is accustomed to act on the directions of another in relation to the affairs of a company, then in relation to that company the two persons are associates of one another. Exempt approved pension schemes and employee trusts are not included in these arrangements (*CTA 2010, ss 1059–1061*).

Connected persons

18.28 A person is connected with a company if he directly or indirectly possesses or is entitled to acquire more than 30% of the issued ordinary share capital, 30% of the combined loan capital and issued share capital, 30% of the voting power or 30% of the assets available for distribution on a winding up.

An interest in loan capital, acquired during the normal course of a money lending business, is disregarded if the person takes no part in the management or conduct of the company (*CTA 2010, s 1062*).

Clearance procedure

18.29 An advance clearance procedure is available under *CTA 2010, s 1044*. A company may make an application before making a payment on the redemption, repayment or purchase of its own shares, and HMRC notify the company whether or not the payment is to be treated as a distribution (*CTA 2010, s 1044*). The application must be in writing, and must contain particulars of the relevant transactions.

Within 30 days of receipt, HMRC can require the applicant to provide further particulars for the purpose of enabling them to make their decision. The Commissioners must notify their decision to the applicant within 30 days of receiving the application, or within 30 days of their request to provide further information. HMRC decisions made in respect of applications that do not fully and accurately disclose all facts and circumstances material for the decision are void. HMRC are not required to make a decision should their request for further information be ignored (*CTA 2010, s 1045*).

The full clearance procedure is set out in Statement of Practice 2 (1982).

Returns

18.30 Where relief under *CTA 2010, s 1033* applies to a payment made by a company on the purchase of its own shares, the company must make a return to HMRC within 60 days after making the payment, giving details of the payment and the circumstances (*CTA 2010, s 1046*).

STRIKING OFF A DEFUNCT COMPANY

Focus

Shareholders wishing to strike off dormant companies that are no longer needed should bear in mind that Concession C16 has been withdrawn.

18.31 If the registrar of companies believes that a company is not carrying on a business, he may strike it off. The procedure involves the registrar writing to the company. If a reply is not received within a month, a second letter is sent within 14 days, this time by registered post. If no reply is received within one month, the registrar may publish a notice in the *Gazette* and will send a notice to the company stating that, within three months from the date of the notice, the company will be struck off the register and dissolved (*CA 2006, s 1000*).

Request for striking off by a private company

18.32 A private company may request that the registrar strike it off. In practice, the company completes a Companies House form DS01, which it sends to the registrar of companies, together with a fee. The form must be signed by all or a majority of the directors. The directors must confirm that in the previous three months it has not carried on any business, or changed its name, disposed of any of its assets or engaged in any other activities apart from making the application, settling its affairs or meeting a statutory requirement. The company must not be involved in any other insolvency proceedings (*CA 2006, s 1003*). The registrar then publishes a notice in the *Gazette*.

Within seven days of sending the form to the registrar, all members, creditors, Crown departments, employees and any directors who have not signed the form should be sent full information as to the company's assets and liabilities, together with a copy of the letter that was sent to the registrar of companies. Creditors should be invited to petition for the winding up of the company as an alternative. In most cases, creditors will not wish to take up this option as to do so would involve them in court costs. If no objections are received, three months after the date of the notice, a further notice will be placed in the *Gazette* and the company will be removed from the register.

Until 29 February 2012, Concession C16 allowed companies being struck off the register to distribute reserves as capital distributions rather than income distributions in the hands of the shareholders. From 1 March 2012 this concession was replaced by new legislation. For further information about Concession C16, see *Corporation Tax 2014/15* (Bloomsbury Professional).

Distributions in anticipation of dissolution

18.33 From 1 March 2012, where:

- the registrar has started the procedure in *CA 2006, s 1000* to strike off a company, or
- a company intends to make or has made an application for striking off under *CA 2006, s 1003*,

and in either event the company makes a distribution in respect of share capital in anticipation of its dissolution under that section, that distribution is not treated as an income distribution for tax purposes if conditions A and B are met (*CTA 2010, s 1030A*).

Condition A is that, at the time of the distribution, the company:

- intends to secure, or has secured, the payment of any sums due to the company, and
- intends to satisfy, or has satisfied, any debts or liabilities of the company.

Condition B is that:

- the amount of the distribution, or
- in a case where the company makes more than one such distribution, the total amount of the distributions,

does not exceed £25,000.

Where two years have passed since the making of any such distribution and:

- the company has not been dissolved during that time, or
- the company has failed;
  - to secure, so far as is reasonably practicable, the payment of all sums due to the company, or
  - to satisfy all of its debts and liabilities,

the favourable tax treatment is withdrawn retrospectively and the distribution is treated as an income distribution for tax purposes (*CTA 2010, s 1030B*).

Note that the legislation treats total distributions of up to £25,000, but no more than this, as capital rather than income if made in anticipation of the striking off of a company. If the distributions made in anticipation of a striking off amounted to £25,001, the entire £25,001 would be treated as income distributions for tax purposes, with no exemption available. In an individual case, there might be difficulty in differentiating between normal distributions before striking off was considered, and distributions made later 'in anticipation of' the striking off. This suggests that a company could benefit greatly from careful recording of its distributions and the reasons why they were made. If there is doubt, or if the £25,000 limit has been exceeded and treatment as capital distributions is definitely required, a formal liquidation may be necessary.

Treatment of assets and liabilities

18.34 Before a company is dissolved, the members should ensure that its assets are transferred out of its ownership. If this is not done, any assets owned at the date of dissolution will become *bona vacantia* and pass into the ownership of the Crown. Assets held in trust by the company for another do not pass to the Crown (*CA 2006, s 1012*).

The company should request well in advance, and whilst the company is still in existence, for any corporation tax repayments to be made to the shareholders or directors. Otherwise, with a closed bank account, the company will not be able to receive the repayment and, with a company no longer in existence, it will not be possible to give alternative payment instructions to HMRC, with the result that the corporation tax repayments will also be *bona vacantia.*

The company's liabilities are extinguished on dissolution, unless the debt is secured on the company's property by a mortgage or charge. The creditor's remedy for unsecured debts is to restore the company to the register, and then bring legal proceedings against the restored company. The time limit for which a company can be restored to the register is six years in the case of striking off under *CA 2006, s 1000* or *1003* (*CA 2006, ss 1024, 1029*).

Bona vacantia

18.35 *Bona vacantia* or 'vacant goods' is ownerless property, which passes to the Crown. The collection of the assets of dissolved companies is dealt with in England, Wales and Northern Ireland by the Treasury Solicitor, and in Scotland by the Queen's and Lord Treasurer's Remembrancer, each as nominee for the Crown. Guidance on *bona vacantia* is updated from time to time on their respective websites.

Unauthorised distribution

18.36 If there is an unauthorised return of the share capital to the members, the company has a right to recover that money from its members. That right of recovery from the members is a 'right' for the purposes of *CA 2006, s 1012*, which would pass to the Crown as *bona vacantia* when the company is dissolved. It follows that, if there was an unauthorised distribution of share capital to the members prior to dissolution, the Crown would be entitled to recover that distribution from the members. The only legal way to avoid this 'right' passing to the Crown as *bona vacantia* is to put the company into formal liquidation prior to dissolution, or to formally reduce the amount of the share capital to a negligible amount prior to the company's dissolution.

SURPLUS ACT

18.37 Before 6 April 1999 a company had to account for advance corporation tax (ACT) when it made a qualifying distribution. ACT was calculated as 1/4 of the dividend paid. The ACT paid was, as its name implies, an advance payment of corporation tax. The advance payment could be set against the mainstream liability up to a 20% limit. Any surplus was carried forward for relief in the next accounting period.

This can still be of relevance where a company wishes to obtain relief for its pre-6 April 1999 surplus ACT against its post-6 April 1999 mainstream corporation tax. It can only do this if it takes account of its 'shadow' or notional ACT (*FA 1998, s 32*; *Corporation Tax (Treatment of Unrelieved Surplus Advance Corporation Tax) Regulations 1999, SI 1999/358*).

The company is required to follow this procedure:

- calculate the ACT that it would have paid on its distributions;
- calculate the maximum ACT set-off;
- calculate the remaining offset capacity after the notional ACT has been used.

This can be used to offset the surplus ACT.

Example 18.5—Set-off of surplus ACT

Facts

Lotus Ltd's profits chargeable to corporation tax for the year ended 31 March 2016 amount to £300,000. The company paid a dividend of £80,000 during the year. Surplus ACT brought forward at 1 April 2015 amounts to £125,000.

Analysis

The position is as follows:

	£
Maximum ACT set-off £300,000 × 20%	60,000
Less 'shadow' ACT £80,000 × 20/80	20,000
Surplus ACT set-off	40,000
Surplus ACT brought forward	125,000
Less set-off for accounting period ended 31 March 2016	40,000
Surplus ACT carried forward	85,000

The final corporation tax liability is:

Corporation tax @ 20% × £300,000	60,000
Less surplus ACT set-off	40,000
Final tax liability	20,000

18.38 If a company wishes to make large payments to shareholders, it may choose to do so in the form of a return of share capital rather than as a distribution. However, non-qualifying distributions are included with qualifying distributions for the purposes of calculating shadow ACT.

DIVIDENDS RECEIVED BY COMPANIES

18.39 Dividends and other distributions are generally exempt from corporation tax in the hands of a recipient company unless anti-avoidance provisions apply. Where foreign dividends are not eligible for exemption, or if the company elects for them not to be exempt, relief may be available for underlying foreign tax, ie tax charged on the profits out of which the dividends were paid.

In *First Nationwide v HMRC* [2012] STC 1261, the Court of Appeal found in favour of the taxpayer on a question concerning manufactured overseas dividends paid in respect of a stock loan of shares in a Cayman Islands company, and this cast doubt on how HMRC would characterise distributions. On 21 November 2012, HMRC published guidance on the tax treatment of payments to UK companies from companies registered in overseas territories (see tinyurl.com/l53mhek).

EXEMPTION OF DISTRIBUTIONS RECEIVED

General provision

> **Focus**
>
> The general rule is that income distributions received by a company are chargeable to corporation tax unless exempt. In practice, most are exempt.

18.40 There is a general rule that a company is chargeable to corporation tax on all the income distributions that it receives unless the distribution is exempt. The exemptions depend on whether the recipient company is small or large, and can only apply to distributions made from income (*CTA 2009, s 931A*).

Even where a dividend is exempt from corporation tax, it can still be taken into account in the calculation of chargeable gains (*CTA 2009, s 931RA*).

Small company exemption rules

What is a small company?

18.41 A company is small if, in that accounting period, it meets the micro or small enterprise criteria, as defined in the *Annex* to *Commission Recommendation 2003/361/EC* of 6 May 2003 (see **21.11**). A company is not small if, at any time during the accounting period, it is an open-ended investment company (OEIC), an authorised unit trust scheme, an insurance company or a friendly society (*CTA 2009, s 931S*).

Exemption

18.42 The dividend received by a small company is exempt (*CTA 2009, s 931B*) if:

- the payer is UK resident or resident in a qualifying territory at the time that the distribution is received; dual residence with a non-qualifying territory is not permitted;
- the distribution does not result from an interest payment in excess of a normal commercial rate of return (see **18.7**);
- in the case of a dividend paid by a non-UK resident, the payer is not entitled to a deduction for that dividend under the laws of that foreign jurisdiction; and
- the distribution is not made as part of a scheme that is designed to gain a tax advantage.

Qualifying territory

18.43 For these purposes, in general, a qualifying territory is a territory that has a double tax treaty with the UK where this treaty contains a non-discrimination provision which broadly ensures that foreign concerns are taxed no less fairly than national concerns. However, this rule is subject to HM Treasury override. A company that is liable to tax under the laws of a territory by reason of its domicile, residence or place of management is resident in that territory. A company is not resident in that territory just because it has income arising or capital situated there (*CTA 2009, s 931C*). If, however, the company is excluded from the benefits of the double tax relief arrangements, the territory is non-qualifying (*Distributions (Excluded Companies) Regulations 2009, SI 2009/3314*).

Large or medium-sized company exemption rules

18.44 The dividend received by a company that is not a small company is exempt (*CTA 2009, s 931D*) if:

- the dividend falls within one of the statutorily exempt classes of distributions (see **18.45**);
- the distribution does not result from an interest payment in excess of a normal commercial rate of return (see **18.7**); and

- in the case of a dividend paid by a non-UK resident, no deduction is available for that dividend under the laws of that foreign jurisdiction.

Statutorily exempt distributions

18.45 Classes of distributions that are statutorily exempt are:

- distributions paid to a parent company that controls the company making the distribution. Control is defined by reference to the controlled foreign company (CFC) control rules (see **20.26**) but with some differences (*CTA 2009, s 931E*);
- distributions paid in respect of non-redeemable ordinary shares (*CTA 2009, s 931F*); for the meaning of ordinary shares, see **18.46**;
- distributions in respect of portfolio holdings, if the recipient holds less than 10% of the holding by reference to share capital, income rights and capital distribution rights on a winding up. The evaluation is made for each class of share held, and shares are not treated as of the same class if the amounts paid up on them (otherwise than by way of premium) are different (*CTA 2009, s 931G*);
- distributions derived from transactions that are not designed to reduce tax (*CTA 2009, s 931H*) (prior to *F(No 3)A 2010, Sch 3, para 3*, the term 'dividends' was used instead of 'distributions'); or
- dividends in respect of shares that would be accounted for as liabilities under the loan relationship rules but for the exclusion in *CTA 2009, s 521C(f)*, ie because the investing company does not own the share for an unallowable purpose, being the gaining of a tax advantage (*CTA 2009, s 931I*).

Meaning of ordinary and redeemable shares

18.46 Ordinary shares are those which carry no present or future preferential dividend rights and no rights to assets on the company's winding up. Redeemable shares are those that, as a result of their terms of issue or any collateral arrangements, either require redemption or entitle the holder to require redemption, or entitle the issuing company to redeem them (*CTA 2009, s 931U*).

Large or medium-sized company anti-avoidance

Anti-avoidance rules of general application

18.47 Anti-avoidance rules have been introduced to ensure that the exemption rules are not abused. In general, a dividend received by a company that is not a small company is not exempt if it falls artificially into an exempt class because it forms part of a tax advantage scheme. A scheme is defined as any scheme, arrangement or understanding of any kind whatever, whether or not legally enforceable, that involves a single transaction or two or more transactions. A tax advantage scheme is a scheme the main purpose, or one of the main purposes, of which is to obtain a tax advantage, other than a negligible tax advantage (*CTA 2009, s 931V*).

Separate anti-avoidance rules apply to schemes or arrangements designed to gain a UK tax advantage by exploiting the double tax relief rules in respect of foreign tax, including underlying tax (*TIOPA 2010, ss 81–95*).

Particular exemption anti-avoidance rules

18.48 As regards the statutorily exempt distributions listed in **18.45**, dividends paid to a parent company are not exempt if they fall into an exempt class because they form part of a scheme or arrangement and are paid in respect of pre-control profits, ie profits that arose before the company was part of the group. If a dividend is paid only partially out of pre-control profits, it is treated as two separate dividends (*CTA 2009, s 931J*).

Distributions paid in respect of non-redeemable ordinary shares are not exempt where the rights obtained under an avoidance scheme are equivalent to the rights of either a preferential shareholder or a holder of a redeemable preference share (*CTA 2009, s 931K*).

Distributions are not exempt if made as part of an avoidance scheme designed to bring them into the exemption for portfolio holdings (*CTA 2009, ss 931G, 931L*; see **18.45**).

Further anti-avoidance rules

18.49 There are further anti-avoidance rules for:

- schemes that yield a return economically equivalent to interest (*CTA 2009, s 931M*);
- situations where a deduction is given in respect of the distribution (*CTA 2009, s 931N*);
- situations where a person connected to the recipient makes a payment or gives up income in return for a distribution (*CTA 2009, s 931O*);
- schemes involving payments not on arm's length terms, which prevent the supply of goods and services on terms for a reduced payment that is then compensated for by the payment of a dividend (*CTA 2009, s 931P*); or

- schemes that divert trade income, whereby a dividend is received by another company in respect of the trading income reduction (*CTA 2009, s 931Q*).

Election that a distribution should not be exempt

18.50 A company can elect, within two years of the end of the accounting period in which the distribution is paid, for it to be non-exempt (*CTA 2009, s 931R*). A company might wish to elect that the dividend be non-exempt in rare cases where, for example, the terms of the double tax treaty with the source territory means that this could lead to a reduced rate of overseas withholding tax.

RELIEF FOR UNDERLYING FOREIGN TAX ON DIVIDENDS

18.51 Where a company receives a dividend that is not exempt from corporation tax under *CTA 2009, Pt 9A*, it may be able to claim relief for the underlying tax on dividends. Underlying tax is the tax charged in the non-UK territory on the profits out of which the dividend is paid.

The calculation of the underlying tax varies according to whether the dividend:

- is paid by a non-UK resident company to a UK resident company (see **18.52**); or
- is not paid by a non-UK resident company to a UK resident company (see **18.53**).

Relief for underlying tax is not available if relief is given in the non-UK territory (*TIOPA 2010, s 57*).

Dividend from non-resident to resident company

18.52 If there is a need to take underlying tax into account where a dividend is paid by a company resident outside the UK to a company resident in the UK, the underlying tax is calculated in six steps (*TIOPA 2010, s 58*):

Step 1

Calculate the amount of the foreign tax borne on the relevant profits by the company paying the dividend.

Step 2

Calculate how much of that amount is properly attributable to the proportion of the relevant profits represented by the dividend.

Step 3

Calculate the amount given by:

$$(D + PA) \times M$$

where:

- D is the amount of the dividend
- PA is the amount given by the calculation at Step 2
- M is the rate of corporation tax applicable to profits of the recipient for the accounting period in which the dividend is received or, if there is more than one such rate, the average rate over the whole of that accounting period.

Step 4

If, under the law of the non-UK territory, the dividend has been increased for tax purposes by an amount to be:

- set off against the recipient's own tax under that law, or
- paid to the recipient so far as it exceeds the recipient's own tax under that law,

calculate the amount of the increase.

Step 5

If the amount given by the calculation at Step 2 is less than the amount given by the calculation at Step 3, the underlying tax is the amount given by the calculation at Step 2 but reduced by any amount calculated at Step 4.

Step 6

If the amount given by the calculation at Step 2 is equal to or more than the amount given by the calculation at Step 3, the underlying tax is the amount given by the calculation at Step 3 but reduced by any amount calculated at Step 4.

Relevant profits are the profits out of which the dividend is paid and are derived from transactions not designed to reduce tax (*TIOPA 2010, s 59*).

Example 18.6—Underlying tax: non-resident to resident company

Facts

England Ltd, a UK resident company, receives a dividend of £9,000 net of 10% withholding tax from Overseas Ltd, a foreign company, in respect of the accounting period ended 31 March 2016.

Extracts from Overseas Ltd's profit and loss account for the accounting period in question (converted to sterling) show the following:

	£
Profit before tax	450,000
Provision for corporation tax	90,000
Distributable profits	360,000

The company paid foreign corporate income tax of £140,000. It is necessary to compute the underlying tax.

Analysis

Computation of underlying tax

Step 1

Calculate the amount of the foreign tax borne on the relevant profits by the company paying the dividend: £140,000

Step 2

Calculate how much of that amount is properly attributable to the proportion of the relevant profits represented by the dividend: £140,000 × £10,000 / (£360,000 + £140,000) = £2,800

Step 3

Calculate the amount given by:

$$(10,000 + 2,800) \times 20\% = £2,560$$

Step 4

No local dividend increases.

Step 5

The amount given by the calculation at Step 2 – £2,800 – is more than the amount given by the calculation at Step 3 – £2,560. Therefore, the underlying tax is £2,560 (*TIOPA 2010, s 58*).

Dividend other than from non-resident to resident company

Basic relief under TIOPA 2010, s 61

18.53 If there is a need to take underlying tax into account where a dividend is not one paid by a company resident outside the UK directly to a company resident in the UK but is paid in other circumstances (eg by one non-resident company to another non-resident company), the underlying tax is calculated as follows (*TIOPA 2010, s 61*):

Step 1

Calculate the amount of the foreign tax borne on the relevant profits (see **18.54**) by the body corporate paying the dividend.

Step 2

Calculate how much of that amount is properly attributable to the proportion of the relevant profits represented by the dividend.

Step 3

If, under the law of the non-UK territory, the dividend has been increased for tax purposes by an amount to be:

- set off against the recipient's own tax under that law, or
- paid to the recipient so far as it exceeds the recipient's own tax under that law,

calculate the amount of the increase.

Step 4

The amount of underlying tax to be taken into account is the amount given by the calculation at Step 2 but reduced by any amount calculated at Step 3.

Example 18.7—Underlying tax: non-resident to non-resident company

Facts

Foreign SA receives a net dividend from Overseas Inc of £9,000 net of 10% withholding tax for the accounting period ended 31 March 2016. Distributable profits of Overseas Inc amount to £50,000 and the underlying tax paid amounts to £10,000. It is necessary to compute the underlying tax.

Analysis

Computation of underlying tax

Step 1

Calculate the amount of the foreign tax borne on the relevant profits by the body corporate paying the dividend: £10,000

Step 2

Calculate how much of that amount is properly attributable to the proportion of the relevant profits represented by the dividend: £10,000 × £10,000 / (£50,000 + £10,000) = £1,667

Step 3

No local dividend increases.

Step 4

The amount of underlying tax to be taken into account is £1,667 (*TIOPA 2010, s 61*).

Meaning of 'relevant profits' for TIOPA 2010, s 61

18.54 The meaning of 'relevant profits' for this purpose depends on whether or not the dividend is paid for a specified period (abbreviated here to SPD), whether it exceeds that period's distributable profits (EDP), and whether it is paid out of specified profits (SPR), and can be determined according to the following table in which these arbitrary acronyms are used (see *TIOPA 2010, s 62*):

Dividend payment criteria

	SPD	EDP	SPR	Relevant profits
1(a)	Yes	No	No	Specified profits of the specified period
(b)	Yes	Yes	No	Profits of that period plus profits of preceding period up to the amount of the excess
2	No	N/A	Yes	The specified profits
3(a)	No	No	No	Profits of the last accounting period ending before the dividend became payable
(b)	No	Yes	No	Profits of the last accounting period ending before the dividend became payable plus profits of preceding periods up to the amount of the excess

Extended relief where dividend received by 10% investor

18.55 Credit against corporation tax in respect of underlying tax may be extended where the profits out of which a non-UK company pays a dividend have suffered tax in a third country (ie a territory other than the UK and the country of residence of the paying company) if:

- the recipient company:
  - controls directly or indirectly, or
  - is a subsidiary of a company which controls directly or indirectly,
- at least 10% of the voting power in the overseas company, and

either

  - the recipient company is UK resident,

or

– the recipient company is non-UK resident and the dividend forms part of the profits of its UK permanent establishment.

For this purpose, a subsidiary of the recipient company is one in which it controls, directly or indirectly, at least 50% of the voting power (*TIOPA 2010, s 63*).

Meaning of 'dividend-paying chain' of companies

18.56 Relief is available for the underlying tax for a dividend paid in a dividend-paying chain of companies. A dividend chain exists where a succession of dividend payments are made by companies which are each 10% associates of the recipient company.

Such a chain exists if a dividend is received by one company (the first company) from another company (the second company) and is followed by any of the following circumstances:

- the second company receives a dividend from its 10% associate (the third company);
- the second company receives a dividend from its 10% associate (the third company) and the third company receives a dividend from its 10% associate (the fourth company); or
- the second company receives a dividend from its 10% associate (the third company), and the third company receives a dividend from its 10% associate (the fourth company), and the fourth company receives a dividend from its 10% associate (the fifth company), and so on.

For this purpose, a 10% associate of a recipient company is one in which the recipient company or its subsidiary controls, directly or indirectly, at least 10% of the voting power or ordinary share capital. A subsidiary of the recipient company is one in which it controls, directly or indirectly, at least 50% of the voting power (*TIOPA 2010, s 64*).

Subject to the double tax treaty, the underlying tax of a company lower down in the dividend paying chain can be relieved against the first company's income if the second company is an overseas company (*TIOPA 2010, s 65*; see **18.53**). The underlying tax must represent corporation tax or the like (*TIOPA 2010, s 66*).

Relief for the underlying tax on a dividend paid by an overseas company to a UK resident company is restricted to the corporation tax rate applying, if the underlying tax rate is higher than this.

The same restriction applies if the underlying tax results from a dividend paying chain (*TIOPA 2010, s 67*). There are also restrictions if schemes exist to avoid tax (*TIOPA 2010, s 68*). If two or more companies (eg a group) are treated as a separate taxable entity in the foreign jurisdiction, they will also be treated as such in calculating the underlying tax (*TIOPA 2010, s 71*).

Where a dividend is paid by an overseas company to a UK company from profits earned in other jurisdictions, on which tax has already been charged, the underlying tax is calculated as if all the profits were earned by the paying company (*TIOPA 2010, s 69*). Special rules apply for dividends paid to banking companies (*TIOPA 2010, s 70*).

In *Peninsular & Oriental Steam Navigation Company v Revenue and Customs Commissioners* [2015] UKUT 312 (TCC), the Upper Tribunal rejected a claim to double tax relief on grounds that no tax had been paid by the UK subsidiary which paid the first dividend in the chain of dividends comprised in the scheme undertaken by the group, so there was no underlying tax which could be relieved.

Credit relief for overseas permanent establishments

18.57 If an election is not made in respect of qualifying income of an overseas permanent establishment to be exempt (see **20.33**), any unrelieved credit for foreign tax in respect of the company's qualifying income from the permanent establishment can be carried forward and set against the qualifying income of that permanent establishment for the next accounting period. This is only possible if the permanent establishment continues to exist. For this purpose, an overseas permanent establishment is a permanent establishment through which the company carries on a trade outside the UK (*TIOPA 2010, s 78*).

Alternatively, a claim can be made to set any unrelieved credit for foreign tax against:

(a) the qualifying income of that permanent establishment for the next accounting period;

(b) the qualifying income of that permanent establishment for accounting period beginning within the previous three years, setting it against income of a later period before income of an earlier period; or

(c) a combination of (a) and (b) in the amounts specified in the claim (*TIOPA 2010, ss 73, 74*).

For the purposes of claiming credit relief, two permanent establishments are treated as one if they are treated as such by the overseas jurisdiction (*TIOPA 2010, s 75*). If a permanent establishment is closed and a new one opened in the same overseas jurisdiction, they are treated as different permanent establishments when claiming credit relief (*TIOPA 2010, s 76*).

Amounts claimed must be specified, and the claim must be made no more than four years after the end of the accounting period concerned, or (if later) one year after the end of the accounting period in which the foreign tax is paid (*TIOPA 2010, s 77*).

Qualifying income is the profit from the overseas establishment of a trade carried on partly but not wholly outside the UK (*TIOPA 2010, s 72*).

Chapter 19

Liquidations

SIGNPOSTS

- Background to insolvency laws in the UK, and insolvency proceedings for insolvent and solvent companies (see **19.1–19.3**).
- Administration proceedings – including the appointment of a receiver and the effect on corporation tax and the trade (see **19.4–19.8**).
- Liquidation proceedings – including the effects of winding up, tax liabilities of office holders and liquidation of subsidiaries (see **19.9–19.16**).
- Dissolution by striking off (see **19.17**).
- Disincorporation relief (see **19.18**).

INSOLVENCY

Background to insolvency laws in the UK

19.1 Within the UK, there are three separate jurisdictions with their own respective laws relating to the conduct of insolvency matters: England and Wales (collectively), Scotland, and Northern Ireland.

The majority of the corporate provisions of *Insolvency Act 1986* apply equally to Scotland (*IA 1986, s 440*), the main exception being those provisions that relate to receivership, for which Scotland has its own system. Scotland also has its own personal insolvency laws.

The majority of the provisions of *IA 1986* do not apply to Northern Ireland but, under separate provisions which apply, the insolvency laws of Northern Ireland are broadly in line with those of England and Wales.

A general principle of insolvency legislation as regards compulsory liquidation is that a company may only be wound up by a court with jurisdiction in the part of the UK in which it is registered.

The same corporation tax repercussions of insolvency and liquidation apply throughout the UK, and the insolvency law terminology used throughout this chapter is primarily that relating to England and Wales.

Note that the HMRC Insolvency Manual does not appear in the gov.uk list of Manuals. It can be accessed in the archives at tinyurl.com/ybpzwx2f. The Manual appears to have been last updated in 2014; however, HMRC still appear to rely on it (see CTM36205 and *Lomas and others v HMRC* [2016] EWHC 2492 (Ch), paras 80–84).

Insolvent company

19.2 If a company becomes insolvent, it may turn out that the only option is to 'wind up' or liquidate the company. However, there are various courses of action that might be taken, or in some cases a mixture of these could be appropriate.

First, the company can enter into a 'voluntary arrangement' with its creditors.

Second, a secured creditor with either a fixed or floating charge, such as a bank, may appoint a receiver who then assumes control of the company's business and becomes an administrator or (exceptionally) an administrative receiver. In Scotland a receivership arises when an insolvency practitioner is appointed to control the whole or a major part of a company's assets and property for the benefit of a creditor holding a floating charge.

Third, the court may make an administration order, and an administrator will then take control of the company; an administrator has similar powers to a receiver.

Finally, a compulsory liquidation may take place, with the company being wound up by a court order under *IA 1986, s 73*, or a voluntary liquidation may take place following a resolution passed at a general meeting of the company.

Solvent company

19.3 A company may be put into liquidation even when it is not insolvent.

A solvent company may be put into liquidation when there is no further use for the company, eg in a group reconstruction or when the shareholders of a family company want to extract their capital. When such a course is contemplated, the company directors, or a majority of them, must make a statutory declaration of solvency to the Registrar of Companies to the effect that the company will be able to pay or provide for all of its debts (including interest) within 12 months. Within five weeks of that declaration, the directors must pass a resolution to wind up the company (*Insolvency Act 1986 s 89*). A members' voluntary winding up starts on the day the resolution to wind up the company is passed.

ADMINISTRATION PROCEEDINGS

> **Focus**
>
> A company within administration proceedings remains chargeable to corporation tax, and there is no change in directors' duties. A new accounting period begins with the date of the administration order.

Administration order

19.4 An administration order is a court order placing a company that is, or is likely to become, insolvent under the control of an administrator following an application by the company, its directors or a creditor. The purpose of the order may be to preserve the company's business, allow a reorganisation, or ensure the most advantageous realisation of its assets whilst protecting it from action by its creditors.

Receivers and administrators

19.5 A receiver takes his appointment from a secured creditor. Sometimes this is through a court order on behalf of the creditor. The receiver is assigned to take control of the secured assets on behalf of the creditor and sell them if need be to pay off the creditors. If the receiver succeeds in this work, the directors continue with their duties and responsibilities. If the receiver is unable to discharge the secured debt, it normally follows that the company is put into liquidation.

Before 15 September 2003 a receiver normally assumed control of the company's business as an administrative receiver with statutory powers. An administrative receiver is an insolvency practitioner. Administrative receivership was abolished for floating charges created on and after 15 September 2003, with certain exceptions (such as financial market transactions and public private partnerships). Under the *Enterprise Act 2002*, lenders appoint administrators in situations that would previously have been dealt with by administrative receivership. From 15 September 2003, an administrative receiver in post must vacate office on the appointment of an administrator (HMRC Insolvency Manual at INS1203).

The administrator may be appointed by the court, the creditors or the directors to manage the affairs, business and assets of the company. Essentially, the administrator seeks to rescue the company and, if possible, secure better results for the creditors. Eventually the administrator may realise assets in order to make a distribution.

Effect of appointment

19.6 The appointment does not affect the corporate existence of the company. The directors and officers retain their respective positions and are not relieved of their duties and liabilities, although the administrator has effective control of the company.

Corporation tax in administration

19.7 A new accounting period begins when the company enters into administration (*CTA 2009, s 10(2)–(5)*), and an accounting period ends when it ceases to be in administration (*CTA 2009, s 10(1)*). Within this period, each successive accounting period will not exceed 12 months. The original accounting date may be used if so required.

If the company is to be dissolved at the end of the administration period, the corporation tax will be charged at that time on the company's profits for the final year based on the corporation tax rate already fixed or proposed for that year or, failing this, the rate fixed or proposed for the previous year (*CTA 2010, s 628*). If the company receives any interest on overpaid tax in the final accounting period, then provided that it does not exceed £2,000 it will not be subject to corporation tax (*CTA 2010, s 633*).

When a company enters into administration, it does not cease to be the beneficial owner of its assets. Therefore, the reconstruction and amalgamation reliefs described in **17.5–17.13** may still apply.

Whether the company may claim group relief is a debatable point. As the administrator or receiver is effectively controlling the company, the company's shareholders cannot secure that the affairs of the company are conducted in accordance with their wishes (*CTA 2010, s 1124*). It is thought that HMRC would generally accept that a parent company in administration could still be grouped with its subsidiaries for group relief purposes, in the absence of arrangements for them to leave the group as outlined in **5.21**, whereas a subsidiary company in administration would not be treated as a member of the group because it is not under the effective control of its parent.

In determining the claims of creditors, corporation tax liabilities are fixed as at the date of the administration and not at the date of the creditors' meeting (*HMRC v Maxwell and anor* [2010] EWCA Civ 1379).

Effect of cessation of trade

19.8 A company may continue to trade during its administration or liquidation period. The date of cessation of all its trading activities, whenever it occurs, marks the end of an accounting period (*CTA 2009, s 10(1)*).

The cessation of a trade has various corporation tax implications:

- Trading stock, if sold to an unconnected UK trade, is valued at sales price. In other circumstances, such as a sale to a connected party or an overseas trader, it is valued at market value. If the parties are connected, they may jointly elect in writing, within two years of the end of the accounting period in which the trade ceased, to substitute the higher of the cost and the sales price (*CTA 2009, s 167*). But see **Chapter 21** for possible adjustments where transfer pricing applies.

- The company should provide for all known bad debts and impairment losses. If trading ceases and a debt that had not been provided for proves to be irrecoverable, it can only be relieved against post-cessation receipts. Similarly, all known expenses should be provided for.

- For capital allowances purposes, the permanent cessation will give rise to a balancing charge or balancing allowance in the final period (*CAA 2001, s 65*). Disposal proceeds will be the sale price if sold to an unconnected third party, or market value in any other case. If the parties are connected and the plant and machinery is used in a qualifying activity which is transferred, the parties may jointly elect in writing, within two years of the end of the accounting period in which the trade ceased, to substitute the higher of the sales price or the actual cost price (*CAA 2001, ss 266, 267*).

- When a company ceases to carry on a trade, its unrelieved trading losses are not available to carry forward. It may still offset its non-trading deficits against its non-trading credits. A trading loss incurred in the final accounting period can be utilised in a group relief claim (see **5.10**). Trading losses incurred in the last 12 months of a trade, or carried forward to the final accounting period from previous years, can be carried back in a terminal loss claim (see **4.22–4.23**). Unrelieved trading losses may be set against post-cessation receipt income (*CTA 2009, s 196*).

LIQUIDATION PROCEEDINGS

> **Focus**
>
> A company within liquidation proceedings remains chargeable to corporation tax, but the liquidator assumes responsibility for the company's affairs. A new accounting period begins with the date of the winding-up order, and the company loses beneficial interest in its assets, so that group relief is denied.

Winding up

19.9 The winding up of a company may be 'voluntary', by company or creditor's resolution, or 'compulsory' by order of the court (*IA 1986, s 73*). Following the winding-up resolution or order, a liquidator is appointed to 'wind up' the affairs of the company; namely to realise the assets and settle outstanding liabilities. The liquidator will then apply to have the company dissolved and removed from the Register at Companies House, and at that point the company will cease to exist. In a member's voluntary winding up, the company is dissolved three months after the date on which the Registrar of Companies is advised that the winding up is complete.

Liquidator

19.10 A liquidator can be appointed by the creditors, the members or the court, depending on the type of liquidation. The role of the liquidator is to realise all company assets within his control and apply the proceeds in payment of the company's debts in order of priority. If any surplus funds remain, the liquidator will repay the members the amounts paid up on their shares, or a proportionate part thereof, in accordance with the rights attaching to the shares. If any further surplus remains, he will distribute the surplus amongst the members according to their entitlement.

Commencement

19.11 A voluntary winding up commences on the date that the resolution is passed, or the date that the company went into administration if the liquidation follows an administration. A compulsory winding up commences on the date that the resolution is passed, or the date of the order, when the company has applied for an administration order, or the date of the petition in any other case. On hearing a petition, the court will make an order for the winding up of the company if all necessary conditions have been followed and the court is satisfied that the company is unable to pay its debts (INS1520, INS1612).

Corporation tax

19.12 The date of the winding-up order marks the end of one accounting period and the beginning of the next. Thereafter, an accounting period ends at the end of each 12-month period or, if earlier, when the winding up is completed (*CTA 2009, s 12*). The profits during the winding up remain chargeable to corporation tax on the company and not on the liquidator (*CTA 2010, s 942*).

If the company receives any interest on overpaid tax in the final accounting period, provided that it does not exceed £2,000, it will not be subject to corporation tax (*CTA 2010, s 633*).

The liquidator will provide HMRC with a provisional date for completion of the winding up. The corporation tax will be charged at that time on the company's profits for the final year based on the corporation tax rate already fixed or proposed for that year or, failing this, the rate fixed or proposed for the previous year (*CTA 2010, s 628*). If it transpires that the winding up continues beyond the provisional date notified to HMRC, an accounting period is deemed to end on that date and a new one commences (*CTA 2010, s 629(4)–(6)*).

Effect of winding-up order

19.13 When a company has entered into liquidation, it loses the beneficial interest in its assets (*Ayerst v C & K (Construction) Ltd* [1975] STC 345). Hence, group relief and consortium relief are no longer available (*CTA 2010, s 154*) and the tax advantages afforded to a reconstruction hive-down under *CTA 2010, s 940A* onwards (see **Chapter 17**) are also denied. The company remains a group member for chargeable gains purposes (*TCGA 1992, s 170(11)*); therefore, the liquidator may transfer assets to group members, with *TCGA 1992, s 171* continuing to apply (see **16.26**).

Distributions of assets may still be made to shareholders (*CTA 2010, s 1020*; see **18.4**), and the close company distribution rules continue to apply (*CTA 2010, s 1064*). However, a distribution made strictly 'in respect of share capital' during the winding up is not a distribution for the purposes of the *Corporation Tax Acts* and is therefore capital in the hands of a recipient (*CTA 2010, s 1030*).

Loans to participators

19.14 Loans to participators of a close company may either be called in, in order to pay out the shareholders, or else written off. The normal tax repercussions will follow, as described in **10.14–10.26**.

Tax responsibilities during liquidation

19.15 Although a receiver deals with all preferential claims, the corporation tax arising during receivership remains the responsibility of the company and will be dealt with by any subsequent liquidator either as an unsecured claim or, to the extent that the income and gains arose after the commencement of winding up, as a liquidation expense.

When appointed, a liquidator or an administrator becomes the proper officer of the company dealing with its corporation tax affairs (*TMA 1970, s 108(3)*).

Corporation tax arising prior to appointment is an unsecured claim; post appointment, it is an administration or liquidation expense and, strictly speaking, must be paid ahead of the liquidator's remuneration (*Re Mesco Properties Ltd* (1979) 54 TC 238, [1979] STC 788).

Under the Insolvency Rules, any surplus remaining after the payment of debts must be applied in paying interest on those debts (Insolvency Rules 1986, r 2.88(7) Insolvency Rules 2016, r 14.23(7)). Such payments constitute yearly interest and must be made on deduction of basic rate income tax under *ITA 2007, s 874* (*HMRC v Lomas and others* [2017] EWCA Civ 2124). The *Lomas* case reverses the previous understanding that statutory payments could be paid gross (INS 7433 and see comments of the judge at first instance in *Lomas* at [2016] EWHC 2492 (Ch) paras 80-84 though the case was overturned in the Court of Appeal)

Other tax aspects of liquidation

19.16 The substantial shareholdings exemption (*TCGA 1992, Sch 7AC*) prevents a chargeable gain or an allowable capital loss from accruing where a UK company (the 'investing company') holds a substantial shareholding in a trading company, and has held the shares throughout a 12-month period beginning not more than six years before the date of disposal (see **16.18–16.23**). For a shareholding to be substantial, either:

- the investing company must hold a stake of at least 10% of the ordinary share capital of the investee company, together with the associated entitlement to profits available for distribution and assets on a winding up; or
- at least 25% of the investing company must be in the ownership of qualifying institutional investors and the investing company has invested at least £20 million in the investee company.

The exemption also applies to holdings in non-trading companies where the qualifying institutional investor conditions are met (see **6.23–6.25**).

The appointment of a liquidator to the investing company or a member of the latter's group does not affect the tax position. Although, on liquidation, assets of the company are vested in the liquidator, for the purpose of the substantial shareholding exemption, the company remains the beneficial owner (*TCGA 1992, Sch 7AC, para 16*). Accordingly, the exemption will still apply on a disposal of shares in the investee company, provided the relevant conditions are satisfied.

If the exemption does not apply and the shares in the investee company are standing at a loss, the holding company may be able to make a negligible asset claim under *TCGA 1992, s 24* (see **16.5**).

During the liquidation period, it is unlikely that the company will be carrying on a trade or business. Therefore, the liquidator's costs will not be relievable. They may form part of the incidental costs of disposal of certain assets, but, apart from that, no relief will be given.

A close company in liquidation may be treated as a close investment-holding company, a status which lost much of its relevance for corporation tax (but not for income tax) after 31 March 2015 (see **10.29–10.31**). For corporation tax purposes, where a close company commences liquidation, *CTA 2010, s 34(5)* provides that it is not to be treated as a close investment-holding company in the accounting period immediately following the commencement of winding up if it was not such in the accounting period immediately before liquidation commenced. In any subsequent accounting period, a close company in liquidation will be excluded from being a close investment-holding company only if it then meets the usual conditions of *CTA 2010, s 34* (see **10.30**).

There may have been a short gap between the end of a period in which a close company was not a close investment-holding company and the commencement of winding up, so that, strictly speaking, the company did not have the benefit of *CTA 2010, s 34(5)*. This may cause difficulties in some cases, and HMRC have undertaken to review the position in any individual case where a company has not been able to avoid a short gap and would suffer significantly if not given the protection of *CTA 2010, s 34(5)* (HMRC Company Taxation Manual at CTM60780).

DISSOLUTION BY STRIKING OFF

19.17 Where a company has ceased business, it may apply to be dissolved as an alternative to a formal liquidation. To achieve this, it may ask the Registrar of Companies to strike it off under *CA 2006, s 1003*. The Registrar also has power to strike off a company if it appears that it is not carrying on any business, eg if it is failing to submit accounts and annual returns.

In either case, a company that has been struck off may be restored to the Register if it transpires that it should not have been struck off. For shareholders who wish to end the life of a company permanently, a formal liquidation offers a more certain means of doing so, because it is only in exceptional circumstances that it could be restored after liquidation.

Until 29 February 2012, HMRC could apply Concession C16, which allowed companies being struck off the Register to distribute reserves as capital distributions rather than income distributions in the hands of the shareholders. From 1 March 2012, Concession C16 was replaced by new legislation which is more restrictive in its application (see **18.31–18.36**).

DISINCORPORATION RELIEF

19.18

> **Focus**
>
> Disincorporation relief was available from 1 April 2013 to 31 March 2018 only. The relief offered an opportunity for small companies to

> disincorporate, but stopped short of what some small companies required and left others with unacceptable uncertainties.

FA 2013 introduced a time-limited tax relief to make it easier for very small companies to disincorporate. It does this by allowing them to postpone or remove tax charges which they might otherwise face as a result of disincorporation.

A claim for disincorporation relief may be made where a company makes a qualifying transfer of its business to some or all of its shareholders during the five years from 1 April 2013 to 31 March 2018. For this purpose, where the business is transferred under a contract, the transfer date is taken to be the date of the contract or, if there is more than one, the date of the contract transferring the goodwill (*FA 2013, s 58*).

There is no requirement for the business transferred to be a trade. For the business transfer to qualify, the following conditions must be met (*FA 2013, s 59*):

- the business is transferred as a going concern;
- the business is transferred, together with all of the assets of the business, or together with all of those assets other than cash;
- the total market value of the qualifying assets of the business included in the transfer does not exceed £100,000. 'Qualifying asset' means goodwill, or an interest in land which is not held as trading stock;
- all of the shareholders to whom the business is transferred are individuals, which may include an individual acting as a member of a partnership but not as a member of a limited liability partnership (LLP); and
- each of those shareholders held shares in the company throughout the period of 12 months ending with the transfer date.

Where a claim for disincorporation relief is made, any qualifying asset (apart from post-*FA 2002* goodwill) is treated as disposed of and acquired for consideration equal to the lower of cost (for chargeable gains purposes) and market value (*TCGA 1992, ss 162B, 162C*). Likewise, any post-*FA 2002* goodwill is treated as disposed of and acquired at the lower of its tax written-down value under the intangible assets regime and its market value (*CTA 2009, s 849A*). As a result, no corporation tax will be payable by the company on chargeable gains, or credits arising under the intangible fixed assets regime, on transfer of the qualifying assets.

A claim for disincorporation relief must be made jointly, within two years beginning with the transfer date, by the company and all the shareholders to whom the business is transferred, and the claim is irrevocable (*FA 2013, s 60*).

Shareholders to whom the assets are transferred will inherit the reduced acquisition values for the purpose of their future tax liabilities.

Disincorporation relief does not relieve the tax on distributions which shareholders may face when assets are distributed to them at below market value in the course of a disincorporation where there is no formal liquidation. It fails to allow tax losses of the company to be carried forward, and fails to provide protection against balancing charges for capital allowances purposes. It also creates uncertainty for companies, particularly those with goodwill, who may find it difficult to assess in advance whether the value of their qualifying assets will fall below the £100,000 threshold.

It may be assumed that a small company, having transferred its business with the benefit of disincorporation relief, is unlikely to go through a formal liquidation but would seek to be struck off (see **19.17**). This would leave former shareholders with the uncertainty that anyone wishing to pursue a claim against the company might seek to have it restored to the Register.

HMRC's guidance on disincorporation relief is at tinyurl.com/mctfrn6. During the Autumn Budget 2017 it was announced that the relief would not be extended beyond 31 March 2018 (Autumn Budget 2017 Overview of Tax Legislation and Rates para 2.23).

Chapter 20

Foreign matters

SIGNPOSTS

- Background introduction to foreign matters (see **20.1**).
- Company residence – meaning of residence and overview of double tax treaties (see **20.2–20.3**).
- UK resident company with overseas income (see **20.4**).
- Non-UK resident company trading in UK – including the meaning of a permanent establishment (see **20.5–20.8**).
- The liability of a non-UK resident company liable to UK corporation tax – including assessment and responsibility of the UK representative (see **20.9–20.10**).
- The tax liability of a non-UK resident company with non-trading UK income (see **20.11**).
- The international movement of capital – including conditions and excluded transactions (see **20.12–20.15**).
- UK company becoming non-UK resident – including notifying HMRC and exit charges (see **20.16–20.23**).
- Double tax relief (see **20.24**).
- New rules for controlled foreign companies – including new definition, determining which income passes through the gateway, exempt profits, safe harbours, self-assessment requirements and calculation of chargeable profits (see **20.25–20.32**).
- Foreign branch exemption – including anti-diversion rule, opening negative amount, streaming and special cases (see **20.33–20.47**).
- Foreign currency accounting – including rules for currency conversion and losses (see **20.48–20.55**).
- Diverted profits tax (see **20.56–20.59**).

INTRODUCTION

20.1 In recent years, the UK has moved from a system that taxed UK companies on their worldwide profits to one that is more territorial in its approach, focusing primarily on taxing profits earned in the UK. Key elements of this are a reformed regime for controlled foreign companies (CFCs), an elective exemption for foreign branches, and a dividend exemption. Interest expense has historically been generally allowable for tax purposes, subject to some important limitations. The current debt cap regime is being replaced by a new corporate interest restriction from 1 April 2017.

New CFC rules (see **20.25** onwards) have applied since 1 January 2013. They aim to protect the UK from the artificial diversion of domestic profits to overseas companies controlled from the UK but located in low-tax jurisdictions, while exempting profits earned in controlled overseas companies that have not been diverted in such a way. Special rules apply to overseas finance profits earned by a CFC from loans to overseas companies. Multinationals moving to the UK are allowed a year to carry out any restructuring necessary for them to be able to take advantage of available exemptions.

An elective tax exemption allows UK companies with overseas trading branches to choose between having the profits of these taxable in the UK (with double tax relief) and corresponding losses allowable, or having all such profits and losses exempt from UK tax (see **20.33** onwards).

The UK allows deduction of interest expense, with no specific restriction for the funding of overseas investment. The rules are subject to the arm's length principle where finance comes from related parties. There is a limitation where the deductions claimed in the UK are excessive compared with worldwide third-party interest expense (the 'debt cap'; see **5.31** onwards), and there is also provision to protect against abuse.

From 1 April 2015 a new diverted profits tax (DPT) was introduced to deter and counteract the diversion of profits from the UK by large groups, typically multinational enterprises (see **20.56–20.59**).

COMPANY RESIDENCE

> **Focus**
>
> Place of incorporation, place of control, or a relevant treaty will determine a company's place of residence. All must be reviewed carefully.

20.2 It is important to know whether a company is UK resident. If it is, it will be chargeable to UK tax on its worldwide income and gains, subject to elections for the foreign branch exemption. Non-UK resident companies may be subject to UK corporation tax only if they have a permanent establishment in this country. Anti-avoidance provisions, such as the CFC regime and the diverted profits tax, have been enacted to avoid the artificial diversion of profits from the UK. The legislation in respect of foreign branch income and foreign dividends has been overhauled, as HMRC seek to levy tax primarily on UK source profits.

The basic rule is that, if a company is incorporated in the UK, it is resident in the UK for corporation tax purposes (*CTA 2009, s 14*).

Even if a company is not incorporated in the UK, it is still resident in the UK if it is centrally managed and controlled in the UK. One of the leading cases on this issue, *De Beers Consolidated Mines Ltd v Howe* (1906) 5 TC 198, involved a company that was registered in South Africa where it worked diamond mines. The company's head office and shareholders' general meetings were held in South Africa, but the directors' meetings took place in both South Africa and the UK. The majority of directors who made the key decisions lived in the UK.

In his judgment the Lord Chancellor, Lord Loreburn, stated:

> 'A company resides … where its real business is carried on … and the real business is carried on where the central management and control actually abides.'

Therefore, even though the company was incorporated in South Africa and its main trading operations were there, the House of Lords held that the company was UK resident because the majority of the directors who had the overall control were situated in London.

Since *De Beers Consolidated Mines Ltd v Howe*, the place where the central management and control of the company are exercised has been interpreted as the place where the effective management decisions are taken and not necessarily where the company is constitutionally managed. In *Wood v Holden (Inspector of Taxes)* [2006] STC 443, although a company's board meetings took place in London, the authority given by those board meetings was usurped by the overseas parent, and the Court of Appeal held that the company was non-UK resident. Thus it is necessary for the courts to apply two tests: first, the *situs* of the management and control of its own constitutional organs (ie the board of directors or the general meeting); and, second, whether that control is usurped.

In 1981, HMRC considered introducing a statutory test for determining a company's residence, based on its place of effective management, but they decided not to do so because they found it difficult to come up with a suitable test.

For HMRC guidance on determining company residence, see HMRC International Manual at INTM120000 onwards.

Dual resident companies

20.3 As stated above, if a company is incorporated in the UK it is UK resident. However, a company can, at the same time, be tax resident in another country if the rules for determining residence in the other country are different from those in the UK. Such companies are known as dual resident companies.

To resolve how a dual resident company is to be taxed, reference is made to the double tax treaty (if any) that the UK has with the other country. Most double tax treaties have a tie-breaker clause to determine which country has the taxing rights – ie whether the company is 'treaty UK resident' or 'treaty non-UK resident'. If the tie-breaker clause gives the taxing rights to the other jurisdiction, the company is treated as non-UK resident for the purposes of the *Corporation Tax Acts* (*CTA 2009, s 18*). HMRC provide a list of UK double tax treaties (in the Double Taxation Relief Manual at DT2140PP onwards), which will allow readers to identify those with tie-breaker clauses and those without.

A 'standard tie-breaker' follows the example of the Organisation for Economic Co-operation and Development (OECD) Model Tax Convention (see *OECD Model Convention with respect to Taxes on Income and on Capital*) by using an objective test which can be applied unilaterally by HMRC – typically by reference to the state in which the company's place of effective management lies. Other tie-breakers are non-standard and depend upon agreement between the competent authorities of the two states, so they cannot be applied unilaterally by HMRC.

Whilst awaiting a determination, a dual resident or potentially dual resident company should submit self-assessment corporation tax returns in the normal manner, based on its view as to the location of its place of effective management. Tie-breakers that depend on agreement between the competent authorities are more complex in practice, and the company should consider all relevant information, including any criteria set out in the treaty or related documents, and self-assess accordingly (INTM120080).

If a company claims that it is treaty non-UK resident, and hence to be regarded as resident in the other state, it should obtain a certificate of residence from the overseas tax authority. HMRC must be satisfied that the company is regarded as resident in the other country under the tie-breaker clause and that its business is carried on in the other country. Insufficient evidence will result in the company continuing to be treated as UK resident.

If a company is resident in the UK and in an overseas territory under their respective domestic laws, in some cases either a double tax treaty may not be in place or the tie-breaker clause in the treaty may be unable to resolve whether the company is 'treaty UK resident' or 'treaty non-UK resident'. In such cases the company remains dual resident.

In the past, some companies have used their dual residence to gain a tax advantage. To combat this, the following anti-avoidance provisions apply to a 'dual resident investing company' (as defined in *CTA 2010, s 949*):

- a dual resident investing company cannot surrender group relief (*CTA 2010, s 109*; see **Chapter 5**);
- for chargeable gains purposes, transfers of assets intra-group cannot be made on a no gain/no loss basis (*TCGA 1992, s 171(2)(d)*), and roll-over relief on replacement of assets is not available on a group basis (*TCGA 1992, s 175(2)*; see **Chapter 16**); and
- for capital allowances purposes, acquisitions from connected persons are treated as taking place at market value (*CAA 2001, s 61(4)(b)*), transfers of trades cannot be dealt with on a continuing basis (*CAA 2001, s 266(1)(c)*; *CTA 2010, s 949(1)*), and transfers of assets intra-group cannot be made at tax written down value (*CAA 2001, s 570(2)(b)*; see **Chapter 3**).

UK RESIDENT COMPANY WITH OVERSEAS INCOME

20.4 A company resident in the UK is chargeable to corporation tax on all its profits, wherever the income arises and wherever the assets giving rise to gains were situated, and whether or not the profits were received in or transmitted to the UK. Trading income earned abroad in the course of a UK trade is included within the trading profits computation. Foreign branch income may be exempt if an election is made (see **20.33** onwards).

NON-UK RESIDENT COMPANY CARRYING ON A TRADE IN THE UK

Focus

If an overseas company trades through a permanent establishment in the UK, any profits arising within the UK permanent establishment will be chargeable to UK corporation tax.

Circumstances in which chargeable to UK corporation tax

20.5 A non-UK resident company is chargeable to corporation tax if, and only if, it carries on a trade in the UK through a permanent establishment, in which case the following becomes chargeable (*CTA 2009, ss 5, 19*; *TCGA 1992, s 10B*):

- any trading income arising directly or indirectly through or from the permanent establishment;
- any income from property or rights used by, or held by or for, the permanent establishment; and
- chargeable gains accruing on the disposal of assets situated in the UK used for the purposes of the trade of the use of the permanent establishment.

Meaning of 'permanent establishment'

20.6 Non-resident companies are assessed to UK corporation tax (subject to treaty override: see **20.3**) if they have a permanent establishment in the UK. A permanent establishment can be a branch or agency, or other establishment. A company has a permanent establishment in a territory if, and only if (*CTA 2010, s 1141(1)*):

- it has a fixed place of business there through which the business of the company is wholly or partly carried on, or
- an agent acting on behalf of the company has and habitually exercises there authority to do business on behalf of the company.

It is likely that some aspects of the definition of a permanent establishment will change as a result of the implementation of the decisions arising from the base erosion and profit shifting (BEPS) project. However, no such changes have been announced for *Finance Bill 2017*.

A fixed place of business

20.7 A fixed place of business can be a place of management, a branch, an office, a factory, a workshop, an installation or structure for the exploration of natural resources, a mine, an oil or gas well, a quarry or any other place of extraction of natural resources, or a building site or construction or installation project (*CTA 2010, s 1141(2)*).

Circumstances in which there is no permanent establishment

20.8 A company is not regarded as having a permanent establishment if it carries on business there through an independent agent acting in the ordinary course of the agent's business (*CTA 2010, s 1142*).

A company is not regarded as having a permanent establishment if it maintains a fixed place of business for the purpose of carrying on activities that have not yet commenced. Neither will the company be regarded as having a permanent establishment if an agent carries on preparatory or auxiliary activities in relation to the business of the company as a whole. For these purposes, the legislation provides examples of preparatory or auxiliary activities, in relation to the business of the company as a whole, which will not be considered sufficient business activities to constitute the existence of a permanent establishment. The list is not exhaustive but includes (*CTA 2010, s 1143*):

- the use of facilities for the purpose of storage, display or delivery of goods or merchandise belonging to the company;
- the maintenance of a stock of goods or merchandise belonging to the company for the purpose of storage, display or delivery;
- the maintenance of a stock of goods or merchandise belonging to the company for the purpose of processing by another person; and
- purchasing goods or merchandise, or collecting information, for the company.

Readers should be aware that the perceived abuse of some of these boundary conditions means that the definition of a permanent establishment is likely to be amended as a result of the OECD's BEPS project and, in particular, Action 7.

NON-RESIDENT COMPANY: UK TRADING INCOME

Assessment, collection and recovery of corporation tax

20.9 When an overseas company commences trading in the UK through a permanent establishment, it must notify HMRC that it is within the charge to corporation tax (see **22.3**). This will be the commencement of an accounting period (see **22.5**).

When it comes within the charge, the permanent establishment is treated as a distinct and separate entity ('the separate enterprise principle'), acting at arm's length from the non-UK resident company of which it is a part, and entitled to broadly the same corporation tax treatment, reliefs and exemptions as would apply to a UK resident company (*CTA 2009, s 21* onwards).

Only where the UK has a tax treaty with the overseas company's home country, and there is a conflict between the treaty and the UK corporation tax domestic law, will the effect of the treaty be to modify or prevent the application of UK corporation tax principles. Relevant treaty provisions take precedence over domestic legislation (*TIOPA 2010, s 6*).

As the UK permanent establishment is treated as a separate enterprise, profits are attributed to it on the basis that it is a distinct entity dealing at arm's length with the non-resident company (*CTA 2009, s 22*).

When calculating the profits, it is assumed that the permanent establishment has the same credit rating as the non-resident company of which it is a part and has such equity capital and loan capital as it could reasonably be expected to have in regard to its circumstances (*CTA 2009, s 21(2)*).

A deduction is given for expenses, wherever they are incurred, if they are incurred for the purposes of the UK permanent establishment and if they would be deductible if incurred by a company resident in the UK. These include executive and general administrative expenses (*CTA 2009, s 29(1)*).

The non-resident company may supply its UK permanent establishment with goods and services. If the supplies are at arm's length and within the non-resident company's normal business, they are treated as a trading or business transaction to which the separate enterprise principle applies; otherwise, they are treated as an expense incurred by the non-resident company for the purposes of its UK permanent establishment (*CTA 2009, s 23*).

From 1 April 2015 the small profits rate of corporation tax has been abolished for most companies as a result of unification of the corporation tax rates (**Chapter 23**). To determine the rate at which a permanent establishment of a non-UK resident company pays corporation tax for periods before 1 April 2015, it is necessary to establish at what rate the non-UK resident company would have had to pay corporation tax on its worldwide profits had it been UK resident, and the same rate is then applied.

Responsibility for UK corporation tax

20.10 The UK representative of the overseas company is responsible for the permanent establishment's corporation tax affairs (*CTA 2010, s 970*). The company, in turn, is bound by the acts or omissions of its UK representative. However, a non-resident company is not bound by mistakes in information provided by its UK representative in pursuance of an obligation imposed on the representative by *CTA 2010, s 970* unless the mistake is the result of an act or omission of the company itself, or to which the company consented or in which it connived. Therefore, the UK representative of a non-resident company can only be prosecuted for a criminal offence if the representative committed the offence or consented to or connived in its commission (*CTA 2010, s 971*).

NON-RESIDENT COMPANY: UK NON-TRADING INCOME

Liability to income tax

20.11 A non-resident company not carrying on a trade in the UK through a branch or agency is chargeable to income tax at the basic rate on any UK income. Therefore, a UK property investment business operated by a non-resident company will be subject to income tax at the basic rate on its profits. The profits are computed according to income tax rules (see *Income Tax 2016/17* (Bloomsbury Professional)).

Where tax is deducted at source from such income, the tax payable is limited to the tax deducted at source. This includes savings and dividend income (*ITA 2007, s 815*).

INTERNATIONAL MOVEMENT OF CAPITAL

Reporting rules

20.12 An issue of shares in excess of £100 million by a foreign subsidiary must be reported to HMRC within six months of its occurrence. Other similar types of transaction must also be reported unless they are excluded transactions (*FA 2009, Sch 17, paras 4, 8*).

The reporting body is responsible for making the report. A reporting body is a UK corporate parent that meets one of the following conditions (*FA 2009, Sch 17, para 5*):

Condition A

- it is not controlled by a foreign parent;

Condition B

- it is the only relevant UK parent or body corporate that is controlled by the foreign parent; or

Condition C

- the foreign parent controls the UK parent and other UK parents, but it has not nominated a single reporting body, or the foreign parent controls the UK parent and other UK parents and it is the nominated group reporting body.

Control of a company means a person's ability, or a group of persons, to guarantee that the company's affairs are carried out in accordance with their wishes. This can be achieved through shareholdings or voting power or through powers conferred by the articles of association or other document (*FA 2009, Sch 17, para 12*).

Two or more UK corporate parents can select one of their number to be the reporting body (*FA 2009, Sch 17, para 6*).

A UK corporate parent is essentially a totally independent UK resident company that controls one or more non-resident companies, and is not itself controlled by another UK resident company or companies (*FA 2009, Sch 17, para 7*).

The purpose of the report is to enable HMRC to establish whether any person gains a direct or indirect tax advantage from the transaction (*FA 2009, Sch 17, para 4*). If a company fails to comply, it is chargeable to a special returns penalty under *TMA 1970, s 98*.

Reportable events and transactions

20.13 An event or transaction is reportable to HMRC (*FA 2009, Sch 17, para 8(1)*) if:

- it exceeds £100 million,
- it is covered by specific provisions relating to foreign subsidiary holdings (see **20.14**), and
- it is not an excluded transaction (see **20.15**).

Conditions applying to foreign subsidiaries

20.14 The reportable events or transactions relating to foreign subsidiary holdings, referred to in **20.13** are (*FA 2009, Sch 17, para 8(2)*):

- an issue of shares or debentures by a foreign subsidiary;
- a transfer of shares or debentures of a foreign subsidiary in which the reporting body has an interest;
- a transfer of shares or debentures of a foreign subsidiary, to which the reporting body is a party and in which the transferor has an interest;
- a circumstance that results in a foreign subsidiary becoming, or ceasing to be, a controlling partner in a partnership, or
- a circumstance of a description specified in regulations made by the Commissioners.

A foreign subsidiary is a controlling partner if it controls the partnership alone or with other subsidiaries (*FA 2009, Sch 17, para 8(3)*).

Excluded transactions

20.15 A transaction is excluded from the reporting rules (*FA 2009, Sch 17, para 9*) if:

- it is carried out in the ordinary course of a trade;
- all the parties to the transaction are resident in the same territory at the time that the transaction is carried out;
- it is a security payment given to the bankers of a foreign subsidiary in the ordinary course of banking business;
- it is a security payment given to an insurance company by a foreign subsidiary in the ordinary course of banking business; or
- it is of a description specified in regulations made by HMRC.

UK COMPANY BECOMING NON-UK RESIDENT

HMRC notification and outstanding liabilities

20.16 Before a company ceases to be resident in the UK, it must comply with the requirements set out in *TMA 1970, s 109B*. It must notify HMRC of the date that it intends to become non-resident, provide a statement of all amounts owing, and provide details of the arrangements it will make for payment. HMRC will require security and the arrangements must be approved by HMRC or else they are void. Security and approval are not required to the extent that there is an exit charge payment plan under *TMA 1970, Sch 3ZB* (see **20.23**).

If a company becomes non-resident without HMRC approval, the company and its directors, and any controlling company and its directors, may be liable to a penalty based on its outstanding tax liabilities (*TMA 1970, ss 109C, 109D*). Outstanding amounts of tax may also be recovered from such persons (*TMA 1970, s 109E*).

The company's ceasing to be UK resident causes the cessation of an accounting period (see **22.5**). Trading stock is treated as disposed of on migration under *CTA 2009, s 162*, unless it is left in a UK permanent establishment. Likewise, balancing adjustments are calculated for capital allowance purposes unless the assets in question continue to be used by a UK permanent establishment.

Exit charges

Introduction

20.17 When a company ceases to be UK resident, there are circumstances in which certain assets are deemed to be disposed of and reacquired, giving rise to 'exit charges' for corporation tax purposes. There are specific exit charges in respect of chargeable gains, intangible fixed assets and loan relationships. These exit charges will also arise where a company becomes treaty non-UK resident (*CTA 2009, s 18*).

It may be arguable that these exit charges breach the EU right of freedom of establishment and are therefore discriminatory. Consequently, they may be the subject of future challenges before the ECJ and possible future changes to UK tax legislation.

Chargeable gains exit charge

20.18 When a company ceases to be UK resident, the company will be deemed to have disposed of all its chargeable assets at market value, thus creating chargeable gains or capital losses. Roll-over relief is not available where a company disposes of its qualifying assets before ceasing to be UK resident and acquires replacement assets after it has become non-UK resident (*TCGA 1992, s 185*).

If, after ceasing to be UK resident, the company carries on a trade in the UK through a permanent establishment, any chargeable assets that are used by the permanent establishment will not be deemed to have been disposed of (*TCGA 1992, s 185(4)*).

If a non-resident company is trading in the UK through a permanent establishment and uses a chargeable asset located in the UK for the purposes of that trade, there is a deemed disposal of the asset on discontinuance of that trade or if the asset is transferred out of the UK without such discontinuance (*TCGA 1992, s 25*).

Note that an ATED-related capital gain or allowable loss (see **7.24**) does not arise on cessation of UK residence, but will arise instead on subsequent disposal of the asset in question (*TCGA 1992, s 187A*).

Postponement of chargeable gains exit charge

20.19 Postponement of the exit charge on chargeable gains may occur if, immediately after the relevant time (see HMRC's Capital Gains Manual at CG42390):

- the assets are situated outside the UK and are used in or for the purposes of a trade carried on outside the UK ('foreign assets'),
- the company is a 75% subsidiary (by ordinary shares) of a UK resident company (the 'principal company'), and
- both companies make an election within two years of the company becoming non-resident.

The postponed gain becomes a chargeable gain of the principal company, in whole or in part, if:

- the asset is disposed of within six years of the company becoming non-resident; or
- at any time:
  - the company ceases to be a 75% subsidiary of the principal company on the disposal by the principal company of ordinary shares of the company;
  - after the company has ceased to be a 75% subsidiary of the principal company for any other reason, the principal company disposes of such shares; or
  - the principal company ceases to be UK resident.

HMRC do not consider that the issue of new shares by the principal company to a third party will bring the gain into charge. However, any subsequent disposal of shares in the subsidiary by the principal company would result in a recovery of some or all of the postponed charge under *TCGA 1992, s 187(4)(b)* (CG42400).

Intangible fixed assets exit charge

20.20 When a company owning assets within the intangible fixed assets regime ceases to be UK resident, or when a non-UK resident company ceases to use such intangible assets for the purposes of a UK permanent establishment, there will be a deemed realisation of those intangible fixed assets at market value, with the result that intangible fixed assets debits and credits may arise (*CTA 2009, s 859*).

Postponement of intangible fixed assets exit charge

20.21 Postponement of the exit charge on an intangible fixed asset may occur if (*CTA 2009, s 860*; see HMRC Corporate Intangibles Research & Development Manual at CIRD47040):

- the deemed realisation at market value gives rise to a gain,
- the assets are held for the purposes of a trade carried on outside the UK through a permanent establishment,
- the company is a 75% subsidiary of a UK resident company, and
- both companies make an election within two years of the company becoming non-resident.

The company must bring the postponed gain into account as a credit under the intangible fixed assets regime, in whole or in part, if (*CTA 2009, ss 861, 862*; CIRD47050):

- the asset is disposed of within six years of the company becoming non-resident; or
- at any time:
  - the company ceases to be a 75% subsidiary of its parent company on the disposal by the parent company of ordinary shares of the company;
  - after the company has ceased to be a 75% subsidiary of the parent company for any other reason, the parent company disposes of such shares; or
  - the parent company ceases to be UK resident.

Loan relationships exit charge

20.22 When a company ceases to be UK resident, the company will be deemed to have disposed of all the assets and liabilities representing its loan relationships, and these disposals are regarded as taking place at fair value as defined in *CTA 2009, s 313(6)*, with the result that loan relationship debits and credits are likely to arise (*CTA 2009, s 333*; see HMRC's Corporate Finance Manual at CFM33300).

However, loan relationships will not be deemed to have been disposed of under these provisions:

- if, immediately after ceasing to be UK resident, the company carries on a trade in the UK through a permanent establishment and those loan relationships are held for the purposes of that permanent establishment (*CTA 2009, s 333(2)*); or
- in certain other circumstances (see *CTA 2009, ss 333, 334*).

Deferral of exit charges generally

20.23 Following a ruling by the European Court of Justice in November 2011 in *National Grid Indus* (Case C-371/10), *FA 2013* introduced new provisions allowing a company incorporated in the UK or another EEA territory to defer payment of corporation tax exit charges arising under any or all of:

- *TCGA 1992, ss 25, 185, 187(4)*: on deemed disposal of assets on ceasing to be UK resident, or when assets held for the purposes of a trade carried on by a UK permanent establishment cease to be situated in the UK, or when a UK permanent establishment ceases to use or hold assets for the purposes of its trade;
- *CTA 2009, ss 859, 862*: on deemed realisation of intangible fixed assets on ceasing to be UK resident or ceasing to hold assets for the purposes of a trade carried on by a UK permanent establishment;
- *CTA 2009, ss 333, 334, 609, 610*: on deemed disposal of loan relationships and derivative contracts immediately before ceasing to be UK resident or ceasing to hold assets for the purposes of a trade carried on by a UK permanent establishment;
- *CTA 2009, s 162*: on revaluation of trading stock on ceasing to trade in the UK (see **20.16**);

when the company becomes a resident of, and established in, another EU or EEA member state.

Before 11 December 2012, corporation tax triggered by the above exit charges was payable nine months and one day after the end of the accounting period (*TMA 1970, s 59D(1)*).

From 11 December 2012 and subject to certain conditions, a company ceasing to be UK resident or a non-resident company with a UK permanent establishment may elect – within nine months of the end of the accounting period for which the charges arise (subject to transitional provisions) – to apply to enter into an exit charge payment plan (*TMA 1970, s 59FA, Sch 3ZB*).

An exit charge payment plan may be based on:

- the standard instalment method. This involves spreading the payment of tax over six years;
- the realisation method. This is more directly related to the economic life of individual assets, with tax on chargeable assets and trading stock becoming payable annually in respect of actual realisations or, if sooner, after 10 years. For intangible assets, derivatives and loan relationships, the useful economic life of each asset is determined at the point of migration, and tax is payable in equal annual instalments over the useful life of each asset; or
- a combination of both the above methods.

In all these cases, tax deferred on exit charges is subject to interest under the normal rules (see **23.26** onwards).

DOUBLE TAX RELIEF

20.24 If a UK resident company has foreign profits, those profits are subject to UK corporation tax. However, that income may also have suffered tax in the foreign jurisdiction, and a double tax treaty should usually ensure that double tax relief is available so that the income is not taxed twice.

To avoid any income being taxed in both jurisdictions, the double tax treaty between the UK and the country concerned may exempt the income in question from corporation tax. For this reason, the treaty should be examined in every case. (Double tax treaties can be viewed in HMRC's Double Taxation Relief Manual at DT2140 onwards.)

Credit relief for overseas corporate tax paid is available against UK corporation tax payable. A claim should be made according to the terms of the double tax treaty (*TIOPA 2010, s 25*).

HMRC v FCE Bank plc [2012] EWCA Civ 1290 concerned group relief (under superseded legislation) between two UK companies with a common US parent company. HMRC had rejected the claim on alternative grounds that the parent company was non-UK resident, or that it was not liable to UK corporation tax. The Court of Appeal found in favour of the taxpayer, citing the non-discrimination article in the then UK/US double tax treaty. The case highlights the importance of such non-discrimination articles.

Where there is no entitlement to relief under a double tax treaty, unilateral relief (*TIOPA 2010, s 18*), together with relief for withholding tax, may be claimed. The general rule is that income is calculated according to UK principles (as determined by the High Court in *George Wimpey International Ltd v Rolfe* [1989] STC 609), and the credit given against the UK corporation tax liability cannot exceed the UK corporation tax which is imposed on the overseas income.

The time limit for making a claim against corporation tax is four years after the end of the accounting period to which the claim applies or, if later, one year after the end of the accounting period in which the foreign tax was paid (*TIOPA 2010, s 19*). Credit relief is only available to UK resident companies, and companies can elect not to receive a credit (*TIOPA 2010, ss 26, 27*).

The credit relief available cannot exceed the credit which would be allowed had all reasonable steps been taken under the law of the non-UK territory, and under double tax arrangements made in relation to that territory, to minimise the amount of tax payable in that territory. The company is expected to claim or secure all the benefits, reliefs, deductions, reductions or allowances available in the non-UK territory and to make all available elections for tax purposes (*TIOPA 2010, ss 33, 44*). It follows that the credit is reduced by any tax refund given by the tax authorities of the non-UK territory (*TIOPA 2010, s 34*).

There is a limit on the amount of credit available against corporation tax to which a company is liable in respect of any income or chargeable gain.

The credit must not exceed:

$$R \times IG$$

where:

- R is the rate of corporation tax payable by the company, before credit for income or chargeable gains of that accounting period
- IG is the amount of the income or gain (*TIOPA 2010, s 42*).

From 5 December 2013 the limit on double tax relief for foreign tax on a non-trading credit from a loan relationship or intangible fixed asset applies to the net amount of the credit after deducting related debits, to combat avoidance schemes that had sought to exploit mismatches between the amounts of UK and foreign income (*TIOPA 2010, s 49B*).

Also from 5 December 2013 a restriction is imposed to prevent over-allowance of double tax relief where a repayment is made by a foreign tax authority and there are arrangements in place which enable another person to receive the repayment of foreign tax (*TIOPA 2010*).

A further anti-avoidance rule was introduced with effect from 22 November 2017. This is designed to counter abuse where the foreign tax losses of a non-UK PE can be relieved against the taxable profits of another entity. In such cases, the double tax relief available in the UK is to be restricted (*FA 2018, s 30* introducing *TIOPA 2010, ss 71A* and *71B*).

CONTROLLED FOREIGN COMPANIES

Background

> **Focus**
>
> The CFC regime is an anti-avoidance measure designed to ensure that UK profits diverted into low-tax jurisdictions remain taxable in the UK.

20.25 The controlled foreign companies (CFCs) legislation was originally introduced in 1984 to protect against the artificial diversion of UK profits into low tax jurisdictions. However, by 2010 the government had recognised that the CFC rules needed to better reflect the way that businesses were operating in a globalised economy, as the CFC rules in force at that time were seen as going further than was needed to protect the UK tax base. Accordingly, *FA 2012* completely rewrote the CFC legislation, although many definitions and concepts were carried over from the previous CFC regime.

This book covers the new CFC rules now contained in *TIOPA 2010, Pt 9A*, which took effect for accounting periods beginning on or after 1 January 2013. See also HMRC's CFC guidance on the new regime at INTM190000 onwards.

Please refer to *Corporation Tax 2011/12* (Bloomsbury Professional) for details of the CFC regime which applied before 1 January 2013 and for accounting periods that straddle that date, including interim improvements that were made by *FA 2011*; see also INTM254100 onwards.

FA 2013 and *FA 2014* made a number of changes to the CFC regime, removing tax avoidance opportunities and making other technical amendments to ensure that the rules operate as the government had intended.

HMRC offer a non-statutory clearance service which may be used to help provide certainty on the application of the CFC legislation where there is a material doubt or difficulty to be resolved. For HMRC's general guidance on non-statutory clearances, see tinyurl.com/pvc4j2h.

Definition of a CFC

20.26 The CFC regime potentially applies to any non-resident company which is controlled by a UK resident person or persons. A company is a CFC if it meets the following conditions (*TIOPA 2010, ss 371AA, 371BA*):

- the CFC has chargeable profits for an accounting period;

- none of the CFC exemptions apply; and
- a UK company has a relevant interest in the company. For these purposes, a UK company has a relevant interest if it is entitled, directly or indirectly, to at least 25% of the CFC's chargeable profits.

Note that a CFC charge is only imposed on UK resident companies which have a relevant interest in a CFC (*TIOPA 2010, s 371BC(1)*, Step 1).

To determine whether a non-resident company is controlled by another person (or persons), the definition of control is found in *TIOPA 2010, ss 371RB, 371RE,* as amended by the *Taxation (International and Other Provisions) Act 2010 (Amendment to Section 371RE) (Controlled Foreign Companies) Regulations 2014, SI 2014/3237,* to reflect FRS 102 (see **Chapter 26** regarding changes to UK GAAP).

Broadly, a person (P) controls a company (C) if any one of the following applies:

- either through its shareholding or voting power, P can ensure that the affairs of C are conducted in accordance with P's wishes;
- on the disposal of C's share capital, P would be entitled to over 50% of the proceeds;
- if the whole of C's income was distributed, P would be entitled to more than 50% of the distributed amount; or
- in the event of a winding up of C, P would be entitled to receive over 50% of C's assets.

TIOPA 2010, s 371RC introduces an alternative control test in determining whether a non-UK resident company is a CFC. The test applies when two persons control the company and one of those persons is non-UK resident. The test is mainly applied to joint venture companies. If conditions X and Y are both met, the non-UK resident company is deemed to be a CFC:

- Condition X is met if the UK resident person has interests, rights and powers that represent at least 40% of the holdings giving control of the company; and
- Condition Y is met if the non-UK resident person has interests, rights and powers representing at least 40%, but not more than 55%, of the holdings giving control of the company.

The CFC charge gateway

Focus

A feature of the CFC regime is the 'gateway test', which is intended to catch only those profits which have been diverted into low tax jurisdictions.

20.27 The CFC charge only applies to a CFC's chargeable profits. A CFC has chargeable profits for a period only if any of its profits pass through the CFC gateway (*TIOPA 2010, s 371BB*). Therefore a company needs to check whether any of its profits are caught by the tests set out in *TIOPA 2010, Pt 9A, Chs 3–8*. The tests in *TIOPA 2010, Pt 9A, Ch 3* tell a company whether it needs to consider the tests in *TIOPA 2010, Pt 9A, Chs 4–8* inclusive. Each of *TIOPA 2010, Pt 9A, Chs 4–8* deals with a different type of profit. In most cases, a company only has to consider the tests in *TIOPA 2010, Pt 9A, Ch 3* and may disregard the tests in *TIOPA 2010, Pt 9A, Chs 4–8*.

The following are the steps to take in considering whether a CFC charge applies:

Step 1

Is the foreign company a CFC?

Step 2

If the answer to the above is yes, does any UK company have a relevant interest and, if so, does the CFC have any chargeable profits? Even if it does, do any of the CFC exemptions detailed in *TIOPA 2010, Pt 9A, Chs 10–14* apply?

If none of the exemptions apply, a CFC charge applies to any UK company with a relevant interest.

The exemptions

If any of the following exemptions apply, the profits of the CFC are exempt from a CFC charge.

The exempt period exemption (TIOPA 2010, Pt 9A, Ch 10)

This exemption applies to foreign companies becoming CFCs for the first time, for example if a non-resident company is acquired by a UK parent, or the parent company becomes UK resident. A 12-month exemption period is available to enable the group to undertake any restructuring necessary so that a CFC charge will not subsequently apply. This could be achieved by relying on one of the other exemptions.

If it is not practicable to restructure within 12 months, an application may be made to HMRC to extend the length of the exempt period.

The excluded territories exemption (TIOPA 2010, Pt 9A, Ch 11)

This exemption applies where CFCs are resident in certain excluded territories and, for this purpose, two special definitions of 'residence' are used.

The exemption applies if a CFC is resident for the accounting period in a territory shortlisted as excluded under *Controlled Foreign Companies (Excluded Territories) Regulations 2012, SI 2012/3024, reg 4*, namely:

- Australia;
- Canada;
- France;
- Germany;
- Japan; or
- the United States of America.

For this purpose, *TIOPA 2010, s 371TA(1)(b)* can be used to apply treaty residence or territory of incorporation as the territory of residence in certain circumstances, only if the CFC (or persons with interests in it) are 'subject to tax' under the law of the territory in question on all of the CFC's income arising during the accounting period.

The exemption also applies if:

(a) a CFC is resident for the accounting period in a territory included in a much longer list of excluded territories under *Controlled Foreign Companies (Excluded Territories) Regulations 2012, SI 2012/3024, reg 3*;

(b) the sum of four specified categories of income does not exceed the greater of 10% of the CFC's accounting profits and £50,000; and

(c) the CFC meets a condition relating to its intellectual property; care should be taken to ensure that, if the CFC wishes to take advantage of this exemption, it has not exploited intellectual property transferred to it by related UK persons in the previous six years.

By contrast, residence for this purpose is determined by reference to *TIOPA 2010, s 371KC(3)*, so *TIOPA 2010, s 371TA(1)(b)* can be used to apply treaty residence or territory of incorporation as the territory of residence in certain circumstances, but in this case only if the CFC (or persons with interests in it) are 'liable to tax' under the law of the territory in question on the CFC's income arising during the accounting period.

In HMRC's view, the difference between the definitions of 'residence' is significant. The meaning of 'subject to tax', used in the definition for the purposes of the shortlist of excluded territories, is more restrictive than 'liable to tax', in that profits are only 'subject to tax' if they are actually charged to tax (subject to any deductions for losses, allowances, etc). If profits or the person receiving them are exempt, those profits are not 'subject to tax' (see INTM242200).

The excluded territories lists include those where the rate of corporation tax is not significantly lower than that of the UK. See *Controlled Foreign Companies (Excluded Territories) Regulations 2012, SI 2012/3024, reg 3* and *Sch, Pt 1* for details of these.

The four categories of income referred to at (b) above are as follows (*TIOPA 2010, ss 371KD–371KI*):

(a) Category A income is exempt income arising in the CFC, or income taxed at a reduced tax rate arising out of, say, an incentive scheme;

(b) Category B income relates to the CFC's non-trading income where a deduction can be made by treating some of the income as a notional interest expense;

(c) Category C income includes income from a settlement to which the CFC is a beneficiary or settlor, or the CFC's share of partnership income where the CFC is a partner; and

(d) Category D income applies where, for example, due to related party transactions, the income of the CFC is reduced but there is no corresponding increase in the other party's income.

The low profits exemption (TIOPA 2010, Pt 9A, Ch 12)

If a CFC's accounting or taxable profits in a 12-month accounting period is not greater than £50,000, its profits will be exempt from a CFC charge. The exemption also applies where the accounting or taxable profits do not exceed £500,000 and the non-trading income included in those profits does not exceed £50,000. This is subject to anti-avoidance rules (*TIOPA 2010, ss 371LB, 371LC*).

The low profit margin exemption (TIOPA 2010, Pt 9A, Ch 13)

This exemption applies in an accounting period if a CFC's accounting profits for that period do not exceed 10% of the CFC's operating expenditure. For this purpose, the accounting profits are calculated without taking a deduction for interest payable. This is subject to anti-avoidance rules (*TIOPA 2010, ss 371MB, 371MC*).

The tax exemption (TIOPA 2010, Pt 9A, Ch 14)

If the local tax paid by a CFC is at least 75% of what it would have had to pay were the CFC subject to UK tax, this exemption applies. To determine whether this exemption applies, the following three steps need to be taken (*TIOPA 2010, s 371NB*):

(a) determine the country in which the CFC is resident (broadly, the territory in which the CFC is liable to tax throughout the relevant accounting period by reason of domicile, residence or place of management; see *TIOPA 2010, s 371TB*);

(b) calculate the local tax payable in respect of the CFC's local chargeable profits; and

(c) calculate the amount of the corresponding UK tax that would have been payable. If the local tax liability is at least 75% of the corresponding UK tax calculated, this exemption applies.

In this context, the local tax amount may need to be reduced in two circumstances (*TIOPA 2010, s 371NC*):

(a) first, when a CFC has any income that is included in its local chargeable profits but is not taken into account when calculating the taxable profits; and

(b) secondly, where a CFC has incurred expenditure which is not included in calculating its local chargeable profits but is brought into account in calculating the taxable profits.

If HMRC believe that companies in certain jurisdictions can exercise significant control over the amount of tax they pay, they may by regulation classify the local tax rate as made under the 'designer rate tax provisions', which means that a company cannot rely on the tax exemption to avoid a CFC charge (*TIOPA 2010, s 371ND*).

If none of the exemptions detailed in TIOPA 2010, Pt 9A, Chs 10–14 apply

If none of the above exemptions apply, the company needs to refer to *TIOPA 2010, Pt 9A, Ch 3* to determine whether a CFC charge applies (*TIOPA 2010, s 371BB*). By reference to *TIOPA 2010, Pt 9A, Ch 3*, a company should be able to establish whether any of *TIOPA 2010, Pt 9A, Chs 4–8* should be considered in determining whether any of a CFC's profits pass through the CFC charge gateway. The aim of the gateway is to assess whether the profits of a CFC have arisen as a result of profits being diverted from the UK. If the profits have not been artificially diverted, the profits should be outside the scope of the CFC regime.

Does TIOPA 2010, Pt 9A, Ch 4 apply? (*TIOPA 2010, s 371CA*)

If *TIOPA 2010, Pt 9A, Ch 4* (profits attributable to UK activities) applies for a CFC's accounting period, there is a CFC charge. *TIOPA 2010, Pt 9A, Ch 4* applies unless any one of conditions A, B, C and D is met:

(a) Condition A is met if a CFC does not hold assets or bear risks under an arrangement where:

  (i) one of the main purposes is to reduce, or eliminate, its UK tax liability; or

  (ii) as a consequence of the arrangement, the CFC expects its business to become profitable by more than a negligible amount.

(b) Condition B is met if the CFC does not have any UK managed assets or bear any UK managed risks.

(c) Condition C is met if the CFC itself has the capability to ensure that the CFC's business would be commercially effective if its UK managed assets and risks were to cease being managed in the UK.

(d) Condition D is met if the CFC's profits consist only of non-trading finance profits (see *TIOPA 2010, Pt 9A, Ch 5* below) and/or the CFC has profits from a property business (see safe harbours, **20.29**).

Does TIOPA 2010, Pt 9A, Ch 5 apply? (TIOPA 2010, s 371CB)

If *TIOPA 2010, Pt 9A, Ch 5* (non-trading finance profits) applies for a CFC's accounting period, there is a CFC charge. *TIOPA 2010, Pt 9A, Ch 5* applies only if a CFC has non-trading finance profits. The following profits are generally excluded from *TIOPA 2010, Pt 9A, Ch 5*:

(a) any profits which fall within *TIOPA 2010, Pt 9A, Ch 8* below (solo consolidation);

(b) profits arising from the investment of funds held for the purposes of a trade and none of the trading profits pass through the gateway; and

(c) profits arising from the investment of funds held by the CFC for its UK or overseas property business.

Incidental non-trading finance profits – the 5% rule

TIOPA 2010, Pt 9A, Ch 5 is excluded from applying if:

- one or both of the following requirements are met:

  (a) the CFC has trading or property business profits (or both); or

  (b) the CFC has exempt distribution income, and a substantial part of its business is the holding of shares of its 51% subsidiaries; and

- the CFC's non-trading finance profits are not greater than 5% of the relevant amount where:

  (i) if the requirement in (a) above is met, the relevant amount is the total of the CFC's trading and property business profits without taking a deduction for interest payable;

  (ii) if the requirement in (b) is met, the relevant amount is the total of the CFC's exempt distribution income; and

  (iii) if both these requirements are met, the relevant amount is the aggregate of the amounts in (i) and (ii) above.

Does TIOPA 2010, Pt 9A, Ch 6 apply? (TIOPA 2010, s 371CE)

If *TIOPA 2010, Pt 9A, Ch 6* (trading finance profits) applies for a CFC's accounting period, there is a CFC charge. *TIOPA 2010, Pt 9A, Ch 6* applies only if a CFC has trading finance profits and the CFC has funds (or other assets) which have arisen from UK capital contributions.

If the CFC is a group treasury company, it can elect for its trading finance profits to be treated as if they were non-trading finance profits. If such an election is made, *TIOPA 2010, Pt 9A, Ch 6* does not apply. Subject to transitional rules that applied from 1 January 2013 to 19 March 2013, *FA 2013* introduced a new definition of 'group treasury company' for CFC purposes, aligned with that which applies from 11 December 2012 for debt cap purposes (*TIOPA 2010, s 371CE*; see **5.59**).

Does TIOPA 2010, Pt 9A, Ch 7 apply? (TIOPA 2010, s 371CF)

If *TIOPA 2010, Pt 9A, Ch 7* (captive insurance business) applies for a CFC's accounting period, there is a CFC charge. *TIOPA 2010, Pt 9A, Ch 7* applies only if the main part of the CFC's business is insurance business and the CFC's total profits include amounts arising from a contract of insurance which is entered into with one of the following:

(a) a UK resident company connected with the CFC;

(b) a non-UK resident company connected with the CFC and acting through a UK permanent establishment; or

(c) a UK resident person where the contract is linked to the provision of goods or services to the UK resident person.

Does TIOPA 2010, Pt 9A, Ch 8 apply? (TIOPA 2010, s 371CG)

If *TIOPA 2010, Pt 9A, Ch 8* (solo consolidation) applies for a CFC's accounting period, there is a CFC charge. *TIOPA 2010, Pt 9A, Ch 8* only applies if either condition A or condition B is met:

(a) Condition A is that the CFC is a subsidiary undertaking which is the subject of a solo consolidation waiver under section BIPRU 2.1 of the PRA Handbook, and the CFC's parent undertaking in relation to that waiver is a UK resident company.

(b) Condition B is that the CFC is controlled by a UK resident bank which holds shares in the CFC. The bank must meet the requirements of the PRA Handbook in relation to its capital. Any fall in the value of the CFC shares are ignored in determining whether the bank has met the PRA requirements.

Exemptions for profits from qualifying loan relationships (TIOPA 2010, Pt 9A, Ch 9)

Certain intra-group non-trading finance profits which would otherwise be caught by *TIOPA 2010, Pt 9A, Ch 5* above may be eligible for a full or 75% exemption. The exemption applies to qualifying loan relationships. In addition, the business premises condition has to be met to qualify for the exemption (*TIOPA 2010, s 371IA* onwards).

A qualifying loan relationship is one where the CFC is a creditor and the ultimate debtor is a company connected with the CFC and controlled by the UK resident person who controls the CFC (*TIOPA 2010, ss 371IG–371II*). If the ultimate debtor is a non-UK resident company, the loan cannot be a qualifying loan relationship if the borrower's debits are:

(a) brought into account for determining the company's profits attributable to a UK permanent establishment, or

(b) taken into account for calculating the company's profits of a UK property business.

The business premises condition is met if the CFC has premises, with some degree of permanence, in the country in which it is resident. In addition, the CFC's activities in that country must mainly be carried on from those premises (*TIOPA 2010, s 371DG*).

From 5 December 2013, anti-avoidance provisions apply on a loan-by-loan basis to prevent groups from moving profits from existing intra-group lending – being profits which would otherwise be taxable in the UK – into offshore finance companies within the exemption for certain non-trading finance profits (*TIOPA 2010, s 371IH(9A)–(9E);* see INTM217610).

Also from 5 December 2013 a loan cannot be a qualifying loan relationship where it is used to repay third party debt of a non-UK resident group company and that debt is effectively replaced by new UK debt as part of an arrangement where one of the main purposes is to obtain a tax advantage for any person (*TIOPA 2010, s 371IH(10)(c)*; see INTM217850).

In January 2014, HMRC published a guidance note at tinyurl.com/np5emmv on the interaction between CFC financing arrangements and the loan relationships unallowable purpose rule (see **11.21**).

Summary of the impact of the rules on finance profits

20.28 *Non-trading finance profits*

Profits derived from lending may be subject to a CFC charge under *TIOPA 2010, Pt 9A, Ch 5* above if:

(a) the activities are undertaken in the UK;

(b) the lending is derived from UK capital investment or UK capital contribution; or

(c) the loans are made to UK residents.

There are some exemptions. Profits derived from loan relationships may qualify for full or partial exemption under *TIOPA 2010, Pt 9A, Ch 9*.

Trading finance profits

Profits which arise from trading activities may be subject to the CFC charge under *TIOPA 2010, Pt 9A, Chs 4* and *6* above.

The *Controlled Foreign Companies (Excluded Banking Business Profits) Regulations 2012, SI 2012/3041*, provide that, if certain conditions are met, no CFC charge will arise in respect of banking profits of a CFC.

Safe harbours

20.29 Certain types of profits are outside the scope of the CFC charge. The government has stated that a company can rely on these 'safe harbours' to show that the types of profits listed below are outside the regime's scope.

These include:

(a) profits from a property business;

(b) incidental non-trading finance profits where the total of such profits does not exceed 5% of its total profits;

(c) incidental non-trading finance profits derived from the investment of funds held for the purposes of a trade or property business, where the profits of the trade would not themselves fall within the CFC charge; and

(d) incidental non-trading finance profits where a CFC's business is holding shares and securities in its 51% subsidiaries.

Self-assessment requirements

20.30 Under self-assessment, a company is required to self-assess any CFC charges on which it is taxable and report these on supplementary form CT600B, included within its corporation tax return.

The information that is required is:

- a calculation of the profits chargeable to tax on a UK corporation tax basis (excluding capital gains);
- an apportionment of the profits among those with a relevant interest in the company; and
- corporation tax self-assessment where 25% or more of the total taxable profits are allocated.

A CFC's accounting profits are its pre-tax profits for an accounting period. Where the accounts are prepared in accordance with an acceptable accounting practice, the CFC's pre-tax profits are to be based on the amounts disclosed in the accounts. Any of the following is an acceptable accounting practice:

- international accounting standards;
- UK generally accepted accounting practice; and
- accounting practice which is generally accepted in the country in which the CFC is resident.

Where accounts have not been prepared under either UK GAAP or international accounting standards, those parts of the CFC provisions which require consideration of accounting treatment are determined by reference to international accounting standards (*TIOPA 2010, s 371VIA(4)*). See **Chapter 26** regarding changes to UK GAAP.

Before 8 July 2015, certain UK losses and expenses could be set off against profits assessable under the CFC rules, reducing the amount of UK tax payable in respect of those diverted profits. For accounting periods beginning on or after 8 July 2015 (subject to transitional provisions):

- no such relief is available (*TIOPA 2010, s 371UD*, before and after repeal by *F(No 2)A 2015, s 35*); and
- the rules on tax avoidance involving carried-forward reliefs (see **4.30**) are extended to ensure that they apply also to arrangements involving the avoidance or reduction of a CFC charge (*CTA 2010, ss 730G, 730H*, as amended by *F(No 2)A 2015, s 36*).

Corporation tax assumptions in computing taxable profits

20.31 In the case of a CFC, the profits chargeable to corporation tax are calculated in the normal way, with the following added assumptions:

- The company is UK resident at all times during the relevant accounting period, and continues to be UK resident for subsequent accounting periods until it ceases to be a CFC (*TIOPA 2010, s 371SD*).
- The company is not a close company (*TIOPA 2010, s 371SE*).
- The company makes full use of any claims or reliefs under the *Corporation Tax Acts* within the applicable time limits (*TIOPA 2010, s 371SF*). However, this assumption does not apply to the following claims or reliefs:

  (a) exemption for profits of foreign permanent establishment;

  (b) relief for unremittable income;

  (c) designated currency of a UK resident investment company; or

  (d) election for lease to be treated as a long funding lease.
- Any intangible fixed asset acquired or created by the CFC before its first accounting period was acquired or created at the beginning of that accounting period (*TIOPA 2010, s 371SK*).
- The CFC is neither a member of a group nor a member of a consortium (*TIOPA 2010, s 371SL*).
- If the CFC incurred any plant and machinery capital expenditure before it became a CFC, the plant and machinery was brought into use at the beginning of the first accounting period (*TIOPA 2010, s 371SM*).

Apportionment of chargeable profits and creditable tax

20.32 The basic rules for how an apportionment of a CFC's chargeable profits is calculated are set out in *TIOPA 2010, s 371QC*. If all three conditions in this section are met, *TIOPA 2010, s 371QD* applies to apportion chargeable profits and creditable tax to all relevant persons in proportion to their ordinary shareholdings in the CFC.

The three conditions are as follows:

- Condition X is that the relevant persons have relevant interests in the CFC only through their holding, whether directly or indirectly, of ordinary shares in the CFC;
- Condition Y is that each relevant person is either only UK resident or only non-UK resident throughout the accounting period; and
- Condition Z is satisfied provided a company with an intermediate interest in the CFC only has that interest from holding, directly or indirectly, ordinary shares in the CFC.

FOREIGN BRANCH EXEMPTION

> **Focus**
>
> Some of the features of the new CFC regime were adopted from 1 January 2013 for the purposes of the foreign branch exemption.

Exemption for profits or losses of foreign branches

20.33 *FA 2011* introduced new rules in respect of foreign permanent establishments of UK companies. Additional changes were made by *FA 2012*, adopting some of the new CFC provisions for the purposes of the foreign branch exemption. HMRC guidance on the foreign branch exemption is at INTM280000, and guidance on the CFC regime is at INTM190000.

If a company has any foreign permanent establishments, it can elect for the profits and losses arising from all of them not to be chargeable to UK corporation tax. Chargeable gains are treated in the same way. Capital allowances are included when calculating profits and losses to be attributed to the foreign permanent establishment. An election can only be made in respect of accounting periods beginning on or after 19 July 2011. From 1 January 2013, such an election may be made by a non-UK resident company, in which case it takes effect from the date on which the company becomes UK resident (*CTA 2009, s 18A*).

Once a company has made this election, all of its foreign permanent establishment profits arising from all foreign territories will be exempt, subject to a transitional rule, namely an anti-avoidance, anti-diversion rule. The profits are exempted by means of exemption adjustments to the company's total taxable profits for each relevant accounting period. The profits attributable to the foreign permanent establishment are known as the 'foreign permanent establishments amount' (*CTA 2009, s 18A*).

Once an election is made, it will apply (for UK resident companies) from the start of the next accounting period. For a non-UK resident company, the election will take effect from the day the company becomes UK resident. The election can be revoked at any time before the start of the first accounting period for which it would have effect, but thereafter it is irrevocable. The only other circumstance in which the election can be revoked is if the company ceases to be UK resident (*CTA 2009, s 18F*).

The foreign permanent establishments amount is the aggregate of the relevant profits amount and the relevant losses amount for each relevant foreign territory. A relevant foreign territory is any foreign territory where the company is carrying on, or has at any time carried on, business through a foreign permanent establishment (*CTA 2009, s 18A(5)*).

Where there is a full treaty in existence between the UK and a relevant foreign territory, the relevant profits amount and the relevant losses amount are determined in accordance with that treaty. A full treaty is in existence if there is a double tax treaty between the UK and the territory in which the branch operates and the treaty contains a relevant non-discrimination provision. Such a provision exists where a treaty provides that the permanent establishment is not to be taxed less favourably than other enterprises carrying on the same activities in the other territory (*CTA 2009, s 18R*). If no full treaty is in existence, the relevant profits amount and the relevant losses amount are defined by reference to the 2010 version of the Organisation for Economic Co-operation and Development (OECD) Model Tax Convention (*CTA 2009, s 18S*; see also *OECD Model Convention with respect to Taxes on Income and on Capital*).

In either case, the relevant profits amount is the amount which would be attributable to the permanent establishment in the foreign territory (if the profits had not been exempt) for the purpose of calculating the tax credit that would have been allowed under the UK's credit regime for tax paid under the law of that territory (*CTA 2009, s 18A(6)*).

For accounting periods beginning on or after 1 January 2013, income from immovable property used for the business of the permanent establishment is included in the relevant profits amount. However, any profits or losses arising from the making of investments cannot be part of the relevant profits amount (*CTA 2009, ss 18CA, 18CB*).

Chargeable gains

20.34 Any chargeable gains or losses that arise on the disposal of assets are taken into account when making the exemption adjustments (*CTA 2009, s 18B(1)*). Gains or losses on immovable property are to be included in relevant profits or losses amounts, to the extent that the property has been used for the permanent establishment (*CTA 2009, s 18B(2)*). Gains and losses are not to be included if they would be attributable for the purposes of ascertaining credit to be allowed in respect of tax payable under the law of the territory before the election has effect (*CTA 2009, s 18B(3)*).

Capital allowances

20.35 Once the exemption applies, there is a deemed disposal of the permanent establishments' plant and machinery. The disposal value is called the 'transition value' and is an amount where neither a balancing charge nor a balancing allowance arises. The transition value is used in calculating notional plant and machinery allowances which are to be taken into account automatically in any calculation of profits or losses attributable to the permanent establishments for each accounting period after an election has been made (*CTA 2009, s 18C(1)*). All other claims and elections are assumed to have been made (*CTA 2009, s 18C(5)*).

There is an exception to this rule: market value applies instead of transition value where an item of plant or machinery (or a group of assets of which it forms part) has an historic cost greater than £5 million and the company has used the plant or machinery other than for the purposes of the permanent establishment at any time during a 'relevant preceding accounting period' – ie the accounting period in which the election is made or any earlier accounting period ending less than six years before the end of that period, but not before 19 July 2010 (or, where cost exceeds £50 million, 19 July 2005) (*CAA 2001, s 62A*; *FA 2011, Sch 13, para 36*).

Profits or losses arising from plant or machinery leases are left out of account for the purpose of calculating any relevant profits amount or relevant losses amount (*CTA 2009, s 18C(3)*). See *CAA 2001, s 70K* for the definition of a plant or machinery lease.

Payments subject to deduction

20.36 Profits or losses referable to any transaction between a person who is UK resident and any of the permanent establishments in question are to be excluded from any relevant profits or relevant losses amount if there would be an obligation to deduct non-repayable income tax at source under *ITA 2007, Pt 15* (*CTA 2009, s 18D*). This exclusion does not apply to banks, unless the transaction is part of arrangements with a main purpose of avoidance of an obligation to deduct income tax.

Employee share acquisitions

20.37 Relief in respect of employee share acquisitions (see **2.45**) is to be taken into account in determining the relevant profit or loss amounts of any exempt foreign permanent establishment, to the extent that those employees are linked to it. The relief is calculated on a just and reasonable basis with respect to the contribution made to the purposes of the business carried on by the workers concerned (*CTA 2009, s 18E*).

Anti-diversion rule

Diverted profits excluded from exemption

20.38 *FA 2012* introduced anti-diversion provisions to align the rules for foreign permanent establishments with certain of the CFC rules discussed above.

The effect of these rules is to identify whether the profits which would otherwise be exempt under the permanent establishment rules include any diverted profits. If there are any diverted profits, they cannot benefit from the exemption.

Diverted profits are those profits that pass through the gateway under the CFC rules other than *TIOPA 2010, Ch 8*. For these purposes, the CFC charge gateway (see **20.27**) is to be referred to as the 'diverted profits gateway'.

Diverted profits gateway

20.39 Diverted profits means those profits of company X's which pass through the diverted profits gateway. To determine which of company X's profits pass through the diverted profits gateway in accounting period X, the following steps are to be applied:

- Company X needs to check whether any of the permanent establishment's profits are caught by the tests set out in *TIOPA 2010, Pt 9A, Chs 3–7*. The tests in *TIOPA 2010, Pt 9A, Ch 3* tell a company whether it needs to consider the tests in *TIOPA 2010, Pt 9A, Chs 4–7* inclusive. Each of *TIOPA 2010, Pt 9A, Chs 4–7* deals with a different type of profit. In most cases, a company only has to consider the tests in *TIOPA 2010, Pt 9A, Ch 3* and may disregard the tests in *TIOPA 2010, Pt 9A, Chs 4–7*.
- Company X is assumed to be a CFC, resident in territory X and its accounting period X is assumed to be the CFC's accounting period. It is

also assumed that company X's total profits of period X are the CFC's total profits for the accounting period.

As with the CFC rules, if company X meets one of the exemptions in *TIOPA 2010, Pt 9A, Chs 11–14*, ie the excluded territories exemption (with some modifications for these purposes), the low profits exemption, the low profit margin exemption and the tax exemption, the company is exempt from the anti-diversion rule.

Companies with total opening negative amount

Calculation of opening negative amount

20.40 Rules are in place not to exempt profits that are set against an opening negative amount at the start of the first accounting period to which the election applies.

A total opening negative amount includes any loss arising in a company's foreign permanent establishments during the six-year period ending at the end of the accounting period in which the election is made, unless it is reduced or eliminated by a subsequent profit arising from the foreign permanent establishments in that period.

CTA 2009, s 18J(1) introduces the rules which apply when an election for exemption has been made and there is a total opening negative amount at the start of the first accounting period to which the election applies.

A total opening negative amount is determined as follows:

Step 1

The adjusted foreign permanent establishments amount, in relation to the earliest affected prior accounting period in relation to which that amount is negative, is taken.

Step 2

The adjusted foreign permanent establishments amount, in relation to the next affected prior accounting period, is added to the result at Step 1. (If the result exceeds nil, it is ignored.)

Step 3

The adjusted foreign permanent establishments amount, in relation to each remaining affected prior accounting period starting with the earliest, is added to the result at Step 2. (If the result exceeds nil, it is ignored.)

If (after the application of Step 3) there is a negative amount for the last affected prior accounting period, there is a total opening negative amount at the beginning of the company's first relevant accounting period of an amount equal to that negative amount.

An affected prior accounting period is the accounting period in which the election for exemption is made and any accounting period ending less than six years before the end of that accounting period (*CTA 2009, s 18J(3)*). This six-year limit may be extended – if a company has losses exceeding £50 million in relation to any relevant foreign territory for any accounting period beginning within the period of six years ending on 18 July 2011, that accounting period and certain later accounting periods become affected prior accounting periods (*FA 2011, Sch 13, para 34*).

The adjusted foreign permanent establishments amount is the foreign permanent establishments amount without reference to chargeable gains or allowable losses (*CTA 2009, s 18J(4)*).

Total opening negative amount matching

20.41 The opening negative amount must be reduced where it is matched by subsequent aggregate relevant profits amounts. In such an event, those aggregate relevant profits amounts are not exempt. In the last accounting period in which the opening negative amount can be matched by an aggregate relevant profits amount, exemption is disapplied only to the extent of the opening negative amount at the start of that accounting period. The company may specify, in its corporation tax return for the period when the opening negative amount is used up, to which part of the aggregate relevant profits amount the exemption from UK tax applies (*CTA 2009, s 18K*).

Example 20.1—Total opening negative amount

Facts

Multinational plc has the following profit and loss figures in the year of election and the preceding five years:

Year	*Profit/(loss)*	*Loss carried forward (if any)*
Year –5	100	0
Year –4	(100)	100
Year –3	300	0
Year –2	(500)	500
Year –1	100	400
Year of election	100	300

Analysis

The earliest affected year with a negative amount is Year –4, and the adjusted foreign permanent establishments amount for that year is –100. After the corresponding amount for Year –3 is added, the result exceeds nil so it is ignored.

The next affected year is Year –2 with an amount of –500. After adding the amounts for the succeeding two years, the total opening negative amount of Multinational plc is 300.

Note that it does not matter whether the net losses of the permanent establishments have been offset sideways (eg against profits of the UK part of the company) or carried back or surrendered as group relief. The computation proceeds as if they are always carried forward.

Streaming instead of negative amount matching

20.42 The company may elect for streaming to apply instead of negative amount matching. The election has to be made at the same time as the foreign profits exemption election, and has the advantage that the rules are applied separately to losses in each particular territory, so that they do not delay the application of exemption to other territories. A streaming election, once made, becomes irrevocable at the start of the first exempt period.

The amount that can be streamed to a territory is what the opening negative amount of the company would be if the territory were the only territory in which the company has carried on business through a permanent establishment. In order for a streaming election to become effective, the company must specify in its tax return, for the first accounting period to which the election for exemption applies, how much of the opening negative amount is to be streamed for each territory (*CTA 2009, s 18L*).

Streamed opening negative amount matching

20.43 The streamed opening negative amount must be reduced where it is matched by subsequent aggregate relevant profits amounts for the territory. In such an event, those aggregate relevant profits amounts are not exempt. In the last accounting period when the streamed opening negative amount can be matched by an aggregate relevant profits amount, exemption is disapplied only to the extent of the streamed opening negative amount at the start of that accounting period. The company may specify, in its corporation tax return for the period when the streamed opening negative amount is used up, to which part of the aggregate relevant profits amount the exemption from UK tax applies (*CTA 2009, s 18M*).

Example 20.2—Matching of streamed opening negative amounts

Facts

Worldwide plc has the following profit and loss figures in the year of election and the preceding five years:

Year	*Territory 1*	*Territory 2*	*Territory 3*	*Territory 4*	*Aggregate*
Year –5	100	0	0	(500)	(400)
Year –4	200	(200)	(100)	100	0
Year –3	(100)	(500)	200	100	(300)
Year –2	300	200	100	(100)	500
Year –1	100	(1,000)	(200)	(100)	(1,200)
Year of election	100	100	100	100	400
Residual negative amount	0	(1,400)	100	(400)	(1,000)

Analysis

If Worldwide plc elects for territory 2 to be streamed, the streamed loss for that territory is the lower of the residual negative amount for that territory (ie 1,400) and the aggregate residual negative amount (ie 1,000), and is thus 1,000. The company streams no other territory, so the unstreamed loss is the difference between the aggregate pool of losses (1,000) and the streamed pool (1,000), which is nil.

Therefore, Worldwide plc has a streamed opening loss of 1,000 for territory 2 and no other opening negative amount. This means that the first 1,000 of profits arising in territory 2 after the accounting period of election is excluded from exemption. All other profits and losses are included in the exemption.

Unstreamed opening negative amount matching

20.44 Where there is an election for streaming, any unstreamed residual opening negative amount is to be reduced, but not below nil, where it is matched by subsequent aggregate relevant profits amounts. The residual opening negative amount of a company is the total opening negative amount less the total streamed opening negative amounts. When a residual opening negative amount is reduced by a residual aggregate relevant profits amount, the aggregate relevant profits amount is not exempt. In the last accounting period in which the residual opening negative amount can be reduced by matching it with a residual aggregate relevant profits amount, exemption is disapplied only to the extent of the residual opening negative amount at the start of that accounting period. The company may specify, in its tax return for the period when the residual opening negative amount is used up, to which part of the residual aggregate relevant profits amount the exemption from UK tax applies (*CTA 2009, s 18N*).

Transfers of foreign permanent establishment business

20.45 When a business or part of a business carried on through a foreign permanent establishment is transferred to a connected company which is or later becomes a UK resident company, and the foreign profits exemption is disapplied due to the opening negative amounts, the transferee company is given the same treatment as the transferor (*CTA 2009, s 18O*).

Special cases

Exclusions

20.46 If a company is a micro or small enterprise, as defined in the *Annex* to *Commission Recommendation 2003/361/EC* of 6 May 2003 (see **21.11**) at any time during a relevant accounting period, no relevant profits amount or losses amount in relation to any foreign territory that is not a full treaty territory is deemed to arise (*CTA 2009, s 18P(1)*).

If a company is a close company (see **Chapter 10**) at any time during a relevant accounting period, so much of the profits that are derived from chargeable gains are not taken into account in computing relevant profits or relevant losses amounts (*CTA 2009, s 18P(2)*).

Insurance companies

20.47 Profits and losses arising from basic life assurance and general annuity business are generally excluded from relevant profits and relevant losses amounts, and are thereby excluded from exemption within the regime (*CTA 2009, s 18Q*).

FOREIGN CURRENCY ACCOUNTING

Tax calculation currency

20.48 A company is required to calculate and express its income and chargeable gains for corporation tax purposes in sterling (*CTA 2010, s 5*).

This rule applies to a UK resident company that:

- operates in sterling as its functional currency, but prepare accounts in another currency (*CTA 2010, s 6*). The functional currency of a company or of part of a company's business are references to the currency of the primary economic environment in which the company or part operates – essentially the currency that it uses to record its daily transactions (*CTA 2010, s 17(4)*, as substituted by *F(No 2)A 2015, s 33(13)*);
- operates in a currency other than sterling as its functional currency and prepares accounts in another currency (*CTA 2010, s 7*); or
- prepares accounts in a currency other than sterling (*CTA 2010, s 8*).

This rule also applies to a non-UK resident company carrying on a trade through a UK permanent establishment that prepares accounts in a currency other than sterling (*CTA 2010, s 9*). Special rules apply in all three circumstances above to UK resident investment companies, for periods of account beginning on or after 1 April 2011.

From 1 September 2013, to ensure closer alignment between tax and economic outcomes for companies that do not use sterling as their functional currency, a company is required to compute its chargeable gains and losses on disposals of ships, aircraft, shares or interests in shares in its relevant currency. This is the currency which is its functional currency (or, if it is a UK resident investment company which has made a designated currency election under *CTA 2010, s 9A*, that designated currency) at the time of the disposal. The chargeable gain or allowable capital loss must be calculated first in the company's relevant currency at the time of the disposal, and then translated into sterling at the spot rate of exchange on the day of the disposal (*CTA 2010, s 9C*).

Conversion rules for companies other than UK resident investment companies

20.49 **Rule 1**: Where a UK resident company operates in sterling as its functional currency but prepares accounts in another currency, the profits or losses of the company for the period that fall to be calculated in accordance with GAAP for corporation tax purposes must be calculated in sterling as if the company prepared its accounts in sterling (*CTA 2010, s 6(1), (2)*).

Rule 2: Where a UK resident company operates in a currency other than sterling as its functional currency and prepares accounts in another currency other than sterling, the profits or losses of the company for the period that fall to be calculated in accordance with GAAP for corporation tax purposes must be calculated in sterling as follows:

- *Step 1*: Calculate those profits or losses in the relevant currency (see *CTA 2010, s 7(4)*) as if the company prepared its accounts in that currency.

- *Step 2*: Take the sterling equivalent of those profits or losses (*CTA 2010, s 7(1), (2)–(4)*).

Rule 3: In all other situations where a UK resident company prepares accounts in a currency other than sterling (the 'accounts currency'), the profits or losses of the company for the period that fall to be calculated in accordance with GAAP for corporation tax purposes must be calculated in sterling as follows:

- *Step 1*: Calculate those profits or losses in the accounts currency.
- *Step 2*: Take the sterling equivalent of those profits or losses (*CTA 2010, s 8*).

Rule 4: Where a non-UK resident company carries on a trade in the UK through a permanent establishment and prepares accounts in a currency other than sterling (the 'accounts currency'), the profits or losses of the company for the period that fall to be calculated in accordance with GAAP for corporation tax purposes must be calculated in sterling as follows:

- *Step 1*: Calculate those profits or losses in the accounts currency.
- *Step 2*: Take the sterling equivalent of those profits or losses (*CTA 2010, s 9*).

Basic rule: In taking the sterling equivalents of profits and losses as required above, there is a basic rule that foreign profits and losses arising in an accounting period must be converted into sterling at the average exchange rate for that accounting period. However, if there is only one transaction, an appropriate spot rate should be used for that transaction. If there are a few transactions, a rate derived on a just and reasonable basis from appropriate spot rates for those transactions should be used (*CTA 2010, s 11*).

See **Chapter 26** regarding changes to UK GAAP.

Conversion rules for UK resident investment companies

20.50 Broadly the same rule applies, that income and chargeable gains must be calculated and expressed in sterling, but with some exceptions.

Where a UK resident investment company prepares accounts in accordance with GAAP in a currency other than sterling, and either has sterling as its designated currency or has no designated currency and identifies sterling as its functional currency, the profits or losses of the company for the period that fall to be calculated in accordance with GAAP for corporation tax purposes must be calculated in sterling as if the company prepared its accounts in sterling (*CTA 2010, s 6(1A), (2)*).

Where a UK resident investment company operates in a currency other than sterling and prepares accounts in another currency, and either has another currency as its designated currency or has no designated currency and identifies another currency as its functional currency, the profits or losses of the company for the period that fall to be calculated in accordance with GAAP for corporation tax purposes must be calculated in sterling as follows (*CTA 2010, s 7(1A)–(4)*):

- *Step 1*: Calculate those profits or losses in the relevant currency (see *CTA 2010, s 7(4)*) as if the company prepared its accounts in that currency.
- *Step 2*: Take the sterling equivalent of those profits or losses (see 'Basic rule' at **20.49**).

Foreign exchange gains and losses may arise on translation if a company holds a loan relationship or derivative contract that is denominated in a currency other than its functional currency, as conversion must first be made from the currency in which the assets are held to the functional currency and then to sterling. To avoid such gains and losses arising, a UK resident investment company can elect for a designated currency to be used for tax purposes, other than the functional currency used in the accounts (*CTA 2010, s 9A*, before and after amendment by *F(No 2)A 2015, s 33*).

A UK resident investment company may elect for a currency other than sterling as its designated currency if either of the following two conditions apply:

- Condition A: the company holds a significant proportion of its assets in that foreign currency; or
- Condition B: if the company is a member of a group, it would be reasonable to assume that its results would be consolidated in that foreign currency.

For periods of account beginning before 1 January 2016 (subject to transitional provisions), an election can also be made during the period from incorporation to immediately before the end of the company's first accounting period. The election becomes null and void should neither of the two conditions be satisfied at the start of the first accounting period (*CTA 2010, s 9A(3)*, before repeal by *F(No 2)A 2015, s 33(4)*).

An election under *CTA 2010, s 9A* becomes ineffective if it is formally revoked, if the company no longer satisfies at least one of the conditions, or if the company ceases to be a UK resident investment company (*CTA 2010, s 9B*), as amended by *F(No 2)A 2015, s 33(11)*).

As part of the reform of the tax treatment of loan relationships (**Chapter 11**), these rules have been tightened for periods of account beginning on or after 1 January 2016 (subject to transitional provisions). An election for a particular designated currency only takes effect if the company is a UK resident investment company and the relevant conditions are satisfied at the time when the election is to take effect (*CTA 2010, s 9A(2)*, as substituted by *F(No 2)A 2015, s 33*).

See **Chapter 26** regarding changes to UK GAAP.

Special rules

20.51 Special conversion rules apply in circumstances where losses are carried back or forwards and where adjustments are made to the amounts of those losses carried back or forwards. These rules depend on the company's operating currency in each of the two accounting periods in question.

Special rules for losses carried back

20.52 Where a loss is carried back under *CTA 2010, s 37(3)* (see **4.16–4.20**), or a non-trading loan relationship deficit is carried back under *CTA 2009, s 459(1)(b)* (see **11.30**), the following rules apply:

- If the same tax calculation currency is used for the earlier and the later accounting period, the basic rule applies (see **20.49**).
- If sterling is the tax calculation currency for the earlier accounting period, but a foreign currency is used for the latter period, the spot rate of exchange for the last day of the earlier accounting period must be used to convert the loss into sterling.
- If different tax calculation currencies are used for the earlier and the later accounting period, neither of which is sterling, the loss must first be translated into the earlier tax calculation currency using the spot rate of exchange for the last day of the earlier accounting period. The loss is then converted into sterling at the same rate as is used for the earlier profits against which the loss is to be set. The earlier profits are translated according to the basic rule; see **20.49** (*CTA 2010, s 12*).

Adjustment of sterling losses carried back

20.53 Subject to the three conditions below being met, if there is an adjustment to the sterling loss that is carried back, the loss must first be translated into the earlier operating currency by applying the spot rate of exchange for the last day of the earlier accounting period. The loss is then converted into sterling at the same rate as is used for the earlier profits against which the loss is to be set. The earlier profits are translated according to the basic rule (see **20.49**).

The three conditions that must be met are:

- the company is UK resident and prepares accounts in accordance with GAAP for a period of account in sterling, or in a foreign currency but identifies sterling as its functional currency;
- the loss computed under GAAP is a carried back amount; and
- the operating currency of the earlier accounting period is not sterling (*CTA 2010, s 14*).

See **Chapter 26** regarding changes to UK GAAP.

Special rules for losses carried forward

20.54 Special rules apply where the following types of losses are carried forward:

- carry forward of trade loss against subsequent trade profits (see **4.2**) (*CTA 2010, s 45*);
- UK property business losses (see **4.45**) (*CTA 2010, s 62(5)*);
- company with investment business ceasing to carry on a UK property business (*CTA 2010, s 63(3)*);
- overseas property business losses (*CTA 2010, s 66(3)*);
- losses from miscellaneous transactions (*CTA 2010, s 91(6)*);
- non-trading loan relationship deficits (see **11.27**) (*CTA 2009, s 457(3)*);
- non-trading loss on intangible fixed assets (*CTA 2009, s 753(3)*);
- patent income: relief for expenses (*CTA 2009, s 925(3)*); or
- expenses of management and other amounts (*CTA 2009, s 1223*).

The rules are:

- If the same operating currency is used for the earlier and the later accounting period, the basic rule applies (see **20.49**).
- If sterling is the operating currency for the later accounting period, but another currency is used for the earlier period, the spot rate of exchange for the first day of the later accounting period must be used to convert the loss into sterling.
- If different operating currencies are used for the earlier and for the later accounting period, neither of which is sterling, the loss must first be translated into the earlier operating currency by applying the spot rate of exchange for the first day of the earlier accounting period. The loss is then converted into sterling at the same rate as is used for the later profits against which the loss is to be set. The later profits are translated according to the basic rule; see **20.49** (*CTA 2010, s 13*).

Adjustment of sterling losses carried forward

20.55 Subject to the three conditions below being met, if there is an adjustment to the sterling loss that is carried forward, the loss must first be translated into the later tax calculation currency by applying the spot rate of exchange for the first day of the later accounting period. The loss is then converted into sterling at the same rate as is used for the later profits against which the loss is to be set. The later profits are translated according to the basic rule (see **20.49**).

The three conditions that must be met are:

- the company is UK resident and prepares accounts in accordance with GAAP for a period of account in sterling, or in a foreign currency but identifies sterling as its functional currency;
- the loss computed under GAAP is a carried forward amount; and
- the operating currency of the earlier accounting period is not sterling (*CTA 2010, s 15*).

See **Chapter 26** regarding changes to UK GAAP.

DIVERTED PROFITS TAX

Background to DPT

20.56 From 1 April 2015 a new diverted profits tax (DPT) has been introduced. This seeks to deter and counteract the diversion of profits from the UK by large groups (typically multinational enterprises) which use contrived arrangements to circumvent rules on permanent establishments and transfer pricing.

DPT addresses three situations, namely:

- where a person (to be interpreted widely, as in INTM412030) carries on activity in the UK in connection with the supply of goods, services or other property by a foreign company and that activity is designed to ensure that the foreign company does not create a UK permanent establishment ('UKPE'), and either the main purpose of the arrangements put in place is to avoid UK tax, or a tax mismatch is secured so that the total tax derived from UK activities is significantly reduced (*FA 2015, s 86*);
- where a UK company uses transactions or entities that lack economic substance in order to exploit tax mismatches (*FA 2015, s 80*); or
- where a foreign company with a UKPE uses transactions or entities that lack economic substance in order to exploit tax mismatches (*FA 2015, s 81*).

In HMRC's view, DPT falls outside the scope of relief available under UK tax treaties. As it will only be applied to arrangements designed to exploit the provisions of tax treaties to avoid tax, the arrangements that it targets are of a kind where there is no obligation to provide relief under international law.

Although, in many cases, the arrangements put in place to divert profits will involve non-UK companies, DPT may also apply in circumstances where wholly domestic structures are used.

The DPT legislation is contained in *FA 2015, ss 77–116, Sch 16*. In November 2015, HMRC published guidance on DPT at tinyurl.com/ogwps36. This is expected to be included in HMRC's International Manual in due course, but this had not happened by September 2017.

Exemptions from DPT

20.57 The legislation provides exemptions from DPT where:

- the entities are SMEs. For this purpose the EU definition of SME (see **14.23**, **21.11**) is modified to remove the transition period that otherwise allows retention of SME status until the relevant limits have been exceeded for two consecutive accounting periods (*TIOPA 2010, s 172*; see INTM412080);
- the effective tax mismatch outcome is an 'excepted loan relationship outcome'. This exempts arrangements that give rise only to a loan relationship, or to a loan relationship and derivative contract entered into entirely as a hedge risk in connection with the loan relationship (*FA 2015, s 109*); or
- there are limited UK sales or expenses (*FA 2015, s 87*). DPT will not arise under *FA 2015, s 86* where the sales revenues of the foreign company plus certain sales revenues of connected companies are no more than £10 million, or their collective UK-related expenses do not exceed £1m, in each case in a 12-month accounting period (the limits being reduced *pro rata* for shorter periods).

Calculation of DPT

20.58 Profits which have been diverted from the UK ('taxable diverted profits') are computed using the same principles which apply for corporation tax, including transfer pricing rules, except where the legislation requires arrangements to be re-characterised (in which case, the amount of diverted profit is calculated on a just and reasonable basis).

Where DPT applies, it is charged on a company's taxable diverted profits arising on or after 1 April 2015, and there are apportionment rules for accounting periods that straddle that date. DPT is charged at a main rate of 25%, or on taxable diverted ring fence profits at 55%. Also included as an integral part of the DPT charge is an amount of 'true up interest' – ie interest calculated from six months after the end of the relevant accounting period until the day the charging notice is issued, to ensure broad equity among companies regardless of whether the notice is issued promptly or delayed (*FA 2015, s 79*).

DPT is a separate tax from corporation tax and is not to be taken into account for corporation tax purposes, either as a deduction or for the purposes of any other relief. No amounts paid (directly or indirectly) by anyone in order to meet or reimburse the cost of DPT are to be taken into account or treated as distributions for corporation tax purposes (*FA 2015, s 99*). However, the legislation makes provision for credit to be given against DPT for certain UK and foreign taxes, or controlled foreign company (CFC) charges or foreign equivalents, in defined circumstances (*FA 2015, s 100*).

DPT procedures

20.59 A company has a duty to notify an officer of HMRC, in writing, if it is potentially within the scope of DPT. This notification must be made within three months after the end of the accounting period to which it relates, and must include certain prescribed information (*FA 2015, s 92*). The time limit is extended to six months for accounting periods ending on or before 31 March 2016 (*FA 2015, s 116(3)*).

There is no requirement to notify:

- when it is reasonable for the company to conclude that no charge to the diverted profits tax will arise in the period (other than because a transfer pricing adjustment may be made in the future for corporation tax purposes);
- when an officer of HMRC has confirmed that the company does not have to notify an officer in the current period, because the company has provided information to HMRC and HMRC have examined this information;
- when it is reasonable for the company to assume (in the absence of confirmation from an officer of HMRC) that it has provided sufficient information and HMRC have examined that information; or
- when in the preceding period notification was given (or not required) and there have been no material changes in circumstances in regard to whether DPT may be imposed in the current period.

The subjective nature of these notification exceptions may encourage companies to file protective notifications, placing heavy administrative burdens on them and on HMRC.

The legislation provides for the issue of a preliminary notice to a company (and copied to the UKPE where applicable) if a designated HMRC officer believes the company to be within the scope of DPT. This preliminary notice must be issued within two years from the end of the accounting period, extended to four years in cases where no notice of potential liability has been submitted by the company and a designated HMRC officer believes that an amount of DPT that ought to have been charged in relation to that accounting period has not been charged (*FA 2015, s 93*).

A company receiving a preliminary notice has 30 days in which to make representations to the designated HMRC officer in respect of that notice. Properly made representations must be considered by a designated officer before determining whether to issue a charging notice (*FA 2015, s 94*). Having considered any such representations, a designated HMRC officer must either issue a charging notice or notify the company that no such charging notice will be issued; this must be done within 30 days from the end of the 30 day period allowed for representations (*FA 2015, s 95*).

Where any of the relevant conditions apply, the legislation describes circumstances where no taxable diverted profits arise and how taxable diverted profits are determined when they do arise. Provisions set out how a designated HMRC officer estimates taxable diverted profits when issuing a preliminary notice or a charging notice, broadly by comparing 'the material provision' (ie the transaction or series of transactions actually undertaken) with 'the relevant alternative provision' (ie those that it is just and reasonable to assume would have been made had tax not been a relevant consideration). It is on this basis that the charge to DPT is calculated (*FA 2015, ss 96, 97*).

DPT must be paid within 30 days after issue of the charging notice, and payment may not be postponed on any grounds (*FA 2015, s 98*).

There are provisions which, following full payment of the DPT, require a designated HMRC officer to review a charging notice within 12 months after the end of the 30-day period allowed for payment, and there are circumstances in which one (but only one) supplementary charge notice may be issued, increasing the charge, or one or more amending notices may be issued to reduce an excessive charge (*FA 2015, s 101*).

Within 30 days after the end of the review period, the company may appeal against a charging notice or supplementary charging notice, and the Tribunal may confirm, amend or cancel the notice (*FA 2015, s 102*).

The charge to DPT includes 'true up interest' (see **20.58**). In addition, late payment interest or repayment interest under *FA 2009, ss 101, 102* respectively applies from 1 April 2015 to DPT paid late or DPT repayable (*Finance Act 2009, Sections 101 and 102 (Diverted Profits Tax) (Appointed Day) Order 2015, SI 2015/974*).

Where a company fails to notify that it is potentially within the scope of DPT, it faces a tax-geared penalty, and in these circumstances the time limit for issue of a preliminary notice by HMRC is extended by two years. Furthermore, the penalties regime (eg for failure to make payments of tax on time) and HMRC's information and inspection powers have been extended to DPT (*FA 2015, s 104*).

Chapter 21

Transfer pricing

SIGNPOSTS

- An introduction to transfer pricing and the OECD BEPS project (see **21.1–21.2**).
- The UK transfer pricing rules, including application and control (see **21.3–21.8**).
- Exemption for pre-existing dormant companies (see **21.9**).
- Small and medium-sized enterprise exemptions and other scenarios – including qualification limits, non-discrimination clauses, compensatory relief and interest-free loans (see **21.10–21.16**).
- Miscellaneous rules relating to transfer pricing, including compensating relief and balancing payments (see **21.17–21.25**).
- Self-assessment, including record keeping and enquiries (see **21.26–21.28**).
- Country-by-country reporting (see **21.29**).
- Advance pricing agreements (see **21.30–21.32**).
- Advance thin capitalisation agreements (see **21.33**).
- Arbitrage, including deduction and receipt schemes (see **21.34–21.37**).
- Mutual agreement procedure and arbitration (see **21.38**).

INTRODUCTION

Focus

The transfer pricing rules require groups and other related parties to calculate their taxable profits as though transactions between connected companies or other related parties were carried out at the 'arm's length prices' that would be charged between two entirely independent parties.

21.1 A 'transfer price' is the price charged in a transaction between two parties. The transfer pricing legislation is concerned with the prices charged in transactions between connected parties. In such circumstances the price charged may not necessarily be the same as the 'arm's length' price that would be expected had the parties been unconnected.

Modern business is transacted globally with many business partners and associates. Groups and other connected companies are able to pick the country or regime that best suits their business in order to minimise their corporation tax liabilities. To prevent any loss to the UK Exchequer, legislation requires that the arm's length principle be applied to all relevant transactions. In most cases, other countries have their own comparable domestic legislation. Where double tax treaties exist, the provisions for the interaction between the transfer pricing laws of the respective countries are generally based on the Organisation for Economic Co-operation and Development (OECD) Model Tax Convention (see *OECD Model Convention with respect to Taxes on Income and on Capital, art 9*). The current version of the Convention was published on 15 July 2014 (see tinyurl.com/nz7tm56).

The OECD Transfer Pricing Guidelines for Multinational Enterprises and Tax Administrations provide guidance on the application of the 'arm's length' principle for the valuation of cross-border transactions between associated enterprises (*TIOPA 2010, s 164(4)*). They were last updated in 2010. Multinational enterprises rely heavily on these to limit the risks of double taxation that may result from a dispute between two countries on the determination of the arm's length remuneration for their cross-border transactions with associated enterprises.

For accounting periods starting on or after 1 April 2016, *TIOPA 2010, s 164(4)* is amended by *FA 2016, s 75* to refer to 'The OECD Transfer Pricing Guidelines for Multinational Enterprises and Tax Administrations as revised by the report, Aligning Transfer Pricing Outcomes with Value Creation, Actions 8–10 – 2015 Final Reports, published by the OECD on 5 October 2015'.

A transfer pricing risk to tax authorities arises mainly in cross-border transactions between companies who are members of the same group or otherwise connected. However, to avoid challenges on the basis of discrimination, UK transfer pricing legislation also applies to transactions where both parties are within the UK. Transfer pricing risks are not limited to transactions between companies; for example, a transaction between a company and a controlling individual (see **21.4**) would be within the ambit of the transfer pricing rules.

Transfer pricing has been at the centre of recent debates on global tax avoidance, triggered by high-profile instances where multinational companies (often household names) have successfully ensured that their profits arise in low-tax jurisdictions.

The UK transfer pricing legislation can be found in *TIOPA 2010, Pt 4, ss 146–230*. HMRC's guidance on transfer pricing was substantially rewritten and restructured and then re-issued in August 2012 (see HMRC International Manual at INTM410000 onwards).

BASE EROSION AND PROFIT SHIFTING

The OECD BEPS project

Focus

Globalisation has led to international co-operation, resulting in a tightening of transfer pricing rules as they apply across multiple tax jurisdictions.

21.2 Increasing globalisation in recent years has boosted trade and increased foreign direct investment in many countries, but the interaction of domestic tax systems can lead to double taxation with adverse effects on growth and global prosperity. Countries agree widely on the need to eliminate double taxation by means of agreed international rules that are clear and predictable.

Multinational enterprises operate globally across national borders, and many of them use opportunities for 'base erosion and profit shifting' (BEPS) to justify taking aggressive tax planning positions. Such business faces reputational damage by doing so, while the countries in which they operate lose revenues or incur increased compliance costs and other taxpayers bear a greater share of the fiscal burden.

In response, the G20 finance ministers called on the OECD to develop an action plan to address BEPS issues in a co-ordinated and comprehensive manner, by providing countries with domestic and international instruments that would better align rights to tax with economic activity.

In July 2013 the OECD published its Action Plan on BEPS, addressing perceived flaws in international tax rules and including several action points aimed specifically at transfer pricing. The G20 countries, including the UK, have endorsed the BEPS project.

The OECD BEPS project contains 15 key action points, as follows:

1	Address the tax challenges of the digital economy
2	Neutralise the effects of hybrid mismatch arrangements
3	Strengthen CFC rules
4	Limit base erosion via interest deductions and other financial payments
5	Counter harmful tax practices more effectively, taking into account transparency and substance
6	Prevent treaty abuse

7	Prevent the artificial avoidance of PE status
8	Assure that transfer pricing outcomes are in line with value creation: intangibles
9	Assure that transfer pricing outcomes are in line with value creation: risks and capital
10	Assure that transfer pricing outcomes are in line with value creation: other high-risk transactions
11	Establish methodologies to collect and analyse data on BEPS and the actions to address it
12	Require taxpayers to disclose their aggressive tax planning arrangements
13	Re-examine transfer pricing documentation
14	Make dispute resolution mechanisms more effective
15	Develop a multilateral instrument

The BEPS project is moving forward. Some of the above action points have already influenced recent changes to tax legislation in the UK, while others are still in progress.

THE UK TRANSFER PRICING RULES

Focus

Taxing authorities often require evidence of arm's length trading. The UK government has established its own code of transfer pricing rules.

21.3 The transfer pricing rules cover:

- the purchase and sale of goods,
- the provision of management and other services,
- rents and hire charges,
- transfers of intangible property, such as trademarks, patents and know-how,
- sharing of expertise, business contacts, supply systems, etc,
- provision of finance, and other financial arrangements, and
- interest.

The legislation aims to mitigate the loss of tax arising from non-arm's length pricing, irrespective of a tax motive.

Application of transfer pricing

21.4 Transfer pricing rules apply if a provision has been imposed by means of a transaction or a series of transactions between any two persons (the term 'person' is to be interpreted widely; see INTM412030) where the participation condition is met, and the actual provision made is different from an arm's length provision that would be made between independent parties and gives one of the two affected parties a potential UK tax benefit (*TIOPA 2010, s 147*). For this purpose, the actual provision is that which is made or imposed between two persons ('the affected persons'), either by a transaction or by a series of transactions (*TIOPA 2010, s 149*). A transaction or a series of transactions includes arrangements, understandings and mutual practices, whether or not they are, or are intended to be, legally enforceable (*TIOPA 2010, s 150*).

The participation condition is satisfied (*TIOPA 2010, s 148*) where, at the time of making or imposing the actual provision (or, in the case of financing arrangements, at any time within the previous six months):

- one of the affected persons was directly or indirectly participating in the management, control or capital of the other, or
- the same person or persons was or were directly or indirectly participating in the management, control or capital of each of the affected persons.

For these purposes, a controlling person may be an individual. However, one of the persons must be a body corporate or a firm which is controlled by the other person. The transfer pricing provisions do not apply to transactions between two individuals (*TIOPA 2010, s 157*).

An arm's length provision is to be applied where a provision made or imposed between any two persons is to be taken to differ from the provision that would have been made as between independent enterprises. This also includes the case in which no provision would have been made as between independent enterprises (*TIOPA 2010, s 151*). An adjustment must be made to the taxable profits of the person or persons enjoying the potential tax advantage (*TIOPA 2010, s 147(3)*).

If the actual provision is a security issued by one company (the issuing company) to another, the matters to consider in relation to an arm's length provision include: whether, in the absence of a special relationship, it would have been made at all; the amount of the loan; the rate of interest; and other agreed terms (*TIOPA 2010, s 152*).

If a guarantee is given, similar questions are to be asked: whether, in the absence of a special relationship, a guarantee would have been provided at all; the amount that would have been guaranteed; and the consideration that would have been agreed. Whether or not guarantees are generally provided by the company in question is to be disregarded (*TIOPA 2010, s 153*).

A person receives a 'potential advantage' in making or imposing the actual provision, instead of the arm's length provision, if either a lesser amount or nil would be taxed or greater loss relief would be available (*TIOPA 2010, s 155*).

The current transfer pricing rules only adjust the provision to an arm's length provision, but not the underlying transaction itself, and some of the cash benefit of the original incorrect pricing is not affected. Although there was a consultation on the issue in 2016, no results of the consultation appear to have been published and there are no new provisions in *FA 2017* or the proposals for the second Finance Bill 2017.

Control

21.5 Control is defined by *CTA 2010, s 1124* as the power to secure that the company's affairs are conducted in accordance with a person's wishes. The powers so recognised are voting power, power given by the articles of association, or powers given by any other document.

Indirect participation examines the following issues.

A person participates indirectly in another entity if:

- he would be participating directly had certain rights and powers been attributed to him (*TIOPA 2010, s 159(2)*), or
- he is one of the major participants in the other entity (*TIOPA 2010, s 160(2)*).

The rights and powers that can be attributed are:

- those which the potential participant is or will be entitled to acquire at a future date,
- those exercisable by other persons on behalf of the potential participant or under his direction or for his benefit, and
- those of connected persons (*TIOPA 2010, s 159(3)*).

The same rights and powers are attributed to a person in determining whether or not he is a major participant in a company (*TIOPA 2010, s 160(5)*). A person is a major participant in a company or other enterprise if the participant and another person each have a 40% interest so that, taken together, they control the company (*TIOPA 2010, s 160(3), (4)*).

In a joint venture, transfer pricing only applies to transactions between at least one of the joint venture parties and the joint venture itself, and not between the two parties to the joint venture unless they are under common control.

In cases relating to financing arrangements, a person (P) is indirectly participating in the management, control or capital of each of another (A) at the time of the making or imposition of the actual provision if:

(a) the actual provision relates, to any extent, to financing arrangements for A;

(b) A is a body corporate or firm;

(c) P and other persons acted together in relation to the financing arrangements; and

(d) P, if attributed with the rights and powers of the other persons mentioned in (c), would be taken to have control of A during the period when the persons mentioned in (c) were acting together or six months thereafter.

Financing arrangements include arrangements for providing or guaranteeing, or otherwise in connection with, any debt, capital or other form of finance (*TIOPA 2010, ss 161, 162*).

Thin capitalisation

21.6 A company is said to be 'thinly capitalised' when it has more debt than equity, and many such cases arise where a company takes on more debt than it could or would have borrowed on its own resources, because it is borrowing from or with the support of connected persons.

The interest payable by a company may be excessive for one or more reasons – eg interest rate, excessive duration of lending, or restrictions on repayment. Other less obvious issues are the appropriateness of the currency of the loan (eg the foreign exchange risk) and the presence of guarantees.

When a company operates at arm's length from its sources of funding, commercial factors drive the decisions to raise funds through debt, equity or a mixture of the two. When a company borrows from or with the support of group companies or other connected parties, funding decisions may not be driven by commercial considerations alone. The connection between the parties involved may allow them to change how the funding is obtained, in ways unavailable or unattractive to a borrower at arm's length, or to take on funding risks which an independent borrower would avoid.

Tax planning may often be a factor leading to thin capitalisation, because differences in tax treatment between interest and dividends mean that a company which increases its indebtedness, and thereby increases its interest payments, reduces the corporation tax that it has to pay.

Thin capitalisation is a form of transfer pricing. It is not restricted to companies, but focuses mainly on corporate relationships. Thin capitalisation is addressed within the main transfer pricing legislation now contained in *TIOPA 2010, Pt 4*. HMRC's guidance on the thin capitalisation legislation was updated and re-issued in January 2013 (see INTM413000 onwards), and their practical guidance on the application of the thin capitalisation rules was updated and re-issued in April 2014 (see INTM510000 onwards).

Corporation tax self-assessment

> **Focus**
>
> Companies are required to self-assess with a transfer pricing adjustment if transactions do not follow the arm's length principles.

21.7 Transfer pricing is within the self-assessment regime. It closely follows the *OECD Model Tax Convention, art 9*. Transactions between UK entities are included within the transfer pricing rules. Dormant companies and small and medium-sized enterprises are generally excluded from the legislation.

Companies are required to include the adjustment to profits within their own self-assessment.

The transaction

21.8 The basic transfer pricing rule follows the *OECD Model Tax Convention* rules and guidelines (*TIOPA 2010, s 164*). The Transfer Pricing Guidelines for Multinational Enterprises and Tax Administrations, approved by the OECD on 22 July 2010, apply for accounting periods beginning on or after 1 April 2011 (*FA 2011, s 58*). The latest version of the guidelines was published on 5 October 2015 and applies to accounting periods starting on or after 1 April 2016 (*FA 2016, s 75*).

The meaning of transactions is extremely wide and includes binding and non-binding arrangements, understandings and mutual practices. A series of transactions includes a number of transactions each entered into (whether or not one after the other) in connection with a single arrangement (*TIOPA 2010, s 150*).

In comparing the actual provision with the arm's length provision, it is necessary to look at all of the terms and conditions of the transactions in question and to adjust them to arm's length terms if necessary. A third party can be involved in a series of transactions. A potential advantage arises from a non-arm's length price if, as a result, taxable profits are reduced, or losses, expenses of management or group relief are increased. The transfer pricing adjustment may only increase profits or reduce losses (*TIOPA 2010, ss 147, 155, 156*).

PRE-EXISTING DORMANT COMPANIES

21.9 Dormant companies which would otherwise be potentially advantaged under the transfer pricing rules are excluded if they were dormant during a specified qualifying period in 2004 and have remained dormant since then. A company is dormant during any period in which it has no significant accounting transaction – that is, a transaction that is required to be entered into its books and records. Share subscriptions and registrar fees are ignored (*TIOPA 2010, s 165*; *CA 2006, s 1169*; INTM412110).

SMALL AND MEDIUM-SIZED ENTERPRISES

> **Focus**
>
> Exemptions from transfer pricing adjustments are granted for small and medium-sized companies.

Exemption

21.10 Subject to exceptions, exemptions apply if the potentially advantaged entity is a small or medium-sized enterprise (*TIOPA 2010, s 166*).

In this context, SMEs are defined in the *Annex* to *Commission Recommendation 2003/361/EC* of 6 May 2003 (see **21.11**).

An SME is exempt from the transfer pricing requirements, except in the following circumstances:

- where it elects to disapply the exemption in relation to the chargeable period (*TIOPA 2010, s 167(2)*); or
- where the other affected person or entity, or a party to a relevant transaction, is, at the time when the actual provision is or was made or imposed, a resident of a non-qualifying territory (*TIOPA 2010, s 167(3)*).

If the SME elects to disapply the exemption for a chargeable period, that election is irrevocable for that period.

If the provision is or was imposed by means of a series of transactions, a party to a relevant transaction is a person or entity that is or was a party to one or more of those transactions (*TIOPA 2010, s 167(4)*).

If a person is a resident of a non-qualifying territory, this is irrespective of whether or not that person is also a resident of a qualifying territory (*TIOPA 2010, s 167(3)*). A non-qualifying territory is any territory that is not a qualifying territory and a qualifying territory is either the UK or any territory with which double tax arrangements have been made and which meets either of the following two requirements (*TIOPA 2010, s 173*):

- the double tax arrangements include a non-discrimination provision and the territory is not designated as a non-qualifying territory; or
- the territory is designated as a qualifying territory.

A non-discrimination provision, in relation to any double tax arrangements, is a provision to the effect that nationals of a state which is a party to those arrangements are not to be subject (in any other contracting state) to tax, or any requirement connected with tax, which is more burdensome than that to which nationals of that other state are subject in the same circumstances, in particular with respect to residence (*TIOPA 2010, s 173(4)*; see **21.15**).

A company's 'residence' in these circumstances comes about by domicile, residence or place of management – not merely by being liable to tax from income sources or capital situated in that territory.

Medium-sized enterprises are not exempt from the transfer pricing provisions for an accounting period if, following issue of a notice of enquiry for that period, HMRC issue them with a transfer pricing notice, requiring them to calculate profits and losses on an arm's length basis (*TIOPA 2010, ss 168, 169*). The company can appeal against the decision to issue the notice, but only on the ground that the company is not a medium-sized company (*TIOPA 2010, s 170*). The company can amend its tax return in order to comply with the notice any time before the end of the period of 90 days beginning with the day on which the notice is given or, if under appeal, the day on which the appeal is finally determined or abandoned (*TIOPA 2010, s 171*).

Definition

21.11 The SME definition follows that given by *Commission Recommendation 2003/361/EC* (*TIOPA 2010, s 172(1)*). For the EU definition of SME and user guide, see tinyurl.com/nc2wyog.

The definition applies not only to companies but to any entity engaged in an economic activity, irrespective of its legal form, and includes entities subject to corporation tax or income tax.

An entity qualifies as either small or medium if it falls within the staff headcount ceiling for that class and either one or both of the following respective financial limits:

	Medium	*Small*	*Micro*
If the company has fewer than	250 employees	50 employees	10 employees
and			
either an annual turnover not exceeding	€50m	€10m	€2m
or a balance sheet total not exceeding	€43m	€10m	€2m

This test is made and determined solely by reference to the period for which a return is being made.

Staff includes employees, persons seconded to work for a business, owner managers and partners – apportioned according to the amount of time that they work.

Turnover and balance sheet totals are net of VAT and otherwise have their ordinary meaning for accounting purposes. Balance sheet total means total gross assets without any deduction for liabilities.

Conversion to sterling should be made at the average exchange rate for the period of account whose profit is being computed, or the exchange rate on the date the account was drawn up if this produces a fairer result.

As with any of the thresholds, companies close to the limit should not leave themselves at the mercy of fluctuating exchange rates, but should plan in advance to meet the requirements (if any) which changing designation would impose.

If the entity is a member of a group or has an associated entity, the limits are applied to the whole group. For this purpose, the company is said to have linked or partnership enterprises (see **21.12** and **21.13**).

If the company is in administration or liquidation, the rights of the liquidator are left out of account in determining whether or not the enterprise is an SME (*TIOPA 2010, s 172(4)*).

Linked enterprises

21.12 A linked enterprise is an enterprise which has the right, either directly or indirectly, to control the affairs of another enterprise. Control can be by shareholding, voting rights or contractual rights.

In order to ascertain which is the dominant linked company, the following are taken into consideration:

- majority of the shareholders or members' voting rights in another enterprise;
- the right to appoint or remove a majority of the members of the administrative, management or supervisory body of another enterprise; and
- the right to exercise a dominant influence over another enterprise pursuant to a contract entered into with that enterprise or to a provision in its memorandum or articles of association.

To ascertain whether the SME limits have been exceeded, it is necessary to aggregate the data for the enterprise with all data for any second enterprise that is linked to it, as well as data for any linked enterprises and a proportion of the data for any partnership enterprises of that second enterprise (INTM412100).

Partnership enterprises

21.13 A partnership enterprise is one that holds 25% or more of the capital or voting rights of another company but is not a linked enterprise. If an enterprise has partnership enterprises, a proportion of the data from those enterprises must be aggregated with those of the enterprise when considering the qualifying data. Where enterprises jointly hold rights, these must be aggregated to see if the 25% threshold has been exceeded (INTM412100).

Excluded holdings

21.14 Holdings and investments by the following are ignored for the purposes of aggregation:

- public investment corporations and venture capital companies;
- venture capital companies, individuals or groups of individuals with a regular venture capital investment activity who invest equity capital in unquoted businesses ('business angels'), provided the total investment of those business angels in the same enterprise is less than €1,250,000;
- universities or non-profit research centres;
- institutional investors, including regional development funds; and
- autonomous local authorities with an annual budget of less than €10 million and fewer than 5,000 inhabitants.

The rights of a person in office as a liquidator or administrator are not to be taken into account when considering partnership or linked enterprises (INTM412100).

Appropriate non-discrimination clause

21.15 From 1 April 2004 the exemption from transfer pricing for small and medium-sized companies does not apply where a business has transactions with or provisions that include a related business in a territory with which the UK does not have a double tax treaty with an appropriate non-discrimination article. Such transactions remain subject to the transfer pricing rules.

An appropriate non-discrimination article is one that ensures that the nationals of a contracting state may not be less favourably treated in the other contracting state than nationals of that latter state in the same circumstances (in particular with respect to residence).

HMRC regard the double tax treaties with the following countries (INTM412090) as containing appropriate non-discrimination articles as at 1 April 2004 (or from such later dates as are stated):

Argentina	Luxembourg
Australia	Macedonia
Austria	Malaysia
Azerbaijan	Malta
Bangladesh	Mauritius
Barbados	Mexico
Belarus	Moldova (from April 2010)
Belgium	Mongolia
Bolivia	Morocco
Bosnia-Herzegovina	Myanmar/Burma
Botswana	Namibia
Bulgaria	Netherlands
Canada	New Zealand
Chile (from 21 December 2004)	Nigeria
China	Norway
Croatia	Oman
Cyprus	Pakistan
Czech Republic	Papua New Guinea
Denmark	Philippines
Egypt	Poland
Estonia	Portugal
Falkland Islands	Qatar (from January/April 2011)
Faroe Islands (from April 2009)	Reunion
Fiji	Romania
Finland	Russian Federation
France	Serbia and Montenegro
Gambia	Singapore
Georgia	Slovak Republic
Germany	Slovenia
Ghana	South Africa
Greece	Spain
Guyana	Sri Lanka
Hong Kong (from April 2011)	Sudan

Hungary
Iceland
India
Indonesia
Ireland
Israel
Italy
Ivory Coast
Jamaica
Japan
Jordan
Kazakhstan
Kenya
Korea
Kuwait
Latvia
Lesotho
Libya (from April 2011)
Lithuania
Swaziland
Sweden
Switzerland
Taiwan
Tajikistan
Thailand
Trinidad & Tobago
Tunisia
Turkey
Turkmenistan
Uganda
Ukraine
USA
Uzbekistan
Venezuela
Vietnam
Zambia
Zimbabwe

The Treasury has the power to make regulations adding to the list of territories that qualify even if the double tax treaty in question does not contain an appropriate non-discrimination article, or to exclude territories even if the treaty in question does contain such an article (INTM412070).

Election to remain subject to transfer pricing rules

21.16 There may be occasions where a business wishes to apply transfer pricing rules even though it would qualify for exemption. A business can elect that the exemption will not apply. An election can be made for a specified chargeable period and will cover all transactions or provisions made in that period. It will be irrevocable (*TIOPA 2010, s 167*).

MISCELLANEOUS RULES RELATING TO TRANSFER PRICING

Compensating relief

21.17 Where transactions take place between two UK taxpayers and a transfer pricing adjustment is made in computing the profits of the potentially advantaged taxpayer, the disadvantaged person may generally claim compensating relief if it is within the charge to corporation tax or income tax in respect of profits arising from the relevant activities. This is intended to prevent the same profits from being taxed twice (*TIOPA 2010, s 174*).

However, for amounts arising on or after 25 October 2013 (but not interest accrued before that date) an individual (or other entity within the charge to income tax) is unable to claim a compensating adjustment where the counterparty to the transaction is a company (*TIOPA 2010, s 174A*). Where this restriction applies to interest, the non-arm's length interest that is subject to the transfer pricing adjustment is treated as a dividend paid by the company, and therefore as a qualifying distribution (*TIOPA 2010, s 187A*; for the tax treatment of distributions, see **Chapter 18**).

Where compensating relief applies, the profits and losses of the disadvantaged person are to be calculated for tax purposes as if the arm's length provision had been made or imposed instead of the actual provision (*TIOPA 2010, s 174(2)*). This is without any effect on the value of closing trading stock or work in progress (*TIOPA 2010, s 180*). If the potentially advantaged person is a controlled foreign company (CFC; see **Chapter 20**), this will result in an increased apportionment of profits (*TIOPA 2010, s 179*).

The claimant company is required to indicate on the front of form CT600 if a compensating adjustment has been claimed. The period within which such a claim must be made is two years beginning with the day of the making of the return (*TIOPA 2010, s 177(2)*).

No compensating relief claim can be made if the participatory condition is satisfied as a result of indirect participation and a guarantee has been issued in respect of a security (*TIOPA 2010, s 175*).

Compensating relief can be claimed in respect of a security issued by one company to another. Security is given a wide meaning, and includes:

- interest payable by a company on money advanced without the issue of a security for the advance; or
- other consideration given by a company for the use of money so advanced.

Claims can be made by the disadvantaged or (on their behalf) by the advantaged person, and can be made before the calculation of profits has been made by the advantaged person (*TIOPA 2010, ss 181–183*). The claim must be amended should a relevant notice be issued to the advantaged person (*TIOPA 2010, s 184*). HMRC will give a notice to the disadvantaged person of the particulars of any determination falling upon the advantaged person (*TIOPA 2010, s 185*). No tax is deductible from interest that exceeds the arm's length interest (*TIOPA 2010, s 187*).

Compensating relief may bring about other adjustments, eg to double tax relief. If a disadvantaged person's profits are reduced because of a claim for compensating relief, and this reduces the double tax relief due, appropriate adjustments are to be made, either by credit, by unilateral relief or, accordingly, by way of deduction for foreign tax (*TIOPA 2010, ss 188, 189*).

Balancing payments

21.18 If the disadvantaged party makes a payment or payments to the advantaged party of sums up to the amount of the available compensating adjustment (as distinct from the tax value of that adjustment), this is generally not taken into account in calculating profits or losses of either entity and is not regarded as a distribution for tax purposes (*TIOPA 2010, ss 195, 196*).

Appeal hearings

21.19 Appeals relating to transfer pricing are heard by the First-tier Tribunal (*TIOPA 2010, s 212*).

Capital allowances and chargeable gains

21.20 The transfer pricing rules do not apply to capital allowances (including balancing charges), chargeable gains or allowable capital losses (*TIOPA 2010, ss 213, 214*).

Trading stock and intangible fixed assets

21.21 Where transfer pricing applies in any of the following circumstances, there may also be a further adjustment if necessary to ensure that the full value of stock or intangible fixed assets (as the case may be) is brought into account for tax purposes:

- a disposal or acquisition of trading stock, other than in the normal course of trade, occurring on or after 8 July 2015 unless under an unconditional contractual obligation made before that date (*CTA 2009, s 161(1A)–(1C)*, as inserted by *F(No 2)A 2015, s 37*; see **2.71**);
- a disposal of trading stock on cessation of a trade on or after 8 July 2015 (*CTA 2009, s 162(2A)–(2C)*, as inserted by *F(No 2)A 2015, s 38*; see **2.72**); or
- a transfer of an intangible fixed asset between related parties that are not companies within the same group, occurring on or after 8 July 2015 unless under an unconditional contractual obligation made before that date (*CTA 2009, s 846(1A)–(1C)*, as inserted by *F(No 2)A 2015, s 39*; see **12.30**).

Matching loans and derivatives

21.22 Foreign exchange gains and losses are generally excluded from transfer pricing. However, a corporate group structure may assist with external borrowing facilities for individual group members, and further advantage may be taken of the group structure by one group member taking out a foreign currency loan to match a non-monetary asset acquired by another group member. The loan may then be further lent to the asset-acquiring company interest-free, and the company may enter into a forward exchange contract to cover the forward exchange risk. No transfer pricing adjustment is required for foreign exchange gains or losses on 'matching' loans, but an adjustment is required where a gain or loss from a derivative contract is left out of account because, for transfer pricing purposes, a company's profits or losses are calculated as though the company were not a party to the contract (*CTA 2009, s 694*).

Interest-free loans

21.23 Under the transfer pricing regulations, an interest-free loan between related parties will attract a tax charge on the lender and the possibility of a compensating adjustment for the borrower (INTM440100, INTM413140). For this purpose, the borrowing capacity of a UK company is assessed in isolation without regard to the borrowing capacity of the whole group. This also applies where a guarantee is made by a fellow group company, and any adjustment will be met by a compensating adjustment (INTM413160). The foreign exchange element of these adjustments is ignored for transfer pricing purposes (*CTA 2009, s 694(2)*).

Foreign exchange gains and losses of the company with the debtor loan relationship are excluded from taxable income for corporation tax purposes where they can be matched against gains and losses from an asset. Where an arm's length adjustment is required, only the arm's length element will become chargeable. If the company would not have been able to borrow at all in an arm's length situation, no part of the foreign exchange gain or loss will be recognised for tax purposes.

Foreign exchange gains and losses of the company with the creditor loan relationship are brought into account immediately through the profit and loss account (*CTA 2009, s 328*).

Loans on which interest is charged

21.24 If interest is charged on an intra-group loan, the tax treatment for the company with the debtor loan relationship is exactly the same. This is because the effect of the matching rules is to disregard the foreign exchange gain or loss arising.

As in the case of an interest-free loan, a company with a non-arm's length creditor loan relationship that receives a less than arm's length amount of interest will attract a tax charge on the lender and the possibility of a compensating adjustment for the borrower (see **21.23**).

If the amount of interest receivable on the loan is more than an arm's length amount, the non-arm's length amount of the foreign exchange gain or loss is disregarded. If a group company acts as guarantor, it can make a compensating adjustment claim (*TIOPA 2010, s 192*). Otherwise, the result is that the creditor does not have a symmetrical position, as far as its foreign exchange gains and losses on its lending and borrowing are concerned.

There is no requirement to deduct income tax from interest payments made in excess of an arm's length-amount (*TIOPA 2010, s 187*).

Currency contracts

21.25 In general, the foreign exchange gains and losses on 'matching' currency contracts are also disregarded for transfer pricing purposes (*CTA 2009, s 447*).

However, transfer pricing rules will apply to premium receipts and non-arm's length interest payments. Arrangements to assign, terminate or vary a currency contract may also fall within the transfer pricing conditions. *CTA 2009, s 694* takes effect to tax the amount of the gain that would have been taxed had an arm's length rate applied.

SELF-ASSESSMENT

21.26 There are no supplementary pages to form CT600 in respect of transfer pricing. A company is required to self-assess its corporation tax liability and, unless it is exempt from transfer pricing, it must make computational adjustments to reflect instances where transfer pricing comes into play because transactions recorded in its accounts are not at arm's length.

A small or medium-sized company wishing to make an election to remain subject to transfer pricing rules should do so as part of its computation of profits or losses for the accounting period, within its corporation tax return (see **21.16**).

Incorrect returns will incur penalties (see **Chapter 24**).

Record-keeping

> **Focus**
>
> A company must maintain adequate records to demonstrate that it is complying with transfer pricing guidelines.

21.27 Businesses need to be able to make records and evidence available to HMRC to demonstrate that the results of both cross-border and domestic transactions with related businesses are determined for tax purposes according to transfer pricing rules and comply with the application of the 'arm's length' principle.

HMRC will expect four classes of records and/or evidence to be available:

- primary accounting records;
- tax adjustment records;
- records of transactions with associated businesses; and
- evidence to demonstrate an arm's length result.

Primary accounting records include the daily accounting transaction records, statutory accounting records (see **Chapter 1**) and the value results of the relevant transactions. These are the actual results, that may or may not be arm's length. Tax adjustment records encompass adjustments made by a business, on account of tax rules, in order to move from profits in accounts to taxable profits, including the value of those adjustments and any adjustment of 'actual' results to arm's length results on account of transfer pricing rules. The records of transactions with associated businesses will include records to identify transactions to which the transfer pricing rules apply. Tax adjustment records and records of transactions with associated businesses should come into existence before the tax return is submitted.

Evidence to demonstrate an arm's length result would need to be made available to HMRC in response to a legitimate and reasonable request in relation to a tax return that had been made. Although the business would need to base relevant figures in its tax return on appropriate evidence, the material recording that evidence would not necessarily exist, at the time the return was made, in a form that could be made available to HMRC. Indeed, if HMRC never made a request, the evidence might never exist in such a form (INTM483030).

The records kept will vary according to each country and to each particular company's circumstances. General guidance is given in Chapter V of the OECD Transfer Pricing Guidelines.

If appropriate supporting records are unavailable, the company faces the possibility of penalties for failing to maintain adequate records (see **Chapter 25**).

As regards evidence to support an arm's length policy, HMRC have suggested the following:

- associated businesses should be identified and the form of association;
- description of business activity in which transactions took place;
- details of contractual relationship and understanding between the parties involved;
- description and justification for method used to establish the arm's length result;
- evidence need not be provided where companies do not fall within the UK transfer pricing rules;
- it is useful to provide supporting information regarding the company's general strategy; and
- English translations of documentation should also be given.

In 2006 the European Commission published a Code of Conduct to standardise the documentation that multinationals must provide to tax authorities on their pricing of cross-border intra-group transactions. This recommends that the documentation should consist of two main parts, namely a 'blueprint' master file of the transfer pricing system, together with business information and standardised documents for intra-group transactions (EU Council Resolution 2006/C 176/01). As an alternative to the documents suggested by HMRC in their guidance, HMRC are willing to accept documents prepared in accordance with the EU's Code of Conduct (INTM483030).

Example 21.1—No attempt to justify intra-group pricing

Facts

A company, whose business is to provide services to other group members, charges out its services at cost plus 5%. The 5% accords with a policy in place throughout the group, and is documented in correspondence involving members of the main Board, the Finance Directorate, and the Tax Department; and in a group agreement. It is established in discussion with HMRC that the arm's length range for the services in question is 10%–15%.

Analysis

The company cannot show from its records that it even considered whether its own 5% rate complied with the arm's length principle. HMRC would view any tax lost as a result of the undercharge as having been lost through negligence, and would wish to consider a penalty.

Example 21.2—Inadequate attempt to justify intra-group pricing

Facts

As Example 21.1, except that in the correspondence it is asserted several times that the group's policy is to comply with the arm's length standard, and that 5% is an arm's length price.

Analysis

The company is unable to bring forward any convincing evidence in support of its assertions, while HMRC are able to show that an arm's length price would be in the 10%–15% range. HMRC would wish to consider a penalty.

Example 21.3—Reasonable attempt to justify intra-group pricing

Facts

As Example 21.1, except that the company charges out at cost plus 8%, and can show that, at the time the rate was set, it had run a check of available industry data, and had found what it considered to be a comparable uncontrolled price supporting the 8% rate. In discussion with HMRC, the company agrees that the comparison it made was flawed, and that the weight of evidence points towards a price in the 10%–15% range.

Analysis

HMRC accept that the company had made an honest and reasonable attempt to comply with the arm's length principle. There is an adjustment but no penalty.

Example 21.4—Well-researched attempt to justify intra-group pricing

Facts

A company, whose business is to provide services to other group members, charges at cost plus 5%. As in Example 21.1, 5% accords with a policy in place throughout the group, and is documented in correspondence and a group agreement. The company includes an adjustment in its computation, bringing the effective rate of charge-out up to 8%. It did so after searching available industry data for possible comparable uncontrolled prices, this search being made at the time when the tax computation was being prepared. As in Example 21.3, the company sees this information as supporting its opinion that 8% accorded with the arm's length principle, but it later concedes that the price should have been in the 10%–15% range.

Analysis

HMRC accept that the company had made an honest and reasonable attempt to comply with the arm's length principle, and there is an adjustment but no penalty.

Enquiries

21.28 An enquiry would follow normal HMRC enquiry procedures (see INTM483000 onwards). In particular, HMRC would seek evidence to support the arm's length policy.

Additional guidance published by HMRC on 10 July 2008 ('Guidelines for the conduct of transfer pricing enquiries') explained that cases are normally to be settled within 18 months, with only the most complex cases taking 36 months. The same guidance is applied to determining the attribution of a profit to a permanent establishment (see **Chapter 20**) and to some thin capitalisation cases.

All enquiries commence with a risk assessment, which is based on the quantum risk, the behaviour risk and the transaction risk of the matters that are being enquired into. Following the risk assessment, HMRC may decide to investigate further and develop a business case, whereupon a thorough enquiry into the nature of the transactions, their treatment and the supporting information will take place. HMRC will specify the transactions that are subject to the enquiry.

Example 21.5—Transfer pricing enquiry

Facts

A UK company is engaged to provide research and development (R&D) activities on behalf of its overseas affiliate. The group employs a cost-plus pricing method, under which the overseas affiliate pays the UK company a sum consisting of the UK company's costs plus a mark-up of 10%. This is characterised in the UK company's transfer pricing documentation as a 'contract research arrangement'.

Analysis

HMRC's criteria and the areas for enquiry are as follows:

Criterion	*Area of enquiry*
1. The transactions subject to the enquiry.	The provision of research and development facilities by the UK company to the overseas affiliate.
2. The aspect(s) of the transaction and its pricing to be tested	HMRC will test whether cost-plus is an appropriate method to set the pricing between the UK company and its overseas affiliate.
3. The criteria by which the transaction is to be tested	HMRC will consider whether the actual functions carried out by the UK company are consistent with their respective characterisations as low-risk research provider and research contractor.
4. What HMRC need to understand in order to achieve this.	• How decisions are made concerning the identification and prioritisation of research projects, who makes these decisions and where the people making them are located. • The process for reviewing and assessing R&D projects. Who is involved in this and where are they located. • The ownership of any value, including the intellectual property, arising from the R&D. • Whether the UK company uses the intellectual property it created in its wider range.

COUNTRY-BY-COUNTRY REPORTING

21.29 From 26 March 2015, HM Treasury have the power to make regulations requiring country-by-country reporting by multinational groups with parent companies in the UK. This reflects recommendations coming out of Action 13 of the OECD base erosion and profit shifting (BEPS) project (see **21.2**) and will give HMRC information about multinational companies' global activities, profits and taxes, helping them to better assess international tax avoidance risks. It is intended that the information reported will be shared with other relevant tax jurisdictions so that they too can identify when multinationals have engaged in BEPS activity (*FA 2015, s 122*).

It is expected that multinationals will be required to make an annual country-by-country report to HMRC showing, for each tax jurisdiction in which they do business:

- the amount of revenue, profit before income tax, and income tax paid and accrued; and

- their total employment, capital, retained earnings and tangible assets.

They will also have to identify each entity within the group doing business in a particular tax jurisdiction and provide a broad indication of the business activities of each.

ADVANCE PRICING AGREEMENTS

> **Focus**
>
> An advance pricing agreement may be a practical solution for dealing with HMRC.

21.30 A company with complex affairs can enter into an advance pricing agreement (APA) with HMRC. An APA is a written agreement made between HMRC and the company. It applies to the company, and may extend to any or all of its associates.

Among the matters which may be covered by an APA, as a consequence of an application by a company (A), are (*TIOPA 2010, s 218*):

- the attribution of income to a permanent establishment through which A has been carrying on a trade in the UK or is proposing to carry on a trade in the UK;
- the attribution of income to any permanent establishment of A's, wherever situated, through which A has been carrying on, or is proposing to carry on, any business;
- the extent to which income that has arisen or may arise to A is to be taken for any purpose to be income arising in a country or territory outside the UK;
- the treatment for tax purposes of any provision made or imposed, whether before or after the date of the agreement, as between A and any associate of A's; and
- the treatment for tax purposes of any provision made or imposed, whether before or after the date of the agreement, as between an oil-related ring-fence trade carried on by A and any other activities carried on by A.

Two persons are associates in relation to a provision made or imposed as between them if, at the time of the making or imposition of the provision, one of them is directly or indirectly participating in the management, control or capital of the other, or the same person or persons is or are directly or indirectly participating in the management, control or capital of each of the two persons (*TIOPA 2010, s 219*).

The income identified in the APA is taxable on all parties and non-parties according to the terms of the APA regardless of other rules and practices, but an APA cannot exclude reference to other statutory provisions (*TIOPA 2010, ss 220, 222*).

An APA will have no effect if (*TIOPA 2010, s 221*):

- an HMRC officer has revoked the APA according to the APA terms;
- there has been a failure by a party to the APA to comply with a 'significant' provision; or
- a 'key condition' has not been met or is no longer met.

For this purpose, a provision is 'significant' if, under the terms of the APA, compliance with that provision is a condition of the APA's having effect. Any other condition of the APA's having effect is a 'key condition'.

For HMRC guidance on APAs, see Statement of Practice 2 (2010) at tinyurl.com/objk97k; also INTM422000 onwards.

Application for agreement

21.31 A valid application for agreement must include the following (*TIOPA 2010, s 223*):

- a request for HMRC's clarification of the extent of the company's taxable income when trading in the UK as a foreign concern, or vice versa;
- the company's understanding of the effect, in the absence of an APA, of the provisions in relation to which clarification is sought;
- the issues on which the company seeks clarification in relation to these provisions; and
- a proposal of how the matters should be resolved.

The APA can relate to a chargeable period beginning or ending before the agreement is made but cannot cover a provision relating to chargeable periods ending before 27 July 1999 (*TIOPA 2010, s 224*). Double tax treaties take priority over APAs (*TIOPA 2010, s 229*). The terms of the APA will require a party to periodically provide HMRC with reports and other information. In addition, the terms of the APA may permit an HMRC officer to request such information (*TIOPA 2010, s 228*).

An APA may provide for modification or revocation of the APA by HMRC, and such modification or revocation may be (but need not be) retroactive (*TIOPA 2010, s 225*).

If false or misleading information was provided to HMRC fraudulently or negligently by the applicant at any time before the APA was entered into,

HMRC may notify the company that the APA is nullified, in which case it is treated as never made (*TIOPA 2010, s 226*). A maximum penalty of £10,000 can be imposed on the transgressor (*TIOPA 2010, s 227*).

Sample advance pricing agreement

21.32 HMRC recommend that agreements entered into are bilateral rather than unilateral (subject to exceptions set out below). A bilateral agreement will confirm how the issues are to be resolved, both in the UK and in the other country, whereas a unilateral agreement only deals with the UK side of affairs.

HMRC comment that businesses operating in several countries may wish to seek APAs that involve all the relevant administrations affected by the transfer pricing issues, and the term 'multilateral APA' has been used to describe such agreements, but there is no discrete mechanism for reaching multilateral agreements.

APA applications should be bilateral rather than unilateral, except where:

- applicants are able to persuade HMRC that the extension to a bilateral APA would unnecessarily complicate and delay the process;
- the other party to the transaction is resident in a jurisdiction with which HMRC have no treaty, or where HMRC are aware that the treaty partner has no APA process; or
- there is considered to be little extra to be gained by seeking a bilateral agreement, for example where the UK is at the hub of arrangements with associated enterprises in many different countries and where the trade flows involved with any one particular country are relatively modest in scale.

HMRC's guidance in Statement of Practice 2 (2010) at tinyurl.com/objk97k gives practical advice on drawing up an APA. The wording of a sample APA is given by HMRC (see INTM422150) as follows:

'ADVANCE PRICING AGREEMENT

Between

TAXPAYER

And

H.M. REVENUE AND CUSTOMS

This Advance Pricing Agreement ("APA") is made between **Taxpayer**, and **HM Revenue and Customs** acting through Business International Directorate ("HMRC")

The Taxpayer and HMRC (collectively "The Parties") wish to enter into an APA, and to include in it an appropriate Transfer Pricing Methodology ("TPM") to be applied to the transactions between the Taxpayer and the related party (or parties) identified below.

(This agreement replicates under UK statute on Advance Pricing Agreements the terms of a bilateral/multilateral agreement reached under the Mutual Agreement Procedure Article of the relevant Tax Treaty covering the same transactions between HMRC and (fisc(s))

1. Identifying Information

Taxpayer (typically – a company registered in (country), under registration number XXXXXXXX, Resident in (country), having a tax reference YYYYY YYYYY, (with a Permanent Establishment in (country)) and a Registered Office at (address) (or place of business at (address))

Related Party (similar information as for the taxpayer above – there may be a number of related parties)

Set out relationship between Taxpayer and Related Party – eg one a subsidiary of the other or both companies members of the multi-national group Z headquartered in (country)

2. Covered Transactions

The transaction(s) covered by this APA (the "Covered Transactions") comprise (succinct explanation of all Covered Transactions)

3. Legal Effect

This APA is made pursuant to and for the purposes of S 218 Taxation (International and Other Provisions) Act 2010 ("TIOPA 2010") and binds the Parties, for the term of this APA, to determine questions relating to the transfer pricing (or branch or PE attribution) matters covered by the APA in accordance with its terms.

If the Taxpayer complies with the terms and conditions of this APA then HMRC will not contest the application of the TPM (as defined in Appendix A) to the Covered Transactions and will not make or propose any reallocation or adjustment that would be necessary in order for effect to be given to the provisions of Part 4 TIOPA 2010 with respect to the Taxpayer concerning the transfer prices for the APA term (this will have to be amended or extended if we are/are also looking at a PE issue….and also refer to Rollback years if relevant).

If, for any year during the APA term, the Taxpayer does not comply with the terms and conditions of this APA, or the Critical Assumptions (as defined in Clause 6 below) cease to be valid, HMRC may (subject to clause 9 below) revoke this APA and S.221 TIOPA 2010 shall apply.

(The terms and conditions of this APA may also be modified or amended upon the agreement of the Parties, subject also to the terms of any bilateral/multilateral agreement)

4. Term

Term of APA.

(Rollback period if relevant)

5. Financial Statements and APA Records

(typically – in accordance with S 228 TIOPA 2010 – the taxpayer is required to provide, in addition to Corporation Tax Returns and Audited Financial Statements: Submission of APA information set out by Clause 6 and 7 below.

Compliance with this will constitute compliance with the record maintenance provisions of Section 12B Taxes Management Act 1970 and paragraph 21, Schedule 18 Finance Act 1998 with respect to the Covered Transactions during the APA term.)

6. Critical Assumptions

(with respect to the Covered Transactions are set out in Appendix B)

7. Annual Reports

(unless this requirement can be very simply put are typically set out in a separate Appendix C. Note that some bilateral or multilateral agreements may require a standard report to be sent to all involved tax Administrations and in that case Appendix C may have to cover the same ground and also any specific information – e.g. (say) conversion into UK currency or UK accounts standards so that the HMRC tax team can readily track the numbers through the relevant UK tax computations.)

8. Disclosure

This APA and the information, data and documents related to this APA, are subject to the same rules of confidentiality as any other taxpayer's information provided to HMRC, and any unauthorised disclosure of information by HMRC will be a breach of those rules.

9. Revocation

HMRC will not revoke this APA unless and until it has explained in detail to the Taxpayer why and from when it is considered the taxpayer is in breach of the terms and conditions of this APA and the taxpayer has been given a reasonable opportunity to rectify any breach.

(Note – this clause may need to be aligned with any relevant requirements in a bilateral or multilateral agreement. In a multilateral for instance the possibility of the taxpayer no longer being felt to satisfy the terms of the APA in one territory only may be considered. Or, similarly, the consequences for the agreement between the other Administrations of there no longer being Covered Transactions in one territory may be tackled. HMRC may also want to emphasise that it will be working from the standpoint of seeking the continuance of the APA in the event of any such difficulty.)

10. Treatment of Allocations under the TPM

(typically – this may cover the treatment of ongoing or end-of-year adjustments which may be required under the TRM to align the results on Covered Transaction business with the APA terms.

11. Professional Fees

(as relevant – deductibility)

12. Tax Laws

(typically – general statement along the lines of – notwithstanding any statement in this APA agreement, the taxpayer remains subject to all applicable taxation laws not directly affected by this APA. The Taxpayer is entitled to any benefits or relief otherwise available under all such laws).

13. Governing Law and Effective Date

(typically – laws of England and effective from the later date below)

Signatories

Responsible Officer or Director on behalf of Taxpayer, and dated.

Except in Oil cases (when it will usually be signed by the Competent Authority at Large Business Service Oil and Gas), usually Deputy Director responsible for APA Programme, or APA Co-ordinator, BID, HMRC, and dated.

Notes

Appendix A (the TPM) – see paragraph 3 – is the "core" of the APA. This section may need to be detailed, but it will always be highly tailored to the taxpayer's particular circumstances. HMRC will try and ensure where there is a bilateral or multilateral agreement that Appendix A is expressed in wording which is identical or near-identical with the wording of the transfer pricing methodology in that agreement. If that is not possible, Appendix A will be operated as if it were expressed in identical terms to the methodology set out in the bilateral or multilateral agreement.

Appendix B (Critical Assumptions) – see paragraph 6 – will generally have a clause to the effect that there should be no major commercial changes governing the Covered Transactions. In volatile, dynamic or cyclical businesses this may need some elaboration. Similarly, in cases involving trading or managing portfolios of Financial Products, consideration may be needed at the time of negotiating the agreement as to how it will be clear that "new generation" Products are or are not covered by the APA. In these kinds of situations there will generally be a requirement for relevant information to be automatically reported in Annual Reports, see below. In practice, other Critical Assumptions that have on occasion been agreed with taxpayers have included clauses relating to changes of control, the possibility that acquisitions might impact upon the APA, to profit share and competition issues, and those involving Regulation, or arising from Government Policy or Laws.

Appendix C (Annual Reports) – see paragraph 7. Ideally Annual Reports will include, in addition to any required or mandated information on the Covered Transactions (see, for instance, comment above) a one or two sheet or spreadsheet "proof" document demonstrating that all the conditions of the APA have been met for the Covered Transactions. Where it is agreed that such a "proof" will be provided, its format should be set out in the APA agreement.'

ADVANCE THIN CAPITALISATION AGREEMENTS

21.33 Although the APA is used as the basis for advance thin capitalisation agreements (ATCAs), these cases have their own distinctive features and are therefore negotiated under an entirely separate process. Accordingly, Statement of Practice 2 (2010) and the other HMRC guidance on APAs are of no consequence in relation to ATCAs.

HMRC have published separate detailed guidance about their practice in entering into ATCAs, in Statement of Practice 1 (2012) at tinyurl.com/oao39bt; see also INTM512000 onwards.

TAX ARBITRAGE

21.34 Tax arbitrage is the practice of taking advantage of the differing tax rates or tax rules of different jurisdictions to achieve an overall reduction in tax. Multinational groups can take advantage of the varying tax rates and regimes across the world, and this has been the focus of much of the recent controversy about unacceptable tax avoidance techniques used by large businesses.

There are complex tax arbitrage provisions within *TIOPA 2010, Pt 6* which seek to remove any irregularity in a particular transaction. They can only be activated by a notice from HMRC. There are two types of notice – a deduction notice and a receipt notice – that deal with deduction schemes and receipt schemes respectively.

Deduction schemes

21.35 The main purpose of a deduction scheme is to achieve a UK tax advantage by procuring a greater deduction or set off than would otherwise be possible (*TIOPA 2010, s 233*). If an HMRC officer considers that there are reasonable grounds, and that the transaction is within the deduction scheme conditions, he may issue the company with a deduction notice setting out details of the transaction and the accounting period concerned (*TIOPA 2010, ss 232, 235*).

It is one of the deduction scheme conditions that the amount of the UK tax advantage is more than minimal (*TIOPA 2010, s 233(5)*). For this purpose, 'minimal' is not defined by statute, but HMRC will normally consider the tax advantage arising from a scheme to be minimal if the sum of all the gross UK tax deductions arising from it is less than £50,000 (INTM595080).

A scheme achieves a UK tax advantage for a company if, in consequence of the scheme, the company is in a position to obtain, or has obtained (*TIOPA 2010, s 234*):

- a relief or increased relief from corporation tax;
- a repayment or increased repayment of corporation tax, or
- the avoidance or reduction of a charge to corporation tax.

There are seven types of deduction scheme:

- schemes involving hybrid entities (*TIOPA 2010, s 236*);
- instruments of alterable character (*TIOPA 2010, s 237*);
- shares subject to conversion (*TIOPA 2010, s 238*);
- securities subject to conversion (*TIOPA 2010, s 239*);
- debt instruments treated as equity (*TIOPA 2010, s 240*);
- schemes including issue of shares not conferring qualifying beneficial entitlement (*TIOPA 2010, s 241*); and
- schemes including transfer of rights under a security (*TIOPA 2010, s 242*).

Receipt of a deduction notice will require the company to recalculate its corporation tax liability (*TIOPA 2010, s 243*).

Receipt schemes

21.36 The main purpose of a receipt scheme is to achieve a UK tax advantage by procuring that an amount representing a contribution to capital, received by a UK resident company in a non-taxable form, provides a tax deduction in the UK or elsewhere for the payer (*TIOPA 2010, s 250*). If an HMRC officer considers that there are reasonable grounds, and that a qualifying payment is within the receipt scheme conditions, he may issue the company, providing it is UK resident, with a receipt notice setting out details of the payment and the accounting period concerned (*TIOPA 2010, ss 249, 252*).

Receipt of a receipt notice will require the company to recalculate its corporation tax liability as if an appropriate part of the qualifying payment is chargeable to corporation tax (*TIOPA 2010, s 254*).

Hybrid and other tax mismatches

21.37 The current rules on tax arbitrage were replaced with a new regime on anti-hybrids under *TIOPA 2010, Part 6A* as introduced by *FA 2016, s 76* and *Sch 10*. The new rules target tax mismatches arising from hybrid financial instruments, hybrid entities, and from arrangements involving permanent establishments. The rules provide for the counteraction of tax advantages arising, either where one person obtains a tax deduction in respect of an amount that is not taxable on the recipient or the recipient is under-taxed (referred to as 'a deduction/non-inclusion mismatch', or where the same amount is deductible twice, either for different persons or from a person's income for more than one tax purpose ('a double-deduction mismatch'). Specifically, the new legislation is concerned with payments or quasi-payments under or in connection with financial instruments or repos, stock lending arrangements or other transfers of financial instruments, hybrid entities, companies with permanent establishments or dual-resident companies.

MUTUAL AGREEMENT PROCEDURE AND ARBITRATION

21.38 The UK has a vast double tax treaty network and operates a mutual agreement procedure and arbitration process for resolving transfer pricing disputes. Details of the approach used are set out in Statement of Practice 1 (2011) at tinyurl.com/pj4yu4r.

Chapter 22

Self-assessment

SIGNPOSTS

- Introduction to company tax returns and dealing with HMRC (see **22.1–22.3**).
- Corporation tax record-keeping requirements (including accounting procedures, CT600, filing dates and online filing) (see **22.4–22.14**).
- Routine tax enquiries by HMRC (including time limits for large and medium-sized companies, special time limits for small companies, the course of enquiries and corporation tax amendment procedures) (see **22.15–22.21**).
- The investigation of tax fraud and the 'contractual disclosure facility' (see **22.22**).
- Appeals and related procedures (including HMRC independent reviews and tribunal procedures) (see **22.23–22.30**).
- Resolving tax disputes – alternative dispute resolution and HMRC's litigation and settlement strategy (see **22.31–22.32**).

INTRODUCTION

Focus

Under self-assessment a company is responsible for computing and reporting its corporation tax liabilities, and the penalties for failing to do so correctly can be severe.

22.1 A company is required to report its liability to corporation tax to HMRC through the self-assessment procedures. The company must calculate its own self-assessment (*FA 1998, Sch 18, para 7*).

The main body of legislation relating to corporation tax self-assessment is contained in *FA 1998, s 117, Schs 18–19*. Changes and amendments have been made by subsequent *Finance Acts*. In theory, the basic premise of self-assessment is that, if the company has made adequate disclosure and HMRC have not initiated an enquiry into a return, the company's tax position will normally be regarded as finalised 12 months after the filing date for the return. In practice, the situation is rarely as clear as this because of the rules regarding disclosure and the ability of HMRC to raise discovery assessments (see **25.22**). Penalties for an incorrect return can be severe (see **Chapter 24**), and HMRC are empowered to carry out compliance checks to ensure that the self-assessment rules are adhered to (see **Chapter 25**).

Companies are required to self-assess their tax liabilities, including any liability on loans, advances or benefits to participators in close companies (see **Chapter 10**), and any tax relating to controlled foreign companies (see **Chapter 20**). A company is also required to self-assess any tax liability under transfer pricing (see **Chapter 21**) in accordance with the arm's length principle.

HMRC publish guidance, including much of the material contained in their internal manuals for HMRC personnel (see tinyurl.com/lcyjhnh). Other HMRC guidance may be found at www.gov.uk/government/organisations/hm-revenue-customs. Some of their published guidance can be incomplete, out of date or simply misleading. Those relying on HMRC guidance published online should print or electronically save a copy of the website pages on which they rely, as evidence in the event of a dispute with HMRC.

COMPANY TAX RETURN

22.2 If a company is chargeable to corporation tax for an accounting period, it is required to give notice to HMRC, within 12 months of the end of the accounting period concerned, that it is so liable. If the company fails to do so, it will incur a penalty (*FA 1998, Sch 18, para 2*).

HMRC may, by notice, require a company to deliver a company tax return to the issuing officer, together with any information and reports relevant to the tax liability (*FA 1998, Sch 18, para 3(1)*). Any notice served by HMRC on the company should be served on the 'proper officer', that is the company secretary or the person acting as the company secretary (*TMA 1970, s 108(1), (3)*).

A company must prepare and submit its company tax return in the prescribed format and within the statutory time limits. Online filing is mandatory for almost all companies. A company tax return is not 'delivered' to HMRC unless it is accompanied by 'all the information, accounts, statements and reports required' (*FA 1998, Sch 18, para 4*). Incomplete returns are rejected.

A complete company tax return should include:

- a completed form CT600;
- any appropriate supplementary pages to the CT600;

- financial statements appropriate to the type of company (if registered at Companies House, the statutory accounts required under the *Companies Acts*); and
- a corporation tax computation showing how the figures on the CT600 have been derived from the accounts.

A company tax return includes a declaration by the person making the return that, to the best of their knowledge and belief, the return is correct and complete (*FA 1998, Sch 18, para 3(3)*). Where a liquidator has been appointed, responsibility lies with the liquidator or such other person who has express, implied or apparent authority to act for this purpose (*TMA 1970, s 108(1)*). The treasurer or person acting as treasurer is responsible in the case of an unincorporated association.

The accurate completion of the company tax return is a prime management responsibility. HMRC publish a number of 'toolkits' which provide guidance (primarily to tax agents) on areas of error that they frequently see in tax returns and set out the steps that can be taken to reduce those errors, and some of these relate to issues affecting companies. For example, between March and September 2015 they published updated versions of their toolkits on chargeable gains for companies, company losses, directors' loan accounts, and capital allowances on plant and machinery, business profits, the distinction between capital and revenue, and the now superseded small profits rate and marginal relief. See tinyurl.com/63vn6ts.

The government's online Corporation Tax service at www.gov.uk/file-your-company-accounts-and-tax-return is designed to facilitate joint HMRC and Companies House filing by private limited companies with relatively straightforward financial and tax affairs (see **22.12**).

CONTACTING HMRC

22.3 A company or an organisation must inform HMRC within three months in writing when it comes within the charge to corporation tax (*FA 2004, s 55*). By virtue of the *Corporation Tax (Notice of Coming within Charge – Information) Regulations 2004, SI 2004/2502*, the information required is as follows:

- the company's name and registered number;
- the address of the company's registered office;
- the address of the company's principal place of business;
- the nature of the business being carried on by the company;
- the date to which the company intends to prepare accounts;
- the full name and home address of each of the directors of the company;

- if the company has taken over any business, including any trade, profession or vocation formerly carried out by another:
  - the name and address of that former business; and
  - the name and address of the person from whom that business was acquired;
- the name and registered office of the parent company (if any); and
- if the company is required to register for PAYE, the date from which that obligation arose.

In practice, Companies House will inform HMRC of the formation of a new company, and HMRC then ask the company to submit the above information online. This procedure replaces form CT41G, which has been discontinued, but the information can still be provided to HMRC by letter instead.

If HMRC do not contact the company for this information, it is still the company's responsibility to supply it. Failure to notify will result in a penalty. Penalties cannot be imposed after the failure is rectified (*TMA 1970, s 98(3)*; see **Chapter 24** for details of the penalty provisions).

If a new company fails to inform HMRC to the contrary, HMRC will assume that the first accounting period runs for 12 months from the date of incorporation.

HMRC will maintain the company's details on their database. HMRC use the database to issue returns and other communications to corporate taxpayers, and it is therefore important to ensure that HMRC are informed of any changes in the company's accounting period or registered office address.

Companies House must be notified of changes to the registered name and/or the registered office address, and notifications can be made to them either by post or online. As soon as Companies House have updated their records, they will advise HMRC about the change automatically. There is no requirement to inform HMRC separately.

Except for companies dealt with by specialist teams such as the Large Business Service, HMRC's contact details for corporation tax enquiries can be found at tinyurl.com/oatwcvs.

HMRC publish their contact details for general advice and specialist areas of tax, covering a wide range of topics (see **17.48**).

DUTY TO KEEP AND PRESERVE RECORDS

Focus

Accurate and timely record-keeping by the company is essential, not only to comply with legal requirements but also to ensure that any questions or challenges raised by HMRC can be answered satisfactorily.

22.4 A company is required to keep and preserve records, together with supporting documents, to enable it to deliver a complete and correct corporation tax return for each relevant accounting period.

If a company complies with *CA 2006, ss 386* and *387*, it will maintain sufficient records to prepare its statutory accounts. Good accounting records should, in most cases, form good records for corporation tax purposes. Under self-assessment a company is specifically required to keep records of (*FA 1998, Sch 18, para 21(5)*):

> '(a) all receipts and expenses in the course of a company's activities and the matters in respect of which they arise, and
>
> (b) in the case of a trade involving dealing in goods, all sales and purchases made in the course of the trade.'

The type of records retained will vary according to the industry, but it is important to bear in mind that information must be available on how a matter arises. HMRC are often enabled by tax legislation to look behind a transaction, and it can be important to demonstrate how a business decision or transaction was actioned at the time. When self-assessment was first introduced, HMRC commented that a company meeting the requirements of what is now *CA 2006, ss 386* and *387*, would have satisfied its duty to keep and preserve records for corporation tax self-assessment (*Revenue Tax Bulletin 37*, October 1998, p 587 see tinyurl.com/ir-tax-bulletin-37 and tinyurl.com/ir-tax-bulletin-pdf-37 (for pdf version)). Although that was some time ago, the article is still current.

In recent years, scrutiny of supporting vouchers by professionals acting for the company may have reduced as a result of risk-based audit methodologies and audit exemptions. The onus for maintaining the supporting vouchers rests with the company, and the supporting documents required are identified as 'accounts, books, deeds, contracts, vouchers and receipts' (*FA 1998, Sch 18, para 21(6)*). These, or the information they contain, may be preserved in any form and by any means, subject to any exceptions made by HMRC in writing (*FA 1998, Sch 18, para 22(1)*). However, companies are required to preserve certain records (as distinct from the information they contain) in any form and by any means, and these are records relating to distributions and tax credits, gross and net interest payments, Construction Industry Scheme tax deductions and foreign tax payments (*FA 1998, Sch 18, para 22(3)*).

In general, records must be kept for six years from the end of the relevant accounting period (*FA 1998, Sch 18, para 21*). HMRC may reduce this period below the six-year time limit (*FA 1998, Sch 18, para 21(2A)(b)*). Records should be kept longer if:

- a return is under enquiry more than six years after the end of the accounting period;
- the company makes its return late; or

- the records relate to a continuing transaction that may affect current years.

Additional documentary evidence may be required to support arm's length dealings under transfer pricing legislation. The records required to enable a company to deliver a correct and complete return in this instance go beyond the *Companies Act* requirements. This is discussed in **21.27**.

Penalties can be charged for failing to provide information to support a company tax return (see **25.21**).

ACCOUNTING PERIODS

> **Focus**
>
> A company prepares its financial statements for each 'period of account' but must self-assess its corporation tax for each 'accounting period'. The distinction between these expressions is important.

22.5 Under *CA 2006*, directors of UK companies are required to prepare and file statutory accounts for every accounting reference period, which is usually a 12-month period (*CA 2006, s 441*). In most cases the corporation tax accounting period will be the same as the accounting reference period. Usually, from three to seven weeks after the end of the expected accounting period, HMRC will send the company a form CT603 'Notice to deliver a company tax return'. The notice will specify a 12-month period for which HMRC consider that a return is due (*FA 1998, Sch 18, para 5(1)*). However, for corporation tax purposes there are specific points at which an accounting period will begin or end.

A corporation tax accounting period begins when a company first comes within the scope of corporation tax by acquiring a source of income or becoming UK resident (*CTA 2009, s 9*).

An accounting period will generally last for 12 months and will usually coincide with the period for which the company draws up accounts. If the statutory period of account exceeds 12 months, it is divided for corporation tax purposes into one or more accounting periods of 12 months, with a further accounting period covering the remainder of the period of account (*CTA 2009, s 10*).

An accounting period ends on the earliest of the following events (*CTA 2009, ss 8–12*):

- 12 months from the beginning of the accounting period;
- the date on which the company draws up its accounts;
- if there is a period for which the company does not prepare accounts, the end of that period;

- the company starting or ceasing to trade;
- if the company carries on only one trade, the date on which it begins or ceases to be within the charge to corporation tax in respect of that trade;
- if the company carries on more than one trade, the date on which it begins or ceases to be within the charge to corporation tax in respect of all those trades;
- the company becoming or ceasing to be UK resident;
- the company entering or ceasing to be in administration;
- the company going into liquidation or commencing winding up; or
- after a company commences winding up, 12 months from the beginning of the accounting period or (if earlier) the date on which the winding up is completed.

Each such event will require the preparation of a separate company tax return.

Example 22.1—Commencement of trading

Facts

A Ltd was incorporated on 1 January 2018. It notifies HMRC and commences trading on 1 April 2018. Form CT603 is issued on 1 April 2019. The company prepares accounts for the three months to 31 March 2018, the 12 months to 31 March 2019, and then to 31 March annually thereafter.

Analysis

A Ltd is required to prepare company tax returns from 1 January 2018 to 31 March 2018 and from 1 April 2018 to 31 March 2019. The latest filing date for the 31 March 2018 return will be 30 June 2019, being three months after receipt of form CT603. The latest filing date for the 31 March 2019 return will be 31 March 2020, being 12 months after the year end (see **22.10**).

Example 22.2—Change in accounting date

Facts

B Ltd has always prepared accounts to 30 September each year. In January 2018 it notifies Companies House that it has changed its accounting reference date to 31 December, and in due course it prepares accounts for the 15 months to 31 December 2018.

Analysis

B Ltd is required to prepare company tax returns from 1 October 2017 to 30 September 2018, and from 1 October 2018 to 31 December 2018. The latest filing date for both returns is 31 December 2019, being 12 months after the end of the period of account (see **22.10**).

Apportionment of profits or losses: normal basis

22.6 A period of account of more than 12 months may result in profits or losses being apportioned to individual accounting periods. As a general rule, these should be apportioned on a time basis (*CTA 2010, s 1172*); this is generally done according to the number of days in each accounting period, but might equally well be done according to the number of weeks or months. Chargeable gains are allocated to the period in which they occur (*TCGA 1992, s 8(3)*).

Example 22.3—Apportionment of profits to accounting periods

Facts

A company prepares its statutory accounts for 1 January 2018 to 31 March 2019, a period of 15 months (ie 456 days). The company is trading throughout the whole period. Its total profits chargeable to corporation tax amount to £500,000 and include no chargeable gains.

Analysis

	Days
The company's corporation tax accounting periods are:	
First accounting period (12 months) from 1 January 2018 to 31 December 2018	365
Second accounting period (balance) from 1 January 2019 to 31 March 2019	91

The total profit is apportioned to accounting periods as follows:

	£
First accounting period profit is (£500,000 ÷ 456) × 365	400,219
Second accounting period profit is (£500,000 ÷ 456) × 91	99,781

Apportionment of profits or losses: special basis

22.7 Exceptionally, profits or losses of a long period of account may be attributed to accounting periods by reference to the actual transactions which took place in each accounting period, where this gives a more accurate result than time apportionment. This occurred in the case of *Marshall Hus & Partners Ltd v Bolton* [1981] STC 18, where a property company had allowed its affairs to fall behind and then prepared one set of accounts to cover a period of more than five years. The company proposed to apportion its profits to the six corporation tax accounting periods on a time basis, but the Inland Revenue objected because they had discovered that the first five accounting periods resulted in profits and the last in a substantial loss. The taxation legislation restricts the carry-back of loss relief against profits of earlier periods (see **4.16**). The High Court upheld the Inland Revenue's approach, commenting that it was not obligatory to time apportion profits where a 'more accurate and a fairer estimate of profit or loss' of the chargeable periods was available.

HMRC consider that transactions can only be matched with accounting periods in this way where there are few transactions and these are easily identifiable (HMRC Company Taxation Manual at CTM01405).

FORM CT600

> **Focus**
>
> HMRC's corporation tax return form CT600 changed for accounting periods starting on or after 1 April 2015, and revised guidance notes are available.

22.8 The company tax return form (CT600 (2008) Version 2) applies for accounting periods starting before 1 April 2015; this version, together with related supplementary pages and HMRC's guidance notes, can be found at tinyurl.com/patpr2o.

The company tax return form (CT600 (2015) Version 3) applies for accounting periods starting on or after 1 April 2015; this version and the relevant supplementary pages and guidance notes can be found at tinyurl.com/klek43s.

If relevant to the company's activities, the following supplementary pages must also be submitted together with the main return.

Supplementary pages

22.9 The following is a list of the supplementary pages that may have to accompany the CT600 (Version 2) for accounting periods starting before 1 April 2015:

CT600A	Loans to Participators by Close Companies	See **Chapter 10**
CT600B	Controlled Foreign Companies (and Bank Levy)	See **Chapter 20**
CT600C	Group and Consortium	See **Chapter 5**
CT600D	Insurance	
CT600E	Charities and Community Amateur Sports Clubs (CASCs)	See **Chapter 2**
CT600F	Tonnage Tax	
CT600G	Corporate Venturing Scheme	
CT600H	Cross-Border Royalties	See **Chapter 23**
CT600I	Supplementary charge in respect of ring fence trades	
CT600J	Disclosure of tax avoidance schemes	See **Chapter 25**

The following is a list of the supplementary pages that may have to accompany the CT600 (Version 3) for accounting periods starting on or after 1 April 2015:

CT600A	Close company loans and arrangements to confer benefits on participators	See **Chapter 10**
CT600B	Controlled foreign companies and foreign permanent establishment exemptions	See **Chapter 20**
CT600C	Group and consortium relief	See **Chapter 5**
CT600D	Insurance	
CT600E	Charities and Community Amateur Sports Clubs (CASCs)	See **Chapter 2**
CT600F	Tonnage Tax	
CT600H	Cross-border Royalties	See **Chapter 23**
CT600I	Supplementary charge in respect of ring fence trades	
CT600J	Disclosure of tax avoidance schemes	See **Chapter 25**
CT600K	Restitution tax	See **23.4**

FILING DATE

22.10 The company tax return must be filed no later than the last day of whichever of the following periods is last to end (*FA 1998, Sch 18, para 14*):

- 12 months from the end of the accounting period for which it is made;
- if the company's period of account is longer than 12 months but no longer than 18 months, 12 months from the end of that period;

- if the company's period of account is longer than 18 months, 30 months from the beginning of that period; and
- if the notice to deliver a return is given late, three months after the notice was served.

A company may amend its company tax return within 12 months after the filing date. Therefore, if a company's accounting period ends on 31 December 2015, its filing date is 31 December 2016 and it is permitted to file an amendment to the return at any time up to 31 December 2017. If a company makes a return for the wrong period, it can correct the position at any time up to 12 months after the date which would have been the filing date if the period for which the return was made were an accounting period (*FA 1998, Sch 18, para 15*).

HMRC have the power to correct returns for obvious errors and omissions and anything else they believe is incorrect based on information available to them, but can only do so for up to nine months after the return was filed, or nine months after an amendment was made if the correction follows an amendment. The company can in turn reject the correction within its amendment period or within three months of receipt of HMRC's amendment, if later (*FA 1998, Sch 18, para 16*).

ONLINE FILING

Focus

Companies and their advisers must keep abreast of changes in the rules for online filing. For accounting periods ending on or after 1 April 2014, a company's detailed profit and loss account must be tagged with new profit and loss account iXBRL tags. Accounts prepared under new UK GAAP and submitted on or after 1 April 2015 as part of a company tax return must be tagged in accordance with new taxonomies.

Introduction to the online filing requirements

22.11 Company tax returns and supporting information relating to accounting periods ended on or after 1 April 2010 must be filed electronically. Companies may also amend their returns online, but this is not mandatory; they may submit amendments on paper if they prefer.

HMRC's form CT600 and related supplementary pages must be submitted online in extensible mark-up language (XML) format. These must be accompanied by financial statements and corporation tax computations complying with the iXBRL data format.

Extensible business reporting language (XBRL) is an internationally recognised electronic format for handling business and financial data. Like HTML, it involves 'tagging' data in a report with both a content and an identity. XBRL-enabled systems can automatically extract this data for further analysis. Individual tags are defined by a taxonomy.

Inline XBRL (iXBRL) is the method of delivery mandated by HMRC. iXBRL allows XBRL data to be embedded in human-readable files. More detail can be found at www.xbrl.org.uk. Various software products that meet certain minimum criteria set by HMRC are listed at tinyurl.com/ygmxlze.

The financial statements forming part of the company tax return are the company's individual accounts required under the *Companies Act 2006,* or under similar legislation applying to building societies, friendly societies or miscellaneous insurance undertakings. Where a parent company chooses or is required to prepare group accounts as well as individual accounts, it may deliver consolidated accounts in iXBRL format instead of individual accounts, provided that these contain the same information about the company that would be provided by individual accounts. A company not required to prepare individual accounts under the *Companies Act* etc may use iXBRL format in delivering such accounts as it is required to submit by the 'Notice to deliver a company tax return'.

Note that the following must be delivered in iXBRL format:

- accounts delivered by a UK-resident overseas company as required by notice;
- where a company not resident in the UK carries on a trade in the UK through a permanent establishment, branch or agency in the UK, the trading and profit and loss account and balance sheet of the UK establishment, branch or agency which it is required to deliver; and
- computations showing the derivation of the entries in the company tax return form from the accounts where other software is used, or where a company using the HMRC filing product chooses not to use the integrated computations template.

Online filing and related online payments of corporation tax are regulated by HMRC's electronic filing directions, issued under *Income and Corporation Taxes (Electronic Communications) Regulations 2003, SI 2003/282* (see tinyurl.com/nngbvzc).

The identity of the person sending information online to HMRC is authenticated by the use of a Government Gateway User ID and password, or a digital certificate where available. These can be obtained by applying to register for an HMRC online account at www.gov.uk/file-your-company-accounts-and-tax-return. To file the company's accounts jointly with Companies House, it is necessary to register online separately with Companies House from the same page. Note that it may take a matter of weeks to establish the necessary online access.

For each accounting period, the company must submit a single online transmission which includes all components of the company tax return. Accounts and computations delivered in iXBRL format must be delivered as separate iXBRL instance documents within the overall return. Other information, accounts, statements, reports, claims or correspondence included as part of the return must be sent as portable document format (PDF) files. All parts of the company tax return, including any PDF documents, must be proper and complete, and the content must be open to view by HMRC officers using appropriate software.

Tax agents filing a company tax return on behalf of a client are required to take an electronic or paper copy for their records and obtain the confirmation of the proper officer, or other person authorised to act for the company in this regard, that the information is correct and complete to the best of the knowledge and belief of that person.

HMRC have an Online Services Helpdesk. Telephone and email contact details for this are at tinyurl.com/mdrl9tl.

Online filing software options

22.12 HMRC have made available free of charge an integrated accounts template and corporation tax software product, which can be downloaded at www.gov.uk/file-your-company-accounts-and-tax-return. This has been designed primarily to meet the needs of small unrepresented private limited companies or micro-entities with relatively straightforward financial and tax affairs, to help them prepare any or all of their financial statements, corporation tax computations and form CT600 in the required formats and submit these online.

Where the circumstances of the company allow, the online accounts template may be used to prepare and submit full statutory accounts to HMRC. If the template is not used, either through choice or because it has been found unsuitable for the company concerned, the accounts must be attached in iXBRL format. The template can also be used to submit statutory or abbreviated accounts to Companies House, either jointly with the HMRC submission or independently of it.

Similarly, HMRC's computation template may be used to prepare and submit the corporation tax computation. If the template is not used, a computation in iXBRL format must be submitted.

Only certain supplementary pages can be filed using the HMRC software, and these are:

- CT600A (Loans to participators of close companies);
- CT600E (Charities and Community Amateur Sports Clubs); and
- CT600J (Disclosure of Tax Avoidance Schemes).

HMRC's online integrated accounts template and corporation tax software product was replaced for accounting periods ending on or after 1 January 2016 by new free software (called 'CATO') designed to make it quicker and easier for unrepresented companies with straightforward affairs to file their own annual accounts and company tax returns. This new software will not be available for use by tax agents.

Third party commercial software applications or services are required where the HMRC software is not used. These applications may (variously) produce and submit form CT600 and supplementary CT600 pages as required, in addition to financial statements and corporation tax computations in iXBRL format. They may also have the functionality to include supplementary information as PDF files within the same submission.

Accounts and computations that are not iXBRL-compliant may be converted to iXBRL format. Some vendors provide a 'tagging service' to convert non-iXBRL accounts and computations to iXBRL format. Others provide software to convert word-processor or spreadsheet-based accounts and computations to iXBRL format.

iXBRL tagging requirements

22.13 Accounts and computations forming part of an online corporation tax return must meet a certain minimum iXBRL tagging requirement to ensure that the return will be accepted by HMRC. Partial or inaccurate tagging makes it more likely that a return will be selected for detailed risk analysis, leading to a possible compliance check.

For accounting periods ending on or after 1 April 2014, a company's detailed profit and loss account must be tagged with new profit and loss account tags, whether it appears in the accounts or the tax computations, and improvements have been made to the structure of the computations tags (see HMRC guidance, November 2013, at tinyurl.com/pw9q3w7).

HMRC has published guidance (see tinyurl.com/p2wtnjk) on taxonomies acceptable to them for online filing generally, and specifically for accounts prepared under the new accounting standards. Accounts submitted as part of a company tax return and filed on or after 1 April 2015 must be tagged with the new taxonomy; however, companies that had produced their accounts under new UK GAAP before 1 April 2015 and had tagged them with the IFRS taxonomy can still submit them, regardless of when the company tax return is filed.

When online filing need not be used

22.14 Online filing need not be used:

- where a liquidator has been appointed;
- in circumstances such as a creditors' voluntary winding up with a provisional liquidator appointed;
- where a company voluntary arrangement is in place;
- where a compromise or arrangement within *CA 2006, Pt 26* is in place; or
- where a limited liability partnership (LLP) is being wound up (*Income and Corporation Taxes (Electronic Communications) (Amendment) Regulations 2010, SI 2010/2942*).

Online filing need not be used, and a paper return may be submitted instead, if the directors and company officers are all practising members of a religious society or order whose beliefs are incompatible with the use of electronic methods of communication. (See HMRC guidance at tinyurl.com/kpqd3bt).

ROUTINE ENQUIRY INTO COMPANY TAX RETURNS

Focus

The time limit by which HMRC may, by notice, enquire into a company tax return that was filed on or before the statutory filing date varies according to the type of company in question.

Time limit: single companies and small groups

22.15 If the company is a single company, or a member of a group which is a small group, HMRC may give notice of an enquiry at any time up to 12 months after the date on which the return was delivered (*FA 1998, Sch 18, para 24(2)*; see also *Dock and Let Ltd v Revenue & Customs Commissioners* [2014] UKFTT 943 (TC)). A small group is defined by reference to *CA 2006, ss 383, 474* (see **1.14** and **1.15**).

If the company is a member of a group other than a small group, HMRC may give notice of an enquiry at any time up to 12 months after the statutory filing date (*FA 1998, Sch 18, para 24(6)*). A company is required to indicate on the front of form CT600 if it is a member of a group that is not small.

Where a company tax return is delivered late, a uniform set of rules applies to all companies in determining the time limit by which HMRC may, by notice, enquire into the return. The enquiry time is extended to 12 months after the next 31 January, 30 April, 31 July or 31 October following the date on which the return was delivered (*FA 1998, Sch 18, para 24(3)*). Similarly, if the company has made any amendments to the return, the enquiry time is extended to 12 months after the next 31 January, 30 April, 31 July or 31 October following the date the amendment was made (*FA 1998, Sch 18, para 24(4)*).

The scope of a new enquiry can be limited. If the time limit has expired for enquiry into the main return but not the company's amendments to that return, HMRC may only enquire into those amendments (*FA 1998, Sch 18, para 25(2)*).

The enquiry notice must be received by the company before the time limit. It is assumed that second-class post takes four working days to be delivered and first-class post takes two working days to be delivered. Working days do not include Saturdays, Sundays or Bank Holidays (HMRC Enquiry Manual at EM1506, EM1510). It would seem that notices or assessments received outside the statutory time limit may only be disputed in practice by noting the post-mark on the envelope in which the notice was sent.

Note that expiry of the time limit for a self-assessment enquiry will not necessarily prevent HMRC from making a discovery assessment (*FA 1998, Sch 18, para 41(1)*). See **25.22**.

Time limit: groups which are not small

22.16 In all cases where a company is a member of a group which is not small, HMRC try to open any enquiries within 12 months of the delivery of the last individual company tax return from any member of the group, referred to as the 'group anniversary target'. Nonetheless, they reserve the right to open enquiries until the statutory deadline (EM1514).

For large groups, HMRC's Customer Relationship Managers (CRMs) in the Large Business Service and CRMs and Customer Co-ordinators in Local Compliance (see **22.18**) are encouraged to seek to agree a timetable for delivery of each group's returns that will enable them to open any formal enquiries before the group anniversary target (EM1515).

Groups of companies which are not small may be able to reduce the likelihood of enquiries being opened after the group anniversary target by agreeing such a submission timetable with HMRC and notifying HMRC as soon as the last return is filed (EM1515, EM1516). However, HMRC would still be entitled to open enquiries right up to the statutory deadline.

Procedure

22.17 To begin an enquiry, HMRC will issue a notice in the form of a letter that they intend to enquire into the company tax return (*FA 1998, Sch 18, para 24(1)*). In practice, they copy the letter to the company's agent if one is appointed.

The scope of the enquiry can extend to any item in the return, including any amount that affects the tax payable by the company for another accounting period or the tax liability of another company for any accounting period, together with all claims and elections included in the return (*FA 1998, Sch 18, para 25*).

The enquiry may also extend to consideration by HMRC of whether to serve the company with a notice under any of the following provisions:

- Corporation tax on chargeable gains: avoidance involving losses (*TCGA 1992, ss 184G, 184H*).
- Schemes and arrangements designed to increase relief: anti-avoidance (*TIOPA 2010, s 81(2)*).
- Transfer pricing; medium-sized enterprises: exception from exemption (*TIOPA 2010, s 168(1)*). See **Chapter 21**.
- Avoidance involving tax arbitrage (*TIOPA 2010, ss 232, 249*). See **21.34–21.37**.

If a return is made for the wrong period, HMRC may enquire into the period for which it should have been made (*FA 1998, Sch 18, para 26*).

A company is responsible for its tax affairs. If a professional adviser has been appointed, the company should ensure that the adviser is fully informed of all relevant facts. HMRC will deal with a professional adviser if one has been appointed. If matters are not progressing with the adviser at sufficient speed, HMRC will inform the company and may then deal with the company direct.

Most enquiries deal with one or two issues on a claim or return. However, in-depth enquiries do occur, with HMRC conducting a wide-ranging examination into some companies' tax affairs. In such an event, HMRC will undoubtedly require to see, and have the power to obtain access to, the records from which the return was prepared. Thus the importance of keeping good accounting records manifests itself. Good accounting records are the company's only real defence in disputing HMRC claims. HMRC may ask to examine the records at the business premises or they may ask for these to be sent to them. HMRC have special powers to obtain information and documents (see **Chapter 25**). With the withdrawal of the statutory audit requirement from many companies, the development of risk-based audit methodologies and the increasing reliance on electronic systems, the supporting evidence and vouchers are often ignored.

An astute director will ensure that his company maintains good systems and company records.

In *Ferribly Construction (UK) Ltd v Revenue & Customs Commissioners* [2007] SpC 635, a construction company estimated and declared a profit on its self-assessment corporation tax return, which it later claimed should have been a loss. The company was unable to produce proper books and records to HMRC in support of the loss claim. The assessment therefore remained unchanged.

Whether or not a professional adviser can be sued by a corporate client in the wake of a full-scale HMRC enquiry, for not warning the client to keep better records, is a moot point. Companies must realise that maintaining good records is not just an administration function but also a statutory function.

Course of enquiry

22.18 The manner in which enquiries are conducted has evolved as a result of changes in the way that HMRC interact with companies.

The largest companies with the most complex tax affairs have a Customer Relationship Manager (CRM) in HMRC's Large Business Service. Other large companies with complex tax affairs have a CRM or Customer Co-ordinator in HMRC's Local Compliance (Large and Complex) unit. The CRM or Customer Co-ordinator handles HMRC's ongoing relationship with the company. Whilst HMRC's compliance check powers are the same for all companies, the approach for large companies is focused on individual risk assessment and engagement (including real time dialogue). In these circumstances, an intervention by HMRC may come as no surprise to the company and may even be planned and scheduled in advance by both sides.

Normally, the course of enquiry involves the company and/or the professional agent supplying information and documents to HMRC in response to their queries. There is a period of time over which this happens, and replies to the HMRC officer conducting the enquiry should be given accurately and in good time. In any event, if any enquiry is in progress, it should not hold up the submission of tax returns for subsequent accounting periods, even if best estimated entries are included when preparing those returns.

In addition, HMRC may call a meeting with the directors, company secretary or even certain other employees to discuss the company's business affairs. Many may feel nervous and intimidated in such a situation. HMRC cannot compel those involved to attend a meeting. A professional adviser may attend as well as or instead of the company attendees. In all circumstances, whether or not a meeting takes place, HMRC must be provided with all the information necessary to answer their enquiries. HMRC have powers to call for information (see **25.2**).

If a meeting takes place, HMRC have formal procedures which they must follow.

They may require the company representatives to bring the necessary records, either to support their answers to HMRC's questions or to support their own queries. HMRC will make a written record of what is said at the meeting. The company may ask to see the notes.

HMRC may even go as far as requesting the company to sign a copy of their (that is, HMRC's) notes to signify agreement. HMRC cannot compel the company to do so. The company may, of course, comment on the notes if it wishes. The value to the company of participating in such a meeting must be judged on its own merits in each and every case, but in many instances it will be an important step in demonstrating a willingness to co-operate with HMRC, thus ensuring that the company's tax affairs are in order and helping to keep any prospective penalties to a minimum.

For HMRC's detailed technical guidance on corporation tax enquiries, see the HMRC Enquiry Manual.

HMRC's single compliance process for SMEs

22.19 Early in 2013, HMRC completed a trial of a 'single compliance process' for use when conducting enquiries into the affairs of small or medium-sized enterprises (SMEs). An adapted version of this approach has now been implemented. It does not apply to Local Compliance fraud cases worked under Code of Practice 9 (see **22.22**) and certain types of avoidance work.

The single compliance process is a streamlined process which claims to minimise the impact of an enquiry on the taxpayer company by using:

- openness and early dialogue through early discussions around the risks identified and the information/documents required;
- a collaborative working relationship with the agent or taxpayer at every stage of the enquiry; and
- (where appropriate) an on-site review of business records, including use of sampling techniques.

The single compliance process is designed to have three possible levels of intensity, so as to be proportionate to the risks or behaviours identified for enquiry, as follows:

- *Desk-based*

  for cases that can be worked either by correspondence or over the telephone, where there is no need for a face-to-face meeting.
- *Visits*

to provide a simplified and faster route for those cases where a face-to-face visit is required (visits are distinguished between cases requiring either a one- or a two-day visit).

- *Evasion*

  to address those cases showing evasion characteristics requiring evasion approaches from the outset, such as surveillance or unannounced visits.

Broad estimates of the time that the single compliance process should take range from a day and a half to eight days.

HMRC's stated aims for the single compliance process are that it should:

- allow the enquiry to be driven by the risks or behaviours identified;
- inform the company and its agent (if any) at the outset of the particular risks to be addressed;
- develop a relationship with the agent and/or company for mutual understanding of the benefits of particular approaches and how these may maintain the pace or speed up the process;
- avoid surprises by ensuring collaboration between HMRC and the agent and/or company;
- review records 'on site' where appropriate;
- only address the particular risks identified;
- use sampling techniques rather than a full review where appropriate; and
- work to HMRC's litigation and settlement strategy principles (see **22.32**), particularly that HMRC will not generally enter into a dispute unless the revenue flows potentially involved justify doing so.

There are concerns that HMRC may place too much emphasis on seeking an early meeting, whereas taxpayers and agents are more interested in HMRC being open in explaining their concerns.

Corporation tax return amendment

22.20 HMRC may, by notice, amend the self-assessment calculation during the course of the enquiry if they consider it insufficient. The company has a 30-day time limit to lodge an appeal against the amendment (*FA 1998, Sch 18, para 30*). Similarly, the company may amend its return during the course of the enquiry. This will not restrict the scope of the enquiry, but it may be taken into account. The amendment will not take effect until the enquiry is finished (*FA 1998, Sch 18, para 31*). During the course of the enquiry, if the company considers that it may have additional tax to pay it can make an additional payment to reduce any interest charges that might arise. Overpayments are repaid if it is found that excessive tax has been paid. If, during the course of the enquiry, it is discovered that there is a period for which a return is required but for which none has been submitted, then such a return is required to be submitted within 30 days of the final determination (*FA 1998, Sch 18, para 35*).

Completion of enquiry

22.21 The enquiry is complete when HMRC issue their closure notice to the company stating their conclusions (*FA 1998, Sch 18, para 32*). The closure notice must either state that, in the officer's opinion, no amendments are required as a result of the enquiry, or, if amendments are required, the corporation tax return must be amended accordingly (*FA 1998, Sch 18, para 34*). The additional corporation tax payments will most likely include interest on overdue tax and may include a penalty.

From 16 November 2017, it is possible to conclude discrete matters within an enquiry where more than one issue is open. This is achieved by issuing a Partial Closure Notice ('PCN') which can be issued ahead of the final closure of an enquiry. The taxpayer also has the right to seek a partial closure notice upon application to the tribunal. This right is additional to the existing right to force a complete closure notice if an enquiry seems to be dragging on unnecessarily (*FA 1998, Sch 18, paras 30–35* as amended by *F(No 2)A 2017, Sch 15*). See *BCM Cayman LP and others v Commissioners for HM Revenue & Customs* [2017] UKFTT 226 (TC), decided before the PCNs were introduced.

INVESTIGATION OF TAX FRAUD

> **Focus**
>
> If HMRC instigate steps to investigate suspected tax fraud, the way in which the company reacts and the degree of co-operation that it offers may have a crucial impact on the outcome of the investigation and the level of penalties likely to be charged.

COP9 and the contractual disclosure facility

22.22 HMRC's Code of Practice 9 ('COP9') sets out their civil procedures for investigating cases where there is a suspicion of tax fraud or dishonesty (see tinyurl.com/ntpcoqr).

Where COP9 is used, HMRC give no absolute guarantee at the outset that the taxpayer will not be investigated criminally with a view to prosecution for tax fraud. Instead, such a guarantee is only given to a taxpayer who enters into a contractual arrangement to disclose, and makes an outline disclosure under that arrangement.

COP9 applies once it has been issued to the taxpayer with an offer of a contractual arrangement and a covering letter. This gives the taxpayer 60 days to choose one of the following options:

- co-operate fully with the process and accept the offer of a contract; this is known as the 'contractual disclosure facility';
- formally deny irregularities; or
- make no response.

A taxpayer who accepts the offer must, within the same 60-day period, produce an outline disclosure, containing a brief description of the frauds that they have committed and a formal admission of deliberately bringing about a loss of tax. Following this outline disclosure, the taxpayer must then make progress towards a formal disclosure, including a 'certificate of full disclosure', statement of assets and liabilities, and certificates of bank accounts and cards operated. In most cases, a detailed 'disclosure report' will need to be prepared and adopted first.

Under the terms of the contract, the taxpayer is conditionally immune from any criminal investigation in respect of the matters contained in their outline disclosure. If the taxpayer continues to co-operate fully with the investigation, penalties should be reduced (see **Chapter 24**).

If the taxpayer denies fraud or makes no response, HMRC may start a criminal investigation, but are more likely in most cases to pursue their own civil investigation on the basis of non-co-operation.

HMRC's Code of Practice 8 (COP 8) is used primarily to investigate cases of tax avoidance, but may be used at times to investigate tax evasion in cases where the contractual disclosure facility is inappropriate. COP 8 is generally reserved for HMRC's most serious or complex investigations (see tinyurl.com/oygr6hb).

For further details of HMRC's investigatory powers and procedures, see their Fraud Civil Investigation Manual.

Attitudes against tax avoidance and evasion have been hardening. In some cases where HMRC might previously have used their civil procedures, they might now be more inclined to use their criminal investigation powers instead. Promoters of artificial tax avoidance schemes, and their intermediaries and clients, are targets of new anti-avoidance measures contained in *FA 2014* and *FA 2015*, and companies who use such schemes face an increased likelihood that they will be investigated (see **Chapter 25**). It is also possible for companies to be liable for the criminal acts of employees who encourage or assist tax evasion by others even if senior management was uninvolved or unaware of these acts (*Criminal Finances Act 2017*; see **25.8**).

APPEALS PROCEDURES

Tribunal system

22.23 The courts operate a two-tier tribunal system: the First-tier Tribunal and the Upper Tribunal (*Tribunals, Courts and Enforcement Act 2007*). The two tribunals are organised into Chambers, which have specific functions, to which pre-existing tribunal jurisdictions were transferred (*First-tier Tribunal and Upper Tribunal (Chambers) Order 2008, SI 2008/2684*). The system is administered centrally by HM Courts & Tribunals Service, an agency of the Ministry of Justice.

The First-tier Tribunal is the first-instance tribunal for most jurisdictions. There is a right of appeal to the Upper Tribunal on points of law, except in the case of 'excluded decisions' (*Tribunals, Courts and Enforcement Act 2007, s 11*; see **22.30**). The Upper Tribunal acts in the main (but not exclusively) as an appellate tribunal from the First-tier Tribunal, but it also has power to deal with judicial review work delegated from the High Court and Court of Session. A decision of the Upper Tribunal may be appealed to the Court of Appeal, except in cases where an appeal is 'excluded'. The grounds of appeal must always relate to a point of law (*Tribunals, Courts and Enforcement Act 2007, s 13*). The Senior President of Tribunals maintains judicial oversight of the whole system. The First-tier Tax Chamber has an appointed President, and the Upper Tribunal has an appointed President and Vice-President.

For guidance on the tribunal system, see HMRC's Appeals, Reviews and Tribunals Manual at ARTG1000 onwards.

COMPANY APPEAL

Introduction

> **Focus**
>
> If a company is dissatisfied with a decision by HMRC, a number of different options may be available – including a formal appeal to the Tribunal, an internal review by HMRC, or an alternative dispute resolution process.

22.24 A company can appeal an HMRC decision directly to the First-tier Tribunal. Alternatively, the company can ask HMRC to carry out an internal review of the decision. There is a 30-day time limit for lodging an appeal or requesting an internal review. HMRC will accept late appeals if there is a reasonable excuse; if there is no reasonable excuse, the company has the option to ask the tribunal for permission to make a late appeal. In *Revenue & Customs Commissioners v McCarthy & Stone (Developments) Limited and related appeal* [2013] UKFTT 727 (TC), the Upper Tribunal denied a late appeal by HMRC where they had not established a reasonable excuse for its lateness. In *Greenwich Investments Ltd v Revenue & Customs Commissioners* [2014] UKFTT 822 (TC), the First-tier Tribunal accepted the taxpayer's late appeal, finding that it was reasonable for the taxpayer to have relied on its advisers to appeal in good time.

An appeal to the tribunal is heard in public, unless there are exceptional reasons for doing otherwise (for example, where the personal safety of individuals is threatened). By contrast, an internal review by HMRC remains confidential between the taxpayer and HMRC.

Where an enquiry by HMRC seems to be dragging on for an excessively long time, the company may apply to the tribunal for a direction that an officer of HMRC gives either a closure notice, or a partial closure notice within a specified period (*FA 1998, Sch 18, para 33* see **22.21**).

Company disagrees with an HMRC decision

22.25 If a company disagrees with an HMRC decision, it may appeal to HMRC (*TMA 1970, s 49A*), in which case there are three possible outcomes:

- the company may ask HMRC to carry out an internal review of the matter in question (see **22.26**);
- HMRC may offer to review the matter in question (see **22.27**), or
- the company may notify its appeal to the tribunal (see **22.28**).

Alternatively, the parties may agree to settle by mutual agreement (*TMA 1970, s 54*).

With regard to their internal reviews, HMRC have confirmed that reviews are carried out by review officers who have experience of the subject matter of the appeal but are independent of the decision maker and the decision maker's line management, in order to allow the review officer to remain as objective as possible (ARTG4310). Their stated aim is to check that the appealable decision already made by HMRC is legally, technically and procedurally correct, evidentially sound, and in line with current HMRC policy, practice and their litigation and settlement strategy (see **22.32**). In practice, not all internal reviews conducted by HMRC are perceived by taxpayers to be as balanced and objective as they might have hoped.

Company requests HMRC to carry out an internal review

22.26 The company may request an HMRC review, and in this event HMRC must explain their view of the matter in question within 30 days of receipt of that request or such longer period as is reasonable (*TMA 1970, s 49B*).

HMRC must then carry out the review that they consider to be appropriate in the circumstances. They must take account of all steps taken before the beginning of the review, both by HMRC and other parties, in resolving the matter in question. They must take all company representations into account. HMRC may conclude that the decision is to be upheld, varied or cancelled. HMRC must notify the company of their decision within 45 days from the day when HMRC notified the company of their view of the matter in question, or within such other period as may be agreed.

If HMRC do not give notice of their conclusions within the specified period, the review is to be treated as having concluded that HMRC's view of the matter in question is upheld. Nonetheless, HMRC must notify the company of the conclusion which the review is treated as having reached (*TMA 1970, s 49E*).

HMRC offer to carry out an internal review

22.27 HMRC may offer an internal review, and their review offer must include their view of the matter in question. The company has a period of 30 days (the 'acceptance period'), beginning with the date of the notification document of the offer, to accept the offer of a review or to appeal to the tribunal. If the company does neither of these within the acceptance period, HMRC's view of the matter in question becomes final and the company cannot subsequently repudiate it (*TMA 1970, s 49C*).

If the company has accepted the offer of a review, HMRC must then carry out the review that they consider to be appropriate in the circumstances. They must take account of all steps taken before the beginning of the review, both by HMRC and other parties, in resolving the matter in question. They must also take all company representations into account. HMRC may conclude that the decision is to be upheld, varied or cancelled. HMRC must notify the company of their decision within 45 days from HMRC's receipt of the company's acceptance of a review offer, or within such other period as may be agreed.

If HMRC do not give notice of their conclusions within the specified period, the review is to be treated as having concluded that HMRC's view of the matter in question is upheld. Nonetheless, HMRC must notify the company of the conclusion which the review is treated as having reached (*TMA 1970, s 49E*).

HMRC cannot offer the company a review if, in relation to the matter in question (*TMA 1970, s 49C*):

- a review offer has already been made;

- the company has requested a review; or
- the company has appealed direct to the tribunal.

Company appeal to the tribunal

22.28 If the company has appealed a decision to HMRC, it may notify its appeal to the tribunal for the tribunal to decide the matter in question. However, no such appeal may be notified to the tribunal while a review by HMRC is in progress following HMRC having given notice of their view of the matter at the instigation of either the company or HMRC (*TMA 1970, s 49D*).

If HMRC have carried out a review, and whether or not the 45-day time limit has been adhered to for giving notice of its conclusions, the company may notify an appeal to the tribunal within the post-review period.

The post-review period is:

- *where HMRC give notification of its conclusions within the 45-day time limit*

  the period of 30 days beginning with the date of the document in which HMRC give notice of the conclusions of the review; or

- *where HMRC fails to give notification of its conclusions within the 45-day time limit*

  the period that begins with the day following the last day of the HMRC 45-day notification period (or other period as agreed) and ends 30 days after the date of the document in which HMRC give notice of the conclusions of the review.

Appeals to the tribunal outside the post-review period are subject to the tribunal's permission (*TMA 1970, s 49G*).

Company appeal to the tribunal having declined an HMRC review

22.29 If a company declines the offer of an HMRC review, it may notify its appeal to the tribunal within the acceptance period. Appeals to the tribunal outside the acceptance period are subject to the tribunal's permission (*TMA 1970, s 49H*).

Excluded decisions

22.30 Restrictions are placed on the ability to appeal against certain decisions of the tribunal, referred to as 'excluded decisions' (*Tribunals, Courts* *and Enforcement Act 2007, ss 11(5), 13(8)*; *Appeals (Excluded Decisions) Order 2009, SI 2009/275, art 3*). In particular, a company has no right of appeal against the following decisions of the tribunal:

- *TCGA 1992, s 138(4)* – advance clearance of exchange of securities for those in another company; see **17.10**;
- *ICTA 1988, s 215(7)* – advance clearance of distributions and payments (*CTA 2010, s 1091*); see **18.20**; or
- *CTA 2009, s 833(2), (3)* – gains and losses from intangible fixed assets: transfer of business or trade; see **17.11**.

Where no right of appeal exists because a decision is an excluded decision, judicial review may be available as a remedy.

ALTERNATIVE DISPUTE RESOLUTION

22.31 Alongside taxpayers' legal rights to appeal or to ask for a statutory review, HMRC operate a non-statutory alternative dispute resolution (ADR) service which aims to help resolve disputes or, if that is not feasible, at least reach agreement on which of the disputed issues need to be taken for a legal ruling. Because ADR does not have a statutory basis, neither a taxpayer nor HMRC can insist on its use. However, it offers significant potential benefits to both sides and seems likely to be used to an increasing extent.

ADR involves a neutral third-party mediator working with the company (or its tax agent) and the HMRC officer dealing with the case. Typically, the mediator works with both sides to explore ways of resolving the dispute through meetings and telephone conversations. The mediator may be an HMRC officer not otherwise involved in the case or, in some instances, an independent professional mediator paid for jointly by both sides.

For further details of ADR, see tinyurl.com/be62llx.

HMRC'S LITIGATION AND SETTLEMENT STRATEGY

22.32 HMRC always aim to reach agreement with companies about the right amount of tax due. Where this is not feasible, they will, as a last resort, take the matter to the courts to decide.

HMRC's Litigation and Settlement Strategy sets out the framework within which HMRC seek to resolve tax disputes through civil procedures, consistently with the law, whether by agreement with the taxpayer or through litigation (see tinyurl.com/l6huqyy and HMRC's Compliance Handbook at CH40000 onwards).

Following concerns about the procedures for resolving contentious disputes in high-profile cases, HMRC published a Code of Governance, explaining their processes in greater detail (see tinyurl.com/cjjqwg3).

Chapter 23

Rates and payment of corporation tax

SIGNPOSTS

- Rates of corporation tax, including a table of rates for financial years up to 2020 (see **23.1–23.6**).
- Corporation tax payments, including dates and instalments, short accounting periods and calculation of tax due (see **23.7–23.10**).
- Large company quarterly instalment procedures (see **23.11–23.25**).
- Late payment interest and repayment interest, together with the effect of losses and close company loans and benefits (see **23.26–23.35**).
- Group payment arrangements (see **23.36**).
- Quarterly income tax accounting procedures (see **23.37–23.39**).
- Penalties for failing to pay corporation tax on time (see **23.40**).
- Accelerated payments of tax (see **23.41**).
- Reclaiming overpaid corporation tax from HMRC (see **23.42–23.43**).
- 'Time to pay' arrangements, Business Payments Support Service and managed payment plans (see **23.44–23.46**).
- Proposals to introduce security deposit legislation, requiring high-risk businesses to provide upfront security for their corporation tax obligations (see **23.47**).

RATES OF CORPORATION TAX

Main rate

23.1 The corporation tax chargeable is calculated by applying the appropriate corporation tax rate to the company's total taxable profits of the period (*CTA 2010, s 4*).

The main rate of corporation tax for recent, current and future financial years has been set as follows:

Financial year	*Effective dates*	*Main rate*	*Statute*
2011	1 April 2011 to 31 March 2012	26%	*FA 2010, s 2; FA 2011, s 4*
2012	1 April 2012 to 31 March 2013	24%	*FA 2011, s 5; FA 2012, s 5*
2013	1 April 2013 to 31 March 2014	23%	*FA 2012, s 6*
2014	1 April 2014 to 31 March 2015	21%	*FA 2013, s 4*
2015	1 April 2015 to 31 March 2016	20%	*FA 2013, s 6*
2016	1 April 2016 to 31 March 2017	20%	*FA 2015, s 6*
2017	1 April 2017 to 31 March 2018	19%	*F(No 2)A 2015, s 7(1)*
2018	1 April 2018 to 31 March 2019	19%	*F(No 2)A 2015, s 7(1)*
2019	1 April 2019 to 31 March 2020	19%	*F(No 2)A 2015, s 7(1)*
2020	1 April 2020 to 31 March 2021	17%	*F(No 2)A 2015, s 7(2); FA 2016, s 46*

Small profits rate

Focus

The abolition of the small profits rate from 1 April 2015 substantially alters the approach of many small companies towards tax planning, by removing incentives they had previously to maximise the benefit of the small profits rate and avoid the higher marginal rate.

23.2 For the financial year 2014, the small profits rate of corporation tax was 20%, and the standard fraction for calculating marginal relief was 1/400ths. The small profits rate applied to profits at or below the lower limit threshold. Marginal relief was available where the company's profits fell between the upper and lower limits. For the financial year 2014, the upper limit was £1.5 million and the lower limit was £300,000. See **23.5** for examples of how marginal relief was calculated.

New legislation was introduced to unify the rate of corporation tax chargeable on a company's profits (other than oil and gas ring fence profits) from 1 April 2015. The unified rate of tax is known as 'the main rate' (*FA 2014, Sch 1, paras 1–4*).

Accordingly, for each financial year starting from 2015 there is no small profits rate for non-ring fence profits.

Ring fence profits

23.3 Ring fence profits are a company's profits or gains from oil extraction and oil rights in the UK and the UK Continental shelf (*CTA 2010, s 276*).

The main rate of corporation tax for ring fence profits for the financial year 2014 was 30% (*FA 2013, s 4*). The small profits rate for ring fence profits for the financial year 2014 was 19%, with the ring fence fraction at 11/400ths (*FA 2014, s 6*).

Following unification of the main and small profits rates for non-ring fence profits from 1 April 2015, corporation tax continues to be charged at two rates on ring fence profits (renamed 'the main ring fence profits rate' and 'the small ring fence profits rate'). The legislation relating to these rates and the related marginal relief has been moved (*CTA 2010, Pt 8, Ch 3A*, as inserted by *FA 2014, Sch 1, para 5*).

The new legislation sets the ring fence rates and marginal relief fraction, instead of these having to be set by Parliament for each financial year through a provision in the Finance Bill. For the financial year 2015 onwards, these rates are set at 30% and 19% respectively (*CTA 2010, s 279A(4)*), with a marginal relief fraction of 11/400ths.

The tax treatment of oil activities is a specialist topic and is not covered further in this book.

Other tax rates

23.4 Loans, advances and certain benefits to participators in closely held companies attract tax ('as if it were an amount of corporation tax') under *CTA 2010, ss 455, 464A*, at 32.5% (see **10.15–10.26**).

From 1 January 2016, banking companies are subject to a new surcharge ('as if it were an amount of corporation tax'). This is to be charged on a banking company's profits in excess of its surcharge allowance (*CTA 2010, ss 269D–269DN*, as inserted by *F(No 2)A 2015, s 17*). Bank levy is to be reduced over a number of years (*F(No 2)A 2015, s 16, Sch 2*). These are specialist topics not covered further in this book.

A special new 45% rate of corporation tax is charged on amounts of restitution interest which may be paid by HMRC under a claim relating to the payment of tax on a mistake of law or unlawful collection of tax. There is also an obligation on HMRC to withhold the tax due from a payment of restitution interest when made. These provisions apply to interest (whenever it accrues) if it arises on a court order or final agreement made on or after 21 October 2015 (*CTA 2010, ss 357YA–357YW*, as inserted by *F(No 2)A 2015, s 38*).

Northern Ireland will have power to set its own corporation tax rate at a future date. It had previously been expected that the Northern Ireland rate of 12.5% would apply from April 2018 but, at the time of writing, this measure has not been enacted (see **1.9** and tinyurl.com/hgagw6a).

Marginal relief up to 31 March 2015

23.5 Marginal relief applied to non-ring fence profits for financial years up to and including the financial year 2014. If a company's augmented profits for a 12-month chargeable period were above £300,000 but less than £1,500,000, they were chargeable at the full rate of corporation tax, subject to any reduction due in respect of marginal relief (*CTA 2010, s 19*).

A company's augmented profits are measured as its total taxable profits of the period plus non-group franked investment income (FII) (*CTA 2010, s 32*). FII is the net dividend received plus the related 1/9th tax credit including foreign dividends (*CTA 2010, s 1126*; *FA 2009, Sch 14, para 3*). From April 2016, the tax credit is no longer available (*FA 2016, s 5* and *Sch 1, para 1(2)*). A group for this purpose is the parent and any of its 51% subsidiaries (*CTA 2010, s 32(2)*), and also extends to certain consortium interests (*CTA 2010, s 32(3)*).

The lower and upper limits of £300,000 and £1,500,000 were proportionately reduced for accounting periods of less than 12 months (*CTA 2010, s 24(4)*). The limits were also proportionately reduced where the company had one or more associated companies, by dividing each by one plus the number of associated companies (*CTA 2010, s 24(3)*; see **23.14–23.21**).

Marginal relief was calculated as follows:

$$\text{Fraction} \times \left(\begin{matrix}\text{upper}\\ \text{limit}\end{matrix} - \begin{matrix}\text{augmented}\\ \text{profits}\end{matrix}\right) \times \left(\begin{matrix}\text{total taxable profits}\\ \text{of the period}\end{matrix} \div \begin{matrix}\text{augmented}\\ \text{profits}\end{matrix}\right)$$

Example 23.1—Small profits marginal relief: no associated companies

Apple Ltd's profits chargeable to corporation tax for the accounting period ended 31 March 2015 amount to £350,000. During the year, the company received a dividend of £9,000 from Pear Ltd, a non-group company. There are no associated companies.

Corporation tax payable is calculated as follows:

	£
350,000 @ 21%	73,500
Less marginal relief:	
1/400 × (1,500,000 – 360,000) × (350,000 ÷ 360,000)	2,771
	70,729

Note: FII = £(9,000 × 100/90) = £10,000

See also HMRC's toolkit for small profits rate and marginal relief calculations at tinyurl.com/63vn6ts.

From 1 April 2015 the pre-existing associated company rules have been repealed as a result of unification of the main and small profits rates of corporation tax. However, these rules were also relied upon for ring fence marginal relief (which remains), quarterly instalment payments by large companies and certain other corporation tax purposes. For the financial year 2015 onwards, these rely instead on a new simplified 'related 51% group company' test (*CTA 2010, s 279F*; see **23.22**).

Effective rates of corporation tax

23.6 For periods up to 31 March 2015, in cases where no dividends were received, corporation tax payable could be more simply calculated, where marginal relief was involved, by applying the following effective rates of corporation tax:

	Financial year 2014		*Financial year 2013*		*Financial year 2012*	
	Rate of corporation tax	*Maximum corporation tax payable*	*Rate of corporation tax*	*Maximum corporation tax payable*	*Rate of corporation tax*	*Maximum corporation tax payable*
£	*%*	*£*	*%*	*£*	*%*	*£*
0–300,000	20	60,000	20	60,000	20	60,000
300,001–1,500,000	21.25	255,000	23.75	285,000	25	300,000
1,500,000	21	315,000	23	345,000	24	360,000

Calculation of tax payable

23.7 The calculation of corporation tax payable by a company under self-assessment is summarised in *FA 1998, Sch 18, para 8*:

- Profits (*CTA 2010, s 4*) at the corporation tax rate applicable to the company;

  First deduct:

- Marginal relief (if any) for companies with small profits (*CTA 2010, ss 19–21*). From 1 April 2015, this refers only to marginal relief (if any) for companies with small ring fence profits (*CTA 2010, Pt 8, Ch 3A*) (see *FA 2014, Sch 1, para 6*);
- Community investment tax relief (CITR) (*CTA 2010, Pt 7*; see **6.29**);
- Double taxation relief (DTR) (*TIOPA 2010, ss 2, 6, 18*; see **20.24**);

- Advance corporation tax (ACT) (*ICTA 1988, s 239* or *FA 1998, s 32*; see **18.37**);

  Then add:

- Tax payable on close company loans, advances or certain benefits to participators (*CTA 2010, ss 455, 464A*; see **10.15**, **10.17**);
- Supplementary charges in respect of ring fence trades (*CTA 2010, s 330*);
- Sums chargeable in respect of controlled foreign companies (CFCs) (*TIOPA 2010, Pt 9A*; see **20.25–20.32**);
- Bank levy (*FA 2011, Sch 19, paras 50, 51*);

  Then deduct (from all other amounts before bank levy):

- Income tax suffered by deduction at source (*CTA 2010, ss 967, 968*);
- Advance corporation tax (ACT) paid in respect of foreign income dividend (*ICTA 1988, ss 246N, 246Q*).

HOW TO PAY CORPORATION TAX

> **Focus**
>
> All companies must pay their corporation tax liabilities electronically.

23.8 All corporation tax and related interest and penalties must be paid electronically. HMRC treat the following as acceptable electronic payment methods:

- direct debit by companies that are registered for HMRC's Corporation Tax Online service;
- the taxpayer's own bank or building society services for payment by internet, telephone banking, BACS or CHAPS; and
- Bank Giro payments from own bank.

From 15 December 2017 it is no longer possible to pay at a Post Office.

Payment by cheque alone is not an acceptable payment method. Where (exceptionally) a payment is made by cheque, the funds are treated as received by HMRC on the date when cleared funds reach HMRC's bank account, and not the date when HMRC receive the cheque. HMRC's active bank account details are shown on their website at tinyurl.com/ldpgjlj. If payment is made to an HMRC bank account not listed on the website, it will not be accepted.

Interest is charged on any corporation tax paid late. Interest is earned on any overpaid corporation tax. Interest on tax debts and repayment amounts is brought into account in the company's corporation tax computation as a loan relationship debit or credit (*CTA 2009, s 482(1)*; see **11.8**).

PAYMENT DATES

23.9 Except where quarterly instalment payments are required, corporation tax is generally due and payable nine months and one day following the end of the accounting period concerned (*TMA 1970, s 59D*).

Small and medium-sized companies

23.10 A small or medium-sized company's corporation tax is due and payable nine months and one day after the end of the accounting period (*TMA 1970, s 59D(1)*). Small and medium-sized companies are not required to pay corporation tax by quarterly instalments, but large companies (as defined) are required to do so.

LARGE COMPANIES: QUARTERLY INSTALMENTS

Introduction

> **Focus**
>
> Payment rules for large companies differ from those for small and medium-sized companies.

23.11 Unlike small and medium-sized companies, large companies are required by Treasury regulations under *TMA 1970, s 59E* to pay their corporation tax liabilities in up to four quarterly instalments, based on the company's estimated liability for the accounting period (*Corporation Tax (Instalment Payments) Regulations 1998, SI 1998/3175*).

Interest is charged at the late instalment rate on instalments paid late, and paid by HMRC on quarterly instalment payments paid in advance (see **23.35**).

See **23.8** for acceptable payment methods, and HMRC Company Taxation Manual (at CTM92500 onwards) for more information on quarterly instalments.

Profit limits for quarterly instalments

23.12 A large company with an accounting period of 12 months is required to make payments in months 7 and 10 for the accounting period to which the liability relates, and months 1 and 4 of the next accounting period (*Corporation Tax (Instalment Payments) Regulations 1998, SI 1998/3175 regs 3, 5* see **23.23**).

For these purposes, a company is a large company for quarterly instalment purposes in an accounting period where its 'augmented profits' for that period exceed £1,500,000, but (for accounting periods beginning on or after 1 April 2019) do not exceed £20 million. However, a company is not treated as large for an accounting period if its corporation tax liability does not exceed £10,000.

A company's augmented profits were defined for periods up to 31 March 2015 by *CTA 2010, s 32*, and are defined in identical terms for periods from 1 April 2015 onwards by *CTA 2010, s 279G*. See **23.5** for further details.

A company is not required to pay by instalments in an accounting period where its augmented profits for that period do not exceed £10 million and it was not large for the previous year.

The £20 million, £10 million, £1,500,000 and £10,000 limits mentioned above are reduced proportionately if the accounting period is less than 12 months.

Up to 31 March 2015, the £10 million and £1,500,000 limits are also reduced if the company has associated companies (see **23.14–23.21**), by dividing that limit by one plus the number of associated companies, but the £10,000 *de minimis* limit applies to each company and does not have to be shared (*SI 1998/3175, reg 3*).

From 1 April 2015 the pre-existing associated company rules are repealed as a result of unification of the main and small profits rates of corporation tax. These rules are replaced for ring fence marginal relief and certain other limited purposes by a simplified 'related 51% group company' test (*CTA 2010, s 279F*; see **23.22**). For quarterly instalment payments, the *Corporation Tax (Instalment Payments) (Amendment) Regulations 2014, SI 2014/2409,* provide rules for setting an upper limit for profits above which a company must pay tax by instalments, based on the 'related 51% group company' test.

Quarterly instalments for very large companies

23.13 For accounting periods beginning on or after 1 April 2019, very large companies are required to pay corporation tax in quarterly instalments in the third, sixth, ninth and twelfth months of their accounting period (*Corporation Tax (Instalment Payments) Regulations 1998, SI 1998/3175 regs 3, 5AZA*).

For these purposes, a very large company is a company with annual taxable profits of £20 million or more. As with the rules for large companies, the relevant threshold is adjusted to take into account accounting periods of less than 12 months as well as related group companies.

The effect of the rules for very large companies is to bring forward their payment dates by four months (see **23.12**). This change will impose rigorous forecasting requirements and adverse cash flow impacts.

Associated companies

Consequences

> **Focus**
>
> The complex rules on associated companies have been abolished from 1 April 2015, and replaced by the new and more straightforward concept of 'related 51% group companies'.

23.14 Until 31 March 2015, the existence of associated companies must be taken into account in determining whether or not a company was a large company and therefore obliged to pay its corporation tax by quarterly instalments.

The same rules regarding the existence of associated companies were also relevant up to 31 March 2015 in determining:

(a) eligibility for the small profits rate of corporation tax and calculation of the small profits rate marginal relief until their abolition for non-ring fence profits from 1 April 2015. Companies that were associated shared the small profits rate lower limit and upper limit equally among them (*CTA 2010, ss 24–30*; see **23.5** and Example 23.4);

(b) the amount of the monetary limit in computing capital allowances on long life assets (*CAA 2001, s 99*; see **3.56**); and

(c) the profit limit for companies electing for small claims treatment under the Patent Box legislation (*CTA 2010, s 357CL*; see **13.8**).

Associated company status

23.15 For the purposes of the small profits rate of corporation tax up to 31 March 2015, a company was another company's associated company in an accounting period if the two companies were associated for any part of that accounting period. A company was treated as an associated company of another at a given time if, at that time, one of the two had control of the other, or both were under the control of the same person or persons (*CTA 2010, s 25(1)*). For this purpose, 'control' is defined by *CTA 2010, ss 450–451* (see **10.4**).

For the purposes of corporation tax quarterly instalment payments up to 31 March 2015, the small profits rate rules were used, but the number of associated companies was determined by reference to the number existing at the end of the immediately preceding accounting period of the company or, if there was no immediately preceding accounting period or the immediately preceding accounting period did not end on the day before the accounting period concerned commenced, by reference to the number existing at the commencement of the accounting period concerned (*SI 1998/3175, reg 3(5)*).

In some cases it was also necessary to take account of the rights and powers of a person's associates (*CTA 2010, s 451(4)–(5)*). However, from April 2011, no account was taken of the rights and powers of that person's associates (including spouse, civil partner and business partners) unless there was 'substantial commercial interdependence' between the companies in question (*CTA 2010, s 27*; CTM03750).

A Treasury order prescribed factors to be taken into account in determining whether there was substantial commercial interdependence between companies, and stipulated that account had to be taken of the degree to which the companies in question were financially, economically or organisationally interdependent (*CTA 2010, s 27(3)*; *Corporation Tax Act 2010 (Factors Determining Substantial Commercial Interdependence) Order 2011, SI 2011/1784*; see **23.19**).

This definition of 'associated company' should not be confused with the same expression as used for the purpose of determining whether a company is a close company, where the concept of a person's associates applies more widely (see **10.4–10.7**, **10.13**).

Partners

23.16 The general rule that a shareholder should be attributed with all the powers of his associates became impracticable to apply after 2002, when the limit of 20 on the maximum number of partners in a partnership was removed. From 1 April 2008, business partners within the meaning of *CTA 2010, s 448(1)* (see **10.13**) were only treated as associates in determining whether companies were associated if there were or had been tax planning arrangements in relation to any of the companies (*FA 2008, s 35*, until its replacement by *CTA 2010, s 27*). For those purposes, arrangements included the formation of a company or any agreement, understanding, scheme, transaction or series of transactions (whether or not legally enforceable) other than any guarantee, security or charge given to or taken by a bank.

The situation for business partners was further improved from April 2011, when the general attribution rules were relaxed (*CTA 2010, s 27*; see **23.15**, **23.18**).

Non-trading or dormant companies

23.17 A company that had not carried on any trade or business during the accounting period in question was excluded from the count of associated companies (*CTA 2010, s 25(3)*). This applied in the main to companies that were wholly dormant and holding companies that met certain specific conditions (*CTA 2010, s 26*; CTM03580, CTM03590).

A trading company that had ceased to trade and had placed its surplus funds on a non-actively managed bank deposit account was regarded as dormant (*Jowett (Inspector of Taxes) v O'Neill and Brennan Construction Ltd* [1998] STC 482). A company that had ceased trading but had continued to receive rent from an established source that required little administration was also excluded from the count of associated companies (*Salaried Persons Postal Loans Ltd v HMRC* [2006] STC 1315).

A close company which merely held a bank deposit account fell into the definition of a close investment-holding company and was thus liable to corporation tax at the full rate (see **10.29–10.31**), but had still to be included in the count of associated companies.

A non-trading holding company was excluded from the count of associated companies provided that, throughout the accounting period, all the following conditions applied:

- it carried on no trade;
- its only assets were its shares in its 51% subsidiaries;
- it had no entitlement to a deduction for charges or management expenses; and
- it had no income or gains, other than dividends which it had distributed to its shareholders in the accounting period, and no right to receive the dividends was treated as an asset of the company in the period in question or any earlier accounting period (*CTA 2010, s 26*).

In relation to dormant companies, the following should be noted:

- When a company that has been dormant becomes active, it must provide certain information to HMRC within three months of the beginning of its accounting period. This can be done using HMRC's Online Tax Registration Service, otherwise the company is required to provide the information to HMRC in writing.
- If a company that has been active becomes dormant, it must notify HMRC in writing that it is dormant. A flat management company will normally have to submit a copy of its recent accounts so that HMRC can decide whether or not it can be treated as dormant.
- If a company has become dormant and wishes to be struck off the Register of Companies, it must apply to Companies House. HMRC are

notified automatically and will object if the company's affairs are not up to date. Note that tax repayments cannot be made to a company that has been struck off.

Rights of attribution

23.18 In practice, the attribution of rights and powers, in determining control for associated company purposes, was an important consideration for companies.

As explained above (see **23.15**), from April 2011, a person could only have the rights and powers of their associates attributed to them if there was substantial commercial interdependence between the companies concerned (*CTA 2010, s 27(1), (2)*).

Example 23.2—Rights of attribution: spouses or civil partners

Facts

F Ltd and C Ltd have the following shareholders. Mr F and Mrs F are married to each other. Mr B and Mr C have no connection at all.

F Ltd	*Shares*	*C Ltd*	*Shares*
Mr F	60	Mrs F	75
Mr B	40	Mr C	25
Total issued shares	100	Total issued shares	100

Analysis

Neither Mr B nor Mr C is an associate of Mr F or Mrs F. Mr F controls Company F. Mr F is a participator and, under *CTA 2010, s 451(4)(a)*, Mrs F's rights may only be attributed to him if there is substantial commercial interdependence between the two companies (*CTA 2010, s 27*). In the absence of substantial commercial interdependence, the companies are not associated under the rules that apply post *FA 2011*.

Example 23.3—Rights of attribution: siblings

Facts

The situation is broadly similar to that in Example 23.2, except that Mrs C is Mr F's sister.

F Ltd	*Shares*	*C Ltd*	*Shares*
Mr F	60	Mrs C	75
Mr B	40	Mr C	25
Total issued shares	100	Total issued shares	100

Analysis

Neither Mr B nor Mr C is an associate of Mr F. Mrs C is an associate of Mr F. Mrs C's rights may be attributed to Mr F. However, this will only occur if there is substantial commercial interdependence between F Ltd and C Ltd. In the absence of substantial commercial interdependence, there is no attribution of rights and powers between brother and sister, so the companies are not associated.

Substantial commercial interdependence

23.19 The meaning of 'substantial commercial interdependence' between companies was clarified by Treasury order (*Corporation Tax Act 2010 (Factors Determining Substantial Commercial Interdependence) Order 2011, SI 2011/1784*). When considering whether there was substantial commercial interdependence, regard had to be had to the degree of financial, economic or organisational interdependence between the companies concerned:

- Two companies were financially interdependent if (in particular) one gave financial support (directly or indirectly) to the other, or each had a financial interest in the affairs of the same business.
- Two companies were economically interdependent if (in particular) the companies sought to realise the same economic objective, or the activities of one benefited the other, or the companies had common customers.
- Two companies were organisationally interdependent if (in particular) the businesses of the companies had or used common management, common employees, common premises or common equipment.

In Example 23.2 above, F Ltd and C Ltd would only be associated if there were financial, economic or organisational links between them. Thus, the inter-spousal relationship was ignored.

Guidance on the *FA 2011* legislation can be found at CTM03750–CTM03800. Needless to say, the facts of each case must be examined carefully. It was not necessary for all three types of link to be present. For example, if there was a sufficient financial link, one company could be an associated company of another even if there was no economic or organisational link between them (CTM03780). There was no association if the links had come about by a mere accident of circumstances (CTM03800).

Financial interdependence existed between two companies if one directly or indirectly supported the other, or if each company had a financial interest in the affairs of the same business. Examples are provided by HMRC at CTM03785.

Economic interdependence existed if both companies pursued the same economic objectives or the activities of one company benefited the other company, or both companies had common customers. Examples can be found at CTM03790.

Organisational interdependence arose if there was sharing of management, employees, premises or equipment. Examples can be found at CTM03795.

Control exceptions

23.20 In determining whether companies were associated, control of a company was ignored in certain cases where it was brought about by:

- the ownership of fixed-rate preference shares,
- a loan creditor relationship, or
- a trustee relationship.

Fixed-rate preference shares were ignored if the company holding them was not a close company, took no part in the management or conduct of the company, and had subscribed for the shares in the ordinary course of a business which included the provision of finance. The fixed-rate preference shares had to have been issued wholly for new consideration, carried no rights to conversion into other shares or securities or the issue of further shares or securities, and carried no right to dividend apart from a fixed-rate dividend which, together with any sum paid on redemption, represented no more than a reasonable commercial return on the consideration for which the shares were issued (*CTA 2010, s 28*).

Association through a company that was a loan creditor company was ignored if there was no other connection between the two companies and the loan creditor company either was not a close company or had become a loan creditor in the ordinary course of its business (*CTA 2010, s 29*).

Association through a trustee was ignored where two companies, that otherwise had no previous or current connection, were controlled by the same person by virtue of rights and/or powers held in trust by that person (*CTA 2010, s 30*).

Company tax return

23.21 For accounting periods beginning before 1 April 2015, the number of associated companies must be disclosed on the corporation tax return. This is necessary in order to determine the company's entitlement to the small profits corporation tax rate or marginal relief as appropriate.

Example 23.4—Associated companies: small profits marginal relief

Facts

The following companies are all wholly owned by Bill, but they do not comprise a group for group relief purposes. They each make up accounts to 31 March each year, and the assessable profits or allowable losses for the year ended 31 March 2015 are shown:

A Ltd	*B Ltd*	*C Ltd*	*D Ltd*
£100,000	(£220,000)	£390,000	£20,000

Analysis

The lower and upper relevant amounts of £300,000 and £1,500,000 are divided by 4, being the number of companies that are associated, resulting respectively in bands of £75,000 and £375,000.

The effective corporation tax paid by each company for its accounting period to 31 March 2015 is as follows:

		Tax		*Tax*		*Tax*		*Tax*
	A Ltd		*B Ltd*		*C Ltd*		*D Ltd*	
	£		*£*		*£*		*£*	
Profits	100,000		Nil		390,000		20,000	
20%	75,000	15,000			75,000	15,000	20,000	4,000
21.25%	25,000	5,312			300,000	63,750		
21%					15,000	3,150		
Total corporation tax		20,312		Nil		81,900		4,000

Although B Ltd has made a trading loss, it must still be included in the count of associated companies.

Collectively, the companies' total results amount to a net profit below £300,000, being £290,000, but it is not possible to make full use of the small profits rate, and it should be noted that the top slice of A Ltd's profit is being charged at the marginal rate. Bill may wish to consider restructuring the companies, either by transferring all their activities into one company, or by forming a group for group relief purposes (see **Chapter 4** regarding losses and **Chapter 5** regarding group relief).

Related 51% group companies

Focus

The new concept of a 'related 51% group company' is introduced from 1 April 2015 to replace the much more cumbersome rules on 'associated companies'.

23.22 From 1 April 2015, the £10 million and £1,500,000 limits (see **23.12**) still have to be reduced for the purpose of identifying large companies obliged to pay corporation tax by quarterly instalments. However, the reduction is by reference to 'related 51% group companies', and not by reference to 'associated companies'. The *Corporation Tax (Instalment Payments) (Amendment) Regulations 2014, SI 2014/2409,* provide new rules for setting an upper limit for profits above which a company must pay tax by instalments, based on this new 'related 51% group company' test. The £10 million and £1,500,000 limits are divided by one plus the number of related 51% group companies but, as before, the £10,000 *de minimis* limit (see **23.12**) applies to each company and does not have to be shared.

The expression 'related 51% group company' is defined for the purposes of the new provisions for ring fence marginal relief (*CTA 2010, s 279F*; see **23.3**). This new definition has been added to the list of *Corporation Tax Acts* definitions in *CTA 2010, s 1119* (by *FA 2014, Sch 1, para 16*), and is then applied for quarterly instalments purposes and other corporation tax purposes, namely, in determining the amount of the monetary limit in computing capital allowances on long life assets (*CAA 2001, s 99*; see **3.56**), and the profit limit for companies electing for small claims treatment under the Patent Box legislation (*CTA 2010, s 357CL*; see **13.8**).

A company ('B') is a related 51% group company of another company ('A') in an accounting period if, for any part of that period (*CTA 2010, s 279F(1)*):

- A is a 51% subsidiary of B; for the definition of '51% subsidiary', see *CTA 2010, s 1119*; or
- B is a 51% subsidiary of A; or
- both A and B are 51% subsidiaries of the same company.

These tests apply to each of two or more related 51% group companies, even if they are related 51% group companies for different parts of the accounting period (*CTA 2010, s 279F(2)*).

A related 51% group company is ignored if it is dormant. This applies if it has carried on no trade or business at any time in the accounting period or, if it was a related 51% group company for only part of the accounting period, at any time during that part (*CTA 2010, s 279F(3)*).

A related 51% group company is treated as dormant if (*CTA 2010, s 279F(4)–(6)*):

- it carries on a business of making investments;
- it carries on no trade;
- it has one or more 51% subsidiaries; and
- it is a 'passive' company.

A company is passive throughout an accounting period if it has (*CTA 2010, s 279F(4), (7)–(9)*):

- no assets other than shares in its 51% subsidiaries;
- no income that arises to it other than dividends. Dividends received can be disregarded if they are redistributed to the company's shareholders in the accounting period in which they arise, and neither the dividends received nor any assets representing them are treated as assets of the company in that or any earlier accounting period;
- no chargeable gains;
- no management expenses; and
- no qualifying charitable donations.

Quarterly instalment due dates

23.23 Corporation tax is payable in up to four quarterly instalments, which are normally due as follows (*SI 1998/3175, regs 5, 5AZA*).

For large companies:

Instalment	*Due*
First	Six months and 13 days after the start of the accounting period
Second	Three months after the first instalment
Third	Three months after the second instalment
Final	Three months and 14 days after the end of the accounting period.

Any balance of corporation tax still remaining outstanding must then be paid by the normal due date – ie nine months and one day after the end of the accounting period (*TMA 1970, s 59D(1)*). If the instalments have resulted in an overpayment, the corporation tax overpaid may be reclaimed.

For very large companies (accounting periods beginning on or after 1 April 2019):

Instalment	*Due*
First	Two months and 13 days after the start of the accounting period
Second	Three months after the first instalment
Third	Three months after the second instalment
Final	Three months after the third instalment.

Example 23.5—Quarterly instalments: due dates

Twelve-month accounting period ended 31 December 2020 (large company):

Instalment	*Due*
First	14 July 2020
Second	14 October 2020
Third	14 January 2021
Final	14 April 2021

Twelve-month accounting period ended 31 December 2020 (very large company):

Instalment	*Due*
First	14 March 2020
Second	14 June 2020
Third	14 September 2020
Final	14 December 2020

Quarterly instalments – short accounting periods

23.24 For large companies, if the accounting period is less than 12 months, the final quarterly instalment is due, as normal, three months and 14 days after the end of the accounting period. The earlier instalments only fall due if the payment date falls before the due date for the final instalment.

For very large companies, the process is more complicated. Broadly, the method involves fixing the final installment date to fall within the last month of the accounting period and then fitting the other payment dates around this date, starting with a payment in month 3, with subsequent quarterly payments, so far as this is possible.

Example 23.6—Quarterly instalments: short accounting period

Six-month accounting period ended 30 June 2020 (large company):

Instalment	*Due*
First	14 July 2020
Final	14 October 2020

Nine-month accounting period ended 30 September 2020 (very large company):

Instalment	*Due*
First	14 March 2020
Second	14 June 2020
Final	14 September 2020

Quarterly instalments – calculation of tax due

Focus

Typically, a large company will recalculate its quarterly instalment due for each quarter, based on its most up-to-date estimate of its corporation tax liability for the accounting period.

23.25 A company which considers that it is large (or very large) should calculate its quarterly payment at each due date.

The liability for a quarter is calculated as follows:

3 × (company's total liability ÷ number of months in the accounting period).

The company should recalculate its estimated liability for the year before each instalment becomes due and payable, and should adjust each quarterly payment or claim a repayment accordingly.

Example 23.7—Adjusting each quarterly instalment

In July 2020, Wood Ltd expects its corporation tax liability for the year to 31 December 2020 to be £1,600,000.

For its first instalment, due 14 July 2020, it pays:

3 × (£1,600,000 ÷ 12) = £400,000

As a result of a major industrial dispute over the summer, by October 2020 Wood Ltd has revised its estimate of its corporation tax liability for the year down to £750,000.

On the due date for its second instalment, 14 October 2020, it claims a repayment:

£400,000 – (6 × (£750,000 ÷ 12)) = £25,000

By January 2021, business has recovered and Wood Ltd has revised its estimate of the corporation tax liability for 2015 to £1,200,000.

For its third instalment, due 14 January 2021, it pays:

(9 × (£1,200,000 ÷ 12)) – (£400,000 – £25,000) = £525,000

In April 2021, although Wood Ltd has not yet finalised its accounts and tax computation for the year ended 31 December 2020, it estimates the tax liability at £1,125,000.

For its fourth instalment, due 14 April 2021, it pays:

(12 × (£1,125,000 ÷ 12)) – (£400,000 – £25,000 + £525,000) = £225,000

In August 2021, Wood Ltd submits its corporation tax return for 2020 to HMRC, showing a final tax liability for the year of £1,137,450.

By the normal due date of 1 October 2021, it pays:

£1,137,450 – (£400,000 – £25,000 + £525,000 + £225,000) = £12,450

The liability for the year has therefore been paid as follows:

Instalment	*Due*	*Amount*
First instalment	14 July 2020	£400,000
Second instalment	14 October 2020	£(25,000)
Third instalment	14 January 2021	£525,000
Final instalment	14 April 2021	£225,000
Normal due date	1 October 2021	£12,450
Total		£1,137,450

LATE PAYMENT INTEREST ON CORPORATION TAX

> **Focus**
>
> Interest at current rates is calculated on tax remaining unpaid by the due date.

Late payment interest – general

23.26 If a company, which is not a large company obliged to pay quarterly instalments, pays its corporation tax later than the due date (nine months and one day after the end of the accounting period), it will be charged late payment interest under *TMA 1970, s 87A*. Late payment interest is calculated from the day after the normal due date until the effective date of payment. The interest is simple, not compound – ie HMRC will not charge the company interest on interest paid late. Interest chargeable under *TMA 1970, s 87A* is paid without deduction of income tax and is a non-trading debit under the loan relationship rules in computing taxable profits (*TMA 1970, s 90*; *CTA 2009, s 482(1)*; see **11.8**).

HMRC have no discretion to determine that interest on tax paid late should not be charged, but an interest charge may be reduced:

- as a form of redress in cases where complaints against HMRC are upheld; or
- where a statutory deferral of tax is allowed in response to a national disaster.

A taxpayer may appeal against a charge to interest on unpaid tax on the grounds of reasonable excuse, but there are limited circumstances in which this will be accepted.

Since October 2011, late payment interest rates have been harmonised over most taxes and duties. However, this regime does not as yet apply to corporation tax (*FA 2009, s 101(2)(a)*). It is expected that corporation tax will be brought into the regime by Treasury order, but the relevant legislation is not yet in force (*F(No 3)A 2010, s 25, Sch 9, para 2*). The following text includes statutory references to both the current and future rules).

The rate of late payment interest is fixed at 2.5% above the Bank of England rate (*FA 1989, s 178(2)(f)*;, *Taxes (Interest Rates) Regulations 1989, SI 1989/1297*; *FA 2009, s 103*; *Taxes and Duties, etc (Interest Rate) Regulations 2011, SI 2011/2446*). Bank of England rates can be accessed at tinyurl.com/9qqfudu, while HMRC interest rates for late payment and repayment can be accessed at tinyurl.com/p4el9lo.

Current and previous rates of interest for late payment are shown in the table:

From	*Rate*
21 November 2017	3%
23 August 2016	2.75%
29 September 2009	3%

Different rates of 'debit interest' apply to late payments by large companies required to pay corporation tax by quarterly instalments (see **23.35**).

From 8 July 2015, where HMRC are owed a tax-related judgment debt arising from the High Court or County Court in England and Wales that carries interest under *Judgments Act 1838, s 17*, or *County Courts Act 1984, s 74*, the late payment rate of interest applies (or cannot be exceeded in the case of a non-sterling debt), regardless of the date of the judgment or order in question and whether interest begins to run on or after 8 July 2015 or before that date (*F(No 2)A 2015, s 48*; regarding repayment interest, see **23.30**).

Late payment interest on carry-back of losses, etc

23.27 Where a company claims to carry back a relief to an earlier period, and which has the effect of reducing or extinguishing its corporation tax liability, the general rule is that interest running on any overdue tax of the earlier period is calculated in respect of the adjusted profit.

Example 23.8—Interest on carry-back of losses

Roquet Ltd anticipates a trading loss of £200,000 for the year ended 31 December 2015. For the accounting period ended 31 December 2014 it had a trading profit of £100,000. The company has no other source of income. On 1 October 2015, the directors consider that it is not worth paying the corporation tax due for the year ended 31 December 2014 because of the forthcoming loss.

Roquet Ltd will be charged interest on the corporation tax due on the profit of £100,000 for the period from 1 October 2015 until 1 October 2016.

There are, however, two exceptions. Where a company claims to carry back loss relief arising from:

- a non-trading deficit on the company's loan relationships where the deficit arises for accounting periods prior to 1 April 2017 (*CTA 2009, s 389(1)* or *459(1)(b)*), or

- a trading loss where the earlier period does not fall wholly within the 12-month period immediately preceding the later period (*CTA 2010, s 37*),

and the corporation tax for the period against which the loss has been set has not been paid, the late payment interest runs from the day the corporation tax is due until the expiration of nine months after the end of the loss-making period (*TMA 1970, s 87A(4A), (6), (8)*; *FA 2009, Sch 53, paras 2A–2D*).

Example 23.9—Interest on carry-back of losses – pre-1 April 2017 non-trading loan relationship deficits

The same facts as in Example 23.8 except, this time, Roquet is a property investment company with profits of £100,000 for the year ended 31 December 2014 and an anticipated loan relationship deficit of £200,000 for the following year ended 31 December 2015. The deficit is a pre-1 April 2017 deficit and therefore the general rule on interest does not apply.

Roquet Ltd will therefore be charged interest on the corporation tax due on the profit of £100,000 for the period from 1 October 2015 until 1 October 2016.

Late payment interest – payment of corporation tax by persons other than company assessed

23.28 Where corporation tax is assessed on other parties as opposed to the company itself, the late payment interest start date is the date that the interest becomes payable by the company itself (*TMA 1970 s 87A(3)*; *FA 2009, Sch 53, para 6A*). Such situations will include:

- tax on reconstructions (*TCGA 1992, ss 137(4)* and *139(7)*);
- tax recoverable from another group company or controlling director (*TCGA 1992, s 190*);
- tax payable on withdrawal of group relief (*FA 1998, Sch 18, para 75A(2)*);
- recovery from another group company or director (*CTA 2009, s 795(2)*); and
- tax unpaid by a non-UK resident company recoverable from a related company or a linked person (*CTA 2010, Pt 22, Ch 7*).

Late payment interest – close company situations

23.29 Where tax, as if it were an amount of corporation tax, becomes payable by a close company under *CTA 2010, s 455(2)* (charge to tax on loan to participator; see **10.15**) or under *CTA 2010, s 464A(3)* (charge to tax on arrangements conferring benefit on participator; see **10.17**), late payment interest will be charged if the tax is paid after its due date (*TMA 1970, s 109(3)*).

Where the company recovers any late-paid tax as a result of a claim under *CTA 2010, s 458(3)* (relief on repayment or release of loan made by close company to participator), the late payment interest referable to the amount of the loan repaid, released or written off is not payable in respect of any period after the date on which that repayment, release or writing off occurred (*TMA 1970, s 109(3A)*).

Likewise, where the company recovers any late-paid tax as a result of a claim under *CTA 2010, s 464B(3)* (relief in case of return payment to close company), the late payment interest referable to the amount of the return payment is not payable in respect of any period after the date on which that return payment was made (*TMA 1970, s 109(3B)*).

Repayment interest on corporation tax

Focus

Interest on overpaid tax is set at a minimum of 0.5%. In practice, at this prevailing low rate of interest, little advantage can be obtained by deliberate overpayment of corporation tax.

23.30 If a company has overpaid tax, it may make a repayment claim. Normally, a company is only able to ascertain whether it has made an overpayment when it prepares its corporation tax computation and company tax return.

A repayment of tax attracts repayment interest under *ICTA 1988, s 826* from the material date until the date of repayment. For this purpose, the material date is the later of the normal due date and the date on which the tax was paid, and interest is calculated on the basis that the tax paid last is repaid first. Repayment interest is simple interest, not compound interest. The interest is received by the company without deduction of income tax at source, and is chargeable to corporation tax as non-trading credits under the loan relationship rules (see **11.8**).

HMRC have issued guidance to companies, advising them of ways they can help speed up the repayment process (see tinyurl.com/kvmbmaz and tinyurl.com/qaat9se).

Since October 2011, repayment interest rates have been harmonised over most taxes and duties. However, this regime does not as yet apply to corporation tax (*FA 2009, s 102(2)(a)*). It is expected that corporation tax will be brought into the regime by Treasury order, but the relevant legislation is not yet in force

(*F(No 3)A 2010, s 25, Sch 9, para 3*). The following text includes statutory references to both the current and future rules.

The rate of interest paid on overpayments is fixed at 1% below the Bank of England rate, subject to a minimum rate of 0.5% (*FA 1989, s 178(2)(f)*; *Taxes (Interest Rates) Regulations 1989, SI 1989/1297*; *FA 2009, s 103*; *Taxes and Duties, etc (Interest Rate) Regulations 2011, SI 2011/2446*) and has stood at 0.5% since 29 September 2009. Bank of England rates can be accessed at tinyurl.com/9qqfudu, while HMRC interest rates for late payment and repayment can be accessed at tinyurl.com/p4el9lo.

From 8 July 2015, where HMRC owe a tax-related judgment debt arising from the High Court or County Court in England and Wales that carries interest under *Judgments Act 1838, s 17*, or *County Courts Act 1984, s 74*, a new special repayment rate of interest applies (or cannot be exceeded in the case of a non-sterling debt), regardless of the date of the judgment or order in question and whether interest begins to run on or after 8 July 2015 or before that date. The special repayment rate is equal to the Bank of England base rate plus 2%, subject to future change by Treasury regulations (*F(No 2)A 2015, s 48*; regarding late payment interest, see **23.26**).

Different rates of 'credit interest' apply to overpayments by large companies required to pay corporation tax by quarterly instalments (see **23.35**).

Repayment interest on carry-back of losses, etc

23.31 Where a company claims carry-back of loss relief for:

- a non-trading deficit on the company's loan relationships where the deficit arises for accounting periods prior to 1 April 2017 (*CTA 2009, s 389(1)* or *459(1)(b)*),
- a trading loss where the earlier period does not fall wholly within the 12-month period immediately preceding the later period (*CTA 2010, ss 37, 45F*), or
- an excess of unrelieved foreign tax (*TIOPA 2010, s 72*),

and a corporation tax repayment arises, the repayment interest runs from the day following the expiration of nine months from the end of the loss-making period (*ICTA 1988, s 826(7A)–(7D)*; *FA 2009, Sch 54, paras A1–A4*).

Repayment interest – close company situations

23.32 Where tax is repaid as a result of a claim under *CTA 2010, s 458(3)* (relief on repayment of loan made by close company to participator; see **10.15**), an entitlement to repayment interest may arise. The repayment interest start date is the later of dates A and B (*ICTA 1988, s 826(4)*; *FA 2009, Sch 54, para 9C*), as follows:

Date A is:

- where the loan repayment date (ie the date on which the whole or any part of the loan or advance is repaid, released or written off) is on or after the tax due date, the date nine months after the end of the accounting period in which the loan repayment date falls, and
- in any other case, the date nine months after the end of the accounting period in which the loan date falls.

Date B is:

- the date on which the tax which is to be repaid was paid to HMRC.

There is no statutory provision equivalent to *ICTA 1988, s 826(4)*, providing an entitlement to repayment interest where tax is repaid as a result of a claim under *CTA 2010, s 464B(3)* (relief in case of return payment to company in respect of certain benefits to participators; see **10.17**). However, it is understood that it is HMRC's intention to pay repayment interest under *ICTA 1988, s 826(1)*, where a repayment under *CTA 2010, s 464B* is made late, on the grounds that it would be considered a repayment of corporation tax, and that they would rely on *ICTA 1988, s 826(4)*, in establishing the date from which any such interest would be payable.

Repayment interest incorrectly paid

23.33 If undue repayment interest is paid to a company, it can be recovered by HMRC from the company as if it were late payment interest, if each of the following conditions is met (*ICTA 1988, s 826(8A)–(8C), FA 2009, Sch 54A, paras 1, 2*):

Condition A

The repayment interest has been paid to the company for an accounting period by reason of:

(a) a repayment of corporation tax;

(b) a first-year tax credit (*CAA 2001, Sch A1*);

(c) an R&D tax credit (*CTA 2009, Pt 13, Ch 2* or *7*);

(d) a land remediation tax credit (*CTA 2009, Pt 14*);

(e) a film tax credit (*CTA 2009, Pt 15, Ch 3*);

(f) a television tax credit (*CTA 2009, Pt 15A, Ch 3*);

(g) a video game tax credit (*CTA 2009, Pt 15B, Ch 3*); or

(h) a theatre tax credit (*CTA 2009, Pt 15C, s 1217K*).

Condition B

In a case within (a) above, regardless of whether a previous assessment or determination has been made:

- an assessment, or an amendment of an assessment, of the amount of corporation tax payable by the company for the accounting period is made, or
- a determination of that amount under *FA 1998, Sch 18, para 36* or *37*, unless replaced by a self-assessment.

Or in a case within (b) to (h) above, an assessment, or an amendment of an assessment, is made to recover an amount of the tax credit in question paid to the company for that accounting period.

Condition C

The change to the assessment or tax credit as a result of Condition B above being met is not one which in whole or in part, corrects an error made by HMRC. An error may include a computational error or the incorrect allowance of a claim or election.

Condition D

Only as a result of that change (and not for any other reason such as an error in the calculation of the interest), it appears to HMRC that some or all of the repayment interest (which had been correctly computed at the time) ought not to have been paid.

Common period rule for corporation tax

23.34 Interest on underpayments is offset against interest on overpayments where there is a common period. Common periods arise where there is an amount of corporation tax due and payable by the company by reason of *TMA 1970, ss 59D, 59E* for one accounting period, and an amount which has been paid on account of corporation tax for another accounting period is repayable to the company (see tinyurl.com/h9j8w5j and *FA 2009, Sch 54A, para 3*).

Quarterly instalments

Debit and credit interest

23.35 A large company – that is, one required to pay corporation tax by instalments (see **23.11–23.25**) – will be charged interest on late quarterly instalment payments and will receive interest on quarterly instalment payments paid in advance. To protect the position of a company that pays quarterly instalments in the belief that it is a large company, but finds out later that it is not, any company that is not a large company will receive interest on corporation tax paid in advance of the due date (*SI 1998/3175, regs 7, 8*).

Interest paid under these provisions is known as debit interest, and interest received is known as credit interest. The interest rate formulae are similar to those for late payment interest and repayment interest but result in lower rates. Debit interest is approximately 1% above base rate. Credit interest is approximately 0.25% below base rate subject to a minimum of 0.5% (*FA 1989, s 178(2)(f)*; *Taxes (Interest Rates) Regulations SI 1989/1297*; *FA 2009, s 103*; *Taxes and Duties, etc (Interest Rate) Regulations 2011, SI 2011/2446*). Bank of England rates can be accessed at tinyurl.com/9qqfudu, while HMRC interest rates for late payment and repayment can be accessed at tinyurl.com/p4el9lo

Debit interest is charged from the quarterly instalment due date until the earlier of the date of payment of the tax and the normal due date, being nine months and one day after the end of the accounting period (see **23.9**).

Current and previous rates of debit interest are shown in the table:

From	*Rate*
13 November 2017	1.5%
15 August 2016	1.25%
16 March 2009	1.5%

Credit interest accrues from the date on which the overpayment arises or from the due date for the first instalment payment, if later, to the earlier of:

- the date the overpayment is removed by being utilised as payment for another quarter; and
- the normal due date, being nine months and one day after the end of the accounting period.

The same rates of credit interest apply if corporation tax is paid early by a company not liable to pay by quarterly instalments (*ICTA 1988, s 826*, as amended by *SI 1998/3175, reg 8*). The rate of credit interest has stood at 0.5% since 21 September 2009.

GROUP PAYMENT ARRANGEMENTS

Focus

A group payment arrangement may be used to simplify the payment of corporation tax, interest and penalties within a 51% group.

23.36 Legislation on arrangements for paying tax on behalf of group members allows one company in a group to attend to the administration of the corporation tax payments on behalf of the other group members if it enters into a group payment arrangement (GPA) contract with HMRC (*TMA 1970, ss 59F–59H*). A GPA also covers interest and penalties. However, note that the GPA is an optional administrative convenience, and each individual company remains liable legally for its own corporation tax, interest and penalties.

In order to be eligible, group members must have a 51% group relationship and be up to date with their filing and payment obligations. A company can only be a member of one GPA. If any group member is liable to make quarterly instalment payments, the paying company should enter into the standard contract at least two months prior to the due date for the first payment.

Payments made under a GPA must be made by electronic funds transfer (ie BACS, CHAPS or Bank Giro), using the separate payment reference that HMRC will issue specifically for the GPA. An application for a GPA must inform HMRC which payment method will be used.

Further information about GPAs and a draft of the required documentation can be found at tinyurl.com/pqrhvw8 and CTM97440.

QUARTERLY ACCOUNTING FOR INCOME TAX

CT61 procedures

23.37 Companies are required to make a return to HMRC under *ITA 2007, s 946*, in respect of income tax deducted from certain annual payments, interest and alternative finance payments (*ITA 2007, Pt 15, Ch 15*). Form CT61 is used for this purpose (see HMRC's guidance notes at tinyurl.com/l7estzp).

There are normally four quarterly CT61 return periods (ending 31 March, 30 June, 30 September and 31 December), plus a fifth return period where the end of the company's accounting period does not coincide with the end of one of the calendar quarters. Where such returns are required, the company's first return runs from the start of its accounting period to the end of the relevant quarter; subsequent returns follow a quarterly cycle, and a fifth return (where appropriate) runs to the end of the company's accounting period from the end of the previous quarter (*ITA 2007, s 947*). The completed CT61 return and any tax liability is due 14 days after the end of the return period (*ITA 2007, s 949*).

HMRC consulted during summer 2015 on future options regarding the deduction of income tax from interest and other types of savings income from 6 April 2016 (see tinyurl.com/q4x7vnm) and also, depending on the outcome of that consultation, on possible new requirements to deduct tax at source from interest on peer-to-peer loans from April 2017 (see tinyurl.com/ot3l46q).

Deduction of tax

23.38 Annual interest and other annual payments (eg copyright royalties) are generally paid under deduction of income tax (*ITA 2007, Pt 15*). However, companies are not required to deduct tax from interest, royalties, annuities and annual payments where the recipient is a company which is chargeable to corporation tax in respect of that income. This applies both to UK companies and to non-resident companies trading in the UK through a permanent establishment (*ITA 2007, ss 933, 934*). Accordingly, few UK companies receive income under deduction of income tax. Likewise, companies are not required to deduct tax from qualifying charitable donations (see **2.81** onwards).

Interest and royalty payments by companies in the UK to associated companies in other EU member states are not subject to deduction of income tax at source if the companies are at least 25% associates (*ITTOIA 2005 ss 757–767*; *ITA 2007, s 914*). However, from 17 March 2016, withholding tax applies to royalty payments between connected parties under arrangements which exploit a double tax treaty for avoidance purposes (*ITA 2007, s 917A*). There are also proposals to extend the withholding tax from April 2019 to cases where the payee is a connected party situated in a low- or no-tax jurisdiction (see Consultation Paper 'Royalties Withholding Tax' 1 December 2017 at tinyurl.com/ycw3vjv7).

HMRC must have issued advance authority in the form of an exemption notice before such interest is paid without deduction of tax. It is not possible to obtain an advance authority in relation to royalty payments; instead, the company making the royalty payment must have a reasonable belief that the recipient company is entitled to the exemption (*ITTOIA 2005, s 758*; *ITA 2007, s 914*; and see HMRC Double Taxation Guidance Note 11: Cross Border interest and Royalty payments).

In *Ardmore Construction Ltd v Revenue & Customs* [2014] UKFTT 453 (TC), the First-tier Tribunal held that: interest paid by a UK company to non-UK established trusts was interest 'arising in the UK' within the meaning of *ITA 2007, s 874*; the company should have deducted income tax at source from the interest; and, on its failure to account for this tax, the company was assessable under *ITA 2007, s 957*.

In *HMRC v Lomas and Others (administrators of Lehman Brothers International (Europe))* [2017] EWCA Civ 2124 the Court of Appeal held that an administrator of a company was obliged to deduct basic rate tax on interest paid to the company's creditors in respect of debts proved in the administration. Although the interest only became payable at a single point in time, when the debt had been proved, it was wrong to treat it as a short-term liability. Under the insolvency rules, the obligation of the administrators was unlimited in point of time and was calculated by reference to a per annum rate of interest, which contemplated a period of administration which could, in many cases, last over a prolonged period of time. Accordingly, the interest constituted annual interest and therefore had to be paid under deduction of tax.

The form CT61 return allows for the offset of income tax due on relevant payments against tax deducted from the company's income. Where such payments exceed income, income tax is due only on the excess. Where income exceeds payments for a return period, income tax paid in an earlier return period may be repaid. At the end of an accounting period, if total income exceeds total interest paid and/or annual payments, the balance of tax suffered is offset against the company's corporation tax liability; alternatively, any excess income tax suffered is repaid (*ITA 2007, Pt 15*). No interest will be paid on any repayment arising.

From 6 April 2016, banks and building societies are no longer required to automatically deduct interest from individual customers' accounts ('relevant investments') – thus, interest is now paid gross without any withholding (*ITA 2007, s 851* repealed by *FA 2016, Sch 6, para 1(b)* for deduction of income tax from interest payments and *ITA 2007, ss 875, 876*).

Example 23.10—CT61 return procedure

S Ltd prepares accounts each year to 31 October. S Ltd is not a bank. During the year ending 31 October 2018, it pays the following interest:

		£
21 December 2017	(net of income tax @ 20%)	8,000
4 January 2018	(net of income tax @ 20%)	5,600
9 August 2018	(net of income tax @ 20%)	8,000
21 October 2018	(net of income tax @ 20%)	12,000

All the interest is paid to individuals holding loan notes issued by the company.

S Ltd will enter the following figures into its CT61 returns and account for tax as follows:

Return periods	*Payments*	*Income tax paid*
	£	£
1 November 2017 to 31 December 2017	8,000	2,000
1 January 2018 to 31 March 2018	5,600	1,400
1 April 2018 to 30 June 2018	(no return)	
1 July 2018 to 30 September 2018	8,000	2,000
1 October 2018 to 31 October 2018	12,000	3,000
Total income tax paid		8,400

Interest on income tax

23.39 Late payments of income tax by a company under the quarterly CT61 procedures attract interest on unpaid tax under *TMA 1970, s 87*.

PENALTIES FOR FAILING TO PAY TAX ON TIME

23.40 A penalty may arise if a company fails to pay its corporation tax on time. A new penalty regime is to be introduced by Treasury order, and *FA 2009, Sch 56* gives details of the relevant taxes and the dates from which the penalty will arise. For further details, see **24.27** onwards.

ACCELERATED PAYMENTS OF TAX

23.41 *FA 2014* introduced measures enabling HMRC to require accelerated payments of tax in certain circumstances. For further details, see **25.49**.

CLAIMS FOR OVERPAID CORPORATION TAX

Focus

While a company may reclaim an amount of corporation tax overpaid (see **23.30**), strict rules exist to monitor the recovery of overpaid corporation tax, specifying circumstances in which HMRC are not liable to give effect to a claim.

23.42 If a company has overpaid its corporation tax, or has been assessed to corporation tax that it considers is not due, it may make a claim for a special relief, being the recovery or discharge of that tax as appropriate (*FA 1998, Sch 18, paras 50, 51*).

The legislation identifies seven cases of potential relevance to companies – Case A to Case G – where HMRC are not liable to give relief (*FA 1998, Sch 18, para 51A*):

Case A

Where the amount paid, or liable to be paid, is excessive because of:

- a mistake in a claim, election or a notice;
- a mistake consisting of making or giving, or failing to make or give, a claim, election or notice;

- a mistake in allocating expenditure to a capital allowance pool or a mistake consisting of making, or failing to make, such an allocation, or
- a mistake in bringing a capital allowance disposal value into account or a mistake consisting of bringing, or failing to bring, such a value into account (see **Chapter 3** for capital allowances).

Case B

Where the company is or will be able to seek relief by taking other steps under the *Corporation Tax Acts*.

Case C

Where the company:

- could have sought relief by taking such steps within a period that has now expired, and
- knew, or ought reasonably to have known, before the end of that period that such relief was available.

Case D

Where the claim is made on grounds that:

- have been put to a court or tribunal in the course of an appeal by the company relating to the amount paid or liable to be paid, or
- have been put to HMRC in the course of an appeal that is settled by agreement under *TMA 1970, s 54*.

Case E

Where the company knew, or ought reasonably to have known, of the grounds for the claim before the latest of the following:

- the date on which an appeal by the company relating to the amount paid, or liable to be paid, in the course of which the ground could have been put forward (a 'relevant appeal') was determined by a court or tribunal (or is treated as having been so determined);
- the date on which the company withdrew a relevant appeal to a court or tribunal; and
- the end of the period in which the company was entitled to make a relevant appeal to a court or tribunal.

Case F

Where the amount in question was paid or is liable to be paid:

- in consequence of proceedings enforcing the payment of that amount brought against the company by HMRC; or

- in accordance with an agreement between the company and HMRC in settling such proceedings.

Case G

Where:

- the amount paid, or liable to be paid, is excessive by reason of a mistake in calculating the company's corporation tax liability, and
- the liability was calculated in accordance with the practice generally prevailing at the time,

but this is subject to an exception.

For claims made six months or more after 17 July 2013, Case G does not apply where the amount paid, or liable to be paid, is tax which has been charged contrary to EU law – that is, in the circumstances in question, the charge to tax is contrary to (a) the provisions relating to the free movement of goods, persons, services and capital in Titles II and IV of Part 3 of the Treaty on the Functioning of the European Union, or (b) the provisions of any subsequent treaty replacing the provisions mentioned in (a) (see *Test Claimants in the Franked Investment Income Group Litigation v Revenue and Customs Commissioners* [2012] UKSC 19 (the 'FII GLO litigation'); also *FA 2013, s 231*; *FA 2014, s 299*).

Making a claim

23.43 Legislation introduced from 1 April 2011 replaced a former extra-statutory practice known as 'equitable liability', which recognised that, in exceptional circumstances, HMRC should have the power not to pursue tax under determinations that had resulted in excessive tax being assessed (*FA 1998, Sch 18, para 51BA*; for details of the earlier concession, see *Corporation Tax 2010/11* (Bloomsbury Professional)).

The special relief claim must be in writing and made to an officer of HMRC by the person to whom the relief is due. The claim must state:

- that it is a claim for 'special relief' under *FA 1998, Sch 18, para 51BA*;
- the tax year or accounting period for which relief is claimed;
- the amount of the claim and the amount of tax due for the relevant period;
- the reason why it would be 'unconscionable' for HMRC to collect the sum legally due on the determination, or to withhold repayment of it if it has already been paid;
- that all the person's obligations to HMRC are up to date, ie that all outstanding returns have been filed and all liabilities paid (or satisfactory arrangements are in place regarding payment);

- that relief of this nature has not been sought or granted previously; and
- that there is no other remedy available to the claimant to reduce the determined tax.

The claim must also include relevant evidence in support of it, and a declaration signed by the claimant stating that the particulars given in the claim are correct and complete to the best of their information and belief.

The word 'unconscionable' (above) has been carried over from the previous concession to ensure that claimants are aware that this is a relief of last resort. The relief will only be granted if HMRC are convinced that it would be wholly unreasonable of them to pursue the tax that is legally due.

Overpaid tax being reclaimed may include amounts paid by contract settlement arising on conclusion of a tax enquiry. If the company that paid the amount under the contract settlement ('the payer') and the company from which the sum was due ('the taxpayer') are not the same, and if the grounds for the claim bring about a discovery assessment or discovery determination on the company in respect of any accounting period, HMRC may set any amount repayable to the payer against the amount payable by the taxpayer (*FA 1998, Sch 18, para 51G*).

DIFFICULTIES IN PAYING CORPORATION TAX

> **Focus**
>
> Special payment arrangements may be entered into with HMRC as a result of an enquiry or an inability to pay.

'Time to pay' arrangements

23.44 As emphasised in an HMRC Issue Briefing entitled 'Our approach to debt collection' published in January 2014 (see tinyurl.com/qx9v7h4), HMRC employ aggressive tactics to ensure that taxpayers pay their tax liabilities on time, so it is very important to contact them in good time if extra time is required. Otherwise, tax debts may be put into the hands of third-party collection agencies, and this may involve court costs, seizure of company assets, etc.

All companies are expected to make payment in full by the due date where they have the means to do so. Where a company is unable to pay in full by the due date, HMRC can use their discretion to allow payment over a period, provided certain principles are followed. Such 'time to pay' (TTP) arrangements allow HMRC to collect tax in a cost-effective way. They allow viable companies who cannot pay on the due date to make payment(s) over a period that they can afford. Arrangements are tailored to the ability of the company to pay and are typically for a few months, although they can be longer. TTP arrangements lasting over a year are only agreed in exceptional cases. Most arrangements involve regular monthly payments being made, but in exceptional cases may involve a short period of deferral. Since 3 August 2015, HMRC have required all payments under new TTP arrangements to be made by direct debit.

Under no circumstances can HMRC ever reduce the amount of tax due as part of a TTP arrangement. Applicable interest will always be charged when payments are received after the due date, whether a TTP arrangement has been agreed or not.

Further details about TTP arrangements can be found in HMRC's Debt Management and Banking Manual at DMBM800010 onwards.

Where a company enters into a contract settlement with HMRC on conclusion of a tax enquiry, this frequently involves the payment of a sum representing tax, interest and penalties, payable by instalments on pre-determined dates. If a company due to pay under a contract settlement fails to do so, in most cases HMRC will simply pursue the company for payment. If the company informs HMRC that it is unable to pay the instalments under the agreed settlement because of a change in its circumstances, exceptionally HMRC may consider revising the original instalment offer. For example, HMRC might agree to spread the instalments over a longer period so that the company can pay them, but note that this could involve a recalculation of the interest element included in the contract settlement (HMRC Enquiry Manual at EM6418).

Business Payment Support Service

23.45 A company in financial difficulty may be able to persuade HMRC to vary the timing of its tax payments through the Business Payment Support Service. HMRC provide this service for companies and other businesses that are in genuine difficulty and are unable to pay their tax on time, but are likely to be able to pay if allowed more time to do so. Payment arrangements are agreed on a case-by-case basis. Details of this service are available at www.gov.uk/difficulties-paying-hmrc or by calling the Business Payment Support Line (Tel 0300 200 3835, Monday to Friday 8.00am–8.00pm, Saturday and Sunday 8.00am–4.00pm).

Businesses seeking time to pay tax debts of £1 million or more must, unless HMRC consider that the facts are straightforward, provide an independent business review in support of this request. The review must be carried out by a qualified professional adviser or insolvency practitioner, and HMRC use a panel of industry experts for this review process (HMRC Press Releases, 29 March 2010, 4 May 2010).

Managed payment plans

23.46 *FA 2009* introduced legislation (*TMA 1970, s 59G*) to allow taxpayers (including companies) to spread their tax payments rather than pay them on the normal due date (see **23.8**). A managed payment plan would have allowed a company to pay its main corporation tax liability by instalments, structured so that instalments paid before the due date would be balanced by those paid after it. Group companies within a group payment arrangement (see **23.36**) would not be allowed to make use of a managed payment plan (*TMA 1970, s 59G(3)*).

The general rule was that all instalments paid on time and in accordance with the plan would satisfy the corporation tax liability as if paid on the normal due date (*TMA 1970, s 59G(4)*). Payments made later than envisaged in the plan would attract late payment interest or penalties, which would run from the normal due date (*TMA 1970, s 59G(5)*). If a company were to be charged late payment interest, any payments that it made before the normal due date would attract credit interest (*TMA 1970, s 59G(6)*).

Although this legislation is on the statute book, it was announced in the Budget of 22 June 2010 that managed payment plans would be deferred to a later date (Budget 22 June 2010, para 2.26: see tinyurl.com/y9o56tl9).

SECURITY DEPOSIT LEGISLATION

Focus

There are currently plans to introduce legislation from April 2019 requiring high-risk businesses to provide upfront security in respect of their corporation tax obligations.

23.47 The rules will be targeted at two particular types of business where HMRC believe that there is a serious risk to the revenue:

- non-compliant businesses, where there is a history of persistent late filing or payment, or a failure to pay a large tax liability on time, and where the business has not requested time to pay or does not respond to contact from HMRC to discuss possible ways of managing the debt;
- cases of 'phoenixism', where a business owner has a practice of closing one business down and leaving behind its tax debts, and subsequently beginning a similar business, usually from the same trading premises, with the same personnel and the same clients.

The new rules will not be applicable where the taxpayer has been unable to pay due to financial difficulties or is a party to a 'time to pay' or other debt management arrangement. The rules are targeted at those who are unwilling to pay.

The security need not be limited to cash payments, but may include guarantees in the form of a performance bond issued by a financial institution. It is proposed that criminal sanctions will apply for non-compliance. For further details, see *Consultation Paper: Extension of Security Deposit Legislation* 13 March 2018 at tinyurl.com/y8kp8axg.

Chapter 24

Self-assessment penalties

SIGNPOSTS

- Penalties for incorrect tax returns – including potential lost revenue, procedures and company officer liability (see **24.2–24.12**).
- Failure to notify taxable activities – including penalties assessment procedures, right of appeal and company officer liability (see **24.13–24.18**).
- Failure to deliver a return on time, new and revised rules – including penalties and penalty assessment (see **24.19–24.26**).
- Penalties for failure to pay tax on time (see **24.27–24.35**).
- Penalty procedures generally (see **24.36**).
- Publication of deliberate tax defaulters' details (see **24.37**).
- Managing serious defaulters (see **24.38**).
- Provisions relating to dishonest conduct of tax agents (see **24.39–24.43**).

INTRODUCTION

Focus

The self-assessment regime is unforgiving, and penalties for minor lapses in compliance are commonplace. In more serious cases, the level of penalties can be salutary.

24.1 A penalty system is in operation to penalise taxpayer self-assessment errors and omissions. The quantum of the penalty depends on the seriousness of the error or omission. The main body of the legislation is contained in the *Finance Acts 2007*, *2008*, *2009* and *2010*. The legislation applies in varying degrees to all taxes. The legislation applying to corporation tax is dealt with as follows:

Penalty legislation relating to taxpayer error	*Implementation date and commencement order*	*Paragraph references in this book*
Incorrect tax returns	1 April 2008	**24.2–24.12**
FA 2007, s 97 and *Sch 24*	*SI 2008/568*	
Failure to notify taxable activities	1 April 2010	**24.13–24.18**
FA 2008, s 123 and *Sch 41*	*SI 2009/511*	
Failure to deliver a tax return by the filing date	Not yet in effect	**24.19–24.26**
FA 2009, s 106 and *Sch 55*		
Failure to pay tax on time	Not yet in effect	**24.27–24.35**
FA 2009, s 107 and *Sch 56*		
Publishing details of deliberate tax defaulters	1 April 2010 *SI 2010/574*	**24.37**
FA 2009, s 94		
Tax agents' dishonest conduct	1 April 2013	**24.39–24.43**
FA 2012, s 223 and *Sch 38*	*SI 2013/279* *SI 2013/280*	

HMRC have published penalty guidance: see the compliance check factsheets at tinyurl.com/mklt2nq.

As HMRC increasingly expect taxpayers to interact with them digitally, aspects of compliance have altered. There have been various consultations over the years on possible changes in the way that they apply penalties in order to encourage greater compliance. See **24.26** and **24.33** for further details of the latest consultations on penalties for late submissions and late payment respectively.

PENALTIES FOR INCORRECT TAX RETURNS

Documents

24.2 HMRC will raise a penalty if the company or another person has either carelessly or deliberately supplied a document (from the type listed below) containing an inaccuracy that leads to a tax understatement, or a false or inflated allowable loss, or a false or inflated claim to repayment of tax, or a payment of a corporation tax credit (including a research and development expenditure credit under *CTA 2009, Pt 3, Ch 6A*). Separate penalties are charged for each inaccuracy contained in the document (*FA 2007, Sch 24, paras 1, 1A*).

The types of documents on which a penalty is payable are as follows:

- company tax return (CT600 and/or supplementary pages) as required by *FA 1998, Sch 18, para 3*;
- any return, statement or declaration in connection with a claim for an allowance, deduction or relief;
- accounts in connection with ascertaining liability to tax; or
- any document which is likely to be relied on by HMRC to determine, without further inquiry, a question about:
  - the company's tax liability;
  - the company's corporation tax payments or in connection with corporation tax;
  - any other payment made by the company including penalties; or
  - repayments or any other kind of payment or credit to the company.

Special returns subject to special penalties under *TMA 1970, s 98* are excluded (*FA 2007, Sch 24, para 12*).

Where the company or its officer has been convicted of an offence in respect of an inaccuracy or failure, that person is not liable to any further penalty under these provisions in respect of the same matter (*FA 2007, Sch 24, para 21*).

Provided that the company takes reasonable care to avoid an inaccuracy in the supply of a document to HMRC, the company is not liable to a penalty in respect of any actions or omissions of its tax agent (*FA 2007, Sch 24, para 18*).

These rules were introduced by *FA 2007, s 97* and *Sch 24* (as amended by *FA 2008, Sch 40*) and came into effect for returns or other documents for tax periods commencing on or after 1 April 2008, which were due to be filed on or after 1 April 2009 (HMRC Brief 19/2008, 2 April 2008; *SI 2008/568*).

Circumstances in which a penalty is payable

24.3 If HMRC under-assess the company's corporation tax liability and the company fails to take reasonable steps to notify HMRC within a 30-day period commencing with the date of the under-assessment, HMRC will raise a penalty. In deciding what is reasonable, HMRC will consider whether the company knew or should have known of the under-assessment and, if so, what steps it would have been reasonable to take to notify HMRC. A loss of tax by an under-assessment includes a loss of tax by an under-determination on HMRC's part, and the same rules apply (*FA 2007, Sch 24, para 2*). See **25.22** for determination assessments.

The legislation, which applies for the purposes of a wide range of taxes, provides for three categories of inaccuracy (*FA 2007, Sch 24, para 21A*):

Category 1

- Where the inaccuracy involves a domestic matter; or where it involves an offshore matter and the territory in question is a category 1 territory or the tax at stake is a tax other than income tax or capital gains tax.

Category 2

- For income tax or capital gains tax where the inaccuracy involves an offshore matter, and the territory in question is a category 2 territory.

Category 3

- For income tax or capital gains tax where the inaccuracy involves an offshore matter, and the territory in question is a category 3 territory.

In general, only category 1 will apply to corporation tax matters, for which there are three degrees of culpability, each with increasing degrees of seriousness, on which a penalty may be charged: careless, deliberate but not concealed, and deliberate and concealed. There is only one prescribed rate of penalty if the error is attributable to another person. In all cases, the penalty is based on a percentage of the potential lost revenue, and the relevant percentages are:

Degree of culpability	*Percentage penalty based on potential lost revenue*
Careless	30%
Deliberate but not concealed	70%
Deliberate and concealed	100%
Error attributable to another person	100%

A careless inaccuracy arises when the company fails to take reasonable care when supplying a document to HMRC. For documents submitted on or after 16 November, and which relate to a tax period beginning on or after 6 April 2017, and ending on or after 16 November 2017, the company will be deemed to be careless where the inaccuracy has arisen in relation to a tax avoidance arrangements, unless independent advice was taken from persons who were qualified to give it (*FA 2007, Sch 24, para 3A* inserted by *Finance (No2) Act 2017 s 64*).

A deliberate but not concealed inaccuracy arises when the company wilfully supplies a document containing incorrect information but takes no steps to conceal the fact.

A deliberate and concealed inaccuracy arises when the company wilfully supplies false evidence and takes steps to conceal the fact.

If a company delivered a document to HMRC containing an inaccuracy which was neither careless nor deliberate at the time, but later discovered the inaccuracy, the circumstance is treated as careless if the company has not taken reasonable steps to inform HMRC (*FA 2007, Sch 24, para 3*).

A penalty can be reduced if the company makes an unprompted disclosure. A disclosure is unprompted if it is made at a time when the company has no reason to believe that HMRC have discovered, or are about to discover, the error. In all other cases, the disclosure is prompted (see **24.8** for further details). In calculating the reduction, HMRC will consider the quality of the information provided, the assistance given to HMRC in calculating the additional liabilities, and the access given to the company's books and records.

Companies are expected to take reasonable care, in proportion to their circumstances, when maintaining their books and records. They should seek assistance when dealing with unfamiliar transactions. HMRC have power to suspend a penalty that is invoked for failing to take reasonable care. See HMRC Brief 19/2008, 1 April 2008, 'New penalties for errors in returns and documents' (tinyurl.com/ycle9qyk).

Potential lost revenue: normal rule

24.4 If tax is under-assessed because of a careless error in a company's tax return or related statement, declaration or accounts, the penalty is 30% of the potential lost revenue. The potential lost revenue is the additional tax due or payable (or not repayable) as a result of correcting the inaccuracy in a document, including that attributable to a supply of false information or withholding of information, or a failure to notify an under-assessment (*FA 2007, Sch 24, para 5*).

The following are ignored for the purposes of calculating the potential lost revenue, although inaccurate claims may still attract a penalty (*FA 2007, Sch 24, para 5(4)*):

- group relief; and
- any relief under *CTA 2010, s 458* (relief in respect of repayment or release of close company loan) which is deferred under *CTA 2010, s 458(5)*.

Potential lost revenue: multiple errors

24.5 In the case of multiple inaccuracies in a document, where the calculation of potential lost revenue depends on the order in which they are corrected, careless inaccuracies are treated as being corrected first, followed by deliberate but not concealed inaccuracies, and finally by deliberate and concealed inaccuracies (*FA 2007, Sch 24, para 6(1)*).

For the purposes of calculating potential lost revenue, an overstatement of tax by the company is brought into consideration when calculating the penalty. The set-off is first against understatements for which the taxpayer is not liable to a penalty, then against careless understatements, then against deliberate but not concealed understatements, and finally against deliberate and concealed understatements. No consideration is to be given to any increased tax revenue from another taxpayer as a result of the company's action (*FA 2007, Sch 24, para 6(2)–(5)*).

Potential lost revenue: losses

24.6 If an inaccuracy results in a loss being incorrectly recorded or overstated, the potential lost revenue depends on the extent to which the inflated loss has been used.

The potential lost revenue is the amount of the additional tax due or payable as a result of correcting the inaccuracy or the assessment (*FA 2007, Sch 24, para 7(1)*). If only part of the inflated loss has been used to reduce the amount of tax payable, the potential lost revenue is the additional tax due or payable as a result of correcting the inaccuracy or the assessment for the loss used, plus 10% of the balance of the loss that has not been used (*FA 2007, Sch 24, para 7(2)*).

Group relief may be taken into account if the inaccuracy creates or increases an aggregate loss for the group (*FA 2007, Sch 24, para 7(4)*).

The potential lost revenue in respect of a loss will be reduced to nil where, because of the nature of the loss or the circumstances of the company, there is no reasonable prospect of the loss being used to reduce a tax liability of the company or any other taxpayer (*FA 2007, Sch 24, para 7(5)*).

Potential lost revenue: delayed tax

24.7 Where tax is declared late because of an inaccuracy, but a penalty based on a wrongly recorded loss does not apply, the potential lost revenue is based on 5% of the delayed tax for each year of the delay. Part years are treated on a *pro rata* basis (*FA 2007, Sch 24, para 8*).

Reductions for disclosure

Focus

A potential penalty levied on a company for an incorrect return may be reduced if the company makes a full, accurate and unprompted disclosure of the error to HMRC.

24.8 HMRC will give a penalty reduction for both prompted and unprompted disclosures. The reduction is based on the seriousness of the penalty and the quality of the disclosure.

A company makes a disclosure to HMRC if that company:

- tells HMRC that there is or may be an inaccuracy, a supply of false information or the withholding of information;
- gives HMRC reasonable help in quantifying the inaccuracy, supply of false information or the withholding of information, or the under-assessment; and
- allows HMRC access to records for the purpose of ensuring that the inaccuracy, supply of false information, withholding of information or under-assessment is fully corrected.

An unprompted disclosure can be made at any time when the person making it has no reason to believe that HMRC have discovered, or are about to discover, the inaccuracy or under-assessment. In all other cases, the disclosure is prompted. The quality of the disclosure depends on its timing, nature and extent.

The minimum penalties that generally apply are as follows (*FA 2007, Sch 24, para 10*):

Penalty	*Normal minimum penalty for an unprompted disclosure*	*Normal minimum penalty for a prompted disclosure*
30%	0%	15%
70%	20%	35%
100%	30%	50%

HMRC have separate discretion to apply a special reduction to a penalty if they consider that special circumstances apply. Special circumstances do not include the company's inability to pay, or the fact that a potential loss of revenue from one taxpayer is balanced by a potential over-payment by another. HMRC also have discretion not to bring proceedings in relation to a penalty and to agree a compromise in relation to proceedings for a penalty (*FA 2007, Sch 24, para 11*).

The penalty is reduced by any other penalty or surcharge applied to the same tax liability (*FA 2007, Sch 24, para 12*).

FA 2016 introduced new, increased minimum thresholds in cases of deliberate evasion involving offshore matters, such as transferring assets overseas or using an offshore structure:

Penalty	*Normal minimum penalty for an unprompted disclosure*	*Normal minimum penalty for a prompted disclosure*
30%	0%	15%
37.5%	0%	18.75%
45%	0%	22.5%
60%	0%	30%
70%	30%	45%
87.5%	35%	53.75%
100%	40%	60%
105%	40%	62.5%
125%	50%	72.5%
140%	50%	80%
150%	55%	85%
200%	70%	110%

These new penalties will apply from a date to be appointed by the Treasury (*FA 2007, Sch 24, paras 9(A2), 10A*; *FA 2016, s 163(2), Sch 21*).

Penalty assessment procedures

24.9 HMRC will assess the penalty and notify the company. The notice will specify the tax period for which the penalty is assessed. The assessment will be treated and enforced in the same way as a corporation tax assessment. It may also be combined with an actual corporation tax assessment (*FA 2007, Sch 24, para 13(1), (2)*).

The penalty assessment under these provisions must be made within 12 months of the period beginning with either the end of the appeal period for the decision correcting the inaccuracy or, if there is no assessment of the tax concerned, the date on which the inaccuracy is corrected (*FA 2007, Sch 24, para 13(3)* and *(4)*). An appeal period is a period during which an appeal could be brought, or during which an appeal that has been brought has not been determined or withdrawn (*FA 2007, Sch 24, para 13(5)*). The penalty is due for payment within 30 days of notification (*FA 2007, Sch 24, para 13(1A)*).

See HMRC Factsheets CC/FS7a 'Penalties for inaccuracies in returns or documents' (tinyurl.com/qfbahqg) and CC/FS7b 'Penalties for not telling us about an under-assessment', (tinyurl.com/nnf55rn) which provide practical taxpayer guidance regarding errors.

Suspension

24.10 HMRC have power to suspend a penalty for a careless inaccuracy leading to a tax understatement. The period of suspension must not exceed two years. HMRC must issue a notice specifying the part of the penalty to be suspended and stating the suspension conditions with which the company must comply. HMRC may suspend all or part of a penalty if they think that compliance with a condition of suspension would help the company to avoid becoming liable to further penalties (*FA 2007, Sch 24, para 14*). The conditions of the suspension may specify the action to be taken and a period within which it must be taken. If, on the expiry of the extension period, HMRC are then satisfied that the conditions of the suspension have been complied with, the suspended penalty may be cancelled in whole or in part.

The penalty provisions seek to influence behaviour by encouraging and supporting those who try to meet their obligations and penalising those who do not. In order to suspend a penalty for a careless inaccuracy, HMRC will set at least one specific suspension condition to help the taxpayer to avoid becoming liable to a further careless inaccuracy. They will also require the taxpayer to file all their returns on time during the suspension period (HMRC Compliance Handbook at CH83110).

See also HMRC Factsheet CC/FS10 'Compliance checks – Suspending penalties for careless inaccuracies in returns or documents' (tinyurl.com/osk7ths), which highlights when a penalty for a careless inaccuracy can be suspended and the conditions for agreeing the suspension.

Right of appeal

24.11 The company has the right of appeal to the tribunal against the imposition and the amount of the penalty, and against the denial or terms of a penalty suspension, in which case no penalty is due until the appeal is determined (*FA 2007, Sch 24, paras 15, 16*). The appeal is treated for procedural purposes in the same way as a corporation tax appeal (see **22.22**). The tribunal may affirm the decision, or it may cancel or recalculate the penalty if it finds that HMRC's decision was flawed (*FA 2007, Sch 24, paras 16, 17*).

A company has no statutory right to appeal against a penalty for an incorrect tax return on the grounds of reasonable excuse. Instead, it may be necessary to provide evidence that reasonable care has been taken in order to dispute a penalty for an incorrect return alleged to contain a careless inaccuracy (*FA 2007, Sch 24, para 3*).

Liability of company officers

24.12 In the case of a deliberate inaccuracy attributable to an officer of the company, HMRC may decide that a proportion (up to 100%) of the penalty due by the company should be paid by the officer, and in such a case they will specify this in a written notice to the officer. Where both the company and the officer are liable for portions of the penalty, HMRC may not recover more than 100% of the penalty in aggregate (*FA 2007, Sch 24, para 19*). For this purpose, an officer of the company includes a director, a shadow director (as defined in *CA 2006, s 251*), a manager, a secretary or any other person managing or purporting to manage the company's affairs (*FA 2007, Sch 24, para 19(3)*). There is no liability if the person concerned has already been convicted of an offence by reason of the inaccuracy (*FA 2007, Sch 24, para 21*).

COMPANY FAILURE TO NOTIFY TAXABLE ACTIVITIES

Notification failure

24.13 Where HMRC omit to issue a company with a notice requiring a company tax return, and the company fails to notify HMRC within 12 months of the end of the accounting period concerned that it is chargeable to corporation tax, it will incur a penalty based upon the behaviour of the company in these circumstances (*FA 1998, Sch 18, para 2*).

The amount of the penalty is based on the percentage of potential lost revenue arising. This is any corporation tax that remains unpaid 12 months after the end of the accounting period by reason of the failure (*FA 2008, Sch 41, para 7*).

There are three degrees of culpability: deliberate and concealed; deliberate and not concealed; and any other case. The most serious failure arises where the company intentionally refrains from making its activities known to HMRC and makes arrangements to hide these activities from HMRC. The second most serious is where, although the failure is intentional, there is no attempt to cover it up. The third failure encompasses all other situations (*FA 2008, Sch 41, para 5*).

These rules were introduced by *SI 2009/511* and apply to obligations arising on or after 1 April 2010.

Penalties invoked

24.14 The relevant percentages are (*FA 2008, Sch 41, para 6*):

Degree of culpability	*Percentage penalty based on potential lost revenue*
Deliberate and concealed	100%
Deliberate but not concealed	70%
Any other case	30%

> **Focus**
>
> A company should contact HMRC immediately if it transpires that HMRC have not been informed of a company's taxable activities. Potential penalties are reduced if the omission is corrected swiftly and the correction is unprompted.

Penalty reduction

24.15 The penalty can be reduced if the company makes an unprompted disclosure. A disclosure is unprompted if it is made at a time when the company has no reason to believe that HMRC have discovered, or are about to discover, the failure. In all other cases, the disclosure is prompted. In calculating the reduction, HMRC will consider the quality of the information provided, the assistance given to HMRC in calculating the additional liabilities, and the access given to the company's books and records (*FA 2008, Sch 41, para 12*).

The minimum penalties that generally apply are as follows (*FA 2008, Sch 41, para 13*):

Penalty	*Normal minimum penalty for an unprompted disclosure*	*Normal minimum penalty for a prompted disclosure*
100%	30%	50%
70%	20%	35%
30%	0%*	10%*
30%	10%**	20%**

* Notification less than 12 months after corporation tax becoming unpaid by reason of the failure to notify

** Notification 12 months or more after corporation tax becoming unpaid by reason of the failure to notify

An unprompted disclosure can reduce a 30% penalty to nil if HMRC are made aware of the failure within 12 months of the time that the corporation tax becomes unpaid by reason of the failure. In any other case, the percentage cannot normally fall below 10%.

HMRC have separate discretion to apply a special reduction to a penalty if they consider that special circumstances apply. Special circumstances do not include the company's inability to pay, or the fact that a potential loss of revenue from one taxpayer is balanced by a potential over-payment by another. HMRC also have discretion not to bring proceedings in relation to a penalty and to agree a compromise in relation to proceedings for a penalty (*FA 2008, Sch 41, para 14*).

FA 2016 introduced new, increased minimum thresholds in cases of deliberate evasion involving offshore matters, such as transferring assets overseas or using an offshore structure:

Penalty	*Normal minimum penalty for an unprompted disclosure*	*Normal minimum penalty for a prompted disclosure*
30%	0%*	10%*
30%	10%**	20%**
37.5%	0%*	12.5%*
37.5%	12.5%**	25%**
45%	0%*	15%*
45%	15%**	30%**
60%	0%*	20%*
60%	20%**	40%**
70%	30%	45%
87.5%	35%	53.75%
100%	40%	60%
105%	40%	62.5%
125%	50%	72.5%
140%	50%	80%
150%	55%	85%
200%	70%	110%

* Notification less than 12 months after corporation tax becoming unpaid by reason of the failure to notify

** Notification 12 months or more after corporation tax becoming unpaid by reason of the failure to notify

These new penalties will apply from a date to be appointed by the Treasury (*FA 2008, Sch 41, paras 12(1A), 13A*; *FA 2016, s 163(2), Sch 21*).

The penalty is reduced by any other penalty or surcharge applied to the same tax liability (*FA 2008, Sch 41, para 15*).

Penalty assessment procedures

24.16 HMRC will assess the penalty and notify the company. The notice will specify the tax period for which the penalty is assessed. The assessment will be treated and enforced in the same way as a corporation tax assessment. It may also be combined with an actual corporation tax assessment (*FA 2008, Sch 41, para 16*).

The penalty assessment for a tax understatement must be made within 12 months of the period beginning with the end of the appeal period for the assessment of tax unpaid by reason of the failure or, where there is no such assessment, the date on which the amount of tax unpaid by reason of the relevant act or failure is ascertained.

An appeal period is a period during which an appeal could be brought, or during which an appeal that has been brought has not been determined or withdrawn. The penalty is due for payment within 30 days of notification (*FA 2008, Sch 41, para 16*).

See HMRC Factsheet CC/FS11 'Penalties for failure to notify', (tinyurl.com/opr9cyn) which provides practical taxpayer guidance regarding failure to notify.

Right of appeal

24.17 The company has the right of appeal to the tribunal against the imposition and the amount of the penalty, in which case no penalty is due until the appeal is determined (*FA 2008, Sch 41, paras 17, 18*). The appeal is treated for procedural purposes in the same way as a corporation tax appeal (see **22.24**). The tribunal may affirm the decision, or it may cancel or recalculate the penalty if it finds that HMRC's decision was flawed (*FA 2008, Sch 41, paras 18, 19*).

A company with a non-deliberate failure may be excused a penalty if it satisfies HMRC or (on an appeal notified to the tribunal) the tribunal that there is a reasonable excuse for its failure to notify. A reasonable excuse does not include an insufficiency of funds unless this is outside the company's control, or reliance on a third party unless the company took reasonable care to avoid the failure. If there was a reasonable excuse for the failure, and the excuse then ceases, it will be treated as continuing if the failure is remedied without unreasonable delay after the excuse has ceased (*FA 2008, Sch 41, para 20*).

Liability of company officers

24.18 In the case of a deliberate failure attributable to an officer of the company, HMRC may decide that a proportion (up to 100%) of the penalty due by the company should be paid by the officer, and in such a case they will specify this in a written notice to the officer. Where both the company and the officer are liable for portions of the penalty, HMRC may not recover more than 100% of the penalty in aggregate (*FA 2008, Sch 41, para 22*). For this purpose, an officer of the company includes a director, a shadow director (as defined in *CA 2006, s 251*), a manager, a secretary or any other person managing or purporting to manage the company's affairs. There is no liability if the person concerned has already been convicted of an offence by reason of the inaccuracy (*FA 2008, Sch 41, para 22*).

FAILURE TO DELIVER A RETURN BY THE FILING DATE

Current penalty rules until FA 2009, Sch 55, takes effect

24.19 *FA 2009, Sch 55* introduced new penalty rules regarding the late submission of a company tax return (see **24.20–24.25**). These rules have yet to take effect, and are, in fact, unlikely to be enacted in the light of the Government's new proposals to introduce a penalty points system as part of the Making Tax Digital project (see **24.26**).

Under the existing rules, failure to deliver a return on time incurs a flat rate penalty of £100 if the return is up to three months late and £200 in any other case. These penalties are increased to £500 and £1,000 where failure occurs for a third successive time (*FA 1998, Sch 18, para 17*). These penalties are not tax-related and will not reduce if the tax liability reduces. If a period of account is longer than 12 months and HMRC have not been advised of the change, an automatic late filing penalty will be issued in respect of the return that HMRC would have expected for each accounting period. This will cause the inconvenience of an appeal even where no penalty is ultimately due. Companies should inform HMRC of any changes in accounting date without delay.

If a company fails to deliver a return within 18 months of the end of an accounting period or (if later) by the statutory filing date, then, in addition to the flat rate penalty, it will be liable to a tax-related penalty. The penalty is 10% of the unpaid tax if the return is delivered within two years after the end of the period for which the return is required, or 20% of the unpaid tax in any other case (*FA 1998, Sch 18, para 18*).

There is no flat rate penalty where accounts are required under the *Companies Act 2006* and the return is delivered no later than the last day those accounts are required at Companies House (*FA 1998, Sch 18, para 19*). This can come into play when a company extends its period of account beyond 12 months.

Example 24.1—Return submitted by *Companies Act* deadline

Facts

Renaldo Ltd, a small private company, prepares accounts to 31 March each year. However, the accounting period beginning 1 April 2017 is extended to 30 September 2018. Renaldo Ltd prepared two corporation tax returns: the first to 31 March 2018, and the second to 30 September 2018. The two returns were submitted to HMRC on 30 April 2019, more than 12 months after the end of the accounting period ended 31 March 2018.

Analysis

Renaldo Ltd is not required to submit the accounts for the period to 30 September 2018 to Companies House until 30 June 2019, ie the latest day on which those accounts may be filed at Companies House. Accordingly, no penalty is due. If HMRC raise a penalty notice, the company should appeal under *FA 1998, Sch 18, para 19*.

Penalty rules post FA 2009, Sch 55 – not yet in effect

Introduction

24.20 *FA 2009, Sch 55* introduced new penalty provisions under *FA 1998, Sch 18, para 3* for failure to deliver a company tax return on time. These have not yet been brought into effect for corporation tax purposes, and the date of their introduction is to be notified by Treasury order.

The amount of each penalty depends on the length of time the return is outstanding after the penalty date. The penalty date is the day after the statutory filing date, being the date on which the penalty is first payable. There are unlimited fixed-rate penalties, and there are separate tax-related penalties which may not exceed 100% of the tax at issue (*FA 2009, Sch 55, paras 1(3)* and *17(3)*). The penalties are not inter-dependent. The company has a right of appeal (*FA 2009, Sch 55, para 20*), and no penalty can be charged if the company has a reasonable excuse for its failure.

Penalties invoked

24.21 The legislation, which will apply for the purposes of a wide range of taxes, provides for the withholding of information in three categories (*FA 2009, Sch 55, para 6A*):

Category 1

- Where the information withheld involves a domestic matter; or where it involves an offshore matter and the territory in question is a category 1 territory or the tax at stake is a tax other than income tax or capital gains tax.

Category 2

- For income tax or capital gains tax where the information withheld involves an offshore matter, and the territory in question is a category 2 territory.

Category 3

- For income tax or capital gains tax where the information withheld involves an offshore matter, and the territory in question is a category 3 territory.

In general, only category 1 will apply to corporation tax matters. On this basis, penalties that will be raised if the company fails to meet the company tax return filing deadline are as follows:

Company tax return outstanding for 3 months or less

- a £100 penalty (*FA 2009, Sch 55, para 3*);

Company tax return outstanding for more than 3 months

- HMRC may issue a notice to charge a penalty of £10 per day from the penalty date for a period of 90 days or until the company tax return is filed (*FA 2009, Sch 55, para 4*);

Company tax return outstanding for more than 6 months

- HMRC may charge a penalty amounting to the greater of £300 and 5% of the corporation tax at issue (*FA 2009, Sch 55, para 5*);

Company tax return outstanding for more than 12 months after the penalty date

- the penalty is dependent on whether the failure amounts to a deliberate withholding of information which would enable or assist HMRC to assess the company's liability to tax (*FA 2009, Sch 55, para 6*). For this purpose, there are three degrees of culpability defining the seriousness of the withholding of information.

Nature of the withholding of information

24.22 The penalty depends on whether HMRC consider that the:

- withholding of information is deliberate and concealed – the penalty is the greater of £300 and 100% of any liability to tax which would have been shown in the return in question (*FA 2009, Sch 55, para 6(3), (3A)(a)*);

- withholding of information is deliberate but not concealed – the penalty is the greater of £300 and 70% of any liability to tax which would have been shown in the return in question (*FA 2009, Sch 55, para 6(4), (4A)(a)*);

- in any other case – the penalty is the greater of £300 and 5% of any liability to tax which would have been shown in the return in question (*FA 2009, Sch 55, para 6(5)*).

For this purpose the withholding of information is deliberate and concealed if the company deliberately withholds the information and makes arrangements to conceal the fact that the information has been withheld. The withholding of information is deliberate but not concealed if the company deliberately withholds the information but does not make arrangements to conceal the fact that the information has been withheld (*FA 2009, Sch 55, para 27*).

Reductions for unprompted and prompted disclosure

Focus

Once the new penalty provisions for failure to deliver a company tax return have been brought into effect, penalties will be invoked for a company's failure to file. Penalties will be reduced if the omission is corrected and the correction is unprompted.

24.23 A penalty can be reduced if the company makes an unprompted disclosure. A disclosure is unprompted if it is made at a time when the company has no reason to believe that HMRC have discovered, or are about to discover, the error. In all other cases, the disclosure is prompted. In calculating the reduction, HMRC will consider the quality of the disclosure, including its timing, nature and extent (*FA 2009, Sch 55, para 14*). This depends upon when the company has told HMRC about its failure to make a return, whether it has given HMRC reasonable help in quantifying any tax unpaid as a result, and whether it has allowed HMRC access to the company's books and records.

If the withholding of information is deliberate, irrespective of whether or not it was concealed, the penalty cannot fall below £300. Subject to this, the minimum penalties that generally apply are as follows (*FA 2009, Sch 55, para 15*):

Penalty	*Normal minimum penalty for an unprompted disclosure*	*Normal minimum penalty for a prompted disclosure*
30%	0%	15%
70%	20%	35%
100%	30%	50%

HMRC have separate discretion to make a special reduction to a penalty if they consider that special circumstances apply. Special circumstances do not include the company's inability to pay, or the fact that a potential loss of revenue from one taxpayer is balanced by a potential over-payment by another. HMRC also have discretion not to bring proceedings in relation to a penalty and to agree a compromise in relation to proceedings for a penalty (*FA 2009, Sch 55, para 16*).

These measures will be supplemented by increased minimum thresholds in cases of deliberate evasion involving offshore matters, such as transferring assets overseas or using an offshore structure:

Penalty	*Normal minimum penalty for an unprompted disclosure*	*Normal minimum penalty for a prompted disclosure*
70%	30%	45%
87.5%	35%	53.75%
100%	40%	60%
105%	40%	62.5%
125%	50%	72.5%
140%	50%	80%
150%	55%	85%
200%	70%	110%

These new penalties will apply from a date to be appointed by the Treasury (*FA 2009, Sch 55, paras 14(1A), 15A*; *FA 2016, s 163(2), Sch 21*).

The penalty is reduced by any other penalty or surcharge applied to the same tax liability (*FA 2009, Sch 55, para 17*).

Penalty assessment procedures

24.24 HMRC will assess the penalty and notify the company. The notice will specify the tax period for which the penalty is assessed. The assessment will be treated and enforced in the same way as a corporation tax assessment; it may also be combined with an actual corporation tax assessment (*FA 2009, Sch 55, para 18(1), (3)*).

The penalty assessment under these provisions must be made on or before (*FA 2009, Sch 55, para 19*):

- the last day of the period of two years beginning with the filing date; or
- if it applies and is later, the last day of the period of 12 months beginning with either the end of the appeal period for the assessment of the liability to tax which would have been shown in the return or, if there is no such assessment, the date on which that liability is ascertained or it is ascertained that the liability is nil.

An appeal period is a period during which an appeal could be brought, or during which an appeal that has been brought has not been determined or withdrawn

(*FA 2009, Sch 55, para 19(4)*). The penalty is due for payment within 30 days of notification (*FA 2009, Sch 55, para 18(2)*).

Right of appeal

24.25 The company has the right of appeal to the tribunal against the imposition and the amount of the penalty, in which case no penalty is due until the appeal is determined (*FA 2009, Sch 55, paras 20, 21*). The appeal is treated for procedural purposes in the same way as a corporation tax appeal (see **22.24**). The tribunal may affirm the decision, or it may cancel or recalculate the penalty if it finds that HMRC's decision was flawed (*FA 2009, Sch 55, paras 21, 22*).

A company with a non-deliberate failure may be excused a penalty if it satisfies HMRC or (on an appeal notified to the tribunal) the tribunal that there is a reasonable excuse for its failure to deliver a return by the filing date. A reasonable excuse does not include an insufficiency of funds unless this is outside the company's control, or reliance on a third party unless the company took reasonable care to avoid the failure. If there was a reasonable excuse for the failure, and the excuse then ceases, it will be treated as continuing if the failure is remedied without unreasonable delay after the excuse has ceased (*FA 2009, Sch 55, para 23*).

Proposals to introduce a penalty points system

24.26 The Government is proposing to introduce a new points-based system for the late submission of returns. This system is not limited to corporation tax but will also cover income tax and VAT. It is proposed that the regime for VAT will be enacted first so as to apply from 2020 in accordance with the Making Tax Digital timetable. It is not known when the new rules will come into force for corporation tax purposes (see Consultation Paper 'Making Tax Digital: sanctions for late payment and submission' 1 March 2017, together with a summary of responses (1 December 2017) at tinyurl.com/mzw48de).

Under the new proposals, a company will collect a penalty point on each occasion that it fails to submit a return on time. However, no penalty will be charged until a certain threshold is reached. Once the threshold is reached, a penalty will be charged for each subsequent failure to provide a submission on time. The points will be reset to zero after a period of good compliance. In general, penalty points will expire after a period of 24 months, provided that the threshold has not been reached in that period. The idea is that penalties will be charged for frequent breaches rather than for isolated failures, thereby encouraging companies to improve the standard of their reporting behaviour.

The following thresholds have been proposed:

Submission	*Frequency of breach*
Annual	2
Quarterly	4
Monthly	5

There will also be a 'reasonable excuse' defence. The amount of the penalty has not yet been decided. The government intends to publish draft legislation for further consultation in summer 2018.

PENALTIES FOR FAILING TO PAY TAX ON TIME

Current penalty rules until FA 2009, Sch 56, takes effect

24.27 *FA 2009, Sch 56* introduced new penalty rules regarding the late payment of tax, and these will apply to corporation tax due on company tax returns and the quarterly instalment arrangements that apply to large companies (see **24.27–24.32**). These rules have yet to take effect, and are, in fact, unlikely to be enacted in the light of the Government's proposals to reform the system as part of the Making Tax Digital project (see **24.34**).

Under the existing rules, failure to pay corporation tax on time attracts interest on unpaid tax (see **23.26**) but no penalty, except in the case of quarterly instalments of corporation tax which large companies are required to pay (see **23.11** onwards). Where a charge to interest arises on a quarterly instalment payment because a large company or its agent deliberately or recklessly fails to make the payment, or fraudulently or negligently claims repayment, a penalty is imposed not exceeding twice the amount of the interest charge (*TMA 1970, s 59E(4)*; *Corporation Tax (Instalment Payments) Regulations 1998, SI 1998/3175, reg 13*).

Penalty rules post FA 2009, Sch 56 – not yet in effect

Introduction

24.28 *FA 2009, Sch 56* introduced new penalty provisions for failure to pay tax on time. These have not yet been brought into effect for corporation tax purposes, and the date of their introduction is to be notified by Treasury order. *FA 2009, Sch 56* gives details of the relevant taxes and the dates from which the penalties arise.

Penalties invoked

24.29 The penalty date for an outstanding corporation tax liability or quarterly instalment payment is the statutory filing date for the company tax return for the period for which the tax is due (*FA 2009, Sch 56, para 1*; *FA 1998, Sch 18, para 14*).

If any amount of the tax is unpaid by the penalty date, a penalty of 5% of that amount is charged. If any amount of the tax is still unpaid after the end of the period of three months beginning with the penalty date, a further penalty of 5% of that amount is charged. If any amount of the tax is still unpaid after the end of the period of nine months beginning with the penalty date, a further penalty of 5% of that amount is charged (*FA 2009, Sch 56, para 4*).

If HMRC raise a determination under *FA 1998, Sch 18, para 36* or *37*, the filing date for the company tax return for the period for which the tax is due is also the penalty date.

Special reduction

24.30 If HMRC consider that special circumstances apply, they may reduce any penalty arising. Special circumstances do not include the company's inability to pay, or the fact that a potential loss of revenue from one taxpayer is balanced by a potential over-payment by another. HMRC also have discretion not to bring proceedings in relation to a penalty and to agree a compromise in relation to proceedings for a penalty (*FA 2009, Sch 56, para 9*).

Suspension of penalty

24.31 If a company requests to defer payment of a tax liability before a late payment penalty becomes due and HMRC agree to that request, the company will not become liable to a penalty unless it breaks the terms of the agreement (*FA 2009, Sch 56, para 10*).

Penalty assessment procedures

24.32 In order to collect the penalty, HMRC must raise an assessment, notify the company and give details in the notice of the period in respect of which the penalty is assessed. The company has 30 days, beginning with the day on which notice of the assessment of the penalty is issued, to pay the penalty. For procedural purposes, the penalty is treated in the same way as tax (*FA 2009, Sch 56, para 11*).

HMRC have a time limit for raising the penalty assessment. This is on or before the later of (*FA 2009, Sch 56, para 12*):

- the last day of the period of two years beginning with the tax due date; and
- the last day of the period of 12 months beginning with:
  - the end of the appeal period for the assessment of the amount of tax in respect of which the penalty is assessed, or
  - if there is no such assessment, the date on which that amount of tax is ascertained.

Right of appeal

24.33 The company has the right of appeal to the tribunal against the imposition and the amount of the penalty, in which case no penalty is due until the appeal is determined (*FA 2009, Sch 56, paras 13, 14*). The appeal is treated for procedural purposes in the same way as a corporation tax appeal (see **22.24**). The tribunal may affirm the decision, or it may cancel or recalculate the penalty if it finds that HMRC's decision was flawed (*FA 2009, Sch 56, paras 14, 15*).

A company with a non-deliberate failure may be excused a penalty if it satisfies HMRC or (on an appeal notified to the tribunal) the tribunal that there is a reasonable excuse for its failure to pay on time. A reasonable excuse does not include an insufficiency of funds unless this is outside the company's control, or reliance on a third party unless the company took reasonable care to avoid the failure. If there was a reasonable excuse for the failure, and the excuse then ceases, it will be treated as continuing if the failure is remedied without unreasonable delay after the excuse has ceased (*FA 2009, Sch 56, para 16*).

Proposals to reform the penalty system for late payment of corporation tax

24.34 The government is proposing to reform the penalty system for late payment of tax, covering corporation tax, income tax and VAT (see Consultation Paper 'Making Tax Digital: sanctions for late payment and submission' 1 March 2017 at tinyurl.com/mzw48de, together with Consultation Paper 'Making Tax Digital: interest harmonisation and sanctions for late payment' 1 December 2017 at tinyurl.com/y8skqxab).

The following is a summary of the proposed rules:

- No penalty will be payable if the tax is paid within 15 days of the due date, or a 'time to pay' agreement is agreed within this period (see **23.44**).
- A penalty of 2.5% of the outstanding tax will be payable if payment or a 'time to pay' agreement is made within the period of 16–30 days (inclusive) after the due date.
- This penalty will increase to a penalty of 5% of the outstanding tax if the latter remains unpaid 30 days after the due date. In addition, a second penalty will be charged, calculated as an amount of interest ('penalty interest'). Penalty interest is distinct from late payment interest, which runs from the due date and is calculated by reference to the Bank of England base rate. Penalty interest will run from the 30-day mark until payment is made in full. The rate of interest has not yet been determined, but it will not be calculated by reference to base rates.

These rules will be subject to a 'reasonable excuse' defence.

GAAR-related penalties

24.35 *FA 2016, s 158* introduced a new tax geared penalty in cases where the taxpayer has been involved in arrangements which are later found to come within the scope of the General Anti-Avoidance Rule (GAAR) (*FA 2013, s 212A, Sch 43C*). The amount of the penalty is 60% of the tax due ('the value of the counteraction').

The penalty is triggered when the taxpayer submits a return, claim or document to HMRC that includes the relevant arrangements, and becomes chargeable at the point that HMRC successfully counteracts the arrangements under the GAAR provisions in *FA 2013, s 209*. A successful counteraction is either one where there is no appeal against the decision, or where an appeal has been made, but has not succeeded.

The GAAR-related penalty is supplemental to the standard penalties set out in *FA 2007, Sch 24* (and presumably to the penalties set out in *FA 2009, Sch 59* when the latter comes into force). However, where both the GAAR-related penalty and standard penalty apply to the same amount of tax in question, the total penalty in respect of the disputed tax is restricted. The restriction applies as follows:

- The total penalty is restricted to 100% of the tax in domestic cases.
- For offshore matters, the total penalty is restricted to the highest penalty available under the standard penalty regime.

It is possible for a taxpayer to avoid a GAAR-related penalty by correcting the tax position, provided this is done at any time until the arrangements are referred to the GAAR Advisory Panel.

PENALTY PROCEDURES GENERALLY

24.36 HMRC's computer system (COTAX) automatically issues flat-rate and tax-related penalty notices shortly after the date a penalty is incurred. Additionally, tax-related penalty determinations are automatically amended when the amount of tax payable recorded on COTAX is revised. Details of HMRC's internal penalty processes can be found in the HMRC COTAX Manual at COM100000 onwards.

The question of whether an automatic penalty generated by computer is valid will depend on the particular charging provisions in the tax legislation. In *Khan Properties Ltd v HMRC* [2017] UKFTT 830 (TC), the First-tier Tribunal held that a notice issued in respect of a flat rate penalty for late filing of a company tax return required a 'flesh and blood' HMRC officer to make a decision to impose a penalty before giving instructions which could then be executed by computer. There was no indication that a human being was involved in the process and, accordingly, the notice was declared invalid. The Tribunal made clear that this decision turned specifically on the wording of *TMA 1970, s 100*, which is the relevant provision for late filing penalties for companies under *FA 1998, Sch 18, para 17* (see **24.19**). The same result will not necessarily apply to other penalty provisions, such as those contained in *FA 2009, Schs 55* and *56* (see **24.20**, **24.27**).

If a company receives notice of a penalty with which it disagrees, it should ensure that a notice of appeal is lodged with HMRC within 30 days of the date of issue of the penalty notice.

All tax-related penalties carry interest, and the rates are the same as for interest on unpaid tax: see **23.26** (*TMA 1970, s 103A*).

PUBLISHING DETAILS OF DELIBERATE TAX DEFAULTERS

Focus

Given the current groundswell of opinion against tax avoidance, a company needs to be alert to the reputational damage which could be caused by having its name and details published as a deliberate tax defaulter.

24.37 Provided that they inform the taxpayer in advance, HMRC may publish details of persons (including companies) who deliberately evade tax, if any of the following penalties is incurred and the aggregate potential lost revenue in relation to the penalty or penalties exceeds £25,000. HMRC may publish the details in any manner they consider appropriate, but before doing so they must provide the taxpayer with sufficient time to make representations about whether the details should be published. Within a year after the penalty in question has become final, HMRC may start to publish the details, and they may continue to publish these for no more than a year after first publication. In cases of deliberate offshore evasion, only taxpayers who make full unprompted disclosures are protected from having their details publicised (*FA 2009, s 94,* as amended by *FA 2016, s 164*; see also HMRC's Factsheet CC/FS13 'Publishing details of deliberate defaulters' (tinyurl.com/ov63wwp)).

For this purpose the penalties in question that can arise in relation to corporation tax are:

- deliberate inaccuracy in a taxpayer's document under *FA 2007, Sch 24, para 1*;
- inaccuracy in a taxpayer's document attributable to deliberate supply of false information or deliberate withholding of information under *FA 2007, Sch 24, para 1A*; and
- deliberate failure to notify under *FA 2008, Sch 41, para 1*.

The following information may be published (*FA 2009, s 94*):

- the person's name (including any trading name, previous name or pseudonym);
- the person's address (or registered office);
- the nature of any business carried on by the person;
- the amount of the penalty or penalties and the potential lost revenue in relation to the penalty (or the aggregate of the potential lost revenue in relation to each of the penalties);
- the periods or times to which the inaccuracy, failure or action giving rise to the penalty (or any of the penalties) relates, and
- any such other information that HMRC consider appropriate to publish in order to make clear the person's identity.

For further details, see HMRC Compliance Handbook at CH190000 and published details of deliberate tax defaulters at tinyurl.com/a4zl2kg.

MANAGING SERIOUS DEFAULTERS

24.38 HMRC operate the Managing Serious Defaulters programme (formerly known as the Managing Deliberate Defaulters programme) to deter known defaulters from returning to non-compliant behaviour, effect a permanent shift to compliant behaviour, deter potential deliberate defaulters, and reassure the compliant population that HMRC do take action against serious defaulters. There is no specified monetary limit on the amount of tax that must be evaded to justify inclusion in the Managing Serious Defaulters programme. It includes people:

- charged a penalty for a deliberate offence under specific taxes legislation or otherwise identified, during a civil investigation of fraud, as presenting a continuing high risk to HMRC;
- successfully prosecuted by the Director of Revenue & Customs Prosecutions or another prosecuting authority for a tax matter;
- charged a civil evasion penalty for dishonesty;
- who have given security in respect of VAT, environmental taxes, PAYE or NICs; or
- who try to get out of paying what they owe by becoming insolvent where insolvency practitioners pursue claims for recovery of money or assets on behalf of HMRC.

For further details, see HMRC Factsheet CC/FS14 'Managing Serious Defaulters' (tinyurl.com/pxa8a6b).

TAX AGENTS: DISHONEST CONDUCT

Introduction

> **Focus**
>
> For most companies, a good working relationship with HMRC is helpful, and this could be damaged if a company were to use a tax agent found guilty of dishonest conduct.

24.39 A company seeking or already using a qualified tax agent or adviser should be aware of the very high standards of professional conduct in relation to tax, set out in guidance updated on 1 May 2015 and subscribed to jointly by the following professional bodies: AAT, ACCA, ATT, CIOT, ICAEW, ICAS and STEP (see tinyurl.com/tax-org-professional-standards). In addition, HMRC have their own standards for agents, which ensure that a minimum standard is set for all agents and, in particular, for those that are unaffiliated to any professional body (see tinyurl.com/gov-uk-agent-standards). Using a qualified tax agent may thus provide a degree of comfort and assurance not necessarily available from an unqualified agent.

HMRC have had powers since 1 April 2013 to obtain working papers from tax agents who engage in dishonest conduct, to impose penalties on them, and to publish their details (*FA 2012, s 223, Sch 38*, brought into effect by the *Finance Act 2012, Schedule 38 (Tax Agents: Dishonest Conduct) (Appointed Day and*

Savings) Order 2013, SI 2013/279). The Treasury has wide powers to make any incidental, supplemental, consequential, transitional or saving provision in relation to these measures, to make different provision for different purposes, and to amend, repeal or revoke any statutory provision (*FA 2012, s 223, Sch 38*).

For general guidance on dishonest conduct by tax agents, see tinyurl.com/curc3md. See HMRC Compliance Handbook at CH180000 onwards for technical guidance, and at CH880000 onwards for operational guidance. See also HMRC Factsheet TAFS 'Tax agents: Dishonest conduct', which HMRC issue to tax agents whom they believe have engaged in dishonest conduct.

Definition of a tax agent

24.40 For this purpose, a tax agent is an individual who, in the course of business, assists clients with their tax affairs. Individuals can be tax agents even if they (or the organisations for which they work) are appointed indirectly or at the request of someone other than the client. Assistance with a client's tax affairs includes:

- advising a client in relation to tax,
- acting or purporting to act as agent on behalf of a client in relation to tax,
- assistance with any document that is likely to be relied on by HMRC to determine a client's tax position, and
- assistance given for non-tax purposes if it is given in the knowledge that it will be, or is likely to be, used by a client in connection with the client's tax affairs (*FA 2012, Sch 38, para 2*).

Definition of dishonest conduct

24.41 An individual engages in dishonest conduct if, in the course of acting as a tax agent and whether or not acting on the client's instructions, they dishonestly do (or refrain from doing) something with a view to bringing about a loss of tax revenue, regardless of whether or not such a loss is brought about (*FA 2012, Sch 38, para 3*). Tax includes corporation tax and any other amount assessable or chargeable as if it were corporation tax, and a wide range of other taxes (*FA 2012, Sch 38, para 37*).

A loss of tax revenue would be brought about for these purposes if clients were to (*FA 2012, Sch 38, para 3*):

- account for less tax than they are required to account for by law,
- obtain more tax relief than they are entitled to obtain by law (tax relief meaning any exemption from or deduction or credit against or in respect of tax, and any repayment of tax),

- account for tax later than they are required to account for it by law, or
- obtain tax relief earlier than they are entitled to obtain it by law.

Conduct notice and file access notice

24.42 If HMRC determine that an individual is engaging in or has engaged in dishonest conduct, they may issue a 'conduct notice' stating the grounds on which the determination was made.

The individual may appeal against the determination within 30 days. On an appeal that is notified to the tribunal, the tribunal may confirm or set aside the determination, but setting it aside does not prevent a further conduct notice being given in respect of the same conduct if further evidence emerges (*FA 2012, Sch 38, paras 4, 5*).

Where a conduct notice has been issued and finally confirmed, or where an individual who was a tax agent at the time has been convicted of a tax-related offence relating to tax that involves fraud or dishonesty, and any possibility of overturning this on appeal expired within the past 12 months, HMRC may (with the approval of the tribunal) issue a 'file access notice' to the tax agent and/or any other person they believe may hold relevant documents.

A file access notice must name the tax agent but need not identify the agent's clients, and may require the provision of particular relevant documents specified in the notice, or all relevant documents in the document-holder's possession or power. A recipient other than the tax agent may appeal against the file access notice within 30 days. On an appeal that is notified to the tribunal, the tribunal may confirm, vary or set aside the notice or a requirement in it, and this decision is final (*FA 2012, Sch 38, paras 7–20*).

Penalties invoked

24.43 A tax agent who engages in dishonest conduct is liable to a penalty of no less than £5,000 and no more than £50,000, but this may be reduced below £5,000 (and even to nil) in special circumstances (*FA 2012, Sch 38, paras 26, 27*). Special circumstances do not include the agent's inability to pay, or the fact that a potential loss of revenue from one taxpayer is balanced by a potential over-payment by another (whether or not a client of the agent in question). HMRC also have discretion not to bring proceedings in relation to a penalty and to agree a compromise in relation to proceedings for a penalty (*FA 2012, Sch 38, para 27*).

A person is not liable to such a penalty for anything in respect of which they have been convicted of an offence (*FA 2012, Sch 38, para* 33), nor in respect of anything for which they are personally liable to a penalty for errors, failure to notify or failure to make a return (*FA 2012, Sch 38, para 34*). Where the penalty exceeds £5,000, HMRC may publish information about the individual incurring the penalty and, in certain circumstances, the organisation for which the individual works or worked, subject to some of the provisions that relate to publishing details of deliberate tax defaulters (*FA 2012, Sch 38, para 28*; see also **24.37**).

A person commits an offence if he or she conceals, destroys or otherwise disposes of a material document, or arranges for the concealment, destruction or disposal of a material document. Penalties may be charged for these offences or otherwise failing to comply with a conduct notice or a file access notice (*FA 2012, Sch 38, paras 6, 21–25, 29–35*).

Interest is payable on late payment of penalties assessed under *FA 2012, Sch 38* for dishonest conduct or for failure to comply with a file access notice (*FA 2009, s 101*, brought into effect for this purpose by the *Finance Act 2009, Section 101 (Tax Agents: Dishonest Conduct) (Appointed Day) Order 2013, SI 2013/280*).

Chapter 25

HMRC powers

SIGNPOSTS

- Introduction to HMRC powers (see **25.1**).
- Information and inspection powers, including restrictions, right of appeal and appeal procedures (see **25.2–25.13**).
- Documents and record keeping, including consequences of destruction (see **25.14–25.20**).
- HMRC time limits for raising assessments (see **25.21–25.22**).
- HMRC correction of tax returns (see **25.23**).
- Tax debtors (see **25.24–25.25**).
- Senior accounting officer reporting duties (see **25.26–25.31**).
- Tax avoidance schemes, including DOTAS disclosure procedures and requirements (see **25.32–25.41**).
- General anti-abuse rule ('GAAR') (see **25.42–25.46**).
- Public sector procurement restrictions (see **25.47**).
- HMRC action to counter tax avoidance schemes, including accelerated payments of tax and action against promoters (see **25.48–25.51**).
- Multilateral co-operation (see **25.52**).

INTRODUCTION TO HMRC POWERS

25.1 HMRC are granted powers in order to monitor the accuracy of company tax returns and to ensure prompt collection of tax. Companies are required to comply with additional reporting procedures imposed on their senior accounting officer, and with disclosure requirements in respect of tax avoidance schemes.

The main body of the HMRC powers legislation is contained in *FA 2008*. The legislation applies in varying degrees to all taxes. The legislation applying to corporation tax is dealt with as follows:

Compliance Checks	*Implementation date and commencement order*	*Paragraph references in this chapter*
Information and inspection powers	1 April 2009	**25.2–25.19**
FA 2008, s 113 and *Sch 36*	*SI 2009/404*	
Computer records	21 July 2008	**25.5**
FA 2008, s 114	(Royal Assent)	
Record keeping	1 April 2009	**25.20–25.21**
FA 1998, s 117(1) and *Sch 18, Pt III*	*SI 2009/402*	
Time limits	1 April 2010	**25.22**
FA 2008, s 118 and *Sch 39*	*SI 2009/403*	
Correction of tax returns	1 April 2010	**25.23**
FA 2008, s 119	*SI 2009/405*	
Debtor contact details	21 July 2009	**25.24**
FA 2009, s 97 and *Sch 49*	(Royal Assent)	
Direct recovery of debts (DRD)	18 November 2015	**25.25**
F(No 2)A 2015, s 47 and *Sch 8*	(Royal Assent)	
Senior accounting officer duties	21 July 2009	**25.26–25.30**
FA 2009, s 93 and *Sch 46*	(Royal Assent)	
Tax avoidance schemes disclosure	1 August 2004	**25.32–25.41**
FA 2004, ss 306–319	*SI 2004/1863*	
	SI 2006/1543	

HMRC publish a factsheet explaining their general approach to carrying out compliance checks (see tinyurl.com/ponk48u).

For information on how HMRC investigate suspected tax fraud, see **22.22**.

INFORMATION AND INSPECTION POWERS

> **Focus**
>
> HMRC's information and inspection powers are wide-ranging, and include powers to obtain information from the taxpayer and from third parties.

HMRC powers to obtain information and documents

25.2 In order to check the accuracy of a tax return or other submitted document, HMRC have powers to:

- request supplementary information from the taxpayer and from third parties;
- inspect records; and
- visit premises and inspect records, assets and premises.

These powers were introduced from 1 April 2009 (*Finance Act 2008, Schedule 36 (Appointed Day and Savings) Order 2009, SI 2009/404*).

Supplementary information

25.3 A request for *supplementary* information to either the company or a third party must be made in writing (*FA 2008, Sch 36, paras 1, 2*). A notice to a third party can only be given with the approval of the company or the tribunal, and an application to the tribunal for approval of a taxpayer or third party notice may be heard *ex parte*, that is, without the taxpayer being present (*FA 2008, Sch 36, paras 3(2A), 5(3A)*). A third party request must name the person to whom it relates, unless this has been disapplied by the tribunal (*FA 2008, Sch 36, para 3(5)*). A copy of a third party notice must be given to the taxpayer unless the tribunal disapplies this requirement (*FA 2008, Sch 36, para 4*). Certain of HMRC's powers in relation to an information notice were clarified in *Revenue & Customs Commissioners, ex parte a taxpayer* [2014] UKFTT 931 (TC).

If there are reasonable grounds for believing that a taxpayer has not complied with any provision of tax law (whether of the UK or another territory), an HMRC officer authorised for this purpose may ask the tribunal to approve a notice, even though the identity of the taxpayer is unknown to them (*FA 2008, Sch 36, paras 5, 59*). A decision of the tribunal regarding the approval of a giving of a notice is final (*FA 2008, Sch 36, para 6(4)*). The notice must be complied with in full within such period and at such time, by such means and in such form as is reasonably specified or described in the notice (*FA 2008, Sch 36, para 7*). Where a notice requires production of a document, this can generally be met by production of a copy of the document, except where HMRC specify that they require the original document (*FA 2008, Sch 36, para 8*).

In relation to these powers, the expression 'tax' includes 'relevant foreign tax'. In *HMRC, ex parte certain taxpayers* [2012] UKFTT 765 (TC) the First-tier Tribunal considered the meaning of the expression 'relevant foreign tax' as used in *FA 2008, Sch 36, para 63,* and helped to clarify its scope.

In line with international standards set by the Organisation for Economic Co-operation and Development (OECD) and the Global Forum on Transparency and Exchange of Information for Tax Purposes, HMRC have powers to issue an information notice in a case where identifying information is held (eg a bank sort code and account number) and the information required consists of the name, address and date of birth (if known) of the person to whom the identifying information relates (*FA 2008, Sch 36, para 5A*).

HMRC may issue notices to merchant acquirers and similar bodies that process payment card transactions, requiring them to provide data about business taxpayers (*FA 2013, s 228*). HMRC use this data to check that businesses are declaring all their income (see tinyurl.com/n9862fv).

The UK's automatic exchange of information agreements

Focus

Increasingly, detailed information about taxpayers and their income is being exchanged on a routine basis between HMRC and tax authorities in other jurisdictions.

25.4 Powers exist under *FA 2013, s 222* to enable HMRC and financial institutions to honour international agreements, such as the UK/US intergovernmental agreement signed on 12 September 2012 to implement UK compliance with the US Foreign Accounts Tax Compliance Act (FATCA).

The introduction of reporting requirements under FATCA was delayed, and revised timelines for implementation were announced by the US Internal Revenue Service in their Notice 2013-43 ('Revised Timeline and Other Guidance Regarding the Implementation of FATCA'). The reporting requirements were phased in between 2014 and 2017 and the first reports, for the year 2014, were required by 31 May 2015. New regulations came into effect on 30 June 2014 to allow UK businesses to comply with their due diligence and reporting obligations under FATCA (*International Tax Compliance (United States of America) Regulations 2014, SI 2014/1506*), but were replaced from 15 April 2015 by the *International Tax Compliance Regulations 2015, SI 2015/878*. HMRC's guidance on FATCA can be found at tinyurl.com/nrttyg9 and tinyurl.com/mbcd3sl).

To meet the UK's obligations under the EU Directive on Administrative Co-operation (Council Directive 2011/16/EU), and under Competent Authority Agreements with non-EU jurisdictions for the Common Reporting Standard, the *International Tax Compliance Regulations* referred to above (*SI 2015/878*) also create due diligence and reporting obligations for UK financial institutions from 1 January 2016. Financial institutions are required to identify accounts maintained for account holders who are tax resident in jurisdictions with which the UK has entered into exchange of information agreements, and to collect and report information to HMRC in a specified manner on specified persons.

HMRC powers to obtain information in relation to state aid-approved tax advantaged schemes

> **Focus**
> Under the *Finance Act 2016* HMRC have the power to request information in relation to tax reliefs subject to EU state aid approval. Failure to supply the information could result in the relief being denied.

25.5 From 1 July 2016, HMRC have the power to request information from persons in respect of tax relief granted under any of the various statutory schemes that are subject to EU state aid approval. The purpose of these powers is to collect information in order to comply with the UK's EU obligations (*FA 2016, ss 180–182, Sch 24*). These obligations will cease upon the UK's withdrawal from the EU – however, the powers will remain unless the relevant domestic legislation is specifically repealed.

There are two categories of tax advantaged schemes to which the new information powers apply:

- The first category contains a list of tax advantaged schemes for which the information must be supplied as a pre-condition to the tax relief being granted.
- The second category lists the schemes for which no such pre-condition exists.

For the purpose of corporation tax, all the relevant schemes currently fall into the first category. These are:

- the Business Premises Renovation Allowance (*CAA 2001, Pt 3A*, see **8.2** *et seq*);
- enhanced allowances for zero-emissions goods vehicles (*CAA 2001, s 45DA*, see **3.37**);
- enterprise zone allowances (*CAA 2001, s 45K*, see **3.40**);
- the following creative tax reliefs: film, television, video games, theatre, orchestra relief and the museums and galleries exhibition tax relief (*CTA 2009, Pts 15, 15A, 15C, 15D, 15E* (see **Chapter 15**); and
- R&D reliefs for SMEs including vaccine relief (*CTA 2009, Pt 13, Chs 2, 7*, see **Chapter 14**).

The information that HMRC may request includes:

- information about the person claiming the tax relief or that person's activities;
- information about the subject-matter of the claim for relief; and
- any other information which relates to the grant of State Aid through the provision of the tax advantage in question.

HMRC are also able to publish and disclose such information through a 'legal gateway' for the purpose of complying with the UK's EU obligations. Information will only be published in respect of persons who have obtained state aid worth €500,000.

Computer records

25.6 A person authorised for this purpose by the Commissioners for HMRC may access and inspect the operation of any computer and associated apparatus used in connection with a relevant required document at any reasonable time (*FA 2008, s 114(3), (9)*). It has been held by the High Court that HMRC may lawfully remove computers for inspection purposes (*R (on the application of Glenn & Co (Essex) Ltd) v Revenue and Customs Comrs* [2010] EWHC 1469 (Admin)).

Any person who obstructs the exercise of this power, or fails within a reasonable time to provide assistance required for this purpose, is liable to a penalty of £300 (*FA 2008, s 114(5), (6)*).

Powers to inspect premises and other property

25.7 Subject to at least seven days' notice being given, an HMRC officer may inspect the business premises, and the business assets and business documents that are on the premises, if the inspection is required for checking the company's tax position (*FA 2008, Sch 36, paras 10, 12*).

Business premises in relation to a company consist of any premises that an HMRC officer believes are used in connection with the carrying on of a business by or on behalf of the company, and include any building or structure, any land and any means of transport, but HMRC's powers do not include power to enter or inspect any part of the premises that is used solely as a dwelling (*FA 2008, Sch 36, paras 10(3), 58*).

Business assets consist of any assets that an HMRC officer believes are owned, leased or used in connection with the carrying on of a business by any person, but do not include documents except those which (exceptionally) comprise trading stock or plant (*FA 2008, Sch 36, para 10*; for plant, see **3.7** onwards).

Business documents include any that relate to the carrying on of a business by any person and comprise statutory records for tax purposes. For this purpose, statutory records are documents and information that the company is required to keep and preserve under the *Taxes Acts* or any other enactment relating to tax. Information and documents cease to form part of the company's statutory records once the period for which they are required to be preserved has expired (*FA 2008, Sch 36, paras 10, 62*).

There are circumstances in which an inspection of premises and other property are approved in advance by the tribunal. In such cases, the company has no right of appeal against the decision of the tribunal (*FA 2008, Sch 36, para 13(3)*).

Further powers

25.8 HMRC officers have powers to copy documents produced to them or inspected by them (*FA 2008, Sch 36, para 15*). They have powers to remove and retain documents for a reasonable time if it appears necessary to do so, and are liable to pay the owner reasonable compensation should they cause loss or damage to the documents (*FA 2008, Sch 36, para 16*). In addition, HMRC have powers to mark business assets inspected, and to record assets and documents inspected (*FA 2008, Sch 36, para 17*).

HMRC also have criminal investigation powers (*FA 2007, ss 82–87* and *Sch 23*). *FA 2013, s 224* and *Sch 48* extend certain powers under the *Proceeds of Crime Act 2002* so they can be exercised by officers of HMRC in respect of a limited number of former Inland Revenue functions.

In certain circumstances where there are reasonable grounds to suspect criminal conduct, the National Crime Agency (NCA), formerly the Serious Organised Crime Agency (SOCA), is allowed to adopt certain HMRC functions relating to corporation tax and other taxes (*Proceeds of Crime Act 2002, Pt 6*). *Fenech v Serious Organised Crime Agency* [2013] UKFTT 555 (TC) was a First-tier Tribunal case where SOCA had raised discovery assessments instead of HMRC.

The *Anti-Terrorism, Crime and Security Act 2001* gives HMRC powers to disclose information to assist criminal investigations or proceedings in the UK or abroad, or to help the intelligence services in carrying out their functions. The HMRC Code of Practice for the disclosure of information under these provisions (see tinyurl.com/nt3dut7) describes the controls and safeguards in place.

Under the Criminal Finances Act 2017 a company can be liable for the criminal offence of failing to prevent the facilitation of tax evasion by others 'acting in the capacity of an associated person'. For these purposes, an associated person is not limited to the company's employees but also includes the company's customers or suppliers. Liability is strict and applies even if senior management were not involved or were unaware of the criminal actions of the company's associated persons. It is a defence if the company had reasonable prevention procedures in place (see guidance at tinyurl.com/y8copxsm). The responsibility for investigating this offence is split between HMRC and the Serious Fraud Office (SFO). HMRC are responsible for cases involving UK evasion, while the SFO is responsible for cases involving foreign evasion.

Restrictions on powers

25.9 An information notice only requires a person to produce a document if it is in his possession or power (*FA 2008, Sch 36, para 18*). An information notice may not require a person to produce a document if the whole of the document originates more than six years before the date of the notice, unless the notice is given by, or with the agreement of, an HMRC officer authorised for this purpose (*FA 2008, Sch 36, paras 20, 59*).

Subject to certain exceptions, if a company has made a tax return under *FA 1998, Sch 18, para 3*, a notice may not be given for the purposes of checking the company's corporation tax position. However, a notice may be given where, or to the extent that, any of the following conditions is met (*FA 2008, Sch 36, para 21*):

Condition A

- An enquiry has commenced under *FA 1998, Sch 18, para 24* but has not yet been completed.

Condition B

- An HMRC officer has reason to suspect that there has been an under-assessment or excessive relief granted.

Condition C

- The information or documents in question are required for the purposes of checking the company's position as regards any tax other than income tax, capital gains tax or corporation tax.

Condition D

- The information or documents are required to check the company's position as regards any deductions or repayments of tax or withholding of income under PAYE regulations, the Construction Industry Scheme etc.

Documents protected by legal privilege need not be supplied (*FA 2008, Sch 36, para 23*). The *Information Notice: Resolution of Disputes as to Privileged Communications Regulations 2009, SI 2009/1916*, set out HMRC's approach in regard to documents alleged to be covered by legal professional privilege, and the procedure for resolving disputes where a claim that a document is privileged is not accepted by HMRC.

In *R (on the application of Prudential plc and another) v Special Commissioner of Income Tax and another* [2013] UKSC 1, the Supreme Court decided by a majority of 5:2 that documents prepared by a firm of chartered accountants acting as tax advisers were not covered by legal advice privilege, thereby confirming that legal professional privilege is only available for communications between legal professionals (solicitors, barristers and advocates) and their clients. The First-tier Tribunal case of *Lewis v Revenue & Customs* [2013] UKFTT 722 (TC) provides a useful summary of legal advice privilege and litigation privilege.

A person holding a statutory appointment as auditor cannot be required to provide HMRC with copies of his working papers (*FA 2008, Sch 36, para 24*). A tax adviser cannot be required to supply copies of relevant communications, being communications with his clients or with other tax advisers (*FA 2008, Sch 36, para 25*). The exceptions for auditors and tax advisers do not extend to explanatory material supplied to the client in relation to a document already prepared for HMRC, or (where the identity of the taxpayer is unknown to HMRC) the name and address details of a person to whom the information notice relates or any person who has acted on that person's behalf (*FA 2008, Sch 36, paras 26, 27*).

Right of appeal

25.10 A company has a right of appeal to the tribunal against an information notice. There is no right of appeal if the document formed part of the statutory records (see **25.7**) or if the tribunal approved the information notice (*FA 2008, Sch 36, para 29*). In *Skelly; Jenner; Mehigan v HMRC* [2014] UKFTT 478 (TC), the First-tier Tribunal refused the taxpayers' applications to set aside its earlier decisions to approve the issue of information notices, on grounds that it had no jurisdiction to do so, and held that if there had been procedural unfairness the appropriate remedy would be judicial review.

Any person given a third party notice may appeal to the tribunal on the ground that it would be unduly onerous to comply with the notice or requirement. There is no such right of appeal if the notice relates to the taxpayer company's statutory records or that of its parent or subsidiary (*FA 2008, Sch 36, para 35(3)*), or if the tribunal approved the giving of the notice (*FA 2008, Sch 36, para 30*). Any person given a notice, where the identity of the person is unknown, has a right of appeal to the tribunal on the ground that it would be unduly onerous to comply with the notice or requirement (*FA 2008, Sch 36, para 31*).

Appeal procedure

25.11 Notice of appeal must be given in writing, within 30 days of the date when the information notice was given, to the HMRC officer who gave the notice. The appeal must state the grounds. The tribunal's decision is final, and on receipt of the appeal it may confirm, vary or set aside the information notice or a requirement in the information notice. Confirmations and variations by the tribunal must be complied with within the time limits set by the tribunal or, if not set, within any reasonable time limit specified in writing by an HMRC officer following the tribunal's decision (*FA 2008, Sch 36, para 32*).

Groups of undertakings

25.12 Third party information notices given to any person to check the tax position of a parent undertaking and any of its subsidiaries need only state this and name the parent undertaking. Where notice would otherwise have to be given to the taxpayer, it need only be given to the parent in such circumstances and not to every subsidiary (*FA 2008, Sch 36, para 35*). The information notice restrictions in *FA 2008, Sch 36, para 21* (see **25.9**), in relation to the company tax return and enquiry framework, apply as if the notice was a taxpayer notice given to each subsidiary or to specific named subsidiaries (as the case may be). If a notice is given to the parent to check the tax position of one or more subsidiaries whose identities are unknown to the officer, the approval of the tribunal is not required, and the parent cannot appeal against a requirement to produce documents which are part of the statutory records of the parent or any of its subsidiaries.

The definitions of parent and subsidiary follow those of *CA 2006*. An undertaking is a parent undertaking in relation to another undertaking if (*CA 2006, s 1162*):

- it holds a majority of the voting rights of the other undertaking; or
- it is a member of the undertaking and has the right to appoint or remove a majority of its board of directors; or
- it has the right to exercise a dominant influence over the undertaking:
  - by virtue of provisions contained in the undertaking's articles; or
  - by virtue of a control contract; or
- it is a member of the undertaking and controls alone, pursuant to an agreement with other shareholders or members, a majority of the voting in the undertaking.

Change of ownership of companies

25.13 Where there has been a change in the ownership of a company under *CTA 2010, s 719* (see **4.25**), the seller may be or become liable to be assessed to corporation tax under *CTA 2010, s 710* or *713* (recovery of unpaid corporation tax). In such circumstances the restrictions imposed by *FA 2008, Sch 36, para 21* do not apply (see **25.9**), so an information notice may be issued even if none of the conditions specified in *para 21* is met (*FA 2008, Sch 36, para 36*). Thus, if the company has made a tax return under *FA 1998, Sch 18, para 3*, a notice may still be given for the purposes of checking the company's corporation tax position, even if:

- an enquiry under *FA 1998, Sch 18, para 24* is not in progress;
- the HMRC officer has no reason to suspect that there has been an under-assessment or excessive relief granted; and
- the information or documents in question are not required for the purposes of checking the company's taxes or deductions other than corporation tax.

Destruction of documents

25.14 A person must not conceal, destroy or dispose of a document which is the subject of an information notice addressed to that person. If the document has already been produced to an HMRC officer in accordance with the information notice, the prohibition no longer applies unless the officer has notified the person that the document must continue to be available for inspection and has not withdrawn that notification. Where a copy of a document (rather than the original) has been produced to an HMRC officer in accordance with the information notice, under *FA 2008, Sch 36, para 8(1)*, the original may be destroyed six months thereafter, unless the officer has made a request in writing under *FA 2008, Sch 36, para 8(2)(b)* for the original document (*FA 2008, Sch 36, para 42*).

A person must not conceal, destroy or dispose of a document if an officer has informed the person within the previous six months that the document is likely to be the subject of an information notice (*FA 2008, Sch 36, para 43*).

Penalties

25.15 A penalty of £300 is invoked for (*FA 2008, Sch 36, paras 39, 41–44*):

- failure to comply with an information notice within the specified period or such further time as an HMRC officer may allow; or
- deliberate obstruction of an HMRC officer in the course of an inspection,

For this purpose, failure to comply includes concealment or destruction of a document following an information notice or informal notification that the document is or is likely to be the subject of an information notice (*FA 2008, Sch 36, paras 39(3), 42–44*).

If the failure or obstruction continues after the £300 penalty is imposed, a daily default penalty not exceeding £60 becomes due for each subsequent day of failure or obstruction (*FA 2008, Sch 36, para 40*).

If a person supplies inaccurate information or produces a document that contains an inaccuracy when complying with an information notice, and the inaccuracy is careless or deliberate, HMRC may charge a penalty of £3,000. Similarly, where the person discovers the inaccuracy some time later and fails to take reasonable steps to inform HMRC, a penalty of £3,000 may be charged. If the information or document contains more than one inaccuracy, a penalty is payable for each inaccuracy (*FA 2008, Sch 36, para 40A*).

A penalty under these provisions must be paid within 30 days of the issue of the penalty notice or, if an appeal against the penalty is made, within 30 days after the appeal is determined or withdrawn (*FA 2008, Sch 36, para 49*).

Where a daily default penalty is imposed under *FA 2008, Sch 36, para 40* for a failure beginning on or after 1 April 2012 to comply with an information notice, and the failure continues for more than 30 days after the penalty assessment is issued, there are provisions for HMRC to apply to the tribunal for the imposition of an increased daily default penalty of up to £1,000 per day until payment is made (*FA 2008, Sch 36, paras 49A–49C*).

Reasonable excuse

25.16 No penalty arises if there was a reasonable excuse for the failure or obstruction. Reasonable excuse is not defined, but it does not include an insufficiency of funds unless this is outside the person's control, or reliance on the work of others unless reasonable care is taken to avoid failure or obstruction. Where the person had a reasonable excuse for the failure or obstruction and the excuse has ceased, the person is to be treated as having continued to have the excuse if the failure is remedied or the obstruction stops without reasonable delay after the excuse ceased (*FA 2008, Sch 36, para 45*).

A person liable for a penalty will be assessed within 12 months of the relevant date, being (*FA 2008, Sch 36, para 46*):

- the end of the period in which an appeal against the information notice could have been given;
- the date on which the appeal is determined or withdrawn, if an appeal is given; or
- in any other case, the date on which the person became liable to the penalty.

Right of appeal

25.17 A company has a right of appeal to the tribunal against a penalty notice or against the amount of a penalty (*FA 2008, Sch 36, para 47*). The notice of appeal must be made to HMRC in writing and must state the grounds of appeal. It must be made within 30 days of the day on which the penalty notice was issued (*FA 2008, Sch 36, para 48*).

Tax-related penalty

25.18 Where a penalty is imposed under *FA 2008, Sch 36, para 39* for failure to comply or obstruction, and the failure or obstruction continues after that penalty is imposed, and an HMRC officer believes that a significant loss of tax is at stake, there are provisions for HMRC to apply to the Upper Tribunal for the imposition of an additional tax-related penalty of such amount as the Upper Tribunal shall decide (*FA 2008, Sch 36, para 50*). Such penalty is due for payment within 30 days of its notification (*FA 2008, Sch 36, para 51*).

Offence

25.19 Any person found guilty of an offence is liable, on summary conviction, to a fine not exceeding the statutory maximum. On conviction on indictment, he may be liable to imprisonment for a term not exceeding two years or a fine or both (*FA 2008, Sch 36, para 55*).

A person is guilty of an offence if he conceals, destroys or otherwise disposes of documents required for an information notice which has been approved by the tribunal. This is not the case if the person concerned acted after the document or copy had been produced to an officer, unless an officer notified that the document should continue to be available. Nor is there an offence if the person acted six months after a copy document was produced to an officer, unless an officer had requested the original document within that period (*FA 2008, Sch 36, para 53*).

A person is also guilty of an offence if the person concealed, destroyed or otherwise disposed of a document after an officer had informed the person in writing that that document was likely to be the subject of an information notice and the officer intended to seek the tribunal's approval. There is no offence if the person acts at least six months after the person was so informed (*FA 2008, Sch 36, para 54*).

RECORD-KEEPING

25.20 A company must keep such records as may be needed to enable it to deliver a correct and complete tax return, and is required to retain its records for six years after the end of the accounting period concerned. In most cases, the records or the information contained in them may be kept in any form and by any means, subject to any exceptions made by HMRC in writing (*FA 1998, Sch 18, para 22*). However, companies are required to preserve certain records (as distinct from the information contained in them) in any form and by any means, and these are records relating to distributions and tax credits, gross and net interest payments, payments to sub-contractors and foreign tax payments (*FA 1998, Sch 18, para 22(3)*).

In general, records must be kept for six years from the end of the relevant accounting period (*FA 1998, Sch 18, para 21(3)*). HMRC may reduce this period below the six-year time limit (*FA 2008, Sch 37, para 8(3)*). Records should be kept longer if:

- a return is under enquiry more than six years after the end of the accounting period;
- the company makes its return late; or
- the records relate to a continuing transaction that may affect current years.

Risky Business Ltd v Revenue and Customs Commissioners [2012] UKFTT 751 (TC) demonstrated the way in which assumed profits can be assessed in the absence of adequate accounting records. The onus of disproving such assessments as inaccurate rests on the taxpayer, but the onus of proving negligence rests on HMRC.

HMRC carry out Business Records Checks to review the adequacy of current-year statutory business records being maintained by selected small and medium-sized enterprises. This may involve a visit by HMRC and, if the record-keeping is found to be unsatisfactory, a follow-up visit. Where the inadequacy persists, the business may face a penalty of between £250 and £3,000. For HMRC guidance on how the checks are conducted, see tinyurl.com/cnlmy5j.

Penalties

25.21 A company may be charged a penalty not exceeding £3,000 for failing to keep and preserve such records as may be needed to enable it to deliver a correct and complete company tax return for an accounting period commencing on or after 1 April 2008 that is due to be filed on or after 1 April 2009 (*FA 1998, Sch 18, para 23*).

There is no penalty for failing to keep or preserve records which might have been needed only for the purposes of claims, elections or notices not included in the return (*FA 1998, Sch 18, para 23(2)*). There is no penalty for failing to keep or preserve records relating to distributions and tax credits, or gross and net interest payments, which are adequately proved by other documentary evidence (*FA 1998, Sch 18, para 23(3)*).

HMRC TIME LIMITS FOR RAISING ASSESSMENTS

> **Focus**
>
> In some circumstances, HMRC will estimate the corporation tax liability if the company fails to submit a self-assessment return.

25.22 If a company fails to submit a corporation tax return by the filing date, in response to a notice to deliver a corporation tax return, HMRC may, at any time during the next three years, estimate the amount of corporation tax due in a determination assessment (*FA 1998, Sch 18, para 36*). The period of time allowed was five years for accounting periods ending before 1 April 2010.

Alternatively, if a notice to deliver a corporation tax return is served on a company and a return is filed for an accounting period ending in or at the end of the period specified in the notice, but it appears to HMRC that there is another such period that is or may be an accounting period, HMRC may issue a determination for that period within any time during the next three years (*FA 1998, Sch 18, para 37*). As above, the period of time allowed was five years for accounting periods ending before 1 April 2010.

Such a determination is treated as the company's self-assessment (*FA 1998, Sch 18, para 39*). If a self-assessment return is subsequently filed, it will replace the determination, but the return must be filed no later than three years (or five years for accounting periods ending before 1 April 2010) after HMRC were first able to issue the determination assessment, or one year after the date of the determination assessment (*FA 1998, Sch 18, para 40*).

If HMRC discover that the amount assessed on a company tax return is insufficient, or the relief has become excessive, they may make a discovery assessment within certain specified time limits (*FA 1998, Sch 18, para 41* onwards).

In the absence of any other provisions allowing a longer period, no assessment may be made more than four years after the end of the accounting period to which it relates; before 1 April 2010, this time limit was six years, and transitional provisions applied up to 31 March 2012 (*FA 1998, Sch 18, para 46(1)*, before and after amendment by *FA 2008, s 118, Sch 39, para 42(1)*).

If a company has delivered a return, HMRC may make a discovery assessment or determination in cases where there is a loss of tax that was brought about 'carelessly or deliberately' by the company or by a person acting on its behalf (*FA 1998, Sch 18, paras 42–44*). *FA 2008, Sch 39, para 41* specifies 'carelessly or deliberately'; before 1 April 2010, the wording 'fraud or negligent conduct' applied, and transitional provisions applied up to 31 March 2012.

An assessment for a loss of tax brought about carelessly by the company or a related person may be made at any time not more than six years after the end of the accounting period to which it relates. In cases of loss of tax brought about deliberately by the company or a related person, a failure to comply with an assessment raised because it acted carelessly, or a failure to comply with a tax avoidance scheme obligation (see **25.32** onwards), the period is 20 years from the end of the accounting period, subject to any condition existing at the time which allows a longer period. Before 1 April 2010, the time limit in cases of fraud or negligence was 21 years after the end of the accounting period, and transitional provisions applied up to 31 March 2012. See *FA 1998, Sch 18, paras 42–44, 46(2)–(2B)*, before and after amendment by *FA 2008, s 118, Sch 39, para 42(3)*.

A discovery assessment may also be made at any time, even if the enquiry time has elapsed or HMRC have completed their enquiries into the return, if they could not have been reasonably expected, on the basis of the information made available to them, to be aware of the errors in the return.

In *Langham v Veltema* [2004] STC 544, the taxpayer had entered into a capital loss scheme that involved the purchase from a promoter of an interest in a trust but, when HMRC came to consider the matter, no evidence of the transactions could be provided and the loss could therefore not be substantiated. The taxpayer claimed that HMRC were out of time to raise an assessment, because the enquiry window had closed and no discovery assessment was possible because a full disclosure had been made in the tax return. The Court of Appeal rejected this and found for HMRC, determining that HMRC were excluded from making a discovery assessment only when a taxpayer, in making an honest and accurate return or responding to an inquiry, had clearly alerted them to the insufficiency of the assessment, and not in cases where HMRC might simply have some other information that could shed doubt on the sufficiency of the assessment.

In *Revenue and Customs Commrs v Household Estate Agents Ltd* [2007] All ER (D) 175 (Jul), a company submitted a corporation tax return in accordance with prevailing practice. An employee benefit trust deduction was treated as an allowable deduction from profits, but following a later ruling was no longer held to be allowable. The company made no adjustment to its corporation tax computation. HMRC had opened enquiries into the following two returns and, in the course of those enquiries, asked about payments into the trust. HMRC made a discovery assessment, which the company claimed was precluded by *FA 1998, Sch 18, para 45* (that is, that the return was made in accordance with practice generally prevailing at the time). It was held that HMRC were not prevented from making a discovery assessment, because it would have been reasonable for the inspector, if he had thought about it, to initiate an enquiry, which could have been expected to reveal the full facts. It was further decided that the burden of proof as to whether a taxpayer had made a return in accordance with generally prevailing practice rested on the taxpayer and not HMRC.

In *HMRC v Charlton & Others* [2012] UKUT 770 (TCC) the Upper Tribunal provided further insight on when HMRC can issue a discovery assessment, establishing that:

- no new information, of fact or law, is required for there to be a discovery;
- a 'hypothetical officer' must be assumed to have such level of knowledge and understanding that would reasonably be expected in an officer considering the particular information provided by the taxpayer;
- the more complex the case, the more information might be required to be provided to give rise to a reasonable awareness of the insufficiency; and
- including information in the 'white space' on the return can help defeat a discovery assessment.

Information is regarded as being made available to HMRC if (*FA 1998, Sch 18, para 44*):

(i) it is included in a company tax return or in the documents accompanying the return;

(ii) it is contained in a relevant claim made by the company or in any accounts, statements or documents accompanying any such claim;

(iii) it is contained in any documents, accounts or information produced or provided by the company to HMRC for the purposes of an enquiry into a return or claim; or

(iv) it is information, the existence and relevance of which could reasonably be expected to be inferred by HMRC from the information supplied in circumstance (i), (ii) or (iii) above or is notified to HMRC.

It is therefore important to supply clear information to HMRC to support the return, and in responding to any questions raised by HMRC, in order to avoid the risk of a subsequent discovery assessment.

Similar powers are afforded to HMRC in respect of a recovery of an excessive repayment. The normal time limit is four years; before 1 April 2010, this limit was six years, and transitional provisions applied up to 31 March 2012 (*FA 1998, Sch 18, para 53*, before and after amendment by *FA 2008, Sch 39, para 44*).

HMRC CORRECTION OF TAX RETURNS

25.23 Within nine months after a company delivers or amends its tax return, HMRC may amend the return to correct obvious errors and omissions and anything else in the return that the HMRC officer has reason to believe is incorrect in the light of information available to the officer (*FA 1998, Sch 18, para 16(1)*). HMRC must issue notice of the correction to the company (*FA 1998, Sch 18, para 16(2)*). The company may reject the correction by further amending its return during the period within which such an amendment is permitted (*FA 1998, Sch 18, para 15*) or by notice to HMRC after the end of that period but within three months after the date of issue of the notice of correction (*FA 1998, Sch 18, para 16(4)*).

TAX DEBTORS

Power to obtain contact details of debtors

25.24 A company may receive a written notice from HMRC to supply them with contact details of a debtor. HMRC can make this request only if amounts are owed to HMRC by the debtor and HMRC reasonably believe that the company obtained the details in question when carrying on its business (*FA 2009, Sch 49, para 1*). The company is required to comply with the request within the time limit prescribed in the request. The company has a right of appeal on the ground that it would be unduly onerous to comply with the notice or requirement (*FA 2009, Sch 49, para 4*; see **22.24** onwards for the appeal procedure).

Failure to comply with the notice renders the company liable to a £300 penalty (*FA 2009, Sch 49, para 5*).

Direct recovery of debts (DRD)

25.25 *F(No 2)A 2015, s 51*, gives HMRC new powers for enforcement by deduction from accounts, also known as direct recovery of debts (DRD). This enables HMRC to recover tax debts directly from bank and building society accounts of tax debtors (including companies) that owe more than £1,000 of tax, have the financial means to pay and have been contacted multiple times by HMRC.

DRD applies only in England, Wales and Northern Ireland (*F(No 2)A 2015, Sch 8, para 24*). DRD will not apply in Scotland, where HMRC already have 'summary warrant' powers to recover debts in a similar, though not identical, manner.

Three conditions must be satisfied in order for DRD to apply (*F(No 2)A 2015, Sch 8, para 2*):

- Condition A – the debt is at least £1,000;
- Condition B – the sum is either an 'established debt' or one due under the accelerated payments legislation (see **25.49**); and
- Condition C – HMRC are satisfied that the debtor is aware that they owe the debt to HMRC; this will be achieved by means of a face-to-face meeting, which will also allow HMRC to assess whether or not the debtor is vulnerable and (if appropriate) remove them from the DRD process.

The legislation contains provisions (*F(No 2)A 2015, Sch 8, paras 3–18*) for:

- the issue by HMRC of an information notice to a deposit taker, where it appears the debtor holds one or more accounts with that deposit-taker;
- a requirement that the deposit taker responds to such notice with 'prescribed information' within 10 working days;

- procedures for HMRC to issue hold notices to deposit takers, setting out the specified amount to be held from the debtor (or from joint accounts) within five working days of such notice and the safeguarded amount (HMRC must always leave a minimum of £5,000 across a debtor's accounts above the amount that has been held);
- obligations on the deposit taker to provide prescribed information to HMRC within five working days of the hold, and on HMRC to do likewise to the debtor and other affected parties within five working days thereafter;
- a period of 30 days allowing objections by the debtor or other affected parties, including on grounds of hardship;
- appeal to the County Court following determination of such objections;
- the issue by HMRC to a deposit taker of a deduction notice requiring payment; and
- penalties on deposit takers for non-compliance or tipping off, with related rights of appeal to the First-tier Tribunal.

HMRC have power to vary specified time limits and sums relating to DRD, and to make secondary legislation in relation to the administration of the DRD regime (*F(No 2)A 2015, Sch 8, paras 19–21*). The *Enforcement by Deduction from Accounts (Prescribed Information) Regulations 2015* (*SI 2015/1986*), prescribes the information to be included in a DRD notice.

Consultations before the introduction of DRD raised widespread concerns, not least because of the perceived risks of error and fraud if HMRC were to be given direct access to millions of taxpayers' bank accounts. An Issue Briefing from HMRC on 5 August 2015 (see tinyurl.com/qz57xtc) explained how they proposed to operate DRD.

DUTIES OF SENIOR ACCOUNTING OFFICERS

Focus

Global operations can complicate compliance. Under tax law, the senior accounting officer has responsibilities for ensuring that complete and correct information is supplied to them.

Introduction

25.26 For accounting periods beginning on or after 28 July 2009, the senior accounting officer (SAO) of a qualifying company must take reasonable steps to ensure that the company establishes and maintains appropriate tax accounting arrangements. This means, broadly, that the company's accounting systems must be sufficiently robust to supply HMRC with accurate information. HMRC's guidance on the duties and responsibilities of SAOs is contained in the Senior Accounting Officer Guidance Manual at SAOG01000 onwards.

A company (including a dormant company or a company in liquidation or administration) is a qualifying company for SAO purposes in relation to a financial year if its relevant turnover was more than £200 million in the previous financial year and its relevant balance sheet total (that is, the aggregate of the amounts shown as assets in its balance sheet) was more than £2 billion at the end of the previous financial year, or if it falls to be included as part of a group. If the company was a member of a group at the end of the previous financial year, the aggregate group member totals for turnover and balance sheet are used instead (*FA 2009, Sch 46, para 15*). A group relationship is determined by a 51% holding in another company (*FA 2009, Sch 46, para 18*).

An SAO of a company is the director or officer who, in the company's reasonable opinion, has overall responsibility for the company's financial accounting arrangements. If the company is a member of a group, it is the group director or officer who, in the company's reasonable opinion, has overall responsibility for the company's financial accounting arrangements. A person may be the SAO of more than one company (*FA 2009, Sch 46, para 16*). Within a group of companies, there may be one or more SAOs.

The name of the SAO must be notified to HMRC by the company no later than the date on which the company's accounts are required to be filed with Companies House (*CA 2006, s 442*), or such later time as agreed by an officer of HMRC (*FA 2009, Sch 45, para 3*). HMRC will accept this notification in any recognised paper or electronic format, eg letter, fax, email or shared workspace (where used), but will not accept it by telephone. The company's notification must be provided separately from the SAO certificate described in **25.28** (HMRC's Senior Accounting Officer Guidance Manual at SAOG13300).

HMRC's SAO guidance has been updated on a number of occasions, and specific changes at different times have included the following:

- the SAO regime applies in most cases where insolvency procedures are underway, but HMRC will accept caveated SAO certificates where the SAO (eg the liquidator or administrator) may be unable to provide full sign-off;
- in HMRC's view, the turnover test is based on turnover as defined for *Companies Act* purposes, and therefore the test should be applied to all companies including banks and insurance companies;
- HMRC believe the SAO rules extend to the overseas activities of companies incorporated in the UK but not resident here;
- HMRC believe they can discuss a late or missing SAO certificate with a company without breaching the confidentiality of the SAO as an individual;

- guidance from HMRC on how the SAO rules apply where a company meets the qualifying criteria and its shares are held by a parent on trading account;
- the treatment of dormant companies;
- the application of the SAO rules where a qualifying company has not notified HMRC of the name of its SAO;
- the fact that the main duty of an SAO is to establish and maintain appropriate tax accounting arrangements which may affect returns made in the current year, for previous years or for future years as well as any other 'in year' filings;
- the failure of the SAO in their main duty, where the onus is on the SAO to fulfil their obligations rather than on HMRC's Customer Relationship Manager (CRM) to prompt the SAO into action;
- revised processes that CRMs must follow where they believe there has been an SAO failure; and
- the appeals process.

HMRC do not consider charging penalties where companies and SAOs have followed previous guidance for any period up to the first period commencing after the publication of revised guidance. Additionally, HMRC apply a 'light touch' period to any companies that are brought into the SAO regime by the changed interpretation for the first period commencing after publication of new guidance. HMRC do not charge penalties for previous periods where a penalty would seem to be due under earlier guidance but would not be due under revised guidance (Revenue & Customs Brief 16/12, 11 June 2012, tinyurl.com/pdgs8w4).

Main duty of the senior accounting officer

25.27 The SAO is required to take reasonable steps to ensure that the company establishes and maintains appropriate tax accounting arrangements which may affect returns made in the current year, for previous years or for future years as well as any other 'in year' filings for the taxes within scope of the SAO legislation. In particular, the SAO must take reasonable steps (*FA 2009, Sch 46, para 1*) to:

- monitor the company's accounting arrangements; and
- identify any respects in which those arrangements are not appropriate tax accounting arrangements.

Appropriate tax accounting arrangements are defined as arrangements that enable the company's relevant liabilities to be calculated accurately in all material respects. Relevant liabilities are not only corporation tax and amounts assessable as corporation tax, but also other direct and indirect taxes and levies that may fall upon a company. 'Accounting arrangements' includes arrangements for keeping accounting records (*FA 2009, Sch 46, para 14*).

Certificate to HMRC

25.28 The SAO must provide HMRC with a certificate confirming that the company had appropriate tax accounting arrangements in place throughout the financial year or, if it did not, giving an explanation of the shortfall. This certificate must be supplied by the date on which the company's accounts are required to be filed with Companies House (*CA 2006, s 442*), or such later time as agreed by an officer of HMRC. The certificate can relate to more than one company (*FA 2009, Sch 46, para 2*).

The certificate provided by the SAO must be either an original signed paper certificate, or in electronic format (see Revenue and Customs Brief 12 (2016) at tinyurl.com/j6krmw5). The SAO certificate must be provided separately from the notice from the company notifying HMRC of the name of the SAO (see **25.26**; SAOG15600).

Penalties for non-compliance

25.29 The fixed penalty, to which the SAO would be liable for non-compliance, is £5,000 (*FA 2009, Sch 46, para 5*).

Non-compliance includes not only the failure to provide a certificate, but also the provision of a certificate that contains a careless or deliberate inaccuracy. A careless inaccuracy results from a failure by the SAO to take reasonable care. A careless inaccuracy also arises if the SAO supplied a certificate in good faith but, upon discovery of an inaccuracy some time later, failed to take reasonable steps to inform HMRC. If the SAO fails to provide the required certificate, or provides a certificate that contains a careless or deliberate inaccuracy, he is liable to a fixed penalty of £5,000. It should be noted that this penalty is charged on the SAO as an individual, rather than on the company (*FA 2009, Sch 46, para 5*). If there has been more than one SAO during the year, the penalty falls on the person who became SAO latest in the year (*FA 2009, Sch 46, para 6*).

If a company fails to ensure that the name of its SAO is notified to HMRC as required by *FA 2009, Sch 46, para 3*, the company is liable to a fixed penalty of £5,000 (*FA 2009, Sch 46, para 7*).

Assessment of penalties

25.30 A penalty charged under these provisions on a company or its SAO must be assessed by HMRC within six months after the failure or inaccuracy first comes to the attention of an HMRC officer, and not more than six years after the end of the period for filing the accounts for the financial year. A penalty does not arise if HMRC or (on an appeal notified to the tribunal) the tribunal are satisfied that there is a reasonable excuse for the failure. Where a reasonable excuse existed but has ceased, the excuse is still treated as having continued so long as the failure is remedied without unreasonable delay after the excuse ceased.

The following are not accepted as a reasonable excuse (*FA 2009, Sch 46, para 8*):

- an insufficiency of funds, unless attributable to events outside the person's control; or
- reliance on a third party, unless the first person took reasonable care to avoid the failure.

Where a person is SAO of more than one company in a group, that person will only be charged one penalty if he fails in respect of two or more of those companies. Similarly, where two or more companies in a group have the same SAO, only one of those companies will be charged a penalty if they fail to notify HMRC of the name of their SAO (*FA 2009, Sch 46, para 9*).

A penalty charged under these provisions is due for payment within 30 days of notification (*FA 2009, Sch 46, para 11*).

Right of appeal

25.31 An SAO or a company charged with a penalty under these provisions has the right of appeal to the tribunal against the imposition of the penalty, in which case no penalty is due until the appeal is determined or withdrawn (*FA 2009, Sch 46, paras 10, 11*; see SAOG22000–SAOG22500 for HMRC guidance on the appeals process)

DISCLOSURE OF TAX AVOIDANCE SCHEMES (DOTAS)

> **Focus**
>
> Aggressive tax avoidance schemes are normally complex and artificial, and are used by only a minority of companies operating in the UK. Nonetheless, even relatively simple tax planning arrangements may need to be notified to HMRC at a very early stage if they are expected to bring about tax advantages.

HMRC strategy

25.32 *FA 2004, ss 307–319* introduced procedures in 2004 for the disclosure of certain tax avoidance schemes ('DOTAS') involving employment and financial products, and this was widened in 2006 to include specific taxes including corporation tax. A separate disclosure regime in relation to VAT was introduced in 2004 and is explained in VAT Notice 700/8, but is not covered further in this book.

The government's stated objectives of the disclosure rules are:

- to provide early information to HMRC about tax avoidance schemes, allowing the risks they pose to be assessed and informing legislation to close loopholes;
- to identify the users of those schemes and inform HMRC's compliance work; and
- to reduce the supply of avoidance schemes by altering the economics of avoidance, reducing the returns to promoters and users as schemes are closed down more quickly.

On its own, the disclosure of a tax arrangement has no immediate effect on the tax position of any person who uses it. However, a disclosed tax arrangement may attract swift attention from HMRC. It may also be rendered ineffective by Parliament, possibly with retrospective effect.

HMRC have explained their strategy in relation to tax avoidance schemes as being to:

- discourage taxpayers from using schemes. This includes a critical appraisal of all new legislation to reduce the potential for tax avoidance as well as publicising successes in closing down avoidance schemes;
- identify as early as possible schemes that are being used;
- challenge avoidance schemes by contesting returns and, where necessary, pursuing the matter through the courts; and
- produce legislative changes that will close down avoidance schemes where litigation is not appropriate or where the amount of tax at stake is particularly large.

In recent years, attitudes towards aggressive tax avoidance have been hardening (see **22.22**). With the introduction of HMRC's extended criminal investigatory powers (see **25.8**), companies and their tax advisers need to consider carefully the scope and extent of their tax planning activities and must remain ever-vigilant.

Practical operation of DOTAS

25.33 HMRC's consolidated guidance on DOTAS is updated from time to time, and the latest version can be found at tinyurl.com/ol94cfp. The taxes covered, and the guidance sections describing the detailed rules for each, are as follows:

Taxes	*Sections within DOTAS guidance*
Corporation tax Income tax Capital gains tax Bank levy	4, 6 and 7
Inheritance tax	12 and 13
Stamp duty land tax	8 and 9
Annual tax on enveloped dwellings	10 and 11
National Insurance contributions	5 to 7
Apprenticeship levy	20A

The DOTAS guidance lists primary and secondary legislation governing the scheme, and also identifies parts of the guidance itself which specify the form and manner for providing specified information and have the force of law (see guidance para 1.5).

As far as corporation tax is concerned, a tax arrangement may need to be disclosed even if HMRC are already aware of it or it is not considered to be avoidance. Tax avoidance schemes which are disclosable are prescribed in secondary legislation, and a tax arrangement should be disclosed where (guidance para 2.3.2):

- it will, or might be expected to, enable any person to obtain a tax advantage (see guidance para 6.2);
- that tax advantage is, or might be expected to be, the main benefit or one of the main benefits of the arrangement (see guidance para 6.3); and
- it is a hallmarked scheme, ie a tax arrangement that falls within any of the 'hallmarks' prescribed in the relevant regulations (see guidance section 7).

In most situations where disclosure is required, it must be made by the scheme 'promoter' within five days of one of three trigger events (see guidance para 14.3 for details of the events that can trigger a disclosure). However, the scheme 'user' may need to make the disclosure where:

- the promoter is based outside the UK;

- the promoter is a lawyer and legal professional privilege prevents him from providing all or part of the prescribed information to HMRC; or
- there is no promoter, eg where a person designs and implements their own 'in-house' scheme – in which case, disclosure must be made within 30 days of the scheme being implemented (see guidance para 14.6).

Secondary legislation sets out what information has to be disclosed. Further information on who should disclose and the time limits for doing so can be found in the guidance at sections 3 and 14.

Once a scheme has been disclosed, HMRC will normally issue the person who has made the disclosure and any co-promoters with a scheme reference number (SRN: see **25.35**). This number must then be sent on to clients and, if appropriate, on again to further clients until all final users of the scheme have received it. Each scheme user must report their use of the scheme to HMRC by including the number on their tax return or on form AAG4. There is more on this in the guidance at section 17, including what to do when a promoter's client is not the person expected to obtain an advantage from the scheme.

A promoter must also provide HMRC with periodic lists of persons to whom they become liable to issue an SRN (see guidance section 16).

Recent changes to DOTAS

> **Focus**
>
> Tightening of the DOTAS regime has become more or less an annual event, and companies and their tax advisers need to keep abreast of the changes so that they can ensure that all disclosable arrangements are reported timeously.

25.34 A number of changes have been made to DOTAS in recent years.

From 17 July 2014, where a person discloses a proposal or arrangement under DOTAS, HMRC may require that person to provide documents or more information about the proposal or arrangement within 10 days, or such longer period as may be specified. If they fail to do so, the Tribunal may order the person to provide the documents or information within a further 10 days or such longer period as HMRC may direct. On continuing failure, penalties may be charged under *TMA 1970, s 98C*, as set out at **25.41** (*FA 2004, ss 310A, 310B*).

From 26 March 2015, *FA 2015, Sch 17* has:

- changed the information that employers must provide to employees and to HMRC in relation to avoidance involving their employees;

- given HMRC power to identify users of undisclosed avoidance schemes;
- increased the penalty for users who do not comply with their reporting requirements under DOTAS;
- introduced protection for those wishing to provide information voluntarily about potential failures to comply with DOTAS;
- introduced a requirement under which promoters of tax avoidance schemes must notify HMRC of relevant changes to notified schemes; and
- provided for HMRC to publish information about promoters and schemes that are notified under the regime.

From 16 April 2015, the *Tax Avoidance Schemes (Information) (Amendment) Regulations 2015, SI 2015/948*, specify the revised information that employers must provide to employees and to HMRC in relation to avoidance involving their employees, and extend the prescribed information that introducers must provide to HMRC in relation to avoidance to include information relating to persons with whom an introducer has made a marketing contact.

Notification

25.35 Under DOTAS, 'notifiable arrangements' means anything which falls within any description prescribed by Treasury regulations, enables or might be expected to enable any person to obtain a tax advantage, and is such that the main benefit or one of the main benefits that might be expected is that advantage (*FA 2004, s 306(1)*). 'Notifiable proposal' means a proposal for arrangements which, if entered into, would be notifiable arrangements (*FA 2004, s 306(2)*). A person who is responsible for the design of such arrangements, or who makes a firm approach to another person with a view to making the notifiable proposal available for implementation by that or any other person, or who makes the notifiable proposal available for implementation by other persons, could be a promoter (*FA 2004, s 307*).

A promoter is required to notify HMRC of the scheme within five days of 'the relevant date' – broadly, the date on which the scheme first becomes available (*FA 2004, s 308; Tax Avoidance Schemes (Information) Regulations 2012, SI 2012/1836, reg 5*). Form AAG1 (notification by scheme promoter) is used for this purpose. HMRC will then issue the promoter with an eight-digit scheme reference number (SRN), which the promoter must pass within 30 days to those clients to whom he provides services in connection with the scheme (*FA 2004, s 312*). Promoters must use form AAG6 for the disclosure of the SRN to a client.

Where a client has been notified of SRN details, they must pass these on to any other person who they might reasonably be expected to know is (or is likely to be) a party to the scheme and who might reasonably be expected to gain a tax advantage from it.

The user may be required to notify HMRC if the promoter is based outside the UK (*FA 2004, s 309*), or if there is no promoter (*FA 2004, s 310*), or where the person that would otherwise be the promoter is not required to notify because of legal professional privilege (*Tax Avoidance Schemes (Promoters and Prescribed Circumstances) Regulations 2004, reg 6*). Form AAG2 (notification by scheme user where offshore promoter does not notify) is available for use. A person who designs and implements a hallmarked scheme for their own use (own scheme) must disclose the scheme within 30 days of implementation, and Form AAG3 (notification by scheme user where no promoter, or promoted by lawyer unable to make full notification) is used for these purposes.

Form AAG5 (continuation sheet) is also available.

The company client must include the SRN details from HMRC on the corporation tax return for the accounting period in which the advantage is being obtained (*FA 2004, s 313*). A co-promoter is not required to disclose a scheme to HMRC if another promoter has disclosed the scheme, or a scheme substantially the same, to HMRC (*FA 2004, s 308*). In relation to notifiable arrangements, the promoter may be required to provide HMRC with certain prescribed information relating to the client (*FA 2004, s 313ZA*).

HMRC, at their discretion, may give notice, in relation to any specified notifiable arrangements, that the promoter or clients (as the case may be) are no longer under a duty to notify under one or more of the relevant provisions (*FA 2004, ss 312(6), 312A(4), 313(5)*). On HMRC's website is a list of SRNs and the date from which the duties on promoters and/or clients no longer apply (see tinyurl.com/kpbm6vj).

Disclosable arrangements

25.36 A scheme is disclosable if it meets any one of a series of hallmark tests. 'Hallmarks' are defined as the descriptions prescribed for the purpose of *FA 2004, s 306(1)(a)–(c)* and the *Tax Avoidance Schemes (Prescribed Descriptions of Arrangements) Regulations 2006* (as amended by *SI 2007/2484*, *SI 2009/2033* and *SI 2010/2834*).

Hallmark tests

25.37 HMRC have devised a series of tests to determine whether a hallmarked scheme exists, which, when applied to direct taxes including corporation tax, are as follows:

Test	*Question*	*Consequence for a positive answer*	*Consequence for a negative answer*
1	Are there arrangements (including any scheme, transaction or series of transactions), or proposals for arrangements, that enable, or might be expected to enable, any person to obtain an advantage in relation to income tax, corporation tax or capital gains tax?	Yes: apply test 2	No: not a hallmarked scheme
2	Are those arrangements or proposals such that the main benefit, or one of the main benefits that might be expected to arise from them, is the obtaining of that advantage?	Yes: apply test 3	No: not a hallmarked scheme
3	Is there a promoter of the arrangements or are they devised for use 'in-house'?	Yes: apply test 4	No: apply in-house test 5A
4	Do any of the hallmarks for arrangements where there is a promoter apply?	Yes: a hallmarked scheme	No: not a hallmarked scheme
5A	Does hallmark 9 (employment income through third parties) apply?	Yes: a hallmarked scheme	No: apply in-house test 5B
5B	Do any of the other in-house hallmarks apply?	Yes: apply test 6	No: not a hallmarked scheme
6	Is the tax advantage intended to be obtained by a business that is larger than a small or medium enterprise?	Yes: a hallmarked scheme	No: not a hallmarked scheme

Note: Even where arrangements do not constitute a hallmarked scheme for income tax, corporation tax or capital gains tax, note that the disclosure rules for other taxes may still apply.

A small or medium enterprise is defined by the *Tax Avoidance Schemes (Prescribed Descriptions of Arrangements) Regulations 2006, SI 2006/1543, reg 4*, as a micro, small or medium-sized enterprise in accordance with the *European Recommendation*, as detailed in *CTA 2009, ss 1119(1)–(2), 1120(2)–(7)* and *Sch 2, para 118(1)–(3)*. This is the same as is used for research and development (see **14.23**).

Hallmarks

25.38 The hallmarks for schemes involving corporation tax apply also to those relating to income tax and capital gains tax.

These hallmarks are set out in the *Tax Avoidance Schemes (Prescribed Descriptions of Arrangements) Regulations 2006, SI 2006/1543.* They are numbered by description (some of which have been removed, hence the gaps):

1(a) Confidentiality from other promoters.

1(b) Confidentiality from HMRC.

2 Confidentiality where no promoter involved.

3 Premium fee.

5 Standardised tax products.

6 Loss schemes.

7 Leasing arrangements.

8 Employment income provided through third parties (introduced by *SI 2013/2592* from 4 November 2013).

9 Financial products.

Hallmarks 1(a), 3 and 4 ('confidentiality from other promoters', 'premium fee' and 'off-market terms') are derived from 'filters' that were used to identify disclosable arrangements before August 2006. Hallmark 1(b) ('confidentiality from HMRC') applies to a promoter who would wish to keep matters confidential from HMRC, for example to secure future fee income.

Hallmarks 1(a) and 1(b) were amended from 4 November 2013. The changes aimed:

- to ensure that the test in Hallmark 1(a) ('confidentiality from other promoters') would be answered in the affirmative if an element of the scheme were sufficiently new and innovative that a promoter would want the details to remain secret in order to maintain their competitive advantage and ability to earn fees; and
- to put it beyond doubt that, for the test in Hallmark 1(b) ('confidentiality from HMRC') to be met, there does not need to be an explicit confidentiality agreement between the promoter and user about the arrangement.

Hallmark 5 ('standardised tax product') applies where there is a promoter of a mass-marketed product that needs little or no alteration to suit a client's situation. Enterprise Investment Scheme (EIS), venture capital trust (VCT) scheme and corporate venturing scheme (CVS) arrangements are specifically excluded, as are approved employee share schemes and regulated pension schemes, but Seed Enterprise Investment Scheme (SEIS) is deliberately not excluded.

Hallmark 6 ('loss schemes') can apply where there is a promoter, and is intended to capture various loss-creation schemes used by wealthy individuals.

Hallmark 7 ('leasing arrangements') applies to promoted and in-house arrangements; it applies to certain high-value sale and leaseback arrangements which involve a party outside the charge to corporation tax and a removal of risk from the lessor.

Hallmark 9 ('employment income from third parties') was introduced from 4 November 2013 and applies to promoted and in-house schemes. Unlike other hallmarks for in-house notifiable arrangements, this hallmark applies to all sizes of business. It is designed to identify schemes which seek to circumvent the disguised remuneration rules contained in *ITEPA 2003, Pt 7A*.

Clearances

25.39 Where statutory clearance is available for any aspect of an arrangement that is disclosable under DOTAS, the prescribed five-day notification period for DOTAS still applies. In such cases, it is important that the clearance application makes explicit mention of any related DOTAS disclosures, preferably by including a copy of the disclosure or, where available, by reporting the allocated DOTAS scheme reference number. HMRC have confirmed that clearance applications will be considered in the usual way, and clearance will not be refused merely on the grounds that some part of the proposed transaction involves a disclosable scheme. For guidance on seeking clearance or approval for a transaction, see tinyurl.com/oluslvj.

When submitting a non-statutory clearance application for a transaction for which there is also disclosure under DOTAS of an avoidance scheme which covers all or part of the transaction, it is also important that explicit mention is made of any related disclosures, preferably by including a copy of the disclosure or, where available, by reporting the allocated DOTAS scheme reference number.

For further details of clearance procedures generally, see **17.44–17.50**.

Scheme disclosure on CT600

25.40 Those companies that need to disclose that they are using a tax avoidance scheme are required to indicate this on their corporation tax return and complete the relevant supplementary pages. Details of the scheme number and the accounting periods that benefit are required.

Penalties

> **Focus**
>
> You may incur penalties of up to £1 million if you fail to disclose a scheme that is notifiable under DOTAS.

25.41 Failure to comply with the disclosure requirements may result in the following penalties (*TMA 1970, s 98C*):

1. disclosure penalties, which apply to failure to disclose a scheme. There are variations in cases where the tribunal has issued a disclosure order;
2. information penalties, which apply to all other failures to comply with DOTAS except for those covered by 3 below; and
3. user penalties, which apply to failure by a scheme user to report a scheme reference number to HMRC.

Disclosure penalties and information penalties involve an initial penalty, and a further penalty if non-compliance continues.

Failure to notify incurs the following maximum penalties:

Promoter or taxpayer failing to notify HMRC of a promoted, offshore or in-house scheme	Initial penalty	*£600 per day
	Further penalty	£600 per day
Promoters failing to give registration number to client	Initial penalty	£5,000
	Further penalty	£600 per day
Taxpayer failing to disclose scheme registration number on returns	Initial failure	£100
	Second failure within 36 months	£500
	Third or subsequent failure within 36 months	£1,000

- The legislation provides for an initial penalty of up to £1 million if the maximum penalty otherwise chargeable appears inappropriately low, having regard to the promoter's fees or the taxpayer's tax saving (*TMA 1970, s 98C(2ZC)*).

Subject to a right of appeal, the tribunal will determine the initial penalties for both the promoters and the taxpayers.

No penalty arises where a person has a reasonable excuse for not disclosing a scheme, as the legislation deems that no failure exists (see tinyurl.com/ol94cfp, paras 22.3 and 22.5.3). Where the person had a reasonable excuse for the failure to disclose and the excuse has ceased, the person is to be treated as having continued to have the excuse if the failure is remedied without reasonable delay after the excuse ceased (*TMA 1970, s 118(2)*).

GENERAL ANTI-ABUSE RULE (GAAR)

Focus

FA 2013 fundamentally changed the landscape of UK tax law by introducing a new 'general anti-abuse rule' (GAAR) targeted at artificial and abusive tax avoidance schemes. This applies from 17 July 2013. It does not apply to any tax arrangements entered into before that date.

25.42 In a move to combat unacceptable tax avoidance, *FA 2013* introduced a GAAR, which provides for the counteraction of tax advantages arising from tax arrangements that are abusive. It applies to a range of taxes, including corporation tax and any amount chargeable as if it were corporation tax or treated as if it were corporation tax (*FA 2013, s 206*).

Before counteraction can proceed under the GAAR, HMRC must refer the arrangements to an independent advisory panel for its opinion. The opinion of the advisory panel is not binding, but forms part of the evidence in any subsequent hearing, as does the GAAR guidance approved by the panel. The legislation applies to abusive tax arrangements undertaken on or after 17 July 2013.

Arrangements are 'tax arrangements' for this purpose if, having regard to all the circumstances, it would be reasonable to conclude that the obtaining of a tax advantage was the main purpose, or one of the main purposes, of the arrangements (*FA 2013, s 207(1)*).

Tax arrangements are 'abusive' if they are arrangements the entering into or carrying out of which cannot reasonably be regarded as a reasonable course of action in relation to the relevant tax provisions, having regard to all the circumstances (*FA 2013, s 207(2)*), including:

- whether the substantive results of the arrangements are consistent with any principles on which those provisions are based (whether express or implied) and the policy objectives of those provisions;
- whether the means of achieving those results involve one or more contrived or abnormal steps; and

- whether the arrangements are intended to exploit any shortcomings in those provisions.

Where the tax arrangements form part of any other arrangements, regard must also be had to those other arrangements (*FA 2013, s 207(3)*).

The 'double reasonableness' test in *FA 2013, s 207(2)* (ie whether the arrangements 'cannot reasonably be regarded as a reasonable course of action') is the crux of the GAAR and establishes a high threshold for showing that schemes are abusive (see HMRC's GAAR Guidance (referred to below), para C5.10).

Each of the following is an example, set out in statute, of something which might indicate that tax arrangements are abusive (*FA 2013, s 207(4)*):

- the arrangements result in an amount of income, profits or gains for tax purposes that is significantly less than the amount for economic purposes;
- the arrangements result in deductions or losses of an amount for tax purposes that is significantly greater than the amount for economic purposes; and
- the arrangements result in a claim for the repayment or crediting of tax (including foreign tax) that has not been, and is unlikely to be, paid.

The above examples are not exhaustive, and in each case apply only if it is reasonable to assume that such a result was not the anticipated result when the relevant tax provisions were enacted. Furthermore, the fact that tax arrangements accord with established practice, and HMRC had, at the time the arrangements were entered into, indicated their acceptance of that practice, is an example of something which might indicate that the arrangements are not abusive (*FA 2013, s 207(4)–(6)*).

For these purposes, a 'tax advantage' includes (*FA 2013, s 208*):

(a) relief or increased relief from tax;

(b) repayment or increased repayment of tax;

(c) avoidance or reduction of a charge to tax or an assessment to tax;

(d) avoidance of a possible assessment to tax;

(e) deferral of a payment of tax or advancement of a repayment of tax; and

(f) avoidance of an obligation to deduct or account for tax.

This definition of 'tax advantage' is not necessarily exhaustive. The expression is intended to have a very wide meaning and cover any form of tax benefit, for example: increasing deductions or losses; decreasing income or gains; obtaining timing advantages; obtaining or increasing repayments of tax; or ensuring that a potential tax charge does not arise or is reduced (HMRC's GAAR Guidance (referred to below), para C2.2).

The GAAR Advisory Panel is a panel of individuals chosen by HMRC for their relevant knowledge and experience, and its Chair and members are all stated to be completely independent of HMRC. The Panel has been established to bring an independent and non-HMRC perspective to the application of the GAAR, and to provide a safeguard for taxpayers. Where tax arrangements are carried out in a business context, the Panel also brings a commercial perspective to the application of the GAAR. The Panel has two specific functions: to provide opinions on cases referred to it, and to approve HMRC's guidance on the GAAR.

HMRC's GAAR Guidance,can be found at tinyurl.com/yaanojkl as well as Opinions published by the GAAR Advisory Panel (see **25.43** below). The guidance comprises the following:

- Parts A, B and C: a broad summary of what the GAAR is designed to achieve, how the GAAR operates, and guidance on the interpretation and application of the GAAR, approved by the GAAR Advisory Panel;
- Part D: examples to illustrate when an arrangement might or might not be treated as abusive in the context of the GAAR, approved by the GAAR Advisory Panel; and
- Part E: HMRC's guidance on GAAR procedure, reviewed by the GAAR Advisory Panel but not requiring to be approved by that Panel.

The guidance is kept under review by HMRC and the GAAR Advisory Panel and is updated periodically. When the guidance is amended, the date of the amended guidance is clearly noted. Each edition of the guidance will remain accessible online, to facilitate reference to the particular edition of the guidance which was current at the time when an arrangement was entered into (GAAR Guidance, para A6).

The safeguards incorporated into the GAAR to protect taxpayers, particularly the 'double reasonableness' test, would prevent the GAAR from operating in relation to arrangements entered into for the purpose of avoiding an inappropriate tax charge that would otherwise have been triggered by a more straightforward transaction. Tax charges of this sort (sometimes referred to as 'bear traps') can be encountered from time to time. For example, where a taxpayer has to take what appear to be contrived steps in order to ensure that they are not taxed on more than the economic gain, such an arrangement would not generally be regarded as abusive (GAAR Guidance, para B12.2).

The GAAR applies to all tax arrangements entered into on or after 17 July 2013, but not to any tax arrangements entered into before that date. The term 'arrangements' is given a very broad meaning, so that it can include a transaction or transactions which form part of a larger arrangement. Where the tax arrangements form part of any other arrangements entered into before 17 July 2013, those other arrangements are to be ignored for the purposes of the GAAR, unless taking them into account would show that the arrangements entered into after 17 July 2013 are not abusive (*FA 2013, s 215*).

The GAAR applies in addition to all other pre-existing and subsequent anti-avoidance provisions. It had been argued in some quarters that many of these should be repealed, but this has not been considered appropriate because the GAAR concentrates only on arrangements regarded as 'abusive'.

The GAAR has a narrower application than the broader general anti-avoidance rules found in several overseas jurisdictions, and in Scotland in relation to devolved taxes. Indeed, in 2013 a House of Lords Committee considering the draft Finance Bill stressed that, because the GAAR is so narrow, it will not apply to current issues of public concern about international tax planning by multinational companies; instead, they suggested that these needed to be addressed at EU, OECD, G8 and G20 levels (see tinyurl.com/qb4kl7l).

Note that the GAAR legislation makes no reference to the disclosure of tax avoidance schemes (DOTAS) rules (see **25.32** onwards). DOTAS, which requires early notification of certain tax avoidance schemes to HMRC, has a different function from the GAAR and has no relevance to the operation of the GAAR (GAAR Guidance, para C11.1).

Operation of the GAAR

> **Focus**
>
> When HMRC use the GAAR to counteract arrangements, the most likely alternative would not necessarily be the transaction which would result in the highest tax charge and, in some cases, might be no transaction at all.

25.43 Under the GAAR, counteraction by HMRC must follow certain procedural requirements. It must first be notified by a designated HMRC officer (*FA 2013, Sch 43, paras 3, 4*). The notice must:

- specify the arrangements and the tax advantage;
- explain why the officer considers that a tax advantage has arisen to the taxpayer from tax arrangements that are abusive;
- set out the counteraction that the officer considers ought to be taken. Note that the just and reasonable counteraction would be to select the transaction which a taxpayer would most likely carry out in such circumstances, which might be that no transaction would have been carried out, and to adjust the tax consequences on the basis that this alternative transaction had been carried out or, as the case may be, that no transaction had been carried out at all. It is important to note that

the most likely alternative transaction would not necessarily be the one which would result in the highest tax charge (GAAR Guidance, para B13.3);

- inform the taxpayer of the period of 45 days for making representations (this period may be extended by HMRC on written request from the taxpayer); and
- explain the effect of the arrangements being referred to the GAAR Advisory Panel;
- explain that the taxpayer will be unable to make any GAAR-related tax adjustments in the closed period. This is the period beginning with 31 days following the expiry of the period during which the taxpayer can make representations and ends immediately before the day that the taxpayer receives HMRC's final notice following the decision of the GAAR Advisory Panel; and
- explain the possibility of the taxpayer being subject to a GAAR-related penalty amounting to 60% of the tax in question (see **24.35**).

FA 2016 introduced supplemental rules which permit HMRC to issue a provisional counteraction notice (*FA 2013, s 209A*).

The arrangements must be referred to the GAAR Advisory Panel unless either the taxpayer has taken corrective action, or, having considered representations from the taxpayer, a designated HMRC officer decides that counteraction ought not to apply,. The legislation stipulates what information must be provided to the Panel and the taxpayer. The taxpayer must be advised that they have 21 days to respond; this period may be extended by the Panel on written request from the taxpayer (*FA 2013, Sch 43, paras 5–9*).

The matter is then considered by a sub-panel consisting of three members of the GAAR Advisory Panel (one of whom may be the Chair), and the sub-panel must produce:

- one opinion notice stating the joint opinion of all the members of the sub-panel, or
- two or three opinion notices which, taken together, state the opinions of all the members,

on whether the entering into and carrying out of the tax arrangements is a reasonable course of action, or not a reasonable course of action, or that it is not possible to reach a view. This opinion (or these opinions) will normally be produced within about 60 days, and must be provided to HMRC and the taxpayer (*FA 2013, Sch 43, paras 10, 11*).

A designated HMRC officer who has received such notice must, having considered any opinion of the GAAR Advisory Panel about the tax arrangements, give the taxpayer a written notice setting out whether the tax advantage arising from the arrangements is to be counteracted under the GAAR. HMRC are not bound by the opinion of the GAAR Advisory Panel, but would be unlikely to go against it without very strong justification. If this notice states that a tax advantage is to be counteracted, it must also set out (*FA 2013, Sch 43, para 12*):

- the adjustments required to give effect to the counteraction; and
- if relevant, any steps that the taxpayer is required to take to give effect to it.

A designated HMRC officer may give a notice, or do anything else, under *FA 2013, Sch 43* where he considers that a tax advantage might have arisen to the taxpayer. Any such notice may be expressed to be given on the assumption that the tax advantage does arise (without agreeing that it does) (*FA 2013, Sch 43, para 13*).

Binding other taxpayers to lead arrangements

25.44 A taxpayer that has been subject to a counteraction notice may not be the only person to be using the arrangements in question. This is particularly the case where a scheme has been marketed by a promoter to a range of taxpayers. *FA 2016* introduced new provisions to enable HMRC to issue both 'pooling notices' and 'binding notices' in the following circumstances (*FA 2013, Sch 43A* as amended by the General Anti-Abuse Rule Procedure (Amendment) Regulations 2017, SI 2017/1090):

- HMRC have already issued a counteraction notice to a person P;
- the time limit for P to make representations has expired, and P has yet to receive a final decision by HMRC upon the latter receiving an opinion notice from the GAAR Advisory Panel;
- a person R is involved in tax arrangements that are considered abusive; and
- those arrangements are equivalent, or similar to the same arrangements that are the subject of the counteraction notice to P.

In these circumstances, HMRC will be able to issue either a pooling notice or a binding notice to R.

The pooling of cases is a means by which all cases which are equivalent to or similar to P's tax arrangements (the 'lead arrangements') are treated in a similar manner. From 5 December 2017, it is possible for R and P to be the same person. This allows arrangements to be 'pooled' with lead arrangements even if they give rise to a tax advantage to the same person. Guidance on pooling notices can be accessed at factsheet CC/FS35 (tinyurl.com/y9qhvwjh).

A binding notice effectively binds R to the outcome of any determination made in respect of P's tax arrangements where P has received a final counteraction notice. Guidance on counteraction notices can be accessed at factsheet CC/FS36 (tinyurl.com/ybqclyoo).

Both pooling and binding notices must:

- specify the arrangements and the tax advantage;
- explain why HMRC consider that R's arrangements are equivalent to the lead arrangements that are the subject of P's counteraction notice;
- explain why HMRC consider that R's arrangements are abusive;
- set out the counteraction that HMRC consider ought to be taken;
- explain the effect of the lead arrangements being referred to the GAAR Advisory Panel;
- inform R of the period of 30 days for making representations following receipt of the Panel's opinion notice(s) in respect of the lead arrangements;
- explain that the taxpayer will be unable to make any GAAR-related tax adjustments in the closed period. This is the period beginning with 31 days after the day the notice is given to R and ending (a) (for pooling notices), immediately before the day that a final notice has been given to R upon HMRC's considering the opinion of the GAAR Advisory Panel, and (b) (for binding notices), 30 days after the day that a final notice has been given to R upon HMRC's considering the opinion of the GAAR Advisory Panel; and
- explain the possibility of R being subject to a GAAR-related penalty amounting to 60% of the tax in question (**24.35**).

A designated HMRC officer who has received an opinion notice in respect of the lead arrangements must give a copy of the notice to R. The office must also provide a written notice explaining that R has 30 days to make representations that the opinion notice does not bind R for any of the following reasons:

- no tax advantage has arisen to R from the arrangements;
- R's arrangements are or may be materially different from the lead arrangements or the counteracted arrangements.

If HMRC have already given a final counteraction notice to P in respect of the lead arrangements, a similar notice must also be given to R once the 30-day period for making representations has expired. HMRC must, having considered any opinion of the GAAR Advisory Panel about the lead arrangements, give R a written notice setting out whether the tax advantage arising from R's arrangements is to be counteracted, together with:

- the adjustments required to give effect to the counteraction; and
- if relevant, any steps that R is required to take to give effect to it.

There are also rules which provide that if P, the person whose tax arrangements constitute the lead arrangements takes corrective action, HMRC can continue the GAAR process with respect to the remaining members in the pool (*FA 2013, Sch 43B*).

25.45 The GAAR forms part of the tax laws of each of the taxes to which it applies, and a company is responsible for self-assessing its corporation tax liabilities. It is important to note, therefore, that a company is required to take the provisions of the GAAR into account when completing its self-assessment returns. Accordingly, if it would be reasonable for the company to believe that it has entered into an abusive arrangement that would be counteracted by the GAAR, it is required by law to counteract tax advantages arising from abusive tax arrangements by making just and reasonable adjustments to its return or claim. Failure to do so could leave the company open to penalties for failing to take reasonable care in completing its tax return.

Counteraction must be on a just and reasonable basis and may take a number of forms, appropriate to the particular tax in question. Where counteraction by HMRC has taken place, or counteraction has been taken by the taxpayer and notified to HMRC, and that counteraction has become final, it is possible for the taxpayer to claim within 12 months any consequential relieving adjustments as are just and reasonable (*FA 2013, ss 209, 210*). Where any such claim relates to corporation tax, it falls within *TMA 1970, Sch 1A* (Claims etc not included in returns) and not within *FA 1998, Sch 18* (Company tax returns, assessments etc) (see *FA 2013, s 210(6)(b)*).

In proceedings before a court or tribunal in connection with the GAAR, the onus is on HMRC to show (*FA 2013, s 211(1)*) that:

- there are tax arrangements that are abusive; and
- the adjustments made to counteract the tax advantages arising from the arrangements are just and reasonable.

In determining any such issue, a court or tribunal is required to take into account (*FA 2013, s 211(2)*):

- HMRC's guidance about the GAAR that was approved by the GAAR Advisory Panel at the time the tax arrangements were entered into; and
- any opinion about the arrangements, given by the GAAR Advisory Panel under *FA 2013, Sch 43, para 11*.

In determining any issue in connection with the GAAR, a court or tribunal may (but is not required to) take into account (*FA 2013, s 211(3)*):

- guidance, statements or other material (whether of HMRC, a Minister of the Crown or anyone else) that was in the public domain at the time the arrangements were entered into; and
- evidence of established practice at that time.

Note that any 'priority rule' (ie a rule stating that particular provisions have effect to the exclusion of, or otherwise in priority to, anything else) has effect subject to the GAAR (*FA 2013, s 212*). Examples of priority rules are:

- the rule in *CTA 2009, s 464, 699* or *906* (priority of loan relationships rules, derivative contracts rules, or intangible fixed assets rules for corporation tax purposes); and
- the rule in *TIOPA 2010, s 6(1)* (effect to be given to double taxation arrangements despite anything in any enactment).

For example, where a rule such as *CTA 2009, Pt 5, s 464*, stipulates that tax may only be charged under that Part in respect of the relevant subject matter (in that case, loan relationships), the GAAR can override the effect of this rule, making use of the exception set out in *CTA 2009, s 464(2)*.

Following the consultation on strengthening sanctions for tax avoidance during summer 2015, *FA 2016* includes legislation for imposing penalties for tax compliance cases where the GAAR applies (see **24.35** and the original consultation paper at tinyurl.com/pbbnh3s).

Examples of the operation of the GAAR

25.46 The examples published by the GAAR Advisory Panel (see GAAR Guidance Part D) are wide-ranging, and aim to illustrate when, on the basis of the double reasonableness test, an arrangement might or might not be treated as abusive in the context of the GAAR. They consider situations falling into the following categories:

- straightforward legislative choice;
- long-established practice;
- situations where the law deliberately sets precise rules or boundaries;
- standard tax planning combined with some element of artificiality;
- exploiting a shortcoming in legislation whose purpose is to close down a form of activity (including, for example, a recent targeted anti-avoidance rule); and
- arrangements that are contrived or abnormal and produce a tax position which is in no way consistent with the legal effect and economic substance of the underlying transaction.

Examples relating specifically to corporation tax include the following topics (as numbered in the guidance):

D5 Accessing trapped non-trade deficits carried forward (illustrating a taxpayer making a legitimate choice);

D6 Late paid interest rules (illustrating how some arrangements, despite having contrived or abnormal steps, will not be within the scope of the GAAR because (i) the substantive result of the arrangement is consistent with the principles on which the relevant tax provisions are based, and (ii) they accord with established practice);

D7 *Barclays Mercantile Business Finance v Mawson* [2005] STC 1 (illustrating a complicated arrangement which was found by the courts to comply with the law and did not contain features that could properly be regarded as abusive);

D8 Shares as debt (illustrating that a transaction with a commercial driver (group funding) may be structured in a contrived or abnormal way so as to give rise to an abusive tax result);

D9 Unauthorised Unit Trusts (illustrating a highly contrived transaction that uses existing structures in an inappropriate way to produce a tax result that is clearly contrary to the intended consequences of the law); and

D10 Capital Allowances – Double Dip (illustrating an arrangement which is clearly abusive because it is contrived and seeks to produce tax results which are contrary both to the intended effect of the statute and the economics).

The published examples also contain commentary and a number of illustrations regarding how the commencement provisions of *FA 2013, s 215* operated when the GAAR came into effect on 17 July 2013. These cover the following topics (as numbered in the guidance):

D37 Commentary on the commencement provisions;

D38 Example 1: post-commencement arrangement abusive in its own right (based on Example D8 referred to above);

D39 Example 2: no tax advantage arises from post-commencement arrangement;

D40 Example 3: post-commencement arrangement part of a broader abusive arrangement; and

D41 Example 4: post-commencement tax arrangement abusive in its own right (based on *Mayes v Revenue and Customs Commissioners* [2011] STC 1269; see particularly para 30 of the judgment of Mummery LJ).

PUBLIC SECTOR PROCUREMENT RESTRICTIONS

25.47 To promote tax compliance, anyone bidding for a government contract worth over £5 million, advertised on or after 1 April 2013, must self-certify at the selection stage that, in the previous six years, they have had no 'occasions of non-compliance' with any HMRC-administered tax on or after 1 April 2013 in respect of tax returns submitted on or after 1 October 2012.

Occasions of non-compliance include:

- returns found to be incorrect (whether as a result of litigation or by agreement) under the general anti-abuse rule (GAAR – see **25.42**) or the 'Halifax abuse' principle established by the European Court of Justice in 2006 (Case C-255/02);
- returns found to be incorrect as a result of failure of a scheme notifiable under the disclosure of tax avoidance schemes (DOTAS) rules (see **25.32**);
- unspent convictions for tax-related offences; and
- liabilities to penalties for civil fraud or evasion.

Suppliers with tax obligations in foreign jurisdictions are required to self-certify that there have been no 'occasions of non-compliance' in relation to equivalent foreign tax rules.

Various remedies are available to government departments, including termination of the contract where a supplier either fails to disclose an occasion of non-compliance at the outset, or where such an occasion occurs during the lifetime of the contract.

These arrangements are administered through the government's public procurement guidance. For further details, see 'Procurement Policy Note: Measures to Promote Tax Compliance: Action Note 03/14', Cabinet Office, 7 February 2014 (tinyurl.com/yan4f8te).

HMRC ACTION TO COUNTER TAX AVOIDANCE SCHEMES

25.48 HMRC claim that large businesses are one of the taxpayer groups most likely to engage in tax avoidance. HMRC seek to reduce tax avoidance by developing an open and co-operative relationship with such businesses, using HMRC Customer Relationship Managers (CRMs) in their Large Business Service, and CRMs and Customer Co-ordinators in their Local Compliance (Large and Complex) unit. These CRMs and Customer Co-ordinators are responsible for knowing the taxpayer's business and tax affairs thoroughly, understanding the avoidance risks they pose and co-ordinating HMRC's interventions.

HMRC's aim is that large businesses should strive to ensure that they are rated as a 'low risk' for compliance purposes, so that they receive less attention and fewer interventions. Paradoxically, many large businesses prefer to be designated as medium risk, because the attention they then receive from their CRM or Customer Co-ordinator is generally useful to them in aiding the compliance process by giving them direct access to, and an ongoing dialogue with, HMRC (see the Consultation Paper on the Business Risk Review dated 13 September 2017 (tinyurl.com/y8723swv) where HMRC seek views on whether to expand the range risk categories tailored to the tax risks encountered in the large business population).

HMRC run 'campaigns' from time to time, targeting particular sectors or activities which they believe may be contributing to a loss of tax. These provide opportunities for taxpayers in those sectors to bring their tax affairs up to date in a simple, straightforward way and take advantage of the best possible terms. For examples, see tinyurl.com/pqncgqu.

HMRC publish periodic warnings about the risks of entering into certain marketed tax avoidance schemes, and these can be found on their page of 'Tax avoidance schemes currently in the spotlight' (see tinyurl.com/ccmrrn). HMRC also warn taxpayers that they will be relentless in pursuing those who choose to engage in tax avoidance.

HMRC have offered a limited number of specific settlement opportunities, inviting some participants in particular tax avoidance schemes to settle their tax liabilities by agreement, without the need for litigation. Where taxpayers invited to settle in this way have declined to do so, HMRC increase the pace of their investigations and accelerate disputes into litigation. For details of such settlement opportunities, see tinyurl.com/pacthuj. For details of HMRC's litigation and settlement strategy, see **22.32**.

From time to time, HMRC publish Issue Briefings, some of which explain action they are taking to counter tax avoidance and prevent tax evasion (see tinyurl.com/kktr7t8).

HMRC have consulted on various occasions on new ways of improving large business tax compliance by tackling evasion, avoidance and aggressive tax planning and by increasing tax transparency in relation to large business tax strategies. The following measures were introduced in 2016 (*FA 2016, s 161, Sch 19*):

- Large businesses will have a legal requirement to publish details of their tax strategy (see guidance at tinyurl.com/zpn283e).
- Large businesses that persistently engage in aggressive tax planning, or who fail to engage with HMRC, will be subject to a 'special measures' regime, involving additional reporting requirements to HMRC, increasing penalties and ultimately, the denial of tax reliefs (see guidance at tinyurl.com/hmxkapv).

Accelerated payments of tax

25.49 Where HMRC dispute a taxpayer's tax repayment claim, they may make a provisional repayment pending resolution of the dispute. However, it is HMRC's practice to withhold repayments which they regard as arising from tax avoidance, thus preventing the taxpayer from gaining a tax advantage, even if only temporarily. This stance was reinforced by *FA 2013, s 234*, which made it more difficult for a taxpayer to obtain an interim payment in court where an application for such a payment relates to a tax matter on which a point of law has yet to be finally determined.

From 17 July 2014, HMRC have powers to require accelerated payments of tax in any of the following circumstances (*FA 2014, Pt 4, Ch 3*):

- where a taxpayer for whom there is an open enquiry or appeal has used a tax arrangement which the courts have found to fail. In such a case, HMRC are able to issue a 'follower notice' stating that, in their opinion, a particular judicial decision is relevant to their case and determines their dispute; or

- where a taxpayer for whom there is an open enquiry or appeal has claimed a tax advantage by the use of arrangements that:
  - fall to be disclosed under DOTAS; or
  - HMRC counteract under the GAAR following an opinion of the GAAR Advisory Panel that, in the Panel's opinion, the arrangements are not a reasonable course of action.

In any such case, HMRC are able to issue an 'accelerated payment notice' (APN), requiring the taxpayer to pay the tax in dispute within 90 days, or a further 30 days where the taxpayer requests that HMRC should reconsider the amount of the APN. Where the matter is under appeal, the measure operates so as to remove any postponement of the disputed tax. Penalties apply for late payment.

HMRC guidance on follower notices and accelerated payments of tax is published at tinyurl.com/qdqv55x, tinyurl.com/lb7ygfv and tinyurl.com/moqo2zz. At quarterly intervals HMRC publish a list of the DOTAS SRNs of tax avoidance schemes whose users may be required to make an accelerated payment of tax (see tinyurl.com/m9xdot9).

From 26 March 2015, where a company makes a return asserting a tax advantage from chosen arrangements and then surrenders all or part of that advantage as group relief, HMRC are allowed to issue an APN to the effect that the asserted advantage may not be surrendered while the dispute is in progress (*FA 2015, s 118*).

Serial tax avoiders

25.50 The government has consulted on potential action that could be taken to impose additional financial costs, compliance and reporting requirements on repeat users of known avoidance schemes (see tinyurl.com/pbbnh3s). *Finance Act 2016, Sch 18* includes various measures of increasing severity in respect of taxpayers that have used a tax avoidance scheme which HMRC have defeated. HMRC have the power to issue a notice covering a five-year period during which the taxpayer has the burden of an annual reporting requirement. If the taxpayer continues to use tax avoidance schemes, which are then defeated by HMRC, further sanctions will apply including penalties, publication of the taxpayer's details and even the denial of access to tax reliefs. See factsheet CC/FS38a at tinyurl.com/y8kuu7wo.

There is also a 'special measures' regime for large businesses who have an ongoing history of aggressive tax planning, or who refuse to cooperate with HMRC (*Finance Act 2016, Sch 19*).

Promoters of tax avoidance schemes

25.51 Powers introduced from 17 July 2014 allow HMRC to deter the development and use of high-risk tax avoidance schemes by influencing the behaviour of promoters, their intermediaries and clients (*FA 2014, ss 234–283, Sch 34*).

From 2 March 2015, the *Finance Act 2014 (Schedule 34 Prescribed Matters) Regulations 2015, SI 2015/131*, enable HMRC to issue 'conduct notices' to promoters of tax avoidance schemes where they have triggered certain threshold conditions at any time in the preceding three years (*FA 2014, ss 237–241*).

In certain circumstances, a person is not treated as a promoter (*Promoters of Tax Avoidance Schemes (Prescribed Circumstances under Section 235) Regulations 2015, SI 2015/130*). In other cases, a person is specifically brought within the definition of a promoter (*Tax Avoidance Schemes (Promoters and Prescribed Circumstances) (Amendment) Regulations 2015, SI 2015/945*).

A conduct notice is issued by an authorised officer of HMRC and imposes conditions with which the promoter in question must comply. There is no right of appeal against the issue of a conduct notice, which can last for up to two years.

If a promoter breaches one or more conditions in a conduct notice, an authorised officer of HMRC may ask the First-tier Tribunal for approval to issue a monitoring notice. There is a right of appeal against a decision of the First-tier Tribunal to do so.

If a monitoring notice is issued, the monitored promoter is subject to a more stringent regime that includes (*FA 2014, ss 242–249*):

- publication by HMRC of information about the promoter;
- publication by the promoter of its status, on the internet and in publications and correspondence;
- a duty on the promoter to tell clients that it is a monitored promoter and to provide them with a promoter reference number (PRN);
- a duty on clients to put the PRN on their returns or otherwise to report the PRN to HMRC;
- enhanced information powers for HMRC, backed by new penalties preventing any attempt by a promoter to impose confidentiality on clients in relation to disclosure to HMRC;
- limitations to the defences of reasonable care and reasonable excuse against the imposition of penalties;
- extended time limits for assessment on clients; and
- a criminal offence of concealing, destroying or disposing of documents.

HMRC have published guidance on the regime for promoters of tax avoidance schemes (see tinyurl.com/n6agvp7).

From 26 March 2015, new measures against promoters were introduced by *FA 2015, s 119, Sch 19* to:

- allow HMRC to issue conduct notices to a broader range of connected persons under the common control of a promoter of tax avoidance schemes;
- provide that the three-year time limit for issuing conduct notices to promoters who have failed to disclose avoidance schemes to HMRC applies from the date when the failure comes to the attention of HMRC; and
- ensure that the threshold conditions take account of decisions by independent bodies in matters of all relevant forms of professional misconduct.

From 27 March 2015, the *Finance Act 2014 (High Risk Promoters Prescribed Information) Regulations 2015, SI 2015/549,* impose enhanced disclosure obligations on certain promoters of tax avoidance schemes, as well as their intermediaries and clients.

These measures have been tightened further, following announcements in Budget 2016. HMRC now have the power to issue provisional conduct notices, an even broader range of persons connected with the promoter will be caught, and there is also a new threshold condition applying where a promoter's scheme has suffered three relevant defeats during the previous three-year period (*FA 2014, ss 237A–237D, 241A–241B, Sch 34A*). From 16 November 2017, HMRC's powers to levy penalties are extended to those who enable tax avoidance schemes that have been defeated in the courts (*F(No 2)A 2017, s 65, Sch 16*, see guidance at tinyurl.com/ycd7g6yo).

MULTILATERAL CO-OPERATION

25.52 The UK and many other countries have signed the Multilateral Convention on Mutual Administrative Assistance in Tax Matters, which was developed jointly by the OECD and the Council of Europe in 1988 and amended by Protocol in 2010. The Convention provides for all forms of mutual assistance – exchange on request, spontaneous tax examinations abroad, simultaneous tax examinations and assistance in tax collection – while protecting taxpayers' rights.

The UK and many other countries have also committed to implement the OECD's new Common Reporting Standard for the Automatic Exchange of Information, which reduces the possibility for tax evasion (see **25.4**).

The OECD continues to be the focus of multilateral initiatives aimed at countering unacceptable cross-border tax avoidance through its base erosion and profit shifting (BEPS) project (see **21.2**).

Chapter 26

Accounting and tax

SIGNPOSTS

- Introduction to the standard-setting process, compliance with accounting standards, and changes of accounting basis or policy (see **26.1–26.3**).
- UK GAAP – including the changes in UK GAAP from 1 January 2015, and the terminology for financial reporting frameworks (see **26.4–26.5**).
- New UK GAAP, and transition from old UK GAAP (see **26.6–26.7**).
- FRS 102 – the new financial reporting standard – including a comparison between old UK GAAP and FRS 102, and the transition to FRS 102 (see **26.8–26.10**).
- FRS 101 – the Reduced Disclosure Framework – including a comparison between old UK GAAP and FRS 101, and the transition to FRS 101 (see **26.11–26.13**).
- Accounting for tax under UK GAAP – including current and deferred tax under FRS 102 and FRS 101 (see **26.14–26.20)**
- International GAAP – a list of the current standards (see **26.22**).
- Interaction of accounting and tax principles – discussing a number of accounting standards of particular relevance to corporation tax (see **26.23–26.43**).

ACCOUNTING STANDARDS

The standard-setting processes

26.1 The Financial Reporting Council (FRC) is the UK's independent regulator responsible for promoting high-quality corporate governance and reporting to foster investment, and its declared aim is to rely on principles rather than detailed prescription. On advice from its subsidiary body, the Corporate Reporting Council (formerly the Accounting Standards Board or

ASB), it is responsible for setting accounting standards for the UK (which are adopted also in the Republic of Ireland) for all entities that are not required (and have chosen not) to apply international accounting standards (also known as International Financial Reporting Standards). These UK standards are referred to collectively as UK generally accepted accounting practice (UK GAAP).

Current UK GAAP consists of a set of financial reporting standards (FRSs) which must be applied for all periods of account beginning on or after 1 January 2015 for reporting entities that are not part of the small companies regime (ie medium-sized and large entities), and early adoption was permitted. Small companies and micro-entities were required to report under the new framework mandatorily for periods starting on or after 1 January 2016.

The FRC completed its first comprehensive review of UK GAAP on 14 December 2017 and issued revised FRS 100 to FRS 105 in March 2018. These apply mandatorily for accounting periods starting on or after 1 January 2019.

UK Statements of Recommended Practice (SORPs) are recommendations on accounting practices for specialist industries or sectors. They supplement UK accounting standards and other legal and regulatory requirements in the light of the special factors prevailing or transactions undertaken in a particular industry or sector. SORPs existed under old UK GAAP, and have been revised and reissued for the purposes of new UK GAAP. Further details are at tinyurl.com/ntdtt8r.

The International Accounting Standards Board (IASB) sets the accounting standards to be used for group accounts of UK entities with securities listed on an EU-regulated market (under *Regulation (EC) 1606/2002*) or where market rules or other regulations require their use. These standards consist primarily of International Accounting Standards (IASs) and International Financial Reporting Standards (IFRSs), and are referred to collectively as international generally accepted accounting principles (or international GAAP). The IASB's IFRS Interpretations Committee issues interpretations (IFRIC Interpretations) which serve a purpose equivalent to that of UITF abstracts. IFRIC Interpretations are authoritative documents.

UK companies may not use a standard set by the IASB unless it has been adopted by the European Union (*CTA 2010, s 1127(5)*), and such standards are known collectively as 'EU-adopted IFRS'. The European Commission is advised by the European Financial Reporting Advisory Group (EFRAG), a private-sector body established to hold consultations and provide input into the development of an IFRS issued by the IASB. A proposal from EFRAG to endorse a new IFRS is reviewed by the Standards Advice Review Group (SARG) before being put to the Accounting Regulatory Committee (ARC), where representatives from member states vote on it. Final decisions on whether or not to endorse the IFRS are then taken by the European Parliament and the Council of the EU.

Note that financial reporting standards use company law terminology rather than tax terminology. When they refer to an 'accounting period', they mean an accounting reference period, ie a period of account for which statutory accounts must be prepared. They do not mean an accounting period for corporation tax purposes.

Compliance with accounting standards

26.2 All companies are required to prepare accounts which comply with *CA 2006*. Companies must prepare their accounts in accordance with either UK GAAP or EU-adopted IFRS. Where the EU has adopted an international accounting standard with modifications, then as regards matters covered by that standard it is to be treated as complying with EU-adopted IFRS if it applies the standard with or without the modifications (*CTA 2010, s 1127*).

Where two companies are parties to an intra-group transaction and either of them would obtain a tax advantage as a result of using different accounting practices, UK GAAP is applied to both companies for corporation tax purposes (*CTA 2010, s 996*).

Companies whose securities are traded on an EU-regulated market are required, by *Regulation (EC) 1606/2002* on the application of international accounting standards, to prepare their consolidated financial statements in accordance with EU-adopted IFRS (*CA 2006, s 403(1)*).

Under both old and new UK GAAP, simplified financial reporting standards exist for companies and groups qualifying as small or micro under the *CA 2006* definition (see **1.14–1.15**). Large or medium-sized groups cannot use these.

There is also an international accounting standard for small and medium-sized companies (IFRS for SMEs; see tinyurl.com/bnv8bre). In May 2015 the IASB agreed amendments to this standard, affecting 21 of the 35 sections of IFRS for SMEs and a final version was issued in December 2015. The amendments are effective for accounting periods starting on or after 1 January 2017, and early adoption was permissible.

Compliance with UK GAAP or EU-adopted IFRS is necessary (other than in exceptional circumstances) in financial statements that claim to give a true and fair view. Company directors are prohibited from approving financial statements unless they give a true and fair view (*CA 2006, s 393*).

> **Focus**
>
> Financial statements prepared in accordance with UK GAAP or EU-adopted IFRS and in accordance with *CA 2006* form the basis of the corporation tax computation. Normally, the profits are then adjusted further because, for corporation tax purposes, tax law takes precedence over accounting principles.

A company's financial statements prepared in accordance with UK GAAP or EU-adopted IFRS form the basis of the company's corporation tax computation (see **1.8–1.11**). This rule applies to trading profits, a letting business, an overseas property business, loan relationships, derivatives, intangible fixed assets, management expenses and leases.

Tax law has no authority to impose compliance with *CA 2006* or any requirements as to audit or disclosure (*CTA 2009, s 46(2)*). Financial statements prepared in accordance with the chosen GAAP and complying with *CA 2006* form the basis of the corporation tax computation. In most cases, the profit or loss then has to be adjusted for corporation tax purposes to take account of specific requirements of tax law (see **Chapter 2**).

If a company has drawn up accounts that are not GAAP-compliant, or has not drawn up accounts at all, it will be treated as having drawn up GAAP-compliant accounts for the purposes of corporation tax. Therefore, accounts must be adjusted for tax purposes if they do not comply with GAAP (*CTA 2009, s 717(1)*).

In *Ball UK Holdings Ltd v HMRC* [2017] UKFTT 457 (2 June 2017), the taxpayer (Ball Holdings) entered into an arrangement where it became a party to a derivative contract triggering the right to apply a particular accounting standard, namely FRS 23 *The effects of changes in foreign exchange rates*. FRS 23 required a reporting entity to determine its 'functional currency', defined in the standard as '… the currency of the primary economic environment in which the entity operates'.

Ball Holdings was a US listed public entity that owned an international group of companies, and Ball UK Holdings Ltd was a UK company indirectly owned by Ball Holdings.

Ball UK Holdings Ltd changed its functional currency from that of the Great British Pound (GBP) to US Dollars, resulting in the recognition of a large foreign exchange loss on which Ball Holdings claimed tax relief in their corporation tax computation. HMRC disputed the tax relief on the foreign exchange loss, arguing that Ball Holdings should have used GBP as its functional currency, not US Dollars. Anti-avoidance provisions were introduced in *FA 2011* to counteract this type of arrangement.

The task of the First-tier Tribunal (FTT) was to establish whether Ball Holdings was correct in its application of FRS 23 in changing its functional currency to US Dollars.

The FTT agreed with Counsel for Ball Holdings that it would have been sufficient to show that the entity's financial statements were in accordance with a reasonable interpretation of GAAP. However, the FTT agreed with HMRC that the functional currency should have been GBP and not US Dollars, hence the company's financial statements were not compliant with UK GAAP.

Ball UK Holdings Ltd argued that the test of autonomy in FRS 23 was in relation to decision-making at the entity level. However, this interpretation was incorrect because the main principle in the autonomy test is to search for a 'primary economic indicator', thus the principle of autonomy is much wider. The tribunal judge cited Ball UK Holdings Ltd's argument in respect of the test of autonomy as 'flawed'.

The case itself is significant because the FTT determined that the interpretation of FRS 23 and Ball UK Holdings Ltd's application of the standard, which was also agreed with by the company's auditors and accountancy advisers, was not correct. HMRC acknowledged that financial statements must be prepared to GAAP principles, and the fact that accountants and auditors may misapply or misinterpret the provisions in an accounting standard does not mean that the financial statements comply with GAAP (to achieve compliance with GAAP, GAAP has to be applied correctly).

As regards the accounting practices adopted, HMRC employ accountants with wide auditing and accounting experience to whom they refer accountancy queries (see Tax Bulletin, Issue 58, April 2002). If HMRC open an enquiry into a company's corporation tax return, the HMRC accountants may also enquire into the accounting policies which the company has adopted (see TAXline, ICAEW Tax Faculty, February 2003; Working Together, Issue 13, HMRC, June 2003, tinyurl.com/p75gwzn).

Changes of accounting basis or policy

26.3 A change of accounting policy from one valid basis to another, including a change from UK GAAP to EU-adopted IFRS or *vice versa*, may bring about a prior period adjustment. Positive adjustments (ie those that increase profits or reduce losses) are taxed as receipts, and negative adjustments are allowed as expenses. These prior period adjustments are treated as arising on the first day of the first period of account for which the new basis is adopted.

Tax adjustments of the kind necessary on a change of accounting basis also applied to all changes of accounting policy on or after 1 January 2015, and in particular to accounting transition adjustments arising from changes to UK GAAP. Thus they are likely to arise on a change from old UK GAAP to new UK GAAP.

The following provisions are relevant in determining how such adjustments are treated for corporation tax purposes:

Trading income	*CTA 2009, s 180(4)*
Property income	*CTA 2009, ss 261, 262*
Intangible fixed assets	*CTA 2009, ss 871–879*

Loan relationships with prior period adjustments	*CTA 2009, s 308*, and other specific provisions
Loan relationships with no prior period adjustments	*CTA 2009, ss 315–319*
Loan relationships: the 'COAP Regulations' apply to most transitional adjustments arising in respect of loan relationships or derivative contracts from changes of accounting practice	*Loan Relationships and Derivative Contracts (Change of Accounting Practice) Regulations 2004, SI 2004/3271*, as amended

UK GAAP

Changes in UK GAAP from January 2015 and January 2016

26.4 The vast majority of UK companies apply UK GAAP. In recent years, there have been many changes to UK GAAP, largely due to measures aimed at bringing it into closer alignment with IFRS. Convergence remains an international objective, but is unrealistic in anything but the long term.

Between 2012 and 2015 the FRC revised the UK's financial reporting standards in a step that has brought UK GAAP into closer alignment with IFRS, making the preparation and use of financial reports easier for companies, banks, tax authorities and regulators. The revision has fundamentally reformed financial reporting, replacing all the previous standards (FRSs, SSAPs and UITFs) with a suite of new financial reporting standards (see www.frc.org.uk). The FRC's first comprehensive review of UK GAAP has resulted in the standards being reissued following incremental improvements and clarifications, which reflect implementation feedback, as follows:

- FRS 100 (March 2018) *Application of Financial Reporting Requirements*, which sets out the applicable financial reporting framework for entities preparing financial statements in accordance with legislation, regulations or accounting standards applicable in the UK;
- FRS 101 (March 2018) *Reduced Disclosure Framework (Disclosure exemptions from EU-adopted IFRS for qualifying entities)*, sometimes referred to as 'IFRS with reduced disclosures', which outlines the reduced disclosure framework available for use by 'qualifying entities' that otherwise apply the recognition, measurement and disclosure requirements of EU-adopted IFRS;
- FRS 102 (March 2018) *The Financial Reporting Standard applicable in the UK and Republic of Ireland*, which is the FRS that contains the accounting and disclosure requirements, but with reduced disclosures available for 'qualifying entities' reporting under it. FRS 102 is, to a certain extent, based on the IASB's IFRS for SMEs but with significant

amendments – for example, Section 29 *Income Tax* was rewritten to be UK specific rather than using the text in Section 29 of IFRS for SMEs as the basis;

- FRS 103 (March 2018) *Insurance Contracts*, which applies to an entity using FRS 102 that issues insurance contracts and holds reinsurance contracts, as well as an entity issuing financial instruments which contain a discretionary participation feature;
- FRS 104 (March 2018) *Interim Financial Reporting*, which is not an accounting standard as there is no new requirement for entities to start producing interim financial statements. However, where an entity is required to prepare interim financial statements (for example, due to the requirements of the Listing Rules) and uses FRS 102 to prepare such interim financial statements, the provisions contained in FRS 104 should be followed and a statement of compliance with FRS 104 included in the financial statements; and
- FRS 105 (March 2018) *The Financial Reporting Standard applicable to the Micro-entities Regime*, which is a stand-alone standard for micro-entities, including micro-entities in the Republic of Ireland and limited liability partnerships.

Copies of FRS 100 to FRS 105 and related material can be found on the FRC website at www.frc.org.uk.

Terminology for financial reporting frameworks

26.5 It may help to clarify the terminology used in this book to describe various versions of GAAP.

In addressing the transition from old UK GAAP to new UK GAAP, there is a need to recognise a number of different financial reporting frameworks likely to be relevant, referred to throughout this book as follows:

- *'EU-adopted IFRS'*

  accounts prepared in accordance with IAS within the meaning of *CA 2006, s 395(1)(b)* and *CTA 2010, s 1127(5)*.

- *'New UK GAAP'*

  FRS 100 to FRS 105. Entities applying new UK GAAP will, within the framework of FRS 100, apply one of FRS 101, FRS 102 or FRS 105. FRS 100 effectively adopts the recognition and measurement requirements of IAS, subject to some adjustments to ensure alignment with the UK *Companies Act* and also reduced disclosure requirements. FRS 102 is a suite of accounting requirements which are closely aligned to, but not the same as, IFRS (specifically, IFRS for SMEs). FRS 105 is explained at **26.21**.

- *'Old UK GAAP'*

  substantively the FRSs, SSAPs, UITFs and relevant accepted practice in existence and applied prior to the introduction of new UK GAAP, and the FRSSE (effective January 2015). FRS 26 *Financial Instruments: Recognition and Measurement* and related standards are included within the meaning of old UK GAAP.

- *'FRSSE'*

  the Financial Reporting Standard for Smaller Entities. Entities which met the eligibility criteria were eligible to prepare and file abbreviated accounts (for accounting periods starting on or after 1 January 2016, abbreviated accounts are abolished).

- *'Micro-entities' exemptions*

  exemptions from disclosure granted by the *Small Companies (Micro-Entities' Accounts) Regulations 2013, SI 2013/3008.*

- *'FRS 105'*

  FRS 105, the Financial Reporting Standard applicable to the Micro-entities Regime.

CURRENT UK GAAP

26.6 FRS 100 sets out the overall financial reporting requirements, giving many entities a choice of detailed accounting requirements depending on factors such as size, and whether or not they are part of a listed group. It does not require any entities to apply IFRS if they are not already required to do so. FRS 100 requires UK financial statements (whether consolidated financial statements or individual financial statements) that are within its scope to be prepared in accordance with the following requirements:

- If the financial statements are those of an entity that is eligible to apply FRS 105 (micro-entities), they may be prepared in accordance with FRS 105 (FRS 105 is an optional standard).

- If the financial statements are those of an entity that is eligible to apply FRS 105 (and chooses not to do so) or is eligible to apply FRS 102, Section 1A *Small Entities*, they may be prepared in accordance with FRS 102, Section 1A.

- If the financial statements are those of an entity that is eligible to apply FRS 105 or FRS 102, Section 1A (and chooses not to do so) or of any other entity, they must be prepared in accordance with full FRS 102, EU-adopted IFRS or, if the financial statements are the individual financial statements of a qualifying entity, FRS 101 *Reduced Disclosure Framework.*

FRS 101 aims to reduce the reporting burden on listed groups. It sets out a reduced disclosure framework, providing disclosure exemptions for individual financial statements of subsidiaries and ultimate parents that otherwise apply the recognition, measurement and disclosure requirements of EU-adopted IFRS. New UK GAAP provides non-IFRS reporting entities with options, and FRS 101 might be a sensible choice for subsidiaries within a group that reports under EU-adopted IFRS if they have been using old UK GAAP; however, a group need not be using EU-adopted IFRS to adopt FRS 101 for its subsidiaries.

Certain protocol must be followed before FRS 101 can be used by a qualifying entity. The term 'qualifying entity' is defined in FRS 101 as:

> 'A member of a group where the parent of that group prepares publicly available consolidated financial statements which are intended to give a true and fair view (of the assets, liabilities, financial position and profit or loss) and that member is included in the consolidation.
>
> A charity may not be a qualifying entity.'

A qualifying entity must therefore have its financial statements consolidated with those of a parent. If, for example, the subsidiary is not consolidated because the subsidiary is immaterial to the group, the subsidiary cannot apply FRS 101. In addition, the subsidiary must also comply with *CA 2006* and the Regulations and disclose a brief narrative summary of the disclosure exemptions adopted, as well as the name of the parent of the group in whose consolidated financial statements its financial statements are included.

Focus

There is a similar reduced disclosure framework, at paragraphs 1.8 to 1.13 of FRS 102 (March 2018), for subsidiaries and ultimate parents reporting under that standard.

FRS 102 is a stand-alone financial reporting standard that applies to the financial statements of entities that are not applying EU-adopted IFRS, FRS 101 or FRS 105. It is based, to a certain extent, on the IFRS for SMEs, and modernises and simplifies financial reporting for unlisted companies and subsidiaries of listed companies as well as public benefit entities such as charities. The standard takes account of evolving business practices. FRS 102 might be a sensible choice for UK companies that are not required to report under EU-adopted IFRS and do not foresee that as a possibility. It also includes some key provisions that might simplify the reporting of financial instruments in straightforward cases.

Micro-entities (as defined in legislation) can choose to report under FRS 105. However, FRS 105 should be considered on a case-by-case basis because, while the standard may be appropriate for many micro-entities, it will not necessarily be appropriate for them all. A key issue that should be considered is where a micro-entity may be carrying an asset under the revaluation model, or has an investment property on the balance sheet which is measured at fair value at each balance sheet date. FRS 105 does not allow the use of the revaluation model or fair values and, as such, all revaluation amounts and fair values must be removed on transition. This will clearly have an impact on the micro-entity's balance sheet, and hence an impact assessment should be carried out prior to the transition to establish the effect. If the effect on the balance sheet is significantly adverse, it may be advisable for the micro-entity to report under FRS 102.

Feedback is that current UK GAAP has been generally welcomed, particularly because it should provide comparability with accounts prepared under IFRS without imposing the full burden of IFRS on most UK companies. However, the move from old UK GAAP to the new framework was not easy for all companies and proved challenging in many areas. To that end, the FRC took on board implementation feedback during the recent comprehensive review of UK GAAP.

Also within current UK GAAP are:

- FRS 103, a standard for entities that have insurance contracts (including reinsurance contracts) and are applying FRS 102; and
- FRS 104, a standard on interim financial reporting.

The FRC has published details of SORPs that have been revised and reissued for the purposes of new UK GAAP, and which are expected to be further revised to reflect changes as part of the triennial review (see tinyurl.com/ntdtt8r).

TRANSITION FROM OLD UK GAAP

26.7 Transition from old UK GAAP to new UK GAAP – ie FRS 101, FRS 102, the FRSSE (effective January 2015) or FRS 105 – or EU-adopted IFRS impacts on a company's accounts in two key ways:

- assets and liabilities at the date of transition must be identified, recognised and measured in line with the requirements of the new standards; and
- thereafter, profits and losses must be recognised in accordance with the new standards. These may differ from those profits and losses that would have been reported had old UK GAAP been retained, for example where investment property fair value gains and losses are concerned.

The date of transition is defined by FRS 100 as the beginning of the earliest period for which an entity presents full comparative information under a given standard in its first financial statements that comply with that standard.

Example 26.1—Accounting transition from old to new UK GAAP

Facts

ABC plc, a large UK company with a 31 December accounting date which is not eligible to use the FRSSE, has been preparing its accounts in accordance with old UK GAAP.

Analysis

ABC plc may continue to prepare its 31 December 2014 accounts in accordance with old UK GAAP.

For its 31 December 2015 accounts, it is no longer permitted to use old UK GAAP. Instead, it must choose to apply one of FRS 101, FRS 102 or EU-adopted IFRS.

The company's date of transition is 1 January 2014 – ie the beginning of the first period for which the company presents full comparative information under its chosen new standard in its first financial statements that comply with that standard.

Assets and liabilities at 1 January 2014 will be identified, recognised and measured in line with the requirements of the new standard.

From 1 January 2014, profits and losses will be recognised in accordance with the new standard. These may differ from those profits and losses that would have been reported had old UK GAAP been retained.

Corporation tax law requires that the profits of a trade are calculated in accordance with generally accepted accounted practice, subject to any adjustment required or authorised by law (*CTA 2009, s 46*). Similar rules exist elsewhere in the tax legislation.

For this purpose, generally accepted accounting practice is defined by *CTA 2010, s 1127*, and it means either:

- generally accepted accountancy practice in relation to accounts of UK companies (other than IAS accounts) that are intended to give a true and fair view (ie UK GAAP); or
- in relation to a company that prepares IAS accounts, generally accepted accountancy practice in relation to IAS accounts (ie international GAAP).

Corporation tax depends heavily on the accounting treatment adopted in a company's accounts. The tax legislation contains provisions originally designed to deal with certain issues that arose for companies on transition to international GAAP in their individual accounts. Similar issues are likely to arise for companies on the transition to FRS 101 or FRS 102. For further commentary on changes in the basis of accounting and changes in applicable accounting standards in the context of trading income, see **2.73–2.76**, **26.3** and **26.36**.

Note that GAAP also has to be applied to companies incorporated outside the UK but resident in the UK, and in some cases to non-resident companies – eg controlled foreign companies (CFCs; see **20.25–20.32**). In most cases, the same statutory definition of GAAP applies: where the company prepares IAS accounts, these will be used to calculate profits, and in other cases the profits will be calculated in accordance with UK GAAP.

FRS 102

Focus

FRS 102 (March 2018), *The Financial Reporting Standard applicable in the UK and Republic of Ireland*, is a succinct and simplified accounting framework; it was initially based on IFRS for SMEs, although modified to be UK-specific, and forms the core of current UK GAAP for those companies eligible to use it.

26.8 FRS 102 is a single financial reporting standard for companies which are not applying EU-adopted IFRS, FRS 101 or the FRSSE, and for other entities including those that are not profit-oriented. It is designed to apply to their general purpose financial statements, ie those intended to meet the needs of a wide range of users including shareholders, lenders, other creditors, employees and members of the public.

FRS 102 consists of 36 sections, as follows:

Section	Topic	Commentary
1	Scope	
1A	Small Entities	
2	Concepts and Pervasive Principles	**26.28**
3	Financial Statement Presentation	
4	Statement of Financial Position	
5	Statement of Comprehensive Income and Income Statement (with appendix: Example showing presentation of discontinued operations)	
6	Statement of Changes in Equity and Statement of Income and Retained Earnings	

7	Statement of Cash Flows	
8	Notes to the Financial Statements	
9	Consolidated and Separate Financial Statements	
10	Accounting Policies, Estimates and Errors	**26.36**
11	Basic Financial Instruments	**26.25, 26.34**
12	Other Financial Instruments Issues	**26.25**
13	Inventories	**26.40**
14	Investments in Associates	**26.34**
15	Investments in Joint Ventures	**26.34**
16	Investment Property	**26.34, 26.39**
17	Property, Plant and Equipment	**26.29**
18	Intangible Assets other than Goodwill	**26.33**
19	Business Combinations and Goodwill	**26.33**
20	Leases	**26.34, 26.38**
21	Provisions and Contingencies (with appendix: Examples of recognising and measuring provisions)	**26.31**
22	Liabilities and Equity (with appendix: Example of the issuer's accounting for convertible debt)	
23	Revenue (with appendix: Examples of revenue recognition)	**26.34**
24	Government Grants	**26.41**
25	Borrowing Costs	**26.30**
26	Share-based Payment	
27	Impairment of Assets	
28	Employee Benefits	**26.37**
29	Income Tax	
30	Foreign Currency Translation	**26.26**
31	Hyperinflation	
32	Events after the End of the Reporting Period	**26.27**
33	Related Party Disclosures	
34	Specialised Activities (with Appendix A: Guidance on funding commitments and Appendix B: Guidance on incoming resources from non-exchange transactions)	**26.34**
35	Transition to this FRS	

Note: For further commentary, see **26.9**.

The FRC intends to review and update FRS 102 every four or five years. The first triennial review of FRS 102 was announced in March 2017, and FRED 67 *Draft Amendments to FRS 102 – Triennial Review 2017* contained details of the FRC's proposals. The comment period on FRED 67 closed on 30 June 2017, and the first review was completed on 14 December 2017. The changes arising from the triennial review apply mandatorily for accounting periods starting on or after 1 January 2019, and early adoption is permissible.

A summary of the changes is as follows:

(1) Undue cost or effort exemptions

The undue cost or effort exemption has been removed from FRS 102. For example, paragraph 16.7 of FRS 102 (September 2015) said that, 'Investment property whose fair value can be measured reliably without undue cost or effort shall be measured at fair value at each **reporting date** with changes in fair value recognised in profit or loss'. The undue cost or effort exemption is removed in the March 2018 edition of the standard, having the effect that all investment properties will be measured at fair value at each reporting date (there are some exemptions for groups – see (2) below).

This treatment will mean that Section 16 *Investment Properties* is similar to the requirements found in previous UK GAAP in the FRSSE (effective January 2015) and SSAP 19 *Accounting for investment properties*. The accounting treatment, however, has not changed, and therefore all fair value gains and losses will continue to pass through the profit and loss account (not a revaluation reserve), and deferred tax will also be brought into account.

The FRC has decided on this course of action because feedback suggested that the undue cost or effort exemptions were not being applied with sufficient rigour and were being regarded by some entities as an accounting policy choice – which they were not.

Other areas where undue cost or effort exemptions were removed are as follows:

- Section 14 *Investments in Associates* – paragraph 14.10;
- Section 15 *Investments in Joint Ventures* – paragraph 15.15;
- Section 16 *Investment Property* – paragraphs 16.3, 16.4 and 16.10; and
- Section 17 *Property, Plant and Equipment* – paragraph 17.1(a).

(2) Investment properties within a group

Unlike previous SSAP 19, the scope exemption to treat property occupied by, or let to, group members was not carried over into FRS 102. This meant that groups which rented property out to other group members would have had to reclassify the property as investment property in the separate financial statements and then do a consolidation adjustment in the group accounts to effectively reverse the investment property treatment and treat the property as owned property, plant and equipment. This is because consolidated financial statements have to show the group in line with its economic substance, which is that of a single reporting entity (ie as if the group structure does not exist), hence any intra-group issues are eliminated on consolidation.

This treatment has proved particularly challenging for some groups and, therefore, new paragraphs 16.4A and 16.4B have been inserted into FRS 102 (March 2018) which deal with investment property rented to another group entity. Paragraph 16.4A provides an accounting policy choice for group members to either account for such properties at fair value through profit or loss or transfer them to property, plant and equipment and apply the cost model in Section 17 *Property, Plant and Equipment* in the individual financial statements of a group member. It is likely that the latter option will be the most popular. It must be emphasised that this policy choice is available only for investment properties in a group context; it is not available to stand-alone companies or small companies.

(3) Financial instruments and loans from director-shareholders

Financial instruments are dealt with in Section 11 *Basic Financial Instruments* and Section 12 *Other Financial Instruments Issues*. Previously, to meet the classification of a 'basic' financial instrument the instrument had to meet detailed conditions outlined in paragraph 11.9, which can be extremely difficult to interpret. Paragraph 11.9A of FRS 102 (March 2018) includes a description of a basic financial instrument which is intended to support the detailed conditions. This means that a relatively small number of financial instruments that previously breached the detailed conditions in paragraph 11.9 of FRS 102, and hence were classified as non-basic and accounted for under Section 12, will qualify for treatment as basic and therefore be able to be measured at amortised cost under Section 11.

Directors' loans were also proving a challenge under FRS 102. This is because, invariably, loans from a director-shareholder to a company are often entered into at below market rates of interest or at zero per cent rates of interest.

To provide relief, **for a small company (as defined in the Companies Act) only**, from the requirement to account for loans from a director to the small company at present value, paragraph 11.13A of FRS 102 (March 2018) allows a loan from the director, or a 'close member of the family of that person' (as defined in the Glossary to FRS 102) to be accounted for at transaction price rather than at present value. In an unprecedented move, the FRC brought forward this relief for small companies with a 31 December 2016 year-end, as the proposals in FRED 67 were not finalised until the end of 2017. If the FRC had not brought forward this relief early, small companies with a 31 December 2016 year-end would not have been able to apply the exemption, hence would have accounted for a loan from a director-shareholder at present value, only to then unravel the discounting in the 31 December 2017 year-end, which would have clearly been unfair to a small company with a 31 December 2016 year-end. To eliminate this unfairness, the FRC issued a Press Release on 8 May 2017 confirming that small companies can apply the relief immediately.

The triennial review extended the relief slightly, so that loans from a person who is within a director's group of close family members, when that group contains at least one shareholder, can also take advantage of the concession.

(4) Intangible assets

Paragraph 18.8 of FRS 102 (March 2018) includes an option, on an asset-by-asset basis, to separately recognise additional intangible assets acquired in a business combination if doing so provides useful information to the entity. This has been done so that fewer intangible assets acquired in a business combination will be recognised separately from goodwill.

(5) Financial institutions

The definition of what constitutes a 'financial institution' has been changed to remove references to '… generate wealth' and '… manage risk'. The effect of this change is that fewer entities will meet the definition of a financial institution and should also allow for fewer interpretational difficulties.

(6) Cash flow statement

A net debt reconciliation is reintroduced for the cash flow statement in Section 7 *Statement of Cash Flows* of FRS 102 (March 2018). This is introduced in paragraph 7.22 on the grounds that it gives better information as it takes into account both cash balances and borrowings of the entity. This is a departure from what is required under IFRS, but the FRC believes that a net debt reconciliation meets the overriding objective and, as preparers will be familiar with the net debt reconciliation (as it was required under FRS 1 *Cash flow statements* (Revised 1996), including it as part of the cash flow statement will be cost-effective to apply.

(7) Key management personnel compensation

A new paragraph 33.7A has been inserted into FRS 102 (March 2018) which says that, when there is a legal or regulatory requirement to disclose directors' remuneration (or equivalent), an entity will be exempt from paragraph 33.7 which requires an entity to disclose key management personnel compensation in totality. The exemption will apply where key management personnel and directors are the same.

(8) Gift aid

Where a charitable parent has a trading subsidiary which 'gifts' its profits up to its parent each year, the tax effects of the gift aid payment can be recognised in the financial statements under FRS 102 (March 2018) in profit or loss where it is probable (ie more likely than not) that the gift aid payment will be made within nine months of the reporting date and that payment will qualify to be set against profits for tax purposes.

Unless there is a Deed of Covenant in place, or there is a legal obligation at the balance sheet date to make the gift aid payment, the gift aid payment cannot be accrued; it is only the tax effects that can be recognised. For accounting purposes, the gift aid payment is a distribution; and, for tax purposes, it is a donation. The gift aid payment itself will, therefore, be treated in the same way as a dividend for the purposes of recognition.

(9) FRS 105

Some notable changes made to FRS 105 are as follows:

- The requirement for a micro-entity's financial statements to state:
  - the part of the UK in which the micro-entity is registered;
  - the micro-entity's registered number;
  - whether the micro-entity is a public or private company and whether it is limited by shares or guarantee (this requirement does not apply to micro-entities which are LLPs);
  - the address of the micro-entity's registered office; and
  - where appropriate, the fact that the LLP is being wound up.
- The requirement for off-balance sheet arrangements to be disclosed (as required by *CA 2006, s 410A*).
- The requirement for information about employee numbers to be disclosed (as required by *CA 2006, s 411*).

These amendments are to take effect for accounting periods starting on or after 1 January 2019, and early adoption is permissible. Comments on FRS 102 (and the other FRSs in the suite) are welcomed in order to influence future proposals for change. Comments can be submitted by email to ukfrsreview@frc.org.uk.

Comparison between old UK GAAP and FRS 102

26.9 FRS 102 is based on the IASB's IFRS for Small and Medium-sized Entities (IFRS for SMEs) which was issued in 2009 (the latest edition is the December 2015 edition), and it therefore shares many similarities with FRS 101 which is also based on IFRS. To understand the effects of a transition to FRS 102, it is necessary to look in many cases at the difference between old UK GAAP on the one hand and IFRS (or, more particularly, IFRS for SMEs) on the other. The following is a brief summary of key accounting and tax differences between old UK GAAP and FRS 102:

Old UK GAAP	FRS 102
Reporting financial performance	
Companies Act profit and loss account and balance sheet. FRS 3 *Reporting financial performance*: where applicable, statement of total recognised gains and losses (STRGL).	*CA 2006*-compliant statement of financial position; single statement of comprehensive income, or income statement and separate statement of comprehensive income; statement of changes in equity.
Consolidated accounts	
These are of little relevance for corporation tax purposes except as a source of information.	FRS 102, Section 9 *Consolidated and Separate Financial Statements*: still of little relevance for tax purposes, so there is no change (but see **26.43**).
Accounting policies	
FRS 3: changes in accounting policy are applied retrospectively; cumulative effect of prior period adjustments are shown at foot of STRGL.	FRS 102, Section 10 *Accounting Policies, Estimates and Errors*: changes are recognised in the statement of changes in equity.
For corporation tax, adjustments are treated as receipts or deductions on change from one valid basis to another – eg for trading income, *CTA 2009, ss 180–187* apply.	No change – eg for trading income, *CTA 2009, ss 180–187* continue to apply.
Financial instruments	
There are six possible transition paths. Companies may or may not have adopted FRS 26 *Financial instruments: recognition and measurement* under old UK GAAP, and they have three options, as shown opposite:	(a) FRS 102, Section 11 *Basic Financial Instruments* and Section 12 *Other Financial Instruments Issues*, which provide specific guidance on accounting for 'basic' and 'other' financial instruments
	(b) IAS 39 *Financial Instruments: Recognition and Measurement*
	(c) IFRS 9 *Financial Instruments* (mandatorily effective for periods beginning on or after 1 January 2018, with early adoption permissible)
Companies that have already adopted FRS 26.	No significant difference from IAS 39.

Old UK GAAP	**FRS 102**
Companies that have not adopted FRS 26: current treatment determined by FRS 4 *Capital instruments*, SSAP 20 *Foreign currency translation*, FRS 5 *Reporting the substance of transactions* and general principles in FRS 18 *Accounting policies*, particularly the accruals concept.	Under FRS 102 or IAS 39 options, substantial change in treatment for some assets on move to fair value. Transitional adjustments can be expected to have corporation tax impacts.
Inventories/stock	
SSAP 9 *Stocks and long-term contracts* values stock and work in progress at lower of cost and net realisable value. It permits valuation on a LIFO basis, exceptionally, but emphasises that this would rarely be appropriate and the directors must have justifiable reasons for the use of LIFO.	FRS 102, Section 13 *Inventories*, prohibits LIFO. Stock is valued at the lower of cost and estimated selling price less costs to complete and sell (effectively the same as net realisable value). It excludes work in progress on construction contracts (Section 23 *Revenue*), agricultural produce and biological assets (Section 34 *Specialised Activities: Agriculture*) and financial instruments (Sections 11 and 12). For example, Section 34 will impose fair value. However, value for tax will generally be lower of cost and estimated selling price less costs to complete and sell/net realisable value.
Investment property	
SSAP 19 *Accounting for investment properties*: investment property is carried at open market value; movements in value recognised each period in the STRGL, except for permanent diminutions in value which go to profit and loss account; investment property let to another group entity for its own purpose is exempt from SSAP 19 and treated as fixed asset instead.	FRS 102, Section 16 *Investment Property*: choice of fair value model (with movements recognised in income statement but not distributable to shareholders) or cost model (with depreciation and impairment) where obtaining fair value will incur undue cost or effort (note that the undue cost or effort exemptions have been removed following the FRC's triennial review, hence all investment properties will be measured at cost). Section 16 allows investment property rented to another group member to be measured at historical cost or fair value. Note that accounting treatment of

Old UK GAAP	FRS 102
Investment property (cont.)	
	investment properties does not determine whether the property is an investment property for tax or whether a property disposal is capital or revenue. Income is taxed when recognised, movements in fair value are not taxed, and chargeable gains or losses do not arise until disposal.
Property, plant and equipment	
FRS 15 *Tangible fixed assets*.	FRS 102, Section 17 *Property, Plant and Equipment*, differs because major spare parts are included, cost measured by present value of future payments where beyond normal credit terms, renewals accounting not permitted, and residual values based on current rather than historic prices. However, little impact because capital allowances apply for tax purposes.
Intangible assets including goodwill	
Goodwill: FRS 10 *Goodwill and intangible assets* applies to 'non-financial fixed assets that do not have physical substance but are identifiable and are controlled by the entity through custody or legal rights'. Goodwill and intangibles should be amortised over useful economic life (UEL), with rebuttable presumption that UEL will not exceed 20 years. FRS 10 can override need to amortise goodwill.	FRS 102 (March 2018) defines an intangible asset as an 'identifiable non-monetary asset without physical substance', where 'identifiable' refers to an asset that is separable or arises from a legal contract or other legal right. FRS 102, Section 18 addresses *Intangible Assets other than Goodwill*, and Section 19 deals with *Business Combinations and Goodwill*. Amortised over UEL – maximum ten years where it cannot be reliably estimated. On transition or subsequent business combinations, more intangible assets may be recognised where this is the accounting policy of the entity. FRS 102, Section 19 overrides the *CA 2006* requirement to amortise goodwill. Tax adjustments may be needed on change of accounting policy (*CTA 2009, ss 871–879*).

Old UK GAAP	**FRS 102**
Software costs: those directly attributable to bringing an item of IT into use are part of cost of tangible fixed asset (FRS 10), and website costs may also be treated in a similar way (UITF Abstract 29 *Website development costs*).	FRS 102 does not specify how such costs should be treated. Hence nature of item should be considered in deciding its treatment, and it may be recognised as an intangible asset. Tax adjustments may be needed on change of accounting policy (*CTA 2009, ss 871–879*).
Business combinations	
FRS 6 *Acquisitions and mergers* and FRS 7 *Fair values in acquisition accounting*.	FRS 102, Section 19 *Business Combinations and Goodwill*, is broadly comparable, but there may be some differences.
Leases	
SSAP 21 *Accounting for leases and hire purchase contracts*, UITF Abstract 28 *Operating lease incentives* and FRS 5.	FRS 102, Section 20 *Leases*, is broadly comparable, but some differences may affect timing of income recognition for tax purposes (particularly lease incentives).
Provisions	
FRS 12 *Provisions, contingent liabilities and contingent assets*.	FRS 102, Section 21 *Provisions and Contingencies*. No significant difference expected for accounting or tax purposes.
Revenue recognition	
No specific standard on revenue recognition, but FRS 5 Application note G *Revenue recognition*, SSAP 9 and UITF Abstract 40 *Revenue recognition and service contracts* all provide guidance.	Primarily FRS 102, Section 23 *Revenue*. This is broadly comparable with old UK GAAP, so for many entities there will be no accounting or tax impact.
Government grants	
SSAP 4 *Accounting for government grants*.	FRS 102, Section 24 *Government Grants*, provides more opportunity for systematic recognition, but little difference for tax purposes.

Old UK GAAP	FRS 102
Borrowing costs	
FRS 15 *Tangible fixed assets* allows capitalisation where certain conditions apply.	FRS 102, Section 25 *Borrowing Costs*, is effectively the same. There will be no significant differences for tax purposes.
Share-based payments	
FRS 20 *Share-based payment.*	FRS 102, Section 26 *Share-based Payment*, is similar. Tax deductions for share-based payments are governed by specific legislation.
Employee benefits	
Pensions schemes: FRS 17 *Retirement benefits.*	FRS 102, Section 28 *Employee Benefits*, differs from an accounting perspective. No tax impact is expected.
Holiday pay accrual: many entities did not accrue or provide for holiday pay earned but not yet paid by the balance sheet date.	FRS 102, Section 28, requires holiday pay accrual. For tax purposes, this will be treated as unpaid remuneration under *CTA 2009, ss 1288–1289*.
Employee benefit trusts: UITF Abstract 32 *Employee benefit trusts and other intermediate payment arrangements.*	FRS 102, Section 28, addresses the accounting aspects in a comparable way, but the tax treatment will still follow *CTA 2009, ss 1290–1296*.
Foreign currency translation	
SSAP 20 (where FRS 26 is not applied) or FRS 23 *The effects of changes in foreign exchange rates* (where FRS 26 is applied).	FRS 102, Section 30. Few differences expected for entities that already use FRS 23 and FRS 26. Some other entities may encounter significant differences.
Functional/presentational currency: under SSAP 20, this is the currency of the primary economic environment in which the entity operates.	Under FRS 102, Section 30 *Foreign Currency Translation*, functional currency also requires consideration of the influence of the parent on the entity's operations and activities, and this could have significant accounting and tax impact. Furthermore, under Section 30, functional and presentational currencies can be different (see *Ball UK Holdings Ltd v HMRC* at **26.2**).

Old UK GAAP	FRS 102
Foreign operations (including branches): under SSAP 20, income and expenditure of foreign operations (including branches) are translated into the company's functional currency at actual or average rates.	Under FRS 102, Section 30, at the end of each reporting period, foreign currency monetary items are translated using the closing rate.
Contract rate accounting: allowed by SSAP 20.	Not allowed by FRS 102, Section 30.
Net investment hedging: under SSAP 20, certain exchange differences can be taken to reserves and not immediately brought into account.	There is no equivalent under FRS 102, Section 30. Hedging is dealt with by FRS 102, Section 12 *Other Financial Instruments Issues*, or (optionally) the recognition and measurement provisions of IAS 39.
Permanent-as-equity debt: under SSAP 20, permanent-as-equity loans at arm's length can be carried at historic rates until eventual disposal, and the tax treatment will be similar.	There is no provision for this under FRS 102, Section 30, so such instruments must be retranslated at each year end, with exchange movements being recognised in the income statement.
Liabilities and equity	
FRS 25 *Financial instruments: presentation*.	FRS 102, Section 22 *Liabilities and Equity*. No differences are expected.

Note that FRS 102, Section 34, includes specific guidance on a number of specialised activities such as service concession arrangements, agriculture and extractive industries.

Transition to FRS 102

26.10 The accounting transition from old UK GAAP to FRS 102 is determined by the requirements of FRS 102, Section 35 *Transition to this FRS*. It follows very much the same pattern as the transition from old UK GAAP to FRS 101 (see **26.13**).

Entities applying FRS 102 for the first time must restate their balance sheet (referred to in FRS 102 as their 'statement of financial position') for the beginning and end of the comparative period. Typically, the first period of account of mandatory application is the year ending 31 December 2015, with a requirement to restate both the opening balance sheet as at 1 January 2014 and the comparative balance sheet as at 31 December 2014. This is to ensure the financial statements are both comparable and consistent, and reflect the requirements of FRS 102 as if the framework had always been in place. For small companies transitioning to FRS 102 for periods starting on or after 1 January 2016, assuming a 31 December 2016 year-end, the opening balance sheet position as at 1 January 2015 and closing balance sheet position as at 31 December 2015 will have to be restated, where necessary. This is to ensure that the financial statements are both consistent and comparable.

On transition, FRS 102, Section 35, requires (subject to a number of exceptions) that the balance sheet presented in respect of the date of transition (see **26.7**):

- recognises all assets and liabilities whose recognition is required by FRS 102;
- does not recognise assets and liabilities if FRS 102 does not permit such recognition;
- reclassifies assets, liabilities and equity components to ensure presentation is consistent with FRS 102; and
- measures all recognised assets and liabilities in accordance with FRS 102.

It is expected that, in some cases, on transition, there may be a significant number of adjustments – both to the carrying value of assets and liabilities recognised previously under old UK GAAP, and in terms of newly recognised assets and liabilities (there are likely to be fewer transitional and prior year adjustments for small companies). For accounting purposes, these adjustments will be made to the assets and liabilities as at the date of transition, with corresponding adjustments directly to the opening reserves. The statutory provisions relevant in determining how such adjustments are treated for corporation tax purposes are listed at **26.3**.

On 22 January 2014, HMRC published Overview Papers on the new accounting framework, and these were last updated on 21 July 2017. One of them aimed to assist companies that were thinking of choosing or had already chosen to apply FRS 102 (see www.gov.uk/government/publications/accounting-standards-the-uk-tax-implications-of-new-uk-gaap/frs-102-overview-paper). An Overview Paper outlining income tax implications was updated on 21 July 2017. Also, on 21 July 2017, HMRC issued an Overview Paper outlining the tax implications for micro-entities reporting under FRS 105.

FRS 101

Reduced Disclosure Framework

Focus

FRS 101 *Reduced Disclosure Framework (Disclosure exemptions from EU-adopted IFRS for qualifying entities)*, or 'IFRS with reduced disclosures', has introduced a reduced disclosure framework allowing eligible entities to prepare financial statements using the recognition and measurement requirements of EU-adopted IFRS but without the full disclosures.

26.11 FRS 101 sets out a number of specific disclosure exemptions available for the individual financial statements of subsidiaries, intermediate parents and ultimate parents that otherwise apply EU-adopted IFRS. It does not apply to consolidated financial statements.

The disclosure exemptions may be used where the requirements of *CA 2006, ss 395(1)(a), 396,* have been met – ie that the financial statements qualify as *Companies Act* accounts, given that they are not IAS accounts. The requirement to notify shareholders in writing about the use of FRS 101 was removed for periods starting on or after 1 January 2016. The financial statements must include a brief summary of the disclosure exemptions adopted.

A company which is not a financial institution may take advantage of a range of disclosure exemptions which reduce the disclosures required under:

- IFRS 2 *Share-based Payment*;
- IFRS 3 *Business Combinations*;
- IFRS 5 *Non-Current Assets Held for Sale and Discontinued Operations*;
- IFRS 7 *Financial Instruments: Disclosures*;
- IFRS 13 *Fair Value Measurement*;
- IAS 1 *Presentation of Financial Statements*;
- IAS 7 *Statement of Cash Flows*;
- IAS 8 *Accounting Policies, Changes in Accounting Estimates and Errors*;
- IAS 24 *Related Party Disclosures*; and
- IAS 36 *Impairment of Assets*.

A few of the above exemption disclosures are not available to financial institutions (for example, the disclosure requirements of IFRS 7).

Several of the exemptions apply only where corresponding disclosures equivalent to the requirements of EU-adopted IFRS are included in the consolidated financial statements of the group in which the company is consolidated.

Where FRS 101 is used, a note to the financial statements must state: 'These financial statements were prepared in accordance with Financial Reporting Standard 101 Reduced Disclosure Framework.'

Because FRS 101 is based on IFRS, it is to be updated annually to reflect any changes in exemptions it offers and changes to EU-adopted IFRS. On 14 July

2017 the FRC published amendments to FRS 101 which provide certain disclosure exemptions in respect of IFRS 16 *Leases*. To maintain consistency with company law, FRS 101 has also been amended in line with *EU Directive 2013/34/EU* on the annual financial statements, consolidated financial statements and related reports of certain types of undertakings, as implemented in the UK by the *Companies, Partnerships and Groups (Accounts and Reports) Regulations 2015, SI 2015/980*. The latest version of FRS 101 is the September 2015 edition but should be read in conjunction with the amendments issued in July 2016, December 2016 and July 2017. There will be no changes to FRS 101 in the 2017/18 annual review.

Comparison between old UK GAAP and FRS 101

26.12 FRS 101 is based on IFRS but with specific exemptions. Accordingly, to understand the effects of a transition to FRS 101, it is necessary to look in many cases at the difference between old UK GAAP and IFRS. The following is a brief summary of key accounting and tax differences between old UK GAAP and FRS 101:

Old UK GAAP	**FRS 101**
Reporting financial performance	
Companies Act profit and loss account and balance sheet. FRS 3 *Reporting financial performance*: where applicable, statement of total recognised gains and losses (STRGL).	IAS 1 (amended): *CA 2006*-compliant statement of financial position; single statement of comprehensive income, or income statement and separate statement of comprehensive income; statement of changes in equity.
Consolidated accounts	***Consolidated financial statements***
These are of little relevance for corporation tax purposes except as a source of information.	Still of little relevance for tax purposes; there is no change to this under FRS 101.
Accounting policies	
FRS 3: changes of accounting policy are applied retrospectively; cumulative effect of prior period adjustments are shown at foot of STRGL.	IAS 8: changes are recognised in the statement of changes in equity.
For corporation tax, adjustments are treated as receipts or deductions on change from one valid basis to another – eg for trading income, *CTA 2009, ss 180–187* apply.	No change – eg for trading income, *CTA 2009, ss 180–187* continue to apply.

Old UK GAAP	FRS 101
Financial instruments	
Companies that have already adopted FRS 26 *Financial instruments: recognition and measurement*.	No significant difference from IAS 39 *Financial Instruments: Recognition and Measurement*.
Companies that have not adopted FRS 26: current treatment determined by FRS 4 *Capital instruments*, SSAP 20 *Foreign currency translation*, FRS 5 *Reporting the substance of transactions*, and general principles in FRS 18 *Accounting policies*, particularly the accruals concept.	IAS 39: little change for some items such as cash and trade debtors, but substantial change in treatment for some other assets on move to fair value. Transitional adjustments can be expected to have corporation tax impacts. IAS 39 will be superseded by IFRS 9 *Financial Instruments*.
Inventories/stock	
SSAP 9 *Stocks and long-term contracts* values stock and work in progress at lower of cost and net realisable value. It permits valuation on a LIFO basis, exceptionally, but emphasises that this would rarely be appropriate.	IAS 2 *Inventories* forbids LIFO. It excludes work in progress on construction contracts (IAS 11 *Construction Contracts* (to be superseded by IFRS 15 *Revenue from Contracts with Customers*)), agricultural produce and biological assets (IAS 41 *Agriculture*) and financial instruments (IAS 32 *Financial Instruments: Presentation* and IAS 39). For example, IAS 11 will impose fair value. However, value for tax will generally be lower of cost and net realisable value.
Investment property	
SSAP 19 *Accounting for investment properties*: investment property is carried at open market value; movements in value recognised each period in the STRGL, except for permanent diminutions in value which go to profit and loss account; investment property let to another group entity for its own purpose is exempt from SSAP 19 and treated as fixed asset instead.	IAS 40 *Investment Property*: choice of fair value model (with movements recognised in income statement but not distributable to shareholders) or cost model (with depreciation and impairment in line with IAS 16, except for property held for sale in accordance with IFRS 5). Such property is instead held at lower of carrying value and fair value less costs to sell. IAS 40 contains no exemption for property let to another group entity.

Old UK GAAP	FRS 101
Property, plant and equipment	
FRS 15 *Tangible fixed assets*.	IAS 16 *Property, Plant and Equipment* differs because major spare parts and standby equipment are included, cost measured by present value of future payments where beyond normal credit terms, renewals accounting not permitted, and residual values based on current rather than historic prices. However, little impact because capital allowances apply for tax purposes.
Intangible assets including goodwill	
FRS 10 *Goodwill and intangible assets* applies to 'non-financial fixed assets that do not have physical substance but are identifiable and are controlled by the entity through custody or legal rights'. Goodwill and intangibles should be amortised over useful economic life (UEL), with rebuttable presumption that UEL will not exceed 20 years. FRS 10 can override need to amortise goodwill.	IAS 38 *Intangible Assets* defines an intangible asset (other than goodwill) as an 'identifiable non-monetary asset without physical substance', where 'identifiable' refers to an asset that is separable or arises from a legal contract or other legal right. On transition or subsequent business combinations, more intangible assets may be recognised under FRS 101 than under old UK GAAP. IFRS 3 *Business Combinations* overrides the *CA 2006* requirement to amortise goodwill, which is tested for impairment at each balance sheet date.
Software costs: those directly attributable to bringing an item of IT into use are part of cost of tangible fixed asset (FRS 10), and website costs may also be treated in a similar way (UITF Abstract 29 *Website development costs*).	Nature of item should be considered in deciding its treatment (IAS 38), and it may be recognised as an intangible asset. Tax adjustments may be needed on change of accounting policy.
Business combinations	
FRS 6 *Acquisitions and mergers* and FRS 7 *Fair values in acquisition accounting*.	IFRS 3 is broadly comparable, but there may be some differences.

Old UK GAAP	**FRS 101**
Leases	
SSAP 21 *Accounting for leases and hire purchase contracts*, UITF Abstract 28 *Operating lease incentives* and FRS 5.	IAS 17 *Leases* (to be superseded by IFRS 16 *Leases*) and IFRIC 4 *Determining whether an arrangement contains a lease* (which is withdrawn when IFRS 16 takes effect) are broadly comparable, but some differences may affect timing of income recognition for tax purposes. The accounting treatment for leases under IFRS 16 is significantly different for lessees.
Provisions	
FRS 12 *Provisions, contingent liabilities and contingent assets*.	IAS 37 *Provisions, Contingent Liabilities and Contingent Assets*. No significant difference expected for accounting or tax purposes.
Revenue recognition	
No specific standard on revenue recognition, but FRS 5 Application note G *Revenue recognition*, SSAP 9 and UITF Abstract 40 *Revenue recognition and service contracts* all provide guidance.	IAS 18 *Revenue* and IAS 11 (both to be superseded by IFRS 15 *Revenue from Contracts with Customers*) are broadly comparable, so for many entities there will be no accounting or tax impact.
Government grants	
SSAP 4 *Accounting for government grants*.	IAS 20 *Accounting for Government Grants and Disclosure of Government Assistance* provides more opportunity for systematic recognition, but little difference for tax purposes.
Borrowing costs	
FRS 15 *Tangible fixed assets* allows capitalisation where certain conditions apply.	IAS 23 *Borrowing Costs* requires capitalisation in such circumstances. However, there will be no significant differences for tax purposes.

Old UK GAAP	FRS 101
Share-based payments	
FRS 20 *Share-based payment.*	IFRS 2 *Share-based Payment* is similar. Tax deductions for share-based payments are governed by specific legislation.
Employee benefits	
FRS 17 *Retirement benefits.*	IAS 19 *Employee Benefits* differs from an accounting perspective, but no tax impact is expected.
Holiday pay accrual: many entities did not accrue or provide for holiday pay.	IAS 19 requires holiday pay accrual. For tax purposes, this will be treated as unpaid remuneration under *CTA 2009, ss 1288–1289.*
Employee benefit trusts: UITF Abstract 32 *Employee benefit trusts and other intermediate payment arrangements.*	No specific guidance in FRS 101. Accounting treatment will be similar, and tax treatment will still follow *CTA 2009, ss 1290–1296.*
Foreign currency translation	
SSAP 20 (where FRS 26 is not applied) or FRS 23 *The effects of changes in foreign exchange rates* (where FRS 26 is applied).	IAS 21 *The Effects of Changes in Foreign Exchange Rates*. Few differences expected for entities that already use FRS 23 and FRS 26. Some other entities may encounter significant differences.
Functional/presentational currency: under SSAP 20, this is the currency of the primary economic environment in which the entity operates.	Under IAS 21, functional currency also requires consideration of the influence of the parent on the entity's operations and activities, and this could have significant accounting and tax impact. Furthermore, under IAS 21, functional and presentational currencies can be different.
Foreign operations (including branches): under SSAP 20, income and expenditure of foreign operations (including branches) are translated into the company's functional currency at actual or average rates.	Under IAS 21, at the end of each reporting period, foreign currency monetary items are translated using the closing rate.
Contract rate accounting: allowed by SSAP 20.	Not allowed by IAS 21.

Old UK GAAP	**FRS 101**
Net investment hedging: under SSAP 20, certain exchange differences can be taken to reserves and not immediately brought into account.	There is no equivalent under IAS 21. Hedging is dealt with by IAS 39.
Permanent-as-equity debt: under SSAP 20, permanent-as-equity loans at arm's length can be carried at historic rates until eventual disposal, and the tax treatment will be similar.	There is no provision for this under IAS 21, so such instruments must be retranslated at each year end, with exchange movements being recognised in the income statement.
Liabilities and equity	
FRS 25 *Financial instruments: presentation*.	IAS 32. No differences are expected.

Transition to FRS 101

26.13 The accounting transition from old UK GAAP to FRS 101 is determined by the requirements of FRS 101 itself and IFRS 1 *First-time Adoption of International Financial Reporting Standards*. It follows very much the same pattern as the transition from old UK GAAP to FRS 102 (see **26.10**).

Entities applying FRS 101 for the first time must restate their balance sheet (referred to in FRS 101 as their 'statement of financial position') for the beginning and end of the comparative period. Typically, the first period of account of mandatory application is the year ending 31 December 2015, with a requirement to restate both the opening balance sheet as at 1 January 2014 and the comparative balance sheet as at 31 December 2014.

On transition, IFRS 1 requires (subject to a number of exceptions) that the balance sheet presented in respect of the date of transition (see **26.7**):

- recognises all assets and liabilities whose recognition is required by IAS;
- does not recognise assets and liabilities if IAS does not permit such recognition;
- reclassifies assets, liabilities and equity components to ensure presentation is consistent with IAS; and
- measures all recognised assets and liabilities in accordance with IAS.

It is expected that, on transition, there may be a significant number of adjustments – both to the carrying value of assets and liabilities recognised previously under old UK GAAP, and in terms of newly recognised assets and liabilities. For accounting purposes, these adjustments will be made to the assets and liabilities as at the date of transition, with corresponding adjustments directly in opening reserves. The statutory provisions relevant in determining how such adjustments are treated for corporation tax purposes are listed at **26.3**.

On 22 January 2014, HMRC published Overview Papers on the new accounting framework. One of them aimed to assist companies that were thinking of choosing or had already chosen to apply FRS 101 (see tinyurl.com/p4wpusm). These Overview Papers were last updated on 21 July 2017.

ACCOUNTING FOR TAX UNDER UK GAAP

Introduction

Focus

In a company's financial statements, the accurate measurement and appropriate disclosure of its current and deferred tax liabilities (or assets) are crucial to an understanding of the company's financial position.

26.14 Current year tax and deferred tax are both represented in the financial statements. The accounting treatment of tax under old UK GAAP is examined here, followed by a discussion of tax accounting under FRS 102 and FRS 101 within new UK GAAP.

Tax accounting under FRS 102

Introduction

26.15 Although FRS 102 has been based on the IFRS for SMEs, FRS 102, Section 29 *Income Tax*, has been written to cater more specifically for the UK, and hence there are significant differences between Section 29 in IFRS for SMEs and Section 29 of FRS 102. For the purposes of FRS 102, 'income tax' includes all domestic and foreign taxes that are based on taxable profit, and also extends to taxes such as withholding taxes payable by a subsidiary, associate or joint venture on distributions to the reporting entity.

Current tax under FRS 102

26.16 Current tax is tax payable (refundable) in respect of the taxable profit (tax loss) for the current period of account or past reporting periods.

FRS 102, Section 29, requires a company to recognise a current tax liability for tax payable on taxable profit for the current and past periods. If the amount of tax paid for the current and past periods exceeds the amount of tax payable for those periods, or if the benefit of a tax loss can be carried back to recover tax paid in a previous period, the current tax asset is to be recognised (ie a prepayment).

Although not included in IAS 12 *Income Taxes*, companies reporting under international GAAP generally recognise potential liabilities from uncertain tax positions by using either a probability-weighted average or a single best estimate approach. This follows FIN 48 *Accounting for uncertainty in income taxes*, which provides specific guidance on this topic under US GAAP. Like FRS 16 *Current tax* within old UK GAAP, FRS 102 does not include any guidance on the recognition or measurement of uncertain tax positions.

Focus

On 12 June 2017, the International Accounting Standards Board issued IFRIC Interpretation 23 *Uncertainty over Income Tax Treatments*. This IFRIC Interpretation (which is authoritative) provides requirements that add to the requirements of IAS 12 *Income Taxes* by outlining how an entity is to reflect the effects of uncertainty in accounting for income tax. This IFRIC Interpretation may also provide guidance for reporters under UK GAAP where uncertain tax treatments are concerned.

A current tax liability or asset is measured on the basis of the tax rates and laws enacted or substantively enacted by the reporting date (see **23.1**). The 'reporting date' is defined by FRS 102 as the end of the latest period covered by the financial statements.

Many companies will experience significant distortions to their distributable profits, and likely cash tax impacts, as a result of the transition from old UK GAAP to FRS 102. This could come about from changes to UK accounting profits, and consequently taxable profits, as a result of differing accounting treatments imposed by the old and new financial reporting standards.

Deferred tax and FRS 102

26.17 Deferred tax represents the future tax consequences of transactions and events recognised in the financial statements of the current and previous periods of account, and must also be recognised on assets (except goodwill) and liabilities recognised as a result of business combinations.

FRS 102, Section 29, combines much of FRS 19 *Deferred tax* from old UK GAAP with elements of IAS 12 *Income Taxes* from international accounting standards, and the result for deferred tax is a new approach known as the 'timing differences plus' approach, where deferred tax is provided on timing differences and on the initial recognition of business combinations.

Under FRS 19, no deferred tax was recognised on a revaluation of investment properties taken directly to reserves (ie the revaluation reserve). However, FRS 102 follows international GAAP by requiring that changes in the fair value of investment properties are recognised in the profit and loss account due to the standard's application of the fair value accounting rules in respect of investment properties. It follows that deferred tax is to be provided, in most cases, on an investment property that is measured at fair value, and that deferred tax is generally to be measured using the tax rates and allowances that apply to sale of the asset (FRS 102, para 29.16).

FRS 19 permitted, but did not require, a company to discount its deferred tax assets and liabilities to reflect the time value of money. FRS 102, like IAS 12, prohibits the discounting of any deferred tax balances. In practice, this is unlikely to have any significant impact as many entities do not discount deferred tax balances under FRS 19.

FRS 19 did not require deferred tax to be recognised on revalued assets unless there was a binding commitment to dispose of them. By contrast, FRS 102 requires deferred tax to be recognised on all timing differences, including revaluation gains or losses, regardless of whether they arise on profit and loss account, other comprehensive income, or equity.

FRS 19 prohibited the recognition of deferred tax on timing differences arising where the remittance of a subsidiary's, associate's or joint venture's earnings would cause tax to be payable but no commitment had been made to remit the earnings. Under FRS 102, deferred tax must be recognised where income or expenses from a subsidiary, associate, branch or joint venture have been recognised in the financial statements (eg as undistributed profits of that undertaking), and will be assessed to or allowed for tax in a future period, except where:

- the reporting entity is able to control the reversal of the timing difference; and
- it is probable that the timing difference will not reverse in the foreseeable future.

FRS 17 *Retirement benefits* required the charge in respect of pensions and the associated deferred tax to be presented together. FRS 102 does not take this approach, so it follows that the deferred tax associated with pensions could be presented with other deferred tax items.

FRS 102 requires a company to recognise deferred tax in respect of assets (other than goodwill) and liabilities in a business combination, where the fair value of assets and liabilities acquired differs from the amount attributed to them for tax purposes. This requirement is a departure from the underlying principle that deferred tax is recognised only in respect of timing differences.

> **Focus**
>
> The requirement to recognise deferred tax only applies to 'business combinations' which are accounted for using the purchase method of accounting. It does not apply to group reconstructions applying the merger method of accounting.

Deferred tax liabilities or assets are generally measured for the purposes of FRS 102 using the tax rates that are likely to apply, based on tax rates enacted or substantively enacted at the reporting date (see **23.1**). In practice, the rate of tax used in the calculation of deferred tax will be 17%, as this is the rate which will apply on 1 April 2020.

Tax accounting under FRS 101

Introduction

26.18 FRS 101 is effectively international GAAP with reduced disclosure requirements, so the tax accounting requirements of FRS 101 follow those of IAS 12 *Income Taxes* under IFRS.

Current tax under FRS 101

26.19 IAS 12 *Income Taxes* requires a company to recognise its liability for any unsettled portion of its tax expense, and an asset to the extent that tax amounts paid exceed tax amounts due. It also allows a tax loss which can be used against future taxable income to be recognised as a deferred tax asset.

As regards current tax, IAS 12 is drawn up on broadly similar lines to previous FRS 16 *Current tax*, but with the following notable differences:

- IAS 12 requires current tax to be shown separately on the face of the balance sheet;
- IAS 12 requires items to be charged to equity if they relate to equity;
- IAS 12 requires disclosure of the tax expense relating to discontinued operations; and
- IAS 12 imposes no requirements as to the presentation of outgoing or incoming dividends.

Although not included in IAS 12, companies reporting under IFRS generally recognise potential liabilities from uncertain tax positions by using either a probability-weighted average or a single best estimate approach. IFRIC Interpretation 23 issued by the International Accounting Standards Board in June 2017 provides requirements that add to the requirements in IAS 12 by outlining how to reflect the effects of uncertainty in accounting for income taxes.

Current tax liabilities or assets are measured using the tax rates enacted or substantively enacted at the reporting date (see **23.1**). The 'reporting date' is the end of the latest period covered by the financial statements.

Many companies will experience significant distortions to their distributable profits, and likely cash tax impacts, as a result of the transition from old UK GAAP to FRS 101. This could come about from changes to UK accounting profits, and consequently taxable profits, as a result of differing accounting treatments imposed by the old and new financial reporting standards.

Deferred tax under FRS 101

26.20 IAS 12 *Income Taxes* requires a company to recognise deferred tax liabilities except for those which arise from:

- initial recognition of goodwill;
- initial recognition of an asset or liability that does not affect accounting or tax profit and the transaction is not a business combination; or
- liabilities from undistributed profits from investments in subsidiaries, branches and associates, and interests in joint ventures where the company can control the timing of the reversal.

IAS 12 also provides for the recognition of:

- deductible temporary differences, unused tax losses, unused tax credits to the extent that taxable profit will be available against which the asset can be used, except those from initial recognition of an asset or liability, other than in a business combination, which does not affect accounting or tax profit;
- deductible temporary differences arising from investments in subsidiaries and associates to the extent that it is probable that the temporary difference will reverse in the foreseeable future and that future taxable profits will be available against which these can be used; and
- deferred tax assets in respect of unused tax losses and tax credits carried forward, to the extent that it is probable that future taxable profits will be available against which these can be used.

IAS 12 uses the 'temporary difference approach' in accounting for deferred tax. Temporary differences are differences between the carrying value of an asset or liability in the balance sheet (statement of financial position) and its tax base (effectively the tax written down value). For deferred tax purposes, taxable temporary differences are those which will result in taxable amounts in future when the carrying amount of an asset is recovered or a liability is settled. Deductible temporary differences are those which will result in deductible amounts in future when the carrying amount of an asset is recovered or a liability is settled.

IAS 12 requires deferred tax provisions in the following circumstances:

- on a revaluation of a non-monetary asset, whether or not it is intended that the asset will be sold and whether or not roll-over relief could be claimed;
- on a sale of assets where the gain has been or might be rolled over into replacement assets;
- where adjustments recognise assets and liabilities at their fair values on the acquisition of a business;
- on the unremitted earnings of subsidiaries, associates and joint ventures;
- on exchange differences on consolidation of non-monetary assets; and
- on unrealised intra-group profits eliminated on consolidation, provision is required on the temporary difference rather than on the timing difference of the profit that has been taxed but not recognised in the consolidated financial statements.

For the purpose of calculating deferred tax under IAS 12, there is a rebuttable presumption that, where an investment property is held at fair value under IAS 40 *Investment Property*, the carrying amount of the investment property will ultimately be recovered entirely through sale, regardless of whether or not that is actually the company's intention. This can be rebutted, for investment properties other than land, where the asset is depreciable and is held to be consumed over its life.

Deferred tax liabilities or assets are measured using the tax rates that are likely to apply, based on tax rates enacted or substantively enacted at the reporting date (see **23.1**). IAS 12 prohibits the discounting of any deferred tax balances to reflect the time value of money.

Accounting for micro-entities

26.21 Following the UK's implementation of the EU Accounting Directive provisions relating to micro-entities (see tinyurl.com/ps9jq7s), where the financial statements for a micro-entity's period of account ending on or after

30 September 2013 are filed at Companies House on or after 1 December 2013, a substantially reduced reporting regime is available (*Small Companies (Micro-Entities' Accounts) Regulations 2013, SI 2013/3008*).

A micro-entity that is a parent company can qualify if its group is a small group, and it does not prepare group accounts. However, a subsidiary company cannot qualify if its results have been consolidated in group accounts. The following are excluded (*CA 2006, s 384B*, as inserted by *SI 2013/3008*):

- investment undertakings;
- financial holding undertakings;
- credit institutions;
- insurance undertakings; and
- charities.

For these purposes the company law definitions of micro-entity and small group apply (see **1.14–1.15**).

Although the accounts of micro-entities must comply with UK GAAP, such companies are relieved of significant disclosure obligations.

On 16 July 2015 the FRC issued its new accounting standard for micro-entities (FRS 105 *The Financial Reporting Standard applicable to the Micro-entities Regime*), offering some simplifications in accounting. FRS 105 was revised in May 2016 to widen the scope of the standard to include LLPs. Following the triennial review, FRS 105 (March 2018) was issued which incorporates requirements for micro-entities in the Republic of Ireland, as well as amending the standard throughout for incremental improvements and clarifications.

FRS 105 is a single financial reporting standard that applies to the preparation of individual financial statements of companies that qualify as micro-entities and choose to apply the micro-entities regime. It aims to provide micro-entities with succinct financial reporting requirements and includes requirements for the most common and relevant transactions that they undertake. If transactions are not addressed in FRS 105, either directly or by cross-reference to FRS 102, a micro-entity must not refer to FRS 102 in selecting its accounting policies, as doing so might result in an accounting treatment which is incompatible with the legislation.

FRS 105 includes the presentation and disclosure requirements of the micro-entities regime, combined with recognition and measurement requirements based on FRS 102. FRS 105 assumes that financial statements prepared in accordance with the micro-entities provisions of *CA 2006* and the *Small Companies (Micro-Entities' Accounts) Regulations 2013, SI 2013/3008,* give a true and fair view of the financial position and financial performance of a micro-entity.

FRS 105 consists of sections on the following topics:

Section	*Topic*
1	Scope
2	Concepts and Pervasive Principles
3	Financial Statement Presentation
4	Statement of Financial Position
5	Income Statement
6	Notes to the Financial Statements (Appendix: Company law disclosure requirements)
7	Subsidiaries, Associates, Jointly Controlled Entities and Intermediate Payment Arrangements
8	Accounting Policies, Estimates and Errors
9	Financial Instruments
10	Inventories
11	Investments in Joint Ventures
12	Property, Plant and Equipment and Investment Property
13	Intangible Assets other than Goodwill
14	Business Combinations and Goodwill
15	Leases
16	Provisions and Contingencies (Appendix: Examples of recognising and measuring provisions)
17	Liabilities and Equity
18	Revenue (Appendix: Examples of revenue recognition under the principles in Section 18)
19	Government Grants
20	Borrowing Costs
21	Share-based Payment
22	Impairment of Assets
23	Employee Benefits
24	Income Tax
25	Foreign Currency Translation
26	Events after the End of the Reporting Period
27	Specialised Activities
28	Transition to this FRS

Although a micro-entity is relieved of certain disclosure requirements, it must still provide HMRC with adequate information to support its corporation tax self-assessment. Where HMRC are unsure of certain treatments, they may launch an aspect or a full enquiry into the micro-entity's corporation tax return.

INTERNATIONAL GAAP

26.22 The following is a list of current international financial reporting standards and international accounting standards (see www.ifrs.org):

		Commentary
	International Financial Reporting Standards	
IFRS 17	Insurance Contracts (effective 1 January 2021)	
IFRS 16	Leases (effective 1 January 2019)	
IFRS 15	Revenue from Contracts with Customers (replaces IAS 18 from 1 January 2018)	**26.34**
IFRS 14	Regulatory Deferral Accounts	
IFRS 13	Fair Value Measurement	**26.11**, **26.25**
IFRS 12	Disclosure of Interests in Other Entities (revised 28 June 2012)	
IFRS 11	Joint Arrangements (revised 28 June 2012)	
IFRS 10	Consolidated Financial Statements (revised 28 June 2012)	**26.11**
IFRS 9	Financial Instruments (largely replaces IAS 39 from 1 January 2018)	**26.25**
IFRS 8	Operating Segments	
IFRS 7	Financial Instruments: Disclosures	**26.11**
IFRS 6	Exploration for and Evaluation of Mineral Resources	
IFRS 5	Non-current Assets Held for Sale and Discontinued Operations	**26.11**
IFRS 4	Insurance Contracts (to be superseded by IFRS 17)	
IFRS 3	Business Combinations	**26.11**
IFRS 2	Share-based Payment	**26.11**
IFRS 1	First-time Adoption of International Financial Reporting Standards	**26.13**, **26.33**, **26.42**
IFRS for SMEs	IFRS for Small and Medium-sized Entities	**26.38**
	International Accounting Standards	
IAS 41	Agriculture	
IAS 40	Investment Property	**26.39**
IAS 39	Financial Instruments: Recognition and Measurement (to be largely replaced by IFRS 9 from 1 January 2018)	**26.24**, **26.25**
IAS 38	Intangible Assets	**26.33**
IAS 37	Provisions, Contingent Liabilities and Contingent Assets	**26.31**

IAS 36	Impairment of Assets	**26.11**
IAS 34	Interim Financial Reporting	
IAS 33	Earnings per Share	
IAS 32	Financial Instruments: Presentation	
IAS 29	Financial Reporting in Hyperinflationary Economies	
IAS 28	Investments in Associates and Joint Ventures (2011)	
IAS 27	Separate Financial Statements (2011)	**26.11**
IAS 26	Accounting and Reporting by Retirement Benefit Plans	
IAS 24	Related Party Disclosures	**26.11**
IAS 23	Borrowing Costs	**26.30**
IAS 21	The Effects of Changes in Foreign Exchange Rates	**26.26**
IAS 20	Accounting for Government Grants and Disclosure of Government Assistance	**26.41**
IAS 19	Employee Benefits (2011)	**26.37**
IAS 18	Revenue (to be superseded by IFRS 15 from 1 January 2017)	**26.34, 26.40**
IAS 17	Leases (to be superseded by IFRS 16)	**26.38**
IAS 16	Property, Plant and Equipment	**26.29**
IAS 12	Income Taxes	**26.20**
IAS 11	Construction Contracts (to be superseded by IFRS 15 from 1 January 2018)	**26.34, 26.40**
IAS 10	Events after the Reporting Period	**26.27**
IAS 8	Accounting Policies, Changes in Accounting Estimates and Errors	**26.11, 26.36**
IAS 7	Statement of Cash Flows	**26.11**
IAS 2	Inventories	**26.40**
IAS 1	Presentation of Financial Statements	**26.11, 26.35**

Note: For further commentary, see **26.12**.

INTERACTION OF ACCOUNTING AND TAX PRINCIPLES

Focus

Financial reporting standards deal with accounting treatment. Certain aspects of the accounting treatment are of particular relevance for corporation tax purposes.

26.23 Financial reporting standards should be examined closely to monitor their effect on the tax treatment of a transaction. Certain aspects are discussed below, but the matters mentioned here are by no means exhaustive.

Financial instruments

26.24 Under current UK GAAP, Section 11 *Basic Financial Instruments* and Section 12 *Other Financial Instruments Issues* of FRS 102 are broadly consistent with IAS 39 *Financial Instruments: Recognition and Measurement* under international GAAP (IAS 39/IFRS 9 are mandatory for companies with listed debt or equity). They are not mandatory for other entities, but there is an option to use them in FRS 102.

26.25 Sections 11 and 12 of FRS 102 and IAS 39 require certain assets and liabilities to be measured at fair value.

Fair value is the amount for which an asset could be exchanged between knowledgeable, willing parties in an arm's length transaction. An impairment loss of a financial asset should be recognised only when it is incurred. An impairment loss is the amount by which the carrying amount of an asset exceeds its recoverable amount.

IFRS 13 *Fair Value Measurement* came into effect on 1 January 2013, providing guidance on measuring fair value in cases where other international accounting standards require it. In May 2017, the International Accounting Standards Board requested views on IFRS 13 so that it could carry out a post-implementation review of the standard.

IFRS 9 *Financial Instruments* was developed by the IASB in several different stages and issued in final form in July 2014, largely replacing IAS 39, and was adopted into EU law on 22 November 2016. Under international GAAP, IFRS 9 will apply for periods of account beginning on or after 1 January 2018, and early adoption is permitted. Secondary legislation has been amended for periods of account commencing on or after 1 January 2015 to ensure that all transition adjustments arising on first adoption of IFRS 9 in respect of credit losses (ie expected defaults on financial instruments) will be spread over a period of 10 years, regardless of when the debt falls due to be discharged (see *Loan Relationships and Derivative Contracts (Change of Accounting Practice) (Amendment) Regulations 2015, SI 2015/1541*).

Foreign currency translation

26.26 Under current UK GAAP, FRS 102, Section 30 *Foreign Currency Translation* follows the principles of IAS 21 *The Effects of Changes in Foreign Exchange Rates* and requires foreign currency monetary items to be translated using the closing rate at the end of each reporting period.

For corporation tax purposes, foreign currency must generally be converted at the average exchange rate for the current accounting period or the appropriate spot rate of exchange for the transaction in question (*CTA 2010, s 11*). However, from 1 September 2013, companies must compute chargeable gains and losses on certain disposals in their functional currency (*CTA 2010, s 9C*; see **20.48**).

For corporation tax purposes, accounts must be prepared in sterling (*CTA 2010, s 5*). If a UK resident company operates in sterling and prepares accounts in a currency other than sterling, for corporation tax purposes the accounts must be computed for GAAP in sterling (*CTA 2010, s 6*). If a UK resident company operates and prepares accounts in a currency other than sterling, but then uses another non-sterling currency as its functional currency, that functional currency is used for preparing accounts according to GAAP. The resulting profits or losses are then converted to sterling (*CTA 2010, s 7*).

Similar rules apply if a UK resident company prepares accounts in a currency other than sterling and neither *s 6* nor *s 7* of *CTA 2010* applies, or if a non-resident company prepares its accounts in a non-sterling currency (see *Ball UK Holdings Ltd v HMRC* at **26.2**). The accounts currency is used for preparing accounts according to GAAP. The resulting profits or losses are then converted to sterling (*CTA 2010, s 8*). A UK resident investment company may choose its designated currency (*CTA 2010, ss 9A, 9B* as amended by *F(No 2)A 2015, s 33;* see **20.50**).

HMRC have published guidance on the tax treatment of Bitcoin and similar digital or virtual 'cryptocurrencies'. There are no bespoke rules, and the general rules on foreign exchange and loan relationships apply. Exchange movements are determined between the company's functional currency and the other currency in question, eg Bitcoin. Thus, the profits and losses of a company entering into transactions involving Bitcoin should be reflected in the accounts and taxed under normal corporation tax rules (Revenue & Customs Brief 09/14, 3 March 2014, see tinyurl.com/plgrhso).

Events after the end of the reporting period

26.27 FRS 102, Section 32 *Events after the End of the Reporting Period* and IAS 10 *Events after the Reporting Period* specify the accounting treatment to be adopted (including the disclosures to be provided) by entities for events occurring between the end of the reporting period and the date on which the financial statements are authorised for issue.

FRS 102, Section 32, like previous FRS 21, sets out the recognition and measurement requirements for two types of event after the end of the reporting period:

- **Adjusting events**. Those events that provide evidence of conditions that existed at the end of the reporting period for which the company should adjust the amounts recognised in its financial statements or recognise items that were not previously recognised (adjusting events). For example, the settlement of a court case that confirms the entity had a present obligation at the balance sheet date (FRS 102, paras 32.4, 32.5).

- **Non-adjusting events**. Those events that are indicative of conditions that arose after the end of the reporting period for which the company does not adjust the amounts recognised in its financial statements. For example, a decline in market value of investments between the balance sheet date and the date when the financial statements are authorised for issue (FRS 102, paras 32.6, 32.7). In certain cases, disclosure would be required (FRS 102, paras 32.10, 32.11).

Dividends declared after the balance sheet date must not be reported as liabilities. Instead, FRS 21 and FRS 102, para 32.8, require disclosures in the notes to the financial statements.

FRS 21 and FRS 102 set out other disclosure requirements. These include (FRS 102, paras 32.9, 32.10):

- the disclosure of the date when the financial statements were authorised for issue;
- the disclosure of information received about conditions that existed at the balance sheet date; and
- if non-adjusting events after the balance sheet date are material, and non-disclosure could influence the economic decisions of users, the entity should disclose the nature of the event and an estimate of its financial effect, or a statement that such an estimate cannot be made.

FRS 102 also requires that an entity should not prepare its financial statements using the going concern basis of accounting if management determines after the balance sheet date that it intends to liquidate the entity or cease trading or that it has no realistic alternative but to do so (FRS 102, paras 32.7A and 32.7B; see also **Chapter 19**).

HMRC have expressed concerns in the past that some companies have paid insufficient attention to the need to adjust events after the end of the reporting period as regards stock obsolescence provisions, impairment provisions (where the debts are subsequently recovered in full) and provisions for claims against a company where these were settled for less than had been provided (Working Together Issue 13, HMRC, June 2003, tinyurl.com/p75gwzn).

Accruals basis

26.28 HMRC have raised concerns in the past that, in some cases, work completed before the end of a reporting period has been invoiced after the end of that period but not correctly accounted for on the accrual basis (see FRS 102

Section 2 *Concepts and Pervasive Principles* at para 2.36); Working Together, Issue 13, HMRC, June 2003, tinyurl.com/p75gwzn).

Property, plant and equipment

26.29 For tax purposes, the distinction between capital and revenue expenditure is maintained. Revenue deductions will follow the timing of recognition in the accounts. FRS 102, Section 17 *Property, Plant and Equipment* and IAS 16 *Property, Plant and Equipment* both follow similar patterns (HMRC Business Income Manual at BIM31060).

Renewals accounting is not permitted by FRS 102 under current UK GAAP, nor by IAS 16. Instead, items of property, plant and equipment are measured at cost or fair value and then depreciated over their expected useful lives. On transition to new UK GAAP or IAS, a company that has previously applied renewals accounting will therefore need to determine the cost or fair value of assets and assign a useful economic life to their assets and depreciate accordingly, and this may require a change of accounting policy adjustment under *CTA 2009, s 181*.

Capitalised borrowing costs

26.30 The capitalisation of borrowing costs is permitted by FRS 102, Section 25 *Borrowing Costs* under current UK GAAP as an accounting policy choice, and by IAS 23 *Borrowing Costs* under international accounting standards. However, IAS 23 makes it mandatory to capitalise borrowing costs which are directly attributable to the acquisition, construction or production of a qualifying asset as part of the cost of that asset. Micro-entities reporting under FRS 105 are not permitted to capitalise borrowing costs as this is an accounting policy option and FRS 105 does not allow any accounting policy options. Micro-entities must, therefore, write off such costs to the profit and loss account as they are incurred.

UK tax law departs from accounting standards by allowing relief for capitalised borrowing costs as if they were a profit and loss account item, but only where they relate to a fixed asset or project (*CTA 2009, s 320*; see **11.35**).

Provisions and contingencies

Allowable and disallowable provisions

26.31 There are no significant differences between FRS 102, Section 21 *Provisions and Contingencies* under current UK GAAP and IAS 37 *Provisions, Contingent Liabilities and Contingent Assets* under international accounting standards. These standards are followed for corporation tax purposes, subject to adjustment where the expenditure is capital for tax purposes or where a provision or contingency is otherwise disallowable.

Under FRS 102, a provision must satisfy the definition of a liability, namely '... a present obligation of the entity arising from past events, the settlement of which is expected to result in an outflow from the entity of resources embodying economic benefits' (FRS 102, para 2.15). Mere anticipation of future expenditure, however probable and no matter how detailed the estimates, is not enough in the absence of an obligation at the end of the reporting period. Provisions are defined by FRS 102 as 'liabilities of uncertain timing or amount' (FRS 102, para 21.1; BIM46515).

Under FRS 102, para 21.4, a company should recognise a provision only when:

- the company has an obligation at the reporting date as a result of a past event, and has no realistic alternative to settling the obligation;
- it is probable (ie more likely than not) that the company will be required to transfer economic benefits in settlement; and
- the amount of the obligation can be estimated reliably.

If these conditions are not met, no provision should be recognised.

FRS 102, Section 21 does not apply to trade creditors, accruals, adjustments to the carrying value of assets, insurance company provisions arising from contracts with policy holders, and provisions that are specifically addressed by other sections of FRS 102.

Trade creditors are liabilities to pay for formally invoiced and received goods or services. Accruals are liabilities to pay for received goods or services, not yet formally invoiced.

HMRC have advised that the following provisions are not allowable for tax purposes (BIM46535), and it follows that the same disallowances will apply under new UK GAAP:

- provisions for 'future operating losses', that is, losses that will or may arise from obligations entered into after the end of the reporting period;
- restructuring provisions until the business has a 'detailed formal plan' for restructuring and has created a 'valid expectation' in those affected that it will carry it out;
- provisions where the only event that might require them is an unpublished decision of the directors;
- provisions for future expenditure required by legislation, where the business could avoid the obligation by changing its method of operation, for example, by stopping doing whatever is affected by the legislation; and

- provisions for future repairs of plant and machinery owned by the business.

HMRC have listed the following as examples of provisions which will generally be allowable if they are sufficiently accurate and accord with GAAP (BIM46545):

- in the period of sale, for the cost of work under a warranty which a trader gives on the sale of merchandise (or under consumer protection legislation);
- for commission refundable by an insurance intermediary on the lapse of a policy, where the commission is recognised as income at the inception of the policy; and
- by builders for rectification work, including retentions up to the level that these have been recognised as income within accounts.

HMRC challenges to provisions

26.32 If HMRC wish to challenge a provision, they will first ascertain whether it accords with GAAP and may then look into the accuracy of the provision.

HMRC have reported that, when enquiring into company accounting matters, they have found problems with refurbishment expenditure, onerous contracts and a debtor's ability to pay when applying FRS 12 *Provisions, contingent liabilities and contingent assets* under old UK GAAP. It is to be expected that similar problems may come to light when companies apply FRS 102, Section 21 *Provisions and Contingencies* under current UK GAAP.

Major refurbishment expenditure should only be provided for if it is in excess of normal repairs and maintenance expenditure. For example, if the lining of a furnace needs to be replaced every five years and at the balance sheet date has been in use for three years, there is no present obligation to make a provision. Similarly, no annual provision is required in the accounts of an airline that is required to overhaul its aircraft once in every three years, the cost being expended when incurred.

In contrast, provisions should be made for onerous contracts, but only those that are truly onerous (a contract is onerous when the unavoidable costs of meeting the obligations under the contract exceed the economic benefits expected to be received under it). When providing for onerous leases, for example, the expected rental income or surrender or sale of the lease should be taken into account (see FRS 102, para 21.11A, and example 2 at para 21A.2). If the facts show that there is no real likelihood of having to pay, for example where the creditor company has already been wound up and the liquidator has decided not to pursue the debt, then practically speaking no provision is required.

Finally, provisions will not be allowed for tax purposes if they are made to 'smooth profits' rather than to comply with FRS 102 (Working Together Issue 13, HMRC, June 2003, tinyurl.com/p75gwzn).

Goodwill and intangible assets

26.33 Under international GAAP, IAS 38 *Intangible Assets* allows intangible assets to be recognised at cost less amortisation, or at fair value. For the purposes of amortisation, an intangible asset cannot be regarded as having an indefinite UEL under FRS 102. Under IFRS 1 *First-time Adoption of International Financial Reporting Standards*, a company has the option of keeping goodwill at the amortised cost at the date of the opening comparative balance sheet in a company's first IFRS accounts, and only impairing from that basis figure (goodwill is not amortised under international financial reporting standards, but is instead tested for impairment at each reporting date).

IAS 38 requires the capitalisation of development expenditure in R&D. *FA 2004, s 53* nevertheless permits a revenue deduction.

IAS 38 requires website costs, when capitalised after meeting the recognition criteria for an asset, to be treated as an intangible asset. Where website costs have been the subject of capital allowance claims, but are reclassified as intangible fixed assets under IAS 38, the tax rules for intangible fixed assets are disapplied by *CTA 2009, s 804* so that capital allowances may continue. If intangible fixed asset costs have been written off to the profit and loss account and are then brought into the balance sheet under IAS 38 as an asset, there will be an intangibles credit and possibly an adjustment under *CTA 2009, s 181*. Rules for the transition from UK GAAP to IFRS are within the rules for adjustments on change of accounting policy within the intangible fixed assets regime (*CTA 2009, ss 871–879*; see also HMRC's Corporate Intangibles Research & Development Manual at CIRD25145).

Under current UK GAAP, Section 18 *Intangible Assets other than Goodwill* and Section 19 *Business Combinations and Goodwill* of FRS 102 are broadly consistent with IAS 38.

Where goodwill and intangible assets were acquired before 3 December 2014, tax relief is generally provided on either the amortisation or the impairment of the goodwill and intangibles recognised in the accounts. However, *FA 2015* imposed restrictions on certain goodwill and customer-related intangibles acquired from 3 December 2014 or 24 March 2015 until 7 July 2015, and *F(No 2)A 2015* introduced wider restrictions which apply to such assets acquired or created on or after 8 July 2015 (see **12.14**).

For tax purposes, *CTA 2009, ss 871–879* provide a comprehensive set of rules for adjustments on changes of accounting policy for intangibles, especially for cases where what is included entirely as goodwill under old UK GAAP is disaggregated into different types of intangible property with different amortisation rates or impairment factors under FRS 102. *CTA 2009, ss 871* and *873* ensure that any write-up on the transition from UK GAAP to IFRS will be a taxable credit for the intangible fixed assets regime, and *CTA 2009, s 872* ensures that any such credit is limited to the net amount of relief already given. Any impairment from the written-up cost will be deductible, subject to the new *FA 2015* and *F(No 2)A 2015* restrictions referred to above. The rules in FRS 102, Section 18 relating to the recognition of more intangible assets in a business combination have been changed in FRS 102 (March 2018) which will result in fewer intangible assets being disaggregated from goodwill in a business combination.

The treatment of website development costs is not addressed in FRS 102. As a result, the nature of each item should be considered in deciding its treatment, and it may be recognised as an intangible asset if appropriate. Usually, a website would be capitalised on the balance sheet if it generates future economic benefits for the entity (ie it has functionality for customers to place orders for goods or services) and the cost can be reliably measured. In all cases, assets can only be recognised on the balance sheet if they meet the recognition criteria laid down in FRS 102.

Note that, in September 2013, HMRC and their Valuation Office Agency updated their Practice Note on 'Apportioning the Price Paid for a Business Transferred as a Going Concern', so that it explains the valuation issues that arise where a property is a 'trade related property', eg public houses, hotels, petrol filling stations, cinemas, restaurants, care homes etc, where there can be particular difficulties in identifying the sum attributable to goodwill (see tinyurl.com/ld5hxa4).

Revenue recognition

26.34 Under current UK GAAP, Section 23 *Revenue* of FRS 102 sets out requirements for accounting for revenue arising from:

- the sale of goods (whether produced by the company or purchased for resale);
- the rendering of services;
- construction contracts in which the company is the contractor; and
- the use by others of company assets yielding interest, royalties or dividends.

Accounting for revenue or other income arising from certain transactions and events is dealt with by other sections of FRS 102, as follows:

- lease agreements (see Section 20 *Leases*);

- dividends and other income arising from investments that are accounted for using the equity method (see Section 14 *Investments in Associates* and Section 15 *Investments in Joint Ventures*);
- changes in the fair value of financial assets and financial liabilities or their disposal (see Section 11 *Basic Financial Instruments* and Section 12 *Other Financial Instruments Issues*);
- changes in the fair value of investment property (see Section 16 *Investment Property*);
- initial recognition and changes in the fair value of biological assets related to agricultural activity (see Section 34 *Specialised Activities: Agriculture*);
- initial recognition of agricultural produce (see Section 34);
- incoming resources from non-exchange transactions for public benefit entities (see Section 34); and
- transactions and events dealt with in FRS 103 *Insurance Contracts*.

In international GAAP, IAS 18 *Revenue* and IAS 11 *Construction Contracts* are to be replaced for annual periods starting on or after 1 January 2018 by IFRS 15 *Revenue from Contracts with Customers*, which defines the information that an entity must report about the nature, amount, timing and uncertainty of revenue and cash flows arising from a contract with a customer. IFRS 15 applies to all contracts with customers except for those covered by another international accounting standard, and requires the transaction price to be allocated to performance obligations in the contract and revenue to be recognised when the entity satisfies each performance obligation. IFRS 15 is more onerous than previous IAS 11 and IAS 18 as it addresses many of the inconsistencies and weaknesses in those standards. It also requires more disclosures to be made in the financial statements.

Reporting financial performance

26.35 UK tax law uses the balance on a company's profit and loss account (profit or loss before tax) as the starting point for the company's corporation tax computation for an accounting period. Amounts are recognised for this purpose when they are included in (*CTA 2009, s 308*):

- the company's profit and loss account, income statement or statement of comprehensive income for that period;
- the company's statement of total recognised gains and losses, statement of recognised income and expense, statement of changes in equity or statement of income and retained earnings for that period; or

- any other statement of items taken into account in calculating the company's profits and losses for that period.

Prior period accounting adjustments, estimates and errors

26.36 FRS 102, Section 10 *Accounting Policies, Estimates and Errors* under current UK GAAP, and IAS 8 *Accounting Policies, Changes in Accounting Estimates and Errors* under international GAAP, both deal with prior period accounting adjustments. Where these relate to the company's trade, they are brought into the computation of trading profits on the first day of the first period of account for which the new basis is adopted (*CTA 2009, ss 180, 181*).

Typically, the first period of account of mandatory application of new UK GAAP is the year ending 31 December 2015, with a requirement to restate both the opening balance sheet as at 1 January 2014 and the comparative balance sheet as at 31 December 2014.

Example 26.2—Timing of tax adjustments on change of basis

Facts

RST plc prepares its financial statements to 31 December annually, and has been reporting under old UK GAAP.

The company decides that in future it will report under FRS 102. The first period of account for which it adopts this new basis is the year ending 31 December 2015.

Analysis

RST plc's financial statements for the year ending 31 December 2015 will be prepared in accordance with FRS 102. These will incorporate comparative statements of its financial position at 1 January 2014 and 31 December 2014, both adjusted to reflect the new basis.

Thus, the first day of the first period of account for which the new basis is adopted (see *CTA 2009, s 181(2)(b), 181(3)(b)*) is 1 January 2014. Therefore, any adjustments required on the change of basis will take effect on 1 January 2014.

For another example, involving a company which has changed its accounting date, see Example 26.3 at **26.42**.

Where the company changes the basis on which it draws up its accounts from one valid basis to another and this is a change from a realisation basis to a mark-to-market basis (eg in a financial trade), any resulting receipt (but not an equivalent expense) may be spread over six years (*CTA 2009, ss 185, 186*). Where amounts have been allowed as a deduction on the old basis, they will not be allowed again on the new basis (*CTA 2009, s 183*).

The provisions of *CTA 2009, s 180* for adjustments on a change of basis do not apply to fundamental errors. In such cases, prior accounting periods must be restated, and this requires amendments to corporation tax returns (see **22.10**).

Retirement benefits

26.37 Accounting for retirement benefits is dealt with in FRS 102, Section 28 *Employee Benefits* and IAS 19 *Employee Benefits (2011)* under international GAAP.

The accounts figures for contributions to, and changes in value of, pension schemes are irrelevant for tax purposes. Relief is given on a paid (and sometimes deferred) basis. For pension scheme contributions, see **2.26–2.30**. For non-pension employee benefits, see **2.24** and **2.45–2.46**.

Leases and hire purchase

26.38 UK tax law is not entirely consistent with FRS 102, Section 20 *Leases* or IAS 17 *Leases* (which will be replaced by IFRS 16 *Leases* for accounting periods starting on or after 1 January 2019), all of which (with the exception of IFRS 16) are drawn up along broadly similar lines (see **3.66** onwards).

The move to current UK GAAP from old UK GAAP and the new IFRS 16 to replace IAS 17 were expected for some time, and *FA 2011* introduced a new provision recognising that, if such changes went ahead, pre-existing tax rules might not work as originally intended, or in some situations might not work at all. Accordingly, where any change is made on or after 1 January 2011 to IAS 17, SSAP 21, or the leasing aspects of IFRS for SMEs or the FRSSE, or to any accounting standard which replaces them, other than a change which permits or requires accounting for leases under UK GAAP in a manner equivalent to the way in which leases were accounted for under IFRS for SMEs as it was on 1 January 2011, such changes are disregarded for tax purposes (*FA 2011, s 53*).

HMRC have confirmed that they do not envisage that *FA 2011, s 53*, will apply on transition to FRS 102. It remains to be seen whether *FA 2011, s 53*, will affect tax computations on eventual transition to a new IFRS replacing IAS 17, but it is thought that this might create some unwelcome administrative tax compliance repercussions for companies with large numbers of leased assets.

The IASB issued its new leasing standard on 13 January 2016.

Investment properties

26.39 Under FRS 102, Section 16 *Investment Property* and IAS 40 *Investment Property,* fair value gains and losses on such properties are taken directly to profit or loss. However, the accounting treatment of investment properties is generally of little relevance for tax, as the chargeable gains rules apply.

There may be cases where a property development company reporting under international accounting standards, or following the principles of IAS under FRS 101 within current UK GAAP, holds land for investment purposes before sale and, in such cases, IAS 40 may apply. If the company moves to the fair value basis, an adjustment on change of basis may arise (*CTA 2009, s 180*).

Where a company holds a property interest as lessee under an operating lease and elects to treat it as an investment property under FRS 102, para 16.3 or IAS 40, para 6, it is required to account for it as a finance lease. Where this happens, the tax rules for finance leases will apply (see **3.66** onwards).

Inventories

26.40 Both FRS 102, Section 13 *Inventories* under current UK GAAP and IAS 2 *Inventories* under international GAAP adopt the same basic principle as previous SSAP 9 *Stocks and Long-term Contracts* – that inventories should be measured at the lower of cost and net realisable value (although FRS 102 uses the term 'estimated selling price less costs to complete and sell' rather than 'net realisable value'). FRS 102 and IAS 2 both allow valuation on a FIFO basis or a weighted average cost formula. FRS 102 explicitly forbids valuation on a LIFO basis, as does IAS 2. Alternative stock valuations, such as the retail method, are acceptable.

Regulations made under *CA 2006, s 396* (namely, the *Small Companies and Groups (Accounts and Directors' Report) Regulations 2008, SI 2008/409*, and the *Large and Medium-sized Companies and Groups (Accounts and Reports) Regulations 2008, SI 2008/410*) permit the addition of incidental costs of acquisition to the stock cost. The company may include production costs and interest on funds borrowed to finance the asset's production. Interest should be separately disclosed in a note to the accounts.

Section 13 of FRS 102 was amended in July 2015 due to changes in the law. Stocks may no longer be accounted for under the alternative accounting rules at current cost, but may instead be accounted for using fair value accounting. However, paragraph 13.3 of FRS 102 restricts the use of this option in the law.

UK GAAP is followed for tax purposes. If a trade ceases, the stock is valued at market value. If the stock is transferred to an unconnected party for the purposes of their trade, stock is valued at the consideration given. If stock is sold to a connected party, it is valued at an arm's length value (*CTA 2009, s 166*). If stock is taken for a participator's own use, it is valued at selling price (*CTA 2009, s 157*; *Sharkey v Wernher* (1955) 36 TC 275), but see **21.20** for possible adjustments where transfer pricing applies.

HMRC have reported in the past that they have encountered problems with aspects of SSAP 9. In particular, they have found that, where companies have made stock provisions, these have not always been supported by the facts of the case. Long-term contracts were not always identified and accounted for as such in accordance with SSAP 9, para 22. Companies have sometimes valued stock and work in progress inappropriately at net realisable value on the theoretical basis that it would have to be sold as an emergency sale in its current condition, rather than being sold in the normal course of business in accordance with SSAP 9, App 1, paras 19, 20 (Working Together, Issue 13, HMRC, June 2003, tinyurl.com/p75gwzn). It seems likely that companies could make similar mistakes when applying FRS 102 unless appropriate care is taken.

HMRC have accepted in the past that there are no practical differences between FRS 102, IAS 2 and IAS 11 *Construction Contracts*, except that they do not recognise LIFO for tax purposes (see BIM33100 onwards).

Government grants

26.41 Under FRS 102, Section 24 *Government Grants* and IAS 20 *Accounting for Government Grants and Disclosure of Government Assistance*, grants are recognised as income unless given specifically as contributions towards particular capital expenditure. The same treatment is adopted for corporation tax purposes.

First-time adoption of IFRS

26.42 IFRS 1 *First-time Adoption of International Financial Reporting Standards* requires that differences between the previous GAAP and the current IFRS treatment are recognised in the opening comparative balance sheet. This establishes the date on which any necessary adjustments on change of basis are to be made under *CTA 2009, ss 180, 181*.

Example 26.3—Timing of tax adjustments on first-time adoption of IFRS

Facts

EFG plc has traditionally prepared its financial statements to 30 June annually, but changes its accounting date and prepares financial statements for the 15-month period ending 30 September 2015 and annually thereafter.

The company has been reporting under old UK GAAP, and decides that in future it will report under EU-adopted IFRS. The first period of account for which it adopts this new basis is the year ending 30 September 2016.

Analysis

EFG plc's financial statements for the year ending 30 September 2016 will be prepared in accordance with EU-adopted IFRS. These will incorporate comparative statements of its financial position at 1 July 2014 and 30 September 2015, both adjusted to reflect the new basis.

Thus the first day of the first period of account for which the new basis is adopted (see *CTA 2009, s 181(2)(b), 181(3)(b)*) is 1 July 2014. Therefore, any adjustments required on change of basis will take effect on 1 July 2014.

The 15-month period of account ending 30 September is treated as two separate accounting periods for tax purposes – the 12-month period ending 30 June 2015, and the three-month period ending 30 September 2015 – and the adjustments will fall into the earlier of these two accounting periods.

Had EFG plc decided to move to FRS 101 instead of EU-adopted IFRS, IFRS 1 would still apply and the timing of any required tax adjustments would be the same.

For another example, involving a company which has not changed its accounting date, see Example 26.2 at **26.36**.

Consolidated financial statements

26.43 Consolidated financial statements of a group are generally of little relevance for corporation tax purposes. However, for the purposes of the worldwide debt cap (see **Chapter 5**) the gross finance expenses of the group are calculated by reference to amounts contained in the consolidated financial statements of the group prepared using either international GAAP or UK GAAP.

To avoid distortion, the *Tax Treatment of Financing Costs and Income (Change of Accounting Standards: Investment Entities) Regulations 2015, SI 2015/662*, came into effect from 2 April 2015 for accounting periods beginning on or after that date, or earlier, and increase the measure of a worldwide group's gross finance costs by certain amounts relating to funding from sources external to the worldwide group. These are amounts which are taken into account in the calculation of a UK company's net finance expenses or income, but not in the amount of gross finance costs of the group as a whole for the purposes of the debt cap calculations, as a result of changes to IFRS 10 *Consolidated Financial Statements* under international GAAP from 1 January 2014 or the introduction of FRS 102, Section 9 *Consolidated and Separate Financial Statements*, para 9.9 under new UK GAAP.

Chapter 27

The year end

SIGNPOSTS

- Outline formats of corporation tax and capital allowances computations (see **27.1–27.2**).
- An alphabetical selection of key planning points, cross-referenced by paragraph number to earlier chapters (see **27.3**).

CORPORATION TAX COMPUTATION

27.1 Shortly after the end of each reporting period, the company will prepare its financial statements, whereupon it will be able to prepare its corporation tax computation and self-assessment company tax return for online filing.

The company will aggregate all its income from its various income sources, less allowances, in order to calculate its total taxable profits of the period. The following is an outline computation which is intended to illustrate the approach, but the format provided may not be appropriate or exhaustive in every individual case.

Corporation tax computation for the accounting period of … months ended on …

Statutory refs	Example Ltd	£	£	Chapter refs
	Company Name			
	Company UTR			
	Accounting Period ended			
	Corporation Tax Computation	£	£	
	Total turnover from trade or profession		X	
	Income:			
CTA 2009, Pt 3, Ch 6A	• including R&D expenditure credit			
CTA 2009, Pt 3	**Trading Profits**		X	**2**
CAA 2001	• net of capital allowances			**3**
CTA 2009, Pt 13	• net of R&D enhanced deduction			**14**
CTA 2009, Pt 14	• net of land remediation deductions			**14**
CTA 2009, Pt 15	• net of film tax relief enhanced deduction			**15**
CTA 2009, Pt 15A	• net of television tax relief enhanced deduction			**15**
CTA 2009, Pt 15B	• net of video games tax relief enhanced deduction			**15**
CTA 2009, Pt 15C	• net of theatre tax relief enhanced deduction			**15**
CTA 2009, Pt 15D	• net of orchestra tax relief enhanced deduction			**15**
CTA 2009, Pt 15E	• net of museum and galleries exhibition tax relief enhanced deduction			**15**
	Less			
CTA 2010, Pt 8A	Patent Box deduction		(x)	**13**
	Less			

Statutory refs	**Example Ltd**			**Chapter refs**
CTA 2010, Pt 4, ss 45, 45B	Trading losses brought forward	x		**4**
	claimed against trading profits	x	(x)	
	Net Trading and Professional Profits		X	
	Income from non-trading loan relationships			
CTA 2009, Pt 5	Loan relationships	X		**11**
CTA 2009, Pt 6	Relationships treated as loan relationships	X		
	Less			
CTA 2009, ss 459(1)(b), 463B(1)(b)	Deficit carried back from a later accounting period (relief to be given after current year set off under *CTA 2009, ss 459(1)(a), 463B(1)(a)* and reliefs mentioned in *CTA 2009, ss 463, 463F* as well as after a claim for group relief, *CTA 2010, ss 137, 188CK*)	(x)		
	Net surplus		X	
CTA 2009, Pt 7	Derivative Contracts		X	
CTA 2009, Pt 10, Ch 7	**Other income**			**2**
	Annuities and Annual Payments		X	
	Overseas Income			**20**
CTA 2009, Pt 3	Trading Income	X		
CTA 2009, Pt 4	Property Income	X		7
CTA 2009, Pt 5–7	Investment Income	X		6
CTA 2009, Pt 9A	Company Distributions	X		
CTA 2009, Pt 10	Miscellaneous Income	X		
			X	
	Income subject to income tax			**23**
CTA 2009, Pt 4	**Property Income**		X	**7**

Statutory refs	Example Ltd			Chapter refs
CTA 2009, Pt 8, s 752	**Non-trading gains on intangible fixed assets**		X	**12**
	Any other income			
CTA 2010, s 1173	Miscellaneous charges (except non-trading gains on intangibles)	X		**4**
	Non-exempt dividends or distributions from a company resident in the UK	X		**18**
			X	
	Total Income		X	
TCGA 1992	**Chargeable Gains**			**16**
	Gross chargeable gains	X		
	Less			
	Allowable losses	(x)		
	Losses brought forward	(x)		
	Net Chargeable Gains		X	
	Total income and Chargeable Gains		X	
CTA 2010, Pt 4, s 45A	Trading losses brought forward against total profits		(x)	**4**
CTA 2010, s 46	Losses brought forward against certain investment income		(x)	**4**
CTA 2010, s 68	**Losses on unquoted shares**		(x)	**6**
CTA 2009, Pt 16, Chs 2, 3	**Management expenses**		(x)	**6**
CTA 2009, ss 459(1)(a), 463B(1)(a)	Non-trading deficits from loan relationships etc (current year) (must be made after a claim for group relief, *CTA 2010, ss 137, 188CK*)		(x)	**11**

Statutory refs	**Example Ltd**			**Chapter refs**
CTA 2009, ss 457, 463G–463I	Non-trading deficits from loan relationships carried forward (either against total profits or against non-trading profits only)		(x)	**11**
CTA 2010, s 62	Property Income losses of a UK property business:			**7**
	current period	(x)		
	previous period	(x)	(x)	**7**
CAA 2001, s 253	Capital allowances for the purposes of the management of the business		(x)	**3**
CTA 2009, s 753	Non-trading losses on intangible fixed assets		(x)	**12**
CTA 2010, s 37	Trading loss of current or a later accounting period (must be made after a claim for group relief, *CTA 2010, ss 137, 188CK*)		(x)	**4**
CTA 2001, s 260(3)	Non-trade capital allowances (must be made after a claim for group relief, *CTA 2010, ss 137, 188CK*)		(x)	**3**
	Total of deductions and reliefs		(x)	
	Total Taxable Profits for the Period before group relief		X	
CTA 2010, Pt 5	Group relief		(x)	**5**
	Total Taxable Profits for the Period		x	**23**
	Corporation tax		x	**23**
CTA 2010, Pt 2	Marginal relief (before 1 April 2015)		(x)	**23**
	Corporation tax chargeable		X	

Statutory refs	Example Ltd			Chapter refs
	Reliefs and deductions in terms of tax			
CTA 2010, s 219	Community investment relief	(x)		**6**
TIOPA 2010, s 130	Double taxation relief	(x)		**20**
FA 1998, s 32; SI 1999/358	Surplus Advance corporation tax	(x)		**18**
	Total reliefs and deductions in terms of tax		(x)	
	Net corporation tax liability		x	
CTA 2010, s 455	Tax payable on Directors' Loans		(x)	**10**
CTA 2010, s 464A	Tax payable on arrangements conferring benefit on participator		(x)	**10**
TIOPA 2010, Pt 9A	CFC tax payable		(x)	**20**
	Tax chargeable		x	
	Tax Credit Payable to Company			
CAA 2001, Sch A1	First-year tax credit	(x)		**4**
CTA 2009, Pt 13	R&D tax credit	(x)		**14**
CTA 2009, Pt 14	Land remediation tax credit	(x)		**14**
CTA 2009, Pt 15	Film tax credit	(x)		**15**
CTA 2009, Pt 15A	Television tax credit	(x)		**15**
CTA 2009, Pt 15B	Video games tax credit	(x)		**15**
CTA 2009, Pt 15C	Theatre tax credit	(x)		**15**
CTA 2009, Pt 15D	Orchestra tax credit	(x)		**15**
CTA 2009, Pt 15E	Museums and galleries exhibition tax credit	(x)		**15**
			(x)	
CTA 2010, s 963	Refunds of quarterly instalments		(x)	**23**
	Final Liability		x	

Capital allowances computation

27.2 The company will also prepare its capital allowances claim. The following is an outline computation which is intended to illustrate the approach, but the format provided may not be appropriate or exhaustive in every individual case.

Capital Allowances Computation

*Note			General pool	Special rate pool	Short-life asset
			£	£	£
1	**TWDV b/fwd**		X	X	X
2/3	**Additions not qualifying for AIA or FYA**				
	Main rate car (51–110g/km from 1 April 2018)		X		
	Special rate car (over 110g/km from 1 April 2018)			X	
	Additions qualifying for AIA	X			
	Main rate pool expenditure				
	Less AIA	(x)			
	Transfer balance to main rate pool		X		
	Special rate pool expenditure	X			
	Less AIA	(x)			
	Transfer balance to special rate pool			X	
	Disposal of short-life asset (lower of cost or sale proceeds)				(x)
4	BC/BA				X/(x)
5	WDA @18%		(x)		
	WDA @ 8%			(x)	
	Additions qualifying for FYAs				
	Energy-saving plant and machinery	X			
	Environmentally beneficial plant and machinery	X			

*Note		General pool	Special rate pool	Short-life asset
New and unused vans	X			
Low emission cars (up to 50g/km from 1 April 2018)	X			
Less FYA @ 100%	(x)			
TWDV c/fwd		X	X	
Allowances				
AIA on main rate pool expenditure	(x)			
AIA on special rate pool expenditure	(x)			
BC/BA	X/(x)			
WDA @ 18%	(x)			
WDA @ 8%	(x)			
FYA	(x)			
Total allowances	(x)			

*Note: Key to abbreviations:

1 TWDV Tax written down value
2 AIA Annual investment allowance
3 FYA First year allowance
4 BC/BA Balancing charge/Balancing allowance
5 WDA Writing down allowance

TAX PLANNING

27.3 A company's financial statements are based on its transactions for a period of account, reported in accordance with GAAP. The results thus reported are used to prepare the corporation tax computation for each accounting period.

The time immediately before the company's reporting date (or 'year end') offers a last chance to review the company's corporation tax position for the accounting period that ends on that date, and may provide some opportunities to defer or avoid tax liabilities or sidestep potential tax pitfalls. In a period of account that extends beyond 12 months, the time immediately before the end of a component 12-month accounting period may offer similar opportunities.

Most companies strive to maximise their reported profits and minimise their corporation tax liabilities, and there is a natural stress between these two objectives. Whatever tax planning is undertaken, a priority should be to ensure that the company's self-assessment tax returns are accurate and timely, to avoid interest and penalties and to minimise any adverse consequences arising from an enquiry. A company should also be fully aware of HMRC's extensive powers, and of its own rights and obligations as a taxpayer.

Tax planning has attracted widespread controversy in recent years, and a general anti-abuse rule (GAAR) now exists to counter serious abuse (see **25.42–25.46**). Companies are justifiably concerned about the possible adverse reputational impact of overly aggressive tax planning, while individual tax directors and heads of tax may still wish to be seen by their boards as actively managing tax liabilities downwards.

The following alphabetical list is a summary of some of the areas of tax planning that a company may wish to consider before the year end and at other times (the list is by no means exhaustive):

- **Accounting dates**. If a company pays corporation tax by quarterly instalments, it will pay its first instalment six months and 13 days after the beginning of the accounting period. If the trade is seasonal, the company might not have sufficient funds to pay the corporation tax. Consider changing the accounting date so that the high-earning period falls at the beginning of the year rather than the end. See **23.11–23.25**.
- **Activities**. Consider the type of activities that the organisation carries out and whether some or all of these might qualify for charitable or mutual status. See **2.80** and **2.87**.
- **Annual investment allowance**. The AIA is £200,000 with effect from 1 January 2016. Companies should review their capital expenditure plans to ensure that they maximise their claims to annual investment allowance, and also optimise the benefit of first year allowances where these are available. See **3.19** onwards.
- **Annual tax on enveloped dwellings (ATED)**. The annual ATED charge and its related capital gains tax charge may catch some companies unawares. In view of the progressive lowering of ATED thresholds, de-enveloping of dwellings may be advisable in some cases, but careful planning will be needed to achieve this in a tax-efficient manner. See **7.23–7.24**.
- **Appeals**. If a company disagrees with an HMRC decision, it can appeal directly to the First-tier Tribunal or ask HMRC to carry out an internal review of the decision. Alternative dispute resolution is also available as a possible way forward that may avoid litigation. See **22.23–22.32**.
- **Apportionment of profits**. If a period of account is longer than 12 months, taxable profits are normally apportioned *pro rata* on a time basis

to the component accounting periods. However, an actual basis may be used if this gives a more accurate result, and this could be particularly relevant where there are seasonal fluctuations in the business. See **22.7**.

- **Associated companies**. For periods before unification of the corporation tax rate on 1 April 2015, the existence of associated companies reduced the availability of the small profits rate and also impacted on other matters such as the requirement to pay corporation tax by quarterly instalments. For quarterly instalments and certain other corporation tax purposes, the anti-fragmentation rules from 1 April 2015 onwards are based instead on the number of 'related 51% group companies'. Related companies should review their structure and relationships to ensure that they know how many related 51% group companies they have and whether the separate companies are actually necessary. See **23.12**, **23.22**.

- **Business premises renovation allowance**. This relief expired on 31 March 2017 and is no longer available. However, claims for expenditure incurred before that date may need to be reviewed in the light of the *FA 2014* changes. These changes narrowed the scope of qualifying expenditure and tightened up some of the other conditions for the relief. See **8.2–8.17**.

- **Cars** qualify for capital allowances according to their CO_2 emissions. There are currently three bands, effective from 1 April 2018: 0–50g/km (100% FYA), 51–110g/km (18% WDA), and over 110g/km (8% WDA). The old bands from 1 April 2015 to 31 March 2018 were: 0–75g/km (100% FYA), 76–130g/km (18% WDA), and over 130g/km (8% WDA). The old rules for 'expensive cars' were abandoned on 1 April 2009, but with a five-year transition, so remember that any remaining balance on an expensive car pool should have been transferred to the main pool. See **3.36**, **3.52** and **3.61**.

- **Changes in company ownership**. Changes made from 1 April 2014 introduced new scope for avoiding forfeiture of loss relief when superimposing a new holding company on an existing company or group, and for avoiding restrictions on relief for management expenses on a change of ownership of a company with investment business. These changes may facilitate structural reorganisations within groups. See **4.25** and **6.20**.

- **Claims for overpaid corporation tax**. Even if a company has overpaid its corporation tax or has been assessed to corporation tax that it considers is not due, HMRC are able to refuse repayment claims if they fall within certain criteria. However, HMRC have the power to grant special relief where tax otherwise charged would be excessive. Appropriate evidence is needed to support a claim for this special relief, so good record-keeping is essential. See **23.42–23.43**.

- **Close company benefits to participators**. *FA 2013* introduced provisions to tax close companies on certain benefits (relating to tax avoidance arrangements) made available to participators or their associates. Ensure that there are no arrangements that could fall within the scope of these provisions or, if there are, that the company will be eligible to recover the tax if the benefit is made good. See **10.17** and **10.18**.

- **Close company loans to participators**. Loans outstanding at the year end to a close company participator attract a tax charge if not repaid within nine months and a day after the year end. Ensure there are no outstanding loans or, if there are, that they are repaid promptly without any arrangements that could fall foul of the *FA 2013* rules that outlaw 'bed and breakfasting'. See **10.15** and **10.18**.

- **Close company: release of loans to participators**. Remember that writing off a loan to a participator does not entitle the company to an allowable loan relationship debit. See **11.16**.

- **Community amateur sports clubs**. Bodies claiming the special tax reliefs available to CASCs should review their circumstances in the light of the changes to the qualifying rules, to ensure that they meet the new requirements by 1 April 2016. See **2.88**.

- **Companies in financial difficulties** can agree to vary the timing of their corporation tax payments through 'time to pay' arrangements and the HMRC Business Payment Support Service. These operate where companies are in genuine difficulty but, given time, will be able to pay their corporation tax. See **23.44–23.45**.

- **Company purchase, sale or reconstruction**, combined with a transfer of trade, may trigger the capital allowance-buying anti-avoidance legislation, which was tightened by *FA 2013* and prevents the utilisation of a company's unused capital allowances by its new owners in certain situations. See **17.28–17.39**. In similar situations, regard should also be had to the restrictions of transfer of deductions, introduced by *FA 2013*. See **17.40**.

- **Connected parties**. Assets eligible for capital allowances may be transferred between connected parties at tax written-down value. Both parties must submit an election to HMRC within two years from the date of sale (*CAA 2001, s 569(1)*). See **3.5**.

- **Consortium relief**. Companies should review consortium arrangements. Since the link company in a consortium relief claim no longer needs to be in the UK or the EEA for accounting periods beginning on or after 10 December 2014, there are now no differing requirements between a UK link company and one based in another jurisdiction. See **5.12**.

- **Contaminated land and land in a derelict state** may qualify for land remediation allowance, which gives full relief for capital expenditure and 150% of revenue expenditure against profits. If the company is engaged in building projects on a brown field site, full details of the work should be obtained in order to assess whether the necessary conditions are met. See **14.48–14.67**.

- **Contribution allowances**. Companies receiving contributions towards their capital expenditure may no longer be entitled to capital allowances on the whole of the capital expenditure in question, as a result of a change that was made to the capital allowance rules from 29 May 2013. See **3.65**.
- **Controlled foreign companies (CFCs)**. Companies operating in a low-tax regime may fall within the new CFC anti-avoidance rules. These rules were substantially relaxed with effect from 1 January 2013, compared with the previous regime, but are still extremely complex, and companies affected need to understand the current provisions. See **20.25–20.32**.
- **Creative sector reliefs.** There are various creative sector reliefs, which provide a superdeduction for losses incurred in a creative sector trade. Loss-making companies may claim a repayable tax credit as an alternative to claiming a loss. Companies eligible for these reliefs should ensure that they meet all the necessary conditions and make appropriate claims. See **Chapter 15**.
- **Diverted profits tax (DPT)**. If your company has engaged in any arrangements that might fall within the scope of DPT, check whether any of the exemptions would apply; otherwise, take steps to ensure that the strict time limit for notification is observed. See **20.57**, **20.59**.
- **Dividends: removal of tax credit**. Owner-managed companies should review their distribution and remuneration strategies. See **10.32**.
- **Dividends: timing of interim dividends**. Interim dividends are due and payable on the day they are declared, but not for the purposes of *CTA 2010, s 455*, where it is the payment date that is relevant. For this reason, an interim dividend may not be effective in clearing a director's overdue loan account. See **10.22**.
- **Dormant company**. Check to see if any related companies are dormant throughout the accounting period. If so, they will not be included within the count of associated companies (before 1 April 2015) or related 51% group companies (on or after that date). See **23.14** and **23.22**.
- **Double tax relief**. From 5 December 2013, anti-avoidance rules in *FA 2014* restrict certain claims to double tax relief. Companies should ensure that they have entered into no arrangements that would bring these restrictions into effect. See **20.24**.
- **Duality of purpose**. Expenditure is only deductible from trading profits if it has been incurred wholly and exclusively for the purposes of the trade. If expenditure has been incurred for both trading and some other purpose, no deduction is generally allowed against trading profits. See **2.13**.

- **Employee shares.** Companies should be aware of the *FA 2014* changes extending corporation tax relief for certain employee share acquisitions from 6 April 2015, revising the purpose tests for SIP, SAYE and CSOP schemes, introducing self-certification requirements, and imposing mandatory online filing for all employee share scheme returns and information, including EMI and non-tax advantaged arrangements providing employment-related securities. See **2.45** and **2.46**.

- **Enquiries**. For single companies and small groups, there is no compelling incentive to delay filing the corporation tax return for as long as possible after the end of the accounting period, because the enquiry window closes 12 months after the return has been delivered to HMRC. See **22.15**. On a non-statutory basis, HMRC will endeavour to follow this procedure for all other companies. Groups of companies which are not small should notify HMRC when the last group return is filed. See **22.16**.

- **Energy-saving plant and machinery and environmentally beneficial plant and machinery** qualify for a 100% FYA. Categories of qualifying plant are periodically updated. Loss-making companies may claim a repayable first-year tax credit. See **3.32–3.34** and **4.38–4.43**.

- **Exit charges**. UK resident companies that face corporation tax exit charges, on moving their place of management from the UK to another EU or EEA member state, should consider the possible merits of entering into an exit charge payment plan and, if appropriate, which method of payment best suits their needs. See **20.24**. Remember that tax deferred on exit charges is subject to interest under the normal rules.

- **Fixtures within buildings**. The *FA 2012* fixtures regime, which came into effect partly on 1 April 2012 and partly on 1 April 2014, can restrict the acquisition value of fixtures for capital allowances purposes, and may make it more difficult for a company to ensure that they will eventually be able to pass on entitlement to capital allowances to a subsequent owner. See **3.46–3.51**.

- **Foreign branch exemption**. A company can elect for its foreign branch income and gains to be exempt from UK corporation tax. The election is irrevocable and applies to all of the company's foreign permanent establishments. The rules were substantially changed with effect from 1 January 2013, in line with the new controlled foreign companies (CFC) regime which applies from the same date. Companies affected need to understand these provisions. See **20.33–20.47**.

- **Foreign dividends** that a company receives are, in the main, exempt from tax. Different exemption rules apply to small and large companies. If the dividends are not exempt, relief for underlying foreign tax may be available. See **18.39–18.50**.

- **Furnished holiday lettings** qualify as a trade for corporation tax purposes, if all conditions are met. For accounting periods beginning on or after 1 April 2012, the required number of letting days was increased and a special relief for underlet properties was also introduced. See **2.63**.
- **Goods vehicles**. Expenditure incurred before 31 March 2021 on new zero-emission vans qualifies for a 100% first year allowance. See **3.37**.
- **Group payment arrangements**. Consider whether it would be administratively efficient for one company in a group to attend to the group's corporation tax payments. See **23.36**.
- **Group treasury companies**. Companies concerned with the debt cap or the controlled foreign companies (CFCs) regime need to be aware of the tightened rules that have applied to group treasury companies from 11 December 2012 (for debt cap) and 1 January 2013 (for CFCs). See **5.59** and **20.27**.
- **Intangible fixed assets**. Where debits and credits for corporation tax purposes follow the accounting treatment. Company and group depreciation policies should be reviewed to ensure that they are suitable. Where goodwill or customer-related intangibles are acquired on or after 3 December 2014, 24 March 2015 or 8 July 2015 respectively, new restrictions on relief need to be taken into account. See **12.9** and **12.14**.
- **iXBRL**. Company tax returns, including statutory accounts and computations in iXBRL format, together with supporting information, must be filed electronically with HMRC. Companies should ensure that they comply with the new requirement to tag their detailed profit and loss account from 1 April 2014, and use the new XBRL taxonomies for tagging under new UK GAAP or EU-adopted IFRS from 1 April 2015. Companies that fail to ensure a satisfactory standard of iXBRL tagging may face increased likelihood of intervention by HMRC. See **22.11**.
- **Landlord** companies that were able to claim an allowance of up to £1,500 per dwelling when installing energy-saving items in residential property are no longer entitled to this from 1 April 2015. To avoid errors in computations, make sure that this allowance is not now claimed. See **7.12**.
- **Large companies**. Check if the company is large and, if so, make sure that corporation tax is being paid by quarterly instalments as appropriate, but note that due dates have been brought forward for 'very large companies'. But ensure also that quarterly instalment payments are not being paid if not required, eg where the company's annualised augmented profits for the accounting period do not exceed £10 million and it was not large for the previous year. See **23.11–23.25**.
- **Loan relationships regime**. Companies need to understand the reforms to this regime from 1 January 2016, the circumstances in which the new

corporate rescue exception applies, and the regime-wide anti-avoidance provisions which need to be taken into account. See **11.2**.

- **Losses, etc carried forward.** Where certain conditions are met, steps taken to carry forward trading losses, non-trading loan relationship deficits or management expenses could be challenged as contrived arrangements to convert brought-forward reliefs into more versatile in-year deductions. Ensure that the arrangement is predominantly commercial by making sure that the anticipated tax advantage is no greater than any other expected economic value of the arrangement. See **4.30**.

- **Main rate of corporation tax** has now been enacted until 31 March 2021, and will reduce from 19% to 17% over the intervening period. Companies can now budget for this rate of tax, which also affects the value of loss relief being carried forward. See **23.1**.

- **Non-resident capital gains tax**. A non-UK resident company may be subject to non-resident capital gains tax (NRCGT) on a gain arising on the disposal of UK residential property. Strict time limits apply for reporting disposals to HMRC and paying the NRCGT. See **7.25**.

- **Patent box**. The voluntary patent box regime came into effect on 1 April 2013. This regime is only open to new entrants for accounting periods ending before 1 July 2016, so that elections into this regime must be made by 30 June 2018, in most cases. There is a new regime in place for new entrants from 1 July 2016, which will apply to all claimants from 1 July 2021. See **Chapter 13**.

- **Payments** of all corporation tax and related interest and penalties have to be made electronically, but the choice of possible electronic payment methods is wider than many people think. See **23.8**.

- **Pension contributions**. A company may consider making additional pension contributions on behalf of its directors/employees. In doing so, the company should note the potential impact of the spreading rules, and should also be aware of the possible business purpose test restriction. See **2.26**.

- **Pension contributions, asset-backed**. A company making asset-backed pension contributions needs to be aware of complex restrictions which came into effect (variously) from 29 November 2011, 22 February 2012 and 21 March 2012. See **2.27**.

- **Plant and machinery in enterprise zones.** 100% first year allowances are available on expenditure on certain new fixed plant for use in designated assisted areas within new enterprise zones. The allowance is available for a period of eight years from the date when the area has been designated. It may be worth reviewing the company's plans for expansion, together with the details of these designated areas. See **3.40**.

- **Property businesses**. Both UK and overseas property businesses are treated as though they were trades for the purposes of claiming allowable deductions, but only certain of the *CTA 2009* provisions for computing trading profits apply; see **7.3–7.12**.
- **Research and development – large companies**. From 1 April 2013, as an alternative to the pre-existing enhanced deduction of 130%, a large company can claim an R&D expenditure credit on its qualifying expenditure and this may be payable to the company in certain circumstances. Claims must be made within the normal corporation tax timescale of two years after the end of the accounting period. The expenditure credit superseded the enhanced deduction from 1 April 2016. See **14.40–14.42**.
- **Research and development – SMEs**. An SME can claim an enhanced deduction of 230% of its R&D expenditure against its taxable profits (up from 225% from 1 April 2015). If loss-making, the company may claim a repayable tax credit of 14.5%. See **14.25–14.34**. There are also some circumstances in which an SME may claim an enhanced deduction or R&D expenditure credit under one of the large company schemes. See **14.27**.
- **Residential property**. Capital allowances are not available on residential property, nor on plant or machinery for use in a dwelling. HMRC have confirmed that individual units in a multi-occupancy building are residential property but the common parts are not, thus allowing claims to be submitted on the basis of apportioned costs. See **8.8**.
- **Roll-over relief**. If a company plans to dispose of tangible fixed assets giving rise to a chargeable gain, or intangible fixed assets giving rise to a realisation credit, it should consider whether there is scope to claim rollover relief or reinvestment relief respectively against expenditure on new assets during the period from 12 months before to three years after the disposal. See **16.8–16.15** and **12.22–12.24**.
- **Senior Accounting Officer (SAO)**. It remains essential for the SAO to keep all the accounting arrangements of the company under review, to ensure that they are appropriate tax accounting arrangements. See **25.26–25.31**.
- **Shares subscribed for in an unquoted trading company**. A loss on disposal of an investment of this nature, or a loss on deemed disposal where the asset has become of negligible value, may be claimed against income of an investment company. The claim must be made within two years from the end of the accounting period in which the loss occurred. See **6.22**.
- **Short-life assets**. Companies who favour an immediate balancing allowance (or charge) on an asset's disposal can apply the short-life

election to qualifying assets. From 1 April 2011 the length of time that an asset remains in the short-life pool was increased from four to eight years, making short-life asset treatment more attractive for many assets. See **3.55**.

- **Small profits rate** of corporation tax was 20% for the financial year 2014, but has ceased to apply from 1 April 2015 and the corporation tax rates have been unified at 20%. This simplifies some aspects of planning within groups. See **23.2**.

- **Striking off – *bona vacantia*.** Companies that are going to be struck off without a formal liquidation should be aware that residual assets representing share capital may be claimed by the Crown as *bona vacantia*. Reduction of share capital may be one way of avoiding this. See **18.34–18.36**.

- **Striking off – distributions**. Following the withdrawal of Concession C16 from 1 March 2012, companies that are going to be struck off (and their shareholders) need to understand the £25,000 limit on distributions in anticipation of winding up that will be treated as capital, and the risks of exceeding this. See **18.33**.

- **Substantial shareholdings exemption**. The importance of this exemption should not be overlooked. HMRC offer guidance on whether an investing company and/or the company invested in meet the necessary conditions. From 1 April 2017, the investing company no longer needs to satisfy the trading conditions, and there is a relaxation of this condition for investing companies immediately after the disposal. Furthermore, the relief is now available for certain holdings in non-trading companies (QII exemption). See **16.18–16.22**.

- **Surrenderable losses for group relief purposes**. Trading losses, excess capital allowances and non-trading loan relationship deficits may be set off against the claimant company's profits, even though the surrendering company has other profits for the same accounting period against which they could otherwise have been set. By contrast, qualifying charitable donations, property business losses, management expenses and non-trading losses on intangible fixed assets must be offset first against the surrendering company's other profits before use in a group relief claim. See **5.10**.

- **Tax agents' dishonest conduct**. The *FA 2012* provisions are directed primarily at dishonest tax agents, but could pose reputational risks for companies that employ them. See **24.39**.

- **Tax planning**. In a climate of disapproval of tax avoidance, companies should exercise care in planning how best to minimise their tax liabilities while managing the legal and reputational risks involved. They need to be aware of steps being taken by HMRC to counter tax avoidance schemes, including extension of disclosure requirements under DOTAS, new powers to demand accelerated tax payments and new sanctions against promoters of high-risk tax avoidance schemes. See **25.46** and **25.48–25.51**.

- **Trading status** of a company is important, to retain loss reliefs and investment reliefs. Consideration should be given to the company's long-term plans. Restructuring may be seen as advisable, to separate trading from investment activities. See **Chapter 17** and **18.14–18.21**.

- **Transfer pricing**. Companies affected by transfer pricing rules must retain records, or be able to produce them, to demonstrate that they have adhered to the guidelines and the arm's length principle for all cross-border and domestic transactions with related businesses. At the time the corporation tax return was made, these records do not necessarily need to exist in a form that could be made available to HMRC. See **Chapter 21**.

- **UK GAAP.** New accounting standards are mandatory for periods of account beginning on or after 1 January 2015, and the new FRSSE is replaced for periods of account beginning on or after 1 January 2016. Companies making the transition to new UK GAAP need to understand the corporation tax implications of doing so, including the tax treatment of any adjustments on a change of accounting basis. See **Chapter 26.**

Appendix 1

Retail prices index from March 1982 onwards

	Jan	Feb	Mar	Apr	May	Jun
1982			79.44	81.04	81.62	81.85
1983	82.61	82.97	83.12	84.28	84.64	84.84
1984	86.84	87.20	87.48	88.64	88.97	89.20
1985	91.20	91.94	92.80	94.78	95.21	95.41
1986	96.25	96.60	96.73	97.67	97.85	97.79
1987	100.0	100.4	100.6	101.8	101.9	101.9
1988	103.3	103.7	104.1	105.8	106.2	106.6
1989	111.0	111.8	112.3	114.3	115.0	115.4
1990	119.5	120.2	121.4	125.1	126.2	126.7
1991	130.2	130.9	131.4	133.1	133.5	134.1
1992	135.6	136.3	136.7	138.8	139.3	139.3
1993	137.9	138.8	139.3	140.6	141.1	141.0
1994	141.3	142.1	142.5	144.2	144.7	144.7
1995	146.0	146.9	147.5	149.0	149.6	149.8
1996	150.2	150.9	151.5	152.6	152.9	153.0
1997	154.4	155.0	155.4	156.3	156.9	157.5
1998	159.5	160.3	160.8	162.6	163.5	163.4
1999	163.4	163.7	164.1	165.2	165.6	165.6
2000	166.6	167.5	168.4	170.1	170.7	171.1
2001	171.1	172.0	172.2	173.1	174.2	174.4
2002	173.3	173.8	174.5	175.7	176.2	176.2
2003	178.4	179.3	179.9	181.2	181.5	181.3
2004	183.1	183.8	184.6	185.7	186.5	186.8
2005	188.9	189.6	190.5	191.6	192.0	192.2
2006	193.4	194.2	195.0	196.5	197.7	198.5

Retail prices index from March 1982 onwards

	Jan	Feb	Mar	Apr	May	Jun
2007	201.6	203.1	204.4	205.4	206.2	207.3
2008	209.8	211.4	212.1	214.0	215.1	216.8
2009	210.1	211.4	211.3	211.5	212.8	213.4
2010	217.9	219.2	220.7	222.8	223.6	224.1
2011	229.0	231.3	232.5	234.4	235.2	235.2
2012	238.0	239.9	240.8	242.5	242.4	241.8
2013	245.8	247.6	248.7	249.5	250.0	249.7
2014	252.6	254.2	254.8	255.7	255.9	256.3
2015	255.4	256.7	257.1	258.0	258.5	258.9
2016	258.8	260.0	261.1	261.4	262.1	263.1
2017	265.5	268.4	269.3	270.6	271.7	272.3
2018	276.0	278.1	278.3	279.7		

	Jul	Aug	Sep	Oct	Nov	Dec
1982	81.88	81.90	81.85	82.26	82.66	82.51
1983	85.30	85.68	86.06	86.36	86.67	86.89
1984	89.10	89.94	90.11	90.67	90.95	90.87
1985	95.23	95.49	95.44	95.59	95.92	96.05
1986	97.52	97.82	98.30	98.45	99.29	99.62
1987	101.8	102.1	102.4	102.9	103.4	103.3
1988	106.7	107.9	108.4	109.5	110.0	110.3
1989	115.5	115.8	116.6	117.5	118.5	118.8
1990	126.8	128.1	129.3	130.3	130.0	129.9
1991	133.8	134.1	134.6	135.1	135.6	135.7
1992	138.8	138.9	139.4	139.9	139.7	139.2
1993	140.7	141.3	141.9	141.8	141.6	141.9
1994	144.0	144.7	145.0	145.2	145.3	146.0
1995	149.1	149.9	150.6	149.8	149.8	150.7
1996	152.4	153.1	153.8	153.8	153.9	154.4
1997	157.5	158.5	159.3	159.5	159.6	160.0
1998	163.0	163.7	164.4	164.5	164.4	164.4
1999	165.1	165.5	166.2	166.5	166.7	167.3
2000	170.5	170.5	171.7	171.6	172.1	172.2
2001	173.3	174.0	174.6	174.3	173.6	173.4

	Jul	Aug	Sep	Oct	Nov	Dec
2002	175.9	176.4	177.6	177.9	178.2	178.5
2003	181.3	181.6	182.5	182.6	182.7	183.5
2004	186.8	187.4	188.1	188.6	189.0	189.9
2005	192.2	192.6	193.1	193.3	193.6	194.1
2006	198.5	199.2	200.1	200.4	201.1	202.7
2007	206.1	207.3	208.0	208.9	209.7	210.9
2008	216.5	217.2	218.4	217.7	216.0	212.9
2009	213.4	214.4	215.3	216.0	216.6	218.0
2010	223.6	224.5	225.3	225.8	226.8	228.4
2011	234.7	236.1	237.9	238.0	238.5	239.4
2012	242.1	243.0	244.2	245.6	245.6	246.8
2013	249.7	251.0	251.9	251.9	252.1	253.4
2014	256.0	257.0	257.6	257.7	257.1	257.5
2015	258.6	259.8	259.6	259.5	259.8	260.6
2016	263.4	264.4	264.9	264.8	265.5	267.1
2017	272.9	274.7	275.1	275.	275.8	278.1

Index

[*All references are to paragraph number*]

F

J

K

L

U